Best Practices in School Psychology IV

Volume 2

Contents

— VOLUME 1 —

I. PROFESSIONAL LEADERSHIP ISSUES AND SERVICES

Professional Foundation

Professional Supervision and Leadership

System-Level Supports for Intervention-Oriented Services

Supporting Parents, Families, and Cultural Considerations

II. IMPROVING STUDENT PERFORMANCE

Intervention Design, Decision Making, and Consultation

Academic Performance

— VOLUME 2 —

Behavior Performance

III. FOCUS ON ASSESSMENT DOMAINS AND SPECIAL POPULATIONS

Assessment Within Domains

Working With Special Populations and Special Situations

IV. APPENDICES

58 Best Practices in Promotion of Social Competence in the Schools

Kathy McNamara
Cleveland State University

OVERVIEW

In 1986, Good and Weinstein presented a case for a comprehensive view of school effectiveness, arguing that emotional, social, and moral capacities must join intellectual capacity as proper targets for the educational mission of schools:

> School is a place where children develop or fail to develop a variety of competencies that come to define self and ability, where friendships with peers are nurtured, and where the role of community member is played out, all during a highly formative period of development. Thus, the building of self-esteem, interpersonal competence, social problem-solving skills, responsibility, and leadership becomes important both in its own right and as a critical underpinning of success in academic learning (Good & Weinstein, 1986, p. 1095).

The term "social competence promotion" (SCP) refers to institutional efforts to accomplish this mission, combining the goals of prevention and competence building with problem-focused interventions (Hoagwood & Erwin, 1997). The importance of SCP extends beyond the school years; adaptability, personal management, group effectiveness, teamwork, negotiation, and organizational effectiveness have been cited by potential employers as competencies that are at least as important as academic skills for success in the workplace (Elias et al, 1997).

The magnitude of the challenge facing SCP initiatives is reflected in the range of problems they are expected to prevent and remedy, including school safety concerns, gang membership, academic failure and school dropout, substance abuse, delinquency, youth violence and weapons possession, bullying, sexual harassment, and mean-spirited teasing (Walker et al., 1998). With increasing interest in school-based SCP programs as a response to these concerns, a window of opportunity has been opened for school psychologists to actualize their potential as mental health professionals knowledgeable about programs, interventions, and resources, and how to integrate them into the culture of schools (Nastasi, 1998).

Unfortunately, the many school-based programs and activities that comprise SCP are often provided in a piecemeal manner, with little or no organization or coordination of various program elements, and inadequate evidence of their likely or actual effectiveness. Even those programs deemed effective seldom demonstrate a meaningful impact on attitudes and behaviors identified as critical by the larger community (Masten & Coatsworth, 1998; Walker et al., 1998). Clearly, there is a need to conceptualize and plan school-based SCP programs as a coordinated system of activities where effectiveness has been validated through research and systematic evaluation. Moreover, programs should match the nature, frequency, and intensity of activities and interventions to the differing needs of students, whether on the basis of developmental considerations, student risk status, or the "severity and intractability of students' adjustment problems"

(Walker et al., 1996, p. 196). Success in building a comprehensive SCP program requires a commitment to infusing its goals and principles into the fabric of the school's organization and daily activities; that is, in other words, into the culture of the school.

The role of the school psychologist varies with each element of SCP programs, from disseminating research findings about risk factors and intervention techniques to developing and conducting screening activities. This chapter provides a conceptual framework for comprehensive school-based SCP program development, including important goals and recommended elements, and includes information about several projects whose success has been documented through research.

BASIC CONSIDERATIONS

Factors Affecting the Development of Social Competence

Research has identified three major influences on the development of social competence: *early life experiences*, *social-contextual factors*, and *school experiences*. In contrast to those who have developed adequate self-regulatory skills by the time of school entry, children who have learned maladaptive behavior patterns in their early years often bring these patterns to school in the form of aggressive and antisocial behavior (Patterson, DeBaryshe, & Ramsey, 1989). Parenting practices that have been linked to conduct problems among school-aged children include inconsistent and harsh discipline, low supervision and involvement, and inflexible rigid discipline (Conduct Problems Prevention Research Group, 1999a). "Early starters," or children exposed since infancy to ineffective parenting practices resulting from disruptive family environments or stressors, are at substantial risk for later school dropout and delinquency (Walker, Colvin, & Ramsey, 1995).

Social-contextual factors also affect the development of social competence; among such factors, the Conduct Problems Prevention Research Group (1999a) cite family poverty, family instability, and factors negatively affecting child development, such as criminal victimization of the family, greater number of siblings, and high residential mobility. Children with more stable and advantaged backgrounds typically are exposed to the kinds of literacy-related experiences that facilitate reading and academic achievement in the early school years, and are more likely to receive active monitoring and reinforcement of prosocial behaviors and skills (Walker et al., 1995). Although many contextual factors are not amenable to intervention (particularly by schools), it is important to recognize their cumulative contribution to children's risk for social competence deficits, and to address their effects in prevention and intervention programs.

Schools, as critical socializing institutions, exert profound and lasting influence on children's social competence (Hawkins & Weis, 1985). The explicit curriculum of schools specifies desired attitudes and skills, as well as methods for their attainment, while the implicit curriculum—conveyed in a more subtle manner through rules, enforcement methods, instructional practices, interpersonal interactions, forms of student participation in decision making, and home-school communication—teaches attitudes and skills through modeling and children's own experiences. Many aspects of children's classroom experience influence the development of social competence; these are displayed in Table 1.

Goals of Social Competence Promotion Programs

SCP programs first need to define an intended scope of influence, a task made difficult by the extremely broad conceptualizations of social competence. For example, Masten and Coatsworth (1998) identified three "hallmarks of success" for children during the school years: (a) social competence with peers, (b) socially appropriate conduct, and (c) academic achievement. Walker et al. (1983) view school-aged social competence as the ability to recruit social networks, to meet the demands of teachers (who control classrooms) and peers (who control playgrounds), and to adapt to changing conditions in one's environment. While all of these competencies can be addressed in different ways by SCP programs, planners should ensure that a school program has several explicit goals that are consistent with the school's stated philosophy or mission. For example, a school that has adopted academic achievement and good citizenship as priorities might articulate such SCP goals as "personal responsibility and self-discipline in working toward a standard of academic excellence" and "active and capable participation in individual and group decision making."

Table 1. Classroom variables affecting children's social competence

Variable	*Desirable features*
Teacher expectations for academic and social performance	Explicit, unambiguous, challenging; accommodating differences
Teacher use of authority	Context-appropriate display of authoritative, democratic, or laissez-faire styles; avoidance of authoritarian control; availability of choice
Development, nature, and enforcement of rules	Student participation in rule development; clear, limited number; observable behaviors; consequences for violations consistently applied
Management of time	Task-relevant time promoting student engagement; smooth transitions; generally predictable but flexible schedule
Use of space	Desk and workspace arrangements consistent with task demands; teacher proximity to students to enable monitoring and encouragement
Goal structure	Flexibility in use of individualistic, cooperative, and competitive goals
Instructional context	Variety of one to one adult-student, small/large groups, peer-assisted, independent, and cooperative work
Nature of tasks	Challenging and stimulating; promoting active engagement; incorporate student interests/skills; minimal use of work-sheets for drill and practice
Monitoring of student behavior and performance	Frequent observation and feedback to students; acknowledgment of positive achievement; ongoing assessment by using objective measures sensitive to small changes in performance; encouragement of self-regulation among students
Behavior management strategies	Reactive strategies (punishment, timeout, etc.) used sparingly; emphasis on proactive strategies (contingency plans, goal-setting); minimal use of class time to manage misbehavior; consequences stress alternative behavior and problem solving; students participate in classroom management (e.g., class meetings, conflict mediation)

Source. Adapted from Campbell and Siperstein (1994).

Although planners may be tempted to focus on narrow goals because of recent circumstances or events (e.g., violence prevention in the wake of highly publicized school shootings), it is important to identify broad outcomes that can be attained through a range of components touching on many aspects of children's school experience. For example, a goal might specify "effectiveness in managing personal and interpersonal conflict in a peaceful and respectful manner," rather than "elimination of weapons from the school environment through conflict mediation and a zero tolerance policy." In this way, the school can avoid the fate of many SCP programs that are abandoned when they fail to have an immediate impact on narrowly construed goals, when resources for a specific activity are withdrawn (especially when no institutional "ownership" of the activity has been cultivated), or when the fanfare surrounding a particular bandwagon issue or approach fades.

It is also important to understand the difference between *social competence* and *social skills.* Social skills are the specific strategies and behaviors used to accomplish social tasks such as making requests, making friends, and initiating interaction. Socially skillful behavior is presumed to lead to social competence, which refers to the overall effectiveness and positive social impact of an individual's behavior (Walker et al., 1995). This distinction is important because an effective SCP program requires more than the adoption of a specific social skills training program. It is reflected in many aspects of the school culture, including disciplinary policies, teaching practices, and decision-making procedures. The yardstick for the success of a school's SCP program is the extent to which administrative and instructional practices support the development and display of socially competent attitudes and behavior among students.

School psychologists with training in organizational consultation are especially well prepared to assist school administrators in the process of setting goals that are consistent with the school's stated philosophy, are responsive to community needs, and are sufficiently broad to accommodate a number of specific objectives. Though administrators and teachers may be inclined to bypass planning stages in their eagerness to adopt curricula or plan activities, school psychologists can help them to understand the importance of goal-setting. A set of comprehensive goals devised by members of the school community elicits support for subsequent implementation efforts, legitimizes the use of school resources for SCP activities, assures that a variety of needs is addressed, and serves as a benchmark for program planning and evaluation.

BEST PRACTICES

Elements of School-Based Social Competence Promotion Programs

In contrast to typical practice, which defines social competence promotion in terms of a particular curriculum or program offered in the school, best practice requires a broad conceptualization of social competence as a goal toward which a variety of activities and experiences is directed. Walker et al. (1996) identified four school-based systems in which SCP might occur. The *school-wide system*, which addresses the general school population, establishes school climate or culture through rules and standards for performance, organizational features and practices, and priorities for instructional activities. A *specific setting system* governs behavior in the common areas in which students spend time daily (e.g., cafeteria, playground, buses). The *classroom system* is largely under the control of teachers, who establish and enforce policies and procedures within an instructional setting. Finally, the *individual student system* provides direction for responding to the needs of students who present problematic behavior. SCP programs reflecting best practice will incorporate program elements in each of these four systems.

A comprehensive approach to SCP is based on models of effective prevention, which incorporate three broad functions in program goals and activities. *Primary prevention* is reflected in academic instruction, training for all children in an array of social problem-solving skills, enhancement of school and classroom climate, extracurricular activities, and teaching and disciplinary practices that confer and promote social and personal responsibility. *Secondary prevention*, which targets children at risk for problematic social adjustment, includes early screening and intervention (including social skills training) to interrupt negative behavior patterns and address skill deficits, enforcement of disciplinary policies for infractions of rules, activities to draw at-risk children and youth into the conventional mainstream, and supportive services to families experiencing acute or chronic disruption. *Tertiary prevention* seeks to minimize the harmful impact of established social adjustment problems, and includes academic remediation, training in survival and social skills such as anger management and self-control, career and vocational training, and efforts to reduce the likelihood of school dropout.

Often, schools' SCP efforts consist of primary prevention initiatives (e.g., drug and alcohol awareness programs, weekly lessons drawn from a social skills curriculum), which are offered to students across a wide range of ages, coupled with tertiary prevention activities (e.g., tutoring students with academic deficiencies) aimed at older students with well-established patterns of problem behavior. Drawing on the research literature about effective prevention, school psychologists can emphasize the need for a fit between levels of prevention and student characteristics, such as age, risk status, and developmental levels (McNamara, 1995). For example, a school psychologist, knowing that early intervention is essential for meaningful behavior change, might offer to work with primary grade level teachers to develop classroom interventions for use with children displaying antisocial behavior patterns.

By now, it should be clear that SCP programming is a broad undertaking extending far beyond choosing a social skills curriculum for the primary grades or training a select group of students to serve as peer mediators. A review of the research literature reveals eight major objectives for school-based SCP programs (see Table 2). In the following section, each of these objectives is accompanied by a description of corresponding program elements.

Objectives for Program Design

Identify Children at Risk for Social Performance Deficits at The Point of School Entry

Children whose early life experiences socialize them into negative behavior patterns (i.e., early starters) are unable to make a successful transition to school, where they find it impossible to meet expectations for prosocial behavior and self-management under conditions of greater structure. Ultimately, their problematic behavior leads to rejection by teachers and peers, a condition that is a powerful predictor of later, more severe, life problems (Walker et al., 1995). Although research demonstrates that intervention before age 9 is crucial to effect meaningful change in the patterns of problem behavior exhibited by these children, most school-based programs bypass younger children in the mistaken belief that children will outgrow these negative patterns, reserving intervention resources for pre-adolescents and adolescents. Intervention at younger ages has a greater likelihood of success, but requires a reliable method for identifying children in need of services (Conduct Problems Prevention Research Group, 1999b). A system for screening children for behavior problems in kindergarten or first grade is an important secondary prevention component of a comprehensive SCP program. With widely acknowledged expertise in assessment, school psychologists might contribute to early screening activities by suggesting specific instruments and procedures, providing accurate interpretations of screening results, and supporting appropriate interventions linked to assessment findings.

Several instruments are available for screening purposes, including the Student Risk Screening Scale (Drummond, 1993), which consists of seven items that are rated on a 3-point scale, and can be used by teachers to evaluate large groups of children. Items included in the scale assess stealing; lying, cheating, and sneaking; behavior problems; peer rejection; low academic achievement; negative attitude; and aggressive behavior. The Child Behavior Checklist (Achenbach, 1991) is recommended by Walker et al. (1995) as another instrument that can detect early patterns of antisocial behavior. They describe a screening process in which teachers nominate children whose behavior matches a profile consisting of rule violations, aggression toward others, damaging or destroying property, taking things without permission, and a sullen, agitated emotional state. Teachers and parents then rate the behavior of these students on the aggression subscale of the Child Behavior Checklist. Children whose scores on either teacher- or parent-rating forms fall two or more standard deviations above the subscale mean are considered to be at risk for serious antisocial behavior problems.

The nature and extent of early intervention efforts vary with children's needs and setting characteristics. However, programs such as First Step to Success, available from the Institute on Violence and Destructive Behavior at the University of Oregon, have demonstrated their effectiveness and serve as models for identification and intervention. First Step is designed to divert young children (grades K–2) from problematic behavior patterns through a systematic and collaborative process involving teachers, parents, and "coaches," or consultants. The program is implemented across a 2- to 3-month period in both kindergarten and home settings, providing opportunities for children to learn adaptive patterns of school behavior and for training parents to teach children skills contributing to school success. The classroom component involves monitoring and reinforcing children's prosocial behavior, with signals to indicate the appropriateness or inappropriateness of behavior. The home component teaches parents about a set of six skills that children need to master for success in school: communication and sharing at school, cooperation, limit-setting, problem solving, friendship-making, and developing confidence. Consultants teach one skill per week to parents during hour-long sessions held in the home. Lessons include materials

Table 2. Objectives for school-based social competence promotion programs

- Identify children at risk for social performance deficits at the point of school entry.
- Provide appropriate and intensive intervention to children displaying problematic behavior patterns.
- Develop discipline policies that emphasize rehabilitation over punishment, that provide clear guidelines for behavior, and that are enforced in a consistent and even-handed manner.
- Promote caring and stable interpersonal relationships between students and adults.
- Modify instructional practices to increase active engagement in learning.
- Offer frequent opportunities for students to learn and demonstrate socially responsible behavior.
- Support the role of families in promoting social competence.
- Evaluate the impact of program activities.

and strategies that parents can use to provide opportunities for children to practice newly learned skills (Golly, Stiller, & Walker, 1998).

Provide Appropriate and Intensive Intervention to Children Displaying Problematic Behavior Patterns

It is beyond the scope of this chapter to provide a detailed review of principles underlying effective interventions for children's problematic social performance. However, Walker et al. (1995) have furnished several guidelines pertaining to the structure and delivery of such interventions in school-based SCP programs (see Table 3). First, they recommend that intervention planning occur in context of an individualized, functional assessment of behavior. The purpose of this assessment is to identify the purposes of problematic behavior; that is, what the child intends to accomplish through the behavior, as well as environmental conditions affecting the occurrence of the behavior (e.g., rules or standards for behavior, teacher demands for academic and social behavior, enforcement methods, difficulty level of materials and activities). The process of functional assessment yields information useful in planning behaviorally based intervention approaches, which have been found to be more effective than other, non-behavioral approaches in producing significant positive outcomes (Gottfredson, 1997). Moreover, documentation of behavior intervention plans based on the results of functional behavior assessment may be needed to satisfy the requirements of the Individuals with Disabilities Education Act (1997) for children with disabilities whose behavior interferes with their ability to learn.

Second, interventions for problems related to social competence should always include strategies to promote empathy and responsible decision making, since these keystone skills are frequently deficient among children displaying inappropriate and antisocial behavior. The Positive Peer Culture program described by Vorrath and Brendtro (1985) emphasizes the development of these skills through student participation in small groups (led by adult facilitators, such as school psychologists) where members employ problem-solving methods in a mutual assistance framework.

Third, interventions should promote positive, alternative ("replacement") behaviors that are at least as efficient as the behaviors they are intended to replace. That is, alternative behaviors should be successful in accomplishing the child's purposes at (what the child perceives to be) an equal or lesser cost. For example, a child who employs aggressive behavior to gain a sense of power and control over others might be taught to exercise leadership in a classroom activity. The child will likely adopt the proposed alternative as long as he or she regards it as effective in attaining a sense of power, and does not believe that it will require resources or skills beyond his or her own ability to perform. Equally significant, the "cost" of a behavior also must be assessed in terms of any potential, negative consequences of the new behavior (again, as perceived by the child). If the child fears that classroom leadership activities will elicit teasing from peers, then this alternative to aggressive behavior is likely to be rejected.

Fourth, Walker et al. (1995) advise that only positive strategies be employed at the outset of an intervention plan (e.g., social skills training, limit setting, daily debriefings about problems encountered, self-monitoring, re-statement of rules, incentives), with the addition of aversive strategies (e.g., timeout, suspension, removal of privileges) only if positive strategies fail to produce desired effects.

Table 3. Guidelines for intervention with students displaying problematic behavior patterns

- Use functional behavior assessment as basis for planning interventions.
- Include strategies to promote empathy and decision making.
- Promote functionally equivalent (positive) replacement behaviors.
- Employ only positive strategies at onset, adding negative strategies only if necessary.
- For group interventions, include positive peer models.
- Involve primary caregivers in interventions.

Source. Walker et al. (1995).

Fifth, interventions that are delivered in a group format should provide for participation by peers who demonstrate positive and skillful social behavior, since their participation keeps the group from assuming a negative identity and enables them to serve as models of positive behavior and prosocial attitudes. In this way, the (inadvertent) negative and damaging effects of segregating children for intervention with similarly troubled peers can be avoided (Gibbs, Potter, Goldstein, & Brendtro, 1996; McNamara, 1996; Vorrath & Brendtro, 1985).

Sixth, Walker et al. (1995) recommend that planners attempt to involve primary caregivers in interventions, even when they are reluctant to participate in planning or implementation activities.

Social skills training programs are perhaps the best-known component of school-based SCP efforts (see Gresham's chapter on social skills, this volume). Miller, Brehm, and Whitehouse (1998) cite research indicating that social-cognitive deficits play a significant role in the development of socially problematic behavior over time, and that such deficits reveal themselves in poor problem solving, misjudgments about social situations, and inadequate strategies for managing conflict situations. Efforts to correct these deficiencies cannot be limited to students' participation in the social skills curriculum offered in a preventive context to all students; instead, individually tailored interventions addressing specific social skill deficits must be implemented. By recommending appropriate procedures for assessing social skills, school psychologists can help educators avoid the "one size fits all" approach to social skills training that is especially inappropriate as the secondary prevention intervention needed by at-risk students.

Jones, Sheridan, and Binns (1993) describe a school-wide social skills assessment and training model that provides in-class social skills training for all students and intensive small group training for at-risk students. They review a number of assessment procedures, including direct observation, teacher and parent rating scales, sociometrics, self-report of social skills, teacher and parent interviews, and child interviews. Walker et al. (1995) offer an assessment procedure in which classroom teachers identify social skill problems by using a matrix to rate students across a set of core social skills, including listening, greeting others, joining in, complimenting, expressing anger, keeping friends, doing quality work, following rules, using self-control, offering assistance, disagreeing with others, being organized, and having conversations. The resulting matrix can be examined at several levels:

1. To determine the overall skill level of the class and whether specific skills represent deficiencies for a number of children.

2. To discover sub-groups of children displaying similar skill deficiencies.

3. To identify children who are deficient in a number of core social skills.

Screening results can be used to plan instructional activities, whether for the entire class, for sub-groups of children with similar skill deficiencies, or for individual children requiring more intensive remedial interventions. The Social Skills Rating System (Gresham & Elliott, 1990), a formal instrument designed to evaluate children's social skills for purposes of intervention planning, allows teachers to rate a set of social skills according to their frequency of occurrence, as well as perceived importance of the skill.

Gresham (1986) distinguished between problems arising from skill deficits and those attributable to performance deficits, observing that this distinction is critical to successful intervention efforts. Problems arising from a failure to perform a known skill—or non-fluent performance of the skill—should be addressed through motivational strategies and increased opportunities for practice. Skill deficits, on the other hand, require instructional intervention. For individual children, a functional assessment should be used to reveal whether problems represent a failure to have learned the desired behavior (skill deficit) or a failure to display an already-learned behavior (performance deficit). Commercially available programs for teaching social skills include the PREPARE Curriculum (Goldstein, 1988), Aggression Replacement Training (Goldstein & Glick, 1987), and Social Decision Making and Life Skills Development (Elias, Friedlander, & Tobias, 1995).

Develop Discipline Policies That Emphasize Rehabilitation Over Punishment, That Provide Clear Guidelines for Behavior, and That are Enforced in a Consistent and Even-Handed Manner

A set of core features characterizing effective discipline policy has been identified by a number of researchers (See Table 4). These features include (a) clear communication of rules and expectations for student behavior, (b) willingness to act immediately to deliver appropriate consequences when rules are broken, (c) monitoring of the behavior of students as a group, and (d) a system through which positive behavior is recognized on a routine basis (Gettinger, 1988; Hawkins & Lam, 1987; Mayer, 1995). At an institutional level, Walker et al. (1995) observe that the success of a school discipline policy depends on (a) the presence of strong leadership, (b) commitment on the part of school staff, (c) guidelines specifying circumstances in which administrators (versus teachers) should manage problem behavior, (d) staff development and training, (e) data management and evaluation allowing record keeping for disciplinary actions and outcomes, and (f) structures allowing for periodic evaluations and revisions of the policy.

Walker et al. (1995) describe five general phases in planning a school-wide discipline policy. The first phase requires school staff and other members of the school community to reach agreement or consensus about the basic purposes of the disciplinary policy. A review of the goals that have been articulated for the schools' SCP program can help guide this process. Next, expectations for behavior should be specified, including examples of appropriate and inappropriate behavior related to each expectation. It is important for a school-wide discipline policy to also specify expectations for unique or potentially problematic settings (e.g., cafeteria, buses, library). In the third phase, a plan is devised for teaching students the agreed-upon expectations for behavior (i.e., practices for acknowledging positive behavior; informal instruction in expected behaviors, including reminders, supervision, and feedback; and formal instruction in expected behaviors, including description and modeling, supervised practice, pre-correction for problematic settings and students, and behavior-descriptive praise of expected behavior).

The fourth phase involves the development of procedures for responding to problem behavior, including designating behaviors as minor infractions, serious violations, or illegal behavior. Responses to minor

Table 4. Features of effective discipline policies

- Presence of strong building leadership.
- Commitment on the part of school staff.
- Guidelines for administrator (versus teacher/staff) management of problem behavior.
- Staff development and training.
- Data management and evaluation.
- Structures for periodic policy evaluation and revision.
- Clear communication of rules and expectations.
- Willingness to act immediately to deliver consequences.
- Monitoring of student behavior as a group.
- Routine recognition of positive behavior.

Source. Gettinger (1988); Hawkins and Lam (1987); Mayer (1995); Walker et al. (1995).

infractions, usually managed by individual staff, include removal of attention, redirection, prompts and reinforcement, warnings involving choice, loss of privileges, use of additional resources in the school (administrators, specialists, assistance team), and documentation of the problem and intervention attempts. When minor infractions persist despite the actions of individual staff, Walker et al. recommend that a problem-solving meeting be convened so that a formal intervention plan can be developed.

The zero tolerance position adopted by many schools in the wake of incidents of school violence in recent years is a controversial response to serious rule violations. The removal of students from school often exacerbates problem behavior, since excluded students are deprived of exposure to positive influences and learning opportunities, and are more likely to subscribe to norms of antisocial, non-normative conduct (Walker et al., 1996). Arguments favoring intensive intervention while retaining students in school are especially compelling in light of research showing that 80% of all crimes are committed by high school dropouts (Walker et al., 1995).

The fifth and final phase in planning a school-wide discipline policy involves the development of procedures for keeping records related to policy implementation, and for disseminating the plan to every member of the school community (i.e., students, parents, teachers, staff, community representatives). In summary, discipline policies that employ proactive approaches emphasizing problem solving, in contrast to policies that rely primarily on reactive, punitive procedures, serve as a critical component of an effective SCP program.

Promote Caring and Stable Interpersonal Relationships Between Students and Adults

Research has demonstrated relationships between the quality of student-teacher relationships and variables contributing to school success, such as academic motivation and attitudes toward school (Anderman & Maehr, 1994; Eccles, Wigfield, Midgley, Redman, MacIver, & Feldlaufer, 1993). A caring relationship with one or more adults has been cited as a powerful protective factor for children at risk for a variety of problematic social behaviors, including substance abuse and school dropout (Doll & Lyon, 1998). A program of research conducted by Eccles and her colleagues has identified a trend of increased impersonality and fewer opportunities for sustained contact between students and teachers as students proceed through their school careers. As students reach the middle and secondary school years, social networks are likely to be disrupted as a consequence of greater numbers of students, larger class sizes, and increases in between-classroom ability grouping. Coupled with increasingly greater emphasis on teacher control and discipline and less attention to the behavior and needs of individual students, these trends fail to support—and, in fact, mitigate against—stable, caring relationships between students and their teachers.

There are several methods for improving the stability of relationships as part of a school's SCP efforts. Felner, Ginter, and Primavera (1982) described a plan where the role of homeroom teachers was redefined to allow frequent, sustained contact between students and teachers, replacing the brief, unidirectional, and impersonal communication characteristic of typical homeroom periods. Similarly, grouping students into teams or "houses," sometimes known as schools within schools or small learning communities, provides opportunities for overlap and consistency in teacher and peer contacts over the course of the school day. Mentoring strategies, which pair adult staff with students for advising, academic and behavioral monitoring, and participation in school activities, represent another promising avenue for increasing the frequency of interaction and enhancing the quality of adult-student relationships. The practice of pairing of children with adults is a major feature of the Primary Mental Health Project (PMHP) (Cowen et al., 1996). PMHP assigns "child associates," selected on the basis of their capacity for warmth and empathy, to provide direct, ongoing support services to young children at risk for school adjustment problems. The Child Development Project (Battistich, Watson, Solomon, Schaps, & Solomon, 1991) is a promising approach to school reform that views schools as caring communities. Its components include cooperative learning activities, learning experiences providing opportunities for self-direction and influence over classroom activities, teaching and modeling of prosocial values in daily interactions, disciplinary procedures by using democratic procedures in context of "classroom communities," home-school cooperation, and service activities.

Modify Instructional Practices to Increase Active Engagement in Learning

The development of academic competence is a primary goal of schools, and serves as a benchmark against which the value of innovative programs is often measured. Some have argued that school-based SCP activities serve only to divert educators' attention from this goal, and recommend the elimination of SCP programs in favor of a strong, back to basics academic emphasis. In recent years, however, advocates for school-based SCP programs have pointed to the optimization of academic competence as a major objective of SCP efforts. In Project Achieve—a school-wide approach to addressing the needs of at-risk children—empirically validated components of successful academic intervention (such as curriculum-based assessment and training teachers in effective instructional methods) are emphasized along with social skills training and school climate interventions (Knoff & Batsche, 1995). In an extensive review of the literature, Masten and Coatsworth (1998) cite academic achievement as a key component of competence during the school years, while Kauffman and Burbach (1997) argue that effective instruction is "the first defense against school violence and disruption" (p. 324).

Effective instructional methods lead to students' active engagement in the learning process, whether in the form of silent reading, discussion, responding to questions, or reciting math facts. Active engagement in learning has been established as a powerful predictor of academic achievement, and can be accomplished through the provision of frequent opportunities for students to respond during instructional activities (Lentz, Allen, & Ehrhardt, 1996). Thus, SCP in a classroom might include the use of peer-assisted learning, where the probability of student responding is increased due to the "demand" characteristics of the peer-to-peer condition. Other elements of effective instruction include positive contingencies for accurate performance, immediate feedback and error correction, frequent and direct measurement of academic skill (curriculum-based assessment) to monitor progress, and aspects of the teaching process such as pacing and appropriate use of modeling, prompting, and fading procedures (Lentz, Allen, & Ehrhardt, 1996). These methods are effective both for class-wide instructional purposes and as the basis for planning interventions for students who have been identified as underachieving or mildly disabled learners. School psychologists who have expanded their role to include consultation for intervention planning will find ample opportunities for involvement in this aspect of a school's SCP program, whether through participation in curriculum-based assessment activities, as a source of information and training for teachers and other instructional personnel, or as a member of teams addressing specific academic needs.

Students' attitudes toward work play a powerful role in achieving academic success, and shape their view of themselves as competent and productive members of society (Maehr & Midgley, 1991). These attitudes are undoubtedly influenced by the nature of the work they are given to do, and the manner in which it is presented. If academic assignments consist largely of work that is not matched to students' instructional levels, or if tasks are dreary and repetitive, then active engagement in learning is unlikely to occur.

Research indicates that students' academic motivation declines over time, a finding partly attributable to changes in teaching practices from the elementary grades to middle and secondary levels (Eccles et al., 1993). Many classrooms are characterized by "ability-focused" goals that emphasize judgments about students based on their ability to achieve success and outperform peers regardless of the nature of tasks, in contrast to "task-focused" goals that promote the accomplishment of challenging tasks and the attainment of understanding, insight, or skill. Research demonstrates that a task-focused classroom environment exerts a positive influence on the motivation of students, especially those considered to be at risk for academic failure (Maehr & Midgley, 1991). Classroom practices found to contribute to a task focus include (a) the availability of choices and opportunities for decision making, (b) grouping on the basis of interests and needs rather than on the basis of ability, (c) evaluation practices that define success in terms of effort and improvement, and (d) opportunities for peer interaction and cooperation.

Task-oriented environments also eschew the practice of providing rewards for school attendance, grades, or achievement. Wonderly (1991) asserts that the unnecessary use of rewards undermines intrinsic motivation by focusing attention on the reward that results from task completion, rather than on the sense of satisfaction and enjoyment available in the work itself. Whatever role they play in influencing motivation, incentives should be used with caution and in accordance with best practices as defined in the applied behavior analytic literature. Although the use of programmed incentives is a topic of continuing debate, social expectations often require individuals to perform in the absence of an immediately apparent reward, suggesting that the promotion of intrinsic motivation ought to be an important component of SCP programs.

Offer Frequent Opportunities for Students to Learn and Demonstrate Socially Responsible Behavior

Wigginton (1994) issued a powerful indictment of schools when, as a former teacher serving time in prison, he described the striking parallel between schools and prisons: "In some ways, life inside prison mimics that in the public schools. In both places, the way the institution responds to the individual's desire to seek meaning in life makes all the difference" (p. 64). Wigginton goes on to describe the typical school experience in the form of restricted and monitored physical movement; rules and routines devised, and decisions made, with no student input; and the threat of punishment as a primary means for behavior control. He correctly points out that the hunger to achieve a worthwhile goal can (and will) be fulfilled through socially responsible pursuits, or through antisocial pursuits such as gang membership and delinquent activity. If the best way for students to learn responsibility is for them to be given responsibility, then it appears that typical school practice (which reserves the assignment of responsibility to students already deemed responsible) fails to teach this important quality to those most in need of it.

Social responsibility is revealed in a number of attitudes and behaviors, including a sense of belonging to prosocial peer groups and institutions, endorsement of conventional norms for behavior, avoidance of peers and adults engaged in antisocial behavior, skill in self-regulation (self-discipline), and a willingness to engage in problem solving to obtain desired outcomes. The development of social responsibility is closely related to issues of classroom and school climate. In 1986, Denise Gottfredson reported the results of a study where changes in factors related to school climate (i.e., institutional response to rule violations, availability of teacher support, promotion of prosocial behavior, and recognition of positive, responsible behavior) led to decreases in student misconduct and an enhanced sense of belonging among students. Table 5 summarizes a number of school practices that promote social responsibility, including (a) instruction in self-management strategies as interventions for impulsive or inappropriate behavior, (b) active teaching of social norms and expectations for behavior, (c) promoting group accountability for the behavior of individual members, (d) encouraging student leadership, (e) providing choices in instructional matters, and (f) creating opportunities for prosocial peer interactions and meaningful decision making (Wentzel, 1991; Maehr & Midgley, 1991).

Classroom meetings are powerful devices for involving children in problem solving, addressing class-wide concerns or needs, and fostering a climate of responsibility and mutual respect. A model for class meetings has been described by Nelsen, Lott, and Glenn (1993), and this model promotes positive interaction among peers (e.g., compliment-giving and receiving), emphasizes the importance of accepting responsibility for one's actions (e.g., compliance with agreed-upon consequences for rule violations), and teaches students a respectful procedure for setting standards for behavior and resolving interpersonal differences. The author has observed school psychologists providing training to teachers in the form of modeling, guided practice, and feedback about their performance as a facilitator of classroom meetings.

Table 5. School practices that promote social responsibility

- Instruction in self-management strategies as interventions for impulsive or inappropriate behavior.
- Active teaching of social norms and expectations for behavior.
- Promoting group accountability for the behavior of individual members.
- Encouraging student leadership.
- Providing choices in instructional matters.
- Creating opportunities for prosocial peer interaction and meaningful decision making.

Source. Maehr and Midgley (1991); Wentzel (1991).

The EQUIP model, developed by Gibbs, Potter, and Goldstein (1995), serves as an example of an intervention that incorporates the dimension of social responsibility in efforts to address problematic behavior. EQUIP offers skill training and practice within the context of a supportive, prosocial peer group. Because group meetings are structured so that participants (in groups of seven to nine students) must use their newly learned problem-solving skills to help others solve personal problems, learning occurs within a motivational context driven by the desire to contribute to others. A similar model has been employed on a pilot basis with at-risk youth, who are invited to participate in student-led groups that also include prosocial peers. Groups plan and implement a service project, learning specific social skills as the need for such skills arises (McNamara, 2000).

Support the Role of Families in Promoting Social Competence

Although it may not be possible for school personnel to directly intervene on stressors (e.g., poverty, unemployment) that exacerbate conditions associated with social competence deficiencies (e.g., family instability and ineffective parenting), some forms of support are within schools' ability to provide. The Parent Program component of the School Development Program developed at Yale University (Haynes, Comer, & Hamilton-Lee, 1989) employs several levels of parent involvement to achieve school improvement goals and encourage parent endorsement of educational goals. Parents become involved in the life of the school as participants in social-recreational events, providers of service in daily school tasks, such as cafeteria and playground supervision and material preparation, and as members of school governance committees. Heller and Fantuzzo (1993) found that specific, neutral, and regularly provided information to parents about children's school attendance, homework, and behavior enhances parental monitoring of behavior, and increases their support for children's active engagement in learning and school activities. In some instances, more intensive service to families is required, and may include training in appropriate child behavior management techniques.

The Homebase parent training module of the First Step program (Golly et al., 1998) includes six in-home lessons and regular check-ins to discuss progress in skills taught in the previous lesson. Lessons seek to improve children's performance in following rules, cooperating, listening, and getting along with peers. Homebase also offers group meetings for parents upon conclusion of the six-week training during which implementation issues can be discussed. The services of community-based agencies are also incorporated in the First Step program, affording an additional level of intervention for at-risk children and their families.

The Adolescent Transitions Program (ATP) (Dishion, Andrews, Kavanagh, & Soberman, 1996) includes a strong parent focus where training activities address three key family management skills: prosocial fostering (monitoring and supporting positive behavior at school), limit setting, and problem solving. Activities are conducted across 12 group sessions, augmented by four individual meetings with each participating family addressing specific change-related concerns. The program was found to be effective in engaging parents, improving parent-child relations, and improving student behavior.

Evaluate the Impact and Success of Program Activities

To ensure accountability and to demonstrate student-specific outcomes, evaluation of SCP programs and their components is essential. A review of the literature from 1966 through 1993 yielded only seven studies examining the generalization effects of commercially available social skills curricula (DuPaul & Eckert, 1994), reflecting a troubling tendency to neglect SCP program evaluation. Even those SCP program elements found to be effective have not necessarily been adopted for widespread use, underscoring the need for valid and reliable evaluation procedures whose results inform decisions about program adoption (Miller, 1999). Walker et al. (1998) state the case for the need to evaluate SCP programs by using methods that can examine socially valid outcomes (i.e., answers to questions such as, "How are you going about creating a sense of discipline in schools that are chaotic and are ruled by disruptive youths and in which teachers are afraid of students?") rather than the "details" of positive gains on social skills rating measures or reports of self-esteem.

The success of social skills training (an important component of school-based SCP programs) is generally evaluated through the use of sociometric measures (peer ratings), behavior and overall competency ratings provided by parents and teachers, direct observation of performance in natural settings, and inspection of products reflecting degrees of socially competent performance (e.g., record of disciplinary referrals). Similarly, the overall impact of SCP programs can be evaluated by examining progress toward academic goals at the classroom or school levels by using curriculum-based assessment, and by obtaining an index of school climate through measures such as the Effective Schools Battery, which solicits student and teacher ratings of climate factors such as morale, student influence, race relations, clarity and fairness of rules, respect for students, planning and action, and smooth administration (Gottfredson, 1985). The School Climate Survey (SCS), an instrument administered in the School Development Program to elementary and secondary school staff and parents, can be obtained from Christine Emmons, Ph.D., School Development Program, 55 College Street, New Haven CT 06510. The Learning Environment Inventory (Walberg & Greenberg, 1997), a rating scale administered to students, is recommended for use by teachers who wish to assess the climate of middle and secondary school classrooms.

SUMMARY

Schools influence the development of social competence through an explicit curriculum (e.g., a published social skills training program adopted for use at the primary grades; conflict mediation training for middle school students) and through an implicit curriculum. School psychologists and other educators who are involved in planning for social competence promotion must attend to an array of factors comprising the implicit SCP curriculum, such as school-wide discipline policies, instructional practices, interpersonal interactions, and responses to the need for individualized intervention for students' academic and social problems.

Elements of effective SCP programs are present across the school-wide, specific setting, classroom, and individual student systems, and include

1. A clearly stated mission to which every member of the school community subscribes.

2. Standards for expected behavior and consistent application of enforcement methods.

3. Commitment to early identification and intervention for children at risk for antisocial behavior and skill deficiencies.

4. Pursuit of home-school linkages focusing on the improvement of parenting skills and support for prosocial behavior.

5. Use of empirically validated instructional practices, including strategies for promoting work as positive and intrinsically rewarding.

6. Opportunities for students to practice socially responsible behavior.

The information and suggestions discussed in this chapter address a broad range of program elements and methods. The reader may be overwhelmed at the magnitude of the challenges facing school-based SCP programs, which include adequacy of resources (funding, personnel, materials) and the likelihood of resistance or reluctance on the part of school personnel to adopt a comprehensive view of SCP programming. Although discussion of these critical issues is beyond the scope of this chapter, school psychologists must approach the planning process with an awareness of their importance and impact. The comprehensive conceptualization of SCP presented in this chapter is intended to inspire creative thinking about empirically supported initiatives that hold promise for developing socially competent youth, rather than as a mandate for the inclusion of particular program elements. The effectiveness of school-based SCP programs depends in large measure on the extent to which program values and practices are integrated into the daily life and routines of the school, rather than on the presence of elaborate or costly program elements.

REFERENCES

Achenbach, T. M. (1991). *The Child Behavior Checklist: Manual for the Teacher's Report Form.* Burlington: University of Vermont, Department of Psychiatry.

Anderman, E. M., & Maehr, M. L. (1994). Motivation and schooling in the middle grades. *Review of Educational Research, 64,* 287–309.

Battistich, V., Watson, M., Solomon, D., Schaps, E., & Solomon, J. (1991). The Child Development Project: A comprehensive program for the development of prosocial character. In W. M. Durtines & J. L. Gewirtz (Eds.), *Handbook of moral behavior and development: Vol. 3: Application* (pp. 1–34). New York: Erlbaum.

Campbell, P., & Siperstein, G. N. (1994). *Improving social competence*. Boston: Allyn & Bacon.

Conduct Problems Prevention Research Group (1999a). Initial impact of the Fast Track prevention trial for conduct problems: I. The high risk sample. *Journal of Consulting and Clinical Psychology, 67*, 631–647.

Conduct Problems Prevention Research Group (1999b). Initial impact of the Fast Track prevention trial for conduct problems: II. Classroom effect. *Journal of Consulting and Clinical Psychology, 67*, 648–657.

Cowen, E. L., Trost, M. A., Izzo, L. O., Lorion, R. P., Dorr, D., & Isaacson, R. V. (1996). *School-based prevention for children at risk: The Primary Mental Health Project*. Washington, DC: American Psychological Association.

Dishion, T. J., Andrews, D. W., Kavanagh, K., & Soberman, L. H. (1996). Preventive interventions for high-risk youth. In R. DeV. Peters & R. J. McMahon, *Preventing childhood disorders, substance abuse, and delinquency* (pp. 184–213). Thousand Oaks, CA: Sage.

Doll, B., & Lyon M. A. (1998). Risk and resilience: Implications for the delivery of educational and mental health services in schools. *School Psychology Review, 27*, 348–363.

Drummond, T. (1993). *The Student Risk Screening Scale*. Grants Pass, OR: Josephine County Mental Health Program.

DuPaul, G. J., & Eckert, T. L. (1994). The effects of social skills curricula: Now you see them, now you don't. *School Psychology Quarterly, 9*, 113–132.

Eccles, J. S., Wigfield, A., Midgley, C., Reuman, D., MacIver, D., & Feldlaufer, H. (1993). Negative effects of traditional middle schools on students' motivation. *The Elementary School Journal, 93*, 553–574.

Elias, M. J., Friedlander, B., & Tobias, S. E. (1995, March). *Promoting children's social and life skills, problem solving, character, and self-discipline: Proven techniques for school professionals*. Paper presented at the annual meeting of the National Association of School Psychologists, Chicago, IL.

Elias, M. J., Zins, J. E., Weissberg. R. P., Frey, K. S., Greenberg, M. T., Haynes, N. M., Kessler, R., Schwab-Stone, M. E., & Shriver, T. P. (1997). *Promoting social and emotional learning: Guidelines for educators*. Alexandria, VA: Association for Supervision and Curriculum Development.

Felner, R. D., Ginter, M., & Primavera, J. (1982). Primary prevention during school transitions: Social support and environmental structure. *American Journal of Community Psychology, 10*, 277–290.

Gettinger, M. (1988). Methods of proactive classroom management. *School Psychology Review, 17*, 227–242.

Gibbs, J. C., Potter, G. B., & Goldstein, A. P. (1995). *The EQUIP Program: Teaching youth to think and act responsibly through a peer-helping approach*. Champaign IL: Research Press.

Gibbs, J. C., Potter, G. B., Goldstein, A. B., & Brendtro, L. K. (1996). Frontiers in psychoeducation: The EQUIP model with antisocial youth. *Reclaiming Children and Youth, 4*, 22 – 28.

Goldstein, A. P. (1988). *The PREPARE curriculum*. Champaign IL: Research Press.

Goldstein, A. P., & Glick, B. (1987). *Aggression replacement training: A comprehensive intervention for aggressive youth*. Champaign IL: Research Press.

Golly, A. M., Stiller, B., & Walker, H. M. (1998). First step to success: Replication and social validation of an early intervention program. *Journal of Emotional and Behavioral Disorders, 6*, 243–250.

Good, T. L., & Weinstein, R. S. (1986). Schools make a difference: Evidence, criticisms, and new directions. *American Psychologist, 41*, 1090–1097.

Gottfredson, D. C. (1986). An empirical test of school-based environmental and individual interventions to reduce the risk of delinquent behavior. *Criminology, 24*, 705–731.

Gottfredson, D. C. (1997). School-based crime prevention. In L. Sherman, D. Gottfredson, D. Mackenzie, J. Eck, P. Reuter, & S. Bushway (Eds.), *Preventing crime: What works, what doesn't, what's promising*. College Park, MD: Department of Criminology and Criminal Justice, University of Maryland.

Gottfredson, G. D., (1985). *Effective school battery: User's manual*. Odessa, FL: Psychological Assessment Resources.

Gresham, F. (1986). Conceptual issues in the assessment of social competence in children. In P. S. Strain, M. J. Guralnick, & H. M. Walker (Eds.), *Children's social behavior: Development, assessment, and modification* (pp. 143–179). New York: Academic.

Gresham, F. M., & Elliott, S. (1990). *The Social Skills Rating System (SSRS)*. Circle Pines, MN: American Guidance Service.

Hawkins, J. D., & Lam, T. (1987). Teacher practices, social development, and delinquency. In J. D. Burchard & S. N. Burchard (Eds.), *Prevention of delinquent behavior* (pp. 241–274). Newbury Park, CA: Sage.

Hawkins, J. D., & Weis, J. G. (1985). The social development model: An integrated approach to delinquency prevention. *Journal of Primary Prevention, 7*, 73–97.

Haynes, N. M., Comer, J. P., & Hamilton-Lee, M. (1989). School climate enhancement through parental involvement. *Journal of School Psychology, 27*, 87–90.

Heller, L. R., & Fantuzzo, J. W. (1993). Reciprocal peer tutoring and parent partnership: does parent involvement make a difference? *School Psychology Review, 22*, 517–534.

Hoagwood, K., & Erwin, H. (1997). Effectiveness of school-based mental health services for children: A 10-year research review. *Journal of Child and Family Studies, 6*, 435–451.

Individuals with Disabilities Education Act (1990, 1997). 20 U.S.C., Chapter 33, ¶ 1400, *et seq.*

Jones, R. N., Sheridan, S. M., & Binns, W. R. (1993). School-wide social skills training: Providing preventive services to students at risk. *School Psychology Quarterly, 8*, 57–80.

Kauffman, J. M., & Burbach, H. J. (1997, December). On creating a climate of classroom civility. *Phi Delta Kappan*, 320–325.

Knoff, H. M., & Batsche, G. M. (1995). Project Achieve: Analyzing a school reform process for at-risk and underachieving students. *School Psychology Review, 24*, 579–603.

Lentz, F. E., Allen, S. J., & Ehrhardt, K. E. (1996). The conceptual elements of strong interventions in school settings. *School Psychology Quarterly, 11*, 118–136.

Maehr, M. L., & Midgley, C. (1991). Enhancing student motivation: A school-wide approach. *Educational Psychologist, 26*, 399–427.

Masten, A. S., & Coatsworth, J. D. (1998). The development of competence in favorable and unfavorable environments: Lessons from research on successful children. *The American Psychologist, 53*, 205–220.

Mayer, G. R. (1995). Preventing antisocial behavior in the schools. *Journal of Applied Behavior Analysis, 28*, 467–478.

McNamara, K. (1995). Best practices in substance abuse prevention programs. In A. Thomas & J. Grimes (Eds.), *Best Practices in School Psychology III* (pp. 369–382). Washington, DC: National Association of School Psychologists.

McNamara, K. (1996). Bonding to school and the development of responsibility. *Reclaiming Children and Youth, 4*, 33–35.

McNamara, K. (2000). Outcomes associated with service involvement among disengaged youth. *Journal of Drug Education, 30*, 229–245.

Miller, D. W. (1999, August). The black hole of education research. *The Chronicle of Higher Education*, A17–A18.

Miller, G. E., Brehm, K., & Whitehouse, S. (1998). Reconceptualizing school-based prevention for antisocial behavior within a resiliency framework. *School Psychology Review, 27*, 364–379.

Nastasi, B. (Ed.) (1998). Mental health programming in schools and communities [Special issue]. *School Psychology Review, 27*.

Nelsen, J., Lott, L., & Glenn, H. S. (1993). *Positive discipline in the classroom: How to effectively use class meetings and other positive discipline strategies*. Rocklin, CA: Prima.

Patterson, G. R., DeBaryshe, B. D., & Ramsey, E. (1989). A developmental perspective on antisocial behavior. *American Psychologist, 44*, 329–335.

Vorrath, H. H., & Brendtro, L. K. (1985). *Positive peer culture* (2nd ed.). New York: Aldine de Gruyter.

Walberg, H. J., & Greenberg, R. C. (1997). Using the learning environment inventory. *Educational Leadership, 54*, 45–47.

Walker, H. M., Colvin, G., & Ramsey, E. (1995). *Antisocial behavior in school: Strategies and best practices*. Pacific Grove, CA: Brooks/Cole.

Walker, H. M., Forness, S. R., Kauffman, J. M., Epstein, M. H., Gresham, F. M., Nelson, C. M., & Strain, P. S. (1998). Macro-social validation: Referencing outcomes in behavioral disorders to societal issues and problems. *Behavioral Disorders, 24*, 7–18.

Walker, H. M., Horner, R. H., Sugai, G., Bullis, M., Sprague, J. R., Bricker, D., & Kaufman, M. J. (1996). Integrated approaches to preventing antisocial behavior patterns among school-age children and youth. *Journal of Emotional and Behavioral Disorders, 4*, 194–209.

Walker, H. M., McConnell, S., Holmes, D., Todis, B., Walker, J., & Golden, N. (1983). *The Walker social skills curriculum: The ACCEPTS program (a curriculum for children's effective peer and teacher skills)*. Austin, TX: PRO-ED.

Wentzel, K. R. (1991). Social competence at school: Relation between social responsibility and academic achievement. *Review of Educational Research, 61*, 1–24.

Wigginton, E. (1994, January). A song of inmates. *Educational Leadership*, 64–71.

Wonderly, D. M. (1991). *Motivation, behavior, and emotional health*. Lanham, MD: University Press.

ANNOTATED BIBLIOGRAPHY

Campbell, P., & Siperstein, G. N. (1994). *Improving social competence: A resource for elementary school teachers*. Boston: Allyn & Bacon.

The authors of this text designed it as a practical resource for general education teachers, but its wealth of practical strategies makes it a valuable addition to the library of school psychologists. Chapters address classroom and student variables that are amenable to intervention, such as the use of classroom rules, management of transitions, cooperative learning methods, and social skill development. Detailed descriptions of modeling and coaching activities are provided, along with resources for teacher-administered assessments.

Elias, M. J., Zins, J. E., Weissberg. R. P., Frey, K. S., Greenberg, M. T., Haynes, N. M., Kessler, R., Schwab-Stone, M. E., & Shriver, T. P. (1997). *Promoting social and emotional learning: Guidelines for educators*. Alexandria, VA: Association for Supervision and Curriculum Development.

School psychologists interested in learning more about a comprehensive approach to SCP in schools will find this a valuable resource. The authors describe how social and emotional learning can be incorporated in the curriculum and reflected in school climate, and recommend specific strategies for accomplishing these objectives. In addition to providing a curriculum "scope and sequence" by grade levels, the text identifies key skills (self-regulation, perspective-taking, and relationship skills) that should be embedded in SCP programs, and addresses issues related to organizational change. Finally, the authors provide descriptions and contact information for 23 empirically supported SCP programs, including the Child Development Project; Promoting Alternative Thinking Strategies (PATHS); the School Development Program, Second Step Violence Prevention; and I Can Problem Solve, a curriculum designed for young children.

Walker, H. M., Colvin, G., & Ramsey, E. (1995). *Antisocial behavior in school: Strategies and best practices*. Pacific Grove, CA: Brooks-Cole.

This text goes beyond an emphasis on antisocial behavior to provide a comprehensive, in-depth description of a range of issues and activities related to school-based social competence promotion programs, including school-wide discipline plans, instructional interventions, and proactive strategies for managing disruptive and socially deficient behavior.

NETWORKS

The National Mental Health and Education Center for Children and Families has been created by the National Association of School Psychologists as "an information and action network" that provides leadership and information for schools to address problems of school failure, classroom disruptions, and youth violence. This resource can be accessed via the internet at http://www.naspweb.org/center.html.

The Collaborative for the Advancement of Social and Emotional Competence (CASEL) is a network supporting educational and mental health initiatives in social competence promotion. Its purposes are to promote standards and evaluation practices for SCP programs, to compile and disseminate information about model programs and practices, to increase opportunities for educators to receive training in SCP practices, and to educate public policymakers and government administrators about effective SCP programs. CASEL's mailing address is Department of Psychology, The University of Illinois at Chicago, 1107 W. Harrison St., Chicago, IL 60607-7037. It also can be accessed via the internet at http://www.cfapress.org.casel/casel.html

59 Best Practices in Promoting a Positive School Climate

Camilla A. Lehr
Sandra L. Christenson
University of Minnesota

OVERVIEW

"A school's climate is its atmosphere for learning. It includes the feelings people have about the school and whether it is a place where learning can occur. A positive climate makes a school a place where both staff and students want to spend a substantial portion of their time; it is a good place to be" (Howard, Howell, & Brainard, 1987, p. 5).

"School climate is a relatively enduring quality of the entire school that is experienced by members, describes their collective perceptions of routine behavior, and affects their attitudes and behavior in the school" (Hoy & Miskel as cited in Hoy & Feldman, 1999, p.85).

"In general, school climate refers to the quality and consistency of interpersonal interactions within the school community that influence children's cognitive, social, and psychological development. These interactions include those among staff, between staff and students, among students, and between home and school" (Haynes, Emmons, & Ben-Avie, 1997, p. 322).

Definitions of school climate are many and varied. Researchers who have studied school climate have defined it in different ways. Educators who work to improve school climate describe it in a variety of ways, and when asked about school climate, students and parents tend to focus on different aspects. Nevertheless, students, parents, educators, and researchers sense a school's climate upon entering the building. During the initial contact with a school, first impressions occur, and one comes away with a snapshot of a school and its climate. Repeated encounters with the school and its inhabitants, extended associations with the school, or more active involvement in the day-to-day operations of the school result in the creation of a sharper image of the school's climate. A clear sense of whether the school provides a warm, friendly, and safe learning environment is developed. Questions about whether there is order and discipline, as well as high expectations for learning can be answered. Quality of leadership, degree of collaborative decision making, and respectful interpersonal relations (between students, staff, and parents) can be ascertained. There is strong evidence indicating school climate is indeed a tangible quality with implications for student learning and development.

A review of the literature suggests a variety of components comprise the construct of school climate. Although there is significant overlap across the components, each is also quite distinct. Anderson (1982) conducted a comprehensive review of research studies in the area of school climate and provided a summary of the variables that appeared to be tied to climate and/or positive student outcomes. Her categories and associated variables are listed below:

1. Ecology variables: Physical/material variables in the school that are external to participants, such as building characteristics (e.g., cleanliness, lighting, equipment), school size, and classroom size.

2. Milieu variables: Variables that represent characteristics of individuals in the school, such as teacher characteristics (number of years teaching), satisfaction, teacher morale, student body characteristics (demographic information), and student morale.

3. Social system variables: Variables that concern patterns or rules (formal and informal) of operating and interacting in the school, such as administrative organization, instructional programming, ability grouping, administrator-teacher rapport, teacher shared decision making, communication, teacher-student relationships, student shared decision making, opportunity for student participation, teacher-teacher relationships, and community school relationships.

4. Culture variables: Variables that reflect norms, belief systems, and values of various groups within the school such as teacher commitment, peer norms, cooperative emphasis, expectations, degree of consistency, consensus, and clear goals.

More recently, a review of the literature conducted by staff at the Yale Child Study Center yielded a comprehensive list of 14 components that characterized school climate (Haynes et al., 1997). The important ingredients of a healthy supportive school climate are listed in Table 1.

Most lists of school climate components have significant overlap, and components generally apply to all students. A review of 33 empirical studies of effective schooling for English Language Learners found that schools characterized by a positive school climate emphasized high expectations for students' academic achievement, along with promoting student/family involvement in the operation and activities of the school and recognizing/valuing the linguistic and cultural background of the students and their families (August & Hakuta, 1997).

Table 1. Ingredients of a healthy supportive school climate

Component	*Definition*
• Achievement motivation	The extent to which students at the school believe they can learn and are willing to learn
• Collaborative decision making	The involvement of parents, students, and staff in the decisions affecting the school
• Equity and fairness	The equal treatment of students regardless of ethnicity and gender
• General school climate	The quality of interactions, feelings of trust, and respect that exist within the school community
• Order and discipline	Appropriateness of student behavior in the school setting
• Parent involvement	Frequency of parent participation in school activities
• School-community relations	The support and involvement of the community in the life of the school
• Staff dedication to student learning	The effort of teachers to get students to learn
• Staff expectations	The expectations of staff members that students will do well academically and will lead a successful life
• Leadership	The principal's role in guiding the direction of the school and in creating a positive climate
• School building	The appearance of the school building
• Sharing of resources	Equal student opportunity to participate in school activities, materials, and equipment
• Caring and sensitivity	The extent to which the principal shows consideration for the students, parents, and school staff and cares about their needs
• Student interpersonal relations	The level of caring, respect, and trust that exists among students in the school
• Student-teacher relations	The level of caring, respect, and trust that exists between students and teachers in the school.

Source: Haynes, Emmons, & Ben-Avie. (1997).

What are the Historical Roots of the Study of School Climate?

In her review of the history of school climate research, Anderson (1982) reported that school climate research (theory, instrumentation, and methodology) has been strongly influenced by earlier work on organizational climate in both business and university settings. In the 1950s business researchers were studying situational characteristics impacting individual behavior within organizations. Instruments were developed to assess the organizational environment, and findings were used to help design programs and strategies to improve morale, productivity, and retain employees. Instruments designed to systematically measure college environments assessed various student and school characteristics as well as student perceptions of environmental pressures exerted by a school (academic press) in relation to student performance.

Another chapter in the history of school climate began in the 1960s with an increased emphasis on the study and measurement of classroom climate. Defining, measuring, and promoting a positive climate in classrooms focused more on examining characteristics such as teacher-student relationships in the classroom, the extent to which classrooms could be characterized as individualized to meet student needs, opportunities for student participation, and degree of shared control. In general, the measurement of classroom climate involved soliciting feedback from students about the classroom environment, instructional practices, and the teacher's role. Several instruments have been developed to measure perceptions of classroom climate. On the basis of the information gathered, teachers can reflect on and modify their teaching practices and instruction. For more information the reader is referred to the work of Fraser (1986) and Burden and Fraser (1993). Whereas *classroom* climate is limited to unique features of the climate within a classroom, *school* climate encompasses the psychosocial aspects of the whole school.

Why Should School Psychologists Be Concerned With School Climate?

A Positive School Climate is an Integral Component of an Effective School

School climate is consistently identified as a variable that is a characteristic of effective schools and one that is positively associated with academic effectiveness (Stevens & Sanchez, 1999). For many years, research has been conducted identifying factors that contribute to effective schools. In an extensive review of the research, eight factors characterizing effective schools were identified including leadership, school climate, teacher/student relations, curriculum instruction, resources and finance, physical environment, evaluation, and parent/community involvement (Borger, 1985). Research conducted by Teddlie and Stringfield (1993) across nearly 10 years confirmed several original findings of the effective schools literature including the importance of principal leadership and correlates of effectiveness including clear academic mission and focus, orderly environment, high academic engaged time-on-task, and frequent monitoring of student progress. Purkey & Smith (1983) argued that "an academically effective school is distinguished by its culture: a structure, process and climate of values and norms that channel staff and students in the direction of successful teaching and learning" (p. 68). Psychologists who work in the schools are charged to promote characteristics that comprise effective schools. The mission of the National Association of School Psychologists is "to promote educationally and psychologically healthy environments for all children and youth...." School psychologists can play an active role in creating a positive school climate, one indicator of an effective school.

The Nature of the School Environment Has Been Shown to Have a Strong Influence On the Way Students Develop and Learn

Many studies have documented the association of school climate with improved student outcomes. For example, it is more likely that students will have higher achievement, more positive self concepts, improved behavior, and higher aspirations when the climate of the school is positive (Hoy & Hannum, 1997; Kuperminc, Leadbeater, Emmons, & Blatt, 1997; Rumberger, 1995). In some cases, the link between school climate and student outcomes is relatively direct. In other cases, school climate may have a more indirect effect. For example, a favorable climate may promote a positive sense of belonging, participation in school tasks and activities, and attendance. Current research suggests these factors are more directly linked to school dropout than perceptions of school climate (Finn, 1993; Goodenow, 1993).

School Climate is an Alterable Variable That Can Be Impacted to Affect Various Outcomes

The opportunity to promote a positive school climate is especially encouraging in light of the many unalterable status variables associated with risk of school failure that educators are faced with on a daily basis. Although school psychologists cannot change a student's socioeconomic standing, genetic predisposition to mental illness, or ability level, we can impact the learning environment in ways that can improve student chances for a successful school experience. Furthermore, instruments are available to assess student, staff, parent, and community perceptions of school climate to help stakeholders determine areas of strength and need. From this feedback, responsive interventions can be shaped, developed, and implemented to affect real change.

Improving School Climate is a Preventative Approach Rather Than Reactive or Remedial

The power of an existing positive school climate may lie in the degree to which it is an effective preventive approach. It is a prerequisite condition that facilitates a successful work or learning experience for individuals in the school setting. When high expectations are in place, order and discipline are clear, rules are consistent and fair, caring and sensitivity characterize relationships between staff and students, and reciprocal exchanges of communication with parents occur, the probability that student achievement will improve and disruptive behavior will decline increases. In schools with positive school climate, suspension rates are lower, attendance rates are higher, and students and parents have higher levels of satisfaction (Griffith, 1997; Haynes, Emmons, Ben-Avie, & Comer, 1996).

School Psychologists Are Challenged to be Active in Promoting Systems Change

Blueprint II (Ysseldyke et al.,1997) suggests that school psychologists should be leaders "in developing schools as safe, caring, and inviting places where there is a sense of community." And one of the 10 domains outlined for training and practice of school psychologists is "School Structure, Organization, and Climate." This emphasis on attending to the social context surrounding students is receiving increasing emphasis. For example, Doll (1999) calls for sweeping changes in the purpose, design, and delivery of school mental health services to children, their families, and the school that they attend. Doll and Lyon (as cited in Doll, 1999, p. 1) concluded "resilience to adversity depends as much on the characteristics of the important contexts in which children develop (e.g. family, school, community) as on the characteristics of the children, themselves." School psychologists are challenged to become active change agents initiating, supporting, and evaluating efforts to improve school climate.

BASIC CONSIDERATIONS

Theoretical Models Explaining School Climate

Over the years, several models of school climate have emerged to explain this multidimensional construct. A brief summary of two models helps to provide a better understanding of school climate and a foundation from which to promote positive school environments.

Stockard & Mayberry (1992) proposed a theoretical framework to examine the social and psychological characteristics of schools. The authors argued that the social psychological nature of schools comprising a school's climate can be organized into two broad areas: social order and social action. Social order consists of the norms and values, environmental climate, and organizational structure of the school. Social action includes the day-to-day interactions among members and includes the quality of communication and the planning and implementation of activities within the school. Each of these dimensions has an expressive and an instrumental component. Instrumental actions clarify and maintain goals and provide the necessary material support to accomplish the objectives of the organization (i.e., high academic achievement). Expressive actions promote positive feelings, motivation, and cohesion among school members. When cross-referenced, four components result. These are illustrated in Figure 1.

This model links affective, cultural aspects of school climate with more structural components of the organization including task accomplishment and achievement. Use of the model can guide the development of questions to self-evaluate the relative

Figure 1. A model of school climate in elementary schools

	Social order (School Structure)	Social action (Interactions/Relationships)
Instrumental support (Focus on achievement/task accomplishment)	Social order instrumental e.g., My school is neat and clean; there is enough space.	Social action instrumental e.g., My teachers help me think about new ways to do things; teachers let me know how I am doing.
Expressive support (Focus on promoting positive feelings)	Social order expressive e.g., My principal treats students fairly; there is an adult I can go to when I have problems with my friends.	Social action expressive e.g., I like my class; my classmates are friendly.

Source: Stockard & Mayberry (1992).

emphasis and effects of the structures, relationships, and supports that are in place. For example, do the interactions between staff, students, and parents support a high level of academic performance? Does the school structure promote positive feelings for students and staff? Does interaction between school members promote positive feelings? Is there a balance between the four components or is one emphasized more than the others?

Hoy, Tartar, and Kottkamp (1991) proposed another model, summarized in Table 2, characterizing a school's climate in terms of its health. They conceptualized healthy schools as consisting of three levels (technical, managerial, and institutional) working in harmony to address both instrumental and expressive needs and to achieve the mission or goals of the school. The technical level (morale, cohesiveness, and academic emphasis) is concerned with the teaching-learning process; the managerial level (principal influence, consideration, initiating structure and resource allocation) encompasses the internal administration of the school; and the institutional level (integrity) connects the school with its surrounding environment. When these levels are working harmoniously, the authors speculate that the instrumental goals (reaching high levels of achievement, intellectual growth) as well as expressive goals (emotional growth, high levels of trust and motivation) will be met.

From this list of components, it becomes clear that school climate is best understood as a multidimensional construct. Furthermore, all parts are necessary in order for a profile of a healthy school to be created.

Research on School Climate and Associated Outcomes

Studies have found school climate to be linked with a variety of outcomes, including student achievement, absenteeism, self-concept, behavior, and rate of suspension (Anderson, 1982; Haynes et al., 1997). In reviewing research on school climate, the reader is cautioned to be aware of the variety of attributes used to represent the construct of school climate. These attributes range from structural characteristics, such as school size, to data reflecting conditions of the school, such as the number of disciplinary problems, to student, teacher, or parent perceptions of the degree to which interactions are respectful. Despite the variety of ways that school climate is operationalized in the research, evidence has accumulated to suggest that the nature of the environment does indeed play an important role in student outcomes.

Table 2. Dimensions of organizational health

Technical level

- *Morale* is a collective sense of friendliness, openness, enthusiasm, and trust among faculty members. Teachers like each other, like their jobs, and help each other. They are proud of their school and feel a sense of accomplishment in their jobs.
- *Cohesiveness* is the extent to which the teachers and administrators form a coherent and integrated group. They identify with each other and the school.
- *Academic emphasis* is the extent to which the school is driven by a quest for academic excellence: High but achievable academic goals are set for students, the learning environment is orderly and serious, teachers believe in their students' ability to achieve, and students work hard and respect those who do well academically.

Managerial level

- *Principal influence* is the principal's ability to influence the actions of superiors.
- *Consideration* is principal behavior that is friendly, supportive, open, and collegial.
- *Initiating structure* is principal behavior that is both task and achievement oriented. Work expectations and standards of performance are clearly articulated by the principal.
- *Resource allocation* refers to a school where adequate classroom supplies and instructional materials are allocated to teachers and extra materials are readily supplied if requested.

Institutional level

- *Institutional integrity* is the school's ability to cope with its environment in a way that maintains the educational integrity of its programs.

Source: Hoy, Tartar, & Kottkamp (1991).

In a classic study, Brookover et al. (1978) found that school climate (defined primarily as academic norms and expectations of the school) contributed to the prediction of mean school achievement over and above achievement predicted by socioeconomic status and racial composition. When school climate was entered prior to SES and racial composition in multiple regression analysis, more than 72% of the variance in average school achievement was explained in a statewide random sample of 68 schools. Schools with high proportions of students from low socioeconomic backgrounds and high levels of academic achievement were characterized as having strong positive climates that fostered student self-efficacy, learning, and achievement. Brookover et al. (1978) concluded "that school composition does not necessarily determine school climate and therefore changes in school composition (changes in SES or race) in the absence of changes in climate do not guarantee changes in school level achievement" (p. 316). In their measurement of dimensions of organizational health in middle schools and academic achievement, Hoy and Hannum (1997) found school climate (as indicated by a general health index) was positively associated with student achievement in math ($r = .61$, $p < .01$), reading ($r = .58$, $p < .01$), and writing ($r = .55$, $p < .01$).

Several studies have examined the relationship between characteristics associated with school climate and truancy or dropout rates. Characteristics associated with dropout include weak adult authority, a climate of low expectations, large school size, and an absence of caring adult relationships (Wehlage & Rutter, 1986). Bryk and Thum (1989) found that 67% of the school level variance in rates of absenteeism could be explained by a variety of school level factors. Absenteeism was lower in schools with strong academic press, high student participation in academic pursuits, an orderly environment, few disciplinary problems, less internal differentiation between curriculum, and where perceived quality of teaching was high. Smaller school size contributed to engaging students at-risk, and student attendance was better in schools where adult authority and discipline policies were perceived to be fair and effective (Rumberger, 1995). By using data from the National Education Longitudinal Survey, statistical analyses revealed an increase of one standard deviation in the proportion of students who reported a fair discipline policy reduced the mean odds of dropping out by 21% ($p < .01$). Findings from these studies support the idea that internal features of schools can affect the outcomes of absenteeism and dropout for all students, and especially youth at-risk of school failure.

School climate has been associated with student behaviors and attitudes. Students' perceptions of a positive school climate are moderately correlated with a more positive attitude toward school as defined by motivation for schooling, academic self-concept, sense of control over performance, and sense of instructional mastery (Lehr & Lange, 1999). Two aspects of school climate, commitment to school, and positive feedback from teachers have been found to predict growth in students' global and academic self-esteem (Hoge, Smit, & Hanson, 1990). Boys attending middle schools who have a more positive perception of school climate tend to have fewer externalizing behaviors (e.g., aggression, delinquent behavior). Kuperminc, Leadbeater, Emmons, and Blatt (1997) found that positive perceptions of school climate were related to lower levels of externalizing problems ($r = -.47$, $p < .05$). Although this study does not allow conclusions about the direction of effects, findings suggest student perceptions of middle school climate may impact boys' behavioral and emotional adjustment.

Also, positive school climate has been associated with higher levels of parent and student satisfaction. In a study of 122 elementary schools, Griffith (1997) found parental satisfaction was best predicted by parental perceptions of a positive school climate ($p < .001$), followed by the school's empowering parents ($p < .001$) and informing parents of their child's educational progress ($p < .001$). Student satisfaction also showed a positive correlation with a more favorable perception of school climate ($r = .22$, $p < .05$). School staff who perceives a positive school climate also tended to have higher levels of job satisfaction and showed greater self-efficacy (Hoy & Woolfolk, 1993).

Findings from research examining school climate are particularly encouraging for practitioners because educators *can* effect positive change in the culture of the school if they have informed feedback from students, parents, and staff about the nature of relationships and conditions in the school. Many studies have linked a positive school climate with important student outcomes. School psychologists can share research associated with school climate and highlight its link with important student outcomes. By assessing a school's climate, educators can make informed decisions about what is working well and where change is needed.

BEST PRACTICES

Measuring School Climate

The assessment of school climate is critical to the improvement of the school learning environment. To develop a responsive action plan individualized to the needs of the school, the climate of the school must be clearly described prior to intervention. Theoretically, instruments designed to assess school climate should provide a picture of the relative health or personality of the school. This information can be gathered from multiple people (students, teachers, support staff, administrators, parents, and community members) and from perceptions of activity throughout the school. It is recommended that climate instruments are best used as "benchmarks for growth rather than hammers for change" (Freiberg, 1999, p. 5). The information that is gathered enables stakeholders within the school to highlight relative areas of strength and areas needing improvement. The information can be especially valuable for school staff to use as a means of self-reflection and self-improvement.

There are two basic kinds of climate measures: indirect and direct. Indirect measures are those where data collection does not require direct interactions with individuals. Examples include existing data sources such as student attendance, frequency of discipline referrals, suspensions, teacher rates of turnover, or student mobility rates. Indirect measures may also document physical aspects of the building, including cleanliness, maintenance, lighting, or display of student artwork or academic work. In contrast, direct measures involve gathering information from others. These kinds of measures most often include the use of climate surveys, questionnaires, interviews, or focus groups.

Direct measures of school climate are based on perceptions of others within the school setting or in the surrounding community. School climate is generally thought to be a shared perception of between groups. For example, teachers within the same school probably have a similar view of the school in terms of the general level of discipline, respect for students, level of parent involvement, or quality of leadership. Yet, it is possible that different groups within the school may have differing perceptions of the school climate. For example, we know that dropouts have a less favorable view of school climate as compared to those who persist, and students at risk attending high schools have less favorable views of school climate as compared to students not at risk (Lehr & Lange, 1999). Some may argue that these differences reflect differences between the individuals rather than the climate of the school. However, individuals involved in efforts to improve a school's climate must be cognizant of working to ensure the school is a positive place to be for *all* students.

Currently, a variety of tools designed to measure school climate are in existence. Instruments range from those that are published and have information about technical characteristics to those that have been developed informally to measure one aspect of school climate. In some cases it may make sense to design and implement an instrument based on the climate issues specific to the needs of a particular school. While locally developed instruments lack normative comparisons, and information on reliability and validity, they may provide more individualized feedback on climate factors relative to a school or district. Development of instruments to assess school climate should, nevertheless, be firmly based on theoretical constructs gathered from the relevant literature.

For the purpose of this chapter, five instruments have been selected for further description and explanation. The following criteria were considered in their selection: grounded in a theoretical framework, stated purpose for which instrument was designed, evidence of technical characteristics (reliability and validity), previous use in research and practice, number of items, ease of administration, comparable forms for various age groups or stakeholder groups, sample content, and date of publication. Each instrument has unique features and should be selected for use on the basis of user needs. In addition, these tools are easily accessible, user friendly, and are not expensive to administer. School psychologists are encouraged to share information about these instruments with colleagues, parents, or other educators who are interested in pursuing measurement of school climate using standardized measures. Information about how to obtain copies of these instruments is included at the end of this chapter.

1. Comprehensive Assessment of School Environments (CASE) (National Association of Secondary School Principals, 1986).
   - *Purpose.* Designed to measure the shared perceptions about the characteristics of an organization (school climate). The climate survey can be administered alone or with an accompanying set of satisfaction surveys to be completed by students (grade 6–12), teachers, and parents.
   - *Dimensions.* Teacher student relationships, security and maintenance, administration, student academic orientation, student behavioral values, guidance, student-peer relationships, parent and community-school relationships, instructional management, student activities.
   - *Number of Items.* 55.
   - *Levels/Age Groups.* For use with students in grades 6–12, teachers, parents, or members of the community.
   - *Technical Adequacy.* A technical manual is available containing information on validity and reliability. Dimensions were constructed after extensive exploratory and confirmatory factor analysis was conducted. Content validity is supported through the use of an expert panel in the selection and development of the items. The average internal consistency measure for scales on the Climate Survey is .81 (range of .67 to .92).
   - *Norm Group.* Norms were established based on nearly 7,900 students, 1,800 teachers, and 3,700 parents in 35 schools across the nation.

2. Effective School Battery (ESB) (Gottfredson, 1991).
   - *Purpose.* Designed to assess perceptions of students and teachers about school climate. The instrument also includes scales and items assessing characteristics of the students who attend and teachers who work in the school.

- *Dimensions.* Safety; respect for students; planning and action; fairness of rules; clarity of rules; and student influence (student version); safety, morale, planning, and action; smooth administration; resources; race relations; parent/community involvement; student influence; avoidance of grades as sanctions (teacher version).
- *Number of Items.* 31 items (student); 61 items (teacher).
- *Levels/Age Groups.* For students in grades 7–12, and secondary level teachers.
- *Technical Adequacy.* A technical manual is available containing information about reliability and validity. Estimates of internal consistency using Cronbach's alpha for the individual scales range from .70 to .90. One-year stability coefficients for the individual scales range from .62 to .84. Items and scales were developed through extensive research in the area of school climate and effective schools. In addition, correlations among the psychosocial climate scales suggest further evidence of the instrument's validity.
- *Norm Group.* Norms have been established and profiles of schools can be interpreted by examining percentile ranks. The ESB has been used with hundreds of schools. However, data about the norm sample were not included in the technical manual.

3. Organizational Health Inventory (OHI) (Hoy & Feldman, 1999).
   - *Purpose.* Designed to measure aspects of school climate via ratings of the extent to which specific behavior patterns occur in the school. The scores that are generated provide a health profile of the school.
   - *Dimensions.* Institutional integrity, initiating structure, consideration, principal influence, resource support, morale, academic emphasis, overall health index.
   - *Number of Items.* 44.
   - *Levels/Age Groups.* For use with middle school and secondary grade level teachers.
   - *Technical Adequacy.* Reliability scores (alpha coefficient) for each subtest range from .87 to .95. Construct validity for each of the scales is supported through factor analysis. In addition, each of the dimensions had high factor loadings on the general factor of school health.
   - *Norm Group.* Authors note norms were developed in an earlier study of a large, diverse sample of high schools from New Jersey.

4. School Climate Survey (Haynes et al., 1996).
   - *Purpose.* Designed to assess dimensions of school climate.
   - *Dimensions.* Fairness, order and discipline, parent involvement, sharing of resources, student interpersonal relations, student teacher relations, achievement motivation, school building, general school climate (students), achievement motivation, collaborative decision making, equity and fairness, general school climate, order and discipline, family involvement, school-community relations, staff dedication to student learning, staff expectations, leadership, school building (staff) academic focus, achievement motivation, caring and sensitivity, collaborative decision making, parent involvement, school-community relations, school building, general School climate (parents).
   - *Number of Items.* 53 items (elementary and middle school student survey); 55 items (high school student survey); 79 items (school staff survey); 55 items (parent survey).
   - *Levels/Age Groups.* Four versions of the School Climate Survey are available for use with elementary and middle school students, high school students, school staff, and parents.
   - *Technical Adequacy.* Content validity was established via the use of an expert panel. Factor analysis was used to group items measuring the same constructs. Internal consistency reliability estimates are presented for each dimension by survey. These range from .70 to .97 on all scales except parent involvement (elementary/middle school version), which is .59, and achievement motivation involvement (elementary/middle school version), which is .64.
   - *Norm Group.* National norms are available based on schools randomly selected from a national database of schools. Samples included about 6,500 elementary, 11,800 middle, and 7,200 high school students as well as 1,900 school staff and 1,800 parents.

5. School Level Environment Questionnaire (SLEQ) (Fischer & Fraser, 1991).
   - *Purpose.* Designed to assess teachers' perceptions of psychosocial dimensions of the environment of the school. In addition to a form that measures perceptions of actual or experienced learning environments, the SLEQ has another form to measure ideal or preferred perceptions of the learning environment.
   - *Dimensions.* Student support, affiliation, professional interest, staff freedom, participatory decision making, innovation, resource adequacy, work pressure.
   - *Number of Items.* 56 (seven items per subscale).
   - *Levels/Age Groups.* For use with elementary and secondary grade level teachers.
   - *Technical Adequacy.* Not available.
   - *Norm Group.* Not available.

Programs and Strategies Designed to Promote Positive School Climate

Many programs and strategies designed to foster positive school climates exist in the literature, and undoubtedly there are other important efforts that are occurring across our nation that are not documented. For this chapter, several programs and strategies illustrating the varied forms that climate improvement projects can take are described. These projects vary according to the size of the effort (e.g., comprehensive, single strategy), the targeted components for improvement, and who is primarily responsible for initiating the effort. Although these examples do not speak specifically to the role of school psychologists, it is easy to see how these programs and strategies could have been carried out with a school psychologist as a key participant in the process. All examples use a tool to measure school climate (or an aspect of it) prior to intervening, and an evaluation of the process or final results of the climate improvement effort.

Large-Scale Programs Within the Context of School Reform

The improvement of school climate often takes place as part of a large-scale reform effort. Perhaps the most comprehensive and widely disseminated example of a program that seeks to improve student outcomes largely through initial changes in school climate is The Yale Child Study Center School Development Program (SDP) (Comer, Haynes, Joyner, & Ben-Avie, 1996). The program is now being implemented in over 700 schools nationally and internationally and involves parents, teachers, and students in the management and coordination of all school activities. Creating a positive school climate that nurtures and sustains good psychological development and high levels of academic performance is a key feature of the model.

SDP consists of nine program elements that provide specific ways for adults to manage their relationships and plan activities to improve the climate and academic focus of their school. The nine elements include three teams, three guiding principals, and three operations. The teams include the

1. School Planning and Management Team (SPMT): Responsible for planning, coordinating, and managing the school program with input from the other two teams.

2. Student and Staff Support Team (SSST): Responsible for identifying and addressing school-level and individual student and staff concerns that affect school climate, student adjustment, and performance. This team includes individuals with expertise in child development and mental health (e.g., school psychologists, counselors, speech therapists, special education teachers, nurses) who help to identify or design programs and activities to address children's growth and development.

3. Parent Team (PT): Responsible for supporting the general mission and work of the school through parent involvement in all aspects of school life.

The three principles that guide the functioning of these teams include (a) a *no-fault* approach that requires teams to adopt a problem-solving approach to address issues, (b) a process of *consensus* that allows decisions to be made after ideas and perspectives are shared in an atmosphere of trust and mutual respect, and (c) an emphasis on *collaboration* that includes teamwork, collegiality, and shared responsibility among all team members. The SPMT is primarily responsible for the three operations including (a) the goals and activities to promote student growth for the year (Comprehensive School Plan),

(b) staff development and training, and (c) ongoing assessment and modification to document progress, identify necessary modifications, and measure outcomes.

The creation of a positive school climate is central to the work of the three teams. Effective integration and coordination of the key elements occur within the context of a positive school climate. Haynes (1998) describes the role of school climate in schools that are using the School Development Program.

> The effects of the nine SDP program elements on student performance outcomes are mediated by several essential climate dimensions, including sensitivity and caring, respect and trust, high expectations, high achievement motivation, effective leadership, strong order and discipline, a collaborative spirit, helpful and supportive teacher-student relationships, and positive student interpersonal relationships. If the SDP is implemented well, these dimensions permeate the life of the school, resulting in desirable student outcomes when coupled with effective teaching and learning strategies. An improved climate provides the context in which effective teaching and learning can take root and bear fruit.
>
> In well-functioning SDP school, there is an observable positive quality of life for students, staff, and parents. Mutual trust and positive regard characterize social interactions and students derive a sense of academic self-efficacy. In many SDP schools there is a progression of positive changes in climate, followed by positive changes in students' attitudes and behavior, followed by achievement growth (p. 7).

Goals for improving school climate are based on information gathered from climate scales developed by the Yale Child Study Center (see *School Climate Survey* instrument description). Initial assessments completed by students, staff, and parents provide baseline data that guide the design of strategies to address specific needs. Follow-up assessments help to determine whether change has occurred or whether further intervention is required.

A case study of an elementary school shows how the SDP is implemented and how school climate can be impacted (for a more detailed description see Emmons, Efimba, & Hagopian, 1998). In 1991, Norman S. Weir was described as one of the lowest achieving schools in New Jersey, characterized by student apathy and disinterest in academics, frequent fights, low staff morale, and a building that was in disrepair. The school served about 260 students in grades K–8, with a student body that was 40% African American, 40% Hispanic, 18% other nationalities, and 2% Caucasian. About 83% of the students received a free or reduced lunch over the past 4 years, and about 30% of the students received special education.

Improving the school climate was one of three main goals identified by school staff. Seven committees were formed to address designated areas related to the goals, and representatives from each committee brought issues and concerns to the SPMT through a representative committee member. One committee was designed specifically to address school climate issues. This committee (as well as each of the other committees) was responsible for developing and submitting a list of goals and objectives to improve school climate, activities to implement the objectives, and a way of evaluating when those objectives were met. Several strategies were implemented to improve the school climate. These strategies were implemented in conjunction with other activities generated by other committees to achieve the goals of improving student achievement and increasing parent involvement. Some of these strategies specific to school climate were

1. To improve caring and sensitivity as well as student teacher relations, staff viewed students as their own children and talked with them in ways that encouraged students to share their attitudes and personal issues.

2. To build student teacher relations (and promote achievement and build on student strengths), a looping strategy was incorporated so that students had the same reading teacher, math teacher, and language teacher for three years.

3. To promote achievement motivation and a strong academic press, teachers were asked to identify one or two students per class who would benefit from participating in an after-school phonics program.

4. To promote staff dedication to student learning, poverty, home environment, parent neglect, or urban location of the school were not allowed to be used as excuses for low student expectations or a low-level curriculum.

5. To improve staff expectations and sense of self-efficacy, consistent use of a no-fault approach that converts negative blaming energy to positive, problem-solving strategies was implemented.

6. To increase collaborative decision making and collegiality and feelings of inclusion and ownership, participation of each staff member on at least one committee was required.

7. To improve school building conditions, students took initiative to form a student council, and purchased new gym equipment as one of its first projects.

Efforts to make abstract ideas explicit by stating clear goals with shared contributions and shared accountability reflects and creates a positive school climate. After 5 years of implementation, the school was described as one of the highest achieving schools in the district. It became bright, clean, and well maintained. Staff members became enthusiastic about their work, and collaborated with each other in order to promote the healthy development and academic achievement of their students. Staff was also willing to engage parents as partners in the education process. Students became excited to learn, proud of their work, and volunteered to take part in activities that promoted school improvement. The authors caution that the process of school improvement and promoting positive school climate does not end once promising results have occurred. As new staff members are employed, they must receive training and become participants in the ongoing efforts. The involvement of new parents must be encouraged and nurtured. In addition, veteran staff and parents must be continually stimulated to maintain the focus on sustaining healthy psychological development and high levels of academic performance for all students. This example points to the challenge of implementing a comprehensive program, and school psychologists who are involved in these kinds of efforts must recognize the need for persistence over time in order to observe measurable impact.

Programs Addressing School Climate on a Smaller Scale

The improvement of school climate does not necessarily have to occur in the context of large-scale school reform. An example of promoting positive school climate on a smaller scale has been described by Andringa and Fustin (1991). Implemented in a suburban school serving students in grades K–8, this school climate project was lead by a principal and university researcher but involved the active participation of the entire faculty. A committee was formed consisting of four teachers (who had volunteered to be on the committee) and the principal. This committee served to evaluate, modify, and personalize the model of change that was proposed. In addition, the four teacher volunteers became group facilitators for the remaining 40 teachers in the school.

To begin the process of improving the school climate, each teacher was asked to identify and bring three concerns about the school's climate to the next meeting. Concerns focused on the quality of interaction between school, parents, and community; the quality of interaction between teachers and the administration; and the quality of interaction between teachers and students. The authors described a deliberate process of developing their own measurement instrument rather than using an existing instrument to assess actual concerns of the teachers. Drawing on previous tools developed to measure the discrepancy between what is perceived as the current situation (what is) and what is desired (what should be), the committee developed a 43–item instrument to assess indicators of school climate across the three major areas of concern. After staff completed the measures, four indicators showing the largest mean discrepancies were targeted for change.

According to Andringa and Fustin, an important key to the success of this climate improvement effort was the allocation of eight half days of release time over a 2–year period for collaborative planning (granted by the school board). In addition, a consensus decision-making process was used to ensure the open exchange of ideas, allowing each individual's concerns to be heard, understood, and considered before agreement was reached. Efforts initially focused on developing the collaborative problem-solving teams, and each group selected a recorder and process monitor (separate from the group facilitator). The principal and the university consultant circulated among the groups to further monitor the group process. Prior to each of the half-day meetings, the consultant met with the main committee to present and explain the agenda for the half-day meeting, as well as explain, model, and role play the process. The first three meetings included the entire faculty. Tasks consisted of defining what should be included as part of the indicators; clarification and categorization of ideas into objectives; and ranking of objectives in order of importance. Each group was then charged with developing implementation plans for each of the four identified indicators of school climate. Implementation plans included breaking the activity into steps, identifying who was responsible for the plan, and the anticipated time line for completion.

The four indicators by group are listed below with an activity designed and implemented by each group:

1. Group A Indicator: The community supports the school's teaching program.
   - *Activity*. To recognize and honor students who have achieved academic excellence, the school established criteria for identifying a student of the week, month, and year in each class. Class, school, and public recognition were provided via the newsletter, signs in school, and photographs in a display case. A recognition dinner with parents was held in May for those students with three or more grading periods on the honor roll.

2. Group B Indicator: Teachers feel that they have important input into school decisions.
   - *Activity*. To improve the transition for new teachers, veteran teachers paired themselves with new teachers. In addition, a 1-day in-service was provided and a handbook with all policies and procedures was developed and disseminated.

3. Group C Indicator: Students believe the school program is meaningful and relevant to their present and future needs.
   - *Activity*. To increase student awareness of the importance of their school work, teachers displayed students' work throughout the school, as well as in each classroom. Class activities were described in the newsletter. Positive reinforcement was provided by teachers for efforts to improve and succeed.

4. Group D Indicator: The school supports parent growth through the provision of opportunities to be involved in learning activities.
   - *Activity*. To increase parent and community awareness of school activities, students published a school newsletter and mailed one to every resident of the surrounding community (four times annually).

All activities were carried out over a 2–year period. The teachers agreed that change had occurred in addition to the stated objectives. Specifically, there was evidence of increased communication among faculty, better services for students, intercollegial interaction, and more immediate problem solving. An evaluation assessing teachers' reactions to the change process at the end of the second year revealed a clear understanding of the process and the belief that change needs were collaboratively identified. Loss of instructional time due to half–time release days, nonpayment for planning time beyond the school day, and the perception that not all faculty followed through on implementations were seen as weaknesses by the staff. Despite areas of weakness, faculty agreed to continue to determine needs and monitor implementation of objectives on an ongoing basis.

Strategies Addressing Elements of School Climate

Oftentimes, rather than implementing a plan to address multiple aspects of school climate, one component of school climate is addressed. For example, educators may choose to focus on particular elements of climate such as the school's physical environment, interpersonal relationships, safety issues, or fostering greater parental or community involvement through the creation of welcoming environments. Cooperative learning strategies, programs addressing violence or bullying, in-house suspension programs that focus on incorporating a problem–solving approach, cross-grade level partnerships for children, weekly school meetings, or creating welcoming environments by decorating the school building with student artwork are examples of strategies used to promote positive school climates and learning environments. Freiberg (1998) noted that surveys of students and observations at school can help educators to identify small changes leading to significant improvements. He shared three examples of ways varying aspects of school climate can be measured and addressed.

One example describes a series of questions asking fifth and sixth graders and middle school students to identify their greatest concerns in moving from their current school to the next level. Survey results indicated top ranked concerns for students entering middle school were being sent to the principal, failure, drugs, taking tests, and giving a presentation in front of others. For students entering high school, top-ranked concerns were failure, keeping up with assignments, taking tests, and giving a presentation in front of others. Survey results were used during summer staff development workshops, where teachers and administrators developed action plans based on the information. Several strategies were developed to address student concerns. For example, introductions on the first day occurred in small groups rather than in front of the entire class, teachers helped students with study and test-taking skills, and students were given assignment/project planner books to support time-management skills. It is important to recognize feedback from students can be extremely valuable, and soliciting input helps students realize they have an opportunity to participate in shaping their educational experience.

A second example of measuring school climate is to interview students upon beginning or exiting (graduating from) a school. Questions for students graduating included (a) What do you like about your school? (b) What was your most memorable experience in high school? (c) What area would you like to have improved in your school? (d) What is one message you would like to give your teachers? Many of the students made a point of thanking teachers for making a difference in their lives. Some students made concrete suggestions about course schedules, homework, or social events in the schools. In response to the interviews (which were videotaped) teachers recognized the powerful role they played in students lives and considered modifying school tasks based on their suggestions.

The last example points to the importance of addressing seemingly small concerns as a way of enhancing school climate. The *Ambient Noise Checklist* was used to assess the noise level in the cafeteria of a Chicago school. The cafeteria was described as having excruciatingly high noise levels.

> The machines in the cafeteria were all running, an aide was using the public address system to ask Billy or Sarah to "find a seat and sit down," and the cafeteria workers seemed to be playing the 1812 Overture with the stainless steel pots and pans. Students were emptying their trays by banging them inside a metal trash can. Adults were shouting across the room asking specific students to be quiet. The students talked over this din. Few adults acted as if they were glad the students were there. The tone of the aides and other cafeteria workers was less than positive. I observed no smiles, no "good mornings," no friendly faces. When I said "good morning" to an older child, he looked at me as if I had called him a bad name. After 30 minutes in the cafeteria, I was ready to fight" (Freiberg, 1998, p.25).

A checklist was used by the faculty and administration to identify sources of noise in the cafeteria. From this information, they developed some ideas about how to address the noise levels and proceeded to make changes, including training to help aides relate more positively to children, a teacher greeter at the front of the serving line, and use of a sponge stick to clean plates rather than banging them in the metal trash cans. In addition, students were assigned to eat at regular tables each day and were allowed to talk with any student on either side or directly across from them. Use of the speaker was discontinued, and adults walked over to children to talk with them. After several weeks, results indicated that the noise level decreased dramatically, and daily fights essentially stopped. The cafeteria became a pleasant and peaceful space within the school setting.

Guidelines for Promoting a Positive School Climate

The ingredients for promoting a positive school climate vary from school to school. Each time the recipe must be tailored to meet the needs of the students, staff, parents, and community members who are key stakeholders and participants in the creation of a healthy school environment. Yet, there are some basic guidelines that can help to facilitate a successful process and positive results. For example, Fraser (1999) suggests feedback gathered from instruments assessing school climate can be used as a basis for reflection upon, discussion of, and systematic attempts to improve school environments. He recommends the following steps that have proven effective in school climate improvement projects: (a) use of an assessment tool to gather information about perceptions of school climate, (b) compilation of data in a form that can be used as feedback about perceptions of school climate, (c) reflection and discussion of findings to help clarify implications and identify areas needing change, (d) development and implementation of an intervention, and (e) reassessment to determine whether change has occurred.

According to Freiberg (1999), the challenges of initiating a school climate improvement project can be made less overwhelming by considering five points, listed in Table 3.

Frieberg recommends initial strategies for change should begin quickly and should be visible to all students and staff. For example, at one school, staff decided to improve the faculty restrooms. They added quality paper products, assigned maintenance responsibilities across grade levels every 3 months, added air freshener, new paint, pictures, mirrors, and a bulletin board with the latest information from the school climate committee. This intervention was highly visible, and the changes enlisted the support of more faculty and staff to participate in more extensive interventions suggested by the climate committee. Another example of a quick and highly visible climate improvement strategy was initiated by a group of middle school students. These students decided that greeting students and faculty upon entering the building each morning would help improve the "friendliness" of the school.

Finally, it is especially important to consider initiating school climate improvement within the context of organizational change (Curtis & Stoller, 1995). Effecting change within schools requires changing behaviors and attitudes, as well as school organization and norms (Purkey and Smith, 1983). Change and maintenance of the change will not take place without the support and commitment of teachers who must come to "own" different or new educational ideology and techniques. A strategy of change that promotes collaborative planning, collegial work, and a school atmosphere conducive to experimentation and evaluation is critical. The most effective approach to promoting school climate sees school staff (including teachers, paraprofessionals, custodians, secretaries, etc.) as an integral part of an entire school organization engaged in development activities that take place over time. Similarly, students, parents, and community members must be included in

Table 3. Initiating school climate improvement projects: points to consider

1.	*Trust your own perceptions and think about whether the school is a place where students, staff, and parents like to be.* How does the school look? How would you characterize interactions between staff and students, student and students, parents and staff? What do you feel as you enter the building? Do you sense strong leadership or high academic expectations? What evidence supports your perceptions?
2.	*Consider what direct and indirect climate measures can be used to help document and create a baseline for change.* What existing data sources are available to measure school climate? Whose perceptions of school climate should be measured (students? staff? parents?). What resources are available for purchasing and analyzing surveys? Does it make sense to design and implement an instrument based on climate issues specific to needs of the school?
3.	*Identify initial climate changes that can be made with a high level of visibility and within a relatively short period.* Prioritize a list of changes that will yield noticeable results. What changes do most key members of the school agree need attention? What changes can be made quickly with a minimal initial investment of time and effort?
4.	*Consider what groups or individuals should be involved to encourage and create an environment for sustained school climate improvement.* Who are key players in the school? Who must be on board to help initiate and sustain this school climate improvement effort? Remember to consider membership from all major groups (student, staff, and parents). Remember to enlist the support of those who may not typically be included in school improvement efforts (community members, students considered at-risk of school failure, support staff, parents who may have been alienated in the past).
5.	*Consider what long-term changes are needed to create a healthy environment for all members of the learning community.* Recognize that improving and sustaining a positive school climate is a continuous process requiring persistent and ongoing efforts. Develop a plan to maintain the changes that have been made. Develop a way of educating and including new members in the school climate improvement effort.

Source: Adapted from Frieberg (1999).

projects initiated to address school climate. Inviting a parent or student as a token representative will not suffice; to foster an investment in the project, individual contributions and participation must be welcomed, respected, and valued as part of school-wide efforts.

SUMMARY

School climate is a complex construct that has been recognized as an important component of effective schools. Definitions point to multiple dimensions including a sense of order and discipline, parental involvement, staff dedication to student learning, high expectations for academic performance and behavior, caring relationships, and respectful interactions between students, staff, parents, and community members. Today, models of school climate underscore the varied dimensions and organize the complexity of the construct. School climate is associated with a variety of student outcomes including achievement, absenteeism, self-concept, and behavior. How can school psychologists promote a positive school climate? First of all, best practice suggests that it is necessary to describe and measure school climate before developing and implementing a responsive action plan. Indirect and direct measures of school climate can be used to assess perceptions of students, staff, parents, and community members. Several tools meeting important criteria to enhance their quality (e.g., standardized, grounded in theory, evidence of technical adequacy, used in research) were reviewed in this chapter. Efforts to improve school climate have occurred within the context of national large–scale reform, or on a smaller scale at the individual school or district level. In addition, relatively simple strategies can be developed to address singular elements of school climate. Although each strategy/program will vary, there are guidelines to help ensure a successful process and positive results. It is important to conduct school climate improvement within the context of organizational change and enlist the support and active participation of key stakeholders in the school community.

School psychologists are in key positions to effect positive changes in school climate and help create schools where people like to be. Every school psychologist can begin to make these changes although they will take a variety of forms and occur at a variety of levels given job responsibilities, role definitions, and building, or district–level constraints. At a minimum, all school psychologists as professionals can participate in promoting a positive school climate by modeling desired behaviors including participating collaboratively in decision making, promoting high and achievable expectations for all students, welcoming parents as participants in the learning community, showing care and sensitivity to students as well as staff members, and interacting with others in a respectful manner. Furthermore, school psychologists must take steps to initiate awareness, interest, and programmatic changes that will improve a school's climate. As school personnel or parents become engaged in exploring and implementing change, school psychologists can offer support and bring knowledge about school climate issues (e.g., associated research, potential instruments, examples) to assist in planning. Finally, school psychologists have the training to recognize the importance of collecting data to make decisions and the skills to evaluate program effectiveness. School psychologists cannot sit back and wait for an invitation to participate; rather, school psychologists must be active catalysts for change, collaborative partners, and leaders in reform efforts directed at promoting positive school climates.

It makes sense to put efforts into promoting educationally and healthy environments for all children and youth because it has been shown to be an effective preventive approach. The words of Norris Haynes (as cited in Haynes et al., 1997, p. 322) serve to stimulate our thinking when considering the influence of school climate and student development: "poor school adjustment and school failure are often incorrectly interpreted as manifestations of cognitive ineptitude, deviant value systems, and inadequate development. The complex interpersonal interactions which occur within schools and significantly influence students adjustment and performance are not sufficiently examined". As school psychologists we are indeed challenged to address the conditions of the school environment that can help to foster academic success and healthy development for all students.

REFERENCES

Anderson, C. S. (1982). The search for school climate: A review of the research. *Review of Educational Research, 52*(3), 368–420.

Andringa, J. W., & Fustin, M. (1991). Learning to plan for and implement change: School building faculty responds. *Journal of Educational Research, 84*(4), 233–238.

August, D., & Hakuta, K.(Eds.). (1997). *Improving schooling for language-minority children: A research agenda.* Washington DC: National Academy Press.

Borger, J. B., Lo, C., Oh, S., & Walberg, H. J. (1985). Effective schools: A quantitative synthesis of constructs. *Journal of Classroom Interaction*, 20(2), 12–17.

Brookover, W. B., Schweitzer, J. H., Schneider, J. M., Beady, C. H., Flood, P. K., & Wisenbaker, J. M. (1978). Elementary school social climate and school achievement. *American Educational Research Journal, 15*(2), 301–318.

Bryk, A. S., & Thum, Y. M. (1989). The effects of high school organization on dropping out: An exploratory investigation. *American Educational Research Journal, 26*, 353–383.

Burden, R. L., & Fraser, B. J. (1993). Use of classroom environment assessments in school psychology: A British perspective. *Psychology in the Schools, 30*, 232–240.

Comer, J. P., Haynes, N. M., Joyner, E. T., & Ben-Avie, M. (1996). *Rallying the whole village.* New York: Teachers College Press.

Curtis, M. J., & Stoller, S. A. (1995). System-level consultation and organizational change. In A. Thomas & J. Grimes (Eds.), *Best practices in school psychology III* (pp. 51–58). Washington, DC: National Association of School Psychologists.

Doll, B. (1999). *Making schools resilient: A case for social environments as therapy.* Paper presented at Division 16 Annual Convention of the American Psychological Association, Boston, MA.

Emmons, C. L., Efimba M. O., & Hagopian, G. (1998). A school transformed: The case of Norman S. Weir. *Journal of Education for Students Placed at Risk, 3*(1), 39–51.

Finn, J. D. (1993). *School engagement and students at risk.* U.S. Department of Education, National Center for Education Statistics. Buffalo, NY: State University.

Fischer D. L. & Fraser, B. J. (1991). School climate and teacher professional development. *South Pacific Journal of Teacher Education, 19*, 15–30.

Fraser, B. J. (1986). *Classroom environment.* London: Croom Helm.

Fraser, B. J. (1999). Using learning environment assessments to improve classroom and school climates. In H. J. Frieberg (Ed.). *School climate: Measuring, improving and sustaining learning environments* (pp. 65–83). London: Falmer.

Frieberg, H. J. (1998). Measuring school climate: Let me count the ways. *Educational Leadership, 56*(1), 22–26.

Frieberg, H. J. (1999). Three creative ways to measure school climate and next steps. In J. Frieberg (Ed.), *School climate: Measuring, improving, and sustaining healthy learning environments* (pp.208–218). London: Falmer.

Goodenow, C. (1993). Classroom belonging among early adolescent students: Relationships to motivation and achievement. *Journal of Early Adolescence, 13*(1), 21–43.

Gottfredson, G. D. (1991). *The Effective School Battery.* Odessa, FL.: Psychological Assessment Resources.

Griffith, J. (1997). Linkages of school structural and socioenvironmental characteristics to parental satisfaction with public education and student academic achievement. *Journal of Applied Social Psychology, 27*(2), 156–186.

Haynes, N. M. (1998). Overview of the Comer School Development Project. *Journal of Education for Students Placed at Risk, 3*(1), 3–9.

Haynes, N. M., Emmons, C., & Ben-Avie, M. (1997). School climate as a factor in student adjustment and achievement. *Journal of Educational and Psychological Consultation, 8*(3), 321–329.

Haynes, N. M., Emmons, C. L., Ben-Avie, M. & Comer, J. P. (1996) *The school development program: Student, staff and parent school climate surveys.* New Haven, CT: Yale Child Study Center.

Hoge, D. R., Smit, E. K., & Hanson, S. L. (1990). School experiences predicting changes in self-esteem of sixth and seventh grade students. *Journal of Educational Psychology, 82*, 117–127.

Howard, E., Howell, B., & Brainard, E. (1987). *Handbook for conducting school climate improvement projects.* Bloomington, IN: Phi Delta Kappa Educational Foundation.

Hoy, W. K., & Hannum, J. W. (1997). Middle school climate: An empirical assessment of organizational health and student achievement. *Educational Administration Quarterly, 33*(3), 290–311.

Hoy, W. K., & Feldman, J. A. (1999). Organizational health profiles for high schools. In H. J. Frieberg (Ed.). *School climate: Measuring, improving and sustaining healthy learning environments.* (pp. 84–102). London: Falmer.

Hoy, W. K., Tartar, C. J., & Kottkamp, R. B. (1991). *Open school, healthy school: Making schools work.* Newberry Park, CA: Corwin.

Hoy, W. K., & Woolfolk, A. E. (1993). Teachers' sense of self-efficacy and the organizational health of schools. *Elementary School Journal, 93*(4), 355–372.

Kuperminc, G. P., Leadbeater, B. J., Emmons, C., & Blatt, S. J. (1997). Perceived school climate and difficulties in the social adjustment of middle school students. *Applied Developmental Science, 1*(2), 76–88.

Lehr, C. A., & Lange, C. M. (1999). *Students at risk attending alternative programs and high schools: School climate, attitudes toward school, belonging, participation and enrollment status.* (Research Report 28). Minneapolis, MN: University of Minnesota.

National Association of Secondary School Principals (1986). *School climate survey.* Reston, VA: Author.

Purkey, S. C., & Smith, M. S. (1983). Effective schools: A review. *The Elementary School Journal, 84*(4), 427–452.

Rumberger, R. W. (1995). Dropping out of middle school: A multilevel analysis of students and schools. *American Educational Research Journal, 32*(3), 583–625.

Stevens, C. J., & Sanchez, K. S. (1999). Perceptions of parents and community members as a measure of school climate. In H. J. Frieberg (Ed.), *School climate: Measuring, improving and sustaining healthy learning environments* (pp. 124–147). London: Falmer.

Stockard, J., & Mayberry, M. (1992). *Effective educational environments.* Newberry Park, CA; Corwin.

Teddlie, C., & Stringfield, S. (1993). *Schools make a difference: Lessons learned from a ten- year study of school effects.* New York: Teachers College Press.

Wehlage, G. G., & Rutter, R. A. (1986). Dropping out: How much do schools contribute to the problem? *Teachers College Record, 87*(3), 374–392.

Ysseldyke, J., Dawson, P., Lehr, C., Reschly, C., Reynolds, M., & Telzrow, C. (1997) *School psychology: A blueprint for training and practice II.* Bethesda, MD: National Association of School Psychologists.

ANNOTATED BIBLIOGRAPHY

Anderson, C. S. (1982). The search for school climate: A review of the research. *Review of Educational Research, 52*(3), 368–420.
This article provides an extensive analysis of the literature on school climate, presents theories of school climate, and draws conclusions about research findings. The history of school climate is reviewed, and the article concludes with a summary of methodological issues researchers are faced with when conducting school climate studies.

Freiberg, H. J. (1999). *School climate: Measuring, improving and sustaining healthy learning environments.* London: Falmer.
This book consists of 11 chapters describing approaches to measuring school climate from multiple perspectives. The book discusses issues related to improving school climate and provides examples of many diverse kinds of climate instruments.

Haynes, N. M., Emmons, C., & Ben-Avie, M. (1997). School climate as a factor in student adjustment and achievement. *Journal of Educational and Psychological Consultation, 8*(3), 321–329.

This brief article defines dimensions of school climate and summarizes research on school climate and student outcomes. Examples of positive school climate are also provided.

Publisher/Contact Information for Select School Climate Instruments:

Comprehensive Assessment of School Environments (CASE) (NASSP, 1986).
The instrument can be ordered from the National Association of Secondary School Principals, P.O. Box 3250, Reston, Virginia 22090. Telephone: (616) 383-1961.

Effective School Battery (ESB) (Gottfredson, 1991).
The instrument, information about scoring, and the norm group can be obtained from Gottfredson Associates, Inc., 3239-B Corporate Court, Ellicott City, MD 21042. Telephone: (410) 461-5530.

Organizational Health Inventory (OHI) (Hoy & Feldman, 1999).
A copy of the SLEQ and directions for scoring are available in Hoy & Feldman (1999). APC computer scoring program for the OHI can be purchased from Arlington Writers, 2548 Onandaga Drive, Columbus, OH 43221. The program will automatically score the data and standardize the scores using the current norms.

School Climate Survey (Haynes, Emmons, Ben-Avie, & Comer, 1996).
The instrument can be ordered from Christine Emmons, School Climate Surveys Request, Yale Child Study Center, School Development Program, 55 College Street, New Haven, CT 06510. Telephone: (203) 737-4000.

School Level Environment Questionnaire (SLEQ) (Fischer & Fraser, 1991).
A copy of the SLEQ and directions for scoring is available in Fraser (1999)

60 Best Practices in Health Promotion for School Psychological Practice

Ellis P. Copeland
University of Northern Colorado

OVERVIEW

In past decades, children were susceptible to a host of deadly diseases. Advances in medical science that resulted in medications and vaccines have now largely addressed the ravages once wrought on children by the diseases of the past. Schools, along with other health and social service agencies, played a major role in eradicating infectious diseases through their involvement in immunization, screening, and educational programming. Such involvement needs to continue today yet in a radically different form.

Today's youth are exposed to multiple risk factors, and these risk factors are common antecedents of diverse disorders. Although this chapter will focus on building functional behaviors and reducing or eliminating dysfunctional behaviors in youth, the exacerbation and increase in health and behavior problems have their roots in the significant family, school, and neighborhood changes that have occurred during the past few decades (Consortium on the School-Based Promotion of Social Competence, 1994). These changes include a breakdown of the traditional family and traditional neighborhoods; a devaluing of parenting, of teachers, and of religious life; increased poverty rates among families with children; damaging television and media messages (i.e., sex, violence, and unhealthy dietary behaviors); lack of positive role models and a reduction in meaningful contact with positive adult role models; unsafe environments (often inclusive of the school environment); inadequate housing; and misplaced values where money becomes supreme amongst the unattended societal problems directly affecting the health of our youth.

The societal erosion noted above has affected the behavior of every youth in our nation. Consequently, the focus of our interventions are most closely tied to the behavioral patterns the youth may choose to adopt that too often lead to mental and/or physical disorders. Epidemiological data indicate that 15–25% of children and adolescents have mental health problems that warrant treatment and/ or place them in the "extremely vulnerable" category (Consortium on the School-Based Promotion of Social Competence, 1994). Further, the most serious and expensive health and social problems facing our country today are caused by negative behavioral patterns that were established during the childhood and adolescent years (Kolbe, Collins, & Cortese, 1997). Health problems spawned by negative behavioral patterns (smoking, unhealthy dietary behaviors, drug and alcohol abuse, intentional injury to others and self, sexual behaviors that can result in pregnancy or sexually transmitted diseases, and inadequate physical exercise) fuel unnecessary health care costs. Unattended health and social problems among our country's young people seriously erode their health status, educational achievement, and quality of life (Kolbe et al., 1997).

Still, these health problems/unhealthy behaviors are largely preventable and rigorous studies of health education in the schools have demonstrated that programming has effectively reduced the prevalence of health risk behaviors among youth. For example,

1. Planned, sequential health education resulted in a 37% reduction in the onset of smoking among seventh-grade students.

2. The prevalence of obesity was decreased by half among girls in grades 6–8 who participated in a school-based program.

3. Forty-four percent fewer students who were enrolled in a school-based life skills training program used tobacco, alcohol, and marijuana one or more times per month than those not enrolled in the program (School Health Programs, 2000).

Given these data, it appears that school health programs are becoming one of the most efficient means that the country might use to prevent the major mental and physical health problems as well as social problems that confront our nation.

The idea of delivery of health services to students in schools is an old one. Dryfoos (1994) noted that, in the 1980s, as conditions worsened for young people, school-based clinics began to pop up serendipitously around the country. The early programs were problem-focused (i.e., alcohol and drug, teen pregnancy) and were later superseded by more comprehensive models such as school-based clinics. Dryfoos' (1994) book, *Full-Service Schools: A Revolution in Health and Social Services for Children, Youth, and Families*, was about the transition from school-based clinics to full-service schools (schools in which health, mental health, social, and/or family services might be located). Today, full-service schools or "comprehensive school health education" is seen as the most effective form to promote healthy behaviors and prevent the previously outlined dysfunctional behaviors. However, without a radical change in societal values (society choosing to directly address major issues such as poverty and unsafe environments) and school mission, most of the nation's 100,000 schools will not implement a comprehensive program or a school clinic in the near future (Kolbe et al., 1997).

Although schools, by themselves, should not be expected to address the nation's most serious health and social problems, school health programs could be one of the most efficient means the nation might use to prevent major health and social problems (Kolbe et al., 1997). By reducing the incidence of mental and physical health problems that afflict young people and often continue into adulthood, school health programs should reduce the spiraling cost of health care, improve educational outcomes, and improve productivity and quality of life. Schools are widely acknowledged as the major setting in which activities should be undertaken to promote competence and prevent the development of unhealthy behaviors (Consortium on the School-Based Promotion of Social Competence, 1994). Further, from a primary and secondary prevention perspective, an economic perspective and demographic viewpoint, it appears essential that social initiatives such as health promotion be linked to schools.

Health promotion has been "broadly defined as a combination of behavioral, educational, social, spiritual, economic, and environmental efforts that support the establishment, maintenance, and enhancement of behaviors and life-styles conducive to overall emotional and physical well-being" (Zins & Wagner, 1997, p. 945). The definition is inclusive of mind, body, and spirit. Further, the definition is systemic and directly encourages the mobilization of community resources and the development of environments that will lead to healthy behavioral patterns during the child's and adolescent's formative years. What a challenge! These healthy lifestyles must be as easy to adopt as unhealthy ones and produce greater immediate and long-term rewards.

The challenge is an especially difficult one for the traditionally trained school psychologist. Although we have witnessed extraordinary progress in our improvement of public health (including mental health) through medical science, we know more today about how to treat mental illness than we know with certainty about how to prevent mental illness and promote health (Satcher, 1999). Larson (2000) notes that the various domains of psychology are more articulate about how things can go wrong than how they can go right. We have numerous research-based programs aimed at curbing at-risk behaviors such as violence and drug use, but we lack a rigorously applied psychology of how to promote positive youth development. Yet, our role becomes obvious given the well-established link between learning and health (Satcher, 1999).

Thus, health promotion will require us to be a part of a team of professionals from many fields working cooperatively with teachers, students, community members, and parents to provide comprehensive school health programs. These integrated efforts may include such disciplines as health education, nursing, physical education, nutrition (food) services, counseling, and school psychology (Zins & Wagner, 1997). The integrated approach will be better able to mobilize community resources to enhance health promotion efforts in the schools and society. Further, the comprehensive effort will reach virtually all children and youth and create an environment that builds health upon health in a more integrated manner.

BASIC CONSIDERATIONS

What We Know

We, school psychologists, know risk factors and at-risk behaviors. Smoking, early sexual intercourse, destruction of property, fighting, stealing, use of alcohol and/or drugs, and absenteeism are a few examples. Jessor, Turbin, and Costa (1998) have turned a number of obvious risk factors into health-enhancing behaviors. Noting the ill effects of not eating a healthy diet, not getting enough sleep, not engaging in regular exercise, not practicing good dental hygiene, and not wearing a seatbelt resulted in the Health-Enhancing Behavior Index. Benson (1993) further provides a list of factors that are associated with negative health outcomes.

Much of what we need to know to practice on a school health team was provided in the foundation courses of our accredited training programs. Program evaluation is taught in most of our training programs and is a key element to update, improve, and define the successful school health program. Consultation and behavioral change strategies are critical skills to enable one to effectively practice on a health team. Learning theory and developmental psychology are true assets. For example, developmental psychology is the study of the process of physical and emotional growth and competence, and is a critical sub-domain of social and emotional intelligence. Of course, a course focused on prevention would be most helpful. Still, most of us are able to "reframe" our skills to be more proactive than reactive.

What We Need to Know

Curriculum concerns that must be addressed are well defined in the Comprehensive School Health Program model developed by the School Health Programs (2000). According to the model, a comprehensive school plan provides:

1. Curriculum that addresses and integrates education about a range of categorical health issues at developmentally appropriate ages

2. Programming for grades kindergarten through twelve

3. Instruction for a prescribed amount of time at each grade level

4. Integrative activities to help young people develop the skills they need to avoid use of tobacco, dysfunctional behaviors, engaging in a sedentary lifestyle, etc.

5. Appropriate instruction from qualified teachers, health professionals, and concerned community members

A good curriculum specialist or teacher will be critical to curriculum development.

We need to perceive health promotion as its own set of assets and competencies and not the absence of disease as it is often defined by the medical model. For example, the Surgeon General (Satcher, 1999) defines mental health as

> The successful performance of mental function, resulting in productive activities, fulfilling relationships with other people, and the ability to adapt to change and cope with adversity; from early childhood until late life, mental health is the springboard of thinking and communication skills, learning, emotional growth, resilience, and self-esteem (p.vii).

Physical health is also better defined by competencies than by a lack of physical disease.

Martin Seligman, past president of the American Psychological Association, hopes to see a profound shift in the field of psychology away from pathology and toward positive psychology. In his article with Csikszentmihalyi (Seligman, & Csikszentmihalyi, 2000), they describe the foreground of this approach as prevention. Since the disease model offers little to prevent violence, depression, etc., the major strides in prevention will come largely from a perspective of building competency and not on correcting weakness. Much of the task of prevention in the next century will be on how to foster courage, future mindedness, optimism, interpersonal skill, faith, hope, work ethic, initiative, and honesty (to name several) in youth. The entire issue of the January 2000 *American Psychologist* addresses this topic.

In a related manner, Benson (1993) has identified 30 assets, referred to as protective factors, associated with positive health outcomes. Benson's acknowledged assets include caring about people, displaying assertiveness skills, motivation to achieve, positive orientation to the future, decision-making skills, involvement in church or synagogue, and acknowledgement of family support. Benson further advocates an additive view of assets that is most consistent with health goals and curriculum.

Building an Integrative Program

This section will examine some general ways to introduce and gain support for implementing a health promotion program in your school(s) or in a school district. A number of the ideas presented in the section were drawn from articles by Hightower, Johnson, and Haffey (1995) and Kelly (1995).

In any plan for change, a formal needs assessment is the best way to begin. If such an assessment is not feasible, then following one's "sense of the obvious" might be an option (Hightower et al., 1995). Such an approach involves spending considerable time in open discussion and active listening among staff to delineate a hierarchy of concerns. Once the needs are identified the homework begins. Attending workshops, visiting schools and communicating with personnel invested in a comprehensive school health program, and reading relevant journals and reports helps you to develop the expertise to better present the concept.

Before directly approaching personnel within your schools or district, a system analysis is always necessary (Hightower et al., 1995). Talking to those who know the system regarding managerial styles, communication pathways, allegiances, etc., is informative. Understanding the school board's philosophy, goals, budget for the district, procedures, etc., lets you know how the system operates. Once you know what is happening and how it happens, start at the safest point with the administrator that oversees that particular area. If the person is one of your principals, then they may be able to provide useful cues on how to proceed.

The next step is to identify school personnel that are either stakeholders and/or "customers" (people who are invested in health education) of the idea. Kelly (1995) firmly supports the idea of starting with internal support before moving to external audiences. Then, a school psychologist should obtain the input and approval of all school staff who will be involved, along with principal(s) and other supervisor input before the program is taken to the superintendent (Hightower et al., 1995). When meeting with the superintendent, be clear about what you wish to accomplish and optimistic about the level of support that the idea has achieved.

With the superintendent's blessing and approval, external audiences can be contacted. These include community agencies, parents who may be "customers," churches and synagogues, hospitals, alternative health providers, and the business community. Direct communication is far better than mass communication (i.e., newsletters), which does little to influence opinions or change behavior (Kelly, 1995). Direct communication also enables you to manage issues that may arise if the idea of health promotion is seen as too far afield by some extreme groups. Further, direct communication allows the services provided to be designed around community needs. Responding to local needs and constructing interventions to meet community needs typically results in a positive attitude from both staff and community and subsequently builds support for services to children (Kelly, 1995).

Funding

Without a major change in health care policy, a comprehensive school health program will seldom be funded to fully meet the present needs and growing demand. School-based health programs cost between $100,000 and $300,000 a year, depending on the size of the school and the comprehensiveness of the program (Dryfoos, 1994). As those who govern schools seldom mandate such programs, developing funding sources for school health programs becomes an important issue. Although most school-based centers must seek multiple financing arrangements, obvious places to start would include the local school board and the local private sector. The local school board may provide seed money yet cannot be depended on as a long-term funding source. An exception may be that if the board's hope is to fully integrate health promotion into the existing curriculum then more permanent funding may occur. Otherwise, the private sector, which includes United Way, corporations that wish to maintain and enhance their communities, and private foundations, may be more reliable and permanent resources.

Several states have adopted laws or officially supported the development of school-based clinics (Dryfoos, 1994). States may use either federal block grants or establish their own state block grants to fund such programs. In general, state agency grants tend to be much shorter, less complicated, and less time consuming than federal grants. The grants supported by states almost always follow the "residual model" (a problem causing one to resort to public assistance). Thus, to obtain a grant, one needs to document problems with drug and alcohol, at-risk youth, etc., in order to obtain funding.

Nationally, funding is typically more complex. Federal grants may be more inclusive yet typically more complicated and involved. If a school is providing medically necessary services to children and families that are Medicaid eligible, then the school could be eligible to receive reimbursement from Medicaid for eligible services and administrative supports (Wrobel & Kreig, 2000). These funds can be substantial and should mean that more children have access to health care and the health care programs that could be provided by the schools. Managed care is another option. It is possible that school-based services may overcome the hurdles of managed care in order to ensure that school-based clinics or programs are certified as providers for students whose parents are enrolled in a managed care plan.

The Centers for Disease Control (CDC) provides resources to ensure that their identified curriculum to reduce risk behaviors is available for state and local agencies interested in using them. Presently, the CDC directly funds 16 states for coordinated school health programs (funding for HIV-AIDS prevention in schools alone accounts for approximately $47 million). The Surgeon General is a strong advocate for health care, and although health care reform failed under the Clinton administration, national health care reform remains a vital agenda item on the federal scene. A comprehensive school health curriculum or health education programming is prevention and may be attractive to both the liberal and conservative elected officials.

BEST PRACTICES

In her book, *Common Purpose,* Lisbeth Schorr (1997) outlines the Seven Attributes of Highly Effective Programs, that I believe set the foundation for this chapter. These attributes (pp.5 –10) are as follows:

1. *Successful programs are comprehensive, flexible, responsive, and preserving.* While they do not try to provide everything to everyone, they are flexible, and offer more than a single strand of service or support. They often think beyond professional services and help families to strengthen bonds with neighbors and churches and other natural networks of support.

2. *Successful programs see children in the context of their families.* Effective programs are alert to the family context. They are aware that whether a child's health needs will be met depends on the coping abilities, mental health, and social and economic resources of the parent. Although enlisting the overwhelmed and overstressed parents of today requires more skill than ever before, school programs must recognize the need for deeper parent involvement.

3. *Successful programs deal with families as parts of neighborhoods and communities.* They grow deep roots in the community and respond to the needs identified by the local population. They are not just *in* the community but *of* the community so that "best practices" are often whatever works in a given context.

4. *Successful programs have a long-term, preventive orientation, a clear mission, and*

continue to evolve over time. Successful health promotion programs would primarily focus on the period from pregnancy through elementary school as the most productive time to intervene. They combine a highly flexible mode of operation with a clear sense of mission and don't abandon their fundamental mission for the fad of the moment. They maintain a stable core and share common beliefs yet adapt strategies based on the changing needs of individuals, families, and communities to reach the goals agreed upon.

5. *Successful programs are well managed by competent and committed individuals with clearly identifiable skills.* Directors of successful programs don't do it by magic or charisma but by using identifiable management techniques to create a coherent, outcome-oriented mission. They inspire staff with a shared vision of the program. Their skills are not a mystery and can be learned. They include a willingness to take risks, to tolerate ambiguity, and to win the trust of staff and the public.

6. *Staffs of successful programs are trained and supported to provide high-quality, responsive services.* Needing to be versatile and flexible, a greater discretion is given to staff. Yet, training, monitoring, and supervision are emphasized to ensure that the discretion exercised keeps with mission goals and high standards or quality. Thus, flexibility is built on competence.

7. *Successful programs operate in settings that encourage practitioners to build strong relationships based on mutual trust and respect.* Often a special relationship is at the core of the successful program. Although rarely explicitly stated, caring and relationships are often the most important aspects of a program. Last, the author points out that a spiritual dimension to the relationships contributes to fostering change.

Coordinated School Health Programs

Consistent with the belief that the most effective form of school health education is "comprehensive school health education," the Centers for Disease Control and Prevention conceives of health education as eight interactive components, including health education, physical education, health services, nutrition services, health promotion for staff, counseling and psychological services, healthy school environment, and parent/community involvement (School Health Programs, 2000). The program is consistent with Schorr's (1997) criteria in terms of comprehensiveness, mission, prevention, and utilizing the context of family and community. The program is well documented, planned, and offers a sequential program of health education for students at every grade level, kindergarten through 12. Although Congress has been most keenly focused on the health services and health education components, aside from the obvious focus on counseling and psychological services, the components of health promotion for staff and the healthy school environment are definite inroads for the school psychologist.

Kolbe et al. (1997) note that the CDC is working with other federal agencies, national organizations, and state and local departments of education, health, and social services to improve delivery of the eight components. Their strategies include (a) identifying and monitoring critical health-related events and school interventions affecting those events, (b) integrating and applying research to increase the effectiveness of interventions, (c) providing the means for relevant constituencies to plan and implement interventions, and (d) evaluating the impact of the interventions over time. Working together toward common goals is a thrust of the CDC. In 1992, CDC began providing fiscal and technical support to selected state departments of education and departments of health to jointly help school districts implement the eight components of school health programs (Kolbe, et al., 1997). In the year 2000, CDC is providing assistance to 16 states: Arkansas, California, Florida, Kentucky, Maine, Michigan, Minnesota, North Carolina, New Mexico, New York, Ohio, Rhode Island, South Carolina, South Dakota, Wisconsin, and West Virginia (School Health Programs, 2000). The CDC helps all 50 states and hopes to provide comprehensive support to all states in the near future. As school psychologists are trained across many of the psychological disciplines, they are considered to be "indispensable members of the school health team" (Kolbe et al., 1997, p. 263).

Mental Health Models

This section is written for those of us who wish to focus more on mental health/emotional services rather than on the larger spectrum, which would include physical and spiritual health. It is becoming clear that the current system of providing mental health services is not efficient and is not working effectively. By using a conservative prevalence rate of 9–13% for serious emotional disturbance, O'Day (2000) notes that, in an elementary school of 600 students, between 54 and 102 children would be in need of psychological/mental health services. Even if assigned full-time to one school, the need and the caseload would overwhelm the school psychologist. Using an individual problem-solving model might be an improvement, yet any focus on treatment or individual intervention would eventually overwhelm the psychologist and the system. Thus, a transformation in the delivery of school psychological services will be necessary to address mental health/emotional–related needs.

Zins and Wagner (1997) recognize the full spectrum of health services while providing numerous examples of mental health activities for the school psychologist to choose:

1. Helping with transitions such as moving from elementary to junior high school;

2. Developing interventions with groups of students in areas such as problem-solving, conflict-resolution and social skills, and helping create a supportive, safe environment in which these can occur;

3. Determining the availability of alcohol in the community and identifying establishments that have a history of serving or selling;

4. Implement programs to prevent smoking, alcohol use and/or premature sexual activity;

5. Teaching behavioral self-management skills to reduce violence or loss of control;

6. Providing program evaluation services to assess the outcomes of health promotion efforts;

7. And, providing instruction in stress or time-management (pp. 949 –950).

Even though most of us were trained in many of these areas in terms of pathology or remediation, the promise of the prevention of problem behaviors and promotion of healthy ones must assume greater importance. Zins and Wagner (1997) note that modification in orientation and skill applications is more often required of the traditionally trained school psychologist rather than extensive new coursework.

Two programs that follow a mental health orientation are worthy of note. Communities That Care (Hawkins, Catalano, & Associates, 1992) is a program that was developed for every person concerned about the healthy, drug-free development of our nation's children. The program is noteworthy inasmuch as it examines health promotion from the perspective of protective mechanisms and risk factors. Further, Communities That Care requires the active involvement of whole communities (mayors office, business leaders, police, health professionals, etc.). Its greatest asset is the bringing together of diverse community members with the common mission of making their community a protective environment for the healthy development of its young people.

Social Problem Solving and Social Decision-Making Project (SPS-SDM) has spread from a demonstration project to one that now includes hundreds of classrooms in nearly half of the states (Zins, Elias, Greenberg, & Weissberg, 2000). The original curriculum developed by Elias and Clabby (1989) was focused on classroom-based interventions in which school psychologists and teachers collaborated. The program was awarded the 1988 Lela Rowland Prevention Award and has been designated as a model program in the National Mental Health Association prevention Clearinghouse, the U.S. Department of Education, and the National Educational Goals Panel (Zins et al., 2000).

The core of the project is the building of social and emotional skills in elementary students. Students are taught self-control, group participation and social awareness, and a decision-making strategy that they can use when faced with difficult choices. The program has a strong prevention orientation, and the social and emotional components require students to integrate behaviors (actions), cognition (thinking), and emotions (feelings) to achieve specific goals. Examples of skills associated with social and emotional learning (SEL) include (Zins et al., 2000, p. 76):

1. Being aware of other's feelings

2. Accurately perceiving the perspectives of others (empathy)

3. Possessing assertiveness and a sense of self-efficacy

4. Ability to cooperate with others and resolve conflicts peacefully

In an attempt to help students develop the skills that a socially competent student might possess, the program has developed modules. Examples of these modules are (Zins et al., 2000, p. 89):

1. A program that allows students to create school and community service projects

2. A video program that shows children how to watch and analyze television programming and use their social decision making and problem solving skills to create their own programs, etc.

3. A "FIG TESPN" approach—an acronym for *F*eelings as a clue that a problem exists; *I* may have a problem; *G*oals to guide actions; *T*hinking of things to do; *E*nvisioning outcomes for each identified solution; *S*elect the best solution in relation to one's goal; *P*lan to implement; and *N*ext time will I do the same or try a different approach.

The program has been in existence for nearly two decades, and extensive research has documented the effects of the SPS-SDM program. Results of the studies that have been performed speak highly of the program. Data have shown that children, teachers, and other educators enjoy the program and put its principles to frequent use (Zins et al., 2000). Studies have been conducted in terms of pre-test to post-test gains where children involved in the program were compared with those children who did not participate. In general, examples of gains for children involved in the program include better transitions to middle school, increased self-esteem, and better social awareness (i.e., empathy) and social decision making.

Physical Activity and Diet

Health is a construct and is composed of many complementary behaviors. The separation of mind and body makes little sense to one serious about studying health. Yet, where does one start when organizing a health promotion program? If a community is knowledgeable and sees that health is a construct that includes physical, mental health/emotional, and spiritual components, then the starting point may not be a central question, and, as noted before, a comprehensive approach is best. However, we would argue that the safest point to start in most communities would be in the physical health and nutrition arenas.

David Satcher, U.S. Surgeon General, on March 15, 2000, argued what follows in the "Opinion" section of the *Atlanta Journal-Constitution*:

> I am alarmed by the steady trend we have seen over the last two decades toward decreasing physical education requirements in public schools... fewer schools require students to engage in physical activity at school... currently, no state mandates daily physical education in grades K–12, and participation by adolescents in grades 9-12 in daily physical education has declined dramatically... by about one-third, from 42 percent to 27 percent between 1991 and 1997... combined with an American diet that is too heavy on sweets and fats and too light on fruits and vegetables, have raised obesity to epidemic proportions in the United States.... We need to create environments where healthy lifestyles are as easy to adopt as unhealthy ones (p. A17).

Not surprisingly, children who participate in regular physical activity have more favorable cardiovascular disease risk factors than less active children. Saunders and Pate (2000) make the point that eating habits that begin in childhood contribute to a multitude of chronic diseases in adulthood (e.g., heart disease, cancer, and osteoporosis). Finally, numerous physical and nutritional policy statements call for lifetime physical activity and improved daily nutritional choices, and professional development for those involved in physical education and nutritional education.

Saunders and Pate (2000) identify the Child and Adolescent trial for Cardiovascular Health (CATCH) project as a model program to promote physical activity and healthful eating in a school setting. CATCH is implemented grades 3–5. Their food program (Eat Smart) focuses on reducing the fat and sodium content of food served. Their physical education component is geared to increase the amount of time that students engage in moderate to vigorous physical activity. The project also adds a home component to complement the classroom curricula. In a 3-year follow-up study, students in the intervention group maintained higher levels of physical activity and dietary intentions than those students in a nonequivalent control group.

Physical Focus and Physical Dimensions (2000) are curricula designed for sixth to eighth (Physical Focus) and ninth (Physical Dimensions) graders to promote knowledge and skills to enjoy a physically healthy lifestyle. Physical Focus centers on level of fitness, regular habits of physical activity, cooperative and competitive activities, and life-long skills. Physical Dimensions includes physical activity, diet, and a wellness component. An exciting element of the Physical Dimensions program is the High School Ph.D., a certificate of achievement given to graduates of the program.

Positive Youth Development

High rates of boredom, alienation, and disconnection from meaningful challenge are typically not signs of psychopathology, but rather signs of deficiency in positive youth development (Larson, 2000). Larson makes the argument that one could engage in a similar debate surrounding many cases of problem behavior, such as drug use, premature sexual activity, aggression, depression, and minor delinquency. Larson, as a developmental psychologist, finds the answers to the problems of today's youth more in an absence of a positive life trajectory than in the most common explanations of emotional disturbance, maladaptive cognitions, or as a response to family stress. The Carnegie Council on Adolescent Development (1992) has made positive youth development a hot term on the national scene, yet psychology has been slow to respond. Consistent with our negative focus on how "things go wrong" for youth, psychology has neglected the positive. Larson (2000), however, sees a diffuse body of research on the pathways whereby children and adolescents become motivated, directed, socially competent, compassionate, and take charge of their lives. Positive youth development is a movement that is enabling youth to explore these pathways.

Owing to a plethora of internal and external factors, most schools have also failed to respond to the challenge of the positive youth movement. As alluded to before, today's schools are so focused on the development of academic skills that health promotion and the benefits of extracurricular activity are often ignored. In 1990, the National Educational Longitudinal Study (see Zill, Nord, & Loomis, 1995) noted that the average tenth grade student spent less that one hour a week in an extracurricular activity (sports, music, art, drama clubs, as well as community service). While involvement in extracurricular activities has been clearly demonstrated as beneficial (Carns et al., 1995) in terms of reducing high-risk behaviors, and increasing academic success and building desirable character traits, its benefits are not being promoted or taken advantage of by a significant number of today's youth.

Children and adolescents are often out of school and home unsupervised by 3:00 p.m., and a number of problems have developed. By using juvenile crime rates as an example, the Federal Bureau of Investigation has found that the hours between 3:00 p.m. and 8:00 p.m. are the peak hours for violent juvenile crimes (Fox & Newman, 1997). As an alternative, Zill et al. (1995) have argued that participation in after-school programs can offer children and adolescents a vast number of skill- and character-building opportunities while diverting them away from delinquent behaviors. Thus, the need for after-school programming is clear and becomes a challenge for both schools and communities.

A community-based asset approach to building positive youth development is a joint project of Lutheran Brotherhood and the Division of Congregational Ministries of the Evangelical Lutheran Church in America. The Search Institute (2000) has identified 40 developmental assets that young people need to build to be healthy and successful. The assets are divided into two broad categories: external and internal. External assets are support (e.g., a caring neighborhood), empowerment (e.g., service to others), boundaries and expectations (e.g., positive adult role models), and constructive use of time (e.g., creative activities). Internal assets are commitment to learning (e.g., achievement motivation), positive values (i.e., promoting equality), social competencies (i.e., empathy), and positive identity (e.g., self-esteem). The focus of the program is to build these assets in a congregation, and yet extensive interaction with one's community is encouraged.

The Search Institute makes a convincing case that assets make a difference. Having collected data from almost 100,000 sixth to twelfth grade public school students in 213 towns and cities in 25 states, it is evident that patterns of risk-taking behavior and positive behaviors and attitudes are altered by the number of assets that youth report. For example, youth that report only 0–10 assets have the highest rates of illicit drug use, rates of violent behavior, and depression/suicide attempts. Conversely, students reporting 31–40 assets, have the lowest rates of illicit drug use, aggressive behavior, and rate of depression/suicide attempts. In terms of positive behaviors and attitudes, the findings again strongly favor those youths reporting the greatest number of assets. For example, the more assets, the more likely the youth is to help others, earn high grades in school, maintain good health habits, and value diversity.

The final project to be addressed in this chapter is a more scientific approach to positive youth development. Larson (2000) believes that *initiative* is a core requirement for other positive components of development, such as health choices, leadership, altruism, and civic engagement. Today, images of adult careers do not have enough magnetic pull, in and of themselves, to motivate most youth to begin taking control of their lives. Further, given that the future of many occupations is unstable (many may not exist in 20 years), it is better that youth are motivated by initiative than by anticipated long-term rewards.

Initiative is the dedication of cumulative effort over time to achieve a goal (Larson, 2000) and is composed of three elements. Initiative involves *intrinsic motivation* or wanting to do an activity and being invested in it. Second, a *concerted engagement* or thought and effort toward creating some form of order, synergy, etc., in the environment is required. Third, initiative involves a *temporal arc of effort* or the capacity to re-evaluate and adjust strategies. Larson notes that to become an agentic adult (a person capable of being an agent of change), one needs to be able to mobilize one's attention, one's mental powers, on a deliberate course of action, without being deterred by the first obstacle one encounters. He later further summarizes these terms as intrinsic motivation, concentration, and challenge.

Larson confirms that the great majority of adolescents' time is spent in two opposite experiential domains. In school, they experience concentration and challenge without being intrinsically motivated. In most leisure activities, including watching television, they report experiencing intrinsic motivation but a lack in concentration and challenge. An exception is what he terms structured voluntary activities, including youth organizations and extracurricular activities. The defining criteria for voluntary structured activities were those with rules, constraints, goals, and activities where the youth were highly motivated to be involved. Sports, arts, music, hobbies, and participation in organizations were all perceived as involving high intrinsic motivation, concentration, and challenge. Larson concludes that such activities are critical to positive youth development.

In addition to the development of initiative, Larson reviews a range of research to confirm that structured voluntary activities are associated with multiple positive outcomes including diminished delinquency, greater achievement, and increased self-control and self-efficacy. Next, he reviews research by Heath (1999) that has recorded language use and has found that adolescents participating in structured voluntary activities acquire a new operating language of agency that reflected an increased ability to affect the world. For example, when the youth first joined a structured voluntary activity their statements included little conjecture about future events and a passive and self-defensive orientation that viewed acts of initiative as doomed to failure. Within four weeks, language use that reflected skills to think about the world as a field of action increased.

Larson's research and his review of the research of cohorts examining structured voluntary activities paints a positive picture of early adolescents that are awake, alive, and open to developmental experiences less common in other parts of their lives. He believes that the agentic states developed by voluntary structured activities make for a fertile ground for adolescents to develop and teach themselves a wide variety of positive health competencies. Our challenge is to help find those activities that contain the elements of intrinsic motivation, concentration, and challenge and expose youth to these elements. A further challenge will be to find ways to incorporate those elements into a school health curriculum that will send today's youth toward a future of spiritual, mental/emotional health, and physical health.

SUMMARY

Today's youth are grossly underserved in almost every arena of health promotion. When a decision is made to support an "academic" area or remedial program versus a health area, the health area is far too often the loser. Yet, research demonstrates that we are approaching a time when emotional, physical, social, and spiritual health of our youth is arguably more important than basic cognitive skills and far more cost effective than remedial programming. Children of today are more at-risk and self-report more emotional problems, delinquency, and problem behaviors than the reports of youth from previous generations. The good news is that solutions do exist, and yet the described solutions will require significant changes in our current practice.

In this chapter we have defined health and demonstrated its manifestations. We have explored the present status of health promotion and have offered numerous models for change. In our review we have found that integrative, comprehensive, and primary school level programs are best and that preventative efforts are vastly preferred over reactive or remedial efforts. Schorr (1997) cautions that even highly successful programs cannot be transplanted wholesale from one setting to another and be expected to work. Needs for health promotion must be defined by the local population. Minke (2000) notes that this does not mean, "reinventing the wheel." A number of excellent programs do exist, and their mission statements and/or theoretical orientations are clear. Find the program or philosophy that may work in your school and community. Network with teachers, parents, principals, and community agencies that are committed to implementing a health promotion program in your school or community. Together, envision what comprehensive school health education can be and bring it to fruition.

REFERENCES

Benson, P. (1993). *The troubled journey: A portrait of sixth-twelfth grade youth.* Minneapolis, MN: Search Institute.

Carnegie Council on Adolescent Development. (1992). *A matter of time: Risk and opportunity in the nonschool hours.* New York: Carnegie Corporation of New York.

Carns, A. W., Carns, M. R., Wooten, H.R., Jones, L., Raffield, P., & Heitkamp, J. (1995). Extracurricular activities: Are they beneficial? *Texas Counseling Association Journal, 23,* 37–45.

Comprehensive School Health Education. (2000). Centers for Disease Control and Prevention 2000. http://www.cdc.gov/nccdphp/dash/cshedef.htm.

Consortium on the School-Based Promotion of Social Competence [Elias, M.J., Weissberg, R. P., Hawkins, J. D., Perry, C. L., Zins, J. E., Dodge, K. A., Kendall, P. C., Gottfredson, D., Rotherum-Borus, M. J., Jason, L. A. & Wilson-Brewer, R. J.]. (1994). The school-based promotion of social competence: Theory, research, practice, and policy. In R.J. Haggerty, L. R. Sherrod, N. Garmezy, & M. Rutter (Eds.), *Stress, risk, and resilience in children and adolescents: Processes, mechanisms, and interaction* (pp. 268–316). New York: Cambridge University Press.

Dryfoos, J. D. (1994). *Full-service schools: A revolution in health and social services for children, youth, and families.* San Francisco: Jossey-Bass.

Elias, M. J. & Clabby, J. F. (1989). *Social decision-making skills: A curriculum guide for elementary grades.* Gaithersberg, MD: Aspen.

Fox, J. A., & Newman, S. A. (1997). *After school crime or after school programs: Tuning in to the prime time for violent juvenile crime and implications for national policy. A report to the United States Attorney General.* Washington, D.C.: Fight Crime: Invest in kids. (ERIC Document Reproduction Service No. ED 412319).

Hawkins, J. D., Catalano, R. F., & Associates. (1992). *Communities that care: Action for drug abuse prevention.* San Francisco: Jossey-Bass.

Heath, S. B. (1999). Dimensions of language development: Lessons from older children. In A. S. Masten (Ed.), *Cultural processes in child development: The Minnesota symposium on child psychology* (vol. 29, pp. 59–75). Mahwah, NJ: Erlbaum.

Hightower, A. D., Johnson, D., & Haffey, W. G. (1995). Best practices in adopting a prevention program. In A. Thomas, and J. Grimes (Eds.), *Best practices in school psychology III.* Washington, D.C.: National Association of School Psychologists.

Jessor, R., Turbin, M. S., & Costa, F. M. (1998). Protective factors in adolescent health behavior. *Journal of Personality and Social Psychology, 75*(3), 788–800.

Kelly, C. (1995). Best practices in building-level public relations. In A. Thomas, and J. Grimes (Eds.), *Best practices in school psychology III.* Washington, D.C.: National Association of School Psychologists.

Kolbe, L. J., Collins, J., & Cortese, P. (1997). Building the capacity for schools to improve the health of the nation: A call for assistance from psychologists. *American Psychologist, 52,* 256–265.

Larson, R. W. (2000). Toward a psychology of positive youth development. *American Psychologist, 55,* 170–183.

Minke, K. M. (2000). Preventing school problems and promoting school success through family-school-community collaboration. In K. M. Minke, and G. G. Bear (Eds.), Preventing school problems—Promoting school success. Bethesda, MD: National Association of School Psychologists.

O'Day, J. (2000). School psychologists as mental health providers. *Communiqué, 28*(7), 12–13.

Satcher, D.(1999). *Mental Health: A report of the Surgeon General.* Rockville, MD: U.S. Department of Health and Human Services, Substance Abuse and Mental Health Services Administration, Center for Mental Health Services, National Institutes of Health, National Institute of Mental Health.

Satcher, D. (2000, March 15). Getting physical: Exercising our demons: Sedentary lifestyles and fatty foods leave Americans overweight and unhealthy. *Atlanta Journal-Constitution*, p. A17.

Saunders, R., Pate, R. (2000). Promoting physical health. In K. M. Minke, and G. G. Bear (Eds.), *Preventing school problems—Promoting school success.* Bethesda, MD: National Association of School Psychologists.

School Health Programs. (2000, Aug. 14). Center for Disease Control and Prevention At-A-Glance 2000. http://www.cdc.gov/nccdphp/dash/ataglance.htm. (8/14/00).

Schorr, L. B. (1997). *Common purpose: Strengthening families and neighborhoods to rebuild America.* New York: Anchor.

Search Institute. (2000). *Take it to heart: An asset-based guide to nurturing children, youth, and families in faith community.* [Brochure]. Minneapolis, MN: Author.

Seligman, M. E. P., & Csikszentmihalyi, M. (2000). Positive psychology. *American Psychologist 55,* 5–12.

Wrobel, G., and Krieg, F. J. (2000). Health care and school psychology: Building the bridges. *Communiqué, 28*(7), 8–10.

Zill, N., Nord, C. W., & Loomis, L .S. (1995). *Adolescent time use, risky behavior, and outcomes: An analysis of national data.* Washington, D,C,: Department of Health and Human Services.

Zins, J. E., Elias, M. J., Greenberg, M. T., & Weissberg, R. P. (2000). Promoting social and emotional competence in children. In K. M. Minke, and G. C. Bear (Eds.), *Preventing school problems—Promoting school success.* Bethesda, MD: National Association of School Psychologists.

Zins, J. E., & Wagner, D. I. (1997). Health promotion. In G. G. Bear, K. M. Minke, & A. Thomas (Eds.), *Chil-*

dren's needs II: Development, problems, and alternatives (pp.945–954). Bethesda, MD: National Association of School Psychologists.

ANNOTATED BIBLIOGRAPHY

Dryfoos, J. D. (1994). *Full-service schools: A revolution in health and social services for children, youth, and families*. San Francisco: Jossey-Bass.
Perhaps the most comprehensive book on full-service schools. Makes a strong argument for broad based health promotion and is filled with ideas on how to make a full-service school a reality.

Schorr, L. B. (1997). *Common purpose: Strengthening families and neighborhoods to rebuild America*. New York: Anchor.
Required reading for anyone interested in solutions to the social problems plaguing our nation. Research based, practical, and optimistic.

Search Institute. (2000). *Take it to heart: An asset-based guide to nurturing children, youth, and families in faith community*. [Brochure]. Minneapolis, MN: Author.
One of a number of brochures and newsletters published by the Search Institute. Highlights positive youth development and offers 40 assets that all youth in America need to possess.

U.S. Department of Health and Human Services (1999). *Mental Health: A report of the Surgeon General*. Rockville, MD: U.S. Department of Health and Human Services, Substance Abuse and Mental Health Services Administration, Center for Mental Health Services, National Institutes of Health, National Institute of Mental Health.
The 487 page document makes a convincing argument (using research articles and other documents) that mental health has a direct link to the learning process and to learning outcomes. May be a valuable source to help convince a broader constituency that mental issues must be addressed if our children are to succeed in school and life.

Zins, J. E., & Wagner, D. I. (1997). Health promotion. In G. G. Bear, K. M. Minke, & A. Thomas (Eds.), *Children's needs II: Development, problems, and alternatives* (pp.945–954). Bethesda, MD: National Association of School Psychologists.
Chapter in an earlier NASP publication that focuses on the full spectrum of health–related issues that affect our children. Their definition of health promotion remains the standard. They convincingly argue that our current system is not working effectively and that school psychologists must play a central role in reducing the many health risks faced by today's youth.

61 Best Practices in Developing Exemplary Mental Health Programs in Schools

Kathy Pluymert
West Dundee, IL

OVERVIEW

The need for school-based mental health services has become increasingly apparent in recent years. As school communities, parents, policy makers, and the media have examined factors that may account for incidents in which a crisis has occurred in a school setting, a recurring theme has been the mental health needs of the students involved. High-profile crisis situations are dramatic illustrations of the struggles that school communities encounter daily in trying to help students succeed in school in the face of sometimes overwhelmingly complex personal and social difficulties.

In some situations, a high-profile incident that captures the media spotlight or a crisis in its own community is what propels the school to develop programs to address the mental health needs of students. In the wake of a crisis, members of the community are searching for ways to prevent those kinds of tragedies from ever happening again. The Chinese symbol for crisis, which includes elements of both danger and opportunity, illustrates the challenge to school communities, and to the profession of school psychology in these situations. Members of the National Association of School Psychologists (NASP) National Emergency Assistance Team observed, "Crisis has been frequently recognized as a time of potential danger as well as potential opportunity.... If our profession is able to manage the danger—that is, manage the immediate crisis and quickly return the system to normal functioning—then there exists a tremendous opportunity to stimulate long-term systemic change. Once seen as effective and credible, the psychologist has infinitely more opportunity to move the system in the direction of prevention" (Poland, Pitcher, & Lazarus, 1995, p.446).

While tragic situations may sometimes be the impetus for developing school-based mental health programs, there is a growing body of compelling evidence in our society of the importance of addressing mental health needs of children. Demographic information collected by a host of private and government agencies clearly demonstrate the need for interventions and systematic approaches designed to address child and adolescent mental health needs. Statistics related to poverty, family disintegration, violence, and substance abuse are staggering indicators related to the lack of supportive families and economic resources needed for learning and school success (Knoff, 1996; U.S. Department of Health and Human Services, 1999). These barriers to learning (Adelman, 1996) are a growing concern in our society.

School psychologists can be an outstanding resource to the school community in the development of effective mental health services to address the needs of students and families. The challenge lies in providing excellent service in a crisis and also on a day-to-day basis in the routine matters and small crises that builds the credibility of the school psychologists within the school community.

Providing mental health services, such as group and individual counseling and mental health evaluations, have been a part of school psychological training and professional practice throughout the history of the profession. More recently, a growing body of literature that addresses the role of school psychologists as mental health service providers has emerged. Both literature and practice show that school psychologists are providing mental health services across the spectrum from prevention to treatment. These services can be found on a small scale in a single school and in complex exemplary school-based mental health programs that integrate the services of the school, community agencies, hospitals, and universities (Nastasi, Varjas, Bernstein, & Pluymert, 1998).

There is an increasing level of awareness among mental health professionals across sub-specialties that schools are a logical place for the delivery of mental health services to children and youth. Mental health services offered to students in school settings is a common sense service delivery option because children and youth are required to be in school. Providing mental health services in the school setting affords some excellent solutions to problems that families have in accessing mental health services, including problems with transportation and financial resources needed to obtain these services in the community (Dryfoos, 1994). As Knoff and Batsche (1990) point out, schools also provide excellent settings in which to identify and treat students with mental health needs as the school setting provides many opportunities to integrate and monitor treatments across home, school, and community settings.

Mental health services within school settings have the distinct advantage of presenting an ecologically realistic setting in which interventions can be readily integrated into students' daily activities. This integration allows for opportunities for students to generalize behaviors and skills learned in therapeutic sessions into their daily routines, allowing for greater integrity in their overall functioning (Jackson & Bernauer, 1975). In addition, mental health professionals who work with students in school settings can, in collaboration with teachers, recommend and evaluate the effects of modifications to the classroom environment. It might also be possible to modify the expectations and attitudes of school personnel through consultation, providing data about the student's needs and learning styles, and modeling.

There is an increasing awareness of the value of school settings as important in meeting the mental health needs of children and youth. Many mental health professionals, who 15 years ago would not have considered providing services in schools, are now very interested in school-based mental health because of the benefits to children and disenchantment with more traditional forms of mental health service delivery systems for children (Waxman & Weist, 1999). In addition to the benefits to students of providing mental health services in schools, there are other economic and professional factors that serve to draw professionals previously serving in private practice and clinical settings to the school. The advent of managed care and subsequently limited or reduced funding for mental health services to hospitals and private practices have also resulted in the schools now being perceived as an attractive practice setting to mental health professionals and psychologists of other specializations (Bricklin et al., 1994; Short & Talley, 1997). Unfortunately, many of these professionals have minimal training and experience in working with children and little familiarity with school settings. While there is some acknowledgment among psychologists that there is a specialized set of competencies in school practice (Kubiszyn, 1999), the future of school-based mental health services will likely be much more a matter of well–conceived and collaboratively implemented mental health services delivered in the schools by a group of mental health specialists across disciplines.

From the perspective of both child and professional advocacy, it is vital that school psychologists become proactive in promoting their role as mental health service providers and in the development of exemplary mental health programs in schools (Dwyer, 1996; Gutkin, 1995). Realistically, professionals who are the most versatile, who can provide the most valued and cost-effective services to the district, and who are able to demonstrate the efficacy of their services to decision makers are those who will be asked to serve the school community, without regard to an individual's training or title.

Given the need for school psychologists to be increasingly proactive in the development of exemplary school-based mental health programs and services, the purpose of this chapter is twofold. First, to serve as an introduction to the practitioner on the resources and literature available that describes school-based and school-linked mental health services and programs currently in school settings. The second purpose of the chapter is to provide practical strategies that school psychologists can use to develop an approach integrating mental health services and programming into their own school community to address the unique needs of the local educational agency they serve.

BASIC CONSIDERATIONS

Before a school psychologist can begin to develop a school-based mental health program, there are a number of factors that the practitioner needs to be cognizant of to maximize the likelihood of the long-term success of a program and to minimize frustration and road blocks to the process. These factors include: (a) building a foundation of credibility and trust within the district, (b) knowing how the school functions as a system and understanding its unique needs, (c) building coalitions and networks for comprehensive and coordinated service delivery options, and (d) becoming well prepared to plan, implement, and evaluate the services and/or program. If the practitioner attends to each of these factors, then the program has a much greater chance of institutionalization. That is, the program will be accepted, implemented as designed, integrated, and valued by the school and community and will survive challenges that will come in the form of changes in staffing patterns, funding, and leadership/administration within the system.

Build a Strong Foundation of Trust

One of the questions most frequently asked by school psychology practitioners is, "How can I get my supervisor/principal/school district to let me provide mental health services? It's not part of my job description." The answer to that question is twofold and has to do with providing excellent services and being willing to take a risk to go beyond the stated job description. The most effective advocates for the profession of school psychology are skilled in two ways. First, they are caring, competent school psychologists who provide excellent forward-thinking services to children and the school community. Second, they are skilled in demonstrating the value of their services to the system in which they work and actively do things to build positive relationships with others. It is vitally important that school psychologists raise their visibility in the school community in which they work, because increased visibility can lead to increased opportunities to expand their role and to serve children.

There are several excellent resources that practitioners can use to become intentional about building positive relationships and developing communications activities that will serve to illustrate the value of their services to the school community. For example, NASP members can access several resources from a NASP manual entitled, *Practical Strategies to Expand Services to Children and Families* (Thomas, Pluymert, & Armistead, 1998). This manual includes examples of communications activities such as model newsletter articles, samples of letters, and prepared presentations (including overheads) that can be used as they are or modified to suit the needs of the individual practitioner. As school psychologists use these kinds of communications activities to educate decision makers in the community about their expertise and knowledge base in key areas of mental health service delivery, the better their position will be as new opportunities present themselves. In addition to purposeful communications activities, school psychologists need to make purposeful positive personal contacts with decision makers. It is important not to underestimate these contacts (Curtis & Stollar, 1995).

For example, one school psychologist began by regularly scheduling only 15 minutes each week to talk with the building principal about building-level issues. After a few weeks of such talks, an interesting journal article related to one of the issues discussed would occasionally be given to the principal. Over time, the school psychologist came to be viewed by the principal as a source of information and expertise regarding a broader range of issues, particularly as they pertained to organizational concerns (p. 55).

Understand the School Community as a System and Know What the Community Needs

The long-term success of school-based mental health programming depends largely on the program becoming integrated into and valued by the system. To achieve the goal of institutionalization of mental health programs, it is critically important to attend to systems issues and needs assessment in the development, implementation, and evaluation of these programs.

Developing a Systems Orientation

Curtis and Stollar (1995) offer the following definition of a systems orientation: "a systems perspective involves the ability to understand the reciprocal influence that the various parts of a system, the system itself, and the surrounding system or environment exert on one another" (p.52). When considering the development, implementation, and evaluation of mental health programs, a systems perspective is important for several reasons. One of these is that implementing mental health programs in schools is essentially a form of system-level consultation. A problem-solving approach, collaboration, and systematic planning are critical skills that a practitioner needs to develop mental health services in school settings. Another reason that a systems perspective is vital is that reciprocal effects of the multiple facets involved in mental health programming need to be considered. Factors such as the effects of family environment, the school, and the community on the students, as well as the impact that students have on their respective environments, are important considerations (Meyers & Nastasi, 1999). Including active participation of key individuals who are decision makers, influential in the community, and determine access to financial resources as well as any group that will be involved in the program (or affected by it) is also vital if the program is to be valued and supported by the system. The reader is referred to the chapter on system-level consultation in this volume for further information about these important skills.

Conducting a Needs Assessment

If a mental health program is to be successful, then it is essential that the program be tailored to the unique needs of the school community, students, and families it is designed to serve. The practitioner needs to look for a convergence of information from a variety of sources to establish the real and perceived needs within the school community from a variety of perspectives. There are several needs assessment methods that can be used to gather this kind of critical information. School psychologists have a natural source of information in the kinds of referrals that are a part of their work in the school system. An analysis of formal and informal referrals for consultation services, problem-solving meetings, pre-referral intervention team meetings, case study evaluations, or "hallway consultation" provide a rich source of information about needs in the community. By keeping track of referrals, case load, and investigating the records of building-level team meetings, from Teacher Assistance Teams to multidisciplinary staff conferences, a pattern of needs will emerge. Information from disciplinary referrals, suspensions, and expulsions will add a substantial amount of information available if it is compiled and analyzed carefully. Data can also be collected from community-based or county resources such as the Department of Corrections, Department of Health, and Social Services. The data about rates of violent crimes, juvenile arrests, substance abuse, adjudicated youth, and teen pregnancy are important information about student mental health needs and assist the psychologist in developing the perspective of the school as a part of a larger community.

Additional perspectives can be gained through interviews with parents, policy makers, and other important decision makers in the school community. Those interviews can be informal conversations, formal structured interviews, or in focus groups. The interviews serve not only to provide information, but to demonstrate that the school psychologist is interested in building collaborative relationships. The field of school-based mental health service is changing and developing at a pace somewhat faster than educators typically proceed, which can lead to some resistance. Be sensitive to this during the interviews. Another factor to consider is that there are groups that object strenuously to mental health services delivered in schools (Evans, 1999), and their perspectives also need to be attended to in the development of school-based services.

Finally, surveys can provide a concrete form of gathering information about both real and perceived needs through collecting specific system-level data and attitudinal information from members of the school community. Nagle (1995) provides an excellent overview of needs assessment techniques for school psychologists that could be used to gather the information needed for mental health program development.

Build Coalitions and Networks for Comprehensive and Coordinated Services

Given that programs and services for children and adolescents are provided by a variety of sources, it is common for any individual child to be served by multiple agencies and service providers within the community that are not in communication with each other. To address the problems of streamlining and increasing the efficacy of mental health services, the current watchwords are "coordinated and integrated services" (Bickman & Rog, 1995). Schools provide an excellent setting for collaboration and coordination of services for children and youths. Schools can serve several functions including complement services of outside agencies, serve as a catalyst to coordinate services, and develop programs to improve and expand services delivered in the school setting (Adelman, 1996). As Conoley & Conoley (1991) observed, the nature of referrals and range of presenting problem behaviors are the same for school-based and clinic-based psychologists. Through working together, school, clinic, hospital, and community agency-based mental health practitioners may have the opportunity to improve treatment outcomes by coordinating interventions across the home and school settings.

The development of comprehensive and coordinated mental health service delivery models requires that school psychologists be well acquainted with the services and agencies already available within the community. School psychologists need to know which community agencies, parent and family support groups, and private providers (including pediatricians and pediatric specialists) exist in the community and what functions those agencies and groups provide to students and families. It is also important to begin to build relationships with those groups to open the door to further communication during the planning, implementation, and evaluation of school-based or school-linked mental health services and programs. Getting to know community resources is not only a form of needs assessment, but it is an important aspect of program development through coalition building. Child advocacy and coordination of services require that school psychologists do this kind of networking in serving individual students. Similarly, coordination and coalition building is needed when developing services for the school community. Look for ways in which the needs of children, teens, and families are being met in the community. Conversely, look for unmet needs and ways that existing programs and services could be improved.

Do Your Homework on Effective Mental Health Services

The Scouting motto "be prepared" offers wise counsel to school psychologists who are working to establish or expand mental health services in school settings. Once the practitioner gets a sense of the needs of the students and the school community served in his or her local education agency, and understands the existing supports and services available, it is critical to begin to investigate effective practices, service delivery systems, and programs that work. While there is merit in creative approaches and innovative programs, the stakes for children and families who have significant mental health needs are high. The field of mental health services has evolved to the point where there is an extensive body of evidence about effective interventions and programs to address the mental health needs of students and families that yield good outcomes (Hoagwood & Erwin, 1997) .

The literature of school-based and school-linked mental health has grown tremendously in the last decade, with good material added regularly. It is difficult to recommend one book or journal over another, since there are many equally good sources from which to choose. However, for a good basic orientation to the literature in school-based mental health services, the brief annotated bibliography and list of references at the end of this chapter can serve as a good starting point. The annotated bibliography was chosen to give an overview of some of the theory and practice in school-based mental health with an emphasis on literature outside of material that a typical school psychologist practitioner might read. For information about specific kinds of programs, for example, to address suicide prevention, or crisis intervention, in addition to the resources in this volume, conduct a literature review by using ERIC, PSYCH-INFO, or other similar databases, many of which can be accessed on-line though a school or university library. The information gained through literature review will provide invaluable information about how to design, implement, and evaluate a program or service, and will provide a kind of benchmark, and perhaps rationale, to use as a pattern. This is also an important consideration in funding, because many funding sources may require the replication of an existing program model.

One good resource to obtain information about existing mental health programs is Nastasi, Varjas, Bernstein, and Pluymert (1997). Nastasi et al. (1997) includes information about many programs across the United States. An example of one frequently cited model developed by school psychologists is Project ACHIEVE. A program description can be found in

Knoff and Batsche (1995). Finally, there are several agencies or organizations that can be accessed via the Internet that have information about school-based mental health programs. In addition to NASP's National Mental Health and Education Center for Children and Families, the American Institute for Research, School Mental Health Project/Center for Mental Health in Schools (University of California, Los Angeles), and the Center for School Mental Health Assistance (University of Maryland School of Medicine) have excellent resources. Another resource includes a multi-million dollar grant program funded by the U.S. Department of Education that was designed to address reduction of school violence through a collaborative school- and community-based mental health program. Obtaining a grant from these funds, The National Mental Health Association and NASP, working together with several other agencies, developed a network of school-based mental health programs called, "Safe Schools/ Healthy Students Initiative." This initiative provided many exemplary comprehensive and coordinated school and community mental health programs for a 3-year period, beginning in 1999, and provides examples of many good model programs.

BEST PRACTICES

There are many excellent program models, theories, and best practices in mental health services for children and families. What follows is a summary of a consensus of opinions and theoretical and practical considerations in developing, implementing, and evaluating an exemplary mental health program. The following factors are important best practices in the process: (a) attend carefully to characteristics of exemplary programs (b) choose well-documented models and/or empirically validated interventions, (c) pay close attention to legal considerations, (d) develop a blended funding base, and (e) complete program evaluation and use the data to further develop the program and to promote the program in the school community.

Characteristics of Exemplary Mental Health Programs

According to Nastasi et al. (1997) , there are six hallmarks of exemplary mental health programs:

1. Programming reflects an integration of theory, research, and practice.

2. Programming is framed within an ecological-developmental theoretical model.

3. Program development, implementation, and evaluation reflect a collaborative/ participatory model.

4. A continuum of mental health services is provided, ranging from prevention to treatment.

5. Program evaluation address program acceptability, integrity, and effectiveness.

6. A school psychologist is involved in one or more aspects of mental health programming.

What follows is a summary of the description of each of these factors from Nastasi et al. (1997).

Integration of Theory, Research, and Practice

If a mental health program is to be exemplary, it is essential that there be an integration of relevant theory and research, and application of these into the daily workings of the program. This process is a cycle of learning, planning, implementing, and evaluating practice in light of developing theory, results of evaluation and related research, and subsequent modification of practice. This collaborative action research approach (Meyers & Nastasi, 1999) is a reciprocal process in which research and theory affect practice and the results and application in practice inform further research and is in itself a way of building theory. Nastasi et al. (1997) note that this approach to program development, implementation, and evaluation is consistent with most school psychologist practitioners' training as scientist-practitioners and offers a promising model for integrating the roles of school psychologists that sometimes appear disparate. "That is, an action research model provides the framework for integrating assessment, intervention, consultation, and research. Ideally, this integration also fosters engagement in and dissemination of research by practitioners" (p. 4). The work that a school psychologist has completed in literature review and investigating model programs and empirically supported interventions will provide a good working foundation for accomplishing this aspect of program development.

Ecological-Developmental Model

If a program is to be exemplary, then it is vital that the program meet the needs of the system and the needs of the individuals within the system. In the ecological-developmental model, development is considered to be a progressive and mutual adaptation of the environment and of the individual. Nastasi et al. (1997) states, "... in order to understand and/or change human behavior, one must attend to the ecological contexts in which the individual is socialized (e.g., school, family, community) as well as the interaction of those contexts (e.g. parent-teacher interaction). Furthermore, the individual plays an active role in development, such that one's personal qualities and behavior engender certain interactions with the environment" (p. 5). The background work that the school psychologist has done in systems analysis and needs assessment as described earlier in this chapter should provide a good foundation for looking into these reciprocal factors in program development, implementation, and evaluation. Look carefully at points of interaction and reciprocal influence in the context of the program and services.

Collaborative/Participatory Model

It is essential that the process of designing, implementing, and evaluating the program is a model of collaboration between the program planning team, stakeholder groups, and decision makers and that each of these groups is involved as members of the team. This approach is consistent with school psychologists training in collaborative consultation and problem solving, applied here to a system. This model is also consistent with school reform efforts and best practice with regard to coordinated and integrated service delivery. Collaboration and coalition building is not easy due to inevitable conflicts in different organizations' conceptualization of their roles, conflicts about professional turf issues, potential competition for funding, and other more personal power and control issues. However, without these potentially political negotiations, comprehensive and coordinated services for students and their families will not occur. Adelman (1996) and Knoff (1996) suggest that school psychologists are possible organizational facilitators who can coordinate collaboration across agencies and between schools, families, and community agencies. These collaborative efforts and participatory management approaches are likely to ensure that the program attends to cultural factors, empowers members of stakeholder groups, and facilitates the process of institutionalizing the program (Nastasi et al., 1997).

Continuum of Services

Comprehensive and coordinated mental health services require a broad-based model ranging from prevention programs targeted to the regular classroom to treatment services for individuals with moderate to severe mental health problems. The services vary on a continuum across several factors including population served, referral processes, context for service provision, and staffing requirements. Nastasi et al. (1997) propose four levels of intervention: prevention, risk reduction, early intervention, and treatment:

Level I : Prevention. Prevention services are targeted toward the general populations. They focus on fostering individual development and creating supportive social environments. All students receive this level of intervention that is delivered in the context of an intact group such as the classroom. Examples of these kinds of services include those in which personal-social goals regarding issues such as substance abuse are integrated into the academic curriculum.

Level II: Risk Reduction. Risk reduction services are targeted toward high risk population. These services focus on building competence, teaching coping skills, and modifying social context in which risky behaviors might occur. Students might self-select into this level of service delivery, which would typically be delivered in the context of a small group. An example of this level of service might include support groups for children of alcoholics.

Level III: Early Interventions. Early intervention services are targeted toward individuals with mild adjustment problems and are designed to treat mild adjustment problems, reduce the risk of more severe problems, and modify the context in which the problem behaviors manifest themselves to affect individual adjustment. Students might be referred for early intervention services though screening and/or referral. Services are typically delivered in individual or small group formats. An example of early intervention service is a counseling group for students experiencing mild depression.

Level IV: Treatment. This most intensive level of service delivery targets individuals with moderate to severe emotional disturbance and/or mental health needs. Service focuses on treating identified mental health problems and modifying context to effect the individual's functioning. Students would likely be referred and selected for this level of service through diagnosis by a mental health professional. Direct services are typically delivered in individual or small group contexts by mental health professionals.

Model of Evaluation

Program evaluation is a critical component of mental health services and programs delivered in school settings, which too often is not thoughtfully integrated into program development from the beginning. As illustrated earlier in the discussion about integrating theory, research, and practice, data from program evaluation informs both practice and theory and offers a defensible rationale for program implementation. Nastasi asserts that in order for program evaluation to be complete enough to assess key factors in service delivery and to inform practice, three key elements of program evaluation need to be included in the process.

The first is *acceptability*, which considers the participants' (both recipients and facilitators) perceptions and attitudes about the program's feasibility, efficacy, usefulness, and whether or not the program is consistent with their own world views. Examples of methods for assessing program acceptability include interviews, focus groups, questionnaires, and examining journals.

The second component is *integrity*, which looks at whether or not the program is implemented as designed. One component of this would be to document variations in program implementation by different facilitators or with various recipients to identify modifications needed in how the program is delivered or to address staff development and training issues. Examples of techniques to assess program integrity would be activity logs, observations, interviews, self-evaluation measures, and journals.

The third component is program *efficacy*, which examines program outcomes. This aspect of program evaluation measures the extent to which the program and services meet their stated goals and objectives. It also evaluates unintended program outcomes. Measures of program efficacy might include observation, interviews, self-report measures, rating scales, analog measures, and curriculum-based evaluation measures.

Choose Well-Documented Models and Empirically Validated Interventions

After completing the literature review and examination of programs during the preparation described earlier in this chapter, it is important to carefully examine the models available keeping two important factors in mind. First, is the information provided in light of the proposed model program's outcome and other evaluation data of high quality? Does the program provide outcome data and information about consumer satisfaction? Second, look at the match between your community and the students you serve and the demographic and organizational data reported by the programs you are investigating. There does not have to be a match, but sometimes settings and resources available can have an impact on program outcomes and consumers' perceptions of the efficacy of the program (Pluymert, 2000). A carefully chosen program model with a proven track record assists the practitioner in that the model is defensible on the basis of a track record of research. Practitioners will want to talk with individuals who are implementing the program and with the program originator or author, if possible. The advice and mentoring available in consulting with other professionals who are already immersed in the program that is under consideration can be a tremendous asset to a practitioner who is learning a new set of skills.

Legal Considerations

It is important to implement best legal practices when developing a mental health program in the school setting. Several aspects of law need to be carefully attended to including confidentiality, consent, and, when including students under entitlement provisions, IDEA regulations. It is also important to investigate state law and regulations with regard to mental health services, because consent and confidentiality in matters of mental health services are often different from those within IDEA and other applicable regulations.

Evans (1999) offers a review of the various aspects of consent for school-based mental health services. Consent is sometimes interpreted within the school setting as passive consent. In other words, parents are informed that they have access to information about mental health services and the fact that they have the right to object if they choose to do so. This is often the mechanism that is used for sex education and some prevention programs offered in the school setting. However, it may be best practice to take a more conservative approach and to obtain parental consent for students who will be receiving mental health services at school. Evans argues that there is a significant difference in the concept of consent for a school versus a clinic setting for mental health services. Parents do not send their children to school with the expectation that they will be receiving mental health services. Informed consent is important to protect the rights of the child, the parent, and the practitioner. Without parental consent, Evans warns, the practitioner is exposed to considerable potential liability.

The issue of confidentiality in school-based mental health services should be dealt with carefully in light of professional responsibilities such as duty to warn, typically confronting the school psychologist in the delivery of any mental health services in school settings. A confounding factor for confidentiality emerges because there is increasing collaboration between agencies and professionals to provide mental health services. Finally, as funding sources such as Medicaid and managed care companies become involved in school-based mental health services provisions, confidentiality becomes a consideration with regard to caps on a student's available future coverage, given services that might be provided in the school setting.

Finally, there are several aspects of IDEA that the practitioner needs to keep in mind when developing mental health services in the schools. Schacht and Hanson (1999) provide an overview of case law from across the country that highlights some of the legal aspects of school-based mental health services under IDEA. The authors highlight factors that have an impact on the development of programs and services, including the difference between a student having a DSM-IV diagnosis and the presence of a disability, the difference between incidents of student misconduct and the presence of a disability, least restrictive environments for service delivery, and mental health services as a related service for students who are entitled to special education services.

Develop a Blended Funding Base

One of the factors that contributes more than almost any other factor in the demise of mental health services and programs is discontinuation of the funding source. While school administrators value school-based mental health services, they are generally not equally enthusiastic about the school's responsibility for providing those services (Pluymert, 2000). If a program is going to go the distance over time in serving students and the school community, then it is important to look to a variety of funding sources for the program. There are many sources to investigate for funding mental health programs.

Nastasi et al. (1997) found the following funding patterns among the 103 programs included in the study:

1. 56% of the programs relied on multiple funding sources
2. 52% of the programs received funding from external grants
3. 64% of the programs were funded by schools, with 37% of these using special education funds and 32% funded as non–special education support services
4. 23% relied on Medicaid funds
5. 11% received funds from health insurance companies or HMO's, and 7% were linked to school-based health clinics.
6. 11% were funded by private agencies
7. 37% of the programs relied on some other source of funds

Several of the programs were volunteer efforts under the leadership of school psychologists, and one school psychologist stated that she personally "scrounged for funds." An interesting resource for the practitioner is a book written by a school administrator that retells her experiences in establishing school-based mental health services in her community (Hoover & Achilles, 1996).

Grant dollars through federal agencies, private industry or foundations are a good source of funding, but can also be risky over time as a program that depends heavily on grant monies can be devastated if the grant dollars are time-limited or dependent on the will of federal or state legislators. There are publications and on-line resources available to investigate grant possibilities, but the practitioner needs to be careful to use grant funding in conjunction with other more stable funding sources. Collaboration with other mental health agencies and with community and with parent groups can be a helpful source of both financial and human resources.

Sometimes the most valuable commodity is not dollars, but committed volunteers who receive support and training through the mental health professionals in the program. The inclusion of volunteer support is a good use of resources and also builds a sense of ownership that is an important factor in the institutionalization process. This concept can also be extended to in-kind donations of materials, space, and services that can be obtained from individuals, small businesses, and agencies.

Use Program Evaluation Data to Maximize Benefits to the Program

It is critical to complete program evaluation and to make the results of the program evaluation useful information for further program development, providing information about the program to constituent groups. Program evaluation is an important part of the school psychologist's role as scientist-practitioner, gathering and utilizing data to validate and potentially improve services. These are practices that may not be considered a priority in the light of the urgent matters of daily practice, but they are critical elements in best practice and in the program's ability to provide accountability and to promote its good work to the community.

Nastasi et al. (1997) found that of the 103 programs, most addressed program acceptability (79%), program integrity (66%), and program efficacy (80%). Forty-three percent reported that they conducted follow-up evaluations. Only 42% reported having any results available in writing, and only a handful of these programs actually provided written data after repeated requests.

The importance of program evaluation from a theoretical and program improvement perspective is clear. Without collecting data in a systematic fashion as was discussed earlier, the practitioner is reliant upon making decisions about services for children and youth absent any reliable benchmarks. There is a changing paradigm for service delivery in school psychology such that practitioners are increasingly utilizing resources such as curriculum-based evaluation (Howell & Nolet, 2000) for assessing and creating interventions for social behaviors. As this level of accountability becomes the standard for educational and psychological service delivery to individuals in the schools, mental health services and programs should be held to the same standard.

Program evaluation is not only required from a professional best practice standard, but funding sources and constituent support also call for the practitioner to produce data that demonstrate the efficacy of the program. Much of the excitement and good will generated around the creation of a program can be sustained through the use of data that demonstrate the positive outcomes of the program to the benefit of the community. Many of the communications activities described earlier, such as letters and presentations to community groups and decision makers, reports to constituent groups, articles written for local publications, and press releases, are good mechanisms for spreading the good word about the value of the program, as well as generating interest and support in the community for the important work of the program.

SUMMARY

The need for school-based mental health services has become increasingly apparent in recent years. School psychologists can be an outstanding resource to the school community in the development of effective mental health services to address the needs of students and families that they serve. From the perspective of both child and professional advocacy, it is vital that school psychologists become proactive in promoting their role as mental health service providers and in the development of exemplary mental health programs in schools.

Before a school psychologist can begin to develop a school-based mental health program, there are a number of factors that the practitioner needs to be cognizant of to maximize the likelihood of the long-term success of a program and to minimize frustration and roadblocks to the process. To have the opportunity to develop mental health programming in the school, many practitioners will find that their first priority is to build a foundation of credibility and trust within the district by providing excellent services in the day-to-day events and the crises that occur, and by promoting the value of the work they do through the use of communications activities. A second key to developing a successful mental health program is knowing how the school functions as a system and understanding its unique needs. The school psychologist will need to utilize systems consultation and needs assessment skills to serve as a catalyst for change. Third, the practitioner will need to actively build coalitions and networks for comprehensive and coordinated service delivery options. In addition, the school psychologist will need to become well prepared to plan, implement, and evaluate the service and/or program through research of the literature and a review of empirically supported interventions and existing program models that are well supported and show evidence of positive outcomes for students. If the practitioner attends to each of these factors, then the program has a much greater chance of institutionalization.

When the school psychologist is ready to approach program development, implementation, and evaluation, specific factors should be considered to facilitate the success of the program. Characteristics of exemplary mental health programs are incorporated in the program including theory-research-practice integration; an ecological-developmental approach; collaborative-participatory model; the provision of a continuum of mental health services; program evaluation that addresses program acceptability, integrity and efficacy; and the involvement of a school psychologist. Finally, the practitioner needs to ensure that exemplary programs attend to best practices in program development, implementation, and evaluation including choosing well-documented models and/or empirically validated interventions; giving close attention to legal considerations; developing a blended funding base; and completing program evaluation, utilizing the data to further develop the program and to promote it in the school community.

REFERENCES

Adelman, H. S. (1996). Restructuring education support services and integrating community resources: Beyond the full service school model. *School Psychology Review, 25*(4), 431–445.

Bickman, L., & Rog, D. J. (Eds.). (1995). *Children's mental health services: Research, policy, and evaluation.* (Vol. 1). Thousand Oaks, CA: Sage.

Bricklin, P., Carlson, C., DeMers, S., Paavola, J., Talley, R., & Tharinger, D. (1994). *Schools as health service delivery sites: Historical, current, and future roles for psychology.* Washington, DC: Schools as Health Service Delivery Sites Work Group, American Psychological Association, Committee for the Advancement of Professional Practice.

Conoley, J. C., & Conoley, C. W. (1991). Collaboration for child adjustment: Issues for school and clinic based child psychologists. *Journal of Consulting and Clinical Psychology, 59*(6), 821–829.

Curtis, M., & Stollar, S. (1995). Best practices in system-level consultation and organizational change. In A. Thomas & J. Grimes (Eds.), *Best practices in school psychology III* (pp. 51–67). Washington, DC: National Association of School Psychologists.

Dryfoos, J. (1994). *Full service schools: A revolution in health and social services for children, youth and families.* San Francisco: Jossey-Bass.

Dwyer, K. (1996, February,). School psychologists: Essential partner in health care reform. *Communiqué, 25,* Insert page 1–3.

Evans, S. (1999). Mental health services in schools: Utilization, effectiveness, and consent. *Clinical Psychology Review, 19*(2), 165–178.

Gutkin, T. (1995). School psychology and health care: Moving service delivery into the twenty-first century. *School Psychology Quarterly, 10*(3), 236–246.

Hoagwood, K., & Erwin, H. (1997). Effectiveness of school-based mental health service for children: A 10-year research review. *Journal of Child and Family, 6*(4), 435–457.

Hoover, S., & Achilles, C. (1996). *Let's make a deal: Collaborating on a full-service school within your community.* Thousand Oaks, CA: Corwin.

Howell, K., & Nolet, V. (2000). *Curriculum-based evaluation.* Belmont, CA: Wadsworth.

Jackson, J., & Bernauer, M. (1975). A responsibility model for the practice of professional school psychology: Psychoeducational therapy. *Journal of School Psychology, 13*(1), 76–81.

Knoff, H. M. (1996). The interface of school, community, and health care reform: Organizational directions toward effective services for children and youth. *School Psychology Review, 25*(4), 446–464.

Knoff, H., & Batsche, G. (1990). The place of the school in community mental health services for children: A necessary interdependence. *The Journal of Mental Health Administration, 17*(1), 122 – 131.

Knoff, H., & Batsche, G. (1995). Project ACHIEVE: Analyzing a school reform process for at-risk and underachieving students. *School Psychology Review, 23*(4), 579–603.

Kubiszyn, T. (1999). Integrating health and mental health services in schools: Psychologists collaborating with primary care providers. *Clinical Psychology Review, 19*(2), 179–198.

Meyers, J., & Nastasi, B. (1999). Primary prevention in school settings. In C. Reynolds & T. Gutkin (Eds.), *The handbook of school psychology* (3rd ed.; pp. 764–799). New York: John Wiley.

Nagle, R. (1995). Best practices in conducting needs assessment. In A. Thomas & J. Grimes (Eds.), *Best practices in school psychology III* (pp. 421–430). Bethesda, MD: National Association of School Psychologists.

Nastasi, B. K., Varjas, K., Bernstein, R., & Pluymert, K. (1997). *Exemplary mental health programs: school psychologists as mental health service providers.* Bethesda, MD: National Association of School Psychologists.

Nastasi, B., Varjas, K., Bernstein, R., & Pluymert, K. (1998). Mental health programming and the role of school psychologist. *School Psychology Review, 27*(2), 260–276.

Pluymert, K. (2000). *A comparative investigation of mental health services in the schools: Administrative perspectives on students' mental health needs, efficacy of mental health services, and school psychological services.* Unpublished doctoral dissertation, Loyola University of Chicago.

Poland, S., Pitcher, G., & Lazarus, P. (1995). Best practices in crisis intervention. In A. Thomas & J. Grimes (Eds.), *Best practices in school psychology III* (pp. 445–458). Bethesda, MD: National Association of School Psychologists.

Schacht, T., & Hanson, G. (1999). Evolving legal climate for school mental health services under the Individuals with Disabilities Education Act. *Psychology in the Schools, 36*(5), 415– 426.

Short, R. J., & Talley, R. C. (1997). Rethinking psychology and the schools: Implications of recent national policy. *American Psychologist, 52*(3), 234–240.

Thomas, A., Pluymert, K., & Armistead, L. (1998). *Practical strategies to expand services to children and families.* Bethesda, MD: National Association of School Psychologists.

U.S. Department of Health and Human Services (1999) *Mental health: A report of the Surgeon General - Executive summary.* Rockville, MD: U.S. Department of Health and Human Services, Substance Abuse and Mental Health Services Administration, Center for Mental Health Services, National Institutes of Health, National Institute of Mental Health.

Waxman, R., & Weist, M. (1999). Toward collaboration in the growing education-mental health interface. *Clinical Psychology Review, 19*(2), 239–253.

ANNOTATED BIBLIOGRAPHY

Goldman, R. (Ed.). (1997). Model mental health programs and educational reform [Special issue]. *American Journal of Orthopsychiatry, 67*(3).

This special issue provides an excellent overview of school-based mental health services. There are articles on the history of school-based mental health services, on theoretical approaches to school reform and mental health services, and several practical examples of programs including wraparound services and consultative service delivery by mental health professionals.

Nastasi, B. (Ed). (1998) Mental health services in the schools [Special issue]. *School Psychology Review, 27*(2). This issue focuses on school-based and school-linked mental health services. The articles discuss the role of school psychologists in mental health programs and provide several examples of model mental health programs in schools.

Psychology in the Schools. (2000). *37*(1). This journal provides a focus on the future of school based practice with a focus on mental health services including articles on the future of the profession of school psychology, the effect of violence on mental health services in the schools, and other thought-provoking articles by well-known authors in the field of school psychology.

Weist, M. (Ed.). (1999) Challenges and opportunities in expanded school mental health [Special issue]. *Clinical Psychology Review, 19*(2). This clinical psychology journal presents several articles that provide the practitioner with information about topics in the development of school-based mental health services including articles about policy issues, legal matters, psychologists working with primary care providers as partners in health-care provision, working with managed care companies, and the growing interface between education and mental health professionals in schools, including a discussion of turf issues.

62 Best Practices in School Discipline

George G. Bear
Albert R. Cavalier
Maureen A. Manning
University of Delaware

OVERVIEW

Throughout the history of American education, school discipline has remained a primary concern among educators and the general public. As seen in the 32nd annual Phi Delta Kappa/Gallup Poll of the Public's Attitudes Toward the Public Schools (Rose & Gallup, 2000), a general "lack of discipline" is viewed by the public as the second biggest problem in public schools. "Fighting/violence/gangs," which are more specific and serious forms of discipline problems, are viewed as the fourth biggest problem. The 2000 poll also found that the public believes that the foremost purpose of public schools is "to prepare people to become responsible citizens." Although participants were not asked how educators could best achieve this goal, they were asked if they supported the use of harsh measures for those who fail to act responsibly, specifically in cases involving weapons. Results showed that 87% favor zero tolerance policies in schools.

The above results illustrate the conflicting views that parents and educators have had of school discipline over the years. That is, they have always recognized that the primary aim of education is to develop responsible citizenship, or self-discipline. At the same time, however, they have strongly supported the external use of discipline in order to maintain school environments that are safe, orderly, and conducive to learning. Over the course of American history various strategies and programs, both effective and ineffective, have been used in attempts to achieve both of these aims. Indeed, as seen below, many of the strategies used in the past to promote self-discipline and to maintain order and safety remain popular today. Thus, as one should expect, many of the debates and controversies over their use are not new to education, or to school psychology. This would include debates and controversies over corporal punishment, suspension, expulsion, the systematic use of extrinsic rewards, the placement of disruptive students in alternative education and special education settings, and the effectiveness of strategies and programs designed to promote social and emotional development.

A Brief History of School Discipline: The Shifting Importance of Prevention, Correction, and Remediation

Before the twentieth century, it was believed that self-discipline was best learned through the memorization of moral teachings based primarily on the Bible (McClellan, 1999). In addition to moral knowledge, parents and teachers strove to instill in children a fear of punishment and sense of shame for their wrongdoings. Such fear and shame were often justified, as harsh consequences, especially corporal punishment and public humiliation, were frequently used to teach self-discipline and maintain classroom order. The popularity of punitive techniques was perhaps best captured in Horace Mann's comment that "adults thought of punishment lightly, spoke of it with amusement, and inflicted it liberally" (as cited in Raichle, 1977/1978).

Strategies changed markedly in the early twentieth century. The use of physical punishment and teaching of Biblical scripture declined as a result of improved teacher training, increased national awareness of children's mental health needs, widespread public concern about the moral decay of the nation, and legal challenges (McClellan, 1999). The emphasis on threats, punishment, and religious education was replaced by an emphasis on democratic values, beliefs, and behaviors. The goal of this movement, known as character education, was to promote the growth of the ideal American citizen. Initially, this goal was advanced through direct teaching strategies. For example, teachers continued to depend on moral exhortations and teaching students to memorize what was "right" and "wrong." Instead of Biblical verses, however, children were taught to memorize oaths, codes of conduct, and passages that focused on qualities of moral character. In time, these direct strategies were replaced by more indirect ones. For example, classroom discussions and the active involvement of students in clubs and cooperative learning activities became common strategies for teaching self-discipline. It was believed that honesty, industry, responsibility, respect, moral decision making, and similar character traits were better learned through experience and practice than through memorization. Perhaps more important, it was believed that systematic efforts to teach such traits and values could *prevent* behavior problems, foster self-discipline, and thus allow teachers to devote less time to the correction of misbehavior. By 1935, every state required the teaching of character education (McKown, 1935).

As the emphasis on character education increased, the emphasis on harsh punitive strategies decreased. In particular, educators began to closely examine alternatives to corporal punishment. Behavioral strategies such as time-out and reinforcement of good behavior were used for correcting minor misbehavior, whereas exclusionary strategies such as suspension and expulsion were used for more serious and chronic misbehavior. Schools also began to understand the need for alternative programs that provided a greater range and intensity of mental health and remedial services. As a result, alternative schools for students with serious behavior problems began to appear (McClellan, 1999).

Thus, for almost a century, schools in America have recognized that school discipline should include more than the correction of everyday behavior problems in the classroom. To be sure, the *correction* of behavior problems continues to be an important component of school discipline, but as recognized by educators in the early 1900s, comprehensive school discipline should include two additional components: *prevention* and *remediation and crisis response*. Whereas the former involves all children, the latter targets those children who exhibit the most serious and chronic behavior problems. What has changed most over the years has been the relative emphasis placed on each of these components and the strategies associated with them. For example, as noted above, correction via fear and punishment was popular at the turn of the twentieth century and prevention via multiple methods of character education was popular in the early and mid twentieth century. Since then, the popularity of a kaleidoscope of program models that employ a variety of preventive and corrective strategies has waxed and waned, including models that focus on values and emotional well-being (e.g., Values Clarification; Raths, Harmin, & Simon, 1966), moral reasoning and social decision making (e.g., the Cognitive-Developmental Approach; Kohlberg, 1981), interpersonal communication (e.g., Teacher Effectiveness Training; Gordon, 1974), social problem solving (Shure, 1992), responsibility (e.g., Reality Therapy; Glasser, 1992), and behavior modification (e.g., Assertive Discipline; Canter & Canter, 1992).

There is little research supporting the above models, as well as other models of school discipline that emphasize a single dimension . However, research does support many of the *strategies* used in these models (Bear, 1998). Indeed, research indicates that multiple strategies are needed to promote responsible behavior and that these strategies must target how children *think*, *feel*, and *act* (Zins, Elias, Greenberg, & Weissberg, 2000). Fortunately, there is a wealth of such strategies from which school psychologists can draw when developing and implementing comprehensive school-based programs for preventing, correcting, and remediating school discipline problems.

School Discipline Today: A Return to Fear and Punishment?

Recently, there has been a shift in emphasis from preventing and correcting school discipline problems to remediating and responding to serious discipline problems. In response to fears among legislators and the general public that school violence has increased in recent years (Skiba & Peterson, 1999), crisis response teams have been created and inservice trainings have been held on how school professionals can respond to violent acts. In addition, zero tolerance policies have become increasingly popular, with student misbehavior often resulting in the automatic application of harsh disciplinary consequences such as suspension, expulsion, and placement in alternative school programs. Moreover, rather than preventing behavior problems by promoting the social, emotional, and moral development of children, many schools have elected to "prevent" behavior problems by focusing on the systematic control of environmental factors perceived to be the primary antecedents of discipline problems. That is, many schools have focused primarily on the purchase of increased security measures, the hiring of police (or school resource officers), and the issuing of staff and student identification badges (Skiba & Peterson, 1999). Such strategies, which also characterize prisons, have received little or no empirical support in the schools (Hyman & Perone, 1998), especially with respect to preventing school violence and promoting socially responsible behavior.

Clearly, acts of violence should not be tolerated: Responding to and remediating serious behavior problems *should* be a priority among those schools in which violence is a problem. Contrary to the perceptions of many parents and educators, however, such schools are rare (Hyman & Perone, 1998; Skiba & Peterson, 1999), especially when "school violence" is appropriately defined as serious (i.e., typically criminal) acts of aggression and not milder forms of verbal and physical aggression (e.g., teasing, bullying, and rejecting others). Although the latter behaviors are relatively normative, the former are fairly uncommon. That is, the majority of schools (90%) report no serious violent crimes (i.e., physical attack or fight with a weapon, robbery, murder, rape, or sexual battery; U.S. Department of Education, 1999), and the majority of students (99%) commit no serious violent crimes, at least not at school (National Center for Education Statistics, 1998). Given these statistics, the great amount of emphasis placed on responses to violence is unwarranted in the vast majority of schools. To be sure, efforts to target violence should be one aspect of a school's discipline plan—a plan that should balance all three necessary components. As discussed below, however, it is unlikely that strategies and programs that focus exclusively on reducing school violence will be effective in developing self-discipline and preventing everyday behavior problems, or in creating a positive atmosphere that is conducive to learning.

BASIC CONSIDERATIONS

There are few topics in school psychology that require a broader base of knowledge and skills than that of school discipline, especially when the components of prevention, correction, and remediation are emphasized. Of particular importance to school psychologists is an understanding of the multiple risk and protective factors related to social and emotional adjustment or maladjustment. These include biological and temperamental factors, social, emotional, and academic competencies, teacher-student relations, family functioning, parenting skills and practices, peer associations, school climate and classroom management strategies, and community factors. Such factors influence behavior in a complex, reciprocal, and cumulative fashion. For example, a student who lacks social-emotional competencies and social skills or whose temperament is characterized by hyperactivity, impulsivity, and inattentiveness will be more difficult to teach. In turn, the student is more likely to be subject to harsh and punitive discipline, especially when placed with a teacher who lacks patience, tolerance, and behavior management skills or who lacks the resources that might be necessary to accommodate the student in a class with many other at-risk students. A teacher's punishment-oriented style toward discipline not only fails to promote social-emotional competencies and prosocial behavior in the student, but also provides negative models of behavior, thereby further impeding the student's social and emotional development. The risk for disciplinary problems is even greater when the child experiences academic failure and the lack of family support. Peer rejection and eventual drift toward a deviant peer group often evolve, as well as the risk of other indicators of social and emotional maladjustment, including low self-esteem and criminality (Kupersmidt, Coie, & Dodge, 1990).

A developmental, multi-risk factor view of conduct problems has profound implications for the prevention, correction, and remediation components of school discipline programs. In particular, it highlights the need for each component to address multiple risk and protective factors. It also suggests why past and present programs focusing on only one aspect of behavior (e.g., self-esteem, social problem solving, communication skills, social skills) fail.

In addition to knowledge of multiple risk and protective factors, it is critical that school psychologists possess knowledge and skills in a variety of areas of psychology and education, including problem-solving consultation, classroom management, character education, systems change, applied behavior analysis, behavior therapy, individual and group counseling, parent education, and crisis intervention. General knowledge of children's social, emotional, and moral development also is important, as is knowledge in the more specific areas of socialization, child rearing, self-regulation, internalization, aggression, and juvenile delinquency. Of central importance to the implementation of strategies and programs that draw from the above skills and knowledge is the evaluation of their effectiveness. That is, school psychologists should play a pivotal role not only in guiding schools in the implementation of empirically based strategies and programs, but also in demonstrating whether or not such strategies and programs result in positive short- and long-term outcomes.

Furthermore, given that school discipline has increasingly become the focus of legal challenges and legislative acts, school psychologists must keep abreast in these areas. In particular, they should be aware of current state and federal regulations, case law, and other court rulings regarding provisions in Section 504 of the Rehabilitation Act and in the 1997 amendments to the Individuals with Disabilities Education Act (IDEA) that focus on school discipline and children with disabilities. These provisions should serve as an impetus for school psychologists to reflect upon the preventive, corrective, and remedial components of their schools' discipline policies and practices.

BEST PRACTICES

In this section we highlight school discipline strategies that characterize programs and models of demonstrated effectiveness. It is important to note that although the strategies are grouped under the categories of prevention, correction, and remediation, few strategies are specific to one category. Our dividing lines between categories of disciplinary strategies are somewhat arbitrary. Undoubtedly, the corrective component would include preventive strategies and the remediation component would incorporate both preventive and corrective strategies. As educational intervention research continues to inform practice, it has become increasingly clear that the most effective learning environments are those in which there is a planful, consistent, seamless, and data-based approach to the prevention, correction, and remediation of disciplinary problems. Our separation of these sections is therefore based more on relative emphases than on exclusive distinctions.

Best Practices for Promoting Self-Discipline and Preventing Discipline Problems

Most authorities on the topic of school discipline agree that prevention should be the primary focus of a school's comprehensive discipline plan. This is for good reason. As noted by Walker, Colvin, and Ramsey (1995), when implemented successfully, comprehensive prevention programs solve the adjustment problems of 75–85% of a school's students and they do so in a cost effective manner, costing approximately $5–20 per student compared to at least $25,000 per student for intensive remediation or treatment programs. Preventive programs target all children, employing a variety of strategies designed to achieve two interrelated goals: (a) the development of self-discipline and (b) the establishment and maintenance of school atmospheres that encourage prosocial behavior and inhibit disciplinary problems. These strategies often serve to promote not only appropriate classroom behavior but also academic achievement and interpersonal relationships (Zins et al., 2000).

Self-discipline entails self-directed inhibition of antisocial behavior, assuming responsibility for one's actions, understanding of right from wrong, and an appreciation of the importance of cooperative relationships in the classroom and society. Self-discipline reflects internalization, which is defined as "taking over the values and attitudes of society as one's own so that socially acceptable behavior is motivated not by anticipation of external consequences but by intrinsic or internal factors" (Grusec & Goodnow, 1994, p. 4). As such, self-discipline is most evident when one acts prosocially and inhibits antisocial behavior in the absence of external regulators of behavior, such as the presence of adults. The development of self-discipline, rather than the external control of behavior, should be the long-term goal of all schools.

School-Wide and Classroom Strategies

Several decades of research on school and teacher effectiveness have resulted in the identification of a variety of classroom and school-wide strategies for developing self-discipline and preventing behavior problems (Bear, 1998; Good & Brophy, 2000; Grusec & Goodnow, 1994). A summary of recommendations based on this research appears in Table 1.

Skills and Dispositions of Effective Teachers

The classroom management strategies listed in Table 1 characterize teachers who are "authoritative" in their approach to school discipline (Brophy, 1996).

Table 1. Recommended school-based strategies for developing self-discipline and preventing behavior problems

School-wide strategies

- Develop a commitment on the part of all teachers, administrators, and support staff to work together to improve school discipline and promote a positive school climate.
- In collaboration with teachers, students, parents, and other members of the school community develop and consistently enforce clear and fair rules and sanctions for problem behaviors. Rules should be incorporated into written policies that are distributed to all involved parties.
- Set high, yet realistic, academic and behavioral expectations and communicate that such expectations, and accountability for meeting them, should be shared by students, teachers, and parents alike.
- Implement curricula and school-wide activities designed to promote social and emotional learning. This may include lessons embedded within the general curriculum that highlight prosocial and democratic values such as responsibility and respect for others; lessons designed to teach social problem solving and social decision-making skills; and school-wide assemblies that recognize prosocial behavior and convey prosocial values.
- Ensure that physical facilities are well designed and monitored. Increase supervision of children where behavior problems most often occur (e.g., halls, playground, cafeteria).
- Provide ongoing staff development and supervision.
- Make sure that program components are being implemented with fidelity and are being evaluated as to their acceptability and effectiveness.

Classroom strategies

- Adopt classroom management and disciplinary practices that combine proactive, instructive, and corrective strategies. That is, make sure that teachers work hard to prevent misbehaviors before they occur, emphasize self-discipline (as opposed to external control), and correct behavior problems fairly and consistently.
- Arrange the physical environment of each classroom in ways that reduce congestion and facilitate the smooth and quiet movement of students.
- Beginning with the first week of school, establish clear and predictable routines and actively involve students in the establishment of rules and consequences.
- Reinforce appropriate behavior ("catch 'em being good") and emphasize internal attributions (i.e., focusing students' attention on the internal, rather than external, reasons for their behavior).
- Frequently discuss rules and behaviors with students so they not only recognize what behaviors are "right" and "wrong" but also understand why. Such discussions are particularly effective if they use inductions (i.e., focusing students' attention on the effects of their behavior on others instead of on external consequences).
- Prevent boredom and frustration by employing a variety of teaching methods, developmentally appropriate and motivating materials, and curriculum materials and instructions that are adapted to the needs, interests, and abilities of individual students.
- Promote cooperation among students rather than competition.
- Offer opportunities for students to voice their needs and opinions (e.g., class meetings, student councils) and to solve social problems on their own.

Authoritative teachers set high standards and hold high expectations, enforce rules and standards in a firm, fair, and consistent manner, and promote autonomy by encouraging children's active participation in decisions regarding their behavior (Bear, 1998). Authoritative teachers emphasize strategies that are proactive (i.e., focus on the antecedents of behavior), rather than relying solely upon strategies that are reactive (i.e., focus on the consequences of behavior). Their use of positive, proactive discipline techniques, in combination with more punitive, reactive strategies (when needed), increases the likelihood that students will exhibit appropriate behavior willingly rather than grudgingly (Brophy, 1996).

Another important characteristic of authoritative teachers is that they tend to display warmth and acceptance toward their students (Brophy, 1996). Warmth may be communicated by expressing positive affect, sympathy, and support toward students, as well as interest in each student as a person and enjoyment of each student's company. Decades of research have demonstrated that students tend to internalize the values and standards of adults with whom they share warm relationships. Their compliance may initially be motivated by a desire to either imitate or please the adults, but tends to become more internally motivated over time (Hoffman, 2000). In addition to fostering internalization, communication of warmth may facilitate the development of close, supportive relationships between teachers and students, which in turn have been linked with decreased drop-out, risk-taking, and aggression, as well as increased academic and social competence (see Pianta, 1999, for a review). Like warmth, acceptance is delivered non-contingently and thus is not conditional upon students' behavior. Acceptance may be communicated when teachers draw a distinction between students and their misbehavior, adopt an attitude that "everyday is a new day" by not holding students' previous discipline problems against them, and consider several possible explanations for students' behavior rather than automatically assuming negative intentions (Brophy, 1996). Together, warmth and acceptance tend to form the basis for teacher-student relationships characterized by mutual respect, thus motivating students to comply with teachers out of respect for them rather than out of fear or mere obedience.

Not only do effective teachers strive to develop positive relationships with the students in their classrooms, but they also seek to promote positive relationships and a sense of community among the students themselves. By emphasizing cooperative rather than competitive activities, teachers communicate the idea that the classroom is a community in which students can help, rather than hinder, each other's success. Responsibility for classroom behavior is shared by encouraging students to take others' feelings and perspectives into account; by doing so, teachers foster feelings of empathy and guilt, thereby motivating students to engage in prosocial rather than antisocial behavior (Eisenberg & Fabes, 1997). In addition, their efforts to build a caring classroom community promote a sense of belonging among students and a sense of attachment to school, both of which may reduce students' sense of alienation and potential for violence (Walker et al., 1995). Finally, effective teachers regularly and unobtrusively measure and evaluate the effects of their efforts on students' prosocial and antisocial behaviors. In sum, effective teachers create a classroom climate in which their students follow norms for appropriate behavior, not only out of respect for the teacher but also out of respect for one another.

Strategies and Programs for Developing Responsible Behavior

In addition to identifying teacher characteristics associated with school discipline, a great deal of research in recent years has focused on individual child characteristics that might be targeted in the prevention of behavior problems and the development of responsible behavior. Of particular emphasis has been the identification of cognitions, emotions, and social skills that mediate social and emotional adjustment in the classroom. Considerable attention has been directed toward social information processing, social problem solving, or social decision-making skills, such as interpreting social cues, clarifying goals, generating solutions, evaluating and choosing solutions, and acting upon the solutions chosen (Crick & Dodge, 1994); anger management and impulse control (Lochman, Dunn, & Wagner, 1997); moral reasoning (Bear, Richards, & Gibbs, 1997); social perspective taking, interpersonal understanding, and negotiation strategies (Selman & Schultz, 1990); empathy (Eisenberg & Fabes, 1997); and self-management, including self-monitoring, self-evaluation, and self-reinforcement skills (Shapiro & Cole, 1994).

Given their roles in mediating classroom behavior, the above areas are routinely incorporated into curriculum packages and programs designed to promote self-discipline and to prevent disciplinary problems ranging from tardiness and classroom disruption to violent forms of aggression. Many of these packages and programs have been shown to be effective in improving social cognitive and emotional skills (Bear, Webster-Stratton, Furlong, & Rhee, 2000). Very few, however, meet the empirically rigorous standard of having demonstrated lasting effects on behavior. Three popular programs for which at least one study demonstrated improvements in behavior that were not simply short-term in duration are *BrainPower* (Hudley, 1999), *PATHS* (Greenberg, Kusche, Cook, & Quamma, 1995), and *Second Step* (Grossman et al., 1997). Note that each of these curriculum programs targets a combination of social, emotional, and behavioral skills.

Overall, research supports strategies that teach a combination of social cognitive, emotional, and behavioral skills. However, there is little, if any, empirical research supporting character education programs reminiscent of the nineteenth century that rely primarily on moral appeal, fear arousal, and information dissemination in teaching students *what* to think (as opposed to *how* to think or how to decide *why* certain actions are wrong; Gottfredson, 1997). Unfortunately, many programs that rely primarily on "lecturing" remain popular today. Included among these are deterrence programs such as Scared Straight and law-related education programs such as DARE (Drug Resistance Awareness Education; Gottfredson, 1997). (Note, however, that the curriculum for the DARE program has been revised recently to include social problem solving and resiliency strategies found to be effective in other programs.) Although widely used among school psychologists, programs that focus on the direct teaching of specific social skills also lack empirical support, especially with respect to lasting improvement in behavior (DuPaul & Eckert, 1994). Likewise, little research indicates that peer mediation programs and recreational programs produce changes in behavior that are maintained over time and that generalize across settings (Gottfredson, 1997). It should be noted, however, that such lack of evidence does not warrant the conclusion that the strategies emphasized in these programs are not valuable, but only that they are likely to be ineffective in achieving lasting improvement in behavior unless they are combined with other strategies.

Best Practices for Correcting Discipline Problems

Teachers are most likely to initiate corrective disciplinary measures when they perceive misbehavior as disrupting or threatening the order of a classroom activity or as endangering the student or others, especially if the behavior is highly visible and contagious. Such misbehavior typically includes noncompliance/defiance, tantrums, aggression, and property destruction (Marquis et al., 2000). The goals of corrective strategies are to terminate the problem behavior if it is presently occurring, weaken or eliminate the likelihood that the student will engage in that behavior again, and replace the behavior with more socially appropriate behavior. As mentioned earlier, many of the preventive strategies described above can, and *should*, be used, when correcting problem behavior. Indeed, incidents of behavior problems provide excellent opportunities for children to learn and practice the cognitive, emotional, and behavioral skills targeted in the prevention component. When correcting misbehavior, however, it often is necessary to strategically apply specific punishment and reinforcement strategies that have proven effective in reducing misbehavior (Martens, Witt, Daly, & Vollmer, 1999; Walker et al., 1995).

Punishment

No other topic has generated more controversy and debate among writers and authorities on school discipline than the use of punishment in the schools. Whereas few, if any, experts on school discipline disagree that developing self-discipline should be a primary aim of education, many question if the use of punishment helps to achieve this important goal. Over the years, many of the most popular writers on school discipline, including Glasser (1992), Gordon (1974), and Kohn (1996), have been quite strident in their opposition to punishment. But school administrators, teachers, parents, and legislators have been equally strident in demanding that "discipline problems" be controlled and not go unpunished (Skiba & Peterson, 1999). Support for punitive strategies continues for several reasons: They often result in immediate decreases in behavior, they are quick and easy to use, their use often is expected of teachers and school administrators, and they generate a sense of control, power, and justice among those who administer them (Kohn, 1996).

Technically speaking, punishment refers to the use of an unpleasant consequence to decrease the likelihood that the behavior of concern will occur in the future (Martens et al., 1999). Corporal punishment is the most commonly criticized form of punishment. Indeed, nearly all professional organizations in psychology and education, including the National Association of School Psychologists (NASP), advocate that corporal punishment be banned from the schools. Suspension and expulsion also have been the focus of much criticism. As true with punishment strategies in general, suspension and expulsion have many limitations. Among their limitations are that they (a) fail to address factors, including classroom and school factors, that underlie the student's problem behavior; (b) do not teach replacement behaviors; (c) produce only short-term, non-enduring, decreases in behavior problems; (d) are likely to be harmful to the student-teacher relationship; and (e) are likely to foster resentment, retaliation, and emotions that are counterproductive to learning. Moreover, suspension and expulsion often allow students to avoid or escape from situations they find aversive, such as academic work, peer rejection, and a harsh and non-caring teacher. As a result, their inappropriate behavior is negatively reinforced. These strategies also tend to result in the loss of valuable instructional time as well as in increased exposure to negative role models (Schloss & Smith, 1998).

Other punishment strategies include verbal reprimands, removal of privileges, time-out, over-correction, and response cost. These strategies are much less contentious than corporal punishment, expulsion, and suspension and are among the most popular disciplinary strategies used by teachers (Brophy, 1996). Although widely employed and effective in causing short-term decreases in behavior, they too share many of the limitations presented above. In light of these limitations, we do not recommend that punishment strategies necessarily be eliminated (except for corporal punishment) but rather that they be used only after less restrictive interventions have failed to reduce misbehavior. Moreover, it is recommended that when used, punishment strategies should always be combined with strategies for teaching and reinforcing appropriate behaviors (Brophy, 1996; Martens et al., 1999). Such an approach not only has an ethical basis, but also is supported by research.

Positive Behavioral Interventions for Correcting Behavior Problems

Positive reductive techniques. Although positive reinforcement is defined by its strengthening effect on a behavior, a variety of related techniques apply the principle of *positive* reinforcement, seemingly paradoxically, to reduce or eliminate misbehavior (Webber & Scheuermann, 1991). Positive reinforcement, such as privileges and social or material rewards, is used to reward a student when he or she (a) completely refrains from exhibiting a problem behavior during a specified interval of time (i.e., Differential Reinforcement of Other behaviors; DRO), (b) performs a specific appropriate behavior that is physically incompatible (i.e., mutually exclusive) with the problem behavior (i.e., Differential Reinforcement of Incompatible behaviors; DRI), (c) exercises sufficient control over a problem behavior, keeping its frequency under a preset limit during a specified interval of time (i.e., Differential Reinforcement of Lower rates of behavior; DRL), or (d) performs a specific appropriate behavior that achieves the same function for the student but is not physically incompatible with the problem behavior (i.e., Differential Reinforcement of Alternative behaviors; DRA). Because these procedures employ no aversive stimuli to achieve reduction of the problem behavior, they should be considered the first resort when a school psychologist is planning interventions to correct problem behaviors. Procedures such as DRI are especially valuable because they reduce the frequency of the problem behavior while simultaneously strengthening an appropriate replacement behavior.

Behavioral momentum. To correct noncompliance and defiance, teachers may issue a series of requests with which they know the student is likely to comply. For example, the requested activities may be reinforcing in and of themselves or the teacher may know, based on previous experience, that particular compliant responses have been reinforced in the past. Through this series of compliances, a *momentum* of compliance is built up such that, when the heretofore non-complied-with request is delivered, it has a much higher probability of success (Mace, 1996). Of course, as soon as the student complies with this target request, the student should be rewarded. Again, this behavior intervention strategy employs no aversive stimuli.

School-home contingency notes. As emphasized in the previous (and following) section, home-school collaboration greatly enhances the prospects that an intervention will be effective. A simple strategy for facilitating teacher-parent communication and improving student behavior involves the use of school-home contingency notes. The basic components involve a teacher periodically sending home a brief written report on a child's behavioral performance and a parent reviewing the report, delivering the prescribed consequences to the child, signing the report, and sending it back to the teacher. School-home notes have been described as "one of the most effective techniques for improving a student's motivation and classroom behavior. It also is one of the most mismanaged and underutilized techniques" (Jenson & Reavis, 1995, p. 29).

Group contingencies. Any of the basic behavior analytic intervention principles that are applied to individual students also can be applied to groups of students, including whole classes. Group contingencies tend to cluster into one of three broad categories based on the performance criterion in the contingency (Sulzer-Azaroff & Mayer, 1991). In *dependent group contingencies*, the reward (or punishment) of every student in the class depends on the performance of a selected subset of students. This technique should be considered only if the teacher is certain that peer support rather than peer pressure will be provided to the students in the targeted subset. In *independent group contingencies*, the reward (or punishment) of the student depends only on the performance of that student. The contingency is the same for all students but is applied individually. In *interdependent group contingencies*, the reward (or punishment) of any student in the class depends in some way on the performance of every member of the class. There is evidence that well-designed group contingencies and individual contingencies can achieve comparable reductions in problem behaviors (Sulzer-Azaroff & Mayer, 1991). Since group contingencies are often more efficient, they might be favored by teachers in busy situations.

Group contingency strategies often are used in various game formats. Such formats offer powerful motivational properties to suppress undesirable behaviors and strengthen socially valued behaviors within a positive or "fun" learning environment. Probably the earliest classroom motivational game format, and one of the most popular, is the interdependent group contingency called the Good Behavior Game (Barrish, Saunders, & Wolf, 1969). Although different variations of the game have been investigated, most share the following features: (a) specific classroom rules are listed, (b) the class is divided into two or more teams, (c) each team receives a mark on the scoreboard whenever a member of that team earns a point or breaks a rule during a lesson, and (d) the team(s) scoring points above (or below) a predetermined criterion number are awarded reinforcers (e.g., praise, extra recess, less homework, special status). In addition to being relatively simple to operate and effective when properly designed, the Good Behavior Game is viewed favorably by teachers (Tingstrom, 1994).

Self-management. In many respects, procedures to directly teach and strengthen students' self-management of their behaviors and skills represent the pinnacle of behavior analytic corrective procedures. Interestingly, they also may share more methodological details with cognitive approaches than any other behavior analytic procedure, though the differences in terminology are often pronounced. The objectives of these procedures are typically for students to successfully monitor their own behavior; evaluate the behavior with respect to some standard for appropriate behavior; if the behavior is deemed to be inappropriate, then cease it and replace it with an appropriate alternative; if the behavior is deemed to be appropriate, then maintain it and issue self-feedback and/or, at the proper time, self-rewards (Shapiro & Cole, 1994). The overall goal of self-management is for students to increasingly assume adult-like responsibility for their own proper demeanor by fluidly and seamlessly performing these steps as the situation warrants, thereby eliminating the need for external supervision of their behavior. In most training situations, self-recording is an important skill that is embedded between self-monitoring and self-evaluation. This permits students to become aware of the magnitude of their behavior problem and provides a basis for their objective evaluation of their progress. Self-management procedures have been evaluated across hundreds of empirical research investigations and represent powerful preventive and corrective intervention tools for school psychologists.

Selecting Among Corrective Strategies

Educational research has documented a large number of corrective strategies shown to be effective with some students in some settings under some circumstances (some of which are highlighted here). A school psychologist with knowledge and skills in these strategies might very well confront a dilemma in deciding *which* strategies are the most appropriate for the particular student of concern. Functional behavioral assessment and positive behavioral support provide the school psychologist well-studied principles and processes for making informed decisions resulting in effective interventions.

Functional behavioral assessment. Regardless whether punishment or reinforcement strategies are used to correct misbehavior, the strategies should be chosen on the basis of a functional behavioral assessment (FBA). As seen in the chapter on FBA in this volume, school psychologists can develop more effective and more durable interventions, and develop them more expeditiously, if they first acquire knowledge about the triggers and functions of the problem behaviors and then design the interventions to be responsive to those factors. This conception acknowledges two fundamental beliefs about the nature of problem behaviors: (a) a problem behavior does not occur in a vacuum (it is related to the *context* in which it occurs) and (b) a problem behavior serves some *function* for the student, which makes it logical and reasonable from the student's perspective. A recent large-scale meta-analysis revealed that interventions for problem behaviors were substantially more effective when a functional assessment was conducted first and the outcomes were used to design the intervention (Marquis et al., 2000). Furthermore, when surveyed, most practitioners rated functional assessment procedures as extremely or very useful (Desrochers, Hile, & Williams-Moseley, 1997).

Positive behavioral support. Concomitant with the heightened emphasis on conducting functional assessments, researchers have increasingly endorsed the design and implementation of interventions that provide the student *positive* behavioral support (PBS). This movement has been fueled largely by ethical concerns over the use of intrusive, restrictive, and punitive disciplinary measures and by research documenting negative effects that are frequently associated with their use (Donnellan, LaVigna, Negri-Shoultz, & Fassbender,, 1988). Positive behavioral support has been defined as "the application of behavioral principles within the context of community norms to reduce problem behaviors and build appropriate behaviors that result in durable behavior change" (Marquis et al., 2000, p. 138).

The large-scale meta-analysis by Marquis et al. (2000) showed that PBS interventions have been effective in reducing problem behaviors across a wide variety of student characteristics (including age, gender, degree of handicap, and diagnosis), problem behaviors (including self-injury, tantrums, aggression, and property destruction), and interventions. Also, the use of multi-component interventions to address both the triggers and the functions of a problem behavior appears to be more effective than the use of a single intervention. Their findings substantiate the results of another meta-analysis by Stage and Quiroz (1997), who also reported large effect sizes for behavior analytic interventions. Of the strategies that they studied, the three most effective on average were group contingencies, self-management, and positive-reductive differential reinforcement.

Four factors are responsible for the effectiveness and growing popularity of PBS approaches to disciplinary problems. First, when done well, they are comprehensive. Both the antecedents and the consequences of a problem behavior are addressed. For the first time in the development of the behavior analytic framework, however, the primary emphasis is on the former. In this approach, the antecedents include both non-school factors, such as negative family influences, deficient coping skills, and low self-esteem (sometimes referred to as setting events or slow triggers), and factors in the immediate school environment, such as teacher demands and student provocation. As noted by Marquis et al. (2000), "a key concept in PBS is that deficient contexts must be remediated first in order to reduce problem behavior" (p. 138). Second, after considering the findings of a functional assessment, the selection of an intervention should be guided by the principle of the *least restrictive alternative*. This means that the practitioner always should choose as a first resort the most appropriate intervention strategy that is the least restrictive on a student's personal freedom and the least intrusive on the student's personal space. A valuable aid to a school psychologist in making these selections is the hierarchical ordering of reductive strategies, from least to most restrictive (Schloss & Smith, 1998). Third, whenever interventions are designed to reduce or eliminate a student's problem behaviors, they also must include strategies to teach appropriate replacement behaviors. This serves not only to build the student's behavioral repertoire but also to facilitate the continued suppression of the problem behavior (Marquis et al., 2000). Fourth, prior to changing to a more restrictive, less positive intervention strategy in the hierarchy, a school psychologist first must be informed by data that show that the current intervention is not effective. Such practices are consistent with the behavior analytic tradition of using field data to substantiate clinical impressions and serves to safeguard the student against hasty decisions by interventionists to use more punitive interventions unnecessarily (Schloss & Smith, 1998).

Remediating, and Responding to, Chronic and Serious Behavior Problems

The above preventive and corrective strategies are sufficient for addressing the needs of the majority of children, but more comprehensive and intensive services are necessary for the children who (a) exhibit behavior problems that are chronic and resistant to common classroom-based interventions and (b) exhibit behaviors, irrespective of chronicity, that are of serious harm, or threat thereof, to self and others. Included would be the estimated 2–9% of children whose behavior warrants the diagnosis of conduct disorder and the estimated 6–10% whose behavior warrants the diagnosis of oppositional defiant disorder (McMahon & Wells, 1998). Also included would be children who are targeted in the disciplinary provisions of the 1997 amendments to IDEA, which pertain to cases involving possession of a weapon or illegal drugs, or cases in which the child is determined by an hearing officer to be "substantially likely" to injure self or others.

General Characteristics of Effective Remedial Programs

There is a wealth of research on the effectiveness of various interventions for children with conduct disorders, including those who exhibit violent behavior. Effective programs tend to share certain characteristics (Bear et al., 2000). In general, they are:

1. *Comprehensive*, targeting multiple risk and protective factors
2. *Broad-based*, adopting a systems perspective in which schools, families, agencies, and communities work together in preventing and treating antisocial and aggressive behavior
3. *Guided by theory and research*, using interventions that are conceptually and empirically justified
4. *Intensive and sustained over time*, with a commitment to providing adequate resources
5. *Sensitive to* developmental differences in behavior, the determinants of behavior, and the appropriateness of interventions
6. *Cognizant of the importance of early intervention*. This would include interventions provided at an early age, as well as interventions that are provided when indicators of behavior problems first appear

In particular, there is growing evidence that a parent or family component to intervention is critical to produce lasting improvements in behavior. In combination with parent management training or family therapy, or when these services are not feasible, home-school collaboration and consultation should be provided.

Crisis Intervention

In light of school shootings that have plagued the nation, the responses that schools and communities make to crises are now recognized as critical components of intervention. Readers are referred to two free documents produced by the U.S. Department of Education in collaboration with NASP and the Center for Effective Collaboration and Practice: *Early Warning, Timely Response: A Guide to Safe Schools* (Dwyer,

Osher, & Warger, 1998) and *Safeguarding Our Children: An Action Guide* (Dwyer & Osher, 2000), for useful guidelines and recommendations in developing crisis response teams and in responding to crises.

Alternative Education Programs

The rapid growth in alternative education programs across the nation can largely be attributed to the widespread adoption of zero tolerance policies and to the new provisions in IDEA that stipulate that children with disabilities be placed into an interim alternative educational setting, with or without parent permission, for certain disciplinary infractions. It is beyond the scope of this chapter to review federal regulations that govern when children with disabilities may be placed into such settings or to review related issues and concepts (e.g., manifestation determination). School psychologists are referred to other resources, including the chapter in this volume on Functional Behavioral Assessment and several recent publications by NASP (see Bear, Quinn, & Burkholder, 2001; Telzrow & Tankersley, 2000). Little research exists on the effectiveness of alternative education, particularly interim alternative educational programs (Bear, 1999; Bear et al., 2001). Research that does exist indicates that alternative educational programs that emphasize punishment and control are associated with poor student attitudes and no reduction in delinquent behavior (Gottfredson, 1997). Research also indicates that an atmosphere characterized by a "community of support" is important to program success (Wehlage, 1991). Features of such a community of support include (Bear et al., 2001) (a) qualified teachers and support staff who volunteer to work with challenging students; (b) flexibility in program management, decision making, and role functions; (c) sufficient funding and resources; (d) sensitivity to individual and cultural differences; (e) clear individual-child and program goals; (f) on-site counseling services; (g) a case management approach to student services; (h) program evaluation; (i) research-supported interventions; and (j) networks of additional supports and services. With respect to interim alternative education settings, it is likely that in addition to the above characteristics, a critical element of success will be the provision of research-supported interventions that are linked to assessment and that are implemented in the setting to which the student returns (Bear et. al., 2001).

SUMMARY

Many persons consider the overarching purpose of education to be the preparation of self-disciplined individuals who become responsible citizens. The linchpin in fulfilling this purpose is school discipline. No longer do we rely on moral exhortations and rote memorization of codes of conduct, however, as the backbone of our discipline programs. Since the turn of the twentieth century, substantial empirical research has accumulated to reveal that effective school discipline programs must be comprehensive, sustained, and composed of three major components: (a) preventive strategies for developing self-discipline and socially responsible behavior, (b) corrective strategies for dealing with misbehavior once it has occurred, and (c) remediation programs for addressing chronic and serious behavior problems.

Research indicates that within each discipline component, multiple factors must be targeted, including how children think, feel, and act; student-teacher relationships; the classroom environment and curriculum; and home and community influences. Of particular relevance are the findings on the characteristics of effective teachers, the importance of fostering social problem-solving skills and social competence in children, and the utility of conducting functional behavioral assessments prior to implementing corrective measures. Schools that address the three major discipline components and multiple factors within each component are successful in creating safe and orderly learning environments as well as in developing self-disciplined and responsible citizens.

REFERENCES

Barrish, H., Saunders, M., & Wolf, M. M. (1969). Good behavior game: Effects of individual contingencies for group consequences on disruptive behavior in a classroom. *Journal of Applied Behavior Analysis, 2,* 119–124.

Bear, G. G. (1998). School discipline in the United States: Prevention, correction, and long-term social development. *School Psychology Review, 27,* 14–32.

Bear, G. G. (1999). *Interim alternative education settings: Related research and program considerations.* Alexandria, VA: National Association of State Directors of Special Education.

Bear, G. G., Quinn, M. M., & Burkholder, S. (2001). *Interim alternative education settings for children with disabilities*. Bethesda, MD: National Association of School Psychologists.

Bear, G. G., Richards, H. C., & Gibbs, J. C. (1997). Sociomoral reasoning and behavior. In G. G. Bear, K. M. Minke, & A. Thomas (Eds.), *Children's Needs II: Development, problems, and alternatives* (pp. 13–25). Bethesda, MD: National Association of School Psychologists.

Bear, G. G., Webster-Stratton, C., Furlong, M., & Rhee, S. (2000). Preventing aggression and violence. In K. M. Minke & G. G. Bear (Eds.), *Preventing school problems—Promoting school success: Strategies and programs that work* (pp. 1–69). Bethesda, MD: National Association of School Psychologists.

Brophy, J. E. (1996). *Teaching problem students*. New York: Guilford.

Canter, L., & Canter, M. (1992). *Assertive discipline: Positive behavior management for today's classroom*. Santa Monica, CA: Canter & Associates.

Crick, N. R., & Dodge, K. A. (1994). A review and reformulation of social information-processing mechanisms in children's social adjustment. *Psychological Bulletin, 115*, 74–101.

Desrochers, M., Hile, M. G., Williams-Moseley, T. L. (1997). Survey of functional assessment procedures used with individuals who display mental retardation and severe problem behaviors. *American Journal on Mental Retardation, 101*, 535–546.

Donnellan, A., LaVigna, G. W., Negri-Shoultz, N., & Fassbender, L. L. (1988). *Progress without punishment: Effective approaches for learners with behavior problems*. New York: Teachers College Press.

DuPaul, G. J., & Eckert, T. L. (1994). The effects of social skills curricula: Now you see them, now you don't. *School Psychology Quarterly, 9*, 113–132.

Dwyer, K., & Osher, D. (2000). *Safeguarding our children: An action guide*. Washington, D.C.: U.S. Department of Education and U.S. Department of Justice, American Institutes for Research. Available at: http://www.ed.gov/offices/OSERS/OSEP/ActionGuide.

Dwyer, K., Osher, D., & Warger, C. (1998). *Early warning, timely response: A guide to safe schools*. Washington, DC.: Center for Effective Collaboration and Practice. Available at: http://www.ed.gov/offices/OSERS/OSEP/earlywrn.html.

Eisenberg, N., & Fabes, R. A. (1997). Prosocial development. In W. Damon (Ser. Ed.) & N. Eisenberg (Vol. Ed.), *Handbook of child psychology: Vol. 3. Social, emotional, and personality development* (5th ed., pp. 701–778). New York: Wiley.

Glasser, W. (1992). *The quality school* (2nd ed.). New York: Harper Perennial.

Good, T. L., & Brophy, J. E. (2000). *Looking in classrooms* (8th ed.). New York: Longman.

Gordon, T. (1974). *TET: Teacher effectiveness training*. New York: McKay.

Gottfredson, D. C. (1997). School-based crime prevention. In L. W. Sherman, D. C. Gottfredson, D. MacKenzie, J. Eck, P. Reuter, & S. Bushway (Eds.), *Preventing crime: What works, what doesn't, what's promising: A report to the United States Congress*. Washington, DC: U.S. Department of Justice.

Greenberg, M. T., Kusche, C. A., Cook, E. T., & Quamma, J. P. (1995). Promoting emotional competence in school-aged children: The effects of the PATHS curriculum. *Development and Psychopathology, 7*, 117–136.

Grossman, D. C., Neckerman, H. J., Koepsell, T. D., Liu, P., Asher, K. N., Beland, K., Frey, K., & Rivara, F. P. (1997). Effectiveness of a violence prevention curriculum in elementary school: A randomized controlled trial. *Journal of the American Medical Association, 277*, 1605–1611.

Grusec, J. E., & Goodnow, J. J. (1994). Impact of parental discipline methods on the child's internalization of values: A reconceptualization of current points of view. *Developmental Psychology, 30,* 4–19.

Hoffman, M. L. (2000). *Empathy and moral development: Implications for caring and justice.* New York: Cambridge University Press.

Hudley, C. (1999, April). *Problem behaviors in middle childhood: Understanding risk status and protective factors.* Paper presented at the annual meeting of the American Educational Research Association.

Hyman, I. A., & Perone, D. C. (1998). The other side of school violence: Educator policies and practices that may contribute to student misbehavior. *Journal of School Psychology, 30,* 7–27.

Jenson, W. R., & Reavis, H. K. (1995). Homenotes to improve motivation. In H. K. Reavis, S. J. Kukic, W. R. Jenson, D. P. Morgan, D. J. Andrews, & S. Fister (Eds.), *Best practices: Behavioral and educational strategies for teachers.* Longmont, CO: Sopris West.

Kohlberg, L. (1981). *Essays on moral development: Vol. 1. The philosophy of moral development.* New York: Harper & Row.

Kohn, A. (1996). *Beyond discipline: From compliance to community.* Alexandria, VA: Association for Supervision and Curriculum Development.

Kupersmidt, J. B., Coie, J. D., & Dodge, K. A. (1990). The role of poor peer relationships in the development of disorder. In S. R. Asher & J. D. Coie (Eds.), *Peer rejection in childhood* (pp. 274–305). New York: Cambridge University Press.

Lochman, J. E., Dunn, S. E., & Wagner, E. E. (1997). Anger. In G. G. Bear, K. M. Minke, & A. Thomas (Eds.), *Children's Needs II: Development, problems, and alternatives* (pp. 149–160). Bethesda, MD: National Association of School Psychologists.

Mace, F. C. (1996). In pursuit of general behavioral relations. *Journal of Applied Behavior Analysis, 29,* 557–563.

Marquis, J. G., Horner, R. H., Carr, E. G., Turnbull, A. P., Thompson, M., Behrens, G. A., Magito-McLaughlin, D., McAtee, M. L., Smith, C. E., Ryan, K. A., & Doolabh, A. (2000). A meta-analysis of positive behavioral support. In R. Gersten, E. P. Schiller, and S. Vaughn (Eds.), *Contemporary special education research: Syntheses of the knowledge base on critical instructional issues.* Mahwah, NJ: Erlbaum.

Martens, B. K., Witt, J. C., Daly III, E. J., & Vollmer, T. R. (1999). Behavior analysis: Theory and practice in educational settings. In C. R. Reynolds & T. B. Gutkin (Eds.), *Handbook of school psychology* (pp. 638–663). New York: Wiley.

McClellan, B. E. (1999). *Moral education in America: Schools and the shaping of character from colonial times to the present.* New York: Teachers College Press.

McKown, H. C. (1935). *Character education.* New York: McGraw-Hill.

McMahon, R. J., & Wells, K. C. (1998). Conduct problems. In E. J. Mash & R. A. Barkley (Eds.), *Treatment of childhood disorders* (2nd ed., pp. 111–207). New York: Guilford.

National Center for Education Statistics. (1998). *Violence and discipline problems in U.S. public schools: 1996–1997.* Washington, DC: Author.

Pianta, R. C. (1999). *Enhancing relationships between children and teachers.* Washington, DC: American Psychological Association.

Raichle, D. R. (1977/1978). School discipline and corporal punishment: An American retrospect. *Interchange, 8,* 71–83.

Raths, L. E., Harmin, M., & Simon, S. (1966). *Values and teaching: Working with values in the classroom.* Columbus, OH: Merrill.

Rose, L. C., & Gallup, A. M. (2000). The 32nd annual Phi Delta Kappa/Gallup Poll of the public's attitudes toward the public schools. *Phi Delta Kappan, 82,* 41–66.

Schloss, P., & Smith, M. A. (1998). *Applied behavior analysis in the classroom* (2nd ed). Boston: Allyn & Bacon.

Selman, R. L., & Schultz, L. H. (1990). *Making a friend in youth: Developmental theory and pair therapy.* Chicago: The University of Chicago Press.

Shapiro, E. S., & Cole, C. L. (1994). *Behavior change in the classroom: Self-management interventions.* New York: Guilford.

Shure, M. B. (1992). *I Can Problem Solve: An interpersonal cognitive problem-solving program: Intermediate elementary grades.* Champaign, IL: Research Press.

Skiba, R., & Peterson, R. (1999). The dark side of zero tolerance. *Phi Delta Kappan, 80,* 372–382.

Stage, S. A., & Quiroz, D. R. (1997). A meta-analysis of interventions to decrease disruptive classroom behavior in public education settings. *School Psychology Review, 26,* 333–368.

Sulzer-Azaroff, B., & Mayer, G. R. (1991). *Behavior analysis for lasting change.* Fort Worth, TX: Harcourt College Publishers.

Telzrow, C. F., & Tankersley, M. (1999). *IDEA Amendments of 1997: Practice guidelines for school-based teams.* Bethesda, MD: National Association of School Psychologists.

Tingstrom, D. H. (1994). The Good Behavior Game: An investigation of teachers' acceptance. *Psychology in the Schools, 31,* 57–65.

U.S. Department of Education (1999). *Annual report on school safety, 1999.* Washington, DC: Author. Available at: http://www.ed.gov.

Walker, H. M., Colvin, G., & Ramsey, E. (1995). *Antisocial behavior in school: Strategies and best practices.* Pacific Grove, CA: Brooks/Cole.

Webber, J., & Scheuermann, B. (1991). Managing behavior problems: Accentuate the positive...eliminate the negative! *Teaching Exceptional Children, 24,* 13–19.

Wehlage, G. (1991). School reform for at-risk students. *Equity and Excellence in Education, 25,* 15–24.

Zins, J. E., Elias, M. J., Greenberg, M. T., & Weissberg, R. P. (2000). Promoting social & emotional competence in children. In K. M. Minke & G. G. Bear (Eds.), *Preventing school problems—Promoting school success: Strategies and programs that work* (pp. 71–99). Bethesda, MD: National Association of School Psychologists.

ANNOTATED BIBLIOGRAPHY

Brophy, J. E. (1996). *Teaching problem students.* New York: Guilford.
Based on both research and practice, this book describes strategies that teachers have found effective in promoting self-discipline among students. A variety of behaviors are addressed, including hyperactivity, defiance, and rejection. Specific strategies for preventing and responding to these behaviors are presented, along with more general teacher characteristics.

Elias, M. J., Zins, J. E., Weissberg, R. P., Frey, K. S., Greenberg, M. T., Haynes, N. M., Kessler, R., Schwab-Stone, M. E., & Shriver, T. P. (1997). *Promoting social and emotional learning: Guidelines for educators.* Alexandria, VA: Association for Supervision and Curriculum Development.
More than 100,000 copies of this book have been sold. Based on multiple theories, research, and their experiences in the schools, the authors provide educators with practical guidelines and multiple strategies for developing social and emotional competence.

Jones, V. F., & Jones, L. S. (2000). *Comprehensive classroom management: Creating communities of support and solving problems* (6th ed.). Boston: Allyn & Bacon.
Among the many basic texts on classroom management, this is perhaps the best because it offers a comprehensive and balanced perspective on the prevention and correction of common classroom behaviors. Unlike other texts that present multiple models of school discipline with little supporting research, this text highlights strategies of demonstrated effectiveness.

Poland, S. & McCormick, J. S. (1999). *Coping with crisis: A resource for schools, parents, and communities.* Longmont, CO: Sopris West.
This valuable reference provides practical strategies to school psychologists and others for responding to school crises, including school shootings, suicides, fights, and gang-related violence. Step-by-step guidelines and actual case studies are presented.

63 Best Practices in the Systematic Direct Observation of Student Behavior

John M. Hintze
University of Massachusetts at Amherst
Robert J. Volpe and Edward S. Shapiro
Lehigh University

OVERVIEW

Direct observation is one of the most widely used assessment procedures by school psychologists. In a survey of more than 1,000 school psychology practitioners, Wilson and Reschly (1996) found that of the 26 different types of assessment instruments listed across seven different assessment categories (e.g., ability/intelligence, social/emotional, visual/motor), structured observational methods were ranked highest in terms of frequency of use. Overall, practitioners report that they conduct more than 15 behavioral observations of student behavior during the course of a typical month.

Systematic direct observation refers to observation of behavior other than behavior that has been explicitly elicited by a predetermined and standardized set of stimuli (i.e., test behavior (Salvia & Ysseldyke, 2001)). School psychology practitioners commonly use both naturalistic and systematic direct approaches to observing student behavior. Briefly, naturalistic observation approaches refer to those observational procedures where the observer enters specific situations (e.g., a classroom) and observes all that is going on with no predetermined behaviors in mind. Here, the most common way of recording observations is to keep an anecdotal record of the behaviors that seem important to the observer. In summarizing the information, the observer provides a complete description of the many behaviors and the context in which they occurred.

In contrast, systematic direct approaches to behavioral observation are distinguished by five characteristics (Salvia & Ysseldyke, 2001). First, the goal of observation is to measure specific behaviors. Second, the behaviors being observed have been operationally defined a priori in a precise manner. Third, observations are conducted under standardized procedures and are highly objective in nature. Fourth, the times and places for observation are carefully selected and specified. Fifth, scoring and summarizing of data are standardized and do not vary from one observer to another.

Both naturalistic and systematic direct approaches to observing behavior have proven useful in developing theory and practice related to the assessment and intervention of student behavior. This chapter provides an overview of (a) naturalistic observational procedures, (b) systematic direct observational procedures, and (c) observational instruments as they related to the observation of student behavior in the classroom.

BASIC CONSIDERATIONS

Rationale for the Systematic Direct Observation of Behavior

With the reauthorization of the Individuals with Disabilities Education Act (IDEA, 1997), now more than ever it is absolutely incumbent that school psychologists adopt assessment and evaluation practices that allow for gathering relevant functional information on student behavior and performance patterns. Specifically, sections 300.532(b) and (c) under the *Procedures for Evaluation and Determination of Eligibility* of IDEA indicate that a variety of assessment tools and strategies be used to gather relevant *functional* and developmental information about a child and that they be *validated* for the specific purpose for which they are used. Moreover, section 300.532(d) requires the use of tests and other evaluation materials that include those tailored to assess specific areas of educational need and not merely those that are designed to provide a single general intelligence quotient. Similarly, sections 300.533(a)(1)(ii) and (iii) indicate that as part of the initial evaluation for special education, evaluation data include current classroom-based assessments and *observations* conducted by teachers and related services providers. Once deemed eligible for special education, section 300.347(2)(ii) requires the specification of *measurable* annual goals in the development of the individualized education program that meet each of the child's needs as they pertain to the disability classification. The spirit of IDEA is also seen in the *Principles for Professional Ethics* and *Standards for the Provision of School Psychological Services* of the *Professional Conduct Manual* (National Association of School Psychologists, 2000). Here, school psychologists are required to use assessment techniques and instruments that have established validity and reliability and to adopt assessment practices that increase the likelihood of developing effective educational interventions.

The call for the increased use of systematic direct observational procedures and a movement toward more ecologically sensitive functional assessment practices contrast directly with those of a more traditional approach that have long been the standard in school psychological assessment practices. Table 1 provides a comparison between traditional and behavioral assessment across a number of key fundamentals. Central to the difference between the two is how they view the role and causes of behavior and the type of inferences that can be made from observing behavior. From a behavioral perspective, all behavior is a result of the dynamic interplay between an individual and the environment. Thus, observing a person's behavior is useful only to the extent that it can be used to summarize a person under a specific set of circumstances. Behavior is thought to be specific to a situation. For this reason, assessment needs to be ongoing and direct until a certain level of stability or generalizability is observed. This is in contrast to a more traditional approach whereby observed behavior is assumed to be enduring and stable across all situations and intrapsychic or residing within the individual. For this reason, assessment can be global and static; that is, occurring just once or enough to measure the internal construct.

Table 1. Comparison between behavioral and traditional assessment

	Behavioral	*Traditional*
Causes of behavior	Interaction between individual and environment	Enduring underlying states or traits
Role of behavior	Important as a sample of an individual's behavior in a specific situation	Behavior is important only to the extent that it represents the underlying trait.
Consistency of behavior	Behavior thought to be specific to a specific situation	Behavior assumed to be consistent across time and settings.
Use of data	To describe and quantify behavior under specific conditions. To select appropriate interventions. To monitor effectiveness of interventions.	To describe personality Functioning and etiology. To diagnose and classify. To make prognosis or prediction.
Level of inference	Low.	High.
Comparisons made	Both within and between individual.	Between individual.
Timing of assessment	Ongoing. Before, during, and after intervention.	Before and occasionally after intervention.

Note. Adapted from Goldfried and Kent (1972) and Hartmann, Roper, and Bradford (1979).

BEST PRACTICES IN SYSTEMATIC DIRECT OBSERVATION

Methods of Systematic Direct Observation

Naturalistic Observation

Naturalistic observation refers to the recording of behavioral events in their natural settings at the time they occur, using trained or impartial observers, where descriptions of behaviors require little if any inference beyond that which is observed and recorded (Jones, Reid, & Patterson, 1979). Similar to descriptive, narrative, or anecdotal observations, naturalistic observation employs the recording of salient behaviors and discriminative stimuli as they are observed chronologically in time. For example, a school psychologist might observe a student in the classroom and note the sequence of behaviors or activities that are hypothesized to be important or serve a reinforcing function in maintaining patterns of behavior. If a student is observed to refuse the request of a teacher, then this datum would be noted and recorded as a behavioral observation or event.

According to Wilson and Reschly (1996), naturalistic observation is the most frequently used type of direct observation, used nearly twice as often as other more systematic approaches to observation. The reason for this practice most likely lies in its ease in use and minimal training requirements. In practice, naturalistic observation usually takes the form or makes use of one of two recording methods. The easiest form involves simply observing and noting behaviors and events descriptively or anecdotally as they occur in the natural setting. Typically, such behaviors and events would be recorded in a written fashion, listed chronologically as they appeared in real time. Interpretation is limited to a descriptive account of the types of behaviors and events observed and their temporal ordering in time. Because interpretation is limited, such anecdotal and descriptive accounts cannot be used for making high-stakes decisions. In fact, one of the limitations posed by naturalistic observation is the inclination to "over interpret" the data, or make inferences regarding student behavioral patterns from a limited and unstandardized sample of behavior. Likewise, observers are prone to use confirmatory search strategies whereby increased attention is directed toward those behaviors that confirm the observers' original hypotheses. In both situations, bias in the selection and interpretation of the observation is present.

A second and equally popular method of naturalistic observation involves the use of A-B-C (Antecedent-Behavior-Consequence) observation and recording. Similar to anecdotal or descriptive observational techniques, here the practitioner makes careful note of those environmental arrangements, behaviors, or events occurring just before the behavior of concern is observed (i.e., the antecedent) and what behaviors or events are observed as a result of the behavior (i.e., the consequence). By using the example of refusing a teacher request above, the antecedent would most likely be some type of teacher request or directive, the behavior would be the act of refusing, and the consequence would most likely be a brief description of how the teacher responded to the student refusal. Figure 1 presents an example of the type of recording schedule that is typically used during A-B-C observations. This type of recording schedule can be easily constructed by dividing a sheet of paper into three columns, each of which corresponds to one of the three conditions (i.e., antecedents, behaviors, and consequences). Once constructed, the observer provides a brief narrative of each condition as they are observed in the natural setting. Although listed as A-B-C, the behavior column is generally completed first and then followed by the antecedents and consequences. The reasoning behind this rests on the understanding that without the presence of some salient recordable behavior, there is little use in recording antecedents and consequences. While numerous behaviors will obviously occur, only those of clinical importance are noted. Given this, it is often helpful to specify beforehand those behaviors that will be recorded during the observation period.

Naturalistic observation techniques have become increasingly popular owing in part to their utility as part of an overall functional assessment strategy. Here, descriptive or anecdotal and A-B-C analyses are used as a preliminary step in data collection and serve the purpose of developing testable hypotheses regarding the motivation and maintenance of student behavior. For example, O'Neill et al. (1997) use naturalistic observation strategies as the first step in an overall functional assessment procedure that allows the clinician to operationally define target behaviors and formulate preliminary hypotheses regarding the function of behavior. Once salient behaviors and environmental events are observed naturalistically,

Figure 1. Example of naturalistic observation using A-B-C observation and recording

A-B-C Observation and Recording Sheet

Antecedent	Behavior	Consequence
Teacher asks students to take out paper and pencil.	Target student does not take out paper and pencil. Plays with toy car on desk instead.	Teacher reprimands target student.
Teacher takes paper and pencil out of target student's desk.	Target student pushes paper and pencil off desk and onto floor. Target student puts head on desk with arms folded around head.	Teacher removes request. Teacher picks up paper and pencil and places on desk. Tells target student he can begin work when he calms down.
Teacher continues lesson with rest of class.	Target student begins to play with car on desk again.	Teacher stops lesson and takes car away from target student.
Teacher directs student to put name on top of paper.	Target student kicks desk away. Sits in chair with arms folded across chest.	Teacher ignores target student.

they are observed systematically by using time-sampling procedures.

The advantages of using naturalistic observation procedures to identify target behaviors in this manner are that (a) their importance or social validity of behaviors can be assessed by noting the frequency of their occurrence in the natural setting, (b) their relationship to important environmental antecedents and consequences can be examined systematically, (c) data can be used to develop testable hypotheses regarding the function of behavior, and (d) the data gathered serve an important step in allowing the clinician to make decisions regarding the function of behavior rather than focusing on topographical and descriptive accounts of what is observed. As was previously noted, one of the restrictions of natural descriptive accounts of behavior is their limited utility in decision making. Because the data gathered are purely descriptive in nature, decisions are restricted to summary statements of what was observed and little else. For the most part, such data prove limited in a more problem-solving assessment orientation. Nonetheless, naturalistic descriptive accounts can be extremely useful when used as a preliminary step in a problem-solving functional assessment paradigm. Here the data gathered form the basis for developing initial hypotheses that can be subsequently observed in a more systematic fashion. The next two sections describe such systematic observational methods and the way in which practitioners can use such methods to quantify behavior from an ecological perspective.

Observational Procedures

Observational procedures refer to a set of techniques that school psychologists can use to quantify behavior along one or multiple dimensions (Kratochwill, Alper, & Cancelli, 1980). For example, a school psychologist might be interested in assessing the frequency in which a referred student is out of his seat. After operationally defining the behavior of interest, the target child would be directly observed for a specified length of time with the number of times he got out of his seat noted. Additionally, the length of time spent out of his seat for each occurrence might be noted. If out-of-seat behavior does not appear to be the main issue of concern, then another behavior can be specified and observed in a similar manner. Likewise, multiple behaviors can be identified and observed concurrently. Although the example is oversimplified, here the advantages of using observational procedures are that they are flexible and can be tailored to suit the specific needs of the assessment situation.

Measuring and Recording Behavior Systematically. There are various types of data that can be collected during systematic direct observation. A workable definition of a target behavior is one that provides an accurate description of the behavior that clearly defines the parameters of its existence and nonexistence (Heward, 1987). As such, constructs and reifications do not lend themselves well to direct observation. For example, raising one's hand to be called on is an observable and measurable behavior. Behaving "off the wall" is not something that can be directly observed. In developing explicit behavioral definitions Hawkins and Dobes (1977) offer the following suggestions:

1. The definition should be objective, referring only to observable characteristics of the behavior and environment.

2. A workable behavioral definition is readable and unambiguous such that an experienced observer could read it and readily paraphrase it accurately.

3. The definition should be complete, delineating the boundaries of what is to be included as an instance of the behavior and what is to be considered a non-instance of the behavior.

As such, operational definitions must be objective, ensuring that specific instances of the defined target behavior can be readily observed and recorded. In addition, an operational definition is a technological definition that enables others to use and replicate it (Baer, Wolf, & Risely, 1968). A complete operational definition identifies what is not the target behavior and aids observers in discriminating the target behavior from similar responses.

Once behavior is defined, the calibration of the operational definition is determined by the nature of the data; that is, the frequency of its occurrence and the particular interests of the observer (Hintze & Shapiro, 1995). In addition, practical considerations such as the availability of observers, the amount of time the student is accessible, or any combination of these factors, all dictate the type of data collected. Because each of these data may yield different results, the method of data collection must be clearly understood.

Frequency or Event Recording: The type of data known as frequency or event recording involves counting the number of occurrences of behavior observed during a specified time period. When the time periods in which the behavior is counted vary, frequencies are converted to rates of behavior per unit of time. For example, an observer may report that a target child raised a hand at an average rate of one time per minute during three separate observations conducted over the course of three days, even though the actual duration of each observation period varied. By using rate of behavior allows the practitioner to compare the occurrence of behavior across observational periods (Shapiro, 1987).

Frequency or event recording is most useful when observing behaviors that have a discrete beginning and ending. Throwing paper airplanes, hitting, and the raising of a hand are all examples of such behaviors. Behaviors that are continuous or persist for longer durations sometimes prove difficult to observe by using event recording. For example, pencil tapping, talking, or on-task behavior would be difficult to observe by using such an observational system. As with all recording schedules, a very clear operational definition of the target behavior helps ensure that accurate frequency data are being collected. In instances such as pencil tapping and talking, episodes of the behavior may be defined by using a time dimension as well as a topographical description of the behavior. For example, pencil tapping may be defined as the continuous tapping of the pencil against a physical surface that produces audible noise for at least five consecutive seconds. In this way, the frequency count for pencil tapping is easily recorded rather than the actual number of times the pencil is tapped against a physical surface.

A second consideration when using event recording has to do with the actual length of time each episode of the behavior occurs for. Generally speaking, each episode of the behavior should take approximately the same amount of time for each instance of the behavior (Barton & Ascione, 1984). For example, if an observer is observing occurrences of "noncompliance," the length of time might vary widely from a simple refusal to follow a direction to a knock-down drag-out tantrum that lasts 20 minutes. Because each episode would be coded as the occurrence of one act of noncompliance, each would be weighted equally in terms of the way in which it was quantified. Obviously, the variability in the duration of each episode is lost. For this reason, when the length of time a behavior occurs is important, event recording might not be the most appropriate recording schedule. It may, however, be combined with other recording options (e.g., duration) to capture both frequency and time dimensions of a particular behavior.

Another instance in which frequency or event recording is particularly useful is when behavior occurs at a relatively low rate. Such behaviors often occur infrequently but are of interest because of their intensity or seriousness. For example, running out of the classroom may occur once or twice a day, but may represent significant difficulties for the student. The advantage here is that with low frequency behaviors, observational periods can be continuous and designed in a fashion to be relatively unobtrusive and at low time and cost to the observer. The disadvantage, however, is that if any instance of the behavior is not observed and recorded, the reliability of the observed data is sacrificed.

As can be seen, the methods for frequency or event recording are quite varied. Commonly, the frequency in which behavior occurs is recorded in a written format (e.g., tallies on a piece of paper) with the beginning and ending time of the observational session noted. In addition to simple paper-and-pencil recording, hand-held mechanical recorders such as those used to keep track of attendance at a social function, golf wrist counters, or a wrist abacus can be used. In the end, any device capable of keeping a cumulative frequency count can be used to perform event recording. Figure 2 presents an example of a paper-and-pencil frequency recording schedule.

Duration Recording: Another type of behavioral response that can be recorded is the duration of the behavior. Duration measures may be very helpful with certain types of school-related behaviors. Studying, temper tantrums, social isolation, and aggressive outbursts are good examples of behaviors in which duration is generally important. Duration is also appropriate in cases where changing the duration of the behavior is an important target for intervention. As in the case of event recording, behaviors that have discrete beginnings and endings may be assessed in the length of time the behavior lasts.

The duration of a behavior is usually standardized in two ways (Salvia & Ysseldyke, 2001). First, the average duration of each occurrence may be computed. For example, Gary got up and out of his seat five times during a 20-minute observation. The duration of each episode was 2, 3, 4, 5, and 6 minutes, respectively. In this case the average duration was 4 minutes (i.e., [2 + 3 + 4 + 5 + 6]/5). Second, the total duration may be computed. In this same example, Gary was out of his seat a total of 20 minutes.

The most precise nonautomated instrument for collecting duration data is a stopwatch. The procedure for recording total duration with a stopwatch is to start

Figure 2. Example of frequency recording. Target behaviors include getting out of seat (OS), calling out (CAL), and teacher redirections (TR)

Frequency Observation and Recording Sheet

Date: May 13, 2000

Observer: A. VanDelay

Time	OS	CAL	TR
9:00 a.m.–10:00 a.m.	X X X	XXXXX	XXXXXXX
10:00 a.m.–11:00 a.m.	X	XXX	XXXX
11:00 a.m.–12.00 p.m.	XX	X	XXXXXX

the stopwatch as the behavior begins and stop the timing at the end of the episode. Without resetting the stopwatch, the observer starts the stopwatch again at the beginning of the second occurrence of the behavior and stops timing at the end of the second episode. The observer continues to accumulate the durations of time in this fashion until the end of the observation period and then transfers the total duration of time showing on the stopwatch to a record sheet. Figure 3 presents an example of duration recording for thumb sucking.

When observation sessions are consistent in length (e.g., 20 minutes), total duration can be compared across sessions. However, when observation sessions vary in length, a percent ratio of total duration to observation length must be computed before comparisons across observational sessions can be made. For example, if the total duration of Gary's out-of-seat was 10 minutes in each of three observational sessions but the observational sessions varied from 20-, to 30-, and 40-minute time frames, then the total duration percent that he was out of his seat would be noted as 50, 33, and 25%, respectively.

The procedure for recording duration per occurrence with a stopwatch is to start the stopwatch as the behavior begins and stop the timing at the end of the episode. The observer transfers the duration of time showing on the stopwatch to a data sheet and resets the watch. The stopwatch is started again at the beginning of the second occurrence of the behavior and is stopped at the end. The duration of time for each episode is then summed and divided by the number of occurrences yielding an average duration per episode.

Latency Recording: Latency recording is the measurement of elapsed time between the onset of a stimulus or signal (e.g., a verbal directive) and the initiation of a specified behavior (Cooper, 1987). Latency recording should be used when the major concern is the length of time between an opportunity to elicit a behavior (e.g., after the presentation of the verbal directive) and the actual time it takes to begin performing the behavior. In this case, the response latency would be the length of time between the end of the teacher's directive and initiation of the student's compliance with the directive. As with event and duration recording, when latency is assessed, both the signal and the behavior of interest must have discrete beginnings. The procedure for latency recording is similar to that for duration recording. The observer uses a stopwatch and begins timing immediately after the signal or stimulus is delivered and stops timing at the instant the target behavior is initiated. For each

Figure 3. **Example of duration recording for thumb sucking**

Duration Observation and Recording Sheet

Student: Alex — Observer: B. Matthews
Behavior: Thumb Sucking
Date: August 5, 2000

Time start: 10:10 — Time stop: 10:30

Thumb sucking (separate incidents)	Elapsed time per episode (in minutes and seconds)
1	1' 17"
2	6' 42"
3	2' 11"
4	7' 26"
5	52"
	Total: 18' 28"

Average duration per episode, 3' 42"

episode, the summary datum is the time lapse between the signal and the behavior. The actual time that it takes to complete the target behavior *does not* figure into latency recording. This is because behaviors can vary widely in the time it takes to complete them. For example, the directive of "pick up your pencil and put your name on the top of the paper" and "pick up your pencil and complete the *New York Times* Sunday crossword puzzle" would each be expected to have similar latencies. Obviously, the duration of these two behaviors would vary significantly. If completion times of these two behaviors were of primary interest, then duration would be an appropriate recording schedule. Moreover, like duration, both average and total latency can be used to summarize observed behaviors.

Time-Sampling Interval Recording: Whereas frequency, duration, and latency recording are able to accurately capture the dimensions of behavior each represents, oftentimes it is difficult to use any one of the recording schedules because of practical or measurement concerns. Issues dealing with availability of observers, lack of time, or operational issues (e.g., complications in determining exact beginning and ending of behavior) all contribute to the difficulty in observing behavior continuously. The essential characteristics of time sampling interval recording involve selecting a time period for observation, dividing the observational period into a number of equal intervals, and recording whether or not a specified target behavior has occurred during each interval (Merrell, 1999). For example, a 30-minute observation period might be broken down into 120 15-second intervals. Within each interval, the presence or absence of one or multiple behaviors might be assessed. Presence or absence of the behavior will be determined by one of three, or any combination, of three recording schedules discussed below (i.e., whole, partial, or momentary time sampling recording).

Also, unlike event, duration, and latency recording that provide exact frequency or time dimensions of observed behavior, time sampling interval recording provides only approximates for the behavior as it occurs. That being so, for situations where the exact number of occurrences or time spent engaged in the behavior, or latency of the behavior is of concern, time sampling interval recording might not be the best option. Nonetheless, time sampling interval recording provides an excellent alternative when conditions warrant observing a number of behaviors simultaneously, or for behaviors that occur at a moderate to high rate or steady state.

Whole-Interval Recording: In whole interval recording, the target behavior is scored as having occurred only when it is present throughout the entire interval (intervals are scored usually with a plus sign or other mark to indicate the presence of the behavior, and empty intervals generally denote the absence of the behavior). Since the behavior must be present for the entire interval, whole-interval recording lends itself quite well to behaviors that are continuous or intervals that are of a short duration (Shapiro & Skinner, 1990). One of the drawbacks of whole-interval recording, however, is that has a tendency to underestimate the presence of the behavior in real time. Consider for example, a whole-interval recording schedule where each interval is 15 seconds long. If, for example, off-task behavior were our target behavior and it was observed for 13 of the 15 seconds during the interval, then the interval would not be scored for the presence of off-task behavior since it did not occur for the entire 15-second interval. In essence, it would appear as if the target student was on-task for the entire 15 seconds. Because of this, whole-interval recording is well suited for behaviors targeted for increase through intervention efforts (Sulzer-Azaroff & Mayer, 1991).

Partial-Interval Recording: In contrast to whole-interval recording, with partial-interval recording an occurrence of the behavior is scored if it occurs during any part of the interval. Thus, if a behavior begins before the interval begins and ends within the interval, then an occurrence is scored. Similarly, if the behavior starts after the beginning of the interval, then an occurrence is scored. Finally, if multiple occurrences of the behavior are observed within the same interval, then the interval is simply scored as if the behavior occurred once. Again, in comparison to whole-interval recording, partial-interval recording is a good choice for behaviors that occur at a relatively low rate or behaviors of somewhat inconsistent duration. Also, partial-interval recording tends to overestimate the actual occurrence of the behavior. By using the example above, if the target student were observed to be off-task for only 2 seconds of the 15-second interval, then the interval would be scored for the presence of the behavior as if it occurred for the entire 15-second interval. Because of this, partial-interval recording is well suited for behaviors targeted for decrease through intervention efforts (Sulzer-Azaroff & Mayer, 1991).

Momentary Time-Sampling: Finally, with momentary time-sampling, a behavior is scored as present or absent only during the moment that a timed interval begins. With this technique, the observer notes either the presence or absence of the behavior at a brief instant during the interval. By using the above example, the target student would be considered off-task if at the moment of observation (e.g., very beginning of a 15-second interval) he was observed to be off-task, irrespective of any behavior observed during the rest of the interval. Salvia and Hughes (1990) have summarized a number of studies investigating the accuracy of these time-sampling procedures. As was previously noted, both whole-interval and partial-interval sampling procedures provide inaccurate estimates of the behavior in real time. Momentary time-sampling, although based on the smallest sample of behavior, provides the least biased estimate of behavior as it actually occurs (Suen & Ary, 1989).

Observational Instruments

In contrast to observational procedures, observational instruments have been developed to assess a specific range of behaviors. For example, a school psychologist might choose to use an observational instrument designed specifically to quantify the percentage of time a student is academically engaged or off-task or the frequency with which a teacher provides directives, provides opportunities to respond, or positively reinforces student efforts. Unlike more generic observational procedures, however, the flexibility of observational instruments is typically limited. With standardized administration and scoring procedures, practitioners cannot alter the operational definitions to suit their individual needs. However, because they have been developed with a specific purpose in mind, observational instruments tend to provide a more detailed account of a student's behavioral pattern across a variety of behaviors of common interest to the observer. What is lost in flexibility is gained in breadth of behaviors observed. While school psychologists could certainly develop their own observational instruments individually tailored to particular behavioral constructs, the time spent in development may be cost and labor prohibitive.

Nonetheless, the use of observational instruments continues to gain in popularity. The increased interest in such techniques is due in part to the optimization of laptop computers and hand-held data recording devices. What follows are two examples of published systematic observation codes. The Behavior Observation of Students in Schools (BOSS) (Shapiro, 1996) can be a useful part of an academic assessment in classroom settings. It may also be used in assessments of disruptive behavior, if aggressive behavior is not of principal concern. The Attention Deficit Hyperactivity Disorder School Observation Code (ADHDSOC) (Gadow, Sprafkin, & Nolan, 1996) was specifically designed to assess disruptive child behavior across a number of school settings and includes various measures of aggressive child behavior. These specific codes were selected for review owing to their ease of use, and their differential purposes.

Behavior Observation of Students in Schools. The BOSS is a useful observation code for assessing child academic behavior in the classroom environment. It is a relatively easy code to learn and use. In simple terms, the BOSS assesses levels of "on-task" and "off-task" behavior. The amount of time children are engaged in academic tasks appears to be an important instructional variable (see Gettinger, 1986, for a review). Although several existing observation codes include behaviors that represent academic engagement, the BOSS is unique in that it divides engagement into two categories: (a) active engagement (e.g., writing, raising hand, answering a question) and (b) passive engagement (e.g., looking at a worksheet, listening to teacher directions). Furthermore, off-task behaviors are assorted into three categories: (a) off-task motor (e.g., out-of-seat, fidgeting, playing with pencil), (b) off-task verbal (e.g., calling out, talking to a peer when prohibited), and (c) off-task passive (e.g., looking around, looking out the window). Finally, the BOSS also includes a measure of teacher directed instruction (TDI), which provides an estimate of the amount of time the teacher is engaged in direct instruction. For example, the TDI category would be scored as present if the teacher were lecturing to the class and absent if the teacher were sitting at the desk correcting papers.

The BOSS is administered in 15-second intervals for a period of at least 15 minutes. The on-task behaviors (i.e., active and passive engagement) are scored at the beginning of each interval by using momentary time-sampling. For the remainder of each interval, the off-task behaviors (i.e., motor, verbal, and passive) are noted by using partial interval scoring. In addition, during every fifth interval, rather than observing the target student, the behavior of a randomly selected peer is observed and noted. In doing so, comparisons can be made between the target student and a peer composite that represents "typical" behavior during the observational period. Once the observation is completed, scoring summaries are computed for on- and off-task behaviors of both the target student and the peer composite, as well as an overall estimate of how much time the teacher was engaged in direct instruction.

Attention Deficit Hyperactivity Disorder School Observation Code. According to its authors, the ADHDSOC was developed as both a screening measure and as a tool for evaluating the effects of interventions for children diagnosed with attention-deficit/hyperactivity and related disorders (e.g., oppositional defiant disorder). The ADHDSOC can be used across a number of school settings (e.g., classroom, lunchroom, playground). For example, the following seven behavior categories are scored in classroom situations: (a) interference (e.g., target student calls out when it is inappropriate to do so), (b) motor movement (e.g., target student gets out of seat without permission, (c) noncompliance (e.g., target student ignores verbal direction from teacher or aide), (d) verbal aggression (e.g., target student curses), (e) symbolic aggression (e.g., target student takes another student's pencil), (f) object aggression (e.g., target student kicks chair or desk), and (g) off-task (e.g., target student stops working on assignment and stares out the window). Though the various aggression scores (i.e., verbal, symbolic, object) may be coded individually, the authors suggest collapsing them into a single category termed "nonphysical aggression." For observations conducted in the lunchroom or on the playground the following categories are coded: (a) appropriate social behavior (e.g., target student is observed talking to another child appropriately), (b) noncompliance, (c) nonphysical aggression (this includes both object and symbolic aggression), (d) verbal aggression, and (e) physical aggression (e.g., target student trips another child). Across all settings, target behaviors are scored on a partial interval every 15 seconds.

For diagnostic purposes, the authors recommend selecting three or four average peers to observe for comparison. Selected peers and the target student are then observed in alternating 1-minute intervals. The observer rotates through each peer until all have been observed, and then returns to the initial peer. Specific guidelines for collecting observation data as well as statistical guidelines for comparing the scores of the target student to the peer composite are provided. In addition, guidelines for incorporating the ADHDSOC into treatment evaluation procedures are also presented. Validation of the ADHDSOC is presented in several studies of school-based medication evaluation studies (see Gadow, 1993; Gadow, Nolan, Poalicelli, & Sprafkin, 1991).

Both the BOSS and the ADHDSOC are relatively simple school-based observation codes to learn and use. They offer the opportunity to assess both within-student features of behavior (e.g., across various settings that vary with respect to task demands), and between-student features of behavior (e.g., target student as compared to peer composite). These are only two of the many coding systems available to school psychologists. Other available instruments are listed in Table 2.

General Issues in Systematic Direct Observation

Considerations in Selection of Target Behaviors

Considering the Social Significance of the Behavior. In daily practice, it is not uncommon for teachers and other school personnel to describe a litany of target behaviors that present as possible candidates for change. As most school psychologists are all too well aware, to target each for observation and intervention is likely to prove time and cost inefficient in the long run. As such, assessment information gathered before systematically observing behavior (e.g., interviews) is absolutely crucial to designing a sound observation strategy. In doing so, the school psychologist must determine which elements of a student's behavioral repertoire might serve as socially significant and ecologically valid target behaviors (Hintze & Shapiro, 1995).

Table 2. Other examples of school-based observation protocols

Code	Published	Age group	Setting	Recording schedule	Length of intervals, seconds
Systematic Screening of Behavior Disorders: Peer Social Behavior Code (Walker & Severson, 1990)	Sopris West (pre-school adaptation available[a])	Elementary	Playground	• Partial interval	10
The Preschool Observation Code (Bramlett, 1993; Bramlett & Barnett, 1993)	See references	Preschool	Classroom	• States (momentary time-sample) • Events (frequency of response)	30
State-Event Classroom Observation System (Saudargas, 1997)	Available from author	Elementary	Classroom	• States (momentary time-sample) • Events (frequency of response)	15

[a]Sinclair, Del'Homme, and Gonzalez (1993).

Procedures that affect behavior of one or more persons in ways that increase the probability or magnitude of benefits for any one or all of the persons involved are considered to be socially valid targets for behavior change (Hawkins, 1986). Teaching children to read, pay attention, or make friends with peers are likely to be socially valid, because these efforts generally increase benefits and decrease costs for both the targeted individual and the rest of society (Hawkins, 1991). As such, a goal, outcome, or procedure is valid only to the extent that choosing it as a target for change improves the benefit-to-cost ratio for the individual, for others, or both. A consumer's or professional's opinion about a targeted behavior for change is only valid to the extent that it is consistent with such improved benefit-to-cost ratio (Hawkins, 1991).

Although conceptually the notion of social validity makes sense, in practice it may be difficult to operationalize. At least one objective validation strategy is to use normative data from same age peers as the target student to identify which behaviors are likely to be adaptive, and the extent to which such behaviors are expected to be mastered. For example, observing the rates of academic engaged time of peers of the target child can help establish whether or not a discrepancy is present, in addition to the magnitude of the discrepancy and goals for change (Hawkins, 1991). Similarly, observing those behaviors considered to be associated with targeted behaviors (e.g., escape or avoidance) from a normative reference group may assist in determining which behaviors are of critical importance for success (Hawkins, 1991). Finally, the best validation of which behavior is most adaptive is to test experimentally the outcomes produced by different behaviors and different levels of their performance (Hintze & Eckert, 2000). By definition, those strategies that yield the greatest benefit at the least cost are the most adaptive (Hawkins, 1986).

Prioritizing Possible Target Behaviors. In many assessment situations, decisions must be made regarding the relative priority of possible target behaviors (Hintze & Shapiro, 1995). In a review of the research, Nelson and Hayes (1979) offer four suggestions that can help guide the practitioner faced with a multitude of potential target behaviors:

1. Alter the behavior that is most irritating to the person who has identified the problem (Tharp & Wetzel, 1969).

2. Alter a behavior that may be relatively easy to change (O'Leary, 1972).

3. Alter behaviors that will produce beneficial response generalization (Stokes & Baer, 1977).

4. When behaviors exist as part of a longer response chain, alter the behaviors at the beginning of the chain (Angle, Hay, Hay, & Ellinwood, 1977).

In addition, Hawkins (1986) suggests that:

1. Targeted behaviors should be those that represent "keystone" or pivotal behaviors within a behavioral response hierarchy.

2. Behaviors that have a "general utility" should be considered prior to those with highly specific functions.

3. The construction or acquisition of behavioral response repertoires should take precedence over the pure elimination of specific behaviors.

4. Behaviors that gain a student access to reinforcement in the natural environment should be given high priority.

5. Student choice should be considered when selecting possible target behaviors.

Antecedents and Consequences of Behavior. Both naturalistic observation and systematic direct observation strategies allow the observer to examine interdependencies among functional antecedents, behaviors, and consequences (Alessi, 1988). Careful examination of such functional response chains allow practitioners to develop hypotheses such as:

1. Are there avoidance, escape, or termination behaviors evident, contingent upon requests or demands made by the teacher?

2. Does the magnitude of the behavior change as a function of varying task demands?

3. Does the target behavior lead to accessing social attention or preferred tangibles or activities?

4. Are there particular setting or temporal characteristics associated with the target behavior?

Once developed, such hypotheses can be tested experimentally in a more controlled experimental analysis of the behavior (Iwata, Dorsey, Slifer, Bauman, & Richman, 1982). By using a brief functional analysis (Wacker et al., 1990), hypothesized behavioral functions can be assessed using predetermined analogue assessment strategies. Most assessments include alone, escape, and attention conditions. During the first phase of the analysis, reinforcement (e.g., social attention, withdrawal of a demand) is provided contingent on the occurrence of the target behavior. During the second phase of the brief functional analysis each condition is replicated; however, the reinforcement contingency (i.e., escape, attention) is provided for appropriate behavior rather than inappropriate behavior. By using such a methodology allows the practitioner to validate specific A-B-C chains and target specific environmental contingencies for ongoing assessment and intervention.

SUMMARY

Significant effort has been made over the past decade to shift the role of the school psychologist from one of problem identifier to one of problem solver (Deno, 1995). With a focus on hypothesis testing and scientific accountability, the school psychologist as problem solver seeks to use assessment instruments that provide clear links between assessment and intervention. Systematic direct observation provides one of the most useful strategies for accomplishing this goal. With a focus on socially significant and meaningful behavior change, systematic direct observation changes the approach of the observer from passive to active and reflects technological advances in both the study of human behavior and how behavior is recorded and summarized. Moreover, systematic direct observation procedures are in line with the reauthorization of IDEA and current standards for test use among school psychologists.

As with any new skill, it takes time to become fluent in the use of systematic observations. School psychologists should not be fooled by its apparent simplicity and should expect to devote as much time in training to use such procedures as they typically would in learning any standardized assessment instrument. With continued use, however, school psychologists will find systematic direct observation to be a crucial component of just about any of the services they offer.

REFERENCES

Alessi, G. (1988). Direct observation methods for emotional/behavior problems. In E. S. Shapiro & T. R. Kratochwill (Eds.), *Behavior assessment in schools: Conceptual foundations and practical applications* (pp. 14–75). New York: Guilford.

Angle, H. V., Hay, L. R., Hay, W. M., & Ellinwood, E. H. (1977). Computer assisted behavioral assessment. In J. D. Cone & R. P. Hawkins (Eds.), *Behavioral assessment: New directions in clinical psychology* (pp. 369–380). New York: Brunner/Mazel.

Baer, D. M., Wolf, M. M., & Risely, T. (1968). Current dimensions of applied behavior analysis. *Journal of Applied Behavior Analysis, 1,* 91–97.

Barton, E. J., & Ascione, F. R. (1984). Direct observation. In T. H. Ollendick & M. Herson (Eds.), *Child behavior assessment: Principles and procedures* (pp. 166–194). New York: Pergamon.

Bramlett, R. K. (1993). *The Preschool Observation Code.* Unpublished manuscript, University of Central Kansas.

Bramlett, R. K., & Barnett, D. W. (1993). The development of a direct observation code for use in preschool settings. *School Psychology Review, 22,* 49–62.

Cooper, J. O. (1987). Measuring and recording behavior. In J. O. Cooper, T. E. Heron, & W. L. Heward (Eds.), *Applied behavior analysis* (pp. 59–80). Columbus, OH: Merrill.

Deno, S. L. (1995). The school psychologist as problem solver. In A. Thomas & J. Grimes (Eds.), *Best practices in school psychology III* (pp. 471–484). Washington, DC: National Association of School Psychologists.

Gadow, K. D. (1993). A school-based medication evaluation program. In J. L. Matson (Ed.), *Handbook of hyperactivity in children* (pp. 186–219). Boston: Allyn & Bacon.

Gadow, K. D., Nolan, E. E., Poalicelli, L. M., & Sprafkin, J. (1991). A procedure for assessing the effects of methylphenidate on hyperactive children in public school settings. *Journal of Clinical Child Psychology, 20,* 268–276.

Gadow, K. D., Sprafkin, J., & Nolan, E. E. (1996). *ADHD School Observation Code.* Stony Brook, NY: Checkmate Plus.

Gettinger, M. (1986). Issues and trends in academic engaged time of students. *Special Services in the Schools, 2,* 1–17.

Goldfried, M. R., & Kent, R. N. (1972). Traditional versus behavioral personality assessment: A comparison of methodological and theoretical assumptions. *Psychological Bulletin, 77,* 409–420.

Hartmann, D. P., Roper, B. L., & Bradford, D. C. (1979). Some relationships between behavioral and traditional assessment. *Journal of Behavioral Assessment, 1,* 3–21.

Hawkins, R. P. (1986). Selection of target behaviors. In R. O. Nelson & S. C. Hayes (Eds.), *Conceptual foundations of behavioral assessment* (pp. 331–385). New York: Guilford.

Hawkins, R. P. (1991). Is social validity what we are interested in? Argument for a functional approach. *Journal of Applied Behavior Analysis, 24,* 205–213.

Hawkins, R. P., & Dobes, R. W. (1977). Behavioral definitions in applied behavior analysis: Explicit or implicit? In B. C. Etzel, J. M. LeBlanc, & D. M. Baer (Eds.), *New developments in behavioral research: Theory, method, and application* (pp. 167–188). Hillsdale, NJ: Erlbaum.

Heward, W. L. (1987). Selecting and defining target behavior. In J. O. Cooper, T. E. Heron, & W. L. Heward (Eds.), *Applied behavior analysis* (pp. 36–58). Columbus: Merrill.

Hintze, J. M., & Eckert, T. L. (2000). The use of functional assessment and analysis strategies to reduce the noncompliant behavior of a child with autism. *Proven Practice: Prevention & Remediation Solutions for Schools, 3,* 9–15.

Hintze, J. M., & Shapiro, E. S. (1995). Systematic observation of classroom behavior. In A. Thomas & J. Grimes (Eds.), *Best practices in school psychology III* (pp.

651–660). Washington, DC: National Association of School Psychologists.

Individuals with Disabilities Education Act: Amendments of 1997 (PL 105-17). 20 USC Chapter 33, Sections 1400 et seq. (Statute).

Iwata, B. A., Dorsey, M. F., Slifer, K. J., Bauman, K. E., & Richman, G. S. (1982). Toward a functional analysis of self-injury. *Analysis and Intervention in Developmental Disabilities, 2,* 3–20.

Jones, R. R., Reid, J. B., & Patterson, G. R. (1979). Naturalistic observation in clinical assessment. In P. McReynolds (Ed.), *Advances in psychological assessment, 3,* 42–95. San Francisco: Jossey-Bass.

Kratochwill, T. R., Alper, S., & Cancelli, A. A. (1980). Nondiscriminatory assessment in psychology and education. In L. Mann & D. A. Sabatino (Eds.), *Fourth review of special education* (pp. 229–286). New York: Grune & Stratton.

Merrell, K. W. (1999). *Behavioral, social, and emotional assessment of children and adolescents.* Mahwah, NJ: Erlbaum.

National Association of School Psychologists. (2000). *Professional conduct manual* (4th ed.). Bethesda, MD: Author.

Nelson, R. O., & Hayes, S. C. (1979). Some current dimensions of behavioral assessment. *Behavioral Assessment, 1,* 1–16.

O'Leary, K. D. (1972). The assessment of psychopathology in children. In H. C. Quay & J. S. Werry (Eds.), *Psychopathological disorders of childhood* (pp. 234–272). New York: John Wiley.

O'Neill, R. E., Horner, R. H., Albin, R. W., Sprague, J. R., Storey, K., & Newton, J. S. (1997). *Functional assessment and program development for problem behavior: A practical handbook* (2nd ed.). Pacific Grove, CA: Brooks/Cole.

Salvia, J., & Hughes, C. (1990). *Curriculum-based assessment: Testing what is taught.* New York: Macmillan.

Salvia, J., & Ysseldyke, J. E. (2001). *Assessment* (8th ed.). Princeton, NJ: Houghton Mifflin.

Saudargas, R. A. (1997). *State-Event Classroom Observation System (SECOS).* Unpublished manuscript, University of Tennessee-Knoxville.

Shapiro, E. S. (1987). *Behavioral assessment in school psychology.* Hillsdale, NJ: Erlbaum.

Shapiro, E. S. (1996). *Academic skills problems workbook.* New York: Guilford.

Shapiro, E. S., & Skinner, C. H. (1990). Best practices in observation and ecological assessment. In A. Thomas & J. Grimes (Eds.), *Best practices in school psychology II* (pp. 507–518). Washington, DC: National Association of School Psychologists.

Sinclair, E., Del'Homme, M., & Gonzalez, M. (1993). Systematic screening for preschool behavioral disorders. *Behavioral Disorders, 18,* 177–188.

Stokes, T. F., & Baer, D. M. (1977). An implicit technology of generalization. *Journal of Applied Behavior Analysis, 19,* 349–367.

Suen, H. K., & Ary, D. (1989). *Analyzing quantitative behavioral observation data.* Hillsdale, NJ: Erlbaum.

Sulzer-Azaroff, B., & Mayer, G. R. (1991). *Behavior analysis for lasting change* (2nd ed.). New York: Harcourt Brace.

Tharp, R. G., & Wetzel, R. J. (1969). *Behavior modification in the natural environment.* New York: Academic.

Wacker, D., Steege, M., Northup, J., Reimers, T., Berg, W., & Sasso, G. (1990). Use of functional analysis and acceptability measures to assess and treat severe behavior problems: An outpatient model. In A. C. Repp & N. N. Singh (Eds.), *Perspectives on the use of nonaversive and aversive interventions for persons with developmental disabilities* (pp. 349–359). Pacific Grove, CA: Brooks/ Cole.

Walker, H. M., & Severson, H. H. (1990). *Systematic screening for behavior disorders: Observer training manual.* Longmont, CO: Sopris West.

Wilson, M. S., & Reschly, D. J. (1996). Assessment in school psychology training and practice. *School Psychology Review, 25,* 9–23.

64 Best Practices in Functional Behavioral Assessment for Designing Individualized Student Programs

Timothy P. Knoster
Bloomsburg University of Pennsylvania
Barry McCurdy
Devereux Institute of Clinical Training and Research

OVERVIEW

It is only 8:10 in the morning, and, once again, John is sent to the principal's office for fighting with his classmates. He passes Carmen, who has recently received her fourth disciplinary referral this week (and it is only Wednesday) for disruptive and disrespectful behavior during classroom instruction. Down the hall from Carmen's classroom, Drew's Individual Education Plan (IEP) team is scheduling yet another meeting after school to modify Drew's behavior intervention plan in response to his increasing self-injury (i.e., face slapping and scratching). Last night, the parents of four kindergarten students requested a meeting with the principal concerning a young boy's use of profanity and his intimidation of their sons or daughters.

Everyday, schools in America are faced with complex challenges related to educating increasingly diverse student populations, especially students with chronic problem behavior. Although these students typically represent a small portion of school enrollment (i.e., 1–5%), they often account for more than 50% of the behavioral incidents handled by office personnel and consume significant amounts of time (Sugai et al., 2000; Sugai, Sprague, Horner, & Walker, 2000; Taylor-Greene et al., 1997). It is also likely that many of these same students will require individualized comprehensive behavioral supports that involve family, school, and community participation (Eber, 1996; Eber & Nelson, 1997). Also, only some of these students are likely to be eligible for special education services and programs.

School psychologists are often asked by school personnel or by parents for guidance in treating these students and are in a prime position to facilitate the design and delivery of comprehensive behavior intervention plans based on functional behavioral assessment (FBA).

The specific issue of how FBA should be integrated into the special education decision-making process is a matter that must be addressed by IEP teams (Tilly et al., 1998). FBA is required in the Individuals with Disabilities Education Act (IDEA) only when students with disabilities become the subject of school discipline proceedings. Section 615(k)(1)(B)(i) of the statute states:

> Either before or not later than 10 days after taking a disciplinary action described in subparagraph (A). . . if the local educational agency did not conduct a functional behavioral assessment and implement a behavioral intervention plan for such child before the behavior that resulted in the suspension described in subparagraph (A), the agency shall convene an IEP meting to develop an assessment plan to address that behavior.

While literally accurate, such a narrow interpretation has a series of shortcomings given a broader reading of the statute. Contrarily, a rationale for a broader interpretation can be built on IDEA statutory language for implementing FBA throughout the special education decision-making process. This position stems from a series of interactions between related sections of the statute.

In particular, §614(b)(2)(A) states that in conducting full and individual evaluations for any student suspected of having a disability, "the local education agency shall use a variety of assessment tools to gather relevant functional and developmental information . . . ." While the term "functional" in this passage modifies the word "information," it is not clear how functional information could be collected as part of a full and individual evaluation outside the context of an assessment. In addition, section 614(b)(3)(D), states that "[e]ach local education agency shall ensure . . . assessment tools and strategies that provide relevant information that directly assist persons in determining the educational needs of the child are provided." Thus, regardless of what information is collected to document the presence of a disability, teams must collect information in all relevant domains where the student demonstrates educational need. So, when the requirements of §614(b)(2)(A) and §614(b)(3)(D) are read together, the following implications seem clear: If a student with a disability experiences difficulties with mobility, reading, or other related skill areas that impede learning regardless of specific disability, then a developmental and functional mobility (reading, etc.) assessment is warranted. Given this interpretation, it may then be further inferred that if behavioral issues are of concern, then a developmental and functional behavioral assessment would contribute important information as part of the full and individual evaluation.

In further support of this broader interpretation, the IEP section of the statute states a series of clear expectations that positive behavioral programming be provided to IDEA-eligible students who need it. Section 614(d)(3)(B)(i) of the statutes states that "in the case of a child whose behavior impedes his or her learning or that of others, consider, where appropriate, strategies, including positive behavioral interventions, strategies and supports, to address the behavior." The design of positive behavioral interventions, strategies, and supports are precisely the purpose for which FBA was developed (O'Neill et al., 1997). FBA procedures should be used as part of positive behavioral intervention development for students and, in particular, for students with disabilities whose behavior impedes their learning or the learning of others.

The final reference in the statute that supports the use of FBA in situations beyond discipline comes from the discipline section itself. Section 615(k)(1)(B)(i) states, "if the local educational agency did not conduct a functional behavioral assessment and implement a behavioral intervention plan . . . ." Thus, the law acknowledges the use of FBA beyond the context of the discipline section for students with disabilities who exhibit problem behavior.

In light of this broad interpretation, school psychologists can and should provide proactive leadership by advocating for, and implementing, the FBA process for all students evidencing increasingly significant problem behavior. Further, school psychologists are in a unique position to provide policy guidance in their respective educational agencies concerning promising and best practices (i.e., functional assessment). School psychologists, in responding to this opportunity, should have a thorough understanding of the inter-relationship between research, policy, and practice as it pertains to functional behavioral assessment. Specifically, current knowledge of the literature coupled with a practical understanding of school policy, as well as an understanding of factors that inhibit or enable the implementation of best practice, is required of school psychologists.

BASIC CONSIDERATIONS

Functional behavioral assessment is a problem-solving framework that leads to intervention. The decision-making process employed by an educational team does not change across settings or situations. However, the level of resources and precision needed to effectively intervene will vary based on need and the circumstances confronted by the educational team (i.e., intensity, severity, and durability of the given student's problem behavior across settings).

There are five general considerations that school psychologists should take into account when conducting FBAs in schools. These considerations are presented in Table 1.

Table 1. Basic considerations

Consideration	*Implications for Practice*
FBA: Intervention link	The behavior of the focus student and others in typical routines and settings (contexts) should serve as the focal point of FBA. Information gathered through the FBA should be summarized in the form of specific and global hypotheses to drive intervention design.
FBA procedures: Continuum	No one interview or direct observational protocol will serve all situations. It is important to create the appropriate match between (a) the resource and precision of assessment and intervention procedures selected and (b) the intensity, severity, and/or durability of problem behavior (Tilly et al. 1998).
FBA: Special education decision making process	FBA (in varying degrees and form) should be conducted as a means to design effective teaching strategies for students who present behavior that impedes their learning or that of others. Therefore, FBA may be conducted at varying points in time throughout the special education decision-making process.
FBA: Critical components	Selected FBA procedures should reflect a problem solving process that will help an educational team answer four questions: • What is the problem? (Initial FBA) • Why does the problem exist? (Initial FBA) • What should be done to address the problem? (Initial FBA) • Did the intervention work and what's next? (FBA in progress monitoring)
FBA: Professional development	School psychologists must be aware of current best practices in conducting FBA and have an understanding of policy and practice implications (e.g., process skills). In particular, school psychologists are in a prime position to guide professional development for teachers and other relevant parties on FBA procedures.

FBA and the Link to Intervention

For an FBA to be functional, it must lead to the development of a plan for intervention and support that has a high likelihood of success. An important role for school psychologists is to effectively communicate this expectation among colleagues in schools.

The process of conducting an FBA involves gathering broad and specific types of information. As a standard practice this includes the use of informant methods with people who (a) know the child well, (b) work with the child on a regular basis, and/or (c) will be directly affected by the results of intervention. It is important to involve these same individuals from the onset of the initial FBA through design, implementation, progress monitoring, and program modification phases of the intervention process. Meaningful involvement by relevant parties will not only increase the likelihood that accurate and useful information is obtained, but also facilitate design and implementation of intervention and support that fit naturally occurring routines and settings (e.g., daily classroom routines). Relevant parties should participate (to varying degrees) in each of the five steps in the process, as highlighted in Table 2.

Table 2. Five step planning process for effective behavior support

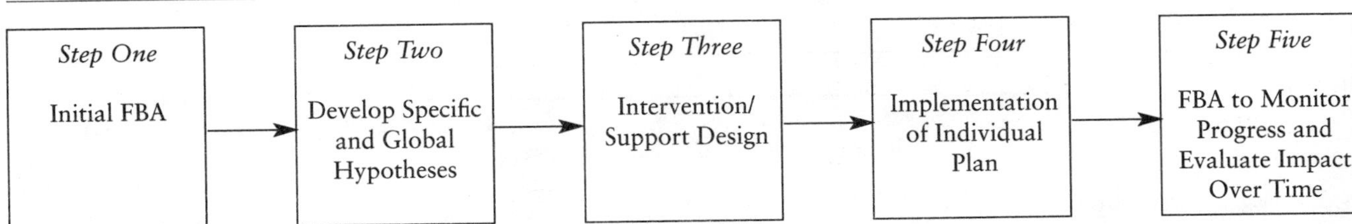

FBA and the Procedural Continuum

The process of conducting FBAs can best be understood as a continuum of integrated assessment procedures that may involve a broad array of data collection tools and procedures. Determining the appropriate level of resource and precision of intervention (including FBA) should be made on a case-by-case basis in relation to the degree of need experienced by the educational team, as depicted in Figure 1.

To illustrate, mild problem behaviors (e.g., occasional and infrequent aggressive actions such as pushing other children on the playground) can be initially assessed through informant methods by simply asking teachers about the setting and circumstances under which the student is aggressive towards others and the consequences that occur after the student has been aggressive. Alternately, an educational team confronted with the need to conduct a more rigorous FBA for a student who engages in high levels of a serious problem behavior that prior interventions and supports have failed to ameliorate (e.g., chronic aggression toward other students in the form of hitting, scratching, and biting), will likely need to employ informant methods (e.g., in-depth interviews) in conjunction with more resource-intensive behavioral observations across settings and time. School psychologists, acknowledging this continuum, are in a unique position to guide team decision making by creating a conducive match between intensity/severity/durability of the student's problem behavior and mitigating circumstances and resources and precision of the assessment procedures employed to design intervention and support.

Figure 1. Conceptual relationship between degree of behavioral problem and resource and precision of intervention

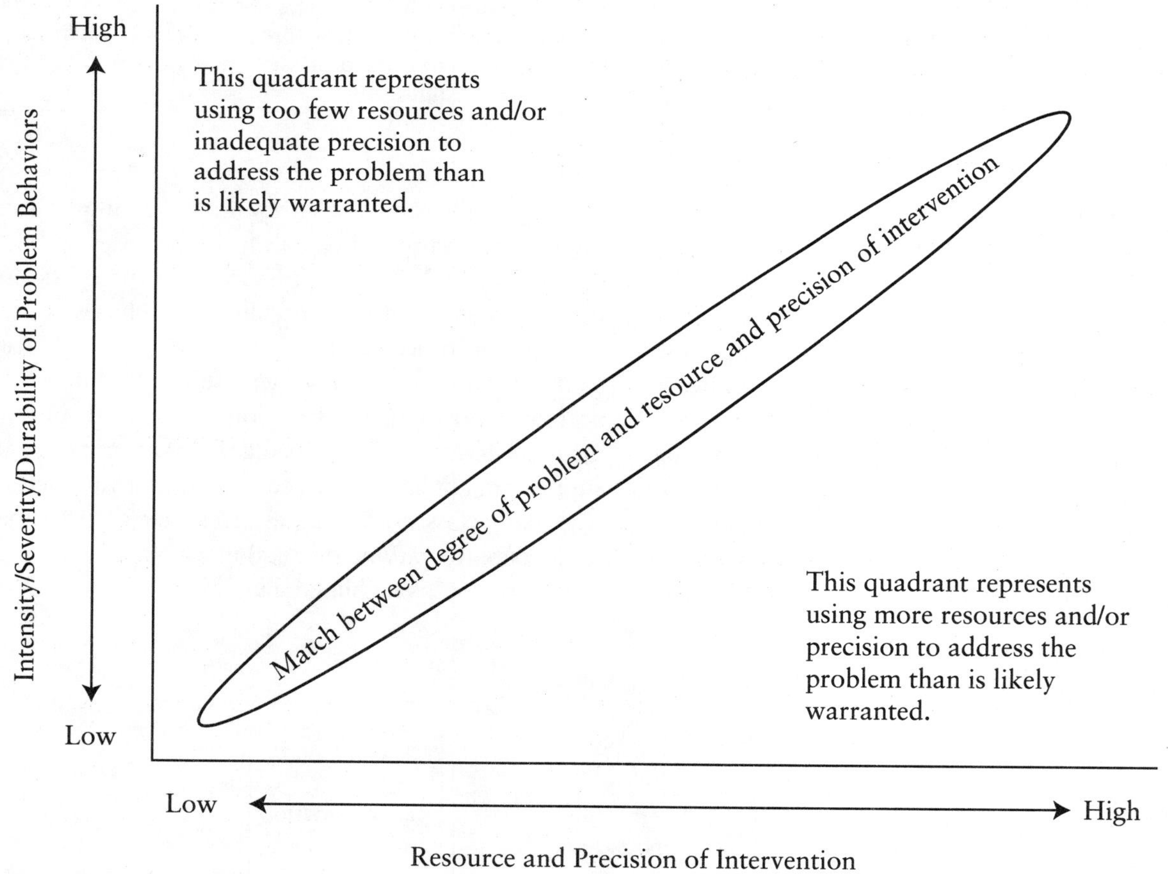

Adapted from Tilly et al., 1998.

In a practical sense, it is important to understand that student-centered teams will likely enter into the process of conducting initial FBAs at varying points in the educational decision-making process ("points of entry"). Two practical illustrations include (a) a third-grade student's persistent tantrums that have prompted a full and individual evaluation for consideration of eligibility and need for special education and (b) an eighth-grade student with an IEP for whom, as a result of Manifestation Determination, the IEP team is initiating a comprehensive functional behavioral assessment.

Given the range of possible points of entry in conducting FBAs, school psychologists are well positioned to guide educational teams in determining educational need in relation to procedural safeguards for the student and selection and use of an appropriate array of tools and procedures to gather relevant information leading to intervention (Tilly, Knoster, & Ikeda, 2000). Further, school psychologists are in an ideal position to sensitize educational teams to the impact of moving to more intensive FBA procedures in tandem with understanding the potential cost implications of more robust data collection procedures. School psychologists should guide educational teams in proceeding along this continuum in a least-to-more intrusive manner, based on student and parent preferences in relation to the success of previous interventions.

FBA and the Special Education Decision-Making Process.

Assessment and intervention for students who display behavior problems should begin at the onset of problems. FBA can be used during pre-referral intervention and in determining eligibility for, and delivery of, special education. Functional behavioral assessment is best used on an ongoing, dynamic, basis with students who display challenging behaviors, as depicted in Table 3.

Effective schools typically incorporate procedures to teach and reinforce expected behaviors and to correct inappropriate behavior. However, even in effective schools, some students will likely require a greater degree of individualization. Typically, initial interventions for this small population of students will be based on good faith and intuitive decision

Table 3. FBA throughout the special education decision-making process

Stages in the Special Education Decision Making Process	*FBA Activities*
Initial concern	• Teacher's/other's intuitive FBA as to why a particular student is exhibiting problem behavior that is based on "sensing" an increasing problem. • Intuitive decision making/intervention-prevention.
Screening/intervention	• Documentation of increasing concerns. • Failure of intuitively based interventions. • Informant methods possibly coupled with direct observation summarized in hypotheses.
Referral/full evaluation	• Continued failure of interventions based on low-tech informant methods. • More comprehensive informant methods coupled with direct observation. • Team/multiple points of input that are summarized into hypotheses.
Individual Educational Program	• Hypotheses generated from FBA serve as focal point for selection of intervention/supports. • Multi-component individualized behavior intervention plan for students whose behavior impedes their learning or that of others.
Progress monitoring and program modification	• Extend methods used during initial FBA to monitor progress. • Assess impact of intervention/supports on reductions in problem behavior, increases in acquisition and use of socially acceptable alternative skills, impact on lifestyle factors, and social validity/consumer satisfaction. • Assess environments in which to teach generalization of alternative skills and to transport necessary supports and interventions.

making. Increasingly, systematic screening and intervention procedures should be employed in instances where intuition-based interventions fail to produce desired results. Screening-level FBA and interventions usually place greater emphasis on preventative strategies in light of identified antecedents (fast triggers) and setting events (slow triggers) that adversely influence student behavior (Knoster & Llewellyn, 1998). The decision as to whether a student should be referred for a full and individual evaluation depends, at least in part, on the student's response to intervention during the screening stage.

FBA serves as a viable assessment process and is based on the requirements for full and individual evaluations in the IDEA. One provision in IDEA regarding lack of instruction is particularly important. Effective instruction for students with problem behaviors includes appropriate academic instruction and individualized behavioral intervention. In essence, the initial evaluation team must appraise the extent to which an appropriate program was in place and whether it was implemented effectively with the particular student.

The evaluation team, in conducting an FBA as part of the full and individual evaluation, provides evidence as to whether the student has a disability and needs special education. A student's response to intervention is a critical indicator of disability and the degree to which special education services are needed (Gresham, 1984, 1991). Students who make little or no progress despite support in general education, or who need extraordinary interventions, may be deemed as needing special education services and programs.

The design of an IEP for a student with problem behavior typically begins with the behavior intervention plan. Behavior intervention should be a part of the IEP if the student's behavior (a) interferes with learning (the student's or others), (b) is a result of an emotional disturbance, (c) persists despite documented interventions, (d) is a risk to safety (the student's or others), (e) results in repeated disciplinary actions that constitute a pattern, or (f) may result in a more restrictive intervention and placement (Tilly et al., 1998).

The identification and selection of well-matched strategies to address the student's needs is accomplished by the IEP team in relation to specific and global hypotheses (Bambara & Knoster, 1995, 1998). Hypotheses summarize assessment results in the form of plausible reasons for the student's problem behavior(s) and provide a foundation from which to logically link interventions addressing (a) short- and long-term prevention strategies, (b) socially acceptable alternative skills, and (c) responses to problem behaviors (including crisis management).

Monitoring student progress toward desired outcomes by IEP teams is required in IDEA. Therefore, IEP teams should employ a similar combination of informant methods and/or direct observation procedures utilized during the initial FBA to monitor progress. Thus, FBA procedures are extended into the progress-monitoring phase of IEP implementation. When extending FBA procedures to evaluate the effectiveness of a behavior intervention plan, school psychologists should guide the IEP team to consider four important questions. First, what type of information is needed to evaluate specific intervention components? Second, how will the IEP team collect this information? Third, how will the IEP team use the information to make decisions? Fourth, how will the IEP team communicate those decisions, to whom, and in what time frame? (Bambara & Knoster, 1998).

FBA Critical Components

School psychologists can significantly influence how FBAs are implemented in school programs. First, the role of the school psychologist in guiding the assessment process can directly influence how students are instructed (i.e., functional assessment). Second, school psychologists, as a result of their expertise in informant methods and direct observational procedures, can influence what information is collected and how that information is used (i.e., gathering information and forming hypotheses). Therefore, it is important for school psychologists to have a thorough understanding of the critical components of FBA, as depicted in Table 4.

It is important to understand the relationship between each critical component of the FBA process and subsequent educational team-related activities associated with intervention. To effectively guide school-based teams in conducting FBAs, school psychologists will need to have a thorough understanding of assessment and intervention practice as well as efficient strategies to engage student support team members in each step of process depicted in Table 4.

Table 4. Critical components of FBA

Step in the Problem Solving Process	*Critical Component of FBA*
Problem identification	• All relevant parties participate (i.e., those who know the student, work with the student, and/or will be affected by results of intervention). • All relevant information is considered. • Problem behaviors are operationally/environmentally defined. • Appropriate resources and precision in intervention is determined in relation to the degree of need presented.
Problem analysis	• Multi-method/multi-informant procedures are employed. • Specific and global hypotheses formulated.
Plan development	• Individualized, multi-component behavior support plan devised that 1. Focuses on measurable outcomes 2. Is based on hypotheses 3. Identifies roles and responsibilities of staff 4. Identifies progress monitoring procedures 5. Identifies necessary supports for school personnel 6. Represents a good contextual fit/social validity
Intervention and evaluation	• Progress monitoring occurs in terms of both fidelity of intervention and impact on student behavior. • Trends in student performance are analyzed. • Ineffective interventions/strategies are modified based on hypotheses. • Interventions/supports are modified to meet emerging needs. • Impact measures are taken concerning behavioral changes, impact on broad lifestyle factors (i.e., quality of life), and consumer satisfaction.

FBA and Professional Development

While the professional development implications for school psychologists relevant to FBA include a thorough understanding of methodologies for data collection, expertise is also required in understanding efficient methods of supporting educational team members in participating in each phase of intervention. Table 5 highlights professional development implications related to FBA for school psychologists.

A comprehensive training curriculum promotes the development of a range of technical skills and competencies focused on creating individualized, assessment-based, interventions that not only improve behavior but also enhance overall quality of life (Dunlap et al., 2000). As can be seen in Table 5, it is important for school psychologists to develop expertise in both the content/practice of FBA and in the process skills as they relate to educating students with problem behavior.

BEST PRACTICES IN FUNCTIONAL BEHAVIORAL ASSESSMENT

A Model for Understanding Behavior in School Settings

School psychologists are well trained to conduct assessments to determine eligibility for special education services. However, assessment for the purpose of addressing student problem behavior requires a different approach, one that is inextricably linked to the intervention process in a formative manner (Lentz & Shapiro, 1986). Functional behavioral assessment refers to a range of strategies intended to identify the variables that influence behavior in the natural environment. The purpose of FBA is to assist school-based teams in identifying the function of problem behavior and to use this information in the design and delivery of a behavior support plan (Horner, 1994; Lewis & Sugai, 1996a; O'Neill et al., 1997). In the process of conducting an FBA, specific antecedent

Table 5. FBA professional development implications for school psychologists

Skill Domain	*Competencies*
Content/practice	• Demonstrates understanding of best practice in the quantification and summarization of student behavior and environmental factors in conducting FBAs. At a minimum, these quantification procedures must include informant methods and direct observational procedures. • Gathers relevant information regarding the student, environments, and problem behavior in a time efficient manner. • Versed in collecting broad (global) and specific information by using a variety of methods. • Translates broad and specific information collected through FBAs into specific and global hypotheses. • Designs interventions with team members that are based on specific and global hypotheses. • Understands, and guides, educational teams in conducting FBA within context of progress monitoring procedures. • Graphically displays data for team interpretation. • Efficiently communicates how effective practice in FBA affects school policy and practices.
Process	• Assesses and effectively influences environmental inhibitors for educational team members as they relate to conducting FBAs and effectively intervening with students. • Collaborates with staff, families, and the student (where appropriate) to design and implement interventions that are derived from hypotheses and create a good contextual fit for the student and the student's support team. • Understands and guides implementation of FBA within context of progress monitoring procedures. • Facilitates effective communication and problem solving among team members.

and consequent events are identified and the relationship of these events to the problem behavior is defined. The FBA is considered complete when (a) the problem behavior is operationally defined, including descriptions of response classes and the sequence of behavior; (b) the antecedent events that predict the occurrence and nonoccurrence of target behaviors, including the influence of establishing operations, are identified; (c) the consequent events that maintain problem behaviors are specified; (d) the hypotheses specifying the setting events, immediate antecedents, and function of the problem behavior are developed; and (e) the direct observational data are collected to provide correlational support for the hypotheses (Bambara & Knoster, 1995; Horner, 1994; Horner, O'Neill, & Flannery, 1993; Kennedy & Itkonen, 1993; O'Neill et al., 1997).

When conducting FBAs in schools, school psychologists have the freedom to choose from a number of assessment strategies to meet the varied demands of the situation. These strategies are encompassed within three general methods, or stages, of the FBA process that vary in intensity and yet are designed to be accumulative of the information collected at each stage. The methods include (a) informant methods, (b) direct observational methods, and (c) experimental or functional analysis (Iwata, Dorsey, Slifer, Bauman, & Richman, 1994; O'Neill et al., 1997; Vittimberga, Scotti, & Weigle, 1999).

Informant Methods

Informant methods refer to indirect measures of behavior that may include the use of questionnaires, checklists, behavior rating scales, and interviews. Informant methods are just that—methods by which one individual or a group share information, in verbal or written form, about the behaviors of a student. Informant methods, although pragmatically useful in a school setting, rely on subjective impression as opposed to observation, which is considered to be more objective and, as such, have been criticized for their psychometric qualities, including inter-rater reliability and predictive validity (Shapiro, 1987). On the other hand, data collected through checklists, behavior rating scales, and interviews typically provide more behaviorally precise information than personality measures and offer opportunities for empirical validation through direct observation.

Questionnaires, checklists, behavior rating scales

There are a large number and wide variety of checklists and behavior rating scales that may be employed as measures of student behavior. These measures are typically used as screening instruments in that they provide useful information and a focus for later interviews. Checklists and behavior rating scales may include simple descriptions of behavior, normative- and criterion-referencing, or even broad and narrow band empirically derived factors. However, to be most useful in the functional assessment process, checklists providing the most precise behavioral descriptors are preferred.

Checklists and behavior rating scales are paper-and-pencil measures usually completed by a teacher or parent and, at times, by the individual student. These measures typically require that informants endorse discrete behaviors from a larger list and/or provide a rating (Likert-type) with regard to the level of acceptability or intensity of the behavior.

There are a number of advantages associated with the use of checklists and behavior rating scales (Merrell, 2000). First, such measures are economical with regard to completion time. Checklists and behavior rating scales usually contain explicit instructions and may be left with teachers or parents for later completion. Second, many of the checklists or behavior rating scales sample low frequency, but significant, behaviors that are not often identified through direct observation (e.g., aggressive and assaultive behaviors). Third, data from checklists and behavior rating scales are more reliable than that obtained through unstructured interviews. Finally, checklists and behavior rating scales provide a comprehensive sampling of behavior, capitalizing on the judgments and observations of those who are familiar with the student in question and have had ample opportunities to observe the student in context over a specified period.

Along with advantages, Shapiro (1987) cites a number of limitations to the use of checklists and behavior rating scales. These limitations often include biases imposed by the indirect measurement format. Most notable are (a) the information obtained may be subject to the demand characteristics, social desirability, and expectations of the respondent; (b) the data are often retrospective; and (c) the information obtained may be influenced by subjective opinion. Nevertheless, checklists and behavior rating scales are considered valuable screening measures.

Two measures of recent development depart slightly from the traditional format for checklists and rating scales: informants are used to rate a singular behavior and to summarize the data across "behavioral functions." The Motivation Assessment Scale (MAS) (Durand, 1990) is a questionnaire designed to identify occurrence patterns for specific behaviors. For each identified target behavior (e.g., hand biting) the informant responds to a series of 16 questions addressing the conditions that may or may not be associated with the behavior. Responses are then summarized according to the perceived function served by the behavior (i.e., sensory, escape, access attention, and access tangible). Durand and Crimmins (1988) report relatively high inter-rater (.80–.95) and test-retest (.89–.98) reliability coefficients for this measure. As well, a strength of the scale is that predictive validity measures were obtained by comparing teachers' ratings on the MAS with students' behaviors observed in analogue assessment conditions. In all cases, teachers' ratings predicted performance in the analogue assessment. It should be mentioned, however, that all psychometric evaluations conducted with the MAS involved students with severe mental retardation or autism who engaged in high rates of self-injurious behavior (Durand, 1990; Durand & Crimmins, 1988).

Similar to (and adapted from) the MAS, the Problem Behavior Questionnaire (PBQ) (Lewis, Scott, & Sugai, 1994) is a 15-item measure designed to assess the degree to which a specific problem behavior is influenced by teacher attention, peer attention, or the occurrence of environmental events. The PBQ is designed as a screening tool to identify initial hypotheses about behavioral function for students with mild learning and behavior problems. The tool is limited, however, in that there has only been one attempt to demonstrate its predictive validity.

Interviews

The purpose of the interview in the FBA process is to narrow the range of factors that influence problem behavior (Horner & Carr, 1997; Schill, Kratochwill, & Gardner, 1996). The interview is a valuable tool for "contextualizing" problem behavior, identifying clearly associated environmental events, and dismissing those variables not likely associated with the behavior of concern. Interviews may be structured, semi-structured, or open-ended, may involve the interviewer and interviewee, or may be completed as a self-interview process. Most importantly, the person interviewed should have direct contact with and knowledge about the student and the student's behavior.

Interviews are one of the more frequently employed techniques in behavioral assessment. There is evidence to suggest that the inter-rater reliability and criterion-related validity of behavioral interviewing is adequate, with the exception of interviews conducted with children (Gresham, 1984). The psychometric qualities of behavioral interviews improve with training and structure (Bergan, 1977; Bergan & Kratochwill, 1990; Bergan & Tombari, 1975). As with all indirect measures, behavioral interviews rely on the subjective impressions of others, which can be influenced by recent and/or salient events (Horner & Carr, 1997).

According to O'Neill et al. (1997), the four main outcomes to be achieved through behavioral interviewing include (a) a complete description of the problem behavior, (b) the identification of antecedent events (including internal processes) that may predict the occurrence and non-occurrence of the problem behavior, (c) the identification of behavioral functions based on maintaining consequences, and (d) the development of summary statements (i.e., hypotheses) to describe the relationships between the problem behavior and associated environmental events. This information can be obtained by school psychologists through the behavioral interviewing process. One sample format for conducting a behavioral interview is the Problem Identification Interview (PII), developed and evaluated by Bergan and colleagues (Bergan, 1977; Bergan & Kratochwill, 1990; Bergan & Tombari, 1975). In conducting the PII, school psychologists request information about antecedent, sequential, and subsequent events surrounding problem behavior. Following from the PII, the Problem Analysis Interview (PAI) is then conducted to validate the problem based on the collection of baseline data and to clarify the behavioral sequence of events, including those factors maintaining the behavior of concern (Schill et al., 1996). From this information, hypotheses about the function of problem behavior are formulated and an intervention plan is developed.

The Functional Assessment Interview (FAI) (O'Neill et al., 1997) is one of the more comprehensive structured behavioral interviews developed. The FAI consists of 10 separate sections, any or all of which may be incorporated into the interview. The FAI differs from Bergan's (1977) PII and PAI formats in that, in addition to clearly defining the target behavior and the events surrounding the behavior, the FAI requests information about the efficiency of the problem behavior (i.e., how readily it leads to reinforcement for the individual), possible functionally equivalent alternative behaviors, and the history of previous interventions. Upon completion, the interviewer is provided with a model to integrate information into "summary" statements or hypothesis statements.

When FBA is used to address the problem behaviors of students, the students themselves may be actively included in the process. Several researchers have examined the possibility of using students as key informants (Kern, Dunlap, Clarke, & Childs, 1994; O'Neill et al., 1997; Reed, Thomas, Sprague, & Horner, 1997). Structured, student-based interviews, including the Student-Assisted Functional Assessment Interview (Kern et al., 1994) and the Student-Directed Functional Assessment Interview (O'Neill et al., 1997; Reed et al., 1997), have been used to gather information from students. Although the psychometric integrity of student-based interviews remains questionable (Gresham, 1984), perhaps the greatest advantage lies in the possibility of discovering unforeseen maintaining consequences, alternative behaviors to be reinforced, or even potential reinforcers. Since the student-based interview process only takes an average of 20–40 minutes, the time may be well spent.

Once interview data have been collected and summarized, it is a good idea to compare information collected across informants. In qualitative research design, this process is known as "triangulation" and is used to corroborate information collected from different sources (Van Acker, 1999; Wiersma, 2000). Given the concerns regarding the reliability and validity of indirect assessment, triangulation helps to ensure the sufficiency of the data collected. When there is little convergence, or agreement, across data sources, additional and more rigorous assessment may be required.

The Initial Line of Inquiry (ILI)

One example of using informant methods to develop initial strategies to intervene on student problem behavior is the ILI (Knoster & Llewellyn, 1998; Lohrmann-O'Rourke, Knoster, & Llewellyn, 1999). The ILI resulted from a collaboration between the

Tri-State Consortium on Positive Behavioral Support (including the states of Pennsylvania, Virginia, and West Virginia) and the Instructional Support System of Pennsylvania, and is used as an initial screening tool for identifying and analyzing patterns of problematic student behavior. The process relies on a team-based interview, which may include several concerned individuals in addition to the child (e.g., teachers, counselors, and administrators as well as family members,, and/or representatives from community agencies). A facilitator, typically a member of the core team who is knowledgeable about the ILI process (e.g., the school psychologist), leads the team through a discussion regarding the relevant factors influencing the child's behavior, including (a) setting events or slow triggers, (b) behavioral antecedents or fast triggers, and (c) behavioral consequences (Lohrmann-O'Rourke et al., 1999). Throughout the process, emphasis is placed on user-friendly language and helping team members to reach consensus.

The facilitator uses a flipchart that is organized with columns to record information. Most times the process can be completed in one session of 60–90 minutes. Occasionally a second session is required. The process ends when the team identifies relevant factors related to the child's problem behavior and generates specific and global hypotheses about behavioral function. Team members then brainstorm a variety of support strategies, selecting those that appear to hold promise for resolving the situation while providing the best contextual fit.

The ILI, like other informant methods, is not intended to replace more comprehensive assessment strategies but, instead, should serve as a good starting point from which initial hypotheses leading to intervention may be developed. In general, when data collected primarily through informant methods is insufficient for hypothesis generation, school psychologists should move to the next stage of information gathering; that is, descriptive or direct observation.

Direct Observation Methods

Conducting a direct observation of the student in the natural setting is often necessary in order to develop and refine hypotheses about problem behavior (O'Neill et al., 1997). In particular, when data from informant methods are inconclusive, the development of hypothesis statements will be dependent upon direct observational data.

Event recording

Methods of implementing direct observation vary along a continuum of structure and complexity. Less structured direct observations may be carried out by teachers and other classroom personnel by asking them to record each occurrence of the behavior.. Adding information about antecedent and subsequent events surrounding the target behavior enhances the data without necessarily complicating the collection process. There are myriad forms for event recording described in the literature. Figure 2 shows one example of a simple event recording form designed to capture information about the target behavior, including the time of occurrence, antecedent, and consequent information.

Another event recording tool that is easily used in a classroom setting is the scatter plot. Use of the scatter plot facilitates the identification of broader environmental events that may occasion problem behavior (e.g., lunch time) and helps to identify an individual's pattern of responding across time (Touchette, MacDonald, & Langer, 1985). Observers record when, during the day, the problem behavior occurs and, once a pattern of occurrence is defined, hypotheses about setting events and specific antecedents are developed. The scatter plot can be adapted to assess the behavior of students in both general and special education programs for a full day, or portions of the day. Figure 3 shows an adapted version of the scatter plot for use in a single classroom setting.

The Functional Assessment Observation Form (FAO) (O'Neill et al., 1997) is one of the more comprehensive tools utilized by teachers or others to organize observational data. The format allows for the recording of behavioral events as well as contextual information (e.g., antecedents and actual consequences). Like the scatter plot, the FAO may be utilized in one or in several different classrooms. It is designed to capture information on one or more behaviors and leads to a summary of the data, including predictors and perceived functions. With all information captured on a single, standard form, data can be collected across several days and summarized for further analysis.

Figure 2. A-B-C event recording form

A- B - C Event Recording Form

STUDENT ____________________ BEHAVIOR ____________________

OBSERVER ____________________ CLASS ____________________

Mark each time the behavior occurs. Baseline _______ Intervention _______

Time	Antecedent	Consequence

Comments:

Descriptive analysis.

A somewhat more complex, yet highly informative, method of collecting direct observational data is through descriptive analysis. A descriptive analysis examines the natural covariation between problem behavior and antecedent/setting and consequent events (Mace, Lalli, & Lalli, 1991). Data from a descriptive analysis highlights potential functional relationships between problem behavior and environmental events, leading to hypothesis development.

Conducting a descriptive analysis in the school setting requires the services of a school psychologist who is adept at conducting structured observations. Although the task can be time consuming, there are several advantages to this form of direct observation, including (a) the opportunity to identify naturally occurring antecedents and/or reinforcers not previously identified via informant methods and (b) the possibility of creating more contextually appropriate analogue conditions should an experimental analysis be required in the future (Mace et al., 1991).

Perhaps the most common form of descriptive analysis is a method involving the continuous recording of naturally occurring antecedent, behavior, and consequent events. Known as anecdotal or A-B-C

Figure 3. **A 30-minute interval scatter plot assessment for behavioral event recording across the school day**

Student: ____________________ Behavior: ____________________

☐ ____________ ◩ ____________ ■ ____________ Date: ________

Date																												
8:00																												
8:30																												
9:00																												
9:30																												
10:00																												
10:30																												
11:00																												
11:30																												
12:00																												
12:30																												
1:00																												
1:30																												
2:00																												
2:30																												
3:00																												

Adapted and reprinted, with permission of the author, from Touchette, MacDonald, and Langer (1985, 18, p. 344). Copyright 1985 by the Society for the Experimental Analysis of Behavior, Inc.

recording, this form of descriptive analysis is designed to provide information about the target behavior, as it occurs in context, and associated antecedent and subsequent events (Bijou, Peterson, & Ault, 1968; Cooper, 1981; Cooper, Heron, & Heward, 1987). Anecdotal recording results in a narrative description of events rather than a frequency count of behaviors. Anecdotal recording requires the full attention of the observer. Generally, anecdotal recording is carried out for short time periods (20–30 minutes), several times weekly, until a clear picture of the behavior and contextual influences emerge.

Several researchers have examined the use of descriptive analysis methods yielding data in the form of conditional probabilities (Gunter, Jack, Shores, Carrell, & Flowers, 1993; Mace et al., 1991; Repp, 1999; Shores et al., 1993; Shores, Wehby, & Jack, 1999). Conditional probabilities reflect the degree or extent to which a particular target event occurs relative to another given event (Bakeman & Gottman,

1986). For example, a conditional probability establishes the likelihood that disruptive behavior (i.e., target event) follows hand raising (given event) for a particular student in a classroom setting (Gunter et al., 1993).

Mace et al. (1991) incorporate an open-ended format for descriptive analysis. Target behaviors are identified and observed, using a 10-second recording interval, while antecedent and subsequent events are identified and recorded during the observation process. Conditional probabilities, then are calculated by expressing the percentage of intervals in which a particular antecedent event (i.e., given event) is followed (within two intervals) by a particular behavior (i.e., target event) or the percentage of intervals in which a particular behavior (i.e., given event) is followed by a particular subsequent event (i.e., target event). Figure 4 shows a sample form for the collection of descriptive data using the method described by Mace et al. (1991).

Shores et al. (1999) as well as Repp (1999) differ slightly from Mace et al. (1991) by incorporating the use of pre-established codes for recording behaviors and antecedent/subsequent events. In their model of naturalistic functional assessment (NFA), Repp and colleagues first operationally define the behavior of concern, then conduct simple, non-structured observations of the student in context, noting the antecedents and consequences for each target behavior(s). Once identified, a code is developed that includes the target behavior (and appropriate alternative behavior), antecedent events (and their opposites), and consequent events, which are typically related to standard functions of behavior (escape/avoidance, attention, sensory regulation). Like Mace et al., observations conducted in the natural environment yield conditional probabilities, summarizing the percentage of intervals in which the target behavior follows specific antecedents and precedes specific consequences.

Direct observation of a student's behavior in the natural environment is an important component of the FBA process because it provides correlational support for hypotheses generated about the behavior of concern. School psychologists must be knowledgeable about, and facile with, direct observational methods. In cases where it becomes necessary to conduct an experimental analysis to determine behavioral function, a prior direct observation, or descriptive analysis, may help the school psychologist to formulate more contextually appropriate experimental conditions.

Experimental Analysis

Experimental, or functional, analysis is a process that involves the systematic manipulation of environmental variables, under contrived or analogue conditions, to determine the variable's effect on problem behavior (O'Neill et al., 1997). The original methodology of functional analysis was pioneered by Iwata et al. (1982, 1994) in the treatment of self-injurious behavior.

Early research efforts exploring the utility of functional analysis focused exclusively on individuals with mental retardation. These early studies clearly demonstrated that problem behavior serves a function for the individual (in some cases multiple functions) maintaining and strengthening the behavior through (a) positive reinforcement, (b) negative reinforcement, and/or (c) stimulation/sensory regulation (Mace et al., 1991; Repp, 1999). Since these early efforts, numerous studies have replicated and extended the work in functional analysis to other populations and problem behaviors.

Until recently, functional analysis has been exclusively implemented in clinical settings. Given the importance of this work, there is much interest in implementing functional analysis in schools. However, constraints imposed by a non-clinical setting limit the viability of conducting an experimental analysis of student behavior. These limitations include the time, expertise, and expense of implementing analogue conditions, including the time to identify and plan the conditions, ethical concerns regarding manipulations (e.g. withdrawal of intervention), and the expense of using additional personnel as observers, confederates, and, in extreme cases (e.g., self-injury), to help in ensuring the student's safety. Moreover, for students who display more complex learning and social behavior, such as students in general education, there is also the concern that controlled manipulations of environmental events, via analogue assessment, would likely result in a high degree of subject reactivity yielding little useful information. Peer attention, for example, is one variable that often serves to reinforce student problem behavior yet is difficult to capture and assess in a contrived assessment situation (Broussard & Northup, 1995; Dunlap et al., 1993; Haring, 1992; Lewis & Sugai, 1996b; Northup et al., 1995).

Figure 4. Sample descriptive analysis data sheet designed for continuous 10-second partial-interval recording

DESCRIPTIVE ANALYSIS DATA SHEET

10 SECOND INTERVALS	1:1	1:2	1:3	1:4	1:5	1:6	2:1	2:2	2:3	2:4	2:5	2:6	3:1	3:2	3:3	3:4	3:5	3:6	4:1	4:2	4:3	4:4	4:5	4:6	5:1	5:2	5:3	5:4	5:5	5:6
Antecedent Events																														
1.																														
2.																														
3.																														
4.																														
5.																														
* Responses*																														
1.																														
2.																														
3.																														
4.																														
Subsequent Events																														
1.																														
2.																														
3.																														
4.																														
5.																														

Reprinted from Mace et al. (1991), with permission from Elsevier Science.

However, despite these concerns, there are times when experimental analysis is necessary, including (a) when plausible hypotheses cannot be formulated based on informant or descriptive approaches and (b) when it is absolutely necessary to have a precise understanding of the nature of the problem behavior, including when, where, and, most importantly, why the behavior occurs (O'Neill et al., 1997). The latter situation is most likely to be encountered when the problem behavior is extreme (e.g. self-injury).

There are two basic approaches to conducting an experimental, or functional, analysis: (a) manipulating structural or antecedent events including instructions, directions, the presence of particular individuals, and/or the absence of all other individuals (i.e., leaving the student alone); and (b) manipulating consequent events, including contingent attention or contingent escape from the demand or task (O'Neill et al., 1997). There are also standard single-case designs that have been employed, including the withdrawal (ABAB) design and the alternating treatments design (Barlow & Hersen, 1984). In the standard model of functional analysis, observations are conducted across several sessions until a clear pattern emerges showing differences in the rate of problem behavior based on condition. However, one of the difficulties associated with this model is the number of observations required that can easily extend to more than 10 per condition depending on data variability and overlap. Recently, an alternative model of conducting functional analysis—brief functional analysis—has been developed and tested as a viable option for applied settings such as schools.

In an early study to explore the feasibility of brief functional analysis, Cooper and associates (Cooper, Wacker, Sasso, Reimers, & Donn, 1990) developed and implemented the model with eight children of normal intelligence, ranging in age from 4 to 9 years, referred to an outpatient diagnostic unit for disruptive behavior. Results showed that for seven out of the eight children, the percentage of appropriate and problem behavior varied substantially based on the assessment condition. Conditions were designed to evaluate the effects of different task demands (easy versus difficult) and parental attention (attention versus no attention). All children were assessed within a time span of 90 minutes, and treatment recommendations were rated by parents as both effective and acceptable.

Replicating and extending the work of Cooper et al. (1990), Northup et al. (1991) evaluated the aggressive behaviors of three individuals with severe disabilities who were referred to an out-clinic service for aggressive and self-injurious behavior at the University of Iowa. Results of the analogue assessment identified clear maintaining contingencies for the target behaviors. The treatment condition, then, was designed to produce that same contingency only for the occurrence of a specific alternative behavior (i.e., contingency reversal). Substantial reductions in aggressive behavior across all individuals were observed during each of the contingency reversal conditions.

The results of Cooper et al. (1990) and Northup et al. (1991) show promise for the implementation of experimental analysis in school-based settings where school psychologists and other personnel have limited time to conduct assessments. However, despite the advantage of time efficiency, conducting brief functional analyses in schools will necessitate that certain conditions be met. For example, because of the short time frame for assessment, the target behavior should occur at a steady and high frequency. Also, analogue conditions should be planned incorporating antecedent or consequent events that will have an immediate impact on the behavior of concern. Finally, school psychologists planning to conduct a brief functional analysis of behavior should be sufficiently skilled in the process to plan and readily adjust analogue conditions as necessary (Cooper et al., 1992; Derby et al., 1992; Vollmer & Northup, 1996).

Hypothesis Development and the Competing Behavior Model

The process of conducting an initial FBA culminates in the development of plausible hypotheses designed to explain the reason for the student's problem behavior. Although considered an important component of the process, hypothesis development is often overlooked by teams (O'Neill et al., 1997). Hypothesis statements are based on the results of the FBA and may emerge at any point in the FBA process. There may be several hypothesis statements developed for each problem behavior. Generally, hypothesis statements are of two types, specific and global (Bambara & Knoster, 1995, 1998).

Specific hypothesis statements are derived from interview and/or observational data. They offer an explanation of the student's problem behavior by identifying the behavioral antecedents and consequences surrounding the behavior. Specific hypothesis statements are developed for each major predictor and for each behavior or class of behaviors serving the same function (O'Neill et al., 1997). Components of a specific hypothesis include statements about (a) distal setting events (slow triggers), (b) immediate antecedents (fast triggers), (c) problem behavior, and (d) maintaining consequences (i.e., function served). Figure 5 shows an example of specific hypothesis statements developed for different predictors, behaviors, and consequences for one student.

Figure 5. Specific hypothesis statements accounting for different predictors, behaviors, and consequences for one student

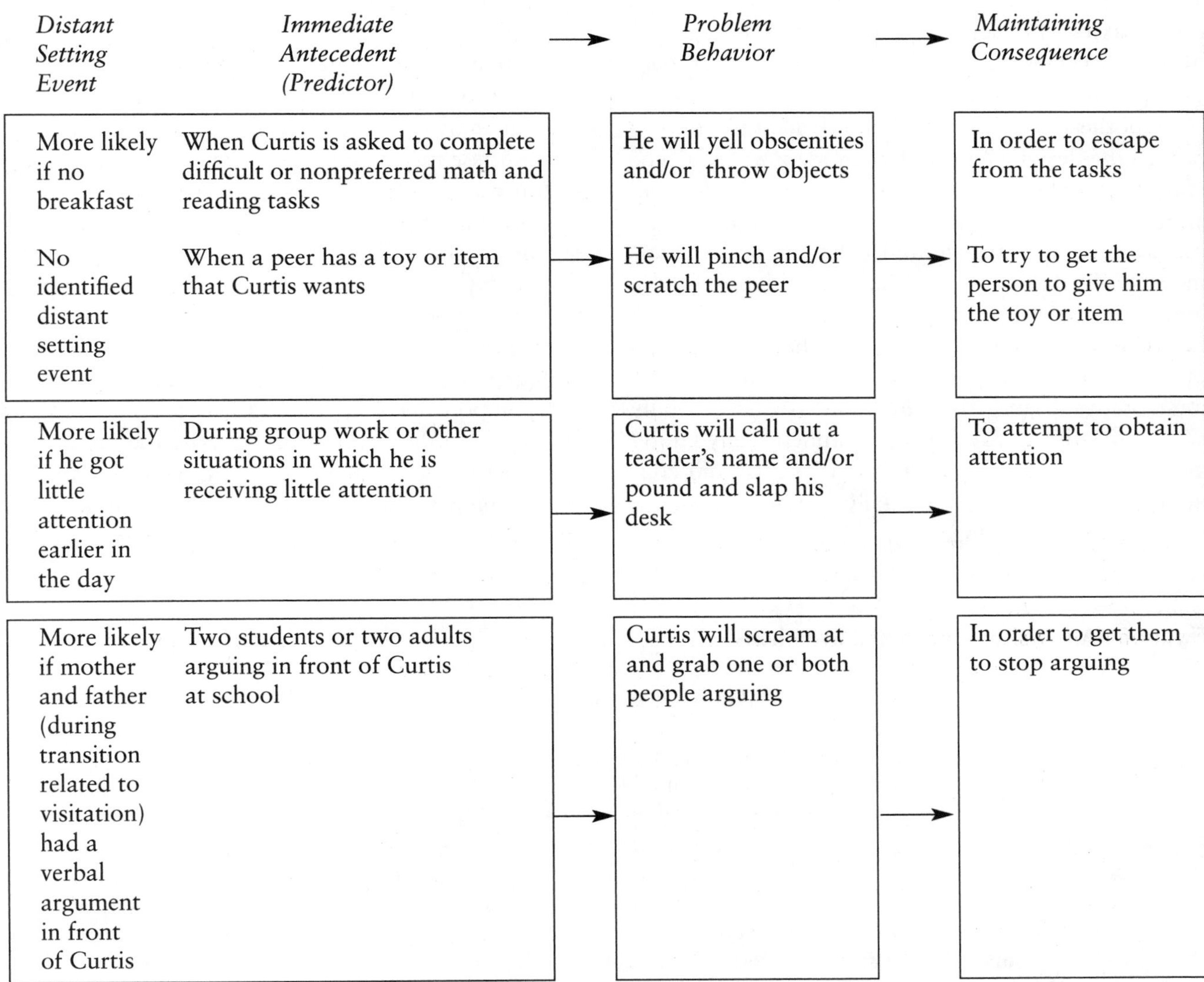

HYPOTHESIS STATEMENTS FOR EACH MAJOR PREDICTOR AND/OR CONSEQUENCE

Distant Setting Event	*Immediate Antecedent (Predictor)*	→ *Problem Behavior*	→ *Maintaining Consequence*
More likely if no breakfast	When Curtis is asked to complete difficult or nonpreferred math and reading tasks	He will yell obscenities and/or throw objects	In order to escape from the tasks
No identified distant setting event	When a peer has a toy or item that Curtis wants	He will pinch and/or scratch the peer	To try to get the person to give him the toy or item
More likely if he got little attention earlier in the day	During group work or other situations in which he is receiving little attention	Curtis will call out a teacher's name and/or pound and slap his desk	To attempt to obtain attention
More likely if mother and father (during transition related to visitation) had a verbal argument in front of Curtis	Two students or two adults arguing in front of Curtis at school	Curtis will scream at and grab one or both people arguing	In order to get them to stop arguing

From *Functional Assessment and Program Development for Problem Behavior: A Practical Handbook* (2nd ed.) by R. E. O'Neill, R. H. Horner, R. W. Albin, K. Storey, J. R. Sprague, and J. Newton © 1997. Reprinted with permission of Brooks/Cole, an imprint of the Wadsworth Group, a division of Thompson Learning.

Global hypothesis statements offer broad explanations for problem behavior and may be more useful for long-term planning (Bambara & Knoster, 1995, 1998). Global hypotheses serve as summary statements that describe the influence of lifestyle, medical issues, and learning history, among other factors, on the student's behavior. This information is usually obtained through the interview process (see the FAI) or through a review of records. Attention problems, communication deficits, medication side effects, and physical and/or mental illness are all conditions that may be described in global hypothesis statements. The long-term prevention of student problem behavior can be addressed by carefully considering the influence of any of these conditions on the behavior of concern. Figure 6 shows an example of a global hypothesis relevant to the same student example depicted in Figure 5.

Hypothesis statements are fundamentally important to the design of the behavior support plan. The competing behavior model, as described by O'Neill et al. (1997) makes use of specific hypothesis statements to identify the desired behavior or "replacement" skills that may serve the same function for the individual. School psychologists skilled in the use of behavioral procedures understand that plans developed for the sole purpose of reducing problem behaviors, without targeting an increase in socially acceptable alternative skills (i.e., functionally equivalent behavior, academic and social skills, and coping/tolerance skills), are not likely to be successful nor promote durable change.

SUMMARY

Functional behavioral assessment is a problem-solving framework that leads to intervention. While required under the IDEA for students with disabilities whose behavior impedes learning, FBA has broader application. School psychologists are in a unique position to guide student-centered teams in applying FBA in schools (inclusive of the special education decision-making process). In conducting FBAs, one interview or direct observational procedure will not serve all situations (no one size fits all). School psychologists should guide teams to select appropriate assessment and intervention tools and procedures in relation to the intensity, severity, and durability of student problem behavior(s).

There are three related approaches to conducting FBAs (informant methods, direct observation, experimental analysis). Various tools and procedures exist within these three approaches that can be imbedded within the continuum of assessment procedures in schools. Functional behavioral assessment can help educators and families to (a) identify the problem behavior; (b) analyze the problem; (c) develop a plan of intervention and support; and (d) intervene, evaluate, and modify the plan of intervention as warranted. School psychologists, when addressing these four components of FBA, must have skills in both the practice of gathering information and the process of constructively engaging other team members important to the process of intervention design and implementation. School psychologists, through their

Figure 6. An example of a global hypothesis

Global Hypothesis: Curtis

Curtis is 7 years old and has been identified as having a specific learning disability in reading coupled with records indicating increasingly problematic behavior. He receives most of his IEP in general education classrooms with itinerant services for reading. Curtis enjoys physical activities (particularly soccer and baseball) as well as playing video games (e.g., Nintendo). Curtis performs best in a structured classroom environment. He seems to have the most difficulty in environments with less structure (e.g., cafeteria, playground). Curtis has had difficulties in establishing relationships with his peers since his arrival at King Elementary School 7 months ago. He lives with his mother and younger brother David. Curtis does have contact with his father (who lives nearby) on weekends and occasionally during the week, based on his father's work schedule. His mother and father are in the process of a divorce. Curtis' problem behaviors generally appear related to his difficulty in gaining attention and/or resolving or escaping difficult situations, disputes, or conflicts in a socially acceptable manner.

endeavors in conducting FBAs, can have a positive influence on policy and practice in school systems by ensuring a direct link between assessment and intervention with students who present problem behavior.

REFERENCES

Bakeman, R., & Gottman, J. M. (1986). *Observing interaction: An introduction to sequential analysis.* New York: Cambridge University Press.

Bambara, L., & Knoster, T. (1995). *Guidelines on effective behavioral support.* Harrisburg: Pennsylvania Department of Education.

Bambara, L. M., & Knoster, T. P. (1998). *Designing positive behavior support plans. Innovations* (No. 13). Washington, DC: American Association on Mental Retardation.

Barlow, D. H., & Hersen, M. (1984). *Single case experimental designs: Strategies for studying behavior change* (2nd ed.). New York: Pergamon.

Bergan, J. R. (1977). *Behavioral consultation.* Columbus, OH: Merrill.

Bergan, J. R., & Kratochwill, T. R. (1990). *Behavioral consultation and therapy.* New York: Plenum.

Bergan, J. R., & Tombari, M. L. (1975). The analysis of verbal interactions occurring during consultation. *Journal of School Psychology, 13,* 209–226.

Bijou, S. W., Peterson, R. F., & Ault, M. H. (1968). A method to integrate descriptive and experimental field studies at the level of data and empirical concepts. *Journal of Applied Behavior Analysis, 1,* 175–191.

Broussard, C. D., & Northup, J. (1995). An approach to functional assessment and analysis of disruptive behavior in regular education classrooms. *School Psychology Quarterly, 10,* 151–164.

Cooper, J. O. (1981). *Measuring behavior* (2nd ed.). Columbus, OH: Merrill.

Cooper, J. O., Heron, T. E., & Heward, W. L. (1987). *Applied behavior analysis.* New York: Macmillan.

Cooper, L. J., Wacker, D. P., Sasso, G. M., Reimers, T. M., & Donn, L. K. (1990). Using parents as therapists to evaluate appropriate behavior of their children: Application to a tertiary diagnostic clinic. *Journal of Applied Behavior Analysis, 23,* 285–296.

Cooper, L. J., Wacker, D. P., Thursby, D., Plagmann, L. A., Harding, J., Millard, T., & Derby, M. (1992). Analysis of the effects of task preferences, task demands, and adult attention on child behavior in outpatient and classroom settings. *Journal of Applied Behavior Analysis, 25,* 823–840.

Derby, K. M., Wacker, D. P., Sasso, G., Steege, M., Northup, J., Cigrand, K., & Asmus, J. (1992). Brief functional assessment techniques to evaluate aberrant behavior in an outpatient setting: A summary of 79 cases. *Journal of Applied Behavior Analysis, 25,* 713–722.

Dunlap, G., Eno-Hieneman, M., Knoster, T., Fox, L., Anderson, J., & Albin, R. (2000). Essential elements of in-service training in positive behavior support. *Journal of Positive Behavioral Intervention, 2,* 22–32.

Dunlap, G., Kern, L., dePerczel, M., Clarke, S., Wilson, D., Childs, K. E., White, R., & Falk, G. D. (1993). Functional analysis of classroom variables for students with emotional and behavioral disorders. *Behavioral Disorders, 18,* 275–291.

Durand, M. V. (1990). *Severe behavior problems: A functional communication training approach.* New York: Guilford.

Durand, M. V., & Crimmins, D. B. (1988). Identifying the variables maintaining self-injurious behavior. *Journal of Autism and Developmental Disorders, 18,* 99–117.

Eber, L. (1996). Restructuring schools through wraparound planning: The LADSE experience. In R. J. Illback & C. M. Nelson (Eds.), *School-based services for students with emotional and behavioral disorders* (pp. 139–154). Binghamton, NY: Haworth.

Eber, L., & Nelson, C. M. (1997). School-based wraparound planning: Integrating services for students with emotional and behavioral needs. *American Journal of Orthopsychiatry, 67,* 385–395.

Gresham, F. (1984). Behavioral interviews in school psychology: Issues in psychometric adequacy and research. *School Psychology Review, 13,* 17–25.

Gresham, F. (1991). Conceptualizing behavior disorders in terms of resistance to intervention. *School Psychology Review, 20,* 23–36.

Gunter, P. L., Jack, S. L., Shores, R. E., Carrell, D. E., & Flowers, J. (1993). Lag sequential analysis as a tool for functional analysis of student disruptive behavior in classrooms. *Journal of Emotional and Behavioral Disorders, 1,* 138–148.

Haring, T. G. (1992). The context of social competence: Relations, relationships, and generalization. In S. L. Odom, S. R. McConnell, & M. A. McEvoy (Eds.), *Social competence of young children with disabilities: Issues and strategies for intervention* (pp. 307–320). Baltimore, MD: Brookes.

Horner, R. H. (1994). Contributions and future directions. *Journal of Applied Behavior Analysis, 27,* 401–404.

Horner, R. H., & Carr, E. G. (1997). Behavioral support for students with severe disabilities: Functional assessment and comprehensive intervention. *The Journal of Special Education, 31,* 84–104.

Horner, R. H., O'Neill, R. E., & Flannery, K. B. (1993). Effective behavior support plans. In M. E. Snell (Ed.), *Instruction of students with severe disabilities* (pp. 184–214). New York: Macmillan.

Iwata, B. A., Dorsey, M. F., Slifer, K. J., Bauman, K. E., & Richman, G. S. (1982). Toward a functional analysis of self-injury. *Analysis and Intervention in Developmental Disabilities, 2,* 3–20.

Iwata, B. A., Dorsey, M. F., Slifer, K. J., Bauman, K. E., & Richman, G. S. (1994). Toward a functional analysis of self-injury. *Journal of Applied Behavior Analysis, 27,* 197–210.

Kennedy, C. H., & Itkonen, T. (1993). Effects of setting events on the problem behavior of students with severe disabilities. *Journal of Applied Behavior Analysis, 26,* 321–328.

Kern, L., Dunlap, G., Clarke, S., & Childs, K. E. (1994). Student-assisted functional assessment interview. *Diagnostique, 19,* 29–39.

Knoster, T., & Llewellyn, G. (1998). *Screening for an understanding of student problem behavior: An initial line of inquiry* (2nd ed.). Harrisburg: Pennsylvania Department of Education.

Lentz, F., & Shapiro, E. (1986). Functional assessment of the academic environment. *School Psychology Review, 15,* 346–357.

Lewis, T. J., & Sugai, G. (1996a). Functional assessment of problem behavior: A pilot investigation of the comparative and interactive effects of teacher and peer social attention on students in general education settings. *School Psychology Quarterly, 11,* 1–19.

Lewis, T. J., & Sugai, G. (1996b). Descriptive and experimental analysis of teacher and peer attention and the use of assessment-based intervention to improve pro-social behavior. *Journal of Behavioral Education, 6,* 7–24.

Lewis, T. J., Scott, T. M., & Sugai, G. (1994). The problem behavior questionnaire: A teacher-based instrument to develop functional hypotheses of problem behavior in general education classrooms. *Diagnostique, 19,* 103–115.

Lohrmann-O'Rourke, S., Knoster, T., & Llewellyn, G. (1999). Screening for understanding: An initial line of inquiry for school-based settings. *Journal of Positive Behavior Interventions, 1,* 35–42.

Mace, F. C., Lalli, J. S., & Lalli, E. (1991). Functional analysis and treatment of aberrant behavior. *Research in Developmental Disabilities, 12,* 155–180.

Merrell, K. W. (2000). Informant report: Rating scale measures. In E. S. Shapiro and T. R. Kratochwill (Eds.), *Conducting school-based assessments of child and adolescent behavior*. New York: Guilford.

Northup, J., Wacker, D., Sasso, G., Steege, M., Cigrand, K., Cooko, J., & DeRaad, A. (1991). A brief functional analysis of aggressive and alternative behavior in an outclinic setting. *Journal of Applied Behavior Analysis, 24,* 509–522.

Northup, J., Broussard, C., Jones, K., George, T., Vollmer, T. R., & Herring, M. (1995). The differential effects of teacher and peer attention on the disruptive classroom behavior of three children with a diagnosis of attention deficit hyperactivity disorder. *Journal of Applied Behavior Analysis, 28,* 227–228.

O'Neill, R. E., Horner, R. H., Albin, R. W., Sprague, J. R., Storey, K., & Newton, J. S. (1997). *Functional assessment and program development for problem behavior: A practical handbook.* Pacific Grove, CA: Brooks/Cole.

Reed, H., Thomas, E., Sprague, J. R., & Horner, R. H. (1997). The student guided functional assessment interview: An analysis of student and teacher agreement. *Journal of Behavioral Education, 7,* 33–49.

Repp, A. C. (1999). Naturalistic functional assessment with regular education students in classroom settings. In A. C. Repp and R. H. Horner (Eds.), *Functional analysis of problem behavior: From effective assessment to effective support.* Belmont, CA: Wadsworth.

Schill, M. T., Kratochwill, T. R., & Gardner, W. I. (1996). Conducting a functional analysis of behavior. In M. J. Breen and C. R. Fiedler (Eds.), *Behavioral approach to assessment of youth with emotional/behavioral disorders.* Austin, TX: PRO-ED.

Shapiro, E. S. (1987). *Behavioral assessment in school psychology.* Hillsdale, NJ: Erlbaum.

Shores, R. E., Jack, S. L., Gunter, P. L., Ellis, D. N., DeBriere, T. J., & Wehby, J. H. (1993). Classroom interactions of children with behavior disorders. *Journal of Emotional and Behavioral Disorders, 1,* 27–39.

Shores, R. E., Wehby, J. H., & Jack, S. L. (1999). Analyzing behavior disorders in classrooms. In A. C. Repp and R. H. Horner (Eds.), *Functional analysis of problem behavior: From effective assessment to effective support.* Belmont, CA: Wadsworth.

Sugai, G., Horner, R. H., Dunlap, G., Hieneman, M., Lewis, T. J., Nelson, C. M., Scott, T., Liaupsin, C., Sailor, W., Turnbull, A. P., Turnbull, H. R., Wickham, D., Wilcox, B., & Ruef, M. (2000). Applying positive behavioral support and functional behavioral assessment in schools. *Journal of Positive Behavioral Interventions, 2,* 131–143.

Sugai, G., Sprague, J. R., Horner, R. H., & Walker, H. M. (2000). Preventing school violence: The use of office discipline referrals to assess and monitor school-wide discipline interventions. *Journal of Emotional and Behavioral Disorders, 8,* 94–101.

Taylor-Greene, S., Brown, D., Nelson, L., Longton, J., Gassman, T., Cohen, J., Swattz, J., Horner, R. H., Sugai, G., & Hall, S. (1997). School-wide behavioral support: starting the year off right. *Journal of Behavioral Education, 7,* 99–112.

Tilly, W. D., Knoster, T. P., & Ikeda, J. J. (2000). Functional behavioral assessment: Strategies for positive behavior support. In C. Telzrow & M. Tankersley (Eds.), *IDEA Amendments of 1997: Practice guidelines for school-based teams.* Bethesda MD: National Association of School Psychologists.

Tilly, W. D., Knoster, T. P., Kovaleski, J., Bambara, L., Dunlap, G., & Kincaid, D. (1998). *Functional behavioral assessment: Policy development in light of emerging research and practice.* Alexandria, VA: National Association of State Directors of Special Education.

Touchette, P. E., MacDonald, R. F., & Langer, S. N. (1985). A scatter plot for identifying stimulus control of problem behavior. *Journal of Applied Behavior Analysis, 18,* 343–351.

Van Acker, R. (1999). *Development of behavioral plans and supports: Changing roles and responsibilities.* Reston, VA: Council for Children with Behavior Disorders.

Vittimberga, G. L., Scotti, J. R., & Weigle, K. L. (1999). Standards of practice and critical elements in educative approach to behavioral intervention, In J. R. Scotti & L. H. Meyer (Eds.), *Behavioral intervention principles, models, and practices* (pp. 47–69). Baltimore, MD: Harris.

Vollmer, T. R., & Northup, J. (1996). Some implications of functional analysis for school psychology. *School Psychology Quarterly, 11,* 76–92.

Wiersma, W. (2000). *Research methods in education: An introduction* (7th ed.). Boston: Allyn & Bacon.

ANNOTATED BIBLIOGRAPHY

Bambara, L. M., & Knoster, T. P. (1998). *Designing positive behavior support plans. Innovations* (No. 13). Washington, DC: American Association on Mental Retardation.

This resource can be used to guide student-centered school-based teams in designing and implementing effective intervention and supports. The booklet is organized chronologically and begins with conducting an FBA, proceeds through intervention design and implementation (inclusive or progress monitoring), and then concludes with a discussion of commonly asked questions.

Cooper, L. J., Wacker, D. P., Sasso, G. M., Reimers, T. M., & Donn, L. K. (1990). Using parents as therapists to evaluate appropriate behavior of their children: Application to a tertiary diagnostic clinic. *Journal of Applied Behavior Analysis, 23,* 285–296.

This article describes the process of conducting a brief functional analysis of eight children with "conduct-type" behaviors in an outpatient setting. Experimental conditions varying task demand (easy versus hard) as well as parental attention are described in detail. Graphic displays show the performance for each subject. The article concludes with a discussion of the advantages of using brief functional analysis and potentially valuable extensions of this work.

O'Neill, R. E., Horner, R. H., Albin, R. W., Sprague, J. R., Storey, K., & Newton, J. S. (1997). *Functional assessment and program development for problem behavior: A practical handbook.* Pacific Grove, CA: Brooks/Cole.

The majority of this book is devoted to strategies that are considered a part of functional behavioral assessment rather than functional analysis. It provides a number of efficient and effective strategies for practitioners and families to employ across school, home, and work settings.

65 Best Practices in Social Skills Training

Frank M. Gresham
University of California-Riverside

OVERVIEW

The ability to interact successfully with peers and significant adults is one of the most important developmental accomplishments of children and youth. The degree to which children and youth are able to establish and maintain satisfactory interpersonal relationships, gain peer acceptance, make meaningful friendships, and terminate negative or pernicious interpersonal relationships defines social competence and predicts adequate long-term psychological and social adjustment (Kupersmidt, Coie, & Dodge, 1990; Parker & Asher, 1987).

The importance of social competence is particularly salient for students demonstrating significant deficits or delays in cognitive, academic, and emotional/behavioral functioning (Gresham & MacMillan, 1997). These students might be classified into one of the high-incidence disability groups specified in the Individuals With Disabilities Education Act (IDEA) and include specific learning disabilities, mental retardation, emotional disturbance, and attention deficit/hyperactivity disorder (eligible for services under Section 504 of the Rehabilitation Act of 1973).

Social competence historically has been a fundamental criterion used to define and classify students with high-incidence disabilities. This is clear in the modern classification criteria for mental retardation, which have consistently emphasized the importance of cognitive and *social competence* deficits (Gresham, MacMillan, & Siperstein, 1995). Likewise, social competence deficits have been used in the identification and classification of students as emotionally disturbed (Forness & Knitzer, 1992; Skiba & Grizzle, 1991). In fact, two of the five criteria specified in IDEA are pivotal in identifying students with emotional disturbance: (a) an inability to build or maintain satisfactory interpersonal relationships with peers and teachers and (b) inappropriate types of behavior or feelings under normal circumstances.

Social competence deficits are critical in the development of several childhood disorders characterized by an externalizing behavior pattern such as oppositional defiant disorder, conduct disorder, and attention deficit/hyperactivity disorder (ADHD) (Achenbach, 1985; Hinshaw, 1987; Kazdin, 1987). For example, students demonstrating an antisocial behavior pattern characterized by aggression, hostility, and violation of social norms are highly resistant to intervention, particularly if intervention does not take place relatively early in the child's educational career (Walker, Colvin, & Ramsey, 1995). Kazdin (1987) suggested that, after about age 8 (Grade 3), an antisocial behavior pattern should be viewed as a chronic condition (e.g., diabetes) that cannot be "cured," but rather controlled and managed with appropriate interventions and supports.

A number of professionals have noted the importance of social competence deficits with students having specific learning disabilities (Gresham, 1992; Gresham & Elliott, 1989, 1990; LaGreca & Stone, 1990). The Interagency Committee on Learning Disabilities (1987) stated that a consensus had developed that social skills deficits represent a specific learning disability. This proposal, however, has not been adopted or widely endorsed (Gresham, 1992). Nonetheless, the literature clearly shows that many students with specific learning disabilities exhibit substantial deficits in social competence, which co-occurs with their academic difficulties (Gresham, 1992).

Finally, students with ADHD exhibit significant social competence deficits and difficulties in interpersonal relationships (Landau & Moore, 1991). Pelham and Bender (1982) estimated that over half of children with ADHD experience substantial difficulties in interpersonal relationships with other children, their parents, and their teachers. Landau and Moore (1991) suggested that these children evoke an extremely negative response from their peer group that, in turn, leads to high levels of peer rejection. These students are perceived by peers and teachers as annoying, boisterous, intractable, and irritating, much of which can be attributed to their behavioral characteristics of impulsivity, inattention, and overactivity.

It is clear that school psychologists require knowledge and skills for conceptualizing, assessing, intervening, and evaluating intervention outcomes for children having social competence deficits. The purpose of this chapter is to present readers with practical information and strategies for the conceptualization of social competence assessment and reviews intervention strategies having the most empirical support. A conceptualization and discussion of generalization and maintenance of social skills concludes the chapter.

CONCEPTUALIZATION OF SOCIAL COMPETENCE

A recent comprehensive review of theories and definitions of social skills by Merrell and Gimpel (1998) indicated that there were 15 definitions that have been used in the literature. Although many definitions and conceptualizations of social competence have been discussed, the *social validity* definition represents a particularly useful way of conceptualizing social competence (Gresham, 1983; Wolf, 1978). A social validity conceptualization defines social skills as socially significant behaviors exhibited in specific situations that predict important social outcomes for children and youth. *Socially significant* behaviors are those behaviors that treatment consumers (e.g., parents, teachers, peers) consider desirable and which predict an individual's standing on socially important outcomes. *Socially important* outcomes are outcomes that treatment consumers consider important, adaptive, and functional (Wolf, 1978). In short, socially important outcomes make a difference in terms of an individual's functioning or adaptation to environmental demands and age-appropriate societal expectations. Socially important outcomes might include peer acceptance and friendships (Newcomb, Bukowski, & Pattee, 1993), teacher and parental judgments of social competence (Gresham & Elliott, 1990; Merrell, 1993), and school adjustment (Walker, Irvin, Noell, & Singer, 1992).

The social validity definition also distinguishes between the concepts of *social competence* and *social skill* (cf., McFall, 1982). In this view, social skills are specific behaviors that an individual exhibits to perform competently on a social task (e.g., starting a conversation or entering an ongoing play group). Social competence is an evaluative term based on judgments that a person has performed competently on a social task. These judgments may be based on opinions of significant others (e.g., teachers, parents, peers), comparisons to explicit criteria (e.g., number of social tasks correctly performed), and /or comparisons to a normative sample. In short, this view of social competence considers social skills to be specific behaviors that result in *judgments* about those behaviors (McFall, 1982). In sum, social skills are behaviors that must be taught, learned, and performed, whereas social competence represents judgments or evaluations of those behaviors within and across situations over time.

BASIC CONSIDERATIONS

Assessment Issues

A comprehensive discussion of social skills assessment methods is beyond the scope of the current chapter. However, several factors should be recognized in linking social skills assessment information to intervention strategies. Social skills assessment takes place in five major stages of the assessment/intervention: (a) screening/selection, (b) classification of social skills deficits, (c) target behavior selection, (d) functional assessment, and (e) evaluation of intervention outcomes. Table 1 presents 12 major goals of social skills assessment. These 12 goals of social skills assessment can also be classified within the four stages of a problem-solving model: problem identification, problem analysis, plan implementation, and treatment evaluation (Bergan & Kratochwill, 1990).

Like all behavioral assessment methods, social skills assessment methods can be broadly classified as *indirect* or *direct* (Gresham, 1998a; Gresham & Lambros, 1998). Indirect behavioral assessment methods assess behavior that is removed in time and place from its actual occurrence. Examples of these methods include functional assessment interviews, ratings by others, peer assessment methods (e.g., peer nominations and peer rating scales), and analogue role-play measures. Direct measures assess behavior at the time and place of its actual occurrence and include naturalistic observations of social behavior (e.g., classroom and playground) and self-monitoring strategies.

SOCIAL VALIDITY OF ASSESSMENTS.
Social skills assessment methods have also been classified on the basis of a social validity criterion (Gresham, 1983). *Type I* measures represent a social valued treatment goal in the sense that social systems (e.g., schools, courts, mental health agencies) and significant others (teachers, parents) tend to refer children for evaluation and intervention based on these measures. Type I measures of peer acceptance/rejection, friendship status, teacher or parent judgments, and some types of archival data (e.g., school attendance, disciplinary referrals, school suspensions, arrests).

Table 1. Goals of social skills assessment

Problem Identification

- Identify social skills strengths
- Identify social skills acquisition deficits
- Identify social skills performance deficits
- Identify social skills fluency deficits
- Identify competing problem behaviors

Problem Analysis

- Conduct functional assessment
- Determine the social validity of specific social skills for treatment consumers
- Select target behaviors for intervention

Plan Implementation

- Develop intervention strategies based on assessment information

Treatment Evaluation

- Select appropriate outcome measures
- Evaluate effects of intervention
- Assessment generalization and maintenance of effects

Type I measures are inherently socially valid. However, a major disadvantage of these measures is that they are not particularly sensitive in detecting short-term treatment effects. Sechrest, McKnight, and McKnight (1996) argued for using the method of *just noticeable differences* (JNDs) to gauge treatment outcomes. In applying the JND approach to social skills interventions, the question is, How much of a difference in social behavior is required for it to be noticed by significant others in the student's environment? For example, large and extended increases in positive social interactions with peers in both classroom and playground settings may be required before these changes are reflected in sociometric ratings of peer acceptance, friendship ratings, and /or teacher judgments of social skills.

Type II measures have demonstrated empirical relationships with Type I measures, and, as such, serve as indicators of one's standing on Type I measures. Type II measures are not socially valid in and of themselves, but they are useful because they predict important social outcomes for students. Common Type II measures are observations of social behavior in natural environments such as classrooms and playgrounds (see Hintz, this volume). These measures have been used frequently in social skills intervention research, and they are used exclusively in applied behavior analytic studies employing single case experimental designs.

Type III measures represent the least socially valid measures in assessing students' social competence, because they show little correspondence to Type I or Type II measures (Bellack, Hersen, & Turner, 1978; Bellack, Hersen, & Lamparski, 1979; Urbain & Kendall, 1980). Several types of measures qualify as Type III measures including behavioral role-play tests, social problem-solving measures, and various measures of social cognition. Gresham (1983) argued that although Type III measures have some face validity, they do not predict important social outcomes for students.

There is little evidence that performance on Type III measures is related to the following: (a) social behavior in naturalistic settings (Type II measures), (b) teacher or parent judgments of social competence

(Type I measures), or (c) peer assessment measures such as indices of acceptance, rejection, or friendship status (Type I measures). Support for this interpretation can be found in the meta-analyses by Beelman, Pfingsten, and Losel (1994) as well as by Denham and Almeida (1987), which showed social problem-solving interventions have a relatively strong impact on social problem-solving skills measured by Type III measures but had little impact on behavior ratings or social interaction skills measured in naturalistic settings.

Taxonomy of Social Skills

A great deal of empirical research has focused on developing a taxonomy or dimensional approach to classifying maladaptive or problem behaviors (see McConaughy, this volume). Achenbach and colleagues have developed a reliable and valid classification system for externalizing and internalizing behavior patterns that are reflected in teacher, parent, and student rating scales (see Achenbach,1985).

A recent synthesis by Caldarella and Merrell (1997) provided such taxonomy in a review of 21 investigations by using 19 social skills rating scales and inventories. Studies in this analysis and synthesis of factor analytic research included 22,000 students ranging from 3–18 years of age with about equal gender representation across studies. Teacher rating scales were used in about three-quarters of the studies, with parent and self-report measures being used in approximately 19% of the studies.

Candarella and Merrell's synthesis included five broad social skills domains: (a) peer relations skills, (b) self-management skills, (c) academic skills, (d) compliance skills, and (e) self-management skills. The taxonomy presented by these authors provides useful directions for selecting target social skills domains for more in-depth and specific assessment and intervention strategies. A number of these social skills domains have been used in published social skills curricula and intervention programs (Elias & Clabby, 1992; Elliott & Gresham, 1992; Goldstein, 1988; Walker, McConnell, Holmes, Todis, Walker, & Golden, 1983). Candarella and Merrell point out that such a taxonomy is useful because it (a) provides a nomenclature to refer to typical social skill patterns, (b) identifies a profile of social skill dimensions on which students may have relative strengths and weaknesses, (c) can be used to design interventions to teach social skills, (d) can be used to measure the outcomes of social skills interventions, and (e) can facilitate theory development concerning the causes, prognosis, and responsiveness of students to social skills intervention procedures.

Classification of Social Skills Deficits

An important step in considering students' social behavioral difficulties is determining the specific type of social skills deficits they may have. Gresham (1981) first distinguished between social skills *acquisition* and *performance* deficits. This distinction is important because different intervention approaches in remediating social skills deficits are required and different settings for carrying out social skills training (e.g., pullout groups versus classroom-based interventions) are indicated. A third type of deficit might be termed a *fluency* deficit in which a student knows how and wants to perform a given social skill, but renders an awkward or unpolished performance of the social skill. A fluency deficit in this sense is not unlike beginning or inexperienced readers who can accurately decode words, but render slow, dysfluent reading performances.

Social skill acquisition deficits refer either to the absence of knowledge for executing a particular social skill even under optimal conditions or a failure to discriminate which social behaviors are appropriate in specific situations. Social performance deficits represent the presence of social skills in a student's behavioral repertoire, but the failure to perform these skills at acceptable levels in given situations. Acquisition deficits can be thought of as "can't do" deficits, whereas performance deficits are "won't do" deficits. Fluency deficits stem from a lack of exposure to sufficient or competent models of social behavior, insufficient rehearsal or practice of a skill, or low rates or inconsistent delivery of reinforcement of skilled performances.

Gresham and Elliott (1990) extended the social skills classification model to include the notion of *interfering* or *competing* problem behaviors. In this scheme, two dimensions of social behavior—social skills and competing problem behaviors—are combined to classify social skills deficits. Competing behaviors can include internalizing or over-controlled behaviors (e.g., anxiety, depression, social withdrawal) or externalizing or under-controlled behavior patterns (e.g., aggression, disruption, impulsivity).

This social skills deficit classification model is pivotal in linking assessment results to interventions for social skills deficits. It is illogical to teach social skills to students already having these skills in their repertoires (i.e., with performance or fluency deficits). Similarly, intervention procedures to increase performance of a social skill (e.g., prompting, shaping, and reinforcement) are not particularly efficient in remediating acquisition deficits. Finally, students having fluency deficits do not require the skill to be re-taught, nor do they need to increase the frequency of its awkward performance. Instead, these students require more practice (opportunities to respond), rehearsal (repetitions), and/or differential reinforcement (shaping) for fluent behavioral performances. Unfortunately, almost all social skills training studies (to be described later) have not distinguished between these types of social skills deficits in delivering interventions to remediate social behavioral difficulties (Gresham, 1998a, 1998b).

BEST PRACTICES IN SOCIAL SKILLS TRAINING

Social skills training (SST) should emphasize the acquisition, performance, generalization and maintenance of prosocial behaviors and the reduction or elimination of competing problem behaviors. A large number of intervention procedures have been identified for teaching social skills to children and youth.

Types of Social Skills Training

The school is an ideal setting for teaching social skills because of its accessibility to children, their peers, teachers, and parents. Fundamentally, social skills intervention takes place in schools and home settings both informally and formally by using either *universal* or *selected* intervention procedures. *Informal* social skills intervention is based on the idea of incidental learning, which takes advantage of naturally occurring behavioral incidents or events to teach appropriate social behavior. Most social skills instruction in home, school, and community settings can be characterized as informal or incidental. Literally thousands of behavioral incidents occur in home, school, and community settings and create rich opportunities for making each of these behavioral incidents a potentially successful learning experience.

Formal social skills instruction can take place in a classroom setting in which the entire class is exposed to a social skills curriculum or in a small group setting removed from the classroom. Walker et al. (1995) refer to these teaching formats as *universal* or *selected* interventions, respectively. Universal interventions are not unlike vaccinations, school-wide discipline plans, or school rules that are designed to affect all children under the same conditions. Universal interventions are designed to prevent more serious problems from developing later in a child's life and, as such, represent primary prevention strategies. Selected interventions are typically conducted with children who have been identified as being at risk for behavior problems and are based on an individual assessment of a child's social skills deficits and competing problem behaviors. These interventions are undertaken to prevent existing behavior problems from developing into more serious behavior problems (i.e., secondary and tertiary interventions).

Objectives of SST

SST has four primary objectives: (a) promoting skill acquisition, (b) enhancing skill performance, (c) reducing or eliminating competing problem behaviors, and (d) facilitating generalization and maintenance of social skills. It should be noted that some children would likely have some combination of acquisition and performance deficits, some of which may be accompanied by competing problem behaviors and some others that are not. Thus, any given child may require some combination of acquisition, performance, and behavior reduction strategies. All children will require procedures to facilitate generalization and maintenance of social skills.

Table 2 lists specific social skills training and behavior reduction strategies for each of the four goals of SST. School psychologists must match appropriate intervention strategies with the particular deficits or competing problem behaviors the child exhibits. A common misconception is that one seeks to facilitate generalization and maintenance *after* implementing procedures for acquisition and performance of social skills. The evidence is clear that the best practice is to incorporate generalization from the beginning of any SST program (Gresham, 1998a).

Table 2. Social skills training objectives and strategies

I. PROMOTING SKILL ACQUISITION
   A. Modeling
   B. Coaching
   C. Behavioral rehearsal
II. ENHANCING SKILL PERFORMANCE
   A. Manipulation of antecedents
      1. Peer initiation strategies
      2. Proactive classroom management strategies
      3. Peer tutoring
      4. Incidental teaching
   B. Manipulation of consequences
      1. Contingency contracting
      2. Group-oriented contingency systems
      3. School/home notes
      4. Verbal praise
      5. Activity reinforcers
      6. Token/point systems
III. REMOVING COMPETING PROBLEM BEHAVIORS
   A. Differential reinforcement
      1. Differential reinforcement of other behavior (DRO)
      2. Differential reinforcement of low rates of behavior (DRL)
      3. Differential reinforcement of incompatible behaviors (DRI)
   B Over-correction
      1. Restitution
      2. Positive practice
   C. Time-Out
      1. Non-exclusionary (contingent observation)
      2. Exclusionary
   D. Systematic desensitization (for anxiety-based competing behaviors)
   E. Flooding/Exposure (for anxiety-based competing behaviors)
IV. FACILITATING GENERALIZATION
   A. Topographical generalization
      1. Training diversely
      2. Exploiting functional contingencies
      3. Incorporating functional mediators
   B. Functional generalization
      1. Identify strong competing stimuli in specific situations
      2. Identify strong competing problem behaviors in specific situations
      3. Identify functionally equivalent socially skilled behaviors
      4. Increase reliability and efficiency of social skilled behaviors (build fluency)
      5. Decrease reliability and efficiency of competing problem behaviors

Promoting Skill Acquisition

Procedures designed to promote skill acquisition are applicable when children do not have a particular social skill in their repertoire, when they do not know a particular step in the performance of a behavioral sequence, or when their execution of the skill is awkward or ineffective (i.e., a fluency deficit). It should be noted that a relatively small percentage of children would need social skills intervention based on acquisition deficits: Far more children have performance deficits in the area of prosocial behavior (Gresham, 1998a).

Three procedures represent pathways to remediation of deficits in social skills acquisition: modeling, coaching, and behavioral rehearsal. Social problem solving is another pathway, but it is not discussed here owing to space limitations and the fact that it incorporates the three procedures discussed in this section. More specific information on social problem solving interventions can be found in Elias and Clabby (1992).

Modeling is the process of learning a behavior by observing another person perform that behavior. Modeling instruction presents the entire sequence of behaviors involved in a particular social skill and teaches how to integrate specific behaviors into a composite behavior pattern. Modeling is one of the most effective and efficient ways of teaching social behavior (Elliott & Gresham,1992; Schneider, 1992).

Coaching is the use of verbal instruction to teach social skills. Unlike modeling, which emphasizes visual displays of social skills, coaching utilizes a child's receptive language skills. Coaching is accomplished in three fundamental steps: (a) presenting social concepts or rules, (b) providing opportunities or practice or rehearsal, and (c) providing specific informational feedback on the quality of behavioral performances.

Behavioral rehearsal refers to practicing a newly learned behavior in a structured, protective situation of role-playing. In this way, children can enhance their proficiency in using social skills without experiencing adverse consequences. Three forms of behavioral rehearsal follow: (a) covert rehearsal, (b) verbal rehearsal, and (c) overt rehearsal. These three procedures can be used in a number of ways and combinations. For example, school psychologists could ask children to imagine being teased by another child and then to imagine how they would respond (covert rehearsal). Next, one might consider combining covert rehearsal with verbal rehearsal by asking children to recite specific behaviors they would exhibit in imagined situations. Finally, one might combine covert and verbal rehearsal with overt rehearsal by asking children to role-play the imagined situation.

Enhancing Skill Performance

Most social skills interventions will involve procedures that increase the frequency of particular prosocial behaviors in specific situations because most social skills difficulties are performance rather than acquisition deficits. This suggests that most social skills interventions for most children should take place in naturalistic environments (e.g., classrooms, playgrounds) rather than small pullout groups. As such, using a consultative framework for intervention can facilitate most SST. Failure to perform certain social skills in specific situations results from two fundamental factors: (a) inappropriately arranged antecedents and/or (b) inappropriately arranged consequences. A number of specific procedures can be classified under the broad rubrics of antecedent and consequent strategies.

Interventions based on antecedent control assume that the environment does not set the occasion for the performance of prosocial behavior. That is, cues, prompts, or other stimuli are either not present or are not salient for the child to discriminate these stimuli in relation to the performance of prosocial behavior.

Two general strategies fall under the category of antecedent strategies: peer-mediated interventions and cueing/prompting. Peer-mediated interventions can include three techniques: (a) peer initiations, (b) peer tutoring, and (c) peer modeling (Kohler & Strain, 1990). With peer initiation strategies, a child's peers are used to initiate and maintain social interactions with socially withdrawn or isolated children. This procedure is effective for children who have performance deficits and who evidence relatively low rates of social interaction, but do not have externalizing behavior problems. Peer tutoring has been used primarily to enhance academic skills (Skinner, 1998), and peer modeling is used primarily in remediating social skill acquisition deficits.

A cueing and prompting procedure uses verbal and nonverbal cues or prompts to facilitate prosocial behaviors. Simple prompts or cues for some children may be all that is needed to signal them to engage in socially appropriate behavior (e.g., "Say thank you" or "Ask Dan to join your group"). Cueing and prompting represent one of the easiest and most efficient social skills intervention strategies (Elliott & Gresham, 1992; Walker et al., 1995).

Interventions based on consequent control can be classified into three broad categories: (a) reinforcement-based strategies, (b) behavioral contracts, and (c) school-home notes. Reinforcement-based strategies assume the child knows how to perform a social skill, but is not doing so because of little or nonexistent reinforcement for the behavior. Reinforcement strategies include attention, social praise, tokens/points, and activity reinforcers as well as group-oriented contingency systems. More extensive discussions of behavioral contracts, school-home notes, and group-oriented contingency systems can be found in more comprehensive treatments of these subjects (Kelley, 1990; Kohler & Strain, 1990; Stuart, 1971).

Removing or Eliminating Competing Problem Behaviors

The focus in SST is clearly on developing and refining prosocial behaviors. However, as was mentioned earlier, the failure of some children to either acquire or perform certain social skills may be due to the presence of competing problem behaviors. In the case of acquisition deficits, the competing problem behaviors may block social skill acquisition. For instance, self-stimulatory behaviors of an autistic child may prevent the development of eye contact and conversation skills. In performance deficits, aggressive behavior may be performed instead of a prosocial behavior because it may be more efficient and reliable in producing reinforcement. Because of space considerations and the author's interest in delivering positive behavioral interventions, only differential reinforcement techniques are discussed in the following paragraphs.

Differential reinforcement derives from the principles of stimulus control in which a behavior is reinforced in the presence of one stimulus and is not reinforced in the presence of other stimuli. After a number of trials of differential reinforcement, a behavior will come under the control of the stimulus associated with reinforcement and thus is said to be under *stimulus control*. Principles of stimulus control can be used to decrease rates of undesirable behavior and increase rates of prosocial behavior. Three types of differential reinforcement are used most frequently: differential reinforcement of other behavior (DRO), differential reinforcement of low rates of behavior (DRL), and differential reinforcement of incompatible behavior (DRI).

DRO refers to the delivery of a reinforcer after any behavior except the target behavior. The effects of DRO are to decrease the frequency of a target behavior and increase the frequencies of all other behaviors. Technically speaking, *any* behavior except the target behavior is reinforced (appropriate or inappropriate). Practically, only *appropriate* behaviors are in a DRO.

Two types of DRO are used: interval DRO and momentary DRO. Interval DRO involves the reinforcement of a behavior if the targeted behavior does not occur in a specified time interval. Thus, an interval DRO 2-minute, the first behavior occurring after a 2-minute interval in which the target behavior (e.g., cursing) *did not occur* is reinforced. If cursing occurs at any time during the 2-minute interval, the timer is reset to the beginning of the interval. In momentary DRO, behavior is *sampled* at the end of a specified time interval. If the target behavior is *not* occurring at the end of the interval, the first behavior occurring after the interval is reinforced. In a momentary 2-minute DRO, a behavior is reinforced if the target behavior is not occurring at the end of the 2-minute sampling time.

Either DRO schedule can be used to reduce the frequency of problem behaviors in a variety of settings. The primary problem with DRO schedules is keeping up with time intervals and resetting the timer. Momentary DRO schedules are more user-friendly than interval DROs and should be more reasonable for practical purposes.

DRL involves the reinforcement of reductions in the frequency of target behaviors in a specified time interval. Two variations of DRL schedules are described: classic DRL and full session DRL. In classic DRL, the time elapsing between behaviors or inter-response times (IRTs) are gradually lengthened. For example, if a child interrupts frequently, interruptions could be reduced in frequency by reinforcing the child waiting 5 minutes between instances of interruptions. If the child interrupted before 5 minutes elapsed (e.g., 2 minutes or 4 minutes), then the timer would be reset and the 5-minute waiting requirement would remain in effect. This would be called a classic DRL-5-minute schedule of reinforcement.

In full session DRL, reinforcement is provided when the overall frequency of a target behavior is reduced by a specified time session. The difference between a full session DRL and a classic DRL is that full session DRLs do not require longer and longer intervals between occurrences of target behavior. Instead, the requirement is that overall frequency of a target behavior in a specified time interval be reduced. For example, a teacher might set a criterion of five or fewer occurrences of disruptive behavior during a 25-minute reading lesson. If this criterion were met, then the child would receive reinforcement. Full session DRLs are more user-friendly than classic DRLs and are easily adapted within the context of group contingency systems.

In DRI, behaviors incompatible with the target behavior are reinforced. Whereas DRO and DRL focus on reducing the frequencies of problem behaviors, DRI emphasizes *increasing* the frequencies of prosocial behaviors. DRI reduces the frequency of competing problem behaviors because prosocial behaviors that are incompatible with problem behaviors are increased in frequency. Several examples should make this clear: sharing behavior is incompatible with stingy behavior, complimenting others is incompatible with teasing others, asking others to borrow a toy is incompatible with grabbing a toy, and compromising with others is incompatible with fighting.

DRIs are not effective because of the incompatibility of behaviors but rather because of the relative rate of reinforcement for each behavior (McDowell, 1982). For example, a child might "choose" to tease others or the child might "choose" to compliment others. Complimenting is incompatible with teasing; however, the child can "choose" to stop complimenting and start teasing at any time. DRI makes particular use of the Matching Law (Herrnstein, 1970), which states that response rate matches reinforcement rate. Based on principles of matching, a child's behavior should follow the Matching Law, and incompatible problem behaviors should decrease and prosocial behaviors should increase using DRI.

Facilitating Generalization and Maintenance

At its most basic level, only two processes are essential to all behavioral interventions: *discrimination* and *generalization* (Stokes, 1992). Discrimination and generalization represent polar opposites on the continuum of behavior change. A major problem confronting social skills trainers is that it is much easier to get some behaviors to occur in one place for a limited period. In other words, SST is somewhat effective in teaching *discriminations*. On the other hand, getting social behavior to occur in more than one place for an extended period has proven to be more difficult to achieve. That is, *generalization* of SST across participants, settings, and behaviors and *maintenance* of these effects over time has been less successful.

Generalization of behavior change is directly related to the phenomenon of resistance to intervention. If social skill deficits at low frequencies, then competing problem behavioral excesses occur at high frequencies, and both of these deficits and excesses are chronic (i.e., they have lasted a relatively long period) and will tend to show less generalization across different non-training conditions and less maintenance over time when SST are withdrawn. (Gresham, 1991). In effect, these children relatively quickly discriminate training from non-training conditions, particularly when training conditions are vastly different from non-training conditions. For example, students exposed to highly structured point system complete with a response cost component for inappropriate behavioral excesses and a reinforcement component for socially appropriate behavior will readily discriminate when the program is in effect and when it is withdrawn. Discrimination being the polar opposite of generalization, behavior will deteriorate rapidly to baseline levels when one returns to non-training conditions.

Students with severe behavior challenges often show excellent initial behavior change, particularly with their competing problem behavioral excesses, but fail to show generalization or maintenance of these behavior changes. One reason for this may be that exclusive attention often is focused on decreasing the momentum of undesirable behavior to the exclusion of facilitating the momentum of desirable behaviors such as social skills. Perhaps the main reason for the lack of generalization and maintenance is that these essential components of behavior change are not actively programmed to occur as a part of SST programs.

Generalization is typically regarded from two perspectives. One emphasizes behavioral *form* or *topography* and the other emphasizes behavioral *function* (Edelstein, 1989; Stokes & Osnes, 1989). The topographical description of generalization refers to the occurrence of relevant behaviors under different, non-training conditions (Stokes & Osnes, 1989). The so-called relevant behaviors (e.g., social skills) can occur across settings or situations (setting generalization), behaviors (response generalization), and/or over time (maintenance). Table 2 presents three categories of topographical generalization strategies. A more detailed treatment of these strategies can be found in Stokes and Osnes (1989). The topographical approach to generalization suggests that relevant behaviors can be made to occur in other settings, that they may lead to increases in collateral behaviors, or that they may be maintained over time. This approach, however, does not indicate *why* generalization and maintenance occurred. Topographical generalization merely describes an observed outcome or correlate of an intervention program, but does not provide a *functional* account of this outcome.

The functional approach to generalization consists of two types: (a) *stimulus generalization*, which is the occurrence of the same behavior under variations of the original stimulus (the greater the difference between the training stimulus and subsequent stimuli, the less generalization) and (b) *response generalization*, which is the control of multiple behaviors by the same stimulus (a functional response class).

One way of understanding generalization errors, functionally, is within the context of competing behaviors. Horner and Billingsley (1988) offered the following scenario: A child has acquired a new, adaptive social skill and demonstrates excellent generalization across new situations. A new situation is presented that contains a strong competing stimulus. This competing stimulus is likely to elicit old, undesirable behavior. This practical effect is that the new adaptive social skill does not generalize to situations containing the strong competing stimulus.

The above scenario would create no problems if the child did not have to encounter environments with the strong competing stimulus. However, it is not always possible to arrange this, such as when the strong competing stimulus is a classmate or teacher. The notion of strong competing stimuli may explain why so many problem drinkers "fall off the wagon" (bars, alcohol, and drinking buddies represent strong competing stimuli for excessive undesirable drinking behavior). One reason, among many, that social skills fail to generalize is that the newly taught behavior is masked or overpowered by older and stronger competing behaviors. This is an important concept for understanding why some behaviors generalize to some new situations, but not others, and why a behavior that has been maintained well for a long time may suddenly deteriorate.

An extremely important goal of SST is to determine the *reliability* and *efficiency* of competing problem behaviors relative to socially skilled alternative behaviors. Competing problem behaviors are often performed instead of socially skilled behaviors because the competing behaviors are more efficient and more reliable than the socially skilled behavior (Horner & Billingsley, 1988). Efficient behaviors are those that (a) are easier to perform in terms of response effort and (b) produce reinforcement more rapidly. Reliable behaviors are those that produce the desired outcomes more frequently than do the socially skilled alternative behaviors. For example, pushing into the lunch line may be more efficient and reliable than politely asking to cut into the lunch line.

Horner and Billingsley (1988) have termed the above the *functional equivalence of behavior*. That is, two or more behaviors can be equal in their ability to produce reinforcement. Thus, grabbing a toy is more efficient than asking for toys or pushing a peer out of the way is more efficient than asking the peer to move. All things being equal, preexisting behaviors are likely to successfully compete with socially skilled behaviors if the preexisting behaviors lead to more powerful or immediate reinforcers or more efficiently produce the same reinforcement as the socially skilled behavior (i.e., they are more cost beneficial).

To program for functional generalization, school psychologists should (a) decrease the efficiency and reliability of competing, inappropriate behaviors and (b) increase the efficiency and reliability of socially skilled alternative behaviors. The latter can be achieved by spending more time and effort in building the fluency of trained social skills by using combinations of modeling, coaching, and, most important, behavioral rehearsal with specific performance feedback.

SUMMARY

Social skills are behaviors that lead to judgments of social competence by significant others such as teachers, parents, and peers, and they are the tools by which children and youth build, maintain, and improve the quality of their interpersonal relationships. From a social validity perspective, social skills can be defined as socially significant behaviors exhibited in specific situations that predict socially important outcomes for children and youth. Social skills deficits were classified as being acquisition, performance, or fluency deficits, which may or may not be accompanied by competing problem behaviors. This classification was described as essential in determining the most appropriate social skills intervention strategies.

Social skills training was viewed as having four fundamental objectives: (a) promoting skill acquisition, (b) enhancing skill performance, (c) removing or reducing competing problem behaviors, and (d) facilitating generalization and maintenance of prosocial behaviors. Specific strategies for accomplishing each of these four objectives were described. Particular emphasis was placed on the notion of functional generalization as it relates to efficiency and reliability of behavior and the resistance of social behavior to intervention.

REFERENCES

Achenbach, T. (1985). *Assessment and taxonomy child and adolescent psychopathology*. Beverly Hills, CA: Sage.

Beelman, A., Pfingsten, U., & Losel, F. (1994). Effects of training social competence in children: A meta-analysis of recent evaluation studies. *Journal of Clinical Child Psychology, 23*, 260–271.

Bellack, A., Hersen, M., & Lamparski, D. (1979). Role-play tests for assessing social skills: Are they valid? Are they useful? *Behavior Therapy, 9*, 448–461.

Bergan, J., & Kratochwill, T. (1990). *Behavioral consultation and therapy.* New York: Plenum.

Caldarella, P., & Merrell, K. (1997). Common dimensions of social skills of children and adolescents: A taxonomy of positive behaviors. *School Psychology Review, 26*, 264–278.

Edelstein, B. (1989). Generalization: Terminological, methodological, and conceptual issues. *Behavior Therapy, 20*, 311–324.

Forness, S., & Knitzer, J. (1992). A new proposed definition and terminology to replace "serious emotional disturbance" in Individuals With Disabilities Education Act. *School Psychology Review, 21,* 12–20.

Gresham, F. M. (1981). Social skills training with handicapped children: A review. *Review of Educational Research, 51,* 139–176.

Gresham, F. M. (1983). Social validity in the assessment of children's social skills: Establishing standards for social competency. *Journal of Psychoeducational Assessment, 1,* 297–307.

Gresham, F. M. (1991). Conceptualizing behavior disorders in terms of resistance to intervention. *School Psychology Review, 20,* 23–36.

Gresham, F. M. (1992). Social skills and learning disabilities: Causal, concomitant, or correlational? *School Psychology Review, 21,* 348–360.

Gresham, F. M. (1998a). Social skills training with children. In T. S. Watson & F. M. Gresham (Eds.), *Handbook of child behavior therapy* (pp. 475–497). New York: Plenum.

Gresham, F. M. (1998b). Social skills training: Should we raze, remodel, or rebuild? *Behavioral Disorders, 24,* 19–25.

Gresham, F. M., & Elliott, S. N. (1989). Social skills as a primary learning disability. *Journal of Learning Disabilities, 22,* 120–124.

Gresham, F. M., & Elliott, S. N. (1990). *Social skills rating system.* Circle Pines, MN: American Guidance Service.

Gresham, F. M., & Lambros, K. (1998). Behavioral and functional assessment. In T. S. Watson & F. M. Gresham (Eds.), *Handbook of child behavior therapy* (pp. 3–22). New York: Plenum.

Gresham, F. M., & MacMillan, D. L. (1997). Social competence and affective characteristics of students with mild disabilities. *Review of Educational Research, 67,* 377–415.

Gresham, F. M., MacMillan, D. L., & Siperstein, G. (1995). Critical analysis of the 1992 AAMR definition: Implications for school psychology. *School Psychology Quarterly, 10,* 1–19.

Herrnstein, R. (1970). On the law of effect. *Journal of the Experimental Analysis of Behavior, 13,* 243–266.

Hinshaw, S. (1987). On the distinction between attention deficit/hyperactivity and conduct problems/aggression in child psychopathology. *Psychological Bulletin, 101,* 443–463.

Horner, R., & Billingsley, F. (1988). The effects of competing behavior on the generalization and maintenance of adaptive behavior in applied settings. In R. Horner, G. Dunlap, & R. Koegel (Eds.), *Generalization and maintenance: Lifestyle changes in applied settings* (pp. 197–220). Baltimore: Brookes.

Interagency Committee on Learning Disabilties (1987). *Learning disabilities: A report to the U.S. Congress.* Bethesda, MD: National Institutes of Health.

Kazdin, A. (1987). Treatment of antisocial behavior in children: Current status and future directions. *Psychological Bulletin, 102,* 187–203.

Kelley, M. L. (1990). *School-home notes.* New York: Guilford.

Kohler, F., & Strain, P. (1990). Peer-assisted interventions: Early promises, notable achievements, and future aspirations. *Clinical Psychology Review, 10,* 441–452.

Kupersmidt, J., Coie, J., & Dodge, K. (1990). The role of peer relationships in the development of disorder. In S. Asher & J. Coie (Eds.), *Peer rejection in childhood* (pp. 274–308). New York: Cambridge University Press.

LaGreca, A., & Stone, W. (1990). Children with learning disabilities: The role of achievement in social, personal, and behavioral functioning. In H. L. Swanson & B. Keogh (Eds.), *Learning disabilities: Theoretical and research issues* (pp. 333–352). Hillsdale, NJ: Erlbaum.

Landau, S., & Moore, L. (1991). Social skills deficits with attention deficit hyperactivity disorder. *School Psychology Review, 20,* 235–251.

McFall, R. (1982). A review and reformulation of the concept of social skills. *Behavioral Assessment, 4,* 1–33.

Merrell, K. (1993). *School social behavior scales.* Austin, TX: Pro-Ed.

Merrell, K., & Gimpel, G. (1998). *Social skills of children and adolescents: Conceptualization, assessment, and treatment.* Mahwah, NJ: Erlbaum.

Newcomb, A., Bukowski, W., & Patee, L. (1993). Children's peer relations: A meta-analytic review of popular, rejected, neglected, controversial, and average children. *Psychological Bulletin, 113,* 99–128.

Parker, J., & Asher, S. (1987). Peer relations and later personal adjustment: Are low-accepted children at-risk? *Psychological Bulletin, 102,* 357–389.

Schneider, B. (1992). Didactic methods for enhancing children's peer relations: A quantitative review. *Clinical Psychology Review, 12,* 363–382.

Skiba, R., & Grizzle, K. (1991). The social maladjustment exclusion clause: Issues of definition and assessment. *School Psychology Review, 20,* 217–230.

Stokes, T. (1992). Discrimination and generalization. *Journal of Applied Behavior Analysis, 25,* 429–432.

Stokes, T., & Osnes, P. (1989). An operant pursuit of generalization. *Behavior Therapy, 20,*337–355.

Stuart, R. (1971). Behavioral contracting with families of delinquents. *Journal of Behavioral Therapy and Experimental Psychiatry, 2,* 1–11.

Urbain, E., & Kendall, P. (1980). Review of social-cognitive problem-solving interventions with children. *Psychological Bulletin, 88,* 109–143.

Walker, H., Colvin, G., & Ramsey, E. (1995). *Antisocial behavior in school: Strategies and best practices.* Pacific Grove, CA: Brooks/Cole.

Wolf, M.M. (1978). Social validity: The case for subjective measurement or how applied behavior analysis is finding its heart. *Journal of Applied Behavior Analysis, 11,* 203–214.

66 Best Practices in Preschool Social Skills Training

Stephen N. Elliott and Brian C. McKevitt
University of Wisconsin-Madison
James Clyde DiPerna
Lehigh University

OVERVIEW

Behaviors such as sharing, helping, initiating relationships, requesting help from others, and saying "please" and "thank you" are examples of socially appropriate behaviors that enable children young and old to successfully function in social settings. Developing these types of social skills is believed to be one of the most important accomplishments of childhood and can lead to successful social relationships and academic functioning. In fact, researchers have established that parents and teachers rank social and language skills as the most important skills needed to transition successfully from preschool to kindergarten (Hains, Fowler, Schwartz, Kottwitz, & Rosenkoetter, 1989; Johnson, Gallagher, Cook, & Wong, 1995).

The process of developing social skills in early childhood, although not fully understood, begins soon after birth and is influenced by person variables (e.g., physical abilities, language, and communication skills) and environmental variables (e.g., family members' and peers' involvement and interactions) (Eisenberg & Mussen, 1989). Unfortunately, some children do not acquire adequate social skills and often experience negative child-adult or child-child relationships as a result. In addition, several researchers have documented that social skills play an important role as academic enablers, or skills that allow students to benefit from instruction (DiPerna & Elliott, 2000; Wentzel, 1993). Thus, the identification and treatment of preschool children who are experiencing delays or deficiencies in social-emotional development warrant the attention of teachers, parents, and psychologists (Elias et al., 1997). This call for attention is congruent with research that documents significant social skills deficits in young students with mild or moderate disabilities (e.g., Cassidy & Asher, 1992; Guralnick, 1986; Strain, Odom, & McConnell, 1984). Briefly, this literature indicates that students with disabilities frequently display fewer positive social and cooperative behaviors, show less initiative in peer interactions, and exhibit lower rates of peer reinforcement than their students without disabilities. If untreated, these social skills deficits have been shown to be relatively stable over time, related to poor academic performance, and may be predictive of social adjustment problems in adolescence and adulthood (Parker & Asher, 1987). Given these potential negative outcomes, it is imperative that psychologists and educators of young children identify social skills difficulties and implement empirically supported interventions as soon as concerns arise.

The purposes of this chapter are to (a) provide an overview of typical social development during the preschool years as well as appropriate parent expectations for preschool children's behavior, (b) briefly review the process of assessing social functioning and identifying skills in need of treatment, and (c) focus on effective methods for promoting social skills in preschoolers. Additional information on each of these topics is provided in the Annotated Bibliography at the end of the chapter.

BASIC CONSIDERATIONS

Identification and Development of Socially Important Behaviors

Social skills may be defined as socially acceptable learned behaviors that enable a person to interact with others in ways that elicit positive responses and to avoid negative responses (Gresham & Elliott, 1984, 1990). When social skills are enacted successfully, the results generally are positive perceptions of social competence. The acronym of CARES has been used to identify, and assist with the memory of, five major behavioral clusters of social skills. These skill clusters are Cooperation, Assertion, Responsibility, Empathy, and Self-Control. Briefly, these clusters of social behaviors can be characterized for preschoolers as follows:

1. Cooperation: Behaviors such as helping others, sharing materials with a peer, and complying with rules.

2. Assertion: Initiating behaviors such as asking others for information and behaviors that are responses to others' actions such as responding to peer pressure.

3. Responsibility: Behaviors that demonstrate ability to communicate with adults and concern about one's property.

4. Empathy: Behaviors that reflect concern for peers' or significant adults' feelings.

5. Self-control: Behaviors that often emerge in conflict situations such as responding appropriately to teasing or to corrective feedback from an adult.

Guevremont (1990) developed an alternative but equally appealing situational approach to characterizing clusters of target skills. Specifically, these skill clusters are referred to as social entry skills, conversational skills, conflict-resolution skills and problem-solving skills, and anger-control skills. Regardless of the terminology or approach one uses to characterize target social skills, the behaviors of interest to most individuals conducting social skills interventions are those observable nonverbal and verbal interpersonal skills that maximize social engagement and social reinforcement.

What is the normal course of social skill development for young children? There is general agreement that older preschool children engage in socially cooperative activities with greater frequency than younger children. Having established that social interaction does indeed increase ontogenetically, with interactive behaviors occurring very early in a child's life, investigators have directed their attention to the behavioral components of successful social interactions. Findings from these investigations are relevant to efforts to remediate social skill deficits in children who have difficulty interacting effectively (cf. Eisenberg & Harris, 1984; Eisenberg & Mussen, 1989).

One area of interest concerns social initiation, that is, the manner in which a child attempts to initiate social interaction. Not surprisingly, Leiter (1977) found requests to play that were accompanied by whining, crying, begging, or coercion were more likely to be denied, whereas friendly, smiling initiations with suggestions for an activity were more likely to be accepted. This is not to say that children who are ingratiating always have successful social initiations. Rather, a judicious balance between assertiveness and accommodation to others' interests constitutes a more successful strategy (Lamb & Baumrind, 1978). Similarly, Hazen, Black, and Fleming-Johnson (1984) found popular children who were successful at entering others' play situations were able to alter their entry communications to fit the demands of ongoing play situations, reflecting not only the knowledge of a wide array of social initiation strategies but also the adaptability to use the strategies appropriately. Further, in contrast with less socially successful children, popular children clearly indicated to whom they were addressing their entry statements, and they communicated to *all* children in the play situation they were trying to enter. Thus, it appears that successful social initiation is characterized by specific nonverbal and verbal communication behaviors that clearly transmit the entering child's desire as well as awareness of contextual accommodations.

A second area of relevant developmental research is concerned with those skills that enhance the maintenance of social interaction. Asher (1978) described the characteristics of maintenance skills frequently used by socially successful children. These include complex perspective-taking abilities, such as adjusting the effectiveness of one's communications to other children's needs. In addition, more straightforward reinforcement strategies may be employed, such as offering other children praise and approval, as well as going along with another child's plan or wishes. Related to these maintenance skills is the manner in which interpersonal conflict is managed by children who exhibit successful interaction styles. In a study of preschool children's friendships, Hartup, Laursen, Stewart, and Eastenson (1988) found that conflicts among friends did not differ from conflicts among nonfriends in situational inducement, frequency, or duration. What did make conflicts distinct between friends and nonfriends was an effort to maintain the interaction with friends in spite of the disagreement. Maintenance of the friendship was accomplished by the children disengaging from each other temporarily, thereby reducing the intensity of the conflict and increasing the likelihood of parity in outcome. This study exemplifies efforts to understand social skills within the context of perspective-taking. That is, behaviors that comprise successful peer interactions may be conceptualized as reflective of a maturing social-cognitive system in which children are developing the abilities to consider and coordinate their own and others' points of view (LeMare & Rubin, 1987).

Our brief review illustrates some key social skills, but does not address the behaviors that are considered to be important to parents and teachers of young children. It is important to consider this issue, because an intervention that addresses goals related to socially valid target behaviors has a greater chance of being used and maintained. Elliott, Barnard, and Gresham (1989) asked the parents and teachers of a heterogeneous group of preschool children to rate the frequency and importance of over 50 discrete social behaviors from the *Social Skills Rating System* (SSRS). The collective ratings of parents indicated the five most important social skills at home for their preschool children were (a) requests permission before leaving the house, (b) reports accidents or minor emergencies to an adult, (c) shows concern for friends' and siblings' feelings, (d) pays attention to parent verbal instructions, and (e) communicates problems to a parent. Similarly, Rubin, Mills, and Rose-Krasner (1989) interviewed mothers of four-year-olds and learned that they expected their children to be able to make friends before their second birthday, share by the time they were two and a half, and successfully lead or influence others before their third birthday. Thus, parents of preschoolers seem to place high value on basic communication skills and behaviors that indicate respect for others.

The teachers of the children in the Elliott et al. (1989) study indicated that the social skills of greatest importance for functioning in their classrooms were (a) attends to teacher's instructions, (b) complies with teacher's directions, (c) appropriately asks questions of the teacher when unsure of what to do in school work, (d) finishes class assignments within time limits, and (e) cooperates with peers without prompting from the teacher. These teachers valued social behaviors that are indicative of compliance, cooperation, and orderliness. Researchers (Hains et al., 1989; Johnson et al., 1995) using a variety of other survey tools have documented preschool and kindergarten teachers value a very similar set of social skills to those identified by Elliott and associates.

Assessment of Social Skills and Identification of Children in Need of Social Skills Training

A number of methods, including rating scales, checklists, and sociometric nomination techniques, have been designed to identify children at risk for behavior problems. Reviews of social skills assessment methods have been published by Gresham and Elliott (1989), Demaray et al. (1995), and Sheridan and Walker (1999). In general, social skills assessments have one of two purposes: identification/classification or intervention/program planning. From a behavioral perspective, the critical characteristic that differentiates assessment methods is the extent to which a method allows for a functional assessment of behavior (i.e., the extent to which an assessment procedure provides data on the antecedent, sequential, and consequent conditions surrounding a specific behavior).

Behavior rating scales have become one of the most common assessment methods given their ease of administration and broad coverage. There are now two published social skills rating scales with preschool norms: the SSRS (Gresham & Elliott, 1990) and the *Preschool and Kindergarten Behavior Scales* (PKBS) (Merrell, 1994). The preschool version of the SSRS comes in parent and teacher forms. For each form, raters evaluate children's prosocial and problem behaviors on a 3-point scale, rating behaviors as never, sometimes, or very often occurring. Despite criticisms that the parent and teacher preschool SSRS forms lack strong correlations (Manz, Fantuzzo, & McDermott, 1999) and have factor structures that differ for low-income populations from those reported in the manual (Fantuzzo, Manz, & McDermott, 1998; Manz et al., 1999), the SSRS has been shown to be a sound, useful, and user-friendly tool for social skills assessment and intervention planning (Demaray et al., 1995). The PKBS also measures social skills and problem behaviors with 76 items rated by parents, teachers, or daycare providers. Like the SSRS, the PKBS has good evidence for reliability and validity, and was developed through a comprehensive review of social skills and psychopathology literature (Holland & Merrell, 1998).

Process of Assessment

As with the psychological assessment of any problem, the process of social skills assessment can be characterized by a series of hypothesis-testing sequences. Hypotheses are generated in an attempt to answer questions regarding identification, intervention, and evaluation of treatment effects. A standard battery of tests or methods for assessing social skills does not exist. Rather, practitioner-generated hypotheses dictate the direction of assessment, the questions to be answered, and the methods to be used. Assessment should proceed from global to specific to allow appropriate planning of interventions. In contrast, evaluation of intervention success typically proceeds in the opposite direction, moving from behavior-specific outcomes to more global analyses of important social outcomes.

Ideally, practitioners should use assessment methods that possess the attributes of reliability (i.e., consistency of measurement), validity (i.e., capability of answering a given assessment question), and practicality (i.e., benefits outweigh costs of collecting information). Unfortunately, few social skill assessment methods meet all of these criteria. Easily administered instruments that are useful for screening purposes generally are of little help in designing interventions. Other methods requiring considerably more effort from assessors and clients (e.g., naturalistic observations and self-monitoring) often have equivocal or unknown psychometric properties (Dodge, Murphy, & Buchsbaum, 1984; Gresham & Elliott, 1990). Moreover, there is a tendency for assessment data obtained from different sources to correlate moderately at best, and more often, to correlate quite low (Ruffalo & Elliott, 1997). As a safeguard, multiple sources of information are considered a best practice when assessing social skills.

To increase the likelihood of accurate identification/classification decisions, we recommend the use of direct observations of the target child and non-target peers in multiple settings; behavioral interviews with the referral source and possibly the target child; rating scale data, preferably norm-referenced, from both a social skills scale and a problem behavior scale completed by more than one source; and sociometric data from the target child's classmates. Regarding intervention decisions, data contributing to a functional analysis of important social behaviors is imperative. These types of data usually result from multiple direct observations across settings, behavioral role-plays with the target child, and teacher and parent/guardian ratings of socially valid molecular behaviors. Behavioral interviews with the treatment agent(s) also will be important to assess the treatment setting, the acceptability of the final treatment plan, and the integrity with which the plan is implemented.

Linking Social Skills Assessments to Interventions

Social skills interventions focus on positive behaviors and most often use nonaversive methods (e.g., modeling, coaching, and reinforcement) to improve children's behavior. Therefore, use of these methods may enhance treatment acceptability and integrity and can rather easily be built into the existing structure of a classroom or home environment (Barnett, Bell, & Carey, 1999). Finally, social skills interventions can be used with individuals or groups of students, and because they primarily concern increasing prosocial behaviors, all students can participate and benefit from the interventions.

The selection of social skills interventions rests heavily on the classification of social skills difficulties as resulting from either deficits in response acquisition or response performance (e.g., Bandura, 1977). Gresham and Elliott's (1990) SSRS extended this two-way classification scheme to include areas of social skills problems, social skills strengths, and potential concurrent interfering problem behaviors. As shown in Table 1, this scheme distinguishes whether a child possesses the ability to perform a target skill, and whether interfering behaviors (e.g., aggression, anxiety) are present. Additionally, Table 1 includes suggested treatments that have been found effective for various types of problems.

Social Skills Acquisition Deficits

This social skill problem characterizes children who have not acquired the necessary social skills to interact appropriately with others, or children who have not acquired a critical step in the performance of a given skill. Training in skill acquisition frequently uses direct treatment approaches, such as direct instruction, modeling, and coaching.

Social Skills Acquisition Deficits With Interfering Problem Behaviors

This social skills problem describes children with emotional (e.g., anxiety, sadness, impulsivity) and/or overt behavioral (e.g., verbal or physical aggression, tantrums, excessive movement) responses that interfere with skill acquisition. Thus, with social skills acquisition deficits accompanied by significant interfering behaviors, the intervention objectives are to teach and increase the frequency of prosocial behaviors while concurrently decreasing or eliminating interfering problem behaviors. Interventions designed to remediate emotional responses typically involve emotional-arousal reduction techniques such as desensitization or flooding, paired with self-control strategies such as self-talk, self-monitoring, and self-reinforcement (Kendall & Braswell, 1985; Meichenbaum, 1977). Interventions that can help reduce overt behaviors often are referred to as reductive procedures (Lentz, 1988). These procedures include the use of differential reinforcement, group contingencies, and mild aversive techniques (e.g., reprimands, time out from positive reinforcement, response cost, and overcorrection). If aversive techniques are used, it is a best practice

Table 1. A classification schema for conceptualizing and linking social behavior problems to interventions

	No interfering problem behaviors	*Interfering problem behaviors*
Social skills acquisition deficits	• Direct instruction • Modeling • Behavioral rehearsal • Coaching	• Modeling • Coaching • Differential reinforcement of a low rate of response (DRL) • Differential reinforcement of other behavior (DRO) • Reductive procedures to decrease interfering problem behaviors
Social skills performance deficits	• Operant methods to manipulate antecedent or consequent conditions to increase the rate of existing behaviors	• Operant methods to manipulate antecedent or consequent conditions to increase the rate of existing prosocial behaviors • Differential reinforcement of a low rate of response (DRL) • Differential reinforcement of other behavior (DRO) • Reductive procedures to decrease interfering problem behaviors
Social skills strengths	• Reinforcement procedures to maintain desired social behavior • Use student as a model for other students	• Reinforcement procedures to maintain desired social behavior • Reductive procedures to decrease interfering problem behaviors

to couple aversives with socially positive procedures.

Social Skills Performance Deficits

Children with social skills performance deficits have appropriate social skills in their behavior repertoires, but do not perform the behavior at acceptable levels and/or at appropriate times or settings. Interventions for social skills performance deficits typically use manipulations of antecedent and consequent contingencies such as peer initiations, social reinforcement, and group contingencies.

Social Skills Performance Deficits With Interfering Problem Behaviors

Children with social skills performance deficits accompanied by interfering problem behaviors have acquired given social skills, but performance of the skills is hindered by emotional or overt behavior responses *and* by problems in antecedent or consequent control. Self-control strategies to teach inhibition of inappropriate behavior, stimulus control training to teach discrimination skills, and contingent reinforcement to increase display of appropriate social behavior often are used to ameliorate this social skill problem. Occasionally, when the interfering behaviors persist, it may be necessary to use reductive methods in addition to positive techniques.

Social Skills Strengths

Many children exhibit social skills strengths that often may be overlooked and may be undermined through lack of attention. Therefore, it is a best practice to take a proactive approach to maintaining those strengths through reinforcement of desired social behaviors. Children with strong social skills also can become part of a treatment strategy for children with social skills deficits by serving as models or as participants in peer pairing and peer initiation strategies.

Procedures for Promoting Social Skills

Teaching children social skills involves many of the same methods as teaching academic concepts. Effective teachers of both academic and social skills model correct behavior, elicit an imitative response, provide corrective feedback, and arrange for opportunities to practice the new skill (Cartledge & Milburn, 1995; Elliott & Gresham, 1993). A large number of intervention procedures have been identified as effective for social skills training with preschool children. These procedures can be classified into three approaches that highlight common treatment features and assumptions about how social behavior is learned. These approaches are (a) operant, (b) social learning, and (c) cognitive-behavioral. In practice, many researchers and practitioners have used procedures that represent combinations of these basic approaches. However, we will use the three groups of interventions to describe the basic procedures and to organize a review of their effectiveness.

Operant Intervention Procedures

Operant intervention procedures focus on discrete, observable behavior and the antecedent and consequent events that maintain that behavior. Behavioral control is achieved most often through the use of reinforcement and/or punishment paradigms that are contingent upon a specified behavior. Many social behaviors, however, can be controlled by manipulating preceding events, such as having a peer ask another child to play or a teacher cueing a child to initiate play.

Young children often fail to interact successfully because of a nonresponsive or inhospitable social environment. Here, the use of antecedent control can serve to facilitate a positive environment and elicit positive social interactions. With these procedures, a teacher or other intervention agent makes wide use of cueing and prompting (Elliott & Gresham, 1991). The key assumption with antecedent control procedures is that a child possesses the necessary social skills, but, however, the child is not performing them at an acceptable rate. Two of the most frequently used antecedent strategies are peer social initiation and cooperative learning.

Peer social initiations have been used by Fenning (1993) and Strain and his colleagues (Strain, Shores, & Timm, 1977) to increase the social interaction rates of socially withdrawn preschoolers. This intervention entails training similar-age peer confederates to initiate and maintain social interactions with a withdrawn or isolated child. Overall, this procedure has been effective in increasing positive social behavior in withdrawn preschoolers. It should be noted, however, that when a child's interaction rate approaches zero, peer initiations are likely to be less effective (Elliott & Gresham, 1991).

Another procedure that focuses on manipulating antecedent events is cooperative learning. Cooperative learning provides a prosocial environment where preschoolers work together to complete specified activities (Doescher & Sugawara, 1989). This procedure requires preschoolers to cooperate, share, and assist each other to complete a task and, as such, represents an effective method for increasing the likelihood of positive social behaviors. When implementing cooperative learning techniques, it is implicitly assumed that children know how to cooperate but are not doing so at optimal levels.

Many operant-learning procedures, that is, the manipulation of antecedents and consequents, have been used to decrease interfering problem behaviors while simultaneously increasing positive social behaviors. These procedures are based on the premise that behaviors are maintained by functional relationships. In other words, reinforcement contingencies (positive or negative) perpetuate low rates of positive social interactions and high rates of negative social interactions. For this reason, it is assumed that a child can perform positive social interaction skills, but does not demonstrate the skills owing to lack of reinforcement. Given the wealth of studies in this domain, only two of the most frequently used methods will be discussed: contingent social reinforcement and differential reinforcement. Group contingencies (e.g., McConnell, Sisson, Cort, & Strain, 1991) also are used frequently. However, because they have much in common with cooperative learning, they will not be discussed here.

Contingent social reinforcement involves publicly reinforcing a child for socially appropriate behaviors. Allen, Hart, Buell, Harris, and Wolf (1964) long ago demonstrated the efficacy of this method when they applied it to a four-year old socially isolated girl. Whenever she interacted with other children, an adult would publicly reinforce her social behavior. This procedure led to a six-fold increase in social interaction rates over baseline levels. Variations of this basic procedure have been successfully extended to children with selective mutism and children with severe and profound mental retardation (Fenning, 1993; Mayhew, Enyart, & Anderson, 1978). Although this procedure has been found effective, it can require an extraordinary amount of time to ensure that the reinforcement is delivered on a consistent basis. Unless reinforcement is given in a consistent manner, it is doubtful the intervention will be as effective. This type of contingent social reinforcement perhaps is best used to maintain social interaction rates established through the use of other social skills interventions.

Other operant-learning procedures used to modify social skills are differential reinforcement of other behavior (DRO), differential reinforcement of alternative behaviors (DRA), and differential reinforcement of low rates of responding (DRL). DRO and DRA are based on the omission of a specific behavior rather than the commission (Barnett, Bell, & Carey, 1999). Therefore, after a certain amount of time, reinforcement is given after any behavior except the target behavior. For example, if one wanted to decrease disruptive behavior while increasing socially appropriate behavior, any behavior exhibited besides disruptive behavior is reinforced after a certain amount of time has elapsed. Hence, this method serves to extinguish undesirable behaviors and increase all other behaviors. Pinkston, Reese, LeBlanc, and Baer (1973) successfully used DRO to decrease a boy's aggressive behavior while at the same time they implemented contingent social reinforcement to increase his positive social interaction. In this study, the teacher differentially reinforced positive peer interaction while she ignored aggressive behavior.

DRL involves reinforcement for reduction in the frequency of a target behavior. Reinforcers may be delivered either for reduction in overall frequency of a response within a particular time period or for increased elapsed time between responses (interresponse time). For example, if the criterion limit for the DRL was six incidents per hour, the target child would receive reinforcement only if six or fewer incidents were emitted in one hour. Dietz and Repp (1973) successfully used a full-session DRL procedure to decrease the amount of inappropriate talking in a classroom for students with mental retardation. The DRL contingency was five or fewer "talk outs" per 50-minute class period. This procedure also was applied as a group contingency because reinforcement was based upon the behavior of the entire class.

The aforementioned studies demonstrate that DRO and DRL are effective in decreasing interfering problem behaviors. These procedures probably are most effective, however, when used in conjunction with other social skills interventions, whereby one decreases socially inappropriate behavior while concurrently teaching or reinforcing positive social behaviors.

Social Learning Intervention Procedures

Social learning procedures can be traced back to the social learning theory of Bandura and Walters (1963) and Bandura (1977). From this perspective, social behavior is the result of two types of learning: observational learning and reinforced learning. Social learning theorists differentiate between the learning and the performance of a response. This distinction enables social learning theorists to advocate the process of modeling as a means to acquire new, socially appropriate behaviors. Modeling also affects previously learned responses through its disinhibitory and/or cueing effects. Therefore, children are vicariously reinforced (positively or negatively) by observing a model receiving reinforcement for a behavioral performance. In essence, observers tend to inhibit responses that they see punished in others, whereas they are likely to perform modeled behaviors that elicit desired reinforcers.

Modeling has substantial empirical support for the promotion of social skills with children and youth (Gresham, 1985; Wandless & Prinz, 1982). For social skills training, modeling can be divided into two types: (a) live modeling, where the target child observes the social behaviors of models in naturalistic settings (e.g., the classroom), and (b) symbolic modeling, in which the target child observes the social behaviors of a model through film or videotape. Both types of modeling have been effective in remediating social skills deficits. However, most research has focused on symbolic modeling owing to the degree of experimental control afforded by videotaped models. Live modeling, however, may be more flexible and efficient in a classroom setting. For instance, Matson, Fee, Coe, and Smith (1991) used peer and puppet models as a novel way to effect a positive change in the social behaviors of preschoolers with developmental disabilities.

A powerful development in the realm of social learning has been peer mediated interventions. These interventions are based on the premise that peers can be effective change agents for other children with social skills performance deficits (Berndt & Ladd, 1989). Empirically, it has been shown that peers can serve to differentially reinforce appropriate social interactions and influence the occurrence of positive social behaviors (Mathur & Rutherford, 1991). Peer-mediated interventions may be more successful than teacher-mediated interventions because peer confederates may be better able to consistently monitor and differentially reinforce their peers. Additionally, peer mediation can be cost effective because it minimizes teacher involvement.

Cognitive-Behavioral Intervention Procedures

Cognitive-behavioral intervention procedures are a loosely bound group of procedures that focus on a child's internal regulation of her or his behavior. In particular, cognitive-behavioral approaches to social skills training emphasize a child's ability to problem solve and to self-regulate behavior. For preschoolers, two of the most frequently used cognitive-behavioral social skills procedures are coaching and problem solving.

Coaching, unlike modeling, is a direct verbal instruction technique that involves a "coach" (usually a teacher or a psychologist, and occasionally a peer) who has knowledge about how to enact a desired behavior. Most coaching procedures involve three basic steps: (a) A student is presented with rules for, or the standards of, a specific behavior; (b) a selected social skill(s) is rehearsed with the coach; and (c) the coach provides specific informational feedback during behavioral rehearsal and gives suggestions for future performances. In some instances, modeling may be included in the coaching procedure to give the child a better understanding of the topography of the social behavior and, if praise is given, reinforcement may occur. Therefore, coaching, although conceptualized as a procedure that requires the child's cognitive skills to translate instruction into desired behaviors, can be enhanced with behavioral and/or social learning procedures.

Coaching has received considerable empirical support as a social skills training procedure (Mize, 1995). For example, Oden and Asher (1977) used coaching to effectively teach participation, communication, cooperation, and peer reinforcement. In addition, sociometric ratings of coached students increased when compared to non-coached students. Ladd (1981) obtained similar results using a coaching procedure as did Gottman, Gonso, and Schuler (1976).

Several interventions have been developed that stress teaching children the process of solving social or interpersonal problems as a way to facilitate socially appropriate behaviors. As Weissburg (1985) pointed out, some of these intervention programs, which are largely classroom-based have been called social problem solving (SPS) programs, whereas others have been called interpersonal cognitive problem solving (ICPS) programs. ICPS programs generally place greater emphasis on cognitions that parallel social problem situations and employ narrower training procedures than SPS approaches. However, both use a similar training sequence to help students identify and cope with social problems. Briefly, the steps can be described as (a) identify and define the problem, (b) determine alternate ways of reacting to the problem, (c) predict consequences for each alternative reaction, and (d) select the "best" or most adaptive alternative. Social problem-solving methods can be used with individual children or with entire classrooms. It should be noted, however, that these methods often are too cognitively complex for most preschoolers and do not focus on discrete social skills training; learning social skills generally requires more skill-oriented, externally-reinforcing procedures than offered by a strictly cognitive approach.

Example of a Class-Wide Social Skills Intervention: The Responsive Classroom

The Responsive Classroom (Charney & Wood, 1981) is an instructional approach that integrates the teaching of social and academic skills as part of everyday school life. This approach has been implemented successfully in preschool and elementary classrooms and is predicated on the belief that classrooms providing socially supportive environments (i.e., facilitate acceptance, positive interpersonal relationships, and responsibility) enable children to learn most effectively. The RC approach is composed of six components: (a) morning meeting, (b) classroom organization, (c) rules and logical consequences, (d) guided discovery, (e) academic choice time, and (f) assessment and reporting.

Morning meeting (MM) begins each day in a Responsive Classroom (RC) and provides children with the opportunity to greet each other, share academic and social news, participate in engaging start-up activities, and learn about the academic goals for the day ahead. This meeting also provides teachers with an opportunity to teach specific social skills and students with an opportunity to practice these skills in role play situations. After introducing a social skill in MM, teachers can provide feedback (and follow-up instruction) regarding the social skill throughout the school day. During MM, children sit in a circle with their teacher in an effort to build a sense of belonging, significance, and fun. The physical environment of the classroom is an important consideration in implementing the RC approach. In RC classrooms, teachers pay particular attention to students' physical skills as well as their academic skills. As a result, RC teachers attempt to match furniture, centers, routines, and time devoted to an activity with the current skills of their students.

Rules and logical consequences is a positive approach to discipline in the classroom. The primary goal of this approach is to help students develop self-control so they can effectively function within social communities like the classroom environment. In addition, developing self-control reduces off-task behavior and increases engaged time. This in turn allows children to receive maximal benefits from instruction. To facilitate students' development of self-control, teachers in RC classrooms emphasize modeling, practice, and role playing of expectations for behavior. In addition, teachers develop and use logical consequences for inappropriate classroom behavior that are fair and consistent with the behavior.

Guided discovery (GD) is an instructional practice designed to introduce students to curriculum materials, learning centers, or processes within a teacher's classroom (Charney, 1992). The primary goal of GD is to excite students about learning while teaching them how to make good choices within the classroom. GD takes children through a carefully planned instructional sequence that begins with an introduction to the applications of knowledge and ends with students extending concepts through small group or independent activities.

The RC approach requires teachers to structure classroom work so that student assignments reflect a balance between teacher-assigned work and work that students choose from an array of possibilities. These choice times allow students to conduct independent and/or cooperative "research" projects. Choice time also enables students to develop study skills, such as producing work to meet a timeline, and provides students with opportunities to share their work with other students in the classroom.

Finally, the RC approach encourages teachers to use alternative methods to assess students' work and to combine these assessments with more common measures of achievement (e.g., classroom tests, standardized tests). The approach also supports reporting student progress to parents on a continuum rather than synthesizing all information into a single grade. RC teachers are expected to engage parents and students in goal setting at the beginning of each year. This establishes a foundation for meaningful communications between teachers and parents regarding the student's social and academic progress throughout the academic year. It also provides an open line of communication regarding the student's classroom behavior and invites parents to become active participants in their child's education.

These six components comprise the RC approach and allow teachers to introduce instruction of social skills in the classroom. Teachers in more than 100 schools in the United States have been trained to implement the RC approach. Evaluation studies conducted with children ages 4–12 by Elliott (1993, 1995, 1998) indicate that the RC approach is an acceptable and effective method for enhancing the social behavior of young children, and appears to create conditions that foster academic achievement. Specific findings replicated across these studies include:

1. The frequency of students' problem behaviors decreases significantly with a year or more exposure to instruction that is organized and delivered within the RC approach.

2. The frequency of students' social skills increases significantly in classrooms where students consistently have been exposed to instruction that reflects the RC approach.

3. The social skills taught and reinforced in the RC approach appear to function as academic enablers, resulting in improved scores on achievement tests.

Although results from these initial studies are promising, it is important to note that these conclusions are based on evaluation projects with moderate samples of students and small numbers of schools.

Effectiveness of Interventions and Suggestions for Practice

The popularity and widespread use of social skills training procedures have resulted in several major reviews of the effectiveness of these procedures with children (see Cartledge & Milburn, 1995; Elliott & Gresham, 1993; Gresham, 1981, 1985; Ladd & Mize, 1983; Schneider & Byrne, 1985). Schneider and Byrne, who conducted a large meta-analysis of social skills training studies, indicated that social skills interventions were more effective for preschoolers and adolescents than elementary children. No gender differences in effect sizes were noted, although few studies have treated gender as an independent variable. In addition, social skills training was found to be more effective for students exhibiting social withdrawal or learning disabilities than for aggressive students.

Based on reviews of research (e.g., Elliott & Gresham, 1993; Mastropieri & Scruggs, 1985; Schneider & Byrne, 1985; Zaragoza, Vaughan, & McIntosh, 1991) there appears to be substantial support for the effectiveness of social skills training procedures in general, and in particular for operant and modeling procedures for preschoolers. Practical suggestions from the research literature for facilitating the development of social skills in young children include the extensive use of operant methods to reinforce existing social skills. These basic operant tactics include (a) manipulation of environmental conditions to create opportunities for social interactions that prompt/cue socially desired behavior in a target child and (b) manipulation of consequences so that socially appropriate behavior is reinforced and socially inappropriate behavior, whenever possible, is ignored rather than punished. In addition, modeling of appropriate social behavior supplemented with coaching, feedback, and reinforcement should be a primary tactic in developing new social behaviors in children.

Facilitating Generalization of Social Skills

Social skills training often results in positive outcomes. However, treatment effects often are short lived and do not generalize to other settings or behaviors (DuPaul & Eckert, 1994). For treatments delivered in social skills training to be considered truly effective and valid, levels of change must evidence treatment generality. Treatment generality is composed of maintenance (behavior change that persists over time) and generalization (behavior changes that occur under nontraining conditions). Although treatment generality often is evaluated as a "hope-for-the-best" side effect of social skills training, maintenance and generalization should be systematic facets of any intervention. Several authors have discussed procedures to enhance treatment generality (e.g., Gresham, 1994; Stokes & Osnes, 1989). These generality facilitators include (a) targeting behaviors that will be maintained by natural reinforcement contingencies; (b) training across different behaviors, settings, and persons; (c) training loosely (i.e., varying stimuli such as reinforcers, tone of voice); (d) systematically withdrawing or fading intervention procedures to approximate the natural environment; (e) reinforcing behavior change in novel and appropriate settings; (f) including peers in training; and (g) providing booster sessions. Programming for generality should occur for both child and treatment agent (e.g., parent, teacher) behaviors. Incorporating as many generality facilitators as possible into social skills interventions should enhance the likelihood of treatment maintenance and generalization.

Evaluation of Intervention Effectiveness

The final leg of the social skills training journey invariably rests with the deceptively simple question, "Was the intervention effective?" Although many practitioners and researchers assess treatment effectiveness as a matter of course, methodologically sound measurement often is overlooked in evaluations of intervention effectiveness. Treatment evaluation extends beyond simply assessing changes in social skills at the completion of treatment. Evaluation should include ongoing assessments of acceptability, integrity, social validity, and generality. Ideally, assessments of intervention effectiveness will be multifaceted, involving multiple settings, informants, and methods.

Important advances in the monitoring and the evaluation of interventions have occurred recently. These advances include the use of goal attainment scaling (Sladeczek, Elliott, Kratochwill, Robertson-Mjaanes, & Stoiber, in press), progress monitoring records (Figure 1) (Elliott & Gresham, 1991), reliability change indexing (Gresham & Noell, 1993), and the integration of visual and statistical analyses (Busse, Kratochwill, & Elliott, 1995). The progress-monitoring record illustrated in Figure 1 often has been used as part of a goal-setting and self-monitoring process with elementary and middle-school students. However, no reports of its use with preschoolers have been published.

SUMMARY

Identifying and using interventions that effectively teach young children social skills may be one of the most important activities for school psychologists given the critical role that social skills play in the academic, social, and emotional development of children. Social skills are clearly one of the key elements in learning about how to care and in caring about learning from other people.

School psychologists involved in school readiness screening or who consult with preschool and kindergarten transition programs will have opportunities to use many of the intervention techniques described in this chapter. Psychologists who also are involved in parenting classes for high school students and/or young parents will find numerous opportunities to translate knowledge about social skills intervention into practice. Finally, whenever possible school psychologists are encouraged to write brief newsletter or newspaper articles describing key steps parents and caregivers can take to facilitate the development of young children's social skills. In all cases, it is important to emphasize the power of positive peer and adult models for young and older learners alike because social skills provide an important foundation for learning and caring at school and in the community.

Figure 1. A social skills intervention progress monitoring record sheet.

A Social Skills Intervention Progress-Monitoring Record

Student's Name____________________ Teacher/Grade____________________

Group Leader____________________ Date Program Began____________________

Skill Domains, Subdomains, and Behavioral Objectives	Progress Assessment				
	Check skills to be taught	No progress	Improvement observed	Mastered in treatment group	Generalized
Cooperation					
1. Ignoring distractions					
2. Making transitions					
3. Using free time					
Classroom interaction skills					
1. Finishing assignments on time					
2. Keeping desk clean, putting away materials					
3. Producing correct work					
4. Paying attention and following directions					
5. Using time appropriately when waiting					
Assertion					
Conversation skills					
1. Giving a compliment					
2. Introducing oneself					
3. Making positive self-statements					
4. Initiating conversations					
5. Telling an adult about unfair treatment					
Joining and volunteering skills					
1. Joining ongoing activities					
2. Volunteering to help peers					
3. Inviting others to join activities					
Responsibility					
1. Asking an adult for help					
2. Paying attention to a speaker					
3. Refusing unreasonable requests					
4. Answering the telephone					
5. Introducing oneself to new people					
6. Asking permission to use property					
7. Asking permission to leave house/property					
8. Reporting accidents to appropriate persons					
9. Questioning rules that may be unfair					
10. Responding to a compliment					

REFERENCES

Allen, K. E., Hart, B. M., Buell, J. S., Harris, F. R., & Wolf, M. M. (1964). Effects of social reinforcement on isolated behavior of a nursery school child. *Child Development, 35,* 7–9.

Asher, S.R. (1978). Children's peer relations. In M. E. Lamb (Ed.), *Social and personality development* (pp. 91–113). New York: Holt: Rinehart and Winston.

Bandura, A. (1977). *Social learning theory*. Englewood Cliffs, NJ: Prentice-Hall.

Bandura, A., & Walters, R. H. (1963). *Social learning and personality development.* New York: Holt, Rhinehart, & Winston.

Barnett, D. W., Bell, S. H., & Carey, K .T. (1999). *Designing preschool interventions.* New York: Guilford.

Berndt, T. J., & Ladd, G. W. (Eds.). (1989). *Peer relationships in child development.* New York: Wiley.

Busse, R. T., Kratochwill, T. R., & Elliott, S. N. (1995). Meta-analysis in single-case consultation outcome research. *Journal of School Psychology, 33,* 269–285.

Cartledge, G., & Milburn, J. F. (1995). *Teaching social skills to children: Innovative approaches* (2nd ed.). New York: Pergamon.

Cassidy, J., & Asher, S. R., (1992). Loneliness and peer relations in young children. *Child Development, 63,* 350–365.

Charney, R. S. (1992). *Teaching children to care: Management in the responsive classroom.* Greenfield, MA: Northeast Foundation for Children.

Charney, R. S., & Wood. (1981). *The Responsive Classroom approach to instruction.* Greenfield, MA: Northeast Foundation for Children.

Demaray, M. K., Ruffalo, S. L., Carlson, J., Olson, A. E., McManus, S., Leventhal, A., & Busse, R. T. (1995). Social skills assessment: A comparative evaluation of published rating scales. *School Psychology Review, 24,* 648–671.

Dietz, S., & Repp, A. (1973). Decreasing classroom misbehavior through the use of DRL schedules of reinforcement. *Journal of Applied Behavior Analysis, 6,* 457–463.

DiPerna, J. C., & Elliott, S. N. (2000). *The Academic Competence Evaluation Scales.* San Antonio, TX: The Psychological Corporation.

Dodge, K., Murphy, R., & Buchsbaum, D. (1984). The assessment of intention-cue detection skills in children: Implications for developmental psychopathology. *Child Development, 55,* 163–173.

Doescher, S. M., & Sugawara, A. L. (1989). Encouraging prosocial behavior in young children. *Childhood Education, 65,* 213–216.

DuPaul, G. J., & Eckert, T. L. (1994). The effects of social skills curricula: Now you see them, now you don't. *School Psychology Quarterly, 9,* 113–132.

Eisenberg, N., & Harris, J. D. (1984). Social competence: A developmental perspective. *School Psychology Review, 13,* 267–277.

Eisenberg, N., & Mussen, P. H. (1989). *The roots and prosocial behavior in children.* New York: Cambridge Press.

Elias, M. J., Zins, J. E., Weissberg, R. P., Frey, K. S., Greenberg, M. T., Haynes, N. M., Kessler, R., Schwab-Stone, M. E., & Shriver, T. P. (1997). *Promoting social and emotional learning: Guidelines for educators.* Alexandria, VA: Association for Supervision and Curriculum Development.

Elliott, S. N. (1993).*Caring to learn: A report on the positive impact of a social curriculum.* Greenfield, MA: Northeast Foundation for Children.

Elliott, S. N. (1995). *The Responsive Classroom approach: Its effectiveness and acceptability* (Final evaluation report). Madison, WI: University of Wisconsin.

Elliott, S. N. (1998). *The Responsive Classroom approach: Its effectiveness and acceptability in promoting social and academic competence* (Final report). Madison, WI: University of Wisconsin.

Elliott, S. N., Barnard, J., Gresham, F. M. (1989). Preschoolers' social behavior: Teachers' and parents' assessments. *Journal of Psychoeducational Assessment, 7,* 223–234.

Elliott, S. N., & Gresham, F. M. (1991). *Social skills intervention guide: Practical strategies for social skills training.* Circle Pines, MN: American Guidance Service.

Elliott, S. N., & Gresham, F. M. (1993). Social skills interventions for children. *Behavior Modification, 17,* 287–313.

Fantuzzo, J., Manz, P. H., & McDermott, P. (1998). Preschool version of the Social Skills Rating System: An Empirical analysis of its use with low-income children. *Journal of School Psychology, 36,* 199–214.

Fenning, P. A. (1993). *A combined peer-mediated and video-modeling social skills intervention for preschool children with developmental delays.* Unpublished doctoral dissertation, University of Wisconsin-Madison.

Gottman, J. M., Gonso, J., & Schuler, P. (1976). Teaching social skills to isolated children. *Journal of Abnormal Child Psychology, 4,* 179–197.

Gresham, F. M. (1981). Social skills training with handicapped children: A review. *Review of Educational Research, 51,* 139–176.

Gresham, F. M. (1985). Utility of cognitive-behavioral procedures for social skills training with children: A review. *Journal of Abnormal Child Psychology, 13,* 411–423.

Gresham, F. M. (1994). Generalization of social skills: Risks of choosing form over function. *School Psychology Quarterly, 9,* 142–145.

Gresham, F. M., & Elliott, S. N. (1984). Assessment and classification of children's social skills: A review of methods and issues. *School Psychology Review, 13,* 292–301.

Gresham, F. M., & Elliott, S. N. (1989). Social skills deficits as a primary learning disability? *Journal of Learning Disabilities, 22,* 120–124.

Gresham, F. M., & Elliott, S. N. (1990). *Social Skills Rating System.* Circle Pines, MN: American Guidance Service.

Gresham, F. M., & Noell, G. H. (1993). Documenting the effectiveness of consultation outcomes. In J. Zins, T. R. Kratochwill, & S. N. Elliott (Eds.), *Handbook of consultation services for children* (pp. 249–275). San Francisco: Jossey-Bass.

Guevremont, D. (1990). Social skills and peer relationship training. In R.A. Barkley (Ed.), *Attention deficit hyperactivity disorder: A handbook for diagnosis and treatment* (pp. 540–572). New York: Guilford.

Guralnick, M. J. (1986). The peer relations of young handicapped and nonhandicapped children. In P. S. Strain, M. J. Guralnick, & H. M. Walker (Eds.), *Children's social behavior: Development assessment, and modification* (pp. 93–142). Orlando, FL: Academic.

Hains, A. H., Fowler, S. A., Schwartz, I. S., Kottwitz, E., & Rosenkoetter, S. (1989). A comparison of preschool and kindergarten teacher expectations for school readiness. *Early Childhood Research Quarterly, 4,* 75–88.

Hartup, W. W., Laursen, B., Stewart, M. I., & Eastenson, A. (1988). Conflict and friendship relations of young children. *Child Development, 59,* 1590–1600.

Hazen, N., Black, B., & Fleming-Johnson, F. (1984). Social acceptance: Strategies children use and how teachers can help children learn them. *Young Children, 39,* 26–36.

Holland, M. L., & Merrell, K. W. (1998). Social-emotional characteristics of preschool-aged children referred for child find screening and assessment: A comparative study. *Research in Developmental Disabilities, 19,* 167–179.

Johnson, L. J., Gallagher, R. J., Cook, M., & Wong, P. (1995). Critical skills for kindergarten: Perceptions from kindergarten teachers. *Journal of Early Intervention, 19 (4),* 315–327.

Kendall, P. C., & Braswell, L. (1985). *Cognitive-behavioral therapy for impulsive children.* New York: Guilford.

Ladd, G. W. (1981). Effectiveness of a social learning method for enhancing children's social interaction and peer acceptance. *Child Development, 52,* 171–178.

Ladd, G. W., & Mize, J. (1983). A cognitive-social learning model of social skill training. *Psychological Review, 90,* 127–157.

Lamb, M. E., & Baumrind, D. (1978). Socialization and personality development in the preschool years. In M. E. Lamb (Ed.), *Social and personality development* (pp. 50–69). New York: Holt, Rinehart and Winston.

Leiter, M. P. (1977). A study of reciprocity in preschool play groups. *Child Development, 48,* 1288–1295.

LeMare, L. J., & Rubin, K. H. (1987). Perspective taking and peer interaction: Structural and developmental analyses. *Child Development, 58,* 306–315.

Lentz, F. (1988). Reductive techniques. In J. C. Witt, S. N. Elliott, & F. M. Gresham (Eds.), *The handbook of behavior therapy in education* (pp. 439–468). New York: Plenum.

Manz, P. H., Fantuzzo, J. W., & McDermott, P. A. (1999). The parent version of the Preschool Social Skills Rating Scale: An analysis of its use with low-income, ethnic minority children. *School Psychology Review, 28,* 493–504.

Mastropieri, M. A., & Scruggs, T. E. (1985). Early intervention for socially withdrawn children. *Journal of Special Education, 19,* 429–441.

Mathur, S. R., & Rutherford, R. B. (1991). Peer-mediated interventions promoting social skills of children and youth with behavioral disorders. *Education and Treatment of Children, 14,* 227–242.

Matson, J. L., Fee, V. E., Coe, D. A., & Smith, D. (1991). A social skills program for developmentally delayed preschoolers. *Child and Family Behavior Therapy, 20,* 227–242.

Mayhew, G., Enyart, P., & Anderson, J. (1978). Social reinforcement and the naturally occurring social responses of severely and profoundly retarded adolescents. *American Journal of Mental Deficiency, 83,* 164–170.

McConnell, S. R., Sisson, L. A., Cort, C. A., & Strain, P. S. (1991). Effects of social skills training and contingency management on reciprocal interaction of preschool children with behavioral handicaps. *Journal of Special Education, 24,* 473–495.

Meichenbaum, D. (1977). *Cognitive-behavior modification: An integrative approach*. New York: Plenum.

Merrell, K. W. (1994). *Preschool and Kindergarten Behavior Scales.* Austin, TX: PRO-ED.

Mize, J. (1995). Coaching preschool children in social skills: A cognitive-social learning curriculum. In G. Cartledge & J. F. Milburn (Eds.), *Teaching social skills to children and youth* (3rd ed) (pp.237–261). Boston: Allyn & Bacon.

Oden, S. L., & Asher, S. R. (1977). Coaching children in social skills for friendship making. *Child Development, 48,* 495–506.

Parker, J. G., & Asher, S. R. (1987). Peer relations and later personal adjustment: Are low-accepted children at risk? *Psychological Bulletin, 102,* 357–389.

Pinkston, E. M., Reese, N. M., Le Blanc, J. M., & Baer, D. M. (1973). Independent control of a preschool child's aggression and peer interaction by contingent teacher attention. *Journal of Applied Behavior Analysis, 6,* 223–224.

Rubin, K. H., Mills, R. S. L., & Rose-Krasner, L. (1989). Maternal beliefs and children's competence. In B. H. Schneider, G. Attili, J. Nadel, & R. O. Weissberg (Eds.), *Social competence in developmental perspective* (pp. 313–331). Dordrecht: Kluwer.

Ruffalo, S. L., & Elliott, S. N. (1997). Teachers' and parents' ratings of children's social skills: A closer look at cross-informant agreements through an item analysis protocol. *School Psychology Review, 26,* 489–501.

Schneider, B. H., & Byrne, B. M. (1985). Children's social skills: A meta-analysis. In B. H. Schneider, K. H. Rubin, & J. E. Ledingham (Eds.), *Children's peer relations: Issues in assessment and intervention.* (pp. 175–192). New York: Springer-Verlag.

Sheridan, S. M., & Walker, D. (1999). Social skills in context: Considerations for assessment, intervention, and generalization. In C. R. Reynolds & T. B. Gutkin (Eds.),

The handbook of school psychology (3rd ed.) (pp. 686–708). New York: John Wiley.

Sladeczek, I. S., Elliott, S. N., Kratochwill, T. R., Robertson-Mjaanes, S., & Stoiber, K. C. (in press). Goal attainment scaling: Establishing treatment goals, monitoring treatment progress, and treatment outcomes of behavioral consultation. *Journal of Educational and Psychological Consultation.*

Stokes, T. F., & Osnes, P. (1989). An operant pursuit of generalization. *Behavior Therapy, 20,* 337–355.

Strain, P. S., Odom, S., & McConnell, S. (1984). Promoting social reciprocity of exceptional children: Identification, target behavior selections, and intervention. *Remedial and Special Education, 5,* 21–28.

Strain, P. S., Shores, R. E., & Timm, M. A. (1977). Effects of peer social initiations on the behavior of withdrawn preschool children. *Journal of Applied Behavior Analysis, 10,* 289–298.

Wandless, R. L., & Prinz, R. J. (1982). Methodological issues in conceptualizing and treating childhood social isolation. *Psychological Bulletin, 92,* 39–55.

Weissberg, R. P. (1985). Designing effective social problem-solving programs for the classroom. In B.H. Schneider, K. H. Rubin, & J. E. Ledingham (Eds.), *Children's peer relations: Issues in assessment and intervention* (pp.225–242).New York: Springer-Verlag.

Wentzel, K. R. (1993). Does being good make the grade? Social behavior and academic competence in middle school. *Journal of Educational Psychology, 85,* 357–364.

Zaragoza, Vaughan, & McIntosh (1991). Social skills interventions and children with behavior problems: A review. *Behavior Disorders, 16,* 260–275.

ANNOTATED BIBLIOGRAPHY

Cartledge, G., & Milburn, J. (Eds.), (1995). *Teaching social skills to children: Innovative approaches.* Elmsford, NY: Pergamon.
Oriented toward social skills training as a part of school curriculum. Part I sets out general assessment and teaching procedures. Part II focuses on specific populations: behavior disordered, young children, and adolescents.

Charney, R. S. (1992). *Teaching children to care: Management in the Responsive Classroom.* Greenfield, MA: Northeast Foundation for Children.
This book lays the foundation for creating a caring school environment and provides specific classroom tactics that facilitate the development of constructive communications among students and teacher. The six components of the Responsive Classroom approach to instruction are described and illustrated with vignettes.

Elias, M. J., Zins, J. E., Weissberg, R. P., Frey, K. S., Greenberg, M. T., Haynes, N. M., Kessler, R., Schwab-Stone, M. E., & Shriver, T. P. (1997). *Promoting social and emotional learning: Guidelines for educators.* Alexandria, VA: Association for Supervision and Curriculum Development.
The authors of this book draw upon research, theories, and successful efforts of educators to provide guidelines to help school officials to design and implement comprehensive programs to enhance the social and emotional development of children preschool through high school. The guidelines are stated in detail and are supported with numerous examples.

Elliott, S. N., & Gresham, F. M. (1991). *Social skills intervention guide: Practical strategies for social skills training.* Circle Pines, MN: American Guidance Service.
This practical guidebook is an extension of the *Social Skills Rating System* (SSRS) (Gresham & Elliott, 1990) and provides lesson plans for 43 of the social skills assessed on the SSRS. The lessons are presented in a tell-show-do instructional group format. Psychologists, counselors, or teachers are considered group leaders. A rich assortment of tables and figures are provided to support implementation of the basic strategies and communication with parents and others.

AUTHOR NOTE

Portions of this chapter are from a chapter by the same title that appeared in *Best Practices in School Psychology III.* The authors would like to thank Joan Ershler, Caroline Racine, and Randy Busse for their contributions to earlier versions of this chapter.

67 Best Practices in Crisis Prevention and Management

Scott Poland
Gayle Pitcher
Cypress-Fairbanks Public Schools
Philip M. Lazarus
Florida International University

OVERVIEW

Since the last edition of this book was published, small towns with names like Paducah, Kentucky; Jonesboro, Arkansas; Littleton, Colorado (Columbine); Santee, California; and El Cajon, California, are now known worldwide as sites where bloodshed has penetrated our schools. Nationwide, parents and teachers and administrators and the local governments have been trying to cope with this violence by intensifying their awareness of crisis intervention and the role it must play in lessening the chance that another child will walk into school one day with a gun. The first author led or served on national crisis teams in Paducah, Jonesboro, and Littleton, and he and the third author were consultants and trainers in Lake Worth, Florida, where a 13-year-old boy with a .25 caliber semi-automatic pistol shot and killed a teacher on the last day of school.

But what can be done to prevent more violence and crisis incidents? Most communities are attempting to answer that question, and varied organizations and government institutions (e.g., National Education Association (NEA), U.S. Department of Justice, U.S. Department of Education, The Center for Effective Collaboration and Practice, and the American Institutes for Research) have joined the National Association of School Psychologists (NASP) in a zealous effort to study and develop recommendations for improving school safety. As a result the recognition of and resources dedicated to crisis intervention are quite vast in comparison with those of a decade ago.

During the recent past many questions have been raised about the role of school psychologists. In the aftermath of school tragedies school psychologists' roles in developing interventions range from very minor to pivotal. There also appears to have been a turnaround in the formal preparation for school psychologists in the area of crisis planning and management. As late as 1993 (Lazarus and Phelps, 1993) professionals were expressing concern regarding the lack of systematic course work in crisis intervention—or psychologist first aid—in most school psychology training programs. As this is being written, however, crisis intervention appears to be rapidly on its way to becoming a more standard part of training and practice in the field of school psychology. A series of workshops offered in the 1990s, together with recently published practical manuals and literature (Poland & McCormick, 1999; National Education Association, 1999), has been used to begin to educate practitioners on how to deliver crisis intervention services and develop crisis response teams.

Some universities offer complete classes in school safety and crisis prevention or intervention (Larson, 1994).

Since the late 1990s there has been increasing attention toward the need to reduce all levels of violence in our schools (Gottfredson, 1997; Guerra & Williams, 1996). In 1998, shortly after the shootings in Paducah, Kentucky, and Jonesboro, Arkansas, President Clinton called for an annual National Report on School Violence and personally conducted a meeting on school violence that the first author attended. During that same year the Principal/School Disciplinarian Survey on School Violence 1996–1997 was released by the National Center for Education Statistics (1998). The report highlighted the following points:

- One in 10 schools reported a violent crime.
- 15% of teachers reported either being threatened or injured.
- 4.2% of secondary students reported being the victim of a violent crime at school.

More than half of the schools reported a crime during the year, and 1 in 10 schools reported a serious violent crime (i.e., rape, robbery, fights with weapons).

Other statistics corroborated the basic tenant that American schools are violent milieus, and that school violence is on the rise. Poland and McCormick (1999) cited governmental statistics that indicated that the number of deaths on school grounds has actually declined since the early 1990s and that fewer than 1% of the violent deaths for children in 1998 occurred at school. The number of multiple homicides at school has increased, and the Columbine shootings was arguably the number one news story of 1999.

Certainly the field of school psychology (along with many professionals in education) appears to be turning its attention to school safety and violence prevention. The number of NASP presentations on school violence and school violence prevention increased significantly in the late 1990s. Several excellent guides are now available that direct attention toward preventing school violence, such as that written by Goldstein and Conoley (1997) and others that are listed in the annotated bibliography.

Overall, crisis preparedness appears to be no less important but much more accepted by most educational systems in the dawn of this new millennium. What remains to be seen is whether the school safety attention, publications, and research will translate into primary prevention programs that will result in safer and healthier educational environments.

BASIC CONSIDERATIONS

Decades ago, Jerome Caplan wrote about primary, secondary, and tertiary prevention (Caplan, 1964). These concepts continue to be paramount in crisis intervention. Primary prevention includes activities that prevent crises from occurring altogether; secondary prevention includes activities that arrest potential crises from escalating; and tertiary prevention aims to repair damage resulting from the occurrence of a crisis (i.e., crisis management). There is much discussion of school safety and crisis planning. There is debate about whether approaches only utilizing hardware such as metal detectors and surveillance cameras are the most effective utilization of resources. The wise principal or school superintendent should form safety task forces that include parents and students to determine what safety and prevention programs should be in place. Will prevention programs be implemented by school systems in an effective manner, and will children learn to solve problems, manage their anger, and get along with others regardless of race? School psychologists will be important players in the resolution of these questions. We can advocate for safety task forces and stress that school safety is an "inside job" that requires a commitment from students, faculty, parents, and the community.

This chapter will outline a practical model for crisis intervention in the schools that will enable school systems to organize and respond effectively in the face of a crisis. The model first establishes competent (prepared) reaction to crises and then offers pointers on the management issues during the aftermath of a crisis and in particular (common) crises. The chapter then moves on to summarize overall knowledge and resources now available to prevent school violence and create safe school environments. Information is summarized from some relatively early works (Pitcher & Poland, 1992) as well as the most recent manuals and compendiums (Poland & McCormick, 1999; National Education Association, 1999; Dwyer, Osher, & Warger, 1998, 2000).

BEST PRACTICES IN PRIMARY PREVENTION: BEFORE THE CRISIS

Safe Schools: Violence Prevention

Should it be surprising that the United Sates has high rates of school violence? School violence appears to be a logical outgrowth of the relatively violent society in which we live. We have high rates of violent behavior in society overall, high rates of family violence (Stark & Flitcraft, 1988) and high rates of television violence (Osofsky, 1997). Can the schools solve all of society's violence problems? Of course not, but schools can positively affect the environment to make it psychologically and physically safer for students (Elliott, Hamburg, & Williams, 1998; Elliott & Mihalic, 1997). American schools, while bearing the brunt of a societal problem, are also potentially a site for learning (and teaching) how to contain and manage societal violence.

Reviews of the literature suggest that there are certain characteristics of schools that appear to be associated with violent behavior (Goldstein & Conoley, 1997). Overall, the information suggests that the more personal and positive the school environment, the lower the level of violence. For example, increased levels of school violence are associated with high levels of arbitrary decision making among school disciplinarians, severe disciplinary actions, large school size, and crowding. We know that large, public, urban schools are typically the educational environments associated with the highest rates of violence. Furthermore, school violence occurs more often in unsupervised, crowded zones such as lockers, restrooms, and hallways.

Conversely, several factors appear to be linked to reduced violence in schools, including educational environments that foster positive academic and social success. Anyone who has worked in educational settings quickly realizes that many of the angriest, most withdrawn students have academic difficulties that predate their behavioral and emotional difficulties. Therefore, the need for effective early intervention programs and a variety of programming alternatives appears even more urgent when taking into account school safety and violence issues.

Fostering positive relationships among students, teachers, and administrators is another factor associated with a safe, well-functioning school. Community involvement and support also helps to personalize a school and is associated with lower levels of student violence. The availability of extracurricular activities to large portions of the student body is another positive contributor to school safety. The factors we know to be associated with safer and less safe school environments are no great surprise for professionals in education. The challenge, however, appears to be in establishing a personal, positive, orderly but supportive educational environment in large (often overcrowded) schools.

There are numerous approaches to violence prevention. Many excellent resources are now available to help schools address these issues and to form a comprehensive preventive program in regard to school violence. As part of the Clinton administration campaign to ensure the safety and well being of school children, the publication *Safeguarding Our Children: An Action Guide* (Dwyer et al., 2000), was intended to be a companion piece to *Early Warning, Timely Response: A Guide to Safe Schools* (Dwyer et al., 1998). These practical and useful guides were developed through the collaborative efforts of the U.S. Department of Justice, the U.S. Department of Education, the Center for Effective Collaboration and Practice (CECP) of the American Institutes for Research (AIR), and NASP, and are highly recommended.

Overall, the interventions recommended throughout the literature in these areas are multiple, and generally emphasize exposing all students to conflict resolution, social problem solving methods, and anger management (Hudley, 1994; Larson, 1994; Loeber & Farrington, 1998). Most importantly, a comprehensive, multifaceted approach that includes media, families, and community members appears to be most effective. A few other promising approaches are considered below.

The Personal Touch: Mentoring Programs

A caring, supportive adult who is concerned for a young person's well-being is essential to healthy emotional development. Lack of these kinds of relationships appears to contribute to violent behavior. As families break up and scatter, schools may find they are the next in line to support children who otherwise have little support. Additional personal attention in the form of mentoring programs in the schools (volunteers to motivate, practice reading on an individual basis) and in the community (Big Brothers, Big Sisters) holds promise. Within the school, smaller classes might be a great way to get started. If this is not a feasible option, then having a climate where each student develops a friendly, positive relationship with at least one adult in the school environment is essential.

Learning Better Social/Life Skills

Several excellent, well-organized curricula have been developed for education of all students (Poland and McCormick, 1999). These lessons should ideally begin in primary grades and continue through high school. At least 10–20 lessons should be included during the first year with 5–10 booster sessions during the following 2 years. The content of these programs should be based on well-established skills such as anger management, social perspective taking, social problem solving, peer negotiation, conflict management, peer resistance skills, active listening, and effective communication. Specific messages should be included, such as it is not right to keep secrets in regard to friends making threats (a familiar message in regard to suicide intervention programs). Most youths that commit violence will have spoken to peers about it prior to taking action.

Improving Environmental Factors

The overall direction of effective interventions in this area is to personalize the environment by making it more pleasant and by encouraging the students. Lower levels of violence emerge when students have some (age-appropriate) ownership of "their" school. For example, displays of students' artwork and projects promote school spirit. Offering merit awards by recognizing at least two students each week for positive behavior has also proven useful in many schools.

Crowd control can make a school environment feel more personal. Staggering class schedules to reduce crowds in the hallways, or providing additional teachers or volunteers to support/supervise in hallways and near lockers during crowded times, can also have a positive effect. Significant improvements in school atmosphere as well as reduced discipline problems have resulted when schools have dress codes that are consistently enforced. Improved lighting and a well-kept facility increase student pride. Reductions in violence are often associated with closer supervision of the contents of student lockers. A proven positive effect in many schools is the use of see-through book bags and/or a complete removal of lockers.

Intervening with At-Risk Students

Studies of violent incidents in schools in the United States noted that most of the youths who committed violent acts in school had a history of emotional disturbance. Some were capable of carefully planning their attacks and also were isolated socially: They were rejected by their peer group, had poor social skills, and lacked parental supervision. Many explicitly told others of their violent plans before following through with those plans, and most of the perpetrators had easy access to weapons.

However, many students who fit this profile will not commit a violent act. The question of how to identify at-risk students is being studied by many researchers and government agencies such as the Federal Bureau of Investigation. Early intervention at the first signs of "at-risk" patterns is the first priority. Fellow students must also learn to report any threatening statements immediately, as many have already learned in suicide intervention programs.

Involving Staff, Students, and Parents

It is important to have these groups involved in building and in system-wide safety task forces. In addition to addressing safety concerns, these task forces can identify priorities and obtain a commitment from participants. It is essential that we implement programs to *end the conspiracy of silence* that allows weapons in schools and threats of violence to go unreported. Our experience has been that peers are almost always aware of threats of violence or suicide. Each student and parent in our school system signs a "safety pledge" in which students are pledging that they will let adults determine the seriousness of threats, immediately report to an adult the presence of a weapon on campus, and work on managing their anger and getting along with others regardless of race or ethnicity.

School staff must also take responsibility to stop violence from escalating by forbidding taunting, teasing, and bullying. All schools have signs that say, "No drugs, no weapons." "No bullying, no teasing" should be added, and all educators should ensure that it is not allowed.

BEST PRACTICES IN PLANNING A SYSTEM-WIDE CRISIS MANAGEMENT PROGRAM

Parents, faculty, and the media frequently ask what's being done to protect our schools? Administrators are expected to prevent and also to prepare for traumatic events. To a greater degree than ever before the schools are coordinating crisis intervention activities, even when a traumatic event occurs outside the school building. Schools are often scrutinized by the entire community for making the "right" decisions under pressure during these circumstances. Developing a plan to manage traumatic events takes much forethought and advanced planning. School districts that have developed crisis event procedures and activities are able to manage crises in a convincing and reassuring manner.

Especially useful is a crisis plan that provides procedures for identifying degrees of hazard and levels of response associated with the hazard. For example, the NEA suggests a monitor level (raising awareness of potential problems), a standby level (when a threatening event may be imminent), and an emergency level (all resources are deployed).

Models for the Formation of a Crisis Team

The sudden flood of demands from every aspect of the school environment is perhaps the most overwhelming characteristic of a crisis: Telephone lines are tied up; all parents need to know what to do; information must be gathered regarding exactly what has occurred; the students must be contained and calmed; victims must be tended to; the media must be managed; and the staff needs assistance, information, and reassurance. In addition, communication lines with the administration must be open. How can all of these tasks be completed in a timely fashion and in orchestration with the others? One element that appears to be ubiquitous in system-wide responses to man-made or natural disaster is the necessity of teams—teams that have been selected and prepared prior to the occurrence of the traumatic event. School psychologists, it is hoped, will be asked to help design the school district/building plan and also to function as a team member.

The overall structure of the teams can be somewhat flexible, based on various demographic characteristics such as size of the school district and resources of the campus staff. Several questions have arisen and been debated in the literature regarding the formation of the building teams (Schoenfeld, 1993; Peterson & Straub, 1992; Pitcher & Poland, 1992). Issues such as the following need to be addressed: How many coordinators are necessary? How many individuals should be identified for each team? Should the individuals be full time campus staff or district wide staff? The resolutions are typically different on each campus. Overall, it appears to be most productive to include personnel from the district level or the community in the case of a more severe incident (campus violence, deaths, etc.). The school district staff are often personally connected to the event and, consequently, highly stressed. Many authors suggest the establishment of two teams: one is the building (front line) team and the other is at the district or local level to assist the building team. District personnel are often better able to manage the media than building personnel. District, state, or national level team members usually have the advantage of less personal involvement (and more objectivity) in addition to having more experience with crisis events. There are some excellent resources for guidance in the annotated bibliography relating to forming teams. One recently published resource book, *Coping With Crisis: Lessons Learned,* is particularly useful in this regard, providing many practical recommendations.

Several roles are almost mandatory in the formation of crisis teams. An overall coordinator (usually the building principal) who reports to the superintendent must be designated in advance. Sub-coordinators must also be pre-designated to manage key service areas including parents, teacher/staff/campus, counseling, medical, security, and media. When these people are selected in advance it allows them to prepare for their role by gathering information and making preparations pertinent to their area of responsibility.

The necessity of school crisis teams and regular review of crisis plans seems so obvious and essential today. However, a new principal recently commented that on his first day at the new school he asked his assistant principals to find the crisis plan. It took them three days to find the plan, and it had not been updated in 11 years. Shakespeare wrote in *Macbeth*, "A false sense of security is mortal's chiefest enemy."

In addition to serving on crisis teams, school psychologists can assure that crisis plans be reviewed annually.

Selection and Training Issues for Team Members

Who should participate on crisis teams? Individuals who have attributes and skills that will enable them to perform well. Team members need to be able to think clearly in circumstances that interrupt normal routine, are likely to escalate in intensity, and are likely to draw attention to the school and jeopardize the school's image. Team members also must be in a position to respond immediately despite their own emotional state, remain as calm as possible, and minimize effects of a disturbing event.

The crisis team should be willing to spend time in training and have time in their schedules to meet, even if a threatening event does not seem to be of immediate crisis proportions (such as a shooting at another school or a death off-campus). Owing to all of these demands, membership on the crisis team should be voluntary and need not necessarily correspond to an individual's job title.

The potential number of preparatory activities is extensive. The crisis response/prevention plans should incorporate input from school administrators, law enforcement agencies, hospitals, the fire department, mental health agencies, parent-teacher organizations, and other community partners. Input from these individuals is vital since, for example, law enforcement personnel will probably control the entire scene immediately during a crisis. School staff will need to have discussions in advance to know how to support the police efforts and rescue crews in the most constructive fashion. All of these individuals should then be informed of the plans. Some districts have generated flip charts where plans for each crisis are summarized beside each labeled crisis tab. Each employee, including substitute personnel, has a copy of the flip chart to guide his or her actions should a crisis occur.

Ruof and Harris (1988) recommend that team members receive as much as 30 hours of training. Certainly each team member should develop a checklist of crisis steps to guide their teams' efforts. Examples of preparatory activities include drafting of general letters to parents or faculty, arranging a calling tree, and arranging for a method to communicate with the teachers if information must be passed on during the school day. The NEA (1999) has listed sample letters and other "tools" for managing crises in the fourth volume of their excellent resource series entitled *Crisis Communications Guide and Toolkit* (volumes 1–4). As a quick review, a summary of the potential training and preparatory activities relevant to each crisis liaison role is listed in Table 1.

Table 1. Possible preparatory activities for crisis team members

Administrative

- Emergency communication to team members/higher-ups
- Overall evacuation plan
- Lock down signal
- Develop a folder for police with important information
- Create a crisis or emergency box
- Develop plans that include after school activities and summer sessions
- Have a website in place for everyday communication with parents and staff
- Design informational display for website in advance to modify at the time
- Designate a "reunion" spot for faculty, students, parents if scattered and plans for transporting large groups to that spot
- Procedures for canceling school, early dismissal, using the school as a shelter
- Instructions, activities for teachers if regular instruction needs to be suspended
- Establish a policy for funerals or memorial services

Staff

- Emergency communication system to warn and inform teachers
- Advance designation of teachers for various duties
- Plan for gathering and disseminating factual information to teachers
- Identification of acceptable substitute teachers (and inservice) subsequent to trauma that affects the teaching staff
- Instructions for managing troubled students in the classroom
- Establish communication channels for faculty to report threatening situations

Table 1. (continued)

• Establish a phone tree, which includes janitors, cooks, bus drivers, etc. • Gather a list of "emergency" substitute teachers that is more extensive
Medical
• Establish emergency communication lines to obtain medical help • Train staff on CPR and emergency medicine • Discuss transportation and potential capabilities with local hospitals • Gather information regarding staff trained in CPR and emergency medicine • Ordering and maintaining emergency medical supplies • Keep track of who is taken for medical treatment and to which facility • Have a plan if school nurse is out • Develop an emergency medical team
Student
• Supervision of emergency containment off campus • Provisions for supervision after school hours (if parents cannot be reached) • Provision of information to students • Specification of disciplinary codes for violent student behavior • Establish communication channels for students to report threatening situations
Parent
• Emergency communication to parents (website?) • Develop a system to make emergency calls or contacts to parents • Develop a system to utilize parent volunteers after a crisis • Sample letter to parents • Setting up/managing parent meeting • Plans for disseminating factual information to parents • Designate a nearby site to receive distraught parents
Counseling
• Designation either of "safe room" for talking after the incident (students and staff) or coordinate sending support personnel to affected classrooms • Discussions with and plans for outside counseling support (short and long term) • Advance preparations for anniversaries of a tragic event or a special remembrance • Periodic screening and checking on those previously affected by a crisis
Media
• Containing and establishing limits for the media during the event • Training staff in media issues, "dos and don'ts" • Clarify district policy about media on campus • Keep records of media requests and contacts • Schedule press conferences
Security
• Establish a method for police to notify schools of dangerous community events • Coordinate plans for students and staff for police operation during an emergency event • Establish a method to notify law enforcement personnel in emergency • Keep roadways clear so that medical and law enforcement personnel can get to the affected school • Build positive relationships with students and implement prevention programs

Preparation of Materials and "Ready" Files

Some materials can be almost fully prepared before a crisis strikes, such as general school information, general information to parents regarding what to expect from shocked children, and a school information fact sheet or contact lists. Samples of letters and handouts are available in the NEA's (1999) *Crisis Communica-*

tions Guide and Toolkit or on-line at www.nea.org/crisis. Many larger districts share materials on a website. Shells and templates that can be prepared in advance are available in the NEA *Crisis Communications Guide and Toolkit* guide and in other resources. These samples include press statements, daily update fact sheets, memos to faculty on media interview, memos to press for pool coverage of funerals, volunteer orientation guides, and media interview request forms.

Emergency Box

Each school should prepare an emergency box of materials and identifying information should an evacuation be necessary. Items that should be included follow:

1. Medical supplies
2. Emergency cards for students and staff
3. Portable phone
4. Bull horn
5. Crisis team badges and/or vests
6. Blueprints and floor plans of the school
7. Maps that locate important shut off valves for sprinklers, gas, electricity, alarms, etc.
8. Master keys for school
9. Flashlights
10. Tools

It might be advisable to have more than one emergency box stored in different locations should an area of the school be inaccessible.

Emergency Signals

All school personnel including substitute teachers should know the separate emergency signals for "lock-down" and "evacuation."

1. Lock-down should be the signal for all staff and students to stay in classrooms away from doors and windows in a protected position until given an all clear signal.

2. Evacuation plans should include teachers taking their class rolls and being able to account for each student in their class. Plans should also include locations to which students would go when evacuating the school. Every school has different surroundings, but plans should include how to utilize nearby businesses, churches, and other schools to safeguard students and staff.

Crisis Drills

Once teams are in place, have received some training, and have prepared their basic materials, the schools should consider conducting crisis drills. Building evacuation, communication lines, and teacher preparedness all need to be tested. There are many examples and suggestions for conducting these drills in previously published manuscripts (Pitcher & Poland, 1992; Poland & McCormick, 1999). Drills should be conducted in such a way that they do not alarm staff and students and should be coordinated with local police and other agencies. It is helpful to place a sign at the front of the building indicating a crisis drill is being conducted.

Training Sessions

The details of the crisis plan should be carefully communicated to all staff, parents, community liaisons, and students. The responsibilities, agreements, and actions should be clearly outlined. Everyone needs to know his or her individual role as well as what to expect. A written summary document or reference flip chart is often useful. Teachers should keep a copy. Parents can be informed of crisis plans and safety activities through school system newsletters and articles in local papers. School psychologists could be involved in writing these articles.

BEST PRACTICES IN SECONDARY PREVENTION: DURING THE CRISIS

Implementing Crisis Intervention: Some Basic Skills

Probably the most pronounced aspect of a crisis in the schools is the intense emotional upset or "dis-equilibrium" experienced by the system immediately when a crisis occurs. With a previously developed plan of action, everyone should be aware of his or her role and have some idea of how the overall team will approach the problem. If there is no prior planning, then it is nearly impossible to form a reasonably well-orchestrated plan of action on the spot.

What To Do

Take Action at Critical Stages

Usually the first issue is how to manage the pragmatic aspects of the crisis. Three waves descend on a school after a crisis:

1. Police and medical
2. Media
3. Parents

The administrator should have school police or assistant principals keep the roadway to the school clear so that police and emergency personnel can access the campus. School psychologists and other crisis team members should make plans for parents who descend on the school to be taken to a specific location, such as a nearby school, to await further information. These parents should be provided with periodic updates and be reunited with their children along with careful record keeping and sign-out procedures. The situation should be assessed, and, if necessary, calls for rescue, law enforcement, or medical help must be made. Next, the immediate needs of affected students and victims must be administered. For all of this to occur, communications must be made among the crisis team members and also to district administrative personnel. The media liaison or designated crisis team member should cooperate with the media but keep them contained off school grounds and away from staff and students. School board policies should be written to clarify the removal of media from school grounds when requested by school administrators. The National Guard in Jonesboro, Arkansas, was very helpful at controlling the media. Our experience has been that local media are usually not as difficult to manage as the national media.

Share Information as It Becomes Available

At the first opportunity, all staff members should be notified and given information and clear directions. The first step when a crisis occurs is to verify the facts. Staff will need to know what happened, where to go for safety, who has been affected, how to get help, and how to provide assistance. Verification can be accepted from eyewitness school staff and from the police or parents of the dead or injured. Once verification has taken place, school administration *must tell everyone the truth* in age-appropriate language and with careful consideration of cultural factors.

Within a few hours a public announcement should be made either in person or through a press release. Include in the message a statement that school officials are working together with law enforcement and medical personnel to manage the situation. Emphasize that there is a plan of action in place, that the information is in the process of being collected, and that further details will be forthcoming. A statement should also be developed for use by personnel answering telephone calls and for any websites.

Meetings

School psychologists should insist that before leaving school the day of the crisis the crisis team members meet and review what is working and support each other. If the issues continue for several days, then team members must meet daily, often in a short session to get organized, establish a to-do list, and assign staff to take action. The teaching staff should also be met with regularly with some unstructured time for informal discussion and emotional support. Too often teachers are not provided the opportunity to vent their emotions and to understand they are not alone.

Supervised Student Areas

Do not send students home to empty houses. If schools must be recessed midday or if the end of the day has come, then students should not be allowed to leave campus unless they will not be alone. Parents and teachers should have been organized to provide a safe place for students to wait for their own parents or to be allowed, with parent permission, to go home with an adult other than their own parent.

Faculty Meeting and Notification

A major subsequent issue is how to cope with the immediate and short-term emotional aftermath of the incident. Much as in personal crises, staff members experience overwhelming feelings of helplessness, denial, inadequacy, and confusion. Following the shock, staff and students continue to be at risk for longer-term effects of crisis: depression or burnout, physical symptoms, and disorganization of functional working relationships. Such long-term effects are thought to be especially pronounced if the crisis is not managed well or if individuals are not given an opportunity to vent, compare notes, let down emotionally, etc.

It is important to provide faculty members the opportunity to confront loss issues and possibly to seek outside support prior to confronting the students and parents. The principal sets the tone for whether the crisis will be dealt with or not. One principal whose school suffered a multiple homicide conducted weekly faculty meetings for 2 years, and it is believed that is why there were few transfers or early retirements. If verification of the death occurs while school is in session, then the most productive course of action involves a written memorandum to be hand delivered to each faculty member. In addition to stating the pertinent information (name of the deceased, cause of death and circumstances surrounding the death) the memo should include suggestions on how faculty members can assist the students.

Teacher Guidance

On the day of the crisis, every effort must be made to reassemble teachers prior to their departure even if just for a few minutes to schedule a faculty meeting the next morning before school. The school's calling tree should be utilized to contact staff members who are not at school and to provide updated information to all. Teachers should be told all known information regarding the incident. They should be provided with clear instructions regarding how and what to share with the students, procedures related to the safe rooms, how much of the traumatic intervention will take place in the classroom, how to manage the media, etc. Teachers should also be allowed time to talk among themselves regarding their personal reactions to the event. If a particularly traumatic event has occurred, then teachers may be tearful and require time to emote. A few back up staff such as familiar, trusted substitute teachers are normally needed since a few faculty members may find themselves unable to teach for part or all of the school day.

The majority of intervention assistance should take place in the classroom. Keeping most students in class, discussing the tragedy as a group, and providing therapeutic activities would be most beneficial. Consider this example: A high school of 800 has a popular student killed in an accident, and 20% of the student body is upset and grieving. The school would not have been built to accommodate 160 students in the counseling office so the majority of those affected will need to receive assistance in the classroom with knowledgeable and empowered teachers.

Schedule a Meeting for Parents

Parents also need to know the facts and be given a chance to discuss them. Following an opportunity for parents to ventilate, information regarding typical childhood reactions to trauma should be disseminated, and strategies should be given to parents on how to handle them. Often the school district sends a letter to all parents listing what happened and what action the district is undertaking to address it. Resources should also be listed for seeking additional help. This is helpful and advised, but should not be a substitute for an actual parent meeting.

Returning to the School Building

When a disturbing incident has occurred at a school building or in the community, students and parents often fear coming to or returning to the school building. Much evidence in the area of community/natural disasters suggests that children and adolescents should be united with their families at the first reasonable opportunity in order to begin the healing process. However, once individuals have had time to get through the initial shock, return to routine (and the school building) is important for healing. School psychologists can help administrators recognize the importance of reopening school as quickly as possible.

Many school community members may be apprehensive about returning to school. However, school provides the one place that is easiest to deliver mental health assistance to all concerned, and it is the only place in many communities where everyone can be together, and that is why we recommend reopening schools as quickly as possible. In Jonesboro, for example, school was closed only one day after the shooting. It was therapeutic to have all students and staff return that quickly. Many of them visited the scene of the shooting and looked at the bullet holes in the walls. The bullet holes were not repaired for several days at the request of the national crisis team. Students have been observed being understandingly cautious about stepping into a room where a death has occurred. Parents should be welcomed to accompany their children. It is not unusual for students to walk around the room touching objects such as desks and chairs while telling their story about where they were and what they were doing when the tragedy occurred.

It is essential that all signs of blood be removed from a school building prior to returning students to school. One school superintendent in a personal conversation (D. Rawls, personal communication) discussed not only the need for a physical cleansing but also a spiritual one. Numerous cultures call for ceremonies of some type to remove bad spirits or karma from a building where a tragedy occurred. School psychologists can assist administrators to consider all cultural aspects.

Curricula Issues

Many professionals who have managed major crises know that curriculum must be set aside during the first days of school after a crisis has occurred. Various techniques have been used that involve incorporation of facing/coping with trauma into the daily lessons. Teachers who have already had some instruction in working with upset students and who are aware of how the use of talking, writing, music, artwork, projects, ceremonies, and rituals can greatly assist students. Teachers should not hesitate to acknowledge their own emotions. School psychologists should provide teachers an inservice on how to assist children in the aftermath of a tragedy.

It is not unusual for teachers to ignore the crisis and want to continue with the scheduled curriculum. While following the schedule of a student who had committed suicide, the first author was astounded when the teacher who was unaware that most of her class was crying asked, "Do you want to talk to them before or after they have their test this morning?" Teachers should be given clear directions from the administration to set aside the curriculum and deal with the emotionality.

Provide Opportunities for the Faculty to Talk

It is important that the faculty express their emotions. The more quickly emotional assistance is offered the better the adjustment. Calling trees are helpful to provide faculty the opportunity to work through their own emotions and to receive assistance from significant others (Poland, 2000). Teachers have repeatedly stated that after tragedies they have not been provided the opportunity to vent their emotions. Post-tragedy meetings for school faculty should be mandatory and should not only provide logistical information but also the opportunity for faculty to share their own thoughts and feelings. School psychologists must attend these meetings and should play a pivotal role, but we must not take any notes about what the faculty says without their permission. Teachers have been very vocal in stating that in the area of school crisis they expect the administrator to

1. Tell the truth and not sweep things under the carpet

2. Be visible and available to all who are affected

3. Seek faculty input

4. Acknowledge their own thoughts and feelings and give others permission to do so

Do Not Underestimate the Impact of the Incident

Attempts to insist that everyone is "just fine" and that they must behave "normally" very often backfire. Staff and students can feel very alone in their grief, and a significant toll is taken on the building tone and camaraderie. Often a faculty or staff meeting following the traumatic incident provides an effective barometer of the level of grieving that is present. The more upset the faculty, the longer it will take the students to readjust. Again, time should be allotted for the venting of emotions with faculty, parents, and students in addition to addressing the more pragmatic or logistical issues. Weekly meetings have greatly assisted faculty in several communities where school shootings resulted in numerous lawsuits. Follow-up meetings held as long as 1 or 2 years after the crisis occurred are useful following many deaths.

Communication

Use of the telephones to place or receive calls is generally impossible during a traumatic event in the community or in the building. The internet is a logical option in such cases or through alternative communication means that should have been established prior to the crisis event (walkie-talkies, a secured line, etc.). Communication to parents is especially problematic. Many parents will descend upon the school, and they should be met and directed to a nearby facility (perhaps the nearest unaffected school) where school crisis team members will give them frequent updates in a calm, professional manner. The parents of students injured or killed should be assigned a staff member to assist them with contacting and gathering family, driving, etc. If their child was injured or killed, then long-term follow-up services will be necessary.

Media Problems

Individuals who have managed major schools crises often speak about the continuing issues surrounding media involvement. Media often return again and again on roughly 12-hour cycles and frequently make mistakes in reporting information accurately. The need for factual information is constant, and the media are persistent. Media coverage can be expected day after day, month after month, and year after year in the more severe incidents. Overall parameters should be set, staff should be coached on how to interact with the media, and overall control should be implemented. School psychologists have served as very effective media spokespersons.

Poland and McCormick (2000) have outlined specific suggestions for managing the media and have emphasized that prior planning and previously developed positive relationships with the media were helpful. Some key points follow:

1. Media coverage goes through stages based on hours:
   - 0–12 hours: Reporters scramble to get facts and answer, "What happened?"
   - 12–24 hours: Question is, "Who are the victims?"
   - 24–36 hours: Focus is on "Why?" and "Who is to blame?"
   - 36–72 hours: Media focus is in-depth analysis.
   - 72 hours forward: Funeral concerns and societal issues.

2. Local media do not normally pose a problem.

3. School board policy should give the principal authority to keep media off school grounds, and local or state police may be needed to enforce the policy.

4. Students should be shielded from interviews, and their parents alone can give permission for interviews.

5. School faculty should defer media requests to the designated spokesperson.

6. The designated spokesperson or persons should have received media training. Written statements should accompany verbal interviews.

7. Schools should cooperate with media requests with definite limits set regarding where the media can go and what they can do.

8. Columbine officials realized they could not control the 750 reporters covering the story, but they could control their reaction to them.

9. Media representatives should be encouraged to refrain from dramatizing, glorifying, or offering simple explanations for the perpetrators' actions.

10. School spokespersons should stress the positive steps taken by the school to help in the coping process and inform media of available assistance services.

11. Specific media guidelines have been outlined for the aftermath of suicide.

12. Research indicates that national news coverage of school violence increases the likelihood that other troubled students will carry out violent thoughts and plans.

13. National media attention should focus more on prevention activities and students and schools who have thwarted or foiled plots of violence.

BEST PRACTICES IN TERTIARY PREVENTION: AFTER THE CRISIS

After a crisis has passed a major job remains: moving beyond the crisis both emotionally and cognitively. Anniversary dates, re-visitation by the media, and the filing of lawsuits continue to contribute to the stress levels during the post-crisis period. Following a crisis, families, students, and faculties often search for a path back to a normal life and routine; however, life will never be quite the same again.

Insisting that everything is fine and avoiding discussion since it dredges up bad memories is not the most constructive approach. Counselors often refer to re-establishing routine after the incident as the "new normal" due to this phenomenon. More specifically, teams and school personnel need to stay involved and be on alert for the following issues:

Student Issues: Maintain the Vigilance

Symptoms of an emotional shock often persist or emerge days and months after the incident(s). It is likely that students will continue to feel "unsafe" for some time or feel that their personal resources are not up to others' expectations.

Unfortunately there appears to be an increase for depression and suicide risk for adolescents following a traumatic event. Drinking and reckless behavior also escalate; therefore, long-term systemic care with periodic mental health screening is essential (R. Pynoos, personal communication).

Parent Issues: Maintaining the Contact

The crisis team should maintain contact with the victims and their families, and the school psychologist is the logical person to do so. Gradually we want to support their understanding of the incident(s) and support their re-entry into the school environment when the time is right. In some instances, questionnaires have been used to assess the emotional needs of staff and students following a traumatic incident and to determine what level of support or counseling was in order.

Increased mental health personnel were assigned to affected schools in Oklahoma City after the bombing and in Littleton, for example, and community mental health workers were assigned to affected families. A collaborative partnership must be formed between school personnel, local mental health agencies, judicial systems, and clergy. A victim advocate assigned to families in Jonesboro, Arkansas, commented, "You are never through assisting the family of a homicide victim." School psychologists are encouraged to develop partnerships with all community caregivers and to advocate for long-term assistance.

Law Enforcement/Security Issues

Additional security is often required for an extended time following a violent incident, since it is often comforting to traumatized individuals and helps them to feel safer. Parent, community, and school task forces are helpful in determining what changes should be made. Most beneficial would be a balance of hardware measures, such as more police, metal detectors, or surveillance cameras, and non-hardware measures, such as more mental health services and prevention programs.

When Is It Not News?

The school community should be prepared for ongoing and predictable media attention. Media coverage will resume when school resumes the next fall and on anniversary dates. Additional incidents of school violence often result in the media's revisiting the sites of previous violence. Court trial dates and release of information from police can also result in a return of the media.

Memorials and Donations

Memorials and donations support the healing process. Often people want to help immediately, and, therefore, decisions regarding therapeutic activities should be made quickly. Such activities include making ribbons, writing songs, and making T-shirts in memory of victims. Many gifts, flowers, and remembrances of all kinds may be brought to a particular location following school shootings and other tragedies. At Columbine, for example, many such objects were taken to the park adjacent to the school. It is recommended that these items left behind be handled carefully. For example, items left at the Vietnam War Memorial in Washington, D.C., are catalogued and warehoused. School communities have taken pictures of remembrance objects left at the informal memorial site and created memory books.

Setting up a foundation or memorial fund is quite complex. A system will need to be established for depositing, warehousing, cataloging, and acknowledging donations. It can be healing for the community to participate in this endeavor. It is important, for example, that how the monies will be spent is agreed upon by a committee consisting of school personnel, students, and parents. Will the money be used for the school, the community, or specifically targeted to the victims of the tragedy? It is hoped these decisions can be made based on consensus and without conflict.

The community is often looking for the "gift of hope" as a sign that something permanent and positive has come from the tragedy. Poland and McCormick (1999) discuss this issue at length. An example is Stockton, California, where the donations were used to build a children's museum.

Permanent physical memorials appear to be best accomplished with time and emotional distance from the incident. It was almost 5 years before the memorial to the Oklahoma City bombing victims was completed. Jefferson County, Colorado, school board president Jon Destefano (personal communication) stressed the need to go slowly in planning memorials and to be prepared for many ups and downs of the recovery process. Issues such as memorial location deserve careful consideration since students should have access but not have to look at it each time they come to school. Students should also be involved in planning the memorial. Schools are often faced with the question of whether or not to have plaques and pictures of deceased students displayed at school. School psychologists can assist school administrators in creating policies that balance the needs of grieving families with that of the school community. A large high school that has a wall containing pictures of all those who have died who previously attended the school will have many such pictures. Caution must be the key word when deciding appropriate memorializing of suicide victims. The American Association of Suicidology guidelines are outlined by Poland (2000).

Anniversary and Benchmark Dates

Anniversaries and other reminders of a traumatic incident often provoke emotional reactions in the survivors, perhaps more than one might anticipate. Possible triggers include the six-month anniversary date, the one-year anniversary date, and the first day of the new school year. Other similar traumas, even if geographically far removed, can trigger severe emotional reactions, even suicidal reactions. Individuals may need additional support during these times. Advanced warning allows individuals to anticipate the emotional shock associated with these events and to have some amount of expectations or control over the situation.

Evaluating Crisis Intervention Services

Crisis has been frequently recognized as a time of potential danger as well as potential opportunity. During and just subsequent to a crisis there is a reduced defensiveness or increased openness on the part of individuals. For educators a sudden shock can be a "teachable moment" to help children and adolescents learn to overcome fears, learn to cope with unsavory events, or revisit troubling experiences from the past that haunt them.

Following any traumatic incident the crisis team needs to meet to review how the plan did or did not work. Revisions, increases or decreases in designated staff, and production of materials are all best accomplished during the first few months back to school. It is hoped this time frame will allow the crisis team enough distance from the event to be objective, but not so much that the specifics of the incident fade from memory.

BEST PRACTICES IN RESPONDING TO COMMUNITY DISASTER AND SCHOOL-WIDE CRISIS

How and When to Utilize Outside Assistance

In many situations it has been constructive for schools to accept outside assistance. Schools often do not have the number of mental health professionals needed to cope with a major loss. Moreover, those they do have may have been personally affected. It is typically a wise move to form a partnership with local agencies, mental health personnel, and clergy. In a severe crisis event, national assistance is available from the American Red Cross, National Organization for Victim Assistance, and NASP's National Emergency Assistance Team (NEAT).

Natural Disasters

Emotional reactions to natural disasters are often severe (Peterson and Straub, 1992; Lazarus & Phelps, 1993) owing to various factors including the unpredictable nature of the event and children having been separated from their families. Knowing about the potential for natural disasters and being aware of how to manage them can be empowering for everyone. Learning about natural disasters that are of a higher probability in your area from a scientific, historic, and geographic perspective as well as safety precautions that can be taken can be incorporated into many curricula. It is important that each school designate the safest locations for staff and students to take shelter in the event of a natural disaster. School administrators should discuss the building's safest areas with the architectural firm that built it.

Signs of post-traumatic stress disorder are often present (see "Crisis Counseling" section for detail and references). During these times schools can often serve as a community resource by conducting meetings for parents, providing parents with information on how best to support their children, and also by providing parents with a forum to compare notes, and this is often a useful service. Resuming a daily routine as soon as is possible and assisting in the clean-up effort are often constructive experiences for those involved. An excellent resource in these areas is the American Red Cross (1999), which produces a *Family Disaster Plan and Personal Survival Guide* that discusses many of these issues. This organization, for example, has outlined four phases of disaster recovery: heroic, honeymoon, disillusionment, and construction. Additional information can be obtained through their website at www.redcross.org.

Managing Emotionality When Death Affects a School

Every school should give specific consideration to the adaptation of their crisis plan for crises involving a death. A plan will be needed that manages emotionality and that provides assistance to everyone concerned with the grieving process. While a death occurring at school is very rare, the death of a child attending a given school is, unfortunately, something all school psychologists are likely to encounter repeatedly during their career. Poland and McCormick (1999) discuss incidence figures from the Center for Disease Control, which estimate annual childhood death rates as follows: 1 in 1200 high school students, 1 in 3000 middle school students, and 1 in 4000 during the elementary school years. What follows are basic principles outlined by the literature on crisis intervention.

1. Suggestions for administrators: Administrators set the tone for the management of any building crisis. They should acknowledge the strong emotions involved when a death occurs and should encourage faculty and students to recognize and express their emotions. Adult willingness to acknowledge the emotional side of the event(s) provides a positive role model for students. The school psychologist should be a consultant to the principal to ensure that those affected have the opportunities to express their emotions.

2. Share as many facts as possible: The first step when a death occurs is to verify the facts. School administrators should contact acceptable sources such as the police and a close family member (deceased child's parents or faculty member's spouse) for verification. The administrator should then utilize the school-calling tree to notify all faculty members if school is not in session.

3. Faculty notification and meeting should be first and mandatory: This is important to provide faculty members the opportunity to confront loss issues and possibly to seek outside support prior to confronting the students and parents (Lieberman, 1998). A faculty meeting before school convenes is optimal. If verification of the death occurs while school is in session, then the most productive course of action involves a written memorandum to be hand delivered to each faculty member. In addition to stating the pertinent information (e.g., name of the deceased, cause of death, and circumstances surrounding the death) the memo should also include suggestions on how faculty members can assist the students. The public address system can be used to deliver sad news, but the wise principal would choose the words carefully, rehearse the message, and recognize that voice tone and inflection will be very important in setting the attitude for the school.

4. Conducting a parent meeting: A major tragedy at school often results in the school being like the epicenter of an earthquake with parents, students, and community members coming to the affected school in search of both answers and assistance. The first author was the main presenter for audiences of hundreds and even thousands following school shootings in Paducah, Jonesboro, and Littleton. Schools should not hesitate to conduct parent meetings as a way of providing information for adults on how we help children the most. Many children and especially younger ones are greatly affected by how adults cope with the tragedy. The following suggestions will help the parent meeting to be effective in assisting the community.

- Hold the meeting as soon as possible after the crisis.
- Publicize the meeting throughout the community with letters of invitation sent to parents and announcements included in television, newspaper, and radio coverage.
- Open the meeting with a review of known and factual information provided by the school administrator and/or local police or prosecutor.
- Provide crowd control with organized parking, seating for all participants, air conditioning, etc.
- Deny media access to the meeting.
- Utilize audiovisual equipment and an effective public address system.
- Provide refreshments.
- Locate an effective speaker who is knowledgeable about crisis intervention, mental health, and schools.
- Recognize the uncertainty, the need to know why the tragedy occurred, and the accompanying anger, but *focus on what can be done now to assist all who are affected.*
- Outline specifically what children's reactions to crisis are and how adults can assist them.
- Encourage the reopening of school as quickly as possible.
- Discourage children from being interviewed by local and national media.
- Stress the commonality of what everyone is experiencing.
- Find the strengths of the community and outline plans for the next few days.

Questions to Estimate the Degree of Trauma After a Death

There are several questions that are useful in designing an appropriate intervention within a school system.

1. *Who was the deceased person?* The death of a popular or well-known member of the school community will have more impact than that of a new or little–known member.

2. *What happened to the deceased?* Unlike an extended illness during which individuals are able to prepare themselves for loss, murder and suicide are unexpected. This aspect makes them more difficult to deal with than a death that is protracted in nature.

3. *Where did the death occur?* Deaths that occur on school grounds are very unexpected and more difficult to deal with. School personnel and students may have actually witnessed the death, and local and national media will likely become involved.

4. *Have any previous occurrences affected the school?* The recent death may bring up unresolved issues from other crisis situations. Mental health professionals should inquire about any previous tragedies that may have affected a particular school and how and if the tragedies were resolved.

5. *Who was the perpetrator?* It is shocking when an acquaintance commits an act of violence, raising many unanswerable Why? questions and individuals questioning whether they might have acted to prevent the tragedy.

It often appears that school personnel underestimate the impact of deaths that occur in the community during holidays and vacation time. A principal questioned why a student suicide during spring break would have much impact on the school when classes resumed. Schools are often the only community environment where teens or adults gather to share the loss and confront emotional issues. One teacher commented in a crisis workshop that 2 days after high school graduation a student of hers lost three classmates owing to a car and train wreck. The student described how she and her surviving classmates met in the school parking lot each evening without any adult assistance, to try to help themselves cope with the loss. School psychologists must be assertive and seek out the grieving students even when school is not in session.

Deaths Due to Suicide

Dealing with suicide is particularly difficult. The American Association of Suicidology's (1998) very important postvention procedures recommend the following for schools :

1. Do not hold a large-scale school assembly or dedicate a memorial to the deceased.

2. Do provide individual and group counseling.

3. Verify the facts, and do treat the death as a suicide.

4. Contact the family of the deceased.

5. Emphasize that no one is to blame for the suicide.

6. Emphasize that help is available, that suicide is preventable, and that everyone has a role to play in prevention.

7. Encourage funerals to be scheduled during non-school hours.

The American Association of Suicidology can be contacted at www.suicidology.org.

Crisis Counseling

One important element in getting over a shock appears to be the opportunity to discuss the event and one's reactions to it (R. Pynoos, personal communication). Although this applies to both children and adults, especially the children should (optimally) be provided an opportunity to process the experience within 24–36 hours after the event (National Association of School Psychologists, 1992). Individuals need help understanding their emotional reactions and reassurance that what they are experiencing is normal. Some individuals become even further distressed since they fear they will "lose their minds" or "be unable to do what others expect of them." Most people benefit from being given time to articulate what they are feeling and thinking. Subsequently, it is beneficial for traumatized individuals to know what to expect (e.g., difficulty sleeping, reoccurring fears, episodes of panic) and how best to confront them.

A properly trained school counseling team is able to provide the necessary short-term support after many types of traumas. For situations involving large groups of students, formation of a community-wide support team is often necessary to manage the numbers of traumatized students, faculties, and parents. Such an experience is labeled a "group crisis intervention" or "debriefing" and specialists in this area are available (for training and intervention) through the National Organization for Victim Assistance (NOVA). Many school psychologists have been and continue to be trained on the NOVA model.

Many practical and age-appropriate strategies are available to assist children (Brooks & Seigel, 1996). However, another significant basic element in crisis counseling is that whenever possible interventions should begin with the faculty and parents. These two groups are in the best position to assist children. The more assistance faculty and parents receive after a jarring event, the greater their ability to help the children.

In addition to helping significant adults cope with their own emotional reactions, it is often useful to be reminded of normal childhood reactions to a disturbing event or loss. Children (and adults as well) should be allowed to discuss/express these emotions as they would discuss more typical emotions under more normal circumstances (Eth & Pynoos, 1985). It can be a temptation for adults to disallow repeated expressions of fears or emotional reactions from children, especially if the adults are attempting to cope with the aversive memories through denial or repression. Many of the typical childhood reactions are not commonly known or understood by many adults. These reactions include:

1. Fears of all sorts

2. Regression academically and behaviorally

3. Nightmares and sleeping difficulties

4. Need to be comforted, reassured or held frequently

5. Easily becoming tearful or angry

6. Over-reactions to small events

Meetings for both faculty and parents can provide an opportunity to outline in a practical manner what reactions to expect from children and how to assist them. Long after a crisis has occurred, individuals tend to continue to ask *"Why?"* and *"What could I have done to prevent it?"* There are no answers, and if these questions persist, then they usually prevent individuals from getting past grief months and years after the tragedy.

Traditional Approaches

Caplan (1964) also wrote about stages typically observed during an emotional breakdown due to personal crisis. Traditionally, crises have been regarded as unfolding in four stages. First there is an initial rise in tension due to the crisis event. Second, in the face of the continued impact of the stressing event, there is a lack of success in the usual problem-solving techniques. During the third stage other problem-solving resources are mobilized, and, following failure of these, tension mounts to the breaking point during the fourth and final phase of severe emotional disorganization (Caplan, 1964; Cohen, 1990).

Community counselors have long advocated crisis counseling, and several authors have written about useful counseling techniques during personal and community-level crises (Faberow & Gordon, 1981; Slaikeu, 1990). There are several different models in the literature. This sort of counseling intervention is specific to crisis. The goals of "psychological first aid" are unlike those of traditional therapies. Rather, they revolve around addressing immediate concerns and helping the distressed individual or "victim" sort out such needs as welfare, safety, shelter, and so on.

In the way of an overview, however, a traditional general approach emphasized by Slaikeu (1990) outlined the following principals of what he called "psychological first aid":

1. Make contact with the victim and give him or her permission to express thoughts and emotions.

2. Explore the problem in terms of the past, present, and future.

3. Identify possible solutions to assist the victim.

4. Take definite actions to assist the victim.

5. Provide follow-up assistance.

NOVA Model

The NOVA (National Organization for Victim Assistance, 1997) model for crisis intervention counseling was developed for community usage and has recently been utilized in educational settings, and has proven effective in the aftermath of school shootings. The model, which is very applicable to the classroom, first recommends that all desks be placed in a circle. One facilitator leads the discussion, and an appointed "scribe" records verbatim key phrases on an easel. The NOVA model suggests the following sequence:

1. Everyone is asked to remember where he or she was when they first became aware of the tragedy.

2. What were their sensory perceptions?

3. What were the accompanying thoughts and feelings?

4. What are they worried about in the near future?

5. What previously helped them when bad things occurred in their lives, and what or who has provided some comfort now?

The facilitator leads the discussion and stresses the commonality among group members in their responses to the above questions. Notes taken by the "scribe" are used to review important points. Based on the group's wishes, the notes are either destroyed or saved at the end of the session.

The model is intended to serve as a starting point in coping with a shocking event. Ongoing or long-term assistance can be delivered subsequently (to those in need) through a partnership or collaboration with community agencies, organizations, and practitioners. The NOVA model has much promise for schools especially with groups of children or adolescents that number fewer than 50 in size. The authors have found that it is difficult for each participant to hear every word spoken when more than 50 chairs are placed in a circle. More information about NOVA is available at www.try-nova.org. The school psychologist should utilize this model with a classroom or small group of traumatized students or staff.

Sanford Model

Developed by Nancy Sanford, The Sanford Model of Debriefing Critical Incident Stress holds much promise for schools especially with groups that have more than 50 people. The Sanford model serves the following purposes:

1. Provides victims the opportunity to sort out thoughts.

2. Identifies what is needed for safety.

3. Provides a guided mental health discussion that fits a 45-minute period.

4. Reduces isolation.

5. Creates empathetic bonds.

The Sanford model format outlined by Wong (2000) is very specific with one facilitator dividing the group into small groups of equal size with four to six participants in each group. Everyone is seated in a small circle with one person chosen to respond first to the four key questions. The following rules must be carefully explained to participants:

1. Everything said is confidential.

2. Each person takes a turn (clockwise).

3. One person speaks at a time and there is no cross talking.

4. Each person has a time limit (e.g., 1 minute) so that the facilitator can conduct this debriefing with large numbers of participants.

5. Group members' responsibilities are to listen and to remain silent if one member does not use the allotted time.

The four key questions that each group member answers in order are:

1. What is your name, and where were you when the tragedy occurred?

2. What was your first thought?

3. What was your worst feeling?

4. What would help you feel safer now?

The first author and Marleen Wong used this model very successfully with Jefferson County school personnel in the aftermath of the Columbine tragedy. School psychologists will find this model particularly helpful with the entire school faculty or with large numbers of high school students. One advantage to the model is that it can be completed during a classroom period or a faculty meeting owing to the defined time limit to respond to each question. One school psychologist can utilize this model with a large number of participants. During the group debriefing the school psychologist should move from group to group so that he or she can summarize important themes and cite the commonality among all in attendance at the conclusion of the debriefing.

NEAT Team

NASP created NEAT in the aftermath of the Oklahoma City bombing so that the organization could be more responsive to national level crises affecting schools (Feinberg, 1998; Zenere, 1998). The specific purposes of the six-member team are:

1. Promote training in crisis intervention.

2. Provide direct on-site assistance when requested at national level crises that affect children and schools.

3. Provide consultation to school officials and students and to school psychologists across the country who are faced with a tragedy either by telephone and through written materials.

4. Support state school psychology associations as they form state level crisis teams as have already been done in Florida and Georgia.

NEAT has formed partnerships with organizations such as NOVA, the American Red Cross, Federal Emergency Management Agency, and state emergency response teams. To contact NEAT, visit NASP's website (www.naspweb.org/NEAT). Specific future activities are to work with the International School Psychology Association to form an international network and foundation for crisis intervention.

Effects of National School Tragedies

Most children in America viewed the extensive and graphic television news coverage of shocking school shootings such as that at Columbine. Reactions to such events often appear to reverberate around the nation and the world. School officials should anticipate increases in feelings of fear for student safety in their school subsequent to such an event. Usually increases in written or verbal threats of violence, bomb threats, bringing weapons on campus, and rumors of copycat attempts also occur. Since the students are already aware of the developments, such incidents can present a "teachable moment" in that the students are more open to discussion about the incidents and are more open to constructive input from adults. If counselors and teachers have been prepared in advance, then such discussions could occur within the confines of the school day, with curriculum very easily being set aside, and students provided with a forum in which to discuss their personal reactions, thoughts, etc. What follows are key points:

1. Conduct faculty meetings to prepare for discussion of the tragedy with students.

2. Make sure discussions are focused on how to make schools safer rather than on glamorizing the perpetrators by mentioning their names and discussing their actions.

3. Assign school police, administrators, and teachers to visible points inside and outside the school where they will greet students and assure them of their safety.

4. Develop a violence prevention and school safety lesson to be utilized in every classroom.

5. Highlight (for both parents and students) prevention programs that are already in place. If there are no such programs, then a task force on school safety and violence prevention should be formed to develop these programs.

Each nationally publicized school shooting in America dramatically affects our children. Too many educators have insisted on sticking to the assigned curriculum when their students needed opportunities to discuss their fears. Many teachable moments to work on school safety and violence prevention have been missed. Students commented that they were told, for example, "The student who made the bomb threat has been expelled," and "There is nothing for you to worry about—get back to work." National news coverage of school violence cannot be simplified or minimized and will affect schools across the country. School psychologists are in a key position to advocate for students to not only have the opportunity to express their own fears but to create opportunities for students to become more involved in prevention activities.

SUMMARY

Major tragedies such as those that occurred in Jonesboro, Arkansas, or Littleton, Colorado, are, thankfully, very rare, but it is still very important that we seek out training in crisis intervention. More university training programs are now including course work in this area. Over the course of a career every school psychologist will encounter a number of deaths or serious injury to students or school faculty. Schools are also greatly affected by tragedies that occur in the surrounding community. Crisis plans can and should be designed to manage the three waves that descend on a school after a crisis, specifically police and medical, parents, and the media. Preventive school and community safety programs must be a central part of the planning.

The school psychologist can be an important member of a building-wide and district-wide crisis team. Throughout the crisis intervention process, school psychologists can make valuable contributions in a number of different areas: advocating for and implementing prevention (school safety) programs and planning for and overcoming traumatic events in schools. Furthermore, school psychologists often coordinate the tremendous support frequently needed during the aftermath of a crisis. Many school psychologists have even served as the school system media spokesman after a tragedy.

Is there opportunity in adversity? Owing to the tragic events of the past, it appears that many administrators are ready to create and improve crisis management plans. How ready are they to put preventive programs in place? Many schools are conducting important crisis drills as a means of establishing readiness, but in a few instances drills have been far too realistic with gunshots and simulated blood. School psychologists can advise administrators and police how to balance the need for preparation while taking care not to scare students. School psychologists are often trained in organizational and community intervention and are particularly oriented toward prevention. School safety can be an issue that unites communities and schools. The attention now directed toward violence in the schools provides school psychologists our opportunity to successfully advocate for prevention programs many of us have read about, discussed, and hoped for over the past few decades.

The American Psychological Association (1993) outlined the origins of youth violence: child abuse, ineffective parenting, violence in the home, media violence, poverty, prejudice, gun access, and substance abuse. School psychologists can advocate at the local, state, and national level for policies and programs that address these origins and specifically programs that prevent the leading causes of death for children, which are accidents, homicides, and suicide. The authors commented in previous editions of *Best Practices* that we hoped that our nation was on the road to safer schools. The recent tragic shootings in schoolyards across the country have made us all wonder what else can be done. There appear to be few if any legislated changes that address any of the origins of youth violence. The philosopher Dac commented, "The future is the past in preparation." School psychologists must learn from these tragic events, increase their skill base in the area of crisis intervention, and advocate for prevention programs.

REFERENCES

American Association of Suicidology. (1998) *Postvention guidelines for the schools: Suggestions for dealing with the aftermath of suicide in the schools* (2nd ed.). Washington, DC: Author.

American Psychological Association. (1993). *Violence and youth: Psychology's response. Volume I: Summary report of the American Psychological Association Commission on Violence and Youth.* Washington, DC: Author.

American Red Cross. (1999). *Family disaster plan and personal survival guide.* Washington, DC: Author.

Brooks, B., & Seigel, P. (1996) *The scared child: Helping kids overcome traumatic events.*

Caplan, J. (1964). *Principles of preventive psychiatry.* New York: Basic Books.

Cohen, R. E. (1990). Post disaster mobilization and crisis counseling: Guidelines and techniques for developing crisis-oriented services for disaster victims. In A. R. Roberts (Ed.), *Crisis intervention handbook: Assessment, treatment and research* (pp. 279–299). Belmont, CA: Wadsworth.

Dwyer, K., Osher, D., & Warger, C. (1998), *Early warning, timely response: A guide to safe schools.* Washington DC: U.S. Department of Education.

Dwyer, K., Osher, D. & Warger, C. (2000) *Safeguarding our children: An action guide.* Washington DC: U.S. Department of Education.

Elliott, D. S., Hamburg, B.A., & Williams, K. R. (1998) (Eds.), *Violence in American Schools.* New York: Cambridge University Press.

Elliott, D. S., & Mihalic, S. (1997). *Blueprints for violence prevention and reduction: The identification and documentation of successful programs.* Boulder, CO: Center for the Study and Prevention of Violence.

Eth, S., & Pynoos, R. S. (1985). Developmental perspective on psychic trauma in childhood. In C. R. Figley (Ed.), *Trauma and its wake.* New York: Brunner/Mazel.

Faberow, N., & Gordon, N. (1981). *Manual for child health workers in major disasters* (DHHS Publication No. [ADM] 81–1071). Washington, DC: U.S. Government Printing Office.

Feinberg, T. (1998, March 22). *NASP/NEAT and NOVA: A crisis partnership that really works.* Bethesda, MD: National Association of School Psychologists. Available online http://www.nasponline.org/office/cq/CQ265NASPNEAT.htm.

Goldstein, A. P., & Conoley, J. C. (1997). Student aggression: current status. In

A. P. Goldstein, & J. C. Conoley (Eds.), *School violence intervention: A practical handbook.* New York: Guilford.

Gottfredson, D. C. (1997). School-based crime prevention. In L. W. Sherman, D. C. Gottfredson, D. MacKenzie, J.

Eck, P. Reuter, & S. Bushway (Eds.), *Preventing crime: what works, what doesn't, what's promising: A report to the United States Congress*. Washington, DC: U.S. Department of Justice, National Institute of Justice.

Guerra, N. G., & Williams, K. R. (1996). *A program planning guide for youth violence prevention: A risk-focused approach*, Boulder, CO: Institute of Behavioral Science.

Hudley, C. (1994). Perceptions of intentionality, feelings of anger, and reactive aggression. In M. Furlong & D. Smith (Eds.), *Anger, hostility and aggression: assessment prevention and intervention strategies for youth*. Brandon, VT: Clinical Psychology.

Larson, J. C. (1994). Violence prevention in the schools: A review of selected programs and procedures. *School Psychology Review, 23*, 151–164.

Lazarus, P. J., & Howard, P. (1993). Hurricane Andrew and the aftermath: The state crisis response team—A humble and necessary beginning. *Communiqué, 21*(6), 18–20.

Lieberman, R. (1998, Fall). Schoolyard tragedies: Coping with the aftermath. *School Safety*, 14–16.

Loeber, R., & Farrington, D. P. (Eds.). (1998). *Serious and violent juvenile offenders: Risk factors and successful interventions*. Thousand Oaks, CA: Sage.

National Association of School Psychologists. (1992). *Helping children grow up in the 90's: A resource book for parents and teachers*. Silver Spring, MD: Author.

National Center for Education Statistics. (1998). *Public school principal survey on safe, disciplined and drug-free schools*. Washington, DC: U.S. Department of Education.

National Education Association. (1999) *Crisis communications guide and toolkit.*Washington, DC: Author.

National Organization for Victim Assistance. (1997). *Community crisis response team training manual*(2nd ed.). Washington, DC: Author.

Osofsky, J. D. (Ed.). (1997). *Children in a violent society*. New York: Guilford.

Peterson, S., & Straub, R. (1992). *School crisis survival guide*. West Nyack, NY: Center for Applied Research in Education.

Pitcher, G. D., & Poland, S. (1992). *Crisis intervention in the schools*. New York: Guilford.

Poland, S. (2000). When death affects your school: A practical guide for administrators. *Inside School Safety, 5*(3), 1–5.

Poland, S., & McCormick, J. (1999). *Coping with crisis: A resource for schools, parents and communities*. Longmont, CO: Sopris West.

Poland, S., & McCormick, J. (2000). *Coping with crisis: A quick reference guide*. Longmont, CO: Sopris West.

Ruof, S., & Harris, J. (1988). How to select, train, and supervise a crisis team. *Communiqué, 17*(4), 19.

Schoenfeld, M. (1993). *Crisis response team: Lessening the aftermath*. Foresthill, CA: Author.

Slaikeu, K. (1990). *Crisis intervention: A handbook for practice and research* (2nd ed.) Boston: Allyn & Bacon.

Stark, E., and Flitcraft, A. (1988). Violence among intimates. In V. B. Van Hasett (Ed.), *Handbook of family violence*. New York: Plenum.

Wong, M. (2000, April). Critical incident stress debriefing: Supporting those who provide support. *National School Safety Center Newsletter*, 1–2.

Zenere, F. (1998, November). NASP/NEAT community crisis response. *Communiqué, 27*(3), 38–39.

ANNOTATED BIBLIOGRAPHY

Brock, S., Lazarus, P., & Jimerson, S. (in press). *Best practices in crisis prevention and intervention*. Bethesda, MD: National Association of School Psychologists.
This is an extremely comprehensive and timely work that covers all aspects of this topic. Many of the authors share their firsthand experience in the aftermath of tragedies at the local, state, and national level. An excellent theoretical model is provided and a wealth of practical strategies.

Canter, A. S., & Carroll, S. A. (Eds.) (1998) *Crisis Prevention and Response: A Collection of NASP Resources.* Bethesda, MD: National Association of School Psychologists.
The authors have compiled a variety of resources that are very useful to NASP members. Contained in this resource are handouts on a wide range of topics and emphasizing key intervention principles.

Dwyer, K., Osher, D., & Warger, C. (1998), *Early warning, timely response: A guide to safe schools.* Washington DC: U.S. Department of Education.
This is a guide developed in collaboration with the U.S. Department of Justice, the U.S. Department of Education, the Center for Effective Collaboration and Practice of the American Institutes for Research to help educators, parents, and community leaders prevent school violence. This guide provides schools with a foundation of principles for recognizing signs of trouble that can lead to violent or destructive behavior.

Dwyer, K., Osher, D., & Warger, C. (2000) *Safeguarding our children: An action guide.* Washington, DC: U.S. Department of Education.
Offers schools specific strategies and programs that have proven effective in getting children the help they need before they become disruptive, disrespectful, or hurtful to themselves or others. This new booklet affirms that teamwork among educators, mental health professionals, parents, students, and community groups and organizations is critical to preventing violent school tragedies. An underlying theme of the publication is the importance of every child being known well by at least one adult. An important balance must be found between responding to a child's early warning signs and doing harm by labeling or over-reacting.

National Educational Association. (1999) *Crisis communications guide & toolkit.* Washington, DC: Author.
There are four very practical, reader friendly volumes including (a) Being Prepared-Before a Crisis, (b) Being Responsive-During a Crisis, (c) Being Diligent-Moving Beyond Crisis, and (d) Hands on Assistance-Tools for Educators. These volumes are useful and practical for principals, counselors, school psychologists, or teachers.

Poland, S., & McCormick, J. (1999) *Coping with Crisis: A resource for schools, parents, and communities.* Longmont, CO: Sopris West.
This comprehensive 460 page book provides step-by-step guidelines for developing both school and community crisis teams. Specific roles for crisis team members are outlined including prevention, intervention, and long-term follow-up assistance. The authors utilize case studies of school shootings in Paducah, Kentucky, and Jonesboro, Arkansas, to illustrate key intervention points. How to manage extensive media coverage is also outlined. Includes a section that discusses the role of parents and community agencies.

Poland, S., & McCormick, J. (2000) *Coping with Crisis: A quick reference guide.*Longmont, CO: Sopris West.
This book provides an excellent summary of all the key points included in the 1999 book to assist schools, communities, and parents not only to cope with crisis but also to organize crisis teams. This book contains many resources for additional information on school safety.

68 Best Practices in School Violence Prevention

Jim Larson
University of Wisconsin-Whitewater

Douglas C. Smith
University of Hawaii

Michael J. Furlong
University of California, Santa Barbara

OVERVIEW

When it comes to evaluating the safety of school campuses and the prevalence of violence-related behaviors at school sites, there are two fundamental truths. First, early pronouncements about schools being "battle zones" or experiencing an epidemic of violence are now generally acknowledged as being alarmist assertions that are not reflective of the day-to-day reality of America's schools. Second, no matter how infrequently it occurs, school violence rightly will always be a matter of concern to both educators and the public. *Phi Delta Kappa* regularly polls the public regarding its attitudes about schools and found that school safety and discipline matters have been the public's top concern about public education for several years (29% of the general public thought that safety matters were school's biggest concern compared to 8% of public school teachers (Langdon & Vesper, 2000)). Despite heightened public concern regarding school violence, recent empirical studies have generally found relatively low levels of risk for serious harm in school settings when compared to other social settings (Brooks, Schiraldi, & Ziedenberg, 2000; Hyman & Perone, 1998; Morrison, Furlong, & Morrison, 1994). Brooks et al. (2000), for example, reported that the odds of a student dying at school was 1 in 2 million during the 1998–1999 school year (which includes the deaths at Columbine high school). Despite this low relative risk level, 71% of the general public believed that a school shooting was "likely" to occur in their community (Brooks et al., 2000).

Against this backdrop of heightened concern about school violence, some investigations are now giving rise to questions about the perception that America's youth are more likely than ever to be prone to extreme violence. In a recent report, the U.S. Department of Justice (2000), in its *Juvenile Justice Bulletin*, presented evidence that dire predictions made in the early 1990s of an uncontrolled wave of predatory juvenile crime has not materialized. What then is the source of the public's concern about youth violence? In part it may be based on the sharp increase in juvenile violent crime arrests in the late 1980s and early 1990s and the high-profile shootings that have recently occurred on school campuses. These are indisputable and undesirable facts. However, the federal government has also conducted high-quality crime victimization surveys since 1973 that provide alternative conclusions. These self-report data indicate that, with the exception of the early 1990s, youth ages 10–17 have reported relatively stable levels of violent crime victimization (these data reflect the reality that not all crimes are reported and of those reported not all are prosecuted). The unexpected conclusion was that, "...despite a temporary increase (in the early 1990s), the rate of serious juvenile offending as of the mid-1990s was comparable to that of a generation ago" (U.S. Department of Justice, 2000, p. 2). Given these patterns of public opinion and empirical research, it is reasonable to conclude that the general public, policy makers, and even some educators and parents have incomplete information about the prevalence and actual risk potential of violence involving school-aged youth. It is also likely that public opinion is driven by a phenomenon known as the availability heuristic, wherein judgments (often erroneous) regarding events and outcomes are based on the availability of recent events in memory (i.e., believing that air travel is becoming unsafe after a recent crash).

Although the data do not support the belief that school violence is increasing, we do not minimize the fear or importance of focusing on violence in the schools. Indeed, with regard to the second truth, expectations that schools should be places of safety, security, and nurturance are fundamental to American educational principles. The desire to create schools that help children to flourish will always mean that attention should be given to evaluating and considering ways to ensure that students are not harmed when attending school or participating in school-sponsored events. Creating safe schools that are also conducive to learning is, in fact, one of America's primary educational objectives (National Education Goals Panel, 1999), and given its status as a fundamental educational goal, concerted efforts have been made in recent years to monitor the prevalence of school violence. We now turn our attention to a brief description of what these surveillance efforts have found.

PREVALENCE OF SCHOOL VIOLENCE

Heightened interest in school violence has motivated investigators to design better instruments to understand its prevalence and patterns. There are some excellent regional data available (e.g., Furlong, Morrison, Bates, & Chung, 1998; Cornell & Loper, 1998) but the Centers for Disease Control's *Youth Risk Behavior Surveillance Survey* (YRBS) (Brener, Simon, Krug, & Lowrey, 1999) is the most widely cited source of prevalence information about school violence-related behaviors and experiences. The YRBS is an epidemiological instrument designed to solicit self-report information from adolescents regarding their involvement in health-risk behaviors including violence-related behaviors and injury-related incidents on school campuses. The YRBS is administered to a random sample of students who are representative of the U.S. school-age population. The most comprehensive questions about school violence were included in the 1993, 1995, and 1997 surveys and provided high-quality estimates of the prevalence of school violence and related behaviors. Given the space limitations of this chapter, we have highlighted salient YRBS patterns and trends along with work by Stephens (2000) exemplifying the national prevalence of school violence in Table 1.

There are several notable trends in school violence-related behaviors. First, since 1992, the number of school-associated deaths (all deaths at school or at school-related events, including suicides and homicides committed by adults) has decreased by more than 50%. Second, fights and weapon possession at school have declined, and their prevalence is higher in the community than on school campuses. Third, males and younger high school students report higher rates of fights and weapon possession at school. Fourth, African-American and Hispanic students tend to report higher rates of weapon possession and fights than do European-American students. Finally, self-reported crime victimization at school does not vary by community urbanization, although urban-school students reported higher rates of gang presence on their campuses. School psychologists who are interested in a closer inspection of these trends will find that the website for the annual school safety report produced by the U.S. federal government provides a comprehensive compilation of school violence information (U.S. Department of Education and U.S. Department of Justice, 1999).

BASIC CONSIDERATIONS

School violence prevention as a meaningful component of every school psychologist's role and function begins with the development of the appropriate competencies. What is it that school psychologists need to "know and be able to do" to be effective in the delivery of these services? At the pre-service level, training content is guided by (a) survey feedback from practitioners, (b) the idiosyncratic preferences and expertise of individual university faculty members, and (c)

Table 1. Prevalence and trends of selected school-site violence-related behaviors and experiences

Violence-related behaviors	*Findings and trends*	*Comment*
School-associated violent deaths are declining (Stephens, 2000)	52.7% decrease from 1992 to 1993 (55 deaths) (first year data available) through 1998–1999 (26 deaths).	This includes suicides and all violence-related deaths on school campuses regardless of the day or time of act. A number of these acts involved adult-generated behaviors (e.g., spouse shooting their teacher-spouse on the school campus).
Physical fights on school property are declining (YRBS; Brener et al., 1999)	Physical fights on school property in past 12 months have declined by 8.6%; 1993: 16.2%; 1995: 15.5%; 1997: 14.8%.	Rates by gender, racial/ethnic identification, and grade level have all been stable or decreasing. Hispanics reported a 6.1% increase in physical fights at school from1993 to 1997.
Possession of any weapon on school property is declining (YRBS; Brener et al., 1999)	Any weapon possession in past 30 days has declined by 28.0%; 1993: 11.8%; 1995: 9.8%; 1997: 8.5%.	Rates by gender, racial/ethnic identification, and grade level have decreased. Weapon possession at school is down for black males (38.7% decrease) and white males (28.4% decrease).
Weapons are carried more often in the community than on school property (YRBS; Brener et al., 1999)	Weapons are carried 2.2 times more often in the community when compared with the school campus; carried in community, 18.3%; carried at school, 8.5%.	Weapon possession in the community and at school has declined steadily since1991. Youths are exposed to more violence-related behaviors and experiences in the community than at school.
Level of concern about school safety is low and stable (YRBS; Brener et al., 1999)	About 1 in 25 students report they stayed home in the previous 30 days because of safety concerns at school and/or going to/from school.	Research has shown that concern about safety at school is not prevalent (Furlong et al., 1997).
Males are most involved in school-associated violence (YRBS 1997 survey, Kaan et al., 1999)	Physical fight on school property in past 12 months: 20% males versus 8.6% females. Any weapon possession in past 30 days: 12.5% males versus 3.7% females.	School violence surveys have focused on overt physical behaviors and have not attended to patterns of behavior and aggression that might be more common among females (e.g., relational aggression).
Violent behaviors vary by grade level (YRBS 1997 survey; Kaan et al., 1999)	Physical fight on school property in past 12 months: ninth grade, 21.3%; tenth grade, 17.0%; eleventh grade, 12.5%; twelfth grade, 9.5%. Any weapon possession in past 30 days: ninth grade, 10.2%; tenth grade, 7.7%; eleventh grade, 9.4%; twelfth grade, 7.0%.	It is generally thought that violence-related behaviors decline with age because of the students' increased maturity and because high-risk youths are more likely to drop out, be expelled, or enroll in alternative school settings.

the mandates of state and national certification and accreditation bodies (Curtis & Batsche, 1991). Recent surveys have obtained information on school violence prevention as a continuing education and pre-service training need. When school violence was defined as "verbal taunting, bullying, sexual and ethnic harassment, gun possession, and more serious forms of physical assault," Olsen, Larson, and Busse (2000) found that, of 221 National Association of School Psychologists (NASP) members, 85% indicated that these issues had emerged as prevention/intervention needs in their districts. Comparatively, Furlong et al. (1996) found that 85.4% of school psychologists indicated that they had received no training in school violence and only 26.8% felt prepared to address the issues. Not surprisingly, the overwhelming percentage of school psychologists endorsed the need for pre-service and continuing education in the area of violence prevention and intervention (Furlong et al., 1996; Larson, 1993; Olsen et al., 2000). The perception of this need is apparently matched by institutions that train at the specialist level. In a survey of 90 school psychology programs, 72% of the respondents agreed or agreed with reservation on the need to provide discrete pre-service education in the area of school violence prevention and 49% indicated that it was already required course work (Larson & Busse, 1998).

NASP guides the content of accredited pre-service training through its *Standards for Training and Field Placement Programs in Psychology* (National Association of School Psychologists, 2000). These most recent standards provide improved latitude for training programs to integrate the necessary practice competencies in school violence prevention. It remains for program faculty to plan internally and work collaboratively with state licensing agencies so that the appropriate competencies can become a part of the general curriculum, although in some states, such as California, the state credentialing agency now mandates specific school safety training standards. Table 2 provides an example of possible school violence training competencies.

Whereas surveys indicate practitioners reported a sense of preparation inadequacy related to the delivery of service in the area of school violence prevention (e.g., Furlong et al., 1996), it can be argued that the gap between training and useful competence is narrower than it may appear. School psychologists, with their current problem-solving orientation and training in assessment, consultation, direct intervention, and program evaluation are well situated to

Table 2. Suggested pre-service training competencies

Domain of training	*Knowledge and practice competencies*
Data-based decision making and accountability	• Construction, implementation and interpretation of local needs assessments • Early screening for children at risk • Threat and suicide assessment • Functional assessment of aggressive behavior
Interpersonal communication, collaboration, and consultation	• Design and leadership skills on school safety collaborative teams
Effective instruction and development of cognitive/academic skills	• Methodologies for increasing academic engaged time to reduce disruptive behavior problems • Designing and monitoring effective alternative instructional settings for high risk students
Socialization and development of life competencies	• Understanding the development of aggressive antisocial behavior • Conflict resolution and social problem-solving methodologies • Small group and individual anger and aggression management skills training • Bully prevention methodologies
School and system structure, organization, and climate	• Organizational development and systems theory to facilitate development of safe schools policies
Prevention, crisis intervention, and mental health	• Primary, secondary, and tertiary prevention as applied to school violence • Violence-related crisis management, including victim support
Home/school/community collaboration	• Parent management training methodologies • Community coalition models for violence prevention
Research and program evaluation	• Evaluation of school violence prevention/intervention at system, school, group, and individual levels • Determining empirically supported prevention/ intervention programs

begin the process of assuming these service delivery obligations. What it means to "understand the issues associated with school violence" subsumes both an array of historically problematic concerns with which most school psychologists have training and skill as well as less familiar, more focused areas. For many practitioners, functional assessment of anger-related student aggression, needs assessment design, classroom/school-wide discipline procedures, and crisis management may be accustomed practice areas, whereas threat assessment and student profiling, primary and secondary prevention procedures, victim support, and school/community coalition building may be comparatively new ground. Although further content and process training in specific violence prevention skills may be needed, most practitioners should possess the baseline training that can be generalized to present needs. The following case example demonstrates the application of traditional professional skills to the implementation of school violence prevention efforts.

CASE EXAMPLE OF APPLYING TRADITIONAL PROFESSIONAL SKILLS TO PREVENT SCHOOL VIOLENCE

At the onset of the school shootings that occurred in the late 1990s and following a series of highly publicized local incidents, the school psychologists of a medium-sized ethnically diverse Midwestern community came together in the fall of the year 1997 to brainstorm possible service delivery options. Whereas each building in the district had or was developing a school safety plan, the school psychologists were concerned with the lack of data-based decision making that was going into the process. Consequently, a decision was made to design and complete a district needs assessment that would provide localized data to each building.

The first step in the initial phase of the project was to secure support from the district administration. A formal presentation, which included a rationale and the proposed procedure, was provided to middle-level program directors. Once support was secured at this level, a full presentation to the Board of Education was made. The Board subsequently adopted school safety as one of the numerous district goals, and the Office of School Psychologists was designated to accomplish the needs assessment.

A decision was made to survey all students in grades 5–12, all teachers and support staff, and a random number of parents, stratified by school. A literature review was completed, and sample survey items were gathered. The school psychologists met over the course of the first semester to refine the survey items. Pilot surveys were constructed, and review copies were sent to a random selection of administrators, teachers, and parents. The reviewers were requested to critique the scale and provide constructive suggestions. The student portion of the survey was a revision of an instrument used previously in a larger urban setting within the state. Specific survey items were modified as a result of feedback from the reviewers.

Surveys were mailed to the randomly selected parents from each school during the late spring. Survey questions were translated for both the Spanish-speaking and Southeast Asian parents who resided in the community. The district administration approved a negative consent procedure, and students, teachers, and support staff completed the survey during a designated 1-week period. Surveys of questionable validity (e.g., clearly patterned or negative response sets) were set aside. By using a popular statistical computer package, descriptive data were completed for each item specific to the parent, student, teacher, and support staff survey versions and localized by building.

By using these local data, the school psychologists were able to function as more effective consultants on their building school safety teams. Among other data, the survey results indicated that despite both national and local high profile school violence incidents, the overwhelming concern across responders was for dimensionally less violent safety issues, such as bullying and harassment. Guided by the survey, the school safety teams utilized a problem-solving framework that the school psychologists had developed to create action plans for each building. Along with facilitating this problem-solving process, the school psychologists helped the building personnel to understand the need for empirically validated prevention/ intervention programs and to design necessary program evaluation protocols (see Berg, Berg, Sutkiewicz, Koras, Schmal, & Larson, 1998).

BEST PRACTICES

Unlike more traditional, historically secure areas of professional practice, school violence prevention is still a comparatively fluid and newly emergent service delivery option. Whereas widespread needs for services at the district level have been identified among school psychologists, training programs differ widely in their efforts at pre-service preparation. Consequently, practitioners seeking to address school violence issues are best served by linking service delivery in this newer area to the more familiar and well-established framework of collaborative problem solving (see Table 3). The remainder of this chapter will emphasize that effective school violence prevention is really little more than the exercise of traditionally established skills—assessment, consultation, intervention, and program evaluation—into a more selective, problem-solving focus.

Step 1: Problem Identification

This initial step includes the two major tasks of creating an organizational structure and identifying needs and concerns through assessment. Central to the potential effectiveness of any school-based violence prevention effort is its strategic location within a conceptually sound organizational framework. Too often, well-meaning efforts are seen to be "floating," independent of a secure, research-supported rationale for implementation. Aggressive publishers hawk their wares, and nervous schools systems start adding "programs" to meet public concerns; that is, an anger management program here, a conflict resolution classroom curriculum there, and so on. Such patchwork efforts may have a certain degree of face validity and offer political cover for those who seek it, but seldom result in positive cost-benefit outcomes for the district or the children it serves (Webster, 1993; Wilson-Brewer, Cohen, O'Donnell, & Goodman, 1991). A critical and natural role for school psychologists, therefore, is to use their training in collaborative and organizational consultation to bring order and focus to this process.

There are three tiers of organization to consider: community, district, and building (see Table 4). There are no data attesting to the strength of beginning at one level over beginning at another, or to the impact of a building-level policy without district or community policies. There are, however, obvious political advantages of obtaining higher level support before embarking at the building level, not to mention possible financial advantages. Nonetheless, there are no hard and fast rules, and school psychol-

Table 3. Problem-solving process in school violence prevention planning

Step 1: Problem identification
- Gather data on current climate and perceptions of school safety from multiple sources and settings.
- Utilize needs assessment surveys, focus groups, and extant discipline and police records.

Step 2: Problem analysis
- Analyze data and communicate findings to stakeholders.
- Facilitate setting of priorities and goals based on data.
- Construct hypotheses to explain current problem(s).

Step 3: Problem response proposals
- Determine primary, secondary, and tertiary prevention responses based on data and empirical research.
- Match prevention strategies to budget and staff capacities for implementation.
- Determine staff training requirements and provide as necessary.
- Develop dimensional rubrics and benchmarks for goal attainment.

Step 4: Response implementation
- Devise evaluation and progress monitoring protocols.
- Implement prevention strategies with high treatment integrity.
- Monitor and adjust strategies for increased effectiveness.

Step 5: Evaluation of prevention strategies
- Monitor goal attainment benchmarks for authentic change.
- Assess social validity: How do the stakeholders perceive the prevention effort?
- Continue, adjust, or discontinue prevention effort.

ogists are advised to consider their own unique circumstances.

Guerra and Williams (1996) identified two primary approaches to organizing community violence prevention efforts: Top-Down Comprehensive Planning and Grassroots Neighborhood Mobilization. The Top-Down model involves the formation of a local task force or planning committee consisting of key community leaders (see Table 4.) The Grassroots model arises out of the concern of local citizens, and leadership emerges out of those efforts rather than from an existing hierarchy. Once formed from either approach, this group is charged with developing a comprehensive strategy to address youth violence through (a) mobilization of community involvement; (b) determining target groups from primary, secondary, and tertiary prevention perspective; (c) assessing current resources and programs; (d) fostering coordination of activities across agencies; and (e) including evaluation components (Guerra & Williams, 1996).

The second and third tiers of organization are at the school district and building levels, and it is here that school psychologists can emerge as a powerful influence in the process. Knoff (1995) addressed the need for school psychologists to understand strategic planning processes and organizational change and urged practitioners to proceed in a systematic, problem-solving fashion. However, in the atmosphere of citizen concern and crisis mentality that currently surrounds the issue of school violence, it is common for the prevention impetus to originate reactively as a hurriedly devised local school board mandate or "safe schools" strategic goal. Whereas this knee-jerk method is not ideal from a strategic planning perspective, such a top-down authorization does serve to create the first stage of the problem-solving process within which school psychologists can use their organizational consultation skills (e.g., Curtis & Stollar, 1996) to help the district develop and implement a systematic response. (Although the remainder of this section will focus on planning for violence prevention at the building level, the problem-solving process is equivalent at the district level.)

In the organizational phase of this step, the school psychologist uses his or her skills in team building and collaborative consultation to create a building School Safety Planning Team (SSPT; Table 4). The SSPT can be formed out of an existing group, such as a school crisis team, and should have wide representation and strong vocal administrative support. This team is charged with moving beyond crisis readiness and response to broad-scale planning for the full range of psychological and physical safety concerns. Importantly, this team must look beyond media-fueled fears about armed intruders and concentrate its efforts on the site-specific needs across the spectrum of safety for all of the students and staff in their building. Prevention planning exclusively focused to offset the potential for a multiple homicide is quite different from planning designed to address imminently more likely events.

The initial task for the SSPT involves defining the problem, and school psychologists can apply skills in data-based assessment to assist in the design and analysis of a comprehensive needs assessment. The results will generate important information from which to begin planning as well as provide a pre-intervention baseline to assist in ongoing program evalua-

Table 4. Three-tier school violence prevention organizational structure

Community organization
- School district superintendent or designee
- School board representative
- Educational staff representative(s)
- Law enforcement
- Business community
- Clergy
- Medical community
- Mental health community
- Municipal government
- Juvenile justice
- Media
- Parents and students

School district task force
- School district superintendent or designee
- Grade level administrator representatives
- Instructional staff representatives
- Supportive services representative
- School security representative
- Classified staff representative
- Parent representatives
- Student representatives

Building-level school safety planning team
- Principal or vice-principal
- Grade level/disability teacher representatives
- Support services representatives
- Students (age appropriate)
- Parents
- Classified staff representative

tion. School violence prevalence studies have utility for forming broad national and regional public policy, but are not as helpful when it comes to helping a specific district or school to evaluate the most pressing needs on *their* school campuses. To plan and implement a school violence prevention program effectively, each school needs to conduct an assessment that is tailored to specific needs of the problem-solving approach. A fundamental requisite of effective problem solving is to clearly identify the client or the primary unit of intervention. As far as school violence is concerned, the overwhelming focus has tended to be on individual students and efforts to reduce their proneness to violence. It is our view, however, that comprehensive school violence prevention programs should include components that examine individual (i.e., student), specific strategies, classroom, and campus-wide influences.

Information should be gathered that can be used for assessing school-wide trends in violence-related behaviors. Such information is initially sought for needs assessment purposes and later provides feedback about the patterns, trends, and correlates of violence-related behaviors. The traditional mechanism used to gather this type of information is self-report surveys of either or both students and staff. Discipline data and assessing the campus settings where reported violence occurs can be useful to augment the validity of self-report data. From a problem-solving perspective, contextual information is important to gather because strategies to prevent or inhibit violent behavior on campus may include modification of setting variables such as the school's physical plant and supervision patterns. Table 5 shows specific instruments and resources that are readily available and can be used as part of an environmental assessment procedure. However, the planning team may prefer instead to develop its own instrument for needs assessment, and school psychologists can provide valuable consultation on assessment domains and item construction.

Understanding the dynamics of school violence also requires obtaining information about how consistently school-wide behavior management and disciplinary practices are being followed. A problem-solving approach to violence prevention will also seek to understand the manner in which student behavior is being reinforced and consequented in the classroom. Strategies developed as part of the problem-solving process may often include elements to change naturally occurring reinforcement patterns.

Table 5. Instruments for assessing the prevalence of school-site violence-related behaviors for needs assessments and program evaluations

Instrument	*Description*	*Source*
Youth Risk Behavior Surveillance Survey	• Used in biennial national, state, and city surveys since 1991. Limited school violence items, but broad coverage of related risk behaviors.	• Centers for Disease Control Brener et al. (1999) (www.cdcp.org). Public domain, no cost.
California Healthy Kids Survey	• Modules provide in-depth coverage of each area, including a safe school module. Includes a detailed resilience module.	• California Department of Education and WestEd (www.wested.org/hks). Questionnaires by module are available at the web site.
California School Climate and Safety Survey	• Includes 102 items assessing school climate and victimization at school. Elementary and secondary versions.	• University of California Santa Barbara (see Furlong et al., 1997) www.education.ucsb.edu/~schpsych).
Multidimensional School Anger Inventory	• 36-item instrument that assesses anger, hostility, and aggression in school context.	• Smith et al. (1998) and Furlong and Smith (1998).
Problem Behavior Frequency Scale	• Compilation of items from surveys such as the YRBS. Inquires about 26 problem behaviors related to drug use, delinquency, and aggression.	• Virginia Commonwealth University Farrell et al. (2000).
Approaches to Assessing Violence Among Youth	• In-depth description of instruments for violence-related behaviors and attitudes. Includes reviews of teacher, parent, and peer instruments.	• Hamilton Fish Institute, George Washington University (www.hamfish.org) (Minogue, Kingery, & Murphy, 1999).

Step 2: Problem Analysis

Data from all sources are analyzed in this step, and the results shared with faculty, students, and the community. An important task for the SSPT is to communicate the results in a manner so that all of the stakeholders understand the problem in the most useful and effective fashion. School psychologists can assume leadership in this area by (a) assisting all parties to understand issues associated with the validity and reliability of surveys and other forms of gathered data, (b) developing data-based conclusions from the information gathered, and (c) ensuring communication of the findings to students and other stakeholders in a developmentally and linguistically sensitive manner.

The task of the SSPT turns now to building a prevention plan based on the knowledge acquired through the needs assessment process. The development of hypotheses linked to the identified problems and concerns is a critical next step, and school psychologists should find this very similar to generating hypotheses for individually based assessment (e.g., Batsche & Knoff, 1995). Looking to the data, the team develops hypotheses or hunches that attempt to explain problems in operational terms. In the previous case example, the problem analysis process revealed that the locale with the highest percentage of victimization was the outside grounds during lunch periods. In addition, poorly trained supervision or an excessively high pupil-to-staff ratio was thought to be a factor contributing to this problem. The collection of needs assessment data led to a useful hypothesis because it was linked to data and offered directions for intervention that could be evaluated.

The final phase of this step involves setting priorities and outcome goals. Limited budgets, competing internal interests, vocal media, and other outside influences can all contribute to the need to approach this task with care and reason. If the school psychologist is not appropriately trained, then it may be helpful to work with an outside facilitator from a local university or consulting group to guide the stakeholders toward consensus and prepare them to take the next step of selecting desired prevention strategies.

Step 3: Problem Response Proposals

The collaborative consultation skills of the school psychologist continue in this step as the SSPT members consider options regarding how the building should address the identified needs. School psychologists can take steps to ensure that a systematic process of consensus-building around an integrated, multisystemic plan is followed as the team examines effective response options. A format such as the one exemplified in Table 6 can aid in this process.

Adapting a public health model, prevention and intervention strategies directed toward reducing violent and antisocial behavior in school settings can be loosely grouped into *primary*, *secondary*, and *tertiary* strategies. At the primary prevention level, *universal* interventions are concerned with providing students with information, strategies, and coping responses designed to prevent the occurrence of negative antisocial behaviors. Usually these programs target the general school audience or groups of students who have not yet manifested problem behaviors. At the secondary prevention level, *selected* intervention programs generally target students who are considered at-risk for violent behavior on the basis of social, familial, academic, or personal characteristics. Frequently, those students considered appropriate for secondary prevention programs have been identified on the basis of emerging patterns of low-level antisocial behavior in school settings. Finally, at the tertiary prevention level, *indicated* programs target students who are already manifesting significant problems in interacting appropriately with others or who have an established history of violent behavior.

Furlong, Pavelski, and Saxton (in press) provide a useful schemata for conceptualizing school-based violence prevention and intervention efforts based on the specific needs of students with regard to their degree of connectedness to the current school milieu. For the majority of students who are reasonably involved in school activities and view school as a positive social and learning experience, the primary task is to *reaffirm* or reinforce their already solid connections. Most primary violence prevention strategies are oriented toward reaffirming students' overall sense of connectedness to school and fostering more positive interpersonal relationships. Often, this goal is accomplished through the development of prosocial and positive coping skills. At a more intense level of need, some students require prevention and intervention services aimed toward helping them *reconnect* or strengthen weakened connections with school. Although those students may be peripherally involved in school, they

Table 6. School violence prevention framework: Sample

	Academic climate	*Primary prevention*	*Secondary prevention*	*Tertiary prevention*	*School discipline*	*Crisis/ security*
Vision or desired outcome	All teachers understand and practice academic engaged time principles.	"Second Step" is taught in all K–5 classrooms within 3 years.	All children are screened for high risk behaviors at school entry.	A wraparound team of school, community, and parents is established.	A Code of Conduct is collaboratively written and taught in all classes.	All staff have been trained in "early warning" behaviors.
Essential questions	Who will provide training? Can we get released time?	What is the training requirement? Is board funding available?	What instruments or procedures have been validated?	Who are the most important members?	What models are currently available?	Can NASP provide training or materials?
Activity: What needs to be done and who will do it?	Contact the university for references and consultation: Mr. Lee.	Call publisher for information: Mrs. Ortega.	Do internet search and contact local university: Ms. Tate.	Contact juvenile justice and mental health association: Mr. Mitchell.	Visit Kohl Elementary and gather facts: Ms. Kwan.	Contact NASP: Dr. Williams.
Evaluation	Current status data are gathered and evaluation design is selected.	Same	Same	Same	Same	Same

Note. Programs, procedures, and names are examples only.

exhibit characteristics and dispositions that place them at-risk for involvement in antisocial behavior. This category of need roughly corresponds to a secondary level of prevention. In addition to the need to acquire prosocial and positive coping skills, those students may benefit from interventions designed to reduce problematic behaviors and to manage negative emotions such as anger and frustration. A third group of students is largely disengaged from school and likely to have a lengthy history of aggressive and violent behavior. In those cases, the task is to *reconstruct* or, in some cases, initially construct positive relationships with school. Such students require more intensive intervention services to rebuild their very precarious connections with school. Those students require comprehensive and multifaceted strategies to reduce their incidence of antisocial behavior, challenge self-defeating attitudes and cognitions, and establish more positive connections with school, home, and community.

School violence prevention and intervention efforts, when viewed from the perspective of the diverse student needs hypothesized by Furlong et al. (in press) must necessarily be multifaceted and complex. Given the multiple pathways through which violent behavior at school may develop, it is also important to consider ecological factors such as family, community, cultural, and other factors that exist outside the school setting. When faced with the difficult task of designing a comprehensive approach to address violence, how do school psychologists choose from among the wide range of alternatives available to them? In part, the decision must be based on both practical and empirical considerations. In the next section we review evidence for best practices for school-based prevention and intervention efforts with specific attention to those strategies that have thus far received the most empirical support.

Best Practices: Primary Prevention

Primary prevention encompasses a host of efforts designed to intervene in a proactive manner with all students to head off the onset of negative developmental outcomes. Strategies may include universal screening of all children for behavioral risk status, education about diversity or alternative conflict resolution procedures, classroom instruction in problem-solving or self-control skills, or the modification of the environment to provide increased security. Walker et al. (1996) pointed that out that as part of a required universal prevention component, every school should have (a) a well-conceived school-wide discipline plan and (b) research-based effective schooling and teaching. School psychologists are aware of the importance of bonding, academic engagement, and increased self-discipline in the general adjustment of children in the school setting. The relationship of those factors to the prevention of school violence cannot be overstated.

One of the most common and potentially serious problems affecting the general school climate is that of bullying, and school psychologists who desire to initiate a primary prevention program are well-served to begin with this issue. Bullying has emerged as a concern not only in schools in the United States but worldwide (Limber & Nation, 1998). As a violence prevention strategy, efforts to curtail bullying most often involve school-wide policies and procedures as well as specific interventions targeting identified bullies and their victims. The primary objective of those programs is to create a school climate of tolerance and respect and to promote positive social interactions among students and adults at school. As defined by Olweus (1993), bullying involves intentional infliction of injury or discomfort on another person that occurs repeatedly over long periods and in which the victim is clearly weaker than the perpetrator. By using this fairly strict criteria, roughly 5–15% of students in U.S. schools are victims of bullying by other students. Boys are more often involved in physical attacks, both as bullies and as victims, whereas girls more typically engage in relational forms of bullying such as social isolation and rumor mongering (Whitney & Smith, 1993).

A best practices approach for bully prevention and intervention must necessarily involve a systems-wide approach that includes the bully, the victim, the school, the family, and the community. At the school level, efforts should include the development of a school-wide code of conduct with clear expectations for what constitutes appropriate and inappropriate social behavior. Batsche (1997) emphasized that students should play a major role in establishing such a code. Additionally, the school should make every effort to establish a climate of respect and mutuality extending from administrators to teachers to students. Such an atmosphere might be reflective of the school's mission statement and can be reinforced through appreciation and recognition of prosocial behaviors. At the family level, parents and their children can be invited to join the school in encouraging a low level of tolerance for bullying behavior. Parent participation in school-sponsored workshops, trainings, and discussion groups can be an important tool for gaining consensus about expectations for appropriate social behavior. Such parent-school partnerships can extend to the community as well.

As members of the SSPT, school psychologists should continue their efforts to encourage school support of empirically based programs and procedures. Whereas innovation and development is ongoing in the area of school-based primary prevention, five programs that have undergone evaluation and merit special attention are: (a) Bully Prevention Program (Olweus, 1993), (b) PeaceBuilders Program (see Embry et al., 1996), (c) Providing Alternative Thinking Strategies (see Greenberg & Kusche, 1998), (d) Resolving Conflict Creatively Program (see Aber et al., 1998), and (e) Second Step Violence Prevention Curriculum (see Grossman et al., 1997). Each of those programs uses teacher-presented curricula along with additional supports to create change in the manner in which all children resolve interpersonal conflict. Addressing needs at the primary/universal level may begin with an examination of the particulars of those five programs to determine if there is a match with the unique needs of the school.

Best Practices: Secondary Prevention

Secondary prevention efforts utilize selected interventions to target those students who have been identified as having multiple risk factors for possible later aggressive or anti-social behavior. Early childhood aggression and peer rejection are both comparatively stable and well-correlated with later antisocial behavior, so risk identification does not necessarily have to be a complex undertaking. Whereas multiple-gate screening and identification procedures are available and useful, school psychologists may find that a veteran teacher can be an invaluable source of highly reliable data in this regard.

Prevention efforts at the secondary/selected level typically involve behavioral self-control skills training in a group or individual format. School psychologists have the requisite training and skills to take the lead in organizing, implementing, and evaluating those programs. What are the essential elements of such efforts? Which students are most likely to benefit from what kinds of treatment? How might those programs be delivered? What is the optimal time frame? What steps must be undertaken to ensure maintenance and generalization of trained skills?

A recent review and meta-analysis of anger management programs for youth by Smith, Larson, DeBaryshe, and Salzman (2000) provides some direction for school psychologists considering such interventions. Although not all programs reviewed were school-based, a major conclusion was that anger management, as a general treatment strategy, is highly effective in reducing antisocial behaviors across several contexts. This conclusion is consistent with the findings of Derzon and Wilson (1999)who identified self-control techniques as among the most promising strategies for modifying students' physical and verbal aggression. In addition to supporting the overall efficacy of such programs, Smith et al. (2000) found that the most effective methods were multi-component interventions that include training in affective self-awareness and regulation, problem solving, and development of alternative means for expressing angry feelings. Those programs that included a strong cognitive component (e.g., problem solving, attribution retraining), appeared especially promising. Given the long-term stability of aggressive and antisocial behaviors, those programs that target younger children and include specific strategies to ensure maintenance and generalization are more likely to demonstrate lasting effects. Additionally, effective interventions should be relevant to a diverse group of students who differ according to such characteristics as gender and ethnicity as well as specific treatment needs.

As always, school psychologists should ensure that the selected skills training program has a strong empirical foundation; however, few well-validated programs exist. Given both the need and the importance of behavioral skills training, the lack of a variety of research-supported programs is disconcerting. Three programs, however, deserve attention and review by practitioners seeking to develop skills training within a multi-component prevention plan: (a) *Anger Coping Program* is a small group 18-session pull-out program for elementary-age students (see Lochman, Dunn, & Klimes-Dougan, 1993), (b) *Positive Adolescent Choices Training* is a culturally sensitive pull-out group for high risk African-American and other adolescents (see Yung & Hammond, 1998), and (c) *First Step to Success* is a promising program that addresses the emerging antisocial behavior of children just entering school in their kindergarten year (see Walker et al.,1996). The *First Step* program involves (a) a universal screening system to identify high-risk children, (b) a classroom-based intervention to teach adaptive behavior and foster effective school relationships, and (c) a parent training component.

Best Practices in Tertiary Prevention

In many schools there are students whose behavioral and emotional disabilities are so pronounced that it is often all the school can do day-to-day just to keep the problem from worsening. Those students frequently are beneficiaries of a variety of services in and out of the school setting in what has come to be called a "wraparound" organizational structure. Multiple supports and services are "wrapped around" the student and, in many cases, the family in an effort to prevent problems from advancing to a more serious level. At the tertiary level, prevention goals are principally a matter of maintaining current functioning strengths, with hopes for significant improvement of self-restraint skills. When explosive anger and aggression are predictable components of the student's behavior, then the SSPT is well advised to develop and monitor an intervention plan. Among the questions to be resolved by the team include:

1. Is there an existing IEP or other behavioral plan and how will the prevention plan interface?
2. Has a functional behavioral assessment been completed, analyzed, and the conclusion shared with appropriate individuals?
3. Is there a need for staff training, including the possibility of de-escalation techniques and restraint/transportation procedures?
4. Is the discipline plan designed to be proactive and educational and not purely reactive and punitive?
5. Is there a need for an alternative educational placement?

Best practices in this step call for comprehensive programs that involve schools, students, their families, and communities. Direct intervention programs should target self-control and regulation and should build social competence, particularly the ability to effectively resolve interpersonal conflict in nonaggressive and prosocial ways. Interventions should occur early, should draw upon developmental theory, and should be presented in culturally appropriate ways. School psychologists have a unique opportunity to use existing skills in consultation, coordination, and provision of direct services at primary, secondary, and tertiary prevention levels.

Step 4: Response Implementation

Whether through consultation or in direct treatment, school psychologists have long recognized the importance of treatment integrity in their work with pupils. In a similar manner, well-conceived, well-designed, but poorly implemented interventions can have disastrous effects on a school violence prevention effort. As teachers and other supportive services staff take on treatment-like roles and responsibilities, it becomes incumbent upon school psychologists to help these individuals to better understand the importance of treatment integrity.

A violence prevention curriculum that has shown promise when provided on a weekly basis is compromised when it is continually set aside in favor of some other "more pressing" curricular need. An anger management program with strong empirical support for an 18-session weekly agenda cannot be reduced to 12 sessions for the convenience of the school calendar with the expectation that anticipated skills will be observed. School psychologists can help support their colleagues in this area by (a) ensuring that the appropriate level of staff training and development has occurred prior to implementation, (b) providing a mini-inservice on the importance of treatment integrity, (c) offering assistance at the implementation level where possible, and/or (d) monitoring the treatment and providing feedback to the principal staff member(s).

The beginning of this step is the opportune time for treatment evaluation protocols to be designed. As data-based decision makers, school psychologists recognize the need to find empirical support for the effectiveness of any school-based program. As protocols for this undertaking are considered, it is important that formative and summative data from both quantitative and qualitative sources be considered. Whereas a complete discussion of the processes involved is beyond the scope of this chapter, three useful resources that school psychologists may have on hand include Bennett (1988), Illback, Zins, and Maher (1999), and Steege (this volume).

Step 5: Evaluation of Prevention Strategies

Ed Koch, when he was mayor of New York City, was fond of asking crowds at every gathering, "So, how am I doing?" Any school psychologist standing by probably replied, "Let's see your data!" Most school psychologists are aware of programs in their districts that "look good" or are otherwise received positively by the stakeholders, but for which there is no evidence that demonstrable positive change is occurring. It is no less so in violence prevention than in other aspects of service delivery that decisions about maintaining, modifying, or discontinuing programs or procedures need to be linked to the continual analysis of acquired data. Occasionally, this can be a politically or socially difficult task, especially when entrenched or popular programs are called on to show authentic outcomes, but answer they must. Few schools would continue a reading curriculum that failed to teach the skill; the same must be true for any aspect of the school violence prevention effort. The time is too short, the resources too limited, and the stakes are too high.

The evaluation protocols designed in the previous response implementation step carry over to this step and guide the SSPT as they monitor the plan. Moreover, seasoned practitioners know that school years tend to flow in "rhythms" of antecedent conditions; that is influences on behavior in April may be qualitatively different than those in December. Consequently, SSPT data analysis should take into consideration data from similar time periods in the previous year. Are the office discipline referrals lower than the similar period last year? Are the number of playground fights fewer than last year? Do the students self-report increased feelings of safety compared to a similar self-report in the previous year?

SUMMARY

The emergence of school psychology as a major force in national policy, research, program development, and service delivery in the area of school violence prevention has been one of the most significant and rapid changes in the profession over the past number of years. Isolated high-profile violence in the schools has caused educational staff in general and school psychology practitioners in particular to struggle with understanding myriad theoretical explanations and has forced them to wade through countless articles, books, conference presentations, and ubiquitous television specials and media hyperbole. Information, official policy, school board rules, and research on "what to do" have come forth at an almost dizzying pace.

School violence prevention involves understanding the multi-systemic pathways that influence the development and maintenance of violent behavior and applying effective prevention strategies. It involves a recognition that single-method approaches that, for instance, hypothesize and target within-child deficits or seek only to prevent a multiple homicide are inadequate. It involves instead a recognition that empirically based, multi-component, multi-level approaches rigorously applied and longitudinally maintained stand the best chances for success. And finally, it involves a sobering understanding that there is little a school can do to completely ensure that a committed individual will not be able to carry out his or her own plan of homicidal violence, yet a heartening realization that the likelihood is statistically very remote.

In this chapter we have attempted to frame the issue of violence prevention in a manner consistent with what practitioners are currently trained to "know and be able to do." At the core are the skills of data-based decision making and collaborative consultation, competencies that allow school psychologists to more accurately assess the needs of the school and to guide their colleagues through the use of a framework of empirically based decisions and research-supported interventions. We have emphasized that violence prevention activities need to be coordinated by a school-based team that possesses a clear understanding of the levels of prevention and can integrate the approaches to meet the needs of all students.

REFERENCES

Aber, J. L., Jones, S. M., Brown, J. L., Chaudry, N., & Samples, F. (1998). Resolving conflict creatively: Evaluating the effects of a school-based violence prevention program in neighborhood and classroom context. *Development and Psychopathology, 10*, 187–213.

Batsche, G. M. (1997). Bullying. In G. C. Bear, K. M. Minke, & A. Thomas (Eds.), *Children's needs, II: Development, problems and alternatives*. Bethesda, MD: National Association of School Psychologists.

Batsche, G. M., & Knoff, H. M. (1995). Best practices in linking assessment to intervention. In A. Thomas & J. Grimes (Eds.), *Best practices in school psychology III*. Bethesda, MD: National Association of School Psychologists.

Bennett, R. E. (1988). Evaluating the effectiveness of alternative educational delivery systems. In J. L. Graden, J. E. Zins, & M. J. Curtis (Eds.), *Alternative educational delivery systems* (pp. 513–524). Silver Spring, MD: National Association of School Psychologists.

Berg, R., Berg, A., Sutkiewicz, F., Koras, P., Schmal, C., & Larson, J. (1998). *Description of a procedural model for conducting a school safety needs assessment: A leadership role for school psychologists*. Poster session presented at the Annual Convention of the National Association of School Psychologists, Orlando, FL.

Brener, N. D., Simon, T. R., Krug, E. G., & Lowry, R. (1999). Recent trends in violence-related behaviors among high school students in the United States. *Journal of the American Medical Association, 282*, 440–446.

Brooks, K., Schiraldi, V., & Ziedenberg, J. (2000). *School house hype: Two years later*. Washington, DC and Covington, KY: Justice Policy Institute and Children's Law Center.

Cornell, D. G., & Loper, A. B. (1998). Assessment of violence and other high-risk behaviors with a school survey. *School Psychology Review, 27*, 317-330.

Curtis, M., & Batsche, G. M. (1991). Meeting the needs of children and families: Opportunities for school psychology training programs. *School Psychology Review, 20*, 565–576.

Curtis, M. J., & Stollar, S. A. (1996). Applying principles and practices of organizational change to school reform. *School Psychology Review, 25*, 409–417.

Derzon, J. H., & Wilson, S. J. (1999, November) An empirical review of school-based programs to reduce violence. Paper presented at the annual meeting of the American Society of Criminology, Toronto, CA.

Embry, D. E., Flannery, D., Vazsonyi, A., Powell, K., & Atha, H. (1996). PeaceBuilders: A theoretically driven, school-based model for early violence prevention. *American Journal of Preventive Medicine, 22*, 91–100.

Farrell, A. D., Ampy, L. A., Meyer, A. L. (1998). Identification and assessment of problematic interpersonal situations for urban adolescents. *Journal of Clinical Child Psychology. 27*, 293-305.

Furlong, M., Babinski, L., Poland, S., Munoz, J., & Boles, S. (1996). Factors associated with school psychologists' perception of campus violence. *Psychology in the Schools, 33*, 28–37.

Furlong, M., Casas, J. M., Corral, C., Chung, A., & Bates, M. (1997). Drugs and school violence. *Education and Treatment of Children, 20*, 263–280.

Furlong, M. J., Morrison, R., Bates. M., & Chung, A. (1998). School violence victimization in California: Grade, gender, and racial-ethnic group incidence patterns. *The California School Psychologist, 3*, 71-87.

Furlong, M. J., Pavelski, R., & Saxton, J. (in press) The prevention of school violence. In S. Brock, P. Lazarus, & S. Jimerson (Eds.), *Best practices in school crisis management*. Bethesda, MD: National Association of School Psychologists.

Furlong, M. J., & Smith, D. C. (1998). Raging Rick to tranquil Tom: An empirically based multidimensional anger typology for adolescent males. *Psychology in the Schools, 35*, 247-258.

Greenberg, M. T., & Kusche, C. A. (1998). *Promoting alternative thinking strategies*. Boulder, CO: Institute of Behavioral Science, University of Colorado.

Grossman, D. C., Neckerman, H. J., Koepsell, T. D., Liu, P-Y., Asher, K. N., Beland, K., Frey, K., & Rivera, F. P. (1997). Effectiveness of a violence prevention curriculum among children in elementary school. *Journal of the American Medical Association, 277*, 1605–1611.

Guerra, N. G., & Williams, K. R. (1996). *A program planning guide for youth violence prevention: A risk focused approach.* (Center Paper F-1491). Boulder, CO: Center for the Study and Prevention of Violence.

Hyman, I., & Perone, D. (1998). The other side of school violence: Educator policies and practices that may contribute to student misbehavior. *Journal of School Psychology, 36*, 7–27.

Illback, R. J., Zins, J. E., & Maher, C. A. (1999). Program planning and evaluation: Principles, procedures, and planned change. In C. R. Reynolds & T. B. Gutkin (Eds.), *The handbook of school psychology* (3rd ed.; pp. 907–932). New York: John Wiley.

Knoff, H. M. (1995). Facilitating school-based organizational change and strategic planning. In A. Thomas & J. Grimes (Eds.), *Best practices in school psychology III* (pp.239–252).Washington, DC: National Association of School Psychologists.

Langdon, C. A., & Vesper, N. (2000). The Sixth Phi Delta Kappa Poll of teacher's attitudes toward the public schools. *Phi Delta Kappan, 81*, 607–611.

Kann, L., Kinchen, S. A., Williams, B. I., Ross, J. G., Lowry, R., Hill, C. V., Grunbaun, J. A., & Kolbe, L. J. (2000). Youth risk behavior surveillance: United States, 1999. *Morbidity and Mortality Weekly Report, 49*, 1–96.

Larson, J. (1993). School psychologists' perception of physically aggressive student behavior as a referral concern in nonurban districts. *Psychology in the Schools, 30*, 345–350.

Larson, J., & Busse, R. T. (1998). Specialist-level preparation in school violence and youth gang intervention. *Psychology in the Schools, 35*, 373–379.

Limber, S. P., & Nation, M. (1998). *Bullying among school children.* Washington, DC: Office of Juvenile Justice and Delinquency Prevention.

Lochman, J. E., Dunn, S. E., & Klimes-Dougan, B. (1993). An intervention and consultation model from a social cognitive perspective: A description of the Anger Coping Program. *School Psychology Review, 22*(3), 458–471.

Minogue, N., Kingery, P., & Murphy, L. (1999). *Approaches to assessing violence among youth.* Rosslyn, VA: Hamilton Fish National Institute on School and Community Violence.

Morrison, G. M., Furlong, M. J., & Morrison, R. L. (1994). From school violence to school safety: Reframing the issue for school psychologists. *School Psychology Review, 23*, 236–256.

National Education Goals Panel. (1999). *The National Education Goals Panel report: Building a nation of learners.* Washington, DC: U.S. Government Printing Office.

National Association of School Psychologists. (2000). *Standards for training and field placement programs in school psychology.* Bethesda, MD: Author.

Olsen, K. A., Larson, J., & Busse, R. T. (2000, April). *Violence and substance abuse in the schools: A survey of school psychologist involvement in prevention and intervention.* Poster session presented at the Annual Convention of the National Association of School Psychologists, New Orleans, LA.

Olweus, D. (1993). *Bullying at school: What we know and what we can do.* Oxford: Blackwell.

Smith, D. C., Furlong, M. J., Bates, M., & Laughlin, J. D. (1998). Development of the Multidimensional School Anger Inventory for males. *Psychology in the Schools, 35*, 1–15.

Smith, D. C., Larson, J. D., DeBaryshe, B., & Salzman, M. (2000). Anger management for youth: What works and for whom? In D. S. Sandhu & C. Aspy (Eds.), *Violence in American schools: A practical guide for counselors.* Reston, VA: American Counseling Association.

Stephens, R. (2000). *School-associated violent deaths report.* Thousand Oaks, CA: National School Safety Center.

U.S. Departments of Education and Justice. (1999). *1999 annual report on school safety.* Washington, DC: Author (available at: http://www.safetyzone.org/pdf/schoolsafety2.pdf).

U.S. Department of Justice. (2000, February). Challenging the myths. 1999 national report series. *Juvenile Justice Bulletin.*

Walker, H. M., Horner, R. H., Sugai, G., Bullis, M., Sprague, J. R., Bricker, D., & Kaufman, M. J. (1996). Integrated approaches to preventing antisocial behavior patterns among school-age children and youth. *Journal of Emotional and Behavioral Disorders, 4*, 194–209.

Webster, D. (1993). The unconvincing case for school-based conflict resolution programs for adolescents. *Health Affairs, 12*, 126–140.

Whitney, I., & Smith, P. K. (1993). A survey of the nature and extent of bullying in junior/middle and secondary schools. *Educational Research, 35*, 3–25.

Wilson-Brewer, R., Cohen, S., O'Donnell, L., & Goodman, I. (1991). *Violence prevention for young adolescents: A survey of the state of the art.* ERIC Document Reproduction Service ED 356 442.

Yung, B. R., & Hammond, W. R. (1998). Breaking the cycle: A culturally sensitive violence prevention program for African-American children and adolescents. In J. Lutzker (Ed.), *Handbook of child abuse research and treatment* (pp. 319–340). New York: Plenum.

ANNOTATED BIBLIOGRAPHY

Elliott, D. S., Hamburg, B. A., & Williams, K. R. (Eds.). (1998). *Violence in American schools: A new perspective.* New York: Cambridge University Press.
This book is an analysis of the problem by a Who's Who list of authors mostly outside of education. Particularly useful are chapters by J. David Hawkins, David Farrington, and Richard Catalano, "Reducing violence through the schools," and Faith Samples and Larry Aber's "Evaluation of school-based violence prevention programs."

Loeber, R., & Farrington, D. P. (Eds.). (1998). *Serious and violent juvenile offenders: Risk factors and successful interventions.* Thousand Oaks, CA: Sage.
A scholarly, yet consumable assembly of everything from screening procedures to gangs and intervention research. The three chapters devoted to risk factors and prediction are worth the price alone.

Pepler, D. J., & Rubin, K. H. (Eds.). (1991). *The development and treatment of childhood aggression.* Hillsdale, NJ: Erlbaum.
Donald Meichenbaum refers to this as a classic in the field, and he is correct. A true library must, this is an outstanding primer on how aggression develops, is maintained, and is treated, authored by major contributors in psychology and child development.

WEBSITES

The Internet has quickly become a major source of useful information and research on school violence prevention. The NASP website (http://www.nasponline.org) and the National School Safety Center website (http://www.nssc1.org) are excellent starting points for links to additional practitioner-friendly sites.

69 Best Practices in Developing Local Norms in Behavioral Assessment

Andrea S. Canter, Matthew Y. Lau, and Allison House
Minneapolis Public Schools

OVERVIEW

The use of local norms in the assessment of academic skills has received considerable attention in recent years, particularly in the professional literature regarding Curriculum-Based Measurement (e.g., Shinn, 1989). This chapter addresses the application of local norms to behavioral assessment, particularly at the school and district level. This overview will be followed by a discussion of basic considerations in the development of locally normed procedures and recommended practices. The chapter concludes with the presentation of three case studies: (a) the development of a locally normed functional skills assessment procedure at the district and state level, (b) the development and normative application of a behavior screening procedure at the district level, and (c) the application of a district behavior screening procedure to norms development at the school level.

For over a century, the practice of assessment in school psychology has been largely characterized by nationally normed procedures used to diagnose and classify intellectual, academic, and behavioral problems. In recent years, researchers and practitioners have implemented significant alternatives to traditional approaches for measuring academic skills, such as Curriculum-Based Assessment and Curriculum-Based Measurement. This new generation of direct assessment procedures is more strongly linked to intervention than to classification, more relevant to instruction than to diagnosis, and more tied to local than to national standards of performance. Further, these procedures offer much promise in reducing ethnic and linguistic bias in assessment outcomes.

While the call to replace traditional approaches with alternative models has been the source of much controversy in the profession (e.g., Braden & Reschly, 1993; Fagan & Wise, 2000), the development of direct and ecological assessment procedures has unquestionably resulted in improved professional practice linked to students' academic outcomes (Reschly, Tilly, & Grimes, 1999). The shortcomings of traditional assessment are certainly as evident in the domains of social and adaptive behavior as in the domains of cognition and achievement: Student performance is compared to statistical national norms regardless of relevance to local cultural norms and home/school expectations and without a direct link to intervention (Reschly & Tilly, 1999; Gresham, 1999).

A Rationale for Local Norms

One alternative approach to traditional assessments is the use of local, rather than national, norms. Local norms have been cited as essential to developing instructionally and ecologically relevant assessments (Bardon, 1988) and as consistent with the concept of "Least Restrictive Environment" and outcomes-driven, problem-solving models (Shinn, Good, & Parker, 1999). Locally normed measures provide a means of overcoming some of the criticisms of traditional procedures, because they can address social standards and environmental contexts, lead to intervention, and reduce ethnic and cultural bias.

Even within the context of traditional assessment purposes of diagnosis and classification, the use of a local frame of reference is essential in addressing functional and social skills that are typically defined in terms of social significance or social validity. Gresham (1983) defines social skills as "situationally specific behaviors that predict important social outcomes for children and youth." Deno (1989) notes the importance of situational specificity in understanding the concept of disability: "Handicaps can only be defined in terms of the relationship between what a person can do and what a person must do to succeed in a given environment . . .. Teachers do not make judgments . . . based only on the universal norms of the culture; instead, their judgments are also based on the behavior of the students in classrooms and schools within which they are working" (pp. 5, 10). To best understand the student's functioning, one must consider the social norms or expectations of the classroom, school, and community in which the student is asked to perform. By addressing an important component of social validity—normative expectations of specific instructional settings—local norms can provide an essen tial contextual perspective to the special education eligibility and placement process (Gresham, 1999).

Local Norms, Expectations, and Intervention

The concept of social validity is closely tied to local expectations or the standards of one's community, culture, neighborhood, school, or peer group. National norms provide information about the individual's functioning relative to what are assumed to be universal standards. Yet, in a diverse society, such assumptions can lead to cultural and regional bias in measurement, one of the strongest criticisms of norm-referenced testing.

Locally developed norms, on the other hand, should reflect what is relevant for success within the local context. Procedures reflecting local standards should more fairly identify individuals in need of intervention in order to perform successfully. Such measures directly relate to referral concerns since teacher referrals likely reflect a discrepancy between student performance and teacher expectationor their perception of "teachability" rather than an absolute deficit in skills (e.g., Gresham, 1999). Furthermore, congruence with teacher expectations for classroom functioning is highly related to mainstream success for at-risk students and those with disabilities (Hersh & Walker, 1983).

Assessment approaches reflecting local standards are more readily applied to designing intervention strategies than are global, nationally normed procedures. Such procedures allow comparison of a referred student with relevant peer groups, facilitating informed decisions regarding (a) the most appropriate and least restrictive placement, (b) the degree of discrepancy between the student's behavior and the expectations of a potential placement, and (c) areas requiring intervention prior to transition to a less restrictive or mainstream placement. These characteristics are consistent with the concept of "template matching" described by Hoier, McConnell, and Pallay (1987), in which assessment information is used to develop a "template" (behavioral profile) of individual classrooms to promote successful transitions from special to regular education classrooms (McConnell, 1987; Horn & Fuchs, 1987). Such applications of local norms help fulfill a critical component of problem-solving models; that is, defining "the degree of discrepancy between the demands of the educational setting and the learner's performance" (Tilly, Reschly, & Grimes, 1999, p. 304).

Importance to School Psychology Practice

School psychologists are generally trained to serve as problem solvers, yet traditional practice tends to emphasize problem identification. School psychologists seeking expanded roles should find that the implementation of locally normed assessment procedures enhances opportunities for problem-solving consultation by directly addressing teacher expectations and referral concerns. By offering alternative or supplemental information that can be interpreted in the local cultural context, local norms also can help alleviate ethical dilemmas created by the potentially discriminatory nature of nationally normed procedures. Furthermore, the design and development of locally normed procedures provides an ideal opportunity for school psychologists to use their training and expertise in measurement and applied research within the practical scope of a single classroom, school, or district.

Limitations of Local Norms

Use of local norms is hardly a cure for all problems associated with traditional measures. Many of the criticisms of nationally normed tests apply to local norms as well. A norm-referenced measure of any sort may not fit the assessment purpose; even a locally normed procedure may not fairly represent a given individual. Technical adequacy also can be a significant problem with locally normed procedures when samples are small. If the behaviors measured vary significantly across settings, then it may be difficult to identify sufficiently consistent environments from which to draw an adequate sample for norming purposes. Furthermore, when data reflect local values and/or local samples, one cannot generalize with much confidence beyond the immediate context.

BASIC CONSIDERATIONS

To effectively design and implement a locally based assessment model, the school psychologist must consider a number of factors, including (a) the purpose of the assessment procedure(s), (b) the "measurement net" or domain(s) of the assessment, (c) the definition and characteristics of the local population, (d) the format of the assessment, (e) data collection procedures, including standardization and psychometric properties, (f) the availability of administrative and technical support for the design and implementation of the procedure, and (g) implementation issues. These factors are addressed sequentially, as presented in Figure 1.

Purpose of Assessment

Before embarking on the development of a locally normed assessment procedure, school psychologists should determine the reasons why the measure is needed and the level of inference to be made from the data. In designing the measure, educators need to consider:

1. What referral concerns/school problems will the measure address?

2. What types of educational decision (eligibility, placement, instructional strategies) will be made?

3. What level of decision making is desired (e.g., screening versus diagnosis)?

4. Is a new tool needed or just local norming of an existing measure?

For reasons noted above, locally normed procedures are well-suited for the assessment of social and functional behaviors, because these are frequently situation-specific and tend to reflect localized cultural and community values and expectations. Normative measures typically are most appropriate for identifying, classifying, and sorting individuals, and are less often appropriate for specific intervention planning or progress monitoring.

The use of locally normed measures enables school personnel to directly address the need for special services as well as eligibility. If most students in a third-grade class are unable to independently exhibit social problem-solving skills and all score below the 25th percentile on a nationally normed scale of social skills, then John's "below average" performance on that scale will not be regarded as discrepant from his classmates. Rather than identify all as in need of remedial or special education, as might be indicated by using nationally normed tests, the locally normed procedure indicates that John is functioning like his classmates or is meeting most of the demands of his current class placement. However, if John's areas of deficit are dissimilar to those of his classmates, then some type of intervention would be warranted to enable him to meet the expectations of his teacher and to avoid referral for more restrictive programming.

Is the procedure intended to serve as a screening device, with students who fall below some set criterion to be referred for more in-depth assessment? Or is the procedure intended to be used to make placement/programmatic decisions? Local norms can be appropriately applied to both purposes, but should not be used in isolation to make diagnostic decisions or special placements. Locally normed measures can help limit the number of students for whom more complete diagnostic information will be obtained by sorting out a group who appears to be at risk relative to the typical students in the local population. Both absolute and relative performance data should be obtained before making placement decisions.

Depending on the format and content of the procedure, some locally normed measures may be appro-

Figure 1. **Developing local norms for behavioral assessment.**

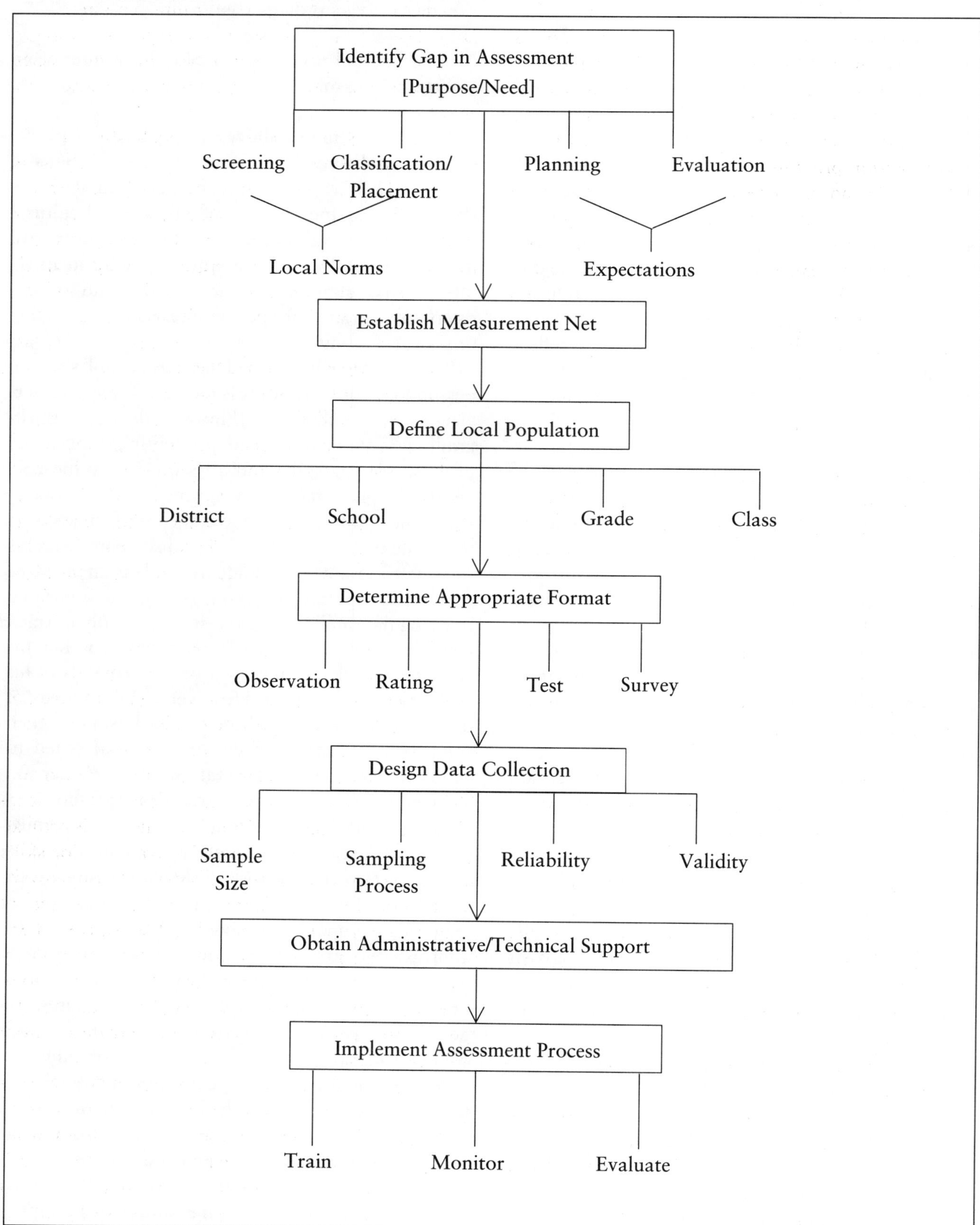

priate for program planning, with the normative data serving as a benchmark or criterion level of performance. Students who fall below this benchmark might be identified for intervention. For example, if most fifth graders are able to use a problem-solving approach to resolving peer conflict, then those who are rated low on this skill might be referred to a conflict resolution program.

Generally, norm-referenced measures cannot be repeated at frequent intervals to measure progress or response to intervention. At annual intervals, or perhaps twice per year, teacher ratings of a student's skills on a locally normed scale might provide useful data regarding the degree of discrepancy between a student and his or her peer group following implementation of intervention services.

The "Measurement Net"

In a problem-solving model, educators develop questions that the assessment will attempt to answer. Questions that might be appropriately addressed by a locally normed measure of social/functional skills include:

1. How do the student's social skills compare to those of his or her classmates?

2. Are the student's deficits in areas where staff expectations are high or low?

3. Has the student's relative performance of locally desired social skills improved following the social skills group training program?

The assessment tool must address the behaviors/skills relevant to the question or problem area. In the examples listed above, "social skills" is the apparent domain of concern. To find answers, both the skill level of the referred student and the expectations of school staff must be addressed by the assessment.

Whatever the area of concern, the skills or behavior of that domain must be clearly defined and adequately sampled within the boundaries of the measure's intended purpose. What skills and behaviors will be included in "social skills?" Is an in-depth, task-analyzed sampling of these skills needed or will a more global sampling of general skills suffice? Are multiple skill areas (domains) needed, such as adult-directed interaction versus peer-directed interaction, or will a single domain such as interpersonal interaction be adequate? Decisions in regard to these questions will help determine the content and length of the measure.

Shinn (1989) describes the establishment of a "measurement net" to identify specific skills to be included in locally normed measures. A pool of possible skills/test items is generated by requesting information from teachers and by surveying available curriculum and research literature. Surveying teachers regarding the behaviors of typical, successful students versus unsuccessful students will provide a starting point for developing a school- or classroom-based behavior rating scale. A review of the objectives of a social skills training curriculum will also contribute tasks/skills to the measurement net. This pool of potential items can then be reviewed by teachers and others, and field tested before final decisions regarding the content of the measure. A similar approach can be taken when considering local norming of an existing test or scale: Reviewing and piloting would be necessary to determine if the tool's content were locally relevant

Defining the Local Population

Who will be the subject of the assessment? Generally, one considers developing local norms or new locally normed procedures because some or all of the population of concern is inadequately served by existing norms and measures of the relevant behavioral domains. Defining the "local" population is critical. When a fair measure of the adaptive behavior skills of Native American students is desired, it makes little sense to randomly sample from the entire school population in a district of only 12% Native American students: The new norms would still reflect a very limited portion of the target group. If the target group is to be "urban midwest children," then the normative sample might be randomly drawn from an entire midwest, urban district.

Some behavioral concerns are so situationally specific that the target population appropriately is an individual classroom or school building. Even in situations where the behavior may have more generalized consequences, intervention may be most appropriate when it addresses skills needed in the immediate environment of the classroom. Gresham (1999) notes that "Students who eventually are classified as EBD often fail to meet teachers' *social behavior standards* and surpass teachers' *tolerance limits* for maladaptive behavior" (p.117); such standards and limits clearly vary across teachers, schools, and communities. Therefore, by using the typical behavior of students in a specific classroom as the "norm," as well as understanding the expectations of their teacher(s), is more likely to lead to effective intervention than would normative comparisons with students in the school or district as a whole. Defining the population to serve as the "standard" is critical to the design of the measure, to the development of reliable and valid norms, and to the ultimate usefulness of the measure as a problem-solving tool.

Appropriate Formats for the Assessment

The format selected for any assessment tool must be appropriate for the assessment's purpose, desired domains, and target population. In behavioral and functional skills areas, observation is often the most practical direct assessment approach. Indirect methods such as checklists and rating scales are commonly used and more easily developed at the local level than standardized individual tests. Rating scales can serve as criterion measures and/or as normative measures in behavioral and functional assessments. While third-party data are inevitably vulnerable to some subjective judgment, parent and teacher ratings of specific behaviors can be highly reliable and valid (e.g., Gresham, 1981; McConaughy & Ritter, 1995). When developed and normed locally, such procedures reflect the community standards and expectations for performance.

An alternative means of establishing local norms is to obtain ratings of expected or preferred performance rather than obtain the direct ratings of individuals from a representative sample. For example, instead of rating the social behaviors of 10 "typical" or randomly selected students, a sample of teachers would be asked to rate the importance or desirability of those social behaviors as related to classroom success. Referred students' behaviors would then be rated and compared to the established expectations for that school or district. This approach could also be limited to one classroom and one teacher's expectations. While teacher expectations are not necessarily realistic or consistent with the rated behaviors of typical students, these expectations tend to be stable over time and are highly related to referral to special education (Hersh & Walker, 1983; Gresham, 1999).

Once the type of measure is determined, the specific format must be considered. Rating scales, for example, can require yes/no responses, ratings of the frequency or severity of problem behavior, or ratings of the degree of independence or success of the individual's performance. The specificity of the ratings and format for responding will vary with the level of inference desired in relation to the scale's purpose: Psychologists must seek the most practical balance between precision and user-friendliness.

For the purpose of classification or screening for more detailed assessment, the most simple and global ratings may be sufficient. However, for intervention planning, effective measures typically differentiate deficits in skill versus deficits in performance (Gresham, 1984). Multipoint rating scales more reliably reflect important differences in the frequency and quality of target behaviors when compared with dichotomous scales (Edelbrock, 1983), although complex ratings can be overly demanding for the rater and possibly limit the usefulness of the results. Furthermore, highly demanding rating tasks could significantly reduce the level of cooperation needed for data collection.

Similar considerations apply to the development of standardized observational systems from which local norms are derived. Complex coding procedures may yield more specific data but also typically require extensive training for reliable use. Systems commonly used in research may be unnecessarily complex for classroom implementation and the intended level of decision making.

Data Collection and Analysis

Developing local norms requires careful consideration of the level of technical adequacy needed for decision making. Special education labeling and placement have obvious long-term implications for the student, and a higher level of technical confidence is necessary than in the case of screening. The general considerations of reliability and validity of norm-referenced procedures apply to the development of locally normed measures. It is typically impractical, however, to hold locally normed measures to the same standards of technical adequacy used to judge nationally normed procedures. Generalization from locally normed data should address inherent limitations of smaller samples, restricted sampling procedures, and situational specificity.

Local norms should appropriately reflect the population of concern, be it a classroom, school building, or school district. The standardization sample should have proportionate representation according to relevant demographic factors such as age, grade, gender, economic status, and ethnicity. Depending on the tool's purpose, students with disabilities may or may not be appropriately included in normative samples. When norms are desired for the entire school district, adequate geographic representation is necessary, as well as sampling across the various curricula and organization options present in the district. The normative group might include all students from that population rather than a random sample, particularly when the norms are to be derived from a single classroom or grade level.

What norms will be available for the interpretation of results? Separate norms for groups known to differ significantly on the target behaviors are preferred for classification and placement purposes, but collecting sufficiently large samples for multiple norming groups is often impractical. Age or grade-level norms tend to be the easiest to construct, assuming that development is a significant factor. Some problematic and social behaviors do not appear to be highly related to age within the school population; therefore, gender-specific norms may be more appropriate for some behavioral domains. Ethnic group norms may also be desirable for some purposes, but often the smaller cultural groups cannot be adequately sampled within a school or district.

What types of normative scores are desired? Percentiles are often the easiest scores to report and interpret, but eligibility criteria often require the use of standard scores. Standard scores can be derived from any distribution, but distributions significantly skewed away from the normal curve yield standard scores that can be misleading.

Sample sizes will dictate reliability of norms and generalizability to similar students in the population. Obviously, larger samples should be more reliable than smaller samples, but how large a sample is necessary for the purpose of the procedure? When percentiles are desired, measurement experts generally recommend that at least 100 individuals be included in each comparison group (e.g., each grade level) so that "true percentiles" can be derived. Smaller groups require "smoothed" percentiles using linear interpolation in order to determine values at each percentile point. Groups of fewer than 100 may nevertheless yield useful norms when sampling is conducted carefully, but the scores should be interpreted with greater caution.

It clearly is impossible to determine true percentiles for single classroom samples, and groups of 25-30 students will certainly not yield the stable normative data possible with significantly larger groups. However, means and standard deviations can be derived and used for screening, planning, and evaluating student progress at the classroom or building level. Such samples can be used effectively for screening purposes and can serve as a practical alternative approach for developing classroom norms for each class or grade level in a school. Samples of 5–10 typical students from each classroom can serve as a standard for comparison with referred students in order to obtain a gross estimate of deviation from the norm. Such data can help teams prioritize referral for more extensive assessment or serve as a first-level screening to identify students for intervention. Depending on the type of measurement, small classroom samples may offer the only practical means of collecting normative data without external funding resources.

Initial piloting of a new measure or new norming procedure with small classroom or building samples may be desirable even when the ultimate goal is district-level norms: The smaller investigation provides a cost-effective means of field-testing materials, procedures, scoring, and decision making. Small investigations can also be effective in establishing teacher expectations as a practical alternative to true norms.

The collection of normative data should, to the extent possible, include data regarding internal consistency, stability of results, and validity relative to the assessment purpose. Depending on sample size, some or all of the sample can serve as a test-retest group. Appropriate criterion measures, such as similar scales or class grades, can be included to examine concurrent and predictive validity. Less formal procedures, such as referral rates, placement rates, and observed response to intervention, can also be useful in validating local norms. With sufficiently large samples, statistical tests of discriminant validity can be applied to determine if the locally normed procedure adequately differentiates groups of students for eligibility or treatment purposes.

When developing normative observation systems and third-party rating scales, one must consider inter-rater agreement. Typically this is determined by comparing the results of two independent observers/raters, such as teacher and parent, reading teacher and math teacher, or two trained observers making simultaneous observations. Behavior scales are often criticized when inter-rater agreement is only moderate. However, when the target behaviors are assumed to be situationally specific, then a high degree of inter-rater agreement may not be realistic. In fact, differences between raters may be of both diagnostic and prescriptive value. Some assessment systems are designed to obtain two or more sets of ratings or observations of the same student in order to provide such comparisons. The degree of acceptable inter-rater difference will of course depend on the purpose of the assessment and level of inference desired.

Administrative and Technical Support

The development of local measures and local norms is typically carried out by school district personnel, such as school psychologists, sometimes with the assistance of grants and in collaboration with university researchers. Regardless of the scope of the project, individuals developing these procedures need the support of school administrators. Professional time must be allocated to the project, and the project must thus be regarded as a priority among the many tasks of the school psychologist. The administration must therefore understand and support the rationale for developing local norms and perceive the proposed project as a cost-effective means of affecting student outcomes.

General support from the school district administration is an essential first step, but support from building principals is critical to implementing data collection. Parents and teachers will ultimately be involved in data collection, either directly by responding to rating scales or by administering tests, or indirectly through the consent process. The endorsement and cooperation of the building principal may help to secure the cooperation of parents, staff, and students, and lend credibility to the project. However, directives from administrators are not sufficient to ensure cooperation of subjects and respondents. Teachers and parents must also perceive that the project leads to better services for students and involves minimal time, effort, and disruption of the normal school routine.

Finally, to successfully implement and complete a local norming project, the school psychologist needs access to sufficient technical support. Very small studies (such as classroom norming projects) may require minimal clerical support, data entry, and data analysis. Larger scale projects such as district-wide norming may require additional funding (such as grants) to secure computer time, data entry personnel, consultants with statistical expertise, and, in some cases, data collection personnel.

Large school districts often have research departments with adequate support for such projects, while smaller districts may have to seek expertise elsewhere. Local universities often offer opportunities for collaboration, shared computer access, and pools of inexpensive labor for data collection.

When external funding is needed, local sources often offer the best opportunities for relatively small grants. State departments of education, local corporations, and private foundations often provide grants for projects directed toward at-risk and special needs populations. Larger school districts often employ one or more individuals to identify such funding sources and to assist staff in applying for grants.

Implementation Issues

The final step in establishing local norms is the development of an implementation plan. The plan should address relevant timelines for training staff in the new procedure(s), a system of monitoring the use of the procedure(s), and methods of evaluating the impact of the procedure(s) in the context of the assessment's intended purpose. Monitoring can be accomplished through periodic surveys or reporting systems that help determine if procedures were appropriately followed. Depending on the assessment's purpose, evaluation plans might address referral and/or placement rates, impact on decision making, teacher satisfaction, and related issues. If resources were available, then evaluation might also include validation through discriminant analysis and replication studies.

BEST PRACTICES

The development and implementation of a locally normed assessment procedure unfolds as a problem-solving approach to decision making (see Figure 1). At each step, the school psychologist is confronted with questions to answer in order to best shape the final measure to the needs of the classroom, school, or district. Regardless of the domains of behavior measured or of the type of measure developed, this sequence of decisions allows the school psychologist to adapt the assessment tool to the identified needs, local population, and available resources.

For the purpose of this chapter, this decision-making sequence will be described in the context of three case-study illustrations, using as the examples the development of the Mainstream Survival Skills Assessment (MSSA) by Canter and Heistad (1990), the development and implementation of a district-wide behavioral screening tool at the district level, and the application of this district screener to the development of norms at one high school.

The Mainstream Survival Skills Assessment Project

While the MSSA is a multimethod system addressing functional and social behavior through ratings, observation, and interviews, this discussion will include only the locally normed rating-scale components.

Purpose of Assessment

During the mid-1980s, school psychologists and other team members repeatedly were frustrated by the apparent discrepancy between the behaviors that prompted special education referral and those behaviors that available tools were designed to assess. Although state and federal rules mandated assessment of adaptive behavior in school as well as home/community settings as part of the identification of "mental handicaps," there were very few measures published and none appeared to be specifically relevant to the diverse local population. School psychologists in a midwest urban school district initiated a project to address this gap in technology through the development of a locally normed rating scale.

After reviewing literature and informally surveying local teachers regarding factors related to school success and failure, "school survival skills" were identified as the general target behaviors for the new assessment. Survival skills were defined as task-related behaviors such as academic engagement, following directions, seeking assistance, and organizing materials, as well as functional academic, personal, and social competencies (Cobb & Hops, 1973; Hops & Cobb, 1974) that have been found to effectively differentiate successful from non-successful mainstream students (McConnell et al., 1984). It was therefore hypothesized that assessment of school-based functional skills would contribute important data to classification and placement decisions, to predicting student outcomes in alternative settings, and to developing more effective, ecological interventions. It was highly desirable that the procedure be sufficiently robust to be useful in eligibility decisions and that student performance be readily compared to teacher expectations.

Establishing the Measurement Net

To be included in the "net," it was essential that items reflect skills related to successful and independent functioning in mainstream classrooms and that the rated behavior was readily observable in school and classroom environments. In addition to an extensive review of relevant literature, K–8 teachers from local schools were surveyed regarding their expectations and observations; currently available measures of functional and problematic behavior were reviewed; and a preliminary set of items was generated and reviewed by a panel of regular and special education teachers, school social workers, and school psychologists. These skills were then organized into four (and later condensed into three) general domains of functional academics, task orientation, personal independence, and social skills.

Defining the Local Population

After trying out items and discussing the procedure with teachers, it was decided to limit the scope of the measure to the elementary (K–6) population. In developing norms, representative samples of all district students who participated in mainstream programs, including those with mild disabilities and with limited English proficiency, were to be included, as well as representative samplings of the district's non-white ethnic populations and economic diversity. To ensure geographic representation as well as sampling of all organizational and curricular structures in the district, students from each grade level at every district K–6 school were included in the normative sample. Norms for each grade level were desired given the documented relationship between adaptive behavior and social skills and age level across the school years.

Determining Appropriate Formats

A three-point scale reflecting independence in typical functioning was selected for both the purpose of cost-effective test development and the ultimate goal of implementing a practical data collection procedure. A second scale was also desired with a subset of identical items for teachers to rate the skills' importance to classroom success. These teacher expectations would provide a template for that classroom.

Data Collection and Analysis

The MSSA rating scales followed traditional test-development procedures, including pilot testing, standardization with a random sample of mainstream students, tests of reliability and validity, and discriminant analyses using special population samples. The normative sample was derived through proportionate random sampling of each elementary school's enrollment lists. To obtain the desired target samples of 100 students per grade level, samples of 140–150 were selected for the norming pool. Subsamples of this total were included in test-retest reliability, inter-rater agreement, and concurrent validity samples, using the Vineland Adaptive Behavior Scales, Classroom Edition as the criterion measure.

Discriminant validity samples were drawn from special education enrollment lists of students in resource and self-contained classroom programs for children with mental impairments, learning disabilities, and emotional/behavioral disorders. Another sample was selected from the Limited English Proficiency program.

The 50 items with the highest degree of technical adequacy and ratings of teacher importance formed the Teacher Expectations Scale. A sample of district teachers at each grade level (K–6) was asked to complete this scale to obtain information about expectations across and within grade levels. Extensive analyses were conducted to examine age, gender, ethnic, and SES differences in teachers' ratings of sampled students, as well as to examine different special education samples. Norms tables were constructed by using smoothed percentiles with linear interpolation for the final normative samples at each grade. Rationale, data collection procedures, norms tables, technical data, and recommendations for applying data to educational decisions were included in a manual published by the district for school personnel (Canter & Heistad, 1990).

Administrative and Technical Support

Many sources of support within the local district were tapped for this project: the Research and Evaluation staff provided technical support; Psychological Services staff provided coordination and professional consultation; principals and special education administrators encouraged teacher participation; and the Minnesota Department of Education awarded a grant totaling approximately $30,000 to fund project coordination, materials, data entry and teacher incentives in the form of small stipends.

Implementation Issues

The MSSA project resulted in a teacher-rating scale that meets accepted standards of reliability and validity and is in fact technically comparable to many published, nationally normed measures of adaptive and social behavior (Canter & Heistad, 1990). The norming population very closely reflects the demographic characteristics of the district, and, as predicted, ratings differentiated disabled from nondisabled and mildly disabled from more severely disabled students. As a contingency for securing funding, the MSSA was normed at the state level in a replication of the district-level norming project. This statewide study served to further validate the data obtained in the earlier project (Canter, Schrot, & Heistad, 1990).

The MSSA scales have been used extensively in the district as components of special education eligibility assessments and as fundamental data in planning interventions and placements for mildly disabled students who participate in inclusion programs or who are making the transition to less restrictive programs. To ensure appropriate implementation, numerous presentations have been made to school personnel, particularly to special education personnel. Over time, additional data have been collected to enhance understanding of survival skills relative to specific groups, including students with severe emotional/behavioral disorders, students with Limited English Proficiency, and Native American students. Of particular value to the Problem-Solving model initiated in the district in 1993 has been the comparison of teacher expectation ratings to teachers' ratings of referred students' performances that have provided the foundation for ecological interventions. At times, these data have also been used to help identify specific classrooms where students are most likely to succeed.

District-Wide Behavior Screener

Whereas the MSSA was developed in response to regulatory as well as population changes of the 1980s, identifying behaviorally at-risk students to better address achievement and school safety became an integral part of many school improvement plans of the 1990s. The primary goal for such a screening process is to identify students who differ significantly from their peers and may need additional support and early intervention to prevent further deterioration of behavior. The challenge of identifying at-risk students is even greater when working with a diverse, urban population in which child rearing practices, cultural expectations, English language proficiency, and socioeconomic status may vary significantly from those of the mainstream Euro-American culture.

Purpose

Traditionally, teachers refer individual students who are felt to be "deviant" from their classmates to the Child Study Team for special education evaluation. This referral approach may reflect possible personal bias and undermine the effort of classroom intervention in the general education setting. Moreover, many teachers vary in their tolerances for, and awareness of, different behavioral problems. Consequently, a systematic, less-biased behavior screening process that provides information about the student's behavior within the context of local social norms and expectations is essential.

During the 1998–1999 school year, school psychologists and staff members of the same midwest urban school district in the above example initiated a project to develop a locally normed behavior screener as a part of the general screening process developed in response to an Office of Civil Rights (OCR) compliance agreement with the district to reduce bias in special education referral and evaluation. The screener was designed to help classroom teachers organize observed information regarding their students' behavior in the classroom and other school environments and, subsequently, to identify at-risk students for early intervention. Further, the screener was designed to complement the existing Problem-Solving model that had been undergoing implementation across the district during the previous 5 years.

The Measurement Net

The evolution of the Behavior Screening Checklist began with a panel of school professionals, including psychologists, social workers, special and regular education teachers, and other personnel, that reviewed relevant literature and conducted an informal staff survey. The panel then generated a set of specific behaviors related to social and behavioral functioning in the classrooms. These behaviors were further organized into three general behavioral categories: Task Management, Physical and Verbal Behavior, and Socialization. In the area of Task Management, teachers were to rate attention to classroom routines, following rules and procedures, completing work independently, and handling change. The Physical and Verbal Behavior Area addresses appropriate versus inappropriate behavior. Target behaviors within Socialization include peer interactions and relationships, classroom participation, and self-image. Classroom teachers were asked to rate their students on a scale from 1 to 5 on these specific behaviors.

Defining the Local Population

The Behavior Screening Checklist was developed as part of the district-wide screening process to identify students at risk for a wide range of problems in learning and behavior. All district students were to be rated through global screening, including those who are English Language Learners (ELL), from kindergarten through twelfth grades. The norming of the Behavior Screening Checklist coincided with the implementation of the OCR compliance guidelines during the 1999–2000 school year. Initially 20 and, later, another 20, schools implemented the screening project during the first year. Norms were developed based on data obtained from 11 of these pilot sites.

Each teacher in the participating pilot schools was asked to complete the Behavior Screening Checklist for all of his or her non-IEP (Individual Education Plan) students in the fall. The normative sample included student ratings from five K–5, four K–6, and two K–8 schools. Although these schools were not randomly selected, they mirrored the district population in terms of geographic location and student population. Furthermore, such selection process allowed a more efficient use of limited resources and larger sample size for each grade level. It was also determined that, at least initially, only grade norms for the K–6 population would be developed because of limited sampling at grades 7 and 8, and that gender-specific norms would not be derived at this time.

Determining Appropriate Formats

For a screening measure designed for district-wide implementation, cost effectiveness and user friendliness are particularly important to assure practical data collection. The 10-item Behavior Screening Checklist is presented as a 5-point Likert-type scale and formatted on a one-sided single page. The behaviors are delineated in neutral descriptors. Teachers are asked to rate their students on a 5-point scale with "1" being the most desirable. The checklist generates three sub-scale scores and a total scale score.

Data Collection and Analysis

The Behavior Screening Checklist was designed to be a global screening device. Yet, an extensive effort was made to ensure acceptable standards of reliability and validity. An internal consistency reliability coefficient of 0.80 as recommended by Salvia and Ysseldyke (1995) for screening devices was adopted. A pilot study using exploratory analyses was conducted on the K–6 data collected from three elementary schools during the 1998–1999 school year. The final normative samples included 500–600 students for each grade level except the sixth grade, which contained 341 students. A subsample of the norm group was used to study internal consistency and to examine agreement of items within each subscale. A separate sample of third-grade students from six classrooms at two elementary schools was used to examine inter-rater reliability. Furthermore, ratings of students with Emotional/Behavioral Disorder ($N = 34$) who were referred for a more restrictive setting during the 1999–2000 school year were examined and compared to those from the normative samples to determine if the checklist differentiated those who required extensive behavioral intervention.

Administrative and Technical Support

The development and implementation of the Behavior Screening Checklist was part of the district's OCR compliance agreement, which provided financial and personnel support for the norming project, as well as administrative support needed to implement the screening procedure. The project personnel are school psychologists with graduate training in research design and statistics who consulted with the Research and Evaluation staff for more advanced technical support in data analyses.

Implementation Issues

At each district site participating in the OCR Screening Project (40 schools as of September 2000), classroom teachers are asked to complete the checklist for each student in their classrooms. Norm tables for each grade level are available for staff members to make a normative comparison for their students. A cutoff score, based on the score distribution in the normative samples, was recommended, which identifies the top 5–10% percent of students as being most "at-risk." Decisions about additional screening, intervention design, and referral for more intensive support or assessment are site-based within the parameters of the district's Problem-Solving model, Guidelines for Reducing Bias in Special Education Assessment, and recommended practice.

The Behavior Screening Checklist provides a systematic process to identify at-risk students within the context of local norms and expectations. It meets acceptable standards of reliability and validity for screening purposes. Although the checklist provides valuable normative information for program planning for target students, it is not intended to be used as a stand-alone measure. Multiple sources of data such as parent interview, staff report, school record, etc., are essential as part of the overall screening procedure and Problem-Solving model. Particularly, additional cultural and socioeconomic data are needed to reduce the danger of biased results.

District Leadership staff and teams from each participating school were trained to use the checklist, using a "trainer of trainers" model, which provides training to a small group of staff members who in turn provide the training to larger groups of building personnel. The checklist complements the district's Problem-Solving model that emphasizes structured pre-referral intervention and functional evaluation procedures. It provides information to help identify target behaviors for intervention and baseline data for progress monitoring.

Development of Local Behavior Norms at a High School Level

The Behavior Screener described in the preceding section was applied to one urban high school in order to establish building norms. The high school has a population of approximately 1,500 students, about 40% of whom speak English as their second language and over 75% of whom receive free or reduced-price lunch. Project components unique to the high school norming project are described below.

Purpose

At one urban high school, local norms using the Behavior Screener were established during the 1999–2000 school year. Beyond addressing a district mandate to reduce ethnic or racial bias in special education referral, the screeners were also intended to direct intervention to students who were experiencing behavior difficulties. As part of a school-wide and district-wide effort to create a more systematic method for addressing behavioral concerns, the screeners were to be used to empirically evaluate trends in behavior referral and intervention at this high school.

Data Collection and Analysis

Each teacher was provided with screeners for all students enrolled in their classes and provided staff development time to complete them. A total of 4,915 screeners were completed for 1,540 students. An average of 75% of each student's teachers completed screeners for each student (generally three of a student's four teachers). Originally, special education students were not intended to be included, but some teachers rated all of their students, including those already receiving special education services.

At the time of the initial ratings, some teachers expressed concern that the screener was directed more toward students who acted out and appeared to ignore some students experiencing high levels of depression and anxiety, as well as some very isolated students who were English language learners. For the purpose of data interpretation, an experimental "internalizing scale" based on 3 of the scale's 10 items was developed to more specifically address the large number of English Language Learners and students with fewer externalizing behaviors. Thus for each Behavior Screener Checklist, two scores were derived: total score based on all 10 items and an internalizing score based on these 3 items alone.

After data entry was completed, a list of "students of concern" was developed. The 95th percentile was used for identification. This cut score was intended to identify a manageable number of students most at need of behavioral support. Additionally, the 95th percentile is two standard deviations from mean, which is generally accepted as being significantly different from the mean of "average" students. Both the Total Score and the Internalizing Score were used to identify students above the 95th percentile. In order to be identified as a "student of concern," two or more teachers' ratings were required to be above the 95th percentile on either scale for identification.

When the list of students of concern was developed, a total of 50 regular education students were identified, with an additional 17 special education students who also had scores above the criterion 95th percentile. This list included a disproportionately large number of ninth graders (55% of total list), which is similar to informal teacher report and referral rates to the student support teams. Gender representation was nearly equal, with 52% boys and 48% girls on the Students of Concern list.

One of the original purposes of the behavior screener was to reduce potential racial or ethnic bias in special education or intervention assistance team referrals. When examining the composition of the list of students of concern, the percentage of African American, Native American, and Hispanic American students were very similar to the percentage of these students at this high school. However, there were proportionately more white students on the list (38%) than are reflected in the building's enrollment (25%), and proportionately fewer Asian American students identified (7%) than enrolled (24%).

Validation of the screening process was accomplished in a number of ways. Initially, the list of students of concern was informally compared with the list of students referred to the school's pre-referral intervention teams. The degree of overlap indicated that some the students on the list were also those about whom teachers had already expressed concerns. An additional informal validation was provided by the inadvertent rating of students in special education, because many of these students who were above the 95th percentile had IEP goals related to some aspect of school behavior. A more formal method of validating the results involved examining the number of student suspensions compared to their score on the screener. A direct positive relationship was found: Students with a higher number of suspensions during the year tended to have higher scores on the Behavior Screener. The Internalizing Scale, however, did not have a similar relationship with suspensions, an expected finding given that students are not generally suspended for internalizing behaviors.

Administrative and Technical Support

Significant supports were needed both at the district and school level to initiate the process of development of the building behavior norms. At the district level, preparation of the screeners and data entry were critically important before and after the teachers actually completed the screeners. At the school level, the administration was fully in support of the process, providing one full day of staff development devoted to training on the purpose and implementation of the behavior screeners, as well as time to complete the screeners. Clerical assistance with gathering information from students' files and organizing the data gathered was also provided. Additional release time for members of the pre-referral intervention teams and the coordinator of the project would have facilitated more timely intervention planning.

Implementation Issues

Once the list of concerns was compiled and initially validated, these students were referred to the pre-referral intervention teams. The teams were to then review the student's files, interview the student's teachers, parents, and the student. With the information gathered by the team and the data gathered on the screener, the team was then to plan interventions and monitor their success.

One of the unexpected consequences of the process of developing these behavior norms was an increased awareness of systems-level changes that needed to occur to better support behavior at the school. These include developments of alternatives to suspension, improved data collection regarding behavior at school, and better understanding of how to address problem behavior at a secondary level and how to structure the school to help increase staff ownership of student success.

In the second year of implementation, students new to the school will be rated by their teachers and the students on the list of concern will be re-rated. The pre-referral intervention teams will work with those students who are above the 95th percentile at the time of the rating. Systemic work on data collection and behavior interventions are continuing. Additional changes are taking place on a larger scale at the school to support students' success, both academically and behaviorally. As data collection continues, it will be possible to evaluate the effects of these changes as they impact student behavior.

SUMMARY

This chapter has presented a rationale for the use of local norms and standards in the assessment of school-based functional and social behaviors, a set of basic considerations in the development of local procedures, and best practice guidelines using case-study examples. School psychologists are ideally suited to the roles of test development consultants and project coordinators: They possess knowledge of educational and psychological measurement and basic research design and intimate knowledge of the purposes of assessment in education and of the gaps between our technology and student/teacher needs.

The use of local norms for identifying and understanding achievement problems has been promoted among researchers and practitioners, particularly regarding implementing Curriculum-Based Measurement strategies. The advantage of locally normed procedures for identifying and understanding behavioral and functional skills problems has been well stated in the literature but appears to be less widely implemented in practice. Even very small projects at the classroom or building level can provide the local frame of reference necessary for appropriate identification of target behaviors that are essential to positive student outcomes. Skills that are basic to daily functioning in significant settings must be identified, analyzed, and directly taught if students are to succeed in mainstream schooling and, ultimately, meet the demands of independent living.

Many published, norm-referenced procedures offer technical advantages over locally developed measures but rely on national norms and assumptions of commonality in their criteria for success. There is no doubt that such general standards for performance should be considered in the assessment process. However, the importance of ecologically valid assessment to effective intervention cannot be overstated. By including local standards and situationally specific performance criteria in the comprehensive assessment plan, school psychologists can help promote better practices in both problem identification and intervention for a broad student population.

REFERENCES

Bardon, J. I. (1988). Alternative educational delivery approaches: Implications for school psychology. In J. L. Graden, J. E. Zins, & M. C. Curtis (Eds.), *Alternative educational delivery systems: Enhancing instructional options for all students* (pp. 563–571). Washington, DC: National Association of School Psychologists.

Braden, J., & Reschly, D. (1993, February). The future of assessment in public schools. *Communiqué, 21*(5), 9.

Canter, A. S., & Heistad, D. (1990). *Mainstream Survival Skills Assessment: Administration and technical manual (Minneapolis Schools Edition).* Minneapolis: Minneapolis Public Schools/Minnesota Department of Education.

Canter, A. S., Schrot, D., & Heistad, D. (1990). *Mainstream Survival Skills Assessment: Administration and technical manual (Minnesota Schools Edition).* Minneapolis: Minneapolis Public Schools/Minnesota Department of Education.

Cobb, J. A., & Hops, H. (1973). Effects of academic survival skills training on low achieving first graders. *Journal of Educational Research, 67*, 108–113.

Deno, S. (1989). Curriculum-Based Measurement and special education services: A fundamental and direct relationship. In M. R. Shinn (Ed.), *Curriculum-Based Measurement: Assessing special children* (pp. 1–17). New York: Guilford.

Edelbrock, C. (1983). Problems and issues in using rating scales to assess child personality and psychopathology. *School Psychology Review, 12*, 293–299.

Fagan, T., & Wise, P.S. (2000). *School psychology: Past, present, and future* (2nd ed.). Bethesda, MD: National Association of School Psychologists.

Gresham, F. (1981). Assessment of children's social skills. *Journal of School Psychology, 19*, 120–129.

Gresham, F. (1983). Social skills assessment as a component of mainstreaming placement decisions. *Exceptional Children, 49*, 331–336.

Gresham, F. (1984). Social skills assessment and training. In J. Ysseldyke (Ed.), *School psychology: State of the art* (pp. 57–80). Minneapolis: National School Psychology Inservice Training Network.

Gresham, F. (1999). Noncategorical approaches to K–12 emotional and behavioral difficulties. In D. Reschly, W. D. Tilly, & J.Grimes (Eds.), *Special education in transition: Functional assessment and noncategorical programming* (pp.107–138). Longmont, CO: Sopris West.

Hersh, R. H., & Walker, H. M. (1983). Great expectations: Making schools effective for all students. *Policy Studies Review, 2*, 147–188.

Hoier, T. S., McConnell, S. R., & Pallay, A. G. (1987). Observational assessment for planning and evaluating educational transitions: An analysis of template matching. *Behavioral Assessment, 9*, 6–20.

Hops, H., & Cobb, J. A. (1974). Initial investigations into academic survival skills training, direct instruction, and first grade achievement. *Journal of Educational Psychology, 66*, 548–553.

Horn, E., & Fuchs, D. (1987). Adaptive behavior in assessment and intervention: An overview. *Journal of Special Education, 21*, 11–26.

McConaughy, S., & Ritter, D. (1995). Multidimensional assessment of emotional or behavioral disorders. In A. Thomas & J. Grimes, *Best practices in school psychology III* (pp.865–878). Washington, DC: National Association of School Psychologists.

McConnell, S. R. (1987, February). *Planning for school transitions*. Paper presented to the Minnesota School Psychologists Association, Brainerd, MN.

McConnell, S. R., Strain, P., Kerr, M., Staff, V., Lenkner, D., & Lambert, D. (1984). An empirical definition of elementary school adjustment. *Behavior Modification, 8*, 451–473.

Reschly, D., & Tilly, W.D. III (1999). Reform trends and system design alternatives. In D. Reschly, W. D. Tilly, & J. Grimes (Eds.), *Special education in transition: Functional assessment and noncategorical programming* (pp.19–48). Longmont, CO: Sopris West.

Reschly, D. , Tilly, W.D. III, & Grimes, J. (1999). *Special education in transition: Functional assessment and noncategorical programming*. Longmont, CO: Sopris West.

Salvia, J., & Ysseldyke, J. E. (1995). *Assessment* (5th ed.). Boston: Houghton Mifflin.

Shinn, M. R. (1989). Identifying and defining academic problems: CBM screening and eligibility procedures. In M. R. Shinn (Ed.), *Curriculum-Based Measurement: Assessing special children* (pp. 90–129). New York: Guilford.

Shinn, M. R., Good, R. H., & Parker, C. (1999). Noncategorical special education services with students with severe achievement deficits. In D. Reschly, W. D. Tilly, & J. Grimes (Eds.), *Special education in transition: Functional assessment and noncategorical programming* (pp. 81–106). Longmont, CO: Sopris West.

Tilly, W.D. III, Reschly, D., & Grimes, J. (1999). Disability determination in problem solving systems: Conceptual foundations and critical components. In D. Reschly, W. D. Tilly, & J. Grimes (Eds.), *Special education in transition: Functional assessment and noncategorical programming* (pp. 285–321). Longmont, CO: Sopris West.

ANNOTATED BIBLIOGRAPHY

Hoier, T. S., McConnell, S. R., & Pallay, A. G. (1987). Observational assessment for planning and evaluating educational transitions: An analysis of template matching. *Behavioral Assessment, 9*, 6–20.
This article reports an observational study of behavioral conditions in mainstream versus special education classrooms that can be linked to intervention. Of particular relevance to local norming efforts is the review of research regarding local contingencies that impact teacher and student behavior and the description of data collection methods.

Shinn, M. R. (1989). Identifying and defining academic problems: CBM screening and eligibility procedures. In M. R. Shinn (Ed.), *Curriculum-Based Measurement: Assessing special children* (pp. 90–129). New York: Guilford.
This chapter, while specifically addressing CBM procedures, has useful applications to the development of local norms in general. Shinn discusses the creation of the "measurement net," alternative approaches to gathering local norms at the classroom/building/district levels, sampling procedures, data collection, and options for establishing norms.

Reschly, D. , Tilly, W. D., III, & Grimes, J. (1999). *Special education in transition: Functional assessment and noncategorical programming*. Longmont, CO: Sopris West.
This edited volume provides both overview and specific discussions of the applications of problem-solving models to the delivery of noncategorical special education services—including discussions of specific student populations, functional behavior assessment, legal parameters, and conceptual frameworks. Of particular relevance to local norming procedures are chapters by Shinn, Good, and Parker (severe academic deficits), Gresham (behavioral disorders), and disability determination (Tilly, Reschly, and Grimes).

70 Best Practices in Classroom Interventions for Attention Problems

George J. DuPaul
Lehigh University
Gary Stoner
Mary Jean O'Reilly
University of Massachusetts-Amherst

OVERVIEW

Problems with attention to classroom instruction and schoolwork are among the most common difficulties exhibited by students in the United States. In fact, a recent survey of teachers indicates that approximately 16% of elementary school children display frequent inattention and/or poor concentration (Wolraich, Hannah, Baumgaertel, & Feurer, 1998). Attention problems often are associated with behavioral difficulties, such as impulsivity, high activity level, and aggression. When attention problems are severe and/or are accompanied by developmentally inappropriate levels of impulsivity and overactivity, the psychiatric diagnosis of Attention-Deficit/Hyperactivity Disorder (AD/HD) may be used (American Psychiatric Association, 1994). Approximately 3–5% of elementary school-aged children in the United States are diagnosed with this disorder, with boys outnumbering girls at about a 2:1 to 5:1 ratio (American Psychiatric Association, 1994; Barkley, 1998). Given that most public school classrooms include 20–30 students, teachers will likely address the needs of at least one student with AD/HD per school year. Further, AD/HD symptoms typically persist from early childhood through at least adolescence for a majority of individuals (Barkley, 1998; Weiss & Hechtman, 1993). Thus, attention and associated behavioral difficulties are likely to affect children's school functioning throughout their educational careers.

Children with attention problems and/or AD/HD are at higher than average risk for a variety of behavioral difficulties including defiance toward authority figures, poor relationships with peers, and antisocial acts such as lying, stealing, and fighting (American Psychiatric Association, 1994; Barkley, 1998). In addition to these behavioral risks, students with AD/HD frequently struggle scholastically, presumably due to their low academic engagement rates and inconsistent work productivity (DuPaul & Stoner, 1994). The results of prospective follow-up studies of children with AD/HD into adolescence and adulthood indicate significantly higher rates of grade retention, placement in special education classrooms, and school drop-out relative to their peers as well as significantly lower high school grade point average, enrollment in college degree programs, and socioeconomic status (Weiss & Hechtman, 1993). Lower than expected rates of work completion may, in part, account for the association of AD/HD with academic underachievement, because up to 80% of students with this disorder have been found to exhibit academic performance problems (Cantwell & Baker, 1991). Further, about 20–30% of children with AD/HD are classified as "learning disabled" because of deficits in the acquisition of specific academic skills (Knivsberg, Reichelt, & Nodland, 1999). Additional students with AD/HD may receive special education services as a function of being classified as "other health impaired." In fact, "other health impaired" is the fastest growing special education category, increasing 280% over the past 10 years, presumably due to an increased identification of students with AD/HD (U.S. Department of Education, 1999).

Research investigating the connection between academic achievement difficulties and disruptive behavior disorders consistently indicates that the presence of attention problems and other AD/HD symptoms is the key variable accounting for poor scholastic outcome (Rapport, Scanlan, & Denney, 1999). The academic achievement problems associated with AD/HD appear to be generic rather than isolated to one particular subject area (e.g., reading or math). In addition, children with attention problems and AD/HD frequently experience difficulties getting along with peers and teachers as well as making friends (Barkley, 1998). Thus, the identification and treatment of academic and social difficulties in this population is critical.

Given the risk for poor academic and social outcomes, school professionals must design and implement interventions to address not only the attention problems endemic to AD/HD, but also the academic underachievement and aberrant social behavior associated with this disorder. The two primary interventions for AD/HD are psycho-stimulant medication (e.g., methylphenidate) and contingency management programming (e.g., token reinforcement and response cost). These intervention strategies have been found to enhance rates of academic productivity and accuracy for most study participants (for review see Barkley, 1998; DuPaul & Eckert, 1997). Further, some children may require the combination of stimulant medication and behavioral intervention to show improvements in academic functioning. Despite their positive effects, these interventions cannot be applied in a generic fashion without considering the individual needs of specific students with AD/HD. Further, given the myriad difficulties exhibited by students with this disorder, interventions must be implemented across home and school settings for an extended period.

The purpose of this chapter is to outline the most effective school-based interventions for attention problems or AD/HD. First, we review basic considerations in designing interventions for this population. Next, specific proactive and reactive intervention strategies are delineated. Finally, a summary of the state-of-the-art in school interventions for students with AD/HD is provided.

Throughout this chapter, we emphasize several key themes. First, to be optimally effective, interventions must be designed based on assessment data gathered before *and* after interventions are implemented. One cannot make informed decisions about treatment without assessment data. Second, interventions must be tailored to meet the unique needs of individual students. The best way to accomplish this is by collecting systematic data about behavioral, social, and academic functioning. Finally, a balanced approach to intervention is necessary wherein both proactive and reactive strategies are included in each student's treatment plan. Teachers should be encouraged to manipulate both antecedent and consequent events to optimize student attention, behavioral functioning, and academic achievement.

BASIC CONSIDERATIONS IN PROFESSIONAL TRAINING

Inherent in the responsibility to design, implement, and evaluate interventions for students with AD/HD is an assumption of appropriate professional training and competence. At a minimum, this includes coursework and supervised experience in diagnostic and educational assessment, developmental psychopathology, interventions for achievement and behavior problems, and professional service delivery models involving collaborative problem solving.

A wide range of assessment skills and strategies are necessary to serve students with AD/HD. For example, assessment for decisions of diagnosis and classification will involve the use of norm-referenced behavior rating scales and systematic direct observations of student behavior. Other necessary strategies will include structured and semi-structured interviews, standardized assessments of achievement, functional behavior assessment, and perhaps assessments of learning aptitude (see Hoff & Landau chapter in this volume for a thorough discussion of these strategies). Some of these same assessment strategies also will be useful for intervention planning and intervention evaluation.

In schools, students with AD/HD often present problems in both the achievement and behavior domains. Thus, school psychologists and other professionals responsible for these students will need to have training in a wide range of empirically supported intervention strategies (Kratochwill & Stoiber, 2000). For example, these students often are treated with psychotropic medications, primarily stimulants. Knowledge of these medications and their effects on children encompass issues of dose-response and time-response relationships, potential side effects, and outcome evaluation monitoring strategies. Additionally, students with ADHD often are involved in behavior and performance management programs. Such programs may be teacher mediated (e.g., token economy and response cost systems), parent mediated (e.g., home-school notes systems), peer mediated (e.g., ClassWide Peer Tutoring), and/or self-mediated (e.g., self-management strategies) (see DuPaul & Stoner, 1994; DuPaul & Power, 2000). Once again, the high quality design of each of these strategies requires specific knowledge, skills, and experiences of the responsible professional.

Finally, the complexities of assessment, diagnosis, and treatment of students with AD/HD result in services that will inevitably involve multiple professionals, parents, and other community members. As such, professional skills in the areas of consultation, collaboration, and coordination of persons and programs are needed for ensuring the quality services delivered. Together, then, this professional set of skills and knowledge in assessment, diagnosis, child development, interventions, and collaboration comprise the foundations of professional service delivery for students with AD/HD.

Conceptual Underpinnings of Interventions for Attention Problems

There are a number of important considerations that underlie best practices in designing interventions for students with attention problems and AD/HD-related difficulties. First, we have observed that all too often, school professionals rely on reactive and punitive procedures in attempting to change the behaviors of inattentive students. In fact, the most common classroom intervention for disruptive behavior is a verbal reprimand from the teacher and/or removal from the classroom. Unless these procedures are used sparingly, with minimal affect, and in the context of a positively reinforcing environment, they are unlikely to be successful. What we believe to be more successful is a balanced approach wherein both proactive and reactive strategies are employed. Specifically, antecedent events that typically precede inattentive behaviors should be manipulated to prevent problematic interactions from arising. In addition, reactive strategies should not be confined to punitive approaches, but should be heavily weighted toward providing positive reinforcement when attentive and appropriate behaviors occur.

Another guiding principle when designing effective interventions for students with attention problems is to intervene at the point of performance (Goldstein & Goldstein, 1998). Stated differently, to be optimally effective strategies must be implemented as close in time and place as possible to the target behavior. For example, if the behavior of concern is attention to and completion of math work, then the most effective intervention strategies will be those that are used in math class at the time when students are expected to complete math work. The further removed the intervention is from the time and place where the behavior of interest occurs, the less effective that strategy will be. This guiding principle is based on growing evidence that impulsivity is the primary deficit underlying the attention difficulties and other symptoms of AD/HD (Barkley, 1998). Thus, interventions need to be implemented in the heat of the moment to have any chance at changing behavior of an impulsive nature.

Intervention strategies for attention problems should be selected on the basis of assessment data and empirical support from the research literature. Rather than choosing interventions on the basis of trial-and-error, school professionals should collect systematic data about a student's academic and behavioral functioning as well as the classroom environment in an effort to make informed treatment selections. For example, data regarding the possible environmental functions of inattentive behavior can be used to develop interventions that directly address the putative function of problematic behavior (for review see DuPaul & Ervin, 1996). In similar fashion, Curriculum-Based Measurement data can be used to set appropriate targets for and assess the value of academic interventions. School professionals also should consult the research literature regarding the most effective interventions for students with AD/HD. There is clear evidence, for example, that manipulating environmental events in the classroom leads to large changes in behavior among students with even the most severe symptoms of this disorder (see meta-analysis by DuPaul & Eckert, 1997). Because the research literature is constantly evolving, educators need to keep abreast of the latest findings relative to effective strategies for attention difficulties.

A final guiding principle in designing interventions for students with attention problems is to avoid a one size fits all approach. Interventions must be individually tailored to meet the needs of each student despite the fact that students may share a common diagnosis or behavioral profile. This process of individualizing intervention plans should take into account (a) the child's current level of academic and behavioral functioning, (b) the possible environmental functions of their inattentive behavior, (c) the target behaviors of greatest concern to the teacher and/or student, and (d) elements of the classroom and/or teaching style that might limit the effectiveness of some interventions. Individualized interventions should be developed through a consultative problem-solving process using assessment data and collaborative interactions among teachers, parents, and other school professionals.

Interventions for students with attention problems can be mediated by a number of individuals, not just the classroom teacher. Specifically, effective strategies can be implemented by parents, peers, or the students with attention difficulties themselves. When available, computers can be used to enhance attention to academic instruction or the completion of drill-and-practice activities. The overriding principle here is that we need to go beyond placing an onus on the teacher to address all difficulties related to attention problems. There are important resources (e.g., peers) in the classroom and home environments that can be used to deliver interventions in a more comprehensive and cost-effective fashion. Table 1 presents some of the most effective intervention strategies in the context of academic setting (i.e., elementary versus secondary level) and mediating agent.

Overview of Interventions for Attention Problems

The most important intervention agent in the school building is the teacher. By using effective instructional and behavior management strategies, the teacher can provide the child with AD/HD and the child's classmates a learning environment that permits all students to fully participate in classroom activities. These strategies also can help provide the class with more instructional time by reducing the time spent coping with behavioral crises. By using effective strategies as part of a well-designed prevention program can allow a teacher to deliver instruction and evaluate student learning without the continual distractions and interruptions that poorly managed problem behavior can provoke.

Designing, implementing, and maintaining strategies does require some extra planning and work, but the benefits are likely to make the extra effort worthwhile. It is important, however, that the intervention strategies are acceptable to the teacher and appear workable. A well-designed intervention that a teacher finds difficult to implement and maintain is not likely

Table 1. Possible mediators for school-based interventions

Intervention type	*Elementary*	*Secondary*
Teacher-mediated	• Instructional strategies • Token reinforcement systems	• Study skills instruction • Contingency contracting
Parent-mediated	• Goal-setting • Contingency contracting • Home-based reinforcement • Parent tutoring	• Negotiating • Contingency contracting • Home-based reinforcement
Peer-mediated	• Peer tutoring	• Peer coaching • Peer mediation
Computer-assisted	• Instruction • Drill and practice	• Instruction • Word processing
Self-directed	• Self-monitoring	• Self-monitoring • Self-evaluation

to be put into action on a consistent basis (DuPaul, Eckert, & McGoey, 1997). Additionally, the constant daily demands made on a teacher's time and energy often become a priority over preventive intervention work that may not show immediate results (Colvin, Kame'enui, & Sugai, 1994).

Teacher-mediated strategies can be used by any adult participant in the classroom, including teacher aides, substitute teachers, or parent assistants. Although most interventions require that each adult carry them out precisely as planned, the strategies are generally simple in design and easily taught to any adults that may be involved in the classroom. Continuity of strategies across adults in a classroom or school serves to reinforce the desired behaviors and to improve management of student behaviors across settings.

Teacher-mediated strategies can be proactive or reactive. A combination of the two generally provides the best results. Proactive strategies typically involve the entire class and are arranged to prevent academic and behavioral difficulties by altering the classroom conditions that allow problems to arise. Proactive strategies can be used throughout the school building and may involve instructional and support staff. These strategies directly benefit all students. Reactive strategies are used in response to problems that arise in the classroom, and may be individually tailored to a particular student's needs. Reactive strategies can be used to respond to both appropriate and problem behavior.

The goal of these strategies is to monitor and improve student performance. To achieve this goal, it is essential to clearly communicate expectations and to provide both positive and corrective feedback to students. Both proactive and reactive strategies require that expectations and feedback are communicated on an ongoing basis. To be successful in the classroom, students with AD/HD generally require frequent opportunities to actively respond to instruction while receiving continual feedback on their performance (DuPaul, Ervin, Hook, & McGoey, 1998). The following strategies delineate ways in which school psychologists and teachers can design classroom routines and instructional delivery to meet the needs of these students while improving outcomes for the whole class.

Proactive Interventions

Proactive or preventive interventions typically involve changing something in the classroom environment *before* a student's inattentive behavior has a chance to occur. If the teacher is able to recognize those situations and cues that are reliably followed by inattentive and disruptive behavior, then a time-efficient way of handling this is to do something beforehand rather than waiting to react to the student's behavior. For many children with attention problems associated with AD/HD, the two primary classroom situations that prompt inattentive behavior are teacher-directed instruction and the presentation of independent academic work. Further, inattentive behaviors can lead to academic difficulties, behavior problems, or both. Thus, in this section, examples of proactive strategies for preventing inattentive behavior associated with academic and behavioral problems are discussed. The selection of proactive interventions for individual students typically is guided by identifying antecedent conditions (i.e., variables related to task, person, time, or setting) that are associated with academic or behavioral difficulty.

Proactive Interventions Focusing on Academic Performance

Proactive interventions that focus primarily on academic performance include adjusting curriculum to student instructional level, ClassWide Peer Tutoring (CWPT), computer-assisted instruction, providing students with task choices, and directed notetaking activities.

A primary consideration in addressing the academic performance of students with attention difficulties is the degree to which the curriculum matches students' instructional levels. More specifically, some students may demonstrate significant levels of inattention and off-task behavior as a function of being exposed to curriculum material that is beyond their instructional level. Curriculum-Based Measurement (CBM) data can be helpful in determining the proper placement of student instruction within the curriculum (Shinn, 1998). In fact, in some cases, an adjustment in instruction based on CBM data can lead to notable improvements in task-related concentration. The vast majority of children with attention problems related to AD/HD, however, will require additional interventions to address their academic and behavioral difficulties.

Peer tutoring is defined as any instructional strategy wherein two students work together on an academic activity with one student providing assistance, instruction, and/or feedback to the other (Greenwood, Maheady, & Carta, 1991). A number of peer tutoring models have been developed which differ as to instructional focus (acquisition versus practice), structure (reciprocal versus nonreciprocal), and procedural components (e.g., number of sessions per week, methods of pairing students, type of reward system used). Despite these differences, all models of peer tutoring share instructional characteristics that are known to enhance the task-related attention of students with AD/HD including (a) working one-to-one with another individual; (b) instructional pace determined by learner; (c) continuous prompting of academic responses; and (d) frequent, immediate feedback about quality of performance (Barkley, 1998).

One of the most widely used peer tutoring programs is CWPT (see Greenwood, Maheady, & Carta, 1991), which has been implemented in general education classrooms to enhance the mathematics, reading, and spelling skills of students of all achievement levels. CWPT includes the following steps: (a) dividing the class into two teams; (b) within each team, classmates form tutoring pairs; (c) students take turns tutoring each other; (d) tutors are provided with academic scripts (e.g., math problems with answers); (e) praise and points are contingent on correct answers; (f) errors are corrected immediately with an opportunity for practicing the correct answer; (g) teacher monitors tutoring pairs and provides bonus points for pairs that are following prescribed procedures; and (h) points are tallied by each individual student at the conclusion of each session. Tutoring sessions typically last 20 minutes with an additional 5 minutes for charting progress and putting materials away. At the conclusion of each week, the team with the most points is applauded by the other team. Points are not usually exchanged for any back-up reinforcement. CWPT has been found to enhance the on-task behavior and academic performance of non-medicated students with AD/HD in general education classrooms (DuPaul, Ervin, Hook, & McGoey, 1998). In the latter study, normally achieving students also showed improvements in attention and academic performance when participating in CWPT. Thus, peer tutoring is an intervention that can be implemented to help *all* students and, thus, offers a practical and time-efficient strategy for meeting the needs of children with attention problems.

There appears to be a variety of ways that computers can be used to enhance the academic achievement of all students, not just those with attention problems. Specifically, computers can promote the initial acquisition of skills through the use of instructional technology and can enhance the mastery of already acquired skills via drill-and-practice software. Some initial research (e.g., Ota & DuPaul, 2000) has provided support for the latter utility by demonstrating increases in the on-task and work productivity of students with AD/HD using computer-assisted instruction (CAI). The instructional features of CAI help students to focus their attention on academic stimuli. Although not always the case, CAI presents activities incorporating specific instructional objectives, provides highlighting of essential material (e.g., large print, and color), utilizes multiple sensory modalities, divides content material into smaller bits of information, and provides immediate feedback about response accuracy. In addition, CAI limits the presentation of nonessential features that may be distracting (e.g., sound effects and animation). More research is needed to determine the uses of specific software to enhance concentration and academic performance among students with attention problems.

Another proactive strategy is choice-making where a student is allowed to choose activities from two or more concurrently presented stimuli. Recent studies have demonstrated the value of providing task-related choices to students with behavior difficulties, including AD/HD, in that on-task behavior and work productivity can increase under choice conditions (e.g., Dunlap et al., 1994). Choice-making typically is implemented by providing a student with a menu of potential tasks in a particular academic subject area from which to choose. For example, if the student is having difficulty attending to independent math work, the child would be presented with several possible math assignments to complete. The child would be expected to choose and complete one of the tasks listed on the menu during the allotted time period. Thus, the student is provided with some control over the specific assignment, while the teacher retains control over the general nature of the assigned work.

Unfortunately, few proactive strategies have been developed specifically for secondary school students with attention difficulties and AD/HD. Adolescents with AD/HD may exhibit inferior organization and study skills, thereby increasing the risk for poor scholastic achievement (Barkley, 1998). Thus, secondary school students with attention problems may benefit from instruction and support in taking organized notes for later study. For example, the Directed Notetaking Activity (DNA; Spires & Stone, 1989) involves teacher-instructed lectures and prompts in an attempt to increase students' on-task behavior, improve comprehension of classroom materials, and reduce the frequency of disruptive behaviors. Specifically, the teacher instructs the students on the notetaking process by illustrating how to outline notes based on main ideas and details. The number of teacher prompts is slowly faded until students are able to independently form an outline based on the presented lecture material. The DNA program has been found to increase the quality of notes and the recording of instructional details by adolescents diagnosed with AD/HD (Evans, Pelham, & Grudberg, 1995). In addition, this procedure led to significant improvements in the classroom on-task behavior and daily academic performance of these students. This study is a good demonstration of the positive relation between enhanced academic skills and appropriate classroom behavior. Thus, targeting an academic skill, such as notetaking, may indirectly lead to improved classroom behavior on the part of students with attention difficulties.

Proactive Interventions Focusing on Social Behavior

Proactive strategies also can be used to enhance social behavior in situations when a specific student has been known to exhibit inattention and/or disruptive behavior. Two examples of interventions designed to prevent classroom behavior difficulties include active teaching of classroom or school rules and altering the structure of the classroom environment.

The degree to which teachers provide cues, prompts, or signals to follow classroom rules ultimately determines the success of those rules in maintaining appropriate student behavior (Paine, Radicchi, Rosellini, Deutchman, & Darch, 1983). Unfortunately, many elementary school-aged children do not fully understand classroom rules presumably because these are not taught to them with clarity and consistency. Not surprisingly, children with attention difficulties and AD/HD are among the students least likely to follow classroom rules. Thus, teachers should be encouraged to go back to basics by actively teaching rules to *all students* throughout the school year. Specifically, teachers should

1. Remind students of classroom rules and actively teach rules by discussion and pointing out examples of children following them (i.e., "catch" students following rules).
2. Maintain eye contact with students as instruction or other activities are in progress.
3. Remind students about expected behaviors *before* the start of the activity not *after* a rule has been broken.
4. Circulate throughout the classroom to monitor student behavior and provide feedback in an unobtrusive fashion.
5. Use nonverbal cues and signals to redirect a student while teaching others.
6. Maintain a brisk pace of instruction.
7. Ensure academic and nonacademic routines are well understood by students.
8. Frequently communicate their expectations about use of class time in a clear manner.

In addition to active teaching of classroom rules, teachers working with children who exhibit significant attention difficulties and AD/HD-related behaviors should consider altering the classroom environment to allow for more careful monitoring of student activities. For example, placing a student's desk near the teacher's may allow easier observation of the student's behaviors and enhance the probability that the student will understand teacher directives (Paine et al., 1983). Teachers also should be encouraged to arrange the classroom so that students with attention problems are more likely to participate in class activities while not restricting opportunities to learn and benefit from instruction. For example, students with attention problems may sometimes be placed in isolated parts of the classroom to decrease potential distractions for the child. Although this can be a successful move, it is important that the student remain accessible to teacher instruction and other class activities.

Reactive Interventions

Reactive intervention strategies typically focus on providing consequences for problem behavior. These strategies often are used on an individual, rather than a class-wide, basis. Individually tailored strategies can help to minimize the impact of disruptive behavior on a classroom, reduce the frequency of negative interactions between the student and the teacher, and teach the child a more appropriate way to get attention from the teacher. The goal of these strategies is to provide an environment that enhances the student's ability to focus on learning and minimizes the rewards for disruptive behavior. These interventions should be designed to fit the needs of the student by changing the conditions that maintain the problem behavior. All children will not respond in the same way to the implementation of these strategies.

Functional Assessment-Linked Strategies

Functional assessment strategies are interviews, observations, and environmental manipulations (e.g., changing a seating arrangement) intended to identify environmental variables that reliably precede or reliably follow problem behaviors of concern. Such variables are then hypothesized, in a behavior analytic formulation, to prompt or promote the occurrence of problem behavior, in the case of preceding variables. And in the case of variables reliably following problem behavior, these are hypothesized to reinforce or maintain problem behavior (see Nelson, Roberts, & Smith, 1998).

Understanding the factors that maintain the problem behaviors, along with the situations that appear to set the stage for those behaviors, is an essential first step in planning successful interventions (DuPaul, Eckert, & McGoey, 1997). For example, consider a target student's out-of-seat behavior that is reliably occasioned by the teacher's presentation of a class-wide, in-seat math work assignment. In this instance one potential intervention could involve provision of teacher assistance at the beginning of that assignment to ensure that directions are understood, the student has all necessary materials, and the student is able to independently complete the work assigned. This would be a preventive or proactive strategy.

Alternatively, consider the same student and behavior but a different formulation of the problem. In this instance, suppose the student's out-of-seat behavior reliably results in teacher attention (e.g., "Allen, do you need help with your math work? Let me see what you are doing."). Here it would be hypothesized that Allen's out-of-seat behavior is being reinforced through teacher-delivered social attention. At least one component of a "functional" approach to intervention would include behavior management strategies intended to strengthen an alternative behavior that would produce the same type of reinforcement—in this case teacher attention. For example, the teacher might use a strategy that included providing attention contingent upon Allen's being in his seat, and/or working on math assignments, and withholding attention when out-of-seat behavior occurs.

In a representative study, Ervin, DuPaul, Kern, and Friman (1998) used functional assessment strategies to guide the development of classroom-based interventions for four adolescents diagnosed with AD/HD. For two of these students, the interventions used were linked to problems hypothesized to serve the functions of escape from written tasks for one student, and access to peer attention for another student. Results of this work suggested that the classroom interventions based on functional assessment strategies resulted in significant improvements in the behavior of both students.

Response Cost

Token reinforcement is a commonly used strategy in which students earn points for meeting behavioral expectations, and the points can be exchanged for privileges. One example of this type of strategy is response cost, a type of token economy system. In this system, students earn tokens based on positive classroom behavior and lose them for inappropriate behavior. Response cost systems require planning and clear communication at the outset. The rules of the system should be taught and reviewed on an ongoing basis. The student should understand when the system will be used, how points may be gained or lost, what privileges are available in exchange for points, and when points may be turned in for privileges. It may be useful to check which privilege a student is working toward before beginning an activity, and to intermittently change the available privileges in order to maintain student interest.

It is essential that the student helps to create the list of possible privileges in this system and gains privileges on a regular basis. Electronic versions of response cost, such as the Attention Training System (ATS; Rapport, 1987) allow the teacher to respond to inappropriate behavior on the part of one child while continuing to work with other children or the whole class. This electronic system is made up of a student module, which sits on the student's desk, and a teacher module. The student automatically accumulates points as he or she works independently or in a group. When the teacher notices off-task or disruptive behavior, then points are easily deducted. This provides immediate feedback on student behavior without interrupting classroom activities or instruction.

A manual version of response cost uses numbered cards held together by a binder ring. The teacher adds and subtracts points by changing the top card on her set of cards as the child demonstrates appropriate or inappropriate behavior. As the teacher changes cards, the student changes the number of points on his or her set of cards to match the teacher's set. These strategies provide the student with frequent and immediate feedback on performance, which is an important factor in helping children with AD/HD meet the behavioral expectations of the classroom. This immediate communication of positive or corrective feedback helps to improve student outcomes in the areas of behavior and classroom achievement. Several studies have supported the use of response cost strategies for children with attention problems associated with AD/HD (see Barkley, 1998).

Time-Out From Positive Reinforcement

Time-out from positive reinforcement is another reactive strategy that can help to minimize problem behaviors in the classroom. This strategy can be used as an effective response to difficult behaviors, but must be applied according to careful guidelines. The teacher or school psychologist should note whether the use of this strategy results in reduced, rather than increased, rates of problem behavior. Continuing use of this strategy can cause the child to miss instruction on a regular basis, which can lead to academic problems. Guidelines in using this strategy include ensuring that the time-out period is brief (i.e., less than 10 minutes) and that it occurs immediately after the problem behavior. It also is essential that there be a reinforcing environment from which the child can be removed. If the environment is not stimulating and interesting to the child, then behavior that results in removal from the environment may increase. If the child's behavior is designed to provoke a response that will allow him or her to escape from or avoid a particular task or situation, then receiving a time-out from the classroom or task may reinforce the behavior.

Parents as Intervention Agents

Other effective strategies that can help improve student performance in the classroom are mediated by parents. Educators can provide an important service to parents of a child with AD/HD by clearly communicating school expectations and by teaching strategies that can be used by parents to promote academic success. Systematic ongoing communication is needed between the parents and teachers in order for parents to effectively support their child's academic performance. Designing a system to support ongoing communication is important, whether it consists of notes sent home on a daily or weekly basis, weekly check-in phone calls or e-mail, brief conversations when a child is picked up after school, or some other system that fits the particular family and school. Maintaining communication allows parents to hear about their child's struggles and successes in school, to communicate about home issues that may be influencing classroom performance, and to build a partnership with teachers with a goal of improving their child's ability to succeed in school.

Contingency Contracting

Home-based reinforcement programs can help to strengthen school-based behavior management systems by allowing the child to earn privileges at home based on positive school behavior. Effective home-based programs require ongoing communication between the teacher and parents; this can be accomplished through the use of a daily note or report that is sent home with the student (Pelham & Waschbusch, 1999). Parents and teachers can negotiate a contingency contract, which specifies the academic performance and classroom behavior that is expected and the privileges that can be earned at home if the child successfully demonstrates the behaviors. This type of contract is most likely to be successful if privileges can be earned each day, rather than on a weekly basis. Long-term success is built on small successes right from the start, so choosing criteria that the child is easily able to meet at the beginning while slowly building up to more challenging goals is an important feature of the contingency contract.

One study of the use of school-home notes with a preschooler with AD/HD showed that classroom on-task behavior increased contingent on home-based reinforcement (McCain & Kelley, 1993). In this study, the preschooler was allowed to color in a happy face on his school-home note when he completed a predetermined amount of time engaged in a task. Eventually, the child was able to set his own timer, engage in the task, then color in the happy face if he had stayed on-task for the full time. In addition, the preschool teacher circled happy, sad, or neutral faces on the school-home note at the end of various activities to provide feedback to the child and his parents about his success in meeting several target behaviors throughout the day. One drawback of home-school notes may be that the success of the system depends on the delivery of the notes, which is usually the responsibility of the child. In the case of a child with AD/HD, home-school communication may be more consistent and accurate if it takes place directly between the teacher and parents. The most effective method of communication should be determined on a case-by-case basis.

Self-Management

A more advanced type of strategy to improve classroom behavior involves self-directed activities that require children to monitor and/or evaluate their own behavior over time. The aspects of a self-management system most likely to actually be managed by the student include observing and evaluating behavior, while the task of identifying problem behaviors and goals is more likely to be done by adults (Fantuzzo & Polite, 1990). Further, interventions with a stronger self-management component may be more effective than those that are managed for the most part by the teacher. When developing interventions that include self-management components, it may be useful to clearly identify which aspects will be teacher-controlled and which will be managed by the student, and to make decisions about these based on the individual student's needs and abilities.

A self-evaluation system generally allows a student to earn points that can be used for privileges (e.g., Rhode, Morgan, & Young, 1983). The teacher clearly identifies the target behaviors and academic performance expected, and provides a written rating scale that states the performance criteria for each rating. The teacher and the student separately rate student behavior during an activity. At the end of the activity or time period, the teacher and student compare ratings. If they match exactly, then the student keeps all points and earns a bonus point. If the student rating is within one point of the teacher rating, then the student keeps his or her points. If the student rating is more than one point away from the teacher ratings, then the student does not receive points for the activity. Eventually, the close teacher involvement is faded, and the student becomes responsible for monitoring his or her own behavior.

Children with AD/HD often lack the skill to be accurate judges of their own behavior. Because they may have a tendency toward recalling their positive behaviors and not recognizing the problem behaviors that affect their ratings, a brief discussion or reminder of the behaviors that led to a lower rating may be useful (Hinshaw & Melnick, 1992). Setting up a self-management system in a classroom involves training the child with AD/HD in the system, providing clear descriptions of the expected behaviors, and drawing up a list of privileges the student would like to earn. The goal of such a system is to eventually train the child to monitor his or her own behavior in the classroom, without constant feedback from the teacher.

SUMMARY

Children with attention problems and/or AD/HD experience myriad academic and social difficulties that are not fully addressed by stimulant medication (i.e., the most common treatment for this disorder). A balanced intervention approach incorporating both proactive and reactive strategies appears optimal for comprehensively addressing the needs of students with attention problems. Several principles should guide intervention design with this population. First, intervention planning should be linked directly to assessment data (e.g., functional behavioral assessment and CBM). Second, a consultative problem-solving process (Kratochwill & Bergan, 1990) should be used to design and modify interventions. Next, maximum treatment effects will be obtained when intervention is implemented at the "point of performance." Fourth, intervention procedures are not written in stone but evolve and are modified on the basis of ongoing assessment data. Fifth, school psychologists must go beyond "train and hope" work with teachers and students to promote generalization and maintenance of behavior change over time and across settings. Specifically, it is insufficient to provide training without appropriate follow-up activities (e.g., modeling, feedback, and ongoing consultation). Sixth, interventions for children with attention problems should not place the entire onus on the classroom teacher. Rather, school psychologists should look to other possible intervention mediators (e.g., peers, parents, and the students, themselves), whenever possible. Finally, one must remember that all behavior serves a purpose, even actions that adults view as inattentive. Thus, whenever possible, interventions should replace inattentive behaviors with functionally equivalent actions that are appropriate for the classroom.

REFERENCES

American Psychiatric Association (1994). *Diagnostic and statistical manual of mental disorders* (4th ed.). Washington, DC: Author.

Barkley, R. A. (Ed.). (1998). *Attention-deficit hyperactivity disorder: A handbook for diagnosis and treatment.* New York: Guilford.

Cantwell, D. P., & Baker, L. (1991). Association between attention-deficit hyperactivity disorder and learning disorders. *Journal of Learning Disabilities, 24,* 88–95.

Colvin, G., Kame'enui, E., & Sugai, G. (1994). Reconceptualizing behavior management and school-wide discipline in general education. *Education and Treatment of Children, 16,* 361–381.

Dunlap, G., dePerczel, M., Clarke, S., Wilson, D., Wright, S., White, R., & Gomez, A. (1994). Choice making to promote adaptive behavior for students with emotional and behavioral challenges. *Journal of Applied Behavior Analysis, 27,* 505–518.

DuPaul, G. J., & Eckert, T. L. (1997). School-based interventions for children with Attention-Deficit/Hyperactivity Disorder: A meta-analysis. *School Psychology Review, 26,* 5–27.

DuPaul, G. J., Eckert, T. K, & McGoey, K. E. (1997). Interventions for students with Attention-Deficit/Hyperactivity Disorder: One size does not fit all. *School Psychology Review, 26,* 369–381.

DuPaul, G. J., & Ervin, R. A. (1996). Functional assessment of behaviors related to Attention Deficit/Hyperactivity Disorder: Linking assessment to intervention design. *Behavior Therapy, 27,* 601–622.

DuPaul, G. J., Ervin, R. A., Hook, C. L., & McGoey, K. E. (1998). Peer tutoring for children with Attention Deficit/Hyperactivity Disorder: Effects on classroom behavior and academic performance. *Journal of Applied Behavior Analysis, 31* , 579–592.

DuPaul, G. J., & Power, T. J. (2000). Educational interventions for students with attention-deficit disorders. In T. E. Brown (Ed.), *Attention-deficit disorders and comorbidities in children, adolescents, and adults* (pp. 607–635). Washington, DC: American Psychiatric Press.

DuPaul, G. J., & Stoner, G. (1994). *ADHD in the schools: Assessment and intervention strategies.* New York: Guilford.

Ervin, R. A., DuPaul, G. J., Kern, L., & Friman, P. C. (1998). Classroom-based functional and adjunctive assessments: Proactive approaches to intervention selection for adolescents with attention deficit hyperactivity disorder. *Journal of Applied Behavior Analysis, 31,* 65–78.

Evans, S. W., Pelham, W., & Grudberg, M. V. (1995). The efficacy of notetaking to improve behavior and comprehension of adolescents with Attention Deficit Hyperactivity Disorder. *Exceptionality, 5,* 1–17.

Fantuzzo, J. W., & Polite, K. (1990). School-based, behavioral self-management: A review and analysis. *School Psychology Quarterly, 5,* 180–198.

Goldstein, S., & Goldstein, M. (1998). *Managing attention disorders in children.* New York: John Wiley.

Greenwood, C. R., Maheady, L., & Carta, J. J. (1991). Peer tutoring programs in the regular education classroom. In G. Stoner, M. R. Shinn, & H. M. Walker (Eds.), *Interventions for achievement and behavior problems* (pp.179–200). Bethesda, MD: National Association of School Psychologists.

Hinshaw, S. P., & Melnick, S. (1992). Self-management therapies and Attention Deficit Hyperactivity Disorder. *Behavior Modification, 16*, 253–273.

Kelley, M. L. (1990). *School-home notes: Promoting children's classroom success.* New York: Guilford.

Knivsberg, A., Reichelt, K. L., & Nodland, M. (1999). Comorbidity, or coexistence, between dyslexia and attention deficit hyperactivity disorder. *British Journal of Special Education, 26,* 42–47.

Kratochwill, T. R., & Bergan, J. (1990). *Behavioral consultation in applied settings: An individual guide.* New York: Plenum.

Kratochwill, T. R., & Stoiber, K. C. (2000). Empirically supported interventions and school psychology: Conceptual and practice issues. Part II. *School Psychology Quarterly, 15*, 233–253.

McCain, A. P., & Kelley, M. L. (1993). Managing the classroom behavior of an ADHD preschooler: The efficacy of a school-home note intervention. *Child & Family Behavior Therapy, 15*, 33–44.

Nelson, J. R., Roberts, M. L., & Smith, D. J. (1998). *Conducting functional behavioral assessments: A practical guide.* Longmont, CO: Sopris West.

Ota, K. R., & DuPaul, G. J. (2000). *Improving mathematics achievement in children with attention deficit hyperactivity disorder: Effects of computer software.* Manuscript submitted for publication.

Paine, S. C., Radicchi, J., Rosellini, L. C., Deutchman, L., & Darch, C. B. (1983). *Structuring your classroom for academic success.* Champaign, IL: Research Press.

Pelham, W. E., & Waschbusch, D. A. (1999). Behavioral intervention in attention-deficit hyperactivity disorder. In H. C. Quay & A. E. Hogan (Eds.), *Handbook of disruptive behavior disorders* (pp. 255–278). New York: Kluwer Academic/Plenum.

Rapport, M. D. (1987). *The Attention Training System: User's manual.* DeWitt, NY: Gordon Systems.

Rapport, M. D., Scanlan, S. W., & Denney, C. B. (1999). Attention-deficit/hyperactivity disorder and scholastic achievement: A model of dual developmental pathways. *Journal of Child Psychology and Psychiatry, 40,* 11–69.

Rhode, G., Morgan, D. P., & Young, K. R. (1983). Generalization and maintenance of treatment gains of behaviorally handicapped students from resource rooms to regular classrooms using self-evaluation procedures. *Journal of Applied Behavior Analysis, 16*, 171–188.

Shinn, M. R. (Ed.). (1998). *Advanced applications of Curriculum-Based Measurement.* New York: Guilford.

Spires, H. A., & Stone, D. P. (1989). The directed notetaking activity: A self-questioning approach. *Journal of Reading, 33,* 36–39.

U.S. Department of Education. (1999). *Twenty-first annual report to Congress: Implementation of the Individuals with Disabilities Act.* Washington, DC: Author.

Weiss, G., & Hechtman, L. (1993). *Hyperactive children grown up* (2nd ed.). New York: Guilford.

Wolraich, M. L., Hannah, J. N., Baumgaertel, A., & Feurer, I. D. (1998). Examination of DSM-IV criteria for attention-deficit/hyperactivity disorder in a county-wide sample. *Journal of Developmental and Behavioral Pediatrics, 19,* 162–168.

ANNOTATED BIBLIOGRAPHY

Barkley, R. A. (Ed.). (1998). *Attention-deficit hyperactivity disorder: A handbook for diagnosis and treatment* (2nd ed.). New York: Guilford.

Provides extensive coverage of AD/HD and its history, as well as clinical perspectives on the developmental course of AD/HD and its assessment. Also, provides excellent coverage of diagnosis and treatment of children and adults with AD/HD, as well as strategies for working with the families/parents of children with this disorder.

DuPaul, G. J., Ervin, R. A., Hook, C. L., & McGoey, K. E. (1998). Peer tutoring for children with Attention Deficit Hyperactivity Disorder: Effects on classroom behavior and academic performance. *Journal of Applied Behavior Analysis, 31*, 579–592.
Demonstrates the use and effectiveness of class-wide peer tutoring with elementary aged students diagnosed with AD/HD in general education settings. The majority of students with AD/HD showed improvements in task engagement. About half of the students with AD/HD also experienced academic performance improvements in math or spelling.

Du Paul, G. J., & Stoner, G. (1994). *AD/HD in the schools: Assessment and intervention strategies.* New York: Guilford
Provides a thorough overview and treatment of research, assessment, interventions, and service delivery issues pertinent to children diagnosed with AD/HD, with a particular focus on school functioning and educational practices. Presents a school-based model of diagnostic assessment, as well as medication treatment issues, and classroom-based interventions for achievement and behavior problems.

Ervin, R. A., DuPaul, G. J., Kern, L., & Friman, P. C. (1998). Classroom-based functional and adjunctive assessments: Proactive approaches to intervention selection for adolescents with attention deficit hyperactivity disorder. *Journal of Applied Behavior Analysis, 31*, 65–78.
Examines the utility of functional assessment strategies applied to two adolescents with challenging behaviors in classroom settings. Provides examples of individualized classroom interventions linked to the individual functional assessments, and documents intervention effectiveness. Shows the utility and acceptability of these approaches to teachers and students.

Repp, A. C., & Horner, R. H. (Eds.). (1999). *Functional analysis of problem behavior: From effective assessment to effective support.* Belmont, CA: Wadsworth.
Provides extensive research and practical information about functional analysis strategies and their linkage to effective interventions. Exhaustive coverage of foundational perspectives, models, strategies, and applications in school and community settings is provided. School focused topics include preventing problem behavior in classrooms, working with students identified with behavior disorders, and assessing variables related to curriculum and instruction.

71 Best Practices in the Assessment of Children With Attention Deficit/Hyperactivity Disorder: Linking Assessment to Intervention

Kathryn E. Hoff
Karla Doepke
Steven Landau
Illinois State University

OVERVIEW

Since the publication of our previous edition chapter (Landau & Burcham, 1995), there have been remarkable professional-practice changes regarding children with Attention-Deficit/Hyperactivity Disorder (ADHD). ADHD is not only the most prevalent disorder of children, involving 3–5% of the school-age population (American Psychiatric Association, 1994), it has also been the focus of more scientific inquiry than any other childhood disorder. As such, new information has appeared at a rapid rate, and there have been many significant changes over the past 10 years that impact the identification of these children. In this chapter we will first discuss the evolving nomenclature and diagnostic/assessment practices that apply to children with ADHD, followed by a brief review of characteristics associated with ADHD. Next, we shall discuss recent important areas of change that impact assessment and intervention with this population, such as increase in medication usage, legal mandates related to ADHD assessment, and the ascension of "functional assessment" in school psychology. Finally, because school psychologists are being called upon to address the multiple needs of children with ADHD, a framework is presented that provides for accurate assessment that can be linked directly to designing effective interventions.

Psychiatric Classification of ADHD

One of the more perplexing issues confronting professionals working with children who present symptoms of ADHD involves confusion (especially in the lay community) resulting from ever-changing diagnostic labels used to denote the disorder (e.g., "My son doesn't have ADHD; he's got ADD!"). Many factors account for this misunderstanding, including extensive albeit misleading ADHD-related discourse in the popular press and Internet. In any case, the most likely explanation for these nomenclature changes relates to improved understanding of the disorder. Historically, ADHD has been portrayed by various diagnostic labels, each one emphasizing differences in hallmark symptoms and inferred loci of the problem.

With the second edition of the *Diagnostic and Statistical Manual of Mental Disorders* (*DSM-II*; American Psychiatric Association, 1968), the field focused on hyperkinesias (i.e., motor excess) as the defining characteristic of the disorder. Thus, these children were considered hyperactive and the disorder became officially known as Hyperkinetic Reaction of Childhood. However, with the time of the publication of *DSM-III* (American Psychiatric Association, 1980), an entirely different perspective of the disorder emerged. Now, a severe deficit in the child's ability to attend was central to the diagnosis instead of the singularly required hyperactive symptoms. The disorder was known as Attention Deficit Disorder (ADD), and subtypes of ADD included ADD/H (with hyperactivity) and ADD/WO (without hyperactivity). Thus, among children with clinically significant attentional problems, it was not necessary to present major- and minor-motor symptoms, such as "always on the go," "squirmy and fidgety," "can't sit still," and "hums and makes other odd noises" to be diagnosed with ADD. Additionally, *DSM-III* recognized that stage-of-development and age of onset were central to diagnostic practices, with ADD requiring a childhood onset.

In spite of the growing recognition of the legitimacy of this new ADD perspective (see Milich, Ballentine, & Lyman, in press), the publication of *DSM-III-R* in 1987 (American Psychiatric Association, 1987) perplexed many by returning to a "polythetic" (Landau, Milich, & Widiger, 1991) criteria set. Subtyping of the disorder was no longer prescribed for classification. Instead, children with ADHD earned a diagnosis by meeting 8 or more of *any* 14 symptoms in the set. The number of symptom combinations was considerable. In the context of *DSM-III-R,* it would be possible to have an ADHD diagnosis in the *absence* of significant attentional difficulties (a questionable assumption based on factor analytic data). The disorder was known as Attention-Deficit/Hyperactivity Disorder, making ADD an anachronistic label as of 1987. Because of this polythetic classification approach, extensive heterogeneity in the symptom pictures of children with ADHD led to difficulties in clinical practice. Indeed, assessment, diagnostic, and treatment protocols that seemed appropriate for many children with ADHD were inappropriate for others.

The current psychiatric taxonomy was introduced in 1994 with the publication of *DSM-IV* (American Psychiatric Association, 1994). In this edition, the label itself remained the same (i.e., ADHD), but there was a return to the subtyping approach described in *DSM-III.* Specifically, children could now be diagnosed as having ADHD-Predominantly Inattentive Type, a disorder that approximates ADD/WO in *DSM-III.* This designation should be applied to those who are easily distracted by irrelevant stimuli and fail to sustain attention, have organizational difficulties and seem forgetful, and appear sluggish. However, by definition, they do not have significant problems with hyperactive and impulsive behaviors. Many of these Inattention criteria pertain directly to the child's performance in school. In addition, children with ADHD-Predominantly Hyperactive/Impulsive Type are diagnosed if they meet a series of acting-out criteria such as "often on the go and acts as driven by a motor," "talks excessively," "fidgets with hands or feet," and "has difficulty awaiting turn." Children in this category do not have significant problems with their attending behavior. Interestingly, both anecdotal and empirical support for this type of ADHD is quite limited (see Milich et al., in press, for a review). Third, children who present a symptom picture that transcends both the Inattentive criteria set and the Hyperactive/Impulsive set are diagnosed as having ADHD-Combined Type (similar to ADD/H in *DSM-III*). Regardless of which subtype is classified, *DSM-IV* also requires documentation that the child's impairment was evident before the age of 7, and that it significantly affected functioning in two or more settings (e.g., home and school).

The Empirical Approach to Classification

By virtue of its subtypic perspective, the *DSM-IV* conceptualization of ADHD reflects a multidimensional or two-factor view of the disorder. In other words, and in contrast to earlier belief (e.g., *DSM-III-R*), factor and cluster analytic studies indicate that symptoms of inattention, hyperactivity, and impulsivity do not necessarily co-occur in samples of children. Although a review of these results is well beyond the scope of this chapter, there are numerous demonstrations (e.g., Lahey, Carlson, & Frick, 1997) that two distinct dimensions, representing symptoms of inattention and hyperactivity/impulsivity, emerge using quantitative methods. Thus, most empirical approaches to the classification of ADHD support the distinction between children whose primary problems reflect inattention and disorganization (i.e., ADHD-Inattentive Type) versus those with symptoms of inattention *as well as* hyperactivity/impulsivity (i.e., ADHD-Combined Type). Results of this empirically derived two-factor conception of ADHD were supported in prepublication field trials of *DSM-IV* (see Frick et al., 1994), indicating that the two ADHD disorders are discrete and unrelated.

The Two ADHD Disorders

Inattention

When examining the actual *DSM-IV* diagnostic criteria for ADHD, it is easy to infer that the symptoms of impaired attention are the same for both Predominantly-Inattentive and Combined subtypes. As such, referred children in either group will have similar symptoms of attentional difficulties, but those in the Combined group will also have problems with hyperactive/impulsive behaviors. Unfortunately, as suggested by Milich et al. (in press), this may not be the case. Even though there have been few investigations designed to examine differences in the topography of inattention as a function of subtype assignment, data indicate children in the two subtypes may differ in their inattention difficulties. Specifically, a sluggish cognitive tempo, paired with slow moving response style, plus drowsiness and lethargy, seem to characterize those in the Predominantly Inattentive group. In addition, these children may have higher scores on Internalizing symptoms and disorders. Unfortunately, this pattern is not without ambiguity. According to Milich et al. (in press), it is possible that those receiving a Predominantly-Inattentive diagnosis also have an insufficient or sub-threshold number of serious hyperactive/impulsive symptoms. As such, the group of Inattentive children may be significantly more heterogeneous than intended by *DSM-IV* diagnostic criteria. In contrast, children in the Combined group seem more likely to have inattention problems such as being distractible, disorganized, irresponsible, sloppy, and intrusive to the classroom environment. Rating scale data indicate they are more likely to present Externalizing characteristics. Given the fact that *DSM* sought to invoke the same Inattention diagnostic criteria for both subtypes, and the paucity of laboratory and observation studies about subtypical inattention differences, it is not surprising that definitive conclusions about the inattention construct have failed to emerge (Milich et al., in press).

Hyperactivity/Impulsivity

The symptoms of motor excess and impulsive responding have been associated with the disorder since its earliest descriptions. This Hyperactive/Impulsive cluster leads to disruptive behaviors in school, rule violations, and difficulty functioning in transitions (Landau & Milich, 1988). Indeed, most school psychologists could comfortably assert "I know it when I see it" when reflecting on the Hyperactive/Impulsive features of ADHD.

To better understand the nature of ADHD represented by hyperactivity/impulsive and inattentive behaviors, Barkley (1997, 1998) has presented an explanation in which all symptoms are attributed to a single phenomenon—known as behavioral disinhibition. According to his theory, the daily demands of academic and social settings place high premium on the child's ability to suppress or delay a response. However, children with ADHD are not able to *inhibit* their behavior at a rate commensurate with agemates. Additionally, Barkley argues that children with ADHD experience difficulties in executive functioning that interfere with working memory, internalization of speech, self-regulation of affect and arousal, and reconstitution (i.e., the ability to rapidly analyze and reconstruct parts of language to constitute meaningful communicative speech). According to his theory, this combination of deficits best explains the syndromal picture of children with ADHD. It should be noted, however, that Barkley has systematically excluded from consideration those with Predominantly Inattentive Type. In his opinion, these children represent a distinct disorder that deserves other explanations.

Although a comprehensive discussion of Barkley's "unifying theory" is beyond the scope of this chapter, a few points are worth mentioning. First, Barkley's hypothesis regarding a deficient working memory is consistent with numerous anecdotal and empirical reports about children with ADHD who fail to efficiently and effectively execute lengthy sequences of goal-directed behavior. This deficiency may explain frequent teacher and parent complaints of forgetfulness, failure to follow direction, and noncompliance.

Second, Barkley (1997) focuses on the self-regulatory and metacognitive applications of language. In this context, language serves as a way for the child to communicate reflectively with self when plans of action are considered, acted out, and evaluated. This portion of his theory borrows heavily from the work of Vygotsky (1934/1987), who asserted that children use speech-to-self (i.e., private speech) as a problem-solving strategy to overcome cognitive challenges and respond to demands of self-regulation. Private speech is initially manifested as externalized thought spoken audibly. However, as children mature, their private speech becomes more internalized and less audible. Empirical investigations by Berk and Landau (1993) and Landau and Berk (2000) suggest that, although the private speech of children with ADHD follows the same maturational path as it does for children without the disorder, it shows a significant delay according to developmental norms. As such, children with ADHD who are expected to "sit quietly at your desk and do your math worksheets!" may be prevented by teachers to engage in a strategy that could be necessary for them (i.e., they may need to solve their problems out loud). Research data indicate that effective use of private speech strongly predicts attention-to-task and motor control (Landau & Berk, 2000).

The third component in Barkley's unifying theory pertains to the ability to self-regulate emotion, motivation, and arousal. According to Barkley (1997), children with ADHD present a significant delay in this ability. Recent data (Mangione & Landau, 2001) support Barkley's assumptions. Poor regulation of affect may also explain why many of these children become excited and distracted by impending rewards used in psychosocial interventions such that performance is disrupted. In the social domain as well, emotional arousal seems to be a contributing factor to the ubiquitous problem of disturbed peer relations (Landau et al., 1998).

The final deficit in executive functioning involves the process of reconstitution, the language-based ability to decompose a stimulus event and then reconstruct an appropriate response to the immediate episode. Verbal discourse, peer communications, story-telling and writing narratives, and the creation of alternative solutions exemplify activities that require reconstituted information (Barkley, 1997). Thus, children who show a delay in their ability to reconstitute events have difficulty developing efficient strategies and seem inflexible or less adaptable to changing environmental demands. For example, numerous anecdotal reports reveal children's difficulties negotiating transitions at school (e.g., returning from recess to quiet desk work quietly; traveling through the hall to go from class to the cafeteria). Additionally, empirical work in the area supports this notion (see, for example, Landau & Milich, 1988).

In the context of understanding the disinhibited characteristics of children with ADHD, the reader is encouraged to consider Barkley's (1997, 1998) unifying theory with several qualifying points in mind. First, as previously indicated, his comprehensive explanation is not applicable to those with ADHD-Predominantly Inattentive Type; these children do not have difficulties with behavioral disinhibition. Second, his theory seems to clarify the important distinction between *skill deficit* versus *performance deficit* as a way to understand the inappropriate behavior of these disinhibited children. Indeed, this distinction should be made regarding all referrals seen by school psychologists, as it is necessary for intervention planning. If children with ADHD experience a skill deficit, one would infer they lack the adaptive skills and knowledge necessary to function in age-appropriate fashion. As such, treatments should take on a skill-development focus (e.g., social skills training). However, if their problems are best explained as a performance deficit, we infer they have the requisite skills and "know how to behave" appropriately. In this latter case, they are simply unable to apply their skills efficiently and effectively in daily situations. Interventions should then focus on developing strategies to assist them in their application of skills already present. If Barkley is correct, and many empirical reports support this contention, then it would be unfair to argue that these children *could* behave properly "if only they tried harder." The final qualifying point to be made about Barkley's theory is it should be viewed as a scholarly guide for future research rather than an unequivocal and valid account of the disorder.

Associated Features

Children with ADHD commonly experience difficulties that go well beyond the *DSM* diagnostic criteria (Jensen, Martin, & Cantwell, 1997). Given the heterogeneity among children diagnosed with ADHD, it is understandable that not all of these children experience additional difficulties, and those who do represent an even more heterogeneous mix of symptoms and disorders. We strongly recommend that assessment of ADHD go well beyond the primary features of the disorder. It should also include a focus of comorbid problems.

Conduct Problems

The most obvious secondary problems include disorders of conduct, with many children with ADHD also meeting the special education eligibility criteria for

Emotionally Disturbed (ED). Although the rates of overlap vary across studies, ADHD is one of the earliest difficulties to co-occur with conduct disorder (CD), and at least one-half of all children with ADHD present comorbid oppositional-defiant and/or conduct disorder diagnoses (Loeber, Green, Lahey, Frick, & McBurnett, 2000). Thus, many can be extremely stubborn, noncompliant, and hostile, and may engage in rule violations, stealing, lying, and aggressive acts (Hinshaw, 1987). This is significant, as follow-up studies of comorbid children with ADHD and CD predict the perseverance of ADHD, and is associated with more serious adolescent and adult adjustment problems (Loeber et al., 2000).

Social Concerns

Many children with ADHD experience disturbed peer relations and are considered by others to be highly aversive playmates (Landau et al., 1998). Many of these children are bossy, loud, intrusive, domineering, disruptive, and easily frustrated while in play situations. Additionally, children with ADHD emit more argumentative statements, and display more explosiveness and defiance than children without ADHD (Barkley, 1998). To make matters worse, the negative reputation earned from exhibiting these behavioral clusters can be established after only brief contact with unfamiliar children (Pelham & Bender, 1982). Given these social interaction patterns, it is not surprising that as many as 50% of children with ADHD are frequently rejected by peers and encounter difficulties making and keeping friends (Landau et al., 1998). Peer rejection is a serious outcome for children with ADHD, as those who experience rejection early in life are known to be at high risk for aggression and delinquency, school maladjustment, later psychiatric disorders, plus adult outcome difficulties, including job dismissals, bad conduct discharge from the military, police contact and incarcerations, and psychiatric hospitalizations (Parker & Asher, 1987).

Achievement Difficulties

Children with ADHD are also at elevated risk for achievement difficulties, and many experience academic skill deficits or meet special education placement criteria as learning disabled (McGee & Share, 1988). Because children with ADHD in the classroom are typically off-task, noisy, disruptive, out-of-seat, and do not finish school work or homework, both parents and teachers complain of underachievement. Their school work can be highly inefficient and disorganized, and performance often shows great fluctuations. Consequently, there may be a grave discrepancy between actual achievement and the child's estimated potential for learning. To make matters worse, there is suggestive evidence that children with ADHD may score an average of one half to one full standard deviation below agemates on standardized tests of intelligence. Even though there are competing explanations for this discrepancy (see Barkley, 1998), there is reason to worry that these children do experience a delay in the development of some cognitive strategies (Whalen, 1989). Because of these academic difficulties, many of these children experience failure in school and grade retentions. This failure, in combination with their problem behaviors and tendency to alienate peers, places them at great risk for negative feedback from parents, teachers, and the peer group.

Additional Concerns

It is little wonder that children with ADHD are also at risk for low self-esteem and depression as they mature, and therefore it is recommended that symptoms of internalizing disorders also be considered during the assessment process. It is worth noting that families of children with ADHD tend to exhibit higher levels of divorce, marital discord, and parent frustration than families without an ADHD child. Therefore, information on these specific family characteristics may provide the school psychologist with valuable information that guides the planning of intervention strategies. An evaluation of the family's strengths and weaknesses round out the assessment picture.

BASIC CONSIDERATIONS

Recent Events

Medication

One change currently receiving considerable attention is the increase of school-based use of medications (e.g., methylphenidate or Ritalin®). Indeed, according to the American Association of Applied and Preventative Psychology, nearly 20 million prescriptions were written last year for the psychopharmacological treatment of ADHD, and various surveys reveal a six- to eight-fold increase in prescriptions during the 1990s. In addition, there is a dramatic increase in the number of preschool-age youngsters who are presently taking psychostimulant medication. Even though efficacy data are encouraging, Ritalin® does not have FDA approval for children under the age of 6, and no long-term safety data are available regarding methylphenidate effects on the developing neurological system of 3- and 4-year-olds. To exacerbate this problem, Campbell (1990) makes it clear that differential diagnoses for hard-to-manage preschool-age children are extremely elusive, leading to numerous false-positives.

Internet postings and the popular press have had a field day with these issues. There is widespread community concern about the cultural shift during the previous two decades regarding a willingness to medicate disruptive or disturbing children. Most school psychologists have had anecdotal experience regarding primary care physicians who have prescribed Ritalin® in the absence of data from school. In addition, we are becoming exposed to the increased comfort many teachers feel asserting, for example, in a parent conference setting "Henry has given me problems since the beginning of school. He won't sit still, constantly annoys other children, and never gets his work done. I really think it would be good for him to be on medication. Please discuss this with your pediatrician." Not surprisingly, the prospect that teachers could or should discuss medication with parents has received attention from some state legislatures. For example, in July 2001, the state of Connecticut enacted the first-in-the-nation law as a backlash to this practice and the apparent over-use of medication to treat these problems. This law prohibits teachers, counselors, and other school personnel (read: school psychologists) from suggesting psychiatric medications to any parent; the intention of the law is to ensure the *first* mention of drugs comes from a physician.

There have been several trends during the 1990s that may account, in part, for the increased use of these medications. According to Kotulak (2000), other psychiatric disorders exist with symptoms that mimic ADHD. Unfortunately, these tend to present to physicians at a much lower base rate (e.g., schizophrenia), leading to false diagnostic conclusions. Second, many professionals would be hard pressed to precisely define the difference between normal and age-appropriate overactive and rambunctious behavior from that indicative of ADHD. As previously indicated, this is a particularly vexing issue for those who work with preschool-age children. Is it the case the child presents clinically significant indicators of a veritable psychiatric disorder or does the mother's request for medication reveal parental intolerance of her high-energy youngster who is actually functioning within normal limits? Third, there is reason to worry that mandatory school-based learning standards adopted across the country have increased performance-focused pressure on educators. Certainly, students with ADHD encounter their own set of learning problems; however, ADHD also can interfere with the learning of others. In a climate of growing teacher accountability, ADHD in the classroom can present difficulties for many. Finally, the prominence of managed care during the 1990s reveals a preference for medication as a "treatment of choice." Insurance companies naturally prefer to authorize this easy, efficient, and inexpensive form of treatment over more time-consuming alternatives (Kotulak, 2000).

Recent Legal Issues

School psychologists should be familiar with the recent changes in the Individuals with Disabilities Education Act Amendments (IDEA '97), and corresponding March 1999 IDEA regulations, especially in relation to an ADHD assessment. The final regulations now explicitly include ADHD under the list of *possible* chronic or acute health problems that may render a child eligible under the Other Health Impairment (OHI) category. This change was not intended to identify more children, but merely to codify the U.S. Department of Education's long-standing position that a child with ADHD may be eligible for special education and related services under the "OHI" designation (Analysis, pp. 12542–12543). However, the diagnosis of ADHD does not automatically entitle that child to receive special education services, nor is it necessary. Children with ADHD are still required to meet the two-pronged eligibility criteria to receive special education services under IDEA '97. First, the child must be identified as having a disability, under 1 of the 13 eligibility categories. If the child is not eligible under OHI, then the child may be eligible under another disability category, such as learning disability or emotional disturbance. The second criteria for receiving special education services is that the child must *need* special education and related services because of the disability. If a child does not qualify for services under IDEA '97, then the child still may be eligible for services under Section 504. Specifically, a child qualifies for services if he or she (a) has a disability that *substantially* limits one or more major life activities (e.g., walking, speaking, learning), (b) has a record or history of having such an impairment, and (c) is regarded as having such an impairment (Zirkel & Aleman, 2000). School psychologists are urged to read Telzrow and Tankersley (2000) or Zirkel and Aleman (2000) for more information regarding student eligibility of services under IDEA or Section 504.

Perhaps a more significant legal change put forth by the IDEA '97 is the required use of functional behavioral assessment (FBA) and positive behavioral interventions and supports. Although this change in law is not specific to students with ADHD, it does pertain to students with possible disabilities who exhibit problem behavior. For example, when a child with disabilities exhibits problem behavior that impedes his or her learning or the learning of others, or if the child's inappropriate behavior is repetitive or anticipated to re-occur, the student's Indivudual Education Plan (IEP) team must address these behaviors with positive behavioral interventions, strategies, and supports. Additionally, IDEA '97 now details specific conditions that trigger conducting a mandatory functional behavioral assessment and completing a behavior intervention plan (e.g., on the eleventh cumulative day of a suspension or placement in an interim alternative educational setting §300.520(b)). The actual procedures required for conducting a FBA and behavior intervention plan are not defined in the regulations. For additional information on the legal issues surrounding functional behavioral assessments, readers are referred to Drasgow and Yell (2001).

Functional Assessments

Numerous experts in the field recently have promoted the use of functional assessment methodologies for assessment and intervention of ADHD and ADHD-related behaviors. In general, functional assessment refers to a range of procedures used to identify functional relationships between the occurrence or nonoccurrence of a behavior, and environmental variables that contribute to the development and maintenance of that behavior. To identify these associations, functional assessment procedures incorporate multiple assessment strategies from a variety of sources, including interviews, rating scales, and direct observations (e.g., Dunlap et al., 1993; O'Neill et al., 1997). Functional assessment extends our assessment methodologies by determining *why* the problem behavior occurs (identifying cause-effect relations) rather than *what* the problem behavior looks like. For a more detailed discussion and description of functional assessment, readers are encouraged to look at several excellent sources for additional information (e.g., DuPaul, Eckert, & McGoey, 1997; Knoster & McCurdy, this volume; Watson, Gresham, & Skinner, 2001).

There are distinct advantages to incorporating functional assessment methods and procedures. First, as mentioned above, functional assessments are now required by mandates in the IDEA 1997 Amendments. Second, best practice requires school psychologists employ assessment techniques that can be directly linked to subsequent interventions. Interventions that are linked to assessment data have a greater likelihood of producing lasting behavior change that is maintained across situations and over time. Additionally, assessment-driven interventions are potentially more cost and time effective than using a trial and error approach to intervention selection, which may enhance treatment acceptability and integrity. Third, functional assessment methods and procedures facilitate individualized interventions (e.g., DuPaul & Ervin, 1996). Because of the extreme heterogeneity among children with ADHD, a mere diagnosis of the disorder has no implications for treatment selection. Specifically, the functions of the ADHD-like behaviors (topography) will vary considerably across students. A functional assessment, or determining *why* a problem behavior occurs, provides invaluable intervention information in a world where "one size does not fit all" (DuPaul et al., 1997). Finally, functional assessment utilizes a problem-solving framework and represents a flexible assessment strategy that school psychologists should use. Although it would be premature to dictate a "best practices in functional assessment" for school psychologists (e.g., Ervin et al., 2001), its methods and procedures can be easily incorporated into the consultative problem-solving paradigm of Bergan and Kratochwill (1990), a model we will describe. As Gresham, Watson, and Skinner (2001) note, “Functional behavioral assessment belongs in the armamentarium of school psychologists.”

Developmental Perspective

Although a developmental approach to assessment is not new, there are increasing numbers of preschoolers and older youth referred for ADHD evaluations. When assessing ADHD, determinations of problem behaviors should be based upon knowledge of developmental norms (i.e., the child was found to behave in age-inappropriate fashion). Without such a perspective, psychologists are at risk of over identifying attention and activity problems among preschool-age children (Hinshaw et al., 1992). Alternatively, ADHD-related behaviors may be under identified among adolescents due to the covert nature of problems in this age group (Barkley, 1998). Thus, the school psychologist must have a sound knowledge of normative or age-appropriate behavior. To determine whether a problem exists, school psychologists need to examine both the frequency and intensity of the problem behavior, and consider whether the problem is typical for a given age group and the problematic environment. It is critical to use assessment procedures that include components with adequate normative data (e.g., norms broken down by age and gender). Further, methods should have high test—retest reliability to help determine whether the problem is merely a transient phenomenon or a more chronic concern. Ultimately, a developmental perspective provides relevant and realistic goals for the intervention plan (i.e., the child will be expected to behave in age-appropriate ways).

BEST PRACTICES

Before undertaking the assessment process, the school psychologist needs to consider the primary goals of the specific evaluation. General purposes of assessment include classification, placement, intervention planning, and intervention evaluation.

Assessment for Classification Purposes

Despite its strong educational impact, ADHD is currently conceptualized as a psychiatric disorder. Family physicians, pediatricians, psychiatrists, and other mental health professionals use the psychiatric taxonomy found in the *DSM-IV* (American Psychiatric Association, 1994). Although simply naming the disorder does not inform intervention efforts, classification may be needed to qualify for treatment services outside the school (medication, parent training, and clinic-based therapy). A school psychologist is in an optimal position to communicate with outside professionals about the child, and thus it is important to know about the terminology and *DSM* requirements. In an assessment for diagnostic purposes, school psychologists should determine whether the child meets the *DSM-IV* criteria for ADHD and rule out other factors or problems that could account for ADHD-like behaviors. Example questions to guide the assessment process include: Does the child exhibit a significant number of ADHD symptoms to meet *DSM-IV* criteria? Did the child exhibit ADHD symptoms prior to age 7, and are these behaviors present across multiple situations? Is the child's functioning significantly impaired in the home, school, or with peers? Are there other factors that may account for the display of ADHD symptoms and behaviors (DuPaul & Stoner, 1994)? Since the focus of this chapter is on linking assessment to effective intervention strategies, the reader is referred to Barkley (1998) or DuPaul and Stoner (1994) for a more complete review of diagnostic assessment.

A second purpose of classification is for placement in school-based services such as special education, and the IDEA and Section 504 supply the foundation for identifying our responsibilities for proper school-based assessment of children with ADHD. The assessment objective for school psychologists is to determine the extent to which attentional and/or hyperactive/impulsive problems are interfering with the child's academic, affective, and social needs. For example, does the child meet the eligibility criteria for a child with a disability? Does the child *need* special education and related services because of his or her disability (e.g., is educational performance significantly affected)? Does the child's disability significantly affect a major life activity, such as learning?

Assessment for Intervention and Evaluation: A Problem-Solving Paradigm

As described in our earlier chapter (Landau & Burcham, 1995), the consultative model of Bergan and

Kratochwill (1990) offers a useful problem-solving paradigm that can be translated into a flexible and dynamic assessment strategy to be directly linked to intervention planning and implementation. Thinking in terms of problem identification, problem analysis, plan implementation, and problem evaluation, school psychologists can collaborate with parents, school personnel, and community professionals to address the needs of children with ADHD. In this way, assessment is extended well beyond classification, and becomes, instead, an on-going, problem-solving process.

Problem Identification

Regardless of whether the referral concern is behavioral, social, or academic, an essential first step is to operationally define (using observable and measurable terms) the problem behavior(s) of concern. For example, concerns may include looking away from the teacher or classroom materials for more than 3 seconds, talking out, touching peers' materials, taking peers' materials, inappropriate noises, throwing things into the air, or getting out of the seat. Likewise, it is also important to define an appropriate replacement behavior, so that the focus of intervention is related to building a desirable behavior rather than solely diminishing an undesirable one. For example, on-task behavior may include 75% work completion or talking to a teacher or peer about the assigned material.

Gathering data from multiple informants can elicit valuable information across situations, help determine precisely which behaviors evoke concern from various significant others, validate the problem, and prioritize areas of concern. Parent, teacher, and child interviews, as well as omnibus rating scales completed by these informants, represent excellent strategies to accomplish this. Additionally, direct observation yields on-line representations of how a child is functioning in various school settings relative to age-mates. Sample questions school psychologists can ask during this stage of the assessment process include: What is the operational definition of the problem behavior and appropriate replacement behavior? How severe is the problem behavior? What percentage of time does the child exhibit off-task behavior? Is the problem validated when comparing targeted behavior to normative behavior of peers?

Problem Analysis

During the problem analysis stage, the school psychologist identifies variables that permit attainment of the problem solution, and develops an intervention plan to meet the stated objectives. Information is gathered and analyzed to determine why a particular behavior is occurring (i.e., its function) and to identify variables related to the problem at hand. By conducting a thorough problem analysis, school psychologists can better design and implement interventions that are matched to the situation (e.g., student ability level or classroom setting). During this phase, there are two major foci of the assessment process. First, the child's present abilities and problem behaviors are analyzed to determine if the concerns are due to a skill deficit or a performance deficit. In this case, individual psychoeducational testing may be warranted—both traditional norm-referenced and nontraditional curriculum-based measures.

Second, after problem behaviors have been operationally defined, the school psychologist continues to gather information from a variety of sources (e.g., structured teacher and student interviews, rating scales, direct observations) to identify environmental variables related to the inception and maintenance of the ADHD-related behaviors (O'Neil et al., 1997). That is, antecedents (e.g., task difficulty, teacher direction, student fight on the bus), consequences (e.g., peer attention, escape from a difficult task), and other environmental variables surrounding the problem behavior(s) (e.g., life stressors, setting events, medication, illness) would be analyzed to determine *why* the problem is occurring. For this purpose, further interviewing of teachers and parents about relevant events (e.g., the nature and timing of eliciting stimuli surrounding the presentation of inappropriate behavior) would be conducted. The reader is referred to O'Neil et al. (1997) and Witt, Daly, and Noell (2000) for some useful interviewing formats.

Additionally, direct observations in the natural setting should be conducted to precisely determine environmental contingencies (i.e., to analyze the ADHD behaviors in relation to antecedent and consequent events). School psychologists should also consider other ecological or contextual factors that may contribute to the development and maintenance of ADHD behaviors. For example, a child may be preoccupied in the classroom (and look inattentive) if the child's parents are getting a divorce or if the child is taking an excessive dose of medication. Additionally, the student may be receiving a higher level of reinforcement for engaging in misbehavior than appropriate behavior.

Once the school psychologist has obtained a sufficient amount of information from a variety of sources related to the onset and maintenance of the problem behavior, the school psychologist should generate hypotheses regarding the functions(s) of the target behaviors. In many cases, it may be difficult to determine why the behavior occurs. Thus, problem analysis is a "cyclical and continuous" process and additional data may be needed to confirm or disconfirm hypothesized functions of behavior (Larson & Maag, 1998). For example, a possible function may be to escape or avoid effortful or challenging tasks, such as difficult math problems or working in a group. A second function may include gaining access to either teacher or peer attention. Common examples may include verbal or nonverbal reactions such as laughter, smiling, or a thumbs-up sign from the student's classmates (DuPaul & Hoff, 1998).

In the case of clear hypotheses, one could move to the next steps in the problem-solving process. By implementing and evaluating an intervention that is *matched* to the behavioral function, school psychologists can infer the operant functions of the behavior (Dunlap et al., 1993). In more complex cases, or situations in which intervention strategies have failed, school psychologists may wish to experimentally test their hypothesis to demonstrate a functional relationship between environmental events and the target behavior (i.e., a functional analysis; FA). The reader is referred to functional analysis resources for specific steps and procedures for this (e.g., Gresham et al., 2001; Knoster & McCurdy, this volume; O'Neill et al., 1997; Sterling-Turner, Robinson, & Wilczynski, 2001; or Witt et al., 2000, for examples of FA methods procedures).

After reviewing data obtained through earlier stages of problem analysis, a specific intervention (optimally based on the functions of the target behavior) should be designed. There are a number of empirically documented intervention strategies for students with ADHD, and the reader is encouraged to consult DuPaul and Stoner (this volume) for more specific information. Sample questions school psychologists could ask during problem analysis are: What are the child's strengths and weaknesses? Is the problem behavior due to a skill deficit (student lacks skills) or performance deficit (student has skills but cannot apply these efficiently and effectively)? What are the situations in which the behavior is most likely and least likely to occur? For example, is the behavior related to a specific time of day (e.g., morning or afternoon), setting (e.g., playground or math class), persons in the environment (e.g., the presence of certain teachers, peers, or siblings), or an activity (e.g., small group instruction or independent seatwork)? What happens immediately before and after the occurrence of the behavior? Have factors, such as major life events or medical conditions that may contribute to the problem behavior, been considered? What are the hypotheses about the purpose or function of the behavior, and what evidence is there to support these hypotheses? What are the objectives for the intervention? What are the optimal intervention strategies? Have the specific steps of the intervention been delineated? For example, where and when is the intervention to be implemented? Who is responsible for implementing the intervention (Ervin, 2001)?

Plan Implementation

During the plan implementation stage, the role of assessment is to ensure the intervention protocol is being implemented as planned, and to permit sensitivity to unintended consequences of the intervention. Thus, for example, child or consultee (i.e., a parent or teacher) behavior should be monitored for the purpose of establishing treatment integrity. Additionally, if the child with ADHD is to receive psychopharmacological treatment in school, a checklist or rating scale designed to assess treatment-emergent symptoms (i.e., medication side-effects) should be used. During this stage, school psychologists may ask: Is the intervention being implemented as planned? If not, what are the barriers to treatment integrity? Are there unintended side-effects to the intervention?

Problem Evaluation

During the problem evaluation stage, assessment continues to determine the extent to which intervention objectives have been met. Thus, assessment data would compare the child's performance at this stage with desired goals previously specified during the problem identification stage (Bergan & Kratochwill, 1990). In the problem evaluation phase, sample questions to guide the problem evaluation assessment process include: What data are being collected to monitor treatment efficacy (e.g., direct observations, permanent products, rating scales, curriculum-based evaluation)? Are procedures for monitoring student outcomes being followed (e.g., percentage of work completion is being tracked on a daily basis)? Have the goals of the intervention been reached?

As before, interviews, rating scales, and direct observations could all be used to assess treatment efficacy. If, however, the assembled data reveal that some goals have not been met, then further assessment would be indicated and the school psychologist should return to the problem analysis phase. We also encourage school psychologists to include a Parent Daily Report (PDR; see Pelham, 1993) as part of the treatment evaluation plan. For this, the school psychologist consults with the teacher and/or parent to identify and operationally define the specific behaviors of concern and targets of intervention. A behavioral report is then constructed in rating scale format, reflecting the specific concerns articulated by the teacher or parent (e.g., frequency of inappropriate verbalizations during class). The teacher then completes the report on a daily basis, providing the school psychologist and parent with on-going evaluations on the target behavior(s). One example is seen in Roberts and Landau (1995), in which the authors developed a PDR as part of their research on the utility of curriculum-based data in medication trials (see Figure 1). In the case of Allen, his teacher was asked to briefly describe specific behavior problems believed to interfere with his academic performance. A behavioral report was then constructed for the behaviors that Allen's teacher considered most dele-

Figure 1. **Example of a Parent Daily Report form**

Parent Daily Report

Date: ______________________________

For each behavior listed below, please check the frequency that best describes Alex's behavior for today.

1. Out of his seat at inappropriate times in the classroom.
   ______ Never
   ______ Sometimes
   ______ Often
   ______ Always

2. Using foul language.
   ______ Never
   ______ Sometimes
   ______ Often
   ______ Always

3. Talking out at inappropriate times in the classroom.
   ______ Never
   ______ Sometimes
   ______ Often
   ______ Always

5. Handling or playing with items from his desk at inappropriate times.
   ______ Never
   ______ Sometimes
   ______ Often
   ______ Always

6. Avoiding eye contact with the teacher.
   ______ Never
   ______ Sometimes
   ______ Often
   ______ Always

Comments: ____
____

terious. These behaviors were evaluated daily by Allen's teacher, and these ratings were subsequently summed and graphed for treatment evaluation.

One of the appealing features of the parent daily report is that it does not rely upon pre-defined concerns that are typically found in published rating scales. Rather, every PDR is individually derived for each student (increasing its social validity). Thus, a PDR may include three target behaviors for one student or five objectives for another. A second advantage to this method of outcome evaluation is that items on the PDR stem directly from the teacher and parent who are consulted during intervention planning. This collaborative effort may facilitate the consultation process, thereby permitting consultees to have a greater sense of ownership of the specific treatment objectives. A third benefit of using the PDR for plan evaluation is that it provides an effective means by which home-school collaboration and communication is improved. Specifically, a teacher daily report can be sent home every evening to the parent, thereby providing the parent with information about school-based progress on a day-by-day basis. This is especially helpful in the case of psychostimulant trials in school. The PDR is a cost-effective and time-efficient way to provide parents with daily teacher information of how their child is responding to treatment.

Assessment of Medication Effects

Since most children with ADHD experience a trial of psychopharmacological therapy sometime during childhood, the school psychologist is in a primary role to conduct an assessment of medication effects during the problem evaluation stage. Knowledge of medication evaluation procedures is especially important, as a given dose of psychostimulant medication may not exert the same therapeutic effect in all domains of functioning for a given child or across children. In the absence of systematically school-based collected data, prescribing physicians are left with few options except to rely on parent anecdotal reports to determine proper dosage. Thus, dose effects should be considered as part of the assessment process for children with ADHD.

The school psychologist is in a unique position to interface with various professionals involved to coordinate data collection and analyze effectiveness of psychostimulant medications. One medication evaluation procedure suggested by Roberts and DuPaul (2000) involves an eight day multimethod protocol, using teacher rating scales (e.g., *ADHD Rating Scale-IV*; DuPaul et al., 1998), academic achievement data (curriculum-based assessment), and direct observations. Their protocol consists of three major phases: pre-medication procedures, medication trial, and interpretation of results. During pre-medication procedures, the school psychologists, in conjunction with the classroom teacher, would determine the appropriate academic materials (level of difficulty matched to student ability level) to be used for assessing medication response. Additionally, a direct observation would be conducted, and a teacher would complete a behavior rating scale. Next, during the medication trial, four medication conditions would be evaluated: 5 mg, 10 mg, 15 mg, and placebo.

Prior to the medication trial, the physician randomly selects the schedule of dose trials (e.g., week one: 5 mg; week two: placebo; week three: 15 mg), and, in the ideal case, only the physician and pharmacist would know the order of conditions. The child would receive medication or placebo each day of the medication trial. Direct observation and academic performance data are collected daily within each condition. Based on these data, the school psychologist can recommend to physicians which condition seems most efficacious. A PDR also can be used to monitor the child's performance on a daily basis, and provide parents feedback regarding the child's medication response. At the same time, treatment-emergent symptoms or side effects should be monitored. The reader is encouraged to consult Roberts and DuPaul (2000) or Northrup and Gulley (2001) for a complete description of a school-based drug evaluation protocol.

Specific Methods of Assessment

Given the view presented earlier, assessment is an ongoing process and progresses with multiple objectives in mind. Throughout this process, school psychologists need to consider the entire range of potential difficulties that could be experienced by a child with ADHD. Thus, it is not sufficient to determine the extent to which the child exhibits inattentive and hyperactive/impulsive behaviors (plus a specification of settings and situations in which these problems present). One must also consider potential secondary problems typically found in samples of these children.

These include conduct disorders, academic difficulties, disturbed peer relations, and internalizing problems (e.g., self-esteem deficits and depression), among others. We will review several methods we consider essential in an ADHD assessment battery.

Rating Scales

Behavior rating scales are a vital component in the assessment of children with ADHD. They allow school psychologists to determine *the degree to which* a child exhibits certain characteristics relative to same-age and same-gender students (i.e., symptom severity from a normative perspective). In addition, they collapse information about how a child functions in naturalistic contexts over extended periods of time (Atkins & Pelham, 1991), and provide insight into concerns experienced by significant others who work and live with the child. They also permit a cost-effective method of data collection on infrequently occurring behaviors that may be missed by more direct methods (e.g., direct observations).

Indeed, the use of rating scales is consistent with a best-practice process described by Power and Eraldi (2000) and Power, Costigan, Leff, Eiraldi, and Landau (2001). This process involves consideration of both categorical and dimensional criteria for ADHD classification. Specifically, it is recommended that we should not only establish that diagnosis-relevant symptoms are actually present (i.e., the child has symptoms indicative of ADHD, the categorical criterion) but also ensure these symptoms are sufficiently severe to warrant classification (i.e., their severity exceeds a cut-off score on a recognized behavior rating scale; the dimensional criterion). To this end, several ADHD-specific rating scales seem appropriate. The first is the *ADHD-IV Rating Scale* (DuPaul et al., 1998). The items from this scale were derived directly from the *DSM-IV* (American Psychiatric Association, 1994) diagnostic criteria for ADHD. Each item can be rated by parents and/or teachers to reveal level of severity of ADHD symptoms. Scores are derived to represent total symptom severity, as well as scores for the two ADHD subtypes. The *ADHD-IV* has sound psychometric properties and has been used by many ADHD research groups for participant selection purposes. Clinical utility is due to its ability to inform school psychologists about the severity of the child's problem from a *DSM* perspective. Finally, there is an Hispanic version of the *ADHD-IV*, which further extends its usefulness. Thus, we consider it an excellent way to provide physicians and child psychiatrists information on the severity of school-based concerns using criteria familiar to medical professionals. Other relevant scales include the *Conner's Rating Scales-Revised* (*CRS-R*; Conners, 1997), the *ADD-H* Comprehensive Teacher's Rating Scale (*ACTeRs*; Ullmann, Sleator, & Sprague, 1997), and the *Behavior Assessment System for Children: Monitor for ADHD* (*BASC Monitor*; Kamphaus & Reynolds, 1998). However, examination of normative, reliability, and validity data regarding these scales encourages us to recommend the *ADHD-IV Rating Scale* and the *CRS-R* for school psychologists. The reader should consult Barkley (1998) for further discussion of these issues.

Despite the ease with which rating scales can be used and the wealth of data they provide, rating scales have some limitations. For example, resulting data simply represent opinions of others and, as such, can be influenced by mood and cognitive, social, or educational characteristics of the rater (e.g., Kolko & Kazdin, 1993). In addition, rating scales reflect the limitations inherent in any retrospective report, including distortions in memory and informant bias. For example, informants differ in their standards for determining problem severity (Reid & Maag, 1994). Finally, rating scales have a pathology focus by highlighting areas of dysfunction without capturing the uniqueness of the child's style or the strengths the child presents. Thus, results of these indirect measures should be interpreted with this caution in mind: They may not portray the child's *actual* behavior but, instead, an informant's impressions of that behavior.

During the first stage of assessment, problem identification, school psychologists should select and utilize rating scales as a strategy to delineate the specific referral concerns. Many of those with direct contact with the student should complete these scales (e.g., teachers or caretakers). This is important, as both ADHD symptoms and rating scales are sensitive to setting effects. Thus, the school psychologist can better understand who views what behavior as problematic, and how perceived differences in degree of deviance vary as a function of setting or situation. During problem analysis, a careful review of rating scale data can be invaluable in developing intervention plans. Not only can these data reveal specific concerns as a function of each informant (e.g., the mother reports significantly more oppositional and defiant behavior than her husband), but differences in symptom severity as a function of various classroom settings may indicate where interventions must be concentrated. For example, a child with ADHD may have difficulty following directions and completing assignments only with the math teacher. This determination would evoke an hypothesis (to be further assessed by other methods) that the problem behavior may be situational, setting, or informant-specific.

For problem evaluation, rating scales are invaluable as an objective measure of the child's response to intervention. By re-administering the same rating scales to informants who previously provided data for problem identification, the school psychologist will be able to make a baseline versus response-to-treatment comparison. Indeed, these scales should be administered intermittently throughout the intervention to evaluate its continued potency.

Cognitive and Educational Assessment

Because the disinhibition and attentional difficulties common in children with ADHD can interfere with the educational process, assessment of academic functioning must be considered. Standardized tests of cognitive ability and achievement can be useful for problem analysis. These norm-referenced tests are important, as many students with ADHD experience learning disabilities, and many states require standardized tests to determine eligibility for special education services. Despite the potential utility in identifying specific patterns of academic difficulties, standardized intellectual and achievement tests have limited value for the development of a remedial plan or for monitoring the effectiveness of treatment.

Criterion-referenced tests and curriculum-based measures show promise in delineating the student's academic needs and strengths, and therefore are useful for problem analysis. Being more sensitive to academic growth, they are also appropriate for designing specific academic intervention strategies (for additional information see Howell, this volume; Shapiro, 1996; Shinn, 1998). A compilation of the academic portfolio (i.e., a collection of work samples over time) will also reflect changes in the student's performance and is, therefore, extremely useful in monitoring progress and evaluating intervention effects.

Interviewing

Interviews are an essential component of all stages of the assessment, intervention, and outcome evaluation process with children with ADHD. Specifically, they can provide critical contextual information regarding rules, expectations, and supports available in the environments in which the children are functioning. Interviews with teachers, parents, and children may yield a wealth of information beyond that obtained from rating scales and standardized cognitive assessments and, as such, serve multiple purposes. It is recommended that school psychologists meet individually with parents, teachers, and the referred child, building rapport with each, and gathering information unique to that person's point of view.

During the problem identification stage, the school psychologist not only gathers information about the problem behaviors but also the child's strengths. In addition, information should be sought regarding behavioral expectations of the classroom and broader school environment, past strategies (both successful and unsuccessful) used to address the problems, and current resources available to parents and teachers. This first interview also sets the tone for future collaborative efforts with the team to establish and evaluate intervention strategies. Here, semi-structured interviews (e.g., SCICA; McConaughy & Achenbach, 1994) and behavioral interviews focused on clarifying the operational definition, frequency, duration, severity, and contextual determinants of problem behaviors should be used. To provide a complete picture of the child, interviews should also carefully identify patterns of appropriate or non-problematic behavior, as the specific contexts may provide clues to intervention strategies.

During the problem analysis phase, school psychologists can use interview information to generate preliminary hypotheses about the functions of target behaviors. Thus, the reported patterns of behavioral difficulties and behavioral successes should be evaluated, particularly looking for conditions under which problematic behavior is almost sure to occur and those under which it is unlikely to occur. The interview also should obtain information on antecedent events (e.g., academic task) and environmental consequences (e.g., peer or teacher attention) associated with the problem behavior. Additionally, other contextual variables, such as the child's social relations, emotional state, and stress level of parents and teachers, as well as and coping strategies, should be considered. The reader is referred to O'Neil et al. (1997) and Witt et al. (2000) for some useful interviewing tools when conducting an FBA.

Interviews may provide critical information for the design of a relevant and practical intervention (e.g., identifying potential reinforcers), and allow the school psychologist to gain better understanding of consultees who may implement the intervention. While there are numerous effective interventions, in practice the intervention will only be as effective as those who implement it. With this in mind, interviews can help the school psychologist discover consultees' attitudes about, and acceptability of, a particular intervention (see Elliott, 1988), thereby having implications for treatment integrity.

After an intervention has been implemented, interviews provide information on treatment effectiveness. It is an excellent opportunity to review data, comment on progress, reinforce the child's and consultees' efforts in implementing the program, and trouble-shoot areas in which the program has not been effective. At this point, sometimes only simple modifications are needed to make a program successful, but without interviews the details of intervention implementation are often missed. For example, a child may respond favorably to an intervention in one situation (e.g., math class) but not in another (e.g., reading lessons). A simple analysis via interviewing may reveal slight differences in the environment, such as seating arrangement, which may have significant impact on treatment efficacy.

At each phase it is important to touch base and interview all participants, keeping in mind the unique contributions of parents, teachers, and children. Specifically, parents are the best informants regarding the child's developmental, medical, and family histories. Equally important, parents can provide details of current family functioning (e.g., response to stressors, marital discord) and the child's role and behaviors in the home context. The reader is advised to consult Barkley (1998) and O'Neill et al. (1997) for detailed guidelines in the development of a parent interview.

Alternatively, teachers may provide information regarding the child's behavior in various academic settings and during social interactions. Teachers can provide details about the child's work habits (e.g., carelessness, disorganization) and style of academic performance (e.g., problems related to inefficiency). In addition, the teacher's interview should pursue the child's ability to follow instructions at school, transition from one activity to another, and establish if there are problems in the peer group. Finally, the interview should permit the school psychologist to assess resources available to the teacher to permit an effective school-based intervention, and special consideration should be made of the teacher's need for collaborative support from the school psychologist and other professionals working with the child.

Finally, some mention should be made of a direct interview with the child. Although the purpose of this interview will depend on the age and maturity of the child, the interview itself will facilitate rapport for subsequent sessions with the child, and permit the school psychologist to observe the child directly (e.g., language usage, ability to follow directions, and overactive/fidgety symptoms, attention). As an interview session is typically a novel, structured, one-on-one interaction, it is important to note the presence or absence of particular behaviors during the interview may not predict the child's behavior outside the psychologist's office. It is also important to remember that children's self-reports are notoriously inconsistent with reports from other informants, as children with ADHD have been found to deny about 50% of the problems their mothers attribute to them (Landau, Milich, & Widiger, 1991). Despite these caveats, interviews with children provide a unique perspective on the problem behavior.

Direct Observation

Based upon informant concerns that emerge from the use of interviews and ratings scales, the school psychologist should also conduct systematic observations of the child with ADHD, as these data will provide unique information about performance in response to various demands of the school setting. If the school psychologist observes the target child and all same-gender classmates engaged in the same activity, then resulting data can contribute to problem identification. For example, if the teacher complains about a boy who "never seems to get his math workbook problems completed; he daydreams constantly instead of doing his work," a duration measure of on-task behavior can be contrasted with average duration of all male classmates. These contrast data will establish if a problem does, in fact, exist, and also suggest a realistic level of performance to serve as the intervention objective. Where time constraints exist, comparisons can be made between the target child's behavior and a small subset of teacher identified representative classmates (e.g., two to three children).

Second, direct observations are necessary for problem analysis. Structured observations can verify information from indirect assessments methods (e.g., rating scales, interviews) and are useful in confirming or disconfirming initial hypotheses regarding causes of problematic behaviors. Structured observations not only clarify *what* the child is actually doing, but also provide important information about the settings and situations in which problem behaviors occur. Because observations can be conducted repeatedly, they also can provide information about the stability and patterns of the child's behavioral strengths and areas of concern. Through direct observation, school psychologists can identify potential antecedent conditions that precede the occurrence of problematic behaviors and consequences that may maintain these behaviors (i.e., identify the potential functions these behaviors serve). Thus, observations represent the best method of identifying controlling variables in the environment and, as a consequence, are necessary for the design of interventions

Third, observation data can be used for plan implementation and evaluation. This is most directly relevant in modifying existing treatment plans and developing the most consistently effective intervention for a child with ADHD. After a plan is implemented, direct observations can provide data about treatment integrity. For example, the school psychologist may observe in the classroom to determine if the teacher is dispensing strategic feedback as prescribed. Direct observations can establish the efficacy of an intervention and, more specifically, the contexts in which the intervention is effective and situations in which it is not. If treatment is not effective, then observational data provide clues to potential contributors to treatment failure and may identify specific aspects that can be changed (e.g., targeting different behavior, changing consequences, providing additional support to teachers and others implementing the intervention).

Thus, direct observations can serve multiple assessment purposes, and offer the most direct and ecologically valid data available to school psychologists. Unfortunately, no single observation system is considered appropriate for all children with ADHD. Instead, the selection of particular code categories, and the recording method to be used (e.g., duration versus event recording), depends on specific informant concerns that emerged during problem identification. Various settings for observation can be identified based on this previously collected information. In any case, it is crucial to observe the child with ADHD in multiple settings and situations. For example, the school psychologist may seek to determine differences in classroom performance as a function of small versus large group activities, teacher-directed versus self-paced academic seatwork, highly structured versus informal classroom settings, and restricted academic versus free play activities. From this perspective, resulting data are always considered in the context of a particular setting, as situational factors account for much of the variance in observed child behavior. In most cases, the system should at least be sensitive to the occurrence of inattention, motor excess, and impulsive responding in the classroom. The reader is encouraged to consult Hintze (this volume) or Platzman et al. (1992) for a discussion of different observation systems.

Computer-Driven Measures of ADHD

Clearly, some mention should be made about the growing use of computer-based assessment of ADHD. There has been a significant proliferation of these methods, most of which are represented by a variant of the Continuous Performance Test (CPT). In these appealing (and expensive) procedures, the child must maintain vigilance and react to the presence or absence of infrequently occurring stimuli while other (distracter) stimuli are presented. For example, the Gordon Diagnostic System (GDS; Gordon, 1991), which has achieved ubiquitous presence in ADHD clinics, provides scores for delay-of-responding, vigilance, and distractibility. Another measure, familiar to many school psychologists, is the Conners Continuous Performance Test (Conners, 1995).

These CPT methods are typically used to facilitate the diagnostic or classification process, and remain seductive because of their putative objectivity. However, they may do no more than provide a false sense of security. Currently, there are no well-established objective measures of ADHD as a diagnostic entity, and one might reasonably ask why one is needed. Indeed, there are no objective measures for other forms of child psychopathology (e.g., autism or child depression). Apparently, the use of an objective procedure makes us feel more comfortable about our diagnostic determination.

Some investigators have recently examined the clinical utility of CPT in the diagnostic process. For example, Rielly, Cunningham, Richards, Elbard, and Mahoney (1999) reported the GDS had such low positive predictive values (PPV) for an ADHD diagnosis the clinician would be "more wrong than right" if assuming an abnormal score was indicative of ADHD. However, their findings did suggest that children who scored within normal limits probably do not have the disorder. Unfortunately, this is useless information unless we are attempting large-scale screening with the GDS (a very expensive undertaking). McGee, Clark, and Symons (2000) had similar concerns about the Conners CPT. In their study, data revealed the CPT had questionable utility because of its failure to distinguish children with ADHD from other clinic referrals.

These studies were designed to examine classification accuracy and involved several indices, such as hit-rate analysis. However, concern with the CPT goes well beyond an alleged ability to correctly classify ADHD in children: These procedures do not have ecological validity (Barkley, 1991). In other words, the child's performance on the CPT in the lab will never inform us of how the child will function in the classroom. In addition, the resulting data (assuming correct classification) cannot be used for the design of interventions. Under the best of circumstances, these procedures may tell us "what the child has," but not "what the child needs." Practitioners who rely on these methods should do so with these important caveats in mind.

Guidelines

The following guidelines are suggested for the multi-informant and multi-method school-based assessment of children with ADHD. These guidelines should not be considered as a rigid chronology for the assessment process but instead as a flexible model for decision making to be linked directly to the planning and evaluation of interventions.

1. Identify the major concerns of referral sources (rating and interviews) and apply a developmental perspective to establish degree of deviance from age-mates (ratings). Begin to cluster specific concerns into areas of developmental domains of functioning (e.g., inattention, hyperactivity/ impulsivity, academic, peer relations, internalizing problems) and into settings or situations of occurrence (e.g., home, school, free play with peers, community).

2. Operationally define target behaviors of concern, as well as appropriate alternative behaviors. Identify the frequency, intensity, duration of misbehaviors, and estimated desired level of functioning. Rank-order the concerns into a hierarchy of troublesomeness/seriousness for this child. This will help establish which interventions should be applied first and which may come later.

3. Conduct direct observations in all settings to identify where problem behaviors do and do not occur. Direct observations are useful to (a) verify informant concerns, (b) further establish degree of deviance by concurrently observing child and same-gender classmates, (c) determine relevant situation/setting effects that account for differences in informant reports, and (d) identify immediate environmental conditions (e.g., antecedents and consequences) and more distal factors (e.g., setting events) hypothesized to be responsible for the inception and maintenance of problem behaviors.

4. Generate hypotheses about the function of behavior. If necessary, conduct a functional analysis of behavior to verify hypotheses and isolate controlling variables in each setting that may provide suitable targets for intervention.

5. Identify unique aspects of the case that have implications for treatment planning. For example, make note of particular features in the classroom environment that could compromise a prescribed behavioral intervention (e.g., teacher reprimand may not be effective in the context of positive peer attention), develop an understanding of parent and teacher acceptance of potential interventions being considered, assess parent and teacher ability to serve as consultees during the intervention process, and establish child characteristics that

could relate directly to the selection of a particular intervention (e.g., social skills training designed to increase rates of interaction will not be suitable for an aggressive child). These unique aspects can be identified through the use of interviews and direct observations.

6. Using information gleaned from functional assessment, list all interventions that seem appropriate to decrease maladaptive behaviors and replace them with alternative, adaptive behaviors. This should be done in collaboration with parents and teachers. Select an intervention based on resources, treatment acceptability attitudes, and strengths noted in the child.

7. Design and apply specific interventions according to a hierarchical list of concerns, the unique features of this case, and the function of behavior.

8. Assess treatment integrity of interventions using direct observations or collaboratively develop a treatment integrity checklist with the classroom teacher.

9. Evaluate intervention effectiveness using multimethod, multi-informant strategies (e.g., parent and teacher rating scales, parent daily report, direct observations, self-reports, academic measures, curriculum-based evaluation).

10. Conduct post-treatment follow-up using previously applied assessment methods.

SUMMARY

Assessing students who exhibit ADHD symptoms represents a daunting challenge for school psychologists. Samples of children with ADHD are extremely heterogeneous, and the prospects for comorbid disorders are high. Clearly, the diagnosis of ADHD per se does not inform intervention planning for any of these youngsters.

A problem solving paradigm, based on Bergan and Kratochwill's (1990) consultation model has been offered to guide the evaluation process for students whose ADHD problems are negatively impacting their functioning in school. During problem identification, the school psychologist determines specific behaviors that are causing concern in the school setting; during problem analysis, focus is on identifying variables that permit attainment of a solution, and may include intervention development; during plan implementation, treatment integrity is monitored; and during problem evaluation, the assessment process continues to determine the extent to which treatment objectives have been met.

The preceding discussion highlights the fact that a comprehensive and efficient assessment of children with ADHD involves procedures that serve *multiple purposes*. Thus, ideal assessments (e.g., interviews, direct observations) are those that may be used at all stages of the problem-solving paradigm (i.e., problem identification, problem analysis, plan implementation, and problem evaluation). Additionally, a comprehensive assessment of children with ADHD must reflect a protocol comprised of several characteristics. First, it must engage *multiple methods* of assessment. Each method (interview, rating scale, or direct observation) can account for only a portion of a description of the child. Thus, a sufficient assessment uses numerous and diverse procedures. Second, assessment should depend on *multiple informants* (parents, teachers, child, peers). Multiple sources are critical in the assessment of children with ADHD because different informants may evoke different behaviors from the same child, informants differ in terms of their respective expectations and demands placed on the child, and finally, because each informant is embedded in a unique environment. Third, children with ADHD should be assessed in the context of *multiple settings*, as data are consistent in documenting that these children do not present the same problem in a trans-situational fashion. Obviously, specific setting differences need to be integrated in the details of problem identification, problem analysis, and ultimately, problem evaluation. Finally, the assessment and intervention process must be *developmentally sensitive*. With a developmental perspective, school psychologists are likely to more accurately identify problems and implement age-appropriate interventions.

REFERENCES

American Psychiatric Association. (1968). *Diagnostic and statistical manual of mental disorders* (2nd ed.). Washington, DC: Author.

American Psychiatric Association. (1980). *Diagnostic and statistical manual of mental disorders* (3rd ed.). Washington, DC: Author.

American Psychiatric Association. (1987). *Diagnostic and statistical manual of mental disorders* (3rd ed., Rev.). Washington, DC: Author.

American Psychiatric Association. (1994). *Diagnostic and statistical manual of mental disorders* (4th ed.). Washington, DC: Author.

Atkins, M. S., & Pelham, W. E. (1991). School-based assessment of Attention Deficit-Hyperactivity Disorder. *Journal of Learning Disabilities, 24*, 197–204.

Barkley, R. A. (1991). The ecological validity of laboratory and analogue assessment methods of ADHD symptoms. *Journal of Abnormal Child Psychology, 19*, 149–178.

Barkley, R. A. (1997). Behavior inhibition, sustained attention, and executive functions: Constructing a unifying theory of ADHD. *Psychological Bulletin, 121*, 65–94.

Barkley, R. A. (1998). *Attention-Deficit Hyperactivity Disorder: A handbook for diagnosis and treatment* (2nd ed.). New York: Guilford.

Bergen, J. R., & Kratochwill, T. R. (1990). *Behavioral consultation and therapy*. New York: Plenum.

Berk, L. E., & Landau, S. (1993). Private speech of learning disabled and normally achieving children in classroom academic and laboratory contexts. *Child Development, 64*, 556–571.

Campbell, S.B. (1990). *Behavior problems in preschool children: Clinical and developmental issues*. New York: Guilford.

Conners, C. K. (1995). *Conners Continuous Performance Test*. Toronto: Multi-Health Systems.

Conners, C. K. (1997). *Conners Rating Scales (Rev.)*. North Tonawanda, NY: Multi-Health Systems.

Drasgow, E., & Yell, M. L. (2001). Functional behavioral assessments: Legal requirements and challenges. *School Psychology Review, 30*, 239–251.

Dunlap, G., Kern, L., dePerczel, M., Clarke, S., Wilson, D., Childs, K. E., White, R., & Faulk, G. D. (1993). Functional analysis of classroom variables for students with emotional and behavioral disorders. *Behavioral Disorders, 18*, 275–291.

DuPaul, G. J., Eckert, T. L., & McGoey, K. E. (1997). Interventions for students with Attention-Deficit/Hyperactivity Disorder: One size does not fit all. *School Psychology Review, 26*, 369–382.

DuPaul, G. J., & Ervin, R. A. (1996). Functional assessment of behaviors related to Attention-Deficit/Hyperactivity Disorder: Linking assessment to intervention design. *Behavior Therapy, 27*, 601–622.

DuPaul, G. J., & Hoff, K. E. (1998). Attention/concentration problems. In S. Watson and F. Gresham (Eds.), *Child behavior therapy: Ecological considerations in assessment, treatment, and evaluation*. New York: Plenum.

DuPaul, G. J., Power, T. J., Anastopoulos, A. D., & Reid, R. (1998). *ADHD Rating Scale-IV: Checklists, norms, and clinical interpretation*. New York: Guilford.

DuPaul, G. J., & Stoner, G. (1994). *ADHD in the schools: Assessment and intervention strategies*. New York: Guilford.

Elliott, S. N. (1988). Acceptability of behavioral treatments in educational settings. In J. C. Witt, S. N. Elliott, & F. M. Gresham (Eds.), *Handbook of behavior therapy in education* (pp. 121–150). New York: Plenum.

Ervin, R.A. (2001). *Checklist for implementing functional assessments in the schools*. Unpublished manuscript.

Ervin, R. A., Radford, P. M., Bertsch, K., Piper, A. L., Ehrhardt, K. E., & Poling, A. (2001). A descriptive analysis and critique of the empirical literature on school-based functional assessment. *School Psychology Review, 30*, 193–210.

Frick, P. J., Lahey, B. B., Applegate, B., Kerdyk, L., Ollendick, T., Hynd, G. W., Garfinkle, B., Greenhill, L., Bierderman, J., Barkley, R. A., McBurnett, K., Newcorn, J., & Waldman, I. (1994). *DSM-IV* field trials for the Disruptive Behavior Disorders: Symptom utility estimates. *Journal of the American Academy of Child and Adolescent Psychiatry, 33*, 529–539.

Gordon, M. (1991). *Instruction manual for the Gordon Diagnostic System, Model III-R*. DeWitt, NY: Gordon Systems.

Gresham, F. M., Watson, T. S., & Skinner, C. H. (2001). Functional behavioral assessment: Principles, procedures, and future directions. *School Psychology Review, 30,* 156–172.

Hinshaw, S. P., Han, S. S., Erhardt, D., & Huber, A. (1992). Internalizing and externalizing behavior problems in preschool children: Correspondence among parent and teacher ratings and behavior observations. *Journal of Clinical Child Psychology, 21*, 143–150.

Jensen, P. S., Martin, D., & Cantwell, D. P. (1997). Comorbidity in ADHD: Implications for research, practice, and DSM-IV. *Journal of the American Academy of Child and Adolescent Psychiatry, 36,* 1065–1080.

Kamphaus, R. W., & Reynolds, C. R. (1998). *Behavior Assessment System for Children: Monitor for ADHD manual*. Circle Pines, MN: American Guidance Service.

Kolko, D. J., & Kazdin, A. E. (1993). Emotional/ behavioral problems in clinic and nonclinic children: Correspondence among child, parent, and teacher reports. *Journal of Child Psychology and Psychiatry and Allied Disciplines, 34*(6), 991–1006.

Kotulak, R. (2000, November 26). Attention disorder: A medical minefield. *Chicago Tribune*, pp.1, 11.

Lahey, B. B., Carlson, C. L., & Frick, P. J. (1997). Attention-deficit disorder without hyperactivity. In T. A. Widiger, A. J. Frances, H. A. Pincus, R. Ross, M. B. First, & W. Davis (Eds.), *DSM-IV source book* (vol. 3), (pp. 163–188). Washington DC: American Psychiatric Association.

Landau, S., & Berk, L. (2000). *Private speech and academic problem-solving in children with ADHD: Implications for classroom behavior*. Paper presented at the annual meeting of the National Association for School Psychologists, New Orleans, LA.

Landau, S., & Burcham, B. G. (1995). Best practices in the assessment of children with attention disorders. In A. Thomas and J. Grimes (Eds.), *Best practices in school psychology III,* (pp. 817–829). Washington, DC: National Association of School Psychologists.

Landau, S., Lorch, E. P., & Milich, R. (1992). Visual attention to and comprehension of television in attention-deficit hyperactivity disordered and normal boys. *Child Development, 63*, 928–937.

Landau, S., & Milich, R. (1988). Social communication patterns of attention-deficit-disordered boys. *Journal of Abnormal Child Psychology, 16*, 69–81.

Landau, S., Milich, R., & Diener, M. B. (1998). Peer relations of children with Attention-Deficit Hyperactivity Disorder. *Reading & Writing Quarterly: Overcoming Learning Difficulties, 14*, 83–105.

Landau, S., Milich, R., & Widiger, T. A. (1991). Conditional probabilities of child interview symptoms in the diagnosis of attention deficit disorder. *Journal of Child Psychology and Psychiatry, 32*, 501–513.

Larson, P. J., & Maag, J. W. (1998). Applying functional assessment in general education classrooms: Issues and recommendations. *RASE: Remedial & Special Education, 19*, 338–349.

Loeber, R., Green, S. M., Lahey, B. B., Frick, P. J. & McBurnett, K. (2000). Findings on disruptive behavior disorders from the first decade of the Developmental Trends Study. *Clinical Child and Family Psychology Review, 3*, 37–60.

Mangione, C., & Landau, S. (2001). *The effect of competitive peer interaction on the emotional reactivity of boys with and without ADHD: A test of Barkley's Unifying Theory*. Unpublished manuscript.

McConaughy, S. H., & Achenbach, T. M. (1994). *Manual for the Semistructured Clinical Interview for Children and Adolescents*. Burlington, VT: Department of Psychiatry, University of Vermont.

McGee, R. A., Clark, S. E., & Symons, D. K. (2000). Does the Conners, Continuous Performance Test aid ADHD diagnosis? *Journal of Abnormal Child Psychology, 28,* 415–424.

McGee, R., & Share, D. L. (1988). Attention Deficit Disorder-Hyperactivity and academic failure: Which comes first and what should be treated? *Journal of the American Academy of Child and Adolescent Psychiatry, 27*, 318–325.

Milich, R. (1994). The response of children with ADHD to failure: If at first you don't succeed, do you try, try again? *School Psychology Review, 23*, 11–28.

Milich, R., Balentine, A. C.. & Lyman, D. R. (in press). ADHD Combined Type and ADHD Predominantly Inattentive Type are distinctive and unrelated disorders. *Clinical Psychology: Science and Practice.*

Northup, J., & Gulley, V. (2001). Some contributions of functional analysis to the assessment of behaviors associated with Attention Deficit Hyperactivity Disorder and the effects of stimulant medication. *School Psychology Review, 30*, 227–238.

O'Neill, R. E., Horner, R. H., Albin, R. W., Sprague, J. R., Storey, K., & Newton, J. S. (1997). *Functional assessment and program development for problem behavior: A practical handbook.* New York: Brooks/Cole.

Parker, J. G., & Asher, S. R. (1987). Peer relations and later personal adjustment: Are low-accepted children at risk? *Psychological Bulletin, 102*, 357–389.

Pelham, W. E. (1993). Pharmacotherapy for children with attention-deficit hyperactivity disorder. *School Psychology Review, 22*, 199–227.

Pelham, W. E., & Bender, M. E. (1982). Peer relationships in hyperactive children: Description and treatment. In D. D. Gadow & I. Bialer (Eds.), *Advances in learning and behavioral disabilities: A research annual* (vol. 1, pp. 365–436). Greenwich, CT: JAI Press.

Platzman, K. A., Stoy, M. R, Brown, R. T., Coles, C. D., Smith, I. E., & Falek, A. (1992). Review of observational methods in attention deficit hyperactivity disorder (ADHD): Implications for diagnosis. *School Psychology Quarterly, 7*, 155–177.

Power, T. J., Costigan, T. E., Leff, S. S., Eiraldi, R. B., & Landau, S. (2001). Assessing ADHD across settings: Contributions of behavioral assessment to categorical decision making. *Journal of Clinical Child Psychology, 30*, 399–412.

Power, T. J., & Eiraldi, R. B. (2000). Educational and psychiatric classification systems. In E. S. Shapiro and T. R. Kratochwill (Eds.), *Behavioral assessment in schools: Theory, research, and clinical foundations* (2nd ed.). New York: Guilford.

Reid, R., & Maag, J. W. (1994). How many fidgets in a pretty much: A critique of behavior rating scales for identifying students with ADHD. *Journal of School Psychology, 32*, 339–354.

Rielly, N. E., Cunningham, C. E., Richards, J. E., Elbard, H., & Mahoney, W. J. (1999). Detecting Attention Deficit Hyperactivity Disorder in a communications clinic: Diagnostic utility of the Gordon Diagnostic System. *Journal of Clinical and Experimental Neuropsychology, 21*, 685–700.

Roberts, M. L., & DuPaul, G. (2000). Evaluating medication effects for students with Attention Deficit/Hyperactivity. *Communiqué, 28*(6), 12–13.

Roberts, M. L., & Landau, S. (1995). Using curriculum-based data for assessing children with attention deficits. *Journal of Psychoeducational Assessment Monograph Ser.: Advances in Psychoeducational Assessment—Assessment of Attention-Deficit/Hyperactivity Disorder*, 74–87.

Shapiro, E. S. (1996). *Academic skills problems: Direct assessment and intervention* (2nd ed.). New York: Guilford.

Shinn, M. R. (1998). *Advanced applications of Curriculum-Based Measurement.* New York: Guilford.

Sterling-Turner, H. E., Robinson, S. L., & Wilczynski, S. M. (2001). Functional assessment of distracting and disruptive behaviors in the school setting. *School Psychology Review, 30*, 211–226.

Telzrow, C. F., & Tankersley, M. (2000). *IDEA Amendments of 1997: Practice guidelines for school-based teams.* Bethesda, MD: National Association of School Psychologists.

Ullmann, R. K., Sleator, E. K., & Sprague, R. L. (1997). *ACTeRS teacher and parent forms manual.* Champaign, IL: MetriTech.

Vygotsky, L. S. (1934/1987). Thinking and speech. In R. W. Rieber & A. S. Carton (Eds.), N. Minick (transl.), *The collected works L. S. Vygotsky: Vol. 1. Problems of general psychology* (original work published in 1934) (pp. 37–285). New York: Plenum.

Watson, T. S., Gresham, F. M., & Skinner, C. H. (Eds.). (2001). Issues and procedures for implementing functional behavior assessments in schools. [Mini-series]. *School Psychology Review, 30*, 153–251.

Whalen, C. K. (1989). Attention deficit and hyperactivity disorders. In T. H. Ollendick & M. Hersen (Eds.), *Handbook of child psychopathology* (2nd ed., pp. 131–169). New York: Plenum.

Witt, J. C., Daly, E. M., & Noell, G. (2000). *Functional assessments: A step-by-step guide to solving academic and behavior problems.* Longmont, CO: Sopris West.

Zirkel, P. S., & Aleman, S. R. (2000). *Section 504, the ADA, and the schools* (2nd ed.). LRP Publications.

ANNOTATED BIBLIOGRAPHY

Barkley, R. A. (1998). *Attention-Deficit Hyperactivity Disorder: A handbook for diagnosis and treatment* (2nd ed.). New York: Guilford.

The most comprehensive and scholarly text pertaining to children with ADHD. Topics are quite diverse, including an exhaustive review of rating scales and an excellent discussion of classroom-based modifications and interventions.

National Organization of Children and Adults with Attention-Deficit/Hyperactivity Disorder (CHADD) website: http://www.chadd.org

This web page is sponsored by the largest parent support group for children with ADHD. The web page offers resources and references school psychologists can use when providing information to parents and teachers regarding assessment, treatment, and legal/placement issues. Additionally, this organization publishes a newsletter, *Attention*, which is accessible from the website.

Witt, J. C., Daly, E. M., & Noell, G. (2000). *Functional assessments: A step-by-step guide to solving academic and behavior problems.* Longmont, CO: Sopris West.

This is an excellent manual that school psychologists can use when conducting functional assessments for academic or behavioral concerns. This resource provides usable data collection forms and practical step-by-step guidelines for collecting functional assessment data and linking the results to classroom-based interventions.

72 Best Practices In Suicide Intervention

Scott Poland
Cypress-Fairbanks Independent School District
Richard Lieberman
Suicide Prevention Unit
Los Angeles Unified School District

OVERVIEW AND SCOPE OF THE PROBLEM

In 1997, 14% of all suicides were committed by people under age 25 (Hoyert et al., 1999). Suicide rates for those 15–19 years old were 300% higher than those same age peers of the 1950s, but have remained largely stable at these higher levels since 1980. Alarmingly, the suicide rates for those between the ages of 10 and14, however, have increased 196% in the last 15 years (Peters et al., 1998; American Association of Suicidology, 1996). This has extraordinary implications for school psychologists who find themselves overwhelmed with referrals of depressed and suicidal students.

The essential first step of the intervention process requires the ability to make an accurate assessment of risk. Because this assessment will guide your actions throughout the referral process, it is important to first understand the developmental and cultural factors of youth suicide relevant to the intervention process.

Developmental Factors

Research shows mortality from suicide, which increases steadily through the teens, is the third leading cause of death for youth between the ages of 15 and 24 and fourth for those aged 10–14 (Hoyert et al., 1999). Among 15–19 year olds, for every female suicide there are 4.4 male suicides. Among 20–24 year olds this ratio increases to 6.8 : 1. Conversely, among the 10–14 year olds this ratio is the smallest, 2.7 : 1 (American Association of Suicidology, 1996). It has been estimated that there are more than 100 youth suicide attempts for every youth suicide (Ramsay , Tanney, Tierney, & Lang, 1996), and, in the 15–19 year old age group, girls make two of every three of these attempts (U.S. Department of Health and Human Services, 1999).

While completed suicides are relatively rare, other forms of suicidal ideation and behaviors are much more common. Data from two risk behavior surveys are presented in Table 1. Simply stated, for every two youths that attempted suicide, one went to the hospital while one went to school. Although rates vary somewhat by geographic location, within a typical high school classroom, it is likely that three students (one boy and two girls) have made some form of suicide attempt in the past year (American Association of Suicidology, 1996).

As the age of the at risk population drops, a cognitive developmental perspective must be explored. Normand and Mishara (1992) suggested that the understanding of the concept of suicide should be clearly related to a child's age as well as their concept of and experiences with death. A more recent paper suggested that all school children have some general knowledge about suicide (Mishara, 1999). While studies of the progression of children's understanding of suicide are rare, there is a more substantial body of literature on the development of ideas about death.

Table 1. **Youth Risk Behavior Surveillance**

	YRBSS-1997[a]	ALT-YRBSS-1998[b]
	Percentage of students responding	
Seriously considered attempting suicide	20.5	25.0
Made a specific plan	15.7	20.5
Made an attempt	4.5	15.7
Made an attempt requiring medical attention	2.6	7.4

[a] Kann et al. (1998).
[b] Grunbaum et al. (1998).

Piagetian theory states that in the formal operational period (age 12 and up), death is seen as not only irreversible but also as personal. However, Orbach and Glaubman (1979) caution that "many children show a split in the death concept: they may have a mature concept of impersonal death, but a rather childish concept of their own personal death. Only the exploration of the emotional and personal aspects of the death concept is of value diagnostically and therapeutically" (p. 677).

In the assessment of suicide risk, the school psychologist is cautioned that when a student is thinking about hurting himself or herself, it is best to assume the student is not thinking realistically. It would not be unusual for any student, sometimes even as old as 16, to view death as magical, temporary, and reversible.

Ethnicity, Cultural Factors, and Sexual Orientation

The suicide rate for white males (15–24) has tripled since 1950, and the rate for white females (15–24) has doubled. Although data regarding suicidal behavior among minority youth are very limited (Roberts, Chen, & Roberts, 1997), recent Centers for Disease Control and Prevention (CDC) studies have identified at-risk populations previously unrecognized. Between 1980 and 1992 the rate for African-American males (10–14) increased 300% while the rate for the white females (10–14) increased almost 240% (Karchur, Potter, James, & Powell, 1995).

Overall, African-American male adolescents (15–24) have shown the greatest increase in suicide completion rates in the 1990's relative to other ethnicities (American Association of Suicidology, 1996). Their rate has risen by 67% from 1980–1995 (American Foundation for Suicide Prevention, 1996). Risk factors for African-American suicide include being male, having a substance abuse problem, having a psychiatric disorder, having antisocial behavior, and being homosexual. Protective factors that mitigate the risks of suicide include religious affiliation and social support (Gibbs, 1997).

Recent data suggest that in 1997 Hispanic students had the highest rates of suicidal ideation and behaviors (Kann et al., 1998) and were more likely than other students to attempt suicide (U.S. Department of Health and Human Services, 1999). However, this has yet to translate into a substantial increase in completed suicides. Heightened levels of acculturative stress may result in critical levels of suicidal ideation in Mexican-American adolescents (Hovey & King, 1996).

The Native American male adolescent and young adult are still the highest risk group in the United States. The rate in Indian Health Service Areas was the highest in the nation at 62.0 per 100,000 (Wallace et al., 1996). The problem of acculturation has been proposed as one of the major causes of depression and suicidal behavior among Native Americans. However, the majority of research reports that Native Americans who attempt or complete suicide mention precipitating causes such as grief over loss and quarrels with relatives and friends (Lester, 1997).

Gay and lesbian youth are 200–300% more likely to attempt suicide than other young people and they may comprise up to 30% of completed youth suicide annually (Gibson, 1989). Recent analyses of the Youth Risk Behavior Survey, Massachusetts (1997) revealed that adolescents who identified themselves as gay, lesbian, or bisexual reported significantly higher rates than their heterosexual peers of considering suicide (54% versus 22%), of making a suicide plan (41% versus 18%), of actually attempting suicide (37% versus 8%), and of requiring medical attention for a suicide attempt (19% versus 3%).

The authors share Moscicki's observation that, in general, research on this issue is complicated by the lack of accurate information on the true rate of homosexuality in the population and the strong emotions it generates in many otherwise objective discussions (Moscicki, 1995). When gay and lesbian students are referred to a professional to assess suicide risk, practitioners are advised this may be a population, similar to the Native American youth, with higher rates of victimization, drug and alcohol abuse, and familial rejection.

Today's school psychologists face a population of referred youth that is growing in racial and cultural diversity. Language and cultural differences will further complicate an already complex referral process. Practitioners will need to familiarize themselves with the many cultures represented in their school districts and to strengthen their cultural awareness skills. School psychologists will also need to utilize language interpreters when necessary and to become aware of appropriate community agencies that focus on the needs of specific populations (Lieberman & Davis, in press).

BASIC CONSIDERATIONS

Youth suicide is a multidimensional and complex behavior with many associated risk factors. These include psychopathological, familial, biological, and situational factors (Davis & Brock, in press; Moscicki, 1995; Berman & Jobes, 1991).

Risk Factors of Youth Suicide

Research indicates similar risk factors for boys and girls (Groholt, Ekebert, Wichstrom, & Haldorsen, 1997). However, marked differences exist in their relative importance (Shaffer et al., 1996). Major depression and/or a previous attempt are the most important risk factors for girls, and for boys the risk factors include a previous attempt, depression, disruptive behavior, and/or substance abuse.

Psychopathological Disorders

There is strong evidence that over 90% of children and adolescents who commit suicide have experienced a mental or emotional disorder before their death (Shaffer et al., 1996; Conwell et al., 1996). The disorders most closely associated with suicide are affective disorder and substance abuse (Brent & Perper, 1995).

Affective Disorder. The most frequently diagnosed mood disorders are major depressive disorder, dysthymic disorder, and bipolar disorder (U.S. Department of Health and Human Services, 1999). Estimates are that 60% of suicide victims are diagnosed with depression. Estimates of depression for youth range from 20 to 55% (Diekstra & Garnefski, 1995). Females are almost twice as likely to experience a major episode of depression (Berman & Jobes, 1995). Roughly two-thirds of children and adolescents with major depressive disorder also have a coexisting or concurrent disorder (Anderson & McGee, 1994). The most frequent concurrent disorders are substance abuse, antisocial/conduct disorder, or anxiety disorder. There is substantial co-morbidity of depression, conduct problems, and drug or alcohol abuse among high school students reporting suicide attempts. Co-morbidity increases the risk of a suicide attempt beyond that found among adolescents who report these disorders in isolation from one another (Wagner, Cole, & Swartzman, 1996).

Substance and Alcohol Abuse. As alluded to above, substance abuse plays a major role in suicide. Intoxication is present in half of all youth suicide (Moscicki, 1995). Those with a history of alcohol abuse are six times more likely to die by suicide than is the general population (Ramsay et al., 1996).

Familial Factors. Family characteristics that increase youth suicide risk include a family history of suicide and of medical and psychiatric illness. Economic stress, significant family strife, and family loss are also associated with increased risk; and suicidal children experience more parental separations, more parental divorces, and more parental remarriages (Davis & Brock, in press; Davis & Sandoval, 1991). Suicidal adolescents perceive their families as being less cohesive and more disengaged, and conflict and violence occur at increased rates within those families (King et al., 1995).

Biological Factors. Neuro-chemical studies have found some evidence of serotonergic dysfunction in adult suicide attempters and completers but the exact relationship has yet to be clarified (Moscicki, 1995).

Situational Factors. Perhaps the strongest of the situational risk factors at least in the United States is the presence of a firearm (CDC, 1997; Brent, Perper, Allman, Moritz, Wartella, & Zelenak, 1991; Kellerman et al., 1992). Firearms are the most common method of suicide (Karchur et al., 1995). Many believe that the increase in rate of youth suicide over the past four decades is largely related to the use of firearms as a method (American Association of Suicidology, 1996). Guns in the home, particularly loaded guns, are associated with increased risk for suicide by youth, both with and without identifiable mental health problems or suicidal risk factors (Brent et al., 1993). Although most gun owners reportedly keep a firearm in their home for "protection or self defense," 83% of gun-related deaths in these homes are the result of a suicide, often by someone other than the gun owner. In general, states with stricter gun laws have lower rates of suicide (American Foundation for Suicide Prevention, 1996).

It is useful to consider suicide as comprising two related factors. The first, an acute factor, is a precipitating event; that is, an event of emotional relevance to this particular adolescent. When this occurs in a child with a second factor (i.e., chronically poor coping skills), then the risk is greatly increased (Lieberman & Davis, in press). Repeat attempters use their behavior as a means of coping with stress and tend to exhibit more chronic symptomology, poorer coping histories, and a higher presence of suicidal and substance abusive behaviors in their histories (American Association of Suicidology, 1996).

It is estimated that 26–33% of adolescent suicide victims have made a previous attempt (American Foundation for Suicide Prevention, 1996). Most adolescent suicide attempts are precipitated by interpersonal conflicts. The intent of the behavior appears to be to effect change in the behaviors or attitudes of others (American Association of Suicidology, 1996). As many as 40% of youth suicidal behaviors appear to have identifiable antecedents (Davis & Brock, in press). Some situational crises are included in Table 2.

Often, in the aftermath of a suicide, these situational factors may be mistakenly viewed as a cause of suicide. Research has shown that situational factors may create the conditions that lead to suicide only when combined with other risk factors (Moscicki, 1995).

BEST PRACTICES IN SUICIDE INTERVENTION

Identifying Suicidal Youth

Individuals who are thinking about suicide usually give signals (Ramsay, Tanney, Tierney, & Lang, 1990). It has been widely written that four of five suicide victims demonstrated identifiable warning signs, often providing verbal clues. Elementary children do not, in general, self-refer; and it is often their behaviors that provide the clues to their intentions. The first step in the identification of a suicidal youth is gaining the knowledge of the indicators of potential suicidal behavior. An effort should be made to keep all gatekeepers of children and adolescents in the school community (peers, parents,

Table 2. Situational crises

- *Loss.* Today's youth seem to possess more avenues to loss in their lives. Among these are loss of a loved one; losses suffered when families break up; losses caused by transience and relocation; and losses of self-esteem, romance, or of devalued life. Traumatic grief heightens vulnerability to suicidal ideation.
- *Disciplinary crisis,* such as fear of incarceration or trouble at school. The rising rate of litigation against schools might indicate need for suicidal assessment after student suspension, expulsion, or exclusion.
- *Stressful life events,* such as poverty and academic and peer pressures.
- *Family crises,* such as family violence, parental arguments, and physical and sexual abuse are associated with suicidal behavior.
- *History of running away.*
- *Suicide completion in community* or the exposure to suicidality in others.

and school personnel) informed of the warning signs of youth suicide and of the referral process for appropriate assessment. The warning signs of youth suicide can be found in Table 3.

General Intervention Strategies

Poland (1989) summarized the responsibilities of the school: detect suicidal students, assess the severity, notify parents, secure the needed mental health services and supervision for the student, and provide follow-up at school. Lieberman and Davis (in press) summarize additional strategies:

Collaboration

School psychologists dealing with suicidal youth should seek support and collaboration from their colleagues (Poland, 1989, 1995). The intervention process is fraught with unexpected developments. Having the support and consultation from an administrator and one other staff member (perhaps the school nurse, counselor, or social worker) is both reassuring and prudent as you make the difficult decisions often necessary when advocating for a suicidal youth.

Assign a "Designated Reporter"

Schools should identify one or more individuals to receive and act upon all reports from teachers and other staff about students who may be suicidal (Davis & Sandoval, 1991). This individual is frequently the school psychologist, but in the event the psychologist is providing itinerant services to that school (which means the psychologist has many schools to whom they provide service), another member of staff should be designated.

Supervise the Student

School psychologists should inform all students they counsel, "There are three pieces of information that if you tell me I must tell someone else in order to help you. Those are (1) if you are being abused, endangered, or neglected in any way, anywhere; (2) if you are planning to harm yourself; or (3) if you are planning to hurt another." In many cases, when a student confesses suicidal intentions, the student is unaware the school psychologist, or any educator for that matter, is not bound by confidentiality and is obligated to report the student's comments or actions to his or her parents (or to protective services, to be discussed later). It is best to always inform the student what you are going to do every step of the way. Solicit the student's assistance where appropriate. Under no circumstances should the student be allowed to leave school or to be alone (even in the restroom). Reassure and supervise the student until a parent can assume responsibility. It may be appropriate to solicit the aid of collaborators to monitor the child while the psychologist seeks a phone in private.

Table 3. Warning signs

- *Threats:* Threats may be direct ("I want to die" "I am going to kill myself") or, unfortunately, indirect ("The world would be better without me" "Nobody will miss me anyway"). In adolescence, indirect clues could be offered through joking or through references in school assignments, particularly creative writing or art pieces. In concrete and pre-operational children, indirect clues may come in the form of acting-out or violent behavior often accompanied by suicidal/homicidal threats.
- *Plan/method/access:* Suicidal thoughts must be distinguished from actual planning (Beebe, 1975). The greater the planning, the greater the potential (Ramsay et al., 1996). In evaluating the suicidal potential of a student, the lethal potential and availability of the means and the level of sophistication of the plan (including the developmental level of the interviewee) must be taken into account (Davis & Brock, in press). Familiar themes for children include running into traffic, jumping from high places, and cutting/scratching/marking the body.
- *Previous attempts:* Adolescent attempters are at increased risk for a variety of negative outcomes, including repeat attempts, psychiatric symptoms, and academic, social, and behavioral problems (Shaffer & Piacentini, 1994); 15% of individuals with a history of one or more suicide attempts will go on to kill themselves (Maris, 1992).
- *Final arrangements:* This behavior may take many forms. In adolescents, it might be giving away prized possessions (e.g., jewelry, clothing, journal). It seems likely that pre-operational elementary children lack the cognitive skills necessary to plan for making final arrangements.
- *Depression:* When symptoms of depression include pervasive thoughts of helplessness and hopelessness, a child or adolescent is conceivably at greater risk for suicide.
- *Sudden changes:* Changes in behavior, friends, or personality.

Mobilize a Support System

In the hierarchy of needs, Maslow (1998) ranks connectedness with caregivers second only to feelings of safety and security. The school psychologist must establish a support system that will carry the child through the difficult challenges ahead long after the student leaves the school. Assessment of that support system will also contribute to evaluating the student's risk. It is often sensible to just ask the student, "Who do you want and who do you think will be there for you now?" and then assist the student in achieving that support. It is important for the student to feel some control over his or her fate.

No-Suicide Contracts

In the authors' experience, no-suicide contracts have been shown to be effective in preventing youth suicide. Figure 1 shows an example of a no-suicide contract (Poland, 1989, 1995). This type of contract helps the student take control over their suicidal impulses and reduces the anxiety of both the student and the school psychologist (Berman & Jobes, 1991; Davis & Sandoval, 1991). In cases where the suicide risk is judged to be low enough not to require an immediate treatment (e.g., there is only ideation and no suicide plan), a no-suicide contract is still recommended to provide the student with alternatives should the student's suicide risk level increase in the future. Such a contract is a personal agreement to postpone suicidal behaviors until help can be obtained. Poland (1989) suggested that "each contract be tailor made for the student. The most official looking school stationery should be used. The contract should be signed by the student and the counselor and the student should be given a copy" (p.82). However, contracts should not be used in isolation (Barrett, 1985). The contract can also serve as an effective assessment tool. If a student refuses to sign, then the student cannot guarantee the student will not hurt himself or herself. The assessment immediately rises to high risk, and the student should be supervised until parents can assume responsibility in taking the student for immediate psychiatric evaluation.

Suicide-Proof the Environment

Whether a child is in imminent danger or not, it is recommended both the home and the school be suicide-proofed (Davis & Sandoval, 1991). Before the child returns home and thereafter, all guns, poisons, medications, and sharp objects must be removed or made inaccessible.

Call Police

All school crisis teams should have a representative from local law enforcement. If a student resists, becomes combative, or attempts to flee, then law enforcement can be of invaluable assistance. In some cases the police can assume responsibility for securing a "72-hour hold," which will place the youth in protective custody up to 3 days for psychiatric observation.

Documentation

Every school district should develop a documentation form for support personnel and crisis team members to record their actions in responding to a referral of a suicidal student. A sample documentation form is pictured in Figure 2. Information should include reasons for referral and actions taken.

Figure 1. This is a sample of a no-suicide contract

I____agree not to harm myself.

If I am having thoughts of harming myself or committing suicide, then I will do the following until I receive help:

- Get assistance from an adult.
- Call the Crisis Hotline at__________________.
- Call the school psychologist/counselor at______________________

I understand the contract that I am signing and agree to abide by it.

______________________________________ (Student signature)

______________________________________ (School psychologist)

Note: From Poland (1995)

Figure 2. This form can be used to document the actions of school personnel when responding to a suicidal student

RISK ASSESSMENT REFERRAL DATA

REFERRAL DATE: :___:___:___: TIME:___________________
MO DAY YR

1. STUDENT'S NAME: :___:___:___:___:___:___:___:___:___:___:___: :___:___:___:___:___:___:___:___: :___:
LAST FIRST MI

2. SCHOOL: :___:___:___:___: :___:___:___:___:___:___:___:___:___:___:___: CLUSTER: _____
LOC. CODE SCHOOL NAME

3. GRADE: :___:___:

4. BIRTHDATE: :___:___:___: 5. AGE: :___:___: 6. SEX: M____ F____ 7. ETHNICITY: ___________
MO DAY YR

8. LIVES WITH: A. ___BOTH PARENTS B. ___MOTHER C. ___FATHER D. ___OTHER GUARDIAN

9. PARENT/GUARDIAN NAME: :___:___:___:___:___:___:___:___:___:___:___: :___:___:___:___:___:___:___:___: :___:
LAST FIRST MI

10 ADDRESS: :___:___:___:___:___:___:___: :___:___:___:___:___:___:___:___:___:___:___:___: :___:___:___:___:
NUMBER STREET APT. NO.

CITY: :___:___:___:___:___:___:___:___:___:___:___:___:___:___:___:___:___:___: ZIP: :___:___:___:___:___:

11. PHONE: HOME (:___:___:___:) :___:___:___:-:___:___:___:___: WORK (:___:___:___:) :___:___:___:-:___:___:___:___:

12. CURRENT EDUCATIONAL PROGRAM:
A. ___REGULAR C. ___RESOURCE SPECIALIST E. ___OTHER (SPECIFY) ___________________________
B. ___GIFTED D. ___SPECIAL DAY CLASS F. ___MAGNET

13. BILINGUAL STATUS A. ___LEP B. ___FEP C. ___ENGLISH ONLY

14 STUDENT REFERRED BY: (CHECK ONE OR MORE)
A. ___SELF D. ___COUNSELOR G. ___NURSES
B. ___PARENT E. ___PSYCHOLOGIST H. ___OTHER (SPECIFY)
C. ___TEACHER F. ___SAAS COUNSELOR I. ___ STUDENT/FRIEND

15. REASON FOR REFERRAL: (CHECK ONE OR MORE)
A. ___DIRECT THREAT
B. ___INDIRECT THREAT
C. ___PREVIOUS ATTEMPT(S) INDICATED
D. ___GIVING AWAY PRIZED POSSESSIONS
E. ___MOOD SWINGS
F. ___SUDDEN CHANGES IN BEHAVIOR
G. ___SIGNS OF DEPRESSION
H. ___TRUANCY OR RUNNING AWAY
I. ___FREQUENT COMPLAINTS OF ILLNESS OR BODILY ACHES
J. ___DRUG OR ALCOHOL ABUSE
K. —OTHER (SPECIFY) ___________________________
L. ___CURRENT ATTEMPT
M. ___COMPLETION: DATE ____________________
N. ___UPDATE OF CURRENT RARD
DATE OF UPDATE: ______________________

16. PREVIOUS RISK ASSESSMENT REFERRAL: ____NO ____YES

17. DATA RECORDED BY (CASE CARRIER):
A. ___COUNSELOR C. ___NURSE E. ___ADMINSTRATOR
B. ___PSYCHOLOGIST D. ___SAAS COUNSELOR F. ___OTHER (SPECIFY) ________________

18. INTERVENTION(S) / OUTCOME(S): (CHECK WHERE APPROPRIATE)
A. ___PARENT CONTACT MADE
B. ___PARENTAL BROUCHURE PROVIDED
C. ___REFFERRAL TO COMMUNITY AGENCY
D. ___CHILD ABUSE FORM FILED (ENDANGERMENT)
E. ___HOSPITALIZATION
F. OTHER (SPECIFY) ____________________
G. ____SCHOOL SUPPORT STRATEGIES
1. ___ GROUP COUNSELING
2. ___ INDIVIDUAL COUNSELING
3. ___ PEER COUNSELING
4. ___ PROGRAM MODIFICATION
5. ___ OTHER (SPECIFY) ____________________

19. SCHOOL TRANSTER (SPECIFY SCHOOL): ______________________________
DATE: ______________________

A Suicide Intervention Model

The intervention component of the Los Angeles Unified School District's (LAUSD) Youth Suicide Prevention Program mandates four steps in responding to the referral of a suicidal student. First, the intervenor must assess the student's risk for suicidal behavior. Such data will determine the course of action. Second, the intervenor has a duty to warn. This will involve notifying the student's parent or a protective service agency. Third, the intervenor has a duty to refer the student to the appropriate community resources. Typically, these will be professional mental health services. Finally, the intervenor must provide follow up and support the family in accessing community resources. Each of these four components of the LAUSD suicide intervention protocol will now be discussed.

Assessment

The experience of talking to a suicidal child can be extremely stressful for the designated reporter. Poland (1989) recommends the use of a Risk Assessment worksheet, and Brock and Sandoval (1996) offer sample questions for interviewing the suicidal student (see Table 4).

School psychologists (or designated reporters), however, are often asked to make critical risk assessments under extraordinary time constraints. Thus, it is impor-

Table 4. Brock and Sandoval's (1996) Student Interview Model

Engagement
- It seems things haven't been going well for you lately. Your parents/teachers have said____. Most teens would find that upsetting.
- Have you felt upset, maybe had some sad or angry feelings you have trouble talking about? Maybe I could help talk about these feelings and thoughts?
- Do you feel like things can get better, or are you worried things will just stay the same or get worse?
- Are you feeling unhappy most of the time?

Identification
- Other teenagers/children I've talked with have said that when they feel sad and/or angry, they thought for a while that things would be better if they were dead. Have you ever thought that?
- Is this feeling of unhappiness so strong that sometimes you wish you were dead?
- Do you sometimes feel that you want to take your own life?
- How often have you had these thoughts?

Inquiry
- What has made you feel so awful?
- What problems have lead you to think this way?
- How do you think your father and mother feel? What do you think will happen to them if you were dead?

Assessment: Current Suicide Plan
- Have you thought about how you would make yourself die?
- Do you have a plan?
- Do you have the means with you now, at school, or at home?
- Where are you planning to kill yourself?
- Have you written a note?
- Have you put things in order?

Prior Behavior
- Has anyone that you know of killed or attempted to kill himself or herself? Do you know why?
- Have you ever threatened to kill yourself before? When? What stopped you?
- Have you ever tried to kill yourself before? How did you attempt to do so?

Resources
- Is there anyone or anything that would stop you?
- Is there someone whom you can talk to about these feelings?
- Have you or can you talk to your family or friends about your feelings of suicide?

Summary
- Use a suicide risk assessment worksheet (e.g., Poland, 1989) to summarize the information gained during the interview(s).

Note. From Brock & Sandoval (1996).

tant for a risk assessment protocol to have a specific set of questions that will quickly and reliably obtain needed information (Ramsay, Tanney, Tierney, & Lang, 1996). Questions often used as part of the LAUSD risk-assessment protocol address the following points:

1. What warning signs(s) initiated the referral?

2. Has the student thought about suicide? (Thoughts or threats alone, whether direct or indirect, may indicate low risk.)

3. Has the student tried to hurt himself or herself before? (Previous attempts may indicate moderate risk.)

4. Does the student have a plan to harm himself or herself now?

5. What method is the student planning to use, and does the student have access to the means? (These questions would indicate high risk.)

6. What is the support system that surrounds this student? (Including the parent in the risk assessment is critical to determining the adequacy of the student's support system.)

Assessment instruments that may assist the school psychologist fall into two categories: those that measure suicide potential and those that measure appropriate risk factors. The efficacy of utilizing any of the instruments listed below has been discussed in the literature (Davis & Brock, in press; Range & Knott, 1997; Davis & Sandoval, 1991; Davis, Sandoval, & Wilson, 1988).

1. MAPS: Measure for Adolescent Potential for Suicide (Eggert, Thompson, & Herting, 1994)

2. Hilson Assessment Profile (Inwald, Brobst, & Morrissey, 1987)

3. Suicidal Ideation Questionnaire (Reynolds, 1988)

4. The Suicide Probability Scale (Cull & Gill, 1982)

5. The Reynolds Adolescent Depression Scale (Reynolds, 1986)

6. The Children's Depression Rating Scale-Revised (Poznanski, Freeman, & Mokros, 1985)

7. The Children's Depression Inventory (Kovacs, 1981)

8. The Hopelessness Scale for Children (Kazdin, Rodgers, & Colbus, 1986)

9. Hamilton Depression Rating Scale for Children (Hamilton, 1960)

Duty to Warn Parents

There is no question that parents must be notified (Poland, 1989). In addressing this aspect of suicide intervention, four critical questions need to be addressed. First, is the parent available? Second, is the parent cooperative? Third, what information does the parent have that might contribute to the assessment of risk? Fourth, what mental health insurance, if any, does the family possess? *If the parent is available and cooperative and the student is judged high risk,* then the psychologist must provide parent(s) with community referral resources specific to where the family resides and based on health insurance status. The school psychologist should contact the community agency after first receiving parental permission and should provide pertinent referral information and then follow up to ensure that the family had arrived at the community agency. If necessary, assist the parent in transporting the student to the community agency. The psychologist should obtain a parent signature on a release of information form and assist school staff in working with parents to develop a school support plan. All actions must be documented.

If a parent is unavailable and the student is judged high risk, then, at the discretion of the school site administrator, two members of the crisis team should escort the child to the nearest emergency mental health facility and coordinate with the community agency's social services on continuing to contact the parent. Alternatively, school law enforcement, local police, or a mobile psychiatric response team may be asked to assist in transporting the suicidal youth.

Some parents are reluctant to follow through on crisis team recommendations to secure outside counseling for the suicidal child and may simplify or minimize warning signals (e.g., "She's just doing this for attention."). Cultural and language issues are frequent. Give the parents appropriate opportunity and encouragement to follow through before collaborating with crisis team members on when to proceed to the next step. The school crisis team must decide when it is appropriate to report a parent to child protective services if the parent's reluctance is truly negligent and endangers the life of the child. If it is determined that a *parent is uncooperative and the student is judged to be at high risk* for a suicidal behavior, then local law enforcement or child protective services should be contacted and a child neglect and endangerment report made. If *the parent is uncooperative and the student is judged low risk* for suicidal behavior, then it is recommended that the parent sign a "Notification of Emergency Conference" form (Poland, 1995). This form, a sample of which is provided in Figure 3, serves to document that the parents have been notified of their child's suicidal assessment in a timely fashion.

There will be occasions *when a student does not want a parent notified.* When children are thinking of harming themselves, they are not thinking clearly and, therefore, may not be the best judge of what might be their parent's response. The crisis team has only one decision to make: Will the child be placed in a more dangerous situation by notifying the parent? In such a situation, child protective services will typically be notified. The parents must still be notified, and it is the challenge of school personnel to elicit a supportive response from parents. School personnel have been found liable in court for failing to notify parents when their child was suicidal (Poland, 1995; Poland & McCormick, 1999).

The parent often has critical information necessary to make an appropriate assessment of risk. Thus it is critical to *include parents in the risk assessment.* This information may include previous school and mental health history, family dynamics, recent traumatic events in the student's life, and previous suicidal behaviors. Interviewing the parent will also assist the psychologist in making an appropriate assessment of the support system that surrounds this student.

Finally, it is important to determine *what mental health insurance the parent/family has.* This information is essential in directing families to appropriate community agencies. All modern mental health intake interviews include questions regarding insurance coverage, and it is wise for the school psychologist to be aware of the various local providers. If a student is directed to an emergency clinic, then the student may later require emergency transport to an appropriate HMO provider. This may not only further traumatize a suicidal student (because most transports must be done under restraints) but also generate great expense for the parent. It is certainly in the best interest of the child and family to limit the trauma of any student in need of emergency action.

Duty to Provide Referrals

It is critical to stress the importance of identifying and collaborating with community agencies before the crisis occurs. It is recommended that the school crisis team representative call the agency to provide accurate information that the parent may omit. School districts have an obligation to suggest agencies that are non-proprietary or that offer a sliding scale of fees.

Figure 3. This is a sample of the form used to verify that parents have been informed of their child's suicidal ideation

I/We____________________, the parents of____________________, were involved in a conference with school personnel on________________. We have been notified that our child is suicidal. We have been further advised that we should seek some psychological/psychiatric consultation immediately from the community. School personnel have clarified the district's role and will provide follow-up assistance to our child to support the treatment services from the community.

____________________ (Parent or legal guardian)

____________________ (School Personnel – Title)

Note: From Poland (1995).

Follow Up and Support the Family

Finally, it is important for school staff to provide ongoing modifications to the student's program, perhaps utilizing student study teams.

Postvention

Schools are frequently not prepared to deal with the aftermath of a suicide, yet few events have greater impact on students, parents, and staff. The primary goal of postvention strategies is to prevent the next suicide. There is considerable scientific evidence that a suicide in the community or exposure to the suicidality in others raises risk in vulnerable children and adolescents. The American Association of Suicidology (1996) and Poland (1989) have provided guidelines to the schools for dealing with the aftermath of a suicide. A summary of these suggestions can be found in Table 5.

Children and adolescents are developmentally at the height of their capacity for imitative behaviors. In addition, there is considerable concern, as well as evidence, for contagion as a result of media reporting of the tragic events that surround a youth's suicide. The American Association of Suicidology also provides guidelines to media and communities to assist in the containment of suicide clusters (CDC, 1992, 1997, 1998). This effort, inevitably, will require a comprehensive collaboration between schools, parents, media, law enforcement, and community agencies.

Legal Issues in Suicide Intervention

Landmark cases, such as *Kelson v. The City of Springfield*, 767 F2nd 651 (1985), have helped to define the responsibilities of schools and their employees when confronted with a suicidal student. School districts have been found liable for not offering suicide prevention programs, for providing inadequate supervision of a suicidal student, and for failing to notify parents when their children were suicidal (*Wyke v. Polk County School Board 11th Cir., 1997)*. The liability issues are foreseeability and negligence. That is, if a child writes or talks about suicide, then adults (particularly trained adults such as school psychologists or counselors) should be able to foresee a potential suicide. It is negligent on the part of school not to notify parents/guardians when students are known to be suicidal and not to supervise the student closely (Poland & McCormick, 1999). Even when a student denies suicidal intent, if the collaborative team suspects the child to be suicidal, then the team has an obligation to notify parents (*Eisel v. Board of Education of Montgomery County 597 A.2nd 447 Maryland, 1991)*.

Although school district personnel should intervene whenever a child threatens suicide or manifests signs of the intent to commit suicide, most courts have recognized that schools are not equipped to do the necessary in-depth counseling and treatment of children. Rather, the courts hold that school person-

Table 5. General suicide postvention guidelines for the schools

- Plan in advance of any crisis.
- Select and train a crisis team.
- Verify report of suicide from collaboration with the medical examiner, police, and family of the deceased.
- Do not dismiss school or do not encourage funeral attendance during school hours.
- Do not dedicate a memorial (i.e., yearbook, tree, bench).
- Do contribute to a suicide prevention effort on behalf of the schools or community.
- Do contact the family, apprise them of the school's intervention efforts, and assist with funeral arrangements.
- Do not release information in a large assembly or over intercom systems. Disseminate information to faculty, student, and parents. *Always* be truthful.
- Follow the victim's classes throughout the day with discussion and counseling.
- Arrange for counseling rooms in the school building, and provide individual and group counseling.
- Collaborate with media, law enforcement, and community agencies.
- Points to emphasize with media and parents: prevention, no one thing or person is to blame, help is available.
- Provide counseling or discussion opportunities for the faculty.

Note: Poland (1989), American Association of Suicidology (1996).

nel are in a position to make referrals and have a duty to secure assistance from others, with parent involvement, when a child is at risk (Davis & Sandoval, 1991).

Districts have a responsibility for providing adequate staff training in suicide prevention. Litigation against the schools has also occurred on the rare occasion of a suicide completion after a student was disciplined (suspended or expelled). Situational crises as precipitating events have already been discussed in this chapter. The school psychologist can play a significant role in providing adequate training for all school staff and in collaborating with administrators when students are involved in serious discipline procedures.

SUMMARY AND FUTURE PERSPECTIVES

The suicide rate for our nation's youth has reached alarming proportions. Research has revealed that youth suicide transcends all boundaries such as gender, age, ethnicity, geographical location, or socioeconomic status. This chapter has discussed the risk factors and warning signs of youth suicide and has provided the school psychologist with general intervention strategies and a school intervention model.

It is encouraging to note that in 1999 the U.S. Surgeon General, Dr. David Satcher, made suicide prevention a priority by issuing a Call to Action to Prevent Suicide. We hope that he can be successful.

However, both authors have attended meetings in Washington involving our higher governmental officials, and it is difficult to see what has changed. Despite alarming indicators, national and state legislators have virtually ignored the problem of youth suicide and have failed to provide the personnel or resources necessary to mandate suicide prevention programs. Few formal suicide prevention units or programs exist in the nation's schools, but those in Dallas, Los Angeles, and Miami are believed to be exemplary.

As schools continue to be overwhelmed with referrals of depressed and suicidal students, the role of the school psychologist in providing leadership has never been so critical. In the future, school psychologists will be challenged to:

1. Promote primary prevention programs that address at-risk youth such as substance/alcohol abuse, violence, dropout, and pregnancy programs.

2. Assist schools in linking with parents, community law enforcement, and mental health agencies.

3. Advocate for school site crisis teams to implement and collaborate on appropriate intervention and postvention strategies.

4. Provide staff development on youth suicide risks factors, warning signs, and referral processes.

5. Advocate for the mental health needs of students who return to school following expulsion, mental health hospitalization, or other traumatic events.

6. Support programs to reduce accessibility to firearms.

No school or community should have to suffer the devastation, confusion, uncertainty, and shock that occur in the aftermath of a suicide. It was Gandhi who said, "Be the difference that you want in the world." School psychologists can make a difference in suicide prevention.

REFERENCES

American Association of Suicidology. 1996.Youth suicide by firearms task force. Available at http://www.suicidology.org/youthsuicidetaskforce.htm.

American Foundation for Suicide Prevention (1996). Available at http://afsp.org

Anderson, J. C., & McGee, R. (1994). Comorbidity of depression in children and adolescents. In W. M. Reynolds & H. F. Johnson (Eds.), *Handbook of depression in children and adolescents* (pp. 581–601). New York: Plenum.

Barrett, T. (1985). *Youth in crisis: Seeking solutions to self-destructive behavior*. Longmont, CO: Sopris West

Beebe, J. E. (1975). Evaluation of the suicidal patient. In C. P. Rosenbaum & J. E. Beebe, III (Eds.), *Psychiatric treatment: Crisis, clinic and consultation.* New York: Basic Books.

Berman, A. L., & Jobes, D. A. (1991). *Adolescent suicide: Assessment and intervention.* Washington, DC: American Psychological Association.

Berman, A. L., & Jobes, D. A. (1995). Suicide prevention in adolescents (age 12–18). *Suicide and Life-Threatening Behavior, 25,* 143–154.

Brent, D. A., Perper, J. A. (1995). Research in adolescent suicide: Implications for training, service delivery and public policy. *Suicide and Life-Threatening Behavior, 25,* 222–230.

Brent, D. A., Perper, J. A., Allman, C. J., Moritz, G. M., Wartella, M. E., & Zelenak, J. P. (1991). The presence and accessibility of firearms in the home of adolescent suicides: A case-control study. *Journal of the American Medical Association, 266,* 2989–2995.

Brent, D. A., Perper, J. A., Moritz, G., Baugher, M., Schweers, J., & Roth, C. (1993). Firearms and adolescent suicide: A community case-control study. *American Journal of Diseases of Children, 147,* 1066–1071.

Brock, S. E., & Sandoval, J. (1996). Suicidal ideation and behaviors. In G. G. Bear, K. M. Minke, and A. Thomas (Eds.), *Children's needs II: Development, problems and alternatives* (pp.361–374). Bethesda, MD: National Association of School Psychologists.

CDC (1997, 1992, 1988). National mortality statistics and Youth Suicide Resource Guide. Available at http://www.cdc.gov/ncipc/osp/usmort.htm.

Centers for Disease Control. (1998). Suicide among black youths, United States, 1980–1995. *Morbidity and Mortality Weekly Report,* 47(10), 193–196.

Conwell, Y., Duberstein, P. R., Cox, C., Hermann, J. H., Forbes, N. T., & Caine, E. D. (1996). Relationships of age and Axis I diagnoses in victims of completed suicide: A psychological autopsy study. *American Journal of Psychiatry, 153,* 1001–1008.

Cull, J., & Gill, W. (1982). *Suicide probability scale manual.* Los Angeles: Western.

Davis, J. M., & Brock, S. E. (in press). Suicide and the schools: Incidence, theory, research, and response. In J. Sandoval (Ed.), Crisis counseling, intervention and prevention in the schools (2nd ed.). Hillsdale, NJ: Lawrence Erlbaum Associates.

Davis, J. M., & Sandoval, J. (1991). *Suicidal youth: School-based intervention and prevention.* San Francisco: Jossey-Bass.

Davis, J. M., & Sandoval, J., & Wilson, M. (1988). Strategies for the primary prevention of adolescent suicide. *School Psychology Review, 17,* 559–569.

Diekstra, R. F. W., & Garnefski, N. (1995). On the nature, magnitude and causality of suicidal behaviors: An international perspective. *Suicide and Life-Threatening Behavior, 25,* 36–57.

Eggert, L. L., Thompson, E. A., & Herting, J. R. (1994). A measure of adolescent potential for suicide (MAPS): Development and preliminary findings. *Suicide and Life-Threatening Behavior,* 24(4), 359–381.

Eisel v. Board of Education of Montgomery County 597 A.2nd 447 Maryland, 1991.

Gibbs, J. T. (1997). African-American suicide: A cultural paradox. *Suicide and Life-Threatening Behavior, 27,* 68–79.

Gibson, P. (1989). Gay male and lesbian youth suicide. In *Report of the Secretary's Task Force on Youth Suicide: Vol. 3.* Washington, DC: U.S. Department of Health and Human Services.

Groholt, B., Ekeberg, O., Wichstrom, L., & Haldorsen, T. (1997). Youth suicide in Norway, 1990–1992: A comparison between children and adolescents completing suicide and age- and gender-matched controls. *Suicide and Life-Threatening Behavior, 27,* 250–263.

Grunbaum, J. A., Kann, L., Kinchen, S. A., Ross, J. G., Gowda, V.R., Collins, J. L, & Kolbe, L. H. (1998) Youth Risk Behavior Surveillance: National Alternative High School Youth Risk Behavior Survey, United States, 1998. *Morbidity and Mortality Weekly Report Surveillance Summary October 29, 1999, 48*(SS07), 1–44.

Hamilton, M. (1960) A rating scale for depression. *Neurology Neurosurgery Psychiatry, 23,* 56–62.

Hovey, J. D., & King, C. A. (1996). Acculturative stress, depression and suicidal ideation among immigrant and second generation Latino adolescents. *Journal of American Academy of Child and Adolescent Psychiatry, 35,* 1183–1192.

Hoyert, D.L., Konanek, K.D., & Murphy, S.L. (1999). Deaths: Final data for 1997. In *National Vital Statistics Report, 47* [DHHS Publication No. (PHS) 99-1120.] Hyattsville, MD: National Center for Health Statistics.

Inwald, R., Brobst, K., & Morrissey, R. (1987). *Hilson adolescent profile manual.* Kew Gardens, NY: Hilson Research.

Kann, L., Kinchen, S. A., Williams, B. I., Ross, J. G., Lowry, R., Hill, C. V., Grunbaum, J., Blumson, D. S., Collins, J. L., & Kolbe, J. L. (1998). Youth risk surveillance-United States, 1997. *Morbidity and Mortality Weekly Report, 47,* 1–89.

Karchur, S. P., Potter, L. B., James, S. P., & Powell, K. E. (1995) *Suicide in the United States 1980–1992.* Atlanta: Centers for Disease Control and Prevention, National Center for Injury Prevention and Control.

Kazdin, A. E., Rodgers, A., & Colbus, D. (1986). The hopelessness scale for children: Psychometric characteristics and concurrent validity. *Journal of Consulting and Clinical Psychology, 54,* 241–245.

Kellerman, A. L., Rivara, F. P., Somes, G., Reay, D. T., Francisco, J., Banton, J. G., Prodzinski, J., Flinger, C., & Hackman, B. B. (1992). Suicide in the home in relationship to gun ownership. *New England Journal of Medicine, 327,* 467–472.

Kelson v. The City of Springfield, 767 F2nd 651 (1985).

King C. A., Segal, H., Kaminiski, K., Naylor, M., Ghaziuddin, N., & Rodpour, L. (1995). A prospective study of adolescent suicidal behavior following hospitalization. *Suicide and Life-Threatening Behavior, 25,* 327–338.

Kovacs, M. (1981). Rating scales to assess depression in school-aged children. *Acta Paedopsychiatry, 46,* 305–315.

Lester, D. (1997). Suicide in America: A nation of immigrants. *Suicide and Life-Threatening Behavior, 27*(1), 50–59.

Lieberman, R., & Davis, J. (in press). Suicide intervention. In S. E. Brock, P. J. Lazarus, & S. R. Jimerson, *Best practices in school crisis prevention and intervention.* Bethesda, MD: National Association of School Psychologists.

Maris, R.W. (1992). How are suicides different? In R.W. Maris, A. L. Berman, J. T. Maltsberger, and R.I. Yufit (Eds.), *Assessment and prediction of suicide* (pp. 65–87). New York: Guilford.

Maslow, A. (1998). *Toward a psychology of being* (3rd ed.). New York: John Wiley.

Massachusetts Department of Education. (1997). *1997 Massachusetts Youth Risk Behavior Survey Results.* Boston: Author.

Mishara, B. L. (1999). Concepts of death and suicide in children ages 6–12 and their implications for suicide prevention. *Suicide and Life-Threatening Behavior, 29,* 105–118.

Moscicki, E. K. (1995). Epidemiology of suicidal behavior. *Suicide and Life-Threatening Behavior, 25,* 22–35.

Normand, C. L., & Mishara, B. L. (1992). The development of the concept of suicide in children. *Omega: Journal of Death and Dying, 25,* 183–203.

Orbach, I., & Glaubman, H. (1979). The concept of death and suicidal behavior in young children. *Journal of the American Academy of Child Psychiatry, 18,* 668–678.

Peters, K. D., Konchanek, K. D. & Murphy, S. L. (1998). In *Deaths: Final data, 1996 National vital statistics report, 47* [DHHA Publication No. (PHS) 99-1120.] Hyattsville, MD: National Center for Health Statistics.

Poland, S. (1989). *Suicide intervention in the schools.* New York: Guilford.

Poland, S. (1995). Best practices in suicide intervention. In Thomas, A. & Grimes, J. (Eds.), *Best practices in school psychology III.* (pp. 155–166). Bethesda, MD: National Association of School Psychologists.

Poland, S., & McCormick, J. S. (1999). *Coping with crisis: Lessons learned.* Longmont, CO: Sopris West.

Poznanski, E. O., Freeman, L., & Mokros, H. (1985). Children's Depression Rating Scale: Revised. *Psychopharmacology Bulletin, 21,* 979–989.

Ramsay, R. F.,Tanney, B.L., Tierney, R. J., & Lang, W. A. (Primary Consultants). (1990). *The California helper's handbook for suicide intervention.* Sacramento: State Department of Mental Health.

Ramsay, R. F.,Tanney, B.L., Tierney, R. J., & Lang, W. A. (1996). *Suicide intervention workshop* (6th ed.). Calgary: Living Works.

Range, L. M., & Knott, E. C. (1997). Twenty suicide assessment instruments: Evaluation and recommendations. *Death Studies, 21,* 25–58.

Reynolds, W. M. (1986). *Reynolds Adolescent Depression Scale (RADS).* Odessa, FL: Psychological Assessment Resources.

Reynolds, W. M. (1988). *The suicidal ideation questionnaire: Professional manual.* Odessa, FL: Psychological Assessment Resources.

Roberts, R. E., Chen, Y. R., & Roberts, C. R. (1997). Ethnocultural differences in prevalence of adolescent suicidal behaviors. *Suicide and Life-Threatening Behavior, 27,* 208–217.

Shaffer, D., Gould, M. S., Fisher, P., Trautment, P., Moreau, D., Kleinman, M., & Flory, M. (1996). Psychiatric diagnosis in child and adolescent suicide. *Archives of General Psychiatry, 53,* 339–348.

Shaffer, D., & Piacentini, J. (1994). Suicide and suicide attempts. In M. Rutter, L. Hersov, & E.Taylor (Eds.), *Child and Adolescent Psychiatry* (3rd ed.). London: Blackwell Scientific.

U.S. Department of Health and Human Services (1999). *Mental Health: A Report of the Surgeon General—Executive Summary.* Rockville, MD: U.S. Department of Health and Human Services, Substance Abuse and Mental Health Services Administration, Center for Mental Health Services, National Institutes of Health, National Institute of Mental Health.

Wagner, B. M., Cole, R. E. & Swartzman, P. (1996). Comorbidity of symptoms among junior and senior high school suicide attempters. *Suicide and Life-Threatening Behavior, 26*(3), 300–307.

Wallace, J. D., Calhoun, A. D., Powell, K. E., O'Neil, J., & James, S. P. (1996). *Homicide and suicide among Native Americans, 1979–1992.* Atlanta: CDC, National Center for Injury Prevention and Control.

Wyke v. Polk County School Board 11th Cir., 1997.

ANNOTATED BIBLIOGRAPHY

American Association of Suicidology, Suite 408, 4201 Connecticut Avenue, N.W.,Washington DC 20008. (202) 237-2280 Website: suicidology.org.
Wealth of information on youth suicide prevention and intervention; Journal with membership: *Suicide and Life Threatening Behavior*; *Suicide Postvention Guidelines* (2nd Ed.) (1999) provides suggestions for dealing with the aftermath of suicide in the schools. Media and community guidelines for the containment of suicide clusters.

Poland, S. (1989). *Suicide intervention in the schools.* New York: Guilford.
The role of the school is defined, and case examples provide step-by-step guidelines for setting up and maintaining a comprehensive program. Issues covered include forces and factors in youth suicide, assessment, parent notification, liability, legislation, curriculum, and dealing with the media. Detailed procedures for intervention following crises are provided.

Poland, S., & McCormick, J.S. (1999). *Coping with crisis: Lessons learned.* Longmont, CO: Sopris West.
The authors provide a wealth of practical suggestions as to how to cope with school crises. Several national school crisis situations are utilized as first hand case examples. The authors thoroughly outline the role of the schools in suicide intervention. The appendices provide a wide array of prevention resources.

U.S. Department of Health and Human Services (1999). *Mental Health: A Report of the Surgeon General—Executive Summary* (1999). Rockville, MD: U.S. Department of Health and Human Services, Substance Abuse and Mental Health Services Administration, Center for Mental Health Services, National Institutes of Health, National Institute of Mental Health.

73 Best Practices in the Assessment of Adaptive Behavior

Patti L. Harrison
Tracy L. Boney
The University of Alabama

OVERVIEW

Adaptive behavior assessment has been emphasized for many years in the definition, diagnosis, and classification of mental retardation. Chapters in previous editions of *Best Practices in School Psychology* have called for the application of the construct of adaptive behavior to assessment and intervention for all students with disabilities (Harrison & Robinson, 1995; Reschly, 1985, 1990). Every person must use daily adaptive skills to function effectively and independently. A person who has deficits in their adaptive skills can experience problems in meeting the various demands of many environments and situations. Children who have major deficits in adaptive skills may have difficulties with important life activities, including interacting with peers, taking care of personal needs, learning new skills, and general functioning in the home, school, and community. Comprehensive assessment of children's adaptive skills by school psychologists is important for identifying children's strengths and needs and for focusing on important goals for intervention programs. The purpose of this chapter is to provide current information about adaptive behavior assessment, including perspectives, assessment methods, and research findings with practical implications for practice in school psychology. The chapter presents adaptive behavior assessment as an important component in data-based decision making for children with disabilities and other learning and behavior problems.

The following sections provide the foundation for using adaptive behavior assessment in decision making: definition and characteristics of adaptive behavior, historical perspectives, current perspectives of diagnosis and classification systems, and adaptive behavior assessment linked to interventions of functional skills.

Definition and Characteristics

Adaptive behavior refers to everyday coping with environmental demands and includes the skills in daily living that people perform to care of themselves and relate to others (Grossman, 1983). The American Association on Mental Retardation (AAMR, 1992) emphasized that adaptive behavior includes an array of important competencies and identified 10 specific areas of adaptive skills: communication, self-care, social, community-use, self-direction, health and safety, functional academics, home living, leisure, and work. The AAMR focused on "adaptive skills," rather than the more global "adaptive behavior." According to the AAMR manual on definition and classification,

> [A]daptive skill limitations often coexist with strengths in other adaptive skills or other areas of personal competence, and the existence of these limitations and strengths in adaptive skills must be both documented within the context of community environments typical of the individual's age peers and tied to the person's individualized needs for support (AAMR, 1992, p. 39).

Adaptive skills have several general characteristics, as summarized by AAMR (1992) and Harrison

(1990). Adaptive skills demonstrate situational specificity, or the ability of a person to match skills to the current environment and to change behavior to fit the specific demands of any situation. Thus, children's adaptive skills are influenced by the demands of specific situations and environments, including home, school, community, and workplace, and by the expectations of important people within the environments. Another concept is the developmental relevance of adaptive skills. Adaptive skills develop across the age range and are associated both with the growth in children's abilities and with the expanded and more complex demands of important environments. Adaptive skills of infancy, early childhood, elementary school years, adolescence, and adulthood are quite different and reflect the development and expectations of individuals in the different age ranges.

The AAMR emphasized that cultural, linguistic, communication, and behavioral factors are important components of a person's adaptive skills. An important assumption about adaptive skills is that with appropriate supports and interventions for a person's adaptive skill deficits, life functioning will generally improve. The general characteristics of adaptive skills listed above illustrate that data-based decision making for adaptive skills must take into account (a) the requirements in a person's specific environments; (b) the developmental expectations for the person's age group; (c) the person's culture and linguistic characteristics, communication skills, and problem behaviors; and (d) the supports and interventions that are needed to improve the person's functioning.

The concept of adaptive behavior has been incorporated into broader models of general competence or personal competence. The Greenspan model of competence has been the most widely utilized. According to one of the latest descriptions of the Greenspan model (Greenspan & Driscoll, 1997), general competence consists of the following:

1. Physical competence, including organ and motor competence

2. Affective competence, including temperament and character

3. Everyday competence, including social and practical intelligence

4. Academic competence, including conceptual intelligence and language

Adaptive skills are important components within everyday competence. The construct of conceptual intelligence, or the skills measured by traditional intelligence tests, is distinguished from everyday competence.

Historical Perspectives

Historically, adaptive behavior assessment has been applied widely in the field of mental retardation. Deficits in adaptive behavior, in addition to subaverage intellectual functioning, were included in the first definition of mental retardation by the American Association on Mental Deficiency in 1959 (Heber, 1961), now called the AAMR, and have been included in every official definition since. Special education legislation, beginning with the Education for All Handicapped Children Act in 1975 and continuing with the current Individuals with Disabilities Education Act (IDEA) and its 1997 re-authorization, also defined mental retardation in terms of limitations in intelligence and adaptive behavior.

Concerns about bias in intelligence testing and use of intelligence test scores to classify children in special education programs have resulted in a number of court cases with implications for adaptive behavior assessment. The use of intelligence tests to classify minority children as having mental retardation and the disproportionate numbers of minority children in special education programs for mental retardation led to a number of lawsuits in the 1960s, 1970s, and 1980s. Although the outcomes of cases such as *Larry P v. Riles* and *Marshall v. Georgia* differed in their opinions about bias in intelligence tests, all cases placed great emphasis on the importance of assessing adaptive behavior in the classification and diagnosis of mental retardation.

The 1960s and 1970s also saw increased emphasis on the use of adaptive behavior assessment for planning and implementing interventions for individuals with mental retardation. Large numbers of individuals in residential facilities for mental retardation were, as a result of many lawsuits, transitioned to less restrictive, community programs. Adaptive behavior assessment became important to identify strengths and limitations in adaptive skills and to plan needed interventions for persons leaving a residential facility and entering a community program.

Current Perspectives

Diagnosis and Classification

Criteria for diagnosing and classifying mental retardation emphasize adaptive behavior. Three definitions of mental retardation currently are used for children and adults: the AAMR (1992) definition, the *Diagnostic and Statistical Manual of Mental Disorders* (DSM-IV) (American Psychiatric Association, 1994) definition, and the definition in the regulations of the Individuals with Disabilities Education Act (IDEA) Amendments of 1997 (1999). Table 1 reports the three definitions.

The 1992 AAMR manual on mental retardation included some changes from previous editions and has been met with some controversies. According to Gresham, MacMillan, and Siperstien (1993, 1995), the current AAMR manual increases the IQ cutoff score to 75 in comparison to a score of 70 used in the previous edition. One concern regarding this change is the possibility of the increase in the number of individuals eligible for the diagnosis of mental retardation. The change in IQ score could also lead to the potential for renewed overrepresentation in programs for children with mental retardation, especially for minority children (Gresham et al., 1993, 1995; Matson, 1995). A second change in the current AAMR definition from previous versions is the identification of 10 adaptive skill areas and an emphasis on limitations in at least 2 of the 10 adaptive skill areas for a diagnosis of mental retardation. However, the AMMR does not specify a criterion or cut-off score for an adaptive skills limitation (Matson, 1995). The current AAMR definition also eliminated the classification of levels of mental retardation (mild, moderate, severe, and profound) and, instead, identifies four possible intensities of needed supports for individuals with mental retardation: intermittent, limited, extensive, and pervasive. Vig and Jedreysek (1996) expressed concern that the elimination of levels of impairment may restrict family understanding of a child's disability and predictions about a child's rate of progress and response to intervention.

In response to the criticisms about the current definition of mental retardation, Luckasson, Schalock, Snell, and Spitalnik (1996) and Reiss (1994) noted that the current, 1992, definition of mental retardation by the AAMR emphasizes a new "support" model of mental retardation, instead of a deficiency model. In addition, they argue that the new definition provides a more flexible role for professional decision making by providing an upper limit range of 70–75 for IQ scores to be used in the diagnosis of mental retardation and not by setting specific scores for adaptive skills limitations. Most important, the cur-

Table 1. Definitions of mental retardation

Source	*Definition*
American Association on Mental Retardation (1992)	"Mental retardation refers to substantial limitations in present functioning. It is characterized by significantly subaverage intellectual functioning, existing concurrently with related limitations in two or more of the following applicable adaptive skill areas: communication, self-care, home living, social skills, community use, self-direction, health and safety, functional academics, leisure, and work. Mental retardation manifests before age 18" (p. 5).
American Psychiatric Association (1994)	"The essential feature of Mental Retardation is significantly subaverage general intellectual function (Criterion A) that is accompanied by significant limitations in adaptive functioning in at least two of the following skill areas: communication, self-care, home living, social/interpersonal skills, use of community resources, self-direction, functional academic skills, work, leisure, health, and safety (Criterion B). The onset must occur before age 18 years (Criterion C)."
Individuals with Disabilities Education Act Amendments of 1997 (1999)	"Mental retardation means significantly subaverage general intellectual functioning, existing concurrently with deficits in adaptive behavior and manifested during the developmental period, that adversely affects a child's educational performance" (p. 12422).

rent AAMR definition focuses on the interaction of a person's characteristics and his or her environments.

As seen in Table 1, the DSM-IV (American Psychiatric Association, 1994) definition is similar to the AAMR (1992) definition. The main criteria for mental retardation in DSM-IV are subaverage general intelligence accompanied by limitations in adaptive functioning in two adaptive skills areas. However, unlike the AAMR criteria, subaverage intelligence is operationalized as an IQ score of approximately 70 or below in the DSM-IV. The DSM-IV also maintains the degrees of severity of mental retardation (mild, moderate, severe, and profound), in contrast to the AAMR use of intensities of support (intermittent, limited, extensive, and pervasive)

In addition to the definitions provided by the AAMR and DSM-IV, mental retardation is a qualifying disability for special education under the IDEA Amendments of 1997. Similar to other definitions, IDEA defines mental retardation as subaverage intelligence existing concurrently with deficits in adaptive behavior, as noted in Table 1. IDEA describes mental retardation as manifested during the developmental period and negatively affecting a child's educational performance. Unlike the AAMR and DSM-IV, the IDEA definition has a broad focus upon adaptive behavior rather than a list of specific adaptive skill areas and does not require deficits in at least 2 of 10 adaptive skill areas.

IDEA Amendments of 1997 also emphasize the importance of adaptive behavior assessment in the definition of developmental delay and identification of needs for services for children experiencing developmental delays. For children aged 3–9, states and local school districts may identify developmental delays in one or more of the following areas: physical development, cognitive development, communication development, social or emotional development, or adaptive development.

Assessment Linked to Interventions for Functional Skills

Assessment of adaptive skills should be an integral part of school psychologists' data collection about children's skills and behaviors in multiple environments. Data from adaptive behavior assessment should be used, along with data from other sources and about other behavior domains, to design, implement, and monitor interventions. The current chapter is based on the ideal that goals of assessment and intervention for children with learning and behavior problems or disabilities should include increases in the daily adaptive skills needed to function more effectively and independently. Although adaptive behavior assessment is a required component of the assessment of children with disabilities such as mental retardation and developmental delays, school psychologists should not use adaptive behavior assessment to merely document a diagnosis. Comprehensive adaptive behavior assessment has implications for important interventions for all children experiencing problems. School psychologists should use adaptive behavior assessment data to plan interventions that actually improve children's independence and expand children's skills.

The AAMR (1992) manual, as well as other resources, focused upon adaptive skills as functional daily living skills that represent important goals of training and interventions. Functional daily living skills are skills that are frequently used during an individual's daily routine and that occur naturally in home, school, work, and community environments (Schleien, Green, Heyne, 1993). Acquisition of functional skills allows an individual to be independent in important environments and settings. Assessment of functional skills should include (a) identification of the individual's strengths, (b) evaluation of the skills needed in the environments in which the person currently participates, and (c) analysis of the skills needed to function in the next, least-restrictive environment to assist in transition. For example, functional skills needed in a preschool setting may be different from skills needed in an elementary school. Assessment requires evaluation of the child's current skills, the skills needed in the preschool setting, and the skills needed in the elementary setting. For an older adolescent student, the demands of the high school setting may be quite different than the demands of the work setting that the student will enter following high school. Assessment requires analysis of the students skills, the high school setting, and the work environment.

The AAMR (1992) addressed the need for assessment of an individual's level of functional skills and identification of supports and services that can be used for an intervention related to functional, daily-living skills. The AAMR recommends that the purpose of assessment should be determined before assessment (e.g., to measure progress of an intervention). Once the function is determined, then a broad assessment should be planned and conducted and assessment information should be analyzed. The assessment can be conducted through a number of methods, including the use of structured interviews, norm-referenced adaptive behavior scales, and direct observation. The assessment information should be translated into a description of needed supports to provide interventions for the student's limitations and weaknesses. While these supports and interventions are being delivered, the student's progress should be monitored for progress or any needed modifications in the intervention.

Interventions to increase functional, daily living skills require prioritizing of goals for interventions. The first step in assessment for identifying intervention priorities is to determine whether the child actually has the skill and chooses not to use it or whether the skill is not in the child's repetoire of behaviors. The next step is to determine if a discrepancy exists between the actual skills of the child and the expected performance in the child's current or next environments, and to then evaluate whether this discrepancy is socially significant in terms of quality of life for the child (AAMR, 1992). The highest priorities for interventions are these skills that have the most social significance for the child.

Depending on the needs and developmental levels of children, different functional skills may be targeted for intervention. For example, interventions for children with milder disabilities in the elementary school tend to focus more on readiness skills such as following directions, developing self-help skills, and interacting with peers. Young children may benefit from interventions that expose them to association with other children in the regular classroom and are more performance-oriented. For children with more severe disabilities, goals for functional skills typically revolve around preparing them to live life as independently as possible. Intervention goals for older children may focus more on functional academics and functional pre-vocational skills. For students leaving secondary programs, transition goals may include adaptive skills needed in job training programs and the workplace. Dunn (1997) concluded that postschool outcomes can be improved for young adults with appropriate assessment and planning for transition.

Several types of interventions have been shown to be effective for increasing functional skills, including the following: modeling, in which the student duplicates a task performed by another person; behavior rehearsal, in which the student practices a learned task over and over; and coaching procedures, which use direct verbal instruction with discussion of the desired behavior (Elliott, Sheridan, & Gresham, 1989). Interventions for older students may include community-based instruction. McDonnell, Hardman, Hightower, Kelfer-O'Donnell, and Drew (1993) found that community-based instruction is an effective technique for generalization of classroom-learned skills to natural settings. Other interventions that may be effective with older students include problem-solving training and self-motivational methods, such as self-instruction, self-management, and self-monitoring (Hughes, 1992; Misra, 1992). The AAMR emphasized that, "Rather than simply scheduled for instruction in discrete blocks of time, basic motor, language, and social skills are taught as they occur or are needed, naturally embedded within routine activities (AAMR, 1992, p. 131).

BASIC CONSIDERATIONS

Assessment Methods

A number of different methods can be used to assess adaptive behavior, including traditional, norm-referenced rating scales, and alternative methods.

Norm-Referenced Instruments

There are a number of standardized, norm-referenced adaptive behavior scales. Table 2 contains brief descriptions of several instruments that are used in school settings. The norm-referenced assessment instruments listed in Table 2 are rating scales used primarily with parents and teachers as informants about children's adaptive skills. Norm-referenced rating scales have a number of advantages in the assessment of daily, adaptive skills. They focus on adaptive skills that occur in naturalistic settings, such as home, school, and community, and they provide comprehensive assessments of a large number of adaptive skills. They obtain information from multiple perspectives and multiple sources of information and include important individuals, such as parents and teachers, in the assessment process. They provide a developmental reference for children's adap-

Table 2. Examples of norm-referenced adaptive behavior scales for use with children in school settings

Scale	*Forms and ages*	*Major areas assessed*	*Norm samples*
Vineland Adaptive Behavior Scales (Sparrow et al., 1984a, 1984b, 1985)	• Survey Form and Expanded Form: Used with parents of children birth through age 18 and low functioning adults. • Classroom Edition: Used by teachers of children ages 3–12.	• Communication, Daily Living Skills, socialization, and Motor Skills.[a] • Adaptive Behavior Composite.	• Standardization samples of children with typical functioning. • Clinical norm samples and validity studies for samples of individuals with mental retardation in residential and non-residential facilities and children with hearing and visual impairments and emotional disturbances in residential facilities.[b]
Adaptive Behavior Scale-School (2nd ed.) (Lambert , Nihira, & Leland, 1993)[c]	• Informants for children aged 3–21.	• Personal Self-Sufficiency, Personal-Social Responsibility, Community Self-Sufficiency, Social Adjustment, and Personal Adjustment.[a,d]	• Standardization samples of individuals with mental retardation and those without mental retardation.
Adaptive Behavior Evaluation Scale-Revised (McCarney, 1995a, 1995b)	• Home Version: Used by parents of children ages 5–18. • School Version: Used by teachers of children ages 5–18.	• Ten specific areas of adaptive functioning as identified by the AAMR • Adaptive Skills Quotient	• Standardization samples of individuals with typical functioning. • Validity study samples included individuals with mental retardation.
Scales of Independent Behavior, Revised (Bruininks et al., 1996)	• Informants for individuals infancy through adulthood.	• Motor Skills, Social Interaction and Communication Skills, Personal Living Skills, and Community Living Skills clusters.[a] • Broad Independence Score.	• Standardization samples of individuals with typical development. • Validity studies samples included individuals with mental retardation and behavior disorders and children receiving different levels of educational services (regular classroom, special education classroom, or special education school).
Adaptive Behavior Assessment System (Harrison & Oakland, 2000)	• Parent Form: Used by parents children ages 5–21. • Teacher Form: Used by teachers of students ages 5–21. • Adult Form: Used by informants of adults ages 16 and older.	• Ten specific areas of adaptive functioning as identified by the AAMR. • General Adaptive Composite.	• Standardization samples of individuals with typical functioning. • Validity study samples included individuals with mental retardation, learning disabilities, autism, attention deficit hyperactivity disorder, and emotional or behavioral disorders.

[a] The Vineland, Adaptive Behavior Scale, and Scales of Independent Behavior also include an assessment of maladaptive behavior.
[b] Supplementary norms were developed by Carter et al. (1998) for use with individuals with autism.
[c] The Adaptive Behavior Scale, Residential and Community (2nd ed.) (Nihira , Leland, & Lambert, 1993) rating scale is available for informants for adults with mental retardation.
[d] Byrant, Taylor, and Rivera (1996) developed an instrument, the Adaptive Areas Assessment, which is a recategorization of the Adaptive Behavior Scale items into the ten adaptive skill areas identified by the AAMR.

tive skills by comparing the adaptive behavior ratings for the targeted child and a norm group of children the same age.

Limitations of Norm-Referenced Scales and Alternative Assessment Methods

In spite of the advantages of rating scales in assessing adaptive behavior, rating scales have a number of limitations that should be taken into account in adaptive behavior assessment, and rating scales should be supplemented with other data collection procedures (Gresham & Elliott, 1990). For example, ratings of informants may simply provide an assessment of the informant's perceptions of a relative summary of the individual's general adaptive behavior, instead of an exact frequency of behaviors. Rating scales may be limited to skills that can be assessed through a rating scale or questionnaire completed by an informant and may not assess all possible adaptive skills. Respondents' ratings on the scales may reflect their own expectations and standards for adaptive skills, and the expectations may differ between respondents and between settings. Respondents also may be influenced by characteristics of the client, including appearance, ability, academic performance, and background.

School psychologists should integrate multiple methods of assessment and collect data from multiple sources of information, given the limitations of norm-referenced rating scales. Alternative methods that may be useful in a comprehensive assessment of adaptive behavior include informal interviews, structured observations, social skills assessment, and sociometric techniques. Parents, teachers, supervisors, and others, as well as children themselves, should serve as sources of information in data collection about adaptive behavior.

Structured, naturalistic observations focus on direct and systematic observation of an individual in a setting, such as the classroom, home, playground, and place of work (see Hintze, Volpe, and Shapiro, this volume). Social skills assessment provides identification of important acquisition and performance deficits that may be affecting children's social interactions (see Gresham, this volume). Sociometric techniques, such as peer rating and peer nominations, can be useful in determining the impact of adaptive behavior deficits on the perceptions of peers. Another assessment technique, direct testing of a client's adaptive skills, may provide objective data about what a child is able to do in a structured testing environment and can supplement rating scales and their focus on an informant's perception of what a child does.

Research suggests that correlations between parent and teacher ratings of individuals' adaptive skills are low to moderate. Research findings suggest that correlations between parent and teacher ratings are higher when disabilities are more severe, but even for children with severe disabilities, parent and teacher scores on adaptive behavior scales may differ significantly (Hundert, Morrison, Mahoney, Mundy, & Vernon, 1997; Voelker, Shore, Hakim-Larson, & Bruner, 1997). The research suggests that both parents and teachers should be used in adaptive behavior assessment and that evaluation of the reasons for differences between parent and teacher ratings would have great value in decision making and planning interventions. Informal interviews with significant others, including parents and teachers, may provide information about factors that may be related to children's adaptive behavior and may impact parent and teacher ratings on adaptive behavior scales. For example, different parenting and teaching styles and expectations or children's behavioral inconsistencies across settings may affect adaptive behavior ratings.

School psychologists should focus on integrating data from multiple methods of assessment and data collection and multiple sources of information in order to obtain the most valid data possible for decision making and planning interventions. For example, a combination of norm-referenced rating scales and informal interviews with parents and teachers may reveal that a child has strengths in self-care skills and weaknesses in communication and self-direction at both home and school. However, parents may report that a child has adequate social skills at home and in the community, and teachers may report that the child has social skills problems in the classroom. Additional interviews with the parents, teachers, and child and systematic observation in the classroom may suggest that the child has fewer social interactions than a typical peer in the classroom and that the limited and infrequent social interactions of the child are characterized by hostile behavior (e.g., raised voice, name calling, shoving) between the child and peers. Thus, the example briefly illustrates the comprehensive nature of the adaptive behavior data provided by multiple assessment methods and sources of information and the implications of the integrated data for prioritizing interventions.

Practical Implications of Research

Much research has been conducted with adaptive behavior assessment. The research findings about the relationship between adaptive behavior and intelligence and the adaptive behavior strengths and limitations of children with disabilities have important implications for school psychologists.

Adaptive Behavior and Intelligence

Given the requirements to assess both adaptive behavior and intelligence for the diagnosis of mental retardation, many studies have investigated the relationship between scores on adaptive behavior and intelligence measures. The majority of the findings demonstrate moderate correlations between the scores from adaptive behavior and intelligence scales, although there is some evidence (e.g., Bruininks, Woodcock, Weatherman, & Hill, 1996; Vig & Jedrysek, 1995) to suggest that the correlations are higher for individuals with more severe disabilities and may vary for different domains of adaptive behavior. The generally modest correlations support the conclusion that adaptive behavior and intelligence are distinct but related constructs. For example, Keith, Fehrmann, Harrison, and Pottebaum (1987) investigated several possible models for the relationship between adaptive behavior and intelligence. Results supported the model that adaptive behavior and intelligence are separate but related constructs.

The AAMR (1992) noted that, although intelligence and adaptive behavior should be applied equally when making decisions about diagnoses of mental retardation, intelligence test scores have been over-emphasized in professional decision making. The AAMR stressed that there should be a balanced consideration of adaptive skills and intelligence measures. The moderate correlations between adaptive behavior and intelligence scales suggest that scores from the two types of scales will provide distinct types of information. Greenspan and Driscoll's (1997) distinction between everyday competence and academic competence supports the importance of considering everyday skills, as assessed by adaptive behavior scales, and academic competence, as measured by conceptual IQ tests.

Adaptive Skills of Children with Disabilities

Children with mental retardation, autism, and other disabilities often are assessed with adaptive behavior assessment measures for diagnosis of the disabilities, evaluation of strengths and weaknesses, and determination of needs for intervention. A number of research studies have investigated the adaptive skills of children in different disability categories.

Mental Retardation. As noted throughout this chapter, deficits in adaptive skills are necessary for diagnosis and classification of mental retardation. Research indicates that individuals with disabilities do have important adaptive skills deficits. Research reported in the manuals for the Vineland Adaptive Behavior Scales (Sparrow, Balla, & Cicchetti, 1984a) and Scales of Independent Behavior-Revised (Bruininks et al., 1996) indicate that individuals with mental retardation have adaptive behavior scores lower than those of individuals with no disabilities. The research also suggests that individuals with moderate to severe mental retardation living in residential facilities have lower adaptive skills than those with mild to moderate mental retardation living in non-residential facilities. Dykens, Hodapp, and Evans (1994) examined the profile of adaptive behavior for children with Down syndrome and found that the children had a weakness in communication relative to daily living and socialization skills. There was also a significant difference between the expressive and receptive abilities in the communication domain. Children with Fragile X syndrome demonstrated weaknesses in adaptive behavior in communication and socialization (Freund, Peebles, Aylward, & Reiss, 1995; Bailey, Hatton, & Skinner, 1998). Bailey et al. (1998) also found that assessment of children with Fragile X syndrome demonstrated strength in the area of motor skills in relation to their weaknesses in communication and cognition.

Autism. Children with autism may have a number of developmental difficulties, including deficits in communication and social interactions, and may exhibit repetitive or stereotyped activities and resistance to change. Research has demonstrated that children with autism typically have weaknesses in the area of socialization when compared with children with mental retardation or typical development (Carpentieri & Morgan, 1996; Loveland & Kelly, 1991;

Rodrigue, Morgan, & Geffken, 1991; Stone, Ousely, Hepburn, Hogan, & Brown, 1999; Vig & Jedrysek, 1995). Individuals with autism also demonstrate a weakness in the adaptive domain of communication (Stone et al., 1999; Vig & Jedrysek, 1995). In addition to specific strengths and weaknesses, Rodrigue et al. (1991) also found that children with autism typically demonstrated overall greater variability in social skills. The research findings support the suggestions of Shriver, Allen, and Mathews (1999) that core areas of assessment and interventions for children with autism should include social competence, play and leisure skills, and self-help/independent living skills.

Other Disabilities. Because many disabilities and disorders can affect adaptive functioning, adaptive skills assessment may be important for identifying strengths and weaknesses of daily functioning for disabilities in addition to mental retardation and autism. For these other disabilities and disorders, it is important to assess adaptive functioning in order to assist with planning appropriate interventions.

Sparrow et al. (1984a) reported that children with emotional disturbances in residential facilities had adaptive behavior scores well below the normative average on the Vineland, and Bruininks et al. (1996) reported that children with behavior disorders demonstrated more maladaptive behaviors on the Scales of Independent Behavior-Revised than did a normal control group. Sparrow and Cicchetti (1987) examined the research related to adaptive and maladaptive functioning of children with emotional disturbances and concluded (1) the severity of adaptive behavior deficits tend to increase with the severity of the disturbance, (2) children with emotional disturbances typically demonstrate the most significant adaptive skill deficits in the areas of socialization and maladaptive behavior, and (3) score patterns in areas such as communication and daily living skills tend to be unpredictable.

Voelker et al. (1997) reported adaptive skills deficits for children with multiple disabilities in cognitive, sensory, and motor areas, and Sparrow et al. (1984a) found adaptive behavior scores well below the normative mean for children with hearing and visual impairments in residential facilities. Given the heterogeneous nature of children with low incidence disabilities, such as sensory or physical disabilities, it is more important to focus on the benefits of adaptive behavior assessment rather than typical adaptive behavior profiles. Many children with sensory or physical disabilities may experience few deficits in adaptive skills. Adaptive behavior assessment for children with physical disabilities, in combination with assessments from other areas such as speech and physical therapy, may offer the most useful information for school psychologists. Although adaptive skills assessment of individuals with hearing and visual impairments may not be necessary for diagnosis or classification of the disability, assessment of their daily adaptive skills may assist in identifying needed goals and supports.

BEST PRACTICES

What follows are eight highlights:

1. School psychologists should consider the routine incorporation of adaptive behavior assessment into a comprehensive data-based decision making framework of providing services for children. Adaptive behavior assessment should be viewed an integral factor in assessment and interventions for daily, functional skills. School psychologists should emphasize that the primary goals of adaptive behavior assessment are to identify needs and develop plans for interventions that enable children to improve their independence and expand important life skills.

2. A number of published, norm-reference adaptive behavior rating scales are available for use by school psychologists and are useful components of comprehensive adaptive behavior assessment. School psychologists should carefully select the scale(s) to be used based on the individual child's needs for assessment and the specific information provided by the scales.

3. Adaptive behavior ratings scales have useful characteristics, but have a number of limitations that should be addressed during decision making. School psychologists should take into account limitations such as the rating scale's reflection of a relative summary of the individual's general adaptive behavior, instead of an exact frequency of behaviors, when respondents rate items. School psy-

chologists must evaluate the impact of respondents' expectations, standards, and perceptions on their adaptive skill ratings of children.

4. School psychologists should use multiple methods of adaptive behavior assessment, given the limitations of norm-referenced rating scales. Methods such as informal interviews, structured observations, social skills assessment, and sociometric techniques, are valuable during adaptive behavior assessment in order to obtain more detailed information about strengths and weaknesses in a variety of settings and to plan and monitor interventions.

5. Information from both parents and teachers should be used in adaptive behavior assessment of a child. Research suggests that parents and teachers may disagree in their adaptive behavior ratings, perhaps because of differing perceptions or expectations of the two informants or actual inconsistencies in the child's behavior across two different settings. Discrepancies between parents and teacher can be of great clinical value in assessment and planning interventions, and discrepancies can be followed by informal interviews with parents and teachers to explore the reasons for the discrepancies.

6. School psychologists should collaborate and integrate adaptive behavior data collected by using multiple assessment methods and sources of information and should never rely only on norm-referenced rating scales. Valid decision making and development of effective interventions require the use of comprehensive, integrated data, instead of a single source of information or assessment method.

7. School psychologists must always use a balanced consideration of adaptive behavior and intellectual assessment results when making decisions about a mental retardation classification. An over-emphasis on intelligence test scores violates legal and professional guidelines and does not meet the needs of children. In addition, research has demonstrated that intelligence and adaptive behavior are distinct, but related, constructs; and consideration of both everyday competence and conceptual intelligence should be included in decision making for children.

8. Although adaptive behavior assessment is required for the diagnosis of mental retardation and has many implications for interventions for individuals with mental retardation, it has many important uses in the assessment and intervention for other children. School psychologists should incorporate comprehensive adaptive behavior assessment into the assessment and data collection plan for all children experiencing learning and behavior problems and difficulties in functional, daily living skills. Many children who are experiencing problems have concurrent deficits in adaptive skills. Increases in adaptive skills represent important intervention goals for many children.

SUMMARY

This chapter has described adaptive behavior assessment as a component of data-based decision making by school psychologists. The current perspective provided by the AAMR (1992) provides a framework for assessing adaptive skills in order to gather information about an individual's functional limitations and needs for services. The primary goal of adaptive behavior assessment should be to plan and monitor interventions for students. A number of norm-referenced rating scales of adaptive behavior are available, and they have many advantages, but a number of limitations. Rating scale assessment should be supplemented with interviews, naturalistic observations, and other techniques for comprehensive adaptive behavior assessment. Research suggests that adaptive behavior and intelligence are distinct, but related, constructs, and supports the need to gather data about both everyday competence and conceptual intelligence. Adaptive behavior assessment is required for individuals before they can receive a diagnosis of mental retardation, but also has important uses for assessment and interventions for children with other disabilities, including children with autism, emotional or behavior disorders, and physical or sensory disabilities.

REFERENCES

American Association on Mental Retardation. (1992). *Definitions, classifications, and systems of supports* (9th ed.). Washington, DC: Author.

American Psychiatric Association. (1994). *Diagnostic and statistical manual of mental disorders* (4th ed.). Washington, DC: Author.

Bailey, D. B., Hatton, D. D., & Skinner, M. (1998). Early developmental trajectories of males with fragile X syndrome. *American Journal on Mental Retardation, 103*, 29–39.

Bruininks, R. H., Woodcock, R. W., Weatherman, R. F., & Hill, B. K. (1996). *Scales of Independent Behavior-Revised comprehensive manual*. Chicago, IL: Riverside.

Bryant, B., Taylor, R., & Rivera, D. (1996). *Adaptive areas assessment*. Austin, TX: PRO-ED.

Carpentieri, S., & Morgan, S. B. (1996). Adaptive and intellectual functioning in autistic and nonautistic retarded children. *Journal of Autism and Developmental Disorders, 26*, 611–620.

Carter, A. S., Volkmar, F. R., Sparrow, S. S., Wang, J. J., Lord, C., Dawson, G., Fombonne, E., Loveland, K., Mesibov, G., & Schopler, E. (1998). The Vineland Adaptive Behavior Scales: Supplementary norms for individuals with autism. *Journal of Autism and Developmental Disorders, 28*, 287–302.

Dunn, C. (1997). Transition assessment for secondary students with mental retardation. In R. L. Taylor (Ed.), *Assessment of individuals with mental retardation* (pp. 173–199). San Diego, CA: Singular.

Dykens, E. M., Hodapp, R. M., & Evans, D. W. (1994). Profiles and development of adaptive behavior in children with Down syndrome. *American Journal on Mental Retardation, 98*, 580–587.

Elliott, S. N., Sheridan, S. M., & Gresham, F M. (1989). Assessing and treating social skills deficits: A case study for the scientist practitioner. *Journal of School Psychology, 27*, 197–222.

Freund, L. S., Peebles, C. D., Aylward, E., & Reiss, A. L. (1995). Preliminary report on cognitive and adaptive behaviors of preschool-aged males with fragile X. *Developmental Brain Dysfunction, 8*, 242–251.

Greenspan, S., & Driscoll, J. (1997). The role of intelligence in a broad model of personal competence. In D. P. Flanagan, J. L. Genshaft, & P. L. Harrison (Eds.), *Contemporary intellectual assessment: Theories, tests, and issues*. New York: Guilford.

Gresham, F. M., & Elliott, S. L. (1990). *Social Skills Rating System manual*. Circle Pines, MN: American Guidance Service.

Gresham, F. M., MacMillan, D. L., & Siperstein, G. N. (1993). Conceptual and psychometric concerns about the 1992 AAMR definition of mental retardation. *American Journal on Mental Retardation, 98*, 3325–3335.

Gresham, F. M., MacMillan, D. L., & Siperstein, G. N. (1995). Critical analysis of the 1992 AAMR definition: Implications for school psychology. *School Psychology Quarterly, 10* (1), 1–19.

Grossman, H. J. (Ed.) (1983). *Classification in mental retardation*. Washington, DC: American Association on Mental Deficiency.

Harrison, P. L. (1990). Mental retardation, adaptive behavior assessment, and giftedness. In A. S. Kaufman (Ed.), *Assessing adolescent and adult intelligence* (pp. 533–585). Boston: Allyn & Bacon.

Harrison, P. L., & Oakland, T. (2000). *Adaptive Behavior Assessment System*. San Antonio, TX: The Psychological Corporation.

Harrison, P. L., & Robinson, B. (1995). Best practices in the assessment of adaptive behavior. In A. Thomas & J. Grimes (Eds.), *Best practices in school psychology III* (pp. 753–762). Washington, DC: National Association of School Psychologists.

Heber, R. F. (1961). A manual on terminology and classification in mental retardation. *American Journal of Mental Deficiency,* 64, Monogr. Suppl. (Rev. ed.).

Hughes, C. (1992). Teaching self-instruction utilizing multiple exemplars to produce generalized problem-solving among individuals with severe mental retardation. *American Journal of Mental Retardation, 97*, 302–314.

Hundert, J., Morrison, L., Mahoney, W., Mundy, F., & Vernon, M. L. (1997). Parent and teacher assessments of the developmental status of children with severe, mild/

moderate, or no developmental disabilities. *Topics in Early Childhood Special Education, 17*, 419–434.

Individuals with Disabilities Education Act Amendments of 1997. (1999). Assistance to States for the Education of Children with Disabilities and the Early Intervention Program for Infants and Toddlers with Disabilities; Final Regulations; 34 CFR Parts 300 and 303; *Federal Register*, *64*(48).

Keith, T. Z., Fehrmann, P. G., Harrison, P. L., & Pottebaum, S. M. (1987).The relationship between adaptive behavior and intelligence: Testing alternative explanations. *Journal of School Psychology, 25*, 31–43.

Lambert, N., Nihira, K., & Leland, H. (1993). *AAMR Adaptive Behavior Scale, School* (2nd ed.). Austin, TX: PRO-ED.

Loveland, K. A., & Kelley, M. L. (1991). Development of adaptive behavior in preschoolers with autism or Down syndrome. *American Journal on Mental Retardation, 96*, 13–20.

Luckasson, R., Schalock, R. L., Snell, M. E., & Spitalnik, D. M. (1996). The 1992 AAMR definition preschool children: Response from the committee on terminology and classification. *Mental Retardation, 34*, 247–256.

Matson, J. L. (1995). Comments on Gresham, MacMillan, & Siperstein's paper, "Critical analysis of the 1992 AAMR definition: Implications for school psychology." *School Psychology Quarterly, 10*(1), 20–23.

McCarney, S. B. (1995a). *Adaptive Behavior Evaluation Scale, Revised: Home version.* Columbia, MO: Hawthorne Educational Services.

McCarney, S. B. (1995b). *Adaptive Behavior Evaluation Scale, Revised: School version.* Columbia, MO: Hawthorne Educational Services.

McDonnell, J., Hardman, M. L., Hightower, J., Kelfer-O'Donnell, R., & Drew, C. (1993). Impact of community-based instruction on the development of adaptive behavior of secondary level students with mental retardation. *American Journal on Mental Retardation, 97*, 575–584.

Misra, A. (1992). Generalization of social skills through self-monitoring by adults with mild mental retardation. *Exceptional Children, 58*, 495–507.

Nihira, K., Leland, H., Lambert, N. (1993). *AAMR Adaptive Behavior Scale, Residential and Community* (2nd ed.). Austin, TX: PRO-ED.

Reiss, S. (1994). Issues in defining mental retardation. *American Journal on Mental Retardation, 99*(1), 1–7.

Reschly, D. J. (1985). Best practices in adaptive behavior assessment. In A. Thomas & J. Grimes (Eds.), *Best practices in school psychology* (pp.353–368). Washington, DC: National Association of School Psychologists.

Reschly, D. J. (1990). Best practices in adaptive behavior. In A. Thomas & J. Grimes (Eds.), *Best practices in school psychology II* (pp.29–42). Washington, DC: National Association of School Psychologists.

Rodrigue, J. R., Morgan, S. B., & Geffken, G. R. (1991). A comparative evaluation of adaptive behavior in children and adolescents with autism, Down syndrome, and normal development. *Journal of Autism and Developmental Disorders, 21*, 187–196.

Schleien, S. J., Green F. P., Heyne, L. A. (1993). Integrated community recreation. In M. E. Snell, *Instruction of students with severe disabilities* (4th ed.) (pp. 526–555). New York: Merrill.

Shriver, M. D., Allen, K. D., & Mathews, J. R. (1999). Effective assessment of the shared and unique characteristics of children with autism. *School Psychology Review, 28*, 538–558.

Sparrow, S. S., Balla, D. A., & Cicchetti, D. V. (1984a). *Vineland Adaptive Behavior Scales, Expanded form.* Circle Pines, MN: American Guidance Service.

Sparrow, S. S., Balla, D. A., & Cicchetti, D. V. (1984b). *Vineland Adaptive Behavior Scales, Survey form.* Circle Pines, MN: American Guidance Service.

Sparrow, S. S., Balla, D. A., & Cicchetti, D. V. (1985). *Vineland Adaptive Behavior Scales, Classroom edition.* Circle Pines, MN: American Guidance Service.

Sparrow, S. S., & Cicchetti, D. (1987). Adaptive behavior and the psychologically disturbed child. *Journal of Special Education, 21*, 89–101.

Stone, W. L., Ousley, O. Y., Hepburn, S. L., Hogan, K. L., & Brown, C. S. (1999). Patterns of adaptive behavior in very young children with autism. *American Journal on Mental Retardation, 104*, 187–199.

Vig, S., & Jedrysek, E. (1995). Adaptive behavior of young urban children with developmental disabilities. *Mental Retardation, 33*, 90–98.

Vig, S., & Jedrysek, E. (1996). Application of the 1992 AAMR definition: Issues for preschool children. *Mental Retardation, 34*, 244–246.

Voelker, S., Shore, D., Hakim-Larson, J., & Bruner, D. (1997). Discrepancies in parent and teacher ratings of adaptive behavior of children with multiple disabilities. *Mental Retardation, 35*, 10–17.

ANNOTATED BIBLIOGRAPHY

American Association on Mental Retardation. (1992). *Definitions, classifications, and systems of supports* (9th ed.). Washington, DC: Author.
The AAMR manual is an excellent resource to obtain information about all aspects of mental retardation, including assessment, diagnosis, and intervention. The manual emphasizes environmental approaches to assessment and intervention.

Reschly, D. J. (1990). Best practices in adaptive behavior. In A. Thomas & J. Grimes (Eds.), *Best practices in school psychology II* (pp.29–42). Washington, DC: National Association of School Psychologists.
The best practices chapter continues to be one of the best resources on adaptive behavior assessment, owing to the outstanding discussion of key issues and the practical recommendations.

Taylor, R. L. (Ed.), *Assessment of individuals with mental retardation*. San Diego, CA: Singular.
In addition to the chapters on intelligence testing and adaptive behavior assessment, this edited text includes outstanding chapters on early childhood assessment and transition assessment for adolescents with mental retardation.

ARTICLES

Series of articles criticizing the 1992 AAMR definition of mental retardation and responses from the team that developed the 1992 definition. A review of the articles will allow school psychologists to explore the key and controversial issues in the field of mental retardation. Outstanding articles include:

Gresham, F. M., MacMillan, D. L., & Siperstein, G. N. (1993). Conceptual and psychometric concerns about the 1992 AAMR definition of mental retardation. *American Journal on Mental Retardation, 98*, 3325–3335.

Gresham, F. M., MacMillan, D. L., & Siperstein, G. N. (1995). Critical analysis of the 1992 AAMR definition: Implications for school psychology. *School Psychology Quarterly, 10*(1), 1–19.

Luckasson, R., Schalock, R. L., Snell, M. E., & Spitalnik, D. M. (1996). The 1992 AAMR definition preschool children: Response from the committee on terminology and classification. *Mental Retardation, 34*, 247–256.

Matson, J. L. (1995). Comments on Gresham, MacMillan, & Siperstein's paper, "Critical analysis of the 1992 AAMR definition: Implications for school psychology." *School Psychology Quarterly, 10*(1), 20–23.

Reiss, S. (1994). Issues in defining mental retardation. *American Journal on Mental Retardation, 99*, 1–7.

74 Best Practices in Promoting Safe Schools

Caven S. Mcloughlin, Robert J. Kubick, Jr., and Melissa Lewis
Kent State University

OVERVIEW

Episodes of school violence occurring in the 1990s and in 2000 have brought violence prevention and intervention strategies to the forefront of every school community's attention. School violence is a topic sensationalized in the media resulting in increasing concern by the general public (Hyman & Perone, 1998a). Contrary to popular perception, the level of violence in schools has largely been stable since the mid-1980s and actually has declined in recent years (Kingery, Coggeshall, & Alford, 1998). In general, school crime data do *not* support the notion that schools are fundamentally violent and unsafe places for students (Hyman & Perone, 1998a). In fact, available data support a contention that typical schools are far from the dangerous and disorderly places that are portrayed by media reports (Hyman & Perone, 1998a ; Hyman, Weiler, Dahbany, Shanock, & Britton, 1996; Miller, 1994). Perceptions that violence is rampant in the nation's schools are not based on verified facts and sometimes have been exaggerated to promote personal gain (Furlong & Morrison, 1994). The perception of schools as unsafe places largely reflects the alarmist images created to portray popular notions of what is "right" or "wrong" about schools and is driven by popular reporting rather than reliance on empirical data (Salkind et al., 2000).

Nonetheless, where a widespread perception prevails, professionals become appropriately concerned. Since school psychologists are likely to be among the only school professionals with training both in atypical behaviors and in developing prevention and intervention programs, it is meaningful for school psychologists to play a central role in the development of safe school plans.

Safe schools, those with a positive school climate, promote optimal academic achievement for all. The National Association of School Psychologists (NASP) promotes the development of effective, safe schools through many forums. NASP has partnered with education, governmental, and mental-health organizations to publish a safe schools guide (*Early Warning, Timely Response*, by Dwyer, Osher and Warger (1998) an implementation manual (*Safeguarding our Children: An Action Guide*, by Dwyer and Osher (2000), and, most recently, *Preventing School Problems—Promoting School Success: Strategies and Programs That Work* (Minke & Bear, 2000), each of which discuss proven prevention programs and specific strategies for at-risk students. Additionally, NASP jointly operates (with the National Mental Health Association) the Safe Schools Healthy Students Action Center, the National Emergency Assistance Team (NEAT) (Helping Schools, Families and Communities Cope with Crisis), and the National Mental Health and Education Center for Children and Families, and provides guidelines for the responsible coverage of school violence to media professionals (all accessible at http://www.naspweb.org).

Incidents of violent behavior are a pervasive concern for school officials, students, and their families. Regrettably, one consequence of the misperception that school violence is on the rise is that schools increasingly have adopted law enforcement rather than educational models to prevent misbehavior

(Hyman & Perone, 1998a). In fact, there is a paucity of evidence supporting the efficacy of most law enforcement prevention efforts, such as metal detectors, increased police presence, searches, identification cards, school uniforms, and boot camps. Furthermore, these law enforcement remedies are often more difficult and expensive to enact than are *educational* programs (American Psychological Association, 1993; Hyman & Perone, 1998b).

Children, particularly minority children, are overrepresented as victims of violence across school and community settings. As settings that house children for a significant portion of their growing years, schools are placed in the position of being legally accountable for ensuring student safety. This is a daunting task that cannot be accomplished by the school alone (Kingery et al., 1998). Sadly, the reluctance of many educators to take ownership of the problem of school violence compounds the problem of keeping students safe (Morrison, Furlong, & Morrison, 1994).

Stephens (1994) contends that it is impossible to complete any of the goals listed in the National Education Agenda Goals 2000 until goal 7 is first accomplished. The seventh National Education goal states that, "By the year 2000, every school in the United States will be free of drugs, violence, and the unauthorized presence of firearms and alcohol and will offer a disciplined environment conducive to learning" (National Education Goals Panel, 1999). Patently, this goal was not achieved by its target date despite the significant political, educational, and financial resources invested. Past and future efforts expended in creating and maintaining safe schools are nonetheless worthwhile. They represent an investment at the individual level and the value of saving even one child from unsafe circumstances is incalculable. If it is accepted that antisocial behavior is largely a learned phenomenon—and thus not an inevitable consequence of childhood regardless of the nurture-characteristics of the child's environment — then school psychologists have an important role to play in "establishing safe environments by developing curricula that focus on violence prevention and reduction of aggression" (Talley, 1995, p. 17). School psychologists have a vital role to play in meeting goal 7 of Goals 2000.

School psychologists can be engaged in developing, implementing, and maintaining safe school plans. This involvement includes facilitating school climate reform, implementing social skills and conflict resolution programs, developing violence prevention and intervention programs, and intervening with victims and perpetrators and responding to crisis situations. This chapter considers the policies and practices that characterize safe schools and recommends procedures for implementing these practices into schools.

BASIC CONSIDERATIONS

Creating a Positive School Climate

Safe schools begin with a positive school climate, one that has the academic achievement of all its students as its central focus. Through school-wide policies and practices, and within every classroom and curriculum, students receive the message that while each child is unique, all are capable of academic achievement and responsible behavior. Safe schools communicate a sense of equal respect for all students.

One of the most important arenas in which this message is communicated to students is in the classroom, through teacher modeling of appropriate behaviors and through the explicit teaching of citizenship and social skills. Safe schools devote inservice training time to the use of prosocial skills in the classroom. In turn, teachers in safe schools incorporate positive themes into their teaching by integrating model conflict resolution, cooperation, respect and responsibility, and problem-solving skills into their lessons.

On a system-wide basis, safe schools are sensitive to the diversity of their students, and this sensitivity is reflected in school policies, programs, and interventions. Further, safe schools incorporate multicultural themes into the curriculum that may help foster a sense of tolerance for diversity. In so doing, many schools have sought to make character education a part of the curriculum in order to promote cooperation, responsibility, and democracy within the school. Such teaching emphasizes the importance of qualities such as commitment and dedication, cooperation, self-control, trustworthiness, tolerance, compassion, work ethic and responsibility, respect for others and self, fairness and justice, and respect for the community and the environment. The incorporation of prosocial practices in schools through character education programs have been cited as causal factors in reducing triggers for conflict, teaching effective interpersonal skills, and avoiding the escalation of conflict into violence. Unfortunately, this widely implemented approach has yet to be subject to the scrutiny of empirical investigation.

Safe schools foster close, caring relationships between students and staff and help adults to identify students needing intervention. Moreover, having close relationships help foster a sense of community among students. Additionally, since research has demonstrated that a supportive relationship with an adult is a primary factor in preventing youth violence, closer relationships between staff and students may, in turn, further reduce the risk of violence within the wider school community.

In a similar vein, research has shown that peers are often alert to the likelihood of dangerous activity within their school. Students are more likely to report dangerous situations to a supportive school staff. Safe schools encourage the participation of families and community members. In such schools, parents and members of community-based organizations feel welcomed and are encouraged to participate in school activities. In this way, students' sense of community is extended beyond the school walls. Students who feel that they are valued by family and community are less likely to be involved in undesirable behavior and more likely to experience academic success.

Schools, families, agencies, and religious groups can work to maintain appropriate examples and offer support, give gentle reminders about desired behaviors, and provide positive affirmations. Positive character traits are not only for display within schools by children, but employers, community agencies and other stakeholders can also model them.

Safe schools encourage each student's active involvement in maintaining their school as a safe community. Creating a positive school climate requires an acknowledgement that children and youth are themselves experts in their own developmental pathway and needs. Safe schools involve students in the creation of school-wide codes of conduct, on safety committees, and as peer mediators to help resolve student disputes nonviolently. The benefits of active student involvement are twofold. First, utilizing student input helps foster a sense that adults respect students' efforts at self-regulation, a critical initial step in developing self-control. Second, working with students to develop safety strategies that will be effective *and accepted* among their peers demands that the students' perspective on the value of each of these activities be considered.

The creation of a positive school climate helps students feel a sense of personal value within their school community. When students feel valued, they are less likely to engage in destructive behaviors and more likely to feel a responsibility to report the dangerous behavior of others to a trusted adult.

BEST PRACTICES IN PROMOTING SAFE SCHOOLS

Steps in Developing a Safe School

Few recent educational phenomena have seen the scope of national attention received at the issuance of *Early Warning, Timely Response* and *Implementing Early Warning Timely Response* (Dwyer, Osher, & Warger, 1998). The focus of these practitioner guides is on providing a practical plan for promoting safe school environments and identifying high-risk students and conditions. A safe school plan comprises a continuing, broad-based, comprehensive, and systematic process to create and maintain a safe, secure, and welcoming school climate, one free of drugs, violence, and fear (Stephens, 1994). The development of a school-wide plan encourages a prevention approach rather than a reactive one. Indeed, violence is often a rather predictable event (Kingery, McCoy-Simandle, & Clayton, 1997). In many cases, the children in the school are aware of its impending likelihood, thus making violence avoidable with appropriate intervention strategies.

Appropriate responses to school violence include student, family, and community initiatives (Baker, 1998; Miller, 1994). The involvement of the community in this process is critical, for school violence is often closely linked to violence in the community at-large (Kingery et al., 1998). Students who demonstrate violent behavior in school are frequently the same students who exhibit behavior problems in their community. A complex array of strategies is necessary to successfully intervene with the problem of school violence (Baker, 1998), including a vision of optimal functioning and an action plan to implement the vision.

Baker (1998) argued that school violence represents a failure of community in schools. In schools that adopt a mission emphasizing community orientation, students feel a sense of belonging, commitment, and shared enterprise of academic achievement. Violence at school may represent a breakdown of this sense of identity, belonging, and community. Baker (1998) has maintained that violence-prone students experience fundamentally different orientations toward, and skills for negotiating, social experiences. The manifestation of violence in such students is the result of a mismatch between (a) the students' developmental capacities and (b) the social context and demand characteristics of the school.

Indeed, it has persuasively been argued that weapons on campuses are not themselves the problem, but rather a symptom of a fundamental interpersonal and structural weakness in the school community (Morrison et al., 1994). When students perceive that school officials are fair and caring, they feel a greater stake in making their own school safe (Hyman & Perone, 1998b). It should be the goal of schools to enact policies and procedures that foster nonviolent attitudes and environments of caring, respect, and acceptance of diversity (Miller, 1994).

Schools may unwittingly contribute to violence when they fail to provide students with meaningful social contexts in which to function. Baker (1998) illustrated that classroom management practices that focus on character development rather than behavior management are more likely to promote affiliation to the school. Baker cited research (Sergiovanni, 1994) supporting the emphasis of personal and civic responsibility, development of skilled and moral decision making, and emphasizing the importance of mutuality and commitment within the community as likely to benefit a sense of belonging. Baker added that this involves an intentional focus on developing personal responsibility, social competencies, and empathy for others, as well as shaping the peer culture toward prosocial interaction.

Historically, when dealing with discipline problems schools have used procedures such as suspension and expulsion reactively, rather than relying on proactive classroom procedures (Larson, 1998). The effectiveness of such punitive procedures has long been questioned in terms of their ability to reduce behavior problems (Larson, 1994). In fact, there are no systematically gathered data that support using suspension for this purpose. Likewise, sanctions such as suspension and expulsion may have the unintended effect of putting even greater distance between disaffected students and their school community (Baker, 1998).

Excessive use of punishers may lead to increases in the very acting-out behaviors they are intended to reduce (Horner, Sugai, & Horner, 2000; Hyman & Perone, 1998b). Unfortunately, a vicious circle is created whereby further acts of violence result in calls for more punishment that simply exacerbate the problem rather than preventing future misbehavior. Such procedures have tended to be used merely as political cover for addressing complaints or to mask disproportionate disciplinary patterns.

Creating a Safe Physical Environment

While maintaining a positive school climate is a crucial element in creating a safe school, safe schools realize that creating a secure physical environment is a prerequisite for students and staff to feel protected. A positive climate promotes and extends a feeling of safety within the school's buildings and in the surrounding school grounds and boundaries, and physical security helps ensure that safety. Physically safe schools with secure boundaries and adequate internal security foster academic achievement and help prevent school violence.

The physical condition of the school plays an important part in establishing children's attitudes toward appropriate behavior and academic achievement. Children who attend clean schools that are in good repair and free of graffiti are significantly less likely to exhibit acting-out behaviors than will their counterparts in derelict surroundings with marginal security.

Safe schools maintain an active relationship with their local police department and may enlist the presence of a uniformed school security officer. Having uniformed law enforcement personnel interact with students may not only deter crime within the school but may also play an important socializing and educative role for students. Since schools are integral elements of the community then Community Policing Initiatives and school-based "resource" police officers have a role to play alongside professional educational staff.

Furthermore, safe schools ensure the physical security of the school campus by

1. Conducting safety analyses of school grounds and buildings in conjunction with local law enforcement and knowledgeable school security personnel.

2. Limiting unsupervised access to the building and grounds and closing the campus when teaching is not being conducted.

3. Arranging supervision before and after school and at other typically unsupervised times (e.g., lunch periods, bus transfers) with adults, including parents and community volunteers, visibly present in the building and on school grounds and in isolated areas.

4. Modifying bell schedules and staggering dismissal and lunch times in order to limit student congregation in unsupervised areas.

5. Sensitively implemented use of enhanced security measures (which at the unwelcome extreme has involved restricted use of book bags, implementation of metal detectors, and regular locker searches and sweeps).

Unfortunately, maintaining the security of the school building and its immediate surroundings is often itself insufficient, and research has repeatedly shown that the primary reason students bring weapons into school is for their personal protection on their *way to and from* school. Violence within our schools is largely a reflection of violence within the greater community. Therefore, schools must develop safety strategies that travel beyond the school's borders. These include enlisting community and family support by encouraging the organization of neighborhood watch programs, establishing volunteer community and parent patrols of the campus and its perimeters before, during, and after school and at school events, and establishing an appropriate referral system for children who are suspected of being abused or neglected.

Creating a School-Wide Team/Task Force

Safe schools develop teams in order to effectively and efficiently plan, execute, and monitor school safety programs and initiatives. Safe schools organize both a violence prevention task force to focus on school-wide safety issues, and an intervention team to focus on individuals with enhanced need for services. A demonstration program reviewed by the National Institute of Justice (Kenney & Watson, 1999) and incorporated into Charlotte-Mecklenberg Schools, North Carolina, provides a comprehensive model for the implementation of such a system-wide approach.

A school's violence prevention task force is made up of individuals from varying (but complementary) backgrounds including the school principal, teacher, guidance counselor, and school psychologist (serving as the school's mental health professional with expertise in prevention and intervention). This core team works with students, non-teaching school staff, parents, and representatives of community organizations (including law enforcement) who serve as its members. This committee develops, implements, and monitors the school's efforts in safety initiatives including (a) the initial school safety analysis, (b) prevention and intervention services, (c) school reform, (d) drafting conduct codes and appropriate consequences, (e) crisis response planning, (f) the facilitation of family and community involvement, and (g) the implementation of prosocial themes within classrooms.

In addition, safe schools establish an intervention team that includes the same core members as the violence prevention task force (the principal, a teacher, and school psychologist) in order to facilitate the sharing of information between the two groups. Additionally, the intervention team collaborates with community agencies to expedite the use of outside services where needed. The intervention team's purpose is to provide direct, individual services to students who may need help. Specifically, the function of the intervention team is to (a) provide diagnostic and evaluation services; (b) conduct functional behavior analyses in order to develop individualized interventions; (c) consult and collaborate with staff, students, and families on issues of safety; (d) ensure that *all* school staff are familiar with early warning signs and ensure prompt service to students demonstrating worrying characteristics; (e) ensure that all students, staff, and families understand the role of the intervention team; (f) adopt policies and procedures regarding the provision of services for referred students; and (g) take immediate action with referrals. The intervention team should be readily accessible to students, staff, and families in order to facilitate timely response to potential dangers.

Teams should openly and objectively examine potentially dangerous situations within the school, and school security should regularly be examined and findings should be shared with the community at large. Additionally, both teams should involve parents-as-experts regarding their children's home life and life history. Moreover, school teams should develop their initiatives with developmental and cultural appropriateness in mind.

Early and Imminent Warning Signs

In most cases school violence does not *just happen.* In retrospect people often can point to troubling signs that preceded the violent event. Unfortunately, the early indicators of violence are often misread or are ignored outright. Safe schools ensure that *all* school staff (including bus drivers, cafeteria, custodial, secretarial, and other non-teaching staff) *and* the greater community are alert to the importance of detection of early and imminent warning signs of violent behavior. Moreover, safe schools make certain that students, staff, and families know the importance of promptly reporting these behaviors to the intervention team and have developed simple procedures for doing so.

Risk-Factors/Warning Signs

There are several *early warning* signs that may signal a troubled child (Dwyer et al. 1998). In addition, there are *imminent warning* signs that indicate a student is very close to behaving in a way that is potentially dangerous to self or others. These imminent warning signs require immediate action from school personnel. This is particularly true when the student (a) has presented a detailed plan (time, place, method) to harm or kill self or others, particularly if the child has a history of aggression or has attempted to carry out threats in the past; or (b) is carrying a weapon, particularly a firearm and has threatened to use it. In these cases, parents should be informed immediately and appropriate community agencies should be enlisted for assistance.

There has been an increase in the development of programs and procedures that assist systematically in identifying violence-prone students *before* crises erupt. Such procedures, commonly referred to as "student profiling" (Fey, Nelson, & Roberts, 2000; Lafee, 2000; Nelson, Roberts, Smith, & Irwin, 2000), have generated considerable controversy. Kingery et al. (1997) argue that singling out potentially violent students is misguided. Instead, they advocate enhanced services to the most vulnerable students to improve their coping resources and school and personal success.

Early warning signs include, but are not limited to, the following:

1. Social withdrawal
2. Poor peer relations, feelings of isolation and/or rejection
3. History of victimization, gang involvement, or intolerance of differences
4. Poor academic performance and school attendance
5. Verbal, drawn, or written expressions of violence or intimidation
6. Uncontrolled or unwarranted anger
7. Serious threats of violence or a history of violent, aggressive, bullying, or disruptive behavior toward peers and others
8. History of discipline problems
9. Access to firearms
10. Drug and alcohol use

In some instances, behaviors are severe enough to warrant immediate response. These behaviors are imminent warning signs signifying that a person is at *very high risk* for causing harm to self or others. Such imminent warning signs include

1. Use or possession of weapons
2. Detailed threats of violence (especially threats mentioning murder or suicide)
3. Serious destruction of property
4. Self-injurious behaviors

5. Intense rage over apparently trivial matters

6. Engaging in serious physical fights with peers or family members

Principles to Guide Practice

Dwyer et al. (1998) advises that, when responding to these warning signs, school officials do no harm, understand violence and aggression within a context, avoid stereotypes, view warning signs within a developmental context, and understand that children typically exhibit multiple warning signs. While the existence of one or more of these warning signs may predict future or imminent violent behavior, it is crucial to remember that these predictors do not, in themselves, unequivocally signify that an individual will become violent. The principles to follow when faced with a child who manifests one or more of these behaviors include

1. Do no harm: The sole aim of any intervention with a fragile or troubled child should be to get the child help in a timely fashion.

2. Understand the antecedents that contribute to violent and aggressive acts: Violence and aggression are triggered differently in each child. It is important to understand the factors within the school, home, and other contexts that exacerbate violence and aggression in the individual at hand.

3. Consider warning signs within a developmental context: In order to avoid misconstruing a child's developmentally appropriate behavior for something deviant, it is important to understand what behaviors are considered normal for the child's developmental level.

4. Avoid stereotyping: Physical appearance, race, socioeconomic status, cognitive ability, academic achievement, and similar features are *not* indicators of the potential for violence and, if acted upon, may cause serious harm to the child. Such profiling is patently destructive to the creation of a sense of community and trust, essential foundational features for a safe-school climate. The FBI, the governmental agency with the longest history of studying school and community-based violence, counsels careful avoidance of profiling (O'Toole, 2000). Recognize that at-risk children tend to exhibit *multiple* warning signs: It is important to not overreact to single unrelated incidents. Typically, children who are at-risk for violence and aggression exhibit multiple warning signs, repeatedly and with heightening severity over time.

Early Intervention

Safe schools make early intervention services available to students at risk of academic failure or behavior problems. The most successful interventions begin as early as possible in order to help the child establish effective, socially acceptable ways with which to handle interpersonal conflict.

In order to be maximally effective, early interventions begin with a functional assessment of the child in various contexts to identify the settings and circumstances that are most and least likely to exacerbate the problem behavior. The team analyzes the reasons for the behavior and then addresses the strengths, weaknesses, and interests of the child prior to selecting an appropriate individualized intervention.

Successful interventions use team approaches that acknowledge the child and the child's family as coequals with team partners. The team chooses an intervention that is appropriate for each child's linguistic capability, developmental level, and culture. In addition, the intervention should utilize a theory-based approach with established efficacy that treats the target-behavior as but one component of a class of antisocial behaviors with each element of the intervention reinforcing another.

Prevention

Unfortunately, not every child is able to get his or her needs met through early intervention. In cases where students are not consistently or persistently violent or seriously violence prone, a primary prevention program that is developmentally appropriate and individualized to the child's strengths and weaknesses, and that promotes the learning and/or use of social and cognitive skills, is in order.

For children who are persistently violent, secondary prevention initiatives become necessary. Such prevention programs typically attempt to educate about the antecedents to aggression, and incorporate sustained multimodal treatments to focus on the individual child's affective, cognitive, and behavioral skills. Furthermore, effective secondary prevention programs continue their involvement of the family as they attempt to modify family members' relationship patterns wherever they are counterproductive to safe and respectful interaction.

Safe schools begin with a positive foundation and utilize intervention and prevention programs to promote prosocial behaviors among at-risk children. Moreover, schools that are supported by the district's administration in their efforts to promote safety become effective schools. Safe schools develop system-wide policies that promote the identification of early warning signs and support early intervention and prevention programs for at-risk students.

Review of Prevention Programs

Larson noted in 1994 that procedures and curricula for violence prevention in the schools were in their infancy. Unfortunately, there are relatively few data available that systematically evaluate the impact of popular violence prevention programs, and there is a clear need for innovation in empirically establishing which programs are effective (Larson, 1998). While it is commonly believed that something must be done, only recently have there been serious efforts to adequately evaluate violence prevention efforts. Clear advances have recently been made in gathering blueprints for the promotion of safe schools, most notably the work of the Center for the Study of Prevention of Violence (http://www.colorado.edu/cspv/) that has evaluated model programs and based on rigorous selection criteria determined some as "promising." This valuable resource even provides an online interactive system for matching a safe-schools program model with a school's local characteristics. Additionally, the National Training and Technical Assistance Center's Safe Schools Healthy Students Action Center (http://www.nttac.org/catalog/projects/nmhaP1.cfm) provides technical assistance to school-based violence prevention activities. This center is operated jointly by the National Mental Health Association and NASP and provides a regularly updated online portal for accessing details of innovative, proven approaches to the promotion of safe schools.

Prevention programs are as varied as the problems that they are designed to address. In general, programs have been chiefly concerned with teaching students responsible behavior (Benson & Benson, 1993). Indeed, it has been argued "the distinction between social skills training and violence prevention is blurred at best" (Larson, 1994, p. 151). Unfortunately, educators too often "have failed to recognize that the teaching of self-discipline, not the external control of behavior, is the ultimate goal of social education" (Bear, 1995, p. 431). Rather than policing students and campuses, school psychologists should be involved in tapping into existing skills and resilience of the student body (Morrison et al., 1994).

There is a need to begin teaching responsible citizenship, effective decision making, conflict resolution skills, cooperation, and simple courtesy early in a student's schooling. While including the use of disciplinary actions to address problem behavior, efforts at school management should also include instruction designed to teach *self-discipline* (Bear, 1995). Such interventions should be implemented system-wide as well as targeted to selected at-risk students.

Because school violence incidents are most prevalent at the middle school level, best practice dictates that violence prevention efforts should begin in the earlier grades. Efforts should be research-based, as well as developmentally and culturally sensitive, in order to address the needs of students *before* they reach the secondary level (Larson, 1998).

Practically useful reviews of school violence prevention programs include Bear (1990, 1995, 1998), Kay and Ryan (2000a, 2000b), Knoff (2000), Larson (1994), McMullen (1996), McMullen, Laurer, McMullen, Troxell, and Goettel (2000), and Shapiro (1999). In addition, best practice guidelines for developing general prevention programs were described by Hightower, Johnson, and Haffey (1990). Reid and Patterson (1991) provide a model social interactional model for the early prevention and intervention of students' conduct problems.

School-Wide Policies That Promote Safety

Within safe schools, there are codes of conduct that reflect the prosocial behaviors that are, in turn, modeled by all school staff. Safe schools include representative members of the staff, student body, and family stakeholders in drafting and implementing rules and regulations that are both culturally sensitive and reflective of the school's academic goals. These codes are not punitively focused on identifying the *don'ts* with elaborations on punishments for infractions; rather they act as the school's standards for living. They teach and emulate appropriate behavior rather than elaborate on the enforcement of punishers for those who defy the code.

In general, effective codes of conduct stress few rules. The codes are, nonetheless, clearly defined, face valid, and relatively uncomplicated. Further, safe schools ensure that their rules are enforceable, realistic, and consistently executed. In addition, safe schools broadcast loudly, and often their *zero tolerance* policy toward the illegal possession of weapons, illegal drugs, and alcohol. The enforcement of zero tolerance reduces future problem behavior among chronic offenders (Uchitelle, Bartz, & Hillman, 1989).

In order to be effective, the consequences for violating the school's standards for living must be defined equally simply, clearly, and without unnecessary elaboration. These consequences should use positive methods of discipline that are proportional in severity to the offense, and that adhere to the conflict resolution skills that are reinforced in every classroom. Finally, if an offense is met with a negative or punishing consequence (e.g., suspension), safe schools assess any antecedent factors that may have exacerbated the behavior so as to incorporate appropriate training in prosocial behaviors congruent with the offense.

What follows are procedures for developing a safe school (after Stephens, 1994):

1. Create a climate of ownership and school pride.
2. Establish a Parent's Center; get parents on your side by establishing collaborative partnerships.
3. Increase safety via school physical design.
4. Make the campus welcoming and safe to students.
5. Establish campus intruder and visitor screening procedures; limit access to school grounds.
6. Establish a vibrant system of extracurricular programs; make certain there is an active student component.
7. Provide adequate adult supervision.
8. Establish inservice training.
9. Implement staff screening process.
10. Establish clear and reasonable dress codes and behavior guidelines.
11. Mandate crime reporting and tracking and establish a closer law enforcement partnership.
12. Establish a crisis response plan.
13. Provide adequate support and protection for victims.
14. Target troublemakers; closely supervise known juvenile offenders.

Another factor becoming especially important is the role of students in reporting to appropriate school personnel their peers' warning signs, and threats from other students (Skiba & Dwyer, 1999). Two factors that often impede the reporting of this information are students' difficulty in determining what constitutes a truly serious threat and their belief that reporting may increase risk to their own safety. The *Early Warning, Timely Response* (Dwyer et al., 1998) guide contains several "Action Steps" for students that encourage them to take ownership of their school's safety, including informing school staff of their observations and concerns. This concept is extended further in the *Implementing Early Warning, Timely Response* practice guide (Dwyer & Osher, 2000) to include a Student Support Team charged with responding to referrals of concerns about individual students.

What follows are characteristics of a school that is safe and responsive to all children (Dwyer et al., 1998):

1. Focus on academic achievement
2. Involve families in meaningful ways
3. Develop links to the community
4. Emphasize positive relationships among students and staff
5. Treat students with equal respect

6. Create ways for students to share their concerns
7. Help children feel safe expressing their feelings
8. Have in place a system for referring children who are suspected of being abused or neglected, or otherwise at-risk
9. Offer extended day programs for children
10. Promote good citizenship and character
11. Identify problems and assess progress toward solutions
12. Support students in making the transition to adult life and the workplace
13. Discuss safety issues openly

Dwyer & Osher, 2000 recommends a three-level implementation approach to preventing violence. The first step involves building a school-wide foundation for all children that incorporates supporting positive discipline, academic success, and mental and emotional wellness. This could be accomplished by developing a caring school environment, teaching appropriate behaviors and problem-solving skills, providing positive behavioral support, and appropriate academic instruction. The second step involves intervening early for selected children. Included in this step would be the creation of services and supports that address risk factors and build protective supports for students at risk for severe academic and/or behavioral difficulties. The third step involves providing intensive interventions for a few children. This entails providing coordinated, comprehensive, intensive, sustained, culturally appropriate, and child- and family-focused services and supports.

Effective Crisis Response Plans

Safe schools take every precaution to prevent violence from occurring within the school. Safe schools do not wait for a disaster. Rather, safe schools anticipate it as a possibility, however remote. In an actual crisis, safe schools are prepared because they have already created prevention and response plans.

Effective crisis prevention and response plans include three levels of organization: (a) policies and practices that are designed to prevent a crisis from occurring, (b) initial response arrangements that deal with response in the immediate aftermath of a crisis in order to minimize the effects of the crisis, and (c) long-term response contingencies that deal with the enduring effects of a crisis.

Whenever planning immediate response strategies, safe schools make the protection of students and staff their primary objective. The most effective crisis prevention and response plans are flexible enough to be quickly modified in order to contend with specific crises. Safe schools develop error-proof ways to contact outside agencies (e.g., direct telephone access to law enforcement with an agreed code to signal emergency status), designate specific roles for key staff members in an emergency, maintain an effective means for *within-building* communication, and develop evacuation contingencies with order and safety as paramount concerns. Additionally, safe schools routinely monitor their immediate response plans by conducting periodic emergency drills to test their system. Finally, safe schools develop procedures to communicate with parents and reunite families and have established and agreed procedures for communicating with the news media and others *outside* the school.

In the aftermath of a crisis—whether natural (weather-related) or human caused (e.g., personal violence) —safe schools continue to support the psychological healing of the entire school community. Effective follow-up plans address the feelings and safety concerns of students as well as faculty and staff and help all their family to readjust following the crisis. The best tertiary prevention plans identify highest-risk participants and provide them with additional counseling, involve outside agencies (e.g., community counseling services) and crisis response teams (such as NASP's National Emergency Assistance Team, NEAT), and educate staff and families about children's typical response patterns to trauma.

Need for Further Training

It is clear that more training in violence prevention for school psychologists is warranted (Cornell & Sheras, 1998). Few school psychology preparation programs place appropriate emphasis on this topic, and school psychologists generally lack sufficient practicum-based training to deal with school violence (Larson & Busse, 1998; Morrison et al., 1994). Most training programs, for example, do not teach skills necessary to assess the degree of danger in students in order to predict the likelihood of violent behavior (Hansen, 2000). Another example of this lack of preparation is evidenced by survey results asserting that 85% of the school psychologists contend they had *no* specific training in school violence, while 73% felt *unprepared* in dealing with school violence (Furlong, Babinski, Poland, Munoz, & Boles, 1996). Furthermore, school psychologists often lack basic knowledge of the myriad of legal issues surrounding the policies and procedures that may be enacted to promote safe schools.

Morrison et al. (1994) have described school safety as an "educational right," one that schools have a legal and moral responsibility to protect. Larson (1994) has argued that continued delay in providing services to children at-risk for, or engaging in, violent behavior is ethically irresponsible. Thomas (1998) stated, "we now have a golden opportunity to expand the scope of our efforts to include prevention activities that directly relate to mental health issues that affect children and youth" (p. 2).

Furlong, Morrison, and Pavelski (2000) asserted that contemporary concerns about school violence provide school psychology a rare opportunity to reinvent itself for the twenty-first century. They maintain "School psychology potentially is facing another watershed social force that has the potential to change fundamentally the ways that school psychologists spend their work days and the types of research they conduct" (p. 82). These authors assert that much is required to increase school psychologists' attention on school violence to become an equal partner with counselors—who have dominated the school violence literature over the last decade.

SUMMARY

Safe schools include students, families, and the greater community in planning and implementing safety initiatives. Safe schools create climates of cooperation and respect in which academic achievement and behavioral responsibility are the focus and a commitment of all stakeholders.

School administrators with the direct involvement of school psychologists can facilitate improved school safety by combining a positive school climate with a secure physical setting and fine-tuning proactive plans for both prevention and intervention. Further, stakeholders who are educated by school psychologists about the early and imminent warning signs for violent behavior are more likely to report them. Likewise, safe schools incorporate access to *both* internal and external supports for referred and high-risk children.

Because violence in our nation's schools is a reflection of violence within the broader society, safe school strategies will not put an end to the incidence or the effects of violence in our schools. Nonetheless, with these strategies school psychologists can help establish schools as appropriately prepared safe havens in the event of a disruption to the school's otherwise safe educational experience.

REFERENCES

American Psychological Association. (1993). *Violence and youth: Psychology's response.* Washington, DC: Author.

Baker, J. A. (1998). Are we missing the forest for the trees? Considering the social context of school violence. *Journal of School Psychology, 36*(1), 29–44.

Bear, G. G. (1990). Best practices in school discipline. In A. Thomas & J. Grimes (Eds.), *Best practices in school psychology II* (pp. 649–663). Washington, DC: National Association of School Psychologists.

Bear, G. G. (1995). Best practices in school discipline. In A. Thomas & J. Grimes (Eds.), *Best practices in school psychology III* (pp. 431–443). Bethesda, MD: National Association of School Psychologists.

Bear, G. (1998). Research reviews: Violence prevention. *Communiqué, 27,* 17.

Benson, A. J., & Benson, J. M. (1993). Peer mediation: Conflict resolution in the schools. *Journal of School Psychology, 31,* 427–430.

Cornell, D. G., & Sheras, P. L. (1998). Common errors in school crisis response: Learning from our mistakes. *Psychology in the Schools, 35,* 297–307.

Dwyer, K., & Osher, D. (2000). *Safeguarding our children: An action guide.* Washington, DC: American Institutes for Research. Available: (http://www.ed.gov/offices/OSERS/OSEP/ActionGuide).

Dwyer, K., Osher, D., & Warger, C. (1998). *Early warning, timely response: A guide to safe schools.* Washington, DC: U. S. Department of Education. Available: (http://www.ed.gov/offices/OSERS/OSEP/earlywrn.html).

Fey, G. P., Nelson, J. R., & Roberts, M. L. (2000, February). The perils of profiling. *The School Administrator,* 12–16.

Furlong, M., Babinski, L., Poland, S., Munoz, J., & Boles, S. (1996). Factors associated with school psychologists' perceptions of campus violence. *Psychology in the Schools, 33,* 28–37.

Furlong, M. J., & Morrison, G. M. (1994). Introduction to miniseries: School violence and safety in perspective. *School Psychology Review, 23,* 139–150.

Furlong, M., Morrison, G., & Pavelski, R. (2000). Trends in school psychology for the 21st century: Influences of school violence on professional change. *Psychology in the Schools, 37,* 81–90.

Furlong, M. J., & Morrison, R. (1995). Status update of research related to National Education Goal Seven: School violence content area. In R. C. Talley & G. R. Walz (Eds.), *Safe schools, safe students* (pp. 85–102). Washington, DC: The National Education Goals Panel and the National Alliance of Pupil Services Organizations.

Hansen, R. G. (2000, May/June). School violence: Assessment of dangerousness in the schools. *The Forensic Examiner,* 20–22.

Hightower, A. D., Johnson, D., & Haffey, W. G. (1990). Best practices in adopting a prevention program. In A. Thomas & J. Grimes (Eds.), *Best practices in school psychology II* (pp. 63–79). Washington, DC: National Association of School Psychologists.

Horner, R. H., Sugai, G., & Horner, H. F. (2000, February). A schoolwide approach to student discipline. *The School Administrator,* 20–23.

Hyman, I. A., & Perone, D. C. (1998a). Introduction to the special theme section on school violence: The ecology of school violence. *Journal of School Psychology, 36,* 3–5.

Hyman, I. A., & Perone, D. C. (1998b). The other side of school violence: Educator policies and practices that may contribute to student misbehavior. *Journal of School Psychology, 36,* 7–27.

Hyman, I., Weiler, E., Dahbany, A., Shanock, A., & Britton, G. (1996). Policy and practice in school discipline: Past, present and future. In R. Talley & G. Walz (eds.), *Safe schools, safe students* (pp. 77–84). Washington, DC: The National Education Goals Panel and the National Alliance of Pupil Services Organizations.

Kay, P., & Ryan, A. (2000a). Prevention strategies for the elementary school classroom. In *Behavioral Interventions: Creating a safe environment in our schools.* Bethesda, MD: National Association of School Psychologists.

Kay, P, & Ryan, A. (2000b). Prevention through school-family-community linkages. In *Behavioral Interventions: Creating a safe environment in our schools.* Bethesda, MD: National Association of School Psychologists.

Kenney, D. J., & Watson, S. (1999). Crime in the Schools: Reducing conflict with student problem solving. Washington, DC: National Institute of Justice.

Kingery, P. M., Coggeshall, M. B., & Alford, A. A. (1998). Violence at school: Recent evidence from four national surveys. *Psychology in the Schools, 35,* 247–258.

Kingery, P. M., McCoy-Simandle, L., & Clayton, R. (1997). Risk factors for adolescent violence: The importance of vulnerability. *School Psychology International, 18,* 49–60.

Knoff, H. M. (2000). Project ACHIEVE: Creating effective building-based social skills, discipline/behavior management, and school safety systems. *Communiqué, 28,* 12–14

Lafee, S. (2000, February). Profiling bad apples. *The School Administrator,* 6–11.

Larson, J. (1998). Managing student aggression in high schools: Implications for practice. *Psychology in the Schools, 35,* 283–295.

Larson, J. (1994). Violence prevention in the schools: A review of selected programs and procedures. *School Psychology Review, 23,* 151–164.

Larson, J., & Busse, R. T. (1998). Specialist-level preparation in school violence and youth gang intervention. *Psychology in the Schools, 35,* 373–379.

McMullen, J. (1996). A prosocial system for improving student discipline and responsibility. *Communiqué, 25,* 22–23.

McMullen, J., Laurer, V., McMullen, R. P., Troxell, L., & Goettel, P. R. (2000). A school-wide plan to unify staff and promote school safety. *Communiqué, 28,* 30.

Miller, G. E. (1994). School violence miniseries: Impressions and implications. *School Psychology Review, 23,* 257–261.

Minke, K. M. & Bear, G. G. (Eds.). (2000). *Preventing school problems—Promoting school success: Strategies and programs that work.* Washington, DC: The National Association of School Psychologists.

Morrison, G. M., Furlong, M. J., & Morrison, R. L. (1994). School violence to school safety: Reframing the issues for school psychologists. *School Psychology Review, 23,* 236–256.

National Education Goals Panel. (1999). *America 2000 goals.* [On-line]. Washington, DC: Author. Available: (http://www.negp.gov/webpg210.htm).

Nelson, R., Roberts, M., Smith, D., & Irwin, G. (2000). The trouble with profiling youth at-risk for violence. *Communiqué, 28,* 10.

O'Toole, M. E. (2000). *The school shooter: A threat assessment perspective.* Quantico, VA: Critical Incident Response Group, National Center for the Analysis of Violent Crime.

Reid, J. B., & Patterson, G. R. (1991). Early prevention and intervention with conduct problems: A social interactional model for the integration of research and practice. In G. Stoner, M. R. Shinn, & H. M. Walker (Eds.), *Interventions for achievement and behavior problems* (pp. 715–739). Washington, DC: National Association of School Psychologists.

Salkind, N., Adams, D., Dermer, C., Heinerikson, J., Jones, B., & Nash, E. (2000). Guns and chewing gum: The perceptions and reality of problem behaviors in public schools. *School Psychology International, 21,* 106–112.

Sergiovanni, T. J. (1994). *Building community in schools.* San Francisco: Jossey-Bass.

Shapiro, J. P. (1999). The peacemakers program: Effective violence prevention for early adolescent youth. *Communiqué, 27,* 6–7.

Skiba, R., & Dwyer, K. (1999). School violence: Listening to the students. *Communiqué, 28,* 1–4.

Stephens, R. D. (1994). Planning for safer and better schools: School violence prevention and intervention strategies. *School Psychology Review, 23*(2), 204–215.

Talley, R. (1995). *Reforming America's schools: A report to the nation's educators.* Washington, DC: American Psychological Association.

Thomas, A. (1998). Golden opportunity for prevention activities. *Communiqué, 27,* 2.

Uchiteele, S., Bartz, D., & Hillman, L. (1989). Strategies for reducing suspension. *Urban Education, 24,* 163–176.

ANNOTATED BIBLIOGRAPHY

Dwyer, K. & Osher, D. (2000). *Safeguarding our children: An action guide.* Washington, DC: American Institutes for Research.

Based on *Early Warning Timely Response: A Guide to Safe Schools*, it presents a plan for implementing safe schools practices, suggesting a three-tiered approach to preventing school violence that includes building a school-wide foundation, early intervention, and intensive interventions. Attention is paid to building an overall positive climate within the school, establishing school-wide teams, responding to the early warning signs of violence, and providing intensive interventions. It emphasizes that safety programs should focus on problem solving, not labeling, and encouraging responsibility and respect for others.

Dwyer, K., Osher, D., & Warger, C. (1998). *Early warning, timely response: A guide to safe schools.* Washington, DC: U.S. Department of Education.

Discusses ways in which the school community may reduce violence and highlights policies for school-wide implementation to prevent violent and destructive behavior within schools. Early and imminent warning signs of violence are presented with procedures for responding to youth. Concludes that school safety must be the priority of everyone in the greater community.

McMullen, J. (1996). A prosocial system for improving student discipline and responsibility. In *Behavioral interventions: Creating a safe environment in our schools* [On-line]. Available: http://www.naspweb.org/center/pdf/nmhec.pdf.
This digest suggests social skills models as promising approaches to addressing problem behavior within the school community, one that simultaneously involves three areas: analysis of overall school atmosphere, addressing specific areas of concern within the school, and promoting discipline and responsibility. The author calls for educative rather than punitive responses to troubling acts, and specific strategies for implementing this system are provided. This web document also contains articles on discipline and management of disruptive behavior, defusing crises, bullying, and disciplining students with disabilities.

National Association of School Psychologists Delegate Assembly (1996, July 14). Position Statement: School violence. In *Behavioral interventions: Creating a safe environment in our schools.* [On-line]. Available: http://www.naspweb.org/center/pdf/nmhec.pdf.
NASP's official position statement discusses the role of the school psychologist in creating a safe school environment including the implementation of intervention strategies for aggressive students and ways to improve school climate. The statement encourages the use of positive methods of discipline including social skills training. It calls for the implementation of school-wide violence prevention programs and for the availability of counseling and supportive services for school violence victims. The parent link also provides access to NASP's 1997 Resolutions on "Children, Guns, and Other Weapons" and "Children and Violence in Media and Toys."

75 Best Practices in Making School Groups Work

Fred Jay Krieg
Marshall University Graduate College
Christine Simpson
Nazareth, PA
Richard E. Stanley
Veterans Administration
David A. Snider
Frontier Local School District
Wirt County Schools

OVERVIEW

The therapeutic application of group counseling has a history that extends over the past 100 years. During this time, the general efficacy of group counseling has been established in empirical literature (Barlow, Burlingame, & Fuhriman, 2000) and also as an intervention strategy for children and adolescents (Hoag & Burlingame, 1997). Interventions include prevention, education, and counseling.

The study of school groups began with the work of Slavson (1940) and has become increasingly popular as school psychologists become more involved with the delivery of mental health services in schools. "The empirical literature supports the power of school groups as a viable intervention for children with emotional, social, and learning dysfunctions ... which can reduce the suffering of children, and prevent impairment in adulthood" (Shectman, Gilat, Fos, & Flasher, 1996, p. 367).

School groups are a cost-effective method to enhance social skills and deliver primary prevention services. Schools have a large captive audience and represent a common place for students to share, talk, and learn. Given the expanded role of school psychologists in drug and alcohol prevention, drop-out prevention, and other at-risk behaviors, it is essential that school psychologists possess the necessary knowledge and skills to lead school groups.

Group counseling offers the opportunity for positive peer experiences as groups provide a method for students to learn universality through feedback from peers under the supervision of a trained professional. School groups provide an opportunity for students to enhance self-esteem and increase their communication skills. For those with greater needs, a school group provides a forum to discuss problems and personal issues that cannot be appropriately aired in the classroom. Used appropriately, school groups serve as a vehicle to identify students who are in need of more intensive services due to difficulties at school, at home, or in the community.

There are a variety of models of group counseling. School groups vary in length from six-session problem-oriented groups—such as divorce groups, children of alcoholic groups, and transition groups—to a 30-session more therapeutic group model. This chapter focuses on skills necessary for effective group leadership in schools and examines how these skills can be utilized so that groups can function as both a prevention and intervention program within the school setting. The authors have used a particular model for over 15 years, and the Adolescent Group Counseling in Schools Program has been recognized by the National Association of School Psychologists as an exemplary mental health program (Nastasi, Varjas, & Bernstein,1998). Also presented is an 8-week model that has been used by the authors in Project YIELD (Youth in Effective Legal Diversion), nationally recognized by the Office of Juvenile Justice and Delinquency Prevention as a model program in 1996. Both of these models use essentially the same leadership style and techniques to enhance social skills, and have resulted in significant behavioral changes in children and adolescents.

Mechanisms of Change in Group Counseling

Whereas in past generations the predominant issues for adolescents were the independent-dependent battle, repressed sexuality, and aggression, today's adolescents experience a lack of hope, fears of abandonment, and rejection, and often lack a sense of intimacy, involvement, and trust (Offer, Ostrov, & Howard, 1981). Group counseling addresses these major life circumstances for students and provides an opportunity for social skill enhancement. There are four major mechanisms that facilitate change through the group process.

1. *Cohesiveness.* By promoting member-to-member interaction and empowering the group members to solve their own issues and problems, the group leader promotes membership, acceptance, and approval as the group builds the cohesiveness essential for the group to be successful (Porter, 1994; Lonergan, 1994). Cohesiveness is the attraction that members have for each other. When a group is cohesive, the members are accepting of one another, supportive, and inclined to form meaningful relationships.

2. *Universality.* The second major mechanism for change is universality, whereby the adolescents learn, perhaps for the first time, that they are not alone in their particular feelings or circumstances. Sharing, ventilation, and insight serve to increase social skills and to clarify adolescent issues while simultaneously instilling a sense of hope and positive expectations for the future. This bond of universality helps lessen feelings of alienation and isolation and also fosters a sense of belonging. Further advantages of group counseling focus on students receiving honest, undeniable feedback from group members (i.e., peers who know each other's "true form" outside of the group). Learning the effect and impact of their behavior from other students assumes greater potency than receiving the identical message from an adult, which in and of itself underscores the strength of group counseling.

3. *Insight times action equals change (I x A = C).* The third mechanism of change is best explained by the mathematical concept "insight times action equals change" (I x A = C). Insight is defined by Phares and Trull (1997) as "...total understanding of the unconscious determinants of one's irrational feelings, thoughts, or behaviors that produce personal misery" (p. 333). Yalom (1995) states that "Insight defies precise description," but goes on to say that "insight occurs when one discovers something important about oneself, about one's behavior, one's motivational system, or one's unconscious" (p. 45). (For a more detail definition of insight, see Yalom, 1995, pp. 45–46.) Students gain insight from the focus on interpersonal dynamics rather than psychodynamic issues. By allowing members to talk through their present problems rather than their personal history, insight is attained. Action is provided by permitting the members to practice new behaviors such as empathy, face-to-face feedback, intimacy, and involvement within the group setting. The group itself becomes the agent of change. Leaders do not play "brilliant analyst" but rather encourage maximum self-direction. Members do not have to tell each other about their problems. The group experience allows each member to observe the issues first-hand. The feedback that members give each other maximizes the energy and the power of the group experience. Leaders discourage advice-giving and questioning by focusing on members' interactions, thoughts, and feelings.

4. *The inside/outside mechanism.* The fourth and perhaps the most meaningful mechanism of change is referred to as "inside/outside." The group leader facilitates the members by using the new perceptions and skills learned in the group to improve the behavior that precipitated their placement in the group in the first place. "Group is a microcosm of the macrocosm" (Yalom, 1995, p. 37). Utilizing their new-found skills outside of the group enhances the overall effectiveness of the group experience when members report to the group their attempts to apply these new skills in the "real" world.

Group is a series of complex processes, not a single curative experience. In order for these mechanisms of change to maximize their effect, the group itself must become the agent of change. The longer the group meets, the greater the likelihood these changes will come to fruition. Group is a process, not an event.

Problems in Group Leadership

Given the information presented in this chapter, and information gathered from experience, and the more one has the opportunity to be a group leader, it is very clear that all group problems fall on a continuum. The more one knows about group, the more one knows about the problems that occur. A group leader has two options, and each of these two options has two bipolar alternatives for consideration. The first thing a leader can do is to let a problem take its natural course; that is, just let a problem happen. If the leader chooses this first option, then the group will have a great deal of anger, frustration, and anxiety, which will provide a source of energy within the group. If the group is able to survive this process, then once it solves its own problem(s) the group will become cohesive more quickly. Hence, cohesiveness is obtained easier and quicker if the group leader allows a problem to happen. On the other end of the continuum is the approach that the leader, knowing the problem, decides to prevent the problem from occurring within the group—an option referred to as "the heading-the problem-off-at-the-pass" approach to group leadership. When a group leader does the latter, he or she identifies the problem to the group before it actually happens; the group then realizes the problem as it is going through it and the group leader is a more active participant in solving the problem. When the latter approach is used, the group will become cohesive; however, because it lacks the energy and frustration derived from the experience of solving its own problem, the group will take longer to build cohesiveness.

The group leader is always faced with the option of allowing a problem to occur or "heading-the-problem-off-at-the-pass." This decision is based on the leader's knowledge of group process and experience as the group leader. The decision-making process faced by a leader is also dependent on the nature of the group itself; that is, whether it be the type of group members (group composition) or the physical location of the group. If a group problem occurs in a situation in which the members have no choice but to attend and cannot leave, then the let-it-happen approach is more appropriate and safe. However, in a situation wherein attendance may be a difficulty or wherein there may be a problem getting members to return to a group, then leadership style must be much more conservative and must not allow problems to be totally solved by the group experience.

The information contained in this chapter gives some of the variables that a leader must think about as he or she functions in the role of primary group leader. Where the group is in its developmental stage, the makeup of the group, the location of the group setting, and how much control over attendance and participation the leader has all affect the leadership style that the leader brings to the group experience. Although a school may appear to be a situation in which a leader has total control of the attendance of the group members, quite the contrary is the case. The fact of the matter is that school groups must be handled by using a very safe structure because you want the students to benefit from the experience, and if there is too much energy early on in the group, then the group will not survive the conflict of the early process.

THE FOUR TASKS OF GROUP LEADERSHIP

All too often, group leaders perceive their roles as providing insight into problem behavior. While facilitating group members' experiencing insight is a very important and meaningful task of group leadership, initially this task takes a back seat to constructing/ structuring the group. In fact, constructing and structuring the group is perhaps the most vital and primary function of the leader. Lack of structure and ambiguous expectations are the most frequently cited reasons for the failure of a group. Unless careful attention is paid to constructing the group and to ensuring that group is a safe place to share, the group will never achieve maximum therapeutic value.

Task One: Constructing the Group

The primary task of group leadership is constructing the group, which requires that several factors be addressed prior to conducting the initial session. Those factors include group composition, physical setting, record keeping, and an initial one-on-one interview with each of the potential group members.

Group Leadership

Consideration of group composition is critical in regard to leaders and members. Much has been written about whether solo leadership or co-leadership is more advantageous (Yalom, 1995; Wheelan, 1997). Although there are many ways a co-leadership model can be implemented, and despite the fact that co-facilitation between equals would be the "politically correct" model, experience has shown that it is better to define one leader as the primary or dominant leader. There are, indeed, various reasons for this. After 15 years of experience, the authors have found that the use of co-leaders, presumed to be equal, results in a power struggle between the two of them to determine who will be the primary leader and who will be the secondary leader. Based on this experience, the authors suggest a model in which there are primary and secondary leaders who are designated these roles at the outset. Based upon the authors' experience, the primary/secondary leader model has been found to provide much greater facilitative value.

The dynamics between the primary and the secondary leader are key and often complex. Since group recapitulates primary family dynamics, the primary/secondary leadership structure resembles the roles parents play and recreates relationship dynamics that all members bring with them to group. In addition, the primary/secondary leadership model avoids rivalry for leadership of the group, which eliminates the competition that occurs in co-leadership models where theoretically equal leaders vie for supremacy until one achieves a primary leadership role and the other a secondary position. Those roles are separate and distinct. Within the group setting, primary and secondary leaders sit directly opposite each other. If the primary leader is absent, then the secondary leader sits in the chair of the primary leader and conducts the group, performing the function of the primary leader. It is important never to have anyone fill-in for an absent leader; therefore, the secondary leader's seat remains vacant when only one leader is present. In addition, the two-person leadership model has a built-in benefit in that the two leaders can lend each other support and double the quality and quantity of observations about the ongoing process and progress of group. Beyond this, during times of intensity and stress, it can prove to be invaluable to have a partner who can step back, analyze, and possibly redirect the action.

The primary leader has overall responsibility for the group, and should be more verbal and active than the secondary leader, and assumes the overall responsibility for the functioning of the group. The less verbal secondary leader is the support person who monitors the process of group. The job of the secondary leader is to broaden the area of interaction, frequently breaking a one-to-one interaction between the primary leader and a student. As the group progresses, the secondary leader becomes more verbal. Secondary leaders are available if there is a crisis situation. For example, if a student leaves the group room, the secondary leader can follow that student so that he or she is not roaming the school without supervision. It is suggested that the school psychologist be the primary leader and that the secondary leader be found among other faculty members within the school.

Choosing a co-leader is much like choosing a spouse: The primary leader must find someone who is not only compatible but who also blends his or her strengths and weaknesses with the strengths and weaknesses of the primary leader. Experience has taught us that the gender of the leaders is inconsequential. Group members will assign "roles" to the leaders consistent with their own family dynamics. What is important is to avoid splitting and not to allow students to play one leader off the other as students often do with their parents.

Members come to the group with their own personal issues to deal with. What a member brings to and takes from group may or may not reflect what is actually discussed within the group, as different students receive different experiences from the group based on their own dynamics and issues. Frequently, the leaders will represent mother and father figures and the other group members siblings and/or peers.

Group Makeup

If the heterogeneous construction of group is followed, and/or if the group is going to be used as a prevention model, then the mix of the group is the key to its success. A careful balance or blend of group members is essential for the proper formation of a group. Eight to ten students, with equal numbers of males and females, is optimum. A specific mix of model, issue, and problem youth is important, with attention given to individual levels of socioeconomic status, levels of verbalization, achievement, socialization, and adjustment, in order to recreate a heterogeneous mixture of the school population. The group should represent a cross-section of the student body of the school (refer to Figure 1).

It is difficult to do group with fewer than 4 members or more than 10 members. Age span should be no more than two grade levels and never more than 48 months (mental age). It is important to take at least two students who have discipline problems, as well as two model students so that the group does not get labeled. One withdrawn child does very well in the group because he or she will learn from listening, and eventually will be drawn out by the other group members. The remaining three to five members of the group can be individuals with academic problems, substance abuse problems, other issues, such as children of divorce. It is important to have at least three or four highly verbal members, including one verbal discipline problem student. These verbal members will keep the group moving and will also provide an opportunity for other students to model their behaviors.

It should be noted that the farther from the above ideal group mix/composition, the longer it

Figure 1. **Demographics of an *ideal* heterogeneous social skills group**

Number of students	*Type of students to select for group*	*Notes*
2	Verbal/model students (but they learn too!)	Unofficial co-leaders
2	Socially/emotionally disturbed students reasonably verbal	One of these two should be
1	Quiet/non-verbal student	
3–5	Students with issues	Issues are academic problems, substance abuse, children of divorce, children of alcoholics, etc.

Additional notes:

- The mix of the group is the key to success. Group should represent a cross-section of the school.
- 8–10 students with equal numbers of males and females is optimum.
- It is difficult to do group with fewer than 4 members or more than 10 members.
- Social/economic status should be: half low to low middle class and half middle class to high.
- Students should be roughly of the same intellectual capacity.
- Limit group to two grade levels and never more than 48 months mental age.
  - Always take seniors by themselves
  - Sixth, seventh, eighth, and ninth graders should be separated by grade level
- Exclude anyone who is clearly too disruptive and/or refuses to consent to the rules.
- The farther that the *ideal* group mix is deviated from, the longer it takes to go through the developmental stages.

will take the group to go through the developmental stages and the more active the leadership style will have to be. For example, if a group is made up of all male socially/emotionally disturbed students, it is obviously a more difficult group to do, and it will be harder for that group to form cohesiveness as compared to a heterogeneous group made up of a cross-section of the school population as outlined above.

There are students who should be excluded from groups: Avoid anyone who is clearly psychotic, too disruptive, and/or refuses to consent to the rules. These types of students are too time-consuming and keep the group from passing through the developmental stages within the allotted time.

Often, groups are organized around a single issue, such as divorce, relocation, transitions, and/or alcoholic parents. Frequently, school psychologists are expected to lead groups composed of students with behavioral disorders, attention deficit hyperactivity disorder, or learning disabilities. Regardless of the initially presented problems, members bring to the group life experiences that are universal and those that make them truly unique. The similarities among the adolescents will bring the group greater cohesiveness, but clearly from their differences these adolescents will develop a greater understanding of the world in which they live. When a group is organized around a homogenous issue, such as children of divorce, the purpose of group (see RAPP described later) should be extended to include learning to cope with their parents' divorce as well as self-esteem, self-responsibility, and interpersonal skills. However, experience has taught the authors that once that unifying issue is addressed, the group functions like a heterogeneous group and only occasionally returns to deal with the initial presenting problem.

When a school psychologist is asked to lead groups composed of students with disabilities who have a primary resource teacher, it is strongly suggested that that teacher be selected as the secondary leader, if at all possible. That teacher will have a better data base and more extensive knowledge of the students, as well as being more aware of interpersonal dynamics and classroom episodes that add a richness to the group.

Since it takes longer for socially and emotionally disturbed students to progress through the developmental stages of group, they should meet more often, perhaps twice a week. The reason to meet more often is that the length of each stage will be extended from the developmental matrix (as explained later in this text). In the instructional stage of a group for behavior disordered students, many more war stories will be told, because these students have a need to establish their territory and to be heard. The telling of stories provides a comfort zone for them. However, the leader's job is still to shift students' focus to the here and now and to the issues that led them to be placed in the group. Individuals with these types of problems tend to blame their problems on other people. Thus the focus always has to be "even if that is true, how can you function in such a way to get these individuals off your back?"

When the mix of the group is not the ideal heterogeneous mix described earlier, leaders will need to be more active and provide more structure and control. The leader needs to model self-disclosure of here and now feelings on a regular basis. It is important not to discipline students within the group. For example, if a school operates on a level system, the students should not be given points or level ratings within the group or based on their behavior in group. Group must be separate and distinct from any discipline system used in the school.

Membership Selection

Prior to admission to the group, each student should participate in an individual interview. The interview can be conducted by either the primary or secondary leader. It should explain the purpose and the rationale for group, identify the leader and the co-leader, explain how students were selected, tell them where and when group will meet, and obtain agreement to participate and abide by the rules. In some cases when a student refuses to give an agreement to abide by the rules during the initial interview, it can be suggested that he or she think about it overnight and then be given a second interview to give his or her final answer before he or she is excluded from the group. The reason for permitting a student to "think about it" is because sometimes he or she will talk to another student who has been interviewed for admission to the group and then decide that it might be cool to be placed in the group. Ultimately, students who will not give an agreement to abide by the rules in the individual interview will create problems once the group begins and should be excluded before the initial session.

Equally important purposes of the interview are to screen for suitability, to obtain some database regarding social skills and the nature of the child's difficulties, and to examine the student's motivation and problem-solving abilities. Attempts should be made to develop a therapeutic alliance by working through the student's resistance to being in group during this time.

Establishing the Contract

During the first session, the primary leader can enhance group function by using a special format called RAPP: Rules, Approach, Purpose, and Phases. RAPP establishes the group contract and helps members better understand the group process. The purpose of the individual interview and RAPP is to create clear expectations, develop the structure, and define acceptable behaviors. In other words, RAPP establishes the group contract.

The most important part of both the initial interview and RAPP is the commitment to abide by the rules. Students will not keep all the rules. However, once members commit to the rules in front of their peers and then break a rule, what remains is an opportunity for students to learn from their mistakes that otherwise is not available to them outside of the group environment. For example, if confidentiality is broken in a relationship, in the world outside of the group, then it often follows that the relationship ceases and the offending person may not be aware of why this happened. Whereas, within the group environment, the breaking of confidentiality is dealt with by the group members who confront the individual who broke confidentiality and make him or her aware of his or her behavior. The end result is therapeutic for the offender. Certainly, given the example above, it can be seen how the processing of a rule break by group members is one of the values of the group experience. The members will deal with any rule breaking through the group process. All group members remember the agreement secured during RAPP and that agreement is indisputable. Therefore, a verbal commitment will be sufficient since the contract is between the group members and not between the member and the leader. The members will deal with any rule breaking through the group process.

By setting clear boundaries, the leader establishes security and a baseline for later behaviors. As nervous as the leaders will be in the first group session, the students in the group are more anxious. Giving them the security of knowing the expectations and the structure of the group will reduce their anxiety, as well as the leaders'. It will also help students understand how they relate to each other and will provide the opportunity to set the stage for further group sessions.

Task Two: Control and Protection

If the first task of group leadership is to construct the group, then the second important task is to maintain control and provide protection for the group members. Most important, the group must identify with the leader, who must establish and maintain a therapeutic leverage while at the same time encouraging maximum group self-direction.

The leader must be authoritative enough to ensure appropriate conduct. By not allowing scapegoating or cruelty to occur, leaders make the group a safe place to share thoughts and feelings. Leaders must be active, since non-directive, passive leadership creates ambiguity and increases anxiety. The leader must protect the individual's right to work on a problem and to use group beneficially. Conversely, the leader must maintain the individual's right not to discuss thoughts and feelings if the student is not ready. Group content and dynamics fall under the professional domain of the leader, who must exercise discretion with regard to the needs of the members and the group.

Monitoring the group's progress while eliciting appropriate behavior through each of the developmental stages of the group is the task of the leader. By ensuring each member's safety, the leader can foster a constructive, non-judgmental atmosphere where an emphasis on the feelings and reasons behind behavior emerges in the later stages of group development.

Task Three: Facilitation of the Processing of Thoughts and Feelings

The third task of group leadership is to facilitate the processing of thoughts and feelings. For this to occur, the group must focus on relationships and member-to-member interaction. Members must become allies in an open and honest atmosphere characterized by autonomy and self-respect. Members have to believe that if growth is to occur, they must bring it about themselves. Therefore, the students, not the leaders, become the "agent of change."

The leader must demonstrate experience and knowledge and is responsible for setting and shaping the group norms. The group leader must model appropriate behavior, giving positive feedback for appropriate on-task behaviors by members. Norms must include giving and receiving appropriate feedback which is specific, direct, timely, and non-judgmental. "Say what you mean, mean what you say, and say it to the person's face." By following this saying in the group, other norms such as risk taking, honesty, openness, and talking in the here and now will be fostered. The leader should discourage individuals taking turns talking and/or allowing members to pass. The emphasis should be on discussing what is occurring within the group, between the members and leaders and not focus on outside events. Advice-giving and repeated questioning should be discouraged because it discourages individuals from bringing forth significant issues in their life. The leader should emphasize that each member is an integral part of the group and each member is as important as any other. The curative factor, cohesiveness, will develop if proper norms are modeled by the group leader.

Trust

The fundamental ingredient in group is the universal issue of trust that surfaces early and is never fully resolved within the group setting. Early in the group, trust relates to trusting the rules and the process of group. Later in the group, trust relates to self-trust and issues of vulnerability. All adolescents come to the group feeling that they are imposters and inadequate. They do not feel that they deserve the recognition for the accomplishments they have received. Many believe that they have "just fooled people" rather than take credit for their successes. Members are afraid of being negatively judged by fellow group members and spend their time attempting to conceal their believed inadequacies. During the group process members will exhibit cover-up behaviors (i.e., attempts by students not to be open and honest) for fear of being rejected or seen as inadequate. What follows is that members will try to fake it or they will not try at all so that they have an excuse for not being successful. In the process of group, members will often try to impress other members or they will attempt to withdraw for fear that they will be seen as imposters. Part of the issue of trust in group is reflected in this concept. Therefore, it obviously follows that everyone has thoughts and feelings he or she is afraid to verbalize. It is the job of the group leader to establish a level of trust so that adolescents can explore these issues in an environment that is accepting and in which they can attempt to resolve these basic issues of the human condition.

Dealing With Anger

The leader must generate feelings, step back, and allow the members to work through these emotions. Anger is the easiest emotion for adolescents to express, but frequently masks sadness and fear. Often leaders worry about anger in the group; however, "norming and storming" is an integral part of the group process. The leader can use anger to enhance the therapeutic value of the group by encouraging the members themselves to confront each other within the group. The leader can help the members be specific about their feelings and the behaviors that generated those feelings and, whenever possible, shift from the cognitive to the affective mode by indicating "I know what you think, but how do you feel?" The more clearly the leader can identify the underlying cause of the anger, the better the opportunity the group has to interpret the behavior appropriately and to relate the behavior exhibited in the group to behaviors outside the group.

Dealing with Resistance

As anger always occurs in a group, so does resistance. Resistance is any behavior that moves a group away from areas causing discomfort. Generally, resistance comes about because members are angry, lack trust, or feel hopeless and helpless. Resistance may take the form of silence (withdrawal), defensive body language, intellectualization, or direct hostility toward leaders or other members. Sometimes resistance takes the form of lack of productive work, individuals changing the subject, or even absence from the group. Other types of resistance include private conversations, subgrouping, outside contact, and testing the rules.

It is important to remember that resistance in the early stages of the group is resistance to the process of group. Resistance later on in the group is a function of psychopathology. Defiance and antagonism usually mask fears. Adolescents are resistant when they feel lonely, scared, or frightened. Frequently, acting out is a manifestation of some type of negative resistance. It is important to set limits on acceptable behavior and to determine whether or not the inappropriate behavior is a deliberate act or a function of the student's emotional difficulties.

Task Four: Providing Insight

The fourth task of group leadership is to provide insight into problem behaviors. The timing of insight is crucial and one of the most important skills the leader must develop. The leader must judge the readiness of members to share their feelings, as well as the level of defenses of each individual in the group.

Leader Interventions

Interventions by the leader provide the "hows and whys," identifying antecedents of behavior and discovering incongruities between emotions and their associated events. Types of intervention include direct feedback, clarification, confrontation, and interpretation. All interventions produce consequences within the group. Some are positive and some are negative. In order to intervene, a leader must decide what is happening in the group, what changes are necessary, and what intervention will bring about those changes. It is best to intervene when there is difficulty with group functioning, when there is unconstructive and/or repetitive material, and when the material is not goal-directed. Not all interventions will be successful, but most will usually move the group in some direction, which is better than no movement at all.

Groups develop at different rates, but they go through predictable stages. Insight given in the working stage is clearly going to be the most beneficial. If an attempt is made by the leader to go too fast, then group resistance will increase, as evidenced by disruptive behavior, silence, or joking. The members will tell the leader by their behavior that the leader is pushing too hard and/or moving too quickly.

Insight is most effective when the leader is able to generalize the insight to more than one member of the group. By generalizing—or going horizontally—the leader reduces resistance and the members' idea that the leader is reading their minds. Leaders should avoid focusing on any one member and try to avoid being perceived as "brilliant analysts." After each successful intervention, the ability of the leader to move the group effectively to a higher therapeutic level is significantly increased. Whenever the leader wants to intervene, it is a good idea to wait (count to10) in the hope that a member will express the same insight. An insight expressed by a group member is always much more powerful than when the same insight is expressed by one of the leaders. It is much more important that students see the leader as their protector than as their "shrink." Always remember that insight provided by member-to-member interaction is more powerful than the identical feedback expressed by the leader.

On a practical level, each leader intervention will generally cause the group to regress until the group absorbs what the leader is teaching. Therefore, timing is crucial so that the group does not regress too far too quickly. After a significant and intense group, it is expected that the level of intensity will be less in the next group. This group behavior is generally due to the feelings generated in the group frightening the group members. The group needs room to breathe before the group can progress through the developmental stages again.

To clarify the above, consider group to resemble a seventh grade square dance. During a square dance the participants "dosi in and dosi back." As they get close to each other, group members will move back because group gets too intimate and too frightening; that is, they fear that they will reveal too much of themselves. It is *a seventh grade square dance* because in the seventh grade participants wait until the end of the dance before they start to become really close and intimate; likewise, the above behavior is analogous to the way members behave in group.

Group Constants

It is important never to remove a student from group for disturbing or misbehaving. In fact, it is not wise to dismiss a student from any group. All students fear rejection and abandonment and dismissing a student generates the feeling "there but for the grace of God, go I" for other group members. The overall effect is to lower the level of trust among all group members. Most of the students who are acting out are doing it with the goal of getting dismissed from group. Their misbehavior is a cover-up for the anxiety and fear that they are experiencing in the group.

There are many specific techniques for dealing with the student other than removal from the group. For example, if it is an individual problem, then the student could be given some individual sessions to deal specifically with a problem behavior that he or she is having in group. Another technique might be to handle the problem as a group problem so members can provide feedback to the student, saying, for example, "You're acting this way to be removed from group, just like you do in class"; and then the inside/outside technique could be used to show how acting out won't work in this case—that the group is going to work with the student so that his or her behavior improves. Note that whenever there is a problem in group functioning (such as illustrated above), the problem can be handled as an individual problem, as a group problem, or as both. Ultimately, how the problem is handled is left up to the discretion of the group leaders. (Additional sources/references are available in the bibliography.)

It is essential to the structure of the group that its setting be consistent. The group must meet in the same location, with the same furniture, on the same day, in the same time period, if at all possible. Groups are best conducted on Tuesday, Wednesday, or Thursday. Mondays and Fridays are more difficult because sometimes schools are closed on these days. All of the chairs in the group should be arranged in a circle and no materials (pencils, paper, books, and backpacks) are allowed in the circle. Desks should not be used. No seats are assigned; students should choose their own seats. Group members enter the group and choose a seat. For the initial session, the primary leader's and the secondary leader's seats should be marked, perhaps by placing a sweater or a coat or a "reserved" sign on their chairs. The leaders will sit opposite each other in the same seats all year long. If a member is absent, his or her chair is left in the circle. However, if a member leaves the group permanently for some reason, such as relocation, then the chair will be permanently removed.

Once everyone is seated, the primary leader asks if there are any questions or concerns and then the primary leader begins by saying, "What do you want to talk about today?" Group then continues for the scheduled length of time until approximately 5 minutes are remaining. Then the group leader says, "How did group go and how did you do?" The leader goes around to each of the group members, asking him or her how he or she did and how the group did. The leader starts with someone who is very verbal and goes around the group in order, then the co-leader goes, then the leader, and group is over. Note that it is important for the leader and co-leader to evaluate the group performance, but not their own; whereas with the group members it is important for each of them to evaluate the group performance as well as his or her own, respectfully, elaborating as much as he or she is able.

Some type of documentation of the events that occur within the group is needed. Generally, a summary of the group is prepared by either the primary leader, the secondary leader, or both together. The shorter the summary, the better. There are at least two options of how to do the summary. The first option is to list everyone's name and make a comment about each person in the group. The second option is to write a paragraph that generally summarizes the material, with limited detail and limited specifics of group processes/content. At a minimum, a copy of the summary can be kept in a locked file cabinet. Some leaders choose to place a summary on the seat of each participant in the group, allow the member to read it, comment, and then collect the copies and destroy them before the leader starts the group with "What do you want to talk about today?"

Notes About the Time-Line of Group Sessions. Leaders must minimize interruptions and disturbances as much as possible. A sign should be placed on the door saying "Group In Session" so that no interruptions occur. It is important that there be a clock in the room so that the students have a sense of when group will end. Groups should always start on time and end on time. Time of the group should not be extended even if important material is being discussed. Attendance in the group is mandatory. Neither leaders nor members will change. Regular attendance is a key to a successful group. Members should be aware that the more conscientious they are about group, the better group will be. This statement is even more true for the leaders.

The sequence of time during a typical group session is as follows: Generally group begins with a little bit of silence, then it moves toward the discussion of current events, then there is a period of a lot of talking with little sustained discussion. With 20 minutes to go group will *actually* begin. It is toward the end of group where the most vital information occurs. This is much like a boxing match in which there is a 3-minute round. If the students know that there is only 20 minutes to go, then they will begin to *fight*, much like a boxer does in the last 30 seconds of the round, because they know that they will be saved by the bell and because they want to talk, but they do not want to dominate the group.

It is an interesting characteristic that all members come to group with the idea that they "would like to go third." They do not want to be the first to speak, nor do they want to dominate group or have all of the attention focused on them. For the reasons given above, the authors know, that as members learn the timing of group, they will learn, as do the leaders, that the last 20 minutes of a session is when the most helpful and productive aspects of group take place. (See Figure 2.)

TWO CONTRASTING MODELS

The information presented in this chapter is based on the Adolescent Counseling School Groups model, which was developed 15 years ago and has been successfully instituted in many school systems with many diverse populations, grades 5–12. After describing that model we will present an eight-session model, which we have implemented over the last 7 years. Both models have been nationally recognized and demonstrate the efficacy of the techniques, and information contained within this chapter.

The goals of the group counseling program are to increase self-esteem, to increase self-responsibility, and to improve interpersonal skills. Each group consists of 8–10 members and two group leaders. Groups are led by school psychologists. Secondary group leaders are volunteers from the faculty, including counselors and teachers. Group members are chosen with regard to their levels of achievement, adjustment, socialization, and verbalization, so that each group represents a cross-section of the entire student population. To this extent, each group should include high academic/low academic, well-adjusted/behaviorally problematic, extroverted/introverted, and verbal/non-verbal adolescents. Originally the program was designed to be preventive and to include all types of students, not merely children at risk or troubled. During the last 15 years the program has been expanded to include students

Figure 2. Time line: How time is spent in a typical group session

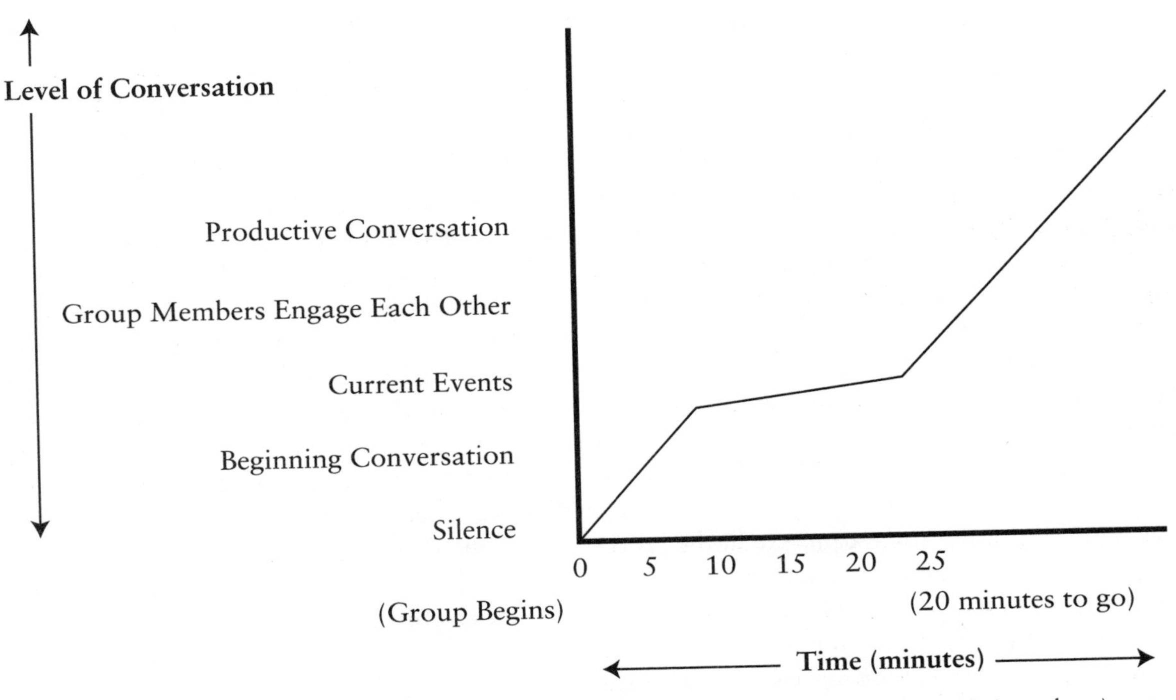

(Note that the 20-minutes-to-go phenomenon applies generally, irregardless if the group is 45 minutes or 1-hour-15minutes long.)

who are socially and emotionally disturbed, as well as groups for individuals with specific kinds of problems (e.g., divorce groups, children of alcoholics groups, and transition groups). The program described in the current chapter is time-proven to work in school systems and eliminates many extraneous variables that keep groups from being successful in a school setting. The nature of the population that is chosen affects the manner in which the leaders operate. In particular, the developmental model that is presented here requires more time if the mix of the group is not the heterogeneous representation of the school population described above. Deviation from the ideal mix requires the leader to be more active and extends the time the group spends in the Instructional Stage.

Students attend group once a week during a regularly scheduled class period for the entire school year. Once group sessions begin in early October, no students are permitted to leave group, and no new students are added. Students recognize their commitment for the full academic year and attend 30 group sessions. By maintaining the group's integrity, group cohesiveness, and mutual trust, salient forces in the success of the group process are fostered.

Structure is provided by the group leaders, but there are no planned activities or lessons. Students are encouraged to focus on thoughts and feelings, troublesome life situations, and other concerns group members may express. Within the confidential group setting, students have a forum to discuss problems and social issues that cannot be appropriately aired in the classroom. Typically, topics originated by group members include academic pressures, personal inadequacies, family concerns, substance abuse, suicide, rejection, peer pressure, and relationships.

Post-testing of all participants indicates that 63% of students with severe and recurrent behavior problems showed improvement in these areas. Parents and teachers state that more than 83% of students alter their behavior in a positive direction. Group members report that 75% felt better about themselves, 74% exhibit better peer relations, and 67% have improved attitudes toward their parents. Most dramatic is the statistic that 79% of the adolescents credit the group counseling program as having impacted favorably on these positive changes (Krieg, 1988).

When the school system and/or the group leader does not desire to do the 30-group session described in this text, the following eight-session group can be implemented using the condensed version of the year-long model. Essentially we find these groups to be more effective if the focus is on a specific issue or problem that results in a member being placed into the group.

Having a cross-section of the student population is less important than being able to identify a specific area for improvement. The shorter-term groups are particularly effective with students who have an issue such as truancy, aggressive behavior, defiance of authority, substance abuse, or any definable problem or issue.

The groups follow the same *Developmental Matrix*, and the group leader's tasks and roles remain unchanged. What does change is the style of leadership from less directive to more directive. The eight group sessions utilize the following format:

- Group I: Dyad technique and a shortened version of RAPP.
- Group II: The focus is on identifying the specific behavior or problem(s) that caused the member to be invited into the group.
- Group III: Functions as the Instructional Stage of Group.
- Group IV: The Rating Game. Using the same format as "taking the chair," the leader chooses a member who will give good and accurate feedback. A second member with a clearly identifiable problem is also selected. The first member using a scale from 1 to 10 picks a number that indicates how likely the second member is to repeat or replicate the same of a similar behavior. The member may choose just to state the number or may explain the justification for that rating. The leader then goes around the group in order, either clockwise or counter-clockwise, asking each member to provide a rating to the designated member. The secondary leader averages the rating saying, for example: "People think that on a scale of 1–10 with 1 being you are unlikely to repeat your problem behavior and 10 being that you are likely to do it, you scored a 4. In my opinion, I think you are more likely to be a 7." The secondary leader then continues on to explain the reason for the higher rating. After the secondary leader, the pri-

mary leader assigns a rating, and explains and offers suggestions for averting a reoccurrence of the problem behaviors. The procedure is used for the entire group so that each member receives feedback from all the other members.

- Group V: Functions as a Working Stage group focusing on the behavior and issues mentioned in the previous sessions. The leaders process thoughts and feelings and provide insight using the leadership techniques described previously.

- Group VI: Same as Group V.

- Group VII: The Rating Game. The procedure is the same as described in Group IV, but the rating for this session is based on "progress made in group." Discussion should focus on insights gained attempting to teach and reinforce positive behavior changes.

- Group VIII: Functions as the Termination Stage. The Group "takes the chair" as described later in this chapter.

The authors have found that through the use of this eight-session model, groups can be highly successful. Members also become more willing participants in future counseling efforts whether in individual and/or a longer term group. The key to success is to select members with as clearly a delineated problem as possible.

BEST PRACTICES

Group Developmental Matrix

Groups progress through predictable developmental stages. The more times the group meets, the more likely each stage will reach its full potential. To maximize the experience of positive personal growth, students should participate in a 30-week group. The 30-week time period permits the developmental stages of group to occur more naturally without the time restraints imposed by shorter term groups. Depending upon the author, these stages are identified by a variety of terms (see Yalom, 1995; and Bernard & MacKenzie, 1994). However, for the purposes of the current model, the stages of development will be termed:

1. Distrust
2. Instructional
3. Working
4. Termination

Each of these developmental stages will require differing leadership styles in accordance with the actions and reactions of group members so that the resulting process maximizes the efficacy of the group experience. (See Shechtman & Ben-David, 1999.) These actions and reactions of the group members will be identified as (a) participation, (b) anxiety, (c) resistance, and (d) cohesiveness (or PARC for short). The leadership styles to be discussed in these various developmental stages can be classified along a continuum. At each end of the continuum stands a definite leadership style. Figure 3 delineates the likely leadership style at each developmental stage of group and lists the likely general behavioral categories of group members at each developmental stage of group.

Like most things in life, little is completely black or completely white. Leadership style is frequently gray. The degree of emphasis that the leader places on each variable of leadership style will fall somewhere between the two extremes, depending on the group's behavior and the stage of group development. From this concept follows the notion of the four essential continuums to be considered when conducting group:

1. *The Content Versus Process Continuum. Content* represents what is said in the group, whereas *process* represents what is happening in the group. These two extremes should be viewed on a continuum from what is being said to what is happening within the group. There will be times when the group leader will focus only on the content and there will be times when the group leader will need to focus upon the process of the group. Depending upon which developmental stage the group is in, the leader will determine which spot along the continuum will be most useful.

2. *The Subjective Versus Objective Continuum.* This particular continuum will represent the level of self-disclosure that the group leader engages in. Subjective disclosure consists of two types: disclosure in the here and now and disclosure of personal

Figure 3. Group Developmental Matrix: Developmental stages, group behavior, and the effect on leadership style

Developmental stage	*Group behavior*	*Leadership style*
Distrust stage (Sessions 1– 6)	• Participation: low • Anxiety: high • Resistance: high • Cohesiveness: low	• Content to process • Subjective (here and now) • Group • Empathy
Instructional stage (Sessions 6–15)	• Participation: moderate • Anxiety: moderate • Resistance: high • Cohesiveness: developing	• Content to process • Subjective • Group • Empathy to clarification
Working stage (Sessions 15–27)	• Participation: high • Anxiety: low • Resistance: low • Cohesiveness: high	• Content • Subjective (personal) • Group and individual • Confrontation (insight)
Termination stage (Sessions 27-30)	• Participation: high • Anxiety: moderate • Resistance: low • Cohesiveness: very high	• Content • Subjective (personal) • Individual (taking the chair) • Empathy and confrontation (insight)

Excerpted from Krieg (1988).

history. There will be times when the group leader may choose to share a here and now feeling and there will be times when the group leader will choose to remain silent within the group. Self-disclosure of the here and now is always positive. Self-disclosure of a personal nature is generally not very helpful except perhaps in the working stage when the leader has gained acceptance from the group members. Group leaders may choose to self-disclose at this time if the topic is one that lends itself to that disclosure. All group leaders should always be careful about self-disclosures because some questions from the group members are really traps. Answering questions such as, "Did you smoke pot when you were our age?" should be avoided. These trap questions can result in much difficulty for group leaders. A good approach to those types of questions would be to respond "What makes you ask?" or "How can my answer to that question help you make your decision?" Leaders should never disclose personal information that may reflect on them poorly.

3. *The Group Versus Individual Continuum.* This particular continuum represents the approach that the group leader might take in deciding whether to deal with the group members as a whole or just one individual group member at a time. This decision will be made based upon the developmental stage of the group and the nature of the disclosure by the group member. For example, suppose that in the third group session, a student indicated that he or she had made a suicide attempt on the weekend prior to that particular group session. Given the preceding scenario happening in the third group session, the leader would want to focus on the process (not the content) by saying, "Isn't it good that Johnny felt confident enough and had enough trust in us to tell us about his experience?" The leader would then lead a generalized discussion about suicide, focusing on the universality of suicidal ideation. The leader would later end the group by saying, "Johnny, you and I need to talk afterwards," so that the group would know that the leader would take care of the problem, fulfilling the role of group protector. However, if the suicide attempt disclosure occurred in the working stage of group, it would be an appropriate time to focus on the individual, work on the issue of suicide as a solution to personal problems, and identify the problems that make individuals think about suicide. The leader could focus on the indi-

vidual, in this case, Johnny, going *vertically*, working on his problem in depth, and also go *horizontally*, relating the issue of suicide to other group members who at one time or another have entertained suicidal ideation (e.g., mentioned above). It is important to note that if the leader focuses on an individual too early in the development of group, such as in the distrust stage, then other members will be afraid to bring up intimate information because if they do that then they believe that the entire group session will focus on them. Although the leader might help the individual student in the third session, by doing so the leader will kill the group process.

4. *The Empathy Versus Confrontation Continuum.* This particular continuum represents how the group leader will respond to any given group situation. The group leader may offer an empathetic response or choose to confront the issue or the group member. The developmental stage of group, the nature of the situation, and the group member or members that are involved will all help to determine where along this continuum the group leader will respond. As a rule of thumb, it is important for the leader to remember: when in doubt, always use empathy. Empathy is always a positive experience. Sometimes confrontation will backfire and work against what the leader is attempting to accomplish. It is also important to know that there are times when group members need confrontation; however, if confrontation is used too early in the development of the group, the leader will find that the members will gang up against the group leader. Whereas if confrontation is used as a method later on in the development of group, then the leader may have a cheering section upon confronting a particular student or, even better, the cohesiveness of the group may allow the students to confront each other offering even greater therapeutic value.

Group Stages/Processes

The Distrust Stage: Weeks 1–6

Limited participation characterizes the distrust stage as the group members do not know one another yet and they have not yet developed enough trust in each other to begin the process of group. Due to the limited participation by members at this stage, the group leaders will necessarily be more active. Group leaders can facilitate increased participation by using the DYAD technique. The DYAD technique serves as an ice breaker and a method to demonstrate that it is much easier to talk about facts than it is to talk about feelings. Group leaders can even use a prepared list of questions to help the students as they complete the DYAD exercise. For example, some possible questions that might be used for the DYAD technique are as follows (i.e., the person interviewing would ask the other person):

1. Tell me a little bit about yourself: Where you are from and what are your hobbies or interests?

2. What is a secret wish that you have?

3. Where do you hope to be 10 years from now?

The DYAD technique is implemented as follows: Group members should be divided into pairs, and they should use the prepared questions to interview each other. At the completion of the interview, group members will then introduce their partners. The purpose of the DYAD technique and the subsequent introduction is that it is easier to introduce someone else than it is to talk about oneself. This technique will reduce anxiety associated with the first group session. Group leaders should first introduce each other, thus giving the group a model of what is expected of each group member. This technique should take a large portion of the first group session—in fact, the longer the better.

Anxiety levels and resistance will be high at this stage of group. Anxiety can be reduced by the DYAD technique, and any resistance can be dealt with by the group leaders. This might mean some degree of coaching a group member through this process. There is also very little group cohesion at this time because the group members do not know one another yet.

During the distrust stage of group, the group leaders will generally be more concerned about what is the content (Establishing the Contract) than what is taking place (Process). Following the above DYAD technique, the group leader will want to use the RAPP sheet in order to help facilitate the content at this stage.

Group leaders will use RAPP as a script to help group members understand the expectations, structure, and process of group and how the group experience will benefit them.

In other words, RAPP is used to establish the group contract.

Rules. Rules have already been discussed in each individual interview. Each group member should already have agreed to the rules in private, but it is also necessary that each group member agree to obey the rules in front of their peers. These are some suggested rules:

1. *Confidentiality.* What is said in group must stay in group. Confidentiality is an extremely important rule because it serves to build trust. If the group members know that what is said will remain in the room, then the group members can be more honest and open with each other. It is important for group members to understand that all group leaders will abide by the confidentiality rule; that is, except where law prohibits confidentiality. This occurs in response to abuse and issues of danger to self or others. Group members need to be informed that disclosure of either of the above will need to be reported to the appropriate authorities. (Please consult local laws about this issue.)

2. *One person talks at a time.* This is an important rule because courtesy must be shown to others' opinions, ideas, thoughts, and feelings. It is very difficult to learn while talking but we can learn while listening. As Covey (1989) teaches, "Seek first to understand, then to be understood" (p.237).

3. *No one leaves group without permission.* This rule is important because there may be times when the group conversation will be uncomfortable. Even if the member is uncomfortable, it will be necessary for that member to remain in the group. Group is a class and a student cannot leave class without permission.

Generally the fewer rules that there are, the better group will be; this is particularly true in the early developmental stages of group. The above are the three stated rules of group. Other rules can be added later as they surface during the group and need to be addressed by the leaders or group members. For example, gum chewing or cursing can be eliminated by saying that group was originally established as a class and those behaviors are not acceptable in class, and such a rule could be added later. The problem is that if there are too many rules initially and the group leader makes an issue out of trying to enforce these rules, then the more testing of these rules will be done by group members. The more rules early on, the more testing that will follow by group members. The rules that are important are the above three main suggested rules because they are reasonable to members and make it possible for group to function.

Approach. The focus of the groups will be about how members feel and how they feel about what happens to them. Students will be talking about here and now feelings, or how they feel about things at this time, not about past feelings or what others may have done at another time. In group any topic is allowed as long as it deals with the three purposes of group: improving self-esteem, self-responsibility, and interpersonal skills.

Purpose. The purpose of group is to improve the three areas listed below and to gain an understanding of the effects of one's behavior on others. Members need to improve their understanding of themselves and how they feel about themselves.

1. Self-esteem
2. Self-responsibility
3. Interpersonal skills

Phases. Groups will go through predictable, necessary phases. These phases are like stages of development when a child learns to walk by crawling first.

- *Phase 1, Distrust.* Group members are nervous because they do not know what to expect. This nervousness will take time to go away, but this time will be well spent. Like building a good friendship, exposing their true selves takes time.

- *Phase 2, Instruction.* Group is like peeling an onion: it gets sweeter toward the inside. In this stage members will feel more comfortable with each other and will begin to talk more openly to each other. Trust will be developed as members learn "A friend is someone who tells you what you need to hear, not necessarily what you want to hear." During this stage members will learn about each other and how group really functions.

- *Phase 3, Working.* In this stage, members will feel much more comfortable talking to each other and will feel more comfortable talking about more important issues. The group will focus on personal issues that are pressing for the member and to each other.

- *Phase 4, Termination.* There is a beginning, a middle, and an end to all groups, and as is the case for the weekly sessions of groups, each group session will have a beginning, middle, and end. Sample script: "When you come into group there will be a summary of the preceding group session on your chair. We will read it to review what happened last week, correct it, and destroy it, so as to keep the group rule about confidentiality. Then, I will begin the group by saying, 'What do you want to talk about today?' Then the group can discuss whatever it chooses as long as it is consistent with the approach and purposes of group. With about 5 minutes to go, the group leader will end each group session by saying, 'How did group go, and how did you do today?' Then each group member and leader will go around the group and answer that question."

RAPP concludes by going around the group and having each group member and leader confirm his or her agreement to abide by the rules of group.

Once RAPP is complete and each member commits to the group to keep the rules, the group leader can move on to a discussion about trust. A discussion about trust might be started by the group leader after asking, "What do you want to talk about today?" and following some silence, and then asking, "Do you trust each other?" Thus, RAPP represents content, and trust will begin the process of group in the early stages.

Trust is the key ingredient for the group at this time, hence the name Distrust Stage. The group leaders should focus upon the entire group at this time because premature concentration on any one individual can escalate the feelings of anxiety within the group. Questions that can be asked at this time include:

1. Why is this stage of group called the distrust stage?
2. How do we learn to trust?
3. Is there trust within this group?

Some answers that are likely to be heard are as follows:

1. I trust everybody in the group.
2. I trust no one in this group.
3. I trust everyone but (name) in this group.
4. It will take some time to learn to trust.

The "correct" answer would be choice 4 because creating trust is like building a friendship. However, the correct answer is less important than allowing as many members to talk in group as possible. Trust is a topic that most students feel comfortable talking about because it is not personal. Therefore, trust is an easy place to start members interacting with each other. The one exception in letting group members talk freely is a situation in which a member would give answer 3, which could result in one student scapegoating another. If a group member is identified as one who cannot be trusted, it will be necessary for the leader to redirect this conversation so that all group members are protected.

In the remaining weeks of this stage, members converse with each other mostly about non-consequential matters in order to reduce anxiety and resistance while building trust and cohesiveness. The group moves from content to process in the distrust stage.

The Instructional Stage: Weeks 6–15

The next 9 weeks of the group are the instructional stage, a period of time when group members are getting to know one another and to be more comfortable with the group process. The group leader is not very concerned about content at this stage, but is more concerned about process. This means that the group leader is pleased that there is conversation rather than silence. It is not important what is being said; what is important is that the group is talking. Group members are learning what is expected of them and what the appropriate norms for behavior and discussion content are to be. The development of cohesion is the key ingredient for the group at this stage. Individual participation will increase to a moderate level as individual resistance begins to decrease. This resistance will decrease because the group members will be more comfortable with the group process.

Anxiety levels will be decreasing as each group member begins to be more actively involved in the group process.

The group leaders will continue to focus upon the group as a whole and not focus upon any one individual. It is still too early to concentrate on any one individual. It is also too early for any confrontation; therefore, the group leaders will maintain an atmosphere of acceptance and empathy. However, inappropriate behavior should be dealt with in an appropriate manner, preferably by ignoring or using another instructional strategy. Group members' misbehavior needs to be addressed in order to protect the group process and to teach group members appropriate group behavior.

At this time the content of group verbalization needs to be narrowed in scope. This process can be characterized as if proceeding through a funnel that narrows the further along the process goes. The large end of the funnel represents an agreement that initially any topic of discussion is permissible.. The narrower area of the funnel represents an attempt by the group leader to guide the group toward more relevant topics which center around the purpose of group: self-concept, self-responsibility, and interpersonal skills. Leaders narrow this focus by asking, "What does that have to do with group?" A new set of norms will be established in regard to topics for discussion which focus on the purposes of group.

Group leaders will attempt to move the group to a discussion about feelings instead of facts. This can be accomplished by stating, "I know what you think about that subject, but how do you *feel* about it?"

The group leaders will keep their own self-disclosure to here and now feelings and not disclose personal history during this stage of group. It is more important that the group members are talking to one another. This stage ends when the group members feel comfortable enough to share meaningful material in appropriate ways, the beginning of the working stage.

The Working Stage: Weeks 15–27

The next weeks of group are characterized as the working stage. This stage of the group is considered the core of the program. It is at this stage of the group that cohesiveness develops and the group functions as a *group* rather than as a set of individuals. During this stage, group members are more willing to deal with fundamental concerns of a personal nature and to deal with issues that require some degree of personal self-evaluation. The group members will be more open, honest, and interactive. Individual resistance and anxiety are much lower at this stage because the group members know each other and what is expected of them in the group process. Group cohesion has formed and will enable group members to be more interactive.

The leadership style at this stage of group can be characterized by more attention to an individual and less focus upon the entire group. The process can be viewed more as individual therapy with a cheering section than as individual therapy with an audience. Confrontation can now be used as an effective intervention because individual members are more ready to receive constructive assistance. Empathy is always a good approach in the group setting, and should not be forgotten at this time.

The Termination Stage: Weeks 27–30

The rule in terminating a group is that 10% of the total number of sessions of a group should be devoted to the group's termination. Translated for the current model, this means that the last 3 weeks of group would be considered the termination stage. There is an equally important beginning, middle, and end to all groups. Termination is often overlooked or ignored, but this is a very important part of the group process. Termination is important because it supplies a concrete ending to the group. The termination stage affords an opportunity to summarize any growth and to demonstrate progress that has been made within the group setting. The termination stage provides an opportunity to give feedback to other group members and to teach/practice skills in being able to give feedback to others. The termination stage is simply a time when group members can learn to express an appropriate goodbye. Group members will reach this stage of group with two differing sets of feelings:

- "I am glad that this is over."
- "I am going to miss group" (meaning they will miss being with their new found friends).

This stage of group is marked by high levels of participation because all members have been part of the group process and know what is expected of them.

Participation may be lessened by the fact that some individuals do not want the group experience to end, but, for the most part, group members will readily participate at this stage. Resistance levels are generally low, except in the case of an individual who does not know how to deliver a goodbye appropriately or to deal with feelings of sadness about leaving the other group members. Anxiety levels will increase some at this stage because of the change that ending group represents. Students have a difficult time with transition, and the termination process provides an opportunity to experience transition in a controlled setting. The group members will continue to have a high level of cohesiveness which will aid in the termination process.

The leadership styles will be characterized by focusing upon the process of termination, as well as on the content of the goodbye statements. The group leaders will be able to focus upon individual group members, as well as upon the entire group. Empathy will be the key ingredient as the group leaders attempt to understand how each group member responds to the termination process. Confrontation should only be used in the event that a group member chooses not to participate appropriately in the termination process.

The group leaders will be free to be very much involved in this stage of group and to express their own subjective feelings about each group member and the degree of growth that has been demonstrated.

The termination exercise "taking the chair" is extremely effective. This exercise serves as a method for each group member to give and to receive goodbye statements and final words of advice or encouragement to and from all group members. This exercise also serves as a "graduation" from the group. This process covers the final three weeks of the group.

Countdown Week 3 (i.e., 2 more meetings until the last session). The group will continue as normal, but the group leaders will inform group members that the time for the group to terminate is coming very close. Members will begin to prepare for termination.

Countdown Week 2 (i.e. the next to last session). The group leaders should be very active at this group session. An attempt to generate a non-specific discussion about termination of the group, feelings about ending, and any perceived progress should be made at this time. This is a sample script: "We have been part of the group for the last 29 weeks. We have all grown in some manner. We have learned to be more responsible, we have learned to get along with each other, and we have learned to feel better about ourselves. We have all benefited from this process. We have learned to share feelings with each other and have discovered that we are more alike than different. We have developed some new skills, and we need to continue using those skills outside of group."

Question: "How do you feel about leaving?"

Wait for answers: "I'm glad it is over." "I will miss group."

Question: "What are some things about yourself that have changed?"

Question: "What do you like or not like about group?"

End this group by suggesting that during the next group we will do something special. There will be an activity designed to say goodbye to each other and to summarize our progress. Do not disclose the nature of the activity.

Countdown Week 1 (Last session). "Taking the chair" is a very important part of the termination process. It gives all group members an opportunity to express their feelings and to share their feelings with each other. Even the most negative things will come out in a positive manner during this process. Feedback from each of the group members and the group leaders demonstrates how much has been accomplished. The purposes of "taking the chair" are to find out how much was accomplished and also to end group on a positive note. This is the procedure:

An important procedure is for the primary and secondary leaders to decide ahead of time which member will receive comments first. They should pick someone who will draw positive feedback from the group. Also important is that a member should be chosen to start giving the feedback in the process, someone who is highly verbal and who will make positive comments.

The primary leader should demonstrate the process by providing feedback to the secondary leader which serves as a model to demonstrate the procedure "taking the chair." The leader could say, "You have been a good co-leader; you have been very supportive and helpful. I think you have done a good job handling the summary sheets, and I really have valued having you in the group with me," thus giving an example of some of the positive things that happened. Then, the leader could add, "I kind of wish that as a co-leader that you would have talked earlier, because I've noticed as this group has progressed you've talked more, and that's been very helpful to me and to the group." By giving both positive feedback and identifying areas to improve, the leader has modeled the process for the group members.

The leader will pick a target person to start the feedback process. That person, again, should be someone who is verbal and will say positive things. Then the process should proceed either clockwise or counter-clockwise, depending on which direction will give more positive information or will offer more time to get to someone who might give negative feedback or who might be very withdrawn and/or nonverbal an opportunity to learn the process. It is important to note that once the pattern/direction around the circle begins, it is locked into. Do not go out of order; do not break the chain. In a situation where the person who receives the feedback first is one seat or two seats away from the person preferred to give it, have two people go and then skip the person receiving the feedback and continue to stay in the same order.

Encourage group members to give honest and constructive comments to each other. If positive or beneficial feedback is not obtained or if members do not understand what is expected of them, stop the process, role model again for them (it is important to teach them what is expected), and then go back and start over. The rules are the following:

1. The person receiving the feedback may not reply to anyone else's comment after the person says it. He or she must wait his or her turn until everyone, including the leaders, has given his or her feedback to make any kind of reply.

2. The members must talk to the person on the chair, not about that person. For example, do not say, "John did pretty well"; instead say, "You did very well."

3. Everyone in the group must say something even if he or she has to wait to think of something, or has to be coached a little bit. Every person *must* talk in turn. The process may take some time, but is absolutely essential. Even the most withdrawn member will say more and more as the process develops.

Primary and secondary leaders need to give feedback last (with the secondary leader going first and the primary leader going last) after each group member has given his or her feedback to the person receiving the feedback and before moving on to the next group member. After all the members have given feedback and before the secondary and primary leader give feedback, the primary leader should ask if anyone has anything else he or she would like to add before the leaders take their turns. The person on the chair may respond and/or answer questions at this time. Then the secondary and primary leaders give their feedback to the person in the chair and go on to the next member (who then *takes the chair*). The process continues until each group member has "taken the chair." The primary and secondary leaders are to receive feedback from the group members (i.e., *take the chair*) only after all of the group members have taken the chair and received feedback. The leaders will find it very beneficial to discover what the group members have to say about them.

SOME IMPORTANT REMINDERS

One of the primary tasks of group leaders is to protect the group members. Therefore, should, for some reason, the process of *taking the chair* go sour and the group gang up or dump on one of the members, then the leader should stop the process, reemphasize the difference between constructive criticism and being cruel, and then begin the process again from that point. Group members are not allowed to scapegoat one another.

This process may run over the allotted time; therefore if the process is running late, a counselor, another school psychologist, or principal must be available to cover leaders' classes. The secondary leader should go out quickly and notify the appropriate person so that arrangements that have been made can be enacted for class coverage.

Spontaneity is the key to making this entire process work. For that reason, in the next to last session do not tell the members exactly what will happen during the last meeting. Both leaders can lengthen or shorten the time it takes to complete this process by the length of the comments they make. They are the key in keeping the timing as appropriate as possible. However, this may be the most meaningful event of the year for group members and/or group leaders, so do not rush this process.

SUMMARY

Of the numerous primary intervention modalities available, school counseling groups certainly should be considered one of the most efficacious and cost effective interventions in terms of how time and financial resources are used. We have presented a brief history of the use of group counseling, as well as an empirical basis for the use of group counseling as a viable intervention for school children with emotional, social, and learning dysfunctions. Two different models of school counseling groups were discussed. First, an 8-week model, followed by a more detailed discussion of a much longer, 30-week model.

Various aspects of the procedures of group counseling and the processes involved were delineated. First a discussion of the *mechanisms of change in group counseling* was presented, which included cohesiveness, universality, insight (i.e., Insight x Action = Change), and the inside/out mechanism.

Next, *problems in group leadership* was discussed, with focus on two primary paths for the leader to consider when conducting a group meeting: (a) permitting a problem to take its course, which builds group cohesiveness quickly, but which also presents with greater difficulty; or (b) the "head-it-off-at-the-pass" approach, wherein the group leader identifies a problem before it happens, thus providing more safety, but must play a more active role in resolving issues presented.

Other areas of group leadership were also considered, including *the four tasks of group leadership*. Task one, *constructing the group* outlined (a) the basics of group leadership, (b) the demographics of group makeup, followed by a discussion of (c) membership selection and (d) initial commitment on the part of the group members and group leaders.

Task two of group leadership was described as providing *control and protection*, which outlined how a group leader creates a safe environment of trust that facilitates group member participation. The third task of group leadership examined was *facilitation of thoughts and feelings*, which overlaps task two, and included delineation of issues of *trust*, *dealing with anger*, and *resistance*. The fourth task of group leadership was entitled *providing insight*, which looked at *leader interventions* and *group behavior*.

The *Group Developmental Matrix* was discussed, including details regarding the four different stages that all groups go through (a) distrust, (b) instructional, (c) working, and (d) termination. Paralleling the Group Developmental Matrix, the chapter reviewed four different variables the group leader must process while leading a group. The four continuums that occur during group counseling are (a) the Content versus Process Continuum, (b) the Subjective versus Objective Continuum, (c) the Group versus Individual Continuum, and (d) the Empathy versus Confrontation Continuum.

It is appropriate to be intimidated by the thought of leading a group of youth through difficult life issues; you learn by doing. Start as a secondary leader and learn the power of the group process. Learning to do group is an apprenticeship skill that can only be learned with adequate supervision. The authors encourage those interested in understanding more about group counseling to review the references and annotated bibliography included as a part of this chapter, and then, do group.

AUTHOR NOTES

The authors gratefully acknowledge the assistance of Patricia S. Gaston, Ph.D., and Claudette Wassil, M.A., in the preparation of the initial drafts of this chapter.

REFERENCES

Barlow, S. H., Burlingame, G. M., & Fuhriman, A. (2000). Therapeutic application of groups: From Pratt's "Thought control classes" to modern group psychotherapy. *Group Dynamics: Theory Research, and Practice, 4*(1), 115–134.

Bernard, H. S., & MacKenzie, K. P. (Eds.). (1994). *Basics of group psychotherapy.* New York: Guilford.

Covey, S. R. (1989). *The seven habits of highly effective people.* New York: Fireside.

Hoag, M., & Burlingame, G. M. (1997). Evaluating the effectiveness of child and adolescent group treatment: A meta-analytic review. *Journal of Clinical Child Psychology, 26*(3), 234–246.

Kazdin, A. E., & Johnson, B.(1994). Advances in psychotherapy for children and adolescents: Interrelations of adjustment, development, and intervention. *Journal of School Psychology, 32*, 217–246.

Krieg, F. J. (1988). Group *leadership training and supervision manual for adolescent group counseling in schools* (3rd ed.). Muncie, IN: Accelerated Development.

Lonergan, E. C. (1994). Using theories of group therapy. In H. S. Bernard and K. R. MacKenzie (Eds.), *Basics of group psychotherapy* (pp.207–208). New York: Guilford.

Nastasi, B. K., Varjas, K., & Bernstein, R. (1998). *Exemplary mental health programs: School psychologists as mental health service providers*. Bethesda, MD: National Association of School Psychologists.

Offer, D., Ostrov, E., & Howard, K. I. (1981). *The adolescent: A psychological self-portrait.* New York: Basic Books.

Phares, E. J., & Trull, T. J. (1997). *Clinical psychology: Concepts, methods, and profession.* Pacific Grove, CA: Brooks/Cole.

Porter, K. (1994). Principles of group therapeutic technique. In H. S. Bernard and K. R. MacKenzie (Eds.), *Basics of group psychotherapy*. New York: Guilford.

Scheidlinger, S. (1994). An overview of nine decades of group psychotherapy. *Hospital and Community Psychiatry, 45*(3), 217–225.

Shechtman, Z., & Ben-David, M. (1999). Individual and group psychotherapy of childhood aggression: A comparison of outcomes and processes. *Group Dynamics: Theory Research, and Practice, 3*(4), 263–274.

Shectman, Z., Gilat, I., Fos, L., & Flasher, A. (1996). Brief group therapy with low-achieving elementary school children. *Journal of Counseling Psychology, 43*(4), 376–382.

Slavson, S. R. (1940). Group psychotherapy. *Mental Hygiene, 24*, 36–49.

Wheelan, A. (1997). Co-therapists and the creation of a functional psychotherapy group: A Group dynamics perspective. *Group Dynamics: Theory Research, and Practice, 1*(4), 306–310.

Yalom, I. D. (1995). *The theory and practice of group psychotherapy* (4th ed.). New York: Basic Books.

ANNOTATED BIBLIOGRAPHY

Corey, G., & Corey, M. S. (1987). *Groups: Process and practice*. Monterey, CA: Brooks/Cole.
This work is the most universally accepted textbook for introductory classes to group counseling.

Krieg, F. J. (1988). *Group leadership training and supervision manual for adolescent group counseling in schools* (3rd ed.). Muncie, IN: Accelerated Development.
A comprehensive training manual for school-based adolescent groups.

Levine, Baruch. (1991). *Group psychotherapy practice and development*. Prospect Heights, IL: Waveland.
This textbook is also considered to be another basic book for introductory psychotherapy group work.

Rutan, J. S., & Stone, W. N. (1993). *Psychodynamic group psychotherapy*, Lexington, MA: Collamore.
This work is the updated second edition. It emphasizes a psychodynamic approach and contains excellent chapters on special topics, such as contracting, transference, and counter-transference, etc.

Yalom, Irvin D. (1995). *The theory and practice of group psychotherapy* (4th ed.). New York: Basic Books .
This book is the classic work in group psychotherapy. Considered essential reading, it contains extensive research and information on many issues and controversies in group psychotherapy.

III.

Focus on Assessment Domains and Special Populations

76 Best Practices in Assessment of Intervention Results With Infants and Toddlers

Charles R. Greenwood, Gayle J. Luze, and Judith J. Carta
Juniper Gardens Children's Project
University of Kansas

OVERVIEW

Public policy (P.L. 99-457, amended by P.L. 102-119) mandates that preschool-aged children with disabilities and their families receive early intervention services, and many states have extended these services to families with infants and toddlers (DEC, 1993). While states vary with regard to the ways in which they identify and serve infants and toddlers with developmental needs, the school psychologist often serves a key role in determining eligibility for services, linking children and families to appropriate interventions, and then determining whether interventions are truly meeting children's and families' needs. This chapter focuses on the role of the school psychologist in carrying out those functions. Specifically, the paper will describe the basic knowledge and skills school psychologists need in addressing the unique challenges in assessing infants and young children. Then the chapter focuses on the emerging area of assessing early intervention results and offers a specific approach for progress monitoring for infants and toddlers being developed by the Early Childhood Research Institute on Measuring Growth and Development (ECRI-MGD).

BASIC CONSIDERATIONS

Infants and toddlers present an array of challenges to the school psychologist who is attempting to determine whether a child is eligible for early intervention services, for what programs the child is best suited, and then whether the early intervention services are making a difference in improving the child's developmental outcomes. These challenges include but are not limited to what follows: first, the difficulty most young children have complying with a predetermined structured protocol in light of the need for comparing children across somewhat standardized conditions; second, the need for assessors to gather representative samples of children's behavior in light of the short amount of time infants and toddlers will stay engaged with a task; third, the need to elicit information about what skills young children can perform in light of the difficulty many young children have with unfamiliar adult assessors or novel situations; and fourth, the need to include the perspective of parents regarding children's skills, needs, and progress in light of the limited amount of time family members have for providing this type of information (Preator & McAllister, 1995; ECRI-MGD, 1998b).

For young children with developmental delays, the critical characteristics and recommended practices of assessment were described in Division for Early Childhood's (DEC) 2000 report, "DEC Recommended Practices in Early Intervention/Early Childhood Education." Among the criteria for evaluating recommended assessment practices cited in this report were the following: (a) They should point to behavioral objectives for change that are judged important and acceptable, (b) they should guide change in treatment activities, (c) they should incorporate several instruments and scales including observation and interviews, (d) they should incorporate input from parents, and (e) they should be used on multiple occasions (Neisworth & Bagnato, 2000). Clearly, psychologists and interventionists qualified to assess infants and toddlers must have a range of specialized knowledge/skills that goes beyond the administration of standardized tests.

Background Knowledge and Skills

Examiners must be knowledgeable about the unique challenges of assessing young children and understand the developmental milestones of early childhood. Because infants and toddlers are just learning to communicate, talk, interact, and move, the behaviors to be assessed and the methods employed to conduct assessments are different and specialized when compared with those of older children. Psychologists' skills using naturalistic observational and play-based assessment are particularly important because they are more likely to engage young children's attention, reduce children's fears, and set the context for children to emit a range of developmentally appropriate skills compared to traditional testing methods. Skills with measures capable of tapping sources of information from the parent and other caregivers are equally important because of their unique and detailed knowledge of what the child in their care knows and what their child can do. School psychologists must also be prepared to work with colleagues across disciplines and settings that typically serve infants and toddlers. Specifically, examiners must be experienced working with parents, early intervention teachers and service coordinators, pediatricians/nurses in the medical center, ancillary staff such as occupational therapists and speech and language pathologists in the clinic, and childcare professionals in community-based settings.

While this set of skills broadly outlines some of the competencies needed by school psychologists in working with infants and toddlers, there is a critical need to move beyond determining eligibility and linking children and families to programs. With the current national focus on accountability for services, taxpayers and policy makers and parents want to know that services provided are effective (Kagan, Rosenkoetter, & Cohen, 1997). In response, states have scrambled to develop accountability systems for children receiving early intervention and preschool services. Thus school psychologists must have the knowledge and skills to assess the results of early interventions.

PROGRESS MONITORING AND PROBLEM-SOLVING CONCEPTS AND SKILLS

School psychologists are often in critical positions to determine whether children are truly benefiting from the early intervention services they receive. Thus, there is a growing realization that psychologists who work with the youngest children and their families must have the competencies to examine whether these children are making progress as a function of these services. The general and specific concepts of progress monitoring and the problem-solving models that are described by Dave Tilly, Roland Good, Scott McConnell, and others elsewhere in this volume are also relevant to work with infants and toddlers. School psychologists need knowledge and skills in nontraditional approaches to assessment that are sensitive to the incremental growth that children will experience within early intervention programs. Three types of assessment particularly relevant to child-based intervention are behavioral assessment, mastery monitoring, and general outcome measurement. *Behavioral assessment* is measurement linked to one or more target behavioral objectives. *Mastery monitoring* is measurement linked to skills in a task analysis hierarchy with skills taught one at a time. In this approach, new assessment is applied to each new skill. *General outcome measurement* (GOM) is assessment linked to a range of key skill elements with the same skill set assessed each time (Deno, 1997). Progress is indicated by change/growth in single behaviors (performance monitoring), or skills (mastery monitoring), or increased proficiency on a set of key skill elements (general outcome) that are repeatedly measured. For infants and toddlers, measures must include the following domains targeted through early intervention: communication/language, motor/movement, social interaction with adults and peers, cognition/problem solving, and adaptive/self-help (e.g., Hebbeler, Simeonsson, & Scarborough, 2000; Priest et al., in press).

Additionally, school psychologists need skills and resources to determine how to change an intervention when it does not appear to be working. They need to be knowledgeable about a range of methods to explore solutions and change intervention strategies designed to affect growth in progress monitoring measures (ECRI-MGD, 1998b). These assessment activities may include observing child-caregiver interaction in natural settings, directly assessing child skills during their typical activities and routines, and/or evaluating features of the particular program(s) in which the child is enrolled. Such measures could then be used to form intervention hypotheses such as changing parent and caregiver interaction to increase growth in language or altering the childcare environment to facilitate more opportunities for communication. Intervention changes such as these may then result in accelerated child progress.

Why is Assessment of Intervention Results Important?

Quite clearly, the assessment of intervention results is important because of the usefulness of this process in providing direction about early intervention for young children. A fundamental tenet of educational psychology is that the success of any instructional intervention should be based on its effect on learning; and that future intervention be modified based on whether the child changes, grows, or learns (Corno & Snow, 1986). Over the last 20 years, the most dramatic methodological advance regarding assessment that is sensitive to instructional interventions has been the development of Curriculum Based Measurement (CBM) (e.g., Shinn, 1989). The CBM measures of reading in school aged children, for example, based on the work of Deno and his colleagues (Deno, 1997) have been demonstrated to be valid, reliable, and sensitive to instructional interventions. Similar measures have recently been developed for use with younger children (e.g., Kaminski & Good, 1996) to assess emergent literacy skills. And, more recently similar measures have been developed for measuring growth of infants and toddlers (Luze, Linebarger, Greenwood, Carta, & Walker, 2000) among others (see Table 1). An example of the application of "CBM-like" measures in the area of expressive communication of infants and toddlers appears later in this chapter.

Why Are Current Measures Not Adequate for Assessing Intervention Results?

According to Bagnato and Neisworth (1991), individual program planning to bring about change in child performance is the ultimate goal of early intervention services for infants/toddlers and their families. Yet, traditional forms of early childhood assessment often do not provide information useful in intervention development and making individual programming decisions. In traditional assessment frameworks, assessment and intervention are often treated as completely separate activities (Meisels, 1996).

For example, *eligibility* for services is the first-order question answered by traditional forms of testing (Bagnato & Neisworth, 1991). While norm-referenced measures are appropriate for comparing an individual child against an established norm group to determine a delay or discrepancy from the norm, they do not provide information appropriate for intervention development. If a child is determined to be eligible, then a new set of assessments is given including criterion-referenced tests, interviews and questionnaires with parents, and formal/informal observations of the child's behavior in home and school settings to determine a child's *needs*. Criterion-referenced tests (e.g., Assessment, Evaluation, and Programming System for Infants and Toddlers (AEPS) (Bricker, 1993) can provide some information

Table 1. Key skill elements in six different general outcome measures for infants and toddlers

Expressive communication	*Social interaction*	*Movement*	*Manipulation*	*Cognition*	*Adaptive behavior*

• Gestures
• Vocalizations
• Single words
• Multiple word utterances
	• Adult social turn
	• Peer social turn
	• Negative interaction
		• Transitional movement
		• Locomotion
		  • Grounded
		  • Vertical
			• Reach/grasp/ release
			• Compound manipulation
				• Attention
				• Problem solving
					• Self-help

for determining a child's specific needs and aid development of the Individualized Family Service Plan (IFSP)/Individualized Education Plan (IEP).

Then, after a need is identified and an intervention developed, a new set of assessment tools is used or developed for *progress monitoring* and *evaluation of growth*. Norm- and criterion-referenced tests are often used to evaluate the effectiveness of a program or intervention. Unfortunately, none of these measures can be used frequently enough by early interventionists to plan and evaluate in an ongoing formative way the interventions used with individual children. These separate steps and sets of tools in the traditional model usually provide information adequate enough to answer the questions being asked (i.e., eligibility, need, progress), but they are not linked in a synergistic and efficient manner. Parents, teachers, support personnel, and children often spend too much time and effort in the collection of all of this information with too little benefit (McConnell, 2000). This often results in a process of information collection that is redundant and not useful for intervention purposes.

School psychologists have been encouraged to help resolve this pervasive problem in the assessment of intervention results for young children. According to Bagnato and Neisworth (1991), the solution encompasses the following: (a) tailoring assessment to the individual needs of each child, (b) determining eligibility for services, (c) linking assessment with early intervention, and (d) communicating assessment results to parents and other professionals. Assessment approaches of this type such as CBM or Dynamic Indicators of Basic Early Literacy Skills (DIBELS) (Kaminski & Good, 1996) for kindergarten and school-aged children have only recently emerged for use with very young children (ECRI-MGD, 1998a; Luze et al., 2000).

One explanation of the late emergence of intervention-linked assessment and decision-making models in early childhood are the unique challenges in working with young children described above. But another reason that this approach has been slow to influence early intervention has been the difficulty in translating the general outcome model of curriculum-based measurement to the relatively unstructured "curriculum" of interaction and play that children experience in their homes, childcare environments, and early intervention settings. For the most part, the curriculum that has been the focus of CBM has been academic/literacy skills. Determining the curricular focus of CBM for very young children in the absence of standardized curricular areas has been puzzling. What key skill elements should be assessed for children 6, 12, 18, 24, 30, or 36 months of age? Which general outcomes and key skill indicators are needed? The emerging solution of this problem has been to measure multiple behaviors known to be indicators of the general outcome and known to change over a particular period of early childhood (ages 0–3) and to evaluate a child's proficiency with these skills at a particular age against peer norms and rate of growth over time. In conclusion, any system used for assessing intervention results for infants and toddlers must address the challenges of working with younger children and at the same time overcome the limited applicability of existing assessment tools.

BEST PRACTICES FOR INTERVENTION RESULTS WITH INFANTS AND YOUNG CHILDREN

Best practices in the assessment of intervention results with infants and toddlers involve use of a decision-making framework with GOM progress monitoring to guide and adapt interventions. The particular advantages of this approach include (a) repeated measurement of progress in the natural setting, (b) graphical representations of the data that provide direction about the intervention, (c) tools that allow improved communication with parents and collaborating professionals, and (d) the ability to assess immediate growth in the absence of a detailed specification of objectives/skills sequences as are needed in both behavioral assessment and mastery monitoring approaches. Use of a decision-making model with GOM progress monitoring also meets the best practice criteria used by DEC (2000) in its selection of recommended practices. DEC criteria include the following: a research- or value-basis, a family centered focus, a multicultural emphasis, cross-disciplinary participation, developmental appropriateness, and a normalized experience.

An example of such a system is one currently being developed by the Early Childhood Research Institute on Measuring Growth and Development (ECRI-MGD, 1998b). It is a decision-making model supported by GOMs and has been specifically designed and validated for use with infants and toddlers (see Figure 1). This system is based on a series of descriptive, correlational, longitudinal, and experimental intervention studies that validated general outcomes and that developed and then established the psychometric properties of the measures of each outcome, including technical adequacy and peer norms (Priest et al., in press; Luze et al., 2000).

Embedded throughout the decision-making model are multiple points of input, choice, and evaluation from the family so that they can participate in decisions regarding the need for the intervention, the type of intervention, the effectiveness, and whether they are satisfied with the intervention (see shaded areas, Figure 1). The model meets the DEC multicultural criteria primarily because it can be used in the context of any language, and the tasks and materials used are those typically available in most modern cultural contexts. In addition, the model and measures were developed with input and participation from a diverse group of families representing a wide range of ethnic and sociodemographic backgrounds. Participation of a range of disciplines and professional practitioners in the program of any one child is supported through specific planning steps, measurement activities, and decision points in the Exploring Solutions section of the model. The model is developmentally appropriate and normalized because the contexts for assessment allow children to engage in toys and interact in unstructured situations that are fun and typical for their age.

The ECRI-MGD decision-making model has several features in common with similar problem-solving models (e.g., Deno, 1989; Kaminski & Good, 1996). Five major steps are completed that lead from identification of a performance problem to the determination of whether or not the problem has been solved. These steps are (a) identifying the problem, (b) validating the problem, (c) developing and implementing a potential solution, (d) evaluating whether or not the solution is working, and (e) evaluating whether or not the problem has been solved. Two distinct forms of assessment are used: Individual Growth and Development Indicators (IGDIs) (the left-most column in Figure 1) and Exploring Solutions Assessments (ESAs) (the right most column in Figure 1). The IGDIs are used to monitor growth and proficiency over time, and the ESAs are designed to inform intervention planning and implementation activities.

Selecting a general outcome of concern and then monitoring its progress by using the appropriate IGDI provides the basic information on an individual's level and rate of growth, thus supporting decisions of problem identification and problem validation. ESA activities fulfill an array of functions from targeting interventions with the highest likelihood of success to measuring their fidelity and ability to accelerate progress as measured by the IGDI (refer to Figure 1).

Case Study: Ray

To illustrate the applicability of the ECRI-MGD decision-making model, we offer the case of Ray. Ray is a 2-year-old boy attending Little Kids, Inc., a community childcare center. His teacher reported that his communication appeared immature and delayed for his age. This was a concern given that expressive communication is a general outcome of early childhood and plays a critical role in cognitive and social development (Acredolo & Goodwyn, 1988; Carpenter, Mastergeorge, & Coggins, 1983; Crais & Roberts, 1996).

While Ray used gestures and vocalizations to communicate with the teacher and his peers, he used only a few words regularly and did not put words together in sentences. The teacher talked with Ray's mother who observed these patterns of behavior at home. The teacher approached the early intervention team and requested an assessment and support services. As a member of this team, the school psychologist came to the center to meet with Ray's teacher and mother and to assess his needs.

Because the concern was in the area of communication, the psychologist decided to assess the child's expressive communication by using an IGDI for communicative expression (Luze et al., 2000). This IGDI involved Ray and his teacher playing with a toy house and people for six minutes while the psychologist recorded the frequency of occurrence of key element skills (i.e., gestures, vocalizations, single words, and multiple word utterances) that have been identified in prior research as important indicators of a child's expressive communication (e.g., Acredolo & Goodwyn, 1988). These tallies were converted to rate per minute and graphed (see Figure 2). During the first assessment Ray produced only five communicative behaviors per minute, and all of these were prelin-

Figure 1. **ECRI-MGD decision-making model**

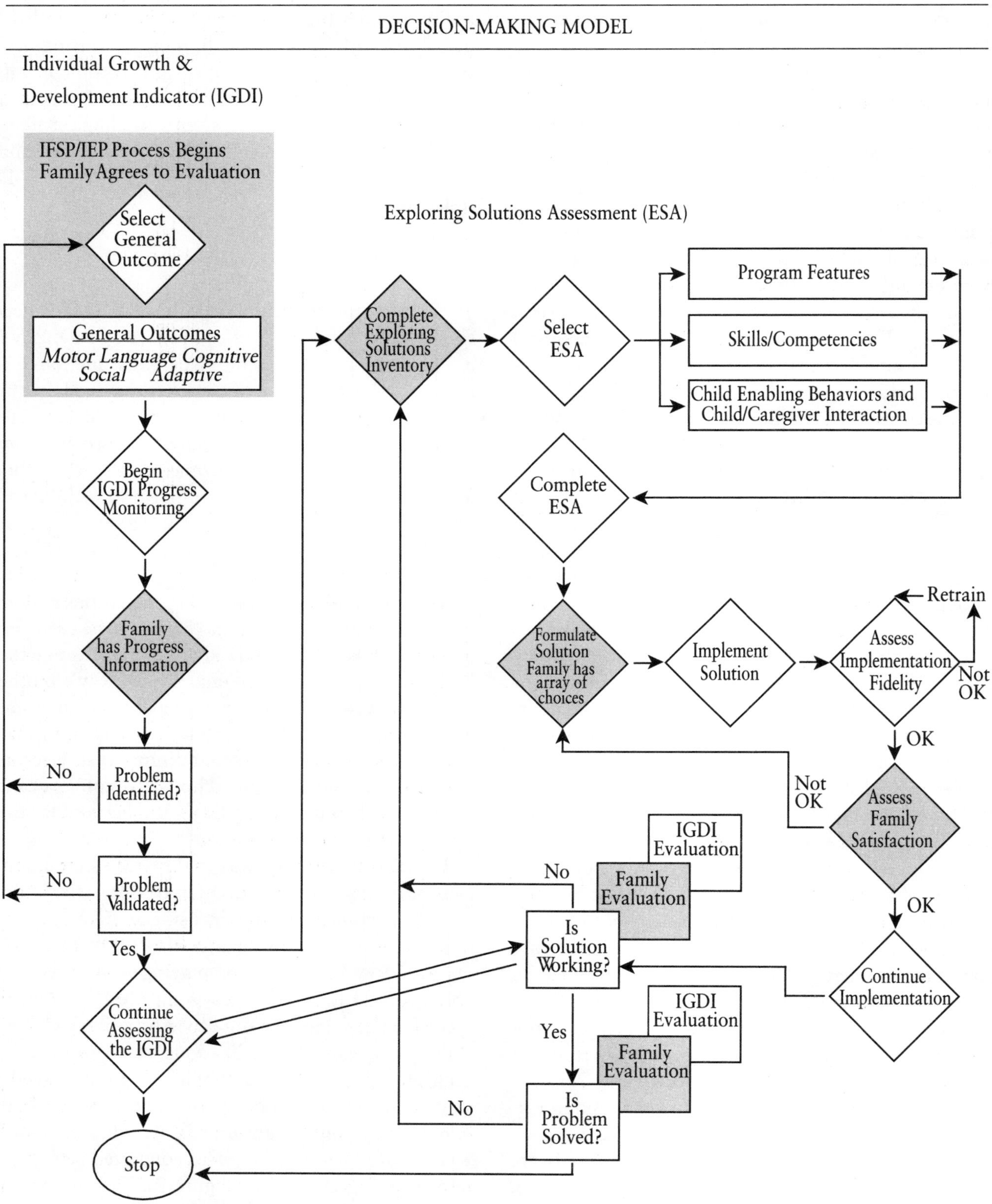

Source: Early Childhood Research Institute on Measuring Growth & Development

Figure 2. Ray's expressive communication measure by using an IGDI

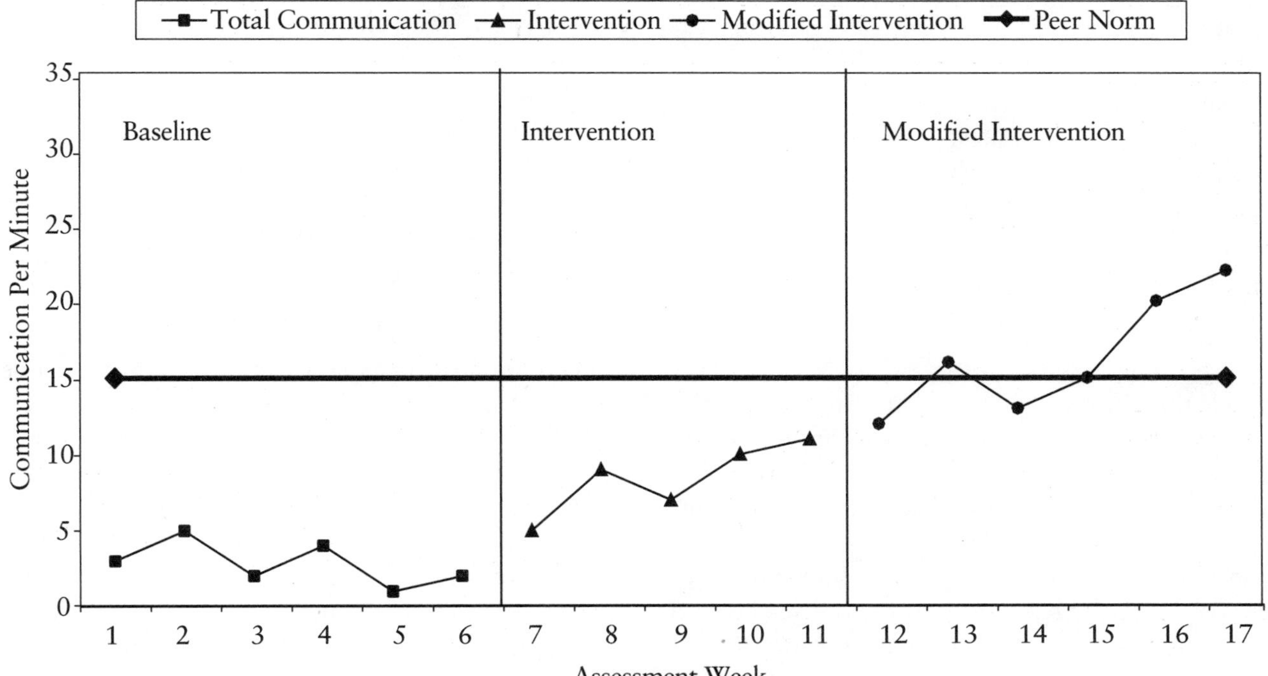

guistic in nature (i.e., gestures and utterances). Because the graph contained a benchmark mean level of 15 communication behaviors per minute (the average for similarly aged children) (Luze et al., 2000), it was clear that Ray's skills were below age-expectancy.

To provide a sense of Ray's rate for growth over time, the psychologist returned five more times in the next several weeks to gather five more assessments of communicative expression. These results documented that his level of communication was lower than his peers and provided an estimate of rate of growth. Furthermore, his results showed that his rate of total communication was actually a decreasing trend line (see Figure 2). The psychologist also gave a standardized language measure, the Preschool Language Scale (Zimmerman, Steiner, & Pond, 1992) to cross-validate information gathered from the IGDI. The standardized language test showed Ray's scores to be below the norm. These data were shared with Ray's mother and his teacher, and because they concurred with the IGDI assessment, the team decided to plan and implement an intervention designed to improve his expressive communication skills.

As part of their intervention planning, the team reviewed an inventory of clinical queries to determine what was already known about Ray's communication delay and what types of information they needed (see Table 2). Working together, they explored issues of possible medical concerns; previous interventions or assessment information; Ray's specific communication skills; the range of settings, activities, routines, and curricula that might prove important in influencing his communicative performance; possible behavior problems potentially interfering with Ray's communication; and potential persons and settings appropriate for inclusion in the intervention.

Completing and ruling out most of these potential concerns, the school psychologist decided to observe Ray in his childcare center, and to examine his communication skills as well as his opportunities to communicate there. She used the Program Features Checklist to determine how the center was organized and how it might be designed to influence Ray's communication. The Program Features Checklist is designed to examine the structural characteristics of the center (caregiver-child ratio, toys accessible), interactions with the caregiver (following the child's lead, asking questions, taking turns, missing opportunities to respond), use of discipline, classroom activities (use of daily creative play, daily reading time, encouraging social interaction, using pre-

Table 2. Clinical concerns guiding exploring solutions assessment decisions

- History with child
- Medical issues
- Family/caregiver concerns
- What child knows and can do
- Settings, activities, routines, curriculum
- Child/caregiver interaction
- Competing or interfering behaviors
- Barriers to intervention implementation
- Fidelity of implementation

dictable transitions), and toys and materials (encourage social and pretend play, exploration, music, and movement exploration). The results showed that Ray's teachers asked relatively few questions, responded infrequently when he used gestures to communicate, and did not provide him with comments or labels for his actions or the objects he used. These features are considered highly important for promoting language development (e.g., McCathren., Warren, & Yoder, 1996; McLean, 1990; Wetherby & Prizant, 1992).

An additional ESA was completed to provide more information about teacher-child interactions in the classroom. This measure, the Code for Interactive Recording of Caregiving and Learning Environments (CIRCLE) (Atwater, et al., 1993), is a behavioral assessment tool that provides information about the ecology of caregiving environments, the behavior of caregivers, and the child's engagement with people and objects within the setting using a time sampling procedure. Use of the CIRCLE indicated that most of the teacher's communication with Ray consisted of verbal instructions or talk directed at him as part of a large group of children. There were few interactions directed exclusively toward him. In addition, teachers did not appear to be expanding on his verbalizations, prompting him to use words, or engaging in much positive feedback. They seemed to miss many opportunities to facilitate his communication. These data also demonstrated that when Ray did communicate with teachers and peers, he used gestures and vocalizations.

Data from these two measures provided the necessary information to formulate a practical and potentially viable solution. The team reconvened, reviewed the information, and decided to implement an intervention with the goal of increasing Ray's imitation of vocalizations and single and multiple word utterances by requiring him to request preferred objects or activities. To meet the goals, the team decided on strategies obtained from a modified Milieu Language Training program (Alpert & Kaiser, 1992; Yoder et al., 1995). Teachers were encouraged to follow Ray's lead during interactions, ask more open-ended questions, expand on his utterances, and use a delay to encourage Ray to fill in the missing words (e.g., When singing a familiar song, pause and then let Ray complete the phrase). The team decided to implement the intervention during snack time. During other times, the teacher could still use the intervention activities, but these activities were targeted for full implementation of the strategies. In addition, the team considered it important to identify what specific steps of the intervention were being implemented consistently and which ones were not. As a result, data were collected about the frequency of use of the intervention strategies during the scheduled time to evaluate fidelity of implementation (Figure 3). This information would be helpful to determine what aspects of the intervention were having the most impact on the rate of growth in Ray's communication.

The intervention was implemented for 5 weeks and then evaluated. At that time, the team examined the IGDI data again and noted that Ray had made some progress (see Figure 2: Intervention), but not as much as had been anticipated to meet the target goal of 15 communications per minute. The Program Features Checklist was used again, and this time the data indicated that the teacher continued to miss opportunities to respond to Ray's communication. The teacher noted that she would try to look for those opportunities in the future and would extend the intervention strategies to Ray's snack and lunch times.

The modified intervention was implemented for another 6 weeks during which weekly progress measures were employed. At the end of the intervention period, the team re-examined the IGDI data and found that Ray had made acceptable progress toward the goal of 15 communications per minute; in fact, he had surpassed the goal (see Figure 2: Modified Intervention). CIRCLE data showed that the teacher was using more open-ended questions, and was providing more frequent comments and labels for Ray's actions and more statements of approval (Figure 4). The CIRCLE data also showed that Ray was using words

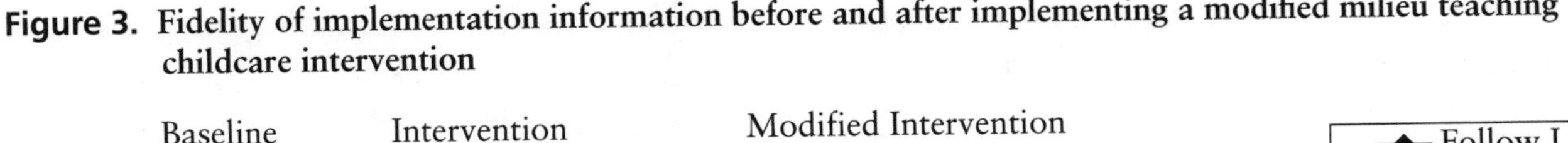

Figure 3. Fidelity of implementation information before and after implementing a modified milieu teaching childcare intervention

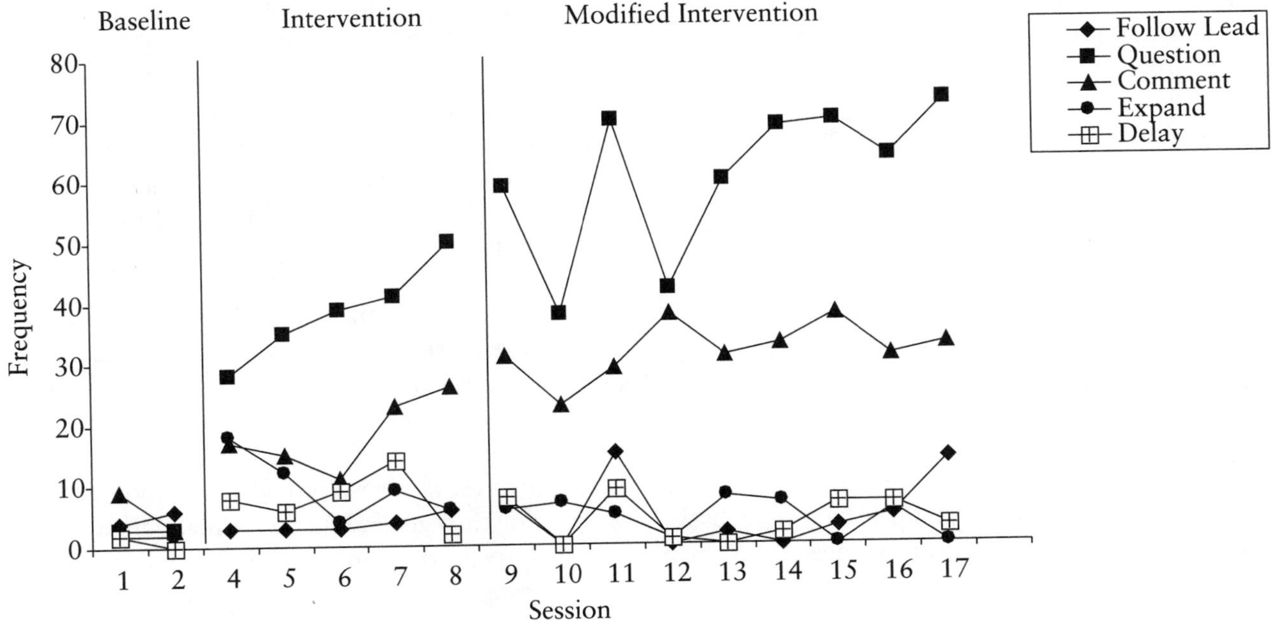

Figure 4. Direct observation of teacher-child interaction before and after implementing a modified milieu teaching childcare intervention

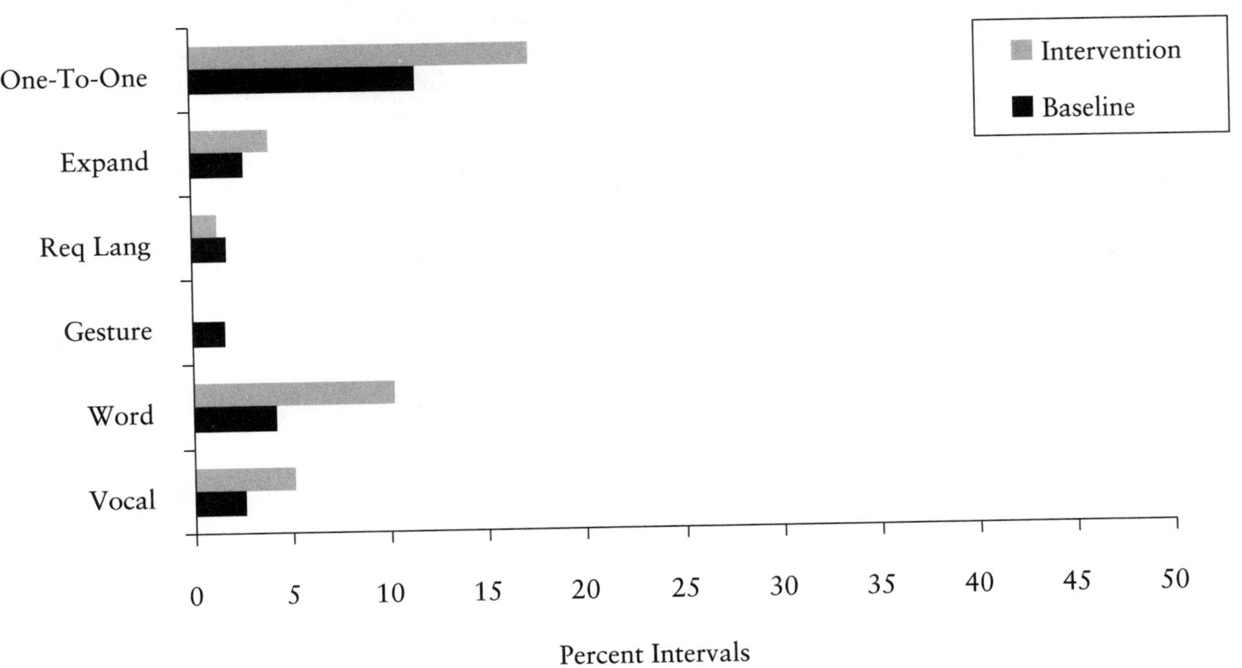

more frequently and using gestures less frequently. The Program Features Checklist data indicated that the teacher was asking more questions, and commenting more on his words and actions. Fidelity of implementation data showed that the teacher implemented more of the steps during the intervention phase compared to baseline, but implemented even more during the modified intervention phase (see Figure 3). The teacher reported that she felt comfortable continuing the intervention and the mother noticed an improvement in his communication at home. The team decided that the solution was working and wished to continue the intervention for an additional 6 weeks.

Illustrated in this case study is the entire decision-making model and the interplay between the separate IGDI and ESA data collection measures. By using a progress monitoring measure on a continual basis, the team was able to determine Ray's needs and when it was necessary to change the intervention. The ESA tools enabled the team to collect data that were directly relevant to the intervention while monitoring variables that could be changed. As a result, they were able to work much more efficiently and effectively than would have been possible with other assessment tools.

SUMMARY

School psychologists play an increasingly important role in the assessment of intervention results for infants and toddlers. Working across a wide range of disciplines, professionals, and settings that cater to the unique needs of this population, school psychologists can use more sensitive tools for identifying needs, implementing interventions, monitoring growth and progress, and adapting interventions for very young children. The background knowledge and skills needed to assess intervention results with this population go beyond that use of standardized testing associated with traditional psychometrics. Two sets of competencies are critical to meet this need: one, the use of observational and naturalistic methods for progress monitoring and problem solving; and two, detailed knowledge of the intervention strategies used to improve the outcomes of young children.

Working with a population of children who are often apprehensive about new people and novel situations requires familiarity and skill using assessment approaches that are highly consistent with the natural and typical experiences of early childhood. Methods for monitoring progress are needed that (a) overcome the difficulty of having younger children follow a predetermined protocol for long periods, (b) incorporate input from parents and caregivers in order to obtain a more complete picture of younger children's abilities, and (c) are capable of obtaining representative samples of children's abilities in a short amount of time.

Best practices in this area, like those of the ECRI-MGD, are currently focused on general outcome measurement approaches used in problem solving models because they facilitate improved communication with caregivers and parents, and are sensitive, efficient, and cost-effective. They also provide a common set of indicators for each general outcome, maintain an individualized focus on current skills and developmental functioning, and support the spirit of IFSP/IEP. Emphasis is on repeated measurement, monitoring rate of progress, and changing intervention when progress is less than expected. Because of their extensive experience and background with the use of progress monitoring and problem-solving models, school psychologists can play a critical role in developing, promoting, and using these approaches in early childhood. In conclusion, the ECRI-MGD decision-making model appears to be a highly useful approach for linking assessment with intervention for infants and toddlers in effective and desirable ways. The approach is consistent with current research, public policy, and DEC recommended practice.

REFERENCES

Acredolo, L., & Goodwyn, S. (1988). Symbolic gesturing in normal infants. *Child Development, 59*, 450–466.

Alpert, C. L., & Kaiser, A. P. (1992). Training parents as milieu language teachers. *Journal of Early Intervention, 16*, 31–52.

Atwater, J. B., Montagna, D., Peterson, P., Creighton, M., Williams, R., & Hou, S. (1993). *Code for Interactive Recording of Caregiving and Learning Environments (CIRCLE 1–2)*. Kansas City, KS: Early Childhood Research Institute on Substance Abuse, Juniper Gardens Children's Project, University of Kansas.

Bagnato, S. J., & Neisworth, J. T. (1991). *Assessment for early intervention: Best practices for professionals*. London: Guilford.

Bricker, D. D. (1993). *Assessment, evaluation, and programming system from birth to three years*. Baltimore: Brookes.

Carpenter, R. L., Mastergeorge, A. M., & Coggins, T. E. (1983). The acquisition of communicative intentions in infants eight to fifteen months of age. *Language and Speech, 26*, 101–116.

Corno, L., & Snow, R. W. (1986). Adapting teaching to differences among individual learners. In M. Wittrock (Ed.), *Third handbook of research on teaching* (pp. 605–629). New York: Macmillan.

Crais, E. R. & Roberts, J. E. (1996). Assessing communication skills. In M. McLean, D. B. Bailey, & M. Wolery (Eds.), *Assessing infants and preschoolers with special needs*, (pp. 334–397), Englewood Cliffs, NJ: Merrill.

DEC (1993). *DEC recommended practices: Indicators of quality in programs for infants and young children with special needs and their families*. Reston, VA: Task Force on Recommended Practices, Division of Early Childhood, Council for Exceptional Children.

Deno, S. L. (1989). Curriculum-Based Measurement and special education services: A fundamental and direct relationship. In M. R Shinn (Ed.), *Curriculum-Based Measurement: Assessing special children* (pp. 1–17). New York: Guilford.

Deno, S. L. (1997). Whether thou goest . . . Perspectives on progress monitoring. In J. W. Lloyd, E. J. Kameenui, & D. Chard (Eds.), *Issues in educating students with disabilities* (pp. 77–99). Mahwah, NJ: Erlbaum.

ECRI-MGD. (1998a). *Research and development of individual growth and development indicators for children between birth to age eight* (Technical Report 4). Minneapolis, MN: Early Childhood Research Institute on Measuring Growth and Development.

ECRI-MGD. (1998b). *Research and development of exploring solutions assessments for children between birth to age eight* (Technical Report 5). Minneapolis, MN: Early Childhood Research Institute Measuring Growth and Development.

Hebbeler, K., Simeonsson, R. J., & Scarborough, A. (2000). *Describing disability in young children: A national study of early intervention eligibility*. Paper presented at the Conference on Research Innovations in Early Intervention, San Diego, CA.

Kagan, S. L., Rosenketter, S., & Cohen, N. (1997). *Considering child-based results for young children*. New Haven, CT: Yale Bush Center in Child Development and Social Policy.

Kaminski, R. A., & Good, R. H. (1996). Toward a technology for assessing basic early literacy skills. *School Psychology Review, 25*, 215–227.

Luze, G. J., Linebarger, D. L., Greenwood, C. R., Carta, J. J., & Walker, D. (2000). *Toward a technology of dynamic indicators of communicative expression for infants and toddlers*. Kansas City, KS: Early Child Research Institute Measuring Growth and Development, Juniper Gardens Children's Project.

McCathren, R. B., Warren, S. F., & Yoder, P. J. (1996). Prelinguistic predictors of later language development. In K. N. Cole, P. S. Dale, & D. J. Thal (Eds.), *Assessment of communication and language* (pp. 57–74). Baltimore: Brookes.

McConnell, S. R. (2000). Assessment in early intervention and early childhood special education: Building on the past to project into the future. *Topics in Early Childhood Special Education, 20*(1), 43–48.

McLean, L. (1990). Communication development in the first two years of life: A transactional process. *Zero to Three*, 13–19.

Meisels, S. J. (1996). Charting the continuum of assessment and intervention. In S. J. Meisels & E. Fenichel (Eds.), *New visions for the developmental assessment of infants and young children* (pp. 27–52). Washington, DC: Zero to Three.

Neisworth, J. T. & Bagnato, S. J. (2000). Recommended practices in assessment, In S. Sandall, M. E. McClean, & B. J. Smith (Eds.), *DEC recommended practices in early intervention/early childhood special education* (pp. 17–23). Reston, VA: Division for Early Childhood.

Preator K. K., & McAllister, J. R. (1995). Best practices assessing infants and toddlers. In A. Thomas & J. P. Grimes (Eds.), *Best practices in school psychology III* (pp. 775–788). Bethesda, MD: National Association of School Psychologists.

Priest, J. S., McConnell, S. R., Walker, D., Carta, J. J., Kaminski, R. A., McEvoy, M. A., Good, R. H., Greenwood, C. R., & Shinn, M. R. (in press). *General growth outcomes for children between birth and age eight: Where do you want young children to go today and tomorrow? Journal of Early Intervention.*

Sandall, S., McClean, M. E., & Smith, B. J. (Eds). (2000). *DEC recommended practices in early intervention/early childhood special education.* Reston, VA: Division for Early Childhood.

Shinn, M. R. (Ed.). (1989). *Curriculum-Based Measurement: Assessing special children.* New York: Guilford.

Wetherby, A. M., & Prizant, B. M. (1992). Profiling young children's communicative competence. In S. F. Warren & J. Reichle (Eds.), *Communication and language interventions series: Vol. 1. Causes and effects in communication and language* (pp. 217–253) Baltimore: Brookes.

Yoder, P. J., Kaiser, A. P., Goldstein, H., Alpert, C., Mousetis, L., Kaczmarek, L., & Fischer, R. (1995). An exploratory comparison of milieu teaching and responsive interaction in classroom applications. *Journal of Early Intervention, 19*, 218–242.

Zimmerman, I. L., Steiner, V. G., & Pond, R. V. (1992). *Preschool Language Scale: 3.* San Antonio, TX: The Psychological Corporation.

ANNOTATED BIBLIOGRAPHY

Deno, S. L. (1997). Whether thou goest . . . Perspectives on progress monitoring. In J. W. Lloyd, E. J. Kameenui, & D. Chard (Eds.), *Issues in educating students with disabilities* (pp. 77–99). Mahwah, NJ: Erlbaum.
This chapter provides fundamental arguments for monitoring the development of individual children. After laying out the rationale for monitoring the progress, one occasion to the next, two approaches are compared: mastery monitoring versus general outcome measurement. These approaches can be highly structured, precise, and lead to improved outcomes and communication.

Luze, G. J., Linebarger, D. L., Greenwood, C. R., Carta, J. J., Walker, D., Leitschuh, C., & Atwater, J. B. (in press). Developing a general outcome measure of growth in the expressive communication of infants and toddlers. *School Psychology Review.*
This article reports the development/technical adequacy of two general outcome measures designed to measure children's growth in expressive communication for children birth to 36 months of age. Results of this longitudinal study of the first 9 months of life include indices of reliability, validity, and sensitivity to growth over time.

McLean, M., Bailey, D. B., & Wolery M. (1996). *Assessing infants and preschoolers with special needs.* Columbus, OH: Merrill.
This book provides a comprehensive discussion of current assessment practices for infants, toddlers, and preschoolers with special needs. In addition to description of practices, emphasis is placed on current practices in the field that are preferred. Just one of these is involvement of families and family-centered practice.

McConnell, S. R. (2000). Assessment in early intervention and early childhood special education: Building on the past to project into the future. *Topics in Early Childhood Special Education, 20*, 43–48.
This article discusses themes likely to mark early childhood special education into this century. Two are relevant to the assessment of infants: intensified attention to assessment of progress and growth of individuals and groups and linkage between assessment and intervention practices reducing the uncertainty about when and how to intervene.

Meisels, S. J. (1996). Charting the continuum of assessment and intervention. In S. J. Meisels & E. Fenichel (Eds.), *New visions for the developmental assessment of infants and young children,* (pp.27–52). Washington, DC: Zero to Three.
This chapter provides an overview of issues related to assessment and intervention with infants and toddlers. After describing different types of assessment and important developmental issues related to assessment, the relationship between assessment and intervention processes (different ways assessment can be tied with intervention) is further specified.

77 Best Practices in Measuring Growth and Development for Preschool Children

Scott R. McConnell, Jeffrey S. Priest, Shanna D. Davis, and Mary A. McEvoy
Early Childhood Research Institute on Measuring Growth and Development
Center on Early Education and Development
University of Minnesota

OVERVIEW

This chapter describes Individual Growth and Development Indicators (IGDIs) for preschool-aged children. IGDIs are quick, efficient, and repeatable measures of correlates or components of developmental performance designed for use with children 30–66 months of age. Preschool IGDIs sample child performance in each major developmental domain (i.e., language, social, cognitive, motor, and adaptive), with a special emphasis on assessment related to long-term developmental outcomes that are common across the early childhood years, are functional, and are related to later competence in home, school, and community settings (Priest et al., in press). Preschool IGDIs are one of a growing class of general outcome measures (like curriculum-based measurement) for monitoring child development and achievement and for producing data that support an ongoing and comprehensive decision-making or problem-solving model of assessment and intervention (c.f., Deno, 1997).

The purpose of this chapter is to provide a broad overview of preschool IGDIs, including foundational information on their development and evaluation and practical information on their application both individually and as part of a decision-making model of assessment and intervention. Preschool IGDIs are still in a fairly early stage of research, development, and evaluation. Readers interested in monitoring recent work on these tools may want to consult http://ici2.umn.edu/ecri.

In the first section of this chapter we will describe how IGDIs can be seen as one part of a comprehensive early childhood education program, the ways in which they contribute to a decision-making approach to assessment and intervention, and the background information and skill needed to use them. In the section on "Best Practices," we will describe preschool IGDIs already developed and those currently under development, and provide some examples of application for these measures. Finally, in an annotated bibliography at the end of this chapter, we provide a few additional references for more information on general outcome measurement and preschool IGDIs.

Overview of IGDIs

As their name suggests, preschool IGDIs are *indicators* of child status in different developmental domains. As indicators, these measures are not considered comprehensive all-inclusive samples of child performance in a particular domain or area of functioning. Rather, these measures are meant to be simpler components or correlates of more comprehensive measures or samples of child performance on the terminal skill in a particular domain.

Preschool IGDIs are specifically designed to help teachers and parents *monitor developmental growth* of individual children over time. This focus on growth will help practitioners identify children needing early intervention, and monitor the effects of such intervention so that long-term outcomes can be improved. Additionally, we expect preschool IGDIs to be used for screening children in potential need of intervention, evaluating programs, and other applications (c.f., Shinn, 1998).

A summary of essential characteristics for individual growth and development indicators can be found in Table 1. Two basic principles underlie these essential characteristics. First and foremost, IGDIs must *represent performance in the presumed developmental domain and general outcome.* Technically, this means preschool IGDIs must demonstrate criterion or construct validity, treatment validity (or sensitivity to the effects of interventions targeting a particular developmental outcome), and social validity (evidence that information helps teachers and parents make decisions about a specific developmental outcome).

Second, preschool IGDIs must also *provide an index of the rate of development or growth over time.* Growth or change is a powerful metaphor for all educational programs, and is especially appropriate for evaluation in early childhood education. Through frequent and repeated assessment, and by using common measurement procedures and metrics, preschool IGDIs (like other general outcome measures) produce empirical "movies" of the rate of change in a particular domain over time. Parents and educational professionals with this information can evaluate the extent to which a child is on a developmental path to achieve desired outcomes at later ages (for instance, whether a preschool child is on trajectory to be an independent reader by the end of third grade).

As depicted in Figure 1, the growth trajectory produced by repeated administration of preschool IGDIs can be used to answer a number of different questions, such as (a) What is the child's current level of performance compared to a normative group of similar age? (b) What is the child's projected rate of growth and development, and on the basis of this information, does it appear likely the child will reach a desired long-term goal by the desired age or date? (c) What is the effect of intervention on the child's rate of growth and development, and does this particular intervention improve the child's chances of reaching the desired long-term goal?

Guidelines for Use

Preschool IGDIs should be used in instances where psychologists, teachers, and other program staff want to measure, record, and act on information about young children's rates of growth and development toward long-term developmentally important goals. This assessment may be completed to monitor children not receiving specialized intervention, to identify children who might benefit from such intervention, and to monitor the effects of such intervention. Preschool IGDIs can be employed in regular early childhood programs with a stable cadre of enrolled students, or in community-based programs where children are seen more periodically by educational or other child service professionals. Further,

Table 1. Essential Characteristics of Individual Growth and Development Indicators

Characteristic	*Rationale*
Assess behaviors related to important outcomes for children	Construct and social validity; likelihood of implementation in range of settings
Efficient and economical administration and scoring	For ease of use, particularly with large samples in repeated fashion
Standardized and replicable procedures	Minimize error due to administration variations
Repeatable over time	Frequent, repeated assessment for monitoring rate of growth
Reliable across occasions, administrators, and stimulus materials	Reliability of assessment information
Sensitive to growth over time	Essential for assessment of developmental progress
Sensitive to the effects of intervention	Essential for monitoring effects of intervention

Figure 1. Sample preschool IGDI

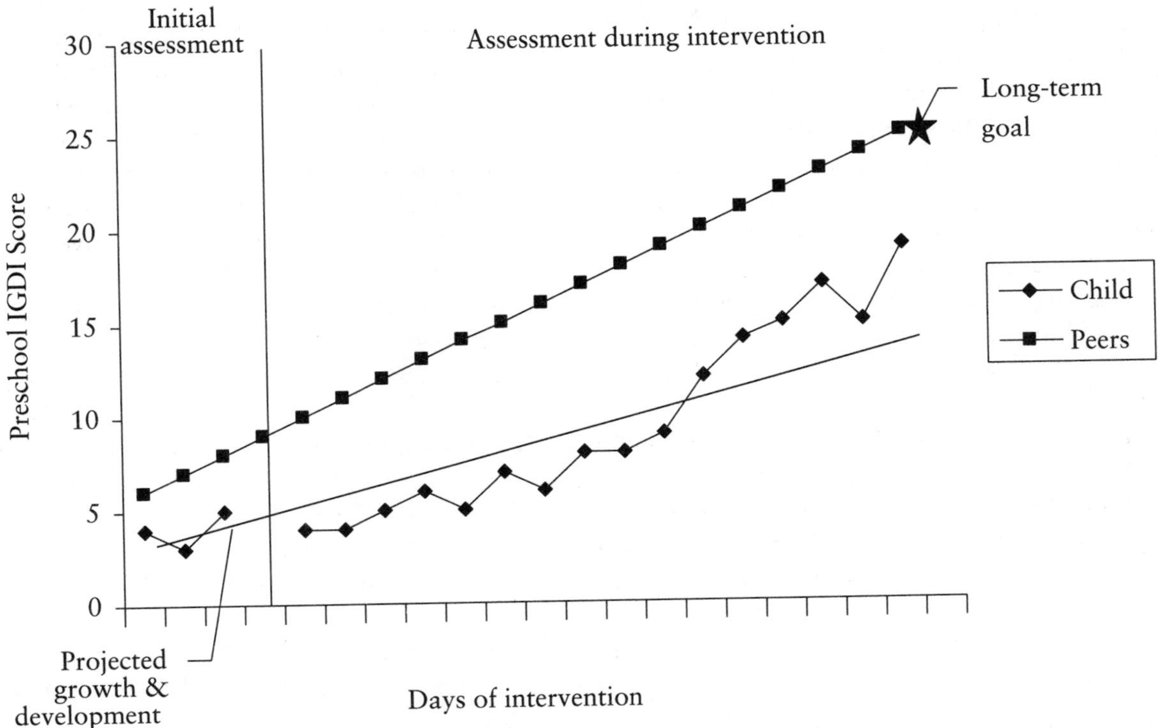

given the standardized and easy-to-use features of these measures, data collection and management can be conducted by psychologists or others with advanced training in child assessment, as well as by teachers, paraprofessionals, volunteers, or others. (When paraprofessionals or volunteers conduct large portions of assessment, an overall plan and ongoing monitoring of assessment results and utilization should be monitored by a professional with more in-depth knowledge and experience.)

To date, preschool IGDIs have only been used experimentally in child-serving programs. We expect, however, that application will include a variety of purposes:

1. Screening and other normative comparisons of children in the general population, or those served in a program or classroom.

2. Identification of need for intervention (or change in intervention), and/or selection of individual children for intervention.

3. Evaluation of effects of intervention.

4. Program evaluation efforts.

In spite of their relative youth, IGDIs build on a strong conceptual and empirical foundation in the design, evaluation, and application of general outcome measures. As a result, by sticking closely to the models provided by earlier research and development (Deno, 1997; Shinn, 1998), we can offer in this chapter an early view of the possible benefits of these measures for preschool-aged children.

BASIC CONSIDERATIONS

Preschool IGDIs, like other general outcome measures, are intended to be both highly replicable and easy to use. Nonetheless, proper application and interpretation of IGDIs requires familiarity with *background information* (including information on assessment in early childhood education, general outcome measurement, and decision-making models). Additionally, skilled use of preschool IGDIs requires specific *background knowledge and skills*, including information on basic test administration, data management skills, and interpretation and treatment planning. These issues are addressed briefly in the following sections.

Background Information

Assessment in Early Childhood Education

Assessment in early childhood education has a shorter history, and more diversity of opinion (and controversy) regarding its scope and appropriateness, than assessment for children in K–12 education. Nonetheless, there is a strong tradition of assessment in early childhood education, particularly for children with special needs (Fewell, 2000; McLean, Bailey, & Wolery, 1996).

Akin to practices for older children, assessment in early childhood education covers a number of different functions. Perhaps most common in early childhood education is *assessment for screening* to identify children who may need additional evaluation or early intervention. Universal preschool screening programs are common in many states, and a variety of checklists, tests, and systems have been developed to support these efforts. Additionally, in the past few decades increased attention has been paid to *assessment for determining eligibility*, especially for special education and related services. Again, a number of checklists, interviews, tests, and systems have been developed to support eligibility evaluations, often in direct response to state and federal laws governing special education.

Other assessment tools for young children have also emerged. Recently, a variety of systems have been developed for *planning intervention programs* (e.g., Barnett, Ehrhardt, Stollar, & Bauer, 1994; Bricker & Pretti-Frontczak, 1996). Generally, these assessment systems relate either to formal or informal developmental sequences, or to explicit curricula (Bricker & Waddell, 1996) for early childhood education.

Closely related, a small number of systems for *monitoring developmental progress and evaluating effects of intervention* have been offered in recent years. In select instances, these monitoring systems are tied directly to program planning and curriculum (as with Bricker's *Assessment and Evaluation Performance System*). In other instances, these systems are free-standing tools based on standard or generic developmental sequences (Meisels, Liaw, Dorfman, & Nelson, 1995). To date, however, most progress monitoring systems for young children represent "critical skills mastery" approaches, with some inherent weaknesses for monitoring progress and evaluating change (McConnell, 2000). In particular, these critical skills mastery approaches are often cumbersome to administer, provide little information for making comparative evaluations of individual children, and provide no information about rate of growth over time nor rate of progress toward long-term desired outcomes.

As we continue to refine assessment practices for young children and their families, several specific conceptual and social-political issues must be confronted. These issues include:

1. *Professionals and parents have a lack of clarity and agreement regarding the developmental goals, or "outcomes," for early childhood education.* Early childhood education has long been saddled with internal debates over the scope and direction of intervention (e.g., "readiness" versus "skills" goals, "child-directed" versus "adult-directed" intervention; cf. Carta, Schwartz, Atwater, & McConnell, 1991). At the same time, there is little conceptual clarity or empirical support for developmental outcomes that prepare children to meet the academic and behavioral standards of early elementary school. Without a clear sense of important functional and developmental outcomes for early childhood education, it will be difficult to develop a monitoring system that is widely accepted and implemented.

2. *There is an associated ambiguity about "curriculum" in early childhood education, and thus ambiguity about standards against which children should be evaluated.* Without agreement and empirical support for particular developmental outcomes, it is impossible to identify specific experiences and opportunities that promote young children's long-term success. And without this information, professionals in early childhood education have little external guidance about what services to provide at any stage of evaluation.

3. *Preschool children do not have universal access to educational services, thus reducing the number of children served in publicly funded programs.* While the United States may be moving toward some version of universal access to educational ser-

vices for preschool-aged children, at the turn of the twenty-first century publicly funded programs are available primarily for children with developmental or other disabilities (served through special education), children living in poverty (served through Head Start and related programs), and children with other perceived special needs or risk factors. There has been tremendous growth in the numbers of children served in congregate care situations such as day care, but there is very little explicit, common, and systematic organization of these services in ways that would support expanded assessment activities.

As a result, any assessment system in early childhood education must address several challenges. First, these assessment systems must be based on explicit definitions of the outcomes of interest, and provide evidence of the construct and social validity of these outcomes (e.g. Priest et al., in press). Second, early education assessment systems must articulate linkages between items or constructs to both earlier and later development and functioning, especially in academic domains considered important for early school success (e.g., reading). Last, assessment systems in early childhood education must be developed, evaluated, and applied across a broad spectrum of children, including those with disabilities, those at risk for learning and behavior problems (including children whose primary language is not English), and those children who are developing typically.

General Outcome Measurement Approach

Two different approaches to assessment for monitoring progress are emerging in early childhood education, similar to what has occurred in elementary and secondary education (McConnell, 2000). These two approaches have been characterized as critical skill mastery approaches and general outcome measurement approaches (Deno, 1997; Fuchs & Deno, 1991).

Critical skills mastery has been the dominant approach to assessment in early childhood education to this point (McConnell, 2000). This approach is characterized by assessment of separate discrete skills that are assumed to be developmentally linked and ordered in a sequence or hierarchy. Critical skills mastery approaches can help practitioners evaluate a child's current developmental status, and can be a strong foundation for program planning assessments. However, these approaches are poorly suited to monitoring the rate of development over time, assessing a child's progress toward long-term goals, or assessing child performance in an integrated, comprehensive, and authentic way.

Conversely, general outcome measurement lends itself to direct assessment of growth and development over time. Instead of breaking skills down into pieces and gathering incomparable measures of these different pieces, general outcome measurement allows the practitioner to continually measure a student's progress over time. General outcome measurement is characterized by the use of standardized prescriptive procedures and long-term measurement that remains constant over time (Fuchs & Deno, 1991). Performance in a particular domain is measured with repeated and direct observations of performance, using common metrics and comparable stimulus materials. Slope of progress over time is used as an indicator of progress in the entire domain or curriculum. Increases or decreases in the slope over time indicate the developmental rate of learning new skills (Fuchs & Deno, 1991). Because general outcome measurement samples a broad domain, growth (or no growth) indicates that the student is or is not making progress toward a specified outcome. General outcome measurement lends itself to treatment or intervention monitoring because of the broad sampling across domains and the measurement of progress over time using slope.

As a result, general outcome measures provide direct assessment of child progress toward a long-term goal. Further, because common metrics are used across time, general outcome measures yield data that index both current level of development and (if administered repeatedly) rate of development. Also, because common measures are employed and tools are explicitly designed for repeated and frequent assessment, general outcome measures are a good match to the task of evaluating the effects of intervention over short periods.

While a variety of critical skills mastery measurement systems have been available in early childhood education for some time (e.g., Bricker & Waddell, 1996; Meisels et al., 1995), general outcome measurement approaches are just beginning to appear (McConnell, 2000). Preschool IGDIs, along with similar measures for infants and toddlers and for early elementary students, and Dynamic Indicators of Basic Early Literacy Skills (Dibels (Good & Gruba, this volume), are examples of these recently-developed general outcome measures.

Decision-Making Model

Preschool IGDIs are part of a more comprehensive decision-making model for monitoring development and providing intervention to children from birth to age 8 (Early Childhood Research Institute on Measuring Growth and Development, 1998). This decision-making model, which is conceptually very similar to other problem-solving models in school psychology and special education (see Tilly, this volume), is designed to identify children in need of intervention, to plan that intervention explicitly, and to monitor the effects of intervention services over time. Figure 2 presents a simplified version of this decision-making model.

This model, like other versions, is *recursive*; that is, individual children typically cycle through different stages or portions of this model. Preschool IGDIs are used to monitor development over time. When performance on one or repeated assessments indicates that children are not making desired rates of progress toward a long-term goal, intervention is designed and implemented (the decision-making variation presented here anticipates future refinement of a new class of assessment tools, "exploring solutions assessments," to provide empirical support for, and reduce the uncertainty in, developing interventions for individual children). As intervention begins, IGDI assessment continues to document the effects of that change in service on the child's development toward the long-term goal. If intervention is successful, then monitoring continues. If intervention does not produce desired results, then the model recycles back to design, implementation, and evaluation of additional intervention.

Figure 2. A simplified version of this decision-making model

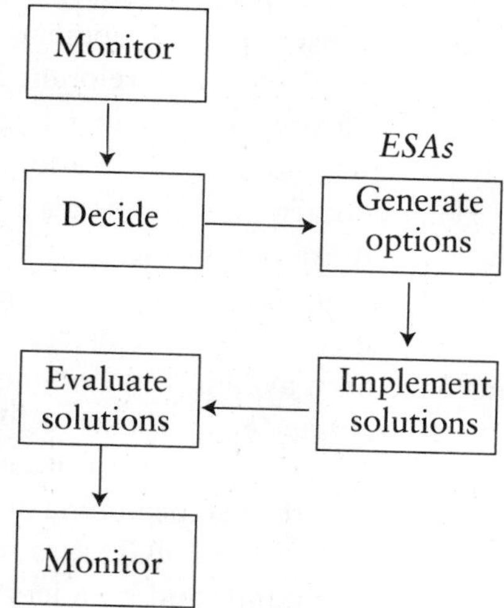

Background Knowledge and Skills

Test Administration

Because preschool IGDIs are specific and precise measures used to indicate progress, an understanding of basic test administration is needed. In particular, administrators of IGDIs must use constant and standardized procedures across children and test occasions. Specific skills include administering procedures in standardized ways, familiarity with administration and scoring procedures, adherence to testing protocols, following standard rules for interpreting and reporting results, and using pace, tempo, and structure to engage the child.

Data Management

While single administration of IGDIs may be useful in some instances, the full power of continuous progress monitoring comes through repeated administration of IGDIs to individual children over extended periods. To obtain the full benefit from this effort, teachers and school psychologists must have efficient and effective tools for storing, managing, and displaying their assessment data to support intervention decision making. Basic management of data consists of recording and graphing the number of correct responses over time (see Figure 1 for example). Time in days or weeks is recorded on the horizontal axis and correct number of responses is recorded on the vertical axis. Individual performance over time can be summarized, typically by calculating and graphing a trend line and interpreting this line based on pre-specified long-term criteria. (At the time this chapter was prepared, we did not yet have sufficient normative data to provide information for evaluating either initial status nor progress over time. Readers are encouraged to check http:www.ici2.umn.edu/ecri for more up-to-date information.)

These tasks can be accomplished with pencil and graph paper or a computer program such as Excel®. A number of professional resources describe procedures for continuous-progress monitoring (e.g., Shinn, 1989; Howell, Fox, & Morehead, 1997; or materials produced at the University of Oregon, Minneapolis (Minn. Public Schools, St. Croix River (Minn. Education District, or Heartland (Iowa) Area Education Agency.)

Interpretation and Treatment Planning

IGDI data collected over time and graphed can be used to answer questions about intervention need (e.g., *Is this child's development on path to meet our long-term goal?*) as well as treatment effectiveness (e.g., *Is my new intervention producing higher rates of growth for this child?*). To answer questions like these, IGDI users must be able to interpret current status and plan changes in treatment when needed.

Normative standards have been developed for some existing general outcome measures, most notably, curriculum-based measures of reading, mathematics, and written expression (Shinn, 1998). Normative datasets have been developed locally, assessing all children in classrooms or districts, and discussions have considered whether more general normative standards can be derived (Shinn, 1988). These normative standards provide one basis for evaluating both the status and developmental trajectory of individual children and groups and may prove helpful for users of preschool IGDIs. To date, however, few formal normative evaluations have been completed, and readers interested in nomothetic comparisons will need to develop local norms, following procedures described elsewhere for curriculum-based measures (c.f., Shinn, 1998).

Interpretation skills for general outcome measures have been described elsewhere (Deno, 1985; Shinn, 1989, 1998). In general, interpretation of IGDIs or other general outcome measures require comparing one child's current rate of development to either predicted long-term status (a "long-term goal") or to a desired rate of growth over time (an "aim line"). As in Figure 1, observed level and trend of child performance can be compared to a long-term goal or a continuous aim line, and teachers or parents can make judgments about whether the child's current rate of development is on-track, given both general and individual-specific goals.

While IGDIs are well-suited to monitoring and evaluating developmental status and treatment effectiveness, they provide little information for planning changes in treatment. Rather, interventionists and support professionals must turn to other data sources, including interviews and observations or curriculum-based assessment to achieve this aim (e.g., Barnett et al., 1994; Bricker & Pretti-Frontczak, 1996). Such "exploring solutions" assessments might detail critical behaviors and skills to be acquired (perhaps in a developmental or skills hierarchy), the naturally occurring or structured situations in which instructional opportunities might be embedded to teach these skills, and opportunities for both generalization programming and inclusion of the child in age-typical activities and settings.

BEST PRACTICES: INDIVIDUAL GROWTH AND DEVELOPMENT INDICATORS FOR PRESCHOOL CHILDREN

As part of the Early Childhood Research Institute on Measuring Growth and Development (see also Greenwood & Luze, this volume, and Good & Guba, this volume), we have been developing and evaluating a set of preschool IGDIs related directly to specific developmental and educational outcomes. In this section we describe specific procedures and evaluation results for IGDIs developed to date, as well as our plans for future development. We also provide an example of how IGDIs can be used in an early childhood education setting.

Expressive Language

Indicators of individual preschooler's growth of expressive language skills have been developed with the following outcome statement as a guide: *Child uses gestures, sounds, words, or sentences (including sign language and augmentative or alternative communication) to convey wants and needs or to express meaning to others.* Two indicators appear promising: (a) Picture Naming Fluency and (b) Semi-Structured Play.

Picture Naming. This preschool IGDI is completed by presentation of photographs and detailed color line drawings of objects commonly found in preschoolers' natural environments (i.e., home, classroom, community) one at a time for 1 minute. The measure of expressive meaning is the number of pictures identified correctly in 1 minute. Categories of objects used in this format include animals, food, people, household objects, games and sports materials, vehicles, tools, and clothing. Each photograph and line drawing is printed on an 8 x 5–inch index card. The examiner demonstrates the task with a set of four cards, looking at each card, naming the object as quickly as possible, and moving to the next card. The child practices the task with the same set of sample cards named by the examiner, ensuring the child understands the importance of speed in naming the pictures. The examiner then shuffles the entire deck of cards, presents the card at the top of the deck, and starts a stopwatch. Acceptable names for each object are printed on the back of each card to help the examiner determine the correctness of the child's labels. Incorrectly named pictures include errors and omissions. If the child does not respond to a picture within 3 seconds of its presentation, then the examiner asks the child, "Do you know what that is?" or "What's that?" If the child does not respond within an additional two seconds, then the examiner shows the next card. After exactly 1 minute has expired, the examiner stops the activity and counts the total number of pictures named correctly.

Studies of the psychometric properties of this measure—total number of pictures named correctly in 1 minute—have generated strong evidence for its use as an indicator of growth of preschoolers' expressive language skills. Results have shown strong concurrent relationships between this Picture Naming measure and norm-referenced measures of preschoolers' language skills, including the *Peabody Picture Vocabulary Test*, (3rd ed.) (PPVT-III) (Dunn & Dunn, 1997) and the *Preschool Language Scale, 3* (PLS-3) (Zimmerman, Steiner, & Pond, 1992), with correlation coefficients ranging from $r = .47$ to .69 (Priest, Davis, McConnell, McEvoy, & Shinn, 1999). Picture Naming also appears sensitive to growth of preschoolers' expressive language skills over time, with significant correlations between children's scores and chronological age ($r = .41$ in a longitudinal study and $r = .60$ in a cross-sectional study), including typically developing children ($r = .63$), children enrolled in Head Start ($r = .32$) and children with disabilities receiving services in early childhood special education classrooms ($r = .48$). Additionally, Picture Naming is sensitive to growth across time ($b_1 = .34$, $p < .01$) and has 1-month alternate form reliability coefficients from $r = .44$ to .78. Picture Naming easily evokes expressive language from preschoolers, and it appears easy for examiners to learn and administer repeatedly across time.

Field testing of Picture Naming is currently underway in a large district in central Iowa and an urban district in Minnesota. These efforts have been undertaken to substantiate continued use of this indicator to track preschoolers' growth of their expressive language skills, as well as expand the normative pool of children to which the measure applies. Eventually this information will help create benchmarks for school psychologists and others to use to make decisions about individual children's growth trajectories and based on comparisons to norm groups.

Semi-Structured Play. In this format, two peers (typically the same age and sex) play in a setting away from others. Each pair is provided with a pre-selected set of materials that can be used in multiple, imaginative ways (e.g., Legos, Duplos, blocks, toy house, toy people). The examiner tells the children to work together to make something with the materials, walks away from the immediate area, and then starts a stopwatch. The examiner does not interact with children during the activity unless one child (or both children) leaves the area or adult intervention is needed to resolve a conflict. After exactly 10 minutes, the examiner stops the activity.

During the activity, the examiner observes one child's verbal behavior by using a 10-second partial-interval observational tool. This tool measures two child-produced behaviors per interval: an intelligible utterance of three or fewer words and an intelligible utterance of four or more words. Once the observer completes the 10-minute observation, the observer calculates two scores: the total number of intervals in which the child produced an utterance of three or fewer words and the total number of intervals in which the child produced an utterance of four or more words.

Research to date suggests that one of these measures—the total number of intervals in which the child produces an utterance of four or more words—is the best measure from this format for use as an indicator of preschoolers' growth in expressive language skills. Concurrent relationships between this measure and norm-referenced measures of preschoolers' language skills—the PPVT-III and PLS-3—appear moderate, with correlation coefficients ranging from $r = .33$ to $.43$ (Priest et al., 1999). However, this measure may not be sufficiently sensitive to growth over time, since correlations between the measure and chronological age range from $r = .25$ for children receiving early childhood special education services to $r = .29$ for typically developing children. One-month alternate form reliability coefficients for the observational measure range from $r = .25$ to $.79$. Learning to score this measure appears straightforward for most observers, based on strong results from tests of inter-observer reliability.

In summary, at least two measures—Picture Naming and an observational measure of four-or-more word utterances—show promise for assessing growth and development of expressive language for preschool-aged children. In particular, the Picture Naming measure shows promise as a logistically simple measure with strong psychometric properties.

Early Literacy

We have begun development of preschool IGDIs specifically designed to assess preschool children's progress in early literacy development. While a broader set of measures will emerge in coming years, three formats have already been developed and evaluated that assess phonemic awareness and analysis of preschool-aged children. Phonemic awareness and analysis is widely seen as a critical element of early reading success (Adams, 1990; Snow, Burns, & Griffin, 1998), and there is clear evidence that development of these skills begins during the preschool years (Lonigan, Burgess, Anthony, & Barker, 1998; Whitehurst & Lonigan, 1998). These three formats assess alliteration, rhyming, and phonemic blending.

Alliteration. Our measure of alliteration was adapted from the work of Lonigan et al. (1998). We identified a set of words commonly known to preschool children, then assembled stimulus cards to present a color line drawing of the stimulus word (e.g., *boat*), and, under that, a row of three randomly ordered line-drawn pictures depicting the correct response (e.g., *butterfly*) and two incorrect responses (e.g., *lamp* and *chair*). During testing the administrator tells the child that the child will be asked to "look at some pictures and find the ones that start with the same sound." The administrator provides a series of sample items, both demonstrating the task and leading the child through it until the child understands the requirements.

Data collection continues for 2 minutes. For each card the examiner labels the stimulus picture and the three possible responses, then asks the child to "point to the one that starts with the same sound as [the stimulus word]." To assess alliteration, the number of correct responses in 2 minutes is counted.

While research continues on this measure, early analyses of psychometric characteristics are quite promising. Our first pilot test, with 38 preschool-aged children, yielded strong correlations to measures of language (with PPVT-III, $r = .57$) and early literacy, including Clay's *Concepts About Print* (Clay, 1977) ($r = .55$), letter identification ($r = .74$), and the *Test of Phonological Awareness* ($r = .75$). Early results also suggest this alliteration measure is sensitive to growth over time, and the number of words identified correctly in 2 minutes correlated significantly ($r = .61$) with children's chronological age. These analyses are being replicated and extended in a larger longitudinal study.

Rhyming. The Rhyming IGDI uses a format similar to the Alliteration measure, and was also adapted from work by Lonigan et al. (1998). Again, we identified a set of words commonly known to preschool children, but then identified rhymes for each of these words. We selected rhyming pairs where both words were likely to be known to preschool children, and assembled cards presenting a color line drawing of the stimulus word (e.g., *hat*) above a line of three randomly ordered pictures depicting the correct response (e.g., *cat*) and two incorrect responses (e.g., *house* and *shoe*).

During testing the examiner teaches the child what "rhyme" means ("Listen to these words: *bat*, *mat*, *hat*, *cat*. They all sound alike; they rhyme. *Cat* and *Sam* don't sound alike; they do not rhyme. Listen: *boy* and *toy* rhyme. Do *boy* and *car* rhyme? (no) Do *car* and *bar* rhyme? (yes)") then tells the child that the child will be asked to "look at some pictures and find the ones that sound alike. They rhyme." The examiner presents a series of demonstration and practice items, continuing until the child understands the task requirements. Data collection continues for 2 minutes. For each card the examiner labels the stimulus picture and the three possible responses, then asks the child to "point to the one that sounds the same as [stimulus picture]." To assess rhyming, the number of correct responses in 2 minutes is counted.

Our early research produced promising, but not quite as strong, evidence of the psychometric properties for this Rhyming measure. The Rhyming IGDI showed strong correlation to the PPVT-III (r = .56) and measures of early literacy, including Clay's *Concepts about Print* (r = .54), letter identification (r = .59), and the *Test of Phonological Awareness* (r = .62). Pilot testing also suggested a significant, but lower, relation to chronological age (r = .44), suggesting this measure might be somewhat sensitive to growth over time. Current research is extending these analyses.

Phoneme Blending. Phoneme Blending is assessed via oral presentation of stimulus words. A shuffled deck of stimulus cards is used to present a list of typically known words. Approximately one third of the items in this list require blending at the level of compound words (e.g., *cow – boy*), one third require blending at the level of syllables (e.g., *ta – ble*), and one third require blending at the level of phonemes (e.g., *r – a – m*). Order of presentation is randomized by shuffling the deck before each administration, so that each examination includes items of all three types, in roughly equal proportions.

The examiner reads previously specified segments, with one-half second pause between segments. The child is told "I'm going to say a word in a funny way and I want you to listen closely and tell me what word I said." Again, the child receives a series of demonstration and training items, and then administration begins. This measure of early literacy is expressed as the number of correct responses in 2 minutes.

Early results for Phoneme Blending, while promising, are not as strong or consistent as those for Alliteration or Rhyming measures. Phoneme Blending is related to performance on the PPVT-III (r = .49) and the early literacy measures (*Concepts about Print* (r = .35), letter identification (r = .28), and *Test of Phonological Awareness* (r = .47)), and significantly but weakly correlated with chronological age (r = .30). It is possible that this measure is too difficult for younger and less-skilled children, and as a result we have obtained floor effects. These issues, and replication of initial findings, are being examined in current research.

Social Interaction

Our work to date has also focused on measures of the development of social interaction skills. Specifically, we have developed indicators for the following outcome: *Child interacts with peers and adults, maintaining social interactions and participating socially in home, school, and community settings.* We are interested in assessing children's success in initiating social interaction with peers, responding to others' interactions, engaging in cooperative play, and knowing how to solve problems. These *key elements* of social interaction were selected based on a comprehensive review of the literature, as well as interviews with practitioners and researchers who had experience working with young children in play settings.

Two IGDI formats—Play Ideas and Joint Play—have been developed to serve as indicators of child-child interaction. For the first, Play Ideas Picture Prompts, the experimenter presents the child with a photo of the child's own playground or classroom. The picture includes areas of the classroom or playground that are typically used for free play. The experimenter asks the child to "pretend that you are going here with a friend." The child is then asked to name "all of the things that you and a friend could do together" in the area. For the second, Play Ideas Verbal Prompts, the experimenter tells the child that "a friend and I are going into your classroom (or playground) to play together." Again the child is asked to name as many things as possible that can be done together. With both the verbal and picture prompts, we count the total number of Play Ideas (number of novel activity ideas and number of novel interactive activity ideas) that a child generates during a 3-minute time period.

Joint Play is measured during a semi-structured play activity. This format includes the target child and one other child, typically of the same sex and comparable age. We have evaluated two different versions of this format. First, we present the children with "silly face" pieces (eyes, ears, nose, mouth, mustache, etc.) and a card with a blank face on it. We ask the children to "work together to make the blank face into a silly face." In a second version, we present the children with a puzzle form, and each child is given one-half of the puzzle pieces. We ask the children to play together to finish the puzzle. In each of the versions, children play for 5 minutes. We record the duration of joint play (defined as a child actively engaging in the same activity as a peer) during this 5-minute period.

Early results of our evaluations of these social interaction measures are promising. Duration of

Joint Play for one format (making silly faces) showed moderate correlations with observer ratings of social competence (r = .40) and teacher ranking of social interaction (r = .43). Additionally, duration of Joint Play in this format was strongly related to child age (r = .58), suggesting its sensitivity to growth over time. Correlations for the second Joint Play format, building puzzles, were generally lower and nonsignificant with all criterion measures (r = .09 to .34), suggesting that the settings in which these data are collected may influence the meaningfulness of scores.

Future research will evaluate the feasibility of using these IGDIs to assess developmental trajectories for young children with identified social interaction deficits, as well as those who may be at-risk for interaction delays. It is anticipated that these indicators will help teachers and families target children who may need additional assessment and possible intervention.

IGDIs Under Development

Future efforts to develop new growth indicators will focus on preschoolers' skills in two domains: motor and adaptive. In the motor domain, the underlying outcome-guiding development of a growth indicator (or indicators) states: *Child moves in a fluent and coordinated manner to play and participate in home, school, and community settings*. Important elements of this outcome for preschoolers include development of locomotion skills, such as walking, running, and jumping, as well as object control skills, such as throwing, catching, and kicking (Burton & Miller, 1998). These elements will be used to formulate potential formats within which preschoolers' movement skills may be observed directly.

In the adaptive domain, the guiding outcome states: *Child engages in a range of basic self-help skills, including but not limited to skills in dressing, eating, toileting/hygiene, and safety/identification.* Factor analyses indicate this outcome represents one component of practical intelligence, which in turn embodies just one of perhaps five dimensions of adaptive skills (Thompson, McGrew, & Bruininks, 1999). For preschoolers, however, these self-care skills may play an even more important role in overall development of personal competence compared to older children, since the construct of adaptive behavior in early childhood appears less differentiated than it is for children beyond preschool (McGrew & Bruininks, 1990). Thus, these self-help skills will serve as essential elements of an indicator of preschoolers' growth in adaptive behavior.

Application Example: Monitoring Progress

Although preschool IGDIs are relatively new, our work to date has given us opportunities to use these measures in several community-based preschool programs. In one example, a school psychologist (the third author) and two classroom teachers implemented a continuous assessment program to monitor progress for children in three early childhood special education classrooms, with eventual focus on three particular children.

Wadsworth Community School is an hypothetical elementary school with a large Early Childhood Special Education program located in a large urban school district. Wadsworth serves 39 preschool children with disabilities in eight classroom sessions. Three classrooms, serving 15 children with developmental delays, participated in baseline data collection using Picture Naming IGDIs. Data were collected in the classrooms twice a week for 5 weeks.

These data were then used to identify individual children who might benefit from some change in their program of intervention. To select participants, the teachers and school psychologist identified children who had flat or decreasing slopes in Picture Naming scores across the 5-week period. Teachers also considered whether students demonstrated potential for growth in expressive communication through a combination of existing preskills, participation in intervention, and absence of competing behaviors.

From this process, the team identified three boys, ages 4-11 to 5-1, for more frequent monitoring and intervention evaluation. All three children were receiving speech and language and other special education services under the category of "Developmental Delay."

The school psychologist collected additional information to plan interventions (c.f., Barnett et al., 1994). Intervention planning data included language samples, information on classroom variables known to contribute to language development, and information on interactions between the boys and their teachers, peers, and classroom materials.

On the basis of assessment of classroom activities, child behaviors, and staff resources, the team designed a peer-mediated language intervention. The three target students were paired with typically developing peers in a structured play setting in 20-minute play groups three times per week. IGDI data were collected twice a week during the 2-month intervention phase to monitor changes in child growth and development. Weekly meetings were held with the two teachers to share data and discuss progress and/or changes.

The results of the progress monitoring can be seen in Figure 3. In two of the three cases, Alex and Ben, students responded positively to the change in intervention. Ben's rate of Picture Naming increased, both in level and slope, after the beginning of intervention; and this result is consistent with a change in developmental trajectory as a function of intervention. Similarly, Alex's rate of Picture Naming increased in slope, with intervention assessments more closely approximating the level demonstrated by typically developing peers. Conversely, Stuart's rate of Picture Naming after intervention showed little reliable change in slope or trend, and change in intervention toward the end of the school year produced little effect on his variable rate of Picture Naming.

Future Directions

In coming years we expect continued development of preschool IGDIs, as well as increased numbers of research studies and practical applications using preschool IGDIs to improve assessment and intervention outcomes for young children with disabilities and other risk factors. After initial development of IGDIs in all developmental domains, we project continued improvement and refinement of existing measures. Indeed, we expect the measures (and results) reported here to be only an initial baseline for the expected quality of these measures. We also hope that others will develop new measures for preschool children, meeting the criteria for general outcome measures outlined by Fuchs and Deno (1991) and summarized in Table 1. Also, we expect applications of preschool IGDIs to follow and replicate the path seen in the use of other general outcome measures, including curriculum-based measurement (c.f., Shinn, 1998).

Two elaborations of preschool IGDIs are already underway. First, our research team is developing *Get it, Got it, Go!, a* web-based application for helping teachers obtain assessment materials, manage resulting data, and collaborate with others on the design and evaluation of intervention programs. Second, we are actively exploring links between preschool IGDIs and general outcome measures in similar domains for infants and toddlers and for early elementary students.

Get it, Got it, Go!

Our work, and that of our colleagues who have developed other general outcome measures, consistently points to the need for a technological infrastructure to support teachers' selection and implementation of these tools. To begin addressing this need, we are developing a multi-component web site for teachers, administrators, researchers, and parents.

The first part of this site, *Get it*, will provide information on the characteristics of general outcome measures, as well as detailed information on implementation in classrooms and programs. This portion of the site will also provide files for downloading and printing that provide both detailed administration instructions and stimulus materials (where needed) for individual preschool IGDIs.

The second portion of this web site, *Got it*, will help teachers who have already begun using preschool IGDIs. The site will provide password-controlled access to a secure area where teachers can enter individual student data, produce reports of child status and/or growth over time, and compare individual results to groups in the teacher's classroom, district, or a national database.

The third portion of this web site, *Go!*, will support teachers interested in using preschool IGDI data to plan and evaluate changes in intervention. Teachers will "invite" others—including parents, colleagues, building and district consultants, or others—to a separate password-protected area where they will view data for a particular individual, and participate in a threaded discussion via email regarding interpretation, planning, and evaluating changes in intervention.

Links to I-IGDIs, E-IGDIs, DIBELS

Preschool IGDIs are one part of an emerging portfolio of general outcome measures, linking outcomes and assessments from birth (see Greenwood & Luze, this volume) to kindergarten and early elementary school (see Good & Guba, this volume) and later grades (see Shinn et al., Fuchs et al., and others, this

Figure 3. Three case studies: using individual growths and development indicators to evaluate intervention

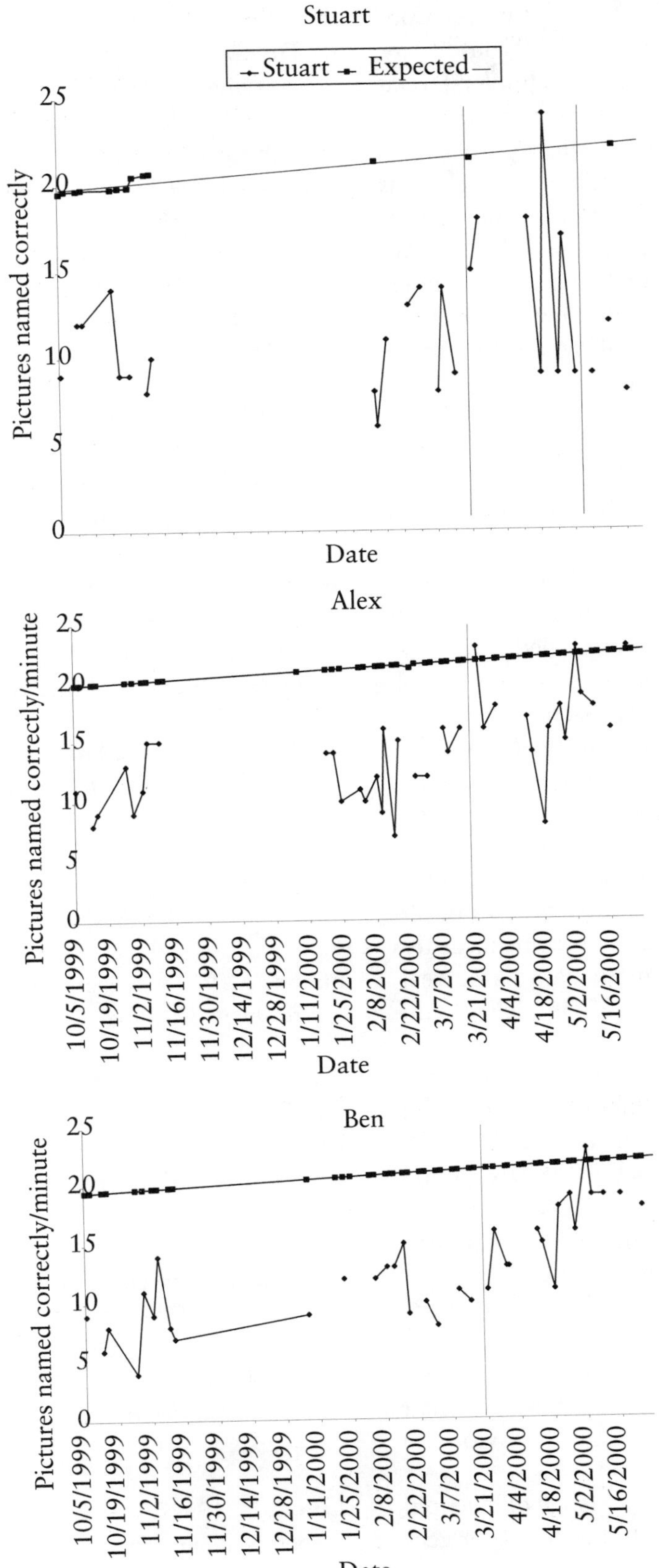

volume). To realize the potential of these measures *as a set*, our research is starting to examine relations between measures for different age groups (say, infants and toddlers compared to preschoolers), relations between *rates of growth* in one set and status on a second (say, relations between rates of growth in Early Literacy IGDIs and later reading), and relations between family and classroom variables and rates of growth within and across IGDIs and age periods. We expect results from this research to extend our understanding of assessment of developmental progress, and to advance our knowledge of the critical dimensions and outcomes of early intervention.

SUMMARY

School psychology researchers and practitioners are developing an expanding portfolio of *general outcome measures* for monitoring the growth and development of children from birth through secondary school. These measures are distinguished by administrative efficiency (they are cheap and easy to collect), psychometric quality (they possess high levels of inter-observer, alternate-forms, and test-retest reliability, as well as high levels of criterion, social, and treatment validity), and enhanced utility in school and community programs. In particular, these measures contribute to empirical evaluation of individual children's growth over time and the effects of different interventions. As such, general outcome measures are an essential component of many data-based decision-making (or "problem-solving") models of education and school psychology.

In this chapter we have described one part of this emerging portfolio of general outcome measures and individual growth and development indicators for preschool children. These preschool IGDIs sample child achievement and growth in developmentally and academically relevant domains, and hold particular promise for linking to similar general outcome measures for infants and toddlers and for elementary-aged students. To date, preschool IGDIs have been developed for expressive communication, early literacy, and social interaction. In the near future, similar measures will be available for adaptive behavior and gross motor functioning.

On the basis of our current knowledge of essential features and application opportunities for other general outcome measures (particularly curriculum-based measurement), we expect these preschool IGDIs to contribute to (a) improving procedures for identifying children with developmental delay, (b) monitoring development over time for individual preschoolers and groups of children, (c) implementing data-based decision-making models of intervention and evaluation for early childhood education programs, and (d) expanding research on developmental continuity in academic achievement, as well as the effects of different child, family, community, and service variables.

REFERENCES

Adams, M. (1990). *Beginning to read: Thinking and learning about print.* Cambridge MA: MIT Press.

Barnett, D. W., Ehrhardt, K. E., Stollar, S. A., & Bauer, A. M. (1994). PASSKey: A model for naturalistic assessment and intervention design. *Topics in Early Childhood Special Education, 14*(3), 350–373.

Bricker, D., & Pretti-Frontczak, K. (1996). *AEPS measurement for three to six years* (Vol. 3). Baltimore: Brookes.

Bricker, D., & Waddell, M. (1996). *AEPS curriculum for three to six years* (Vol. 4). Baltimore: Brookes.

Burton, A. W., & Miller, D. E. (1998). *Movement skill assessment.* Champaign, IL: Human Kinetics.

Carta, J. J., Schwartz, I. S., Atwater, J. B., & McConnell, S. R. (1991). Developmentally appropriate practice: Appraising its usefulness for young children with disabilities. *Topics in Early Childhood Special Education, 11*, 1–20.

Clay, M. M. (1979). *The early detection of reading difficulties: A diagnostic survey with recovery procedures.* Auckland, NZ: Heinemann Educational Books.

Deno, S. L. (1985). Curriculum-based measurement: The emerging alternative. *Exceptional Children, 52*(3), 219–232.

Deno, S. L. (1997). *Whether* thou goest ... Perspectives on progress monitoring. In J. W. Lloyd, E. J. Kame'enui, &

D. Chard (Eds.), *Issues in educating students with disabilities* (pp. 77–99). Mahwah, NJ: Erlbaum.

Dunn, L. M., & Dunn, L. M. (1997). *Peabody Picture Vocabulary Test* (3rd ed.). Circle Pines, MN: American Guidance Service.

Early Childhood Research Institute on Measuring Growth and Development. (1998). *Theoretical foundations of the Early Childhood Research Institute on Measuring Growth and Development: An early childhood problem-solving model* (Tech. Rep. No. 6). Minneapolis, MN: Center for Early Education and Development, University of Minnesota.

Fewell, R.R. (2000). Assessment of young children with special needs: Foundations for tomorrow. *Topics in Early Childhood Special Education, 20*, 38–42.

Fuchs, L. S. (1989). Evaluating solutions, monitoring progress, and revising intervention plans. In M. R. Shinn (Ed.), *Curriculum-based assessment: Assessing Special Children* (pp. 153–181). New York: Guilford.

Fuchs, L. S. & Deno, S. L. (1991). Paradigmatic distinctions between instructionally relevant measurement models. *Exceptional Children, 57*(6), 488–500.

Howell, K. W., Fox, S. L. & Morehead, M. K. (1994). *Curriculum-based evaluation: teaching and decision making* (2nd ed.). Pacific Grove: Brooks/Cole.

Lonigan, C. J., Burgess, S. R., Anthony, J. L., & Barker, T. A. (1998). Development of phonological sensitivity in 2- to 5-year-old children. *Journal of Educational Psychology, 90*, 294–311.

McConnell, S. R. (2000). Assessment in early intervention and early childhood special education: Building on the past to project into our future. *Topics in Early Childhood Special Education, 19*, 43–48.

McGrew, K. S., & Bruininks, R. H. (1990). Defining adaptive and maladaptive behavior within a model of personal competence. *School Psychology Review, 19*, 53–73.

McLean, M., Bailey, D. B., & Wolery, M. (1996). *Assessing infants and preschoolers with special needs* (2nd ed.). New York: Macmillan.

Meisels, S. J., Liaw, F. R., Dorfman, A., & Nelson, R. N. (1995). The Work Sampling System: Reliability and validity of a performance assessment for young children. *Early Childhood Research Quarterly, 10*, 277–296.

Priest, J. S., McConnell, S. R., Walker, D., Carta, J. J., Kaminski, R. A., McEvoy, M. A., Good, R. H., Greenwood, C. R., & Shinn, M. R. (in press). General growth outcomes for children between birth and age eight: Where do you want young children to go today and tomorrow? *Journal of Early Intervention.*

Priest, J., Davis, K., McConnell, S., McEvoy, M., & Shin, J. (1999, December). *Individual growth and development indicators of preschoolers' "expressing meaning" skills: Follow that trajectory!* Paper presented at the annual meeting of the Division for Early Childhood, Council for Exceptional Children, Washington, DC.

Shinn, M. R. (1988). Development of curriculum-based local norms for use in special education decision-making. *School Psychology Review, 17*, 61–80.

Shinn, M. R. (Ed.) (1989). *Curriculum-based assessment: Assessing special children.* New York: Guilford.

Shinn, M. R. (Ed.). (1998). *Advanced applications of Curriculum-Based Measurement.* New York: Guilford.

Snow, C. E., Burns, M. S., & Griffin, P. (Eds.). (1998). *Preventing reading difficulties in young children.* Washington DC: National Academy Press.

Thompson, J. R., McGrew, K. S., & Bruininks, R. H. (1999). Adaptive and maladaptive behavior: Functional and structural characteristics. In R. L. Schalock (Ed.), *Adaptive behavior and its measurement: Implications for the field of mental retardation* (pp. 15–42). Washington, DC: American Association on Mental Retardation.

Whitehurst, G. J., & Lonigan, C. J. (1998). Child development and emergent literacy. *Child Development, 69*, 848–872.

Zimmerman, I. L., Steiner, V. G., & Pond, R. E. (1992). *Preschool Language Scale, 3.* San Antonio, TX: The Psychological Corporation.

ANNOTATED BIBLIOGRAPHY

Early Childhood Research Institute on Measuring Growth and Development. (1998). *Research and development of individual growth and development indicators for children between birth and age eight* (Tech. Rep. No. 4). Minneapolis, MN: Center for Early Education and Development, University of Minnesota (available at http://ici2.umn.edu/ecri).

This report presents the rationale and research and development process for creation of individual growth and development indicators for young children. It is especially for practitioners interested in more detailed evaluation of the quality and utility of IGDIs, and for researchers interested in developing measures of this type.

Early Childhood Research Institute on Measuring Growth and Development (1998). *Theoretical foundations of the Early Childhood Research Institute on Measuring Growth and Development: An early childhood problem-solving model* (Tech. Rep. No. 6). Minneapolis, MN: Center for Early Education and Development, University of Minnesota (available at http://ici2.umn.edu/ecri).

This report describes an early childhood problem-solving model for delivering services to children with disabilities or at-risk. Phases of this model include identifying the need for additional assessment based on a child's lack of growth toward developmental outcomes, validating need for early intervention, exploring possible solutions, evaluating implemented solutions, and monitoring child progress over time.

Fuchs, L. S., & Deno, S. L. (1991). Paradigmatic distinctions between instructionally relevant measurement models. *Exceptional Children, 57*, 488–500.

This article provides a critical conceptual distinction between "critical sub-skill mastery" and "general outcome measurement" approaches to monitoring progress in academic achievement, and outlines the paradigmatic distinctions associated with these two approaches. General outcome measurement is proposed as an approach to monitoring progress toward a single long-term goal, with periodic assessment using common metrics as a means of assessing an individual's progression toward mastery of this long-term goal.

Kaminski, R. A., & Good, R. H. (1996). Toward a technology for assessing basic early literacy skills. *School Psychology Review, 25*, 215–227.

This article describes a study investigating the validity, reliability, and sensitivity of three measures designed to assess three important aspects of early literacy: vocabulary, phonological awareness, and letter naming. The authors describe these measures as "Dynamic Indicators of Basic Early Literacy Skills," or DIBELS. DIBELS are designed to identify kindergarten and first grade students who have not acquired important prerequisites for reading.

AUTHOR NOTE

This research was funded by the U.S. Department of Education, Office of Special Education Programs, as part of the Early Childhood Research Institute on Measuring Growth and Development (Grant H024S600010). The authors thank the co-investigators of this project (Drs. Ruth Kaminski, Roland Good, Karen Rush, Judy Carta, Charles Greenwood, Gayle Luze, and Dale Walker) and our colleagues at the University of Minnesota site who have worked on the research reported here, including Kristen Davis Missal, Julie Good, Na'im Madyun, Stephanie McNeill, Chrisa Nitsiou, Maytali Novack, Allison Shiu, Jongho Shin, Ben Silberglitt, Marie Stadler, Michelle Suedbeck, and Sara Weisser Hall.

78 Best Practices in Early Intervention

David W. Barnett
University of Cincinnati

OVERVIEW

This chapter describes the basics of intervention-based service delivery for young children who would be considered high risk: children who are difficult to parent, teach, or befriend. Behaviors of importance for intervention purposes are individually determined, but rather than based on controversial developmental testing (Macmann & Barnett, 1999), they evolve from an understanding of problem situations. Interventions typically include those that reduce challenges of parenting or teaching, improve developmental functioning, enhance peer or sibling relationships, and help lead to successful transitions to next environments. The analyses of behavior in educational contexts and needed interventions also can provide information for special services eligibility entitled by Federal Law (P.L. 105-17).

The *potential* benefits of early intervention are far reaching and impressive but they are not *givens*. The outcomes for children described as high risk have included relatively immediate gains in development and achievement, and long-term social advantages such as fewer bouts with social services and the law. However, the promising but uneven data result from relatively few experimental programs (Karoly et al., 1998) that may be difficult for communities to replicate. Educators may question how early intervention benefits may be realized through local school and team efforts. The answer is not easy, but in addition to experimental programs, suggestions may be generalized from intervention-based research and practice that has evolved from thousands of single case studies since the 1960s targeting the developmental and behavioral challenges of young children (Baer, Wolf, & Risley, 1968; Barnett, Bell, & Carey, 1999b).

Intervention-based service delivery is guided by problem solving, functional assessments, intervention design principles including positive behavioral support, and strong accountability methods. *Problem solving* describes a step-by-step collaborative process of problem identification and analysis, plan development, and plan evaluation. For some children, continued iterations of problem solving are needed to maintain and generalize adaptive behaviors. *Functional assessments* are based on (a) identifying skills necessary for adaptations to typical environments with increasing independence and on (b) hypothesizing and evaluating the reasons for maladaptive behaviors (e.g., crying may serve the communication function of obtaining attention *or* avoiding a situation) (O'Neill, Horner, Albin, Sprague, Storey, & Newton, 1997). As a guiding principle, naturalistic *intervention design* may be defined as identifying the least intrusive, most robust intervention that will accomplish the goals of change within a natural setting. *Positive behavioral support* is a set of procedures for making environmental changes to reduce the need for reactive interventions and to teach skills for successful adaptations to environments. The key idea is the remediation of deficient setting *contexts* (Carr, Horner, & Turnbull, 1999). *Strong accountability methods* include direct measures of (a) child outcomes, (b) the intervention as carried out, and (c) parent and teacher judgments about the worthiness of the goals, intervention methods, and outcomes.

Related guides for early intervention are inclusion and developmentally appropriate practices. *Inclusion* is a philosophical stance used to help make judgments about the soundness of decisions for placing children in educational programs based on criteria of normality of environments and activities. *Developmentally appropriate practices* require classroom environments that are safe, engaging, orderly, organized, that promote positive social relationships and independence, and that meet individual needs (Bredekamp & Copple, 1997).

Intervention-based service delivery for high-risk children is based on well-established procedures. In the context of problem solving, and through information revealed by functional assessments, targets for change are identified and measured, and interventions are designed, carried out, and evaluated. Intervention designs have natural as well as empirical support in that they are based on actual observations of behavior in context and on research.

BASIC CONSIDERATIONS

Problem Solving With Parents and Teachers

Rather than providing direct services to children, the early intervention consultant engages in problem solving with primary caregivers to develop effective, acceptable intervention strategies for use within natural settings. Other team members are added as needed (i.e., specialized professionals, persons to help achieve cross-cultural problem solving). Teaming goals are (a) the improvement of current problem situations through the development of effective interventions and support and (b) the prevention of future problems through the enhancement of the caregiver's and/or children's skills. Intervention strategies arising out of parent/teacher problem solving and teaming may be developed for the home, community, and school.

When guided by intervention design and a problem-solving model, those involved emphasize the identification of *problem situations*, not problem children. Problem situations are defined by barriers or behaviors that preclude the natural effective roles of parents, siblings, teachers, and peers in children's development. Because the focus is on problem situations, from the outset an expectation is that caregiver behaviors and setting characteristics, as well as the child's behaviors, are frequently the focal points in problem solving. Thus, the units of analyses are reciprocal interactions between child and caregiver behaviors, routines, and activities in natural settings.

Functional Assessments

Functional assessment and intervention components for early intervention settings (school, home, community) have been organized into procedural guidelines termed PASSKey, which stands for Planned Activity, Strategic Sampling, and Keystone variable. PASSKey is used to structure functional assessments and problem solving in early childhood settings. An overview of PASSKey is presented in Table 1. The end result of functional assessments using PASSKey procedures are collaboratively developed intervention *scripts* for resolving problem situations that are then tried out, refined, evaluated, and ultimately faded. The origins of the concepts, descriptions of techniques, as well as evidence for positive outcomes, are summarized in Barnett et al. (1997, 1999a, 1999c).

Activity Analysis

At the core of functional assessment is the contextual analysis of behavior. Planned activities are socially valid ecological units identified and prioritized by care providers (i.e., dressing, transportation to school, shopping, learning activities, free play, etc.). Planned activities of parents and teachers serve as fundamental units of analysis for intervention purposes. Sometimes the entire day is of concern, but prioritized planned activities are still the building blocks of intervention design. There are four basic techniques useful for assessing planned activities and designing interventions.

1. Functional record reviews and developmental histories help teams examine the degree to which health and family issues may be contributing to the reason for referral. Examples of health issues include vision, hearing, medications, and early identified disabling conditions. Examples of family issues include stressors and continuity of care difficulties. While many factors are typically explored, the term "functional" is used to link features of the developmental/medical history to specific influences on important daily activities and routines.

Table 1. PASSKey Steps

- Planned activities in school, home, or community settings
  - Waking-day and problem-solving interviews are used to examine daily schedules important to family and classroom routines
  - Consider especially difficult activities to target *and* successful activities for intervention ideas
- Strategic sampling of child behaviors and activities
  - From planned activities, decide when to observe activities
  - Choose methods for observing and recording behavior (and other intervention variables)
  - Observe sufficiently to determine patterns of interactions
- Keystone behaviors (or variables) are individually determined
  - Safety related (i.e., running from adults)
  - Prerequisites for progress (i.e., communication)
  - Socialization and self-help
  - Behaviors to avoid rejection from adults and peers
  - Behaviors important to parents' and teachers' routines (e.g., compliance with requests)

Overview of PASSKey

- Scripts as intervention plans
  - Written or pictorial personalized and detailed guidelines
  - For providing instructions and managing behaviors
  - Based on natural caregiver-child interactions, research, or learning principles
  - Tried out and adjusted with assistance and support
- Accountability
  - Is the script or intervention plan being implemented as intended?
  - Is the script comfortable and feasible?
  - Are the targeted variables changing in the desired way?
  - What changes need to be made?

2. "Waking day" (and sleep) and problem-solving eco-behavioral interviews provide teams with a detailed description of behaviors across settings and problem situations for caregivers. In separate interview formats to cover the child's waking day, parents and teachers are asked to describe a child's typical day by focusing on planned activities, routines, and behavior from awakening to bedtime. The problem-solving interview is used for an in-depth analysis of problem situations from the waking-day results. Both are used to help select targeted keystone variables, problematic as well as effective planned activities and routines, and needed supports.

3. An observation system is planned to assess and monitor the child's behavior and contextual variables within activities (e.g., responses to specific activities; child-peer or child-adult interactions). Observation systems need to be practical and effective, but there are many possibilities depending on the activity and behavior of interest, including parent, teacher, and consultant observations, and various combinations. A multi-step process is often effective in developing appropriate observations for home, preschool, and community settings.
   - The results of waking-day and problem-solving interviews are used to help define behaviors, places, circumstances, times for observations, and potential intervention roles.
   - Narrative real-time observations are used to document target behaviors, interactions, situations, sequences of events, and possible naturalistic interventions based on contextual features of the observations. The observer records meaningful and complete units of behaviors in lines or sentences and records the clock time for each unit of behavior. Data collected from real-time observations can yield frequency and rate, duration, prevalence, and inter-response time. On successive lines, an observer might record the following series of events:

     11:12 *J* begins to play alone at water table.
     11:13 *J* is approached by another child.
     11:14 *J* leaves to go to blocks.
     11:15 *J* returns to the water table and pushes the other child away.
     11:16 *Miss B* says "clean-up time."
     11:16 *J* continues at water table.

- Decisions about other observation techniques are based on findings from interviews and real-time observations. Relatively high-rate behaviors or those related to parent-child or teacher-child interactions typically will benefit from consultant observation and perhaps from the use of a preschool observation code (e.g., Bramlett & Barnett, 1993). Low-rate behaviors (i.e., infrequent tantrums) usually require that parents or teachers serve as the primary observers. Hypotheses about possible variables that maintain behaviors may be studied through an A-B-C (antecedent-behavior-consequence) analysis. Observation techniques useful for preschool settings are described in more detail in Barnett et al. (1999c).

4. Curriculum-based assessment (CBA) enables ongoing observations of children's performance in preliteracy, communication, social, self-care, and other developmental areas and yields information needed to determine the conditions necessary for competent performance. For intervention decisions, a curriculum must have a wide range of functional, developmentally appropriate and sequenced tasks, ongoing measurement of progress, and suitable group and individualized teaching strategies. Teachers apply the "instructional hierarchy" in building skills, first focusing on accuracy, then fluency, generalization, and finally application/adaptation (Haring & Eaton, 1978). Instructional situations of children whose progress is of concern become the focus of problem-solving efforts.

Strategic Sampling of Activities

A major consideration is how to sample behaviors within activities. Rarely can observations be continuous and complete. *Strategic sampling* refers to collaboratively derived plans to acquire sufficient data about significant planned activities (behavior in context) for intervention decisions. Carefully designed sampling plans are needed (a) to ensure the ecological and technical soundness of assessment and intervention decisions, including generalizations that may be made about behavior and intervention results and (b) to make observations efficient. Based on interviews with teachers or parents, planned activities within the period of interest are identified to create "pools" of potential observation times that are both important for intervention purposes and comparable. Next, sets of planned activities representing the same activity/time across days, or equivalent sets of planned activities (e.g., all large group instructional activities), are identified as potential periods for observation/analysis. From these potential observation times, observation sessions are planned. As an example, perhaps observations should cover morning activities for a child, but this may not be possible owing to the consultant's schedule that allows for brief visits to the classroom once a week. Observations by teachers may be used to supplement the consultant's observations, or, at the very least, the problem-solving team would address the representativeness of data and gaps in allowable inferences.

Keystone Variables

The defining characteristic of a *keystone variable* is selecting a relatively narrow target variable that has widespread positive consequences. Children are often described by a multitude of problem behaviors depending on the preferences of assessors. In contrast, keystone variables emerge from understanding problem situations. Keystone variables are those that, if changed, are likely to positively impact the largest set of other significant behaviors, perceptions, or problem environments to most efficiently provide long term resolution of problem situations. Thus, keystone variables lead to other beneficial child behaviors and other benefits for those with significant child-care responsibilities. While keystone variables are individually determined, examples common in many preschool classrooms and families include communication skills, social relationships, compliance with adult requests, and adaptation to routines.

BEST PRACTICES IN EARLY INTERVENTION

Planned activity analysis and strategic sampling lead to the measurement of keystone variables for change. Intervention scripts are developed to address keystone variables within planned activities. Single-case accountability designs are used to evaluate the interventions. The data from these designs also fit reform efforts in eligibility determination (discussed later).

Intervention Scripts

Naturalistic intervention design applies problem-solving steps toward identifying (in order of possibility or caregiver preference) (a) naturally occurring parent or teacher intervention strategies likely to be successful either as implemented or with minor changes developed through consultation and feedback, (b) research-based interventions adaptable to evident styles of parenting or teaching within a problem context and setting, or (c) other positive interventions that may be acceptable to parents and teachers as well as effective. From functional assessments, generalizations from intervention research, and brief intervention trials, scripts are developed with parents, teachers, and for children that detail intervention steps using the natural language and context of the problem situation. Scripts are personalized guidelines or prompts (written or pictorial) for providing instructions and/or managing behaviors to meet specified goals. Scripts are tried out and refined as necessary, and eventually lead to self-regulated behavior and are ultimately faded. Table 2 identifies major characteristics and advantages of scripts. Our research has shown that scripts are highly acceptable to parents and teachers, even scripts that may seem complex. Figure 1 gives an example of steps that may be scripted for effective requests. This type of intervention is often a component for improving compliance.

Table 2. Intervention scripts

- Scripts are used for describing significant instructional or problem situations in terms of characteristics of actual interactions. They may be highly specific (e.g., how to give effective requests) or more general (e.g., how to do incidental teaching), or class-wide.
- They may be used for identifying natural interactions and specifying their key components, and translating research-based interventions into natural and contextual steps.
- Scripts are used for teaching new behaviors or ways of responding to situations because they address skills or competencies ("how to do it") and self-efficacy ("I can do it").
- Scripts are easily shared across settings as needed; changes may be quickly made and shared.
- Scripts can create expectations for creativity, feedback, and coaching to try out new roles.
- Scripts may improve accountability and research in intervention design by creating more acceptable intervention plans through the script-building process, clarifying the intervention steps, and creating opportunities to note intervention adherence (intervention use "probes").
- The use of scripts may facilitate self-regulated behavior by fading script use as new behaviors are learned in problem situations.
- Scripts may enhance cross-cultural practice and ethnic validity since they are developed and written in everyday language of the care provider.
- Scripts are helpful in fulfilling the ethical requirements of informed consent because all of the relevant intervention components are described without jargon.

Figure 1. Script building example

Effective requests	*Steps observed*
• Get Sam's attention	
• Move close (3 feet)	
• Make eye contact, move to Sam's level.	
• Use short, simple words (e.g., "Come here," "Sit down," "Stop hitting")	
• Use gestures and visual cues (e.g., hands to show "Come here")	
• Thank child (e.g., "Thanks for keeping your feet to yourself")	
• Give frequent positive trials throughout the day (e.g., "It's your turn for art, let's practice what to do")	
• Give planned trials for less preferred activities (e.g., "It's time for clean up"; "You need to put the blocks away")	

Strong Accountability Methods

Evaluation is a continuous process that includes judgments of how reasonable the interventions are, whether they are being carried out as planned, and whether they actually lead to desired changes. The adequacy of intervention design is determined at the individual-case level, and data can be summed to characterize programmatic or agency efforts (Barnett et al., 1999a).

Acceptability

Acceptability refers to judgments by caregivers regarding reasonableness: the appropriateness, fairness, intrusiveness, and normality of interventions. A purpose for evaluating acceptability is to anticipate and avoid rejection of an intervention and to consider information about variables that affect a parent's or teacher's use of an intervention (Schwartz & Baer, 1991). In the PASSKey model, acceptability is sampled throughout the intervention process.

Intervention Adherence: Interpreting Patterns of Script Use

Treatment integrity is the degree to which an intervention is carried out as planned (Yeaton & Sechrest, 1981), but many parents and teachers have not found this term acceptable, and *intervention adherence* is used here instead. Factors affecting intervention adherence include (a) complexity, (b) time, (c) materials/resources, (d) number of persons, (e) perceived and actual effectiveness, (f) competition from other demands, and (g) motivation of change agents. Interventions that require substantial changes in the classroom or home ecology may require additional support.

Scripts are used as intervention adherence measures through direct observation and self-report, but the data need to be properly interpreted. Teams must distinguish between some natural variability in patterns of strong intervention use from difficulties in script use. Problems with intervention adherence without behavioral gains may indicate that the intervention is unreasonable for a situation and that reconsideration of the steps or redesign of the intervention are necessary, additional support needs to be provided, or motivation may be a problem. Intervention adherence with desired behavioral gains, but with missing intervention steps, may indicate that the intervention may be simplified.

Often, aspects of interventions may need to be redesigned to improve plan implementation. These barriers are approached through problem solving (i.e., adding practice steps to promote fluency with the intervention; noting the influence of antecedents, consequences, and setting events on the team member attempting to carry out intervention scripts). Other considerations include finding ways to make plans more acceptable without losing effectiveness, and recycling back through the problem-solving process, checking hypotheses, and possibly redoing a functional analysis. It is critical that problem-solving teams have supportive skills for working with team members who do not carry through with previously agreed upon plans in order to look more closely at barriers to intervention adherence. Alternatively, strong implementation of a script that is difficult to carry out without proper support, even with behavioral gains, may ultimately lead to burn out. In sum, teams need to closely consider intervention adherence patterns. The more complex and time consuming the intervention, the less likely that it will be implemented as intended. Conversely, naturalistic interventions may have greater intervention adherence because they are based on existing caregiver competencies.

Single Case "Accountability" Designs

Basic reasons for selecting single-case research designs are to compare the effects of alternative conditions and evaluate the effectiveness of interventions. These designs emphasize repeated, ongoing measurement of behavior and intervention use, and intervention modification based on data analysis. Data are presented graphically and analyzed visually to determine intervention effectiveness or the need for modification. The A-B design, a baseline followed by an intervention condition, is viewed as a cornerstone of accountability.

Team Progress Monitoring

Much has been written about individual *child* progress monitoring. Described above, teams monitor the child's progress toward goals by using direct measures of performance, and data are organized by single-case accountability designs. Methods for team progress monitoring have evolved from PASSKey early intervention research. *Team* progress monitoring reveals how well teams are accomplishing their goals. Steps include building-level preparation, team composition and responsibilities, legal and ethical procedures, technical adequacy checks, and intervention planning and evaluation routines. Team *fluency* is a critical variable, mostly independent of child-related challenges, predictive of how much time problem solving "takes" (Barnett et al., 1997). Functional intervention-based service delivery steps are detailed in procedural guidelines available from the author.

Empirically Valid Intervention Design: Selecting Likely Interventions

Early intervention consultants are usually needed to help guide teams through a problem-solving process and to expand and help analyze the range of interventions that may be considered by a team. A fundamental question is, "Where do we get these intervention scripts?" Interventions are (a) generalized from developmental studies and intervention research, (b) founded on the realities of settings determined through problem analysis, and (c) based on the predicted success of the least-intrusive intervention likely to accomplish the goals of change. Developmental studies capitalize on the natural interactions of master teachers and successful parents, and these may be scripted as intervention exemplars (i.e., Hart & Risley, 1995).

Interventions are reviewed that have considerable validity support and that have frequently been applied to high-risk problem situations by our early intervention team members, but their use would need to evolve from the problem-solving steps. Antecedent interventions involving environmental restructuring and teaching have been less emphasized in the past but are highly promising in facilitating development and preventing problem behaviors (Luiselli & Cameron, 1998). Most practical interventions are "packages" or combinations of components (antecedents *and* consequences).

Some Intervention Basics

This section builds on interventions found in behavioral texts by describing fundamentals that have proven helpful in early intervention environments.

Interesting and Developmentally Appropriate Environments

One of the most powerful interventions in many preschool environments has been adding interesting activities and guides to their use, teaching children appropriate skills to access them, modifying activities as necessary, giving choices between activities, and rotating or limiting activities to maintain interest (Dunlap & Kern, 1996; Nordquist & Twardosz, 1990; Peters, 1995; Stollar, Dye-Collins, & Barnett, 1994). Peters (1995) found that social behaviors improved across *all* activities when a novel center was introduced and not only within the newly introduced activity.

Scanning: A Key Observation Skill

Adults naturally monitor children's behavior in settings by periodically scanning or "seeing" what is occurring in activities. Effective scanning is often a key to problem analysis and many intervention designs. Scanning skills include (a) moving to strategic locations, (b) visually sweeping the room (Paine et al., 1983) or setting (car, store, playground), and (c) spot checking activities based on predictions from past behaviors or risk appraisals. Scanning is a *foundation* of intervention design because it sets the stage for altering antecedents (e.g., anticipating and guiding a child from an inappropriate act; giving choices) or providing consequences (e.g., attention). Interventions themselves may depend on *positive* scanning (such as noticing improvements in performance, looking for opportunities to provide attention) but *negative* scanning (ignoring positive behaviors while reprimanding disruptive behaviors or rule violations) may be commonplace in problem situations. Many intervention designs focus on altering *patterns* of scanning (e.g., reducing intensive monitoring by teaching self-regulated behaviors; increasing intensive monitoring in interventions for dangerous behaviors). Where aversives such as reprimands are overused, increasing positive scanning may be an effective intervention component (e.g., attending to three positives for every negative).

Guides, Rules (or Limits), and Consequences

Guides, rules, and limits are essential for self-regulation as well as family and classroom management. The basic principle is that carefully selected, positively stated, learned, practiced, and enforced "guides" establish expectations for behavior. Paine et al. (1983) provided a thorough discussion about setting up classroom rules that we have frequently used and have adapted for many parent consultations.

Functional Analysis

Functional analysis is used to test hypotheses about the control of behavior and behavioral change. Functional behavior-environment relationships are not necessarily revealed through observations of natural events (A-B-C analysis), and other procedures may be necessary to determine the function of behavior. Functional analyses are critically significant when problem behaviors may lead to aversive or more intrusive interventions (e.g., removing a child from a classroom due to behavior). The basics include (a) hypothesizing reasons for the inappropriate behavior (e.g., a child is interested in obtaining something like a toy, attention, or stimulation; or a child is interested in avoiding a situation such as a food item or activity); (b) teaching the child a more effective as well as efficient method to communicate (e.g., "Stop!" if another child tries to take a toy); or, if the function cannot be "honored," (c) introducing environmental changes or self-regulated coping behaviors, and requesting greater tolerance from teachers, other adults, and children (Reichle, McEvoy, Davis, Rogers, Feely, Johnston, & Wolff, 1996).

Differential Attention

Differential or systematic attention consists of approval contingent on desired behavior. It may be used to shape new behaviors and maintain or generalize behaviors. By definition, it is brief and may be non-intrusive. However, this intervention may be easily squandered or misapplied. Furthermore, studies show that appropriate behavior is frequently and inadvertently ignored and misbehavior actually may be rewarded. Thus, assessing caregivers' use of attention is often a necessary step for intervention design, a reason for the focus on scanning behavior (above). Assessment for differential attention may be conducted through an A-B-C analysis.

Modeling and Opportunities to Practice

According to Bandura (1986), most behavior is learned through modeling. Thus, modeling appropriate and adaptive behavior, and guiding, prompting, and reinforcing children to perform new or alternative behaviors, are basic intervention strategies. One of the most powerful interventions for preacademics or social behavior is simply increasing "opportunities to practice" skill attainment (Greenwood, Delquadri, & Hall, 1984). Two steps are necessary: (a) analyzing occasions for learning and practice and (b) increasing the chances for practice and feedback.

Sequential and Hierarchical Plans

Problem solving is a step-by-step process, and intervention decisions involve the same considerations. Components of strong interventions may include (a) sequential and hierarchical plans (the easiest, most natural, and promising interventions are tried first and they become progressively more intensive as necessary) (e.g., Harding, Wacker, Cooper, Millard, Jensen-Kovalan, 1994; Porterfield, Herbert-Jackson, & Risley, 1976), (b) the analysis of appropriate replacement behaviors for an inappropriate or disruptive behavior, (c) a plan for teaching and prompting the replacement behavior, (d) the development of increased opportunities for the child to practice new responses, (e) choices and positive contingencies for desirable behaviors (Peck et al., 1996), and (f) planned responses for inappropriate behavior that eliminate its reinforcement.

Examples of Interventions for Language and Literacy

Language and communication referrals are pervasive in early intervention settings. While specialized, several language interventions that fit the roles of parents, teachers, and school psychologists are reviewed.

Milieu Language Interventions

Perhaps the best example of naturalistic intervention is incidental teaching in facilitating language development (Hart & Risley, 1982; Warren, 1992). *Incidental teaching* capitalizes on important exchanges between a child and caregiver in relatively unstructured settings rich in materials or activities. The adult, following the child's lead, focuses attention on the child's verbalizations and encourages elaboration. The power of incidental teaching results from the cumulative effects of numerous brief exchanges between child and caregiver (or siblings, peers).

The use of a brief natural time delay (e.g., 5 seconds) during natural routines when children need assistance or otherwise need to initiate communication has been found to help with the development of language. Halle, Baer, and Spradlin (1981) give an example: The caregiver holds a glass of juice, faces the child, and waits for the child's vocal initiation. Delay can be used with any natural or functional opportunities that occur on a regular basis such as gross motor play (putting hands on the toy car to be moved and waiting before moving it) or when the child needs help with a shoelace or button or with bathroom requests. If the child does not make a response or the response is incorrect, then the adult may model the behavior.

Tirapelle and Cipani (1991) described an intervention termed as *missing-item format* that employs both incidental teaching and brief time delays. Adults provide opportunities to practice and motivation to do so by removing a necessary item from a natural activity. For example, in a game-like fashion, the spoon or cereal may be briefly removed, giving the child an opportunity to make a functional request. Correct responses are prompted after an incorrect response or a delay of a few seconds.

In learning new skills, it is important to maximize the amount of early success. In *errorless teaching*, early teaching tasks are simplified through prompts that are gradually faded. More difficult tasks are introduced slowly based on prior successes. Errorless teaching stresses the control of antecedent teaching procedures to enable the child to perform with no (or few) errors. There are two basic types of procedures. One involves a system of teacher prompts to help children perform. A second (and more elaborate) procedure uses systematic modifications of instructional materials whereby the task is initially made easy and progressively becomes more difficult by fading prompts (Wolery, Bailey, & Sugai, 1988).

Early Literacy

Reading to children is one of the best supported interventions for early literacy skills. A routine for parents *reading to children* (Taverne & Sheridan, 1995; see also Dale, Crain-Thoreson, Notari-Syverson, & Cole, 1996) includes (a) examining a storybook and pointing out its features (author, illustrator) and main parts, (b) labeling and discussing picture content, (c) reading aloud, and (d) pausing to question understanding of the material. Potential benefits include improved attending skills, relationships, and bedtime routines, as well as literacy and language gains.

Examples of Interventions for Challenging Behaviors

Analysis of Aversives

Children referred for behavior or learning problems may be experiencing very negative environments. Reprimands (and more harsh forms of discipline) are frequently overused and ineffective, and thus may be a critical point of problem analysis. One of the additional benefits of consultation reducing the ineffective use of reprimands and harsh discipline, and introducing positive interventions, is to improve family or classroom environment.

High Probability Sequences

Inserting a brief rapid sequence (usually two to three) high-probability requests (likely to be complied with based on observations, i.e., 80% compliance), may be used to increase appropriate responding to a low-probability request (i.e., 50% compliance) when the low-probability request is given soon after reinforcing the high-probability requests (i.e., 5 seconds). As an example, a child may have left a play area without cleaning up. A sequence of requests might be "Come stand by me" and "Point to your picture" followed by "Please put the markers away on the shelf." This sequence may be more likely to lead to compliance than "Put the markers away on the shelf" alone (however, the specifics need to be varied). Numerous studies show effectiveness with many potential referral questions such as compliance and social behaviors and even young peers delivering the requests (Davis & Reichle, 1996).

Teaching Alternative Responses and Functional Communication Training

Differential reinforcement of alternative behavior means a more acceptable behavior is substituted for the maladaptive behavior and occurrences of the acceptable behavior are reinforced. A common example is play engagement as an alternative for unoccupied time. Alternative responses may need to be first taught and practiced. Carr and Durand (1985) argued that communication skills may offer significant possibilities as functional alternative skills for severe problem behaviors. They proposed a "communication hypothesis of child behavior problems" where behavior problems function as "nonverbal communication acts" (p. 124). Durand (1990) presents a detailed guide for professionals to assist with functional communication training (see also the earlier section on "functional analysis").

Choices

Choice making adds quality to interactions (Hart & Risley, 1995), and structured choice making fits the criteria of being a natural and research-based strategy to help manage or modify behavior. It is incorporated into intervention design in many ways: for reinforcement appraisal and goal setting and as a foundation of many other intervention strategies. Procedurally, it may mean that children have (limited) choices over objects or activities, such as when to take a break or get a drink. A thorough illustration of choice making with young children having multiple and severe problems is provided by Peck et al. (1996; see also the special issue on choice, *Journal of Applied Behavior Analysis, 30*(3), 1997).

Timed Positives, Fixed-Time, or Noncontingent Reinforcement (NCR)

This procedure has been in search of a name (Vollmer, 1999), but it has been sufficiently effective to become a "go to" procedure for severely aggressive and self-injurious behaviors in our settings. *NCR* (no longer the accepted name but commonly described in the literature this way) helps resolve the potential problems associated with differential reinforcement (continuous monitoring of behavior, potential side effects due to extinction, and possible low rates of reinforcement because of high rates of inappropriate behavior). The basics are simple. Studies show that when a functional reinforcer (one that is linked to behavioral maintenance) is administered noncontingently, a target response will be reduced. NCR consists of the following components (Marcus & Vollmer, 1996, pp. 43–44): (a) a functional analysis to determine potential reinforcers; (b) NCR, during which a fixed-time schedule determines when the individual will receive access to preferred reinforcers during the session, independent of occurrences of disruptive or adaptive behaviors; (c) extinction, during which the experimenter provides no programmed consequences contingent on the disruptive target behaviors; and (d) fading, in which the schedule of noncontingent reinforcement is gradually decreased from a dense (continuous) to a lean schedule (e.g., one per 5 minutes). A procedure may be added to reduce potential negative effects by omitting reinforcement if the targeted response (i.e., aggression) occurs during a preset interval (i.e., 10 seconds) prior to the scheduled time for reinforcement. We have simplified these procedures greatly, still with effectiveness, in line with teacher's realities and acceptability (e.g., fixed interval schedules of 5 minutes during prioritized activities and 10 minutes for other activities; NCR to more than 1 child).

Correspondence Training

In correspondence training, reinforcement is contingent on a child both agreeing to engage in a target response and then actually performing the desired behavior. It has considerable research support for many applications (Paniagua, 1999). The rationale for correspondence training is straightforward, and involves developing the relationship between "saying and doing." Language is a logical target for self-regulation efforts for several reasons: (a) relatively speaking, it may be a well-developed skill with a pattern that leads to some control over behavior; (b) it can be used readily across different environments; and (c) it may be used conveniently and requires little effort. Although the focus of correspondence training is on verbalizations used to mediate behaviors, the procedures have been used with language delayed or socially withdrawn children.

First, careful consideration must be given to the child's ability to perform the task and to criteria for reinforcement. Baseline information is used to set initial criteria, and level changes are introduced by changing the criteria in planned increments. Final goals are set by peer comparisons through the use of micronorms (Bell & Barnett, 1999). For example, before a play period, the caregiver asks the child, "What are you going to do in play today?" If the child responds with "I'm going to talk to the kids a lot," then the child is sent to play. The criterion for "talking a lot" is set with baseline performance in mind. If the child does not spontaneously respond, then the caregiver prompts the child until the child verbally responds that he or she is ready to play. After the play period, the child is taken aside and given feedback about the play session. If the child "talked a lot," then the child is given positive attention (i.e., a reinforcer). The results of studies suggest the importance of prompts, reinforcement of appropriate behavior, and rule-governed behavior. For some children, learning rules through language use and correspondence training may be quite beneficial.

Differential Reinforcement of Diminishing (DRD) Rates of Behavior

This tactic means that reinforcement is contingent on a preplanned reduction in response rate (Sulzer-Azaroff & Mayer, 1991). Two examples should make it clear why this contingency arrangement may be valuable. A mother may be concerned with excessive yelling or her use of intense reprimands that occur with very high frequency. She may "self-reward" at the end of the planned activity (or day) if self-monitoring demonstrates that 17 "yells" were recorded, down from 18 the day before. As another example, a child may show 10 "complaints" in play with other children; a decrease to 9 "complaints" is reinforceable during the next play period. Thus, on subsequent days, the mother and child in the examples would have to beat the prior days' accomplishments to be reinforced. DRD may be used for eliminating behaviors or reducing behaviors to suitably low levels. As with other differential reinforcement strategies, an important condition is that appropriate alternative behaviors need to be in the person's repertoire or must be taught. (An opposite strategy may be used for increasing desirable behaviors.)

Grandma's Law Revisited (Premack Principle)

High-frequency behaviors (playing with favorite toys) are made contingent on low-frequency behaviors (completing a pre-academic task). Although it has a wicked sounding title, the *response deprivation hypothesis* is a more general statement of Grandma's Law and has many possibilities for reinforcer assessment: Almost any behavior in which children naturally engage may be a potentially effective reinforcer "providing access to that response can be restricted" (Sulzer-Aazaroff & Mayer, 1991, p. 160). In fact, a low-probability behavior can function as a reinforcer for a high-probability behavior if there are restrictions placed on responses as assessed at baseline levels. Stollar, Dye-Collins, and Barnett (1994) reduced the inappropriately high activity levels of two children by placing some very mild and temporary restrictions (and time limits) on free play.

Intervention "Packages" for Challenging Children

The term "package" in this context applies to a multicomponent intervention with strong evidence for wide applicability. Many children have been referred to us for behaviors typically described as conduct disordered. Earlier, we described work by Durand (1990) that falls under this category. Another intervention "package" is provided by Barkley (1997). Sanders and Dadds (1993) also provide a comprehensive model for parent consultation.

Social skills are often targeted for intervention purposes. A "Buddy Skills" program to help develop friendship patterns is another example of an intervention package (English, Shafer, Goldstein, & Kaczmarek, 1997).

In Figure 2, a menu of possible intervention components and scripts for a class wide intervention "package" are shown. We have had numerous referrals for disruptive behaviors in classes where groups of children (e.g., three to five) and entire days were of concern. Through collaboration, problem solving, and functional assessments, the key ideas are generally *adding "positives"* to the classroom and planning *routine sequences*, hierarchically arranged from least to most intrusive and demanding, to help with individual or group disruptions. Steps are used only as necessarily in a sequenced and hierarchical plan (also known as a consequence hierarchy) (Harding et al., 1994). We have found rapid improvements for class wide interventions with infrequent use of more demanding steps.

Using Intervention Data for Eligibility Decisions and Individualized Educational Programs

Problem solving is used to avoid unnecessary labeling. If necessary, the problem-solving approach described above can be used for analyzing developmental delays and making eligibility and Individualized Educational Programs (IEP) decisions. The data from intervention-based assessment and intervention may yield defensible and educationally useful *functional* discrepancies in performance and needed interventions.

These functional discrepancies that describe developmental delays are derived from applying appropriate measurement tactics (child *in* environment) and technical adequacy checks (Macmann & Barnett, 1999), and examining differences in the instructional,

Figure 2. Class-wide plan: Scripting interventions for disruptive behaviors

	Observed
• **Adding Positives**	
— **Positive scanning:** effective movement; scanning, guiding, prompting, and using positive (versus misplaced) attention	
— **Increasing opportunities to practice:** direct teaching of expected behaviors; becoming fluent with rules and expected behaviors; peer "buddy systems" for social learning objectives	
— **High interest activities:** teaching expected behaviors in activities and transitions; setting time limits to sustain interest and promote rule learning leading to self-regulated behavior	
— **Functional communication training:** teaching children to solicit appropriate attention or request assistance	
— **Timed positives:** providing brief social/activity rewards regardless of behavior (surprise box, mystery rewards, brief activities) based on timer set for brief intervals	
— **Additional support for teacher**	
• **Building routine sequences** and **consequence hierarchies**	
— **Prompts, redirection, simple correction**	
— **Clear requests; choices** (to reduce power struggles); **high probability sequences:** (i.e., "Come here," "Stand by me," "Point to something red you're wearing," "Put the blocks away")	
— **Limit warnings, repeat requests; limit activity times** (to maintain interest)	
— **Sit and watch** (contingent observation)	
— **Other safeguards** (for crisis/dangerous situations)	

environmental, or related classroom strategies that are required to meet children's needs (Hardman, McDonnell, & Welch, 1997). On the basis of a review of intervention research, the following measurement tactics, singly or in various combinations, may serve as important targets for observations as well as service delivery, eligibility, and IEP determination: (a) teacher monitoring (amount of time required in proximity, rates of "teacher contacts" or supervision, and quality of interaction); (b) activity engagement (participation in classroom activities); (c) levels of assistance (prompting strategies facilitating learning or adapting to routines); (d) trials to criterion (rate of progress measured by learning trials or practice time); (e) behavioral fluency (differences in accuracy and rate of specific skills); (f) modifying activities (activities or instruction that involve unique or more complex interventions); and (g) curricular adaptations (domains, skill sequences, or instructional techniques that need to be modified) (Barnett et al., 1999b). Many of the techniques are used in conjunction with peer micronorms (Bell & Barnett, 1999).

"Eligibility" decision making is based both on (a) a discrepancy between educational performance in a critical or significant curriculum area of the referred child in comparison to expectancies for the performance of a typical child *and* (b) a desired change in performance that is resistant to planned intervention efforts that are naturally sustainable within the educational service unit. At least three patterns or combinations of patterns derived from direct measurement of "intensity of the need for special support" are used for making decisions (Hardman et al., 1997, p. 64): (a) an intervention may be successful but requires extraordinary effort to be sustained; (b) an intervention may need to be in place extensively or throughout the school day for appropriate inclusion; or (c) interventions carried out by a teacher may be unsuccessful, requiring replanning and special resources to be added to a situation. The performance discrepancy and actual intervention data are used to clarify the special education services or supports needed for a teacher and child in order to meet the needs of the child in the present environment or to establish needed environmental modifications to do so. The data may be used for individual as well as agency progress monitoring (Barnett et al., 1999a).

In summary, rather than a "categorical child label," the stress is on *legally, ethically, and technically defensible data sets* for eligibility decisions based on behavior in context. Singly, or in combinations, the above tactics may be aligned with children's needs expressed as categories used in federal law and by states for eligibility decisions (i.e., child with a disability or traditional categories).

Caution and Encouragement

The early intervention procedures outlined here require hard work, creativity, and a high level of professional preparation, perhaps learning the language of interventions, but the efforts are worth it. Positive outcomes for children may be documented. Capacity building of agencies and schools in providing effective learning environments reduces the need for intensive individualized intervention efforts.

SUMMARY

The many controversies and intractable problems surrounding "testing" for developmental delays and programming based on test results are reasons for emphasizing functional intervention-based service delivery. Intervention-based service delivery meets the intent of the IDEA amendments (P.L.105-17) in bringing proven intervention practices to educational services that will improve outcomes and reduce the need for children's labels. This premise has received a great deal of attention. The data sets produced by intervention-based services for individual children may be used for inclusionary efforts, special services delivery determination, and IEPs. The data is encouraging, but the work is challenging with capacity building and team fluency in problem solving techniques representing the most important variables.

REFERENCES

Baer, D. M., Wolf, M. M., & Risley, T. R. (1968). Some current dimensions of applied behavior analysis. *Journal of Applied Behavior Analysis, 1,* 91– 97.

Bandura, A. (1986). *The social foundations of thought and action: A social cognitive theory.* Englewood Cliffs, NJ: Prentice-Hall.

Barkley, R. A. (1997). *Defiant children: A clinician's manual for assessment and parent training* (2nd ed.). New York: Guilford.

Barnett, D. W., Air, A. E., Bell, S. H., Gilkey, C. M., Smith, J. J., Stone, C. M., Nelson, K. I., Maples, K. A., Helenbrook, K., & Hannum, L. E. (1999a). Evaluating early intervention: Accountability methods for service delivery innovations. *Journal of Special Education, 33,* 177–188.

Barnett, D. W., Bell, S. H., Bauer, A., Lentz, F. E. Jr., Petrelli, S., Air, A., & Hannum, L. (1997). The early childhood intervention project: Building capacity for service delivery. *School Psychology Quarterly, 12,* 293–315.

Barnett, D. W., Bell, S. H., & Carey, K. T. (1999b). *Early interventions: A practitioner's guide* (2nd ed.). New York: Guilford.

Barnett, D. W., Bell, S. H., Gilkey, C. M., Lentz, F. E. Jr., Graden, J. L., Stone, C. M., & Smith, J. J. (1999c). The promise of meaningful eligibility determination: Functional intervention-based multifactored preschool evaluation. *The Journal of Special Education, 33,* 112–124.

Bell, S. H., & Barnett, D. W. (1999). Peer micronorms in the assessment of young children: Methodological review and examples. *Topics in Early Childhood Special Education, 19,* 112–122.

Bramlett, R. K., & Barnett, D. W. (1993). The development of a direct observation code for use in preschool settings. *School Psychology Review, 22,* 49–62.

Bredekamp, S., & Copple, C. (Eds.) (1997). *Developmentally appropriate practices in early childhood programs* (rev. ed.). Washington, DC: National Association for the Education of Young Children.

Carr, E. G., & Durand, V. M.. (1985). Reducing behavior problems through functional communication training. *Journal of Applied Behavior Analysis, 18,* 111–126.

Carr, E. G., Horner, R. H., & Turnbull, A. P. (1999). *Positive behavioral support for people with developmental disabilities: A research synthesis.* Washington, DC: American Association on Mental Retardation.

Dale, P. S., Crain-Thoreson, C., Notari-Syverson, A., & Cole, K. (1996). Parent-child book reading as an intervention technique for young children with language delays. *Topics in Early Childhood Special Education, 16,* 213–235.

Davis, C. A., & Reichle, J. (1996). Variant and invariant high-probability requests: Increasing appropriate behaviors in children with emotional-behavior disorders. *Journal of Applied Behavior Analysis, 29,* 471–482.

Dunlap, G., & Kern, L. (1996). Modifying instructional activities to promote desirable behavior: A conceptual and practical framework. *School Psychology Quarterly, 11,* 297–312.

Durand, V. M. (1990). *Severe behavior problems: A functional communication training approach.* New York: Guilford.

English, K., Shafer, K., Goldstein, H., & Kaczmarek, L. (1997). *Teaching buddy skills to preschoolers.* Washington, DC: American Association on Mental Retardation.

Greenwood, C. R., Delquadri, J. C., & Hall, V. R. (1984). Opportunities to respond and student academic performance. In W. L. Heward, T. E. Heron, D.S. Hill, & J. Trap-Porter (Eds). *Focus on behavior analysis in education* (pp. 58–88). Columbus, OH: Merrill.

Halle, J. W., Baer, D. M., & Spradlin, J. E. (1981). Teachers' generalized use of delay as a stimulus control procedure to increase language use in handicapped children. *Journal of Applied Behavior Analysis, 14,* 389–409.

Harding, J., Wacker, D. P., Cooper, L. J., Millard, T., Jensen-Kovalan, P. (1994). Brief hierarchical assessment of potential treatment components with children in an outpatient clinic. *Journal of Applied Behavior Analysis, 27,* 291–300.

Hardman, M. L., McDonnell, J., & Welch, M. (1997). Perspectives on the future of IDEA. *Journal of the Association for Persons with Severe Handicaps, 22,* 61–77.

Haring, N. G., & Eaton, M. D. (1978). Systematic instructional procedures: An instructional hierarchy. In Haring, N. G., Lovitt, T. C., Eaton, M. D., & Hansen, C. L. (Eds.) *The fourth R: Research in the classroom* (pp. 23–40). Columbus, OH: Merrill.

Hart, B., & Risley, T. R. (1982). *How to use incidental teaching for elaborating language.* Austin, TX: PRO-ED.

Hart, B., & Risley, T. R. (1995). *Meaningful differences in the everyday experiences of young children.* Baltimore: Brookes.

Karoly, L. A., Greenwood, P. W., Everingham, S. S., Hoube', J., Kilburn, M. R., Rydell, C. P., Sanders, M., & Chiesa, J. (1998). *Investing in our children: What we know and don't know about the costs and benefits of early childhood interventions.* Santa Monica, CA: Rand.

Luiselli, J. K., & Cameron, M. J. (Eds.). (1998). *Antecedent control: Innovative approaches to behavioral support.* Baltimore: Brookes.

Macmann, G. M., & Barnett, D. W. (1999). Diagnostic decision making in school psychology: Understanding and coping with uncertainty. In C. R. Reynolds & T. B. Gutkin (Eds.), *The handbook of school psychology* (3rd ed.) (pp. 519–548). New York: John Wiley.

Marcus, B. A., & Vollmer, T. R. (1996). Combining noncontingent reinforcement and differential reinforcement schedules as treatment for aberrant behavior. *Journal of Applied Behavior Analysis, 29,* 43–51.

Nordquist, V. M., & Twardosz, S. (1990). Preventing behavior problems in early childhood special education classrooms through environmental organization. *Education and Treatment of Children, 13,* 274–287.

O'Neill, R. E., Horner, R. H., Albin, R. W., Sprague, J. R., Storey, K., & Newton, J. S. (1997). *Functional assessment and program development for problem behavior: A practical handbook* (2nd ed.). Pacific Grove, CA: Brookes/Cole.

Paine, S.C., Radicchi, J., Rosellini, L. C., Deutchman, L., & Darch, C.B. (1983). *Structuring your classroom for academic success.* Champaign, IL: Research Press.

Paniagua, F. A. (1999). Correspondence training and verbal mediation. In J. K. Luiselli, & M. J. Cameron (Eds.), *Antecedent control: Innovative approaches to behavioral support* (pp. 223–242). Baltimore: Brookes.

Peck, M. S., Wacker, D. P., Berg, W. K., Cooper, L. J., Brown, K. A., Richman, D., McComas, J. J., Frischmeyer, P., & Millard, T. (1996). Choice-making treatment of young children's severe behavior problems. *Journal of Applied Behavior Analysis, 29,* 263–290.

Peters, C. (1995). *Preschool activity centers: Effects on opportunities to engage in social interactions.* Unpublished doctoral dissertation, University of Cincinnati.

Porterfield, J. K., Herbert-Jackson, E., & Risley, T. R. (1976). Contingent observation: An effective and acceptable procedure for reducing disruptive behavior of young children in a group setting. *Journal of Applied Behavior Analysis, 9,* 55–64.

Reichle, J., McEvoy, M., Davis, C., Rogers, E., Feely, K., Johnston, S., & Wolff, K. (1996). Coordinating preservice and in-service training of early interventionists to serve preschoolers who engage in challenging behaviors. In L. K. Koegel, R. L. Koegel, & G. Dunlap (Eds.), *Positive behavioral support: Including people with difficult behavior in the community* (pp. 227–259). Baltimore: Brookes.

Sanders, M. R., & Dadds, M. R. (1993). *Behavioral family intervention.* Boston: Allyn & Bacon.

Schwartz, I. S., & Baer, D. M. (1991). Social validity assessment: Is current practice state of the art? *Journal of Applied Behavior Analysis, 24,* 189–204.

Stollar, S. A., Dye-Collins, P. A., & Barnett, D. W. (1994). Structured free-play to reduce disruptive activity changes in a Head Start classroom. *School Psychology Review, 23,* 310–322.

Sulzer-Azaroff, B. & Mayer, G. R. (1991). *Behavior analysis for lasting change.* Fort Worth, TX: Holt, Rinehart, & Winston.

Taverne, A. & Sheridan, A. M. (1995). Parent training in interactive book reading: An investigation of its effects with families at risk. *School Psychology Quarterly, 10,* 41–64.

Tirapelle, L., & Cipani, E. (1991). Developing functional requesting: Acquisition, durability, and generalization effects. *Exceptional Children, 58,* 260–269.

Vollmer, T. R. (1999). Noncontingent reinforcement: Some additional comments. *Journal of Applied Behavior Analysis, 32,* 239–240

Warren, S. F. (1992). Facilitating basic vocabulary acquisition with milieu teaching procedures. *Journal of Early Interventions, 16,* 235–251.

Wolery, M., Bailey, D. B. Jr., & Sugai, G. M. (1988). *Effective teaching: Principles and procedures of applied behavior analysis with exceptional students.* Boston: Allyn & Bacon.

Yeaton, W. H., & Sechrrest, L. (1981). Critical dimensions in the choice and maintenance of successful treatment: Strength, integrity, and effectiveness. *Journal of Consulting and Clinical Psychology, 49,* 156–167.

ANNOTATED BIBLIOGRAPHY

Bambara, L. M. & Knoster, T. (1998). *Designing positive behavioral support plans.* Washington, DC: American Association on Mental Retardation.
This book provides a brief (43 pages with large print), inexpensive, and easy to read description of positive behavioral support that can be widely used in early intervention programs. Included are assumptions and characteristics of positive behavioral support written to be understood by a general audience. Similarly, the basics of hypotheses development for problem behavior and functional assessments are clearly and succinctly communicated. Last, a check for support plans is provided. The book would be highly suitable for pre-service preparation and staff development.

Barnett, D. W., Bell, S. H., & Carey, K. T. (1999b). *Early interventions: A practitioner's guide* (2nd ed.). New York: Guilford.
This book provides a comprehensive source for early intervention concepts, functional assessments, and empirical intervention methods for home and school settings. It also suggests practical legal, accountability, and technical adequacy checks, and concepts and measures for meaningful eligibility determination. The foundations are based on eco-behavioral analysis, intervention research, and positive behavioral support.

Hart, B. & Risley, T. R. (1995). *Meaningful differences in the everyday experiences of young children.* Baltimore: Brookes.
This book is a must read for early intervention personnel by providing critical insight into environments and

the potential for environmental interventions, however daunting. It describes the results of a recent study by two pioneers in early intervention. Measures include not only children's language growth, but what happens in families (or doesn't!) to promote language as a keystone for later school and social success.

Karoly, L. A., Greenwood, P. W., Everingham, S. S., Hoube', J., Kilburn, M. R., Rydell, C. P., Sanders, M., & Chiesa, J. (1998). *Investing in our children: What we know and don't know about the costs and benefits of early childhood interventions.* Santa Monica, CA: Rand. This book packs much in 159 pages. It includes a succinct summary of major early intervention programs and benefits. The historical review, descriptions of key programs, and especially, program analyses are critical reading for early intervention specialists.

AUTHOR NOTES

Appreciation is greatly felt toward the following individuals who provided feedback to an earlier draft: Steve Coyne (special education preschool teacher), Misty Cresap (preschool teacher and parent), Rachel Dennison (special education preschool teacher), Mary Eaton (kindergarten teacher), Jodi Esterline (school psychology student), Sue Fan Foo (teacher of the deaf), Melanie Horvath (school psychology student), Maggie Jones-Prendergast (early intervention teacher and parent), Tom Knestrict (teacher, doctoral student), Jennifer Morris (school psychology student), Beth Myers (preschool teacher, schoolbus driver), Michelle Struckman (school psychology student), Christina Wronkiewicz (school psychology student).

79 Best Practices in the Use of Play for Assessment and Intervention with Young Children

Roslyn P. Ross
Queens College and the Graduate Center of the City University of New York

OVERVIEW

Preschoolers Do Surgery

This is a story from the field as told to me by Dr. Kirschenbaum, a urologist and the father of 4½ year old Benjy. Benjy's teacher, Ms. Hardin, invited Dr. K to the preschool to explain what he did, an invitation she extended to all parents. Dr. K went because he wanted to please Benjy and participate in his program, but he also had a message to deliver to the children that doctors would help them if they needed an operation and put them to sleep so it would not hurt. "I gave them a little spiel about what I do and why. I just told them a story that a little girl's kidneys failed and her mother decided to give her her own kidney. So I took the kidney from mom and everybody was happy. I told them what the kidney does, that we all have two and that you can live with one. I drew a diagram and showed them how it cleans the blood of all waste products. I also told them when we were in the operating room, we had to put on special gowns and clean our hands and how I work with a whole team—doctors, nurses, an anesthesiologist."

The action then switched to a corner of the room where Ms. Hardin had set up miniature operating and recovery rooms. There were tables, baby dolls of different colors, surgical gowns, masks, gloves, and (improvised) hats. There were three operating tables and Dr. K appointed an anesthesiologist, a nurse, and a surgeon to work at each of the tables. Since there were 20 children, each child took turns, and the teacher supervised the proceedings. Dr. K reported being very busy going from one table to another "to make sure they didn't kill someone." To get his message across, he kept saying things like "Make sure you put the patient to sleep so there is no pain." "We'll make it better." "We'll remove whatever we have to." "We'll give medication that makes it O.K."

Despite Dr. K's focus on enacting successful pain-free operations, other elements did enter the children's play. Steven rushed from the operating table to say, "Dr. K, my patient is bleeding. I'm losing my patient." When told to go to the blood bank, Steven replied, "There's no blood in the blood bank." He did allow Dr. K's next suggestion (to ask one of his colleagues to get blood) to end the crisis on a positive note, and he convinced one of his friends to give blood. Sam, all of a sudden, went to the phone and announced "There's a fire at Mt. Sinai." He kept yelling, "911. Fire. Come to Mt. Sinai." Kristen, a 4½ year old Barbra Streisand look-a-like, with a raspy voice, got into a corner, started to squat, and announced, "I'm having a baby."

This kept the children's attention for about 2 hours. One anesthesiologist wouldn't take his mask off and stayed in role for the entire time. After about 50 operations with a 100% positive outcome, the dolls were gently removed to the recovery room. The teacher then put a picture of a man on the floor. Working with the children who were still interested (about five of them), she had them put cut outs of different organs in place. They could also write the name of the organ with her spelling it. Then she took red and blue thread to explain the passage of the blood through arteries and veins.

The Value of Play

This story illustrates many of the reasons we study children's play. It is charming. It captures the wonderful creativity and spontaneity of children. Though the adults in this vignette initiated the play, the children took to it with delight and stamped it as their own. Because of this, their play serves as a window into their interests, their cognitive functioning, their emotional concerns. The story also illustrates how easily play can be used as a tool for teaching information and values, and how creative, inventive, and hardworking teachers of young children can be.

Indeed, the position of the National Association for the Education of Young Children (Bredekamp & Copple, 1997) is that child-initiated, teacher-supported play is an essential component of developmentally appropriate practice. Early childhood teachers recognize that play is an important vehicle for children's social, emotional, and cognitive development and use play to support and advance development. Vygotsky (1933/1978), a Soviet psychologist whose writings first became available in English in the 1960s, has been influential in this contemporary view of early childhood curricula. He proposed that a child's play, under adult guidance or in collaboration with more capable peers, creates a zone of proximal development, a zone in which the child can jump above the level of his or her normal development. In other words, according to Vygotsky, play actually sets the stage for subsequent development, and it is during play that we may see children at their most competent.

Preschool policymakers usually do not need to be convinced of the value of play for curricula. Primary school policymakers are more likely to need to be convinced, particularly as expectations for academic progress at younger and younger ages become commonplace. The legitimacy of the school recess period has even come into question in some quarters (Pellegrini & Boyd, 1993). There are also cultures in which parents do not value play nor engage in infant-child play (Roopnarine, Lasker, Sacks, & Stores, 1998). Additionally there are periods in history when play has been devalued. Sutton-Smith (2000) describes negativity toward play in agricultural societies needing children's labor and in many cultures of low production throughout Africa and the Americas. Play was also rejected during the several hundred years of European history associated with the arrival of industrial work hours and puritanical attitudes. According to Sutton-Smith, the result of several centuries of viewing play as a useless activity has meant that most twentieth-century theories of play and research have focused on showing how useful play actually is. Generally, those who argue the importance of play for children point to the many developmental assets in cognitive-linguistic and affective-social domains that are associated with play (Fisher, 1992; Pellegrini & Boyd, 1993). Children who engage in sociodramatic play tend to show more social competence, creativity, divergent thinking, language and reading skills, and impulse control, among other things. (Of course, the correlational nature of these relationships does not reveal whether play leads to these developmental advances, whether these other abilities lead to enhanced play abilities, or whether a third factor underlies success in both.)

In this chapter, an overview of how early twentieth century interest in children's play led to its use for intervention and assessment is followed by a section on the advantages of play, particularly play-based assessment, in contemporary school psychological practice with young children. The chapter next takes up the knowledge, skill base, personal qualities, and professional training needed to implement play-based assessment and interventions. A consideration of best practices in play assessment includes different models of assessment and a description of limitations aimed at giving a balanced picture of its potential. Recommendations for practice are made in light of advantages and limitations. The section on play interventions deals with play therapy (interventions aimed at diminishing emotional problems and disturbances) and interventions emphasizing developmental possibilities for children with special needs (in order to teach age-appropriate play activities). Descriptions of various approaches, outcome research, and recommendations for practice are given for both types of interventions.

How Play Came to be Used for Intervention and Assessment

The psychologists who dominated play theory in the first half of the twentieth century, among them Vygotsky, Freud, and Piaget, dealt with play as a secondary topic (Rubin, Fein, & Vandenberg, 1983). Interestingly, they all thought that children sought to express themselves through pretense play and that play results, in part, from wish fulfillment. Freud originally proposed that play provided children with an avenue for wish fulfillment or catharsis; that is, for safely venting unacceptable wishes. Later, he came to see that play also afforded opportunity for the mastery of traumatic events (the repetition compulsion in action). Through repetition in play, the child could spontaneously work over and assimilate anxiety-provoking situations. In play, children are able to exercise control instead of enduring events passively. They may do instead of being done to. They may stop and start the action at will, dealing only with as much of their experience as they can manage at a time. The belief that play can help children deal with traumatic events has lead to its use with hospitalized children and children who have suffered physical and sexual abuse (Gil, 1991).

Although Freud recognized the importance of play, he did not use it in treatment; his own therapeutic efforts were geared toward an adult population. His ideas about how play might aid the development of emotional stability, however, paved the way for its use in clinical and school settings. Play started to be used in psychoanalytic therapeutic work with children by Hug-Hellmuth in the late 1910s, and by Melanie Klein, Anna Freud, and Margaret Lowenfeld in the 1920s and 1930s (O'Connor, 1991).

In the 1940s and 1950s, ego psychologists studying play, most notably Erik Erikson (1950), expanded on its mastery aspects. They came to regard play and fantasy as cognitive skills that could be used to deal with conflict and anxiety and restore a sense of mastery. Difficult experiences could be replayed until a more satisfactory outcome was worked out. Erikson likened play to dreams and saw it as the royal road to the unconscious in children. Play disruptions signaled the breakdown of effective defenses or ego coping in the face of anxiety that was being expressed in the play. To evaluate play, according to Erikson, one needed knowledge of what play was expected of a child of a given age in a given community as well as individual and family dynamics.

Just as with adult treatment, play therapy began to be used by therapists of different theoretical orientations. Virginia Axline's translation of Roger's nondirective client-centered approach into play therapy is one well-known example, partly because of the popular book, *Dibs: In Search of Self*, that she published in 1964. In the 1960s other forms of child treatment began to challenge the analytic movement. Forms of treatment that were behavioral, time-limited, cognitive, and family oriented became important. The function of play changed. For example, in behavioral therapies play is merely a way of engaging the child in behavior that can then be reinforced. Since children enjoy play, play can create a positive relationship that enhances the therapist's reinforcement potential. The play itself is not seen as having particular adaptive or developmental advantages, nor is it a vehicle for communication. The reader who is interested in learning more about different theoretical orientations as well as the history of play theories and play therapy can consult O'Connor (1991), O'Connor and Schaefer, (1994), and Rubin et al., (1983).

Play was primarily thought of as a treatment technique, rather than as an assessment technique, from the early part of the twentieth century to the 1960s (Gitlin-Weiner, Sandgrund, & Schaefer, 2000). It did, however, have an assessment component in the sense that play provided information about emotional functioning that was used in a child's treatment. Play assessment in the form of naturalistic observation continues to be a useful way of obtaining information about a child's emotional functioning both for professionals, such as teachers and school psychologists, who need to be alert to signs of potential problems, and for those who need to understand the children they are formally evaluating or treating. Pretend play that becomes too frightening for the child to continue, play that is perseverative, play that has no benign pretend solutions for conflict or negative feelings, and play that is fragmented as if the child cannot piece things together are examples of pretend play that may be signaling the impairing presence of anxiety (Gordon, 1993) in a child who needs help.

At the same time that play was primarily thought of as a treatment technique, developmentalists were building a body of literature that described children's play within a normative framework. This work eventually became the foundation for using play for diagnosis. The most notable of the developmentalists and play theorists, Piaget (1945/1962), classified play and games along developmental lines and related changes in play to changes in intellectual or cognitive development. He noted that infants first engage in practice play, also known as functional or sensorimotor play, for the first year and a half or so of life, then symbolic or pretense play from about 21 months to 6 years of age, and then games-with-rules from about 7 to 11 years of age. Other play theorists added the categories of constructive play, in which objects are manipulated for the purpose of constructing something, and rough-and-tumble play, which is boisterous, physical, playful action patterns performed at a high pitch of activity. Constructive play begins at about 24 months of age and predominates from 36 months on, and rough-and-tumble play begins at about 36 months but predominates at 4 and 5 years of age. Piaget saw play as assimilation or practice which consolidates initial learnings, not new learning. Since children incorporate experience into existing ways of thinking, their three types of play correspond to sensorimotor, preoperational, and concrete operational intelligence, respectively. He also thought that since the meanings invoked in pretense play include emotional meanings and wishes as well as cognitive aspects, pretense play is also a mechanism for consolidating or working out emotionally discordant experiences.

Among the early scales for assessing play, in addition to Piaget's classification scheme, was one by Parten (1932) for studying normal social development in play. After observing children in a nursery school setting in group free play for over a 9-month period, Parten devised a scale with several categories of social participation. These categories were (a) unoccupied behavior, (b) solitary independent play, (c) onlooker behavior, (d) parallel activity, (e) associative play, and (f) cooperative play. This scale has continued to play a role in research. It has also been updated and adapted for clinical use, most notably in the Play Observation Scale by Rubin (1989), a norm-based, time-sample procedure that evaluates both social participation and, drawing upon the work of Piaget, structural components of free-play behavior.

Another early scale, used in conjunction with psychoanalytic treatment, to determine functioning in a number of areas was developed by Lowenfeld (1939). Lowenfeld used a sand tray and many small objects with children whom she asked to build a series of worlds over the course of several sessions. Their productions were analyzed in terms of a variety of predetermined characteristics. Several diagnostic tools based on Lowenfeld's work were developed in Europe where they enjoy popularity, but they have been overlooked in the United States (Gitlin-Weiner et al., 2000). Until recently, subsequent scales developed here tended to be for purposes of research, and were hard for the clinician to find. Early (and some not so early) scales proposed for clinical work tended to be subjective. Currently, there is increased emphasis on developing reliable and useful play diagnostic tools because of the increased emphasis on assessment of infants and preschool children stimulated by federal legislation committed to extend educational services to the youngest of those who are disabled and at high-risk and because of the perceived need for alternative assessment techniques.

Advantages of Play Assessment With Young Children

The assessment of infants and young children is fraught with difficulties. They are hard to test and often poorly motivated to do "well." Furthermore, the standardized tests that are used are often technically inadequate for them (Bracken, 1987; Bracken, Keith, & Walker, 1994; Flanagan & Alfonso, 1995). Even when technically sound, tests may assess only limited domains and have limited utility in treatment planning (Bagnato & Neisworth, 1994; National Association of School Psychologists Delegate Assembly, 1991). These limitations have prompted the call for alternative strategies to be used to complement traditional assessments. Among the suggested strategies are parent interviews, parent-child interactions, peer interactions, well-known research paradigms such as the strange-situation to assess attachment security or the conditioning paradigm to assess cognitive functioning, clinical judgment rating scales, and curriculum-based assessment. Play-based assessments are strongly recommended. There is consensus among those recommending play-based assessments that it offers many advantages.

Play is the child's language. Long before children can talk about their emotional concerns or express what they know in words, they can express themselves in play. Play also offers this advantage to children with language impairments, to children who are second-language learners, to children with sensory or behavioral impairments that inhibit their expression on standardized tests.

As a window into children's minds, play allows us to gain insight into their emotional concerns and coping strategies. Play has been found to reflect so many other areas of functioning, that it may also be used to gain insight into cognitive development, intellectual capacity, ego functioning, social competence, motor functioning, and handicapping conditions (Fisher, 1992; Hughes, 1998; Rubin et al., 1983). Multiple domains can be assessed from the same data by members of various disciplines.

It is also easier to gain such insights through play than tests because children love to play. They are motivated when it comes to play. It is a pleasurable natural situation with minimum stress. This means that multiple observations can be made without the results being compromised by boredom or practice effects. It also means that we are likely to see children at their most competent during play. Play assessment is also ecologically sensitive. Parents can easily be involved and the child can be seen in various contexts in which he or she operates. An additional advantage to play assessment is that it encourages team cooperation because members of the various disciplines can be involved simultaneously or view the same videotaped samples of behavior. Play-based assessment can also easily be designed to yield information linked directly to intervention planning. The work of Linder (1993a, 1993b) and Lifter (2000) are examples of systems in which as much thought has been given to play-based interventions that may help children at various developmental levels as to the assessment instruments themselves.

Implications for School Psychologists

School psychologists have increasing responsibility for preschoolers as a result of legislation calling for early intervention for children with developmental delays or at risk for such delays. This is in addition to the responsibilities they already bear for young children in elementary school. From this overview, it should be clear that knowledge about the use of play for both assessment and intervention is important. Even psychologists working with older elementary-school youngsters need to understand how some of them may originally have been judged eligible for services while still in preschool or younger. For those who are working directly with young children, the development of actual skills in these areas is essential.

BASIC CONSIDERATIONS

Knowledge and Skill Base

Because play-based assessment and interventions must be selected and used on the basis of their appropriateness for a particular case, the knowledge and skill base needed for their use includes the broad one involved in working with young children and their families in general. In 1991 the National Association of School Psychology (NASP) Delegate Assembly adopted a position paper on Early Childhood Assessment that called for practices that are developmentally appropriate, ecological, family focused, directly linked to intervention strategies, nondiscriminatory, conducted by multi-disciplinary teams, technically adequate, and validated for the purpose for which they are used. Collaborations between professionals and between parents and professionals were also to be stressed. Recognizing that assessment of young children requires specialized training and skills beyond those required for the assessment of older children, the NASP Delegate Assembly (1991) recommended preservice and in-service education to address:

- normal as well as atypical developmental patterns of young children;
- practices, procedures, and instrumentation appropriate for screening and assessment of young children, their families, and their environments;
- the use of empirically sound procedures and technically adequate instruments with demonstrated treatment utility;
- the selection of assessment techniques and utilization of findings from such assessments for the design, implementation, and efficacy evaluation of interventions;
- standards for early childhood psychological and educational assessment, including legal, ethical, and professional issues; and
- noncategorical service delivery for young children and their families (p. 1213).

The importance of knowledge of family systems theory and child-family interactions may also be inferred from this position statement.

Additional specific knowledge that is required for play-based assessment and intervention includes knowledge of the course of play in normal and abnormal development, situational and cultural factors that can enhance or limit play, play typical of children with different disabilities, and play disturbances that indicate a child is experiencing undue stress. Knowledge of various play-assessment instruments and their reliability and validity is needed. Because so many new instruments are being developed, it is important to know how to evaluate technical adequacy. Knowledge of different play interventions, as well as other interventions that exist for young children, along with knowledge of their validity and relative usefulness for different purposes, is also required. Because this is often knowledge in the making, it requires keeping up with the clinical and research literatures.

As far as the personal qualities needed, it really helps if you enjoy working with young children, if you are comfortable engaging in play with them, and if you delight in play and fantasy. It also helps if you have a natural talent for understanding and speaking in the language of play, although this can be learned. Flexibility and creativity will also give you an edge. Among the skills needed are skill in doing and recording naturalistic observations, skill in using one or more play instruments, skill in selecting and planning play interventions, and skill in carrying out one or more of these interventions. Some of the instruments and some of the interventions, such as play therapy, are harder to learn than others, and most require training and supervision to learn.

Professional Training

In order to learn skills, it is necessary to first gain knowledge, then observe the skill in action, and then practice the skill under conditions of being observed and critiqued. This is the reason for field-based practicum and internship experiences in pre-service training programs. However, many school psychologists already in practice have not had pre-service training to work with preschoolers and will need to learn these skills on the job. Whether you seek out continuing professional development within your work setting or postgraduate training, you will need opportunity to read and discuss the literature, to observe someone experienced, model the skills, and to practice new skills while you are observed on a regular on-going basis. This is particularly so if you are inexperienced with young children or if you want to learn to do play therapy. If you have not had pre-service, supervised training in treating young children, it is best to seek out postgraduate training from a university training program or institute to learn play-therapy techniques. Ongoing peer supervision groups are recommended after initial skill mastery.

BEST PRACTICES

Play Assessment

Models of Assessment

Play may be used to assess the young child's skills in a number of domains (e.g., cognitive, language, motor, social). Play may also be used to assess the child's interests and emotional concerns or the nature of the child's typical interactions with caretakers and peers. Play skills themselves may be assessed to plan interventions to facilitate play skills. Play may also be used to help detect sexual abuse. Anatomically detailed dolls have been used when interviewing young children about suspected sexual abuse, though this practice remains controversial and should only be used by interviewers familiar with the legal constraints of providing evidence in such cases.

Obviously, a number of different formats exist for these various purposes, and the selection of an instrument depends upon purpose. Observations may be made of spontaneous play or play elicited by specific toys, situations, or interactions. Observations may be recorded in written anecdotal, narrative, or time-interval form and/or videotaped. Observations may also be coded according to rating scales that differ in terms of specificity. Some formats such as arena assessment (e.g., Linder, 1993a) include the entire professional team who participate as active spectators who record observations and score portions of assessment tools while one of them or the parent or a peer interacts with the child and facilitates play. When one of the professional team members acts to facilitate play, the team member follows the child's lead, encourages,. motivates, and also provides scaffolding for eliciting higher-level behaviors. The child is also observed playing alone. The assessment process is intended to include the family. It is videotaped, when possible, for both professional and parent reference. Team discussion after the assessment allows parents to join with professionals in analyzing what they have seen and to plan interventions. Linder's model of Transdisciplinary Play-Based Assessment is among the most widely used models of play-based assessment. It is designed for children between infancy and 6 years of age and examines performance across four domains of development (cognitive, social-emotional, communication and language, sensorimotor).

Descriptions of assessment procedures can be found in Fewell and Kaminski (1988) and Gitlin-Weiner et al. (2000). In addition to formal procedures, assessment based on play can also be conducted through play observations that are less formal or open-ended. Segal and Webber (1996) call these observations nonstructured because they are open-ended, but they do require structuring by the clinician in the sense that decisions must be made about participants, setting, toys, focus of observation, how to record the data, and how to write up the observation. It is also possible to do targeted observations of play behavior (e.g., how often a child initiates play with other children, how well the child handles frustration while playing) and devise a coding system that would do for interval, event, or ratings recording. To interpret the results of these less formal procedures, it is necessary to know the contextual factors that can elicit and inhibit play processes (see Pellegrini, 1998; Rubin et al., 1983). Three examples of contextual factors that affect play are that children will display the highest level of competence in play in the presence of peers compared to adults, with friends compared to nonfriends, and with gender-consistent toys.

Limitations of Play-Based Assessment

The advantages of play-based assessment are many and have been described in the Overview of this chapter. Despite its great promise, it must be noted that currently there are only a few existing studies that support the reliability and validity of play-assessment instruments. The one scale that is thought to have more evidence of validity than other scales, the Play Assessment Scale by Fewell, has no evidence of reliability and is not available commercially (Athanasiou, 2000). We therefore lack sufficient information to conclude that other observers using the same instruments would come up with the same findings or that the information obtained from play assessment correlates with information from other developmental measures or that the interventions they suggest lead to significant developmental changes, when implemented. With respect to reliability issues, it is particularly difficult to obtain high standards when observations are flexible, naturalistic, or unstructured.

Additionally, most play assessment instruments give qualitative information about the presence or absence of developmental skills. While this may be useful for developing a curriculum for a youngster, it might not be sufficient to gauge the seriousness of a delay or deficit or to determine eligibility for services. Different instruments also measure different skills and give only partial information about a child's development . Play assessments may also be expensive, time consuming, difficult to arrange, require a great deal of skill to conduct and analyze, and be considered intrusive by some parents (Segal & Webber, 1996). At present it makes sense to consider play-based and traditional norm-based methods of assessment as complementary procedures. We need to know with whom play-based procedures work best and how they can be assimilated into practitioners' existing knowledge base (Bracken, 1994).

Recommendations for Practice

The recommendations that follow are consistent with (though not limited to) position statements made by the NASP Delegate Assembly (1991) on early childhood assessment and the Zero to Three Work Group on Developmental Assessment (Greenspan & Meisels, 1994).

1. Use play assessment as one source of data to validate and expand information from other sources. Play data should never be used alone to make diagnostic or placement decisions. It is most likely to have greatest use in identifying instructional strategies and educational goals. As Bracken (1994) has pointed out, those advocating alternative assessment procedures solely need to present evidence that the procedures have at least as much reliability and validity as those they are meant to replace.

2. Whenever possible, use valid and reliable scales to analyze play data. This provides operational definitions for the behavior to be assessed and increases reliability of observations.

3. Carefully record what has been observed.

4. The importance of multiple sources of information applies to play assessment itself. Include structured and unstructured play sessions. Observe on more than one occasion and in more than one kind of situation.

5. Play content is like projective content in that it cannot be interpreted without additional sources of information. Play content may reflect how the child actually responds to events or wishes he or she could respond or has seen others respond. Play content may reflect the expression of impulses typically controlled. It may also reflect turning what has been passively experienced into an active form in order to reassert a sense of control. Get information about the child's actual behavior so that interpretation of play content is more than guesswork.

6. Try to observe play in the child's natural environment to appreciate the influence of the environment. This is also most likely to give a child with disabilities the chance to show his or her best play behavior because he or she will be most at ease and less likely to be distracted than in a classroom or a novel situation.

7. Try to observe the child in play with the parent(s) or other familiar caregivers.

8. Do not do an entire assessment in the space of one day.

9. Give the child time to explore the environment and get comfortable before beginning an observation. Incorporating the child's toys in play sessions will also increase the child's comfort.

10. Children who come from backgrounds that do not value play will need prompting and time to engage in play. Judgments about their play will have to be delayed until they have been given sufficient opportunities to engage in play. If parents have not encouraged play for cultural reasons, then norm-based assessment of cognitive functioning may be more appropriate.

11. Have someone familiar with the child's culture and language on the team when working with culturally different children.

12. Work with families as team members to get information about the child, to determine their needs and resources, to help analyze the play data, and to generate and implement recommendations.

13. View the process of assessment as the first step in a potential intervention process

Play Interventions

Play interventions may be divided into (a) those aimed at diminishing emotional problems and disturbances (play therapy), (b) those emphasizing developmental possibilities for children with special needs in order to teach age-appropriate play activities, and (c) those that are part of general educational curriculum emphasizing cognitive effects (Hellendoorn, van der Kooij, & Sutton-Smith, 1994). Play interventions in the third category also include (a) play-training programs that help young children with environmental disadvantages such as poverty make gains in pretense and sociodramatic play to increase social participation and language, (b) programs training parents to play with their infants to increase parenting skills, (c) teacher interventions in play aimed at influencing specific social behaviors and attitudes, and (d) social-skills training. While social-skills training is not, strictly speaking, a play intervention, with younger children it typically involves training those children in developing positive approach responses so that they may be able to play with peers.

This section will focus on play interventions in the first two categories. Information on play interventions in the third category may be found in Hellendoorn et al., (1994), Singer and Singer (1990), Bredekamp and Copple (1997), and articles on social-skills training in this volume.

Play Therapy

Theories of Play Therapy. Play therapy makes use of the therapeutic aspects of play, just as does any good preschool or kindergarten setting. In addition, it relies on a given theoretical orientation that directs what the therapist does and how the therapist understands what is going on. Although play therapy was first developed in the 1920s by psychoanalysts, it is no longer associated with any one theoretical position. It is used by practitioners with vastly different theoretical positions and methods (see O'Connor & Schaefer, 1994) because it is a natural medium for children. Children engage in play easily and happily, for the most part, and this facilitates the development of a positive relationship between therapist and child. For behavioral therapists, play serves only as a way of engaging the child in behavior that can be reinforced. It has no other intrinsic value.

Most other therapists consider play to be a medium of communication and not just a form of activity in which children will readily participate. The therapy room and its equipment are set up to facilitate that communication. Therapists show active, reflective, listening by reflecting the thoughts and feelings the child expresses in play: at first, by making running comments on the content of the play (e.g., "That doll is playing games by himself and the other dolls are playing together.") and, later, by adding affective or motivational comments about the child's play (e.g., "That doll must feel lonely because no one is playing with him.") and, still later, when the time is appropriate, by tentatively broaching the distance between play feelings and the child's feelings (e.g., "Perhaps you feel like that sometimes."). Questions are also asked in the context of the play (e.g., "I wonder why the doll is playing by himself?") and only later, when appropriate, more directly. The therapist also reflects on the child's verbalizations and feelings.

In humanistic (or client-centered) therapy, reflection rather than interpretation is emphasized. Interpretation is much more important in therapies with a psychoanalytic or psychodynamic orientation because it is thought crucial for bringing about insight and change. The psychoanalytic therapist may also use the play to present information to the child. The therapist delivers an interpretation or information framed to apply to the characters in the play, thus allowing the child to maintain some distance and better tolerate what is being said (e.g., "That doll gets so frightened every time the daddy hits him that he thinks the only way to be safe is to hurt himself first . . . . He doesn't know that he can get other grownups, like his teacher or the doctor, to stop the daddy from hitting him if he tells them about it. I guess he doesn't know that because the mommy never stopped it when he told her, but she's probably scared of the daddy too."). There are a series of steps to follow in giving interpretations that start with interpreting within the play and end with interpreting directly to the child.

In the more cognitively oriented behavioral therapies, emphasis is placed on altering the child's thoughts and beliefs to produce behavior change. It was originally thought that preschool-age children were not developmentally ready for a cognitive approach. Cognitive-behavioral play therapy (Knell, 1998) is an example of an adaptation for younger children. As described by Knell, it is a structured, directive, problem-oriented treatment. The therapist may construct specific play scenarios and model adaptive behavior through the actions of dolls or puppets. The doll or puppet model may verbalize problem-solving skills or solutions to problems that parallel the child's difficulties. Cognitive distortions, even developmentally appropriate ones such as the fear of falling down the toilet, can be corrected. Children may also be provided with positive self-statements as a coping device (e.g., "I will make new friends when I move.") and be helped to label feelings so they can think about them. This all sounds very much like "interpreting within the play." Mastery through repetition in play also seems to be redefined as a desensitization paradigm in cognitive-behavioral play therapy; that is, play is useful as the activity that is incompatible with anxiety. Cognitive-behavioral play therapy is more directive than some psychoanalytic therapies, and its interpretative focus is more on maladaptive thoughts. Despite these exceptions, there seem to be many similarities in what therapists do.

Other models of play therapy stress a corrective emotional experience to repair caregiver/child interactive failures (e.g., Jernberg; see O'Connor, 1991). A number of techniques are used to produce positive interactions between the child and therapist, among them using every opportunity for making physical contact, insisting on eye contact, placing exclusive focus on the child, and keeping the sessions cheerful.

Following the development of a strong bond, the therapist gradually introduces others (caregivers, siblings, peers) into the playroom so that the child's newly developed interactive style will generalize. Although this is a therapist-directed structured approach, the therapist communicates through play, using reflection and interpretation, in a way similar to that described above for psychodynamic approaches.

The developmental, individualized, relationship–based approach to the treatment of "developmentally challenged" children (usually those falling within the autistic spectrum disorders) also emphasizes the development of relationships and communication (Greenspan & Wieder, 1998). Both therapists and caregivers, working individually, become the child's active play partner in a way that encourages the child to interact with them. The child is also encouraged to express feelings or intentions in pretend play and words.

Contexts in Which Therapy Occurs. Play therapy may occur in different contexts. Children may be seen individually or in a group. They may be seen individually by a therapist in their classroom in "push-in therapy" during which they are coached on how to interact with their classmates. They also may have their parent(s) or peers as co- or primary therapists. The number of techniques and contexts is dizzying. Play therapy has also been used in different kinds of situations: in work with children who have been abused, children in crises, traumatized children, autistic children, and children facing medical treatments and/or hospitalization. From the perspective of those who espouse the various therapies, it can be used with children with a wide variety of problems and ages.

Outcome Research. To best serve the mental health needs of children, we need to be able to identify specific interventions for specific problems and diagnoses. We should like to be able to say of play therapy that it has demonstrated efficacy for children with specific problems and demonstrated superiority over other interventions. We should further like to specify what kind of play therapy to use in different situations. All that we can say is that, on average, play therapy has demonstrated efficacy; we lack sufficient information to be more specific. Too few studies of play therapy have been done (Eyberg, 1992), and even fewer of these have been rigorous enough to be included in meta-analytic reviews of therapy outcomes. This is so despite the fact that play therapy is widely used in practice (Tuma & Pratt, 1982).

A recent search turned up only two meta-analyses that either reviewed play therapy studies or included play therapy as a category of treatment to analyze. Both reported an effect size of two-thirds of a standard deviation, or between moderate and large, according to Cohen's (1988) interpretation of effect size. A difference this size would have considerable practical and clinical significance. The difference in the average child treated with play therapy would be normally noticed in daily life. The first meta-analysis (Casey and Berman,1985) compared play and non-play treatments and found them to be equally effective. This means that play treatments were found to be neither more nor less effective than non-play treatments. There was not enough information, however, to tell what kind of play treatment was being compared with what kind of non-play treatment or whether both play and non-play treatment were equally effective for different problems, or for children of different ages. The second review of play therapy research (LeBlanc and Ritchie, 1999), which found a similar effect size, also suggested that modes of play therapy, like filial therapy (a client-centered approach) and parent-child interaction therapy (a behavioral approach), in which parents become additional therapists, may be more effective than other forms of play therapy.

The research base for play therapy is thin, and it gives limited guidance on what type, if any, is most effective for preschoolers, for children of different cultures, or for different problems. It is necessary to turn to the more broadly based psychotherapy and treatment literature for further information. The findings of over 300 outcome studies conducted between 1952 and 1993 have been summarized in meta-analytic reviews. The following conclusions may be drawn (Weisz & Hawley, 1998). First, there are effective interventions for children and adolescents that produce substantial effects. Effect sizes hover around 0.80, the level considered "large" by Cohen (1988). The average child included in an intervention group scored higher on outcome measures than 76–81% of children in a control group. Second, the magnitude of these effects is similar to those found for treatment of adults. Third, child treatments produce effects that are relatively lasting in their impact. Fourth, these effects are relatively specific to the problems targeted in treatment. Fifth, treatment effects are stronger for behavioral and cognitive-behavioral than for non-behavioral techniques.

It is clear that there is strong empirical support for behavioral and cognitive-behavioral interventions. It should be noted that most of the reviewed behavioral and cognitive-behavioral interventions do not involve play. Hopefully, cognitive-behavioral play therapy will also receive empirical support when it is reviewed. In making sense of the demonstrated empirical superiority of behavioral and cognitive-behavioral over non-behavioral techniques, it also should be noted that non-behavioral treatments have not received as extensive an evaluation as behavioral ones. More than 75% of the studies in most child meta-analyses test behavioral and cognitive-behavioral interventions (Weisz & Hawley, 1998). This figure increases for recent meta-analyses. Ollendick and King (1998) did not even bother to review any therapies other than behavioral and cognitive-behavioral ones for childhood phobic and anxiety disorders because of findings that treatment effects, in general, are stronger for behavioral than non-behavioral techniques. This does a disservice to studies that have demonstrated that psychodynamic and client-centered therapies can be effective in treating childhood internalizing problems, including anxiety disorders (e.g., Fonagy & Target, 1994; Kolvin et al., 1981).

It also leaves unexamined the very procedures (e.g., family, eclectic, psychodynamic) that practitioners, including school psychologists, report they frequently use (Kazdin, Siegel, & Bass, 1990). A recent meta-analysis of school-based studies of counseling found 17 studies from 1985 to 1994 that fit (methodologically rigorous) criteria for inclusion (Prout & Prout, 1998). Not one of them included individual counseling, although a national sample of school psychologists reported in 1993 that this was the most frequently used modality in the school (cited in preceding study). Further, all of the school-based studies involved cognitive- behavioral variants of treatment. Empirical research on psychotherapy as it is practiced is needed.

The special issue on empirically supported intervention techniques in the *Journal of Clinical Child Psychology,* 27(2), 1998, is recommended for the information it provides on the benchmarks that must be met by current clinical treatments before they can be as confidently recommended as can certain behavioral and cognitive-behavioral treatments. At present, however, we cannot say with certainty what kind of play therapy is most effective for what kind of problem. Relatively few of the studies included in most meta-analyses involve psychotherapy as it is practiced in most settings. I am afraid we also cannot say with certainty what school psychologists are actually doing when they say they are doing play therapy. It is not unusual to have a recommendation for play therapy on an Individual Educational Plan in the New York metropolitan area. It seems to mean different things in different settings. It can be translated, for example, as a recommendation for psychodynamically oriented play therapy or a developmental recommendation to enhance language skills or enhance play skills or social skills. The only common meaning seems to be that it will be given by a psychologist.

Play Therapy and Aggression. Nondirective play therapies are not considered useful for children who are very aggressive or engage in considerable acting out. The intense structure and quality of limit setting these children require runs counter to the philosophy of nondirective approaches. In addition, aggressive play (or watching filmed aggression) may actually stimulate rather than reduce further aggression in aggressive children who are motorically oriented and reveal much action and little thought or imagination in play activities (Biblow, 1973). Catharsis by itself, without emotional restructuring or reorganization, is not healing. Psychoanalytic treatment (presumably including play therapy for the younger children) was found to be much less effective for children with disruptive behavior disorders than children with neurotic or internalizing disorders, though differences in treatment effectiveness disappeared if the children remained in intensive treatment for 3 years (Fonagy & Target, 1994). However, the percentage of children with disruptive behavior disorder who returned to a level of functioning within the normal range falls far short of rates of improvement for such children who receive a combination of parent-management training and problem-solving skills training (Brestan & Eyberg, 1998).

Recommendations for Practice. Two useful sources of information on handling everyday issues in play therapy and setting up a playroom are Dodds (1985) and Ginott (1961). (I particularly like Ginott's recommendation that a maid be available to put the playroom back to rights after each session.)

There are so many different techniques and theoretical orientations to treatment that fall within the rubric of play therapy that it is impossible to give any but the most general recommendations below.

1. Consider whether simpler interventions in the classroom might help or whether modifying the child's classroom or home environment might be more appropriate.

2. Form collaborative relationships with caretakers. Involve them as much as possible in their children's treatment and in parent-training programs. We need to work with significant adults in the child's world, including teachers, to carry out change in that world.

3. Consider play therapy to help a young child deal with (certain) emotional or developmental problems if the child's communication can be facilitated by play. The range of age for which it should be considered is roughly between 3 and 12 years, with exceptions at both ages. With older children, the play will likely be games, rather than fantasy play, and many preteens may opt for communicating directly through language.

4. Until we have outcome data to the contrary, consider play therapy primarily for helping a child deal with internalizing or overcontrolled problems. Play therapy is not the method of choice for getting the child to change behavior that disturbs others. This may happen as a byproduct as the child feels better emotionally and develops more mature ways of dealing with stress, but it cannot be guaranteed.

5. For children with serious problems in aggression, consider first parent-management training for parents and problem-solving skills training and behavior modification interventions for the children.

6. Any child seen in play therapy in order to ameliorate emotional problems or negative feelings thought to be causing learning problems should receive academic remediation as well. The same may be said about the need for social skills training for a child seen in order to ameliorate emotional problems thought to be causing social ones.

7. Building a positive relationship is important no matter what one's theoretical orientation is. Techniques that convey understanding, respect, and nonjudgmental acceptance work as well with children as they do with adults.

8. Although we may accept all symbolic behavior in play, limits should be placed on behavior that might hurt the child or the therapist, or encroach upon the ability of the therapist to do his or her job. Ginott (1961) is recommended as a good source for how to set limits.

9. Set goals to guide treatment and evaluate whether you are reaching goals.

10. Review your work in ongoing supervision with peers or a supervisor.

Play-Based Interventions for Children With Special Needs

Play in Children With Developmental Disabilities. Play difficulties have been linked empirically with various handicapping conditions. (See Hughes, 1998, and Rubin et al., 1983, for summaries of findings.) Currently, many researchers believe that children with autism have unique, specific, deficits in symbolic play (and language) that cannot be explained by level of cognitive development or degree of mental retardation alone. A paucity of symbolic play is considered characteristic of autism. When it comes to other types of disability, however, it is much less clear that play differences reflect innate deficits in play abilities. For some groups, such as pre-term infants and children with intellectual impairments, the issue is primarily one of delay. Hughes (1998) and others have suggested that the issue for children with physical and social disabilities and for victims of child abuse may be one of lack of opportunity. A blind child, for example, will not explore what he or she cannot see unless adults make special efforts to alert the child to what is available and remove physical obstacles to exploring. A child with limited mobility needs toys brought to him or her, and needs adults sensitive to the slightest cue of interest in a toy or in playing. Deaf children are unable to engage with others in the negotiations necessary to set up sociodramatic play because of their language difficulties and not because of innate difficulties with play. Children with disabilities may have limited social opportunities. This may be so even if they are in early childhood special education programs if such programs group them with similarly handicapped youngsters or put greater emphasis on teaching academic skills and less on play than is found in mainstream programs. They may also have limited social opportunities when they are in inclusion mainstream programs because they lack the social skills to participate in play. Children with mild disabilities are, on average, approximately 1 standard deviation below normally developing children in social skills (Gresham, 1997)

Teaching Developmentally Relevant Play. Play has long been the mainstay of early childhood programs. It is assumed that physical, emotional, and social development, as well as learning, will follow if the child's inherent motivation to play is supported (Bredekamp & Copple, 1997). The teacher provides an environment that is conducive to play and develops a curriculum that supports emerging play skills of the normally developing child. This is not sufficient for children with special needs who need to be helped to compensate for the constraints that limit their play. They need to be helped to learn to play, and they need to be taught the social skills that will enable them to initiate and sustain social play (to actually engage in play with their peers).

There are a number of formal linked assessment/intervention programs that help teachers (and parents) adapt their existing play strategies to meet the unique needs of a child with disabilities that are based on an assessment of where that child is developmentally (e.g., Lifter, 2000; Linder, 1993a, 1993b). Linder's (1993a) system of Transdisciplinary Play-Based Assessment, for example, provides summary worksheets on which observed competencies and deficits are directly translated into goals for the child. She also provides a companion book of suggested play and playful interventions to reach goals for each of the four functional domains that have been assessed (Linder, 1993b). The program of play interventions is planned jointly by the entire team, including parents.

Lifter (2000) also directs interventions toward developmentally relevant activities that she defines as activities that the child is at the threshold of learning; that is, they are the emergent categories of play as determined by quantitative criteria applied to a sample of play activities. Recommended procedures for interventions build on the standard practice in Early Childhood Education of following the child's lead in terms of what he or she appears to be paying attention to and incorporating least-to-most prompting procedures to shape new behaviors (Sulzer-Azaroff & Mayer, 1991). Thus one might comment on a cup that a child was playing with and suggest additional things that could be done with a cup that build upon the child's readiness to learn certain kinds of activities. The assessment and the intervention planning are usually done by one person, typically a teacher. Interventions may be implemented by the classroom teacher, by a home-based therapist, or by a parent.

Children with disabilities have also been taught play activities to (a) compete with the occurrence of maladaptive behavior (e.g., Ballard & Medland, 1986) and (b) to increase prosocial behavior when they have skill deficits (e.g., Stahmer, 1995). The second approach has included teaching symbolic play to children with autism. Generally, these interventions have not employed systematic play assessment procedures. Instead, objectives have been determined based on what could be done with appealing toys for the first approach and a general knowledge of what children do when they play for the second approach.

Outcome Research. Play intervention studies indicate that children with developmental disabilities can learn play activities as a result of systematic procedures (e.g., Stahmer, 1995) and that the ease of learning such activities may be linked to their developmental, rather than chronological, relevance (Lifter, 2000). Studies also suggest that for some children the programs contribute to language development and social interaction (Fisher, 1992). However, most children with autism are still seen as socially unacceptable by their peers following play intervention programs (Schreibman & Koegel, 1996). Children with autism tend to respond less to peers than they do to adults after training procedures conducted solely with adults. Findings from social-skills training research with less handicapped youngsters also indicate that it is easier to change children's social behavior than it is to change their peers' perceptions of them (Kazdin & Johnson, 1994). Because peers and adults may see children differently, information from multiple sources is necessary for outcome data. The answer to how a child responds to an intervention for undercontrolled problems or poor social skills may differ depending on who is asked.

In general, much more research needs to be done before we can be sure that learning play activities leads to progress in overall development for children with disabilities or that play interventions are better than instruction that focuses only on the specific ability in question. While play-based assessment that puts intervention planning in the forefront is an important step in providing a link between assessment and intervention, it remains to be seen whether implementation of these interventions leads to improved functioning above and beyond improved play functioning.

Recommendations for Practice. Linder (1993b) provides the following general recommendations for implementing play interventions that may be useful in a number of different contexts or programs.

1. Intervene in a child's play only when it can be done unobtrusively without disrupting the flow of play. Wait till the child is exhibiting low levels of play or is playing in a perseverative fashion.

2. The child should be allowed to select and lead play activities as much as possible.

3. Determine what engages the child, and use that information to form an interactive relationship.

4. Responsiveness to the child's cues is crucial to enhancing adult-child interactions. Responsiveness is shown by responding to the child's cues and communicative intent, matching language and pace to that of the child, and staying with the child's agenda.

5. Make sure that you give children with disabilities a sufficient wait time (at least 5 seconds) to respond. Lack of wait time can result in the adult's dominating the interactions.

6. Use a variety of language strategies that have been found to increase children's communication efforts.
   - Mirroring: Repeat the child's actions, sounds, or words.
   - Commenting: Comment on what the child is doing or describe the content of the play.
   - Self-talk: Talk about one's own actions.
   - Expansions: Add new words or ideas when restating what the child has said or done.
   - Modeling: Model sounds, words, or language structures. Label actions, feelings, events.
   - Prompting: Prompt responses specific to the situation that the child can make.
   - Open-ended questions: Avoid questions that can be answered with one word.

7. Work collaboratively with significant adults in the child's world to carry out change in that world.

SUMMARY

The history of how play came to be used for assessment and intervention includes views of play as a means of emotional expression for children, a cognitive skill that could be used to deal with conflict and anxiety, a vehicle for learning, and a developmental phenomenon that follows a distinct sequence.

Play-based assessment provides an excellent alternative assessment strategy for young children because play is childhood's language. Children love to play. It is a pleasurable, natural, situation with minimum stress, a situation in which we are likely to see children at their most competent. It is an ecologically sensitive technique that easily involves parents, and it can easily provide information for developing interventions. Play-based assessment also encourages team cooperation because members of the various disciplines can be involved simultaneously or view the same videotaped samples of behavior. A number of different formats exist for the various purposes to which play-based assessment may be put. Play may be used to assess skills in a number of domains or to assess play skills themselves in order to facilitate play skills. It may be used to assess emotional concerns, the nature of the child's interactions, and the possibility of abuse.

Despite all of its advantages, play-based assessment is not an automatic answer for all of the ills of traditional standardized testing with young children.

We lack information on its reliability and validity, among other limitations, and it should be seen as a complement to, rather than a replacement for, existing instruments of proven reliability and validity.

Play is often used to influence development because it has so many important developmental consequences and because it is so easily influenced. Play interventions may be divided into (a) those aimed at diminishing emotional problems and disturbances (play therapy), (b) those emphasizing developmental possibilities for children with special needs in order to teach age-appropriate play activities, and (c) those that are part of general educational curriculum emphasizing cognitive and social effects. This chapter deals with interventions in the first two categories.

Meta-analytic reviews of outcome studies of child and adolescent interventions for emotional problems are coming up with positive findings. They indicate that there are effective interventions for children and adolescents that produce substantial effects, and these interventions include play therapy. There are, however, insufficient data to know what kind of play therapy, if any, is best for what type of problem. This is unfortunate because we need to be able to identify specific interventions for specific purposes and problems in order to best serve the mental health and developmental needs of children. Certain recommendations for best practice can still be made despite the limitations of our knowledge.

Play intervention studies indicate that children with developmental disabilities can learn play activities as a result of systematic procedures. For some children, the programs contribute to language development and social interaction. While these are very encouraging findings, more research needs to be done before we can be sure that learning play activities leads to progress in overall development for children with disabilities or that play interventions are better than instruction that focuses only on the specific ability in question. Some general recommendations for implementing play interventions may be useful in a number of different contexts.

REFERENCES

Athanasiou, M. S. (2000). Play-based approaches to preschool assessment. In B. A. Bracken (Ed.), *The psychoeducational assessment of preschool children* (pp. 412–427). Boston: Allyn & Bacon.

Bagnato, S. J., & Neisworth, J. T. (1994). A national study of the social and treatment "invalidity" of intelligence testing for early intervention. *School Psychology Quarterly*, 2, 81–102.

Ballard, K. D., & Medland, J. L. (1986). Collateral effects from teaching attention, imitation, and toy interaction behaviors to a developmentally delayed handicapped child. *Child and Family Behavior Therapy*, 7(4), 47–50

Biblow, E. (1973). Imaginative play and the control of aggressive behavior. In J. L. Singer (Ed.), *The child's world of make-believe: Experimental studies of imaginative play* (pp. 104–128). New York: Academic.

Bracken, B. A. (1987). Limitations of preschool instruments and standards for minimal levels of technical adequacy. *Journal of Psychoeducational Assessment, 4*, 313–326.

Bracken, B. A. (1994). Advocating for effective preschool assessment practices: A comment on Bagnato and Neisworth. *School Psychology Quarterly*, 9, 103–108.

Bracken, B. A., Keith, L. K., & Walker, K. C. (1994). Assessment of preschool behavior and social emotional functioning: A review of thirteen third-party instruments. *Assessment in Rehabilitation and Exceptionality, 1*, 331–346.

Bredekamp, S., & Copple, C. (Eds.). (1997). *Developmentally appropriate practice in early childhood practice* (Rev. ed.). Washington, DC: National Association for the Education of Young Children.

Brestan, E. V., & Eyberg. S. M. (1998). Effective psychosocial treatments of conduct-disordered children and adolescents: 29 years, 82 studies, and 5,272 kids: Empirically supported treatments for children with phobic and anxiety disorders. *Journal of Clinical Child Psychology*, 27(2), 180–189.

Casey, R. J., & Berman, J. S. (1985). The outcome of psychotherapy with children. *Psychological Bulletin, 98*, 388–400.

Cohen, J. (1988). *Statistical power analysis for the behavioral sciences* (2nd ed.). Hillsdale, NJ: Erlbaum.

Dodds, J. B. (1985). *A child's psychotherapy primer: Suggestions for the beginning therapist*. New York: Human Sciences Press.

Erikson, E. (1950). *Childhood and society.* New York: Norton.

Eyberg, S. M. (1992). Assessing therapy outcome with preschool children: Progress and problems. *Journal of Clinical Child Psychology, 21*, 306-311.

Fewell, R. R., & Kaminski, R. (1988). Play skills development and instruction for young children with handicaps. In S. L. Odom & M. B. Karnes (Eds.), *Early intervention for infants and children with handicaps: An empirical base* (pp. 145–158). Baltimore, MD: Brookes.

Fisher, E. P. (1992). The impact of play on development: A meta-analysis. *Play and Culture, 5*, 159–181.

Flanagan, D. P., & Alfonso, V. C. (1995). A critical review of the technical characteristics of new and recently revised intelligence tests for preschool children. *Journal of Psychoeducational Assessment, 13*, 66–90.

Fonagy, P., & Target, M. (1994). The Efficacy of psychoanalysis for children with distruptive disorders. *Journal of the American Academy of Child and Adolescent Psychiatry, 33*(1), 45–55.

Gil, E. (1991). *The healing power of play: Working with abused children.* New York: Guilford.

Ginott, H. M. (1961). *Group psychotherapy with children.* New York: McGraw-Hill.

Gitlin-Weiner, K., Sangrund, A., & Schaefer, C. (Eds.). (2000). *Play diagnosis and assessment.* (2nd ed.). New York: John Wiley.

Gordon, D. E. (1993). The inhibition of pretend play and its implications for development. *Human Development, 36*, 215–234.

Greenspan, S. I., & Meisels, S. (1994). Toward a new vision for the developmental assessment of infants and young children. *Zero to Three, 14*(6), 1–8.

Greenspan, S. I., & Wieder, S. (1998). *The child with special needs.* Reading, MA: Addison-Wesley.

Gresham, F. M. (1997). Social skills. In G. G. Bear, K. M. Minke, & A. Thomas (Eds.), *Children's needs II: Development, problems, and alternatives* (pp. 39–50). Bethesda, MD: National Association of School Psychologists.

Hellendoorn, J., van der Kooij, R., & Sutton-Smith, B. (Eds.). (1994). *Play and intervention.* Albany, NY: State University of New York Press.

Hughes, F. P. (1998). Play in special populations. In O. N. Saracho & B. Spodek (Eds.), *Multiple perspectives on play in early childhood* (pp. 171–193). Albany, NY: State University of New York Press.

Kazdin, A. E., & Johnson, B. (1994). Advances in psychotherapy for children and adolescents: Interrelations of adjustment, development, and intervention. *Journal of School Psychology, 32*, 217–246.

Kazdin, A. E., Siegel, T. C., & Bass, D. (1990). Drawing upon clinical practice to inform research on child and adolescent psychotherapy: A survey of practitioners. *Professional Psychology: Research and Practice, 21*, 189–198.

Knell, S. M. (1998). Cognitive-behavioral play therapy. *Journal of Clinical Child Psychology, 27*(1), 28–33.

Kolvin, I., Garside, R. F., Nicol, A. R., MacMillan, A., Wolstenholme, F., & Leitch, I. M. (1981). *Help starts here: The maladjusted child in the ordinary school.* London: Havistock.

LeBlanc, M., & Ritchie, M. (1999). Predictors of play therapy outcomes. *International Journal of Play Therapy, 8*, 19–34.

Lifter, K. (2000). Linking assessment to intervention for children with developmental disabilities or at-risk for developmental delay: The developmental play assessment (DPA) instrument. In K. Gitlin-Weiner, A. Sangrund, & C. Schaefer (Eds.), *Play diagnosis and assessment* (2nd ed.) (pp. 228–261). New York: John Wiley.

Linder, T. W. (1993a). *Transdisciplinary play-based assessment: A functional approach to working with young children* (Rev. ed.). Baltimore: Brookes.

Linder, T. W. (1993b). *Transdisciplinary play-based intervention: Guidelines for developing a meaningful curriculum for young children.* Baltimore: Brookes.

Lowenfeld, M. (1939). The world pictures of children: A method of recording and studying them. *British Journal of Medical Psychology, 18*, 65–101.

National Association of School Psychologists Delegate Assembly (1991). Position statement: Early childhood assessment. In A. Thomas & J. Grimes (Eds.) (1995), *Best practices in school psychology III* (pp. 1213–1214). Washington, DC: National Association of School Psychologists.

O'Connor, K. (1991). *The play therapy primer: An integration of theories and techniques.* New York: John Wiley.

O'Connor, K., & Schaefer, C. (Eds.). (1994). *Handbook of play therapy: Vol. 2, Advances and innovations.* New York: John Wiley.

Ollendick, T. H., & King, N. J. (1998). Empirically supported treatments for children with phobic and anxiety disorders. *Journal of Clinical Child Psychology, 27*(2), 156–167.

Paiget, J. (1945/1962). *Play, dreams, and imitation in childhood.* New York: Norton.

Parten, M. B. (1932). Social participation among preschool children. *Journal of Abnormal Psychology,27*, 243–269.

Pellegrini, A. D. (1998). Play and the assessment of young children. In O. N. Saracho & B. Spodek (Eds.), *Multiple perspectives on play in early childhood* (pp. 220–239). Albany, NY: State University of New York Press.

Pellegrini, A. D., & Boyd, B. (1993). The role of play in early childhood development and education: Issues in definition and function. In B. Spodek (Ed.), *Education of young children* (pp. 105–121). New York: Macmillan.

Prout, S. M., & Prout, H. T. (1998). A meta-analysis of school-based studies of counseling and psychotherapy: An update. *Journal of School Psychology, 35*, 121–136.

Roopnarine, J. L., Lasker, J., Sacks, M., & Stores, M. (1998). The cultural contexts of children's play. In O. N. Saracho & B. Spodek (Eds.), *Multiple perspectives on play in early childhood education* (pp. 194–219). Albany, NY: State University of New York Press.

Rubin, K. H. (1989). *The Play Observation Scale (POS).* Waterloo, ON: University of Waterloo.

Rubin, K. H., Fein, G. G., & Vandenberg, B. (1983). Play. In P. H. Mussen (Series Ed.) & E. M. Hetherington(Vol.Ed.), *Handbook of child psychology: Vol. 4, Socialization, personality, and social development* (4th ed.) (pp 693–774). New York: John Wiley.

Schreibman, L., & Koegel, R. L. (1996). Fostering self-management: Parent-delivered pivotal response training for children with autistic disorder. In E. D. Hibbs & P. S. Jensen (Eds.), *Psychosocial treatments for child and adolescent disorders: Empirically based strategies for clinical practice* (pp. 525–552). Washington, DC: American Psychological Association.

Segal, M., & Webber, N. T. (1996). Nonstructured play observations: Guidelines, benefits, and caveats. In S. J. Meisels & E. Fenichel (Eds.), *New visions for the developmental assessment of infants and young children* (pp. 207–230). Washington, DC: ZERO TO THREE: National Center for Infants, Toddlers, and Families.

Singer, D. G., & Singer, J. L. (1990). *The house of make-believe: Children's play and the developing imagination.* Cambridge, MA: Harvard University Press.

Stahmer, A. C. (1995). Teaching symbolic play skills to children with autism using Pivotal Response Training. *Journal of Autism and Developmental Disorders, 25*, 123–141.

Sulzer-Azaroff, B., & Mayer, G. R. (1991). *Behavior analysis for lasting change.* New York: Holt, Rinehart & Winston.

Sutton-Smith, B. (2000). Play. In A. E. Kazdin (Ed.), *Encyclopedia of psychology: Vol. 6* (pp. 213–218). Washington, DC: American Psychological Association and New York: Oxford University Press. .

Tuma, J. M., & Pratt, J. M. (1982). Clinical child psychology practice and training: A survey. *Journal of Clinical Child Psychology, 11*, 27–34.

Vygotsky, L. S. (1933/1978). The role of play in development. In M. Cole, V. John-Steiner, S. Scribner, & E. Souberman (Eds.), *Mind in society* (pp. 92–104). Cambridge, MA: Harvard University Press.

Weisz, J. R., & Hawley, K. M. (1998). Finding, evaluating, refining, and applying empirically supported treatments for children and adolescents. *Journal of Clinical Child Psychology, 27*(2), 206–216.

ANNOTATED BIBLIOGRAPHY

Gitlin-Weiner, K., Sangrund, A., & Schaefer, C. (Eds.). (2000). *Play diagnosis and assessment* (2nd ed.). New York: John Wiley.

This second edition contains a collection of updated and recent contributions to play assessment. It will be of interest to researchers as well as to clinicians. The book presents techniques used for developmental play assessments, diagnostic play assessments, parent-child interaction play assessments, family play assessments, peer interaction play assessments, and projective play assessments.

O'Connor, K., & Schaefer, C. (Eds.). (1994). *Handbook of play therapy, Vol. 2: Advances and innovations*. New York: John Wiley.

This book serves as an introductory source for different approaches to play therapy, especially recent applications.

Rubin, K. H., Fein, G. G., & Vandenberg, B. (1983). Play. In P. H. Mussen (Series Ed.)& E. M. Hetherington (Vol. Ed.), *Handbook of child psychology: Vol. 4, Socialization, personality, and social development* (4th ed.) (pp 693–774). New York: John Wiley.

Although the review of research needs updating, this remains the classic reference for understanding children's play and the issues that are still being considered. It has an excellent section on the history of theories of play.

Singer, D. G., & Singer, J. L. (1990). *The house of make-believe: Children's play and the developing imagination.* Cambridge, MA: Harvard University Press.

This book is a good resource for parents as well as professionals. Recommending a book explaining the importance of play in a child's life may help parents appreciate intervention efforts. The authors manage to cover important research at the same time that they unfold a wonderful tale: "the special mystery of how we develop our human capacity for mental travel through time and space."

80 Best Practices in Personality Assessment

Howard M. Knoff
University of South Florida

OVERVIEW

The assessment of child and adolescent personality remains an important activity for school psychologists given the mandate of the Individuals with Disabilities Education Act (IDEA) to identify and provide services to emotionally disturbed (ED) students. Beyond IDEA, however, the personality assessment process helps us to better understand the significant number of social-emotional and behavioral problems that *non-special education* students manifest in today's schools and communities. Clearly, through personality assessment, school psychologists can provide parents and educators with insight and direction into such problems as truancy, drug abuse, dropping out, teenage pregnancy, suicide, and the emotional impacts of divorce, poverty, rejection, and academic failure. But, most importantly, school psychologists can provide these individuals with recommendations and action plans that decrease or resolve current child and adolescent problems such that they can be prevented in the future. This is the bottom line of personality assessment. Personality assessment is a process of collecting valid data to explain the causes for or contingencies relevant to a child's social-emotional, behavioral, or affective difficulties. This assessment is useless in isolation; it must be linked with viable, acceptable, and socially valid interventions that are successfully implemented with ongoing attention to treatment integrity and evaluation.

Within a context of comprehensive school psychological service delivery, it is essential that school psychologists understand normal and abnormal personality development and apply this information to empirical models that explain children's social-emotional, behavioral, and affective development. In addition, school psychologists must identify what they want to accomplish from the personality assessment process as well as what their school districts and multidisciplinary teams want from this process and whether these two sets of goals converge. While the ultimate personality assessment goal is to develop and implement effective intervention programs for referred students, other goals for the school psychologist might be (a) to determine who "owns" a specific referred problem (e.g., the referred child, a referring teacher or parent, a dysfunctional system, or a combination thereof); (b) to validate hypotheses explaining how a referred child's behaviors are being caused, encouraged, reinforced, or supported; (c) to create a sound baseline of data so that interventions can be evaluated from an appropriate context so that an accurate presenting history can be documented; and (d) to identify the referred child's behavioral assets and the home and school's resources so that they might be integrated into an intervention program.

Relative to the school district, the primary goal of personality assessment often is to determine a student's *eligibility* for special education services. This is unfortunate when it becomes the district's exclusive focus, because it reinforces the serious misconception that finding one eligible for special education is, in and of itself, an intervention. In total, special education represents an integrated spectrum of services needed by a student that are delivered in the most appropriate, least restrictive, setting possible such that the student is able to academically and/or socially and behaviorally progress. Moreover, special education decisions, relative to both eligibility and programming, must be made within the context of a functional behavioral assessment (FBA). Finally, given the prerequisite and the results of a student's functional assessment, the interventions needed by the student should guide the decision on *where* (i.e., the setting) services should be delivered. That is, the setting should not determine the program or services, and the student's functional needs should influence that decision.

School psychologists must discourage their colleagues and child study teams from requesting personality assessments primarily as a means to qualify students for a placement into a class for the emotionally disturbed. More appropriate district-related uses of personality assessment might be (a) to identify and analyze recurring patterns of student behavior or affect so that effective preventive programs can be developed, (b) to understand the severity and demands of students' social-emotional problems so that optimal staffing patterns can be organized, (c) to investigate the relationship between unrealistic academic expectations and inappropriate student behavior so that curricular restructuring as appropriate can occur, and (d) to address student problems that do not require formal referrals or special education placements through teacher consultation, staff development, and pre-referral interventions. Ultimately, the best reason to initiate an assessment to determine a student's eligibility for ED services is the lack of sufficient progress in resolving specific social, emotional, or behavioral concerns through systematic, classroom-based intervention. If this criterion were used, then the personality assessment process would begin with a focus on the need for more intensive intervention approaches for a specific, functionally defined and assessed "problem," and not on a process geared to evaluating a student against eligibility criteria that are difficult to operationalize and measure (see below).

Conversely, school psychologists must *encourage* their colleagues and child study teams to look at students from an ecological perspective. While initially this will involve the ecology of the classroom (or other settings) where a student's social, emotional, or behavioral problems exist, it also should include the student's broader ecology that includes peers, home, and community. Thus, school psychologists need to extend an assessment process that may focus heavily on just a student's educational (or school) context to one that considers and integrates a "psychology by education" context. While this may create some tension within certain child study team members, the "psychology by education" context is necessary in order to most effectively and functionally assess the intervention needs of a student. Critically, once these needs are identified and intervention components are determined, the child study team *then* can determine which components are the responsibility of the school and under what circumstances these components should be delivered. Thus, once again, students' needs drive the (potential) special education and intervention process, and it is not assumed that the school will be responsible for every facet of a needed program.

The need to analyze referred students from a "psychology by education" perspective is a best practice behavior for school psychologists. Children's behavior and affect are the interdependent products of the many institutions, settings, people, and contingencies with which they interact. Personality assessment must reflect these interactions through multitrait, multisetting, and multimethod analyses that necessarily involve data collection from home, school, and community sources. Once again, school psychologists must look at a student's entire ecology. The school setting is but one part of that ecology (Knoff, 1983).

BASIC CONSIDERATIONS

Given the discussion above, it seems crucial that school psychologists work from an empirical-based model that explains children's social, emotional, and behavioral development in a "psychology by education" and ecological context. Critically, this model should focus on children's skills and assets, the ways that they develop resilient responses to challenging events and environments, and the enabling conditions that facilitate their growth and development. This model, then, provides information that can help psychologists and educators to differentiate the reasons why one student is making good social, emotional, or behavioral growth and another is making slower or atypical growth. This model also must be sensitive to situation- and setting-specific behavior, and it should guide the school psychologist's thinking so that personality assessment becomes an empirically based problem-solving process that links assessment directly to intervention and that integrates referred problems and their needed solutions into a realistic and holistic context.

Significantly, a number of empirically derived models have been developed that synthesize the research literature and explain certain specific student outcomes (Knoff & Batsche, 1991a; McKee & Witt, 1990; Wang, Haertel, & Walberg, 1990). These models have been synthesized into a single, summary model with four primary student outcomes involving: (a) academic skills, (b) cognitive/metacognitive skills, (c) social/behavioral skills, and (d) adaptive behavior skills. While students' cognitive/metacognitive and social/behavioral skill difficulties generally prompt most personality assessments, the other two outcome areas also may be affected by problems in these first areas (e.g., when a student's poor problem-solving or on-task behavior skills interfere with academic or social engagement and, therefore, interfere with academic or adaptive behavior learning) or they actually may contribute the antecedent or moderator conditions that are influencing these problems (e.g., when a student's academic failure causes depression or withdrawal or when a student's poor adaptive behavior causes social skill problems because of peer rejection). Thus, at times, these four outcome areas are interdependent, and the conditions that influence them are dynamic.

While it is usually very easy to identify student's outcomes in the four areas (and, thus, the specific social, emotional, or behavioral concerns with a specific, referred, student), it is not always easy to determine *why* students are being successful or not. As can be seen in Figure 1, research has shown that the four outcome areas are directly and indirectly affected (by the arrows shown) by eight different conditions or domains that exist in most students' worlds: family, neighborhood, and community conditions; school/school district conditions; within school/classroom conditions; teacher characteristics or conditions; teacher performance/teacher effectiveness conditions; curricular characteristics and conditions; student characteristics and conditions; and student academic behavior conditions. By using this figure, hypotheses explaining why a student is successfully or unsuccessfully attaining specific outcomes can be generated, and, once confirmed, they can be directly linked to specific interventions. Relative to personality assessment, this figure facilitates a functional assessment of behavior, within an ecological and problem-solving context, that links assessment directly to intervention.

Briefly, the six areas of the empirical model, as described previously and as related especially to cognitive/metacognitive and social/behavioral skill outcomes (Knoff & Batsche, 1991b, pp. 177–180), involve the following points:

1. Family, neighborhood, and community conditions: These involve characteristics or conditions of a referred student's family, neighborhood, and community as they relate ultimately to effective discipline and behavior management approaches and students' social skills, self-esteem, and self-management outcomes. They emphasize the importance of a positive and proactive home environment, the strengthening of conditions that teach and encourage resiliency, and the direct and indirect interactions that affect students' school readiness, social-emotional development, and success.

2. Within classroom/school/district conditions: These involve favorable and/or unfavorable characteristics and conditions within students' classrooms and school buildings such as the physical plant, the pupil-teacher ratio, the presence of mental health resources (e.g., school psychologists and guidance programs), professional development opportunities for staff, the administrative and instructional organization of the building, the range of same-age or same-grade students' academic and social skill levels, school and classroom climate, the presence and effective use of technology, and other conditions that explain teacher effectiveness. This area also extends to policies and procedures within the school district that affect classroom management and instruction and successful student achievement. These may include (a) the district's policies, for example, on multicultural education and tolerance, on student harassment and violence, and on grade retention; (b) the district's curricular support for social skills, conflict resolution, and other areas of health and mental

Figure 1. Summary of ecological characteristics and conditions that impact student learning outcomes

TEACHER/INSTRUCTIONAL CHARACTERISTICS

TEACHER CHARACTERISTICS
Qualifications
Experience
Aptitudes
Knowledge of Subject
Knowledge of Teaching
Values and Attitudes
High, Yet Realistic Expectations
Social Class

TEACHER/PERFORMANCE EFFECTIVENESS
Presence/Absence of Effective Teaching Skills
Continuous Evaluation of/Feedback to Students
Provision of Student Incentives for Learning
Effective Instructional Presentation
Effective Classroom Management
Productive Use of Time/Academic Engaged Time
Emphasis of Developing Student Thinking Skills
Use of Relevant Student Practice Techniques
Ability to Adapt Instruction to Individual Needs

CURRICULAR CHARACTERISTICS/CONDITIONS
Adaptability/Flexibility to Meet Individual Teacher and Student Needs
Written for Optimal Teacher Understanding and Implementation
Instructional/Drill Lessons Consistent with and Relevant to Stated Instructional Goals/Expectations
Sufficient Opportunities/Materials for Practice to Student Mastery
Sufficient Opportunities/Materials for Reteaching and Remediation
Research/Empirically-Based and Proven

STUDENT CHARACTERISTICS/CONDITIONS
Social Class, Race, Parental Influence
Aptitudes and Prior Learning
Values and Attitudes
Expectations
Cognitive Capacity
Differential Learning Styles
Adaptive Behavior Capacity
Presence of Prerequisite Skills and Conceptual Readiness for New Learning

SCHOOL/SCHOOL DISTRICT CONDITIONS
School Size
Fiscal Resources, Salaries
Pupil-Teacher Ratio
Administration-Teacher Ratio
Professional Staff Services
Facilities (labs, books, etc.)
Average Class Size
Urbanism of School's Location
Student Social Class
Racial Composition
Effective Clinical Supervision Programs
Effective Staff Development Programs
Clear Criteria for Professional Accountability
Use of Achievement-Oriented School Improvement Goals/Programs

WITHIN SCHOOL/CLASSROOM CONDITIONS
Administrative Organization
a. Administration-Teacher Ratio
b. Degree of Control, Authority
c. Reward Mechanism
Instructional Organization
a. Tracking
b. Team Teaching
c. Open vs. Traditional
Student Peer Group Influence
Class Size
Quantity of Schooling
School Climate
Clear Staff and Student Roles and Expectations
Degree of Staff/Student Collaborative Decision-Making
Learning-Conducive Physical Plant Characteristics
School-Based Incentive for Achievement/Success
Principal Involvement in Academic Program

ECOLOGICAL/INSTRUCTIONAL ENVIRONMENT CHARACTERISTICS

FAMILY, NEIGHBORHOOD, COMMUNITY CONDITIONS
Parent Involvement in Home/School Reinforcement of Instruction
Business Involvement in School Program
Social Class of Neighborhood
Social Service/Public/Other Agencies/Resources
Presence of Significant Community Crises
Family/Child Health History and Health Characteristics
Presence/Absence of Family Life Crises (e.g., divorce, separation, deaths, financial strains, unemployment)
Family Mobility/Moves

STUDENT ACADEMIC BEHAVIOR CONDITIONS
Use of Allocated Time for Practice/Mastery
Academic Engaged Time/Time-on-Task
Active Participation in Instructional Program
Demonstration of Basic Academic Skills
Evidence of Self-Competence Skills:
Responsibility for Learning Outcomes
Evidence of Internal Attributions for Learning Outcomes
Motivation
Task Persistence
Expectations of Success
Positive Self-Reinforcement
Evidence of Cognitive/Metacognitive Skills:
Ability/Understanding of How to "Learn How to Learn"
Use of Higher Order Cognitive Strategies
Use of Planning Skills
Use of Monitoring Skills
Use of Self-Regulation Skills
Use of Checking/Review Skills
Use of Attentional and Memory Strategies
Use of Cognitive Behavior Modification Approaches
Evidence of Effective Social Skills:
Effective Peer Interactions
Peer Acceptance
Classroom Adjustment
Ability to Work in Groups
Ability to Seek Assistance
Effective Adult Interactions

STUDENT LEARNING OUTCOMES
Academic Skill Outcomes
Cognitive/Metacognitive Outcomes
Social Skill Outcomes
Adaptive Behavior Skill Outcomes

STUDENT-SPECIFIC CHARACTERISTICS

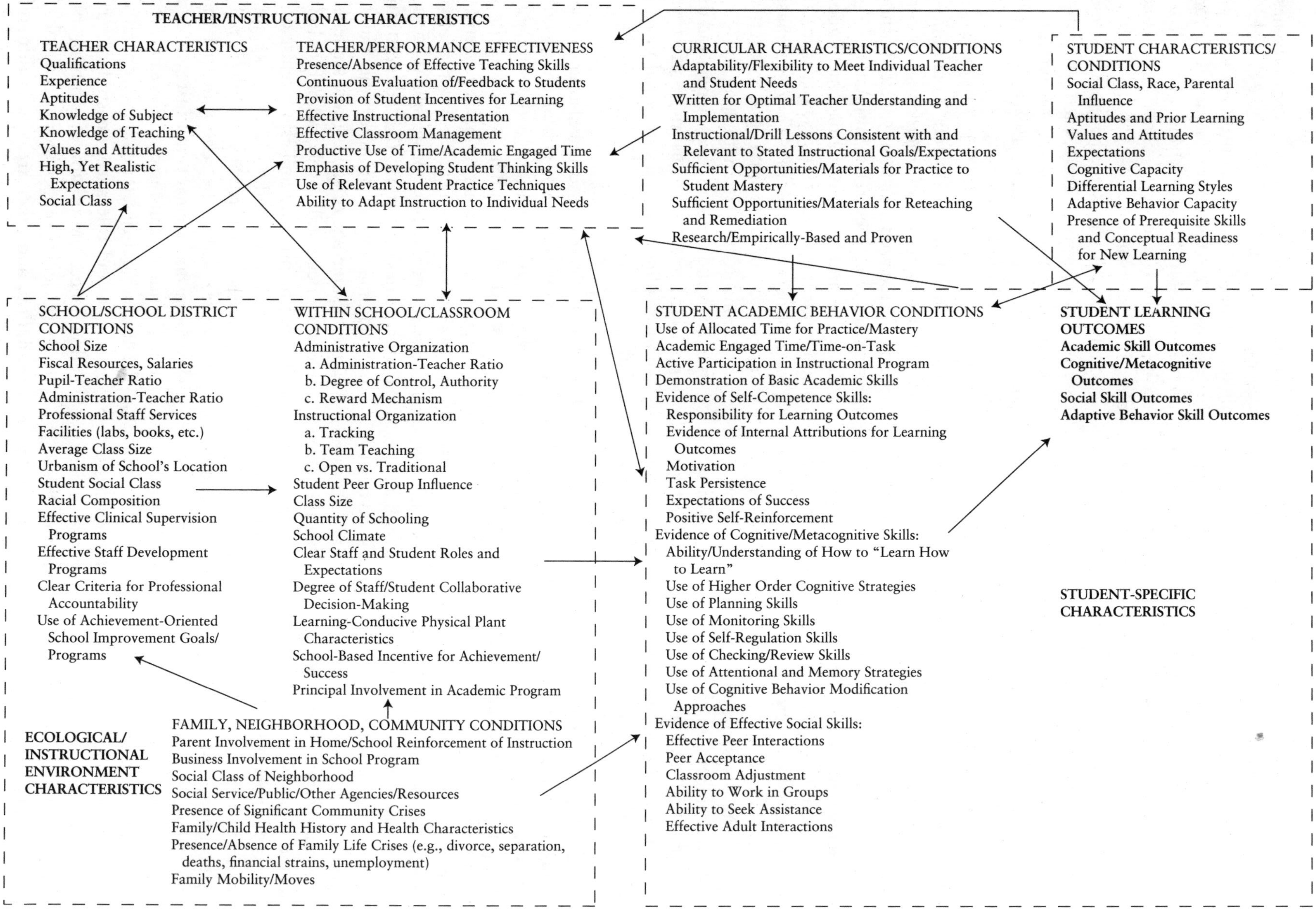

health instruction; and (c) the district's outreach to the community such that preventive programs and approaches are prioritized over reaction ones.

3. Teacher characteristics/performance/effectiveness conditions: These involve characteristics and conditions that teachers bring to the classroom that ultimately translate into the effective management and instruction skills and behaviors that support student learning and development (e.g., background characteristics, professional training). Also included are those empirically identified skills, activities, and conditions that teachers demonstrate or create that make their instruction effective (e.g., their ability to adapt instruction, their use of social skills curricula and behavior management techniques). Finally, this area includes the strategies or approaches that teachers' use to motivate students' skills development and their consistency when interacting with students. When effective, these create positive instructional environments that are structured, predictable, and nurturing.

4. Curricular characteristics/conditions: These involve characteristics and/or conditions of the curricula being used and include the content as well as the process that is used to ensure student learning and mastery. Curricula here include those self-esteem, social skills, and other behavior management curricula that lead to student "learning" in the areas of self-control, self-management, and self-efficacy. In addition, this area also reflects the ability of these curricula to flexibly adapt to different types of students such that appropriate student-curricula matching occurs.

5. Peer characteristics/conditions: These involve characteristics and/or interactions within a school or classroom's formal and informal peer groups that influence student attitudes, perceptions, and behaviors toward a school's expectations and norms, climate and safety, and inclusiveness or exclusiveness. Relative to specific student situations, the conditions that permit a peer group to determine positive or negative student outcomes (or to encourage prosocial versus antisocial behavior) are important. Thus, this area helps to identify the links between certain antecedent or consequent peer control conditions and specific student outcomes. While these peer characteristics or conditions may be real or simply perceived by one or more students, they do, nonetheless, have some impact on these individuals.

6. Student characteristics/conditions: These involve often pre-existing characteristics and conditions, including neurological, physiological, genetic, and biochemical conditions, that relate primarily to a student's behaviors, emotions, affects, and cognitions. Cognitions here include a student's attitudes, expectation, beliefs, attributions, thoughts, and internal processes. All of the characteristics or conditions in this area should directly link to the social-emotional development of students and their ability to conform to social and situational demands. These characteristics and conditions also involve those behaviors that students exhibit that directly support their academic and social learning and progress such as their motivation, their self-competence skills, and their use of appropriate social skills.

In looking at the pathways outlined in Figure 1, school psychologists must differentiate between causal pathways and correlational pathways. Causal pathways involve conditions and characteristics that directly cause specific student outcomes. Critically, many of the characteristics and conditions within the student, teacher, and curricular areas above tend to be causal to student outcomes—although there are more correlational relationships within the latter two areas. Correlational pathways involve conditions and characteristics that influence student outcomes, increasing or decreasing the probability of their attainment depending on their positive versus negative impact. Many of the characteristics and conditions in the peer, classroom, school, district, family, and community areas above tend to be more correlational than causal.

Critically, the presence of causal versus correlational pathways has a direct influence on the functional assessment of student behavior. Indeed, while FBA tends to focus on classroom-based behavior (or the specific settings where referred, problematic behavior occurs) and to look for causal relationships that explain why problematic behavior is occurring (Gable, Quinn, Rutherford, & Howell, 1998; Tilly et al., 1998), school psychologists performing FBA must still acknowledge correlational influences that often occur in parts of students' ecologies outside of the classroom. Nonetheless, in the typical FBA model, a problem-solving process is used to (a) functionally identify a referred problem; (b) collect and analyze existing background information about the student and then the specific problem of concern; (c) gather contextual information that explains the circumstances, situations, or conditions that are associated with the existence *and the absence* of the problem behavior; (d) generate and then assess the hypotheses that empirically confirm the accuracy of these explanations; (e) link confirmed hypotheses to functional intervention plans that ideally emphasize the development, building, or strengthening of skills and positive behavioral supports; and (f) evaluate the impact of these interventions on problem resolution and student success.

From a problem identification perspective most referrals for personality assessment involve problems involving extreme or excessive amounts of behavior, inappropriate or unnecessary behavior, the absence or not enough of an appropriate behavior, or situationally inappropriate, irrelevant, or bizarre or idiosyncratic behavior. Critically, these problems influence students' social (or interpersonal), emotional (or affective), and/or behavioral (externalized or internalized) interactions; they may exist in isolated though pervasive settings or situations; and they may have a brief (or acute) or extensive history.

From a problem analysis perspective, seven basic questions are important as the FBA begins (Gable et al., 1998; Tilly et al., 1998):

1. When is the student most likely to engage in the problem behavior?

2. What specific people, events, factors, or conditions appear to be present and/or contributing to the student's problem behavior? Which of these people, events, factors, or conditions appear to precede or trigger the problem behavior, and which appear to follow the problem behavior?

3. Does the problem behavior involve a skill deficit or a performance deficit? If a performance deficit, does the problem behavior occur more or less often in the face of certain incentives and/or consequences? If a performance deficit, is the problem behavior a result of inconsistent expectations or the inconsistent delivery of incentives and/or consequences?

4. What function(s) does the problem behavior serve for the student?

5. What might the student be communicating through the problem behavior?

6. When is the student most successful and, therefore, less likely to engage in the problem behavior? Or, are there times when certain circumstances exist that either discourage or eliminate the problem behavior or encourage or introduce other behaviors that are incompatible with the problem behavior?

7. What other factors might be contributing to the student's problem behavior?

Ultimately, problem analysis moves to the generation and then the assessment of hypotheses that explain *why* the problem behavior occurs or does not occur. Given the questions above and using the ecological/empirical model discussed earlier, four primary areas of characteristics or conditions may functionally explain the existence of the problem behaviors, for example, in a classroom. These involve the referred student, the teacher or instructional process, the curriculum, and classroom or peer factors. That is, a student might be verbally aggressive toward a teacher and/or classroom peers during reading instruction in the morning (problem identification) *because* (hypothesis) the student

1. Is feeling uncertain or insecure about his reading skill and gets angry when put in situations when he might fail, especially when it occurs in front of his peers (student condition)

2. Has a teacher who focuses only on the correct answer, never provides instructive or positive feedback, asks questions without providing enough reflective time to answer them, and who uses competition amongst peers to "facilitate and motivate" instruction (teacher/instructional condition)

3. Is presented with reading material that is two grade levels above his instructional level and that

often involve content or stories that are not culturally sensitive or relevant (curricular condition)

4. Is grouped in a cooperative peer group that is focusing more on answers than understanding, that is frustrated with him because of his past failures, and that includes a number of students who have been grouped in an accelerated group for the past 3 years (classroom or peer conditions)

Taking a more positive view of this student and situation, it should also be recognized during this problem identification and analysis that the referred student demonstrates appropriate and prosocial interactions in all other academic areas and times during the school day, that he has a group of friends who accept him, that his reading "problem" is not affecting other curricular areas, and that the referred concern has not occurred in previous years.

As hypotheses are assessed, utilizing a FBA and problem-solving orientation, personality assessment focuses primarily on answering specific questions that confirm or reject the hypotheses generated. That is, personality assessment here maintains the functional assessment process, and it does not shift to a random search for student pathology or a narrow, test-by-test, determination of the students' eligibility for special education. If school psychologists make this "paradigm shift" and maintain the functional assessment focus, then the personality assessment process will lead to functional interventions that address the reasons for the referred behavior and that have a high probability of success in the natural environment where they occur. If this shift is ignored, then personality assessment will remain a random, subjective, and disconnected process that is student (not ecologically) centered, results in either global descriptions of behavior or labels of "pathology," and does not lead to effective or defensible interventions or functional services.

In summary, the considerations cited above create a foundation for sound personality assessment. Below, these approaches are extended and operationalized by focusing on the classification systems, pragmatic beliefs, applied approaches, and fundamental procedures that translate into effective personality assessment. After reading this chapter, school psychologists should not only have an updated perspective as to how to link personality assessment and intervention, but they also should have a working model that helps them to implement this important process.

Classification Systems Affecting Personality Assessment

Assuming a psychological and educational perspective of personality assessment, school psychologists must attend to the available classification systems that are used to categorize referred child and adolescent behavior. While the functional assessment of a students' behavior and affect will be more relevant to planning viable and effective intervention programs, the presence of these classification systems cannot be ignored given their widespread use and their determination of much of our diagnostic nomenclature. Three different classification systems, with their strengths and weaknesses, briefly will be reviewed: the IDEA definition of emotional disturbance, *Diagnostic and Statistical Manual of Mental Disorders* (DSM-IV), and empirically based classification approaches.

The IDEA Definition

Most states (approximately 75%) use the actual or an adapted IDEA definition of ED despite the fact that they may or may not use the ED label. Despite the apparent consensus, the fact remains that the IDEA definition (a) is predominantly an educational definition that does not lend itself to psychological differentiation or analysis, (b) requires behavioral operationalization in order to be used in a consistent manner, (c) necessitates only a *yes* or *no* "diagnostic" decision, (d) encourages a "medical-model" perspective of disturbed behavior; (e) still excludes (without definition) "socially maladjusted" students, and (f) ignores the co-occurrence of two or more behavioral or affective disorders in many students.

Expanding briefly, the IDEA definition focuses on conditions that "adversely affect educational performance," desensitizing our schools to children who progress educationally but still need socialization or mental health services. The definition leaves such characteristics as "inappropriate types of behaviors or feelings," "under normal circumstances," "over a long period of time," and "to a marked degree" to the state, school district, or individual multidisciplinary team to operationalize. This creates, at best, a great potential for inconsistency across referred children and, at worst, conditions allowing unchecked bias, inequity, and prejudice. Finally, the definition permits a simplistic "yes, the child qualifies as an ED child," or "no, the child does not qualify" mentality, which suggests that the child owns or does not own the causal pathology. This discourages an ecological perspective that focuses more on functional assessment, intervention, and problem resolution.

Over the past decade, many experts and a number of professional associations and coalitions have critiqued IDEA's ED definition, some proposing their own definitions and improvements (e.g., Forness & Knitzer, 1992; Gresham, 1998). In general, these new definitions addressed many of the cultural, normative, clinical, developmental, situational, and behavioral problems of the current ED (and past seriously emotionally disturbed (SED)) definition. And, they advocated a more multimethod, multisource, multisetting orientation and functional approach to assessment. Nonetheless, IDEA's ED definition persists, as does the need to operationalize the personality assessment process *at the school level* regardless of what definition is used. Thus, school psychologists must take a leadership role at the district and individual multidisciplinary team level to operationalize and systematize the ED definition currently in use. This will require discussions with all team members as to (a) what is typical and expected behavior in the classroom and school building from both a developmental perspective and a normative (school or community) perspective; (b) what types of behaviors, affects, and interactions fall under the ED definition, thereby requiring programmatic intervention (regardless of its setting); (c) what curricular, instructional, and mental health support services are available to "wraparound" an ED student such that a regular classroom placement can continue; and (d) what behavioral frequencies, intensities, and durations are needed for regular versus special education classroom placement decisions. Only by having clear ED procedures and definitions can a multidisciplinary team make consistent, objective, and functional decisions, simultaneously overcoming the weaknesses of the current IDEA definition. Only by operationalizing at a local level can a multidisciplinary team evaluate referred children; be sensitive to the community's individual strengths, weaknesses, history, and problems with these students; and determine what constitutes ED behavior for a specific community.

DSM-IV

The current version of the *Diagnostic and Statistical Manual of Mental Disorders* is the DSM-IV (American Psychiatric Association, 1994). Continuing its attempts to describe disorders as behaviorally as possible, the DSM-IV describes the following specific disorders of infancy, childhood, and adolescence: mental retardation, learning disorders, motor skill disorders, pervasive developmental disorders and specific disorders, disruptive behavior and attention-deficit disorders, feeding and eating disorders of infancy or early childhood, tic disorders, communication disorders, elimination disorders, and other disorders of infancy, childhood, or adolescence. Critically, there are other disorders that extend from infancy, childhood, and/or adolescence *through* adulthood that are classified elsewhere in the DSM-IV.

Despite the research reviews and clinical trials completed prior to its publication, the problems that existed in the previous DSM systems persist in the DSM-IV. Among the most critical problems are the DSM-IV's (a) dependence on a medical model perspective of behavior and pathology; (b) focus on signs, symptoms, syndromes, and diseases that more describe a referred student's problem than functionally assess why it is occurring; (c) excessive differentiation of different mental disorders; that is, moving from more than 100 diagnoses or labels in the first DSM to now more than 350 diagnoses or labels in the fourth DSM; (d) lack of improvement in the areas of diagnostic agreement among clinicians, test-retest reliability, and validity; (e) lack of clear applicability, for some diagnoses, in school versus home or community settings and given IDEA's definition and approach to ED (Atkins, McKernal, McKay, Talbott, & Arvanitis, 1996; Gresham, 1998).

As an example of many of these points, the inattention subset of DSM-IV's attention-deficit/hyperactive disorder (AD/HD) diagnosis is made for a disturbance of at least 6 months duration, beginning no later than the age of 7, and *involving at least six of nine specific manifestations*. Critically, the psychologist does not need to specify *which* six of the nine behaviors exist such that the diagnosis can be made, and some of these behaviors (e.g., often has difficulty organizing tasks and activities, often forgetful in daily activities, often does not seem to listen to what is being said to him or her) are behaviorally imprecise and dependent, at times, on situation-specific subjectivity. Thus, one ADHD "diagnosis" could be functionally different from another, and there would be no way for a psychologist to determine which of the various AD/HD behaviors were present unless they were specified in a psychological report. Without specifying the behaviors of concern, then, the AD/HD diagnosis is of limited use, especially in the development of appropriate intervention strategies and programs. When the diagnosis' behavioral manifestations *are* specified, then the AD/HD label is basically unnecessary. School psychologists' interventions will address these problematic behaviors, *not* the so-called "diagnostic" labels.

In summary, there are few, if any, compelling reasons why school psychologists need to use the DSM system. While some feel that their ability to label a referred problem means that they understand it and are ready to successfully resolve it, this has never been empirically demonstrated. What has been demonstrated is that the identification of behavioral skill deficits, performance deficits, and self-management deficits and their behavioral contexts and contingencies can be successfully addressed, and that these approaches are often more parsimonious, efficient, and well-accepted by referral sources and referred individuals.

Empirically Based Classification Approaches

An empirically based classification system can be developed from the factor analytic results of the many researchers who have analyzed the characteristics of emotionally disturbed and behaviorally disordered children and adolescents over the years (Achenbach & McConaughy, 1996). At a broad-band level, two factors—internalizing or over-controlled and externalizing or under-controlled—have consistently been identified. These factors broadly describe children who demonstrate depressed, withdrawing, or uncommunicative behavioral styles versus hyperactive, aggressive, or delinquent behavioral styles, respectively. At a narrow-band level, many different behavioral clusters have been identified, some of which vary developmentally across age, sex, and research sample. To date, the following narrow-band factors have been most consistently identified: aggressive, delinquent, attention problems, thought problems, social problems, anxious/depressed, somatic complaints, and withdrawn behavior (Achenbach, 1991), and conduct disordered, socialized aggression, attention problems-immaturity, anxiety-withdrawal, psychotic behavior, and motor excess (Quay, 1983).

From a psychometric perspective, the factor analytic approach, and the resulting broad-band and narrow-band factors, represent a very sophisticated approach to classifying behavior. However, this classification approach does not facilitate an accurate identification of all problems or the development of appropriate interventions in every case. In fact, it must be emphasized that, when factors are generated by a factor analysis, individual factors sometimes consist of items that are included for more theoretical than statistical reasons, these factors often represent clusters of correlated behaviors or characteristics that may or may not clearly define a clinical disorder, and these factors ultimately are named by the researcher. By way of implication, this suggests (a) that some factors may be multidimensional in nature despite the fact that a single factor is presented, (b) that the presence of an item within a factor does not imply a causal relationship relative to the diagnostic label of the factor, and (c) that there is a level of subjectivity involved in finalizing or naming any factor, especially at the narrow-band level.

While the empirically based classification approaches have some limitations, they do provide a functional framework from which to organize a sound, school-based, classification system that differentiates among referred students' primary social-emotional problems and that facilitates a link between assessment and intervention. This has been demonstrated in Iowa, which applied the outcomes from empirically based classification research into a state special education definition and approach for behaviorally disordered students that recognized four clusters of such students, the developmental and situational nature of their problems, the importance of problem solving and FBA, and the need for intervention-based services. While any ED definition and empirically based assessment approach needs further operationalization at the school and school psychological level, this approach to classification offers some distinct advantages over the DSM and IDEA-exclusive approaches to both personality assessment. Integrating FBA, an ecological perspective, comprehensive problem solving, and empirically based classification increases the potential for the most effective services for referred and identified students.

BEST PRACTICES IN PERSONALITY ASSESSMENT

Given the discussions above, five pragmatic beliefs are essential to a best practices approach to personality assessment. These beliefs, critical both to the conceptualization and operationalization of the assessment process, involve what follows:

1. The need for an ecological/environmental orientation to personality assessment suggests that referred students are best understood by investigating the family, school, and community systems in which they grew up and now with which they interact. In most cases, these systems have determined and/or influenced referred students' developmental progress, and analyses of the interdependent relationships between these systems and students may explain certain behaviors, affects, and interactions of concern. Clearly, a child's anxious or phobic behavior toward school is best understood when it is known that the child has been corporally punished and embarrassed in full view of his or her peer group for forgetting to bring in homework. Similarly, a child who never attended preschool and has been in four different kindergartens and first grades owing to frequent moves may never have learned appropriate play or socialization behavior. The ecological/environmental assessment helps to efficiently explain many referred problems while decreasing the tendency to assume that the child should be the exclusive focus of the assessment process. This perspective also increases the probability that the ecological/environmental contingencies that explain referred problems are recognized and directly addressed with appropriate intervention approaches.

2. The need for multimethod, multisource, multisetting assessments suggests that the identification and analysis of referred problems are more accurate when the assessment procedures used involve multiple techniques and approaches from multiple informants who have interacted with the referred student in multiple situations and settings (Gresham, 1983). This process minimizes diagnostic and analytical errors and poorly developed intervention programs that have occurred because (a) only one assessment technique was used (e.g., a projective test) to the exclusion of a more comprehensive assessment battery (e.g., behavioral observations plus behavior rating scales plus home and school interviews plus appropriate developmental scales); (b) only one assessment source (e.g., the mother) was used, when multiple sources might indicate that the mother has excessively high expectations for the child; and/or (c) the child was evaluated in only one setting, when a multiple setting evaluation might indicate that the child experienced a traumatic event in a different setting and generalized the emotional response across settings. While some problems are legitimately related to specific individuals or settings, the multimethod, multisource, multisetting process increases assessment and intervention reliability and validity while assuring the ecological/environmental considerations described above.

3. The need for a developmental context to assessment suggests that school psychologists must be knowledgeable and sensitive to the typical and atypical developmental characteristics that occur for the independent variables of age, gender, multicultural status, and socioeconomic status, and that all personality assessment data be analyzed and interpreted from this perspective. For example, it makes no sense to interpret projective drawings as "psychologically significant" when a child has obvious visual-motor deficiencies or when developmental norms for certain-aged students indicate that they cannot form meaningful, interactive, figures in their drawings. It is also somewhat dangerous for school psychologists to depend on their own, or others', subjective interpretations of *any* assessment method if no sound empirical base exists to guide and support those conclusions. Finally, it is important to consider referred children's cognitive-developmental status when interpreting any personality assessment data gathered directly or indirectly. Clearly, a mildly retarded child's social skills and emotional reaction to frustration may be closely related to his or her cognitive skills and developmental status. In

this context, it is important to note that much of the projective drawing literature depends on clinically based, rather than empirically based, studies and case examples (Knoff, 2001). While projective drawings may provide insight into a student's behavioral cognitions and belief systems, their results can only be interpreted as *hypotheses* that are in need of objective and multimodal validation. In contrast, even though a common set of narrow-band scales were created, the various Achenbach (1991) behavior rating scales have been factor analyzed across age and gender, and the problems scales are scored separately by gender and age (4–11 and 12–18).

4. The need for a problem-solving and hypothesis-testing approach to assessment suggests that the personality assessment process should systematically involve a problem identification, problem analysis, intervention, and evaluation sequence so that problems are accurately (and ecologically) identified and then comprehensively analyzed (using multimethod, multisource, multisetting assessments) *before* any intervention is attempted. This process explicitly and logically links assessment results with intervention programs, and ensures that these programs are not implemented until an explanation as to *why* a referred problem or situation is occurring has been found. Inherent in this process is the belief that changes in students' educational settings or placements are needed only if intervention programs in the regular classroom (with "pull-in" resources if needed) are not successful. Moreover, personality assessment is completed to answer specific questions and not to describe or identify student pathology or to affix labels to unnecessary diagnoses.

5. The need for objective and observable assessment strategies emphasizes that all assessment hypotheses must be validated objectively and, ideally, through observable means. While objectivity is clearly relative, school psychologists must use instruments and techniques that have demonstrated their ability to validly and reliably generate the desired data and information. Thus, the psychometric properties of all personality assessment instruments must be investigated on an ongoing basis, and only the most sound instruments should be used among those that advertise similar assessment purposes or domains. Beyond objectivity, comprehensive behavioral observation is still the best way to assess the presence of specific social-emotional skills or deficits. Behavioral observation requires a clear operationalization of targeted skills or deficits, and the results include the frequency, intensity, and duration of a referred student's behavior and the antecedent, consequent, and ecological conditions that occur when these behaviors are exhibited. Collecting accurate and useful data through behavioral observation requires training, organization, and practice. It is a learned skill. But when done effectively, behavioral observation becomes the cornerstone of any personality assessment, and the source of the objective data that can confirm or reject many important hypotheses about a referred student.

The Referral Question Consultation Process

Rather than describing the various personality assessment approaches, tools, and techniques in a somewhat random, categorical, form, this section will discuss the assessment process from the beginning to the end using the Referral Question Consultation (RQC) process (Knoff & Batsche, 1991a). Assumed throughout this entire discussion are the beliefs that school psychologists have the professional training and autonomy to determine what personality assessment procedures are necessary for any ED (or related) referral; that school psychologists ultimately identify and implement intervention programs that offer the highest probability of treatment success; and that service delivery is provided within the context of consultee acceptability, social validity, treatment integrity, and transfer of training and generalization. While some states and school districts require the completion of certain personality assessment techniques (e.g., projective tests) with any ED referral *regardless* of the circumstances surrounding the referral, this is *not* a best practices approach. Personality assessment is an individualized process that should be fully in the hands of the professional school psychologist, and the requirement that certain techniques be used is personally and professionally appalling and potentially unwise or even damaging to the referred student.

The RQC process involves 10 interdependent steps after an individual student has been referred.

1. Review all existing data available on the referred student and collect any additional background data as appropriate.

2. Meet with the referral source in a *consultative interview* to behaviorally define his or her initial concerns, to identify the need for additional data to finalize the behavioral operationalization of these concerns, to initiate the functional assessment process and informally test some initial hypotheses, and to determine the referral source's assessment goals and commitment to the RQC process and classroom-based interventions if appropriate.

3. Develop hypotheses to explain the initial concerns as behaviorally operationalized.

4. Develop prediction statements from the generated hypotheses.

5. Develop data-based referral questions that will guide the assessment process and confirm or reject the generated hypotheses.

6. Select multi-trait, multi-method assessment procedures that will specifically answer the referral questions, continue the functional assessment process, and facilitate the link between assessment and intervention.

7. Apply the assessment and background data so as to answer the referral questions and to confirm or reject the generated hypotheses.

8. Select and implement intervention strategies consistent with those hypotheses that have been confirmed.

9. Monitor change in the area of the initial concern to determine the impact of the intervention.

10. Develop a written report that documents the RQC process, the interventions tried, and the intervention outcomes as they relate to the resolution of the initial, referred concerns.

Review of the Data

When a school psychologist receives a referral from a teacher, the first step in the RQC process is to review essential information about the referred student and to collect any additional background data that may be important to know before interviewing the teacher. The review of essential information typically centers around an analysis of five possible existing student areas or "folders": (a) the student's cumulative folder; (b) the student's health and attendance folder; (c) the administrative/ discipline folder; (d) relevant teachers' academic portfolio, running record, authentic assessment, and work sample folders; and (e) the special education/remedial education (e.g., Title I/Chapter I) folder. In addition to the information available in already-existing records and student folders, it may be time- and cost-efficient to collect other data from teachers and other sources (e.g., parents and significant others) prior to an initial consultation interview. This information may be collected through behavior checklists, behavior rating scales, ecological or developmental status surveys or questionnaires, or objective personality scales or inventories; and it may provide the answers to routine developmental (and other) status questions so that precious interview time can focus on the areas most relevant to the referral concerns. Significantly, this information also may facilitate a more accurate and in-depth behavioral operationalization of the teacher's initial concerns, identify possible correlates of those concerns, identify possible student assets and strengths, and generally prepare the school psychologist more thoroughly for the consultation interview and the teacher's (and others') perception of the referral problem.

Behavior Rating Scales

Behavior rating scales are one of the most efficient, sound, and effective ways to identify a referred student's behavioral strengths and weaknesses, to validate a referral source's initial concerns, to evaluate the severity of a wide range of specific behaviors, to assess for atypical patterns of behaviors or clinical entities, and to complete one facet of a multisource, multisetting evaluation. With hundreds of rating scales on the market, school psychologists' ability to choose the rating scales that will best accomplish their assessment goals without sacrificing psychometric quality is critical. To that end, Edelbrock (1983) noted that behavior rating scales differ dramatically across a number of critical dimensions, and he provided the following suggestions to help school psychologists become better behavior rating scale consumers:

1. School psychologists need to match their RQC and assessment goals to the results that a particular behavior rating scale actually provides. Some behavior rating scales (a) assess clinical, home, and/or school concerns; (b) are descriptive, prescriptive, or diagnostic; (c) evaluate specific behaviors or simply provide a checklist indication that they exist; (d) are unidimensional or multidimensional in scope; (e) rate actual student behaviors or characteristics that correlate with certain behavioral conditions; and (f) focus exclusively on behavioral deficits or problems, while others assess both behavioral deficits and assets. School psychologists must consider these rating scale characteristics, the referred problem, and the diagnostic and intervention questions to be answered. Clearly, behavior rating scales must be chosen in an informed manner with due consideration of their purposes and intended uses.

2. School psychologists need to recognize that behavior rating scales' technical adequacy vary greatly and need to be analyzed prior to their use. Among the variables to evaluate are (a) how items were selected during the development of the behavior rating scale, (b) what response scaling approach was used (e.g., "true/false," "often/sometimes/never"), (c) how the scale was developed and constructed, (d) the scale's standardization and norming procedures, and (e) the scale's validity and reliability data.

3. School psychologists need to evaluate whether behavior rating scales evaluate global or specific levels of manifested behavior, the time frames within which referred students are evaluated (e.g., 1, 3, or 6 months), and who the optimal respondent should be. To clarify this latter point, some behavior rating scales require that the informant be the referred student's mother or teacher. Other rating scales are completed simply by an individual who genuinely knows the student or who has interacted with the student over a long period.

4. Finally, school psychologists must assess how behavior rating scales control for response bias, for example, for halo effects, leniency or severity effects, and/or central tendency or range restriction effects. Without sufficient controls for bias, a behavior rating scale's results are of extremely limited use.

From an RQC perspective, school psychologists must strategically use all of the potential information generated by a behavior rating scale. School psychologists also must recognize that behavior rating scales measure *the perceptions of the scale's respondent* and that these perceptions must be validated. Finally, and too often, school psychologists simply use the broad- and narrow-band results of a behavior rating scale concluding and writing in their personality assessment reports, for example, that a referred child "has significantly high externalizing or acting-out tendencies, and that he manifests hyperactive, aggressive, and delinquent behavior" by virtue of elevated scores on those scales. Unfortunately, conclusions such as these are simplistic at best and downright inaccurate and damaging at worst. A best practices approach to behavior rating scale interpretation (a) begins at the individual item level to determine what specific behaviors and/or behavioral correlates are of greatest concern to the scale respondent; (b) continues at the narrow-band scale level, first to determine if the significant items are consistent with the label of the specific scale that contains them, and then to determine if the scale's scores indicate a statistical or clinical problem; and (c) ends at the broad-band scale level where the most global interpretations of a referred student's behavior are considered. Significantly, the data generated in this manner are compared with other information at this first step of the RQC process and then integrated into the consultation interview for further confirmation and analysis.

Objective Personality Scales

Objective personality assessment scales assess specific diagnostic areas (e.g., self-concept, anxiety, depression) or multidimensional areas of referred children's personality functioning. At this RQC stage, it may be best to use the latter type of objective scale so that a broad range of psychological problems or concerns can be sampled for later, more in-depth investigation. Currently, a number of multidimensional objective scales are available, including the Personality Inventory for Children and for Youth, the Children's Personality Questionnaire, the Early School and High School Personality Questionnaires, the Minnesota Multiphasic Personality Inventory-Adolescents, and the Millon Adolescent Personality Inventory. The Personality Inventory for Children, for example, has 12 clinical scales focusing on Achievement, Intellectual Screening, Development, Somatic Concerns, Depression, Family Relations, Delinquency, Withdrawal, Anxiety, Psychosis, Hyperactivity, and Social Skills, all of which can stand alone as separate clinical entities.

Like behavior rating scales, the development and psychometric properties of all objective scales must be investigated, and only those scales that have clinical (as opposed to research) validation and utility should be used. Also, like the behavior rating scales, analyses of individual items on these instruments, as opposed to unconditional acceptances of scale and profile results, are more likely to facilitate the development of effective interview questions and hypotheses for later validation through the RQC process.

The Consultative Interview

The consultation interview(s), involving those individuals referring and relevant to a specific child, is the most important activity in the RQC process. While the long-term impact of the consultation interview focuses on intervention planning and implementation, the interview has a number of goals as the second step of the RQC process:

1. To engage the teacher (and/or parents) in the comprehensive problem-solving process such that they are committed to the entire process and to the service delivery directions that result from the process.

2. To obtain additional relevant information beyond that already collected during the Review of Data step and to integrate and apply all of the data to the next steps of the RQC process.

3. To use all the data collected to clarify the initial concerns of the referral source resulting in a behavioral definition and operationalization of the behavior(s) of concern.

4. To determine what interventions have already been attempted and to evaluate the treatment integrity and impact of those interventions.

5. To initiate/continue the functional assessment process by asking some or all of the problem analysis questions noted earlier in this chapter.

6. To begin to generate tentative hypotheses that explain the clarified concern and to outline the remainder of the RQC assessment process for the consultee.

Armed with the teacher- and parent-completed referral and background information forms, behavior rating scales, and objective rating scales, the school psychologist can begin the diagnostic interview process at a much higher level of sophistication than when starting the process with a simple statement of concern. In fact, with the social, behavioral, developmental, educational, behavioral, and familial history of the student already documented by both teachers and parents, a great many background questions are unnecessary, and the school psychologist need only pursue those questions that are directly or indirectly related to the referral problem. Thus, the school psychologist now can listen to teachers' and parents' descriptions of the referral problem, match them to the behavior and objective rating scale data that has already been completed, behaviorally define and operationalize the stated problems and the behavioral ecology where they exist, and begin to generate hypotheses that explain the referred behavior or situation.

Development of Hypotheses

After completing the needed consultation interviews and collecting the necessary relevant information, the RQC process proceeds to the development of hypotheses that explain the now-clarified and behaviorally operationalized referral concerns. At this point in the process, the school psychologist and others have a great deal of information about the referred behavior, about the settings within which this behavior occurs, and about other significant ecological environments and contexts that are related to the referred student and the referral situation. Now, it is time to integrate all of this information and generate hypotheses that answer the question, *Why is this referral situation happening?* These hypotheses are generated by using the variables and conditions in Table 1 (adapted from Batsche & Knoff, 1995), and they conform to the principle that hypotheses must be relevant, predictive, and measurable.

Development of Predictions

The next step in the RQC process is the development of predictions. Predictions are statements, developed from specific hypotheses, that identify what should or should not happen if a hypothesis is true or untrue,

Table 1. Conditions that relate directly/indirectly to student learning

1. Child characteristics/conditions

Cognitive areas
- Adequate/inadequate short and long-term memory (auditory, visual)
- Length of attention span
- Self-monitoring and self-management skills
- Self-control/impulsivity (ability/inability to delay long enough to think/behave)
- Ability/inability to integrate visual/motor/auditory tasks
- Presence/absence of prerequisite academic skills for task
- Cognitive/metacognitive ability and skills

Behavioral areas
- Self-control and self-management skills
- Attributions, beliefs, expectations, attitudes
- Social skills (interpersonal, problem-solving, conflict resolution skills)
- Adaptive behavior skills
- Academic engagement

Health areas
- Hearing, motor, vision skills
- Presence of specific health conditions
- Physical and motor (fine and gross) capacity
- Medication cycle not appropriate for school day/activities
- Side effects of medication
- Speech/language difficulties
- Metabolism
- Fatigue/persistence resulting in higher activity, less ability to focus, etc.

Other
- Excessive absences or moves
- Lack of sensory stimulation during early childhood
- Language other than English

2. Peer characteristics/conditions

- Degree of cohesion between students relative to sharing common interests, values, and goals
- Peers support/reinforcement of appropriate/inappropriate behavior
- Peers providing/not providing appropriate/adequate models
- Social/academic skills of peers significantly higher (lower) than referred student
- Peer influence over student's appropriate/inappropriate behavior (e.g., supporting versus taunting and instigating)
- Expectations/values of peer group that influence student

3. Curriculum characteristics/conditions

- Curriculum too easy or difficult
- Curriculum relevant/not relevant to child experiences/understanding
- Curriculum flexible/inflexible in its ability to be adapted to students' learning styles or individual needs
- Curriculum presented in a way that relates to child strengths/weaknesses (lecture/auditory, etc.)
- Curriculum presented too fast or slow for student learning rate
- Sufficient/insufficient opportunity to practice skills

(Table continues on the following page.)

Table 1. (continued)

- Length of curriculum assignments too long/too short for attention/concentration skills of student
- Philosophy of curriculum presentation too narrow or broad (e.g., phonics only)
- Curriculum empirically based or not relative to student learning outcomes

4. Teacher characteristics/conditions

- Teacher expectations too high/too low for skills of student
- Feedback to student frequent/not frequent enough
- Rate of reinforcement too high/too low for student needs
- Presence/absence of assessment as an integral component of instruction
- Student and teacher physically too far apart or too close
- Sufficient/insufficient rehearsal time, direct instruction time, teacher guided practice
- Teacher energy, fatigue, or tolerance resulting in higher positive/negative or more/less frequent feedback and interaction
- Teacher familiar/unfamiliar or experienced/inexperienced with curricular methods necessary for child
- Level of supervision (frequency/rate) too high/low for student needs
- Teacher teaching style related to child strength or weakness areas

5. Classroom/school/district characteristics/conditions

- Classroom seating arrangement fosters problems (too close/near to peers, too far from/close to teacher, near window or distractions, etc.)
- Rules/expectations in class/building far exceed skills of student to be successful
- Presence/absence of a school-wide discipline approach
- School and staff (staff to student) ratio
- Sufficient/insufficient school materials (books, labs, other learning resources)
- Satisfactory/unsatisfactory professional development programs for staff
- Areas in building that are supervised adequately/inadequately
- Consistent/inconsistent discipline programs/philosophies/differences between staff who interact with students
- Temperature of building/classrooms
- Schedule of the daily activities
- Bus ride (length, problems on bus carry over to school, etc.)

6. Family/neighborhood/community characteristics/conditions

- Parent discipline adequate/inadequate (e.g., too severe/passive, teaches child prosocial or aggressive strategies)
- Presence of conflict/physical aggression between parents/guardians
- Presence/absence of appropriate/inappropriate levels of parent supervision
- Parents support/non-support of homework completion
- Discrepancy in values/expectations between home/school
- Parent academic skills adequate/inadequate to help child
- Reading and related academic and appropriate extracurricular activities present/absent in or supported by the home
- Parent difficulties (substance abuse, etc.) result in inconsistent parenting, low levels of supervision, negativity
- Parent able/unable or willing/unwilling to reinforce school-related academic/behavior strategies in the home
- Parent expectations too high/too low for child along with too much/too little pressure
- Parent willing/unwilling or able/unable to meet health/nutrition/basic needs of child resulting in potential school absences, tardiness, ability of child to concentrate on school tasks, etc.
- Parent supervision of student relative to the presence/absence of appropriate/inappropriate adults/peers in community, neighborhood, and home settings

respectively. For example, if we hypothesize that *A child aggresses because his peers verbally taunt him*, then our prediction statements would be *When peers verbally taunt the child, then the child will aggress against the peers* and *When peers do not verbally taunt the child, then the child will not aggress against the peers.*

Prediction statements are set up to evaluate the hypothesis *and its converse*. That is, it is necessary to demonstrate that the referral concern exists when our explanatory hypothesis is true, and it is also necessary to demonstrate that the concern *does not exist* in the absence of our hypothesis. For example, given the example above, we need to demonstrate that the child aggresses only when his peers verbally taunt him. If he aggresses when the peers ignore him, then our hypothesis is not true in that the verbal taunting is not consistently related to an aggressive response.

Another important point about predictions is that they must be evaluated without changing the student's "natural" environment whenever possible. That is, predictions should be tested, as much as possible, without implementing new interventions and, thus, without changing the referral setting. If a student, for example, is referred because he is out of his seat a great deal of the time, and your hypothesis is that he gets out of his seat during unstructured times in the classroom, then your prediction statements would say that *When unstructured time occurs in the classroom, then the student will get out of his seat* and *When structured time occurs in the classroom, then the student will stay in his seat.* To evaluate these prediction statements in a naturally occurring way, we would need to observe during times when the teacher routinely allows the classroom to be structured and unstructured, respectively. If we asked the teacher to artificially plan special structured and unstructured times, then this would constitute an intervention that changes the normally occurring classroom routine. When such changes occur, in the absence of baseline data and a multiple baseline or reversal research design, we cannot truly be sure whether the referred student's behavior is a function of the classroom structure (or lack of structure) or the change in the classroom routine.

Technically, this is the difference between a functional behavioral *assessment* and a functional behavioral *analysis*. The former is completed under naturally occurring conditions in the behavioral ecology. The latter involves some manipulation of the environment in order to test a specific and hypothesized contingency between two events (Tilly et al., 1998).

Development of Referral Questions

Referral questions are data-based questions, derived from the prediction statements, that quantitatively confirm or reject the original hypotheses related to a referral concern. More specifically, referral questions are typically yes or no questions, or questions related to frequency, duration, latency, or intensity. Referral questions are important for a number of reasons. First, referral questions actually drive the assessment and decision-making process. While assessment procedures must be reliable, valid, and psychometrically sound, the form and format of the referral questions actually determine what assessment methodologies must be used. Second, referral questions provide an internal check for the RQC process to insure that the parents' or teachers' referral concerns still are being addressed. Third, referral questions help to organize the report writing process. In fact, reports documenting the confirmation of hypotheses, the development of interventions, and the successful results of those interventions can be structured in a question-and-answer format around the referral questions. Thus, reports should do more than describe the referred student, they should answer questions that lead to and relate to interventions.

To write effective and appropriate referral questions, they must have the following characteristics:

1. Referral questions must be clearly defined, they must be directly related to the previous prediction statements, and they must require data that are observable and measurable.

2. Referral questions must be agreed upon by the referral source and other evaluation team members, and they must lead to or have the potential to lead to interventions, not labels.

3. Referral questions should result in clear, definitive answers regardless of whether they are testing causal or correlational relationships. Ideally, referral questions should be answered in a "yes" or "no" or other data-based format, and they should be able to directly confirm or reject hypotheses generated to explain the referred problem.

Given the scenario above relative to the aggressive child, the referral questions should be:

1. Do the peers verbally taunt the child? (Yes or No?)

2. Is the child aggressive with the peers? (Yes or No?)

3. Do the peers ignore or leave the child alone? (Yes or No?)

4. Is the child aggressive with the peers? (Yes or No?)

To confirm the hypothesis in this situation, questions 1, 2, and 3 would have to be answered "yes," and question 4 would have to be answered "no."

Once referral questions are developed, assessment begins. It is important to note that *only those assessment instruments and processes* needed to answer the referral questions are necessary. This discourages the random use of personality assessment tools in a "search for pathology," and it makes the RQC process both efficient and effective. In this context, most RQC referral questions will be answered jointly by the school psychologist and the classroom teacher, and they will most likely involve direct assessment *in the setting where the referred student's behavior or problem is occurring*. These assessments involve low inference procedures (e.g., the use of behavioral observation), they use multi-trait, multi-method assessment procedures, and they directly link assessment and intervention.

Briefly, there are four behavioral observation approaches commonly noted in the literature (O'Neill et al., 1997): naturalistic free behavior, naturalistic role play, analog free behavior, and analog role play observations.

Naturalistic observation involves observing referred students in the actual settings where their behaviors of concern and/or the conditions that most influence those behaviors are exhibited. When used to confirm hypotheses generated to explain well-identified behaviors, naturalistic observations are both time- or cost-efficient. In addition, they are the most ecologically sound of the behavioral approaches, and they are the least inferential relative to interpretation within the personality assessment context.

Analog observation involves observing referred students in controlled situations that simulate particular environments or circumstances of behavioral concern. These situations are used to objectively evaluate *a priori* hypotheses that explain referred behaviors or situations and to provide detailed and comprehensive functional analyses of significant facets of a referred student's behavior. Significantly, analog observations attempt to maximize the ecological accuracy of simulated situations so that interpretation requires as little inference as possible. They are also very time-efficient given their intent to elicit behaviors that test the referral-related hypotheses.

Free behavior observations occur when referred students are allowed to freely react and interact within environments that are either unmanipulated and naturalistic or simulated and analog. No artificial rules or constraints are placed on the students, and they respond to situations in any way that they choose.

Role play observations occur as referred students are requested to follow pre-conceived and semi-structured scripts that focus on interactions or situations relevant to particular hypotheses. These observations involve more inference than free behavior observations, because the student's role played behavior is assumed to represent behavior that would be exhibited if the situation actually occurred in a real-life situation. Once again, role play observations can occur in both naturalistic or classroom-based settings and analog or simulated settings; and naturalistic observations are assumed to require less interpretive inference than analog observations.

While behavioral observations may appear to be the easiest and most objective of all personality assessment approaches, they actually involve very complex processes. Beyond choosing which observation approach to use, school psychologists still must decide which recording method to use (e.g., narrative, interval, event, ratings) and how to best assess the antecedent conditions, environmental characteristics and interactions, overt and covert contingencies, planned and unplanned consequent conditions, and unintended effects of a referred behavior within its unique ecology. Though one of the most effective ways to validate hypotheses generated during the problem identification phase of the personality assessment process, behavioral observation also can be misused or abused. School psychologists must recognize that it is a learned skill that requires training, practice, and more practice.

Once data are collected, then the referral questions can be answered, and the original hypotheses can be confirmed or rejected. At this point, the multidisciplinary team can take the confirmed hypotheses, begin to develop intervention plans, and outline a formative report organized around the hypotheses tested, the referral questions generated, and the data collected.

Other Assessment Techniques

Beyond behavioral observation, there are a number of other personality techniques that can be used during the assessment process to answer specific RQC questions: for example, objective personality assessment techniques that focus on single diagnostic dimensions when needed (e.g., self-concept, anxiety, depression) and family assessment techniques. Projective instruments, to a large degree, *cannot* validate *a priori* hypotheses; and they only generate additional hypotheses that need subsequent validation, and thus, are only useful (if at all) in the earliest stages of the RQC process. The reader is strongly encouraged to read Knoff's (1993, 2001) research review and analyses of projective drawing approaches. The primary conclusions from these reviews are that projective instruments do not have sufficient empirical validation for clinical use, that they are both time- and cost-inefficient, and that their use necessitates additional assessments to validate their assertions.

A BRIEF RQC CASE STUDY

To quickly illustrate the RQC process in action, let us consider a fourth-grade male student (Jason) who has been referred by his regular classroom teacher because of a number of incidents where he becomes verbally angry, pushes his desk violently away from himself and toward other students, and refuses to calm down and follow teacher directions. Typically, we would behaviorally operationalize this problem in more specific detail by completing a series of consultative interviews, by some classroom observations, and, perhaps, by having the teacher complete a behavior rating scale or two. But, for the purposes of this example, let us just generate one hypothesis in each of the six hypothesis areas that conform to Figure 1 that potentially explain this behavior. Putting these hypotheses in the recommended format, we would say that Jason becomes verbally angry, pushes his desk violently away from himself and toward other students, and refuses to calm down and follow teacher directions *because*:

1. *Family-oriented hypothesis*: He sees his father respond similarly to his mother when she asks him to do something around the house.

2. *Classroom-oriented hypothesis*: There is so much noise in the classroom that he can't attend to and complete his work.

3. *Teacher-oriented hypothesis*: The teacher constantly orders him around giving him five negative comments for every one positive comment.

4. *Curriculum-oriented hypothesis*: His mathematics text and assignments are above his instructional level.

5. *Peer-oriented hypothesis*: His peers reinforce him with attention and laughter each time this occurs.

6. *Student-oriented hypothesis*: He forgets to use the "stop and think" steps of his prosocial skills/problem-solving self-management intervention.

At this point, we would generate prediction statements and referral questions for each of these hypotheses, and then proceed to collect the data to confirm or reject each hypothesis. Continuing our example for just one of the hypotheses above, we would say that

7. *Curriculum-oriented predictions*: *When* Jason's mathematics assignments are above his instructional level, *then* he will become verbally angry, push his desk violently away from himself and toward other students, and refuse to calm down and follow teacher directions. *Conversely, when* Jason's mathematics assignments are at his instructional level, *then* he will not become verbally angry, push his desk violently away from himself and toward other students, or refuse to calm down and follow teacher directions.

The data-based *referral questions* needed to assess this hypothesis, drawn from the prediction statements, include

1. Are Jason's mathematics assignments above his instructional level?

2. Does Jason become verbally angry, push his desk violently away from himself and toward other students, and refuse to calm down and follow teacher directions?

At this point, the school psychologist and/or the teacher can collect the data to answer these questions (a) through an assessment of the instructional level of Jason's math assignments over time and (b) through observations of Jason's behavior during math. If the data demonstrate that Jason acts out when math assignments are above his instructional level, but does not act out, is calm, and appropriately follows teacher directions when math assignments are at his instructional level, then the hypothesis has been confirmed. If the data do not support one or both of these situations, then the hypothesis should be rejected. For the confirmed hypothesis, the intervention program would focus on (a) ensuring that current math assignments are at Jason's instructional level, (b) working with Jason to increase his mathematics skill and confidence levels such that he progresses more successfully through the math curriculum's goals and objectives, and/or (c) teaching Jason coping skills such that he is able to more adaptively handle the academic and personal frustration that occurs when he receives a mathematics assignment above his instructional level. If the hypothesis is rejected, then another hypothesis must be generated, assessed, and validated; that is, intervention programs cannot be developed without one or more confirmed hypotheses.

SUMMARY

Personality assessment is most effective when referred problems are comprehensively identified and analyzed from an ecological, developmental, and environmental perspective using a hypothesis-testing, problem-solving process where hypotheses are evaluated using objective, multimethod, multisource, multisetting methods. Once accomplished, school psychologists then are ready to develop effective intervention programs. Intervention should be clearly linked to the assessment process, the referral concerns identified and confirmed by the personality and behavioral assessments, and the factors that interact and influence the referral concerns. As was noted earlier, intervention is useless unless viable, acceptable, and socially valid approaches are successfully implemented with ongoing attention to treatment integrity and treatment evaluation. In the end, the success of the personality assessment process will be evaluated most clearly on the behavioral and treatment changes resulting from the intervention program.

To summarize, personality assessment is a process, not a product. It is simply not enough to *describe* or even *understand* a child's behavioral or social-emotional problems. School psychologists must move from problem analysis to interventions that resolve these problems and that facilitate children's normal development and positive mental health. This chapter has been dedicated to this ultimate best practice. It is hoped that we will soon see the day when school psychologists provide comprehensive services, when intervention success is valued over special education placement, and when social, emotional, and behavioral success is an explicit educational goal and emphasis in every classroom.

REFERENCES

Achenbach, T. M. (1991). *Manual for the Child Behavior Checklist and Revised Child Behavior Profile*. Burlington, VT: University of Vermont Department of Psychiatry.

Achenbach, T. M., & McConaughy, S. (1996). Relations between DSM-IV and empirically based assessment. *School Psychology Review, 25*, 329–341.

American Psychiatric Association. (1994). *The diagnostic criteria from DSM-IV*. Washington, DC: Author.

Atkins, M., McKernal, M., McKay, M., Talbott, E., & Arvanitis, P. (1996). DSM-IV diagnosis of conduct disorder and oppositional defiant disorder: Implications and guidelines for school mental health teams. *School Psychology Review, 25*, 274–283.

Batsche, G. M., & Knoff, H. M. (1995). Linking assessment to intervention. In A. Thomas & J. Grimes (Eds.), *Best practices in school psychology III* (pp. 569–585). Washington, DC: National Association of School Psychologists.

Edelbrock, C. S. (1983). Problems and issues in using rating scales to assess child personality and psychopathology. *School Psychology Review, 12*, 293–299.

Forness, S. R., & Knitzer, J. (1992). A new proposed definition and terminology to replace "Seriously Emotional Disturbance" in Individuals with Disabilities Education Act. *School Psychology Review, 21*, 12–20.

Gable, R. A., Quinn, M. M., Rutherford, R. B., & Howell, K. W. (1998). *Assessing student problem behavior, Part II: Conducting the functional behavioral assessment*. Washington, DC: American Institutes for Research, Center for Effective Collaboration and Practice.

Gresham, F. M. (1983). Multitrait-multimethod approach to multifactored assessment: Theoretical rationale and practical application. *School Psychology Review, 12*, 26–34.

Gresham, F. M. (1998). Noncategorical approaches to K–12 emotional and behavioral difficulties. In D. J. Reschly, W. D. Tilly, & J. P. Grimes (Eds.), *Functional and noncategorical identification and intervention in special education*. Des Moines: Iowa Department of Education.

Knoff, H. M. (1983). Personality assessment in the schools: Issues and procedures for school psychologists. *School Psychology Review, 12*, 391–398.

Knoff, H. M. (1993). The utility of human figure drawings in personality and intellectual assessment: Why ask why? *School Psychology Quarterly, 8*, 191–196.

Knoff, H. M. (2001). Evaluation of projective drawings. In C. R. Reynolds & R. W. Kamphaus (Eds.), *Handbook of psychological and educational assessment of children: Vol. 2. Personality, behavior, and context*. New York: Guilford.

Knoff, H. M., & Batsche, G. M. (1991a). *The Referral Question Consultation process: Addressing system, school, and classroom academic and behavioral problems*. Tampa, FL: Author.

Knoff, H. M., & Batsche, G. M. (1991b). Integrating school and educational psychology to meet the educational and mental health needs of all children. *Educational Psychologist, 26*, 167–183.

McKee, W. T., & Witt, J. C. (1990). Effective teaching: A review of instructional and environmental variables. In T. B. Gutkin & C. R. Reynolds (Eds.), *The handbook of school psychology* (2nd ed.) (pp. 821–846). New York: John Wiley.

O'Neill, R. E., Horner, R. H., Albin, R. W., Sprague, J. R., Storey, K., & Newton, J. S. (1997). *Functional assessment and program development for problem behavior: A practical handbook*. Pacific Grove, CA: Brooks/Cole.

Quay, H. C. (1983). A dimensional approach to behavior disorder: The Revised Behavior Problem Checklist. *School Psychology Review, 12*, 244–249.

Tilly, W. D., Kovaleski, J., Dunlap, G., Knoster,T. P., Bambara, L., & Kincaid, D. (1998). *Functional behavioral assessment: Policy development in light of emerging research and practice*. Alexandria, VA: National Association of State Directors of Special Education.

Wang, M. C., Haertel, G. D., & Walberg, H. J. (1990). What influences learning? A content analysis of review literature. *Journal of Educational Research, 84*, 30–43.

ANNOTATED BIBLIOGRAPHY

Knoff, H. M., & Batsche, G. M. (1991a). *The Referral Question Consultation process: Addressing system, school, and classroom academic and behavioral problems*. Tampa, FL: Author.
An introductory manual to the RQC process, which utilizes a systematic problem-solving process to address referred problems. By using consultation processes as a foundation, this process ensures a direct link between case-related assessment and intervention by generating hypotheses that explain the referred behavior, confirming behavioral predictions based on these hypotheses, and developing interventions that address these behavioral explanations. This manual describes this decision-making process and relates it to use by support teams, team reports, and triennial re-evaluations. It also provides a step-by-step teaching of the RQC process complete with numerous case examples and practice exercises to facilitate reader mastery.

Knoff, H. M. (2001). Evaluation of projective drawings. In C. R. Reynolds & R. W. Kamphaus (Eds.), *Handbook of psychological and educational assessment of children: Vol. 2. Personality, behavior, and context*. New York: Guilford.
A critical chapter in an important edited volume devoted to personality assessment and sound clinical and school practice. The chapter reviews all of the current research on projective drawings and concludes that much of the "evidence" is provided through case studies or research that has serious methodological flaws. Projective drawings are put into a problem-solving context that suggests limiting their use while increasing their accountability—for those who still want to use them. While the debate on projectives rages on, this chapter provides an objective and empirical perspective in the midst of the storm.

O'Neill, R. E., Horner, R. H., Albin, R. W., Sprague, J. R., Storey, K., & Newton, J. S. (1997). *Functional assessment and program development for problem behavior: A practical handbook*. Pacific Grove, CA: Brooks/Cole.
Very practical book that provides comprehensive, step-by-step, approaches and strategies for completing FBA of students with problem behaviors. The book contains a number of pragmatic forms that can be used during a FBA and that can be applied to educational settings. In addition, discussions are presented to help the assessment to intervention process relative to the development of behavior support plans.

Sattler, J. M. (2001). *Assessment of children: Behavioral and clinical applications*. San Diego: Author.
The fourth edition of Sattler's comprehensive work (now arranged in two volumes, the other volume addressing cognitive applications) covers all facets of the behavioral and clinical assessment process with children and adolescents and has some critical chapters related to personality, behavioral, and functional assessment. Included is information on the assessment of adaptive behavior and behavior problems, assessment of behavior by interview methods, assessment of behavior by observational methods, assessment of ethnic minority children, and others related to consultation, conferencing, and report writing. Sattler balances theory, empirical research, and pragmatic best practices approaches in a way that facilitates appropriate assessment processes and a clear assessment to intervention linkage.

81 Best Practices in Multidimensional Assessment of Emotional or Behavioral Disorders

Stephanie H. McConaughy
University of Vermont
David R. Ritter
Burlington (Vermont) School District

OVERVIEW

When the district school psychologist read the referral for evaluation, it was clear that the student's classroom behavior warranted concern. Teachers reported that the student's moods and behavior seemed unpredictable from day to day. On "good" days, the student seemed generally happy, but often clowned around and disrupted class activities. Other days, the student came into school looking angry and sullen and sometimes depressed. When asked to do school work on the "bad" days, the student became defiant and disrespectful or simply shut down and refused to do anything. The student was often sent out of class as a disciplinary procedure. As a result, the student missed instruction and was falling behind in academic performance. On the playground, the student frequently fought with others, though it was not always clear who initiated the fights. The student seemed to have no real friends. The student's behavior was understandably disturbing to teachers. The school psychologist was aware that many regular education teachers feel that they lack the necessary skills and training to cope with such problems (Kauffman & Wong, 1991; Scruggs & Mastropieri, 1996). The school psychologist also knew how important it was to identify emotional and behavioral problems early before they become irreversible (Walker et al., 1998).

In formulating an assessment plan, the school psychologist considered four perspectives on emotional or behavioral disorders. One perspective views *child psychopathology* as the basis for a disorder. This viewpoint seeks to identify emotional and behavioral problems that are symptoms or characteristics of psychopathology. This perspective uses a classification system to describe and label different patterns of problems exhibited by the child. It also acknowledges that familial and environmental factors may contribute to the development of child psychopathology. Examples are mental illness in a parent, parental alcohol or drug abuse, low socioeconomic status, life stress, and divorce (Jensen, Bloedau, Degroot, Ussery, & Davis, 1990).

A second perspective focuses on *behavioral-environmental interactions* as the basis for disorder. Instead of identifying symptoms or characteristics of psychopathology in the child, this perspective emphasizes reciprocal interactions between the child's behavior and the environment (Bandura, 1986). Behavioral excesses or deficits are then thought to constitute emotional or behavioral disorders. This viewpoint considers family factors as well, but from a different angle, such as incompatibility between parents' and children's interactional styles, parents' maladaptive reactions to the needs or problems of children, and parents' attributions about intentionality, consequences, and circumstances surrounding behavior (Grotevant, McRoy, & Jenkins, 1988). Aspects of the school environment and interactions with teachers are equally important considerations within this perspective (Ysseldyke, Christenson, & Thurlow, 1987).

A third perspective seeks to identify the *functional relationship* between environmental events and problem behavior. This viewpoint is similar to the behavioral-environmental perspective. It assumes that behavior occurs within a context of antecedent and consequent events and that most behavior is a function of the reinforcing aspect of consequent events. The consequent events can provide either positive reinforcement (social attention or pleasant situations) or negative reinforcement (escape or avoidance of unpleasant situations). Functional behavioral assessment identifies the antecedent and consequent events surrounding problem behavior. Interventions are then designed to change reinforcing relationships to extinguish problem behavior and substitute desired behavior (see McComas, Hoch, & Mace, 2000; Knoster & McCurdy, this volume; Kratochwill, this volume).

Yet a fourth perspective emphasizes the *effectiveness of interventions* for emotional or behavioral disorders, directly linking assessment of problems to intervention planning (see Batsche, this volume). This viewpoint defines emotional or behavioral "disorders" by the extent to which the child's behavior proves to be resistant to interventions (Gresham, 1991).

In our case example, the school psychologist recognized that the four perspectives were not mutually exclusive. Each perspective needed to be considered in evaluating the referred student's problems and determining the extent to which such problems constituted a disorder. The school psychologist also recognized that the primary goals for assessment should be to identify students' needs and to assist in developing and implementing interventions when they are warranted (National Association of School Psychologists, 1993). To accomplish these general goals, school-based assessments of emotional and behavioral disorders can serve several purposes. These include:

1. Helping teachers to cope with behavior problems in regular education classrooms

2. Helping students to reduce their problems and improve their competencies

3. Determining whether a student is eligible for special education services

4. Referring children (and perhaps families) for mental health services outside of the school setting

Depending on the purposes of assessment, the school psychologist may emphasize each of the four perspectives to different degrees. To help teachers cope with classroom behavior problems, the behavioral-environmental interaction or intervention-focused perspectives are likely to offer the most effective strategies. In such cases, the school psychologist could employ behavioral consultation methods to determine specific excesses or deficits in the student's behavior (see Kratochwill, this volume; Zins, this volume). Specific antecedents and consequences of the problem behaviors would be identified. In consultation with teachers, the school psychologist could then evaluate the effectiveness of prior interventions and the feasibility of alternative interventions in the regular education setting. The behavioral-environmental interaction or intervention-focused perspectives are also likely to be effective for working directly with students to reduce their problems and improve their competencies and school performance. In such cases, the school psychologist may provide individual or group counseling to students as well as consult with teachers and parents. For these purposes, it is usually not necessary to label or classify a student's problems into categories.

Determining eligibility for special education services or Section 504 accommodations, on the other hand, often involves classifying students' problems according to categories of "disabilities," as defined in federal and state laws. Providing mental health services outside of school may also require classification of problems, for example, in order to obtain third-party insurance payments. Making appropriate classifications involves assessing the severity and patterning of problems, as well as considering environmental circumstances. Other chapters in this volume describe assessment best practices from the perspectives of behavioral-environmental interactions, functional relationships, and effectiveness of interventions. To assist school psychologists in assessment of child psychopathology, this chapter describes best practices for identifying and classifying patterns of children's emotional and behavioral problems. The following section covers basic considerations regarding classification systems. A subsequent section describes best practices for multidimensional assessment of emotional and behavioral disorders.

BASIC CONSIDERATIONS

Two different approaches have been taken toward classifying children's emotional or behavioral problems: categorical classification and empirically based taxonomies (Achenbach & McConaughy, 1997). Categorical systems classify problems in a *dichotomous* present versus absent fashion. In a categorical system, specific criteria are listed to describe features of a disorder. If all of the required features are met, an individual is judged to have the disorder. If all of the required features are not met, the individual is judged not to have the disorder.

In empirically based taxonomies, statistical procedures, such as principal components or factor analysis, are employed to derive "syndromes" or groupings of problems that tend to co-occur. Individuals are scored according to the *degree* to which they manifest a given problem. Rather than judging features as present or absent, problems are rated on quantitatively graded scales that represent frequency, duration, and/or intensity. Scores for each problem item are then summed to produce an overall score for the relevant syndrome. Standard scores derived from raw scores for each syndrome then indicate how high or severe an individual's score is compared to large normative samples. Standard scores can also be derived for total problems and broad groupings of internalizing problems (e.g., withdrawal, anxiety, and depression) and externalizing problems (e.g., aggressive and delinquent behavior).

Empirically based taxonomies and categorical classification systems are not incompatible. Scores on quantitative scales can be dichotomized to define normal versus clinical ranges. However, quantitative taxonomies do not assume that a particular syndrome represents a distinct or separate disorder. Instead, different patterns of problems are reflected in profiles of high and low scores across a set of syndromes. In this way, quantitative taxonomies provide a more differentiated method than categorical systems for assessing the severity and patterning of problems.

The DSM-IV Classification System

The American Psychiatric Association's *Diagnostic and Statistical Manual of Mental Disorders-Fourth Edition* (DSM-IV) (American Psychiatric Association, 1994) is one of the most widely used categorical systems for classifying adult and childhood psychopathology. The DSM-IV lists specific features, or symptoms, for some 40 numerically coded disorders of childhood and adolescence. Several adult disorders are also considered applicable to children. For each disorder, evaluators must judge whether the defining symptoms are present or absent over a specified time period (e.g., the past 6 months). They must also determine whether the symptoms produce functional impairment in relevant settings (e.g., home, school, or work), and they must rule out other diagnoses with similar symptoms. Children judged to meet the requisite number of symptoms and qualifying conditions are diagnosed as having a DSM-IV disorder. Common childhood diagnoses include conduct disorder (CD), oppositional defiant disorder (ODD), attention deficit hyperactivity disorder (ADHD), and separation anxiety disorder. Examples of adult diagnoses that can be applied to children include major depression, dysthymia (a chronic form of sad affect), obsessive compulsive disorder (OCD), generalized anxiety disorder, phobias (which can include school phobia), and schizophrenia.

While the DSM is commonly used to classify individuals for mental health services, it has questionable utility for special education and school psychological services (Gresham & Gansle, 1992). Moreover, DSM diagnoses are *not* required by federal law for determining eligibility for special education. However, DSM diagnoses do provide a descriptive system for communicating with mental health professionals and other non-school service providers. In addition, DSM diagnoses are usually required for third-party insurance reimbursement and other mental health administrative purposes. For these reasons, it is helpful for school psychologists to familiarize themselves with the current DSM-IV classification system.

Special Education Classification System

The Individuals with Disabilities Education Act (IDEA, P. L. 101-476, 1990; P. L. 105-17, 1997) represents another form of categorical classification. The IDEA defines 10 types of disability that can entitle children to special education services. The law describes general criteria for each disability area. Children with emotional or behavioral problems are most likely to qualify for special education under the IDEA category of emotional disturbance (ED), defined as follows:

(i) The term means a condition exhibiting one or more of the following characteristics over a long period of time and to a marked degree, which adversely affects educational performance:

A. An inability to learn which cannot be explained by intellectual, sensory, or other health factors;
B. An inability to build or maintain satisfactory interpersonal relationships with peers and teachers;
C. Inappropriate types of behavior or feelings under normal circumstances;
D. A general pervasive mood of unhappiness or depression;
E. A tendency to develop physical symptoms or fears associated with personal or school problems;

(ii) The term includes children who are schizophrenic. The term does not include children who are socially maladjusted unless it is determined that they have an emotional disturbance (20 U.S.C. § 1401 [a] [1]; 34 C.F.R § 300.7 [g]).

To meet the criteria for ED according to the above definition, a child must exhibit *one or more* of the five characteristics A through E *or* have a diagnosis of schizophrenia. In addition, *all three* qualifying conditions listed in paragraph (i) must apply to at least one of the identified characteristics. That is, the characteristic(s) must exist over *a long period of time, to a marked degree*, and *adversely affect educational performance.* A child exhibiting at least one of the five characteristics, or having a diagnosis of schizophrenia, and meeting all three qualifying conditions, is judged to have ED. A child who does not meet criteria for ED is judged to be ineligible for special education on the basis of emotional or behavioral disorders. Like the DSM-IV system, special education classification requires a categorical decision regarding the presence or absence of a given disability.

Professionals and advocacy groups have criticized the IDEA definition of ED as being overly restrictive and not supported by legal precedent or educational and clinical research (Forness, 1992; Skiba & Grizzle, 1992). In the early 1990s, a national coalition of mental health and special education professionals and advocacy groups launched an effort to substitute a new definition of "emotional or behavioral disorder (EBD)" for the IDEA definition of ED (*Federal Register*, 1993, Vol. 58, No. 26, p.7938). The National Association of School Psychologists endorsed the coalition's proposed definition (National Association of School Psychologists, 1993). However, after receiving public comments, Congress opted to retain the IDEA definition, but later removed the word "serious" from the label for the ED category. Many states have adopted the federal definition of ED, while other states have framed their own definitions modeled on the federal definition. A few states do not require categorical classifications for special education. In evaluating ED, school psychologists must follow the rules and regulations for their own particular state. In subsequent sections, we will use the federal definition of ED as a guideline for defining best practices for assessment of children's emotional and behavioral problems. However, for consistency, we will use the abbreviation "ED/EBD" to encompass all terms for emotional disturbance and emotional and behavioral disorders or disabilities.

Empirically Based Taxonomies

The Achenbach System of Empirically Based Assessment (ASEBA) provides a good example of an empirically based taxonomy (Achenbach, 1991a). The ASEBA includes the *Child Behavior Checklist* (CBCL) (Achenbach, 1991b) and its related forms. The CBCL is designed to obtain parents' ratings of emotional or behavioral problems of children aged 4–18. Parents rate their child on 118 problem items for how true the item is over the past 6 months. Each item is rated on a 3-point scale: 0 = not true (as far as you know); 1 = somewhat or sometimes true; and 2 = very true or often true. The *Teacher's Report Form* (TRF) (Achenbach, 1991c), covering ages 5–18, is a parallel form for obtaining teachers' rating of children's problems over the past 2 months. The *Youth Self-Report* (YSR) (Achenbach, 1991d), covering ages 11–18, is designed to obtain adolescents' ratings of their problems. The CBCL and YSR also include items for measuring social competencies, while the

TRF includes items for rating academic performance and school adaptive functioning. Other ASEBA forms are available for parent and teacher ratings of preschool children, direct observations in group settings, and child clinical interviews. (Forms for observations and child clinical interviews are discussed in later sections.)

The CBCL, TRF, and YSR are scored on profiles containing eight empirically based cross-informant syndrome scales: Withdrawn, Somatic Complaints, Anxious/Depressed, Thought Problems, Social Problems, Attention Problems, Delinquent Behavior, and Aggressive Behavior. The profiles also provide scores for higher-order groupings of Internalizing and Externalizing and Total Problems. In this taxonomic system, the names of the syndrome scales describe the problems they represent, and are not considered to be "diagnostic" labels. (For details of the derivation of syndromes, see Achenbach (1991a) and McConaughy (1993a)). Cut points for defining normal, borderline, and clinical range scores on the problem scales can be used for judging the severity of a child's reported problems relative to nationally representative normative samples.

Several other rating scales are also scored on empirically based syndromes for assessing children's emotional or behavioral problems. For example, the *Behavior Assessment System for Children* (BASC) (Reynolds & Kamphaus, 1992) is scored on 10 clinical syndromes: Aggression, Anxiety, Attention Problems, Atypicality, Conduct Problems, Depression, Hyperactivity, Learning Problems (teacher form only), Somatization, and Withdrawal. The BASC also contains four scales for assessing positive traits: Adaptability, Leadership, Social Skills, and Study Skills (teacher form only). The *Revised Behavior Problem Checklist* (RBPC) (Quay & Peterson, 1983) is scored on six syndromes: Anxiety-Withdrawal, Attention Problems-Immaturity, Motor Tension-Excess, Psychotic Behavior, Socialized Aggression, and Conduct Disorder. The *Walker Problem Behavior Identification Checklist* (WPBIC) (Walker, 1983) is scored on five syndromes: Acting Out, Distractibility, Disturbed Peer Relations, Immaturity, and Withdrawal. Other rating scales, such as the *Behavior Evaluation Scale-2* (BES-2) (McCarney & Leigh, 1990), provide quantitative scores for problems, but do not contain syndrome scales derived through empirically based procedures.

BEST PRACTICES FOR ASSESSMENT OF ED/EBD

Because school psychologists continue to have key roles in assessing ED/EBD to determine eligibility for special education, this type of assessment will be our primary focus. Assessment of ED/EBD as a defined disability is also relevant for accommodations under Section 504 of the Rehabilitation Act of 1973 (29 U.S.C. § 706, 1996; § 504 [30 C.F.R Part 104]). A multidisciplinary team is required for special education and Section 504 evaluations. School psychologists are particularly well qualified to serve as members of multidisciplinary teams for assessing ED/EBD. (Other team members may include special educators, classroom teachers, speech/language pathologists, guidance counselors, parents, and other non-school professionals.) In practice, school psychologists often become involved with children exhibiting emotional or behavioral problems long before they are referred for evaluations. For example, a school psychologist may have already consulted with teachers to develop classroom interventions, or may have provided counseling to such children and their families. The school psychologist's role in assessment of ED/EBD may involve any or all of the following procedures:

1. Reviewing referral and screening information
2. Consulting with teachers and other school staff
3. Planning assessment procedures
4. Conducting screening and assessment procedures
5. Interpreting assessment data and preparing reports
6. Linking assessment data to intervention planning, implementation, and evaluation (National Association of School Psychologists, 1993)

Professional ethics require that all evaluators be familiar with the relevant instruments and procedures and select only those they can administer and interpret with confidence. It is especially important that evaluators understand the limits of reliability and validity of each instrument or procedure. Evaluators must be aware of the advantages and limitations of various assessment procedures and report their findings accordingly. Not all procedures are standardized, nor do they all produce quantifiable data. However, whenever possible, standardized instruments are preferable over non-standardized procedures. Standardized instruments should also be used in conjunction with non-standardized procedures. No single measure or procedure should be considered definitive in providing evidence of ED/EBD. Instead, determination of ED/EBD must be based on an integration of findings from a multidimensional assessment, as discussed below.

Multidimensional Assessment of ED/EBD

Children's behavior often varies from one setting to another, such as home versus school or one classroom versus another. Perspectives or judgments of children's behavior can also vary from one person to another. For these reasons, agreement between informants in different situations is likely to be moderate at best (Achenbach, McConaughy, & Howell, 1987). Differing perspectives about children's behavior do not mean that one informant is right and the other wrong. Instead, differing perspectives underscore the need for multiple information sources to assess children's functioning across settings. For best practice in assessing ED/EBD, information should be obtained from three major sources, as outlined in Table 1: parent reports, teacher reports, and direct assessment of the child.

Standardized parent, teacher, and self-report rating scales provide quantitative scores for measuring different patterns of problems and competencies. Interviews can corroborate rating scale results, as well as provide new information and opportunity to evaluate interaction patterns. Direct observations can further corroborate information obtained from other sources, as well as add information about the child's functioning in a particular setting. Observations are essential for functional analysis of problems, as discussed by Hintze (this volume) and Knoster and McCurdy (this volume). The next sections describe instruments and procedures for each data source listed in Table 1.

Standardized Rating Scales

Standardized rating scales provide efficient methods for obtaining parent and teacher reports of children's problems and competencies. Numerous rating scales have been developed for this purpose. Some instruments are "omnibus" measures that assess a wide range of potential problems. Examples are the CBCL, TRF, BASC, RBPC, and WPBIC. Other instruments are narrower in focus, such as the Conners (1997) scales for assessing attention deficits and hyperactivity. Narrow measures can be used in conjunction with omnibus measures to assess particular problems. It is also important to assess children's competencies or strengths. The *Behavioral and Emotional Rating Scale* (BERS) (Epstein & Sharma, 1998) is one

Table 1. Components of multidimensional assessment of ED/EBD

Parent Reports	*Teacher Reports*	*Direct Assessment of the Child*
Standardized Rating Scales	Standardized Rating Scales	Standardized Self-Reports
Parent interview a. Details of presenting problems b. History related to problems c. Other possible problem areas d. Feasibility of interventions e. Family factors and stressors	Teacher interview a. Details of presenting problems b. History related to problems c. Feasibility of interventions d. Initial goals and intervention plans	Child clinical interview a. Activities, school b. Friends c. Family relations d. Fantasies e. Self-perception, feelings f. Child's view of problems g. For adolescents: somatic complaints, alcohol, drugs, trouble with the law
Questionnaires/Forms	Questionnaires/Forms	Direct Observations
	School Records	Personality Assessment

omnibus measure for assessing emotional and behavioral strengths. The BERS is scored on five empirically based scales: Interpersonal Strength, Family Involvement, Intrapersonal Strength, School Functioning, and Affective Strength. Other omnibus measures, such as the CBCL and TRF, also measure competencies, such as the child's involvement in activities and social organizations, school performance, and school adaptive functioning.

Standardized self-report rating scales have also been developed to obtain children's own views of their problems and competencies. Respondents are usually asked to rate lists of feelings or behaviors on dichotomous (e.g., true/false) or multi-point scales. The YSR is an example of an omnibus self-report scale for youth aged 11–18. The YSR has 102 problem items similar to those on the CBCL and TRF, except that items are worded in the first person. The YSR also has 16 socially desirable items and items for assessing the youth's involvement in activities and social organizations. The YSR is scored on the same eight empirically based syndromes as the CBCL and TRF, plus Internalizing, Externalizing, and Total Problems. The BASC system also has a self-report rating scale for ages 11–18. Other standardized self-report scales focus on particular types of problems, such as depression or anxiety. Examples are the *Child Depression Inventory* (CDI) (Kovacs, 1992), the *Reynolds Adolescent Depression Scale* (RADS) (Reynolds, 1987), and the *Revised Children's Manifest Anxiety Scale* (Reynolds & Richmond, 1985).

In multidimensional assessment, evaluators should compare scores on self-report rating scales to similar scores obtained from parent and teacher rating scales. The ASEBA Windows® computer scoring program was designed to facilitate such comparisons for the CBCL, TRF, and YSR. The program provides printouts of cross-informant comparisons for 89 common problem items as well as syndrome and broad scale scores. The program also provides Q correlations for judging the level of agreement between pairs of informants, such as two parents, a parent and a teacher, or the youth and a teacher/parent. When interpreting results from self-report rating scales, evaluators should consider how responses might be affected by a child's reading ability, insight, motivation, and willingness to disclose sensitive personal information. It is also important to consider the age and cognitive ability of the child. In general, older children are better able to reflect on their own emotions and behavior than are younger children. However, even some adolescents have difficulty adopting a personal perspective on their functioning.

Research has revealed low agreement between children's self-ratings and ratings from other informants, such as parents and teachers (Achenbach et al., 1987; Achenbach, 1991a). Again, this does not imply that only one perspective is the right one. For example, low problem scores from self-ratings, in contrast to high problem scores from parent and/or teacher ratings, may indicate a child's lack of awareness of problems or an unwillingness to disclose problems. High problem scores on self-ratings, in contrast to low problem scores from parents and/or teachers, may indicate the child's heightened sensitivity to problems that are not apparent to adult informants. Evaluators need to consider all of these possibilities when interpreting results from children's self-reports in comparison to reports from other informants.

Advantages of Standardized Rating Scales

For best practice, school psychologists are encouraged to select standardized rating scales with empirically based syndromes and large normative samples covering a wide age range for both genders. Standardized rating scales meeting these criteria have the following advantages:

1. Information is quantifiable and thus amenable to psychometric tests of reliability and validity.

2. Multiple items on omnibus measures provide data on a broad range of potential problems, rather than limiting the focus only to referral concerns or behaviors in one area.

3. Information is organized in a systematic way by aggregating problems into groupings of different syndromes and broad scales.

4. Empirically based syndromes cluster problems that co-occur in large samples of referred children, rather than being based on assumed diagnostic categories.

5. Normative data provide a standard for judging the severity of problems by comparing an individual to large samples of non-referred children.

6. Rating scales are economical and efficient, since most can be completed by the relevant informant in 10–15 minutes and can be scored quickly by hand or computer.

7. Sets of related rating scales can be used to compare similar data from multiple informants, such as parents, teachers, children themselves, and observers.

When choosing a standardized rating scale, it is important that it meet acceptable psychometric standards of reliability and validity. It is equally important that the scale provide useful information for assessing ED/EBD and planning appropriate interventions. To accomplish these goals, the following criteria should be considered:

1. Do the items on the rating scale pertain directly to the child's observable behavior (e.g., gets into fights) rather than consequences of behavior (e.g., often in trouble), inferences about behavior (e.g., lacks social skills), or family situations (e.g., on welfare)?

2. How are the items scaled? Simple yes/no scaling is less effective than multi-point scales, since most behaviors vary in degree. In general, 3- or 4-point scales have shown better discriminatory power than dichotomous scales (e.g., yes/no or true/false), or scales where zero equals "never."

3. Are the items on the scale appropriate for the particular situation? For example, some behavior is more likely to be observed by teachers (e.g., cannot follow directions), while other behavior is better observed by parents (e.g., has nightmares).

4. Do the forms and scoring procedures allow comparisons among multiple raters who observe the child under different conditions in and outside of school?

Limitations of Standardized Rating Scales

While standardized rating scales provide quantitative data on children's problems and competencies, they also have limitations. These include:

1. Rating scales do not identify the etiology or causes of children's problems. Most rating scales assess current functioning over a limited time frame, such as 2 or 6 months. To identify factors that may precipitate and sustain identified problems, evaluators must obtain additional information on such factors as biological conditions, earlier development, social interactions, and environmental circumstances.

2. Rating scales do not dictate choices for interventions. While results are useful for identifying specific areas of concern, additional data are necessary to determine appropriate and feasible interventions.

3. Rating scales are not "objective" measures of children's problems. Like most other assessment procedures, rating scales involve people's perceptions of problems. Perceptions can vary from one rater to the next and can be influenced by the rater's memory, values, attitudes, and motivations, as well as situational factors.

As best practice for school-based assessment of ED/EBD, an omnibus standardized rating scale should be obtained from at least one parent and one teacher who know the child well. If a child has multiple teachers, then it is useful to obtain ratings from several teachers to compare problems across different school environments. A standardized self-report rating scale can also be obtained from older children. Rating scale results must then be integrated with data from other procedures, including interviews and direct observations.

Interviews

In both clinical and school settings, interviews have long been a standard method for assessing children's emotional and behavioral problems (Busse & Beaver, 2000; McConaughy, 2000a, 2000b). For assessment of ED/EBD, interviews should be conducted with parents (or parent surrogates), teachers, and the child, whenever possible. Interview formats can vary from highly structured to semistructured and unstructured approaches.

Parent and Teacher Interviews

Several structured diagnostic interviews have been developed for interviewing parents about their children's problems. Most structured diagnostic interviews have parallel forms for parents and children, and some have been adapted for teacher interviews. Structured diagnostic interviews require strict adherence to standard procedures for asking questions, rating responses, and ordering items. An example is the NIMH *Diagnostic Interview Schedule for Children-Fourth Edition* (NIMH DISC-IV) (Shaffer, Fisher, Lucas, Dulcan, & Schwab-Stone, 2000). Other structured diagnostic interviews also utilize standard question formats, but allow the interviewer to adjust the length and order of items to create a more conversational approach. Examples are the *Child Assessment Schedule* (CAS) (Hodges, Gordon, & Lennon, 1990) and the *Schedule for Affective Disorders and Schizophrenia for School-Age Children* (K-SADS) (Ambrosini, 2000) (for a review, see McConaughy, 2000b).

A disadvantage of structured diagnostic interviews is their exclusive focus on psychiatric diagnoses, which may not be necessary to address the child's problems in the school setting. However, a structured diagnostic interview with a parent can be useful when a diagnosis is needed to facilitate referrals for mental health services or to make referrals for programs targeted at specific types of disorders, such as ADHD, CD, or anxiety disorders. However, because they contain questions covering many different disorders, structured diagnostic interviews can be very time consuming. Their rigid pattern of questioning can also seem unnatural and tedious for the interviewer and interviewee.

In contrast, unstructured interviews do not follow a standard format. They have the advantage of flexibility, since they can be tailored to specific problems and concerns raised by the interviewee. However, unstructured interviews may fail to address other important issues, such as other possible problem areas, family factors and stressors, what interventions have already been tried, and what interventions are feasible in a given setting. Unstructured interview formats also make it difficult to compare information across parents, teachers, and children.

For school-based assessments, semistructured behavioral interviews are especially appropriate for parents and teachers (e.g., see Busse & Beaver, 2000; Kratochwill, this volume). If standardized rating scales are obtained from the same informants, then parent and teacher interviews can focus on information not readily assessed by rating scales.

The first and second columns of Table 1 list general areas to be covered in parent and teacher behavioral interviews. Each interview begins with questions regarding details of a child's presenting problems. Once specific problem behaviors have been identified, the interviewer then asks about antecedent, sequential, and consequent conditions that precipitate and sustain the behaviors. The interviewer should also inquire about parents' and teachers' feelings regarding targeted problems, their usual responses to the problems, and their expectations and preferences regarding the child's behaviors. While the focus of parent and teacher interviews is primarily on a child's current behavior, historical information about identified problems should be obtained as well. It is also important to explore other possible problem areas. This can be accomplished by discussing scores and profile patterns obtained from standardized rating scales, assuming these instruments were completed before the interviews. To assess the feasibility of different interventions, it is useful to ask parents and teachers about their typical strategies for coping with identified problems, such as rewards, punishments, and other procedures.

Parents should also be asked about family factors and stressors that may be related to their children's problems. Examples are:

1. Changes in family structure or relationships, such as divorce or a death in the family

2. Upsetting events or changes at home or school for the child

3. Changes in residence or economic status of the family

4. Psychological or psychiatric problems of family members and mental health services for such problems

5. Significant losses experienced by the child, such as death or loss of a loved one, loss of a pet, or breakup of peer or romantic relationships

6. Medical traumas, hospitalizations, or serious illnesses of the child or family members

7. Alcohol or drug use/abuse by the child or family members

8. Traumatic episodes experienced by the child or family members, such as a suicide attempt, sexual or physical abuse, violence, or serious accident

9. Trouble with the law or involvement with the justice system or social service agencies by the child or family members

Child Clinical Interviews

Semistructured formats are usually most appropriate for child clinical interviews. Unstructured interviews are the least useful, because it is difficult to quantify their results and clinicians vary widely in their interpretations of children's responses. Unstructured interviews are also less amenable to psychometric tests of reliability and validity than are semistructured interviews. Structured diagnostic interviews are also not recommended as best practice for interviewing children in the school setting, because they are often too long and tedious and the information they provide can usually be obtained more reliably from parents (see McConaughy, 2000b).

Semistructured child clinical interviews offer unique opportunities for evaluating children's patterns of problems, their coping strategies, and their perceptions of significant persons and events related to their problems (Hughes & Baker, 1990; McConaughy, 2000a). They also provide opportunities for directly observing children's behavior and interaction styles, especially behavior that may impinge on different treatment options. Hughes and Baker (1990) cited several important behaviors to note during child clinical interviews, such as response to limit setting, impulsivity, distractibility, reaction to frustration or praise, language skills, responsiveness to the interviewer, emotional reactions, nervous mannerisms, and range of affect. Observations of the child's behavior and responses during the interview can then be compared to reports from other informants, such as parents and teachers. A well-conducted child clinical interview can also serve as the initial step for establishing rapport necessary for treatment. In this respect, the child clinical interview can serve as a bridge between assessment and intervention.

The *Semistructured Clinical Interview for Children and Adolescents* (SCICA) (McConaughy & Achenbach, 1994) is an example of a standardized interview for children ages 6–18. The SCICA utilizes a semistructured protocol covering the different content areas listed in the third column of Table 1. Similar areas are often covered in other semistructured child interviews. A unique feature of the SCICA is the use of structured rating scales for scoring the interviewer's observations of the child's behavior and problems reported by the child during the interview. The SCICA rating scales contain 120 observation items and 114 self-report items to be scored on a 4-point scale for ages 6–18. Eleven additional self-report items are scored for adolescents, covering somatic complaints, alcohol, drugs, and trouble with the law. The 1994 SCICA scoring profile contains eight empirically based syndrome scales for ages 6–12, plus broad scales for Internalizing, Externalizing, Total Observations, and Total Self-Reports. The SCICA profile offers the advantage of separate syndromes for scoring observations (Anxious, Withdrawn, Attention Problems, Strange, Resistant) and the child's self-reports (Anxious/Depressed, Family Problems, Aggressive Behavior). A revised SCICA profile to be released in 2001 will contain scales for ages 6–11 and 12–18. As part of the ASEBA system, quantitative scores from the SCICA profile can easily be compared to similar scores on the CBCL, TRF, and YSR profiles.

Besides providing additional information on problem patterns, the child clinical interview can be a key source for assessing feasibility of different interventions and deciding whether to refer the child for mental health or social services outside of school. Along with questions related to the topics listed in Table 1, other questions can also be added to address specific referral issues, such as suicidal risk, danger to others, or possible physical or sexual abuse.

Direct Observations

Direct observations are another important data source for assessing ED/EBD. Direct observations are also an essential data source for functional behavioral assessment (see Knoster & McCurdy, this volume). For some children with emotional or behavior problems, direct observations may have already been conducted by the school psychologist as part of behavioral consultation with teachers. After a child has been referred for evaluation, additional direct observations should be conducted. These can once again be done by the school psychologist, or by other members of the school staff who have been trained in observational techniques. Observations should occur in relevant settings where problems are occurring. It may also be useful to observe the child in other less problematic situations for comparison.

Because children's behavior is apt to vary from day to day, it is important to obtain more than one observation over different days. It usually is better to conduct observations of relatively short duration (e.g., 10–20 minutes) on different days than to rely on one single lengthy observation. Observing one or two randomly selected "control" children in the same setting provides a comparison with peers in the same environment. Finally, the validity of direct observations may become suspect if the target child is aware of being observed. This problem can be reduced by using an observer who is not known by the child or who is a regular visitor to the classroom. If the observer is also one of the evaluators, then it is advisable to observe the child before interviewing or testing.

Direct observations require an independent observer who can record overt behaviors and environmental conditions surrounding the behaviors (see Hintze, this volume; Skinner, Rhymer, & McDaniel, 2000). For optimal effectiveness, direct observations should focus on target behaviors amenable to change. Antecedent and consequent events should also be noted. Observations may utilize narrative recording or empirical methods.

To obtain narrative recordings, an observer writes a description of events that occurred within a given time frame. Methods for narrative recording include descriptive time sampling, antecedent-behavior-consequent (A-B-C) analysis, or daily logs. Narrative recordings are then used to operationally define behaviors that can be targeted for intervention.

Empirical methods require operationally defined behaviors that can be recorded or rated by an observer. Once operational definitions have been established, several different techniques can be employed. Continuous recording methods count the number of times a behavior (or event) occurs within a given period or record the duration of time in which the behavior (or event) was observed. Continuous recording is most effective when behaviors have discreet beginnings and ends, low to moderate rates of occurrence, and are present only briefly. Time sampling records the presence or absence of operationally defined behavior within short specified time intervals. Time sampling is useful when multiple simultaneous target behaviors hinder continuous recording, or when samples of behavior are observed across several different settings.

The *Direct Observation Form* (DOF) (Achenbach, 1986) is an example of a standardized rating scale for obtaining time samples. The DOF contains 96 items scored over a 10-minute interval. The DOF scoring profile contains six empirically based syndromes, plus Internalizing, Externalizing, and Total Problem scales. Children's on-task behavior is also rated at 1-minute intervals over each 10-minute sample. As part of the ASEBA system, the DOF has a scoring profile similar to profiles for the CBCL, TRF, and YSR, which facilitates comparisons of observations with reports from other informants. Hintze (this volume) and Skinner et al. (2000) discuss examples of other procedures and formats for obtaining direct observations.

Personality Assessment

Personality assessment can provide additional information on aspects of social-emotional functioning. Personality assessment, in its broadest context, can include some of the procedures already discussed in this chapter, such as self-report rating scales and child clinical interviews. Other commonly used instruments are the *Minnesota Multiphasic Personality Inventory for Children-Adolescents* (MMPI-A) (Butcher et al., 1992) and *Personality Inventory for Children* (PIC) (Wirt, Lachar, Klinedinst, Seat, & Broen, 1990) described in detail by Knoff (this volume). It should be noted, however, that while standard scoring procedures exist for many personality measures, the interpretation of results still relies heavily on clinical judgment. Moreover, normative data, reliability, and validity are limited for certain types of procedures, such as projective techniques. Personality assessment, therefore, should be conducted only by school psychologists or clinical psychologists specifically trained in this methodology. Even then, results should be interpreted with caution. Since different examiners often disagree in their interpretations of personality measures, such procedures should *not* be used as the primary or sole data sources for assessment of ED/EBD.

Social Skills and Social Reasoning

Many children with emotional or behavioral problems have difficulties in social interactions. Therefore, assessing social skills and social reasoning is important for evaluating ED/EBD and designing interventions. Methods most frequently used include behavior observations, rating scales, children's self-reports, and sociometric techniques (see Gresham, this volume). Several standardized rating scales have been specifically developed to measure social skills. Examples are the *School Social Behavior Scales* (Merrell, 1993), *Social Skills Rating System* (Gresham & Elliott, 1990), and the *Walker-McConnell Scale of Social Competence and School Adjustment* (Walker & McConnell, 1988).

Observations of children's behavior with peers and adults in natural settings, such as the regular education classroom or at recess, can also provide information about social skills and relationships. Observing children's behavior during social skills instruction or role-playing situations provides a more direct method for assessing specific areas of social reasoning, such as empathy or problem solving, and specific social behaviors, such as giving and receiving praise or criticism.

Co-Occurring Conditions

Emotional or behavioral problems can overlap or co-occur with other types of problems. Children with ADHD or learning disabilities, for example, frequently display emotional or behavioral problems (Barkley, 1990; McConaughy, Mattison, & Peterson, 1994). Children with chronic or acute medical conditions, such as allergies, seizure disorders, traumatic brain injury, and Tourette's syndrome, may exhibit co-occurring emotional or behavioral problems, as can children with intellectual or communication impairments. In certain cases, children with other identified disabilities may also be determined to have ED/EBD, according to IDEA criteria. However, emotional or behavioral problems that are clearly a function of another medical, learning, cognitive, or communication disorder should not automatically be classified as ED/EBD. Knowledge of the child's educational and medical history, coupled with direct observations, should help evaluators judge the presence or absence of co-occurring conditions.

Etiology or Causes of Problems

Multidimensional assessment does not require uncovering the etiology or underlying causes of emotional or behavioral problems. Instead, it is more a process of identifying barriers (emotions and behaviors) that impede children's optimal functioning. One may hypothesize about why a child behaves in a certain way, or the way in which a pattern of behavior is understandable from an etiological perspective. Such hypotheses can contribute to a greater understanding of the child and can be helpful in designing interventions. An example would be distinguishing between an acquisition deficit (the absence of a skill) versus a performance deficit (where the skill is clearly evident but the child fails to use the skill) (see Gresham, this volume). Distinguishing between acquisition versus performance deficits is important because it implies different ways of intervening: teaching the skill itself in the former instance versus teaching a replacement behavior or encouraging generalization in the latter instance. Forming hypotheses about the impact of antecedent and consequent events on behavior can be equally useful for functional assessment and intervention planning. At the same time, the origins of emotional and behavioral problems are usually complex, making it difficult to identify clear links between specific causes and effects. For this reason, searching for specific etiologies, except perhaps clear medical problems, is likely to be an unproductive undertaking for most ED/EBD assessments.

Achievement and Educational Performance

All special education evaluations require assessment of a child's current academic achievement and educational performance. For ED/EBD classifications, evaluators must determine whether the identified emotional or behavioral problems adversely affect educational performance as one of the qualifying conditions for special education eligibility. Standardized tests, curriculum-based assessment, grade reports, and work samples can all provide evidence regarding academic achievement. Evaluation of broader educational performance can focus on school adaptive functioning and academic behaviors, such as productivity and success. The *Academic Performance Rating Scale* (APRS) (DuPaul, Rapport, & Perriello, 1991) is a standardized instrument designed for this purpose. Standardized teacher rating scales, such as the BASC, SSRS, and TRF, also provide scores for academic performance and school adaptive functioning, as well as scores for problems. Evaluators can use these measures along with other achievement data to judge adverse effects on educational performance.

Social Maladjustment

Paragraph (ii) of the IDEA definition of ED/EBD specifically excludes "children who are socially maladjusted unless it is determined that they are seriously emotionally disturbed." The social maladjustment clause was added to the original definition of ED/EBD to exclude adjudicated delinquents from special education (Skiba & Grizzle, 1991). However, certain authors (e.g., Slenkovich,1992a, 1992b) have argued that children with externalizing disorders, such as DSM diagnoses of ODD and CD, are socially maladjusted, and therefore should be excluded from special education. Others disagree, arguing there is no theoretical or empirical basis to exclude youth with externalizing disorders from special education (Forness, 1992; Skiba & Grizzle, 1991, 1992). Furthermore, research studies have shown high co-occurrence or "co-morbidity" between externalizing and internalizing problems (McConaughy & Skiba, 1993).

All of the above issues muddy interpretations of the social maladjustment clause. To guide best practice, school psychologists and other evaluators are encouraged to focus first on assessing the IDEA (or state) defined characteristics for ED/EBD. If a child exhibits one or more of the defined characteristics, and all three qualifying conditions, then that child can be considered to have ED/EBD (assuming other possible explanations for the problems have been ruled out). Once ED/EBD criteria are met, further evidence of social maladjustment is irrelevant for purposes of determining eligibility for special education or Section 504 accommodations. The presence of social maladjustment along with ED/EBD, however, is an important factor to consider in planning interventions, since children with such problems often require mental health and/or social services in addition to educational services to meet their needs.

Need for Special Education Services

To qualify for special education services, it is not sufficient that a child exhibit a specific disability, such as ED/EBD. *Need* for special education must also be documented. That is, the multidisciplinary team must demonstrate that the child *needs* specially designed instruction or other interventions that cannot be accomplished through remedial education or related services. For many children with emotional or behavioral problems, interventions may have been already been undertaken prior to referral for evaluation. If pre-referral interventions have done little to reduce the child's problems or to improve school performance, then such resistance to change could be evidence of the need for special education services. School psychologists who have been involved in pre-referral and regular education interventions can play a key role in multidisciplinary team decisions regarding need for special education and other more intensive interventions.

Written Reports

After data gathering has been completed, evaluators must integrate relevant findings into a written report. The report should provide specific information that addresses the characteristics and qualifying conditions of the ED/EBD definition. It is not sufficient to merely state that a child has an "ED/EBD." The report should provide clear and specific descriptions of the child's emotional or behavioral problems, as reported by parents and teachers and directly assessed through child clinical interviews, observations, self-reports, and other measures. Scores on standardized rating scales and self-reports, in particular, can provide quantitative evidence of the extent to which a child exhibits characteristics of ED/EBD. Accordingly, Table 2 outlines relations between the IDEA criteria for ED/EBD and empirically based syndromes scored from the CBCL, TRF, & YSR, BASC, RBPC, and WPBIC. For each instrument, Table 2 lists the syndromes containing problem items that are most closely related to each ED/EBD characteristic (see McConaughy (1993b) and Achenbach & McConaughy (1997) for applications of CBCL, TRF, and YSR scores to the IDEA criteria for ED/EBD).

The written report should provide information on the duration and severity of identified problems. Standard scores and clinical cut points derived from normative samples can be examined to determine the degree to which a child's identified problems deviate from those typically reported for children of the same age and gender. It is also important to discuss how the identified problems may adversely affect academic

Table 2. Relations between IDEA Criteria for ED/EBD and Empirically Based Syndromes

IDEA Criteria for ED	*CBCL, TRF, and YSR*	*BASC*	*RBPC*	*WPBIC*
Inability to learn	• Attention Problems	• Attention Problems	• Attention Problems-Immaturity	• Distractibility
Inability to build or maintain relationships	• Social Problems • Withdrawn	• Withdrawal	• Anxiety-Withdrawal	• Withdrawal • Disturbed Peer relations
Inappropriate types of behavior or feelings	• Aggressive Behavior • Thought Problems	• Aggression • Atypicality	• Conduct Disorder • Psychotic Behavior	• Acting Out • Immaturity
General pervasive mood of unhappiness	• Anxious/Depressed	• Depression	—	—
Tendency to develop physical symptoms or fears	• Anxious/Depressed • Somatic Complaints	• Anxiety • Somatization	• Anxiety-Withdrawal	• Immaturity

Note: CBCL, Child Behavior Checklist; TRF, Teacher's Report Form; BASC, Behavior Assessment System for Children; RBPC, Revised Behavior Problem Checklist; WPBIC, Walker Problem Behavior Identification Checklist; YSR, Youth Self-Report.

achievement and other aspects of educational performance. In most cases, additional evidence regarding educational performance will be provided by other evaluators.

Finally, as best practice, the written report should contain specific recommendations that link assessment results to interventions. Examples include recommendations for consultation with teachers, home-school collaboration, behavioral interventions with students, classroom accommodations, schedule alterations, adaptations in teaching strategies, social skills instruction, and individual, group, or family counseling. The report may also contain recommendations for monitoring the student's behavioral and academic progress, evaluating outcomes of chosen interventions, and making adjustments in interventions to ensure efficacy. The school psychologist may be directly or indirectly involved in several of the recommended activities.

SUMMARY

Best practice procedures were presented for assessing children's emotional or behavioral disorders. A multidimensional approach was recommended that requires gathering and integrating information from multiple data sources. Multidimensional assessment assumes that no single method or informant can capture all relevant aspects of a child's emotional or behavioral functioning. While school-based assessments can serve several purposes, a major emphasis in this chapter was assessing ED/EBD as a disability classification for special education or Section 504 accommodations.

Procedures were described for obtaining parent reports, teacher reports, and direct assessment of the child. As best practice, some combination of the following procedures was recommended: standardized rating scales, standardized self-reports, parent and teacher interviews, child clinical interviews, direct observations of the child, and reviews of relevant background information. Some cases may require additional assessment of intellectual ability and communication skills, social skills, or broader aspects of personality. All special education evaluations require assessing the impact of an identified disability on academic achievement and educational performance.

After all necessary data have been gathered, the evaluator must integrate information in a written report. For special education evaluations, the report should present specific findings that address the criteria for ED/EBD, as defined in the IDEA or specific state regulations. Empirically based syndromes scored from standardized rating scales and self-reports can provide quantitative evidence of the characteristics of ED/EBD. Parent and teacher interviews, child clinical interviews, and direct observations can contribute additional evidence of ED/EBD. Normative comparisons on standardized rating scales and self-reports can determine whether identified problems deviate from expected behavior "to a marked degree." Duration of problems and their adverse effect on educational performance must also be documented. Recommendations in written reports should link assessment results to interventions as much as possible.

Although major emphasis was placed on assessment of child psychopathology, or ED/EBD, many of the best practice procedures described in this chapter can be used for other purposes, such as school-based behavioral consultation and functional behavioral assessment. Once interventions have been implemented, similar assessment procedures can be used to monitor children's progress and to evaluate outcomes. For example, standardized rating scales, interviews, and direct observations can provide baseline and follow-up data for children with ED/EBD. Comparing Time 1 and Time 2 data on the same measures can determine whether there has been any change in identified problems. It is also necessary to obtain similar data for comparable individuals or groups who have not received the interventions to determine whether changes are associated with specific interventions. Single subject designs can also be used to evaluate the effectiveness of interventions with specific individuals. Monitoring progress and evaluating outcomes are essential steps for ascertaining which interventions are most effective for which types of problems.

REFERENCES

Achenbach, T. M. (1986). *Direct Observation Form of the Child Behavior Checklist* (rev.). Burlington, VT: University of Vermont, Department of Psychiatry.

Achenbach, T. M. (1991a). *Integrative Guide for the 1991 CBCL/4-18, YSR, & TRF Profiles*. Burlington, VT: University of Vermont, Department of Psychiatry.

Achenbach, T. M. (1991b). *Manual for the Child Behavior Checklist/4-18 and 1991 Profile*. Burlington, VT: University of Vermont, Department of Psychiatry.

Achenbach, T. M. (1991c). *Manual for the Teacher's Report Form and 1991 Profile*. Burlington, VT: University of Vermont, Department of Psychiatry.

Achenbach, T. M. (1991d). *Manual for the Youth Self-Report and 1991 Profile*. Burlington, VT: University of Vermont, Department of Psychiatry.

Achenbach, T. A, & McConaughy, S. H. (1997). *Empirically based assessment of child and adolescent psychopathology: Practical applications*. Thousand Oaks, CA: Sage.

Achenbach, T. M., McConaughy, S. H., & Howell, C. T. (1987). Child/adolescent behavioral and emotional problems: Implications of cross-informant correlations for situational specificity. *Psychological Bulletin*, *101*, 213–232.

Ambrosini, P. J. (2000). Historical development and present status of the Schedule for Affective Disorders and Schizophrenia for school-aged children (K-SADS). *Journal of the American Academy of Child and Adolescent Psychiatry*, *39*, 49–58.

American Psychiatric Association. (1994). *Diagnostic and statistical manual of mental disorders* (4th ed.). Washington, DC: Author.

Bandura, A. (1986). *Social foundations of thought and action: A social cognitive theory*. Englewood Cliffs, NJ: Prentice-Hall.

Barkley, R. A. (1990). *Attention deficit hyperactivity disorder: A handbook for diagnosis and treatment*. New York: Guilford.

Busse, R. T., & Beaver, B. R. (2000). Informant report: Parent and teacher interviews. In E. S. Shapiro & T. R. Kratochwill (Eds.), *Conducting school-based assessments of child and adolescent behavior* (pp. 235–273). New York: Guilford.

Butcher, J. N., Williams, C. L., Graham, J. R., Archer, R. P., Tellegen, A., Ben-Porath, Y. S., & Kaemmer, B. (1992). *Minnesota Multiphasic Personality Inventory for Children—Adolescents*. Minneapolis, MN: National Computer Systems.

Conners, K. C. (1997). *Conners' Rating Scales (Rev.) Manual*. North Tonawanda, NY: Multi-Health Systems.

DuPaul, G. J., Rapport, M. D., & Perriello, L. M. (1991). Teacher ratings of academic skills: The development of the Academic Performance Rating Scale. *School Psychology Review*, *20*, 284–300.

Epstein, M. H., & Sharma, J. M. (1998). *Behavioral and Emotional Rating Scale*. Austin, TX: PRO-ED.

Forness, S. (1992). Legalism versus professionalism in diagnosing SED in the public schools. *School Psychology Review, 21*, 29–34.

Gresham, F. (1991). Conceptualizing behavior disorders in terms of resistance to intervention. *School Psychology Review, 20*, 23–36.

Gresham, F. M., & Elliott, S. N. (1990). *Social Skills Rating System.* Circle Pines, MN: American Guidance Service.

Gresham, F. M., & Gansle, K. A. (1992). Misguided assumptions of the DSM-III-R: Implications for school psychological practice. *School Psychology Quarterly, 7*, 79–95.

Grotevant, H., McRoy, R., & Jenkins, V. (1988). Emotionally disturbed adopted adolescents: Early patterns of family adaptation. *Family Process, 27*(4), 439–457.

Hodges, K., Gordon, Y., & Lennon, M. (1990). Parent-child agreement on symptoms assessed via a clinical research interview for children: The Child Assessment Schedule (CAS). *Journal of Child Psychology and Psychiatry, 31*, 427–436.

Hughes, J. N., & Baker, D. B. (1990). *The clinical child interview.* New York: Guilford.

Jensen, P. S., Bloedau, L., Degroot, J., Ussery, T., & Davis, H. (1990). Children at risk: I. Risk factors and child symptomatology. *Journal of the American Academy of Child and Adolescent Psychiatry, 29*, 51–59.

Kauffman, J. M., & Wong, K. L. (1991). Effective teachers of students with behavioral disorders: Are generic teaching skills enough? *Behavioral Disorders, 16*, 225–237.

Kovacs, M. (1992). *Children's Depression Inventory Manual.* North Tonawanda, NY: Multi-Health Systems.

McCarney, S. B., & Leigh, J. E. (1990). *Manual for the Behavior Evaluation Scale, 2.* Columbia, MO: Hawthorne.

McComas, J. J., Hoch, H., & Mace, F. C. (2000). Functional analysis. In Shapiro, E. S., & Kratochwill, T. R. (Eds.). *Conducting school-based assessments of child and adolescent behavior* (pp. 78–120). New York: Guilford.

McConaughy, S. H. (1993a). Advances in empirically based assessment of children's behavioral and emotional problems. *School Psychology Review, 22*, 285–307.

McConaughy, S. H. (1993b). Evaluating behavioral and emotional disorders with CBCL, TRF, and YSR cross-informant scales. *Journal of Emotional and Behavioral Disorders, 1*, 40–52.

McConaughy, S. H. (2000a). Self-report: Child clinical interviews. In Shapiro, E. S., & Kratochwill, T. R. (Eds.), *Conducting school-based assessments of child and adolescent behavior* (pp. 170–202). New York: Guilford.

McConaughy, S. H. (2000b). Self-reports: Theory and practice in interviewing children. In E. S. Shapiro & T. R. Kratochwill (Eds.). *Behavioral assessment in schools: Theory, research, and clinical foundations* (pp. 323–352). New York: Guilford.

McConaughy, S. H., & Achenbach, T. M. (1994). *Manual for the Semistructured Clinical Interview for Children and Adolescents.* Burlington, VT: University of Vermont Department of Psychiatry.

McConaughy, S. H , Mattison, R. E., & Peterson, R. (1994). Behavioral/emotional problems of children with serious emotional disturbance and learning disabilities. *School Psychology Review. 23*, 81–98.

McConaughy, S. H., & Skiba, R. (1993). Comorbidity of externalizing and internalizing problems. *School Psychology Review*, 22, 419–434.

Merrell, K. W. (1993). Using behavior rating scales to assess social skills and antisocial behavior in school settings: Development of the School Social Behavior Scales. *School Psychology Review*, 22, 115–133.

National Association of School Psychologists. (1993). *Position statement on students with emotional/behavioral disorders.* Silver Spring, MD: Author.

Quay, H. C., & Peterson, D. R. (1987). *Manual for the Revised Behavior Problem Checklist.* Coral Gables, FL: University of Miami, Department of Psychology.

Rehabilitation Act of 1973, Section 504. (1973). 29 U.S.C. § 706, 1996; § 504 [30 C.F.R Part 104].

Reynolds, C. R., & Kamphaus, R. W. (1992). *Behavior Assessment System for Children (BASC)*. Circle Pines, MN: American Guidance Service.

Reynolds, C. R., & Richmond, B. O. (1985). *Revised Children's Manifest Anxiety Scale*. Los Angeles, CA: Western Psychological Services.

Reynolds, W. M. (1987). *Reynolds Adolescent Depression Inventory*. Odessa, FL: Psychological Assessment Resources.

Scruggs, T. E., & Mastropieri, M. A. (1996). Teacher perceptions of mainstreaming/inclusion, 1958–1995: A research synthesis. *Exceptional Children, 63*, 59–74.

Shaffer, D., Fisher, P. Lucas, C. P., Dulcan, M., & Scwab-Stone, M. E. (2000). NIMH Diagnostic Interview Schedule for Children, Version IV (NIMH DISC-IV): Description, differences from previous versions and reliability of some common diagnoses. *Journal of the American Academy of Child and Adolescent Psychiatry, 39*, 28–38.

Skiba, R., & Grizzle, K. (1991). The social maladjustment exclusion: Issues of definition and assessment. *School Psychology Review, 20*, 577–595.

Skiba, R., & Grizzle, K. (1992). Qualifications v. logic and data: Excluding conduct disorders from the SED definition. *School Psychology Review, 21*, 23–28.

Slenkovich, J. (1992a). Can the language of "social maladjustment" in the SED definition be ignored? *School Psychology Review, 21*, 21–22.

Slenkovich, J. (1992b). Can the language of "social maladjustment" in the SED definition be ignored? The final words. *School Psychology Review, 21*, 43–44.

Skinner, C. H., Rhymer, K. N., & McDaniel, E. C. (2000). Naturalistic direct observation in educational settings. In E. S. Shapiro & T. R. Kratochwill (Eds.), *Conducting school-based assessments of child and adolescent behavior* (pp. 21–54). New York: Guilford.

Walker, H. M. (1983). *Walker Problem Behavior Identification Checklist*. Los Angeles, CA: Western Psychological Services.

Walker, H. M., & McConnell, S. R. (1988). *Walker-McConnell Scale of Social Competence and School Adjustment*. Austin, TX: PRO-ED.

Walker, H. M., Kavanagh, K., Stiller, B., Golly, A., Severson, H. H., & Feil, E.G. (1998). First step to success: An early intervention approach for preventing school antisocial behavior. *Journal of Emotional and Behavioral Disorders*, 6, 66–80.

Wirt, R. D., Lachar, D., Klinedinst, J. E., Seat, P. D., & Broen, W. E. (1990). *Multidimensional description of child personality: A manual for the Personality Inventory for Children*. Los Angeles, CA: Western Psychological Services.

Ysseldyke, J., Christenson, S., & Thurlow, M. (1987). *Instructional factors that influence student achievement: An integrative review* (Monograph 7). Minneapolis: University of Minnesota, Instructional Alternatives Project.

ANNOTATED BIBLIOGRAPHY

Breen, M., & Fiedler, C. (Eds.) (1996). *Behavioral approach to the assessment of youth with emotional/behavioral disorders: A handbook for school-based practitioners*. Austin, TX: PRO-ED.
Describes behaviorally oriented procedures for assessing children's emotional and behavioral disorders. Early chapters address theoretical and legal requirements for school-based assessment of emotional and behavioral disorders, including eligibility for special education services. Later chapters cover empirically based behavioral rating scales; direct observation methods; parent, teacher, and child interviews; and consultation strategies. A comprehensive and practical resource for school-based practitioners involved in assessment and programming for children with emotional and behavioral problems.

Hughes, J.N., & Baker, D.B. (1990). *The clinical child interview*. New York: Guilford.
Describes various procedures for interviewing children and adolescents for clinical and school-based assessments. Early chapters cover developmentally sensitive interviewing techniques for children of varying ages. Later chapters describe different interviewing procedures, including structured diagnostic interviews, psychodynamic approaches, behavioral interviewing, and

problem-specific interviews. An excellent resource for school-based practitioners and clinicians involved in child assessment and therapy.

Shapiro, E. T., & Kratochwill, T. R. (2000a). *Behavioral assessment in schools: Theory, research, and clinical foundations*. New York: Guilford.
Describes the theoretical and empirical underpinnings of multidimensional behavioral assessment. Eleven chapters present theory, research, and clinical foundations of different methods of behavioral assessment. Additional chapters examine conceptual foundations, professional practice issues, legal and ethical concerns, assessment of individuals from culturally and linguistically diverse backgrounds, and educational and psychiatric classification systems. A companion volume for the practical guidelines offered in Shapiro and Kratochwill (2000b).

Shapiro, E. T., & Kratochwill, T. R. (Eds.) (2000b). *Conducting school-based assessments of child and adolescent behavior*. New York: Guilford.
A hands-on companion volume to Shapiro & Kratochwill (2000a). The initial chapter reviews goals and methods of multidimensional assessment of emotional and behavioral problems. Subsequent chapters guide readers through direct and indirect methods of assessment, including direct observation, analogue assessment, functional analysis, child self-reports, teacher and parent interviews, standardized rating scales, and self-monitoring procedures. Many chapters include practical recommendations and case illustrations. The concluding chapter provides recommendations for effective work with culturally and linguistically diverse students. An excellent how to guide for K–12 practitioners in regular and special education settings.

82 Best Practices in Nondiscriminatory Assessment

Samuel O. Ortiz
St. John's University

OVERVIEW

The concern with fair and equitable psychological assessment is a mirror of the values in our culture. As the nature of those values has changed, so have our concerns (Oakland & Laosa, 1976; Sandoval, 1998). The late 1950s and 1960s saw the rise of the civil rights movement, which brought to the forefront issues of discrimination that had remained entrenched but largely unspoken and unacknowledged in our nation's people and its systems. The rights of many diverse groups of people were upheld time and again by the U.S. Supreme Court, which affirmed equal protection under the law and the unconstitutionality of systematic and deliberate discrimination on the basis of race, creed, color, gender, or national origin (Irons & Guitton, 1993). During this dramatic shift in our country's cultural values, individuals with disabilities, including the parents of children with disabilities, were no less reticent to assert their rights (Jones, 1988; Laosa, 1976; Oakland & Laosa, 1976; Valdés & Figueroa, 1994). The passage of the landmark P.L. 94-142, the Education of Handicapped Children Act (later re-authorized and renamed the Individuals with Disabilities Education Act; IDEA) stands as testimony toward eliminating longstanding bias and discriminatory practices in education. IDEA contains a clear directive regarding the potentially discriminatory aspects of assessment, in that "tests and other evaluation materials used to assess a child...are selected and administered so as not to be discriminatory on a racial or cultural basis; and are provided and administered in the child's native language or other mode of communication" (§300.532, Evaluation Procedures).

Attention to the attenuating effects of racial, cultural, and linguistic differences on test performance is evident in the wording. Moreover, this same section of IDEA requires the use of a "variety" of tools and strategies, emphasizing the fact that tests alone are unlikely to provide an accurate picture of functioning. Thus, nondiscriminatory assessment is not defined as a single procedure or test, but as a wide range of approaches that collectively seek to uncover as fairly as possible relevant information and data upon which decisions regarding functioning and performance can be equitably based. In other words, nondiscriminatory assessment is not a search for an unbiased test but rather a process that ensures every individual, not just those who are different in some way, is evaluated in the least discriminatory manner possible. To live up to its very name, nondiscriminatory assessment should be applicable to everyone, not just those from a particular group. In the most basic sense, "it is recognized that nondiscriminatory assessment may be considered one dimension of the more general problem of valid assessment of any child" (Oakland, 1976, p. 1).

Completely unbiased assessment, however, is an illusion. It is impossible to eliminate every single instance of bias or every potentially discriminatory aspect of assessment. Even with the most objective means and methods, bias exists in some form or another. Because elimination is unrealistic, the goal of nondiscriminatory assessment should be viewed as an effort to reduce it to the maximum extent possible.

Nondiscriminatory assessment is, however, much more than the sum of its parts. Although many discrete methods for reducing bias in assessment have been presented (Gonzalez, Brusca-Vega, & Yawkey, 1997; Gopaul-McNicol & Thomas-Presswood, 1998; Hamayan and Damico, 1991; Sandoval, Frisby, Geisinger, Scheuneman, & Grenier, 1998; Valdés & Figueroa, 1994) much less attention has been paid to the development of a broad, comprehensive framework for nondiscriminatory assessment. Application of a comprehensive framework designed to guide the general collection and interpretation of data in a systematic manner seems key to the process of equitable assessment. Engaging in assessment without the benefit of a guiding approach produces unrelated and disconnected activities and procedures that will likely fail to address important areas of bias and will produce data that are ambiguous and difficult to interpret. Nondiscriminatory assessment is much more than considering which standardized tools should be used and which should not. There is no simple answer or prescription, and standardized tests represent only one element of concern with bias. The use of one method or one procedure that may reduce bias is hardly enough to constitute unbiased assessment (Jones, 1988; Sandoval et al., 1998; Valdés & Figueroa, 1994). The use and application of a comprehensive, systematic framework comprising a broad range of methods and procedures is critical to engaging in best practices in nondiscriminatory assessment.

BASIC CONSIDERATIONS

The increasing diversity of the U.S. population, especially in the public schools, has caused service and professional organizations to recognize the implications for change in both practice and training of its members. For example, in 1990, the American Psychological Association (APA) published *Guidelines for Providers of Psychological Services to Ethnic, Linguistic, and Culturally Diverse Populations* (American Psychological Association, 1990) in an effort to encourage psychologists to (a) consider the influence of language and culture on behavior when working with diverse groups, (b) consider the validity of the methods and procedures used to assess minority groups, and (c) make interpretations of resultant psychological data within the context of an individual's linguistic and cultural characteristics (Lopez, 1997).

Many researchers have outlined certain procedures or methods related to compliance with these directives (e.g., Gonzalez et al., 1997; Gopaul-McNicol & Thomas-Presswood, 1998; Hamayan & Damico, 1991; Samuda, Kong, Cummins, Pascual-Leone, & Lewis, 1991; Sandoval et al., 1998; Valdés & Figueroa, 1994). Many of these methods revolve primarily around the modified use of or alternatives to standardized tests rather than specification of a comprehensive approach to nondiscriminatory assessment. The focus on reducing or avoiding bias related to the use of standardized, norm-referenced tests by these methods is not surprising given that tests are ubiquitous in psychoeducational assessment and often carry significant implications with respect to questions regarding diagnosis and intervention (e.g., special education eligibility). School psychologists are quite familiar and comfortable with this form of assessment, and it usually forms the bulk of their skills in assessment (Reschly & Grimes, 1995). However, the training of school psychologists often fails to provide sufficient competency regarding what might make their use biased or discriminatory and even less about how to use them in a less biased or discriminatory manner (Geisinger, 1998; see also Flanagan & Ortiz, in this volume).

Despite the need for information and guidance regarding the manner in which school psychologists may apply equitably or find alternatives to standardized tests, the varied and numerous recommendations offered in the literature for nondiscriminatory assessment have not gained wide acceptance in general school psychology practice. One possible reason is the lack of a comprehensive framework for nondiscriminatory assessment that guides the manner in which effective methods for reducing bias can be integrated into practice in a deliberate and systematic way. Indiscriminant and uninformed use of bias reduction techniques is a poor foundation upon which to claim fairness. Assessment activities that seek to reflect equity need to be undertaken within a broad framework built upon systematic and informed procedures that are brought together to form a valid context for interpretation. Apart from discussion of the main issues involved in nondiscriminatory assessment, the significance of the lack of a comprehensive and guiding model is underscored by the delineation of "best practices" in the latter portion of this chapter that is presented within the structure of just such a framework.

Hypothesis Testing

Nondiscriminatory assessment should incorporate the notion of hypothesis generation and testing. Although psychometric data are often viewed as objective, they have no inherent meaning and derive significance only from interpretation. Personal and professional bias often leads to idiosyncratic interpretations of the same data, in particular when assessment was begun with preconceived ideas. Consciously or unconsciously, bias on the part of the evaluator affects interpretive decisions and is known as confirmatory bias (Matsumoto, 1994; Sandoval, 1998). The chances of making incorrect inferences about data on the basis of preconceived ideas can be reduced through an approach that utilizes hypothesis generation and testing.

When a school psychologist or other evaluator conducts an assessment with pre-conceived notions regarding what the data will show (e.g., expected patterns of performance on a test), confirmatory bias can occur both in the type of data that are collected and the manner in which the data are interpreted (Matsumoto, 1994; Sandoval, 1998). For example, learning problems in the classroom may be erroneously ascribed to attention difficulties and thus subsequent data gathering efforts will tend to focus only on examining issues related to attention at the expense of other potential factors, such as limited English proficiency, that may be related to the learning problem. Conversely, attributions of behavior that are made on the basis of stereotyped or pre-conceived notions can often steer assessment away from the real cause of many school-related problems. Indeed, if there exists a belief that a student's learning problems or behavior are attributable to personality, environmental, cultural, or linguistic differences, then no assessment may even be undertaken in cases where the learning difficulties may in fact be related to factors that can be readily ameliorated (e.g., instructional mismatch, health problems, sensory dysfunction, and so forth). These preconceptions can be particularly discriminatory whenever standardized tests are used. Believing that an individual is disabled can directly affect the manner in which the test is administered and scored (benefit of the doubt will tend toward expectancies of dysfunction and disability) and the manner in which data are interpreted. The evaluator will tend to look for patterns and results in the data which support the pre-conception and is predisposed to perceiving only those patterns consistent with the a priori beliefs. Moreover, there is a tendency to ignore, minimize, or reject data counter to the assumption (Matsumoto, 1994; Sandoval, 1998).

Bias related to preconceived notions of dysfunction or discriminatory misattributions of performance or behavior tend to influence the very nature and range of data that will be collected. The questions asked during interviews, the behaviors observed in the classroom, and the work samples chosen for analysis will all be influenced by such preconceptions. Asking a parent when their child first learned to walk is different than asking if their child was in fact a late walker. School psychologists may reduce this form of bias by avoiding attempts to confirm presumptions of pre-existing deficits and testing hypotheses instead. The process of assessment should begin with the hypothesis that the examinee's difficulties are not intrinsic in nature, but rather that they are more likely attributable to external or environmental problems. When standardized tests are used, the same assumption of normality should be used. In other words, the individual being tested is not impaired and general ability, performance, or functioning in any specific area is within normal limits. This assumption forms, in essence, a null hypothesis that can be evaluated with both quantitative and qualitative data to determine if it should be retained or rejected in favor of an alternative hypothesis (i.e., that performance is not average or within normal limits). When the process of evaluation is initiated with a presumption of normality, it reduces the tendency to search for data or "see" patterns of dysfunction where none may exist.

Another nondiscriminatory benefit of testing hypotheses that are not based on preconceptions is achieved by using the process for intervention in a proactive rather than reactive manner. For example, evaluation that seeks to determine the particular conditions under which a student's learning may be improved or accelerated leads to the collection of data that are directly tied to intervention. The very purpose of the evaluation in such cases is to enhance learning rather than simply diagnose the causes of poor performance. Even when there may be a diagnostic component to evaluation, assessment should always be linked to intervention and the potential discriminatory influence of confirmatory bias can be reduced significantly when the focus is on identifying ways to improve school performance and learning rather than attempting to simply pinpoint the underlying cause of observed problems.

In sum, although it may be difficult not to entertain preconceived notions regarding the reasons for learning difficulties, particularly if efforts at intervention and treatment have failed, evaluation of data must remain squarely focused on whether hypotheses, not opinions, attitudes, or beliefs are or are not supported. Unless and until the data suggest strongly to the contrary, the null hypothesis that an individual's school problems are related to situational, not intrinsic variables, or that behavior or performance are normal and intact, must not be rejected. In addition, the alternative hypothesis should not be considered as providing de facto support for any preconception. The reasons why an individual may be having true problems learning in the classroom or why performance on any given test might fall outside of the normal range are numerous. Nondiscriminatory assessment seeks to ensure that the vast array of potential causes for learning difficulties, behavior problems, or low performance (e.g., low motivation, physical illness, anxiety, cultural or linguistic difference) have been ruled out as primary causes for any observed learning problems or patterns of deficit in the collected data. The act of developing and using hypotheses that affirm normality to guide the collection and interpretation of data remains central to reducing confirmatory bias and establishing defensible practices in nondiscriminatory (i.e., less discriminatory) assessment.

Cultural and Linguistic Competency

Nondiscriminatory assessment represents a collection of approaches; each designed to systematically reduce bias within the broader framework. Cultural and linguistic competence is fundamental to that process. Cultural competence reflects a knowledge base of, or direct experience with, the values, attitudes, beliefs, and customs of a particular culture that can be used as both guide and context for collecting and evaluating any and all assessment data (Leigh, 1998). Psychologists need not be raised natively in a particular culture in order to derive such competence, but the necessary skills will not develop by reading a book or taking a trip (Frisby, 1998). Those not fortunate enough to receive direct experience and education toward development of cultural competence from their training programs will need to embark on a focused process that includes a variety of professional development activities (Geisinger & Carlson, 1998; Leigh, 1998). In some cases cultural advocates from the community can assist in providing consultation regarding the particular aspects of culture that may be relevant to the evaluation.

Linguistic competence is reflected in two distinct ways: the ability to communicate effectively in an individual's native language (eliminating the need for an interpreter) and possession of a knowledge base related to first and second language development and instructional methodology and pedagogy (Sandoval & Durán, 1998). Possession of the ability to communicate effectively in an individual's native language does not automatically imply competency in first and second language development, instructional methodology, and pedagogy. Research has demonstrated that both cultural (not race, but acculturation) and linguistic (proficiency) differences are significant factors that can influence an individual's performance on psychological, language, and achievement tests (Comas-Diáz & Grenier, 1998; Cummins, 1984; Frisby, 1998; Sandoval et al., 1998; Valdés & Figueroa, 1994). Ortiz and Flanagan (1998) note, "mere possession of the capacity to communicate in an individual's native language does not ensure appropriate, nondiscriminatory assessment of that individual. Traditional assessment practices and all their inherent biases can be quite easily replicated in any number of languages" (p. 426). The entire process of assessment is subject to bias whenever there is a failure to account for culturally based influences including conceptions of time, world views, patterns of acculturation, normative behaviors, beliefs, values, attitudes, and expectations (Frisby, 1998; Salvia & Ysseldyke, 1991).

In general, the combination of cultural and linguistic competence may be defined as possession of the following: (a) skill and competence in selecting and using culturally appropriate methods, procedures, and tools that are designed to reduce bias systematically in assessment; (b) knowledge of, and familiarity with, cultural factors relevant to the individual being assessed and the ability to evaluate data within the context of that culture; (c) knowledge of language development, second language acquisition, models of bilingual or English as a Second Language education and their relationship to achievement and school based learning; and (d) the ability to communicate effectively and competently in the native language of the individual being evaluated (Cummins, 1984; Hakuta, 1986; Krashen, 1985; Leigh, 1998). Within these general definitions, it is important to recognize that culture-specific knowledge and linguistic ability are secondary to the knowledge bases involving nondiscriminatory assessment practices and multi-language development and instruction. Linguistic or cultural similarity between examiner and examinee does not guarantee that the examiner possesses the requisite knowledge bases. A psychologist who has acquired the knowledge and skills described above is, with the assistance of an interpreter or a cultural advocate or both, much better equipped to conduct assessments that are far less discriminatory than an individual who possesses none of these skills but "matches" the child in terms of language or culture.

Using Standardized Tests

Because their training may not have provided direct education and supervision in nondiscriminatory assessment or cultural and linguistic competency, school psychologists may resort to utilizing procedures and tests that are not suitable or appropriate for measuring cognitive abilities or intellectual functioning in equitable ways (Flanagan & Halsell Miranda, 1995; Geisinger & Carlson, 1998; Lopez, 1997). Use of standardized tests within the context of nondiscriminatory assessment requires knowledge of (a) the adequacy of representation of each norm or comparison group, (b) the full range of abilities that are being measured and those that are not, and (c) the inherent linguistic demands and cultural loading of each test (Flanagan & Ortiz, 2001; McGrew, Flanagan & Ortiz, 2000; Ortiz, 2001; Valdés & Figueroa, 1994). Whenever tests are selected, administered, and interpreted in a manner that is not systematic or guided by research, decisions and conclusions based on resulting data may be invalid or largely indefensible (Sandoval, 1998). In general, use of well-constructed, technically sound, native language tests (for individuals who are evaluated in a language other than, or in addition to, English), where available, is preferable to tests with limited, poor, or unknown technical properties even if available in the native language (Geisinger, 1998). Oakland and Laosa (1976) reinforce this notion by stressing that "test misuse generally occurs when examiners do not apply good judgment or do not adhere to well-established professional procedures...governing the proper selection and administration of tests" (p. 17). In order to reduce bias that may arise from the use of standardized tests, knowledge regarding the ways in which such bias might operate and to what extent is required (Frisby, 1998; Valdés & Figueroa, 1994)

Bias in Testing

The issues surrounding the nature of bias in standardized (in particular intelligence) tests have been discussed at length in the literature (e.g., Figueroa, 1990; Kamphaus & Reynolds, 1987; Oakland, 1976; Sandoval et al., 1998; Sattler; 1992; Valdés & Figueroa, 1994). With respect to the nature of bias, as operationalized in these investigations, the results have been rather unanimous: the majority of major intelligence batteries are not psychometrically biased (Valdés & Figueroa, 1994). Tests have been examined for bias related to item content, factor structure, mean group IQ differences, and prediction, all with the same result—no bias found (Jensen, 1974, 1980; Sandoval, 1979; Sandoval, Zimmerman, & Woo-Sam, 1983; Valdés & Figueroa, 1994). This is not surprising, however, because decades of test development have succeeded in creating instruments that measure quite well what they purport to measure. In the case of native English-speaking individuals raised in mainstream U.S. culture, they measure intelligence, or different facets of cognitive ability, or they predict achievement as well if not better than anything else irrespective of race or ethnic origin (Niesser et al., 1996). However, in the case of individuals whose experiential backgrounds (not race, ethnicity, or even culture per se) differ from the mainstream, bias may well operate. Oakland and Matuszek (1976) provide an eloquent synopsis of such bias and their comments deserve to be quoted in full:

> The acculturation patterns governing the development of many children from racial-

> ethnic minority groups or from lower socioeconomic homes also may be sufficiently different to warrant our judgment that the test is inappropriate. We must avoid the notion that all minority or lower socioeconomic children are, by definition, significantly different from those in the standardization sample. This position is prejudicial and unwarranted. However, we must be sensitive to the fact that important difference exist with respect to child-rearing practices, expectations and aspirations, language experiences, an availability of and involvement in informal and formal learning experiences, and that these and other factors may result in acculturation patterns which are not directly comparable to those which are more typical in the United States. The decision as to whether a child's acculturation patterns are similar to those generally reflected in the test's standardization sample can be made individually and only after a thorough knowledge of the child's background (p. 28).

Although bias has long been equated with differences in race, ethnicity, and culture, identifiable inequity lies less in these factors than it does in unique patterns of experience that may include either varying levels of acculturation or English language proficiency or both. The structure and design of intelligence and cognitive ability tests and the construction of representative norm groups are based on the notions of equivalency in levels of acculturation for both the individuals on whom the test was standardized and on whom the test will be used. In the assessment of any individual in today's diverse society, the validity of this assumption must be carefully evaluated. According to Salvia and Ysseldyke (1991), a fundamental principle within test development relevant to notions of bias is called "assumption of comparability." They write:

> When we test students using a standardized device and compare them to a set of norms to get an index of their relative standing, we assume that the students we test are similar to those on whom the test was standardized; that is, we assume their acculturation is comparable, but not necessarily identical, to that of the students who made up the normative sample for the test. When a child's general background experiences differ from those of the children on whom a test was standardized, then the use of the norms of that test as an index for evaluating that child's current performance or for predicting future performances may be inappropriate (p. 18).

The biasing effect from the use of psychometric instruments, therefore, operates whenever tests of intelligence and cognitive ability (developed and normed in the United States) are given to individuals whose cultural background, experiences, and exposure are not similar to or consistent with that of the individuals comprising the norm group against whom performance will be compared. Tests will likely measure a lower range of ability in such diverse individuals because they sample only the cultural content related to mainstream experience and not the full or range of cultural content possessed by the individual, and incorrect inferences may be drawn (Valdés & Figueroa, 1994). Tests may not be psychometrically biased, but they are culturally loaded and linguistically demanding to varying degrees (Sattler, 1992). In citing Jensen (1980), Frisby (1998) comments that "it is more accurate to characterize tests as falling along a continuum from 'culture reduced' to 'culture specific' or 'culture loaded.'" The same may be said for experience with respect to language proficiency requirements. Tests can be placed along a continuum from language reduced (i.e., nonverbal) to language embedded (e.g., a test of oral vocabulary). At the very center of nondiscriminatory assessment lies the need to recognize that incorrect inferences may be made on the basis of test scores that reflect performance as a function of measured variables not related to actual ability or aptitude. Moreover, reduction of bias in the use of tests can come only from knowledge regarding where a given test lies along these continua.

Native Language Testing

Individuals involved in the assessment of linguistically diverse individuals should appreciate and recognize the difference between "bilingual assessment" and "assessment of bilinguals." The difference is not semantic, but rather represents two different research traditions that have concomitant differences in application for nondiscriminatory assessment.

Bilingual assessment implies an approach to assessment that is conducted in a bilingual manner whereas assessment of bilinguals does not necessarily seek to gather information in a bilingual manner. Tests like the Bilingual Verbal Abilities Test (BVAT; Muñoz-Sandoval, Cummins, Alvarado, & Ruef, 1998) should be recognized as real, technical advances in "bilingual assessment." Because this is an area of research that is relatively new, the underlying methods are neither complete nor without flaw. For example, despite the use of the term "bilingual" in its name, proficiency is still measured by the BVAT one language at a time which is quite different than the manner in which bilinguals are able to use both languages in an integrated manner (Bialystok, 1991; Grosjean, 1989). Aggregation of an individual's language abilities into a bilingual composite after being measured separately is unlikely to be the most accurate operationalization of what bilingual ability actually is, yet it does manage to surpass previous methods in this respect. True bilingual sampling of an individual with standardized tests remains to be accomplished. Nevertheless, in time and with sufficient empirical support, these approaches to assessment may prove to have greater accuracy in measurement or practical utility. Indeed, they stand at the forefront of a relatively new line of research.

Assessment of bilinguals is the line of inquiry where the vast majority of research and practice exists and it has been conducted almost exclusively with tests given in English to people with varying levels of English language proficiency but rarely in a systematic way (Cummins, 1984). Therefore, a great deal more is known about how people who are non-native English speakers will perform on standardized tests given in English, than is known about how they perform on tests given bilingually or in their native language. The use of translated tests with unknown technical characteristics or limited norm group samples (e.g., WISC-R-M, WISC-R-PR) has provided little insight into the performance of bilinguals. In the future, the emergence of outstanding native language tests with superior technical qualities (e.g., Bateria-R, Woodcock, & Muñoz-Sandoval, 1996) will serve as the vehicles by which this distinct research question is addressed.

The distinction between bilingual assessment and assessment of bilingual individuals carries important and distinct implications for nondiscriminatory practices. To engage in bilingual assessment, a psychologist must possess the requisite linguistic (and cultural) competency. Even when the competency requirement is met, the potential for bias is not fully diminished because there are no established procedures or guidelines to guide the process in a fair and equitable manner. How children growing up bilingual and bicultural in the United States should perform on tests that are normed on children raised in monolingual, single culture environments is unknown. Consequently, the vast majority of assessments to be conducted by psychologists will fall under the tradition of assessment of bilinguals, where the cultural and linguistic knowledge bases can be applied systematically within the context of a comprehensive framework for nondiscriminatory assessment.

BEST PRACTICES IN NONDISCRIMINATORY ASSESSMENT

Apart from the considerations that have been discussed, in order to draw valid and defensible inferences from assessment data, nondiscriminatory assessment practices should be multi-faceted and guided by a comprehensive framework that integrates efforts to reduce bias in a cohesive and systematic manner. For any such framework to prove useful it must be practical and easily accommodated within the school or other applied setting. The following framework is designed to meet these criteria and is offered as a reasonable and efficient means for accomplishing reduction in the various aspects of the assessment process and its various steps are summarized in Table 1. The framework represents an initial attempt to coalesce the more salient and promising procedures and recommendations for nondiscriminatory assessment offered by both researchers and practitioners in school psychology and related fields. The framework is both linear and recursive in that a return to already completed steps in the process may well be necessary as new data are uncovered and new hypotheses formed, evaluated, and re-evaluated. The framework accommodates both individual and assessment team activities. Collaborative assessment, where members of an assessment team (including parents) work together and where information is shared and decisions rendered jointly, significantly improves the likelihood of success of any and all nondiscriminatory efforts.

Table 1. A comprehensive framework for nondiscriminatory assessment

1. Assess and evaluate the learning ecology.
2. Assess and evaluate language proficiency.
3. Assess and evaluate opportunity for learning.
4. Assess and evaluate educationally relevant cultural and linguistic factors.
5. Evaluate, revise, and re-test hypotheses.
6. Determine the need for and language(s) of assessment.
7. Reduce bias in traditional testing practices.
8. Utilize authentic and alternative assessment procedures.
9. Evaluate and interpret all data within the context of the learning ecology.
10. Link assessment to intervention.

1. Assess and evaluate the learning ecology. School psychologists should recognize that there exist an infinite number of reasons why any given individual is having learning difficulties and that intrinsic factors form only a small fraction of these possibilities. Nondiscriminatory evaluation begins with directing initial assessment efforts toward exploration of the extrinsic causes that might be related to any observed learning difficulties. Hypotheses should be developed that revolve around the individual's unique experiential background within the context of the learning environment. When assessment is conducted on culturally and linguistically diverse individuals, in particular, there are many reasons related to these experiential factors that can adversely affect classroom performance or behavior.

Very often it is the systemic interaction between these factors and those that exist in the learning environment that simply do not or are not able to accommodate them that creates a mismatch between instruction delivered and instruction needed. Although cultural or linguistic differences are probably two of the most common factors that are evaluated relative to the learning ecology, they are by no means the only ones and the learning ecology should not be ignored simply because a student's background is not characterized by diversity on these two dimensions. In addition, a student's learning ecology should not be thought of as being restricted solely to the classroom environment. Although focus on the classroom environment is central to the evaluation of learning problems, students learn a great many things in contexts other than the classroom. Comparison of behavior, performance, or functioning between these contexts (e.g., physical education, non-academic instruction, recess, home, community) is crucial in conducting nondiscriminatory assessment.

Data that inform evaluation of hypotheses related to ecological and systemic factors may be obtained via a variety of methods, including review of educational records, direct observation of instruction and teaching, review of the content, level, relevancy and appropriateness of the curriculum, analysis of the match between the curriculum and the student's needs, interview with parents, teachers, or the individual, and medical records. Often culture and its concomitant experiences most dictate the unique history of an individual but they should not be equated to or measured simply by skin color or ethnic heritage. Evaluation of cultural difference should be viewed as examination of relatively unique circumstances or learning experiences that can not be considered comparable to the experiences of individuals raised in the U.S. mainstream. Some examples that may be consistent with this definition include poverty, deafness or other disability, bicultural students, students with childhood trauma or abuse, and students from dysfunctional families. Although culture tends to be the major factor that influences an individual's development, it need not be thought of as being neatly circumscribed. Evaluation of the extent to which a student's experiences differ from that of mainstream students may not even be a function of culture, but simply the result of unusual or highly idiosyncratic experience. Specification of hypotheses should be "null based" (i.e., performance, behavior, or learning problems are due to extrinsic factors such as differences in experience, not intrinsic factors like ability) in order to prevent bias in the collection and interpretation of data.

2. Assess and evaluate language proficiency. In cases where the individual is a dual-language learner, it will be necessary to determine current levels of language proficiency in both languages, especially with respect to Basic Interpersonal Communicative Skills (BICS) and Cognitive Academic Language Proficiency (CALP) (see Cummins, 1984). This information is often necessary in order to properly evaluate many of the ecological elements of the learning context related to dual-language experiences. Questions regarding opportunity to learn, the level and manner of instruction, the curriculum's linguistic relevancy and appropriateness, expected level of functioning or performance relative to English language development, and others are answerable only with this information. Thus, knowledge of an individual's proficiency in each language is crucial to nondiscriminatory assessment and interpretation. It provides the required context within which academic difficulties can be properly evaluated and forms the basis for the development of instructional interventions that are appropriate linguistically. Such data are usually gathered through any one of the various, standardized language tests available on the market today. Of particular note is the BVAT (Muñoz-Sandoval et al., 1998), which is available in 15 different language versions. The data may already exist in school districts where there are bilingual or English as a Second Language (ESL) programs. If the information is available but is out of date (older than 6 months), then new data should be collected. The impact of language experiences is profound, particularly in the preschool and early primary grades, and exposure to a second language no matter how small can have a significant impact on patterns of academic performance and basic skills development or acquisition (Cummins, 1984; Krashen, 1985). As such the presence of a language other than English in the home should not be minimized in the face of even considerable exposure to the English language.

3. Assess and evaluate opportunity for learning. The school setting provides perhaps the most significant context for learning. However, it is by no means perfect, and an individual may become a "casualty" of the educational system's failure to provide an effective or appropriate instructional program. The educational institution itself, including the curriculum, personnel, policies, and even the instructional setting, must be carefully evaluated to determine whether the individual has been provided with adequate "opportunity to learn" particularly in the case where significant cultural or linguistic differences exist. Again, the usual methods for collecting this type of data include evaluation of classroom environment and teaching methods, direct observation of academic performance, review of the content, level, relevancy and appropriateness of the curriculum, analysis of the match between the curriculum and the student's needs, interviews with parents, current and previous teachers, interview with the individual, and review of existing educational records and progress reports. Specific factors that should be examined include: regularity of school attendance; experience with the school environment and setting; match between individual's native language and the language of instruction; parent's ability to support language of instruction; years (duration) of instruction in the native language and English; quality of native language and English instruction in ESL or bilingual programs; cultural relevance of the curriculum; frequency of changes in schools; relative consistency in and across curricula; teaching strategies, styles, attitudes, expectations; system attitude regarding dual language learners; and socialization with peers versus isolation from peers.

4. Assess and evaluate educationally relevant cultural and linguistic factors. Learning does not take place only in school but occurs throughout the broad scope of an individual's complete social milieu. Many factors outside and apart from the educational setting can significantly affect the learning process, and careful evaluation of the extent to which such factors might be present and might be affecting learning in the school is necessary in order to evaluate data from a nondiscriminatory standpoint. In cases where the individual is culturally or linguistically diverse, it will be necessary to assess and evaluate the experiential aspects of these particular variables and their relative influence on school-based learning, language development, and educational progress. The effect of small amounts of exposure to two or more cultures or languages during early childhood development may create circumstances that cause the individual to have experiences that differ markedly from that of other individuals within the U.S. mainstream and that can negatively affect school performance. In short, the ability to draw valid conclusions regarding school dysfunction from the whole of assessment data rests squarely on proper identification and understanding of the individual's total linguistic history as well as other factors that may have influenced the development of both languages. This information is most commonly collected via observations across multiple settings, interviews with parents, teachers, and the individual, and review of existing educational records. Additionally, home visits are particularly effective for gathering this type of data. Factors that should specifically be examined include: current language(s) of the home, the individual's initial or primary language, the individual's total informal experience with the native language and English, individual's birth order or relative impact of siblings and their language development, individual's fluency in the native language and English, individual's and parent's level of acculturation, parent's fluency in the native language and English, parent's level of literacy in the native language and English, parent's level of education, and parent's socio-economic status.

5. Evaluate, revise, and re-test hypotheses. School psychologists should ensure that all reasonable and viable factors that could be related to an individual's observed learning difficulties have been thoroughly evaluated and ruled out as the "primary" cause of them. Within the school setting, it is only when enough confidence exists in the belief that there are no plausible or demonstrable external factors that can account for an individual's learning difficulties and that consideration of possible intrinsic factors should be entertained. This is necessary primarily to reduce confirmatory bias. Additionally, there should also be evidence that systematic and appropriate efforts to improve the student's classroom performance were undertaken but proved to be unsuccessful. The litmus test here is whether there is one or a combination of external factors present that can be reasonably presumed to be the primary cause of the individual's learning difficulties. If so, then the null hypothesis regarding normal behavior, performance, or average functioning (albeit, inhibited by the identified external constraints) should be maintained and the individual's learning problems should not be ascribed to intrinsic factors. The reduction of potentially discriminatory attributions regarding learning, behavior, or performance is further attenuated by returning to the development of additional interventions to address academic need within the classroom setting. In some cases, however, external factors may be present, but might only be contributing to and not directly causing the student's observed learning problems. When difficulties learning in the classroom setting or behavioral problems can not be reasonably ascribed to the primary influence of any such extrinsic factors, assessment may proceed appropriately to explore potential intrinsic factors with confidence that the process is operating in a fair and equitable manner.

6. Determine the need for and language(s) of assessment. The course of assessment may be significantly affected in cases where the individual is not a native English speaker (e.g., is limited English proficient) or uses an alternative mode of communication. This is particularly true for special education evaluations where IDEA mandates that assessors consider the individual's primary language ability (in addition to his or her ability in English) in the development of the assessment plan (§§300.532-330.534(b)). As assessment moves logically toward the use of standardized tests it becomes important to recognize that testing need not be conducted solely in the primary language or English. Moreover, nothing in IDEA or any other regulatory guideline mandates "parallel" testing in both languages. Exactly what should be assessed and in what language it will be assessed are decisions that rest with the assessor or assessment team. Factors that affect the selection of linguistically appropriate tools and techniques come from examination and review of existing pre-referral data, the unique background variables of the individual, and relevant referral concerns. Because each case is unique, and because the foundation of IDEA rests on the notion of "individualization" in both evaluation and instruction, it is inappropriate to make specific guidelines or rules with respect to decisions about the most appropriate language or combination of languages for testing. Within the framework of nondiscriminatory assessment, these decisions may be guided by the following general statements that represent only the most basic of guidelines: (a) individuals who are not proficient in English should be assessed in their primary language or native mode of communication in addition to any English language testing that may be appropriate; (b) individuals who are proficient in English may be assessed in their primary language or native mode of communication in addition to any English language testing that may be appropriate; and (c) all individuals, whether proficient in English or not, whose histories and backgrounds are not comparable to the U.S.

mainstream, should be evaluated by an assessor who possesses knowledge regarding the factors relevant to the individual's unique experiences and how they may affect learning and development.

A criticism often leveled at nondiscriminatory assessment suggests that it is not practical and involves considerable expenditures in terms of time and effort. To the contrary, the six steps that have already been delineated above can be accomplished well within the scope of any pre-referral intervention and assistance process. Use of a pre-referral process coupled with attendance at such meetings by professionals with the relevant knowledge and competencies (school psychologists are very well suited for this role) creates a system that is highly efficient by eliminating time wasted conducting inappropriate evaluations. Not only does creation and involvement in an effective pre-referral process reduce time and effort spent in evaluations, but it also helps to streamline compliance with legal mandates by facilitating scheduling and documentation. Nondiscriminatory assessment need not wait to begin upon formal referral.

*7. **Reduce bias in traditional testing practices.*** As discussed previously, bias in traditional testing occurs primarily when individuals whose backgrounds and experiences differ significantly from those on whom the test was normed. This is not an uncommon situation, and the issues of acculturation and English language proficiency significantly affect the validity of interpretations drawn from results of performance on such tests. Even where native language tests are available, potential bias remains. The process of nondiscriminatory assessment in using tests is represented by two distinct options: (a) administer tests in a standardized way and attempt to evaluate the results in a nondiscriminatory manner or (b) modify the testing process in a way that is less discriminatory initially.

In pursuing the first option, maintaining standardization has the advantage of allowing application of systematic methods for reducing bias. This includes use of existing (Mercer, 1979) or locally developed pluralistic norms that provide more appropriate comparison groups or use of information regarding the linguistic demand and cultural loading dimensions of the tests given (Flanagan, McGrew, & Ortiz, 2000; Flanagan & Ortiz, 2001; Ortiz & Flanagan, 1998). Because there is considerable research surrounding the nature and manner in which various groups of diverse individuals perform on a wide range of available English language tests, maintaining standardization provides a foundation for nondiscriminatory assessment based directly on this body of empirical evidence. The CHC Culture-Language Matrix developed by Flanagan and Ortiz (2001) capitalizes directly on this research and provides practitioners with a systematic method that can assist in determining the relative impact of cultural and linguistic differences on test performance. Deviations from standardization would produce results that are unknown and unpredictable, as does use of native language tests for which an extensive literature base does not exist. Both approaches within this option provide the means for basing interpretation relative to more representative peers as well as expected patterns of performance as a function of acculturation and language proficiency. Moreover, knowledge of test properties relative to cultural loading and linguistic demand creates a basis for test selection that may also be less discriminatory without violating standardization.

The second option in using standardized tests involves modification and adaptation in ways that attempt to reduce acculturative or linguistic bias directly. Any such modifications, however, represent significant violations of standardization and automatically impugn the validity and interpretability of obtained results. The major drawback in applying modifications is the elimination of empirically established baselines for comparison or performance. Unlike performance on tests administered in English following standardization, how much any given modification or adaptation affects performance is not well known or defined. Consequently, the major benefit that may be derived in using tests in non-standardized may rest more in the collection of qualitative versus quantitative data. Even in this respect administration and scoring should remain systematic.

Standardized norm-referenced tests, both in English and the native language, can be modified in a variety of ways including bilingual administration, use of extended and expanded instructions on sample items, mediation of concepts to ensure comprehension prior to administration of items, repetition of items to facilitate comprehension, extension or elimination of time limits, acceptance of alternative responses (e.g., in a different language, culture-specific responses, through non-verbal gestures), and additional probing and querying of incorrect responses. When carefully adapted and interpreted within the context of the individual's unique experiential background, the use of standardized tests can provide valuable qualitative information about functioning. Such data are often much more useful in instructional planning than the quantitative results that are derived. Despite the limitations, use of tests as tools that provide rich clinical or behavioral information should not be discounted as a basis for drawing less discriminatory inferences about ability or performance.

8. Utilize authentic and alternative assessment procedures. Nondiscriminatory assessment represents a collection of related and systematic procedures designed to reduce bias and implies the collection of a broad range of information. Non-standardized methods and information should not be excluded from the process. Whereas standardized, norm-referenced tests are driven mainly by questions and needs related to classification, diagnosis, and legal eligibility, authentic assessment is geared more toward answering questions regarding instructional needs and interventions—something that standardized tests do not address well. Examples of such procedures and methods include informal analysis of work samples, curriculum or criterion based measurement, performance-based assessment, portfolio assessment, and various test-teach-test frameworks such as dynamic assessment (Fischer & King, 1995).

When properly applied, non-standardized, alternative assessment strategies can provide valuable information especially in school-based and special education evaluations. In educational settings, authentic assessment often utilizes material that has already been provided through direct instruction. Evaluation of learning and performance through use of the curriculum-based materials and content reflects an authentic nondiscriminatory approach. Accordingly, comprehensive assessment should include information and data obtained through such methods. Examples include curriculum-based assessment or authentic measures of academic achievement and skill development, performance-based assessment that evaluates more by task completion within context than answering of factual questions out of context, criterion-referenced assessment using minimum levels or standards of performance, portfolio assessment that documents development of skills learning and academic progress, informal analysis of actual work completed in the classroom setting, symbolic dynamic assessment of learning propensity using abstract stimuli, and authentic dynamic assessment of learning propensity using actual materials from the curriculum. Dynamic assessment is a particularly useful culture-reduced method that can be accomplished by using a wide variety of materials that provides relevant and useful information about performance that is directly applicable to instructional intervention and planning (Lidz, 1997).

9. Evaluate and interpret all data within the context of the learning ecology. All data collected in the course of nondiscriminatory assessment should be evaluated in an integrated manner utilizing the information obtained regarding the student's unique experience and background as the appropriate context. Knowledge of factors that may have played a part in creating significant differences between the experiences of the individual in terms of acculturation or language development provides the least discriminatory framework with which to evaluate and assign meaning to the patterns seen in the data. Although less obvious and more difficult to judge, information related to differences in acculturation are every bit as important as the more overt differences seen in language, and should not be minimized or ignored. Very often the meaning of the data will depend in large part on an understanding of the environmental influences (generally most associated with cultural and linguistic differences) that have transpired to shape the individual in unique ways and set the stage for observed and measured performance. In the final analysis, successful nondiscriminatory assessment is contingent upon application of this information. An effective method for ensuring equity in this process is based on the notion of convergence. The data collected in the course of assessment should cut across procedure or method and come together in a cohesive and convincing manner that supports the plausibility of final conclusions. Although in practice, a preponderance of evidence would be sufficient to provide validity to conclusions, care should be taken not to assign unwarranted importance or significance to any single piece of information or datum. Use of single scores, combinations or products of scores, and unduly favoring certain data over other data will lead to discriminatory inferences and outcomes. Equivocal data support the null hypothesis that functioning is within normal limits and that any observed difficulties are the result of factors other than internal disability.

*10. **Link assessment to intervention.*** Assessment and evaluation are not interventions. Even when an individual has been assessed and it has been determined that no disability exists, the original problems that prompted the referral do not cease to exist automatically. Similarly, that a disability has been correctly identified does not make the best or most appropriate remedial methods instantly apparent. Assessment of any kind, nondiscriminatory included, is of little value unless it can be extended to incorporate appropriate interventions and treatment options. In school-based evaluations, modifications to the instructional program and the provision of specific remedial strategies are necessary whether the individual qualifies for special education services or not. Because the process of nondiscriminatory assessment has generated information regarding both relative performance as well as causal and contributory factors, it has considerable value in guiding the development of appropriate interventions and treatment strategies. As with use of the hypothesis-driven approach, awareness of the need to link assessment to intervention significantly affects the manner in which activities are conducted and the type of data that are collected. Failure to generate data for the purpose of intervention can be construed as the most discriminatory aspect of assessment as it affects all individuals equally.

SUMMARY

No assessment is unbiased and no evaluation can ever be wholly nondiscriminatory. Attempts to be completely unbiased are doomed to failure. A more practical approach is to recognize the various sources of potential bias and use systematic procedures that will reduce it as much as possible. Nondiscriminatory assessment is not limited to individuals who are distinct from the cultural or linguistic mainstream. Rather, in keeping with the egalitarian implications of its name, nondiscriminatory assessment can provide fair and equitable evaluation of any individual regardless of background. Nondiscriminatory assessment is not a single tool or procedure that is applied in isolation or without consideration of differences in individual experience and development. It is a collection of activities brought together in comprehensive fashion and used in a systematic way to address a variety of issues related to bias or discrimination. Nondiscriminatory assessment is broad and includes a wide variety of data generated from review of records, interviews, observations, standardized tests, and authentic methods. Bias is not a function of technical or psychometric deficiencies in tests but rather differences in experience between an individual taking the test and the individuals on whom the test was normed. Differences in race, ethnicity, or culture do not always reflect significant experiential differences. Direct training and education in nondiscriminatory assessment assists in drawing fair and correct inferences regarding patterns of, and reasons for, learning or behavior problems. There is no one right way to reduce bias, and there are no strict procedural specifications for which adherence is required. Nondiscriminatory assessment is, however, best carried out within the provisions of an overarching framework that brings bias reduction procedures together in a cohesive and logical manner and which assists not only in interpreting data fairly but also the collection of data in ways that are similarly less biased. Additionally, testing hypotheses regarding factors that are not child-centered but rather problem-centered and which affirm normality assists in reducing the discriminatory aspects of assessment and leads directly to the development of appropriate interventions. A general framework for nondiscriminatory assessment that achieves these goals was proposed. The process outlined in the previous section provides a structure whereby more than half of the components essential to nondiscriminatory assessment can be accomplished within the scope of general education and prereferral activities. These activities provide data that inform the development of appropriate instructional interventions and guides subsequent assessment activities. Should assessment of learning or behavioral difficulties proceed to formal evaluation of the presence of an underlying disability, the remaining components in nondiscriminatory assessment that are often required in such cases can be completed efficiently in approximately the same amount of time and with no more effort than would be required in any other type of assessment. Ultimately, nondiscriminatory assessment should be "undertaken with the intentions of improving children's development and helping persons make wise and informed decisions" (Oakland, 1976, p. 3). When data collection and interpretation are guided by responsive methods embedded in a systematic framework, the likelihood of fair and equitable decisions are increased.

REFERENCES

American Psychological Association. (1990). *Guidelines for providers of psychological services to ethnic, linguistic, and culturally diverse populations*. Washington, DC: Author.

Bialystok, E. (1991). *Language processing in bilingual children*. New York: Cambridge University Press.

Comas-Diáz L., & Grenier, J. R. (1998). Migration and acculturation. In J. Sandoval, C. L. Frisby, K. F. Geisinger, J. D. Scheuneman, & J. R. Grenier (Eds.), *Test interpretation and diversity: Achieving equity in assessment* (pp. 213–239). Washington, DC: American Psychological Association.

Cummins, J. C. (1984). *Bilingual and special education: Issues in assessment and pedagogy*. Austin, TX: PRO-ED.

Figueroa, R. A. (1990). Best practices in the assessment of bilingual children. In A. Thomas & J. Grimes (Eds.), *Best practices in school psychology II*. Washington, DC: National Association of School Psychologists.

Fischer, C. F., & King, R. M. (1995). *Authentic assessment: A guide to implementation*. Thousand Oaks, CA: Corwin.

Flanagan, D. P., & Halsell Miranda, A. (1995). Best Practices in working with culturally different families. In A. Thomas and J. Grimes (Eds.), *Best practices in school psychology III* (pp. 1049–1060). Washington DC: National Association of School Psychologists.

Flanagan, D. P., McGrew, K. S., & Ortiz, S. O. (2000). *The Wechsler intelligence scales and Gf-Gc theory: A contemporary approach to interpretation*. Boston: Allyn & Bacon.

Flanagan, D. P., & Ortiz, S. O. (2001). *Essentials of cross-battery assessment*. New York: John Wiley.

Frisby, C. L. (1998). Culture and cultural differences. In J. Sandoval, C. L. Frisby, K. F. Geisinger, J. D. Scheuneman, & J. R. Grenier (Eds.), *Test interpretation and diversity: Achieving equity in assessment* (pp. 51–73). Washington, DC: American Psychological Association.

Geisinger, K. F. (1998). Psychometric issues in test interpretation. In J. Sandoval, C. L. Frisby, K. F. Geisinger, J. D. Scheuneman, & J. R. Grenier (Eds.), *Test interpretation and diversity: Achieving equity in assessment* (pp. 17–30). Washington, DC: American Psychological Association.

Geisinger, K. F., & Carlson, J. F. (1998). Training psychologists to assess members of a diverse society. In J. Sandoval, C. L. Frisby, K. F. Geisinger, J. D. Scheuneman, & J. R. Grenier (Eds.), *Test interpretation and diversity: Achieving equity in assessment* (pp. 375–386). Washington, DC: American Psychological Association.

Gonzalez, V., Brusca-Vega, R., & Yawkey, T. (1997). *Assessment and instruction of culturally and linguistically diverse students with or at-risk of learning problems: From research to practice*. Needham Heights, MA: Allyn & Bacon.

Gopaul-McNicol, S., & Thomas-Presswood, T. (1998). *Working with linguistically and culturally different children: Innovative clinical and educational approaches*. Needham Heights, MA: Allyn & Bacon.

Grosjean, F. (1989). Neurolinguists beware! The bilingual is not two monolinguals in one person. *Brain and Language, 36*, 3–15.

Hakuta, K. (1986). *Mirror of language: The debate on bilingualism*. New York: Basic Books.

Hamayan, E. V., & Damico, J. S. (1991). *Limiting bias in the assessment of bilingual students*. Austin, TX: PRO-ED.

Irons, P., & Guitton, S. (1993). *May it please the court*. New York: The New Press.

Jensen, A. R. (1974). How biased are culture-loaded tests? *Genetic Psychology Monographs, 90*, 185–244.

Jensen, A. R. (1980). *Bias in mental testing*. New York: Free Press.

Jones, R. L. (Ed.). (1988). *Psychoeducational assessment of minority group children: A casebook*. Berkeley, CA: Cobb & Henry.

Kamphaus, R., & Reynolds, C. (1987). *Clinical and research applications of the K-ABC*. Circle Pines, MN: American Guidance Services.

Krashen, S. D. (1985). *Inquiries and insights: Second language teaching, immersion and bilingual education, literacy*. Englewood Cliffs, NJ: Alemany.

Laosa, L. M. (1976). Historical antecedents and current issues in nondiscriminatory assessment of children's abilities. In T. Oakland (Ed.), *Non-biased assessment of minority group children: With bias toward none*. Paper presented at a national planning conference on nondiscriminatory assessment for handicapped children, Lexington, KY.

Leigh, J. W. (1998). *Communicating for cultural competence*. Boston: Allyn & Bacon.

Lidz, C. S. (1997). Dynamic assessment approaches. In D. P. Flanagan, J. L. Genshaft, & P. L. Harrison (Eds.), *Contemporary intellectual assessment: Theories, tests, and issues* (pp. 281–296). New York: Guilford.

Lopez, E. C. (1997). The cognitive assessment of limited English proficient and bilingual children. In D. P. Flanagan, J. L. Genshaft, & P. L. Harrison (Eds.), *Contemporary intellectual assessment: Theories, tests, and issues* (pp. 506–516). New York: Guilford.

Matsumoto, D. (1994). *Cultural influences on research methods and statistics*. Pacific Grove, CA: Brooks/Cole.

Mercer, J. R. (1979). *System of Multicultural Pluralistic Assessment: Technical manual*. New York: The Psychological Corporation.

Muñoz-Sandoval, A. F., Cummins, J., Alvarado, C. G., & Ruef, M. L. (1998). *The Bilingual Verbal Ability Test*. Chicago: Riverside.

Neisser, U., Boodoo, G., Bouchard, T. J., Boykin, A. W., Brody, N., Ceci, S. J., Halpern, D. F., Loehlin, J. C., Perloff, R., Sternberg, R. J., & Urbina, S. (1996). Intelligence: Knowns and unknowns. *American Psychologist, 51*, 77–101.

Oakland, T. (Ed.) (1976). *Non-biased assessment of minority group children: With bias toward none*. Paper presented at a national planning conference on nondiscriminatory assessment for handicapped children. Lexington, KY.

Oakland, T., & Laosa, L. M. (1976). Professional, legislative, and judicial influences on psychoeducational assessment practices in schools. In T. Oakland (Ed.), *Non-biased assessment of minority group children: With bias toward none* (pp. 15-26). Paper presented at a national planning conference on nondiscriminatory assessment for handicapped children, Lexington, KY.

Oakland, T., & Matuszek, P. (1976). Using tests in nondiscriminatory assessment. In T. Oakland (Ed.), *Non-biased assessment of minority group children: With bias toward none* (pp. 27–34). Paper presented at a national planning conference on nondiscriminatory assessment for handicapped children, Lexington, KY.

Ortiz, S. O. (2001). Assessment of cognitive abilities in Hispanic children. *Seminars in Speech and Language, 22(1)*, 17-37.

Ortiz, S. O., & Flanagan, D. P. (1998). *Gf-Gc* cross-battery interpretation and selective cross-battery assessment: Considering referral concerns and the needs of culturally and linguistically diverse populations. In K. S. McGrew & D. P. Flanagan (Eds.), *The intelligence test desk reference (ITDR): Gf-Gc cross-battery assessment*. Boston: Allyn & Bacon.

Reschly, D. J., & Grimes, J. P. (1995). Best practices in intellectual assessment. In A. Thomas & J. P. Grimes (Eds.), *Best practices in school psychology III* (pp. 763–773). Washington, DC: National Association of School Psychologists.

Salvia, J., & Ysseldyke, J. E. (1991). *Assessment* (5th ed.). New York: Houghton Mifflin.

Samuda, R. J., Kong, S. L., Cummins, J., Pascual-Leone, J. & Lewis, J. (1991). *Assessment and placement of minority students*. New York: C. J. Hogrefe/Intercultural Social Sciences.

Sandoval, J. (1979). The WISC-R and internal evidence of test bias with minority groups. *Journal of Consulting and Clinical Psychology, 47*, 919–927.

Sandoval, J. (1998). Critical thinking in test interpretation. In J. Sandoval, C. L. Frisby, K. F. Geisinger, J. D. Scheuneman, & J. R. Grenier (Eds.), *Test interpretation and diversity: Achieving equity in assessment* (pp. 31–50). Washington, DC: American Psychological Association.

Sandoval, J. & Durán, R. P. (1998). Language. In J. Sandoval, C. L. Frisby, K. F. Geisinger, J. D. Scheuneman, & J. R. Grenier (Eds.), *Test interpretation and diversity: Achieving equity in assessment* (pp. 181–211). Washington, DC: American Psychological Association.

Sandoval, J., Frisby, C. L., Geisinger, K. F., Scheuneman, J. D., & Grenier, J. R. (Eds.). (1998). *Test interpretation and diversity: Achieving equity in assessment.* Washington, DC: American Psychological Association.

Sandoval, J., Zimmerman, I. L., & Woo-Sam, J. M. (1983). Cultural differences on WISC-R verbal items. *Journal of School Psychology, 21*, 49–55.

Sattler, J. (1992). Assessment of children (3rd ed.). San Diego, CA: Sattler.

Valdés, G., & Figueroa, R. A. (1994). *Bilingualism and testing: A special case of bias.* Norwood, NJ: Ablex.

Woodcock, R., & Muñoz-Sandoval, A. (1996). The Bateria-R: Pruebas de habilidades cognitivas. Chicago, IL: Riverside.

ANNOTATED BIBLIOGRAPHY

Cummins, J. C. (1984). *Bilingual and special education: Issues in assessment and pedagogy*. Austin, TX: PRO-ED.
A classic text in the area of bilingual assessment especially with respect to the issue of language proficiency. Cummins discusses the concepts of language proficiency including Basic Interpersonal Communicative Skills and Cognitive Academic Language Proficiency that are critical to understanding the effect of language development on learning.

Flanagan, D. P. & Ortiz, S. O. (2001). *Essentials of cross-battery assessment*. New York: John Wiley.
In addition to providing a modern, theoretical framework for cognitive assessment, this book contains classifications of tests according to cultural loading and linguistic demand as well as a culture-language matrix that can assist practitioners in determining the relative influence of level of acculturation and English language proficiency on test performance. In addition, specific guidelines for nondiscriminatory interpretation of test results are provided, and the text is written specifically for practitioners in the field.

Sandoval, J., Frisby, C. L., Geisinger, K. F., Scheuneman, J. D., & Grenier, J. R. (Eds.). (1998). *Test interpretation and diversity: Achieving equity in assessment.* Washington, DC: American Psychological Association.
This is perhaps the most up-to-date and comprehensive volume on equitable assessment. The chapters are written by leading researchers who present a broad range of issues involving diversity with a balanced perspective and attention toward practical issues.

Valdés, G. & Figueroa, R. A. (1994). *Bilingualism and testing: A special case of bias.* Norwood, NJ: Ablex.
This volume is the definitive treatise on the issue of bias in the assessment of culturally and linguistically diverse children. Although not intended as a guide to assessment, the extensive review of empirical findings, judicial influences, and recommendations for assessment are crucial to the complete understanding of issues of bias.

83 Best Practices in Intellectual Assessment

Daniel J. Reschly
Vanderbilt University
Jeffrey P. Grimes
Heartland Area Education Agency 11

OVERVIEW

School psychology was born in the prison of the IQ test. A prominent American psychologist in a commentary advanced this controversial thesis on school psychology over 25 years ago (Sarason, 1975). In this chapter, the appropriate role for intellectual assessment will be considered as school psychology emerges from this prison. Although our analysis will suggest a diminished role for intellectual assessment in the future, we recognize the necessity of best practices when intellectual assessments are conducted because these results typically are used in crucial decisions about children and youth.

Surveys over the last 50 years have verified the importance of assessment in general and the key role of intellectual assessment in particular regarding school psychology roles. Although there is increasing evidence for greater diversity in assessment practices and some school psychologists and the systems in which they work have abandoned intellectual assessment entirely, typical school psychologists at the turn of the century continue to use individually administered, standardized tests of intellectual functioning several times per week in their practice (Hosp & Reschly, in press; Reschly, 2000a). The changes over the last 25 years suggest, at best, the possibility that school psychology may be on parole from the prison of IQ tests. There are several reasons for the prominence of the IQ test in the history of school psychology.

Historical Influences

History is a powerful influence on current school psychology roles (Fagan, 1992). The earliest roots of school psychology were in a university-based clinic where psychological studies of children with learning problems were conducted. As school psychology developed from these early roots, services were provided most often by itinerant professionals in clinic-like settings, that is, children were brought to psychologists who studied them individually *outside* of the natural setting in which behaviors of concern occurred. This pattern of service continues today. Standardized measures of intelligence and achievement are administered today in clinic-like settings, outside of natural classroom and home environments, as part of evaluations to estimate expected level of achievement, make inferences about the cause(s) low achievement, and determine eligibility for disability diagnosis (e. g., learning disability) and special education placement. Each of these uses of intellectual assessment has become increasingly controversial over the last decade.

Graduate Education

The clinic-like practice established in the early roots of school psychology was and is reinforced by much of graduate education in which individually administered measures of intellectual assessment are taught first and more thoroughly than any other kind of assessment or intervention competency. This occurs despite the nearly universal claim by graduate program faculty that intellectual assessment is but one of many emphases in programs and that other competencies are equally important. Nevertheless, what is taught first and most thoroughly has a powerful influence on students and future practice. Our impression is that some programs today, perhaps 15–20%, a proportion that we think is increasing, truly do provide as much or more emphasis on other assessment and intervention competencies. For the majority, however, cognitive assessment dominates other competencies

Legal Regulations

Arguably, legal requirements are the most important single influence on school psychology practice today (Reschly, 2000a, 2000b). Legal requirements are a two-edged sword in that they have established in most places a secure funding base for school psychology. The other edge of the sword is that the highest priority service according to many school officials is the determination of eligibility for special education services. A full and individual evaluation (legal language), comprehensive case study or comprehensive evaluation (school psychology language), is guaranteed to every student considered for special education placement. Moreover the evaluation must meet certain crucial criteria that are specified in the Protection in Evaluation and Eligibility Determination regulations of federal law (Individuals with Disabilities Education Act (IDEA)1997, 1999). In most states school psychologists have key and, often, dominant roles in conducting the mandated full and individual evaluation.

Compliance with legal requirements is an ethical obligation. The meaning of many legal requirements, however, is ambiguous. For example, consider the following provision from federal law. "The child is assessed in all areas related to the suspected disability, including, *if appropriate*, health, vision, hearing, social and emotional status, general intelligence, academic performance, communicative status, and motor abilities" (IDEA, 1997, 1999) (emphasis added). The words "if appropriate" are crucial in this regulation. Professional judgment must be exercised in designing an *individual* evaluation, including whether information on general intellectual functioning is needed. For many cases referred to school psychologists, intellectual assessment is not needed while other domains of behavior and other assessment approaches yield information that is more relevant to referral issues.

Classification Criteria

Legal requirements for classification criteria exert vast influences on whether intellectual assessment is needed in full and individual evaluations. Most states have legal requirements that define learning disability (LD) and mental retardation (MR) in ways that necessitate intellectual assessment information (Mercer, Jordan, Allsopp, & Mercer, 1996; Luckusson et al., 1992). A substantial proportion of the use of intellectual assessment measures today occurs in the context of determining whether referred students meet the classification criteria for MR or LD. If the classification criteria change for LD or MR, or if states move to non-categorical, functional assessment systems, then the need for intellectual assessment is likely to change significantly.

Progress has occurred in efforts to reconceptualize MR in terms of functional skills and necessary supportive services (Luckusson et al., 1992); however, these alternatives are not sufficiently well developed to replace IQ testing in the MR diagnosis in schools and other settings. We expect that intellectual assessment will continue to be a major component of MR classification criteria in contexts that use disability categories such as the Social Security Administration and the courts. The situation in LD, which constitutes over half of all comprehensive individual evaluations by school psychologists, is markedly different. Current thought among the leading reading disability researchers contends that the widely used IQ-achievement discrepancy method of determining LD classification is invalid and harmful to many children (Fletcher et al., 1998). Fletcher et al. (1998) concluded:

> Classifications of children as discrepant versus low-achievement lack discriminative validity.... However, because children can be validly identified on the basis of a low-achievement definition, it simply is not necessary to use an IQ test to identify children as learning disabled (p. 200).

Fletcher and colleagues strongly advocate the use of direct measures of reading and language skills, particularly phonemic awareness, and the elimination of IQ in the diagnosis of LD. Elimination of IQ as part of the LD full and individual evaluations would have an enormous impact that could be extremely positive or extremely negative depending on the degree to which alternative assessment and decision-making approaches are mastered and adopted by school psychologists. On the one hand these changes could liberate school psychology from the prison of the IQ test, clearing the way for more effective roles that have a more direct positive impact on children and youth. Resistance to change in intellectual assessment requirements as LD classification is brought more in line with research could, on the other hand, increasingly isolate school psychologists from the cutting edge of developments in services to students with learning and behavior problems. The next decade is likely to be very challenging to our profession as we leave old and familiar methods behind that have undocumented benefits and embrace changes toward more effective practices.

Non-Categorical and Functional Assessment Systems

One way that intellectual assessment is likely to decline is through changes in classification criteria, especially in LD. Another avenue of change has occurred and, we think, will expand, involving reform of special education and school psychology through changes in the overall special education classification/placement system accompanied by commitments to enhance the effectiveness of general and special education interventions (Reschly & Tilly, 1999; Reschly, Tilly, & Grimes, 1999;Tilly, Reschly, & Grimes, 1999). Although several versions of these basic reforms have been implemented in some districts in at least 20 states, and statewide in at least one state, a set of basic principles characterize all of these reforms (see Reschly & Ysseldyke, this volume).

The key reform principles involve less emphasis on disability categories to establish special education eligibility and more emphasis on direct measures of skills and behaviors in natural settings. Curriculum-based academic measures and behavioral assessment procedures are emphasized in these systems. Eligibility is determined in part by the existence of large differences between the student's level of performance and that of peers using direct, ecologically valid measures of performance in natural settings. Once low performance is documented, research-based interventions are designed, implemented, and evaluated to determine the degree to which specialized instruction and additional resources are needed to produce significant improvements in performance (Tilly et al., 1999; Tilly, this volume). Special education eligibility occurs when there is a large performance gap between current level of performance and grade/age expectations *and* the resources required to produce an effective intervention are beyond the scope of general education.

As reform plans are implemented, we anticipate declining use of intellectual assessment. The current pattern of administration of an intellectual assessment measure several times each week already has changed for some school psychologists and, we think, will change for many more school psychologists in the next decade due to system reforms and changes in LD classification criteria. It is likely that intellectual assessment will continue in MR and, perhaps, as part of the comprehensive individual evaluations of a limited number of other students. When used, intellectual assessment must be carried out in ways that are consistent with theory, research, and best professional practices. It is to these topics that the rest of the chapter is devoted.

BASIC CONSIDERATIONS

The voluminous literature pertaining to intellectual assessment cannot be reviewed in detail in this chapter. Thousands of journal articles, hundreds of book chapters, and scores of books have been written on topics related to intellectual assessment. In this section of the chapter we will review only general findings that relate directly to best practice considerations. Readers are referred to other sources for further information on theories of intelligence, developmental patterns, and reliability and validity of instruments, and group differences (Flanagan, Genshaft, & Harrison, 1997; Neisser, 1998; Sattler, 2001; Sternberg, 1994).

Nature of Current Measures

The intellectual measures used most frequently in school psychology are composed of a variety of complex tasks ranging from items requiring simple memory to abstract problem solving. Until recently, nearly all were theoretical in the sense that the items and scales were not derived from applications of theories of cognitive development or information processing. Several recently developed tests are derived from theory, although it is too early to determine if these tests will be used frequently by school psychologists (Naglieri & Das, 1997a; Woodcock & McGrew, 2000). Most analyses of the psychometric structure of the new and traditional tests such as the Wechsler Scales and the Stanford-Binet yield a general factor, not unlike the concept of Spearman's "g," with one to four group factors (Kranzler & Keith, 1999). Interpretations of scores beyond the composite or overall score and two or three group factor scores typically are less reliable and often invalid.

Meaning of Current Measures

Academic Performance

Intellectual measures are useful because of their relationship to other critical indices of human functioning. The most common use is to attempt to estimate likely level of performance in educational settings or to attempt to identify causes of poor school performance. This use of intellectual measures is supported by the well-known substantial correlation between intellectual functioning and school achievement. This relationship, ranging from a correlation of about .4 to about .7 depending on the achievement criterion measure, reflects a substantial, but by no means perfect, association between intellectual functioning and school performance.

Occupational attainment

Intellectual measures are also correlated with occupational attainment. Although there is a broad range of ability associated with each occupational category (e.g., attorney or carpenter), there is a clear relationship with the average level of ability in occupational categories. Generally, the more prestigious the occupation the higher the average level of ability. This fundamental relationship rarely has direct applicability to school psychology decision making.

Cognitive Processes

Performance on intellectual measures is also related to a variety of indices of cognitive processing. The classic Campione, Brown, and Ferrara (1982) chapter summarized evidence that performance on intellectual measures is positively related to the speed and efficiency of information processing, to the individual's knowledge base, to the spontaneous use of appropriate strategies in problem solving tasks, to metacognitive operations whereby the individual exerts control over approaches to problem solving, and to the transfer of problem solving skills to novel situations.

Perhaps the most salient result in the Campione et al. (1982) review was the interpretation of intellectual differences in terms of the capability of profiting from incomplete instruction. In general, the higher the level of measured ability, the greater the individual's capability of learning through indirect or incomplete instruction. The latter bears strong relationships to the concept of incidental learning, cited earlier as the process through which much of the knowledge or problem solving strategies on intellectual measures are learned.

Measured Intelligence Versus Intelligent Behavior

The discrepancy between what is assessed on intellectual measures and effective, intelligent behavior has been recognized for many decades. In a 1921 symposium on the meaning of intelligence, E. L. Thorndike suggested three major facets of intelligence: social, mechanical (practical), and abstract thinking. He noted that the tests at that time, like most current measures, focused primarily on abstract thinking (Intelligence and its measurement, A Symposium, 1921). A similar insight was offered by David Wechsler in his emphasis on intelligent behavior as the overall capacity to think rationally, act purposely, and deal effectively with the environment (Wechsler, 1955). Sternberg (1985) has identified different components of intelligent behavior including social and practical intelligence (an aspect of which is tacit knowledge).

The above formulations recognize the distinction between what is measured on current measures and intelligent behavior. Intelligent behavior, if defined simply as the effectiveness in dealing with the environment, clearly involves a variety of intellectual and nonintellectual competencies. The IQ score from a well-standardized instrument such as one of the Wechsler scales represents some, but by no means all, of these competencies. It is critical for users of measures of general intellectual functioning to understand this distinction and to communicate the distinction to consumers of test result, (i.e., students, teachers, and parents). As Wechsler pointed out, a high level of measured intelligence, perhaps reflecting primarily abstract thinking capabilities, is rendered quite useless in the absence of goal-directedness, motivation, persistence, or sufficient emotional stability to allow concentrated effort.

Variations in Performance: Intra-Individual Differences

Intellectual measures are designed to identify individual differences. Two perspectives can be used in examining these variations: (a) intra-individual differences involve variations within the individual over different tasks or items and (b) inter-individual differences involving variations between persons on the same tasks or items. Both types of differences have been used widely in intellectual assessment.

Intra-individual differences over subtests have often been used in making diagnostic decisions about individuals. For example, it was widely believed that larger subtest variations or unique patterns were typical of persons with various disabilities or neuropsychological deficits. It turns out that these assertions were and are still almost certain to be incorrect because a high degree of variation across item types or tasks is typical of normal persons; that is, profile scatter is typical of normal individuals (Macmann & Barnett, 1997; McDermott, Fantuzzo, & Glutting, 1992; McDermott, Fantuzzo, Glutting, Watkins, & Baggaley, 1992; Sattler, 2001). If large subtest differences or verbal-performance scale differences occur frequently, then it is a statistical impossibility for subtest patterns to be a unique or defining characteristic of a disorder or neurological deficit that presumably occurs infrequently.

Difference scores are nearly always less reliable than the separate scores on which the difference is based. This fact explains to a large degree why the intra-individual differences used in profile or scatter analysis are not useful bases for diagnoses or specification of treatment. If the reason for difference scores being less reliable is not immediately apparent, then consider this analogy. If one is uncertain about when a vacation period begins and also uncertain about when the vacation ends, then, there must be even greater uncertainty about the length of the vacation. Similarly, if we are somewhat uncertain of the individual's short-term memory score since it is not perfectly reliable and, also, somewhat uncertain about the individual's auditory processing score for the same reason, then we are, by necessity, even less certain of the difference between the two scores.

Norms for subtest and scale differences are available for the most widely used tests (Sattler, 2001). The norms often are organized around the size of the difference between two scores that is statistically significant at the .05 or .01 levels. These results are widely misunderstood. For example, on a Wechsler scale the Verbal-Performance Scale difference of about 15 points is statistically significant at the .01 level. Does this mean that only 1% of the standardization sample obtained Verbal and Performance scores at that magnitude of difference? No! In fact, nearly 25% of persons in the standardization obtained Verbal and Performance scores that were different by 15 points or more. The statistical significance indicates the likelihood that a difference of that magnitude would occur by chance. The .01 or .05 levels indicate that the difference is likely to be real, not whether the difference is unusual or unique. It is essential to keep in mind that real differences in score profiles do occur frequently.

Developmental Changes

The performance of individuals also varies over time. IQ test results are relatively stable for most individuals after approximately age 5–7; however, the IQ scores for a significant percentage of individuals (at least 20%) change by 15 points or more between age 6 and maturity, and considerably larger changes of 30 or 40 points have been reported in a few cases. When large changes do occur, they tend to be associated with significant changes in the individual's environment or overall adjustment (McCall, Apelbaum, & Hogarty, 1973). The fact that IQ test results do change as a function of changes in the individual or the environment can be seen as evidence to support the most common interpretation of test results as reflecting *current* intellectual functioning. We need to be conscious of the fact, and inform others, that scores do change, and that inferences about future intellectual status of the individual are tentative.

Measures of Cognitive Processes

As noted earlier, well-standardized intellectual measures reflecting theoretical formulations of cognitive processes appeared recently, sometimes accompanied by claims that the processes should be used as intervention targets (e.g., Naglieri & Das, 1997b), as a means to prescribe instructional methodology (Kaufman & Kaufman, 1983; Reynolds, 1992), or to provide a more complete description of cognitive abilities (Woodcock & McGrew, 2000). The assertions regarding the value to academic achievement of training weak cognitive processes or matching teaching methodology to presumed cognitive or neurological strengths typically do not have any empirical support (Kavale & Forness, 1999). In other cases exaggerated claims are made on the basis of studies with weak methodologies and very small sample sizes (e.g., Naglieri & Johnson, 2000). Although these notions are intuitively attractive, there is little evidence to date that their application confers benefits to children.

A second use of cognitive process measures is represented by dynamic assessment procedures that attempt to identify strengths and weaknesses in the individual's problem solving strategies. Attempts are then made to overcome deficits in strategies through direct cognitive training (Lidz, 1987). Thus far, dynamic assessment and cognitive training have not had much impact on the practice of school psychology in part because the dynamic assessment procedures have not been well standardized and the effectiveness of interventions related to improving cognitive processing are as yet unproven.

Inter-Individual Differences

The central purpose in most administrations of individual IQ tests is to determine how the individual performs in relation to a group of persons with similar characteristics. The standard scores and percentile ranks that give meaning to the performance and form the basis for the interpretation are based on the normative group. Obviously, the quality of the norms is crucial to the usefulness of the test. When we interpret the performance of individuals using the common scores such as IQs and percentile ranks, we are implicitly concluding that the normative group on which these scores were based constituted an appropriate comparison group for that individual. Careful consideration of whether that group is appropriate is crucial to accurate interpretation of measures of intellectual performance.

Perhaps the most controversial finding related to intellectual assessment is that sociocultural groups differ in level and pattern of performance on measures of standardized tests. These findings have appeared for many years (Kaufman & Doppelt, 1976; College Board, 1999; Smith et al., 1995). The variations in level typically are confounded with group differences in socioeconomic status, rendering difficult interpretation of the source(s) of level and pattern differences. For that reason, we urge extreme caution in attributing causality to group differences as well as additional care in interpreting the results of intellectual test performance for persons from groups that are culturally different or economically disadvantaged. We note with favor Mercer's (1979) excellent discussion of conditions that must be met before attributing intellectual test differences to hereditary causes. In fact, those criteria cannot be met for individuals, and estimations of their effects for groups are fraught with many possible sources of error. For these reasons, we strongly admonish against making inferences about causation in our everyday interpretations of inter-individual differences on measures of intellectual functioning.

Bias and Litigation

Allegations of bias against minority students are perhaps the most controversial and unresolved issues regarding the use of IQ measures by school psychologists. Considerable research was devoted to topics of bias in the 1970s and 1980s. The voluminous results generated from this research led to complex conclusions about intellectual assessment with minority students (Reynolds, Lowe, & Saenz, 1999). First, there are multiple definitions of bias with varied meanings. The results of studies of bias depend heavily on the definition used. Definitions of bias include the following conceptions: (a) mean differences, (b) item bias, (c) psychometric characteristics of tests, (d) factor analysis of underlying test structure, (e) atmosphere or examiner/examinee interaction effects, (f) prediction, (g) selection ratios or disproportionate classification of students, and (h) social consequences, particularly use of test results to support racist interpretation of differences.

Most conventional tests are not biased according to the conventional definitions related to properties of items, psychometric characteristics, factor analysis, examiner-examinee effects, and prediction (Jensen, 1980; Reynolds et al., 1999). Specifically, there is no evidence that conventional tests underpredict the actual performance of minority students. Conventional tests typically are found to be biased on the less well accepted definitions such as mean differences, selection ratios-disproportionate classification, and social consequences.

The mean differences and disproportionate classification definitions, along with several conventional definitions, were key features of extremely costly and divisive litigation over the past 20 years. Four trials over these issues occurred in federal district courts between 1979 and 1986 (Reschly, Kicklighter, & McKee, 1988a, 1998b). Three of the trials concluded that conventional measures of intellectual functioning were not biased, despite overrepresentation of minority students in special education programs, *if* certain crucial standards were met; that is, (a) rigorous implementation of procedural safeguards in the referral, classification and placement process, (b) implementation of a multifactored assessment designed to identify specific educational needs by a group of professionals, and (c) classification, placement, and programming decisions made by a team that included professionals and parents. The initial *Larry P* (1979, 1986) decisions in California resulted in a ban on IQ tests with African-American students, but the most recent decisions in that case rescinded the IQ test bans (*Larry P.*, 1992, 1994). Nevertheless, the perception of unfairness to minorities persists for a number of reasons such as the concerns that different environments provide differential preparation for the test, narrow item content, and negative outcomes associated with the use of IQ tests. It is doubtful that IQ testing will ever be acceptable to many minority educators and social scientists regardless of the results of empirical studies of bias.

Treatment Validity

We anticipate considerably reduced use of intellectual assessment because the results of intellectual measures are not related closely to treatment selection, planning, or evaluation. Witt and Gresham's evaluation of the treatment validity of the most widely used scale summarizes our views on this matter: "In short, the WISC-R lacks treatment validity in that its use does not enhance remedial interventions for children who show specific academic skill deficiencies.... For a test to have treatment validity, it must lead to better treatments (i.e., better educational programs, teaching strategies, etc.)" (Witt & Gresham, 1985, p. 1717).

We acknowledge that others in school psychology whom we respect may disagree with our view on treatment validity, and we wish more space were available here for a full representation of our and their views. We note that the principal use of intellectual measures has been disabled child classification leading to placement in special education. We also refer the reader to Kavale and Forness' (1999) analysis of the efficacy of special education programs organized around disability labels. From these results, as well as the negative findings on matching instruction to cognitive or neuropsychological strengths, we have concluded that alternatives must be considered.

Appropriate Uses of Intellectual Assessment

Intellectual assessment may have a positive or negative impact on the individual depending on the context that leads to assessment and the outcomes of decisions made using intellectual assessment information. The importance of these context and outcome conditions was emphasized in a report of the National Research Council on equity in special education placement (Heller, Holtzman, & Messick, 1982). Consideration of alternatives to special education referral, classification, and placement and, if these steps are necessary, focusing on the outcomes of classification and placement, moves the discussion of bias beyond arguments about test items and prediction equations (Reschly, 1979; Reschly et al., 1988b). Consideration of alternatives and outcomes is the central focus of system reform efforts now underway.

Context

The typical context of intellectual assessment for school psychologists often involves determination of eligibility for possible special education classification and placement. A two-pronged classification-placement process is established in federal and state special education legislation: (a) determination of need for special education and (b) determination of eligibility for classification. All too often the eligibility determination, rather than the need for special education, is addressed in the multifactored assessment that precedes classification and placement.

The least restrictive environment (LRE) principle from federal and state legislation places emphasis on attempts to resolve problems and to provide necessary services in regular education settings. Application of this principle implies that intellectual assessment and eligibility determination should not be the first choice in efforts to address learning or behavior problems.

The first phase of a system within which intellectual assessment can be used appropriately involves concerted efforts to resolve problems in regular education settings. This phase must involve careful consideration of prior efforts to resolve the problem and systematic, high quality interventions. Intervention quality at the pre-referral stage, as indicated by the presence of essential features such as behavioral definition of the problem, collection of baseline data, design of systematic interventions, and intervention implementation, monitoring, and evaluation, typically is very poor. School psychologists have critical roles and essential contributions to ensuring the delivery of high quality pre-referral interventions (Tilly, this volume).

Choice of Measure and Decision Making

If the problem behavior is pervasive and persistent, and beyond the purview of regular education, even with high quality pre-referral interventions, then consideration of special education eligibility is appropriate. At this stage, depending on state rules concerning classification of students as disabled, intellectual assessment may be part of the multifactored assessment. Intellectual assessment should not dominate the assessment process; rather, it should be one component of a comprehensive evaluation that is tailored to the referral problem and oriented to determining specific intervention need(s). Consideration of other aspects or dimensions of behavior should receive equal or more attention and decision making about eligibility and placement should reflect a clear balance between intellectual assessment and other important information.

The choice of intellectual assessment measure(s) must be based on the characteristics of the student. Student characteristics such as age, sensory status, language competencies, and acculturation are crucial factors that must be considered carefully when professionals select specific intellectual measures. For some students, few if any good choices exist due to various combinations of language differences, sensory impairments, and acculturation. In some of these cases, intellectual assessment should be avoided. In other cases, interpretations should be extremely cautious and decisions considered highly tentative.

The best measures available should be used when intellectual assessment results are part of significant decisions such as disability classification. Practitioners should base instrument choices on published critical reviews in authoritative sources such as the Buros Mental Measurement Yearbooks (also see Salvia & Ysseldyke, 2001) as well as their thorough study of the available technical information. Instruments that are short forms of more comprehensive measures, tests with a single item type, and measures with dubious technical adequacy should be avoided.

Additional challenges arise when the effects of various disabilities such as sensory impairments or complex conditions such as autism or traumatic brain injury have to be considered in instrument choice and interpretation. Familiarity with a variety of instruments and knowledge of various disabling conditions are essential to the choice of measures and the interpretation of results in these complex cases.

Decision Making

Information on intellectual functioning is used most often in decisions about classification of students as MR, LD, or gifted and talented. Most students considered for these classifications will be performing near the margins of the classification criteria; that is, they will perform at levels where they are just eligible or just ineligible for classification. For example, an IQ of less than 70 or 75 is used frequently as part of the criteria for a diagnosis of MR. The majority of the persons for whom an MR diagnostic decision is necessary will perform within a few points of the cut off score of 70 or 75. There are, for example, more students with IQs between 70 and 75 than have IQs below 70! Of course the same holds true for IQs of >130 and 125–130. A substantial proportion of cases will be within one standard error of measurement of the cutoff established by the state rules.

The mechanical application of scores to classification criteria is inappropriate in MR, LD, and gifted-talented eligibility decisions. Complex judgments are required rather than mechanical application of scores. These complex judgments should reflect application of the convergent validity principle described by Gresham (1985); that is, the consistency of information over settings, sources, and data collection methods. Application of the convergent validity principle provides a means to integrate information from the multifactored assessment. For students performing near cut-off points, a pattern of information consistent with the underlying diagnostic construct should lead to classifying the child as disabled. On the other hand, one or more sources of information that are not consistent with the diagnostic construct should lead to consideration of alternatives to classifying the student as disabled.

Inappropriate or Questionable Uses of Intellectual Assessment

An array of inappropriate or questionable uses of measures of general intellectual functioning will be described briefly in this section. An obvious inappropriate use is to reach conclusions about the individual using only the results from a measure of intellectual functioning, without considering a wide variety of other information. We are aware of no information on how frequently this inappropriate practice occurs, but it was of sufficient concern to merit a special sentence in federal regulations pertaining to assessment of students [IDEA, 34 CFR 300.532(b)]. We suspect that the results of an intellectual measure overshadow other important data quite frequently, and the other data often are more useful in developing interventions.

Profile Analysis

One of the most frequent inappropriate uses is to conduct a profile analysis for the purpose of differential diagnosis (e.g., determining whether or not the student is learning disabled or emotionally disturbed). As noted previously, a considerable degree of subtest score variation is typical. Differences between scales or subtests, because they occur frequently, simply cannot be a unique feature of any diagnostic category, nor the basis for distinguishing between diagnostic categories.

Group Differences

Applications of the results from studies of groups of students also need to be interpreted cautiously with individuals. For example, the WISC-R ACID profile has been reported frequently in contrasts of learning disabled and normal achieving students (2001). However, these findings are based on mean differences, developed from distributions of scores for normal achieving and LD groups. The overall distributions overlap considerably. Therefore, a specific normal achieving child may obtain the ACID profile and a specific student accurately characterized as learning disabled may not obtain that profile. Therefore, conformance or nonconformance with the particular profile reported for groups is not an accurate indicator of the appropriate diagnosis for an individual child.

Personality or Neuropsychological Status

Profile analyses for the purpose of determination of neurological strengths or weaknesses or psychodynamic personality characteristics are also fraught with significant errors of logic and probable unreliability. These interpretations have a long history in applied areas of psychology including school and clinical. The empirical basis for the interpretations typically is weak or nonexistent. In virtually all instances, careful studies have not been done with individuals known to possess the underlying neurological or psychodynamic characteristic inferred from the test profile. Rather, analogical reasoning of the form, *What would this most likely mean*, has been applied to analysis of the profile resulting in largely unsubstantiated inferences about the meaning of various subtests or scale discrepancies. These interpretations in the absence of empirical support are likely to be inaccurate, unreliable, and, in any case, not related to effective intervention methodology or techniques (Kavale & Forness, 1999; Reschly & Gresham, 1989).

Structured Observations

One of the most frequent justifications for administering an IQ test to nearly all students with learning and/or behavioral problems is the opportunity provided for structured observations. The problem with this use is that the observations occur in an unnatural setting, on a one-to-one basis, with an adult who may have little continuing involvement with the child, using tasks that do not reflect directly the difficulties that prompted the referral. Most important, the behavioral observations in the testing setting do not predict accurately behavior in other settings (Oakland, Broom, & Glutting, 2000; Glutting, Oakland, & McDermott, 1989).

In contrast, structured observations in natural settings are enormously useful *if* gathered through use of direct measures of the behavior of concern and related to crucial environmental or instructional variables that can be used in interventions. The question is, in large part, whether we adapt to the client's setting or whether we require the client to adapt to our setting. Use of the IQ test for structured observations is also time consuming, usually requiring 3–4 hours for test administration, scoring, interpretation, and report preparation. Time is precious, our time as well as the time of students. Time devoted to IQ testing inevitably reduces or eliminates the opportunity to conduct other assessment activities.

Inferences About Group Differences

The final inappropriate use relates to the use of results on measures of general intellectual functioning to support inferences about innate abilities of individuals or groups. Although these questions are investigated, sometime rigorously and sometimes not, the varied and controversial inferences from this research have little relationship to our day-to-day practice with diverse groups of students. The most popular conclusions from this research have varied during our careers and will likely continue to be modified as new information is generated and more sophisticated investigative techniques are developed and applied. Our concern with accurate interpretation for individuals must include efforts to protect individuals from unwarranted inferences about innate abilities that may further diminish efforts to remediate problems and to intervene effectively.

Surgeon General's Warning

A kind of "surgeon general's" warning can be formulated to protect children and youth from unwarranted inferences about their intellectual abilities and to remind all of us, especially consumers of our work, of the developmental nature of measured abilities (Reschly, 1979). This "surgeon general's" warning is far from perfect. Concerned practitioners can develop appropriate modifications. However, the essential ideas are to protect students from inappropriate inferences such as the beliefs that (a) intellectual abilities are determined by genetic factors, (b) intellectual abilities are unitary, (c) IQ scores reflect all of intelligent behavior, and (d) performance on intellectual measures is fixed, or unchanging. We recommend the use of a statement such as the following in test reports and as attachments to test protocols.

> IQ tests measure only a portion of the competencies involved with human intelligence. The IQ results are best seen as estimates of likely performance in school and reflections of the degree to which children have mastered the middle class cultural symbols and broad culturally rooted facts, concepts, and problem solving strategies. This information is useful but limited. IQ tests do not reflect innate genetic capacity and the scores are not fixed. Some persons do exhibit significant increases or decreases in their measured intellectual abilities. (Reschly, 1979, p. 224).

BEST PRACTICES

Best practices considerations require careful judgments about (a) *when* and *how* intellectual assessment instruments are used; (b) the selection, administration, and interpretation of measures; and (c) prevention of misuses and misconceptions.

1. Appropriate use requires a context that emphasizes prevention and early intervention rather than eligibility determination as the initial phase in services to students with learning and behavior problems. The context within which the intellectual assessment occurs is crucial. The typical context is the investigation of the causes and correlates of learning problems. Special education eligibility may be a concern, but that concern should be investigated after, not before, the development, implementation, and evaluation of interventions within regular education settings.

2. Intellectual assessment should be used when the results are directly relevant to well-defined referral questions, and other available information does not address those questions. Evaluations should be goal directed. The goal of the evaluation should be to address significant questions developed jointly

between the psychologist and the referral agent. Some referral questions require consideration of current intellectual functioning, many others do not.

3. Mandatory use of intellectual measures for all referrals, multifactored evaluations or reevaluations is not consistent with best practices. It is not uncommon for all referred students to receive IQ tests, regardless of referral questions or behavioral problems. IQ test results simply are not relevant to many referral questions or reevaluation issues. A critical question is, *How would the intervention, classification decision, or selection of placement option change if an IQ test is or is not administered?*

4. Intellectual assessment must be part of a multifactored approach, individualized to a child's characteristics and the referral problems. The practice of using a standard battery, often dominated by IQ tests, for all children regardless of referral questions must be avoided. Standard batteries provide superficial information over very limited areas of functioning. In most instances, the standard battery does not relate directly to referral problems and is not well matched to characteristics of the child.

5. Intellectual assessment procedures must be carefully matched to characteristics of children and youth. A variety of instruments are available. No instrument is appropriate for all students. Special consideration needs to be devoted to choices of instruments with students exhibiting sensory or motor handicaps, language differences or significant cultural differences. Basal and ceiling problems need to be considered. For example, an instrument may not assess a low functioning youngster close to the bottom age of the test norms adequately because very few items will be administered due to ceiling rules and insufficient numbers of items for low-scoring persons.

6. Score reporting and interpretation must reflect the known limitations of tests, including technical adequacy, measurement error, and general performance ranges. Test scores should always be presented as ranges around an obtained score using confidence intervals. Furthermore, limitations in the norms for the test, in reliability or stability of scores, and questionable or undemonstrated validity, must be carefully considered and communicated to consumers of test information. Finally, the overall performance needs to be interpreted within broad categories, established by the test developer or established by other sources (e.g., state special education rules).

7. Interpretation of performance and decisions concerning classification must reflect consideration of overall strengths and weaknesses in intellectual performance, performance on other relevant dimensions of behavior, age, family characteristics, and sociocultural background. Present behavior is described. Interpretations and descriptions of likely future performance are inferred from the sample of current behavior. The sample of current behavior may need to be regarded with varying degrees of tentativeness depending on age, family characteristics, and sociocultural background. Furthermore, overall pattern of strengths and weaknesses in intellectual performance as well as the individual's performance on other relevant dimensions such as adaptive behavior and social skills must be incorporated in interpretations and recommendations.

8. The newest revision and most recent norms for a test should be used because recent studies show that the stringency of norms changes over time and more recent norms typically are tougher than older norms. The now well-known Flynn Effect must be considered to avoid the undue effects of out-of-date norms (Flynn, 1998).

9. Professionals should adopt strategies to prevent misuse and misconceptions about the results of intellectual measures. Many consumers of test results including teachers and parents often view the findings as reflecting a predetermined characteristic and regard the results as fixed. Many do not see the distinction between the results of measures of intellectual measures and the much broader construct of intelligent behavior. A "Surgeon General's Warning" should appear on test protocols and reports as a means to reduce the likelihood of misuse and misconceptions (see previous section).

SUMMARY

Intellectual assessment continues to be prominent in the services of school psychologists. That prominence depends in profound ways on the conceptual definitions and classification criteria for disabilities in educational settings. Changes that are underway regarding disability conceptions and criteria may change markedly the prominence of intellectual assessment in special education and school psychology. These changes are likely to be uneven across the United States. Where intellectual assessment continues, it must be carried out competently, implementing the best practices formulated in this chapter.

REFERENCES

Campione, J. C., Brown, A. L. & Ferrara, R. A. (1982). Mental retardation and intelligence. In R. J. Sternberg (Ed.), *Handbook of Human Intelligence* (pp. 392–490). New York: Cambridge University Press.

College Board. (1999). *Reaching the top: A report of the national task force on minority high achievement.* New York: College Board Publications. (Available:www.collegeboard.org).

Fagan, T. K. (1992). Compulsory schooling, child study, clinical psychology, and special education: Origins of school psychology. *American Psychologist, 47,* 236–243.

Flanagan, D. P., Genshaft, J. L., & Harrison, P. L. (Eds.). (1997). *Contemporary intellectual assessment: Theories, tests, and issues.* New York: Guilford.

Fletcher, J. M., Francis, D. J, Shaywitz, S. E., Lyon, G. R., Foorman, B. R., Stuebing, K. K, & Shaywitz, B. A. (1998). Intelligent testing and the discrepancy model for children with learning disabilities. *Learning Disabilities Research and Practice, 13,* 186–203.

Flynn, J. R. (1998). IQ gains over time: Toward finding the causes. In U. Neisser (Ed.), *The rising curve: Long-term gains in IQ and related measures* (pp. 25–66). Washington, DC: American Psychological Association.

Glutting, J. J., Oakland, T., & McDermott, P. A. (1989). Observing child behavior during testing: constructs, validity, and situational generality. *Journal of School Psychology, 27,* 155–164.

Gresham, F. (1985). Behavior disorder assessment: Conceptual, definitional, and practical considerations. *School Psychology Review, 14,* 495–509.

Heller, K., Holtzman, W., & Messick, S. (Eds.). (1982). *Placing children in special education: A strategy for equity.* Washington, DC: National Academy Press.

Hosp, J. L., & Reschly D. J. (in press). Regional differences in school psychology practice. *School Psychology Review.*

Individuals with Disabilities Education Act (1997, 1999). 20 U. S. C. Chapter 33, Sections 1400-1485. (Statute), 34 C.F.R. 300 (Regulations).

Intelligence and its measurement: A symposium (1921). *Journal of Educational Psychology, 12,* 123–147, 195–216.

Jensen, A. R. (1980). *Bias in mental testing.* New York: Free Press.

Kaufman, A., & Doppelt, J. (1976). Analysis of the WISC-R standardization data in terms of stratification variables. *Child Development, 47,* 165–171.

Kaufman, A., & Kaufman, N. (1983). *Kaufman Assessment Battery for Children (K-ABC).* Circle Pines, MN: American Guidance Service.

Kavale, K. A., & Forness, S. R. (1999). Effectiveness of special education. In C. R. Reynolds & T. B. Gutkin (Eds.), *The handbook of school psychology* (3rd ed.) (pp. 984–1024). New York: John Wiley.

Kranzler, J. H., & Keith, T. Z. (1999). Independent confirmatory factor analysis of the Cognitive Assessment System (CAS): What does the CAS measure? *School Psychology Review, 28,* 117–144.

Larry P. v. Riles (1979, 1986, 1992, 1994). 495 F. Supp. 926 (N. D. Cal. 1979) (decision on merits). Order modifying judgment, C-71-2270 RFP, September 25, 1986. Memorandum and Order, August 31, 1992. aff'd F. (9th Cir. 1994).

Lidz, C. S. (Ed.) (1987). *Dynamic assessment: An interactional approach to evaluating learning potential.* New York: Guilford.

Luckasson, R., Coulter, D. L., Polloway, E. A., Reiss, S., Schalock, R. L., Snell, M. E., Spitalnik, D. M., & Stark, J. A. (1992). *Mental retardation: Definition, classification, and systems of support* (9th ed.) Washington DC: American Association on Mental Retardation.

Macmann, G. M., & Barnett, D. W. (1997). Myth of the master detective: Reliability of interpretations for Kaufman's "intelligent testing" approach to the WISC-III. *School Psychology Quarterly, 12*, 197–234.

McCall, R., Appelbaum, M., & Hogarty, P. (1973). Developmental changes in mental performance. *Monographs of the Society for Research in Child Development, 38*, 1–83.

McDermott, P. A., Fantuzzo, J. W., & Glutting, J. J. (1992). Just say no to subtest analysis: A critique on Wechsler theory and practice. *Journal of Psychoeducational Assessment, 8*, 289–302.

McDermott, P. A., Fantuzzo, J. W., Glutting, J. J., Watkins, M. W., Baggaley, A. R. (1992). Illusions of meaning in the ipsative assessment of children's ability. *Journal of Special Education, 25*, 504–526.

Mercer, C. D., Jordan, L., Allsopp, D. H., & Mercer, A. R. (1996). Learning disabilities definitions and criteria used by state education departments. *Learning Disability Quarterly, 19*, 217–232.

Mercer, J. (1979). *System of Multicultural Pluralistic Assessment technical manual.* New York: Psychological Corporation.

Naglieri, J. A., & Das, J. P. (1997a). *Cognitive Assessment System.* Itasca, IL: Riverside.

Naglieri, J. A., & Das, J. P. (1997b). *Cognitive Assessment System interpretative handbook.* Itasca, IL: Riverside.

Naglieri, J. A., & Johnson, D. (2000). Effectiveness of a cognitive strategy intervention in improving arithmetic computation based on the PASS theory. *Journal of Learning Disabilities, 33*, 591–597.

Neisser, U. (Ed.) (1998). *The rising curve: Long-term gains in IQ and related measures.* Washington, DC: American Psychological Association.

Oakland, T., Broom, J., & Glutting, J. (2000). Use of freedom form distractibility and processing speed to assess children's test-taking behaviors. *Journal of School Psychology, 38*, 469–475.

Reschly, D. (1979). Nonbiased assessment. In G. Phye & D. Reschly (Eds.), *School Psychology: Perspectives and issues* (pp. 215–253). New York: Academic.

Reschly, D. J. (2000a). The present and future status of school psychology in the United States. *School Psychology Review, 29*, 507–522.

Reschly, D. J. (2000b). Assessment and eligibility determination in the Individuals with Disabilities Act of 1997. In C. F. Telzrow & M. Tankersley. (Eds.), *IDEA amendments of 1997: Practice guidelines for school-based teams* (pp. 65–104). Bethesda, MD: National Association of School Psychologists.

Reschly, D. J., & Gresham, F. M. (1989). Current neuropsychological diagnosis of learning problems: A leap of faith. In C. R. Reynolds & E. Fletcher-Janzen (Ed.), *Child neuropsychology techniques of diagnosis and treatment* (pp. 503–519). New York: Plenum.

Reschly, D. J., Kicklighter, R. H., & McKee, P. (1988a). Recent placement litigation, Part II, Minority EMR overrepresentation: Comparison of Larry P. (1979, 1984, 1986) with Marshall (1984, 1985) and S-1 (1986). *School Psychology Review, 17*, 20–36.

Reschly, D. J., Kicklighter, R. H., & McKee, P. (1988b). Recent placement litigation, Part III: Analysis of differences in Larry P., Marshall, and S-1 and implication for future practices. *School Psychology Review, 17*, 37–48.

Reschly, D. J., & Tilly, W. D. III. (1999). Reform trends and system design alternatives. In D. J. Reschly, W. D. Tilly III., & J. P. Grimes (Eds.), *Special education in transition: Functional assessment and noncategorical programming* (pp. 19–48). Longmont, CO: Sopris West.

Reschly, D. J., Tilly, W. D. III., & Grimes, J. P. (Eds.). (1999). *Special education in transition: Functional assessment and noncategorical programming.* Longmont, CO: Sopris West.

Reynolds, C. R. (1992). Two key concepts in the diagnosis of learning disabilities and the habilitation of learning. *Learning Disability Quarterly, 15*, 2–12.

Reynolds, C. R., Lowe, P. A., & Saenz, A. L. (1999). The problem of bias in psychological assessment. In C. R. Reynolds & T. B. Gutkin (Eds.), *The handbook of school psychology* (3rd ed.) (pp. 549–595). New York: John Wiley.

Salvia, J., & Ysseldyke, J. (2001). *Assessment* (8th ed.). Boston: Houghton-Mifflin.

Sarason, S. (1975). The unfortunate fate of Alfred Binet and school psychology. *Teachers College Record, 77*, 579–592.

Sattler, J. M. (2001). *Assessment of children: Cognitive applications* (4th ed.). San Diego: Sattler.

Smith, T. M., Perie, M., Alsalam, N., Mahoney, R. P., Bae, Y., & Young, B. A. (1995). *The condition of education, 1995.* Washington DC: Office of Educational Research and Improvement, U.S. Department of Education.

Sternberg, R. J. (1985). *Beyond IQ: A triarchic theory of human intelligence.* New York: Cambridge University Press.

Sternberg, R. J. (Ed.). (1994). *Encyclopedia of human intelligence.* New York: Macmillan.

Tilly, W. D. III., Reschly, D. J., & Grimes, J. P. (1999). Disability determination in problem solving systems: Conceptual foundations and critical components. In D. J. Reschly, W. D. Tilly III., & J. P. Grimes (Eds.), *Special education in transition: Functional assessment and noncategorical programming* (pp. 285–321). Longmont, CO: Sopris West.

Witt, J. C., & Gresham, F. M. (1985). Review of the Wechsler Intelligence Scale for Children-Revised. In J. Mitchell (Ed.), *Ninth Mental Measurements Yearbook.* Lincoln, NE: Buros Institute.

Wechsler, D. (1955). *The measurement and appraisal of adult intelligence* (4th ed.). Baltimore: Williams & Wilkins.

Woodcock, R. B., & McGrew, K. S. (2000). *Woodcock-Johnson Psycho-Educational Battery-Third Edition (WJ-3).* Chicago: Riverside.

ANNOTATED BIBLIOGRAPHY

Flanagan, D. P., Genshaft, J. L., & Harrison, P. L. (Eds.). (1997). *Contemporary intellectual assessment: Theories, tests, and issues.* New York: Guilford.
This is an excellent volume edited by persons with deep knowledge of school psychology practice.

Neisser, U. (Ed.). (1998). *The rising curve: Long-term gains in IQ and related measures.* Washington, DC: American Psychological Association.
This edited volume provides excellent chapters on the puzzle of rising IQ scores, but stable achievement scores as well as possible hereditary and environmental influences on score trends.

Sattler, J. M. (2001). *Assessment of children: Cognitive applications* (4th ed.). San Diego: Sattler.
Sattler provides an excellent text as well as an essential reference for individuals responsible for conducting intellectual assessments of children. Extensive information is provided on the most commonly used intellectual assessment measures with suggested guidelines for interpretation.

Sternberg, R. J. (Ed.). (1994). *Encyclopedia of human intelligence.* New York: Macmillan.
Sternberg's edited volume has extensive information on various facets of intelligence including theory, research, and future prospects.

84 Best Practices in Intellectual Assessment: Future Directions

Dawn P. Flanagan and Samuel O. Ortiz
St. John's University

OVERVIEW

The first chapter of the previous edition of this volume recognized the emergence of a "paradigm shift" in school psychology service delivery toward a foundation based on a problem-solving approach (Reschly & Ysseldyke, 1995). This new and promising focus, however, seems to have found no more stubborn ground from which to spring to life than that involving intellectual assessment and the use of standardized tests (Reschly & Grimes, 1995). Although advances in theory and research are sometimes given their proper, albeit brief, consideration, nothing seems to stir the passion of a school psychologist more than the publication of a new test. The brightly colored images with more realistic depictions of people and things, the more durable, precise, and carefully engineered blocks, the utilitarian aspects of the folding manual, the precision sheen of the protocol, and, of course, the crisp smell of those current norms, are enough to send the pulse of the average school psychologist racing into orbit. Tests, it seems, have become an indelible part of the character of school psychologists and a nearly indispensable tool within their intellectual assessment repertoire. To be sure, any discussion involving "best practices" in intellectual assessment would appear incomplete if it did not focus heavily on issues of standardized tests and testing. Yet, virtual neglect of the underlying and fundamental theoretical notions regarding intelligence and cognitive abilities in the same discussion would not likely result in much of a protest from the field. Despite the fact that it is the very guiding force behind both *measurement and interpretation*, theory has seldom been something to which school psychologists have paid much attention (McGrew & Flanagan, 1998). Perhaps the paradigm shift that needs to occur in school psychology with respect to intellectual assessment is not necessarily that we adopt any *particular* paradigm, but rather that we actually use one.

Can we really say that current school psychology practice, in particular the use of standardized tests, is guided by modern, empirically supported theory? Can it be said that all school psychologists are trained and educated in issues of modern theoretical formulations of intelligence and cognitive abilities and their relevance to measurement and interpretation? The truth may be painful, but the answers are evident—many practitioners are driven primarily by the inertial heritage of test kits, the pretty packages they are wrapped in, and their familiarity with them, and not by the science or technology that underlie them or that should underlie them.

Not surprisingly, the criticisms surrounding standardized intelligence tests and their use have been far ranging and form a substantial body of literature. The spectrum tends to be polarized with many advocates in staunch defense of tests and their benefits on one end and those who see no merit in continuing to use them on the other. Most of us are probably somewhere in between, and the controversy seems to ensure only one thing—that tests are unlikely to disappear from the repertoire of the applied school psychologist anytime soon. But notions regarding best practices have, in the past, tended to be based on finding and applying solutions and remedies to the problems inherent in popular intelligence tests identified by researchers and scholars in the field (Kamphaus, Petoskey, & Morgan, 1997).

For example, it was found that individual subtest score interpretation is invalid, so one solution was to interpret composites only (see Flanagan, Andrews, & Genshaft, 1997, for a review). However, composites tend to wash out meaningful differences in the specific abilities that comprise them, so we were advised to evaluate clinical profiles (e.g., Verbal IQ – Performance IQ differences on the Wechsler Scales) (Sattler, 1992, 2001). Then we learned that clinical profile analysis is too subjective and unreliable, so it was recommended that we interpret profiles using stringent statistical methods and procedures (e.g., Kaufman, 1979, 1994; Kaufman & Lichtenberger, 1999). The identification of these problems and their solutions could very well continue ad nauseum. However, such "remedies" appear to do little with respect to advancing intellectual practice in any meaningful way. The reason is that the litany of recommendations concerning what to do or what not to do with standardized tests may well be important and proper, but it does not begin to address the most basic and severe maladies that have plagued the practice of assessing intellectual abilities since the inception of IQ measures to our field. Promoting best practices in intellectual assessment through piecemeal methods is like making incremental navigational changes to a vessel that has already gone astray so that it will arrive more precisely at an unknown destination. As applied psychologists making high stakes decisions, it is imperative that we know exactly where we are going (viz., in terms of measurement and interpretation) when we select and use standardized tests. The only map that seems likely to guide us in a meaningful direction is theory.

Intelligence Theory in Perspective

The assessment practices adopted by the field of school psychology have roots dating back a century or more (Fagan & Wise, 2000). From both an historical and contemporary perspective, there has perhaps been no greater influence on the practice of assessment than the psychometric tradition (Neisser et al., 1996). The very process of analyzing, classifying, and assigning meaning to the variety of human cognitive abilities, in particular, "has intrigued scientists for centuries" (Kamphaus et al., 1997, p. 33). At the core of this tradition rests the development and refinement of the ubiquitous intelligence test, which has become nearly synonymous with the profession. This association has not, however, been universally affirmed by the passage of time. But more and more, school psychologists are beginning to understand what Sarason meant when he asserted that "school psychology was born in the prison of the IQ test" (1975; as cited in Reschly & Grimes, 1995).

It is widely known that Binet's original scales were created for the purpose of identifying a section of the general school population who were performing much lower than average and who might, therefore, benefit most from specialized instruction. His intent was not to measure intelligence but rather to identify individuals whose academic performance fell significantly below that of the majority of their peers and provide them with remedial instruction (Gould, 1996). H. H. Goddard brought Binet's scales to the United States and extended their application from finding those in need of help to include finding those who were not able or "feeble-minded." Goddard essentially sanctioned the IQ as a measure of nothing less than intelligence itself as a single, innate entity. He also championed the idea that his adaptation of the Binet Scales could identify, reliably, individuals who should be segregated from society because of their inability to contribute meaningfully to the common welfare—a notion that continues to drive educational decision making to the present day (Zenderland, 1998).

L. M. Terman revised Binet's Scales in 1916 to form the Stanford-Binet, which quickly set the standard against which all subsequent IQ tests were measured. Terman succeeded in popularizing the notion that intelligence could be measured reliably, and thus, individuals could be classified according to their ability for a wide variety of socio-psychological purposes (e.g., employment aptitude, predicted scholastic achievement, college admissions). In 1917, R. M. Yerkes developed the Army Alpha and Beta Tests (in collaboration with Goddard, Terman, and others) that were used to place individuals in military positions for which they were "best suited." Yerkes demonstrated the fact that mass mental testing could be accomplished, and with it a whole new vista for ability testing was born. Shortly after the end of World War I, the relative success of Yerkes' mass testing efforts resulted in the emergence of commercial and educational interest in IQ testing. This is perhaps exemplified best by the advent of the Educational Testing Service (ETS) founded by C. C. Brigham, an assistant to Yerkes who helped to administer the Army tests. It did not take long for mental testing to become a multimillion-dollar industry. The evolution of ETS, and many other companies involved in the development and publication of IQ tests, attests to their economic value (Lemann, 1995).

Although monetary gain may not have been the driving force behind the development of IQ tests, it certainly was not a trivial issue. Furthermore, much of the intent behind the science involved in test development was subject to the deeply rooted cultural values and beliefs that prevailed in society during the early twentieth century, including the notion that non-whites were innately less intelligent than whites and that females were innately less intelligent than males (Gould, 1996). On both a conscious and unconscious level, intelligence tests were developed and constructed with these (and other) ideas in mind that unfortunately took precedence over the more substantive issues of scientific theory. Fueled by a socio-political climate, ripe for the very notions espoused by test developers and mesmerized by intoxicating possibilities regarding mass mental ability testing, an industry was born with such passion and inertia that it continues to plow under any of those who oppose it. Indeed, the roots of intelligence testing had every bit as much to do with economics and opportunism as they did science and psychology (Lemann, 1995). For too long now, the latter have been sacrificed in favor of the former. If we as a profession are to emerge from the prison of the IQ test, it will be theory that provides the key to unlocking the cell door.

BASIC CONSIDERATIONS

Theory Comes First

Perhaps the single most critical problem with intelligence tests and their use is that historically they have been based on either decades old theory or no theory at all. Failure to put theory first is unacceptable because such practice runs counter to all notions of good science and the scientific method. Strict adherence to the basic tenets of good science simply cannot yield to issues of expediency or convenience. A prime example of this problem can be seen in the history of the Wechsler scales. In 1939, David Wechsler developed the Wechsler-Bellvue (W-B) (see Flanagan, McGrew, & Ortiz (2000) for a brief history of the development of the Wechsler scales). Among his more notable contributions as a result of that effort were the deviation IQ, measurement of intelligence through both verbal and nonverbal means, and developmental scaling of items within each subtest rather than across subtests. Wechsler's intentions in creating the W-B were driven less by a need for precision in measurement of cognitive ability constructs than by practical reasons related to his clinical practice (Kaufman, 1990; Zachary, 1990). Wechsler was more interested in being able to distinguish clinically between an acutely psychotic individual out of touch with reality and someone who was simply incompetent to understand the nature of their behavior. But Wechsler fell prey to the very same problem that befell many of his predecessors—he did not concern himself much with theory (Flanagan et al., 2000; Kamphaus et al., 1997).

In 1904, Spearman had already published on the nature of general intelligence, or *g*, measured through factor analytic techniques, which he more or less invented. The *g* factor quickly gained wide acceptance as the predominant theory of intelligence. When Goddard turned the Binet Scales into an intelligence measure, IQ was thought to be a measure of this *g* construct (Gould, 1996; Lemann, 1995). The Stanford-Binet held much to the same basic theoretical conceptualization and naturally, so did Wechsler's W-B. For the most part, as reflected in the structure of his tests, Wechsler never really attempted to develop or advance any particular theoretical viewpoint beyond that of *g*. Because the W-B, and its subsequent iterations, such as the WAIS (1955), WISC (1949), and WPPSI (1967), were oriented toward the needs of practitioners, its user friendly nature gave it tremendous clinical appeal and eventually allowed it to surpass the venerable Stanford-Binet as the preeminent IQ test in the United States. From the very beginning, from the Army Mental Tests to the Stanford-Binet to the W-B and beyond, theory has been a rather minor concern in test development. For whatever reasons, some of which have already been discussed, the problems created by the failure to adhere to modern theory have been and remain largely ignored.

The problems inherent in the lack of a specific theoretical framework to guide assessment are seen in the "Verbal-Performance" dichotomy that continues to underlie the Wechsler Scales. The historical dominance of the Wechsler Scales and the central position granted to them in training programs has resulted in a wide ranging cadre of assessment professionals who have internalized the belief that a verbal/nonverbal dichotomy is one of the best models for understanding cognitive test performance. Yet, the Wechsler verbal/nonverbal model is not based on any empirically derived theory of intelligence and from the perspective of contemporary psychometric theory, this model operationalizes only a small portion of the multiple, empirically supported, broad cognitive abilities known to exist. For example, Carroll (1993a, 1993b) concluded that the Wechsler Verbal scale is an approximate measure of crystallized intelligence (*Gc*), and the Performance scale is an approximate measure of both broad visual perception (*Gv*) and, somewhat less validly, fluid intelligence (*Gf*). In support of Carroll's conclusion, recent research has shown that the Wechsler Performance scale is predominately a measure of *Gv*, and not *Gf* (Elliott, 1994; Kaufman & Kaufman, 1993; McGrew & Flanagan, 1998; Woodcock, 1990). Carroll (1993a) provided a succinct judgment regarding the atheoretical Wechsler Scales when he concluded, "presently available knowledge and technology would permit the development of tests and scales that would be much more adequate for their purpose than the Wechsler Scales" (p. 702).

Not all test developers, however, have treated the issue of theory casually. While some test developers continue to pay little attention to theory, Richard Woodcock took a courageous step in modernizing test technology. For example, the Woodcock-Johnson—Revised: Tests of Cognitive Ability (WJ-R; Woodcock & Johnson, 1989) emerged as perhaps the first test ever to be designed expressly to operationalize current, empirically supportable theory. Built around Horn's extension of Cattell's original *Gf-Gc* theory, Woodcock clearly placed theory at the center of the development and construction of the WJ-R. In other words, he fit a battery of tests to the theory, not theory to the battery. It is interesting to note that although the Cattell-Horn *Gf-Gc* theory has been used loosely as the theoretical basis for a number of tests (e.g., Kaufman Assessment Battery for Children [K-ABC], 1983; Kaufman Adolescent and Adult Intelligence Test [KAIT], 1993; Stanford-Binet: 4th edition [SB:IV], 1986), the *Gf-Gc* conceptions underlying these instruments tend to refer to Cattell's two-factor, fluid and crystallized intelligence dichotomy that is now upward of 50 years old. Modern *Gf-Gc* theory encompasses multiple cognitive abilities and is now known as the Cattell-Horn-Carroll theory, or CHC theory.

Another theoretical model, an information processing one, has also been used recently in test development. Specifically, the PASS model (planning, attention, simultaneous, sequential) forms the basis for the Cognitive Assessment System (CAS; Das & Naglieri, 1997). Although current research has demonstrated that the PASS model is not the best explanation of the factorial structure underlying the CAS (Keith, Kranzler, & Flanagan, 2001; Kranzler & Keith, 1999; Kranzler, Keith, & Flanagan, 2000), the authors' placement of theory as both the central and comprehensive element in the design of their test is noteworthy. Although the trend toward making theory central in test development is admittedly slight, it is nonetheless quite perceptible. The Woodcock-Johnson (3rd edition) (WJ III; Woodcock, McGrew, & Mather, 2001) exemplifies the success attainable by test developers in efforts to incorporate theory from the earliest to the latest stages of test development and at every point in between. We can only hope that this trend will continue to strengthen in the future.

Theory Guides Instruction

Despite the meager theoretical beginnings of IQ tests, very little has stood in the way of IQ (and, indeed, the Wechsler-based IQ) in its unrelenting ascension to a position of unparalleled power and supremacy in intellectual testing, intellectual assessment courses, and decision making. IQ has taken on a life of its own, credited with properties unheard of in any theoretical formulation, and has remained largely unquestioned by applied practitioners and those who train them. Lezak (1995) noted:

> [It] has been suggested that examiners retain IQ scores in their reports to conform to the current requirements of...various other administrative agencies...this is not merely a

case of the tail wagging the dog but an example of how outdated practices may be perpetuated even when their invalidity and potential harmfulness has been demonstrated. Clinicians have a responsibility not only to maintain the highest—and most current—practice standards, but to communicate these to the consumer agencies. If every clinician who understands the problems inherent in labeling people with IQ scores ceased using them, then agencies would soon cease asking for them (p. 691).

It is easy enough to blame the test development industry for their decision to relegate theory to secondary status (e.g., Flanagan et al., 2000), and it is equally easy to blame applied psychologists for failing to realize this serious error and take appropriate action. However, training programs must shoulder much of the blame for perpetuating the practice of psychological assessment in the absence of modern theory and research. As creatures of habit, subject to inertia and innately disdainful of change, it is a natural tendency to adhere closely to the methods and procedures first taught to us. If school psychology training programs are to effect any real paradigmatic change in the practice of intellectual assessment, then recognition of the central role of theory in measurement and interpretation will have to supersede the lock-step, test-kit–focused instruction that is all too common and which perpetuates antiquated, unsupportable, and largely inappropriate assessment practices. If school psychology training programs ceased the teaching of atheoretical methods of assessment and interpretation, then practitioners would soon cease the practice. It has been and continues to be the case that practicing school psychologists spend more time in assessment-related activities than any other activity. Yet training programs have a single course on intellectual assessment that focuses mainly on administration and scoring of the Wechsler Scales (Alfonso, Oakland, La Rocca, & Spanakos, 2000). Is it any wonder that school psychologists and their Full Scale IQ are losing (or have lost) credibility in a number of assessment related arenas (e.g., evaluation of learning disability; see Kavale & Forness, 2000; Siegel, 1999; Stanovich, 1999). When theory plays no role in instruction, practice remains invalid.

Theory Drives Interpretation

Kamphaus et al. (1997) described the history of intelligence test interpretation as being composed of four waves: (a) quantification of a general level, (b) clinical profile analysis, (c) psychometric profile analysis, and (d) applying theory to intelligence test interpretation. The first wave was driven by the basic intentions of the IQ test founders—the classification of individuals into separate groups according to general ability. Because intelligence was being measured via IQ, it was easy enough to establish descriptive ranges of functioning for various types of groups. Early labels for those believed to have inferior abilities included "moron" and "feeble-minded" (Goddard's terms) whereas those at the opposite end of the spectrum were greeted with cries of "genius" and "superior." Even Wechsler (1944) argued that labels should correspond to medical and legal terminology and thus included such terms as "idiot" and "imbecile" in his descriptive schemata. With some refinements, primarily with respect to the pejorative connotations of many of the terms, modern IQ tests retain this type of descriptive and labeling classification system.

Theory played a role in the initial development of classification schemata only to the extent that it was believed that a single, innate quality (i.e., general intelligence) could be measured in all people, and thus grouping individuals was a simple exercise in statistics. The second wave of interpretation, however, made no pretenses to be connected with theory at all. Kamphaus et al. (1997) describe the second wave as clinical profile analysis. It was, perhaps, the popularity of the W-B scales that drove much of this form of interpretation primarily because the organization of the test lent itself readily to partitioning, albeit in ways Wechsler never originally intended. In combination with the second order IQs (VIQ and PIQ), the Wechsler scaled subtest scores seemed to offer the promise of understanding intellectual functioning beyond the simple measurement of general ability. Thus was born the idea of the "profile" based on the assumption that "patterns of high and low subtest scores could presumably reveal diagnostic and psychotherapeutic considerations" (Kamphaus et al., 1997, p. 36). Research by Rapaport, Gill, and Schafer (1945–1946) is largely credited with bringing this practice to practitioners. The intuitive clinical appeal of profile analysis may have seemed, on the surface, to represent a more sophisticated approach to intelligence test interpretation as compared to quantification of general functioning, but it was a flawed approach. The flaws rested in the fact that profile analysis made it easy to fit the obtained profile with the known functional patterns of any individual and did little to inform intervention. Despite these problems, and without theory to guide the process, this form of interpretation remains the dominant interpretive method to date (Kamphaus et al., 1997; Keith, 2000).

The advent of microcomputers and inexpensive statistical software helped to give rise to the third wave of interpretation, known as psychometric profile analysis (Kamphaus et al., 1997). Like the second wave, theory plays virtually no role in helping practitioners make sense of their data. Rather, techniques such as factor analysis, albeit a rigorous scientific method, were applied to an already misdirected interpretive practice. For example, Cohen (1959), among others, showed that interpretation of subtests as reliable measures of a presumed construct was not empirically supportable (nor theoretically, for that matter). In 1974, Bannatyne applied psychometric techniques to reorganize a complete WISC profile in an attempt to improve diagnostic interpretation. Although it did improve reliability somewhat, the problems with validity remained. Kaufman (1979, 1994) tried desperately to dispel the notion that simple application of psychometrics to profile analysis constituted a valid interpretive framework. He combined psychometric approaches with basic notions of measurement theory and common sense techniques (e.g., logical decision making, top-down procedures, supplemental testing as necessary, and so forth) in order to emphasize flexibility in interpretation and bring meaning to an individual's scaled score profile. More recently, it has become increasingly clear that profile analysis, with or without the application of psychometric theory, is largely without empirical support and therefore should be abandoned. In the words of the researchers who brought the fallibility of the third wave of test interpretation to the forefront, "until preponderant and convincing evidence shows otherwise, we are compelled to advise that psychologists just say 'no' to subtest analysis" (McDermott, Fantuzzo, & Glutting, 1990, p. 299).

In order to understand an individual's functioning across multiple, specific cognitive abilities, vis-à-vis current theory and research, it is necessary to adopt measurement and interpretation approaches that are psychometrically defensible—approaches other than subtest or profile analysis. Kamphaus et al. (1997) believe that interpretation must emanate from theory if it is to become a reliable and valid practice. These authors see the next and fourth wave of IQ test interpretation as mainly comprising the need to integrate research and theory. Even during the third wave of interpretation, Kaufman (1979) had noted that interpretive problems with intelligence tests might be traced back to a lack of a specific theoretical base. Kaufman extended this argument further, suggesting that perhaps interpretation could be enhanced if subtests were reorganized not just through exploratory factor analysis methods but into constructs specified by a particular theory. What is key in Kaufman's ideas and those proposed by Kamphaus et al. (1997) with respect to the next wave of interpretation, is that theory must play a central role in guiding the interpretive process and that the need to adhere to this requirement may well necessitate conforming assessment instruments to theory. This premise formed the foundation of the "CHC Cross-Battery" approach, which places theory at the heart of the assessment and interpretation process (Flanagan et al., 2000; Flanagan & Ortiz, 2001; Flanagan, Ortiz, Alfonso, & Mascolo, 2002; McGrew, 1997; McGrew & Flanagan, 1998). Indeed, success in advancing current intellectual assessment practice to a level commensurate with current knowledge and research is likely to emerge only from the application of modern theory. By framing interpretation within the context of theory and by extending Kaufman's notions regarding "intelligent testing," the fourth wave of interpretation may well be best described as "intelligent interpretation" (Flanagan et al., 2000). When theory plays no role in interpretation, conclusions are ambiguous.

Lack of Theory Precludes Validity

Despite Wechsler's dramatic improvement in many ways over the Stanford-Binet, it is unlikely he would have gotten far with the W-B and its subsequent descendants (WAIS, WISC, WPPSI, etc.) had he not validated it through correlation with the Stanford-Binet. After all, Terman had already decreed that the Stanford-Binet was a valid measure of intelligence (quantity and quality of empirical evidence notwithstanding). As such, it was reasoned that any measure that correlated with it must also measure intelligence. Thus, the lineage that established a large portion of the validity for virtually all IQ tests that came afterward essentially began with the Stanford-Binet and the W-B. In almost every case, validity of a new IQ test was and still is established through positive correlation with one or both of these hallmark tests and virtually no attempt is made to provide any independent confirmation for the proposition that the test actually does measure intelligence. One only needs to consider the unfair criticism endured by the WJ-R for having only moderate correlations with the Wechsler as evidence of the influence and power of this heritage. Even when the lack of validity for IQ tests is pointed out, it does little to sway the minds of publishers and users alike. With respect to the WAIS-R, Salvia and Ysseldyke (1995) express it rather succinctly, "no evidence for the validity of the WAIS-R is included in the manual. Instead, the authors argue that (1) the WAIS-R and WAIS overlap considerably in content, (2) there are many studies of the validity of the WAIS, and (3) the WAIS-R will no doubt correlate with other measures of global intelligence as well as the WAIS did" (p. 182–183). We imagine that "other measures of global intelligence," in this context, is no doubt the marketing euphemism for the Stanford-Binet. Nevertheless, the same argument can be applied to the relationship between the WISC-R and the WISC-III where most of the information presented in the WISC-III manual in support of its validity consists of information on the validity of the WISC-R .

Historically, IQ tests have paid only marginal lip service to issues of validity. Apart from the positive intercorrelations among a collection of cognitively based tasks, there appears to be little if any other support for the notion that we are indeed measuring intelligence. The very concept of *g* remains the best example of this issue. On one side, Jensen (1998) argues that *g* is a "ubiquitous superfactor…appropriately called *general mental ability*" (p. 115; italics in original) for which he claims there is a great deal of empirical evidence, although he stated that it is primarily, if not exclusively manifested by "positive intercorrelations among diverse measures of cognitive ability" (p. 115). On the other side, Horn argues that "there is no contrary evidence, no evidence supportive of *g*. The only thing that gets treated as evidence is positive manifold of the intercorrelations among measures of cognitive abilities and a string of correlations with other variables that reflect this positive manifold. But this is evidence that Thurstone showed many years ago does not support a structural hypothesis of *g*, much less a developmental, genetic, neurological, educational, social, anthropological—in general, a construct validity—hypothesis" (CHC listserv, August 1999).

The controversy regarding the existence of a general intelligence construct is only one aspect of concern about the validity of IQ tests. Perhaps a more significant problem has been the failure of test developers to provide validity evidence related to the subordinate constructs. One of the most striking illustrations of this practice can be seen in the Freedom From Distractibility (FFD) factor found on the WISC-III (and originally called the "third factor" on the WISC-R). In short, FFD is an artifact of the factor analysis of a severely limited battery of tests and should not be considered a basic primary factor in mental organization (Carroll, 1993a). As such, the external validity evidence for the FFD index is, not surprisingly, very limited, extremely confusing, and contributes little in the way of explanation or prescription. The replacement of the FFD label with *working memory* in the recent third edition of the WAIS is a welcomed step in the direction toward linking test indicators (i.e., subtests) to well-defined and validated cognitive constructs.

Even the more established Performance IQ (PIQ) factor is not without validity problems. It has become rather common to refer to PIQ as "nonverbal ability" when in fact there is no such thing as "nonverbal" abilities—only abilities that are expressed nonverbally (Kamphaus, 1993; Reynolds & Kamphaus, 1990). As mentioned previously, one of Wechsler's main contributions to IQ test development was the organization of a set of tests, some of which were meant to quantify intelligence through verbal means and some through less verbal means. Wechsler never regarded the Verbal-Performance dichotomy as representing two different types of intelligence. Rather, his intent was to organize the tests to reflect the two different ways (i.e., two different "languages" or channels) through which intelligence could be expressed (Kamphaus, 1993; Reynolds & Kamphaus, 1990; Zachary, 1990). Recent factor analyses, however, have shown that two traditional subtests comprising the PIQ domain (Picture Completion and Picture Arrangement) have significant correlations with tests that measure both visual-spatial skills and acquired knowledge suggesting that both visual processing and crystallized intelligence play a part in determining success on these tasks (Flanagan et al., 2000; McGrew & Flanagan, 1998). The PIQ domain is also confounded by speed of processing (i.e., the Coding subtest) and, most recently, has been confounded further by fluid reasoning (i.e., the Matrix Reasoning subtest on the WAIS-III). In addition, the characterization of PIQ as being "nonverbal" is also misleading because although the underlying subtests do not require any oral or expressive language ability, they do quite often demand a high level of receptive language skill from the examinee in order to comprehend the test's instructions and examiner's expectations. To say that PIQ is a good representation of nonverbal ability is to be ignorant of contemporary theory and of the facts regarding construct validity. When theory plays no role in test development, validity remains elusive.

Theory Guides Intervention

Implicit in the title of school psychologist is the notion of relevance to education and instruction. For what purpose do we justify the use of standardized tests of intelligence in the school setting if not for informing the development of effective remedial strategies? Even as early as 1922, Lippman (as cited in Gould, 1996) recognized the problems with mental testing when he wrote:

> The danger of the intelligence tests is that in a wholesale system of education, the less sophisticated or the more prejudiced will stop when they have classified and forget that their duty is to educate. They will grade the retarded child instead of fighting the causes of his backwardness (p. 209–210).

The Full Scale IQ (FSIQ) that is included in nearly every psychoeducational evaluation report ever written reveals little in the way of diagnostic meaningfulness and yields virtually no information relevant for the purpose of intervention planning. Given that a great majority of school psychologists' time is spent in assessment, particularly with respect to learning disabilities, the continued use of global scores only reinforces their lack of utility. According to Kaufman (1990), "the individual tested makes an unspoken plea to the examiner not to summarize his or her intelligence in a single, cold, number; the goal...should be to respond to that plea by identifying hypothesized strengths and weaknesses that extend well beyond the limited information provided by FSIQ, and that will conceivably lead to practical recommendations that help answer the referral questions" (p. 422). Kaufman's comments were echoed by Lezak (1995) who, when discussing the Wechsler FSIQ, stated that,

> average scores on a WISC battery provide just about as much information as do averaged scores on a school report card. There is no question about the performance of students with a four-point average: they can only have had an A in each subject. Nor is there any question about individual grades obtained by students with a zero grade point average. Excluding the extremes, however, it is impossible to predict specific disabilities and areas of cognitive competency or dysfunction from the averaged ability test scores (p. 691).

Solid links to intervention are unlikely to ever spring spontaneously from global scores generated with largely atheoretical tests. The limited relevance of FSIQ to the diagnosis of many conditions as well as to intervention has been highlighted by recent research that investigated the relations between *g* and specific cognitive abilities and general and specific reading achievement (e.g., Flanagan, 2000; McGrew, Flanagan, Keith, & Vanderwood, 1997; Keith, 1999). It was found that auditory processing (*Ga*) abilities (among others) were strongly related to reading above and beyond the explanation provided by *g*. Although the effect of *g* was larger than that for *Ga*, recent research has shown that intervention directed at specific *Ga* abilities (e.g., phonetic coding) improves reading performance (e.g., Felton & Pepper, 1995; McGuiness, McGuiness, and Donohue, 1995; Wagner, Torgesen, & Rashotte, 1994). Conversely, attempts to modify general intellectual ability have not resulted in long-standing changes (Gustafsson & Undheim, 1996), with the available research suggesting that specific abilities may be most amenable to modification (Carroll, 1993a). Thus, the probability of developing successful interventions lies not at the apex of the hierarchy of cognitive abilities (i.e., *g*) but at lower levels (see Flanagan et al., 2000; Flanagan et al., 2002; Kaufman, 1994).

In all fairness, IQ tests were developed precisely for the purpose of classification, not intervention or problem solving. Thus, it seems hardly fair to criticize them for doing exactly what they were originally intended to do. Recall, however, that Binet sought to identify individuals who might benefit from some form of special or remedial education, solely on the basis that they were performing quite poorly in the classroom compared to their age or grade level peers. Ability tests, at their earliest inception were indeed meant to have intervention links and designed to have practical use in solving real world (school and classroom) problems. But when Binet's scales were adapted as a tool for evaluating intelligence only, apart from any other concern, the hope of creating and maintaining a bridge to treatment or intervention planning was all but lost. Yet, the advent of school psychology as a modern profession in the early 1970s appears to have brought us back full circle to the very predicament Binet faced. Use of IQ tests in the school setting most often revolves around the need to identify and diagnose disability specifically for the purpose of providing special education services. Whereas today's federal and state legislative codes mandate the need to identify a disability as part of the condition for eligibility for services, Binet, of course, had no such legal constraints. However, because current regulations call for the generation of data that will assist in developing an appropriate instructional program for any individual who is identified as being disabled and otherwise qualified to receive special education services, it seems clear that the need to link testing with intervention has returned full force.

The key to linking assessment with treatment must therefore lie in recognition of the fact that intervention, not classification, is the main focus of evaluation. If assessment begins with the notion that what is being done is simply quantifying an ability, then that is all that will be done. Assessment should begin with deliberate efforts to gather relevant information for the purpose of developing appropriate and effective instructional strategies that will assist in educating the individual. This can happen readily when theory remains central to the process and when it is combined with empirical research in a systematic way that highlights the relationship between ability constructs and academic skills. An innovative example of the manner in which theory and research can be integrated in order to produce information that guides intervention is seen in the comprehensive framework for learning disability (LD) determination put forth by Flanagan et al. (2002). By taking the latest LD research and combining it with theory driven, cross-battery assessment methods within the context of a systematic diagnostic process, these authors have operationalized learning disability in a way that is likely to improve the reliability of the diagnosis and yield data that link the disability to specific underlying cognitive processing deficits. Knowledge of the root cause of a learning disability is part and parcel of the process of developing instructional methods to deal with it (see Das, Naglieri, & Kirby (1994) and Naglieri (1997) for additional examples of linking theory to intervention). Although the practice of IQ testing has never been much concerned with intervention, there is no reason why it cannot be a more salient component of the process of assessment. When theory plays no role in the assessment-intervention link, the development of appropriate and effective instructional strategies is difficult.

Theory is Transdisciplinary

For too long the IQ has been the sole province of the applied psychologist and has even been encoded into legal statutes to keep its derivation and assignment of meaning well within the scope of trained practitioners of psychology. We have come to believe that intelligence, and all constructs which relate to it, belong solely to the field of mental testing as if it were a pure and quantifiable entity. Never mind that cognition and language tend to be so interrelated that it is, for example, virtually impossible to distinguish between a severe language delay and mental retardation in a 5-year-old child. Never mind that one of the three core academic subjects, arithmetic, appears on both IQ and achievement tests. Never mind that common definitions of learning disability rely heavily on the concept of global ability and its hypothesized relationship to academic skills. Intelligence is not an isolated construct. It does not exist independent or irrespective of other constructs, such as language or academic achievement. If intellectual assessment is to remain a vanguard in the assessment repertoire of the applied school psychologist, then the arrogance of the IQ test mentality must be relinquished.

The idea that intellectual assessment rarely occurs in a territorial vacuum is evident in the concepts of ability and achievement. Despite the distinctions drawn between these concepts on a daily basis in the schools, surprisingly, there is no ability-achievement dichotomy recognized or supported in the cognitive psychology literature. The difference between ability and achievement appears to be primarily a verbal, not theoretical, one. For example, both Carroll (1993a) and Horn (1991) include reading and writing (*Grw*) and quantitative knowledge (*Gq*) ability constructs in their theoretical formulations of intelligence and the structure of cognitive abilities. These two abilities are routinely found on achievement tests and many commonly used intelligence tests either include measures of reading/writing (*Grw*) and math (*Gq*) or involve these "achievement-like" abilities. According to prominent theorists (e.g., Carroll, 1993a; Horn, 1988), the ability-achievement distinction is primarily semantic; that is, measures of cognitive abilities are every bit as much measures of achievement as measures of achievement are measures of cognitive abilities. Rather than being mutually exclusive, cognitive and academic abilities can be thought of as lying on a continuum with those abilities that are more dependent on and tend to develop largely as a function of formal education and direct learning and instruction at one end (e.g., *Grw*, *Gq*) and abilities that are less dependent on and tend to develop less as a function of formal education and direct learning and instruction at the other end (e.g., Processing Speed [*Gs*]). Thus, "abilities are achievements from past learning just as they are at the same time aptitudes for future learning. Most abilities develop from extensive experience across learning history. . . . And ability differences are influenced by genetic factors as well as by experience" (Snow, 1994, p. 4). Others have been more to the point in their views on the relation between IQ and achievement. According to Lemann (1995) in reference to an article that appeared in *The Scientific Monthly*:

> Without mentioning the SAT specifically, the article treated academic-aptitude and IQ tests as closely related—which in fact, they were and still are. IQ tests have always heavily stressed reading comprehension and vocabulary items like analogies and antonyms, and so does the verbal section for the SAT. Back in the early days Carl Brigham published a scale for converting intelligence test scores to SAT scores. Paul Diederich, a contemporary of Henry Chauncey's [first president of ETS] who was for decades a researcher at ETS, expresses a view common in the field: "IQ tests are reading comprehension and vocabulary doctored up to look like reasoning. To change the SAT to an IQ you'd simply divide the score by an age measure. Basically they're the same thing" (p. 86).

If something like vocabulary, for example, is a part of IQ tests, part of achievement tests, part of language tests, and part of classroom instruction, it would seem that communication regarding the concept and meaning of vocabulary among the various disciplines would be straightforward. Unfortunately, this is rarely the case. Although there are many ability constructs that overlap the various fields involved in studying one or another aspect of human cognitive functioning, each discipline has chosen to use and define the very same construct in very different ways, thereby complicating matters of communication. For example, vocabulary on the WISC-III for the school psychologist might be interpreted as a measure of lexical knowledge—a narrow ability subsumed by Crystallized Intelligence (*Gc*). For the speech language specialist, vocabulary from the Peabody Picture Vocabulary Test (Dunn, Dunn, & Williams, 1997) is seen as a measure of receptive language ability. And for the educational specialist, vocabulary from the Wide Range Achievement Test (Wilkinson, 1993) is viewed as a measure of reading ability. If there is to be any benefit in working collaboratively during the assessment and evaluation process, school psychologists will need to recognize the substantial degree of construct overlap that exists with other fields and vice versa. Moreover, if the various professionals involved in assessment can use and apply a theory that specifies the relationship between the various shared constructs, the process of measurement and interpretation will likely become significantly more complementary. The current CHC theoretical formulation represents one such viable choice because it provides not only a practical and empirically supported taxonomic model from which to understand and interpret human cognitive, academic, and language abilities but also provides a common set of names or terms for the components of the theory (i.e., a standard nomenclature) (see Carroll, 1997; Flanagan et al., 2000; Flanagan & Ortiz, 2001; Flanagan et al., 2002; Kaufman, 2000; McGrew & Flanagan, 1998). Because of the comprehensiveness of CHC theory, it is equally applicable to practitioners who study and assess cognitive, academic, and language abilities. Thus, adoption of the established CHC theoretical nomenclature would increase the precision in communication among practitioners and researchers and provide a useful foundation whereupon a nonproprietary and shared "knowledge base [could] be accumulated" (Reynolds & Lakin, 1987). When theory plays no role in communication among professionals across disciplines, assessment is territorial.

In summary, it has been noted that an unfortunate by-product of the Wechsler Scales' success is that it has served to constrain practice and in many respects limit growth and progress. The staying power of its antiquated taxonomy—in particular the verbal/performance dichotomy—is at variance with modern taxonomies that are more supported, comprehensive, and evolving. "The premature 'hardening of the taxonomy categories' can result in a deformation of the scientific process through the 'hermetically sealing of the boundaries of knowledge'" (Prentky, 1994, p. 507; cited in Flanagan et al., 2000). It also seals the boundaries between disciplines. Continued reliance on outdated, static and invalid taxonomies will no doubt eventually seal school psychology in the prison of our IQ tests.

BEST PRACTICES IN INTELLECTUAL ASSESSMENT

Up to this point we have attempted, with all the subtlety of a sledge hammer, to reinforce the notion that theory is quite literally "everything" when it comes to intellectual assessment and more specifically, the measurement of human cognitive abilities. Although at times we may have seemed to favor one theory over another, in truth it matters little as to what theory is utilized as long as it is current, empirically supported, and provides the necessary specifications for operationalizing its constructs in the course of practical, school-based or clinical assessment. The application of theory, however, cannot occur in a haphazard way. Successful and effective use of theory must be accomplished logically and systematically within the context of a comprehensive framework that guides each step in the assessment process and that specifies the manner in which theory is integrated. Poorly conducted assessment even with theory at the center is no better than methodically appropriate assessment conducted in the absence of theory. Only when sound assessment practices are augmented and guided by theory is the evaluation process enhanced significantly. It is in this spirit that we offer a proposal for an assessment and interpretation framework wherein theory is at the core of all activities.

The flow chart illustrated in Figure 1 depicts the general steps within the framework. Each step was developed in direct response to the specific problems described previously and that are inherent in any assessment conducted from an atheoretical or poorly supported theoretical basis. As will become evident, issues related to measurement, validity, interpretation, and intervention are all accommodated within the framework, precisely because theory is applied.

Step 1: Decide Whether Standardized Tests are Appropriate

The very act of deciding whether or not to use standardized tests of intelligence or cognitive ability represents a crucial step in intellectual assessment. Because of their convenience and efficiency, standardized tests represent perhaps the most common instruments and methods in cognitive evaluations. Nevertheless, adoption of these tests for evaluation purposes must be made carefully because administration of a standardized test to any individual is not a benign action. The decision as to the appropriateness or suitability of standardized tests for any given evaluation should be based on several broad criteria including the intended purpose for evaluation and specific referral concerns. Moreover, careful evaluation of individual case history information (e.g., educational records and authentic measures of achievement, medical records), consideration and appraisal of data from other relevant sources (e.g., parents, siblings, teachers, friends, employers), and reframing of an individual's difficulties within the context of their unique educational, cultural, or linguistic experiences should also enter into the decision

Figure 1. Framework for best practices in intellectual assessment

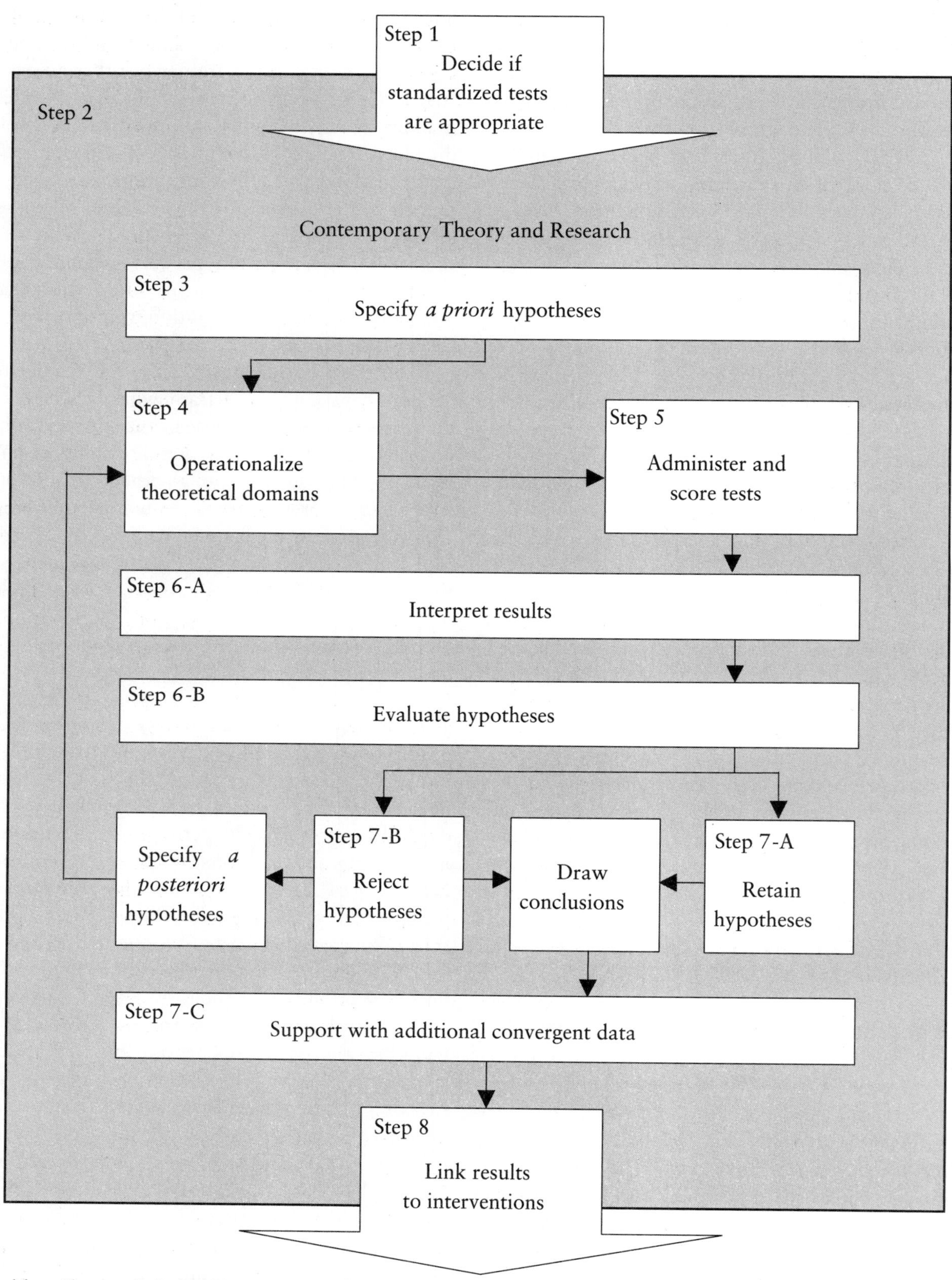

Adapted from Flanagan & Ortiz, 2001.

equation. There are potentially many instances where the use of standardized instruments may be unnecessary, inappropriate, or questionable at best. Examples include assessment of individuals with perceptual disabilities, motor impairments, cultural or linguistic differences, and so forth.

Step 2: Apply Contemporary Theory and Research

Utilization of theory occurs at the outset of assessment. If school psychologists are to conduct assessment in a way that facilitates accurate measurement and meaningful interpretation, then it will come from a substantial knowledge base related to a modern and valid theory of intelligence. The process of assessment is guided by theory through knowledge or understanding of (a) the literature on the relations between cognitive abilities specified by the theory and specific academic and occupational outcomes, (b) the principles and philosophies that underlie the theoretical approach to assessing cognitive functioning, and (c) the network of validity evidence that exists in support of the structure and nature of abilities within the theory. In the early stages of assessment, this research knowledge base is crucial to understanding the specification of and relationships among the various constructs of interest. The correspondence between deficits in academic skills or performance and suspected underlying cognitive impairments is perhaps one of the more common issues informed by theory because it relates to learning disabilities assessment—the most common reason for assessment encountered by school psychologists. The ability to relate constructs to one another in ways predicted by actual theory and supported by empirical findings, provides a defensible basis for the formation and subsequent testing of *a priori* hypotheses related to the original referral concerns.

Step 3: Specify A Priori Hypotheses

Gathering data for the purpose of psychological evaluation is systematic when the data are used to evaluate *a priori* hypotheses. Use of an *a priori* approach "forces consideration of research and theory because the clinician is operating on the basis of research and theory when the hypothesis is drawn" (Kamphaus, 1993, p. 167). When case history data and current information are combined with knowledge of theory and research (or even information from other fields such as the literature on learning disabilities), defensible connections between various cognitive constructs can be made (e.g., between academic achievement and cognitive ability). For example, in the case of reading problems, a theoretically established research knowledge base can assist in identifying the most salient cognitive abilities related to reading achievement (e.g., phonological processes, working memory, naming facility or rapid automatic naming, lexical knowledge). Research and theory guide the development of assumptions that, in this situation, relate and connect particular cognitive constructs to manifest reading difficulties. Specification of this relationship provides both the logical target for evaluation and the basis for constructing hypotheses to test the expected predictions (see Flanagan & Ortiz, 2001).

Inferences regarding the relationships between various cognitive constructs set the stage for testing by allowing and guiding the creation of theoretically based predictions. The gathering of standardized test data not only allows for a test of these relationships but also relationships with respect to performance in directions that may be known or implied. However, there is a tendency in the development of hypotheses to couch them in terms of dysfunction or deficiency. Although we may suspect that an individual is disabled, the use of an hypothesis that predicts poor performance in one or more cognitive domains as a consequence or cause of a deficit in some other ability area (e.g., reading) too often leads to confirmatory bias. Confirmatory bias occurs whenever an evaluator collects data in an effort to support some preconception regarding the expected pattern of performance and is thus predisposed to see only those patterns in the data which support the preconception (Sandoval, 1998). To avoid this type of bias in assessment, hypotheses should be stated in null form and tested accordingly. For example, irrespective of any suspicions or other evidence regarding dysfunction, an individual's performance on any given standardized test should be predicted to fall *within normal limits*. Thus, unless and until the data show convincingly otherwise, individuals being tested should be accorded the very tangible benefits that accompany assumptions of normal functioning (see Flanagan & Ortiz (2001) and Flanagan et al. (2002) for a complete description of an hypothesis-driven approach to assessment and interpretation).

Step 4: Operationalize Theoretical Domains

In the previous step, theory provided a foundation for specifying relationships among and between constructs that could be readily tested via an hypothesis-driven approach. In this step, theory serves to guide the manner in which the specified constructs are operationalized in assessment. Historically, the test-kit mentality entrenched in the field of school psychology has resulted in the use of tests that were either atheoretical or based on outdated or vague theoretical notions. It is at this point that intellectual assessment must move in some way toward instruments or procedures that bring modern theory to the forefront of measurement.

One way in which Step 4 can be accomplished is through the use of an instrument that was developed specifically to operationalize the guiding theory selected at the outset (i.e., in Step 2). Unfortunately, the bleak history of test development with respect to theoretical issues and its over-reliance on rather nebulous and largely unsupported conceptions of *g* will make this step difficult to carry out unless the practitioner selects either CHC or PASS theory. To date, only the WJ III operationalizes CHC theory well and only the CAS purports to operationalize PASS theory. With the lack of available theory-based tests notwithstanding, these two instruments represent viable options for use in assessment. Unlike the new CAS, however, the WJ III is accompanied by a solid body of research. Its predecessor, the WJ-R, has been in use for over a decade and its underlying cognitive ability constructs, along with their counterparts on the WJ III, have been well validated. Although no battery of tests provides measurement of every construct specified by its base theory, and even though some constructs may not be well represented, use of standardized tests that are based on a guiding paradigm for assessment nonetheless represents a significant advance in the science of assessment of cognitive abilities.

An alternative to using a specific theory-based test in order to fulfill the requirements of Step 4 is the CHC Cross-Battery approach (Flanagan & Ortiz, 2001; Flanagan et al., 2002; Flanagan et al. 2000; McGrew & Flanagan, 1998). In recognition of the virtual lack of theoretically based tests, these authors developed a method for "crossing" batteries that is not limited by the parameters of any single test kit or tool. The need to provide adequate representation of the theoretical constructs relevant to the referral is an area where CHC Cross-Battery methods display particular merit. The loose theoretical heritage of most modern day tests creates a situation where use of a single battery very often fails to measure one or more constructs central to the need for assessment. By classifying tests in accordance with CHC theory, and by utilizing the extensive and comprehensive literature base that supports its development, the CHC Cross-Battery approach provides an innovative and viable method for ensuring that appropriate and sufficient data are collected with respect to the constructs of interest, in an efficient and defensible manner. The psychometric rigor of the approach, combined with the integration of modern intelligence theory creates a reasonable foundation for both psychological measurement and interpretation.

Irrespective of the method used to operationalize the theory selected to guide the assessment process, it is imperative that constructs be adequately represented with respect to construct validation principles (e.g., Messick, 1995). When such measurement is accomplished, interpretation of data is greatly facilitated and the derivation of meaningful conclusions is enhanced (Flanagan & Ortiz, 2001).

Step 5: Administer and Score Tests

Once Step 4 has been accomplished, the next step simply involves administration of the selected battery or cross-battery and scoring it in accordance with the specifications provided by the publishers of the tests or authors of the approach. Although it may seem that Step 5 is obvious, its delineation as a concrete step helps to reinforce the notion that it is a necessary component of the overall assessment process and that the generation of data is for the purpose of testing hypotheses. Application of theory in assessment represents an integrative, and as will be discussed, possibly recursive effort. In the initial phase of assessment, Step 5 activities relate to testing of the initial or *a priori* hypotheses specified in Step 3, but in subsequent phases of assessment, Step 5 may relate to testing of *a posteriori* hypotheses that emanate from Step 7. The process of assessment may become iterative and recursive as a function of the findings and the patterns in the data that either support or fail to support initial hypotheses. When it becomes necessary to conduct further testing, either to clarify ambiguous findings or investigate functioning more in depth or in alternate areas, it would not be unusual for administration and scoring to be accomplished more than once. Although administration and scoring of a selected battery of tests typically represents the final step in the assessment process, as far as standardized testing is concerned, more often than not it is necessary to gather additional data following evaluation of initial findings. Because follow-up testing is not common practice, diagnostic and placement decisions are often made in the absence of conclusive findings.

Step 6: Interpret Results and Evaluate Hypotheses

Step 6 is composed of two major interpretive activities: psychometric and theoretical interpretation of results and evaluation of hypotheses. Psychometric interpretation of test results forms Step 6-A (see Figure 1), and it is at this point where evaluation of numerical data collected within the context of the theory-guided assessment is conducted. Although each test battery provides its own system and criteria for evaluating the meaning of results, especially with regard to classification or descriptions of performance, it is crucial that school psychologists not lose sight of the importance of evaluating performance against a normative standard. Test batteries have, of course, their norms readily available for making comparisons based on real, normal distributions corresponding to age or grade. The CHC Cross-Battery assessment approach utilizes the properties of the normal probability curve for making these evaluative judgments in the absence of a true norm group. In either case, the utility of the normal distribution is evident because it "has very practical applications for comparing and evaluating psychological data in that the position of any test score on a standard deviation unit scale, in itself, defines the proportion of people taking the test who will obtain scores above or below a given score" (Lezak, 1976, p. 123). Theoretical interpretation of results involves applying the validation research that specifies the relations between cognitive and academic abilities as well as other research pertinent to the referral (from the theoretical and research knowledge base that comprises Step 2).

Step 6-B in Figure 1, evaluation of hypotheses, actually represents an activity that is distinct but related to the interpretation of results conducted in Step 6-A. In order to test *a priori* hypotheses, a determination must be made as to whether the collected data are in line with performance expected to be within normal limits. Use of normative standards for evaluating these expectations is the only appropriate metric. Based on the evaluative judgments derived from normative comparisons completed in Step 6-A, school psychologists should decide whether the data suggest that the null hypothesis is supported, and should therefore be retained, or whether the data suggest that the null hypothesis is not supported, and should be rejected in favor of an alternative hypothesis. When the data are not seen to fall clearly and convincingly outside of normal limits, it must be concluded that performance is, as expected, within normal limits. When the data are seen to fall clearly and convincingly outside the normal range of functioning, it can be concluded that performance is not, as expected, within normal limits. The fact that performance may fall outside and below the normal range of functioning cannot, however, be used as *prima facie* evidence of dysfunction. Rather, the hypothesis-driven approach leads only to the conclusion that performance is not within normal limits. The reasons for this performance need to be clearly articulated within the context of theory and relevant research. The presence of a disability is but one possible reason out of many (e.g., motivation, attitude, anxiety, poor instruction, cultural and linguistic factors) for why the patterns observed in the data appear the way they do. Support for any hypothesis related to deficient performance must be established on the basis of convergent data culled from a wide variety of sources and should never be based solely on the results of standardized testing.

Step 7: Draw Conclusions or Specify *A Posteriori* Hypotheses

When assessment data are interpreted and evaluated according to theoretically specified *a priori* hypotheses, there are two broad possibilities with respect to the results. First, it is possible that functioning in all areas operationalized and measured according to theory fall within normal limits or higher, *as expected* (Step 7-A). If the theoretical constructs were appropriately constructed and adequately represented, then it can be reasonably concluded that there are no measured impairments in functioning and that performance is within normal limits. This is not to say, however, that no disability exists. Rather, it is only an indication that standardized test data simply do not provide support to conclude that performance is deficient in any way. Deficient performance may, of course, be established through other means and other types of data that do in fact converge to support particular conclusions (Step 7-C). With respect to inferences that may be drawn from standardized test data in this case, the only valid conclusions that can be made are that the standardized test data support hypotheses related to normal functioning.

Evaluation of standardized test data in isolation is problematic because there is no logical reason to assume that only these type of data will provide relevant information upon which to base conclusions. Moreover, theory-driven assessment is not solely dependent on findings generated from the use of tests. Performance along any process or ability dimension of theory-driven assessment may well be evaluated and established through the collection and evaluation of any available data (Step 7-C). Standardized test data represent but one element of information that should be integrated with other data in order to understand and evaluate performance as it relates to both direct observations and evaluation of hypotheses regarding functioning. If indeed there are sufficient other data that provide a clear convergence toward substantiating conclusions about performance and these data are consistent with standardized test data that reveal normal functioning, there would be little reason to engage in any further assessment or specification of *a posteriori* hypotheses.

The second, and perhaps more probable, outcome from assessment is that one or more areas of functioning are found to be outside of and below normal limits. This outcome is likely because the referral process itself is selective and the decisions to engage in assessments are generally based on preliminary evidence of problematic performance. Other than efforts directed at identifying gifted or talented individuals, assessment activities usually revolve around determinations regarding dysfunction or disability. When the data suggest that performance cannot be construed as average or within normal limits, then the null hypothesis is rejected and the practitioner may either draw conclusions and support them with additional convergent data or specify *a posteriori* hypotheses (discussed next). When the data provide contradictory, ambiguous, or insufficient evidence upon which to base such evaluative decisions, the process of theory guided assessment becomes iterative due to the need for additional assessment.

In cases where it is deemed necessary to investigate anomalous or ambiguous findings, practitioners need not abandon the hypothesis-driven approach but rather should continue its use in the specification of *a posteriori* hypotheses (Step 7-B). Perhaps the most common situation where the need for additional testing may arise occurs when there is a significant difference between two measures of a particular cognitive ability that fail to converge as might be predicted or expected according to theory, research, and the construct validation literature (e.g., Messick, 1995). On occasion, and for a wide variety of reasons (differences in narrow ability performance, differences in task demands, administration influences, cultural or linguistic factors, chance, error, and so forth), convergence may not be found and there may in fact be an unexpected significant difference between scores. Nonconvergence of indicators (i.e., subtests) that are expected to converge is virtually impossible to interpret in the absence of the administration of additional tests (Flanagan & Ortiz, 2001).

Supplemental testing, just as with initial testing, is guided by the specification and testing of hypotheses. These *a posteriori* hypotheses are constructed in the same manner as the *a priori* hypotheses. That is, they are based on assumptions of normalcy and, in order to test these hypotheses, it is necessary to return to Step 4 in the assessment process where operationalization of the relevant theoretical domains is conducted a second time. The assessment process proceeds much the same as before, returning eventually to Step 7. This iteration in assessment assists in "narrow[ing] down the possibilities" or reasons for the existence of a particular finding (Kamphaus, 1993, p. 166) and can be continued until all hypotheses are properly evaluated and valid conclusions may be drawn. At this point in the assessment process, the meaningfulness of the conclusions drawn from standardized test data can only be realized fully when such conclusions are supported with additional convergent data (see Step 7-C in Figure 1). In other words, evaluation of data and the process of drawing conclusions represent an integrative effort that is accomplished via examination of all available data that extends, in many cases, well beyond standardized test data.

Step 8: Link Results to Intervention

The process of theory-driven assessment does not require adherence to any particular report format or template. Nevertheless, the application of theory will modify the manner in which results are interpreted and translated into recommendations for interventions primarily because the predictable nature of the relationships among and between constructs now represents a central component in establishing greater validity for conclusions (see Flanagan & Ortiz (2001) and Flanagan et al. (2002) for case study examples). Whatever the selected guiding theory, the report should include at a minimum a clear explanation of the basis for assessment, the reasons why specific constructs may have been evaluated and others not, the relationship between substantiated deficits in cognitive ability and any presenting or referral concerns or manifest skill deficits (e.g., academic functioning). More importantly, however, because the application of modern theory provides a defensible platform for both measurement and interpretation, stronger statements regarding causal links and avenues for appropriate remediation and logical intervention can be made (e.g., Mather, 1991).

The greater precision achieved in measuring constructs inherent in theory-driven assessment as well as the specification of empirically supported relationships between and among constructs lends itself readily to the development of recommendations for intervention. For example, when a weakness in an academic skill is identified, it can probably be construed according to theory and research as being reasonably due to the presence of a weakness in a related area of cognitive ability. Remedial instruction can therefore either target the area of weakness in efforts to improve functioning both directly (at the academic skill level) and indirectly (at the ability level) or provide strategies that capitalize on any strengths that may have been identified, or both. It is important to remember that knowledge regarding the probable causes of poor performance is half the battle in guiding and informing the development of appropriate instructional modifications. Without an understanding of probable causes, planning remedial strategies is difficult. For example, remedial instruction for a young child with reading difficulties presumably caused by poor instruction and attendance will likely differ from instructional strategies developed for a child with reading difficulties that are presumably caused by phonetic coding and working memory deficits.

SUMMARY

There is perhaps no other area of school psychology that has changed as little as that of intellectual assessment, and the time has come for more significant strides in improving the practices of the past. If indeed the paradigm shift toward problem solving as the foundation for school psychology service delivery is to be realized fully within the context of intellectual assessment, then the pace will need to quicken. Current practices in intellectual assessment have long roots and a grand history, but progress seems almost measurable in geological units. We have discussed many of the diverse reasons that account for such slow incremental change in intellectual assessment, including the role of tests in professional identity, neglect of theoretical issues in guiding test construction and interpretation, stagnation of instruction in training programs, perpetuation of clinical lore and other atheoretical interpretive methods, and failure to link assessment to intervention and problem solving activities in the schools. Each of these will require attention. However, foremost among them will be the requisite attention that must be paid to placing theory at the center of all intellectual assessment activities. As has been noted, the lack of theory to guide practice is unacceptable given the impressive advancements that have been made in theories of intelligence and the structure of human cognitive abilities. Theory is required, not merely because it maintains the sanctity of the scientific process, but because it provides the basis for accomplishing every aspect of intellectual assessment that is crucial to the practice of school psychology. Theory guides instruction, test selection, and interpretation as well as intervention and problem solving. Theory is transdisciplinary. Lack of theory precludes validity. Yet, theory is not enough. Best practices in intellectual assessment will not emanate from the development or application of a great new theory of intelligence any more than it will result from publication of a great new "IQ" test. Best practices in intellectual assessment (as with any type of assessment) will come from the application and use of a systematic, comprehensive assessment and interpretation framework that integrates the various issues we have highlighted in this chapter. School psychology may have been born in the prison of the IQ test, but the cell door has been unlocked. The time has come for us, as a profession, to emerge from the confines of the prison cell's dark and decrepit walls into the light of a new era.

REFERENCES

Alfonso, V. C., Oakland, T. D., LaRocca, R., & Spanakos, A. (2000). The course on individual cognitive assessment. *School Psychology Review, 29*, 52–64.

Bannatyne, A. (1974). Diagnosis: A note on recategorization of the WISC scaled scores. *Journal of Learning Disabilities, 7*, 272–274.

Carroll, J. B. (1993a). *Human cognitive abilities: A survey of factor-analytic studies*. New York: Cambridge University Press.

Carroll, J. B. (1993b). What abilities are measured by the WISC-III? *Journal of Psychoeducational Assessment*, 134–143.

Carroll, J. B. (1997). The three-stratum theory of cognitive abilities. In D. P. Flanagan, J. L. Genshaft, & P. L. Harrison (Eds.), *Contemporary intellectual assessment: Theories, tests, and issues* (pp. 122–130). New York: Guilford.

Cohen, J. (1959). The factorial structure of the WISC at ages 7-7, 10-6, and 13-6. *Journal of Consulting Psychology, 23*, 285–299.

Das, J. P., & Naglieri, J. A. (1997). *Cognitive Assessment System*. Itasca, IL: Riverside.

Das, J. P., Naglieri, J. A., & Kirby, J. R. (1994). *Assessment of cognitive processes: The PASS theory of intelligence*. Needham Heights, MA: Allyn & Bacon.

Dunn, L. M., Dunn, L. M., & Williams, T. K. (1997). *Peabody Picture Vocabulary Test* (3rd ed.). Circle Pines, MN: American Guidance Service.

Elliott, C. D. (1994, April). The measurement of fluid intelligence: Comparison of the Wechsler scales with the DAS and the KAIT. Paper presented at the annual meeting of the National Association of School Psychologists, Seattle, WA.

Fagan, T. K., & Wise, P. (2000). *School Psychology: Past, present, and future* (2nd ed.). Bethesda, MD: National Association of School Psychologists.

Felton, R. H., & Pepper, P. P. (1995). Early identification and intervention of phonological deficits in kindergarten and early elementary children at risk for reading disability. *School Psychology Review, 24*, 405–414.

Flanagan, D. P. (2000). Wechlser-based CHC cross-battery assessment and reading achievement: Strengthening the validity of interpretations drawn from Wechsler test scores. *School Psychology Quarterly, 15*, 295-229.

Flanagan, D. P., Andrews, T. J., & Genshaft, J. L. (1997). The functional utility of intelligence tests with special education populations. In D. P. Flanagan, J. L. Genshaft, & P. L. Harrison (Eds.), *Contemporary intellectual assessment: Theories, tests, and issues*. New York: Guilford.

Flanagan, D. P., McGrew, K. S., & Ortiz, S. O. (2000). *The Wechsler intelligence scales and* Gf-Gc *theory: A contemporary approach to interpretation*. Boston: Allyn & Bacon.

Flanagan, D. P. & Ortiz, S. O. (2001). *Essentials of cross-battery assessment*. New York: John Wiley.

Flanagan, D. P., Ortiz, S. O., Alfonso, V. C., & Mascolo, J. (2002). *The achievement test desk reference (ATDR): Comprehensive assessment and learning disability*. Boston: Allyn & Bacon.

Gould, S. J. (1996). *The mismeasure of man*. New York W. W. Norton.

Gustaffson, J. E., & Undheim, J. O. (1996). Individual differences in cognitive functions. In D. C. Berliner & R. C. Cabfee (Eds.), *Handbook of educational psychology* (pp. 186–242). New York: Macmillian.

Horn, J. L. (1988). Thinking about human abilities. In J. R. Nesselroade, & R. B. Cattell (Eds.), *Handbook of multivariate psychology* (Rev. ed., pp. 645–685). New York: Academic.

Horn, J. L. (1991). Measurement of intellectual capabilities: A review of theory. In K. S. McGrew, J. K. Werder, & R. W. Woodcock, *Woodcock-Johnson Technical Manual* (pp. 197–232). Itasca, IL: Riverside.

Horn, J. L. (1999). CHC listserv.

Jensen, A. R. (1998). *The g factor: The science of mental ability*. Westport, CT: Praeger.

Kamphaus, R. W. (1993). *Clinical assessment of children's intelligence*. Boston: Allyn and Bacon.

Kamphaus, R. W., Petoskey, M. D., & Morgan, A. W. (1997). A history of test intelligence interpretation. In D. P. Flanagan, J. L. Genshaft, & P. L. Harrison (Eds.), *Contemporary intellectual assessment: Theories, tests, and issues* (pp. 32–51). New York: Guilford.

Kaufman, A. S. (1979). *Intelligent testing with the WISC-R*. New York: John Wiley.

Kaufman, A. S. (1990). *Assessing adolescent and adult intelligence*. Boston: Allyn and Bacon.

Kaufman, A. S. (1994). *Intelligent testing with the WISC-III*. New York: John Wiley.

Kaufman, A. S. (2000). Foreword. In D. P. Flanagan, K. S. McGrew, & S. O. Ortiz (eds.), *The Wechsler intelligence scales and Gf-Gc theory: A contemporary approach to interpretation*. Boston: Allyn & Bacon.

Kaufman, A. S., & Kaufman, N. L. (1993). *The Kaufman Adolescent and Adult Intelligence Test*. Circle Pines, MN: American Guidance Service.

Kaufman, A. S., & Lichtenberger, E. O. (1999). *Essentials of WAIS-III assessment*. New York: John Wiley.

Kavale, K. A., & Forness, S. R. (2000). What definitions of learning disability say and don't say: A critical analysis. *Journal of Learning Disabilities*, *33*(3), 239–256.

Keith, T. Z. (1999). Effects of general and specific abilities on student achievement: Similarities and differences across ethnic groups. *School Psychology Quarterly, 14,* 239–262.

Keith, T. Z. (2000). Research methods for profile analysis: Introduction to the special issue. *School Psychology Quarterly*, *15*(4), 373–375.

Keith, T. Z., Kranzler, J. H., & Flanagan, D. P. (2001). What does the Cognitive Assessment System (CAS) measure? Joint confirmatory factor analysis of the CAS and the Woodcock-Johnson Tests of Cognitive Ability (3rd ed.). *School Psychology Review, 30,* 89–119.

Kranzler, J. H., & Keith, T. Z. (1999). Independent confirmatory factor analysis of the Cognitive Assessment System (CAS): What does the CAS measure? *School Psychology Review, 28,* 117–144.

Kranzler, J., Keith, T. Z., & Flanagan, D. P. (2000). Independent examination of the factor structure of the Cognitive Assessment System (CAS): Further evidence challenging the construct validity of the CAS. *Journal of Psychoeducational Assessment, 18*, 143–159.

Lemann, N. (1995, August). The structure of success in America. *The Atlantic Monthly*, 41–60.

Lezak, M. D. (1976). *Neuropsychological assessment.* New York: Oxford University Press.

Lezak, M. D. (1995). *Neuropsychological assessment* (3rd ed.). New York: Oxford University Press.

Mather, N. (1991). *An instructional guide to the Woodcock-Johnson Psycho-Educational Battery-Revised.* Brandon, VT: Clinical Psychology Publishing.

McDermott, P. A., Fantuzzo, J. W., & Glutting, J. J. (1990). Just say no to subtest analysis: A critique on Wechsler theory and practice. *Journal of Psychoeducational Assessment, 8,* 290–302.

McGrew, K. S. (1997). Analysis of the major intelligence batteries according to a proposed comprehensive Gf-Gc framework. In D. P. Flanagan, J. L. Genshaft, & P. L. Harrison (Eds.), *Contemporary intellectual assessment: Theories, tests, and issues* (151–180). New York: Guilford.

McGrew, K. S., & Flanagan, D. P. (1996). The Wechsler Performance Scale debate: Fluid intelligence (Gf) or visual processing (Gv)? *Communiqué, 24*(6), 14–16.

McGrew, K. S., & Flanagan, D. P. (1998). *The intelligence test desk reference (ITDR): Gf-Gc cross-battery assessment.* Boston, MA: Allyn & Bacon.

McGrew, K. S., Flanagan, D. P., Keith, T. Z., & Vanderwood, M. (1997). Beyond g: The impact of *Gf-Gc* specific cognitive abilities research on the future use and interpretation of intelligence tests in the schools. *School Psychology Review, 26*, 189–210.

McGuiness, D., McGuiness, C., & Donohue, J. (1995) . Phonological training and the alphabet principle: Evidence for reciprocal causality. *Reading Research Quarterly, 30*(4), 830–852.

Messick, S. (1995). Validity of psychological assessment: Validation of inferences from persons' responses and performances as scientific inquiry into score meaning. *American Psychologist, 50*, 741–749.

Naglieri, J. A. (1997). Planning, attention, simultaneous, and successive theory and the Cognitive Assessment System: A new theory-based measure of intelligence. In D. P. Flanagan, J. L. Genshaft, & P. L. Harrison (Eds.), *Contemporary intellectual assessment: Theories, tests, and issues* (pp. 247–267). New York: Guilford.

Neisser, U., Boodoo, G., Bouchard, T. J., Boykin, A. W., Brody, N., Ceci, S. J., Halpern, D. F., Loehlin, J. C., Perloff, R., Sternberg, R. J., & Urbina, S. (1996). Intelligence: Knowns and unknowns. *American Psychologist, 51*, 77–101.

Prentky, R. A. (1994). Teaching machines. In R. J. Corsini & E. Lieberman (Eds.), *Concise encyclopedia of psychology* (2nd ed., vol. 3). New York: John Wiley.

Rapaport, D., Gill, M. M., & Schafer, R. (1945–46). *Diagnostic psychological testing.* Chicago: Year Book Publishers.

Reschly, D. J., & Grimes, J. P. (1995). Best practices in intellectual assessment. In A. Thomas & J. P. Grimes (Eds.), *Best practices in school psychology III* (pp. 763–773). Washington, DC: National Association of School Psychologists.

Reschly, D. J., & Ysseldyke, J. E. (1995). School psychology paradigm shift. In A. Thomas & J. P. Grimes (Eds.), *Best practices in school psychology III* (pp. 17–31). Washington, DC: National Association of School Psychologists.

Reynolds, C. R., & Kamphaus, R. W. (Eds.). (1990). *Handbook of psychological and educational assessment of children: Intelligence and achievement.* New York: Guilford.

Reynolds, M. C., & Lakin, K. C. (1987). Noncategorical special education: Models for research and practice. In M. C. Wang, M. C. Reynolds, & H. J. Walberg (Eds.), *Handbook of special education: Research and practice.* (Vol. 1): *Learner characteristics and adaptive education* (pp. 331–356). New York: Pergamon.

Salvia, J., & Ysseldyke, J. E. (1995). *Assessment* (6th ed.). Boston: Houghton Mifflin .

Sandoval, J. (1998). Critical thinking in test interpretation. In J. Sandoval, C. L. Frisby, K. F. Geisinger, J. D. Scheuneman, & J. R. Grenier (Eds.), *Test interpretation and diversity: Achieving equity in assessment* (pp. 31–49). Washington, DC: American Psychological Association.

Sarason, S. (1975). The unfortunate fate of Alfred Binet and school psychology. *Teachers College Record, 77*, 579–592.

Sattler, J. (1992). *Assessment of children* (3rd ed.). San Diego, CA: Sattler.

Sattler, J. (2001). *Assessment of children: Cognitive applications* (4th ed.). La Mesa, CA: Sattler.

Siegel, L. S. (1999). Issues in the definition and diagnosis of learning disabilities: A perspective on *Guckenberger v. Boston University. Journal of Learning Disabilities, 32*(4), 304–319.

Snow, R. E. (1994). Abilities and aptitudes. In R. J. Sternberg (Eds.), *Encyclopedia of human intelligence* (pp. 3–5). New York: Macmillan.

Stanovich, K. E. (1999). The sociopsychometrics of learning disabilities. *Journal of Learning Disabilities, 32*(4), 350–361.

Wagner, R. K., Torgesen, J. K., & Rashotte, C. A. (1994) . Development of reading related phonological processing abilities: New evidence of bi-directional causality from a latent variable longitudinal study. *Developmental Psychology, 30*(1), 73–87.

Wechsler, D. (1944). *The measurement of adult intelligence* (3rd ed.). Baltimore: Williams & Wilkens.

Wilkinson, G. S. (1993). *Wide Range Achievement Test* (3rd ed.). Itasca, IL: Riverside.

Woodcock, R. W. (1990). Theoretical foundations of the WJ-R measures of cognitive ability. *Journal of Psychoeducational Assessment, 8*, 231–258.

Woodcock, R. W. & Johnson, M. B. (1989). *Woodcock-Johnson psycho-educational battery-Revised*. Itasca, IL: Riverside.

Woodcock, R. W., McGrew, K. S., & Mather, N. (2001). *Woodcock-Johnson III*. Chicago: Riverside.

Zachary, R. A. (1990). Wechsler's intelligence scales: Theoretical and practical considerations. *Journal of Psychoeducational Assessment, 8*, 276–289.

Zenderland, L. (1998). *Measuring minds: Henry Herbert Goddard and the origins of American intelligence testing*. New York: Cambridge University Press.

ANNOTATED BIBLIOGRAPHY

Flanagan, D. P., McGrew, K. S., & Ortiz, S. O. (2000). *The Wechsler Intelligence Scales and Gf-Gc theory: A contemporary approach to interpretation*. Boston: Allyn & Bacon.

This book presents cross-battery assessment and interpretation principles and procedures as a means to modernize the use of the Wechsler Intelligence Scales. In this book, the Wechsler Scales are described in terms of their contributions to research and practice and are placed firmly in the current, theory-based trend of intelligence-test interpretation. The Wechsler Scales are described according to the extent to which they operationalize prominent abilities specified in contemporary theory on the structure of intelligence. This book shows how contemporary theory can be linked to the applied measurement of cognitive abilities using the Wechsler Scales. More specifically, it imposes a strong substantive framework to the interpretation of the Wechsler Scales via Flanagan and McGrew's cross-battery approach. The end result is the derivation of more valid inferences from Wechsler test scores. The Wechsler-based cross-battery approach to assessment described in this book provides practitioners with the knowledge and skills necessary to ground cognitive ability assessment and interpretation with the Wechsler Scales in strong theory and research, and to conduct assessments in a more psychometrically and theoretically defensible manner.

Flanagan, D. P., & Ortiz, S. O. (2001). *Essentials of cross-battery assessment*. New York: John Wiley.

This book presents a general overview of cross-battery assessment and interpretation principles in an easy-to-follow format. Two cross-battery methods are offered: comprehensive cross-battery assessment, which ensures that the widest range of broad cognitive abilities and processes is represented in assessments in accordance with contemporary psychometric theory and research; and selective cross-battery assessment, which ensures that the abilities and processes that are most closely related to well-defined referral issues are assessed thoroughly. In this book, the authors also extend their cross-battery procedures further in order to address issues of interpretive bias and nondiscriminatory assessment that often arise when assessing individuals with cultural and linguistic backgrounds that differ from those of the U.S. mainstream. Through their provision of easy-to-follow steps, data summary sheets, and worksheets, these authors demonstrate how practitioners can improve upon reliability and validity in assessment and use current theory and research to enrich and inform interpretations of cognitive function and dysfunction.

Flanagan, D. P., Ortiz, S. O., Alfonso, V. C., & Mascolo, J. T. (2002). *The achievement test desk reference (ATDR): Comprehensive assessment and learning disability*. Boston: Allyn & Bacon.

A useful companion to McGrew and Flanagan's *Intelligence test desk reference (ITDR): Gf-Gc Cross-battery assessment*, this book provides comprehensive information about the most important psychometric, theoretical, and qualitative characteristics of the major achievement batteries, including the WIAT-II, WJ III ACH, DAB-3, DATA-2, KTEA/NU, and PIAT-R/NU. In addition, test characteristics are summarized for brief/screening measures as well as special-purpose batteries that are used to assess specific academic skill areas such as reading, math, writing, oral language, and phonological processing. This information, contained in an easy-to-read, visual-graphic format, is a foundational source that is invaluable to practitioners who conduct academic assessments. In addition, this book offers a comprehensive framework for LD determination and provides practitioners with a step-by-step decision making process in responding to learning-related referrals. Therefore, it offers an in-depth discussion and presentation of the theory and research relating to LD assessment and diagnosis.

McGrew, K. S., & Flanagan, D. P. (1998). *The intelligence test desk reference (ITDR): Gf-Gc Cross-battery assessment*. Boston: Allyn & Bacon.

This book provides comprehensive information about the most important psychometric, theoretical, and qualitative characteristics of the major intelligence batteries, including WISC-III, WAIS-III, WPPSI-R, KAIT, K-ABC, SB:IV, DAS, and WJ-R. In addition, test characteristics are summarized for more than 20 special-purpose cognitive ability tests that are used to assess the cognitive capabilities of diverse populations and to supplement intelligence tests (e.g., Leiter-R, UNIT, CAS, C-TONI, WRAML, etc.). This information, contained in an easy-to-read, visual-graphic format, is a foundational source that is invaluable to practitioners, particularly those who employ cross-battery techniques. In addition, this book was the first to introduce formally cross-battery assessment to practitioners. Therefore, it offers an in-depth discussion and presentation of the theory and research underlying cross-battery assessment.

85 Best Practices in Interventions for School Psychologists: A Cognitive Approach to Problem Solving

Jack A. Naglieri
George Mason University

OVERVIEW

The purpose of this chapter is to illustrate how interventions can be linked to cognitive assessment within a problem-solving context. The chapter focuses on cognitive assessment methods as a means of understanding the nature of the problem and what might be done to solve the problem (instructions that are rooted in cognitively based educational principles). The approach combines a way of thinking about intelligence as specific cognitive processes and a way of teaching that places emphasis on the cognitive activities involved in academic tasks, sometimes referred to as cognitive education. In order to place this new approach to intervention within a larger context, the chapter begins with a brief look at the current state of the art of using results from traditional IQ tests. Next, cognitive education will be defined and illustrated and the steps needed to go from cognitive assessment to cognitively based interventions will be discussed. An illustration of using a cognitive approach to assessment and intervention will be provided along with instructional handouts that school psychologists could give to a teacher or parent. This illustration is intended to show how the connections between cognitive assessment and cognitively based educational methods may be achieved and how it may be conducted within a problem-solving context.

BACKGROUND

The concept of using results from an intelligence test to guide educational recommendations and interventions is intuitively appealing, yet traditional IQ tests have been criticized for providing limited information for intervention design (Reschly & Grimes, 1995). This limitation has been recognized for some time. For example, Kaufman and Kaufman took a historically important step about 20 years ago when they suggested that tests of intelligence like their Kaufman Assessment Battery for Children (K-ABC; Kaufman & Kaufman, 1983) could be used for instructional decision making. While the K-ABC made many important contributions to the assessment of intelligence, the suggestion that their measure of ability could be used to guide intervention is one of the ways in which that test distinguished itself. More recently, Ashman and Conway (1997) have suggested that tests like the K-ABC or the more recent Cognitive Assessment System (CAS; Naglieri & Das, 1997a) could be combined with cognitively based educational approaches to aid in the development of interventions to provide more effective instructional environments for children.

Peverly (1994) noted the value of a cognitive approach in a review of the potential impact of cognitive psychology on school psychology. He wrote that instructional "programs that include the knowledge of cognition and the regulation of cognition have proven to be very successful in improving students' academic performance, especially in the domain of reading and especially for poorer learners" (p. 304). Perverly also stated that methods that carefully evaluate the child's knowledge of the curriculum (e.g., curriculum-based assessment), although useful, are limited and should be "supplemented by knowledge of the cognitive processes that underlie competency in those skills" (p. 301). In this chapter cognitively based educational intervention approaches will be offered as viable methods for improving academic outcomes for children, especially when they are tied to the results of cognitive assessment that informs the school psychologist about the child's underlying cognitive competencies as suggested by Peverly (1994).

LINKING ASSESSMENT TO INTERVENTION

When intelligence test scores are used to guide the selection of interventions to help a child with poor academic performance, the concept of an aptitude-treatment interaction (ATI) is being used. The concept, which is intuitively attractive and logical, assumes that individual differences in abilities (aptitude or underlying cognitive competencies) need to be taken into account when interventions or treatments are being planned (Snow, 1991). Snow defined aptitude as "a complex of personal characteristics identified before and during treatment that accounts for a person's end state after a particular treatment" (p. 205). That is, there are child characteristics that are assumed to be relevant to the extent to which a child benefits from one type of intervention over another resulting in an interaction between the aptitude and the treatment. Although the term aptitude is not limited to intelligence (it could include variables such as personality or motivation), in this chapter the focus will be on non-traditional intelligence tests that measure cognitive processing. In this discussion the way in which aptitude, or in this case intelligence, is defined takes on critical importance.

School psychologists have traditionally defined aptitude by using IQ tests, particularly the Wechsler intelligence scales. This test is built on the concept of general ability developed in the early part of the last century. The vagueness of the concept is apparent in Wechsler's (1939) definition of intelligence: "the aggregate or global capacity of the individual to act purposefully, to think rationally, and to deal effectively with his environment." Interestingly, when writing about the origin of the concept of general intelligence, Pintner (1925) wrote, "we did not start with a clear definition of general intelligence... [but] borrowed from every-day life a vague term implying all-round ability and knowledge, and ... we [are] still attempting to define it more sharply and endow it with a stricter scientific connotation" (p. 53). This statement, although written more than 75 years ago, is as true today as it was then.

Many practicing school psychologists have attempted to obtain information that can be used within an ATI conceptualization by going beyond the composite IQ scores from the Wechsler. To do so they have interpreted the Wechsler subtests, scales, and indices in many ways to extract meaning out of this test of general intelligence. School psychologists and other professionals have often relied on authoritative books like *Intelligent Testing With the WISC-III* by Kaufman (1994b) and *Assessment of Children* by Sattler (1988). These books are important attempts to help school psychologists do something with the Wechsler scales that goes well beyond its capabilities because intervention design demands more than the IQ scores a test of general intelligence provides. In order to further examine this problem, a brief review of where the test came from is needed.

Kaufman and Lichtenberger (2000) and Naglieri (1999) describe sources from which Wechsler developed his tests. Verbal subtests like Vocabulary, Similarities, and Comprehension were largely based on the Stanford-Binet whose work also influenced the U.S. military testing program. Reading the book *Army Mental Tests* by Yoakum and Yerkes (1920), provides an enlightening look at the sources of Wechsler's subtests. There are striking similarities between the task names, descriptions, and instructions included there and the present day Wechsler scales. The Army tests were organized into verbal and nonverbal portions so that a wide variety of persons could be effectively assessed. The verbal and nonverbal tests could be effectively given to those who could speak English, but for those with limited English language skills only the nonverbal tests were used. This is an obvious and simple idea that formed the basis for the partition of the Army Alpha and Beta tests and the Wechsler-Bellevue Scales (Wechsler, 1939). Nonverbal tests provide an efficient solution to the problem of assessing general intelligence for persons from diverse cultural and linguistic populations and are still used today, as illustrated by the recent publications of nonverbal individual (Universal Nonverbal Intelligence Test by Bracken and McCallum (1998)) and group (Naglieri Nonverbal Ability Test by Naglieri (1997)) tests. Thus the organization of tests into Verbal and Performance Scales on the Wechsler tests can be considered a dichotomy of convenience rather than a representation of two different types of intelligence. Many have published important works to help us interpret these verbal and nonverbal tests in a variety of ways, each designed to go beyond the overall IQ scores.

There have been many attempts to find theoretical explanations for the Wechsler subtests. Kaufman (1994a, 1994b) and Kaufman and Lichtenberger (2000) provided outstanding texts for interpretation of the various Wechsler scales so that practitioners may extract meaning from the many scores the test yields by using a mixture of psychometric analysis, knowledge of the research, and clinical judgment. Others have provided similar texts to better understand the results of the Wechsler, and other tests of general intelligence (e.g., Sattler's 1988 text), and there have been many published papers on how to interpret the subtests. Among the most recent attempts to provide school psychologists with still another way to interpret the Wechsler is the cross-battery approach (McGrew & Flanagan, 1998), which applies a Gf-Gc model. This reinterpretation in particular has a basic limitation noted by Kaufman (2000) when referring to Horn's Fluid/Crystallized approach and the related Carroll model:

> There is no empirical evidence that these approaches yield profiles for exceptional children, are directly relevant to diagnosis, or have relevance to eligibility decisions, intervention or instructional planning—all of which are pertinent for school psychologists (p. 27).

It is becoming more apparent that while there are many possible ways to interpret the Wechsler scales, these methods have not resulted in improvements in diagnosis or interventions for children with academic problems (Naglieri, 1999; Reschly & Grimes, 1995). It is reasonable, therefore, to suggest that the quest for obtaining meaning from the various Wechsler scores does little to help practitioners move from assessment to intervention. This is not as much a criticism of the general intelligence approach as recognition that this way of conceptualizing ability is better used as an overall estimate of ability rather than as a tool for differential diagnosis and treatment planning.

The view that Wechsler's scales are not based on firm theoretical concepts of verbal and nonverbal intelligence but rather on the vague concept of general intelligence (e.g., a global aggregate or all-round ability and knowledge concept) with subtests that contain verbal and nonverbal content helps us see why this approach does not lend itself to being useful within the ATI context. In order to have an interaction between a child's underlying ability and some instructional method, there needs to be a clear conceptualization of what the underlying ability is. There also must be a good understanding of the underlying component of the instructional method using the same theoretical basis. That is, in order to show an interaction between an aptitude and performance in the classroom, the same underlying cognitive component should be involved in both. This will be illustrated later in this chapter by using methods that come from the cognitive education literature. It is, however, important to understand the basic elements of a cognitive approach to education.

Cognitive Education

One important purpose of education is to provide children with the knowledge and skills they need in order to be productive members of a society. Considerable emphasis has been placed on teaching children facts like who discovered America, how to solve a math word problem, what sounds each letter and letter combinations make, what the components of a proper sentence are, and so forth. Knowledge and skill acquisition has been and continues to be essential to success. It is becoming apparent, however, that in addition to teaching students knowledge and skills that seem important today, teachers also need to help children learn how to effectively manage situations that they will face well after schooling is completed. Modern instruction should help children acquire knowledge and skills, but, more importantly, "to plan and control, to think and inquire, to evaluate and reflect" (Scheid, 1993, p. 3). This means that knowledge and skills as well as the cognitive dimensions of learning are relevant in the classroom. A cognitively based educational approach teaches children knowledge and skills as well as effective ways of *thinking*.

Ashman and Conway (1997) describe cognitive education as an approach to improve outcomes for children that is based on the merging of education and cognitive psychology based upon theories of human thinking and intelligence applied to instruction. Scheid (1993) stated that "cognitive instruction emphasizes the development in students of a reflective, self-reliant learning style" (p. 2) which is markedly different than a behaviorist point of view. Miller, Galanter, and Pribram (1960) noted that a behavioristic approach discourages the psychologist from speculating or examining (through the use of a test, for example) about the processes used by a learner. Instead, the behaviorist deals with how the teacher structures the environment and provides reinforcement and punishment, for example, to obtain desired student behaviors and reduce unwanted behaviors. The cognitive psychologist directs efforts toward careful observation and testing of the learner's abilities to, for example, work with spatial tasks, situations that demand different types of attention, and problem solving to explain performance. The cognitive approach is one "which explicitly tries to describe what is going on in the brain, in addition to observing what behavior that brain produces" (Kirby & Williams, 1991, p. 52).

Cognitive and behaviorally oriented approaches to learning, while both interested in behavior of the organism, depart considerably in basic assumptions. The behavioral approach takes the position that a child learns from practice and reinforcement making memorization of facts and rules a fundamental way of learning (Scheid, 1993). Students are viewed as recipients of information whose role is to absorb facts delivered and organized by the teacher. In contrast, in a cognitive education approach the child is seen as an active participant who interprets information that is received, relates it to previously acquired facts, organizes and stores it for later use, develops ways of doing things, and critically examines information. From this approach "learning is perceived as a complex process that does not proceed in a neat, linear manner, but rather in recursive phases. What students are capable of learning is influenced by developmental factors, by the amount of expertise they have about a subject or topic, and by what they know and understand about how to approach learning strategically" (Scheid, 1993, pp. 3–4).

Reading is an excellent skill to illustrate the cognitive perspective. Children with reading problems often struggle with word recognition and devote so much of their efforts to decode words that little time is left for other important aspects of reading. Some educators have focused on teaching children word recognition skills through drill and practice to increase automaticity. "While word recognition automaticity is clearly important, it is not sufficient to guarantee successful reading" (Scheid, 1993, p. 5). It is well documented that success in reading comprehension requires, for example, the use of strategies such as looking back at the information given, focusing on the relevant from irrelevant information provided, using good methods to analyze the passage, and paying special attention to answer the specific questions that were asked (Pressley, 1998; Pressley & Woloshyn, 1995). A cognitive education approach to reading instruction aims to help students develop strategies for reading decoding using their prior knowledge and skills. It also helps them construct mental images or pictorial representations of the text (e.g., Story Maps), learn to summarize as they read, and be active participants in the activity of reading.

The cognitive education approach puts emphasis on both the academic skills the child must learn as well as the cognitive processes the child uses in the act of learning. Additionally, this approach views teaching and learning as an ecosystem in which the characteristics of the teacher, the setting, the curriculum, and the child interact to lead to academic success or failure. Knowing the cognitive competencies or deficiencies of a learner is, therefore, a critical element in a complex process that leads to effective learning (Naglieri & Ashman, 1999). Instructional design as well as intervention can be most efficiently conducted, therefore, when a child's knowledge and skills as well as levels of competence in basic psychological processes are known (Peverly, 1994). The question then becomes, *What are the basic psychological processes that are important for children's academic success?*

Basic Psychological Processes

The cognitive processes related to academic skill acquisition need to be clearly understood if the connection between a child's cognitive processing competence and academic performance can be understood (Peverly, 1994). This demands a strong theoretical perspective and assumes that the school psychologist has a working knowledge of the cognitive processes. This is important because the cognitive demands of the academic tasks need to be determined and these demands related to a theory of cognitive processing. One approach to defining cognitive processes is the PASS (Planning, Attention, Simultaneous, Successive) theory, which is measured using the CAS (Naglieri & Das, 1997a). This theory is well supported by a considerable amount of research summarized in the *Cognitive Assessment System Interpretive Handbook* (Naglieri & Das, 1997b) and in *Essentials of CAS Assessment* (Naglieri, 1999). The CAS provides the most extensively validated way to measure the four processes defined as follows:

1. Planning is a mental activity that provides cognitive control, use of processes, acquisition of knowledge and skills, intentionality, and self-regulation.

2. Attention is a mental activity that provides focused, selective cognitive activity over time and resistance to distraction.

3. Simultaneous is a mental activity by which the child integrates stimuli into inter-related groups.

4. Successive is a mental activity by which the person integrates stimuli in a specific serial order to form a chain-like progression.

The four processes measured by the CAS have been found to have a greater correlation with achievement than do traditional IQ tests; yield profiles of PASS scores that are sensitive to the cognitive problems experienced by children with, for example, Attention Deficit/Hyperactivity Disorder and reading disabilities (Naglieri, 1999); yield the smallest differences between white and African-American children (Wasserman & Becker, 2000); and relate to intervention (Naglieri & Gottling, 1995, 1997; Naglieri & Johnson, 2000). Additionally, extensive research evidence that supports the validity of the separate PASS scales is provided. For example, Naglieri and Das (1997b) reported that the standardization sample children who used strategies to solve the planning tests earned good scores on those subtests while the children who did not use strategies earned low scores. Importantly, strategy use (Planning) has also been related to interventions that improve performance in mathematics calculation (Naglieri & Gottling, 1995, 1997; Naglieri & Johnson, 2000). The relationship between PASS and academic improvement found in these research papers in combination with research on differential diagnosis provides ample support for the use of CAS for building interventions, especially when a child has a cognitive weakness (which will be described in greater detail later in this chapter) in one of the PASS scales.

Evidence That Cognitive Interventions Can Work

Perhaps the research most relevant to using cognitive processing information to improve educational outcomes is the planning facilitation research most recently illustrated by Naglieri and Johnson (2000). This research, which is based on the work of Cormier, Carlson, and Das (1990) and Kar, Dash, Das, and Carlson (1992), utilized a method that stimulated children's use of planning, which had positive effects on performance. The method was based on the view that planning processes should be facilitated rather than directly taught so that children discover the value of strategy use without being specifically told to do so.

The studies reported by Cormier et al. (1990) and Kar et al. (1992) demonstrated that students differentially benefited from a technique intended to facilitate planning. They found that participants who initially performed poorly on measures of planning earned significantly higher scores than those with good scores in planning. The method encouraged a planful and organized examination of the demands of the task, and this helped those children that needed to do this the most (those with low planning scores). These studies were the basis for three experiments by Naglieri and Gottling (1995, 1997) and Naglieri & Johnson (2000) that focused on improving math calculation performance.

The two research studies by Naglieri and Gottling (1995, 1997) demonstrated that an intervention that facilitated planning led to improved performance on multiplication problems for those with low scores in planning, but minimal improvement was found for those with high planning scores. In that study learning disabled students benefited differentially from the instruction based on their cognitive processing scores, which suggested that matching the instruction to the cognitive weakness of the child was important. Naglieri and Johnson (2000) followed up on these studies and expanded the methodology by identifying children in the study who had a cognitive weakness in one of the four PASS processes as well as a no cognitive weakness group. A cognitive weakness was defined as an individual child's PASS score that is significantly lower than that child's average PASS score and a standard score less than 85. The results showed that children with a cognitive weakness in Planning improved considerably in math calculation problems that is very similar to the regular curriculum over math calculation performance during baseline while those with no cognitive weakness improved only marginally. Similarly, children with a cognitive weakness in Simultaneous or Successive or Attention also showed substantially lower rates of improvement in math performance. These results suggested that the PASS characteristics of the child showed a relationship to the response the child had to the instruction. Thus there was an interaction between the aptitude (PASS) and the treatment (planning facilitation).

The results of these studies are clear: Children who are low in planning improve considerably when given instruction that teaches them to be more strategic. In contrast, children who are not low in planning do not improve as much. What is important in this conclusion for the practicing school psychologist is that information about the PASS characteristics of the child was helpful when interventions were applied. The most improvement in a math activity that involved much planning was found for those who were disorganized and non-strategic (those low in planning). These children improved the most because they needed to be more organized, more strategic, and more planful. These findings for the planning facilitation method are also important from a more theoretical perspective because they are the *opposite* of what would be expected from past ATI research. Traditional ATI research has shown that children who are low in ability usually benefit the least from instruction while children who are high benefit the most. What these results most strongly indicate is that the PASS characteristics of a child need to be considered in relation to the PASS demands of an academic task when interventions are selected. In the remainder of this chapter some ways to link assessment to intervention will be described in more detail.

FROM COGNITIVE ASSESSMENT TO COGNITIVE EDUCATION

Four-Step Method

Naglieri and Ashman (1999) describe how the connection between cognitive assessment and intervention can be made. They suggested that for teaching and learning to be efficient, the process must include a careful examination of what is to be learned and how it will be taught in relation to the cognitive characteristics of the child. Using the PASS theory as a guide, they state that "knowing about the PASS cognitive competencies or deficiencies of a learner is a critical element in a complex process that leads to effective teaching and learning (p. 153)." Their approach involves four steps, each of which will be described below:

Step 1

Assessment is the first step of a cognitive approach to instruction and intervention. Assessment is a complex task that involves many individuals such as teachers, parents, and perhaps the learner. The initial evaluation may be informal observations by the teachers that may lead to initial attempts to deal with the learning problem. When further efforts are required, more formalized methods such as norm-referenced or criterion-referenced assessments may be needed to determine if there is an academic weakness and/or cognitive explanation for the learning problems. Based upon the severity of the academic need different magnitudes of intervention may be indicated. The greater the academic need the more effort will be required and the closer the setting, curriculum, teacher, and learner dimensions should be examined. At this stage it can be important to carefully examine the child's cognitive competence in PASS cognitive processes and their connection to academic performance.

In order to take this cognitive assessment/cognitive intervention approach the school psychologist would work with the teacher to detect when the child's weakness in some area of PASS cognitive processing is related to academic difficulty. When a child's academic skill deficit has an associated cognitive processing deficit, then an intervention that takes into consideration the connection between these two dimensions is needed. If, however, a child has an academic skills deficit without a cognitive deficit, nor an emotional or behavioral or some other child-based problem, then the best intervention may be to provide additional instruction of the academic skill, make alterations to the environment, ensure that the child is exerting effort to learn, and so forth.

When a child has an academic problem and is weak in some area of cognitive processing and the cognitive demands of the academic tasks have been carefully examined, one option is to consider interventions that help the child use a different process when doing the academic work. For example, suppose that a child has difficulty learning basic math addition facts such as 9 x 6 = 54, and the teacher's instructional method is to make the child recite the phrase "nine times six equals fifty-four" or write the statement many times until the facts are remembered (become automatic). This task demands recall of information in a specific order, which demands considerable Sequential (from K-ABC) or Successive (from CAS) processing. If a child is poor in this type of processing, recall of the string of words could be very difficult. Thus, the problem may be that the processing demand of the task as presented by the teacher has a heavy reliance on Successive processing and the child has a cognitive weakness (Naglieri, 1999) in that area. Instruction that takes into account the underlying processing demand of the academic task needs to be selected or prepared. That is, it may be helpful to use a different instructional approach that has a different cognitive processing demand (this will be expanded in the description of step 2). At this point in the procedure, the child's knowledge and skills as well as cognitive competencies have been examined.

Step 2

Preparation of the best teaching method is the second step in the instructional cycle described by Naglieri and Ashman (1999). This phase includes selection of the content, examination of the various methods available to help the child acquire the content, selection of the best materials, and consideration of the processing demands vis-à-vis the academic demands of the activity. Continuing from the example given previously, the teacher and school psychologist might collaboratively determine that the child needs to be taught basic math facts using a method that does not put so much emphasis on successive processing. One way to do that is to teach the child to use strategies for obtaining the correct answer (i.e., use more planning processing and less successive). When a strategy or plan is used in this way, the correct answer is arrived at by thinking about the problem (being strategic or planful) rather than by rote memory (which demands much successive processing). This alteration in the methods used changes the cognitive demands of the task considerably.

There are many strategies or plans that can be used to change the processing demands of a task like memorization of facts. When the teacher switches instructional methods in this manner the use of strategies (plans) for remembering basic math facts can have very positive results (Pressley & Woloshyn, 1995). Geary (1994) also stressed the importance of teaching children strategies for remembering math facts, and Goldstein and Mather (1998) provided a comprehensive list of strategies for remembering math facts. For example, in order to learn the 9 times tables the child may use a system of obtaining the answer as follows: For the problem presented above (9 x 6 = 54) the strategy works like this. Take 1 away from the multiplier (6), then add a number to that one which equals 9. For example, to calculate 9 x 6, you would say: 6 – 1 = 5, so 5 goes in the 10s place, and 5 + 4 = 9, so 4 goes in the 1s place making the answer 54.

Another example, using more basic math might involve the "doubles plus one rule." This rule teaches children that if they know the sum of two same numbers (7 + 7 = 14), then a problem like 7 + 8 is one more than 7 + 7. This strategy for obtaining the answer shifts the cognitive demand from one that demands recall of the specific series of words—"7 plus 8 equals 15" (which demands much successive processing)—to a planning rich activity where the child thinks to arrive at the answer. The child might say "7 + 8, I know 7 + 7 is 14, 8 is 1 more than 7, so the answer has to be 1 more than 14 which is 15." Shifting the cognitive processing demand of a task is an excellent intervention because not only does it help the child perform a task in a way that does not rely on his or her cognitive weakness but it gives the child a chance to be successful using strategies or plans as suggested by Geary (1994) and Pressley (1998).

Step 3

The next phase in the cycle is *instruction*, which relates directly to the decisions made during the preparation phase. Here the identified methods are applied. This phase also includes elements of the final instructional cycle: *evaluation*. During instruction and at the end of the instruction phase the teacher should carefully monitor progress made by the child to fine tune the instruction as well as to evaluate the progress of the child.

Step 4

After completion of the instruction, more formal evaluation should be accomplished. This might include a thorough curriculum-based analysis or formal standardized testing procedures. If the latter are used, then the treatment effectiveness evaluation method described by Naglieri (1999) should be applied because it provides a psychometrically sound approach that takes into account measurement issues such as regression to the mean and reliability of the measures.

Instructional Planning and Eligibility Decisions

The instructional cycle described here could be conducted within many different contexts that may or may not involve questions of eligibility. School psychologists might work with a teacher to assist in the instructional process on an informal basis. In some instances assessment may include a formal test such as the CAS, not for the purpose of eligibility determination, necessarily, but for the purpose of instructional planning. If, however, eligibility is to be determined, then a comprehensive assessment must be conducted and then the assessment of cognitive processes should be used within that context. When the academic skills are poor enough to be described as a deficit and differences between the tests of achievement and cognitive processing are sufficiently large vis-à-vis state guidelines, then it may be possible to establish eligibility (e.g., learning disabled) as well as a cognitive plan for intervention. Naglieri and Sullivan (1998) showed how this could be accomplished. They suggested that when a discrepancy between the academic skill deficit and some adequate areas of PASS cognitive processing are found, evidence for a discrepancy is obtained. The discrepancy, alone, however, provides little information about the nature of the child's cognitive problem (if one exists). When a child also has significant variation in cognitive processing scores, and the low processing score is below normal, then a cognitive weakness has been found. The child with a significant difference between his or her high levels of cognitive processing and achievement and, in addition, a cognitive weakness accompanied by similarly low achievement scores should be considered within Individuals with Disabilities Education Act Amendments of 1997 (IDEA 97) regulations as potentially learning disabled (see Figure 1). That is, the determination of a discrepancy (processing and achievement) consistency (processing and achievement) can be used to determine if (a) the child meets eligibility requirements and (b) that a cognitive intervention may be appropriate.

The discrepancy/consistency approach can be used to help classify children as learning disabled when there is an academic failure and poor cognitive processing scores using the guidelines provided in IDEA 97. Naglieri and Sullivan (1998) wrote that using the PASS theory can provide evidence of a "disorder in one or more of the basic psychological processes [i.e., PASS constructs] involved in understanding or in using language, spoken or written, which disorder may manifest itself in imperfect ability to listen, speak, read, write, spell, or do mathematical calculations" (p. 46). When a processing disorder has been found and there is cognitive variation within the child (i.e., a cognitive weakness is found) and academic problems, then in addition to relevant eligibility issues a cognitive education method may be appropriate.

The cognitive education approach presented here should be applied when a child has a discrepancy between a high cognitive processing score and a low academic score as well as similarity between the low academic score and a low cognitive processing score. Cognitive variation may be of two types: a relative weakness or a cognitive weakness. A relative weakness is found when at least one PASS scale standard score is significantly lower than the child's mean PASS score. Because the PASS scores are compared to the individual child's average (and not the normative mean of 100), this tells us about "relative" strengths or weaknesses. For example, if a child has scores of 114 (Planning), 116 (Simultaneous), 94 (Successive), and 109 (Successive), the Successive score, which is 14.25 points below the child's mean of 108.25, is a "relative weakness." This approach

Figure 1. Relationships among CAS and K-TEA scores

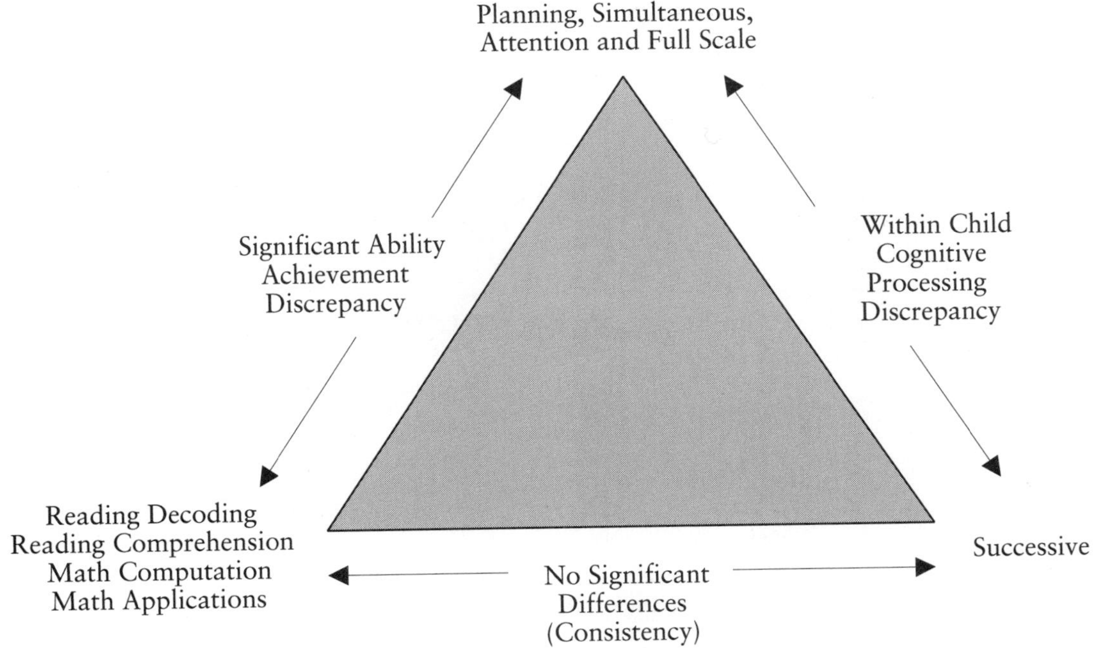

has been used in intelligence testing (see Kaufman, 1994a , 1994b; Naglieri, 1993; Sattler, 1988) for some time. In contrast, there are two requirements for a child to have a "cognitive weakness." The first is that a relative weakness is present, and the second is that the low cognitive processing score should be below normal limits (e.g., a standard score of 85, representing one standard deviation below the mean). Additionally, some area of academic skills deficit similar in level to the cognitive weakness should be present to indicate that some intervention is necessary. This distinction is important because Naglieri (2000) found that children with a cognitive weakness were more likely to have significant academic problems and have been previously placed in special education settings while children with a relative weakness were less likely to have experienced academic problems.

Illustration of the Cognitive Education Approach to Intervention

Step 1: Assessment

The examination of a child's academic problems is, as described above, multifaceted and may or may not involve decisions about eligibility. When initial attempts to solve educational problems did not meet with success or the severity of the problem warrants an in depth examination of the entire situation, it will be important to determine if a child has a cognitive weakness. In this illustration it is assumed that the academic problem detected by a teacher was not solved by initial pre-referral intervention efforts and the child was administered a test of cognitive processing (CAS) and achievement (K-TEA) as well as other relevant assessment methods not summarized here. The data presented in Table 1 are illustrative rather than actual.

The data provided in Table 1 are first analyzed by computing the child's PASS standard score mean and comparing each of the four PASS scores to that mean (see Naglieri, 1999, for more details). This allows the school psychologist to determine if a cognitive weakness is present. In this illustration the child's Successive Scale standard score is significantly lower than the mean of 94.25 and below a cut-score of 85 used to designate below normal functioning. This means that the child has difficulty with tasks that require the use of information in a specific series, the memory of serial information, and comprehension of information based on linearity (see Naglieri, 1999, for more information about interpretation of this process).

Table 1. PASS and K-TEA standard scores, comparison of PASS scales with the child's PASS mean, and comparison of CAS and K-TEA standard scores

CAS	Standard scores	d	Values needed at p = .05	Sig/NS
Planning	98	3.75	10.8	
Simultaneous	102	7.75	9.6	
Attention	96	1.75	11.1	
Successive	81	–13.25	9.5	Sig
PASS mean	94.25			
CAS FS	92			

K-TEA	Standard scores	K-TEA versus each PASS and Full scale: Plan	Sim	Att	Succ	FS
Reading Decoding	79	Sig	Sig	Sig	NS	Sig
Reading Comprehension	84	Sig	Sig	NS	NS	NS
Spelling	81	Sig	Sig	Sig	NS	NS
Math Computation	80	Sig	Sig	Sig	NS	NS
Math Application	83	Sig	Sig	NS	NS	NS

Note: Differences required for significance between the CAS and K-TEA are provided by Naglieri (1999).

Next, the separate PASS scale scores are compared to achievement. Each PASS score is compared to the K-TEA standard scores using tables of significance provided by Naglieri (1999). The results showed that Planning and Simultaneous scores are significantly higher than all of the K-TEA scores. This provides evidence of a *discrepancy* between ability (Planning and Simultaneous) and achievement (which could be used for eligibility determination). The Attention score is significantly higher than Math Computation and Math Application scores. The CAS Full Scale and Attention scores are also significantly higher than the child's Reading Decoding score. Importantly, there is no significant difference between the Successive score and the poor achievement scores. That is, there is *consistency* between the cognitive weakness in Successive and poor academic scores.

The lack of a significant difference between Successive and Reading Decoding (a relationship anticipated from previous research summarized in Das, Naglieri, & Kirby (1994)) provides a reasonable explanation for the academic problem. A strong relationship between word decoding and successive processing is reported in the literature (Das, Naglieri, & Kirby, 1994; Kirby & Williams, 1991). The poor reading comprehension is likely related to these decoding problems because the child's understanding is blocked by failure to adequately determine the words that are included in the sentences. Finally, the problems with math are related to the child's difficulty with mastery of basic math facts. This would be expected when a repetition of basic facts is used as the instructional method (e.g., the child writes or says the facts repeatedly until they are recalled quickly).

The relationships among the cognitive and academic measures are illustrated in Figure 1. At the base of the triangle are the weaknesses, those in achievement (Reading and Math) and one in cognitive processing (Successive). At the top of the triangle are the child's high scores. This includes the Planning, Simultaneous, and Attention scales as well as any other areas of achievement for which the child is competent. When this relationship is found, the practitioner has data indicating that a significant cognitive weakness and associated academic weakness have been detected.

Step 2: Preparation

The methods available to help the child acquire the academic content are selected with careful consideration of the processing demands of the academic tasks. Continuing from the above example of a child with low successive processing, the demands of the current reading instruction need to be determined. This example illustrates a case where the PASS Remedial Program (PREP; Das, 1999) intervention would be appropriate because it teaches children things like the importance of attending to the sounds of events in order and helps the child apply good successive processing to reading. Other interventions that do not require the teacher to use a pre-packaged program include strategies for reading decoding and reading comprehension that the regular or special education teacher could apply.

A child with a successive processing weakness but adequate planning could be taught to utilize strategies to decode words as an alternative to sounding out the letters and the sounds that go with them. This is illustrated in Appendix 1, which is a handout developed by Naglieri and Pickering (2000). This intervention is a strategy (a plan) that can be used by children who have trouble decoding words, perhaps due to a successive processing weakness. Another appropriate intervention would be to utilize strategies to improve reading comprehension (Appendix 2). This method is designed to teach children the strategies used by good readers to obtain information from text. This includes teaching children how to integrate their prior knowledge with what is read, how to look for cues that help define the meaning of the text, and how to approach reading comprehension questions. In both these illustrations, the successive processing weakness is being addressed by teaching the child to approach the task with strategies, or plans, which engage planning processing. Thus, the processing demands of the task initially might have been very successive but with these interventions there is a shift toward a more strategic (planful) way of approaching the material. The same approach would be used to help the child be more successful in math calculation.

Two math calculation interventions are suggested. First, one strategy that helps a child with successive processing weakness learn facts without rote memory of a linear statement like 8 + 7 = 15. The child who is taught to memorize these facts by repeatedly saying or writing the string of numbers and signs uses successive processing to commit the statement into memory. In contrast, the "Using Plans to Learn Math Facts" handout (Appendix 3) encourages teachers to help children use strategies for obtaining the correct answer. This intervention helps the teacher instruct the child to arrive at the answer using a strategy that changes the dominant cognitive process from successive (memory of the sequence of facts) to planning (obtaining the information via a strategy that is based on what was previously known). There are several strategies for math facts that are presented by Naglieri and Pickering (2000).

Steps 3 and 4: Implementation and Evaluation

Once the teacher and school psychologist have developed a plan, the methods are implemented. During this time the teacher should follow the concepts developed in the intervention plan in a flexible way and modify the method as the situation demands. Although frequent monitoring of progress is an important component of this step, evaluation of the effectiveness of the intervention (step 4) should occur after the treatment has been completed. Naglieri (1999) recommends that the effectiveness of the overall program of interventions should be made in comparison to initial results from standardized achievement tests. In this example, a K-TEA Reading Decoding score of 89 is needed to demonstrate reliable improvement over the initial standard score of 79. Refer to that source for more information and values needed for significance to demonstrate significant improvement over time.

PROBLEM-SOLVING MODEL

The use of a cognitive processing approach to evaluate a child's competence described here fits within a problem-solving model. For example, Deno's (this volume) description of the IDEAL problem-solving model includes five components: identify the problem, define the problem, explore alternative solutions to the problem, apply a solution, and look at the effects of that application. Clearly, the steps described earlier in this chapter fit these problem-solving components. For example, the first two components are a part of step 1 (Assessment) where the nature of the problem is identified (cognitive and academic difficulties) and if so then define the problem within the PASS theory. In the illustration provided above, the child was found to have a cognitive weakness in Successive processing and similarly poor performance in Successive processing. Thus the problem has been identified and carefully defined. Step 2 (Preparation) is accomplished in the third component of the problem-solving model – exploring solutions. Continuing with the illustration, at this point possible interventions such as PREP or those provided by Naglieri and Pickering (2000) are considered and a plan for intervention is prepared. Step 3 (Instruction) is the same as the fourth (apply a solution) and step 4 (Evaluation) is the same as the last component (look at the effects of that application).

The cognitive approach to understanding educational problems also fits with the problem-solving approach discussed by Tilly (this volume). He asks four basic questions: *What is the problem?* . Using the cognitive approach one might answer the questions as follows: The problem is that the child has not learned well from a phonics instruction because (why is it happening) she has considerable difficulty dealing with stimuli in order (poor successive processing) and does not use effective strategies while reading (poor planning). Instruction that takes into account processing weaknesses need to be applied so that instruction does not rely so heavily on successive processing and strategy instruction is provided for better reading. Finally, assessment of the effectiveness of the intervention will be needed. Thus, a cognitive approach to problem solving is illustrated.

CONCLUSIONS

School psychologists have long recognized the potential value of intelligence tests to examine children's abilities that may have relevance to instruction and interventions designed to overcome academic problems. Although widely used, the research on traditional IQ tests has not been supportive of use of these tests for understanding the cognitive problems associated with academic failure (a pre-requisite for development of an effective intervention) and therefore attempts to tie IQ test results to instructional design have been difficult to achieve. With the reconceptualization of intelligence as cognitive processes (e.g., the CAS), school psychologists can go beyond general intelligence (e.g., Wechsler's scales) and factor analytic models (e.g., Woodcock-Johnson III; Woodcock, McGrew, & Mather, 2001) for which evidence of instructional utility is lacking (Kaufman & Lichtenberger, 2000). In contrast, recent research has shown that cognitive processing results can provide important information relevant to cognitively based interventions (Naglieri & Gottling, 1995, 1997; Naglieri & Johnson, 2000). These positive results warrant further examination and continued field-testing, but when integrated with other cognitive educational methods, this collection of literature offers school psychologists valuable options. Taken as a whole, the results of these efforts to help children achieve better using cognitive assessment and cognitive educational interventions provide school psychologists with modern approaches that should be within every professional's repertoire.

In the book *Assessment of Cognitive Processes*, Das, Naglieri, and Kirby (1994) urge readers to recognize that progress in the field of human intellectual assessment and educational remediation "cannot be achieved if improvements consist mainly of revisions of old tests or reconceptualizations of the tasks included in old measures" (p. 12). They recognize that the time has come to move beyond the Wechsler scales and statistically derived approaches that do not have a theory base and more toward cognitive measures of basic psychological processes. This chapter provides some information about how the relationship between assessment and intervention might change if practitioners used measures of cognitive processing. This chapter has also illustrated how the application of information about a child's cognitive processes can be an important part of what school psychologists do when they translate assessment information into intervention plans. This method represents the merging of cognitive assessment and cognitive educational methods that require change on the part of school psychologists. Das, Naglieri, and Kirby (1994) noted this need for change when they wrote: "We are on the edge of a major transition from old theories that limited us to new approaches that offer alternatives (p. 204)." The time has come for practitioners to consider new ways of measuring intelligence so that they move from cognitive assessment to cognitive intervention.

REFERENCES

Ashman, A. F., & Conway, R. N. F. (1997). *An introduction to cognitive education: Theory and applications.* London: Routledge.

Bracken, B. A., & McCallum, R. S. (1998). *Universal Nonverbal Intelligence Test.* Itasca, IL: Riverside.

Cormier, P., Carlson, J. S., & Das, J. P. (1990). *Psychological testing and assessment.* Mountain View, CA: Mayfield.

Das, J. P. (1999). *PASS Reading Enhancement Program.* Deal, NJ: Sarka Educational Resources.

Das, J. P., Naglieri, J. A., & Kirby, J. R. (1994). *Assessment of cognitive processes.* Boston: Allyn & Bacon.

Geary, D. C. (1994). *Children's mathematical development: Research and practical applications.* Washington, D.C.: American Psychological Association.

Goldstein, S., & Mather, N. (1998). *Overcoming underachieving: An action guide to helping your child succeed in school.* New York: John Wiley.

Kar, B.C., Dash, U.N., Das, J. P., & Carlson, J. S. (1992). Two experiments on the dynamic assessment of planning. *Learning and Individual Differences, 5,* 13–29.

Kaufman A. S. (1994a). *Assessing adolescent and adult intelligence.* Boston: Allyn & Bacon.

Kaufman, A. S. (1994b). *Intelligent testing with the WISC-III.* New York: John Wiley.

Kaufman, A. S. (2000). Seven questions about WAIS-III regarding differences in abilities across the 16 to 89 year life span. *School Psychology Quarterly, 15,* 3–29.

Kaufman, A. S., & Kaufman, N. L. (1983). *Kaufman assessment battery for children.* Circle Pines, MN: American Guidance.

Kaufman, A. S., & Lichtenberger, E. O. (2000). *Essentials of WAIS-III assessment.* New York: John Wiley.

Kirby, J. R., & Williams, N. H. (1991). *Learning problems: A cognitive approach.* Toronto: Kagan and Woo.

McGrew, K. S., & Flanagan, D. P. (1998). *The intelligence test desk reference: Gf-Gc cross-battery assessment.* Boston: Allyn & Bacon.

Miller, G., Galanter, E., & Pribram, K. (1960). *Plans and the structure of behavior.* New York: Henry Holt.

Naglieri, J. A. (1993). Pairwise and Ipsative WISC-III IQ and Index Score comparisons: Psychological Assessment. *A Journal of Consulting and Clinical Psychology,* 5, 113–116.

Naglieri, J. A. (1997). *Naglieri Nonverbal Ability Test.* San Antonio: The Psychological Corporation.

Naglieri, J. A. (1999). *Essentials of CAS assessment.* New York: John Wiley.

Naglieri, J. A., & Ashman, A. A. (1999). Making the connection between PASS and intervention. In J. A. Naglieri (Ed.), *Essentials of CAS assessment.* New York: John Wiley.

Naglieri, J. A., & Das, J. P. (1997a). *Cognitive Assessment System.* Itasca, IL: Riverside.

Naglieri, J. A., & Das, J. P. (1997b). *Cognitive Assessment System interpretive handbook.* Itasca, IL: Riverside.

Naglieri, J. A., & Gottling, S. H. (1995). A cognitive education approach to math instruction for the learning disabled: An individual study. *Psychological Reports, 76,* 1343–1354.

Naglieri, J. A., & Gottling, S. H. (1997). Mathematics instruction and PASS cognitive processes: An intervention study. *Journal of Learning Disabilities, 30,* 513–520.

Naglieri, J. A., & Johnson, D. (2000). Effectiveness of a cognitive strategy intervention to improve math calculation based on the PASS theory. *Journal of Learning Disabilities, 33,* 591–597.

Naglieri, J. A., & Pickering, E. (2000). *Handouts for teachers: PASS theory to practice.* Available: www.mypsychologist.com.

Naglieri, J. A., & Sullivan, L. (1998). IDEA and identification of children with specific learning disabilities. *Communiqué, 27,* 20–21.

Peverly, S. T. (1994). An overview of the potential impact of cognitive psychology on school psychology. *School Psychology Review, 23,* 292–309.

Pintner, R. (1925). *Intelligence testing.* New York: Henry Holt.

Pressley. M. P. (1998). *Reading instruction that works: The case for balanced teaching.* New York: Guilford.

Pressley, M. P., & Woloshyn, V. (1995). *Cognitive strategy instruction that really improves children's academic performance* (2nd ed.). Cambridge, MA: Brookline.

Reschly, D. J., & Grimes, J. P. (1995). Best practices in intellectual assessment. In A. Thomas & J. Grimes (Eds.), *Best practices in school psychology III* (pp. 763–773). Washington, DC: National Association of School Psychologists.

Sattler, J. M. (1988). *Assessment of children* (3rd ed.). San Diego: Jerome M. Sattler.

Scheid, K. (1993). *Helping students become strategic learners*. Cambridge, MA: Brookline.

Snow. R. E. (1991). Aptitude-treatment interaction as a framework for research on individual differences in psychotherapy. *Journal of Consulting and Clinical Psychology, 59*, 205–216.

Wasserman, J. D., & Becker, K. A. (2000, August). *Racial and ethnic groups mean score differences on intelligence tests*. Paper presented at the annual convention of the American Psychological Association, Washington, DC.

Wechsler, D. (1939). *Wechsler-Bellevue Intelligence Scale*. New York: Psychological Corporation.

Woodcock, R. W., McGrew. K. S., & Mather, N. (2001). *Woodcock-Johnson III Tests of Cognitive Abilities*. Itasca, IL: Riverside.

Yoakum, C. S., & Yerkes, R. M. (1920). *Army mental tests*. New York: Henry Holt .

Appendix 1. Example of a teacher handout for reading decoding

IMPROVING READING DECODING USING THE READING BY ANALOGY STRATEGY

Jack A. Naglieri, Ph.D.
George Mason University

Eric Pickering
The Ohio State University

Background

Fluent reading requires good reading decoding, which involves making sense out of printed letters and words including understanding letters, what they represent, how they work together, and how they relate to sounds. Decoding involves several cognitive processes but particularly successive processing. Knowing what order letters, letter sounds, and words must be in to make sense requires successive processing. Understanding how letters and word parts relate to one another requires simultaneous processing. Using strategies for decoding involves planning. Attention is needed for recognition of details such as letter orders (ie or ei), punctuation, focus on the story line, etc.

Decoding is important for basic reading as well as for fluent and successful comprehension. Good readers are able to decode words quickly and easily and therefore can devote more attention to comprehending what is read. A strategy like comparing known words to new words with similar spelling patterns may be helpful for the student having trouble decoding a word or text for the first time. The strategy, Reading by Analogy, may be helpful for a student having difficulty decoding new words and who may be poor in successive or planning on the CAS.

Reading by Analogy Strategy

Words that sound the same often are spelled similarly. This can be used to help a child who knows how to pronounce a word such as "tank" to make a reasonable guess at "rank." The same student might also have a good chance at pronouncing "bank," "Frank," and "thank" if he or she were to use the Reading by Analogy strategy. In Reading by Analogy students are taught to compare words they do not know to similar words they do know.

One way to present the Reading by Analogy strategy is to explicitly teach it and then introduce new target words along with five to six new words that can be related to words the students already know. In this method, students are encouraged to learn the new words by analogy and are asked why and how the strategy helps them. Each word is presented on a sheet of paper and the students are instructed to write two or three other words that share the same spelling pattern. After this stage, the students are asked to read passages containing the new words and are encouraged to use analogies to decode them. The teacher should model the use of analogies while reading and provide feedback for the student independently using the strategy.

Once the strategy is taught, modeled, and the students have practiced it, they may be simply encouraged to use the strategy whenever they encounter new words. It may be helpful for the teacher to post a list of words the students know by sight that they may refer to when they encounter a new

Appendix 1. (continued)

word. It is important to consider that reading by analogy need not be confined to simple words or comparisons such as "bug," "hug," and "rug." More complex words and analogies can be made, for example, the words "at," "tent," and the suffix "–tion" may be put together or "analogized" to form attention. Although not a direct combination, this analogy can serve to help the student approach the word thoughtfully and independently.

The Teacher Role

- Discuss the rational or helpfulness of the strategy
- Use and model the strategy
- Provide the student ample opportunity for practice
- Provide feedback
- Encourage the use of the strategy

Use

Children who are poor in successive processing will likely have decoding problems (Das, Naglieri, & Kirby, 1994) and those with planning weakness will have few plans to help them learn how to decode. This strategy for reading decoding using the analogy method should be applied when the child has a successive and/or planning weakness along with reading decoding failure.

Resources

Das, J. P., Naglieri, J. A., & Kirby, J. R. (1994). *Assessment of cognitive processes.* Boston: Allyn & Bacon.

Kirby, J., & Williams, N. (1991). *Learning problems: A cognitive approach.* Toronto: Kagan & Woo.

Naglieri, J. A. (1999) *Essentials of CAS assessment.* New York: John Wiley.

Pressley, M. P., & Woloshyn, V. (1995). *Cognitive strategy instruction that really improves children's academic performance* (2nd ed.). Cambridge, MA: Brookline.

Appendix 2. Example of a teacher handout for reading comprehension

IMPROVING READING COMPREHENSION WITH STRATEGIES

Jack A. Naglieri, Ph.D.
George Mason University

Eric Pickering
The Ohio State University

Background

Expert readers use a variety of strategies to understand what they read. They combine their background knowledge with context cues to create meaning, monitor their ongoing comprehension solving comprehension problems as they read, and they evaluate what they have read (e.g., Is the content believable? Does it make sense?) (Pressley & Woloshyn, 1995). This thoughtful approach to reading takes planning, which is why teachers should instruct children to be planful when they read. Good comprehension instruction should incorporate not only decoding (see Reading Decoding Strategy handout) and understanding of what is read but also the systematic planful approach to comprehending what is read.

When students encounter difficult text the consistent use of multiple comprehension strategies is essential for good comprehension (Pressley & Woloshyn, 1995). Students who are taught to be planful in reading are more successful. Teachers should make the strategies and mental processes for good comprehension explicit in their instruction by thinking aloud to the students when they teach and model strategy use. The key is teaching students a variety of strategies and encouraging them to use all of them when appropriate (which includes teaching *when* a strategy is appropriate). This will be very important for all children but especially those who are poor in planning (see Naglieri & Gottling, 1995; Naglieri, 1999).

Strategies

The following strategies can be easily taught and may be very helpful for the reader who is struggling with comprehension, especially those with poor planning scores on the CAS:

- *React* to text, by relating ideas in text to prior knowledge. This can be achieved by encouraging students to activate background knowledge related to text.
- *Predict* upcoming content by relating prior knowledge to ideas already encountered in text. This includes teaching students to check whether the predictions they made were consistent with text content.
- *Construct images* representing the ideas in text.
- *Slow down*, reading more carefully, and check back in text when unsure.
- *Generating questions* in reaction to text, perhaps by using specific question-asking methods, with the answers then pursued by reading groups.
- *Summarization,* including construction of notes capturing the important ideas in a text (see Summarization Strategy for Improving Comprehension).

Appendix 2. (continued)

The Teacher's Role

The teacher's role in strategy use includes explanation, modeling and providing feedback. Pressley and Woloshyn (1995) suggest the following teacher behaviors:

- Use strategy terms (e.g. Summarizing or Question Generation) including defining such terms when necessary.
- Model strategies by thinking aloud while applying the strategy during reading, including explaining the reasoning for applying particular strategies.
- Emphasize that strategies are coordinated with one another before, during, and after reading the text, with different strategies appropriate at different point in a text.
- Tell students the purpose of the strategy lesson (e.g., to understand stories by using the imagery strategy along with other strategies).
- Tell (discuss with?) students how they benefit from strategies use (i.e., how strategies help their comprehension), emphasizing that strategies are a means for obtaining comprehension and learning goals.

Uses

Comprehension strategies can be useful for all students. However, students having difficulty in comprehension who show deficits in planning may find the direct instruction and support of these strategies particularly helpful. Because these students may not be able to generate their own planful strategies for comprehension, they may find success when provided with specific and multiple strategies as well as an environment that suggests and supports their use.

Resources

Kirby, J., & Williams, N. (1991). *Learning problems: A cognitive approach*. Toronto: Kagan & Woo.

Naglieri, J. A. (1999) *Essentials of CAS assessment*. New York: John Wiley.

Naglieri, J. A., & Gottling, S. H. (1995). A cognitive education approach to math instruction for the learning disabled: An individual study. *Psychological Reports, 76*, 1343–1354.

Naglieri, J. A., & Gottling, S. H. (1997). Mathematics instruction and PASS cognitive processes: An intervention study. *Journal of Learning Disabilities, 30*, 513–520.

Pressley, M., & Woloshyn, V., (1995). *Cognitive strategy instruction that really improves children's academic performance*. Cambridge, MA: Brookline.

Appendix 3. **Example of a teacher handout for learning math facts**

USING PLANS TO LEARN MATH FACTS

Jack A. Naglieri
George Mason University

Eric Pickering
Ohio State University

Background Information

There are many ways to learn math facts: Some involve rote memory while others rely more on an understanding of how math works. Students are often encouraged to memorize math facts so they can be produced automatically. Sometimes they are encouraged to say or write the basic facts in order to learn them (for example, the fact 7 + 8 = 15). Writing or saying this sequence of numbers puts the task into a linear order with at least five steps as shown in the figure. Whenever a child has to learn something that is arranged in a specific linear order, the task demands considerable successive processing (using the PASS theory as a guide). If a child is poor in successive processing, then memorization of the statement 7 + 8 = 15 can be very difficult.

7	+	8	=	15
1	2	3	4	5

Memorization, however, is not the only way children can learn math facts. In order to reduce the heavy reliance on successive processing, children can be taught to use strategies (plans) for getting the correct answer. When a child uses a strategy to remember a math fact, the answer is obtained by thinking (using the plan or method) rather than by relying on remembering the string of numbers and signs (successive processing). For example, if a child is taught the "Doubles Plus One" rule, then the answer can be obtained by using this strategy as follows: "7 + 8 ... well, 7 + 7 is 14, so 7 + 8 has to be one more than 14, so the answer is 15." Alternatively, the child may reason: "7 + 8 is the same as 7 + 7 + 1 so the answer is 14 +1, which is 15." This strategy changes the cognitive processing demands of the task from one that relies on successive processing to one that involves planning. Children who are poor in successive processing and who have problems memorizing math facts should be taught to use strategies like the illustrations that follow.

Strategies for Multiplication and Division

Multiplication by:

0s – 0 x any number is always 0 (0 x 9 = 0).
1s – 1 x any number is always that number (1 x 7 = 7).
2s – 2 x a number will end in a zero or an even number (0, 2, 4, 6, or 8).
5s – 5 x any number, the answer must end in 0 or 5.

- 5 x any number involves counting by fives, as when telling time from a standard clock.
- 5 x an even number is half that number with a 0 added (4 x 5 = 20, 5 x 8 = 40).

6s – 6 x any number is half that number in front of the 6, so 6 x 8 = 48. Half of 8 = 4 (which goes in the tens place with the 8 in the 1s place) and remember the answer must be even.

9s - 9 x any number can be solved by a plan: take one away from the multiplier and then add a number to make 9, those two numbers are the answer. For example, for 9 x 8, take 1 from 8 = 7, 7 – 9 = 2, those two numbers (7 and 2 or 72) make the answer.

- 9 x any number is that number times 10 minus the number (9 x 7 is 10 x 7 = 70 then 70 – 7 = 63). Of course the 10s rules are best to have mastered before this one.

Appendix 3. (continued)

- 9 x any number, adding the digits of the answer equals 9 (9 x 4 = 45, 4 + 5 = 9).

10s – The answer will end in 0.
Simply put a 0 on the end of the multiplier.

Remaining Multiplication Facts

After learning all the above multiplication rules, only the following facts must be specifically memorized: 3 x 3; 3 x 4; 3 x 6; 3 x 7; 3 x 8; 4 x 4; 4 x 7; 4 x 8; 6 x 7; 7 x 7; 7 x 8; 8 x 8.

Division

2s – The answer must be an even number, ending in 2, 4, 6, 8, or 0.
3s - The sum of the digits of the number must be divisible by 3.
4s - The number must be even and the last two digits of the number are divisible by 4.
5s - The number must end in 0 or 5.
6s - The answer must be even and the sum of its digits must be divisible by 3.
7s - You must be able to drop the 1s' digit, and subtract 2 times the 1s' digit from the remaining number. If that number can be divided by 7, the original number can be, too.
8s - The number formed by the last three digits of the number can be divided by 8.
9s - The sum of the digits must be divisible by 9.
10s - The number must end in 0.
11s - First add the alternate digits, beginning with the first digit. Next you must add the alternate digits, beginning with the second. Subtract the smaller sum from the larger. If the difference is divisible by 11, the original number is divisible by 11.
12s - The number must be divisible by both 3 and 4.

Teacher Guidelines

- Use direct explanation: teach why, when, and where to use these rules
- Model skills: talk through examples, showing how the skill is applied
- Provide practice with feedback
- Phase out teacher direction and phase in student use throughout instruction
- After these rules have been learned post them in the classroom for independent use

When To Use This Technique

Students who have a successive processing weakness may have a particularly difficult time committing math facts to memory. This technique may be used to help the students approach multiplication and division in a different strategic way that is specific and engaging. Because the method teaches a plan, it may also be useful for children who are poor in planning.

Resources

Goldstein, S., and Mather, N. (1998) *Overcoming underachieving: An action guide to helping your child succeed in school.* New York: John Wiley.

Muschla, J. A., & Muschla, R. G. (1995) *The math teacher's book of lists.* Englewood, NJ: Prentice Hall.

86 Best Practices in Program Planning for Children Who Are Deaf and Hard-of-Hearing

Jennifer A. Lukomski
Rochester Institute of Technology

OVERVIEW

In the last 20 years educational programming of students who are Deaf (a capital "D" will be used for "Deaf" to acknowledge the cultural perspective of deafness) and hard-of-hearing has shifted from the residential schools to the public schools (Schildroth & Hotto, 1996). With this shift in educating Deaf and hard-of-hearing students in the public school system, more school psychologists are faced with the challenges of providing services to students who have a hearing loss. The complexity of the educational programming for Deaf students is daunting because it involves the interaction of academic, linguistic, social, and cultural issues. The primary task for school psychologists is how to make Deaf and hard-of-hearing students' educational programming in the public school system the most appropriate and the least restrictive.

This chapter is written for school psychologists who have limited knowledge in working with children who are Deaf or hard-of-hearing. Although the focus of the chapter is on the practical elements to consider when planning the educational programming of Deaf students who use sign language and who rely on interpreters for communication, planning issues for students who are oral are also addressed. These issues pertain to Deaf or hard-of-hearing students in partial programs, fully integrated programs, or a separate program within the regular school system. Although assessment concerns will be mentioned, this chapter is not an in-depth focus on assessment issues.

BASIC CONSIDERATIONS

Specialized Training

The fundamental consideration regarding the best practices for providing services for Deaf learners is to know one's limitations. Sign language proficiency and specialized training in the area of school psychology and deafness are necessary in order to work with Deaf and hard-of-hearing students. The current law and professional standards stipulate that students must be assessed by using their native language or primary mode of communication unless it is clearly not feasible to do so (e.g., Individuals with Disabilities Education Act Revisions of 1997: Section 3.4.4.1, NASP Standards for the Provision of School Psychological Services, 1997). Often for Deaf learners that native language is American Sign Language (ASL). Unfortunately, a majority of school psychologists reported that when assessing Deaf and hard-of hearing students they had no specialized training in deafness and either no, or poor, sign language skills (Weaver & Bradley-Johnson ,1993). One solution to this ethical and legal mandate is to use a certified sign language interpreter when providing psychological services to a Deaf learner. The use of interpreters, however, may result in misinterpretations or misunderstandings in communication (Raifman & Vernon, 1996). Another solution to this dilemma is contacting the psychologist at a Deaf residential school system in the state. Often psychologists at the residential schools are able to provide information and direction in the psychological and educational aspects of deafness.

Heterogeneous Nature

Another basic consideration regarding the educational programming of Deaf and hard-of hearing students is understanding the heterogeneous nature of the Deaf and hard-of-hearing population. The Deaf and hard-of-hearing population is as diverse as the hearing population in regards to gender, religion, ethnicity, home languages spoken, and sexual identity. In addition, within the Deaf and hard-of-hearing population there is considerable range and diversity of hearing loss type, etiology of deafness, and degree of hearing loss. Other factors such as when the child was identified with a hearing loss, when the loss actually occurred, the child's early language intervention background, the family's hearing status and communication modes, the child's cultural identification, the child's language development, whether the child's hearing is progressive or stable, the child's use of speech, cued speech and/or sign language, and the child's use of hearing aids and/or cochlear implant contribute to the uniqueness of each Deaf and hard-of-hearing child. Those variables need to be thoroughly assessed and taken into account when planning the child's educational programming. Furthermore, a sensory deficit such as a hearing loss does not mean that the Deaf or hard-of-hearing child may not be gifted, have a learning disability, or have mental retardation. With so many factors to consider when working with a Deaf and hard-of-hearing child the "individual" in Individualized Education Plan is bold.

Cultural Considerations

A third consideration is that Deafness is often viewed as a distinct culture rather than as a disability (Padden, 1980). This cultural identification of the child is not based on degree of hearing loss but rather on ASL fluency and with interaction with the Deaf community. For many Deaf and hard-of-hearing children the residential school is the place where they develop their cultural identity. For students who have minimal contact with other Deaf individuals this identification may not happen until later in life. Often this identity may not fully be initiated until adolescence (that is, depending on the student's family and educational background) and exposure to other deaf individuals (Calderon & Greenberg, 2000).

Sensitivity to these cultural differences is essential for correct interpretation of the Deaf and hard-of-hearing child's behaviors. Deaf children's behavioral norms are often dictated by their communication mode. Some of these behavioral examples are vigorous waving of one's hand to get a person's attention, scanning the classroom periodically to see who is talking, use of peripheral vision to alert to the environment, maintaining intense and continual eye contact, touching to gain attention, or use of animated and affect-laden sign. These behaviors, the norm for children who are Deaf or hard-of-hearing, when misinterpreted can lead to misidentification of behavioral disorders in Deaf and hard-of-hearing children (Morgan & Vernon, 1994).

Collaboration With Family

The importance of considering the cultural perspective of deafness highlights another important consideration regarding educational programming of Deaf and hard-of-hearing children: that is, collaboration with the Deaf or hard-of-hearing student's parents as well as the student. The majority of Deaf and hard-of-hearing children are born to hearing parents. Often these hearing parents have limited knowledge about deafness, about the Deaf culture, and about the language and educational options available for their child. Complicating matters is that in the midst of hearing parents' grief regarding having a child with a hearing loss they may hear conflicting opinions about the most appropriate and effective communication and educational method for their Deaf child. Researchers and experts in the field agree that early childhood identification and early intensive language intervention is critical (Downs & Yoshinaga-Itano, 1999). However, debated speech topics include whether a child should have a cochlear implant, be educated in an oral setting, learn ASL, and/or use cued speech. Parents need information and professionals need to collaborate with parents in evaluating the options for the child as a unique learner.

Deaf and hard-of hearing children are also integral members of the educational programming team. For example, a school psychologist who had limited knowledge about working with Deaf and hard-of-hearing students consulted with me regarding a 17-year-old "hearing impaired" student on her caseload. She had not yet met with the student and asked me for some direction planning his transition services. She added that this student was the only Deaf student in the school building. She reported that she was worried that the adolescent was too dependent on "his" interpreter and she was thinking about recommending that the interpreter be phased out of the student's educational programming. She added that the student was passing all his classes and that he had been accepted at a local college. Although she reported no behavioral concerns or adaptation issues, she was worried about how he was managing his daily living skills and how he would manage at college. She was surprised to hear that most Deaf and hard-of-hearing individuals manage daily life demands as independently as hearing individuals. For instance, they drive cars, use TDDs or the state relay system for phone communication, have flashing doorbells, and may use flashing or vibrating alarm clocks. On the basis of the information she provided, I recommended that she contact the student and have a frank discussion with him about his life plans and goals. Linking him up with Vocational Rehabilitation Services may be one of the transition services with which she could assist him. Regarding her thoughts to phase out the interpreter, I explained that removing the interpreter, thereby removing the student's access to language and communication, would be like taking away someone's glasses because that student was successful in class work while wearing glasses.

The main point of this story is that the children/adolescents and families often have information that will help with the planning of the student's educational programming. Problems encountered are compounded by a lack of comfort on the part of both the school personnel and the family/student in dealing with deafness either by ignoring problems or by minimizing the differences (Foster & Holcomb, 1990). To maximize solutions and to encourage a productive learning environment there must be open communication and information sharing. These are essential components in the educational programming for the Deaf and hard-of-hearing student.

Assessment Issues

A critical element in the design and selection of the educational programming for a Deaf and hard-of-hearing student is a thorough and ongoing assessment of the student's learning strengths and weaknesses. The components of this assessment depend on the current academic, social, and emotional development of the student. As for most students, testing is not sufficient for educational planning of the Deaf and hard-of-hearing student. Rather, a problem-solving multiple assessment approach that documents norm-referenced test results, interviews, direct observations, and analyses of informal assessment tasks is the starting framework for a comprehensive assessment. Owing to the limitations of most of the current test instruments for use with Deaf and hard-of-hearing students, the examiner needs to be sensitive and knowledgeable regarding the interpretation and integration of both the quantitative and qualitative information the student provides. Specifically, the areas that need to be addressed in a psychoeducational assessment of Deaf and hard-of-hearing students are the developmental history and educational background of the student, language background, classroom interactions and behaviors, work samples, and teacher and parent perspective of the child's adaptive behavior skills. Whether the child is a Deaf child fluent in ASL or a hard-of-hearing child who is oral or a child with a hearing loss who has limited language fluency, a section in the assessment report needs to address the child's language development. Additionally, the assessment report should specify what communication mode the examiner used to assess the child.

Owing to the language differences for the Deaf and hard-of-hearing, a verbal intelligence test is not an assessment of a Deaf and hard-of hearing student's verbal cognitive potential or problem-solving ability. Rather it is an assessment of the student's ability to *understand* verbal material. Instead of using verbal intelligence measures, the recommended practice for assessing deaf and hard-of-hearing persons' intelligence is to use nonverbal scales of intelligence, usually two different nonverbal measures (Sullivan & Vernon, 1979). A helpful document in determining the most appropriate tests to use with Deaf and hard-of-hearing students is a review of tests that Spragins and Mullen (1998) have compiled and which can be accessed on the Internet.

BEST PRACTICES IN PROGRAM

Three interconnected domains that need to be thoroughly addressed when designing the instructional programming for the student who is Deaf or hard-of-hearing are the student's communication needs, learning needs, and social interaction needs. A common theme across these three domains is the child's language development.

Communication

Communication is a process by which information is exchanged between individuals through a common system of symbols, signs, or behavior. Communication can happen on many different levels: emotionally, socially, and linguistically. When considering the appropriate learning environment for a Deaf or hard-of-hearing child, how the child communicates and the opportunities available to the child to share in communication should be examined and developed. Additionally, to determine the readiness of the student who is Deaf or hard-of hearing to participate within a specific setting, some assessment must be made of the communicative demands required of the students within the placement (Ying, 1990).

Probably the most controversial area within the communication domain for children who have a hearing loss is what is the best communication mode for a Deaf and hard-of-hearing child. Questions exist regarding whether the child and or adolescent should attend speech classes, have a cochlear implant, use a FM system, use sign language, or use cued speech. Although there is conflicting evidence in the literature and differences of opinion concerning language development and the best language method for all children with a hearing loss, experts agree that early language intervention and ongoing rich language exposure is critical (Marschark, in press). Signed and spoken language are not necessarily exclusive approaches. A combination of methods can be the most effective approach to language development. Furthermore, sign language is the most naturally accessible language to Deaf and hard-of-hearing children and for most Deaf children have a vital and valuable place in the student's life. The best practice approach is to be knowledgeable about the options and the pros and cons of each option for the specific student.

For Deaf and hard-of hearing children who are not blind, the visual field will be the student's primary sense used to orient to the environment whether he or she uses sign language or speech. This reliance on the visual field dictates that for instructional purposes, lighting and seating arrangements are of paramount importance. The classroom needs to be well lit, and glare on windows and the positioning of the teacher when lecturing in relation to the lighting needs to be examined. The student needs to be seated close to the teacher, so that the student can visually track the teacher without any visual obstructions. One of the best seating arrangements for the classroom is placing tables or seats in a horseshoe shape. When the seating arrangement is in a horseshoe, the Deaf and hard-of-hearing student can visually locate students who are participating in class discussion as well as track class activity.

Another consideration for students who rely on the visual field for communication is that the student's attention is divided among the various tasks presented in the classroom. To begin communication, the teacher first needs to gain the child's visual attention either by a tap on the student's shoulder, a hand movement in the child's visual field, or a flick of the overhead lights. Then the teacher needs to allow the child to orient visually to the teacher or object of discussion. The student has to shift visual attention from the environment to the communicator in order to receive a person's message. Often teachers present material and talk about the material at the same time. For example, teachers lecture while writing on the blackboard, or explain points during a movie. For a Deaf student this simultaneous presentation, rather than complementing the material presented, may compete with the salient information to be learned. Taking notes is another activity that for Deaf or hard-of-hearing students can become a competing rather than a supplementing task. Daily interactions in the classroom, such as rapid rate of discussion, rapid turn taking, rapid change of topics, and more than one student talking at a time, are also difficult for the student to follow (Stinson, Liu, Saur, & Long, 1996). To facilitate communication, classroom activities need to be structured in a manner that allow the student to fully participate. The best practice approach is for the teacher to limit simultaneous presentation of material, allow for pauses in presentation of activities, identify speakers, and monitor turn-taking. Depending on the student's age, a notetaker may be necessary.

Another environmental factor to consider for children who use hearing aids or cochlear implants is background noise. Many Deaf children who use hearing aids or have cochlear implants are sensitive to background noise. Any extraneous noise can be extremely distracting and the student's concentration can be affected.

Speech and Language

Owing to the heterogeneous nature of the Deaf population, Deaf and hard-of-hearing students vary considerably with respect to hearing and communication skills. The documentation that a child has a hearing loss is the child's audiogram. Audiograms should be completed and reevaluated annually to help determine the student's amplification needs and needs for programming. However, the audiogram is a gross starting point to determine the child's communication needs. Two children with identical audiograms can have dramatically different functional hearing (Ying, 1990). Similarly children with poorer auditory skills do not necessarily have the greater degree of hearing loss (Ying, 1990). In addition, frequent ear infections affect the child's hearing, as does the stability of the child's hearing loss. For example, when the student has a progressive hearing loss, a proactive approach to the student's future communication needs should be incorporated into the educational planning, and the school psychologist has to be sensitive to the student's and family's psychological needs for coping with a progressive hearing loss.

Not only will two children with identical audiograms have different functional hearing, two children with identical audiograms will also have different family attitudes toward amplification and speech training. Speech training, not to be confused with language development, can be time-intensive and may exclude the child from other valuable learning experiences. Whether speech training is enhancing the child's education or detracting from the child's learning experiences needs to be assessed and determined in conjunction with the parent's concerns, the child's motivation, the child's age, and the child's most effective mode of communication. In general, many children with mild-to-moderate hearing losses benefit from amplification and speech training. While children with severe-to-profound hearing losses may also benefit from amplification and speech training, most often they additionally need sign language as their primary mode of input and output.

Assistive Listening Devices

There have been many advances in the technology relating to assistive listening devices (ALDs) and other communication devices. Most of the ALDs help the student make the most out of residual hearing and make speech or noises more audible, if not clearer. No device, however, restores the hearing to normal or typical hearing. The traditional ALDs are FM systems and hearing aids, which are used primarily by children who have moderate hearing losses to amplify the loudness and the clarity of the sender's voice. The FM system is used in the classroom. The teacher wears the microphone and transmitter, and the child wears the receiver. Recent technological advances in ALDs include transposers, programmable hearing aids, and cochlear implants (Copmann, 1996). Hearing aids that are programmable are devices programmed specifically to fit the user's hearing loss. Transposers are devices that change the high pitched sounds that the child cannot hear into low pitched sounds the child can hear.

In comparison, the cochlear implant is one of the newest technologies now used in "treating" children with a sensorineural hearing loss. Considered a more invasive ADL, the cochlear implant has seven components. A receiver is surgically implanted under the skin near one ear and fine electrode wires are inserted into the cochlea. Additionally the child wears a microphone at ear level that picks up sound signals. These signals are then processed into appropriate electrical signal that travels by a cable to a radio frequency transmitter that is placed on top of the area of the skull where the receiver has been implanted. The receiver then delivers the electrical signal to the afferent auditory nerves within the cochlea.

The controversy revolving around the cochlear implant stems primarily from professionals and members of the Deaf community who view deafness as a rich culture with its own language. In contrast, cochlear implants are perceived as representing a medical perspective of deafness, implying that deafness is a deficit that needs to be fixed. In addition to being seen as a threat to the vitality of Deaf culture, another concern pertaining to cochlear implants is that medical professionals appear to be recommending to parents that they have their child implanted without providing deliberation of the ramifications, complications, and realistic outcomes.

Recent studies have shown that children with cochlear implants have continued improvement in speech perception and production as long as 4 years postimplant (Brookhouser, Beauchaine, & Osberger,

1999). Cochlear implants, however, do not restore hearing to normal nor are there reliable factors that accurately predict which children will benefit most from implantation (Epstein, 1996). Furthermore, the auditory and speech rehabilitation is extensive, requiring that the child and family be highly motivated for the child to learn how to make sense out of the sounds the child is hearing.

For a school psychologist working with a Deaf child whose parents are considering a cochlear implant, it is important to stress to the parents the need for a preoperative psychological evaluation to thoroughly examine the motivation and expectations as well as extensive rehabilitative efforts required of this treatment (Pollard, 1996). As more children with cochlear implants enter the schools, school psychologists will need to be aware that these children need extensive auditory and speech training. And perhaps most important, owing to the visible nature of these cochlear implants, children with cochlear implants may also need special support in coping with ridicule from other hearing children and Deaf children.

Other assistive technology that can be used to accommodate students with hearing losses are telecommunication devices (i.e., TDD, TTY), captioned films and media materials, and computers. The TTY is a device that is hooked up to the telephone so that the student can communicate with other TTY users or communicate via the relay system with hearing individuals. Deaf and hard-of-hearing students need to have access to a TTY in the school and be encouraged to use the TTY rather than rely on others to make phone calls for them. For example, if the student's hearing aid is broken, the student can learn how to advocate for himself or herself by learning how to contact the hearing aid center and request repair services.

Another more omnipresent technological device that can be used for instruction as well as to facilitate communication and interaction among students is the computer. The computer is a more sophisticated form of the pencil and pad method of communication. This method of communication presupposes that students have minimum literacy level and keyboard skills. Both these skills can, however, be further developed as students communicate via the computer.

Cued Speech

Cued speech is a visual representation of English that can help a child who is Deaf become aware of speech sounds. Different hand shapes that represent sounds or phonemes are positioned around the speaker's mouth while the speaker talks. Cued speech stems from an oral approach to language, and the hand shapes support spoken language making sounds that look alike on the lips in English more distinguishable to lip-read. Research, primarily in Europe, found that deaf children who used cued speech consistently at home and at school from an early age showed increased performance in reading skills (Marschark, in press). Parents and educators, therefore, need to at least consider the possible incorporation of cued speech as a supplemental support system to help the child in learning phonetics and reading subskills.

American Sign Language (Sign Language Systems)

For children with severe to profound hearing losses, exposure to spoken language usually is not sufficient for successful communication. For these Deaf students, communication has to depend on visual cues (Marschark, in press). ASL or other forms of manually coded English provide an effective means of communication. ASL is a natural language that has its own grammar and rules of syntax. In contrast, other manually coded sign languages use hands to convey language rather than voice, yet are artificial signing systems that adopt and adapt ASL signs to fit the grammatical structure of English. The degree these signing systems adhere to the grammatical structure of English lies on a continuum with Pidgin Sign English (PSE) on the end of most flexible in use of ASL structure as well as English word order. On the other end of the continuum are more rigid manually coded systems such as Signed Exact English (SEE1, SEE2). Total Communication—using a combination of methods to communicate to the child—is effective for facilitating communication; however, it is not a real language and does not develop a language base for the child.

Considering the varied language enrichment backgrounds of Deaf and hard-of-hearing children the assumption that Deaf children will automatically learn and become fluent in ASL is optimistic. Interaction with ASL Deaf role models facilitates the learning of ASL. Nonetheless, many Deaf children who have limited exposure to Deaf role models at early ages would benefit from formal instruction in ASL to enhance their communication skills.

Interpreters

For those students whose preferred mode of communication is sign language, an educational interpreter should be provided to facilitate communication for the Deaf student. Often the function of the educational interpreter in the public school system is not clearly defined, and school personnel have misunderstandings regarding the role of the interpreter and who can interpret. The mere ability to sign does not qualify one to be an interpreter. Especially in a formal setting where an interpreter is the voice for the teacher, the interpreter must have specialized training and be certified by the state or the national Registry of Interpreters for the Deaf . Additionally, the interpreter must not only be a certified interpreter, but also qualified to interpret in the sign language form used by the child. Another misunderstanding regarding the role of the interpreter pertains to when the interpreter's support is no longer needed. That a Deaf student demonstrates success in the classroom does not mean that the student no longer needs the interpreter. One of the reasons why the student is successful is because the interpreter facilitates communication. If the interpreter is removed, than the student no longer has the access to communication.

The other roles an educational interpreter may assume must be clearly defined with all members of the educational team. First, and foremost, the interpreter is a facilitator of communication in class and out of class (i.e., extracurricular activities). In the school setting, educational interpreters are also members of the educational team. Educational interpreters can assume other responsibilities if they have the qualifications, background, and time. School psychologists, understanding that some teachers may believe that the interpreter is either an interruption or a glorified teacher's aide, can facilitate the team's discussing these obstacles and clarifying roles.

When a classroom uses an interpreter, a few unique communication dynamics occur. The lag time between the spoken and signed message affects the ability of the Deaf student to fully participate in classroom discussion. Teachers, therefore, need to allow extra time before calling on students, to allow for the Deaf student to catch up. Sometimes the interpreter may also need extra time to provide explanations and define terms.

Learning Issues

Educators are often concerned that deaf and hard-of-hearing learners are not achieving to the level of their potential, especially in reading and writing. Overall, Deaf and hard-of-hearing individuals have average intellectual abilities; however, their academic achievement often falls below average. Many Deaf students leave high school reading on a third- or fourth-grade level. Specifically many Deaf and hard-of-hearing students have a low reading vocabulary, limited background knowledge/experience, poor English syntax, weak processing ability, difficulty understanding figurative language, and problems with inferencing skills (Paul & Quigly, 1994). No doubt the development of literacy skills needs to be the focus of education planning for Deaf and hard-of-hearing students, especially in the elementary years.

The area that has to be first considered in developing these literacy skills is the student's language development. Many Deaf and hard-of-hearing students are challenged to learn to read when they have not yet acquired and internalized any formal language (McAnally, Rose, & Quigley, 1994). This delay in language is partly due to delays in diagnosis of the hearing loss and lack of exposure to early enriched language experiences, pointing to the importance of early hearing loss diagnosis and language intervention. Owing to the critical aspects of having a foundation in language before learning to read, Deaf and hard-of-hearing students need a thorough language assessment. This language assessment may include both an assessment of the child's ASL development as well as the child's English development. It is recommended that an interactionist approach to a comprehensive language assessment for Deaf and hard-of-hearing children be used that focuses on identifying the strategies the student is using to accomplish certain language tasks and to evaluate the success of these strategies (Yoshinaga-Itano, 1997). Developmental profiles then can be created and information can be evaluated concerning the context in which the language is used.

It is possible for deaf students with profound hearing losses to achieve reading skills commensurate with those of their hearing peers. Although Deaf children of deaf parents tend to read better than most Deaf and hard-of-hearing children of hearing parents, many Deaf children of hearing parents who learn to sign also have reading abilities that are higher (Marschark, in press). The crucial issue is that children who have access to language at home and have more language experiences have an increased proficiency and automaticity in processing meaning from the written word (Bebko & Metcalfe-Haggert, 1997).

A concern has been raised that reading instruction for Deaf students focuses on teaching them the basic decoding skills of how to read, without encouraging active participation or teaching individual strategies for reading to learn for comprehension (Strassman, 1997). Deaf students greatly benefit from instruction in metacognition about reading (Strassman, 1997). Instruction that focuses on basic skills such as using worksheets, answering teachers questions, or memorizing vocabulary words without developing metacognitive knowledge of reading for meaning and authentic purposes is not effective. Additionally, strategies that encourage attention to text elements as well as relations among those elements are most effective in optimizing text comprehension (Marschark & Lukomski, in press).

Making implicit the connections and relationships between words in the text as well as across experiences should be an instructional goal. Teachers can select stimuli for exposure, control environmental events, and focus the child regarding salient aspects of the task. A qualitative interactive feedback format or mediated learning experience is recommended to be used with Deaf and hard-of-hearing students (Das & Ojile, 1995).

Another instructional approach is to use existing resources that are used with children who have difficulty with reading, such as strategies borrowed from the learning disability field (Marschark & Lukomski, in press). This is not to suggest that these children should be labeled or diagnosed with a learning disability, but rather that there are teaching methods available in the learning disability domain that can be successfully applied with Deaf and hard-of-hearing learners. Many strategies used with children who have reading disabilities involve interactive and direct instruction, emphasize pictorial materials, and use repetition and incorporate multi-sensory information sources, all of which enhance the learning experience for Deaf and hard-of-hearing children.

Parents also should be advised concerning the importance of reading with their young children and instructed on methods by which they can combine sign language and spoken language or sign-supported spoken language. Early reading experience can directly facilitate language development and literacy in children with hearing loss, as well as provide a structured interaction between a child and the parent.

Another component to interactive learning is teaching the student about his or her hearing loss. Similar to children who have learning disabilities, Deaf and hard-of-hearing students need to be taught about their hearing loss and how it affects learning and the strategies needed to compensate for the differences. This understanding of learning style, strengths, and weaknesses allows the student to become a self-advocate. Many Deaf and hard-of-hearing college-age students remember being tested by the school psychologist. In comparison, few are able to explain the results of the testing, know how to read their own audiogram, or understand what learning strategies work for them. Informing students about their strengths and weaknesses is significant in empowering students, thereby enhancing their self-esteem and motivating them to become more active in the learning process.

Social Interaction

Informing students about the impact that their hearing loss has on their learning is one component in helping students to have clearer perceptions of their hearing loss. Another component that influences students' perceptions of their hearing loss is the students' interaction with family members, peers, and others.

The proponents of mainstreaming believe that proximity to hearing children will actually promote social interaction. Unfortunately, owing to the language constraints for Deaf and hard-of-hearing children, this social interaction happens infrequently. Furthermore, many Deaf and hard-of-hearing students have limited contact with other Deaf children because often only one or two students in a school or school district may be Deaf. Coping with hearing loss in the mainstream becomes more stressful without the variety of social interaction that can help combat some of the stress.

School psychologists know how important friends are for mental health and overall adjustment. Additionally, students with positive social interactions in school tend to have higher academic achievement and are more likely to succeed in their careers (Marschark,

1997). The lack of close friendships for Deaf and hard-of-hearing students in the mainstream setting has critical implications for program planning for their development. Program planning should include their feelings of isolation and loneliness that may increase through the school years as peer influences increase. Considering the significance of social interaction, children may do best with an educational plan that recommends or supports different placements at different times during their development. Some children benefit from attending a separate program designed for Deaf children part of the day in addition to mainstream classes for identified courses.

Social interaction, however, is not just about having friends, socializing at school, and minimization of isolation or belonging to a group. Social settings provide rich learning opportunities for language development and also for incidental learning that illuminates the aspects of daily life (Yoshinago-Itano, 1997).

There is considerable overlap between communication, language, and social interaction. A shared language does not necessarily guarantee good communication; however, without a shared language limited communication can happen, and without social interaction language development is hampered. Social interaction activities such as teaching others sign language and teaching Deaf and hard-of-hearing children how to ask questions, take turns, and listen should be planned in the child's educational program. For the most part, small group activities are better than large social groups; dyad cooperative exercises are the best for an equal interaction to take place.

To foster and promote the Deaf and hard-of-hearing child's social emotional development, home-school collaboration is also critical. As with other disabilities, the family's coping and adjustment to the hearing loss often is a good predictor of the student's adjustment. Some suggestions are to involve parents in the education process and to provide them with resources regarding advanced sign language classes, family weekend retreats, exposure to deaf adults, and problem-solving groups to address deaf adolescent issues (Calderon & Greenberg, 2000). The importance of providing Deaf and hard-of-hearing children opportunities to learn about cultural aspects of deafness and socialize with other Deaf and hard-of-hearing students and adults needs to be brought to the attention of the child's family.

SUMMARY

School psychologists who are sensitive to the complex and interconnected nature of the communication, literacy, and socialization issues related to hearing loss can play a vital role in the planning of a Deaf and hard-of-hearing student's educational programs. A dominant theme and focus must be the child's language development. Early language intervention is a key element in the planning of the child's educational programming. In the role of consultant, school psychologists can facilitate collaboration among the regular education teacher, special education teacher, interpreter, speech and language specialist, and family. Especially in the domain of socialization, which pertains primarily to the socioemotional well-being of the child, it is necessary for school psychologists to be proactive in advocating for the child's welfare.

REFERENCES

Bebko, J. M., & Metcalfe-Haggert, A. (1997). Deafness, language skills, and rehearsal: A model for the development of a memory strategy. *Journal of Deaf Studies and Deaf Education, 2*, 131–139.

Brookhouser, P., Beauchaine, K., & Osberger, M. (1999). Management of the child with sensorineural hearing loss: Medical, surgical, hearing aids, cochlear implants. In N. J. Roizen & A. O. Diefendorf (Eds). *The pediatric clinics of North America: Hearing loss in children* (pp.121–142). Philadelphia: W.B. Saunders.

Calderon, R., & Greenberg, M. (2000). Challenges to parents and professionals in promoting socioemotional development in deaf children. In P. E. Spencer, C. J. Erting, & M. Marschark (Eds.), *The deaf child in the family and at school* (pp. 123–167). Mahwah, NJ: Erlbaum.

Copmann, K. (1996). The audiological assessment. In S. Schwartz (Ed.), *Choices in deafness: A parents' guide to communication options* (2nd ed) (pp.17–38). Bethesda, MD: Woodbine House.

Das, J., & Ojile, E. (1995). Cognitive processing of students with and without hearing loss. *The Journal of Special Education, 29*, 323–336.

Downs, M. & Yoshinaga-Itano, C. (1999). The efficacy of early identification and intervention of children with hearing impairment. In N.J. Roizen & A. O. Diefendorf (Eds). *The pediatric clinics of North America: Hearing loss in children* (pp. 79-88). Philadelphia: W.B. Saunders.

Epstein, S. (1996). The cochlear implant. In S. Schwartz (Ed.), *Choices in Deafness: A Parents' guide to communication options* (2nd ed) (pp. 39–52). Bethesda, MD: Woodbine House.

Foster, S., & Holcomb, T. (1990). Hearing impaired students: A student-teacher-class partnership. *Special Educational Needs Review, 3*, 150–169.

Marschark, M. (1997) *Raising and educating a deaf child.* New York: Oxford University Press.

Marschark, M. (in press). *Psychological development of deaf children* (2nd ed.). New York: Oxford University Press.

Marschark, M., & Lukomski, J. (2001). Understanding language and learning in Deaf children. In D.Clark, M. Marschark, & M. Karchmer (Eds.) *Context, cognition and deafness* (pp.71-86). Washington, DC: Gallaudet University Press.

McAnally, P., Rose, S., & Quigley, S. (1994). *Language learning practices with deaf children* (2nd ed.). Austin, TX: PRO-ED.

Morgan, A., & Vernon, M. (1994). A guide to the diagnosis of learning disabilities in deaf and hard-of-hearing children and adults. *American Annuals of the Deaf, 139*, 358–370.

Padden, C. (1980). The Deaf community and the culture of Deaf people. In C. Baker & R. Battison (Eds.), *Sign language in the deaf community: Essays in honor of William C. Stokoe* (pp 89–103). Silver Spring, MD: National Association of the Deaf.

Paul, P. V., & Quigley, S. P. (1994). *Language and deafness* (2nd ed.). San Diego: Singular Publishing.

Pollard, R. (1996). Conceptualizing and conducting preoperative psychological assessment of cochlear implant candidates. *Journal of Deaf Studies and Deaf Education, 1*, 45–81.

Raifman, L. J., & Vernon, M. (1996). Important implications for psychologists of the Americans with Disabilities Act: Case in point, the patient who is deaf. *Professional Psychology: Research and Practice, 27*, 372–377.

Spragins, A., & Mullen, Y. (1998).Reviews of four types of assessment instruments used with deaf and hard-of-hearing students [On-line]. Available from: http://www.gallaudet.edu/~catraxle/reviews.html.

Schildroth, A. N., & Hotto, S. A.(1996). Annual survey of deaf and hard-of-hearing children and youth: Changes in student characteristics, 1984–85 and 1994–95. *American Annuals of the Deaf, 141*, 68–71.

Stinson, M. S., Liu, Y., Saur, R., & Long, G. (1996).Deaf college students' perceptions of communication in mainstreamed classes. *Journal of Deaf Studies and Deaf Education, 1*, 140–151.

Strassman, B. (1997). Metacognition and reading in children who are deaf: A review of the research. *Journal of Deaf Studies and Deaf Education, 2*, 140–148.

Sullivan, P. M., &Vernon, M. (1979). Psychological assessment of deaf and hard-of-hearing children. *School Psychological Digest, 8*, 271–290.

Weaver, C. B., & Bradley-Johnson, S. (1993). A national survey of school psychological services for deaf and hard-of-hearing students. *American Annuals of the Deaf, 138*, 267–274.

Ying, E. (1990). Speech and language assessment: Communication evaluation In M. Ross (Ed.), *Hearing-impaired children in the mainstream* (pp. 45–60). Parkton, MD:. York Press.

Yoshinaga-Itano, C.(1997). The challenge of assessing language in children with hearing loss. *Language, Speech and Hearing Services in School, 28*, 362–373.

ANNOTATED BIBLIOGRAPHY

Marschark, M. (in press). *Psychological development of deaf children* (2nd ed.). New York: Oxford University Press.
The second edition of this book is a comprehensive review of the most recent research in the areas of mental health,

cochlear implants, assessment and educational placement issues, support services such as interpreting and captioning, the impact of technology in development and education, language development, alternative communication methods, and cutting-edge treatment of literacy issues.

National Institute on Deafness and Other Communication Disorders (NIDCD), Bethesda, MD 20992-3456. (1-800-241-1044 or www.nih.gov/nidcd)
The clearinghouse is a resource for health information on hearing, balance, smell, taste, voice, speech, and language. The section on hearing and balance includes information and materials on American Sign Language, cochlear implants, captioning, and links to other helpful sites such as the National Association of the Deaf and the Alexander Graham Bell Society.

Ramsey, C.L. (1997). *Deaf children in public schools.* Washington, DC: Gallaudet University Press.
This book addresses the theoretical and strategic questions of the educational programs for Deaf and hard-of-hearing students in public schools. The author shares her extensive sociolinguistic data on classroom contexts and language use in an elementary school mainstreaming program for deaf children.

Ross, M. (Ed.). (1990). *Hearing-impaired children in the mainstream.* Parkton, MD: York Press.
This is a good reference book with its diverse selection of chapters written by professionals of different backgrounds regarding Deaf and hard-of-hearing children education. For example, chapters included cover the audiological evaluation, speech and language assessment, psychoeducational assessment, developing an IEP, managing classroom amplification, and communication and behavior management issues.

Schwartz, S. (1996). *Choices in deafness: A parents guide to communication options.* Bethesda, MD: Woodbine House.
An overview of the range of communication choices available to Deaf and hard-of-hearing children. Chapter selections range from cochlear implants, oral approach, cued speech, and a total communication approach. Each section includes a brief overview of the communication mode followed by testimonials of Deaf and hard-of-hearing individuals who have made the choice.

Spragins, A., & Mullen, Y. (1998). Reviews of four types of assessment instruments used with Deaf and hard-of-hearing students [On-line]. Available from: http://www.gallaudet.edu/~catraxle/reviews.html.
The four categories of cognitive assessment, adaptive behavior and social emotional assessment, developmental/criterion-based scales, and academic/readiness assessment are reviewed. The specific instruments advantages and disadvantages for use with Deaf and hard-of-hearing students are outlined. Recommendations for use with Deaf students are presented.

87 Best Practices in Planning Effective Instruction for Students Who Are Visually Impaired or Blind

Sharon Bradley-Johnson
Sandra K. Morgan
Central Michigan University

OVERVIEW

Students whose visual loss, even with corrective lenses, interferes with educational performance are eligible for special education services under the category of visual impairment. This group of students is a very heterogeneous group because of differences in the severity and type of loss, environmental factors, and whether or not there are additional impairments. Few students with a visual impairment are totally blind. Most, even those classified as legally blind, are able to perceive light and see details to some extent.

The classification *legally blind* makes one eligible for government benefits. Individuals who are classified as *legally blind* have a visual acuity of 20/200 or less in the better eye with correction or a restricted visual field with a diameter of no more than 20 degrees. Visual acuity describes distance vision measured on a standard eye chart, where 20 indicates the distance at which vision is measured and 200 the distance at which someone with normal vision could identify the largest symbol on the eye chart. The restricted visual field refers to the amount of visual field one uses to view something from the side. The amount is described in degrees and typically the visual field extends to 180 degrees (Sacks, 1998). The definition of *legally blind* is of little help in educational planning because often these students can use visual material (Scholl, 1985). For clarity in this chapter, the term *blind* will be used to refer to students who must use senses other than vision for learning in the classroom.

Students who are blind will need tactile and auditory input for instruction. They require special equipment and materials such as computer hardware and software with speech or Braille output, talking calculators, recorded material, or raised-line paper for writing. For eligibility for special education services, these students would be classified as *visually impaired*. *Visually impaired* refers to students whose visual loss, even when corrected, interferes with their educational performance.

Other students classified as visually impaired, but who are not blind, include those needing more than glasses to function well in the classroom. The classification of visual impairment used in schools includes students with *low vision*. These students have severe vision losses even after correction, and their vision is improved by the use of vision aids, changes in the environment, and use of other procedures (Corn, 1983). Examples of low vision equipment include book stands, magnifiers, and closed circuit television (CCTV) where text is magnified electronically and displayed on a monitor. Some students classified as visually impaired may require large type, whereas others may be able to read regular-size type. Even though some students have sufficient vision for reading, they may require tactile and auditory material for instruction. Thus, students classified as visually impaired are a very diverse group requiring many different types of adaptations to enable them to function well in the classroom setting.

Incidence

A report from the National Plan for Training Personnel to Serve Children with Blindness and Low Vision

(NPTP), a project funded by the U.S. Department of Education's Office of Special Education Programs, estimated the number of students with visual impairments who received special education services in 1998 (Kirchner & Diament, 1999). The estimate for students between birth and 21 years of age was 93,600. These students consisted of 32,700 (35%) whose only impairment was vision; 50,100 (53%) who had at least one additional impairment other than deafness; and 10,800 (12%) who were deaf-blind. These data support the fact that many students with a severe vision loss also have additional impairments.

The American Printing House for the Blind (APH) annually compiles a registry of legally blind individuals. Estimates by the NPTP were somewhat more than double the number of students reported in the census completed a few years before for APH. This was not surprising, however, because the NPTP study was based on the functional definition of visual impairment used in schools to determine eligibility for special education services, whereas the APH census is based on individuals classified as legally blind.

Etiology

The many types and degrees of vision loss are a result of numerous etiologies. Most visual losses are congenital for school-age students (Scholl, 1985). Congenital losses may be a result of inheritance, genetic malformation, or prenatal damage. Acquired vision losses can result from factors such as anoxia at birth, head injury, infection of the central nervous system (e.g., meningitis), or reactions to medications.

Examples of congenital losses include albinism and retinitis pigmentosa. Albinism involves partial or total lack of pigment and results in abnormal development of the optic nerve. Classroom adaptations needed for this condition may include sunglasses, magnification, holding objects and materials close, and special lighting. Retinitis pigmentosa involves degeneration mainly of light-sensitive cells in the retina, sometimes resulting in total blindness. Adaptations required may include use of closed-circuit television, special lighting, and avoidance of glare.

Examples of acquired vision losses include retrolental fibroplasia and retinal detachment. Retrolental fibroplasia can be caused by factors such as low birth weight or early gestational age. Adaptations might include telescopes to see material at a distance, magnifiers for desk work, high illumination, and closed-circuit television. Retinal detachment can occur as a result of factors such as diabetes or trauma to the head. Adaptations needed are similar to those used for retrolental fibroplasia.

Consultation with a student's medical specialist, teacher, and the consultant for students who are visually impaired should be helpful in understanding a particular student's condition. A multidisciplinary approach is essential in order to work effectively with these students.

Onset and Progression

Age at onset of the vision loss has implications for instruction. When the onset is after 5 years of age, children typically retain visual memories such as memories for color and visual images. These memories facilitate acquisition of language concepts and other skills. For example, learning the meaning of words such as *mountain, castle,* or *fish* for sighted children usually is largely dependent on visual input. However, children who have a severe loss of vision prior to age 5 must depend on verbal explanations and definitions to understand such words. This reliance on verbal explanations may make it more difficult for those students to acquire a thorough understanding of such concepts. Furthermore, some students with a vision loss may use certain concepts correctly in their speech, but do so only because they have learned the concepts by rote. It is wise to probe any questionable responses to ensure that students with a vision loss have an adequate understanding of concepts they use.

Whether the onset of the loss of vision is gradual or sudden also has implications for instruction. When the loss is gradual, it is important to teach as much information requiring vision as possible while a student is still able to use visual input. In either case, students and their families are likely to benefit from support and counseling to help cope with this dramatic change in their lives. Those whose vision loss leaves them with little usable vision will need to adapt to the use of tactile and auditory input for instruction and, in many cases, to a new mode for written expression. Counseling or therapy may be needed to help students and their families understand the student's vision loss, comprehend what adaptations can be made, and address their fears.

BASIC CONSIDERATIONS

Multidisciplinary by Necessity

In nearly all cases it is impossible to plan a comprehensive, effective instructional program for a student who is visually impaired without using a multidisciplinary approach. In addition to parents and teachers, school psychologists must work with consultants certified in working with students who are visually impaired, medical specialists, and orientation and mobility instructors.

Consultants certified in working with students who are visually impaired or blind may carry out a functional vision assessment, the results of which have important implications for classroom instruction. How a particular student uses his or her vision when performing various academic and daily living tasks is assessed. Utley, Roman, and Nelson (1998) cited the example of a student with monocular dominance who might need to turn his or her head, or position himself or herself off center from a task to engage useful vision. Uninformed members of a multidisciplinary team might choose the mid-line position as best for viewing the task because they lack an understanding of the effects of vision loss on learning. A consultant certified in this area, however, would be able to conduct an assessment taking into consideration the student's type of vision loss and factors such as position, lighting, contrast, and glare. On the basis of these results the consultant could make recommendations for positioning and environmental modifications to enhance visual efficiency. Reports from functional vision assessments can include information regarding appropriate illumination, viewing distance for materials, type of media for reading and writing, size of type, and low-vision equipment. Functional vision assessments are carried out with students ranging in age from infancy through adolescence.

Reviewing medical reports is critical to understanding a student's loss of vision. Ophthalmologists' and optometrists' reports will include a description of medical interventions needed, prescriptions, prognosis of progression, and any required restrictions on eye use.

Reading a medical report can be a daunting task because of the terminology and abbreviations. Commonly used abbreviations and their meaning appear in Table 1.

Information in a medical report includes a description of visual acuity measured separately for each eye. In addition, acuity will be measured with and without correction, that is, with and without glasses. Typically such information is given for both near-vision and distance viewing.Because vision conditions change frequently, resulting in changes in the needs of students, it is important that vision assessments are current (i.e., no more than a year old). Not only should vision assessments be current, but hearing reports also should be up to date. Students who are visually impaired or blind rely so heavily on what they hear that it is important to ensure that hearing ability is maximized.

Table 1. Commonly used medical abbreviations

C.C.	With correction.
C.F.	Counts fingers. If unable to read letters on the eye chart, vision may be measured by the ability to count fingers held up at varying distances.
H.M.	Hand movement. If unable to read letters on the eye chart or count fingers, vision may be measured by the ability to see hand movement at varying distances.
L.P.	Light perception
N.L.P.	No light perception (totally blind)
N.V.	Near vision
O.D.	Ocular dexter (right eye)
O.S.	Ocular sinister (left eye)
O.U.	Oculi unitis (both eyes)
P.P.	Near point
P.R.	Far point
S., S.S., or S.C.	Without correction
V.A.	Visual acuity
V.F.	Visual field
W.N.L.	Within normal limits

Recommendations from a medical report, however, may not apply to the classroom context. Anxiety and the unfamiliar environment of a medical office may affect a student's use of vision during a medical examination. Thus, information from a functional vision assessment conducted within the school environment also is needed to plan instruction.

An orientation and mobility (O & M) instructor has special training in facilitating safe and independent travel for students who are visually impaired or blind. An untrained observer may think that the student moves about quite well considering the vision loss. An orientation and mobility specialist making the same observations, however, may be able to suggest several options that could increase independent functioning considerably. Thus, assessment and instructional planning by a specialist in this area is an important component of an educational program for those students. Training in orientation and mobility skills often begins as early as infancy (Leong, 1996).

An O & M assessment will include evaluation of a student's skills relevant to moving about safely, such as balance, posture, and gait, and consideration of factors in the environment in which the student travels, such as obstacles, traffic flow, and support received from others for the student's independence. An O & M instructor may teach a student directly, working on skills such as travel indoors or outdoors (including both urban and rural areas), concept development, use of a cane, low-vision equipment, electronic travel devices, and public transportation. This specialist also may work with family members and other professionals who are able to help students practice skills as well as arrange experiences where the skills will be needed (Fazzi, 1998).

Thus, school psychologists must collaborate with other professionals to develop comprehensive, effective educational programs that maximize the benefit of services provided to students who are visually impaired or blind. Work with teachers certified in this area, medical specialists, and orientation and mobility specialists is particularly important.

BEST PRACTICES

Working With Families

Adjusting to the diagnosis of a child's severe vision loss can be particularly difficult for family members who have had little or no contact with persons who are visually impaired or blind. Family members may go through various stages of grieving when first informed of the condition. Parents may be very concerned or frightened about raising a child with a severe vision loss. School psychologists can, however, do several things to help the family adjust to the diagnosis and aid in planning the child's educational program. When sharing information with students and their families, encourage conversation and provide an environment that is conducive to students asking questions. Preparing the student and family members on ways to answer others' questions about the vision loss may be helpful (Sacks & Corn, 1996).

Besides providing support and counseling, school psychologists can arrange for members of the family to talk with adults who are visually impaired or blind. These adults can share their experiences, discuss concerns the parents have, and serve as role models for the families and the child. The fact that most children who are visually impaired or blind grow up to be happy, productive adults should be emphasized. Arranging for the family to participate in parent support groups and talk with other families with children with severe vision losses can be very helpful.

Because of vision loss, certain skills may be delayed in development, especially for infants, toddlers, and preschoolers. Many of these delays amount to only a few months, and some can be lessened or eliminated with instruction. If parents are aware that certain skills may take longer to develop for these children, then they are less likely to become upset when their child does not meet a developmental milestone when sighted children do. Also, if parents are aware of these possible delays, then they can target such skills for practice that should help to minimize delays. Examples of developmental delays that may occur for children who are visually impaired or blind include play and self-help skills that require fine motor movement (scooping food is particularly difficult); walking, which appears at approximately 20 months (Scott, Jan, & Freeman, 1985); social skills (discussed later in this chapter); and some language skills including use of pronouns and recognizing one's name.

Families of children from infancy to age 5, or whose children are developmentally delayed, may find the *On the Way to Literacy* (Stratton & Wright, 1993) program helpful. This program provides a framework for interaction and helps parents teach important language concepts and early book-handling skills. A print handbook is provided for parents and 10 tactile/visual storybooks are included for reading to children. The books are in Braille and print and include tactile and visual illustrations. These materials also might be helpful for teachers who have little or no experience with children with a severe vision loss. Also, a video and brochure package, *Discovering the Magic of Reading*, is available from APH for parents and teachers of children from birth to age 5. This material addresses methods for involving children with a vision loss in a story and choosing books that are likely to be of interest to those children.

For children who will become Braille readers, family members may benefit from learning some basic information about Braille. Encouraging family members to observe their child in the classroom may help the family members better understand how their child functions in this setting and understand how they can be of help. Discussing the importance of organization (covered later in this chapter) and different learning strategies may aid parents in helping children with homework.

Families also may benefit from information regarding computer technology, including voice input/output, scanners, and Braille printers that help Braille readers share information with others.

As Chen and Dote-Kwan (1998) suggested, "The simplest way to identify what is important for the family is to ask them" (p. 318). Parents must be closely involved in educational planning for their child, and their interests and concerns must be solicited and used in planning programs. Communication with parents will be enhanced during this process if school psychologists avoid using jargon when talking with family members.

Infants, Toddlers, and Preschoolers

Studies comparing interactions of parents of sighted infants and parents of infants with visual impairments indicate that parents of infants with visual impairments may need assistance in recognizing and interpreting the signals of their infants (Chen, Friedman, & Calvello, 1990). Because infants with a severe vision loss do not make eye contact or direct their gaze toward someone speaking to them, parents may be disappointed or feel rejected when attempting to interact with their infant. The lack of eye contact results in a decrease in the frequency of parents' visual and vocal responsiveness to the child (Rogers & Puchalski, 1984).

Another factor interfering with parent-child interaction is that smiles are difficult to evoke from infants who are visually impaired. Frequently vigorous physical play is required to make these infants smile (Baird, Mayfield, & Baker, 1997). Without visual feedback, children's smiling behavior diminishes (Teplin, 1995). Thus, verbal feedback (e.g., "What a beautiful smile!") can be used to reinforce smiling.

Further, when auditory stimulation is present, infants with a visual impairment tend to decrease their movement, which parents may interpret as a lack of interest in interaction. The motor inhibition, however, is actually used as a means to attend better to the auditory stimulation (Ferrell, 1985).

Consequently, parents of young children with a severe visual impairment must make more of an effort than parents of sighted infants to evoke interaction with their infants. Often these parents need help recognizing behaviors that indicate their infant is responding to their initiations, is signaling to initiate an interaction, or is needing a break from interaction. Infants who are visually impaired have a limited number of signaling behaviors for communicating (Baird, Mayfield, & Baker, 1997), and these behaviors can be subtle or difficult to interpret. Other than eye contact and smiles, communicative behaviors can involve any fairly consistent change in behavior. Examples include quieting, squirming, changing facial expression, and other increases or decreases in activity level. Helping parents identify these responses, and modeling back-and-forth interaction with the baby, can facilitate positive interactions between these parents and their infants. Such assistance can prevent a negative pattern of interaction where the infant's signals are ignored, the parent perceives the infant as uninterested in interacting, and initiations from both parent and infant decrease.

Because some children are unable to see when someone is approaching, their parents may need guidance on how to avoid startling those children when initiating an interaction. Reminding the parent to talk as he or she approaches the child will be helpful.

Physical contact aids learning in young children, especially for those with a severe vision loss. Physical contact contributes to the development of language, social skills, cognition, and motor skills. If young children with a visual impairment learn to find physical contact pleasurable, this will help prevent the passivity and isolation that frequently characterize these children. Thus, encouraging physical contact between parents and infants or young children can be very beneficial. For infants, the use of sling carriers makes physical contact easy for parents to provide. The carriers also keep the infant in an upright position enhancing alertness and allowing the baby to be up at a level where most activities take place.

Physical contact from parents in the form of guided exploration can be helpful for several reasons. Some infants with a visual loss may be quite passive as a result of extended hospital stays where they have been restrained for medical reasons. Passivity limits learning opportunities. Also, because infants and children with little or no useful vision are not enticed by visual stimulation, this may limit exploration of the environment. Furthermore, because these children cannot visually scan their environments, without assistance from others they may be unaware of their choices and opportunities (Recchia, 1997). To familiarize children with various choices and opportunities, parents can physically guide their child to encourage movement, manipulation and exploration of objects, and search for objects that fall out of reach. Such guidance aids learning.

Whereas safety is an issue when vision is severely impaired, frequent interaction with the environment is critical to reduce passivity and enhance learning. Often these infants and young children need more opportunities to explore the environment than sighted children in order to learn. Hence, a balance needs to be found between encouraging exploration of surroundings and ensuring safety. Parents with children with a disability may tend to be overprotective and may inadvertently inhibit learning. Teaching these children to avoid hazards and to respond appropriately to "No" are critical skills to target for instruction.

Play skills may require some instruction, and provision of appropriate toys is helpful. Toys that are large and make noise are easier for children with a severe vision loss to locate. Toys that respond to simple motor movements, such as roly-poly toys, wrist rattles, or bells on booties help an infant learn that his or her behavior affects the environment. This is an important lesson, especially for a child with a physical or mental impairment.

Parents of preschoolers with a severe vision loss report that their children prefer to play with household objects, musical toys, and other noise-making objects (Troster & Brambring, 1994). Several activities to enhance orientation, play, and social skills of preschoolers with vision impairments are described in Zanandrea (1998). These activities are designed for use with groups of children including those with vision losses and their sighted peers.

Having a particular place for storing toys and other items belonging to the child, and teaching the child to put things back when finished with them, helps teach organization skills. The sooner these skills are taught to children who are visually impaired or blind the better. Developing the habit of keeping things organized will be very beneficial once children reach school age.

Because of vision loss, language development may be slower in some areas than it is for sighted children. Parents can help with language development by routinely naming objects and describing their own actions, even with infants. Providing rich verbal descriptions of children's exploration of the environment can help integrate experiences in a meaningful way (Recchia, 1997). Daily reading to the infant and young child also is important.

Encouraging parents to develop the habit of using their child's name before saying something to the child is helpful for two reasons. These children often are delayed in learning to respond to their names. Frequent use of the child's name provides needed practice in name recognition. Second, use of the child's name lets the child know that what is about to be said is directed to her or to him.

Social skills, unfortunately, are delayed for many children who are visually impaired or blind. Often these infants and young children miss nonverbal cues such as gestures, facial expressions, and eye contact. Preschoolers with vision impairments have a tendency to spend most of the time playing alone. Their difficulty in interpreting nonverbal messages may cause a breakdown in communication with peers (Erwin, 1993). Rather than making eye contact, Chen and Dote-Kwan (1998) suggested that these children tend to use physical contact, which may not be positively received by their peers. Hence, social skills often should be targeted for instruction.

Sleep problems is another area where families of young children with a severe vision loss may require assistance. Blind individuals are particularly prone to disturbances in circadian rhythms. Without visual input, circadian rhythms in body temperature, hormone levels, and alertness may not coincide with a 24-hour cycle. Sleep problems have been reported in from 34 to 80% of blind adults (Sack, Blood, Hughes, & Levy, 1998). In a study comparing blind and sighted children from 4 through 36 months of age, Mindell and DeMarco (1997) found that children who were blind had significantly more problems at bedtime and during the night. Children who were blind tended to sleep about an hour less at night because they went to bed later and were awake longer during the night. Early intervention is important as sleep problems tend to continue into later childhood (Mindell, 1993). Behavioral interventions typically used with sighted children may help children with severe vision loss (Mindell, Goldberg, & Fry, 1996). The establishment of consistent bedtime routines helps to cue the body that it is time to sleep (Ferber, 1987). Children should be awakened at a consistent time in the morning as well in order to establish a normal cycle (Weissbluth, 1982). Other behavioral strategies that have been helpful for sighted children include progressive delayed responding (Ferber, 1987) and "crying it out." The effectiveness of these procedures for children with severe visual impairments, however, has not been systematically evaluated. Espezel, Jan, O'Donnel, and Milner (1996) suggested that oral melatonin alleviates sleep disturbances in children who are visually impaired. School psychologists working with children with visual impairments can help to lessen the stress sleep problems place on families by working with parents to develop effective treatments.

School-Age Students

Classroom Behavior

When planning instruction for students who are visually impaired or blind, consideration of several classes of behavior is more critical than for most sighted students. Students with a severe vision loss are likely to require more assistance from others than their sighted peers. Consequently, it is important that they are able to request help, accept help, and refuse help appropriately. If this is not the case, then these behaviors need to be taught. Some students may benefit from counseling to ensure that they are asking for help when needed.

To function efficiently, and to avoid frustrating and unnecessary searches for materials, students who are visually impaired or blind need good organizational skills. By using the *Social Skills Rating System* (Gresham & Elliott, 1990), Buhrow, Hartshorne, and Bradley-Johnson (1998) surveyed 21 regular-education teachers of elementary-level students who were blind. Teachers rated 81% of these students as having difficulty at least sometimes in keeping their desks clean and neat without being reminded. Teaching students to keep their desks well organized and to put things away where they belong will enable these students to function more independently as well as more efficiently.

Because students with a severe loss of vision must rely heavily on auditory input, good listening skills are especially important. Good listening skills enhance independence. Yet, Buhrow et al. (1998) found that teachers rated 76% of the students who were blind as having difficulty sometimes or always in attending to teachers' instructions. For these students, praising them when they attend well, and asking them to repeat directions before beginning an assignment, should improve their listening skills.

Another concern of teachers in the Buhrow et al. (1998) study was that 62% of students who were blind did not finish their assignments in a timely fashion. This problem may be a result of several factors. First, Braille reading usually takes about two and a half times longer than reading regular type (Duckworth & Caton, 1986) and reading large type also takes longer than regular type. Fatigue is more of a factor when reading Braille or large type. Some regular education teachers may be unaware of the amount of extra time and fatigue involved and may set unrealistic time limits for these students. Problems with organization and listening may make these students less efficient in completing assignments. Teachers indicated that at least on some occasions 71% of the students who were blind were not using their time appropriately when waiting for assistance (Buhrow et al., 1998). Thus, if students who are visually impaired or blind are not completing assignments in a timely fashion, then consideration of the appropriateness of teacher expectations as well as students' organization skills, listening skills, and ability to use time effectively while waiting for help should help resolve the problem.

Social Skills

Visual information helps in monitoring social interaction, especially when nonverbal communication (e.g., gestures and facial expressions) is used (Erwin, 1993). Thus, it is not surprising that for students with limited visual input, social interaction may sometimes be difficult. Results of several studies of adolescents with visual impairments indicate that these students have fewer friends than their sighted peers (Kef, 1997; Hurre & Aro, 1998) and spend more time alone engaging in passive activity (Wolffe & Sacks, 1997). Though Buhrow et al. (1998) found that both parents and teachers rated the overall social skills of elementary-age students who were blind in the average range when compared to the sighted sample for the Social Skills Rating System (SSRS), they found that some specific social skills were problematic. Because of the potential for problems in this area, instructional planning for these students should include an examination of both the frequency and quality of interaction with others. Participation in clubs, sporting events, and other after-school activities should be encouraged as well.

Several factors specific to students with a severe visual loss may contribute to problems in social interaction. Students with little or no vision may need to be taught to turn to face someone who is speaking. Without this skill, interactions with others will be awkward. Orienting to a speaker may be particularly difficult when several people are speaking at the same time.

The use of prompts, feedback, reinforcement, peer mediation, and modeling have been helpful in teaching students with a severe vision loss specific social skills including eye gaze, initiation of social interaction, and joining activities. These skills have generalized and been maintained over time (e.g., Raver, 1987; Sacks & Gaylord-Ross, 1989). In addition, well-researched social skill training programs for sighted students can be helpful such as the *Social Skills Intervention Guide* (Elliott & Gresham, 1991), the ACCEPTS Program (Walker et al., 1983), and the ACCESS Program (Walker, Todis, Holmes, & Horton, 1988).

Although everyone engages in self-stimulation to some degree, students who are visually impaired or blind may self-stimulate at a higher frequency or engage in unusual behaviors. This is most likely to occur when a student is bored or stressed. Eye pressing and body rocking are the most frequent forms of self-stimulation for young blind children, and they tend to be quite stable behaviors (Brambring & Troster, 1992). These behaviors interfere with learning. Because these behaviors can make a child appear strange to others, they may negatively affect acceptance by peers. If these behaviors are observed, then intervention is needed to eliminate them. Brambring and Troster (1992) observed that when these behaviors occur in children over 4 1/2 years of age they are particularly stable even if they occur at a low frequency. Thus, intervention to eliminate body rocking or eye pressing should begin as early as possible.

Several different interventions have been effective in eliminating eye pressing including differential reinforcement of incompatible behavior (e.g., Raver and Dwyer, 1986), over-correction using arm exercises (e.g., Wesolowski & Zawlocki, 1982), and time out (e.g., Simpson, Sasso, & Bump, 1982). Likewise, different interventions have been effective in eliminating body or head rocking including head-band mechanisms (e.g., Felps & Devlin, 1988), restraint and time out (e.g., Barton & LaGrow, 1985), and verbal and physical prompts as well as praise (e.g., Ross & Koenig, 1991). Results of several studies, such as McHugh and Pyfer (1999) and Powers, Thibadeau, and Rose (1992), suggest that vigorous physical activity can decrease the occurrence of such stereotypical behavior. Results from studies designed to eliminate these behaviors are encouraging, though long-term follow-up and studies with older students in integrated settings are needed (DeMario & Crowley, 1994).

Effective procedures have been found for increasing positive behaviors that facilitate social interaction as well as procedures to decrease stereotypic behaviors that interfere with successful social interaction. An extensive and useful discussion of these procedures for different types of emotional and behavior problems for students who are visually impaired or blind is provided by Mar and Cohen (1998).

Oral Language

Students who are blind are not able to receive information conveyed by others through their facial expressions and gestures, which can interfere with their learning and communication. Unless someone is speaking to them or touching them, students who are blind cannot tell when someone is attending to them.

As was noted previously, a thorough understanding of some concepts typically learned primarily through visual input also may be lacking.

Students with a severe vision loss sometimes have problems with articulation and in using pronouns correctly. Roland and Schweigert (1998) noted that students with vision use their vision to monitor activities around them, but students without vision may use their speech for this purpose. They do this by repeating information (words or phrases), by frequently asking questions, and by using their speech to attract others' attention more so than sighted students.

Reading

Prior to formal reading instruction, exposure to books and reading with adults are important for all children (Stratton, 1996). The *On the Way to Literacy* and *Discovering the Magic of Reading* programs noted earlier promote parent and child interaction while using books. Students who read Braille and those who read print both have to learn the same beginning skills (e.g., phonics, structural analysis, and recognition of whole words). Students who must read large-type material can be taught with regular basal readers where print is enlarged or magnifiers are used. When teaching Braille, a systematic approach should be employed such as *Patterns* (Caton, Pester, & Bradley, 1980), a basal program that goes through the third-level reader.

The movement to teach children with visual impairments in the general classroom may hinder access to daily, quality instruction in Braille (Johnson, 1996). It is important to ensure that all relevant materials within a student's classroom can be available to the student with visual impairment either through enlargement or Braille. When this is not the case, students miss valuable instructional time. To monitor progress in learning to read, use of a modified version of Curriculum-Based Measurement (CBM) can be very useful. Morgan and Bradley-Johnson (1995) found that use of a 2-minute rather than 1-minute probe, and use of 6 seconds in place of 3 seconds to prompt unknown words, was as reliable and valid for Braille readers as the standard CBM method is for sighted students.

A concern about Braille reading is speed. In a study by Trent and Truan (1997), the factor most related to reading speed was age at onset of blindness. No relationship was found between speed and degree of vision, comprehension, methods of instruction, age, attitude toward Braille, reading for pleasure, or type of school attended. The authors found that to develop speed, students need to read Braille on a daily basis for a considerable amount of time. They also concluded that Braille instruction should be done early, especially for students whose vision is such that eventually they will no longer be able to read print. Residual vision makes learning Braille easier than if it is learned when there is little functional vision, and the sooner a student begins learning Braille the more they will practice. Trent and Truan (1997) also found that those who begin to learn Braille in grade three or later usually do not catch up to those who begin Braille reading upon entering school.

Because Braille reading typically takes two and a half times longer to read than regular print, even the fastest Braille reader will not read at a rate commensurate with that of print readers. Trent and Truan (1997) concluded that because of the amount of required reading in regular classrooms, students with low or medium reading rates will require both listening to orally read or audiotaped material and access to Braille.

Layton and Koenig (1998) found that having students with low vision repeatedly read a short paragraph until they met a fluency standard increased oral reading fluency rate. This procedure has been effective with sighted students. Repeated reading is relatively simple to use, and children typically enjoy reading as they gain confidence. Increasing fluency is important so that students with low vision can be exposed to similar amounts of instructional material as their sighted peers.

Arithmetic

Because children between 5 and 9 years of age who are blind frequently have more difficulty solving simple arithmetic problems than their sighted peers, Ahlberg and Csocsan, (1999) examined how these students experience numbers. Results showed that these children did not spontaneously use their fingers to solve arithmetic problems, and had trouble showing a given number of fingers. This finding was consistent with results from a study by Ahlberg and Csocsan (1994), which found that children who are blind do not use their fingers to model numbers or to count. The authors hypothesized that this lack of finger counting occurs because children who are blind only perceive the finger most recently counted by touch without simultaneously experiencing the group of fingers. Instead, the authors found that grouping elements to be counted with both hands is important to the children's understanding of numbers. By grouping elements they can experience the elements as units to compose and decompose. They concluded that young children who are blind should be given opportunities to group elements through hearing and touch, rather than focusing on finger patterns or counting on their fingers.

Written Language

Students who have lost their vision after having learned to write may be able to use script writing on raised-line paper. This paper is available from the American Printing House for the Blind (see address in the Bibliography). For students who cannot use script writing, however, another method will be needed. Some students will use a brailler (similar to a typewriter, but for Braille) or a more portable slate and stylus. Writing in Braille is very time consuming. Others will use a computer system with speech output, print, or Braille.

It seems that spelling skills of students who are blind are superior to those of sighted students. Layton and Koenig (1988) compared spelling skills of seventh and eighth grade students who were blind with those of their sighted peers and found the performance of students who were blind to be superior. Likewise, Grenier and Giroux (1997) found that spelling skills of ninth, tenth, and eleventh grade students who were blind and used grade 2 Braille were superior to those of their sighted peers. Though further studies in this area are needed with larger samples, it appears that spelling skills of Braille readers typically are well developed.

SUMMARY

To effectively meet the psychological and academic needs of infants, children, and adolescents with a severe vision loss, the school psychologist must work closely with the family and a variety of other professionals. A student's type of loss, degree of loss, and age at onset can have important implications for this educational planning.

Families may need assistance in understanding and coping with a student's vision loss, information on effective methods for reading to their child, or strategies to help with classroom performance. School psychologists can assist parents of infants, toddlers, and preschoolers who are visually impaired or blind by recommending procedures shown to enhance interaction with their child and facilitate the child's development. Issues of particular concern with young children include play skills, social interaction, language development, organizational skills, and sleep patterns. With school-age students a number of concerns often need to be addressed including organizational skills, listening skills, use of language, social skills, reading rate, and other issues relevant to Braille and large print. Fortunately there are many resources to assist in these areas.

REFERENCES

Ahlberg, A., & Csocsan, E. (1994). *Grasping numerosity among blind children* (Report No. 1994-4). Goteborg, Sweden: Institute for Special Pedagogy, University of Goteborg.

Ahlberg, A., & Csocsan, E. (1999). How children who are blind experience numbers. *Journal of Visual Impairment & Blindness, 93*, 549–560.

Baird, S. M., Mayfield, P., & Baker, P. (1997). Mothers' interpretations of the behavior of their infants with visual and other impairments during interactions. *Journal of Visual Impairment & Blindness, 91*, 467–483.

Barton, L. E., & LaGrow, S. J. (1985). Reduction of stereotypic responding in three visually impaired children. *Education of the Visually Handicapped, 16*, 145–151.

Brambring, M., & Troster, H. (1992). On the stability of stereotyped behaviors in blind infants and preschoolers. *Journal of Visual Impairment & Blindness, 86*, 105–110.

Buhrow, M., Hartshorne, T., & Bradley-Johnson, S. (1998). Parents' and teachers' ratings of the social skills of elementary-age students who are blind. *Journal of Visual Impairment & Blindness, 92*, 503–511.

Caton, H., Pester, H., & Bradley, W. J. (1980). *Patterns: The primary Braille reading program.* Louisville, KY: American Printing House for the Blind.

Chen, D., & Dote-Kwan, J. (1998). Early intervention services for young children who have visual impairments with other disabilities and their families. In S. Sacks & R. K. Silberman (Eds.), *Educating students who have visual impairments with other disabilities* (pp. 303–334). Baltimore: Brookes.

Chen, D., Friedman, C. T., & Calvello, G. (1990). *Parents and visually impaired infants*. Louisville, KY: American Printing House for the Blind.

Corn, A. L. (1983). Visual function: A theoretical model for individuals with low vision. *Journal of Visual Impairment & Blindness, 77,* 373–377.

DeMario, N. C., & Crowley, E. P. (1994). Using applied behavior analysis procedures to change the behavior of students with visual disabilities: A research review. *Journal of Visual Impairment & Blindness, 88,* 532–543.

Duckworth, B. J., & Caton, H. (1986). *Basic reading rate scale: Braille edition or large type*. Louisville, KY: American Printing House for the Blind.

Elliott, S. N., & Gresham, F. M. (1991). *Social skills intervention guide*. Circle Pines, MN: American Guidance.

Erwin, E. J. (1993). Social participation of young children with visual impairments in integrated and specialized settings. *Journal of Visual Impairment & Blindness, 87,* 138–142.

Espezel, H., Jan, J. E., O'Donnel, M. E., & Milner, R. (1995). The use of melatonin to treat sleep-wake rhythm disorders in children who are visually impaired. *Journal of Visual Impairment & Blindness, 90,* 43–50.

Fazzi, D. L. (1998). Facilitating independent travel for students who have visual impairments with other disabilities. In S. Z. Sacks & R. K. Silberman (Eds.), *Educating students who have visual impairments with other disabilities* (pp. 441–467). Baltimore: Brooks.

Felps, J. N., & Devlin, R. J. (1988). Modification of stereotypic rocking of a blind adult. *Journal of Visual Impairment & Blindness, 82,* 107–108.

Ferber, R. (1987). *Solve your child's sleep problems*. New York: Simon & Schuster.

Ferrell, K. A. (1985). *Reach out and teach: Meeting the training needs of parents of visually and multihandicapped young children*. New York: American Foundation for the Blind.

Grenier, D., & Giroux, N. (1997). A comparative study of spelling performance of sighted and blind students in senior high school. *Journal of Visual Impairment and Blindness, 91,* 393–400.

Gresham, F., & Elliott, S. (1990). *Social Skills Rating System*. Circle Pines, MN: American Guidance Service.

Hurre, T., & Aro, H. (1998). Psychosocial development among adolescents with visual impairment. *European Child & Adolescent Psychiatry, 7,* 73–78.

Johnson, L. (1996). The Braille literacy crisis for children. *Journal of Visual Impairment & Blindness, 88,* 276–278.

Kef, S. (1997). The personal networks and social supports of blind and visually impaired adolescents. *Journal of Visual Impairment & Blindness, 91,* 236–244.

Kirchner, C., & Diament, S. (1999). Estimates of the number of visually impaired students, their teachers, and orientation and mobility specialists: Part 1. *Journal of Visual Impairment & Blindness, 93,* 600–606.

Layton, C. A., & Koenig, A. J. (1998). Increasing reading fluency in elementary students with low vision through repeated readings. *Journal of Visual Impairment & Blindness, 90,* 276–291.

Leong, S. (1996). Preschool orientation and mobility: A review of the literature. *Journal of Visual Impairment & Blindness, 88,* 145–153.

Mar, H. H., & Cohen, E. J. (1998). Educating students who have visual impairments and who exhibit emotional and behavior problems. In S. Z. Sacks & R. K. Silberman (Eds.), *Educating students who have visual impairments and other disabilities* (pp. 263–302). Baltimore: Brookes.

McHugh, E., & Pyfer, J. (1999). The development of rocking among children who are blind. *Journal of Visual Impairment & Blindness, 93,* 82–95.

Mindell, J. A. (1993). Sleep disorders in children. *Health Psychology, 12*, 152–163.

Mindell, J. A., & DeMarco, C. M. (1997). Sleep problems of young blind children. *Journal of Visual Impairment & Blindness, 91*, 33–39.

Mindell, J. A., Goldberg, R., & Fry, J. M. (1996). Treatment of a circadian rhythm disorder in a blind 2-year-old child. *Journal of Visual Impairment & Blindness, 86*, 162–166.

Morgan, S., & Bradley-Johnson, S. (1995). Technical adequacy of curriculum-based measures for Braille readers. *School Psychology Review, 24*, 94–103.

Powers, S., Thibadeau, S., & Rose, K. (1992). Antecedent exercise and its effects on self-stimulation. *Behavioral Residential Treatment, 7*, 15–22.

Raver, S. (1987). Training blind children to employ appropriate gaze direction and sitting behavior during observation. *Education and Treatment of Children, 10*, 237–246.

Raver, S., & Dwyer, R. C. (1986). Using a substitute activity to eliminate eye poking in a 3 year old visually impaired child in the classroom. *The Exceptional Child, 33*, 65–72.

Recchia, S. L. (1997). Play and concept development in infants and young children with severe visual impairments: A constructivist view. *Journal of Visual Impairment & Blindness, 91*, 401–406.

Rogers, S., & Puchalski, C. B. (1984). Social characteristics of visually impaired infants' play. *Topics in Early Childhood Special Education, 3*, 52–56.

Roland, C., & Schweigert, P. (1998). Enhancing the acquisition of functional language and communication. In S. Z. Sacks & R. K. Silberman (Eds.), *Educating students who have visual impairments and other disabilities* (pp. 413–438). Baltimore: Brookes.

Ross, D. B., & Koenig, A. J., (1991). A cognitive approach to reducing stereotypic head rocking. *Journal of Visual Impairment & Blindness, 85*, 17–19.

Sack, R. L., Blood, M. L., Hughes, R.J., & Levy, A. J. (1998). Circadian-rhythm sleep disorders in persons who are totally blind. *Journal of Visual Impairment and Blindness, 90*, 145–161.

Sacks, S. Z. (1998). Educating students who have visual impairments with other disabilities: An overview. In S. Z. Sacks & R. K. Silberman (Eds.), *Educating students who have visual impairments with other disabilities.* (pp. 3–38). Baltimore: Brookes.

Sacks, S. Z., & Corn, A. L. (1996). Students with visual impairments: Do they understand their disability? *Journal of Visual Impairment & Blindness, 88*, 412–422.

Sacks, S. Z., & Gaylord-Ross, R. (1989). Peer-mediated and teacher-directed social skills training for visually impaired students. *Behavior Therapy, 20*, 619–638.

Scholl, G. T. (1985). Visual impairments. In G. T. Scholl (Ed.), *The school psychologist and the exceptional child* (pp. 203–218). Reston, VA: Council for Exceptional Children.

Scott, E. P., Jan, J. E., & Freeman, R. D. (1985). *Can't your child see?* Austin, TX: PRO-ED.

Simpson, R. L., Sasso, G. M., & Bump, N. (1982). Modification of manneristic behavior in a blind child via a time-out procedure. *Education of the Visually Handicapped, 14*, 50–55.

Stratton, J. M. (1996). Emergent literacy: A new perspective. *Journal of Visual Impairment and Blindness, 90*, 117–183.

Stratton, J. M., & Wright, S. (1993). *On the way to literacy: Early experiences for visually impaired children.* Louisville, KY: American Printing House for the Blind.

Teplin, S. W. (1995). Visual impairment in infants and young children. *Infants and Young Children, 8*, 18–51.

Trent, S. D., & Truan, M. B. (1997). Speed, accuracy, and comprehension of adolescent Braille readers in a specialized school. *Journal of Visual Impairment and Blindness, 91*, 494–500.

Troster, H., & Brambring, M. (1994). The play behavior and play materials of blind and sighted infants and preschoolers. *Journal of Visual Impairment & Blindness, 88*, 421–432.

Utley, B. L., Roman, C., & Nelson, G. L. (1998). Functional vision. In S. Z. Sacks & R. K. Silberman (Eds.), *Educating students who have visual impairments and other disabilities.* (pp. 371–405). Baltimore: Brookes.

Walker, H. M., McConnell, S., Holmes, D., Todis, B., Walker, J., & Golden, N. (1983). *The ACCEPTS program: A curriculum for children's effective peer and teacher skills.* Austin, TX: PRO-ED.

Walker, H. M., Todis, B., Holmes, D., & Horton, G. (1988). *The ACCESS program: Adolescent curriculum for communication and effective social skills.* Austin, TX: PRO-ED.

Weissbluth, M. (1982). Modification of sleep schedule with reduction of night waking: A case report. *Sleep, 5,* 262–266.

Wesolowski, M. D., & Zawlocki, R. J. (1982). The differential effects of procedures to eliminate an injurious self-stimulatory behavior (Digito-Ocular Sign) in blind retarded twins. *Behavior Therapy, 13,* 334–345.

Wolffe, K., & Sacks, S. Z. (1997). The lifestyles of blind, low vision, and sighted youths: A quantitative comparison. *Journal of Visual Impairment & Blindness, 91,* 245–257.

Zanandrea, M. (1998). Play, social interaction and motor development: Practical activities for preschoolers with visual impairments. *Journal of Visual Impairment & Blindness, 90,* 176–189.

ANNOTATED BIBLIOGRAPHY

Levack, N., Stone, G., & Bishop, V. (1994). *Low Vision: A Resource Guide with Adaptations for Students with Visual Impairments* (2nd ed.). Austin, TX: Texas School for the Blind and Visually Impaired.

This book contains a listing of eye conditions and diseases that may be helpful in understanding the needs of individual students.

Sacks, S. Z., & Silberman, R. K. (1998). *Educating students who have visual impairments with other disabilities.* Baltimore: Brookes.

This is an excellent text describing research-based interventions. Because so many students with serious vision loss have additional impairments, this text is a very useful resource. Collaboration among professionals is emphasized. Many topics are addressed including orientation and mobility, functional vision, transition planning, communication, and use of technology. Chapters are included for students with a vision loss in addition to other impairments such as emotional problems, learning disabilities, hearing impairments, and neurological disabilities.

ORGANIZATIONS

American Foundation for the Blind (AFB), 11 Penn Plaza, Suite 300, New York, NY 10001 (212-620-2000 or 800-232-5463) (www.afb.org).

AFB provides technical assistance services to individuals who are visually impaired and to their families and to professionals and organizations. The AFB also publishes books, periodicals, pamphlets, videos, and talking books for professionals and consumers.

American Printing House for the Blind (APH), P.O. Box 6085, Louisville, KY 40206.
(1-800-223-1839) (www.aph.org).

APH publishes educational materials and assessment instruments, including materials adapted and transcribed in Braille or large type as well as recorded books and magazines.

Blind Children's Center, 4120 Marathon Street, Los Angeles, CA 90029. (1-800-222-3566).

The Center publishes booklets for parents of infants and preschoolers who are visually impaired or blind. Some topics include play, language, and movement. Most are available in English or Spanish.

88 Best Practices in Working With School Interpreters to Deliver Psychological Services to Children and Families

Emilia C. Lopez
Queens College, City University of New York

OVERVIEW

A significant number of students in our schools speak languages other than English and demonstrate limited proficiency in English. The U.S. Department of Education (1998) estimated that between 1996 and 1997 approximately 8% of students enrolled in grades K–12 were English language learners (ELL), defined as students whose first language is not English and who are in the process of learning English. The families of many of our ELLs are also limited in their abilities to communicate in English. Cambodian, Cantonese, Hmong, Korean, Laotian, Navajo, Spanish, Tagalog, Vietnamese, and Russian are some of the most common languages spoken by linguistically diverse students and their families (Fleischman & Hopstock, 1993).

As a result of the large influx of immigrants from diverse cultural backgrounds, statistical projections indicate that the number of immigrant children and adults who speak languages other than English will increase in the twenty-first century (U.S. Department of Education, 1998). As the number of ELLs increase, there is a greater need for bilingual school personnel. The reauthorization of Individuals with Disabilities Education Act (IDEA) Amendments of 1997 states that students who are referred for special education evaluations should be assessed in their native languages. IDEA also states that the parents of children who are referred for special education assessment or services must be notified of their rights in their native languages either in written format or via oral translation. However, a frequent problem encountered in our schools is a shortage of bilingual personnel who can communicate with such a linguistically and culturally diverse student population.

In an effort to communicate with ELLs and their families, school psychologists sometimes use the services of school interpreters (Lopez, 2000; Ochoa, Gonzalez, Galarza, & Guillemard, 1996). The purposes of this chapter are to discuss the process of using interpreters and to provide some recommendations for school psychologists working with interpreters.

Definitions and Background

The term *translation* refers to the process of changing messages produced in one language to another language. The language from which one translates is referred to as the source language whereas the language into which the translation is made is the target language (Frishberg, 1990). The translation literature differentiates between the roles of interpreters and translators. Translators engage in the process of translating the *written* language as when, for example, translating books or legal documents (Frishberg, 1990). Translators are hired in school districts to translate documentation such as district policies and special education guidelines that are made available to students and parents who speak languages other than English (e.g., referral forms, Individual Educational Plans (IEPs)).

Interpreters are professionals who demonstrate expertise in translating the *spoken* language (Frishberg, 1990). In schools, interpreters work with a variety of school professionals to translate oral communication. Interpreters typically use two styles of oral translations referred to as simultaneous and consecutive translations (Frishberg, 1990). In simultaneous translation, the interpreter's translation is delivered a couple of seconds behind the speaker. Two common forms of simultaneous translation are whispered translation, in which the interpreter whispers the translation to the listener, and soundproof booth translation, where the interpreter speaks into a microphone and the message is delivered to the listener's ear via earphones.

The process of simultaneous translation is demanding for the interpreter because the interpreter is simultaneously listening to the speaker of the source language, understanding the message being delivered in the source language, converting the message into the target language, and delivering the message in the target language (Barik, 1973). The process is also difficult for the recipients of the translation because they are simultaneously hearing the original message in the source language and the interpreter's translation in the target language.

In consecutive translation, the speaker delivers his or her message in the source language and stops to allow the interpreter to deliver the message in the target language (Frishberg, 1990). There are two forms of consecutive translation, continuous and discontinuous. In continuous translation, the interpreter waits until the speaker has finished his or her entire message before delivering the translation. In discontinuous translation, the interpreter delivers the translation at periodic breaks.

According to Barik (1973), the faster the speech rate of the speaker in translation, the greater the number of errors made by interpreters. The translation research also indicates that the more pauses the speaker makes, the less likely the interpreter is to omit words from the message being translated. Finally, Barik reported that less qualified interpreters make more errors in translation, omit more information when translating, and engage in more literal translation.

Interpreters in School Settings

Several recent surveys have explored the use of interpreters in school settings. Lopez and Rooney (1997) surveyed interpreters who provided translation services in school settings in New York State. Lopez (1995) and Ochoa et al. (1996) surveyed school psychologists working with interpreters in several states throughout the country with significant numbers of ELLs (e.g., Texas, Florida, California). In general, the surveys indicated the following results:

1. School psychologists reported working with interpreters to deliver psychological services to a diverse group of ELLs. For example, Ochoa et al. (1996) reported that the school psychologists in their survey had assessed students from 85 different language groups through interpreters.

2. The school interpreters reported working with school psychologists during such activities as parent interviews, parent conferences, student interviews, and student assessments (Lopez, 1995).

3. The majority of the school psychologists indicated having little or no training to work with school interpreters during parent conferences and assessment sessions (Lopez, 1995; Ochoa et al., 1996).

4. The majority of school psychologists reported working with interpreters who had little or no training in translation and in issues relevant to working in schools (Lopez, 1995; Ochoa et al., 1996).

5. Individuals serving as interpreters in school settings have a wide range of backgrounds and experiences and include professionally trained interpreters, bilingual school personnel (e.g., teachers, secretaries), bilingual students, family members, and individuals from the community (Lopez and Rooney, 1997).

6. The school psychologists encountered a number of problems when working with interpreters to deliver psychological services in school settings, including miscommunications, interpreters delivering inaccurate translations, interpreters lacking an understanding of the assessment process, and interpreters violating confidentiality (Lopez, 1995).

Presently, there are no research data describing the translation styles most frequently used in school settings by interpreters. In the author's experience, consecutive translations are more frequently used in schools than simultaneous translations. Simultaneous translations require well-trained interpreters, and the interpreters being used in schools may not have the skills to deliver simultaneous translations. There are also no empirical investigations indicating what styles of translation may be most helpful when communicating with different speakers (e.g., preschool children versus older children or adults) within a variety of school-related situations (e.g., parent conferences, clinical interviews). Research investigating those areas will help school psychologists in the future to understand how to work with school interpreters to reduce errors in translation and to improve all communications with ELLs and their families.

BASIC CONSIDERATIONS

Understanding the Process of Working With Interpreters

As school psychologists continue to work with interpreters to provide psychological services to ELLs and their families, there is a call to develop an awareness of the complexities involved in the translation process. Many words and concepts cannot be directly translated from one language to another (Langdon, 1994). Metaphors, puns, and jokes tend to lose their meaning when literally translated. The meaning of words and concepts can also change when translated because they may have more than one meaning in the target language. Variations in vocabulary due to regional difference can also be challenging because the interpreter must have knowledge of the lexical variations used in specific regions or geographical areas (e.g., many Puerto Ricans call kites "cometas" whereas many Cubans call them "papalotes"). The developmental level of concepts can also change when translated from one language to another. All these difficulties are inherent to the process of translation and can result in miscommunications if interpreters are not competent communicators and if school psychologists are not aware of the impact of translation on the communication process.

It is often assumed that the interpreter is merely a tool that the school psychologist can use to communicate with ELLs and their families and that as long as we ask the right questions and probe for clarification, we will obtain valid and reliable information through interpreters. However, because interpreters are human beings and are not merely translation machines, the quality of the outcomes obtained from the process of using interpreters will depend on the interpreters' skills and their understanding of the psychological services provided by school psychologists. Information can easily be lost in translation if interpreters do not demonstrate bilingual and bicultural competence (Cokely, 1987). The presence of the interpreter can substantially change the quality of the interaction between school psychologists and their clients. Thus, the interpretations derived from those interactions need to be cautiously examined in all situations where interpreters are used. In essence, all information obtained through interpreters must be questioned because of the mere fact that the information is filtered through the interpreters and the school psychologists are in no position to judge the quality of the translation because of their limited proficiency in the ELLs native languages. As the chapter continues, issues relevant to the assessment process, and to competencies needed by interpreters and school psychologists are explored.

Translation and the Assessment Process

Perhaps one of the most controversial issues is the use of interpreters in the practice of translating tests. Lopez (1995) found that school psychologists often ask interpreters to translate test questions either on the spot or before the testing session. On-the-spot translations involve the school psychologist reading testing questions to the interpreter during the testing session and the interpreter translating them during the session for the student being assessed. The interpreter then translates the student's responses to the school psychologist.

In an investigation designed to explore the types of translation errors that can occur when untrained interpreters conduct on-the-spot translations, Lopez (1994) asked interpreters with little or no experience and training in translation or in assessment issues to translate questions from the Wechsler Intelligence Scale for Children-Revised (WISC-R) into Spanish. Lopez chose the WISC-R because it has an equivalent version that was translated and pilot tested in Spanish called the Escala de Inteligencia Wechsler Para Niños-Revisada (EIWN-R). The equivalent version in Spanish was used to examine the quality of the interpreters' translations and to code the types of translation errors that the interpreters made when translating the test questions. A translation error classification scheme developed by Barik (1971) was used to code the interpreters' errors. The results indicated that the interpreters sometimes omitted, added, and substituted words and phrases that significantly changed the content and the meaning of the questions and directions. There were even situations in which the interpreters were not at all able to translate specific words because they did not have the appropriate vocabulary in Spanish.

Another practice used by school psychologists is to provide the interpreter with the manual before the translation session begins so that the interpreter can translate the test questions prior to the assessment session (Lopez, 1995). The assumption made is that if the translation is conducted prior to the testing session, then the quality of the translation will be better because the bilingual interpreter has more time to work on a more accurate translation. However, the additional time factor will not necessarily result in a better product because the practice of translating tests is problematic for several reasons. As previously discussed, equivalent words or concepts may not be found when translating from the source to the target language. Thus, the content of test items may change substantially. The developmental level of an item or question may also change when the item is translated into the target language (Langdon, 1994). Examples can be found in the translation of the WISC-R to the Spanish EIWN-R. When the questions in the Information subtest of the WISC-R were translated into Spanish and the translation was pilot tested, the test publishers found that the developmental level of some of the questions changed based on the performance of the children who participated in the pilot testing. Neither the school psychologist nor the interpreter will be able to accurately judge the developmental level of the items simply based on their practical experience (Bracken & Barona, 1991).

Bracken and Barona (1991) add that the process of simply translating test items is problematic because test directions are frequently too "psychotechnical" or difficult to allow for easy translation and versions of translated tests produced by practitioners and interpreters are rarely "sufficiently perfected" to provide equivalent meanings across language. Furthermore, test adaptation experts argue that test translation can result in significant changes in the underlying psychological constructs assessed by the translated version of the test (Bracken & Barona, 1991; Geisinger, 1994). Thus, test translation can alter test validity for ELLs.

According to Geisinger (1994), merely translating a test is not sufficient when the "the new target population differs appreciably from the original population with which the assessment device is used in terms of culture or cultural background, country, and language" (p. 304). In such situations, the test must be adapted through the following procedures: (a) translating the test questions, (b) reviewing the translated version through an editorial review committee, (c) adapting the draft instrument on the basis of the comments made by the editorial review committee, (d) pilot testing the instrument, (e) field testing the instrument, (f) standardizing the scores, (g) obtaining validation data, (h) developing a manual and documentation, (i) training users, and (j) collecting reactions from users (Geisinger, 1994). In regards to the establishment of validation data, Geisinger points out that the validity and reliability of the adapted measure must be established to "demonstrate that the instrument continues to assess the same qualities with the same degree of accuracy in the new population" (p. 308). That recommendation is supported by the Standards for Educational and Psychological Testing (American Educational Research Association, American Psychological Association, National Council on Measurement in Education, 1999) which state that when a test is translated from one language or dialect to another, its reliability and validity should be established for the uses intended with the linguistic groups to be tested.

The problems of using interpreters during assessment sessions are not limited to loss of validity in the process of translating test questions. Once the interpreter translates the test question, the interpreter also translates the student's response for the benefit of the school psychologist, and miscommunications can also occur at that stage of the translation process. How is the school psychologist to know that the interpreter's translation is an accurate representation of the student's message in terms of content, grammatical organization, and emotional intent? Because of the nature of the translation process, the interpreter must avoid delivering a literal translation and must filter the message so that the translation conveys the original intent of the sender. Thus, the school psychologist must solely rely on the interpreter's rendition of the student's message.

How is the school psychologist to know if the speech patterns demonstrated by the student in the native language are a function of a speech impairment or are due to dialectical/regional differences? For example, Spanish speaking Caribbean children tend to drop the "s" sound, signifying plural, from the ends of words. That is a speech pattern that is not considered a function of impairment and is viewed as a function of the children's regional origin (i.e., Caribbean countries such as Puerto Rico and Cuba). One can argue that the school psychologist will make those judgments based on carefully crafted questions directed at the interpreter such as, Did the student have difficulty making any sounds in his/her native language? Are those speech sounds typical of individuals from the child's region? However, the reality is that the answers to these questions will be largely dependent on the skills of the interpreter in translating the student's messages and in their thorough understanding of the rules and functions of their native language. The competent interpreter will be able to help the school psychologist to examine the children's language skills from a developmental perspective.

The competent interpreter will also be helpful to the school psychologist in examining the student's responses and behaviors from a cross-cultural perspective. Lopez (2000), for example, found that the interpreters used in her study to communicate with high school ELLs helped the consultants to understand that the Mandarin- and Polish-speaking students were having difficulties viewing portfolio assessment assignments as assessment tools and working collaboratively with peers to complete their portfolio work. For those students, being assessed meant sitting in a room, working individually to answer a series of test questions, and obtaining grades based on the product they produced on the test. The students' attitudes toward the portfolio assessment process were affecting their performance because they did not view portfolio assessment as a legitimate form of assessment and because they did not understand the process of working cooperatively to receive grades. In these cases, the interpreters' familiarity with the students' educational experiences in their native countries, and the interpreters' abilities to communicate those issues with the consultants, were instrumental in examining the students' behaviors from a cross-cultural perspective.

In the examples cited above, school psychologists are dependent on the interpreters to translate the students' messages, express the students' intent, and examine behavior cross-culturally. As such, anything less than a well-trained interpreter will result in miscommunications and erroneous analyses of behaviors. Ultimately, because the school psychologist is so dependent on the skills of the interpreter, too much is left to chance if school psychologists assume that they can conduct valid assessments by relying on the translations and judgments of inexperienced or poorly trained interpreters.

Competencies for School Interpreters

Translation is a complex and demanding process that requires highly competent interpreters. It is widely agreed within the field of interpreter training that interpreters must possess a number of important competencies that include high levels of proficiency in the source and target languages; knowledge of the cultural backgrounds of the clients they are translating for; knowledge and skills in the different types of translation styles (e.g., simultaneous and consecutive translations); professional conduct as in understanding their roles, behaving ethically, and adhering to confidentiality; excellent listening skills; and excellent long-term and short-term memory (Castle, 1984).

In addition, interpreters must possess sufficient knowledge of the situations in which they are translating to deliver messages that are contextually appropriate because what is not understood cannot be translated and what is incorrectly understood will be incorrectly translated (Castle, 1984). Ultimately, the goal of the translation process is to convey the message originally expressed in such a way that the content of the message remains accurate when translated into the target language, retains the original meaning, and evokes the same emotional response as the original message (Cokely, 1987).

For interpreters who translate in school settings, understanding the educational context is crucial. For example, school interpreters must be familiar with the education system, district policies, and school policies to be able to understand and translate accurate information to children and parents (Langdon, 1994). Interpreters must be knowledgeable of technical vocabulary used by school psychologists such as diagnostic categories (e.g., learning disabilities, emotionally disturbed), educational programs (e.g., special education, acceleration, inclusion), and psychological terms (e.g., cognition, assessment, exceptionality).

The interpreters' ability to understand the cultural context of communication is also important given the need to work with families who are culturally diverse. In an investigation designed to explore how culturally different families view exceptionality, Harry (1992) reported that Puerto Rican families in her study tended to view the mild mentally retarded label as being synonymous with severe forms of mental handicaps. When first introduced to the concept of mild retardation, many of the parents in the investigation responded with confusion and distress because they associated the terms with "loco" or crazy. In time, some of the parents became more accepting as they began to equate the mentally retarded classification with other terms such as "slow." In these situations, interpreters and school psychologists must be prepared to help the families to understand the labels within the families' own cultural framework. For interpreters, it is particularly important to have a repertoire of vocabulary in the target language that will help them in the process of explaining diagnostic categories and psychological concepts that are more culturally congruent with culturally diverse families.

Interpreters' knowledge of developmental and psychological issues is imperative in situations where interpreters work with school psychologists to provide translation services to children of different age groups and to students with mental health, behavioral, and medical problems. Marcos (1979), for example, found that when interpreters were asked to translate for patients who had thought disorders, the interpreters often changed the client's statements so that they sounded like they made more sense. School psychologists who provide services to handicapped populations must use interpreters who have knowledge of the different types of behaviors and disorders that children with mental health, educational, and behavioral difficulties exhibit so that the interpreters are better prepared to deliver accurate translations and to respond appropriately to situations where the students exhibit unusual behaviors (e.g., seizures, inappropriate verbalizations, conduct problems).

Our work as school psychologists entails establishing rapport with our clients and gaining their trust to create an environment that is conducive to collaboration and problem solving. Thus, interpreters must possess excellent interpersonal skills and skills in establishing rapport with children and families. The presence of an interpreter might serve as a barrier as well as a facilitator in the process of establishing rapport with clients. In a qualitative investigation where interpreters were used within the instructional consultation process, Lopez (2000) found that the interpreters were often very helpful in establishing a trusting relationship with the students and families because the students and parents viewed the interpreters as facilitating their communication with the consultants and consultees. In contrast, a student from Ethiopia who spoke Amharic felt inhibited by having to communicate through an interpreter who was part of the student's community. The student felt inhibited in discussing many issues related to his family because he feared that the interpreter would not keep the information confidential. This case exemplifies how the presence of the interpreter can interfere with the establishment of rapport with students. Interpreters who understand the social context of the translation process can serve as facilitators in the process of examining the dynamics involved in providing psychological services through interpreters and can work collaboratively with school psychologists to overcome barriers in establishing rapport with ELLs and their families.

According to Anderson (1976), because the interpreter holds the key to the communication process in situations where individuals from different language backgrounds cannot communicate with each other, the interpreter's position is pivotal and has the advantage of power. Anderson adds that the interpreter's position of power "is inherent in all positions which control scarce resources" (p. 218). As such, the interpreter may exert control by translating all that is said or part of what is said. Lopez (2000), for example, found that one of the interpreters working in the case study of a Polish student who was receiving instructional consultation services was unwilling to translate everything said in the interviews with the student and parents because the interpreter felt it was too time consuming. The interpreters' feelings toward the clients and their reactions toward the issues being discussed may also interfere with their ability to deliver accurate translations. Nida (1964) acknowledges that interpreters may not be able to avoid a certain degree of personal involvement in their work and may attempt to change the content of the messages they translate to fit their own personal, political, social, or religious preferences. Thus, school interpreters must develop a clear understanding of their roles along with the ability to reflect on how their own feelings and actions influence the delivery of psychological services to ELLs and their families.

Competencies for School Psychologists

Figueroa, Sandoval, and Merino (1984) have outlined the competencies needed by school psychologists to work with ELLs. The competencies outlined by Figueroa and his colleagues include cross-cultural awareness, skills in non-discriminatory assessment, knowledge of language development and second language acquisition, and knowledge of interventions appropriate for ELLs.

Those competencies are the basic prerequisites for any school psychologist working with interpreters to communicate with ELLs. In addition, school psychologists must demonstrate specific competencies to work with interpreters. Among the competencies needed by school psychologists are skills in establishing rapport with ELLs and families through interpreters, skills in interviewing clients through interpreters, skills in conducting meetings with clients through interpreters, and skills relevant to reporting results obtained through interpreters (Lopez, 1999; Rogers et al., 1999).

An understanding of the problems inherent in the translation process is also pivotal for school psychologists. Since many concepts and vocabulary words cannot be directly translated from the source language to the target language, school psychologists must communicate clearly with interpreters so that interpreters can understand what information needs to be conveyed in their translations. The more information the school psychologist provides the interpreter, the better prepared the interpreter will be to deliver translations that convey the intent of the original message.

The school psychologists' awareness of the emotional and social aspects of using interpreters is another important skill. For example, the child may identify with the interpreter because he may see the interpreter as the protective one or simply because the interpreter is able to communicate with him in the native language. As a result of such interactions, school psychologists can often feel resentful, frustrated, guilty, left out, or powerless when working with interpreters. An awareness of such issues can be helpful to school psychologists when examining the social interactions observed during the process of using interpreters.

Skills in training interpreters to deliver psychological services are additional competencies for school psychologists. Given the breadth of information that school interpreters must have to work effectively in the delivery of psychological services, school psychologists must provide training for school interpreters to work in such situations as meetings, interviews, and assessment sessions. Finally, school psychologists must have a clear understanding of the limitations of assessing students through interpreters. An understanding of those limitations should help school psychologists to advocate for students in situations where interpreters should not be used and to make cautious interpretations when interpreters are used.

RECOMMENDED PRACTICES

At the present time, school psychologists are working with interpreters during a variety of activities including interviews, conferences, and assessment sessions. However, there is an absence of policies and guidelines at the systemic level to guide our practice in the use of school interpreters. The recommendations made in this chapter address systemic and practitioner issues. At the systemic level, the need to provide guidelines for the practice of using school interpreters is addressed. A number of recommendations are also made for school psychologists involved in the delivery of psychological services through interpreters.

Systemic Recommendations

At the present time, the practice of using interpreters continues despite the absence of clear guidelines for practitioners. Ochoa et al. (1996) argue that the National Association of School Psychologists and the American Psychological Association need to provide criteria as to how to work with interpreters during assessment situations. However, the need for clear guidelines extends beyond assessment. Our professional organizations must also address the guidelines that should be followed when working with interpreters during conferences, interviews, and other activities in schools. Furthermore, national and state policies should be created outlining the procedures that should be used for working with interpreters in school settings and the qualifications for school interpreters. State education agencies and districts need to develop guidelines for training and credentialing competent school interpreters. The guidelines should address the need to hire interpreters with adequate training in translation, and with high levels of proficiency in English and the second language. The need for guidelines and policies is imperative given the current practice of using interpreters with little or no training to assess, classify, and place ELLs for special education programs (Lopez, 1995).

Plata (1993) proposed a management system to coordinate the services offered by school interpreters. He recommended that districts develop a roster of qualified interpreters; guidelines for outlining interpreters' roles; guidelines and procedures for selecting and working with interpreters; a system for monitoring the interpreters' practices; a plan for interpreter and school personnel training; a reward system for compensating interpreters; procedures to help interpreters to improve their performance; plans for conducting formative and summative evaluations relevant to the interpreters' programs; and a plan to employ bilingual school personnel to diminish the need to hire interpreters. Given the absence of national, state, and local policies addressing the use of school interpreters, school psychologists can work with district administrators to implement the management plan recommended by Plata (1993). At the systems level, school psychologists can also advocate for ELLs and families by working with other school personnel to develop guidelines as to the kind of credentials, training, and experiences school interpreters must demonstrate.

Local school districts and school psychology training programs need to work collaboratively with interpreter training programs in universities across the nation to develop preservice and inservice training programs for school interpreters. Interpreter training programs expose their trainees to a number of courses that target basic principles in translation, verbal expression, professional roles, and ethics (Castle, 1984). In addition, interpreter training programs offer courses that target setting-specific situations such as translating during conferences and legal proceedings (Cokely, 1987). The training programs use a variety of tools to sensitize interpreters to the psychological and social contexts of translation including practicum experiences; analysis of video tapes and audio tapes; and role playing (Frishberg, 1990). Given our expertise in educational and psychological issues, school psychologists have a pivotal role in training interpreters to deliver translation services to ELLs and their families in schools. School psychologists can be instrumental in developing courses and workshop experiences that can help interpreters to acquire specific knowledge and skills to deliver translation services in schools. The use of role plays and the examination of video tapes and audio tapes of different situations where interpreters are needed can also be helpful in training interpreters to acquire specific skills such as translating during clinical interviews and parent meetings. Practicum experiences can also be created for interpreters to receive practical experiences in working in school settings with a variety of professionals.

Recommendations for School Psychologists

When working with ELLs and their families during such activities as consultation, clinical interviews, and special education assessment activities, school districts should make every effort possible to obtain the services of bilingual school psychologists who are familiar with the language and culture of the clients. The *Directory of Bilingual School Psychologists* (National Association of School Psychologists, 2000) should be a useful resource at the national level. Local directories should also be developed at the state and district levels so that districts can share interpreters. When bilingual school psychologists are not available, school psychologists should work with interpreters who demonstrate the competencies outlined earlier in this chapter, including bilingual as well as bicultural competencies.

When professionally trained interpreters cannot be located, school psychologists may find themselves in the position of having to use bilingual school personnel with educational expertise to provide translation services. Among the bilingual school personnel who may provide assistance are teachers, social workers, counselors, teacher's aides, and trained paraprofessionals. School psychologists should provide the bilingual school personnel with the necessary training to prepare them for their roles as interpreters. If bilingual school personnel are not available, then the school psychologist may want to locate individuals from the community who demonstrate bilingual proficiency and who are familiar with the cultural backgrounds of the students. Community members serving as school interpreters may be in need of extensive training if they are unfamiliar with the educational and psychological issues that they will encounter in their roles as interpreters (Lopez, 2000).

Trained interpreters, school personnel, and community members who have dual relationships with specific clients should not be placed in the position of providing translation services for those clients. As such, placing school children and family members in the roles of interpreters is not recommended (Lynch, 1998). The confidential and sensitive nature of the issues we discuss with children and parents precludes bilingual peers from acting as interpreters during interviews, conferences, and assessment situations. Peers and family members who are placed in the roles of interpreters can have difficulty delivering accurate translations because they may lack the language skills needed for the task. In addition, their personal involvement with the student and family may interfere with their ability to remain objective during the translation process. As such, they may refrain from translating everything that is said because they do not agree with the content of the discussion or because they may wish to protect the student or family member they are helping.

Providing psychological services through interpreters is time consuming because of the many barriers that can be encountered during the process. Lopez (2000) reported that consultation activities took longer than expected because of the difficulties in locating qualified interpreters and the need to provide interpreters with adequate training to translate during consultation sessions. In addition, the time consuming factor is inherent in the process of translation because of the need to filter all communication through a third party (i.e., the interpreter). School psychologists should acknowledge and expect that activities conducted through interpreters will take additional time. That factor should be shared with other school professionals involved in the activities where interpreters will be used so that time constraints are acknowledged early on during the process and steps can be taken to prevent the violation of any explicit or implicit deadlines.

Opportunities for interpreters to establish rapport with clients help clients to feel comfortable with the interpreters (Lopez, 2000). Thus, school psychologists may want to ask interpreters to meet with ELLs and their parents prior to translation sessions. School psychologists should discuss rapport building sessions with interpreters to establish the parameters of the encounter. For example, during those rapport sessions interpreters should abstain from discussing any issues that will be brought up during conferences, interviews, or assessment sessions.

A number of practices recommended in the literature for school professionals working with interpreters are provided in Table 1. The practices were adapted from the existing literature on interpretation and translation (Fradd & Wilen, 1990; Langdon, 1994; Lopez, 2000; Lynch, 1998). It should be noted that the practices recommended in Table 1 assume that the interpreters have adequate competencies and high levels of language proficiency in English and the second language.

Before working with interpreters, school psychologists should conduct briefing sessions with them. If other school personnel are joining the school psychologist for activities such as meetings and interviews with parents, then the briefing session should be conducted with all relevant personnel. Briefing sessions provide school psychologists with the opportunity to discuss with the interpreters the background information needed to prepare for the translation session such as procedures that will be used (e.g., interviews, meetings, assessment) and topics that will be discussed (i.e., special education issues, technical vocabulary). The briefing session is also the time when the school psychologist may want to explore the cultural issues that he or she needs to be aware of to work with ELLs from diverse cultural backgrounds. Table 1 also provides a list of recommendations that should be followed during translation sessions as well as during debriefing sessions. Debriefing sessions are held after translation sessions for school psychologists and interpreters to discuss issues and problems that surfaced during the translation process.

Table 1. Recommended practices for school psychologists working with interpreters

The following recommendations apply to such activities as interviews, conferences, and assessment sessions. The recommendations are made with the assumptions that the interpreters have adequate training to work in schools and demonstrate high levels of proficiency in English and the second language.

During briefing sessions:

- Establish sitting arrangements. Stansfield (1980) recommends that the clinician and the interpreter sit next to each other with the interpreter sitting slightly behind the clinician. According to Stansfield, this sitting arrangement allows the clients to see both the interpreter and the clinician, the client can look at both the clinician and the interpreter to receive verbal and nonverbal messages from both, and the clinician will be in a position of facing and directly talking to the client.
- Provide the interpreter with an overview of the purpose of the session. The overview should include a description of the activities that should take place such as interviews, discussions, and questions. The interpreter should be apprised of the purpose of the translation session (i.e., to obtain information about the student's developmental background; to provide parents with feedback regarding the student's functioning).
- Provide the interpreter with any information that the interpreter needs to understand the context of the situation. For example, inform the interpreter of any unusual behaviors or verbalizations that may be characteristic of the student based on the diagnostic classification.
- Address issues related to confidentiality and describe boundaries of confidentiality.
- Decide what type of oral translation will be used. Since the translation research supports the use of translation styles that provide frequent breaks for the interpreter to deliver messages with fewer translation errors, discontinuous consecutive translations may be most appropriate for school settings.
- Provide the interpreter with the opportunity to examine and translate any documents that may need translation during the session (i.e., IEPs, letters).
- Discuss technical terms that will be used during the session (i.e., diagnostic categories, special education terms, psychological terms), and encourage the interpreters to ask questions about any vocabulary or concepts that they need more information about.
- Discuss cross-cultural issues form the perspective of communication and behaviors. For example, the school psychologist may want to greet cross-culturally different families in ways that are culturally appropriate. Also, explore with interpreters the pragmatic rules pertinent to the students' cultures (Plata, 1993).
- Discuss with the interpreter the expectation that everything said will be translated to the clients and that the interpreter should translate all communication from clients.
- If the appropriate tools are available and prior to the assessment session, the interpreter should review all assessment materials and should have the opportunity to ask questions relevant to the assessment materials. Discuss with the interpreter concepts related to standardization, validity, reliability, and conduct during assessment sessions (e.g., do not coax students).
- Fradd and Wilen (1990) suggest developing an agenda to follow during the translation session. The agenda should list all the issues that will be covered during the session. The agenda should be reviewed by the school psychologist and the interpreter during the debriefing session.

During sessions when interpreters are being used:

- Take the time to welcome the children and parents. The interpreter should introduce herself or himself, you (that is, the school psychologist), and any other school professional present during the session. If sitting arrangements have been predetermined, then you should be specific as to where everyone should sit.
- Take time to establish rapport with the clients. Speak directly to the clients and direct your attention to the clients when they are speaking. Avoid the ping-pong effect of darting your eyes and attention back and forth from the clients to the interpreter.
- Figueroa (1989) recommends the use of audiotapes during translation sessions. The audiotapes can provide school psychologists and interpreters with opportunities to review the session at a later point. If audiotapes are used, then permission must be obtained from parents and other participants. The permission should be obtained in writing. The decision to use audiotapes must be made taking into consideration that the presence of tape recorders may inhibit clients to discuss sensitive or confidential issues.
- Speak in short sentences and allow time for the interpreter to translate everything said during the session. Communicate to the clients that they need to stop periodically to allow the interpreter to translate their messages. The interpreter should be ready to ask the client to slow down or to speak in short sentences if the rate of speech is too fast or if the client is not stopping frequently enough to allow the interpreter to translate their messages. In situations where the inter-

Table 1. (Continued)

preter and the clients become involved in long discussions, then be ready to remind the interpreters and the clients that all communications must be translated.
- Avoid idioms, slang, and metaphors because they are difficult to translate.
- Take notes relevant to any issues that need to be discussed during debriefing. The interpreter should also take notes. For example, terms that were difficult to translate or cross-cultural issues relevant to communication can be noted and discussed during debriefing sessions.
- During conferences and interview sessions, periodically ask the client questions to establish that they are understanding the content of the communication. Asking clarifying questions is helpful in situations where information was lost as a result of the translation.

During debriefing sessions:
- Discuss with the interpreter the outcomes of the translation session. In addition, discuss any translation problems that may have surfaced during the session and their implications.
- After assessment sessions and student interviews, discuss cross-cultural issues relevant to the student's responses and behaviors. Acknowledge cultural differences and discuss their role in the assessment process.
- Encourage the interpreter to ask questions regarding the translation session. Also, encourage the interpreter to discuss his or her perceptions of the translation session and the cultural issues that surfaced during the session.

Recommendations Relevant to Assessment Sessions

The need for a special education referral should be carefully examined for all ELLs. Pre-referral alternatives such as consultation and prevention services (e.g., changes in instructional program) should be implemented before referring ELLs to special education. Bilingual psychologists who are proficient in the students' native languages should assess ELLs who are referred for bilingual evaluations. Trained interpreters should be used only when all resources have been exhausted to locate bilingual school psychologists and when a referral is imperative.

If an interpreter is needed to perform the evaluation, then multiple procedures should be used to collect the assessment data. When interviews are used as assessment tools, the school psychologist should consult the practices listed in Table 1. On-the-spot translations of standardized achievement and cognitive tools are not recommended. The first choice should be using testing tools that have been translated and validated for the population being tested. If such tools are available, then the school psychologist must provide the interpreter with training to assist in the assessment process. Among the applicable recommendations are providing interpreters with the opportunities to familiarize themselves with the testing tools and to practice administering the test. Once interpreters are familiar with testing procedures, they are better able to understand the assessment process and to follow the school psychologists' directions.

School psychologists assessing Spanish-speaking students can utilize the Bateria Woodcock-Muñoz (Woodcock & Muñoz-Sandoval, 1996) if they feel it is appropriate for the cultural and language background of the students being assessed. If the student's academic skills must be assessed in the first language and adequately normed tools are not available, then the school psychologist can work with a bilingual teacher or other qualified bilingual personnel to develop informal curriculum-based assessment procedures such as informal reading inventories and writing sample tasks. Newspapers and developmentally appropriate books in the native language can also be used for informal assessment purposes.

Informal translations of cognitive assessment tools are not recommended. The Universal Nonverbal Intelligence Test (UNIT) is a recent cognitive assessment tool that provides school psychologists with the means to assess ELLs nonverbally (McCallum & Bracken, 1997). The instructions for the test are delivered through pantomime and do not require any verbalizations from the students. Although more validity data are needed at this time to establish its utility with ELLs, the UNIT seems to be a preferable alternative to using interpreters to translate testing questions.

The Bilingual Verbal Ability Tests (BVAT; Muñoz-Sandoval, Cummins, Alvarado, & Ruet, 1998) is another tool that school psychologists can consider when working with interpreters to assess students' language skills. The BVAT is available in 15 languages, including Arabic, Chinese, English, French, German, Haitian-Creole, Hindi, Japanese, Korean, Polish, Portuguese, Russian, Spanish, Turkish, and Vietnamese.

Any reports generated for the purposes of describing data obtained through interpreters should include a number of points. In addition to any language and cultural data pertinent to the student's background, the report should clearly indicate that an interpreter was used. A clear description should also be included of the extent to which the interpreter was needed. For example, school psychologists should indicate if the interpreters were needed for the entire assessment or interview session or only infrequently. In addition, the report should indicate the style of translation that was used (e.g., simultaneous, consecutive) and a clear description of any assessment procedures that involved the use of interpreters. The report of any evaluation data collected through interpreters should address the validity and reliability of the findings. When necessary and appropriate, results should be presented in qualitative formats. All assessment data should be interpreted within the context of the students' cultural backgrounds. If the findings are questionable because the process of working with the interpreter did not yield valid assessment data, then the test report should clearly state so and the recommendations should address the need for a bilingual evaluation by a qualified school psychologist.

SUMMARY

This chapter makes a number of recommendations for school psychologists working with interpreters. Interpreters were defined as professionals who provide translation services in the context of spoken communication. In school settings, school psychologists work with interpreters during a variety of activities including interviews, conferences, and assessment sessions. School interpreters facilitate the communication between school psychologist and ELL children.

The process of translation is complex and demanding. School interpreters must exhibit a number of important competencies. Their bilingual and bicultural competencies are important because of their involvement in providing psychological services to ELLs and their families. A number of practices were recommended targeting systemic and practitioner issues. The information provided here does not answer all the questions about the practices of working with interpreters. Literature relevant to the use of interpreters is scarce, and little research has been conducted in this area.

Despite the fact that there are many unanswered questions, school psychologists often find themselves in the position of working with interpreters in a variety of situations. The pressures of providing services to diverse groups of students and their families should not mean that school psychologists should engage in such questionable practices as using untrained interpreters to translate tests on the spot. Our practices should always be guided by the ethical and professional principles dictated by our profession. Because of our expertise in human behavior and functioning, school psychologists should play a critical role in defining the competencies and practices of school interpreters providing services to ELLs and their families. School psychologists must also develop competencies to work with school interpreters. The profession of school psychology needs to begin to establish a dialogue about the practice of using interpreters to provide psychological services. Guidelines and policies must be developed at the national, state, and local levels to support the use of recommended practices when working with interpreters. Without guidelines for recommended practices we are inadvertently sanctioning the use of untrained interpreters and ignoring questionable practices that have a negative impact on the ELLs with whom we work.

REFERENCES

American Educational Research Association, American Psychological Association, National Council on Measurement in Education (1999). *Standards for educational and psychological testing*. Washington, DC: American Educational Research Association.

Anderson, R. B. W. (1976). Perspective on the role of the interpreter. In R. Brislin (Ed.), *Translation: Application and research* (pp. 208–228). New York: Gardner.

Barik, H. (1971). A description of various types of omissions, additions, and errors encountered in simultaneous interpretation. *Meta, 16*, 199–210.

Barik, H. C. (1973). Simultaneous interpretation: Temporal and quantitative data. *Language and Speech, 16*, 237–270.

Bracken, B. A., & Barona, A. (1991). State of the art procedures for translating, validating, and using psychoeducational tests in cross-cultural assessment. *School Psychology International, 12*, 119–132.

Castle, D. L. (1984). Effective oral interpreters: An analysis. In W. H. Northcott (Ed.), *Oral interpreting: Principles and practices* (pp. 169–185). University Park, MD: University of Maryland.

Cokely, D. R. (1987). The morning after the night before: Thoughts on curriculum sequencing. In M. L. McIntire, (Ed.), *New dimensions in interpreter education: Curriculum and instruction* (pp. 9–14). Northridge, CA: California State University.

Figueroa, R. (1989). Psychological testing of linguistic-minority students: Knowledge gaps and regulations. *Exceptional Children, 56*, 145–152.

Figueroa, R., A., Sandoval, J., & Merino, B. (1984). School psychology and limited-English-proficient (LEP) children: New competencies. *Journal of School Psychology, 22*, 131–143.

Fleischman, H. L., & Hopstock, P. J. (1993). *Descriptive study of services to limited English proficient students.* Arlington, VA: Development Associates.

Fradd, S. H., & Wilen, D. K. (1990, Summer). Using interpreters and translators to meet the needs of handicapped language minority students and their families. *NCBE Program Information Guide Series, No. 4.*

Frishberg, N. (1990). *Interpreting: An introduction* (3rd ed.). Silver Spring, MD: Registry of Interpreters for the Deaf.

Geisinger, K. F. (1994). Cross-cultural normative assessment: Translation and adaptation issues influencing the normative interpretation of assessment instruments. *Psychological Assessment, 6*, 304–312.

Harry, B. (1992). Making sense of disability: Low-income, Puerto Rican parents' theories of the problem. *Exceptional Children, 59*, 27–40.

Langdon, H. W. (1994, May). *Working with interpreters and translators in a school setting.* Paper presented at the Fordham University Bilingual Conference, New York.

Lopez, E. C. (1994, March). *Errors made by interpreters during on the spot translation of WISC-R questions.* Paper presented at the annual meeting of the National Association of School Psychologists, Seattle.

Lopez, E. C. (1995, August). *Survey of school psychologists: Training and practice issues in the use of interpreters.* Poster session presented at the meeting of the American Psychological Association, New York.

Lopez, E. C. (1999, August). *What competencies are needed for the delivery of psychological services through interpreters? Advances in the field.* Paper presented at the annual meeting of the American Psychological Association, Boston.

Lopez, E. C. (2000). Conducting instructional consultation through interpreters. *School Psychology Review, 29*, 378–388.

Lopez, E. C., & Rooney, M. (1997). A preliminary investigation of the roles and backgrounds of school interpreters: Implications for training and recruiting. *Journal of Social Distress and the Homeless, 6*, 161–174.

Lynch, E. W. (1998). Developing cross-cultural competence. In E. W. Lynch & M. J. Hanson (Eds.), *A guide for working with children and their families: Developing cross-cultural competence* (2nd ed.) (pp. 47–89). Baltimore: Brookes.

Marcos, L. R. (1979). Effects of interpreters on the evaluation of psychopathology in non-English-speaking patients. *American Journal of Psychiatry, 136*, 171–174.

McCallum, R. S., & Bracken, B. A. (1997). The Universal Nonverbal Intelligence Test. In D. P. Flanagan, J. L. Genshaft, & P. L. Harrison (Eds.), *Contemporary intellectual assessment: Theories, tests, and issues* (pp. 268–280). New York: Guilford.

Muñoz-Sandoval, A. F., Cummins, J., Alvarado, G. G., & Ruet, M. L. (1998). *The Bilingual Verbal Ability Tests.* Chicago: Riverside.

National Association of School Psychologists (2000). *Directory of bilingual school psychologists*. Bethesda, MD: Author.

Nida, E. A. (1964). *Toward a science of translating*. Leiden: E. J. Brill.

Ochoa, S. H., Gonzalez, D., Galarza, A., & Guillemard, L. (1996). The training and use of interpreters in bilingual psycho-educational assessment: An alternative in need of study. *Diagnostique, 21*(3), 19–40.

Plata, M. (1993). Using Spanish-speaking interpreters in special education. *Remedial and Special Education, 14*(6), 19–24.

Rogers, M. R., Ingraham, C. L., Bursztyn, A., Cajigas-Segredo, N., Esquivel, G., Hess, R. S., Nahari, S. G., & Lopez, E. C. (1999). Best practices in providing psychological services to racially, ethnically, culturally, and linguistically diverse individuals in the schools. *School Psychology International Journal, 20*, 243–264.

Stansfield, M. (1980). Psychological issues in mental health interpreting. In F. Caccamise, J. Stangarone, & M. Mitchell-Caccamise (Eds.), *Century of deaf awareness* (pp. 102–114). Silver Spring: MD: Registry of Interpreters for the Deaf.

U.S. Department of Education (1998). *Summary Report of the Survey of the States' Limited English Proficient Students and Available Educational Programs and Services, 1996–1997*. Washington, DC: Office of Grants and Contracts Services.

Woodcock, R. W., & Muñoz-Sandoval, A. F. (1996). *Bateria Woodcock-Muñoz: Pruebas de Habilidad Cognitiva-Revisada*. Chicago: Riverside.

ANNOTATED BIBLIOGRAPHY

Langdon, H. W. (1994). *The interpreter translator process in the educational setting: A resource manual* (ERID Document Reproduction Service No. ED383155).

Dr. Langdon is a pioneer in issues related to the use of interpreters in educational settings. This manual provides an overview of issues relevant to using interpreters and translators in school settings.

Lopez, E. C. (2000). Conducting instructional consultation through interpreters. *School Psychology Review, 29*, 378–388.

This is a qualitative investigation that explored the practice of using interpreters during instructional consultation activities. The findings address the facilitators as well as barriers encountered when using interpreters in consultation

Lynch, E. W. (1998). Developing cross-cultural competence. In E. W. Lynch & M. J. Hanson (Eds.), *A guide for working with children and their families: Developing cross-cultural competence* (2nd ed.) (pp. 47–89). Baltimore: Brookes.

This chapter provides guidelines for interventionists working with interpreters. Lynch discusses the characteristics of effective interpreters, cautions in using family and nonfamily members as interpreters, stress factors for interpreters, and interpreter training, guidelines.

Plata, M. (1993). Using Spanish-speaking interpreters in special education. *Remedial and Special Education, 14*, 19–24.

This article addresses the use of interpreters in special education settings. The author discusses the roles of interpreters, problems in using interpreters, training needs, and recommendations for managing the use of interpreters in school settings.

89 Best Practices in Working With Students With Traumatic Brain Injury

J. Michael Havey
Eastern Illinois University

OVERVIEW

Imagine that in a school you serve there is a child who is bright, active, and well behaved. Imagine that the child changes radically in a short period of time, and he is no longer capable and well behaved. What was once a teacher's dream student is now the student who needs more teacher attention and help than anyone else in the classroom. This scenario, unfortunately, is not rare. It describes an all-too-common situation following a traumatic brain injury (TBI). Although it is only within recent years that TBI has received legal recognition as a distinct category within special education, the disability is not new and nor is it rare. In fact, TBI is the number one killer and disabler of children and young adults in this country. According to the Brain Injury Association, traumatic brain injury is the most frequent cause of disability and death among children and adolescents in the United States. Each year, more than 1 million children sustain brain injuries ranging from mild to severe trauma. Of those, more than 30,000 endure permanent disabilities as a result of their brain injuries. Moreover, according to the National Pediatric Trauma Registry, about one third of all pediatric injury cases in the United States are related to brain injury (Brain Injury Association, no date). The tragedy of this condition is intensified because it is unforeseen and unexpected.

As medical technology has improved, so have survival rates of those who have sustained this type of injury. Also, the trend toward limited hospital stays has increased the focus on post-acute school and community programs (Gerring & Carney, 1992). The results of these trends are that increasing numbers of children with TBI are returning to schools, and schools are called upon to be major providers of long-term rehabilitation for these individuals. School psychologists who are knowledgeable about this disability can play a meaningful and important role in providing these services.

Educationally, TBI is defined as:

> an acquired injury to the brain caused by an external physical force, resulting in total or partial functional disability or psychosocial impairment, or both, that adversely affects a child's educational performance. The term applies to open or closed head injuries resulting impairments in one or more areas, such as cognition; language; memory; attention; reasoning; abstract thinking; judgment; problem solving; sensory, perceptual and motor abilities; psychosocial behavior; physical functions; information processing; and speech. The term does not apply to injuries that are congenital or degenerative, or brain injuries induced by birth trauma (34 C.F.R. 300.7 (c) (12)).

As do other categories of educational disability, this definition excludes some children. The present educational definition includes children who are adversely affected by "an external physical force." It explicitly excludes those children whose brains may have been affected by congenital or degenerative conditions (e.g., hydrocephaly, microcephaly) as well as those whose brains may have been injured by birth trauma. The definition also omits mention of those children who might suffer from an "internal" incident such as a vascular accident (stroke). Children who, because of the congenital or degenerative nature of their conditions, are excluded from special education eligibility under the TBI category, may still be eligible for special education and related services under another category, or they may be eligible for accommodations under Section 504.

Brain injury caused by external physical force is typically divided into two major classes: open and closed. Open brain injury is the result of an injury in which the brain is penetrated from the outside. Examples include a gunshot wound or a crushing of the skull. Damage from such an injury tends to be localized (focal) and to result in fairly predictable impairments. Closed brain injury, the most common type among children, results when a moving object (e.g., baseball bat) strikes the stationary head causing a sudden jolt (acceleration injury) or when the moving head is abruptly stopped or slowed (deceleration injury) by a stationary object (e.g., car dashboard) . In contrast to penetrating or open head injury, damage resulting from closed head injury is almost always diffuse (widespread) owing to both the nature of the physical agent involved and the characteristics of the human brain and central nervous system. The brain is of a gelatin-like consistency. Strong impacts cause the brain to move in a rippling manner inside the skull. Twisting and tearing of tissue often results from this movement. This damage is exacerbated by the fact that the inner surface of the skull is rough and rigid. The movement of the brain across this surface causes additional tearing. Damage obviously occurs at the point of impact (coup) in a closed head injury. Additional damage also occurs to the area of the brain opposite the site of actual contact (contra-coup). In addition to the mechanisms described above that are collectively known as "primary" brain damage, closed head injury also often results in "secondary" injuries that can occur subsequent to the initial injury. These include bleeding, swelling of tissue, decreased blood flow, elevated pressure, and infection. Because tissue damage from closed head injury can affect such widespread areas, predicting functional impairment can be especially difficult.

The etiology of TBI is heterogeneous. Although closed brain injury is more common among children than open brain injury, cause of injury tends to vary with age. Bruce and Mira, Tyler, and Tucker (as cited in Blosser & DePompei, 1994b) categorized causes of injury by age as follows:

Age	*Cause of Injury*
Infants	Mishandling by caregivers, accidental dropping, rolling from changing tables, physical abuse
Toddlers	Falls, motor vehicle accident (MVA), physical abuse
Preschoolers	Falls, MVA, physical abuse
Elementary School Children	MVA, bicycle accident, falls, injuries during play
Adolescents	MVA (including alcohol or drug misuse), sports injuries, assault, risk-taking behaviors

In recent years increasing attention has been paid to sports-related injuries. Although sports- and recreation-related injuries account for 3% of hospitalized persons with TBI, approximately 90% of sports-related TBIs are mild and may go unreported. Sports-related TBI occurs most frequently among people ages 5–24, many of whom will return to public education settings (National Institute of Health, 1998).

Although young people in the 15- to 24-year-old range are most at risk for TBI, children under 15 are afflicted at almost the same rate (Kalsbeek, McLaurin, Harris, & Miller, 1980; Rosen & Gerring,1986). TBI occurs in males at a rate approximately twice that in females. Incidence rates are similar for whites and nonwhites. Motor vehicle accidents and falls are the most common causes for school-age children (Kalsbeek et al., 1980).

BASIC CONSIDERATIONS

Issues of severity

Because the forces responsible for TBI vary significantly, the severity of the injury varies from individual to individual. A convention among medical personnel is to rate TBI as mild, moderate, or severe based on length and depth of coma and duration of post traumatic amnesia. Although common usage suggests that a dichotomy exists between coma and consciousness, reality is better represented as a continuum of degrees of consciousness. A metric frequently utilized to measure the severity of coma is the Glasgow Coma Scale (GCS). This technique grades eye, motor, and verbal responses within the first 24 hours following trauma. Numerical values are assigned to different levels of response, and a total score (15 points possible) is obtained. Lower scores represent a lesser degree of response and are indicative of more severe injury. In addition to providing an indication of initial severity, the GCS is also employed for monitoring change. Post traumatic amnesia (PTA) is defined as the period of time following trauma when the patient is incapable of reliable, consistent, and accurate memory for ongoing events. Under a common classification system, PTA of less than 1 hour is considered mild, PTA of 1–24 hours is considered moderate, PTA that continues from 1 to 7 days is considered severe, and PTA of greater than 7 days is considered very severe. A standard measure of PTA in children is the Children's Orientation and Amnesia Test (COAT) (Ewing- Cobbs, Levin, Fletcher, Miner, & Eisenberg, 1990).

Although ratings of coma and PTA are often employed to provide an estimate of severity of injury and physiological disruption, an important consideration for school psychologists and other school personnel to remember is that they often do not correlate well with future recovery or provide information that is useful in predicting outcome. For example, Savage (1991) cited a study that found many of the children with mild head injury to be experiencing serious problems in a variety of contexts. Also cited were many children with severe injury who, with the exception of motor difficulties, were doing as well as the mildly to moderately injured children. Traumatic brain injury is a complex phenomenon, and recovery is affected by a variety of factors. Other variables such as age, causal agent, extent of damage, site of injury, and quality of rehabilitation all interact to influence outcomes for individuals (Begali, 1992).

A related issue of importance to school psychologists who might work with children with TBI is the concept of "plasticity." This term has been applied to the long-held notion that because children's brains are not completely developed they can recover more rapidly and more completely from brain insult than can adults. Although some evidence does exist that suggests that children may recover language functioning more easily than do adults, there is other research evidence suggesting that trauma to a brain that is incompletely developed prevents the development of a complete and competent behavioral repertoire (Berg, 1986). Age may be an important variable in recovery prospects. Kolb and Whishaw (1996) contended that lesions incurred before 1 year of age produce disproportionately greater impairment than those incurred later. They also contended that lesions incurred between 1 and 5 years of age allow reorganization of brain function, but lesions incurred later than 5 years of age allow little or no sparing of function. Current beliefs about the limits of cerebral plasticity in children argue against complacency in rehabilitation efforts.

Psychological Sequelae/Consequences of TBI

As was discussed above, TBI can vary greatly in severity and the rating of the severity of injury and physiological disruption does not provide a great deal of insight about recovery. The potential often exists for sending children back to school with little if any academic or social support before they have recovered sufficiently. Although apparently well, children who have sustained TBI often experience psychological sequelae (pathological consequences following traumatic insult or disease) that may not be apparent until they are returned to a school setting. Memory disorders are common and persistent psychological consequences of TBI. Problems of attention and concentration as well as problems with language production and processing (e.g., word finding, verbal fluency, reading comprehension, and writing) are also frequently experienced by these children (Begali, 1992). In addition to these cognitive difficulties, psychosocial sequelae such as emotional volatility, anxiety responses, and depression are frequent results from even mild head injury (Frey, 1994).

Educators should also be aware that anticonvulsant medication is often prescribed as a prophylactic measure to reduce the possibility of seizures and that other medications may be prescribed to help manage behavioral excesses. Cognitive side effects that could have an impact on learning may result from these medications. Educators should always know what medications have been prescribed for a child and any possible side effects. School psychologists can play an important role in alerting educators to the possibility of those effects and in monitoring the student's behavior.

A number of physical deficits can also result from TBI. Rigidity of movement, loss of muscular control, weakness, and loss of balance and coordination are not uncommon sequelae of TBI. School psychologists need to be particularly aware of those factors because of their potential impact on assessment results and classroom performance.

BEST PRACTICES

Best Practices in Assessment for Intervention

Because of the varied sequelae that can follow a head injury, broad-based, multidisciplinary assessments are essential in order to make the best educational plans and develop the best educational programs for children who have sustained TBI (Telzrow, 1991). TBI affects each child differently, and any aspect of the child's functioning can be affected. TBI can have an impact on cognitive processes, language, social behavior, and/or sensory and motor functioning. The expertise of a variety of professionals may be needed to develop a comprehensive picture of the child's abilities and needs.

Because post-trauma functioning is often markedly different from pre-trauma functioning, the school psychologist and other school personnel must take care to gather information to allow pre- and post-trauma comparisons to be made. Information regarding pre-trauma functioning, by providing a baseline against which post-trauma behavior can be judged, is important in determining the educational impact of trauma. This information will also allow teachers to understand the source of frustration that many children with TBI display and to incorporate knowledge about any "lost" skills into daily instruction (Madigan, Hall, & Glang, 1997).

Since the likelihood exists that a child who has experienced TBI will not have had a complete psychoeducational assessment prior to injury, this component of the evaluation will focus primarily on a review of the child's educational record and interviews with adults knowledgeable about the child's previous level of functioning. Madigan, Hall, and Glang (1997) provide a brief, 11-item questionnaire to assist in comparing pre- and post-trauma academic functioning and behavior. These authors also stress the importance of information about the speed with which the child mastered therapy skills and how well the child followed directions while in the hospital. Group achievement scores, report cards, anecdotal records, and work samples are additional important sources of data.

A review of medical records and/or interviews with medical personnel and parents can provide valuable information about the severity of the trauma and the overall medical situation surrounding the injury. Moreover, many children will have been evaluated by a hospital psychologist shortly before returning to school. A review of the report and personal contact with the hospital psychologist can also provide helpful information.

In most cases the school psychologist will need to be directly involved with a complete case study evaluation conducted by school personnel. Gerring and Carney (1992) suggest that assessments be completed as close as possible to the date of school reentry because this is usually a time when the child is no longer experiencing rapid recovery of function.

Telzrow (1991) recommends that assessment of children with TBI should include contextual assessment. This includes a focus on "moderator" variables: social, environmental, and motivational factors that influence and affect the child's ability to cope and adjust to the presenting disorder (Ewing-Cobbs & Fletcher, 1990). It is important that school psychologists not ignore these important factors that may not be obvious, but yet may have an important impact on the child's functioning in the school setting. Telzrow (1991), in addition to several other authors (e.g., Ewing-Cobbs & Fletcher, 1990; Obrzut & Hynd, 1990), suggests that school psychologists take a domain-specific approach to the assessment of children who have sustained TBI. This approach involves the identification and examination of several specific areas or domains of functioning. Although the nomenclature varies somewhat from author to author, domains typically specified include intelligence, language, memory and concentration, sensory recognition and perception, academic achievement, and behavior and personality (see Telzrow (1991) for lists of major assessment domains suggested by seven experts or teams of experts).

Although some domains may appear to be only marginally related to performance in school, they may provide information about factors that might interfere with the child's progress. The main focus of the assessment should, however, remain on those factors most closely related to performance in school. An overemphasis on domains may lead school personnel to ignore information directly related to interventions that can improve school performance and to shift their attention to areas of processing deficit that may provide little information useful for intervention.

During the recovery process the child's level of functioning can change rapidly. For this reason, optimal assessment of the child with TBI needs to be periodic and ongoing. This does not mean that a complete psycho-educational assessment needs to be administered on a frequent basis. Indeed, many standardized assessment measures are subject to practice effects and tend to be insensitive to small but important changes in skill level (Kranzler & Shaw, 1992). A methodical system for closely monitoring progress of the child will be important, however. Curriculum-based assessment (CBA) or curriculum-based measurement (CBM) techniques that are designed for ongoing assessment and for measuring discrete changes in functioning can be important tools in assessing and program planning for children with TBI (Kranzler & Shaw, 1992; Cohen, 1996). In addition, CBA and/or CBM techniques can be useful in documenting the adverse impact of the trauma on academic functioning (Shaw & Yingst, 1992) and in helping children and parents understand the need for a gradual and systematic return to school (Ylvisaker, Hartwick, & Stevens, 1991). By comparing performance on post-trauma measures with pre-trauma placement in the curriculum the school psychologist can determine if functioning has deteriorated. Shaw and Yingst (1992) recommend starting the CBA at the place within the curriculum where the child was placed prior to the trauma and testing through progressively lower levels until an instructional level is reached if evidence of decline is apparent.

Regardless of technique utilized, school psychologists who assess children who have sustained TBI need to be alert for signs of the cognitive and behavioral difficulties that are frequent sequelae of TBI. There are, however, several steps that school psychologists can take to surmount this problem. Spreading the assessment over more than one session will probably be appropriate with a child who has difficulty maintaining attention and concentration. "Testing the limits" procedures may also allow greater insight into a child's abilities and skills when test performance is impeded by one of the sequelae discussed above. Information gained through observation and interview methods will be especially important in the assessment of a child whose behavioral limitations interfere with testing and interpretation of results. Kaplan (as cited in Begali, 1994) suggested a process approach to assessment, in which the student's behavior and problem-solving strategies are the focus of assessment rather than conformity to standardized procedures. This approach has been incorporated into the recently published *WISC-III* as a Process Instrument (WISC-III PI; Kaplan, Fein, Kramer, Delis, & Morris, 1999). Finally, utilization of non-standardized measures such as CBA that allow for greater flexibility in administration can be valuable sources of information.

Best Practices in Educational Planning and Academic Consultation

For many children with TBI the first step in the educational planning process is the transition from a medical environment (hospital or rehabilitation center) to an educational environment. The differences in philosophy, outlook, and system structure all too often contribute to inadequate communication and poorly coordinated services. The type and amount of interagency cooperation will depend on the severity of the injury and the length of stay in a medical/rehabilitation facility. Moreover, the return of a student with TBI to a school setting is not a one-time process and may take several weeks. Savage and Carter (1988) identified four steps that are crucial to ensure a successful transition:

1. Involvement of the school-based special education team in the hospital or rehabilitation facility

2. In-service training for all school-based staff who will have contact with the student

3. Short- and long-term planning for the support services needed for the student

4. Continued follow up by the rehabilitation professionals

Ongoing communication between medical and school staff that begins early in the recovery process may help avoid frustration and failure that can result from inappropriate expectations based on inadequate information. School psychologists are especially suited to serve as effective liaisons between schools and medical/rehabilitation facilities. Many school psychologists are knowledgeable about clinical and medical issues and have served as transition facilitator for children who have been hospitalized for psychiatric reasons. Moreover, school psychologists are experts at communicating with children. They can serve the child with a traumatic brain injury by serving as a liaison for classmates and peers as well as adults in the school environment.

Not only is early communication between medical and school staff important, school personnel also need to reach out to the family. Not only is this an ethical step to take, but increasingly authors are stressing the important role that the family plays in the rehabilitation and return to school of children with TBI (DePompei & Blosser, 1994). Early and sustained contact is important because it facilitates the establishment of positive relationships and alliances that will be important for successful reentry. This contact also allows school personnel to develop an understanding of the family's potential for help and to solicit parental input concerning their needs and wishes for their child, and their attitudes toward school and the child's injury. All of these must be incorporated into reintegration plans in order for these efforts to be successful.

Students who make the transition back to a school setting are in the later stages of recovery. Although many of them may be medically stable and display no physical needs, cognitive and psychosocial effects that can interfere with school performance may continue (Gerrin & Carney, 1992). To help school personnel establish appropriate expectations, Begali (1994) listed 20 questions that should be answered prior to re-entry. These included, What was the child's estimated cognitive and educational status before the injury? What are the child's strengths? Which functions remain intact? How long is the child's attention span? Is the child at risk for seizures?

School psychologists who have developed expertise about TBI may also serve the transition process by providing in-service presentations for school personnel. Tyler (1997) provided the following objectives for an awareness-level inservice program:

1. Becoming familiar with federal and state definitions of TBI

2. Developing an understanding of the incidence and causes of TBI

3. Gaining an awareness of the mechanisms of TBI

4. Becoming aware of the recovery pattern of students with TBI

5. Developing an understanding of the immediate and long-term effects of TBI

6. Gaining an awareness of the medical, rehabilitative, and therapeutic interventions students with TBI require

7. Becoming familiar with techniques used to aid in the school reentry of students with TBI

8. Becoming familiar with educational modifications and instructional strategies used for students with TBI

If practitioners do not feel completely competent to conduct an in-service, then prepared training materials, such as those developed by Tyler (1992), can be employed. In addition to the above topics, DeBoskey (1996) suggested that teachers need to be aware of the fact that they will experience emotional and/or behavioral changes as a result of interaction with a student with TBI. Typical negative reactions include over-optimism/unrealistic expectations, frustration, and anger.

Although much of the discussion thus far has addressed issues central to the development of appropriate expectations for returning students, the school psychologist must assist school personnel in addressing questions designed to ensure that interventions are appropriately individualized and likely to succeed. The need for a carefully tailored, truly individualized IEP is paramount. Brain injury affects each child differently. Some children will be only mildly affected and will need only minimal services while others will need both a significantly greater intensity and variety of interventions. School psychologists can help schools engage in Savage and Carter's (1988) step 3, short- and long-term planning, by attending to the questions that follow:

1. What instructional techniques are most likely to be appropriate?
2. What does the student find to be reinforcing?
3. What motivates the student to learn in a sustained way?
4. What kind of rest periods will the student need?
5. What curricular modifications will need to be made?
6. What interventions or accommodations will the student need to help the student cope with residual physical problems?
7. What assistive devices will be necessary?
8. What kind of school/classroom environment will provide the appropriate amount of structure to facilitate learning?

A key concept in the development of an IEP for a child with TBI is flexibility. Students with TBI often make rapid progress in the first few months following their injury. Future performance levels often are not consistent with nor can they be inferred from current levels of performance. Because the student's needs may change rapidly during the early stages of the recovery process, the recommendation has been made (e.g., Savage, 1991; Ylvisaker, Hartwick, & Stevens, 1991) that the initial IEP should be written for a short period of time (i.e., 6–8 weeks) rather than the more customary 1-year period. Because TBI often affects more than academic functioning, it is important that IEPs contain provisions for addressing the child's other needs as well. The IEP must view academic progress as a part of the process of achieving independent functioning and should include provisions to foster the development of adaptive and effective behaviors that will enable the child to meet with educational, social, and vocational success (Roth, Harley, Havey, Probst, & Vaal, 1993). Cohen (1996) advocated a "Who" (the student, education staff, family), "What" (program components), "When" (time of reentry), "Where" (program location: school and classrooms), "Why" (clarification of program adaptations), and "How" (development of techniques to implement the adaptations) approach to program development. Ylvisaker et al. (1991) also assert that the unique characteristics and possible rapid recovery of children with TBI make the ongoing success of their educational programs dependent on careful case management.

The wide variety of outcomes subsequent to TBI mandates that educators consider the complete continuum of services and placements as they plan educational programs for children with TBI. Students returning to school after a brain injury are often at a disadvantage in two ways. Not only have they missed whole units of instruction, but they also are returning with limited functional abilities that reduce the likelihood they can learn at the same pace as they did before their injuries (Gerring & Carney, 1992). These students will need placements that will allow them time to make up what has been missed. They might also require extended time for tests and assignments. Extra time may be required of teachers for repetition and extra assistance. Finally, these students may also need extra time to get from one place to another in the school building (Gerring & Carney, 1992).

Educators need to be flexible and allow for changes in placement as the recovery process progresses. Two areas in which flexible programming can be important include length of school day and length of time in a "regular" education classroom. Many children with TBI become fatigued easily. For many of these children a gradual return to a complete school day might be more appropriate than an abrupt reentry. In addition, as children recover they will need less restrictive educational environments and will be able to spend more time in "regular" classrooms. A structured, self-contained placement that provides close supervision may, at least initially, be most appropriate for the child with a TBI (Gerring & Carney, 1992; Telzrow, 1987). An extended school year may be an appropriate way to provide extra learning time. Blosser and DePompei (1994a) suggested that placement decisions should also be based on considerations of physical, social, and psychological environments most conducive to learning.

They advocated that educators should be mindful of environmental barriers, availability of resources, and classroom structure when making placement decisions.

Teaching methods and techniques that are uniquely beneficial for children with TBI have not been identified, and teaching practices helpful for students with TBI are also beneficial for other students. An approach to instruction that stresses process as well as product has, however, been stressed for students with TBI (Cohen, 1996; Blosser & DePompei, 1994a). This approach is based on the idea that teaching should focus on both products to be completed (assignments) and the strategy needed to complete the task. Students may need instruction in such metacognitive processes as organization, summarizing, and attending and following directions and other skills necessary for success in school. Blosser and DePompei (1994a) also suggested that IEPs may need to contain goals to address potential problems with social interaction and communication. Depending upon individual needs, the IEP may contain accommodations and supplementary aids and/or services to help the child function in his or her least restrictive environment. Kraemer and Blacher (1997) provided a list of suggested accommodations to address the following areas of potential difficulty: attention, orientation, information processing, sensory, organization and planning, memory and learning, reasoning and problem solving, behavior, and motor.

Educational programs based on behavioral instructional strategies also appear to be most successful. Task analysis and systematic progression from goal to goal are key components. Cohen (1996) proposed that by providing clear expectations, frequent reminders, direct instruction, and individualized reinforcers and reinforcement schedules teachers can increase odds for the accomplishment of goals.

Because many children who have sustained TBI require related services as well as modified instruction, an integrated program that provides coordinated instructional and therapeutic services is viewed as preferable to a more segregated approach. One method of ensuring this integrated approach is to deliver related services in the primary instructional setting rather than through a "pull out" design.

Programming for Behavioral and Emotional Needs

Post-traumatic cognitive difficulties can interfere with social as well as academic adjustment. Children who have sustained TBI often exhibit behavioral and emotional problems that can be further compounded by cognitive impairments. School psychologists may, therefore, be called on to provide behavior management consultation or direct counseling as a part of the intervention package for children who have sustained TBI. Although each person who has incurred TBI displays a unique constellation of behaviors, enough commonality exists for Feeney and Ylvisaker (1997) to identify a common clinical picture of a student who appears lazy and unmotivated when not directed by others, may exhibit irritating or explosive behaviors that can be inhibited by neurologically intact students, and does not change behavior in response to the contingencies that are often effective in managing the behavior of peers.

Deaton (1994, 1997) and Feeney and Ylvisaker (1997) stressed the importance of functional analysis in developing behavioral interventions with students who have sustained a TBI. Feeney and Ylvisaker (1997), however, emphasized that because the problem behavior of a child with TBI may be the result of neurologic factors that are unrelated to environmental events, conducting an analysis of the behavior can be very complex. These authors concluded that "in most cases, challenging behavior is a complex mix of preinjury behavior patterns, physiological triggers, reduced initiation or inhibition, and newly learned behaviors" (Feeney and Ylvisaker, 1997, p. 234). Deaton (1994) cautioned that maladaptive behaviors can easily and inadvertently be reinforced because of feelings of over protectiveness, guilt, or pity on the part of adults. Maladaptive behavior can also be reinforced when teachers or parents give in or give up because of fatigue or convenience.

Because of diminished self control and ability to modify behavior in response to feedback, Feeney and Ylvisaker (1997) suggested that behavior programs should focus more on the manipulation of antecedents rather than consequences. They specifically recommended creating familiar routines, reducing frustration by ensuring that tasks can be completed successfully, and allowing students to make choices, thereby avoiding confrontation. They also recommended that the principle of behavioral momentum (i.e., positive and successful behavior increases the likelihood of subsequent positive and successful behavior and negative, unsuccessful behavior has the opposite result) be considered when establishing expectations and making assignments.

Deaton (1997) offered suggestions for specific behavior problems that frequently occur after a TBI. For lack of initiation she suggested that once a target behavior has been identified by the teacher and the student, positive reinforcement and shaping of successive approximations should be attempted. Disinhibition can be addressed by responding to the behavior the same way each time it occurs. If classmates are of sufficient maturity, then they can help with implementation. An aide can also be employed to help monitor and cue the student. Deaton also advised that impulsivity and poor anger control can best be controlled by providing additional environmental cues and structuring the environment by decreasing triggers for anger. Her suggestions for these latter two behaviors are similar to Feeney and Ylvisaker's (1997) emphasis on antecedent manipulation.

Deaton (1997) also offered general suggestions for behavioral interventions with students with TBI. First, collaboration among educator, parent, and student is important. Second, salient and obvious reinforcers should be used at least initially. Third, cognitive and communication difficulties that underlie behavior problems should be addressed. Fourth, care should be taken that expectations and work load are realistic and appropriate.

In addition to the provision of indirect, behavioral consultation services, school psychologists may need to provide direct psychotherapeutic services to the student with TBI. A theme that runs through much of the literature dealing with emotional issues surrounding TBI is "loss." The person recovering from a traumatic injury to the brain is, in many ways, different from the person who sustained the injury. Children who have sustained this type injury may have particular difficulty adjusting to this circumstance because outwardly they may appear to be perfectly normal. A major goal of school psychologists and others who counsel children with TBI should be to help the individual accept the trauma, its consequence, and the new set of circumstances posed by the injury. Deaton (1997) contended that individual counseling is most appropriate with students with relatively intact insight and memory. Deaton (1997) and Begali (1994) suggested that periodically videotaping students may be a useful supplement to counseling because this can provide the basis for insight into the severity of the injury as well as evidence of progress and recovery.

Working With Families and Peers

Although TBI is sustained by individuals, the changes that it causes in that individual's functioning extend its impact to other people with whom the individual with TBI interacts. Nowhere is this impact more obvious and pronounced than within the family. A child's TBI is an intrusive shock to the functioning of a family. The impact of TBI on the family is important to consider because the family is such a vital part of any child's life and because the family's support and cooperation are essential for the child's success in school.

A TBI can leave family members confused and prone to feelings of guilt, sorrow, and anger. Family members are confronted with the fact that the child is not the same as before the injury. Denial is often part of the adjustment process and may continue for months or years. Changes in family dynamics and functioning can compound the stresses associated with adjusting to changes in the child with the injury. Children who require long-term rehabilitation present their families with a different set of responsibilities and demands. The amount of time and energy expended simply transporting the child can be daunting. Adding the new and extra demands for care in the home presented by the child can prove overwhelming. Another source of stress for the parents of a child severely disabled by a head injury is the realization that their responsibility for the child will be ongoing and continue much longer than previously expected. The financial strain of providing for the needs of the child can also be a source of substantial stress. The new circumstances of the family of a child who has sustained a TBI often result in at least some social problems involving isolation, loss of emotional support, and restricted independence (Lezak, 1988). In fact, many couples seek counseling for the problems that emerge from coping with all of the changes in the family (DePompei & Blosser, 1994).

In addition to the stresses and strains encountered by the parents of the child with TBI, specific problems are also associated with being the sibling of such a child. Because parents must focus so much time and energy on the child who has been injured, siblings often feelings of abandonment, guilt over those feelings, and a need for special attention (DePompei & Blosser, 1994). The TBI of a sibling can also bring about changes in the school environment as well. The injured sibling may engage in behaviors that are difficult to understand and that may embarrass uninjured siblings, but which these siblings may feel compelled to defend or explain. Withdrawal and self-imposed isolation, which can be interpreted by parents as a lack of concern, are common reactions. Moreover, the increased demands associated with coping with a child with TBI may prevent siblings and/or parents from participating in typical activities, therefore decreasing social contacts and support.

School psychologists can assist families with their adjustment in several ways. Listening carefully and providing an empathic ear can provide an important service to family members. Oftentimes parents encounter professionals who are so intent on conveying information and directions that they do not take the time to listen to the concerns of the parents. A sensitivity to the stage of the adjustment process of the parents can lead the school psychologist to tailor the presentation according to the needs of the parent at the time. For example, parents who are still in a state of shock may need information to be presented in small amounts and on more than one occasion. On the other hand, parents who are feeling great sorrow at their child's condition may need assistance dealing with feelings of guilt.

The provision of information is an important role for the school psychologist. Parents may need information about potential cognitive and behavioral consequences of TBI and how these might affect school performance. Parents also will likely need information about the school reintegration process and special services. Because the personal and financial demands of caring for a child who has sustained a severe head injury can be so draining, school psychologists can effectively serve by providing parents with information regarding respite care services. Referrals to rehabilitation facilities that operate with sliding payment schedules may help ease the family's financial burden. Hall (1989) offered suggestions that are helpful in working with parents of children who have incurred a TBI. These include giving important news to both parents simultaneously; providing a quiet, distraction-free environment for discussion; allowing ample time for questions; and encouraging parents to bring another adult for support and to reinforce the information provided by the professional.

Their location in the schools and subsequent availability to children provides school psychologists with a unique opportunity to help siblings adjust to their new family circumstances. Serving as a source of information about TBI and its effects can be helpful to many siblings. Others may experience greater adjustment difficulties and require therapeutic intervention. Group counseling may be a particularly effective method of providing support, but the low incidence of TBI may make the establishment of a group difficult.

TBI to a child can also prove disruptive to a classroom environment. Peers are frequently uninformed about the TBI of a classmate. School psychologists can provide an important service by informing children (in accordance with family wishes) of the nature and extent of the injury to their classmate. Communication with classmates should begin early in the recovery process to help dispel rumor and to lay the groundwork for reentry. Children may not understand the extent of injury nor be prepared for the changes that may be apparent in their classmate. As a result, peers may be likely to withdraw and unintentionally isolate the returning child. In addition to providing information and answering questions about the child's injury and its effects, school psychologists can help the reentry process by recruiting peers and school personnel to form a team for the purpose of ensuring social reintegration. Cooley, Glang, and Voss (1997) describe several formal and informal methods to facilitate this process.

SUMMARY

The two key concepts central to effective service to children who have sustained traumatic brain injury are variability and flexibility. Children sustain TBI in any number of ways. Moreover, the effects on the child's physical, cognitive, and behavioral functioning are completely idiosyncratic, and the child's level of functioning can change from one day to the next. Finally, the school and home environments to which children must return following a head injury vary widely. Although some generalizations can be made and guidelines offered, flexibility must be a key principle guiding intervention efforts, and effective service can be provided only by tailoring the efforts of the professional to the needs of the individual student. Despite the fact that the need for flexibility is important when working with all children, it is especially important when working with children with TBI because of the variability of needs among the population and the rapidity with which functioning levels can change.

Another concept important in working with children with TBI is coordination. Because TBI can affect all aspects of children's functioning and development, effective services can only result from the coordinated efforts of representatives of different disciplines. In addition to acknowledging the contributions of a variety of professionals, increasing attention has been paid to the role family members play in the recovery process. Coordinating services and roles can require much effort, but the unique needs of these children can only be met if educators, allied professionals, and family members function cooperatively to carry out the educational program.

School psychologists can play key roles in providing appropriate educational services to these children. One important function that the school psychologist can perform is to ensure that broad-based, comprehensive, and timely assessment provides a valid picture of the child's assets and deficits that can be incorporated into appropriate psychoeducational interventions. School psychologists can also serve the population with TBI by providing in-service presentations about the nature of the disability and the needs of the children to teachers and other educators. Providing ongoing consultation to teachers to help them effectively meet the educational and behavioral needs of these children is another important service that the school psychologist can render. Direct intervention in the form of counseling to help the child with TBI to come to terms with the disability may also be necessary. Finally, school psychologists need to be sensitive to the effects that TBI can have on the family and social environment and provide support for parents, siblings, and peers.

REFERENCES

Begali, V. (1992). *Head injury and adolescents: A resource and review for school and allied professions* (2nd ed.). Brandon, VT: Clinical Psychology Publishing.

Begali, V. (1994). The role of the school psychologist. In R. C. Savage & G. F. Wolcott (Eds.), *Educational dimensions of acquired brain injury*. (pp. 453–474). Austin, TX: PRO-ED.

Berg, R. A. (1986). Neuropsychological effects of closed-head injury in children. In J. E. Obrzut & G. W. Hynd (Eds.), *Child neuropsychology: Clinical practice*. Orlando, FL: Academic.

Blosser, J. L., & DePompei, R. (1994a). Creating an effective classroom environment. In R.C. Savage & G.F. Wolcott (Eds.),*Educational dimensions of acquired brain injury*. (pp. 413–452). Austin, TX: PRO-ED.

Blosser, J. L., & DePompei, R. (1994b). *Pediatric traumatic brain injury: Proactive intervention*. San Diego: Singular Publishing.

Brain Injury Association. (No Date). Kids Corner [Online]. Available: http://www.biausa.org/children.htm [2000, April 20].

Cohen, S. B. (1996). Practical guidelines for teachers. In A. L. Goldberg (Ed.), *Acquired brain injury in childhood and adolescence: A team and family guide to educational program development and implementation* (126–170). Springfield, IL: Charles C. Thomas.

Cooley, E. A., Glang, A., & Voss, J. (1997). Making connections: helping children with ABI build friendships. In A. Glang, G. H. S. Singer, & Todis, B. (Eds.), *Students with acquired brain injury: The school's response* (pp.203–228). Baltimore: Brookes.

Deaton, A. V. (1994). Changing the behaviors of students with acquired brain injuries. In R. C. Savage & G. F. Wolcott (Eds.). *Educational dimensions of acquired brain injury*. (pp. 257–276). Austin, TX: PRO-ED.

Deaton, A. V. (1997). Understanding and overcoming the challenging behaviors of students with ABI. In A. Glang, G. H. S. Singer, & Todis, B. (Eds.), *Students with acquired brain injury: The school's response* (pp.203–228). Baltimore: Brookes.

DeBoskey, D. S. (1996). *An educational challenge: Meeting the needs of students with brain injury*. Houston: HDI Publishers.

DePompei, R. & Blosser, J. L. (1994). The family as collaborator for effective school reintegration. In R. C. Savage & G. F. Wolcott (Eds.), *Educational dimensions of acquired brain injury*. (pp. 257–276). Austin, TX: PRO-ED.

Ewing-Cobbs, L., & Fletcher, J. M. (1990). Neuropsychological assessment of traumatic brain injury in children. In E. D. Bigler (Ed.), *Traumatic brain injury*. Austin, TX: PRO-ED.

Ewing-Cobbs, L., Levin, H. S., Fletcher, J. M., Miner, M. E., & Eisenberg, H. M. (1990). The Children's Orientation and Amnesia Test: Relationship to severity of head injury and to recovery of memory. *Neurosurgery, 27,* 684.

Feeney, T. J. & Ylvisaker, M. (1997). A positive, communication-based approach to challenging behavior after ABI. In A. Glang, G. H. S. Singer, & Todis, B. (Eds.), *Students with acquired brain injury: The school's response* (pp.229–254). Baltimore: Brookes.

Frey, W. F. (1994). Psychotherapeutic interventions for mild traumatic brain injury. In R. C. Savage & G. F. Wolcott (Eds.). *Educational dimensions of acquired brain injury*. (pp. 453–474). Austin, TX: PRO-ED.

Gerring, J. P., & Carney, J. M. (1992). *Head trauma: Strategies for educational reintegration*. San Diego: Singular Publishing.

Hall, D. (1989). Understanding parents. In D. Johnson, D. Utley, & M. Wyke (Eds.), *Children's head injury: Who cares?* Hillsdale, NJ: Erlbaum.

Hynd, G. W. (1988). *Neuropsychological assessment in clinical child psychology*. Newbury Park, CA: Sage.

Kalsbeek, W., McLaurin, R., Harris, B. S., & Miller, J. D. (1980). The national head and spinal cord injury survey: Major findings. *Journal of Neurosurgery, 53*, 19–31.

Kaplan, E., Fein, D., Kramer, J., Delis, D., & Morris, R., (1999). *WISC-III PI Manual*. San Antonio, TX: The Psychological Corporation.

Kolb, B. & Whishaw, I. Q. (1996). *Fundamentals of neuropsychology* (4th ed.). New York: W.H. Freeman.

Kraemer, B. R., & Blacher, J. (1997). An overview of educationally relevant effects, assessment, and school reentry. In A. Glang, G. H. S. Singer, & Todis, B. (Eds.), *Students with acquired brain injury: The school's response* (pp.3–32). Baltimore: Brookes.

Kranzler, J. H., & Shaw, S. S. (1992). *The application of the techniques of mental chronometry to the study of learning disabilities*. Paper presented at the convention of the National Association of School Psychologists, Nashville, TN.

Lezak, M. D., (1988). Brain damage is a family affair. *Journal of Clinical and Experimental Neuropsychology, 10*, 11–123.

Madigan, K. A., Hall, T. E., & Glang, A. (1997). Effective assessment and instructional practices for students with ABI. In A. Glang, G. H. S. Singer, & Todis, B. (Eds.), *Students with acquired brain injury: The school's response* (pp. 123–184). Baltimore: Brookes.

National Institutes of Health (1998, Oct. 26–28). Rehabilitation of Persons With Traumatic Brain Injury. *NIH Consensus Statement, 16*, 1–41.

Obrzut, J. E., & Hynd. G. W. (1990). Cognitive dysfunction and psychoeducational assessment in traumatic brain injury. In E. D. Bigler (Ed.), *Traumatic Brain Injury*. Austin, TX: PRO-ED.

Rosen, C. D., & Gerring, J. P. (1986). *Head trauma: Educational reintegration*. San Diego: College Hill Press.

Roth, G., Harley, R., Havey, M., Probst, J., & Vaal, J. (1993). *Reference manual for determining eligibility and best practices in assessment of traumatic brain injury (TBI)*. Addison, IL: Illinois School Psychologists Association.

Savage, R. C. (1991). Identification, classification, and placement issues for students with traumatic brain injury. *Journal of Head Trauma Rehabilitation, 6*, 1–9.

Savage, R. C., & Carter, R. R. (1988). Transitioning pediatric patients into educational systems: Guidelines for rehabilitation professionals. *Cognitive Rehabilitation, 6*, 10–14.

Savage, R. C., & Wolcott, G. F. (Eds.) (1988). *An educator's manual: What educators need to know about students with traumatic brain injury*. Southborough, MA: National Head Injury Foundation.

Shaw, S. S., & Yingst, C. A. (1992). Assessing children with traumatic brain injuries: Integrating educational and medical issues. *Diagnostique, 17*, 255–265.

Telzrow, C. F. (1987). Management of academic and educational problems in head injury. *Journal of Learning Disabilities, 20*, 536–545.

Telzrow, C. F. (1991). The school psychologist's perspective on testing students with traumatic brain injury. *Journal of Head Trauma Rehabilitation, 6*, 23–34.

Tyler, J. S. (1992). *Traumatic brain injury preservice training module.* (Available from University of Arkansas Medical Center, Department of Special Education, 3901Rainbow Boulevard, Kansas City, KS 66160-7335).

Tyler, J. S. (1997). Preparing educators to serve children with ABI. In A. Glang, G. H. S. Singer, & Todis, B. (Eds.), *Students with acquired brain injury: The school's response* (pp. 323–342). Baltimore: Brookes.

Ylvisaker, M., Hartwick, P., & Stevens, M. (1991). School reentry following head injury: Managing the transition from hospital to school. *Journal of Head Trauma Rehabilitation, 6*, 10–22.

ANNOTATED BIBLIOGRAPHY

Begali, V. (1992). *Head injury and adolescents: A resource and review for school and allied professions* (2nd ed.). Brandon, VT: Clinical Psychology Publishing.
A useful and informative overview of brain injury and its effects on children. Provides chapters concerning basic brain functions, mechanisms of brain injury, sequelae of brain injury, assessment of children with TBI, and treatment rationale and strategies for educational settings.

Bigler, E. D. (Ed.). (1990). *Traumatic brain injury: Mechanisms of damage, assessment, intervention, and outcome*. Austin, TX: PRO-ED.
The subtitle explicitly states the sections of this edited volume. Although many of the topics of discussion are similar to the Begali book described above, the presentation is more detailed and technical. Early chapters provide excellent photographs of CT scans and actual brains that depict effects of brain injury.

Glang, A., Singer, G. H. S., & Todis, B. (Eds.) (1997). *Students with acquired brain injury: The school's response.* Baltimore: Brooks.
The focus of this edited volume is intervention with children with TBI after they have left rehabilitation facilities and moved back to school. The book addresses educational issues that occur in typical school settings and describes, in some detail, effective school-based educational and behavioral interventions.

Savage, R. C., & Wolcott, G. F. (Eds.) (1994). *Educational dimensions of acquired brain injury.* Austin, TX: PRO-ED.
This edited volume was written specifically for school personnel and contains chapters addressing several aspects of intervention. In addition to chapters of interest to school psychologists, the book contains chapters especially targeted toward teachers, administrators, speech language pathologists, and parents.

90 Best Practices in Considering Gender Differences in Providing Psychological Services to Children and Adolescents in Schools

Linda M. Raffaele Mendez
Deanne Gale
University of South Florida

OVERVIEW

It is well known that there are some important behavioral differences between boys and girls (see Maccoby & Jacklin, 1974; Berk, 2000). Research has shown that, on average, boys tend to be more physically aggressive, more competitive, have higher activity levels, and be greater risk-takers than girls, while girls tend to be more empathic, more compliant, more anxious about failure, and more likely to seek help than boys (Berk, 2000). With regard to learning and achievement, girls tend to develop language skills more quickly and show advantages over boys in reading achievement throughout the school years. Boys tend to have better developed spatial skills by middle childhood and begin to outperform girls in mathematical reasoning beginning in adolescence (Berk, 2000).

Whether such differences are biologically based or result from differential treatment is still a matter of debate, although most child development experts would agree that both nature and nurture play a role in producing differences in behavior between the two genders. Regardless of the origin of these differences, it is important that school psychologists understand the unique development and needs of each gender. This chapter will provide school psychologists with an overview of the most important differences between males and females for the practice of school psychology as well as some guidelines to follow in best addressing such differences in providing psychological services to children in schools.

BASIC CONSIDERATIONS

Most school psychology training programs are becoming increasingly aware of the need to infuse diversity into the curriculum. Diversity training often is focused mainly on race and culture, although issues of language, religion, disability, sexual orientation, learning style, and gender are an important part of diversity as well. It is likely that most school psychologists, though aware of differences between males and females, are not well versed in the implications of these differences for practice.

Although certain differences in behavior between boys and girls are to be expected based on differences in biology and deeply entrenched differences in treatment, educational opportunities for the two genders should be similar. Title IX, a federal law passed in 1972, mandates that no person be discriminated against on the basis of sex in any educational program receiving federal funds. Despite the fact that this law was passed almost 30 years ago, there is considerable evidence that gender equity continues to be more of an ideal than a reality (see Bailey, 1993). For the most part, those working in this area have focused attention on the ways in which girls are underserved in schools (e.g., American Association of University Women Educational Foundation, 1992). Frequently noted concerns include girls receiving less teacher attention than boys (Sadker & Sadker, 1994), biased curricular materials presenting women in subordinate roles to men and/or failing to recognize the significant accomplishments of women (e.g., Scott &

Schau, 1985), attitudes toward sexual harassment that accept such behavior as being a normal part of the adolescent school experience (American Association of University Women Educational Foundation, 1993), and stereotypes indicating that girls are less able than boys in mathematics and the sciences (U.S. Department of Education, 1997).

More recent literature has begun to note concerns about boys' educational experiences as well (e.g., American Association of University Women Educational Foundation, 1998; Gurian, 1998; Pollock, 1998). For example, Pollock (1998) noted that boys are more likely than girls to be criticized by teachers for expressing feelings of fear (e.g., on the first day of school) or affection (e.g., hugging another child). Male peers also are likely to chastise boys for any behavior that is perceived as feminine or as being "like a girl" (e.g., boys whose athletic skills are not well-developed might be criticized as "throwing like a girl"). These observations exemplify the fact that although there has been increasing freedom for girls to adopt traditionally male characteristics and interests (e.g., playing physical contact team sports), boys still are restricted by what Pollock calls "the boy code," which stipulates that boys must act tough, independent, and confident even in situations where they feel frightened or unsure. Additionally, Bailey (1993) noted that boys' school experiences do not prepare them well to make contributions (or to think they should make contributions) to the traditionally female tasks of homemaking, childrearing, or community building. And yet, with more than 70% of women currently employed outside of the home, it is clear that men are needed to participate in these activities. It is notable, too, that the fact that so many more boys than girls (particularly African-American boys) experience disciplinary action at school each year may suggest that the types of educational environments currently existing in our schools are not meeting boys' unique educational needs.

With regard to the practice of school psychology, it is important for school psychologists to examine the ways in which they work with students, parents, teachers, and administrators to ensure that they are addressing the unique needs of each gender. Much of what school psychologists can do to enhance gender equity in schools is related to training and education of staff, although an examination of assessment and intervention strategies is important as well. There are three major areas in which school psychologists should be aware of differences between boys and girls in schools: (a) differences in the types of problems experienced and rates of diagnosis, (b) differences in the likelihood of receiving assistance when problems are identified (e.g., in special education programs), and (c) differences in congruency between teaching materials/ methods and how students of each gender learn best.

With regard to the types of problems boys and girls experience, a review of DSM-IV (American Psychiatric Association, 1994) shows that there are clear differences in rates of diagnosis of psychopathology between the genders. For example, boys with attention-deficit/hyperactivity disorder (ADHD) outnumber girls with ADHD by a ratio of 4:1 to 9:1 depending on whether the data are collected from the general population or from a clinic setting (American Psychiatric Association, 1994). Boys also are much more likely than girls to be suspended or expelled from school. A recent study by Raffaele (2000) found that more than 70% of all out-of-school suspensions in one large Florida district were of males. Studies in other communities (e.g., Nichols, Ludwin, & Iadicola, 1999) have reported similar findings. In general, boys tend to be over-represented in externalizing disorders and disciplinary actions. They are far more likely than girls to engage in antisocial behavior or violent crime and/or to be diagnosed with Conduct Disorder (American Psychiatric Association, 1994; Berk, 2000). Boys who are diagnosed with Conduct Disorder also display a different clinical picture than girls with this disorder, with boys engaging in more violent behaviors (e.g., fighting, stealing, vandalism, school disciplinary problems) and girls displaying more defiant behaviors (e.g., lying, truancy, running away, substance abuse, prostitution) (American Psychiatric Association, 1994). Additionally, data from the 1995 U.S. census showed that boys were twice as likely as girls to be identified by their parents as having a learning disability, speech impediment, or emotional disturbance (U.S. Department of Education, 2000b). Boys also are more likely than girls to repeat a grade. In 1995, 7.7% of boys versus 5.3% of girls repeated a grade (U.S. Department of Education, 2000b).

In contrast to boys, girls are more likely to be diagnosed with internalizing disorders, particularly as they move into adolescence. In fact, in childhood, boys and girls are equally likely to experience depression (Nolen-Hoeksema & Girgus, 1994); however, in adolescence, girls are more than twice as likely as boys to meet the criteria for a major depressive disorder or dysthymic disorder (Kashani et al., 1987). One longitudinal study of students assessed in grades 6–8 and again in grade 12 found that girls showed significantly more depressed affect and poorer emotional tone than boys in grade 12, although differences began to emerge as early as grade 8 (Petersen, Sargiani, & Kennedy, 1991). Such a finding is consistent with research suggesting that girls experience a decline in self-esteem in the early adolescent years. For example, Gilligan and her colleagues (e.g., Brown & Gilligan, 1992), through their ethnographic research, noted a tendency for girls transitioning into adolescence to become unsure of themselves, to disconnect from their true feelings, and to fear speaking their minds. They referred to such changes as "losing one's voice." Adolescent girls, in comparison with their male peers, also are much more likely to experience disordered eating (including anorexia, bulimia, and subclinical eating problems) and disturbances of body image (Berk, 2000). Additionally, they are much more likely than adolescent boys to make a suicide attempt (although males greatly outnumber females in completed suicides, primarily because they use more lethal methods) (Lonnqvist et al., 1995). Importantly, the types of problems that girls experience, while clearly detrimental to their development, often do not come to the attention of teachers or other school personnel because they tend not to disrupt classroom activities.

In addition to differences in the types of problems experienced, there also are differences in the frequency with which boys and girls receive intervention to help them deal with these problems. As previously noted, since boys are over-represented in externalizing disorders and girls are over-represented in internalizing disorders, boys' problems are more likely to cause classroom disruptions and thus be brought to the attention of the school psychologist. It has been well documented that there are more boys than girls in special education programs. Recent figures indicate that boys make up about two-thirds of special education students (Jans & Stoddard, 1999). One national report noted that males composed 73.4% of students receiving services for a learning disability and 76.4% of students receiving services for an emotional disturbance (Jans & Stoddard, 1999). Interestingly, a 1998 report by the U.S. Department of Education found that girls in special education programs were identified as having disabilities earlier and scored lower on tests of intelligence than their male counterparts, indicating that girls in special education were likely to have more severe disabilities than boys in those programs (Jans & Stoddard, 1999). Parent reports from the 1995 U.S. census also indicated that 50.4% of boys identified as having a disability were receiving special services at school compared to 39.4% of girls (U.S. Department of Education, 2000b).

Finally, in addition to having an awareness of gender differences in the types of problems experienced and the likelihood of receiving assistance for these problems, it is important for school psychologists to be knowledgeable about differences in boys' and girls' experiences in the classroom setting. Several publications from the early 1990s (e.g., American Association of University Women Educational Foundation, 1992; Sadker and Sadker, 1994) did much to raise awareness of gender inequity in schools. For example, the American Association of University Women Educational Foundation (1992) summarized research indicating that teachers give more classroom attention and more esteem-building encouragement to boys than to girls. Similarly, Sadker and Sadker (1994) noted that boys stand out (receiving both more positive and negative attention than girls), while "girls blend in, do their work, wait their turn, and become the supporting cast" (p. 199). Importantly, when Sadker and Sadker (1994) videotaped teachers in their classrooms and played back the tapes for them, they reported that teachers were "stunned to see themselves teaching subtle gender lessons" (p. 46), indicating that many of the teacher behaviors observed by Sadker and Sadker were not intentional. It is likely that the discrepancy in the way teachers treat boys and girls is related to gender differences in activity level and interactional style, with boys demanding more attention through their behavior than girls. Nonetheless, it is likely that differences between boys and girls in teacher attention could be reduced if teachers were more aware of these issues. Unfortunately, a recent national survey found that pre-service teachers receive little or no training in gender equity (Campbell & Sanders, 1997).

In addition to patterns of interaction between teachers and students, concerns also have been raised about the degree to which current teaching materials and methods are meeting the needs of both boys and girls. It has been widely recognized that girls, women, and people of color are underrepresented in roles of importance in textbooks and other educational materials. Bailey (1993) noted that the majority of lead characters in books read to their classes by elementary teachers are male. She also noted that the books used most frequently in high school English classes are written by men. Others (e.g., American Association of University Women Educational Foundation, 1992) have noted that teaching methods fostering competition continue to be used in many classrooms despite research showing that girls—and many boys as well—learn better through cooperative projects and activities. Of particular concern are teaching methods in science, mathematics, and technology, academic areas in which, by grade 12, girls often have less confidence and enjoy less than do boys (e.g., American Association of University Women Educational Foundation, 1998; U.S. Department of Education, 2000b).

Concerns exist for boys as well. In particular, despite the high level of attention that boys receive in the classroom, girls earn better grades than boys throughout elementary and secondary school (Berk, 2000; Sadker & Sadker, 1994). Whether such grade differences reflect greater mastery of the curriculum across subjects or better behavior in the classroom is unclear. What is clear is that girls show advantages in reading and writing performance compared to their male peers. Results of the 1996 National Assessment of Educational Progress (NAEP) (U.S. Department of Education, 2000a) showed that girls outperformed boys in reading and writing at the elementary (grade 4), middle (grade 8), and high school (grade 12) levels. On the other hand, boys outperformed girls in mathematics in grades 4 and 8, although—in contrast to scores from previous years—the performance of boys and girls was similar in grade 12. Boys and girls also were equally likely to score at the highest levels (at or above 300) on the NAEP in mathematics, although boys were more likely than girls to score at this level in science. Research has shown as well that boys are more likely than girls to take the three core science courses in high school (biology, chemistry, and physics) and to aspire to careers in the sciences or engineering (U.S. Department of Education, 1997).

Additionally, with regard to differences in boys' and girls' experiences in the classroom, it is important to consider the research on sexual harassment in schools. One survey (American Association of University Women Educational Foundation, 1993) found that 85% of girls and 76% of boys in grades 8–11 indicated that they had experienced "unwanted and unwelcome sexual behavior that interferes with their lives" (p.7) while at school. This behavior included sexual jokes, comments, gestures, or looks; touching, grabbing, or pinching in a sexual way; being forced to do something sexual at school other than kissing; and having their clothes pulled off or down. Another survey found that 39% of girls reported being harassed at school on a daily basis (Wellesley College Center for Research on Women, 1993). Outcomes of harassment reported most frequently by students included not wanting to go to school; not wanting to talk as much in class; finding it hard to pay attention in school; feeling embarrassed, self-conscious, or less confident; avoiding particular people or places at school; avoiding particular activities or sports; and changing one's group of friends (American Association of University Women Educational Foundation, 1993). Gay and lesbian youth report even higher rates of harassment and are much more likely than heterosexual youth to make a suicide attempt (see Henning-Stout, James, & Macintosh, 2000).

BEST PRACTICES

In order to assist in minimizing gender bias in schools, it is important first for school psychologists to be aware of the unique problems confronting boys and girls in the education system. Taking action to alleviate these problems involves (a) assuming a consultative role in helping to raise awareness of these issues among others in the school system (including administrators, educators, students, parents, and the larger community) and (b) making changes in one's own practice to assure that decisions that are made reflect an understanding and appreciation of the unique needs of each gender. In this section, we discuss best practices in considering gender in three critical areas of the practice of school psychology—prevention, assessment, and intervention.

Prevention

School psychologists can do much to prevent common problems for both girls and boys by helping school personnel to design learning environments that are sensitive to the needs of each gender. This work, the majority of which will be done at the systems level through consultation, in-service training, and participation on school planning teams, includes addressing issues in (a) the curriculum, (b) behavior management, (c) school climate, and (d) classroom dynamics and instructional styles.

The Curriculum

To begin with the curriculum, it is important that educational materials used in schools (e.g., textbooks, posters, media, Internet resources) represent the diversity of the human experience. In terms of gender, this includes depicting both men and women of various ethnic and racial backgrounds in positions of leadership and achievement. Students should have the opportunity in schools to learn about the important contributions that both women and men have made to society and to see depicted in their educational materials role models who help them to envision possibilities for themselves that defy gender role stereotypes (see Denmark, 1999). This might include, for example, watching a video of a science experiment conducted by a woman or reading a book about a man who gave up his job to care for his infant. It also includes balancing the number of books or other educational materials created by men and women as well as the gender of the strong central figure in these materials. School psychologists can affect the decisions teachers and administrators make about educational materials through in-service presentations that bring the importance of these issues to their attention. Resources that might be incorporated in preparing such an in-service include Roberts (1993), Horgan (1995), and the American Association of University Women Educational Foundation (1998). Other materials are readily accessed on the Internet by searching under the term "gender equity."

At the middle and high school levels, it is particularly important for schools to find proactive ways to address the problems of teenage pregnancy, sexual harassment, and sexual violence (see American Association of University Women Educational Foundation, 1998). These are concerns that many school administrators (and parents and teachers as well) do not believe should be discussed in schools. Nonetheless, research demonstrating the disproportionate negative impact of these issues on young women's schooling experiences is cause for concern. For example, although the average high school completion rate for girls in 1998 was 94%, girls who gave birth prior to their senior year of high school had a graduation rate of only 54% (U.S. Department of Education, 2000b). Unfortunately, research has shown that girls who drop out of school are less likely than boys to return to finish their education or to earn a GED (American Association of University Women Educational Foundation, 1998).

Behavior Management

It has been noted that boys are greatly over-represented in school disciplinary actions. Thus, in order to meet boys' unique needs, it is very important, from a preventive standpoint, to put in place behavioral strategies that attempt to curtail disruptive classroom behavior. Most school suspensions—which have a disproportionate impact on boys—are for classroom disruptions and disobedience (Raffaele, 2000; Rosen, 1997). Research summarized by Kay (1999) has shown that such behaviors can be reduced through preventive programs that involve positive behavior management, social skills instruction, a unified discipline approach (involving partnerships between schools, families, and communities), and shared expectations for socially competent behavior. As an example, Project ACHIEVE (Knoff & Batsche, 1995), a comprehensive school reform process involving building-wide in-service training in and implementation of problem-solving assessment and intervention skills (including classroom-based social skills training), was shown to significantly decrease discipline referrals to the office (both from the bus and the classroom) and student suspensions over a 3-year period. School psychologists can take a leadership role in helping administrators to select programs that meet the needs of their particular schools and to design evaluation strategies to determine the degree to which such programs are successful. Examples of other promising programs can be found in Kay (1999).

School Climate

With regard to school climate, there are a number of gender-related issues to be considered. The most important of these are specific programs and policies that (a) reflect a valuing of individual differences and encourage each student to develop his or her strengths independent of traditional gender role stereotypes, (b) foster a sense of belonging among both boys and girls, and (c) provide protection for students against gender-related forms of discrimination, harassment, and violence.

There are many ways for school administrators to reflect to students, staff, and the larger community that students at their school will not be limited by traditional gender role stereotypes. Decisions about the curriculum have been discussed above. Other strategies involve developing nontraditional career-mentoring programs, providing similar levels of financial support for girls' and boys' athletic teams, and establishing awards programs that recognize (a) teachers for excellence in promoting gender equity and (b) students for significant accomplishments in areas traditionally considered to be more appropriate for the opposite gender (e.g., girls in science or math, boys in writing or the arts).

School psychologists can help administrators to become aware of areas of inequity through conducting an analysis of issues on gender (see Sheridan & Henning-Stout, 1994). For example, interviews, observations, and record reviews can be employed to examine issues such as the percentage of boys and girls in special education programs (including gifted programs), communication patterns among staff, and bias in curricular materials. The findings of the analysis then can be shared with the school staff. Sheridan and Henning-Stout (1994) noted that awareness of inequity often is enough to incite a change in practice. However, when it is not, school psychologists should be prepared to address the staff's resistance to change and be aware that depending on the degree to which the stereotypes are imbedded, school-wide change in attitudes and practices may be slow.

As for fostering a sense of belonging among both boys and girls, it is important to consider the consistency between gender-specific developmental needs and the day-to-day operation and management of the school. Henry (1996) has criticized U.S. schools for operating according to rigid bureaucratic structures that give little importance to the development of positive, caring, collaborative relationships among people. Although this clearly is not the case in every school, it is true that many schools—particularly at the middle and high school level—are large and impersonal. Given the findings of Brown and Gilligan's (1992) research on the importance of relationship in girls' development, it must be questioned whether such a learning atmosphere is consistent with the needs of girls (and boys for that matter, as well). Approaches to school reform that emphasize an ethic of care (see Noddings, 1992) seem to have the potential to meet the needs of both girls and boys for acceptance and belonging. School psychologists should become familiar with this approach to school reform (see Baker, Terry, Bridger, & Winsor, 1997, for a recent review) so that they can assist administrators and teachers in applying these principles to enhance the climate of schools.

Finally, to provide protection for students against gender-related forms of discrimination, harassment, and violence, it is important for school psychologists to be aware of the frequency of these types of behaviors in their schools and to help school staff develop appropriate strategies for dealing with them. All schools receiving federal funds are required to have a written policy prohibiting sexual discrimination. School psychologists should be familiar with the particular policies at their schools. Although not required by Title IX, it also is recommended that schools have a policy prohibiting sexual harassment. School psychologists whose schools do not have such a policy may help to develop it. It is particularly important that this policy include student-to-student sexual harassment given the findings of the 1993 American Association of University Women Educational Foundation study. Guidelines for developing a student-to-student sexual harassment policy can be found in Webb, Hunicutt, and Metha (1997).

Classroom Dynamics/Instructional Style

Finally, school psychologists, in their role as consultants, can help to educate teachers about gender equity in classroom dynamics and instructional style. For example, Sheridan and Henning-Stout (1994) suggested that school psychologists can (a) educate teachers about the truths and myths of gender differences (e.g., boys are *not* inherently better at math and science than girls), (b) train teachers directly in gender-fair teacher-student interactional practices (e.g., through modeling and/or role-playing gender-fair expectancies, practices, and attitudes), and (c) observe and provide feedback on the degree to which teachers are engaged in gender-fair teaching methods and strategies.

According to Sheridan and Henning-Stout (1994), when modeling is ineffective with a teacher, it may be necessary for the school psychologist to address the teacher's attitudes and beliefs. This can be done through direct or indirect confrontation and/or reframing. As an example of confrontation, the school psychologist might share with the teacher data he or she has collected through an observation (e.g., the teacher responded to 80% of the boys with raised hands and only 20% of the girls with raised hands). These authors caution that this approach should be attempted only after the school psychologist has already established a trusting relationship with the teacher. A more subtle approach is reframing. Using this strategy, if, for example, a young girl is struggling with math and the teacher attributes this to girls' inherent inability in math, the school psychologist could reframe the young girl's difficulty as due instead to possible environmental or curricular factors such as biased texts or different societal expectations.

Assessment

In addition to assisting school personnel to better understand gender differences, it also is important for school psychologists to examine their own practice. With regard to assessment, it is notable that the rates of diagnosis of academic, emotional, and behavioral problems differ by gender (see Basic Considerations). While this may reflect biological differences between the genders (e.g., the two X chromosomes in females appear to protect them against some genetic disorders) or differences in behavioral expectations for boys and girls, the possibility also exists that such differences stem from biases in the referral and/or assessment process (i.e., how problems are conceptualized and/or how they are measured).

It is clear that, in schools, problems that cause disruption in the classroom are those that are most likely to be recognized and further assessed. Thus, the fact that boys demonstrate more externalizing behavior problems while girls demonstrate more internalizing behavior problems means that boys' problems come to the attention of teachers more often than girls'. Boys are thus more frequently referred to the school psychologist for assessment. For example, one problem in boys that tends to be responded to frequently is aggression. Historically, aggression has been conceptualized as including physical or verbal attacks, such as hitting, kicking, cursing, and yelling. Such behaviors are significantly more common in boys than in girls (Berk, 2000). Until recently, it was believed that girls were less likely than boys to engage in aggressive behavior (e.g., Maccoby & Jacklin, 1974). However, in recent years, research conducted by Crick and her colleagues (see Crick & Rose, 2000) has shown that, if aggression is defined as the intent to hurt or harm, boys and girls are equally likely to engage in aggressive acts, albeit of different types. The type of aggression in which girls are more likely to engage is relational aggression, which includes acts designed to damage the victim's personal relationships (e.g., spreading rumors, threatening to dissolve a friendship if the victim does not comply with a request) (Crick & Rose, 2000). Relational aggression has been shown to result in negative consequences for both victims and aggressors, including low peer status, difficulty with peer relations, anxiety, and depressed affect for victims (Crick, 1996), and immediate peer rejection, increasingly less acceptance from peers over time, and future social maladjustment for aggressors (Crick, Casas, & Ku, 1999). Unfortunately, relational aggression is less likely than physical aggression to be recognized in the classroom because it is more covert. As a result, children who engage in relational aggression are less likely to be identified as having a problem, receive further assessment, or—most importantly—be targeted for intervention.

Relational aggression is just one example of gender bias in the types of problems that are conceptualized as requiring further assessment from the school psychologist. Others include learning problems that occur in the absence of behavioral problems, depression, and eating disorders, all of which are more common in girls. School psychologists need to help teachers and administrators become more aware of the types of problems that girls experience, the warning signs associated with these problems, and the necessity of involving members of the student support team in intervening with girls in these situations.

In terms of how problems are assessed and diagnosed, it is important to consider whether the instruments that are administered to understand children's functioning are biased against either gender. At the level of the test, some of the questions to be addressed in determining if a measure is appropriate for both genders are (a) *Were boys and girls equally represented in the normative sample?* (b) *Have girls and boys been shown to obtain similar average scores (where it is expected that they would be similar on the construct being measured)?* and (c) *Has the instrument been shown to be equally reliable and valid for girls and boys?* Most of the major cognitive assessment instruments currently used by school psychologists (e.g., WISC-III, Stanford-Binet: FE, Woodcock-Johnson Tests of Achievement-III) provide evidence in their manuals that similar numbers of boys and girls were included in the normative sample. However, few test manuals provide evidence of similar average scores across gender or report reliability or validity by gender. The technical manual of the Stanford-Binet: FE does show that boys and girls in the normative sample obtained similar average scores on each of the scale's factors. But not all intelligence test manuals report this information. In fact, several investigations have found boys to score significantly higher than girls on the Wechsler scales. For example, Quereshi and Seitz (1994) found that, in their sample of 72 children selected from nine elementary schools, boys scored an average of 8.8 points higher than girls on the Verbal Scale score of the WPPSI-R. Similarly, in examining scores on the WISC-III, Slate (1998) found that among 366 students who had been referred for special education testing but did not meet eligibility requirements, boys scored an average of 4.0 points higher than girls on the Verbal Scale score and 5.7 points higher than girls on the Full Scale score. These differences in average scores are particularly notable when one considers that relatively small differences on measures of intelligence often determine the outcomes of major educational decisions (e.g., special education program eligibility).

In addition to looking at measures of intelligence at the level of the test, one also can examine gender bias in tests at the item level. Differential item functioning (DIF) provides a means for determining whether particular items on a measure are of equal difficulty for boys and girls who are similar on the construct being measured (e.g., intelligence, self-esteem). Very few of the major assessment tools that are currently being used by school psychologists have been examined for gender DIF. The few studies that do exist (e.g., Maller, 1997) indicate that this is an area in which more research is needed. Additionally, more research is needed on the gender-related predictive bias of frequently used measures of intelligence and achievement. One recent study found that Curriculum-Based Measurement (CBM) over-predicted reading comprehension (as measured by the California Achievement Test) for fifth-grade girls and under-predicted reading comprehension for fifth-grade boys (Kranzler, Miller, & Jordan, 1999). Glutting, Hyeon-Joo, Ward, and Ward (2000) also reported evidence of bias against boys in using the Verbal, Performance, and Full Scale IQs from the WISC-III to predict Reading, Mathematics, Language, and Writing Composite scores on the WIAT. Although definitive conclusions cannot be drawn from these few studies, school psychologists should be aware of these issues, stay abreast of research in this area, and be aware of potential gender bias in the measures they use.

Designing norm-referenced measures to assess the severity of behavioral problems equally well in females and males also has proven to be a formidable task. Most behavior rating scales use separate norms for females and males to reflect differences between the genders in the severity of various behaviors. Recent investigations have supported such an approach (e.g., DuPaul et al., 1997; Reid at al., 2000). For example, Reid et al. (2000), using the ADHD-IV Rating Scale, found that although the same two-factor model of ADHD (i.e., Hyperactivity/Impulsivity and Inattention) held across gender, there were significant differences between teachers' ratings of the severity of symptoms among girls versus boys. Boys were rated as having more severe symptoms than girls. This finding was true across both the Caucasian and African-American samples, although gender differences were larger in the Caucasian sample. School psychologists should be aware that behavior rating scales frequently show significant differences between boys and girls in the normative sample and should supply separate norms for each gender when such differences are found.

Behavioral measures also can be examined at the item level, and several investigations of gender DIF in behavioral measures have been conducted. For example, Brown, Greenbaum, and Maller (1998), who examined the Teacher Report Form of the Child Behavior Checklist, found that, when rating boys' behavior, teachers were more likely to endorse statements describing overt externalizing behaviors (e.g., destroying property, clowning around). In contrast, when rating girls' behavior, teachers were more likely to endorse statements describing covert externalizing behaviors (e.g., easily jealous, moody). Such findings are consistent with Crick's work (e.g., Crick & Rose, 2000), which suggests that girls and boys demonstrate aggressive behavior in different ways.

The findings of the Brown, Greenbaum, and Maller study (1998) in combination with Crick's work (e.g., Crick & Rose, 2000) suggest that gender-specific measures of aggression may be more appropriate than those that are currently used. Notably, when measures that conceptualize problems in a way that is more descriptive of one gender than the other (e.g., aggression = physical aggression) are used, problems may fail to be detected when they truly do exist. As an example of this, Henning-Stout's (1998) qualitative review of the Child Behavior Checklist, the Social Skills Rating System, and the Behavior Assessment System for Children found that none of these instruments addressed concerns for girls often noted in the literature, including a tendency to question the validity of one's own perceptions, the impact of interpersonal crises on daily functioning, vulnerable sexual boundaries, pregnancy history, and exploration of sexual identity. Additionally, Henning-Stout noted that particular items on behaviors presumed to be positive (e.g., tries to bring out the best in people) might, in some girls, actually be maladaptive if they are associated with girls' compromising their own thoughts and desires to be pleasing to others (see Brown & Gilligan, 1992). Further work in this area is necessary to understand what is missed—such as problems with vulnerable sexual boundaries or relational aggression—when assessment instruments that do not include the experiences of historically marginalized groups are employed. In the absence of norm-referenced measures to detect these types of problems, school psychologists should be cognizant of gathering such information through interviews and observations of the student.

It is important, as well, for school psychologists regularly to engage in assessment activities that help to detect mental health problems among youth that may not come to the attention of classroom teachers. For example, Stark (1990) described a multiple-gate assessment approach for detecting internalizing disorders among children in the schools. This approach involves screening large numbers of children with a paper and pencil measure and then following up with children who twice score above a cutoff point with a clinical interview, such as the Schedule of Affective Disorders and Schizophrenia for School-Age Children (K-SADS). Upon screening 720 elementary-aged children with a paper and pencil measure of depression, Stark found that 77 scored above the cutoff point twice. Follow-up interviews with the K-SADS found that 33 of these children met DSM-IV diagnostic criteria for a depressive disorder. These children were then targeted for intervention. Such large-scale screenings—which do require prior parent permission—could be introduced to detect other mental health problems that may not be easily recognized in the classroom, including eating disorders and other internalizing problems.

Intervention

The intervention activities in which school psychologists are involved also are informed and enhanced by an understanding and appreciation of gender differences. In particular, gender has implications for (a) individual and group counseling with students, (b) the design and monitoring of academic and behavioral interventions, and (c) recommendations for special education placement and educational programming.

In counseling students, it is important to recognize that there are gender differences in the degree to which boys and girls feel comfortable sitting down with an adult to discuss their thoughts and feelings. Pollock (1998) noted that boys have been socialized to believe they should handle their problems on their own rather than reach out to others for help. Additionally, it is common for boys to "feel it is necessary to cut themselves off from any feelings that society teaches them are unacceptable for men and boys—fear, uncertainty, feelings of loneliness and need" (p. 5). As a result, it is less likely that boys, as compared to girls, will enter the counseling process prepared to share their innermost thoughts and feelings. This may be particularly true when the school psychologist is female and/or of a different racial background. Pollock's (1998) research suggests that, in counseling situations, boys may feel more comfortable focusing on an activity (e.g., counseling games, role plays) and having discussions of thoughts and feelings arise out of the activity rather than simply being asked to share what is on their minds.

In group counseling, it is important to consider whether single gender or mixed gender groups are most appropriate. This will vary depending on the nature and purpose of the group. Elementary aged children are more likely than adolescents to feel comfortable in mixed gender groups. Adolescents may prefer same gender groups, particularly when issues related to relationships or sexuality are a focus of the group. When mixed gender groups are used, school psychologists should be aware of giving equal attention to boys and girls and not allowing children of one gender to dominate the discussion (see Sadker & Sadker, 1994). In mixed gender groups, it also is important not to allow gender-stereotyped statements to go unchecked and to recognize that differences in boys' and girls' communication styles may need to be explored with the group openly to facilitate the most productive interactions.

School psychologists should exercise caution in assuming that interventions that are successful with one gender will be successful with the other gender as well. Research by Kavanagh and Hops (1994) supports the notion that there is a need for further research to investigate how gender affects the likelihood of success of behavioral interventions. These authors found that although parent training was effective for adolescent boys with externalizing disorders, peer training was more effective for girls. They noted that most of the research examining interventions for children with externalizing disorders has been conducted with boys. Importantly, these authors emphasized that the social-interactional context of the student's development must be considered in designing interventions. Thus, for example, because girls are likely to have more difficulty than boys in establishing independence from their parents in adolescence (because parents typically allow boys greater independence earlier in life) and because females are more likely than males to experience separation as a hostile act (Brown & Gilligan, 1992), it may be particularly important for family-based interventions with adolescent girls to include training in conflict resolution. Considerably more research is needed in this area to guide gender-specific intervention strategies.

It also is important to consider the gender of the student in making decisions about educational placement. Because boys with emotional or behavioral disorders greatly outnumber girls in the special education system, a problem that arises in this area is the dilemma of placing a girl with an emotional or behavioral disorder into a special education class that is composed mainly of boys. Within such a classroom, girls have limited opportunities to develop friendships with other girls and may be more likely to be subject to harassment. Similar concerns arise in placing girls in alternative education programs or centers (e.g., as an alternative to expulsion) in that these programs often are dominated by boys. There is a considerable amount of research showing that youth naturally gravitate toward same-gender friendships (see Maccoby, 1988). Placing students in classrooms that do not contain many students of the same gender should be done with considerable caution. This is particularly true when a girl with an internalizing disorder is being considered for placement in a classroom composed mainly of boys with externalizing disorders. If other accommodations are feasible, then these should be attempted first. Interestingly, Minnesota (see Ryan & Lindgren, 1999) has developed an all-girls program for adolescents with emotional or behavioral disorders who spend more than 60% of their day in a special education setting. The program, referred to as UNITE, incorporates a number of gender-specific practices including a relationship-based approach (versus a highly structured token economy), a strengths-based model for developing personal goals and objectives, and a procedure for resolving problems and conflicts with restorative measures to re-establish connections (as opposed to traditional punitive measures). This program provides an excellent example of how research on gender can be used to directly inform program development.

Finally, when making recommendations for programming, it is important to think beyond traditional stereotypes. This is particularly true in the area of vocational programming. Despite many efforts to expand nontraditional vocational programming for girls, most high school girls enrolled in vocational education programs are in one of a few traditional areas of study (e.g., hairdressing) (American Association of University Women Educational Foundation, 1998). Girls need to be educated that male-dominated vocational areas (e.g., construction, mechanics) tend to be higher in pay than female-dominated vocational areas and that women can be successful in these areas as well. This is particularly important when one considers that young women in special education programs, upon graduation, have been found to be less likely than their male special education peers to be employed or to enroll in postsecondary training or education. Those who are employed earn lower wages than their male special education peers (U.S. Department of Education, 1998).

SUMMARY

This chapter has summarized best practices in considering gender in providing psychological services to children and adolescents in schools. As noted, school psychologists' greatest opportunity to assist schools in meeting gender-specific needs is through raising awareness of the most important issues in this area among administrators, teachers, parents, students, and the larger community. These include differences in the ways girls and boys are treated in the classroom, the degree to which the types of problems they encounter are recognized and treated, and the sensitivity of the school environment to their particular needs. School psychologists also must consider their own practices in assessment and intervention. In particular, they need to be reflective about the types of problems that are most likely to be referred to them (and what types of problems are not referred to them), the degree to which the assessment instruments they use are sensitive to problems and issues faced by both genders, and the extent to which their intervention strategies take into account the needs of boys and girls as documented in the research literature. Greater consideration of gender issues in practice can help school psychologists to create and nurture school environments that encourage all students—regardless of gender—to achieve their personal best.

REFERENCES

American Association of University Women Educational Foundation. (1992). *The AAUW report: How schools shortchange girls*. Washington, DC: Author.

American Association of University Women Educational Foundation. (1993). *Hostile hallways: The AAUW survey on sexual harassment in America's schools*. Washington, DC: Author.

American Association of University Women Educational Foundation. (1998). *Gender gaps: Where schools still fail our children*. Washington, DC: Author.

American Psychiatric Association. (1994). *Diagnostic and statistical manual of mental disorders* (4th ed.). Washington, DC: Author.

Bailey, S. M. (1993). The current status of gender equity research in American schools. *Educational Psychologist, 28*(4), 321–339.

Baker, J. A., Terry, T., Bridger, R., & Winsor, A. (1997). Schools as caring communities: A relational approach to school reform. *School Psychology Review, 26*(4), 586–602.

Berk, L. E. (2000). *Child development* (5th ed.). Boston: Allyn & Bacon.

Brown, E. C., Greenbaum, P. E., & Maller, S. J. (1998). *Externalizing behavior in children with serious emotional disturbance: Gender differences in item functioning*. Paper presented at the annual meeting of the Florida Educational Research Association, Orlando, FL.

Brown, L. M., & Gilligan, C. (1992). *Meeting at the crossroads: Women's psychology and girls' development*. New York: Ballantine.

Campbell, P., & Sanders, J. (1997). Uninformed but interested: Findings of a national survey on gender equity in preservice teacher education. *Journal of Teacher Education, 48*(1), 69–75.

Crick, N. R. (1996). The role of overt aggression, relational aggression, and prosocial behavior in the prediction of children's future social adjustment. *Child Development, 67*(5), 2317–2327.

Crick, N. R., Casas, J. F., & Ku, H. (1999). Relational and physical forms of peer victimization in preschool. *Developmental Psychology, 35*(2), 376–385.

Crick, N. R., & Rose, A. J. (2000). Toward a gender-balanced approach to the study of social-emotional development. In P. H. Miller & E. K. Scholnick (Eds.), *Toward a feminist developmental psychology*. New York: Routledge.

Denmark, F. L. (1999). Enhancing the development of adolescent girls. In N. G. Johnston, M. C. Roberts, & J. Worell (Eds.), *Beyond appearance: A new look at adolescent girls* (pp. 377–404). Washington, DC: American Psychological Association.

DuPaul, G. J., Power, T. J., Anastopoulos, A., Reid, R., McGoey, K. E., & Ikeda, M. J. (1997). Teacher ratings of attention-deficit/hyperactivity disorder symptoms: Factor structure, normative data, and psychometric properties. *Psychological Assessment, 9,* 436–444.

Glutting, J. J., Hyeon-Joo, O., Ward, T., & Ward, S. (2000). Possible criterion-related bias of the WISC-III with a referral sample. *Journal of Psychoeducational Assessment, 18*(1), 17–26.

Gurian, M. (1998). *A fine young man: What parents, mentors, and educators can do to shape adolescent boys into exceptional men.* New York: Tarcher/Putnam.

Henning-Stout, M. (1998). Assessing the behavior of girls: What we see and what we miss. *Journal of School Psychology, 36*(4), 433–455.

Henning-Stout, M., James, S., & Macintosh, S. (2000). Reducing harassment of lesbian, gay, bisexual, transgender, and questioning youths in schools. *School Psychology Review, 29*(2), 180–191.

Henry, M. (1996). *Parent-school collaboration: Feminist organizational structures and school leadership.* Albany, NY: State University of New York Press.

Horgan, D. D. (1995). *Achieving gender equity: Strategies for the classroom.* Boston: Allyn & Bacon.

Jans, L., & Stoddard, S. (1999). *Chartbook on women and disabilities in the United States.* Washington, DC: U.S. National Institute on Disability and Rehabilitation Research.

Kashani, J. H., Beck, N. C., Hoeper, E. W., Fallahi, C., Corcoran, C. M., McAllister, J. A., Rosenberg, T. K., & Reid, J. C. (1987). Psychiatric disorders in a community sample of adolescents. *American Journal of Psychiatry, 144,* 584–589.

Kavanagh, K., & Hops, H. (1994). Good girls? Bad boys? Gender and development as contexts for diagnosis and treatment. In T. H. Ollendick & R. J. Prinz (Eds.), *Advances in clinical child psychology: Vol. 16.* New York: Plenum.

Kay, P. J. (1999). *Prevention strategies that work: What administrators can do to promote positive student behavior.* Burlington, VT: The School Research Office, Department of Education.

Knoff, H. M., & Batsche, G. M. (1995). Project ACHIEVE: Analyzing a school reform process for at-risk and underachieving students. *School Psychology Review, 24*(4), 579–603.

Kranzler, J. H., Miller, M. D., & Jordan, L. (1999). An examination of racial/ethnic and gender bias on curriculum-based measurement of reading. *School Psychology Quarterly, 14*(3), p 327–342.

Lonnqvist, J., Aro, H., Heikkinen, M., Heila, H., Henriksson, M., Isometsa, E., Kuurne, K., Marttunen, M., Ostamo, A., & Pelkonen, M. (1995). Project plan for studies on suicide, attempted suicide, and suicide prevention. *Crisis, 16*(4), 162–175.

Maccoby, E. E. (1988). Gender as a social category. *Developmental Psychology, 24*(6), 755–765.

Maccoby, E. E., & Jacklin, C. N. (1974). *The psychology of sex differences.* Stanford, CA: Stanford University Press.

Maller, S. J. (1997). *Differential item functioning in the WISC-III: Item parameters for boys and girls in the national standardization sample.* Paper presented at the annual meeting of the American Educational Research Association, Chicago, IL.

Nichols, J. D., Ludwin, W. G., & Iadicola, P. (1999). A darker shade of gray: A year-end analysis of discipline and suspension data. *Equity & Excellence in Education, 32,* 43–55.

Noddings, N. (1992). *The challenge to care in schools: An alternative approach to education.* New York: Teachers College Press.

Nolen-Hoeksema, S., & Girgus, J. S. (1994). The emergence of gender differences in depression during early adolescence. *Psychological Bulletin, 115*(3), 424–433.

Petersen, A. C., Sargiani, P. A., & Kennedy, R. E. (1991). Adolescent depression: Why more girls? *Journal of Youth and Adolescence, 20*, 247–271.

Pollock, W. (1998). *Real boys: Rescuing our sons from the myths of boyhood*. New York: Henry Holt.

Quereshi, M. Y., & Seitz, R. (1994). Gender differences on the WPPSI, the WISC-R, and the WPPSI-R. *Current Psychology, 13*(2), 117–123.

Raffaele, L. M. (2000). *An analysis of out-of-school suspensions in Hillsborough County*. Tampa, FL: The Children's Board of Hillsborough County.

Reid, R., Riccio, C. A., Kessler, R. H., DuPaul, G. J., Power, T. J., Anastopoulos, A. D., Rogers-Adkinson, D., & Noll, M. B. (2000). Gender and ethnic differences in ADHD as assessed by behavior ratings. *Journal of Emotional and Behavioral Disorders, 8*(1), 38–48.

Roberts, P. (1993). *Gender positive! A teachers' and librarians' guide to non-stereotyped children's literature, K-8*. Jefferson, NC: McFarland.

Rosen, L. (1997). *School discipline: Best practices for administrators*. Thousand Oaks, CA: Corwin.

Ryan, C., & Lindgren, S. (1999). How to work effectively with girls: Promising practices in gender specific interventions. *Reaching Today's Youth, 3*(3), 55–58.

Sadker, M., & Sadker, D. (1994). *Failing at fairness: How our schools cheat girls*. New York: Touchstone.

Scott, K. P. & Schau, C. G. (1985). Sex equity and sex bias in instructional materials. In S. S. Klein (Ed.), *Handbook for achieving sex equity through education* (pp.218–232). Baltimore: The Johns Hopkins University Press.

Sheridan, S. M. & Henning-Stout, M. (1994). Consulting with teachers about girls and boys. *Journal of Educational and Psychological Consultation, 5*(2), 93–113.

Slate, J. R. (1998). Sex differences in WISC-III IQs: Time for separate norms? *Journal of Psychology, 132*(6), 677–679.

Stark, K. (1990). *Childhood depression: School-based intervention*. New York: Guilford.

U.S. Department of Education. (1997). *Findings from the condition of education 1997: Women in mathematics and science* (NCES Publication No. 97-982). Washington, DC: National Center for Education Statistics.

U.S. Department of Education. (1998). *Twentieth annual report to Congress on the implementation of the Individuals With Disabilities Education Act*. Washington, DC: Office of Special Education and Rehabilitation Programs.

U.S. Department of Education. (2000a). *The condition of education 2000* (NCES Publication No. 200-062). Washington, DC: National Center for Education Statistics.

U.S. Department of Education. (2000b). *Trends in educational equity of girls and women* (NCES Publication No. 2000-030). Washington, DC: National Center for Education Statistics.

Webb, D. L., Hunnicutt, K. H., & Metha, A. (1997). What schools can do to combat student-to-student sexual harassment. *NASSP Bulletin, 81*(585), 72–79.

Wellesley College Center for Research on Women. (1993). *Secrets in public: Sexual harassment in our schools*. Wellesley, MA: Wellesley College Center for Research on Women.

ANNOTATED BIBLIOGRAPHY

American Association of University Women Educational Foundation. (1998). *Gender gaps: Where schools still fail our children*. Washington, DC: Author.

This follow-up to the 1992 AAUW Educational Foundation publication entitled *How Schools Shortchange Girls* provides an update of the status of gender equity in U.S. schools. The Executive Summary of this document, which provides a good overview of the major issues in this area, is available on the Internet at www.aauw.org.

Henning-Stout, M. (1998). Assessing the behavior of girls: What we see and what we miss. *Journal of School Psychology, 36*(4), 433–455.

This article describes how three frequently used behavioral assessment systems (i.e., the Child Behavior Checklist, the Social Skills Rating System, and the Behavioral Assessment Scale for Children) fail to reflect the significant experiences and concerns of girls in late childhood and early adolescence. This is an excellent article for those interested in understanding more about how behavioral assessment tools might be examined to determine if they address the experiences of historically marginalized groups.

Pollock, W. (1998). *Real boys: Rescuing our sons from the myths of boyhood.* New York: Henry Holt.
This is one of a few recently published books to examine the challenges that boys face during their formative years. This would be a good book to recommend to teachers and parents who want to know more about what they can do to minimize the impact of negative gender role stereotypes and help boys develop into productive, caring, well-adjusted adults.

Sadker, M., & Sadker, D. (1994). *Failing at fairness: How our schools cheat girls.* New York: Touchstone.
This frequently cited book describes the Sadkers' extensive observational research on gender bias in the classroom. Despite the title, it also contains a chapter describing how boys are shortchanged in schools. More recent work by David Sadker and information on Myra Sadker Day can be found on the Internet at www.sadker.org.

U.S. Department of Education (2000b). *Trends in educational equity of girls and women* (NCES Publication No. 2000-030). Washington, DC: National Center for Education Statistics.
This is one of many documents examining educational equity available through the National Center for Education Statistics. This particular report summarizes the latest findings on gender equity in 11 educational areas, including preprimary, achievement, curriculum issues, and students at risk. It can be ordered at no cost over the Internet at www.nces.ed.gov.

91 Best Practices in Assisting Relocating Families

Frederic J. Medway
University of South Carolina

OVERVIEW

This chapter provides a framework and a description of the best professional practices for school psychologists to follow in order to aid students and families faced with relocation. The chapter will clarify the impact of relocation on children and their parents, and provide guidelines and resources for intervention. The chapter examines the concept of mobility, describes variables associated with a family move, and presents research on the effects of moving on indices of children's adjustment. Finally, ways that school psychologists can help reduce the potential negative effects of family mobility on children are considered.

Background

Yearly approximately 16% of American families and nearly 9 million school-age children change residence (U.S. Census Bureau, 2000). Although the percentages of families changing residence has declined about 3% in the past 30 years, the total number of individuals moving has increased. Mobility is most likely to affect families of preschool children, families facing divorce and separation, and military families. The latter relocate as often as every 2 years. Mobility rates are particularly high (21.2%) among people of Hispanic origin.

Sixty-three percent of relocating families stay within the same county (van Vliet, 1986; U.S. Census Bureau, 2000). However, the primary impact of residential mobility is not so much a function of the distance moved but rather whether an increase or decrease in family income or change in family composition precipitates the move. Residential moves are made by both those who seek larger or more luxurious housing and by those forced to move because of economic circumstances including family separations and job loss. Even a move of relatively short geographical distance can be associated with a significant life change. For children, these moves can involve changes in children's familiar surroundings including their school. About one in six moves are to a different state or country. A number of occupations such as sales, the clergy, government service, and the military often require frequent relocation. Family migration also characterizes migrant families. Some individuals relocate many times just during their school years alone. Norford (1991) found that 5.5% of more than 7,000 high school students surveyed had moved seven or more times.

Even one act of relocation places many demands and challenges on individuals. It is difficult to leave friends, family, and familiar environments, and develop new relationships. Feelings of anxiety, loneliness, a sense of loss, and uncertainty are common. For children, these worries typically involve losing friends and making new ones (Norford, 1991). This is true throughout the school years. A stable reference group of friends serves many important functions, such as aiding in the formation of self-concept, providing feedback on one's abilities, and providing opportunities for positive socialization.

Research conducted up through the mid 1950s concluded that high residential mobility was associated with suicide, homicide, juvenile delinquency, and mental health problems. However, the more recent literature reviews conclude that moving per se is not necessarily problematic. Children who are well adjusted prior to relocating tend to be well adjusted after relocating. Additionally, children with academic or adjustment deficits preceding a move tend to be at risk for similar or greater problems after a move (DeWit, Offord, & Braun, 1998; Tucker, Marx, & Long, 1998). If anything, the evidence shows that there is considerable variability in how families handle relocation (Cummings, 1999).

In summary, as will be documented subsequently, there is little evidence to support the widely held belief that moving has negative effects on *average* children. This belief is based on case study reports, clinical impressions, and methodologically flawed studies (e.g., small and selected samples, lack of experimental controls). It further is compounded by media accounts of moving as "traumatic" for children, and numerous well meaning self-help books (e.g., Dickinson, 1983; Olkowski & Parker, 1993) with tips to deal with moving related problems in children. Although exaggerated fears regarding the negative effects of mobility on children have been challenged before (Goldsmith & Clark, 1987), school professionals continue to be unduly concerned about the unpleasant side of relocation. This chapter examines relocation as a family transition process and provides suggestions for increasing the probability that the transition will be a smooth one.

BASIC CONSIDERATIONS

The Process of Moving and Relocation

There is general consensus that family relocation should be considered as one of many life transitions and adjustment situations faced by children. With this view, relocation potentially can have either positive or negative effects on families and, in most instances, involves some combination of the two. Those effects can be short-term and transient or long-term and affect behavior patterns for a number of years. The impact of mobility may be associated with the geographical, social, and environmental changes faced by children, or the effects on children may be mediated by changed behavior patterns of parents and caregivers and how they deal with relocation. Most likely, the impact of a relocation experience reflects the family's adaptability (DeWit, Offord, & Braun, 1998; Tucker, Marx, & Long, 1998) in conjunction with the number of times a family has faced this potential stressor. There also is general support for the notion that moving is not a discrete event but rather involves a series of stages and challenges facing families from the time that relocation becomes an option to the time that the family is fully settled in a new environment. Each of these stages may demand adjustment and, accordingly, at each stage, there are opportunities for school psychologists to provide assistance. These stages are described below and the accompanying school psychological intervention opportunities described in the concluding section of this chapter.

Stages of Family Relocation

Stage One: Anticipation and Preparation

This stage involves families facing a potential relocation, and weighing the advantages and disadvantages of it. This stage involves all aspects of initial decision making regarding relocation (possibly including solicitation of the child's input), parents' attitudes, and ultimately communication of the decision to the child. Early research confirmed the public's view that many children are unhappy, sad, or scared when they learn that they may have to move (Khleif, 1978). Children typically focus on the negative side of moving and minimize the positive aspects. This is especially true of children in elementary school who have great difficulty considering themselves in a new community and with new friends. Thus, an essential first step to ease the anxiety of children is to be reassuring, to clearly explain the reasons for the move, and to be optimistic and positive about the benefits of relocation. Many of the books and resources about moving targeted for children that are listed at the conclusion of this chapter can be very valuable in dealing with children's initial apprehension.

Stage Two: Planning

This stage involves all actions necessary to change the physical environment with the least amount of personal distress. This may involve elements related to house sale, selection of neighborhoods and schools, inquiries about community resources, and transfers of school records. Without proper planning parents may feel irritable, overwhelmed, and fatigued. Those feelings often affect child behavior.

Stage Three: Moving Day

Moving day is characterized by the actual geographic transportation of the family and its possessions. Since three out of four families move without the help of relocation professionals, this day can be highly stressful and physically exhausting. Young children may be particularly upset during this time as they watch prized possessions loaded by strangers on a moving truck.

Stage Four: Initial Adjustment

This stage, lasting upward to 6 months, is characterized by those actions taken by the family, child, and community resources to deal with the stresses associated with environmental change. This may involve increased financial responsibilities, securing new employment for family members, and adjusting to changing work or travel schedules of the employed adult(s). Families hope that the child's behavior in the new home, school, and neighborhood will be similar to (or in some cases better than) the prior location. There is little disagreement among clinicians and researchers that initial adjustment difficulties are normal and expected.

Stage Five: Later Adjustment

This stage involves the impact of a move or series of relocations on individuals usually after an initial period of adjustment lasting 6 months to a year.

Many families feel relatively well equipped to deal with Stages Two and Three. Some are ably assisted with these issues by their employers and by relocation specialists. By contrast, Stages One, Four, and Five have been the concern of social scientists.

Mobility Dimensions

Beyond acknowledging that moving represents a series of activities and subsequent adjustments, it is important to recognize that the events themselves vary dramatically from one moving situation to another. For example, a military move from one base to another, although *superficially* similar, can involve considerable adjustment. Family moves vary on different dimensions, and each of these, either singly or in combination with others, will influence moving-related reactions. These dimensions are presented in Table 1. Each of these can have an impact on various aspects of children's social adjustment, including their peer relations and friendship networks, participation in social activities, mental health and anxiety, self-concept, age-appropriate behavior, loneliness and susceptibility to depression, and school performance.

Mobility Characteristics

Several variables associated with the move itself have the potential to impact directly on children although not all have been subjected to research scrutiny. Three important and researched characteristics are the distance moved, the degree of perceived choice, and the

Table 1. Variables associated with family mobility

Mobility Characteristics

- Distance of move
- Timing of move
- Degree of choice in move
- Reason(s) for move
- How recent was the move
- Cultural similarity between old and new community
- Number of prior moves
- Pattern of prior moves

Child Characteristics

- Age
- Gender
- Personality
- Preexisting achievement or adjustment problems

Family Characteristics

- Family size
- Family support mechanisms
- Family structure
- Family mobility history
- Family attitudes about moving
- Availability of parents

School Factors

- Time of entry into classroom
- Curriculum
- School size
- Amount of student turnover
- Programs to address relocation and other support services
- Degree of student grade retention

Community Factors

- Availability of child and family social services
- Availability of community supports
- Economic climate

reason for the move. Although distance as measured by miles from old to new residence has little consistent impact on children, it must be recognized that even short moves can potentially exaggerate existing problems if they involve significant life changes such as an extended commute or a school change. Moving usually is hardest on family members who have had little say in the decision to move as well as those with minimal choice of new community, including the new house and school. Typically, this describes young children and even spouses in corporate and military families. Transplanted spouses are likely to experience loneliness, depression, and feelings of loss. These feelings may affect their attitudes toward the move and their actions in relation to their children. In short, moving often affects children because primary caregivers become less functional in carrying out parental roles. In some households the relocated spouse may attempt to use the child as emotional support to deal with their own loneliness and discomfort.

Research also shows the important role of the reason for the move. Families may move because of financial hardship, the requirements of military duty, separation, or divorce, because of occupational necessity, or simply to secure more adequate housing. Single-parent families move more often than two parent-families. These higher rates of mobility are directly associated with low income. Children who do not reside with both parents suffer more moving-related stress than children who do (Tucker, Marx, & Long, 1998). Children who move as a result of divorce report less involvement in school social activities in the years following a move when compared with non-movers, even when stressful life events are controlled (Norford, 1991).

Child Characteristics

The stresses associated with moving affect different children in different ways, and this appears to be influenced by developmental levels, gender, and psychological risk factors. Although there is not a clear developmental pattern, the more carefully designed studies point to both the preschool years and early adolescence as vulnerable ages to moving-related stresses (Cummings, 1999; Vernberg, 1990). This is contrary to the prevailing common notion that the best time to move a family is before children start school and contrary to the notion that moving is hardest on students in their last years of high school. Preschoolers have difficulty dealing with the changes in familiar surroundings, lack the coping skills of older children, and have trouble cognitively understanding the need for the move. Also, they are less likely than older children to understand abstract concepts of time such as "in 6 months," which may relate to when the move will occur. Early adolescents report about three times as much difficulty forming friendships as do children in the primary grades (Barrett & Noble, 1973). Gender does not appear to have consistent effects on mobility reactions. Some have argued that males react more negatively to relocation and other life transitions (cf. Rutter, 1981) than females (van Vliet, 1986; Vernberg, 1990). Males reportedly have a harder time leaving old friends and making new ones, and experience more peer rejection, than do females (Donahue & Gullota, 1983). On the other hand, Brown and Orthner (1990) found that recent moves and a history of frequent moves were more strongly associated with low life satisfaction among female than male adolescents. Finally, it has been recognized that children with existing academic and behavioral problems require structure, consistency, and special attention. Thus, it is not surprising that environmental changes would affect children who have pre-existing problems more than children who do not. Kantor (1965), in one of the few studies to assess children both before and after a move, found that negative mobility effects were attributable to initial behavioral differences between children, not mobility per se.

Family Characteristics

It is virtually impossible to disentangle the effects of family variables from the impact of relocation. It is the parents who inform the child of the future move, deal with children's associated concerns and anxieties, make the important relocation-related decisions, and interact closely with children throughout the transition period. If the family attitude toward moving or toward this particular move is negative, then it is likely that the child's attitude will be negative as well. Several studies have underscored the importance of the mother's attitude toward the move on children. Norford (1991) reported that more than 60% of mothers who had relocated their children an average of seven times reported that family moving was either "moderately" or "very" stressful. Further, if either parent becomes overanxious, withdrawn, physically stressed, or intolerant, then this, as well, will affect the child, particularly if the child connects this behavioral change to the move. In corporate families the needs of the head of the household may so overshadow the needs of other family members that problems develop. Several studies indicate that moving can result in depression but only when family support and social cohesion is low. For example, the negative effects of relocation on children are considerable when fathers are uninvolved and mothers are unsupportive (Hagan, MacMillan, & Wheaton, 1996). By contrast, in the military community, relocation is a necessary part of life, and families are supported throughout the transitions to new locations in the states and overseas.

School Factors

School factors are an important, although unstudied, moderator of moving-related reactions. School size, quality of teacher-student interactions, opportunities for leadership roles, curriculum demands, policies and norms, and the nature of support services all would appear to have an impact on mobility adjustment. Occasionally school experiences can exacerbate moving reactions. For example, considering the effects of group cohesion, it is not surprising that elementary age males who enter school late in the year are less likely to be accepted socially than those who enter early in the year. Schools characterized by existing cliques create challenges for the newly relocated adolescent. However, in most cases, relocation as an issue for children has not been systematically addressed by school systems. One early review found only two large-scale school intervention programs to help children who relocate (Blair, Marchant, & Medway, 1984). One program, known as the Summer Visitation Program, used school counselors to (a) conduct home visits with new school families, (b) involve those families in school and community activities by sponsoring various outings and social opportunities for them, and (c) develop support groups for recently relocated children. This program was successful in increasing social contacts and happiness, and in reducing absenteeism in participating students as compared with nonparticipating controls. A second program, Students Assimilated Into Learning, also sought to increase parental involvement in the school. This program made use of staff development activities and special learning centers to quickly assess the educational status of students moving into the school and provided children assistance with academic deficiencies. Data obtained from this program indicated that targeted students showed increased achievement scores. There is no indication that such school-wide programs are in operation in schools today.

The fact that schools have historically viewed the child who is relocating as a deficit when compared with children with a stable residence has led some educators to encourage grade retention of incoming students as a way to aid their school adjustment. Indeed, research shows that highly mobile children are retained more often than non-mobile children. *Light's Retention Scale* includes mobility as a factor to consider in deciding whether or not to retain a child. Yet, there is little evidence to indicate that moving harms school achievement. In one study (Norford, 1991) only 15% of adolescents who had moved at least six times reported that they were academically behind their new classmates. Given that retention itself is a practice of questionable educational value and given research showing that mobility effects can be effectively minimized by proper home and school support, there is little evidence to support the practice of routinely retaining a child based solely or even primarily on their relocation.

Community Factors

Conventional wisdom suggests that it is easier to adjust to a new community with characteristics similar to an old community. Moves that subject children to cultures and subcultures different from those to which they are accustomed are presumed to demand greater adjustment on the child's part. Along these lines it is often assumed that moving from one military base to another is generally not highly stressful since bases tend to be similar and because the base tends to insulate the military family from the surrounding community. In addition, relocation support services are available through Family Service Centers and military assistance centers associated with service branches. While this may be true, there is no empirical evidence that children in military-related moves do any better (or worse) than children in corporate moves (Norford, 1991).

The Impact of Relocation on Children

In attempting to understand the impact of relocation on families it is not only important to consider the stages of moving and the various elements associated with the process but also to realize that the public generally views relocation as emotionally trying and resulting in anxiety. Empirical research does not bear out this negative view. The following three excerpts are typical of how mobility is perceived by many citizens and by the media. The first is from Rouhana (1990):

> Samantha and Robert Brown had been preparing for moving day for weeks. On the big day Samantha left her 1-year-old son with a neighbor while she and her husband supervised the movers. Eight hours later it was time for one last look around. With the baby in her arms, Samantha entered his now-bare room. He took one startled look and began to bawl. [Samantha] was surprised at the force of her infant's reaction: "There was no question. He knew something was terribly wrong." Like most infants, [Samantha's] baby suffered only momentarily, because the real center of his world was his parents.... But for most kids, be they toddlers or teens, moving can be stressful.

The second is from the *Boston Globe* ("Helping kids handle the stress of moving," 1992):

> Whether you are relocating across town or across country, moving is traumatic for children of any age. The change in routine, parents' preoccupation with the move, giving up friends—these are all losses for the child. The worst mistake parents can make is to underestimate their importance.

The third is from *The New York Times* ("A move can shake a child's confidence," 1988).

> Daniel and Gerry Barnett hadn't expected their children to react so strongly to the family's move from Oklahoma to suburban Chicago. Twelve-year-old Helen told her parents that she looked forward to the move because it was, "a neat thing to do...," but as the move approached, she became more obstinate when adults asked her to do something. She would overreact to ordinary events. Helen's school grades dropped slightly in the next marking period

In short, both the popular press and general opinion is of the belief that moving is a potential traumatic event that can have long-term consequences on children's mental health and school performance. By contrast, although research suggests that there may be some short-term impact of mobility on children, data obtained from more than one hundred studies of children's relocation indicates that there is little evidence of any long-term negative impact. What follows is a brief overview of research in this area drawn from earlier reviews by Humke and Schaefer (1995), Norford (1991), and van Vliet (1986).

Academic Achievement

Numerous studies have looked at the achievement levels of mobile children and comparison groups. Across 18 of the most methodologically sound studies (out of more than 40 conducted) there is virtually no effect of mobility on school achievement once initial achievement levels are controlled. Mobility does appear to hurt the achievement of students with academic problems prior to a move.

Social Adjustment

Does frequent relocation undermine self-image, peer relations, participation in extracurricular activities, and other areas of social adjustment? Most research suggests that it does not. High frequency and low frequency movers have not been found to differ on traditional scales of self-concept and personality. There is some evidence that depression may be associated with higher levels of mobility in young adolescents. However, it is not clear in these studies if the depression arose after the move or during earlier preparatory stages. In one well-controlled study (Norford, 1991) there were no differences in depression and perceived social support among high school students varying in mobility history, including nearly 100 students who have moved seven times on average. Norford did find that frequent mobility after seventh grade did significantly affect participation in extracurricular activities. Norford measured potential positive adjustment indicators as well and found no consistent positive effects associated with high mobility.

BEST PRACTICES

With familiarization with the research on family relocation and with appropriate training in assessment, child development, and intervention, school psychologists, possibly working along with school counselors, should be able to apply best practices to family relocation issues. School psychologists are likely to encounter mobility concerns in two primary contexts. First, in their capacities as school consultants, school psychologists occasionally are asked to provide information about the effects of relocation on children to various sources. Those seeking this information may be parents (those considering relocation or those who have recently relocated), teachers (faced with making decisions about newly transferred students), school administrators, and, occasionally, the media. For example, an article on family relocation could be written for a school newspaper or a presentation can be made at a teacher or parent meeting. Parents may be prone to worry about mobility effects far more than is warranted. Norford (1991) found that 27% of approximately 95 adolescents who had moved more than six times viewed frequent moving as "very positive" compared to 15% of their mothers. Only 3% of the students viewed moving as "very negative" compared to 10% of their mothers.

Typically, however, families new to a community probably are not likely to turn to school psychologists with these questions. If their child hasn't had school problems in the past or if the parents aren't familiar with school resources it is unlikely that psychologists will be consulted. Best practice, therefore, dictates that school psychologists take the lead in informing those in the community such as doctors, the clergy, and key people in school district administration of their knowledge in this area and their desire to provide assistance.

Second, in their roles of providing intervention services, school psychologists may be called on directly to (a) develop programs to ease mobility transitions or (b) work with children having difficulty with mobility-related adjustments. The following section reviews several best practices and helpful sources to aid in both capacities.

Parent Consultation

Parents who contact school psychologists for information about moving may do so at any stage of the relocation process. Typically, these parents fear that moving will upset their child in some way, and desire practical tips and resources to make the move easier. Table 2 provides some practical tips designed for parents. Further tips are presented in books specifically designed for parents, listed in Table 3, and in resources such as *Mobility* magazine. Many books written for the lay audience are useful, although some overstate the negative effects of mobility. Additionally, school psychologists can encourage parents to use one or more of the storybooks listed in Table 3 with their children to clarify relocation feelings and let children know that their feelings are not unique. A number of real estate agents and most major moving companies have resources and activities to aid families with many aspects of moving (e.g., North American Van Lines, Mayflower Transit, United Van Lines, and Ryder Truck Rental) including moving with children. Useful websites include virtualrelocation.com and MoversNet.com.

Consultation With School-Based Professionals

School psychologists should share information and research regarding family mobility with schools, teachers, counselors, and administrators. Useful tips for teachers are presented in Table 4. School psychologists can routinely be given the names of all families who have recently moved into the school district in order to offer family and academic assistance if necessary. Particular attention should be given to families with children that have some of the identified risk factors, such as preexisting problems, economic and family distress, and difficulty with social skills.

Program Development

School psychologists can take the lead in developing school-based preventive programs focusing on relocation issues. In particular, aspects of the well-validated Summer Visitation Program reviewed earlier can be developed by special service teams, particu-

Table 2. Tips for parents about moving

1. Discuss the move openly and honestly with children once the decision to move is definite. Elementary school-age children and older youth should be given at least 3 months notice, if possible, to prepare for the move. Preteens and teenagers should also be given some input into family decisions. For preschool children it is preferable to wait until moving day is closer such as when moving-related activities change family routines. For these children, reading storybooks about moving may stimulate questions, elicit feelings, and ease any anxiety. Toys, such as trucks and wagons, can be used in "moving games" to illustrate the concept of moving to the 2- and 3-year-old child. Be clear the move is final, and avoid promises you may not be able to keep.
2. Attempt to delay a move during other upheavals in the life of a child such as right after a sibling's birth or immediately following a divorce or parent's death. Such moves may compound the stress and adjustment demands placed on children.
3. Get children involved in the move. Encourage children to take on projects designed to gather information on the new community. Subscribe to the newspaper in the new community and do virtual community tours using the Internet.
4. Start building a new community network before the move. Inquire about religious groups, medical and social service facilities, educational opportunities, newcomers' assistance, and children's activities such as scouting. If relocation is due to corporate or military transfer, then inquire about special assistance offered.
5. Recognize your own stress level, and do not take on more than you can handle. Moving yourself, looking for a house without an experienced real estate agent, or moving into a home requiring repairs and renovation can serve as added stressors. Recognize that your stress level as well as your attitude about moving will affect your child's behavior.
6. Make sure that all medical and school records are sent ahead in advance. These should include a birth certificate, achievement tests, immunization records, and relevant school correspondence including all records relating to special education.
7. Take responsibility for orienting your child to the new school and community. Have a meeting with your child's new teacher to discuss the placement. Inquire about any special programs or assistance provided by psychologists and counselors for relocated students. Do not allow your child to repeat a grade just on the basis of a move. If retention is recommended, then insist on a full individually administered evaluation and, if necessary, a second opinion.
8. Although a move during the summer is less likely to be disruptive to a child's school performance, a move during the school year brings children into immediate contact with others their age. Also, teachers and classmates are more likely to treat children as special when they enter during the year than at the start of a new school year.
9. On moving day reassure children that their possessions are going to the new home. Allow children to pack a small suitcase to carry with them, including such things as special playthings, mementos, and pictures. Load the furniture of young children last so that these items are first to be unloaded and placed in the new home. Once in the new home allow the child some say in how the room will be decorated, or arrange the new room to match the child's old room. Make the first night in the new home special by having some kind of party.
10. Formal good-byes, such as going-away parties, should be encouraged. Help children make scrap books with pictures of old friends, and encourage them to correspond with old friends using letters and e-mail.
11. Take the initiative, especially during the initial weeks of a move, to actively explore the new environment. Make an effort to meet people. Invite neighbors over and volunteer at the school.
12. Avoid staying indoors and devoting all your time to unpacking and arranging the new house. Be sure to spend quality time with your children.
13. Try to find positive things in moves required by financial hardship.
14. Moving may diminish teenagers' feelings of independence. Therefore, aid teenagers in exploring social opportunities in the new environment. Resist the temptation to be overprotective because of unfamiliarity with the new community.

larly in areas of high family mobility and transience. In addition to interventions with students just entering school, counseling groups can be organized for elementary school children whose families will soon be moving to other communities. In such groups, children can be given an opportunity to share feelings about moving and practice the social skills involved in leaving old friends and making new ones. Programs also can be developed for parents to help them understand the impact of family mobility as it relates to their own specific circumstances and the developmental status of their own child.

Counseling and Therapy

As was previously indicated, it is unlikely that school psychologists will encounter very many children whose family mobility, in and of itself, results in serious mental health problems such as depression, withdrawal, physical ailments, or academic problems that

Table 3. Bibliography and readings on relocation

Suggested Books for Parents

Artenstein, J. (1990). *Moving: How to be sure that your child makes a happy transfer to a new home*. New York: TOR.

Carlisle, E. (1999). *Smooth moves: The relocation guide for families on the move*. New York: Teacup Press.

Dickinson, J. (1983). *Jan Dickinson's complete guide to family relocation*. Portland, OR: Wheatherstone.

Goodwin, C. (1999). *Making the big move: How to transform relocation into a creative life transition*. Oakland, CA: New Harbinger.

Kalb, R., & Welch, P. (1992). *Moving your family overseas*. Yarmouth, ME: Intercultural Press.

Miller, Y. F., & Cherry, J. W. (1992). *Kids on the move*. Laurel, MD: National Association of School Psychologists.

Olkowski, T. T., & Parker, L. (1993). *Moving with children: A parent's guide to moving with children*. Littleton, CO: Gylantic.

Porter, O. (1992). *From here to there: The workbook for families on the move*. Portland, OR: Niche.

Books for Children: Preschool and Primary Grades

Asch, F. (1989). *Goodbye house*. New York: Aladdin.

Banks, A., Evans, N., & Kelley, T. (1999). *Goodbye, house: A kids guide to moving*. New York: Crown.

Berenstain, S., & Berenstain, J. (1981). *The Berenstain Bears' moving day*. New York: Random House.

Biale, R. (1996). *We are moving: Lets make a book about it*. Berkeley, CA: Tricycle Press.

Carlstrom, N. W., & Wickstrom, T. (1999). *I'm not moving mama!* New York: Aladdin.

Cuddy, R., & Zoehfeld, K. (1999). *Tigger's moving day*. New York: Disney Press.

Mayer, M. (1995). *Little monster's moving day*. New York: Cartwheel.

McGeorge, C. W. (1994). *Boomer's big day*. San Francisco: Chronicle.

Packard, M., & Lopez, S. (1998). *Kitty's moving day: Fisher-Price Little People little pockets playbooks*. New York: Readers Digest.

Sharmat, M. W. (1996). *Mitchell is moving*. New York: Aladdin.

Stimson, J., & Rutherford, M. (1997). *A new home for Tiger*. New York: Barrons Juveniles.

Books for Children: Elementary Grades

Davis, G. (1997). *The moving book: A kid's survival guide*. New York: Little, Brown.

Hurwitz, J., & Wallner, J. (1997). *Aldo Applesauce*. New York: Morrow.

Milord, S., & Milord, J. (1985). *Maggie and the goodbye gift*. New York: Lathrop, Lee, & Shepherd Books.

O'Donnell, E. L., & Schwartz, A. (1990). *Maggie doesn't want to move*. New York: Aladdin.

Schulman, J., & Hoban, L. (1990). *The big hello*. Keighley, England: Mulberry.

Sharmat, M. W. (1999). *Gila monsters at the airport*. Chicago: Econo-Clad.

Books for Adolescents

Anderson, P., & Strecker, R. (1992). *First day blues*. Seattle, WA: Parenting Press.

Lipson, S. L. (2000). *Knock on wood*. New York: Leba House.

Walsh, J. P. (1991). *Gaffer Samson's luck*. New York: Farrar, Straus, & Giroux.

Videotapes for Elementary Grade Children

Let's get a move on! (1990). Newton, MA: Kidvidz.

Table 4. Tips for educators about moving

1. Present children who are moving with photo albums of classmates and friends. Consider having a going-away party for moving students.
2. Announce the arrival of new students. Make sure they are included in yearbooks, etc.
3. Assign buddies to new students. Buddies may also serve as school guides and peer tutors.
4. Encourage recently moved students to do presentations on the places they have lived.
5. Be sensitive to family stresses that may be associated with mobility. Provide families in need with information about support services or make an appropriate referral.
6. Do not routinely retain new school enrollees. Retention decisions, if made at all, should not be based on family mobility history or the ability of the child to adjust to new school routines. If academic or behavior problems are present, then consult the school psychologist.
7. Maintain particularly close contact with newly relocated families to ensure good school-home communication and parent involvement.
8. Participate in and encourage school-sponsored meetings and social events for parents of newcomers to acquaint them with school policies and community services.

necessitate extended counseling. Some adjustment problems are normal during the first 6 months after relocation and typically can be handled through family or teacher consultation. Unusual withdrawal, anxiety, anger, stress-related reactions, acting-out, or academic problems, however, should not be ignored and do require early intervention. In addition to family therapy, several non-behavioral techniques (cf. Medway, 1985) are particularly appropriate. These include play therapy, role playing to bring conflicts into awareness, and bibliotherapy. There is a wealth of good children's books on the topic of moving and relocation. Some excellent sources are listed in Table 3. These books are designed to help work through some of the emotional issues surrounding relocation and provide a vehicle for parent-child communication. Additionally, social skills training can be used to aid in building friendship networks and dealing with negative remarks made by others.

SUMMARY

Each year one out of five families relocate in the United States. The process of relocation involves several adjustment stages. A child's adjustment during each stage is influenced by many contextual variables such as reason for the move, the child's individual characteristics, and particulars of the new school and community. Because moving does involve changes and interruptions in children's schooling and friendships, there is concern among the public and school professionals about the effects of moving on children and their families. Despite this concern, research indicates that family relocation is far less stressful on children than many people believe it to be. Although relocation to a new community can cause children to be anxious, to develop behavior problems, and to have academic problems in the classroom, those problems typically are short-lived. Most normal children ultimately handle moving transitions well. Those who do not handle moving well typically have problems that are present before the move rather than as a result of the relocation. Within 6 months to a year it is virtually impossible to distinguish movers and non-movers on traditional measures of personality and achievement. Successful child relocation depends heavily on the behavior and attitudes of the adults in the home and on children's opportunities to make new friends within a supportive environment. Although the school environment can aid the relocation transition, with the exception of some isolated efforts, schools often have ignored their important role as a key community resource in aiding mobile families (Blair, Marchant, & Medway, 1984). School psychologists can serve an important function in both advocating for school-wide efforts and broadening their roles and functions to include aiding relocating families.

Family mobility is an integral part of the American lifestyle. By providing planned consultation and intervention services focused on relocation issues, school psychologists can bring to bear a variety of assessment, consultation, and intervention skills to a potential family dilemma.

REFERENCES

A move can shake a child's confidence. (1988, July 8). *The New York Times*, p. 21.

Barrett, C. L., & Noble, H. (1973). Mother's anxieties vs. the effects of long distance moves on children. *Journal of Marriage and the Family, 35*, 181–188.

Blair, J. P., Marchant, K. H., & Medway, F. J. (1984). Aiding the relocated child and mobile family. *Elementary School Guidance and Counseling, 18*, 251–259.

Brown, A. C., & Orthner, D. K. (1990). Relocation and personal well-being among adolescents. *Journal of Early Adolescence, 10*, 366–381.

Cummings, B. W. (1999). *A review of books, studies, and journal articles published in the U.S.A. from 1955–1995 relating to the sociological impact of corporate relocation on the family system*. Parkland, FL: Dissertation.com.

DeWit, D. J., Offord, D.R., & Braun, K. (1998). *The relationship between geographic relocation and childhood problem behavior.* Canada: Human Resources Development.

Dickinson, J. (1983). *Jan Dickinson's complete guide to family relocation*. Portland, OR: Wheatherstone.

Donahue, K. C., & Gulotta, T. P. (1983). The coping behavior of adolescents following a move. *Adolescence, 18*, 391–401.

Goldsmith, D. F., & Clark, E. (1987). Moving. In A. Thomas & J. Grimes (Eds.), *Children's needs: Psychological perspectives* (pp. 372–378). Washington, DC: National Association of School Psychologists.

Hagan, J., MacMillan, R., & Wheaton, B. (1996). New kid in town: Social capital and the life course effects of family migration on children. *American Sociological Review, 61*, 368–385.

Helping kids handle the stress of moving. (1992, May 29). *Boston Globe*, pp. 67, 71.

Humke, C., & Schaefer, C. (1995). Relocation: A review of the effects of residential mobility on children and adolescents. *Psychology: A Journal of Human Behavior, 32*, 16–24.

Kantor, M. B. (1965). Some consequences of residential and social mobility for the adjustment of children. In M. B. Kantor (Ed.), *Mobility and mental health* (pp. 86–122). Springfield, IL: Charles C. Thomas.

Khleif, B. B. (1978). The military dependent as a stranger in the public schools. *Sociologia Internationalis, 16*, 153–161.

Medway, F. J. (1985). Direct therapeutic intervention in school psychology. In J. R. Bergan (Ed.), *School psychology in contemporary society: An introduction* (pp. 207–229). Columbus, OH: Merrill.

Norford, B. C. (1991). *The relationship of repeated geographical mobility to social adjustment and depression in high school students*. Unpublished doctoral dissertation, University of South Carolina, Columbia.

Olkowski, T. T., & Parker, L. (1993). *Moving with children: A parent's guide to moving with children*. Littleton, CO: Gylantic.

Rouhana, K. (1990, June). Smooth moves. *Sesame Street Magazine: Parent's Guide*, 19–20.

Rutter, M. (1981). Stress, coping, and development: Some issues, some questions. *Journal of Child Psychology and Psychiatry, 22*, 323–356.

Tucker, C. J., Marx, J., & Long, L. (1998). "Moving on": Residential mobility and children's school lives. *Sociology of Education, 71*, 111–129.

U.S. Census Bureau. (2000). *Annual geographical mobility rates*. [On-line]. Available from: http://www.census.gov/population/socdemo/migration.

van Vliet, W. (1986). Children who move: Relocation effects and their context. *Journal of Planning Literature, 1*, 403–426.

Vernberg, E. M. (1990). Experiences with peers following relocation during early adolescence. *American Journal of Orthopsychiatry, 60*, 466–472.

ANNOTATED BIBLIOGRAPHY

Carlisle, E. (1999). *Smooth moves: The relocation guide for families on the move*. Charlotte, NC: Teacup Press.
Based on her experiences moving eight times in 17 years, Carlisle shares a number of tips to reduce the stresses of relocation. The book includes tips related to the sale of the home to tips for choosing schools and neighborhoods to tips to maintaining family harmony. This is a positive and upbeat book that has received excellent reviews from readers.

Humke, C., & Schaefer, C. (1995). Relocation: A review of the effects of residential mobility on children and adolescents. *Psychology: A Journal of Human Behavior, 32*, 16–24.
This article reviews research on children and moving, and discusses those factors that contribute to poor adjustment following a move including negative parental attitudes toward the move and moving due to financial disruption.

Miller, Y. F., & Cherry, J. W. (1992). *Kids on the move: Meeting their needs*. Laurel, MD: National Association of School Psychologists.
A comprehensive source designed for professionals who work with children who encounter a variety of relocation-related problems, including both routine family moves and divorce-related changes.

Olkowski, T. T., & Parker, L. (1993). *Moving with children: A parent's guide to moving with children*. Littleton, CO: Gylantic.
This is a practical book on family moving written by a psychologist and social worker.

92 Best Practices in Interdisciplinary Service Delivery to Children With Chronic Medical Issues

Steven R. Shaw and Doris Páez
Department of Developmental Pediatrics
The Children's Hospital
Greenville, SC

OVERVIEW

Children with chronic medical issues are a large and growing population (Brown, 1999). Improvement in health care means that children's chronic medical issues are more frequently addressed at home or at school rather than during lengthy hospitalizations (Brown, 1999). Despite advances in medical care, academic and social problems are common in children with chronic medical issues (Brown & DuPaul, 1999). Academic and social issues that may be affected directly or indirectly by medical problems or treatments include cognitive ability, personality, adaptive behavior, motivation, school functioning, emotional disturbance, attention, memory, language, school absenteeism, family dynamics, and academic skills (Power, DuPaul, Shapiro, & Parrish, 1998; Tarnowski & Brown, 1995). Because children are surviving chronic and serious medical issues in greater numbers than in the past, effectively addressing the complex and reciprocal academic and social factors is a necessary role for school psychologists to embrace (Tarnowski & Brown, 1995).

Increasingly, school psychologists are addressing health-related issues in school and medical settings (Drotar, 1998). Among the roles that may be filled are parent training, child advocacy, assessment, service coordination, counseling, program development, and research (Brown, 1999; Power et al., 1998). Despite the variety of roles, there are common issues to be addressed for effective interdisciplinary delivery of psychological and educational services. Addressing the needs of children with medical issues is an interdisciplinary task. The ability to function well as a team member is as important as is clinical skill for effective service delivery. School psychologists, given their knowledge of school systems, consultation expertise, clinical skills, and research training, are well positioned to be leaders in interdisciplinary service provision to children with chronic medical issues.

Psychologists may be involved at one or more of four general levels of service delivery for children with medical issues: prevention, acute, chronic, and rehabilitation. The level of service delivery at which the psychologist is involved dictates role and function.

Prevention

Preventative care has two distinct definitions (Kaplan, 2000). The first definition refers to a child who is experiencing medical issues, and the goal is to prevent psychological or educational problems. Children with medical concerns are at-risk for future psychological or educational difficulties (Talley & Short, 1995). A school psychologist may review school, mental health, social, and medical records to determine potential problem areas. Additional assessment may be conducted to determine which areas of functioning may benefit from early intervention. For example, pre-maturity is a medical condition with well-documented risk factors and established efficacy of early intervention. Among the other medical issues that may warrant assessment for purposes of preventative care are injury, allergies, diabetes, exposure to toxins, alcohol and drug abuse, otitis media, and somatic complaints.

The second definition of prevention involves the reduction of the occurrence of chronic medical conditions. Examples of this type of preventative health care include violence prevention, problem–solving skills, social skills training, sex education, injury prevention, and alcohol and drug intervention. In addition, there are risky behaviors that, if not prevented, have long-term health consequences, such as smoking, poor nutrition, substance abuse, and eating disorders. Because many pediatric medical conditions involve health risk behaviors, psychologists frequently are included in preventative health care. Psychologists, especially those working in schools, are in a prime position to engage in primary prevention (Shaw, Kelly, Joost, & Parker-Fisher, 1995).

Acute

Acute care refers to health issues requiring emergency room care or immediate first aid. Injuries, life-threatening illnesses, asthma attacks, poisoning, and other urgent health needs fall under the category of acute care. Suicide attempts, pain management, psychotic episodes, grieving, and family issues may involve psychologists. Expertise in crisis counseling and grief and bereavement counseling can be of great value in emergency rooms and other locations addressing acute medical issues.

Chronic

Chronic illnesses are conditions of long duration that require some level of ongoing medical management and accommodations in life functioning. Physicians and psychologists recognize the educational and mental health consequences of many chronic pediatric medical conditions, providing multiple opportunities for medical and psychological collaboration (Frank et al., 1998). Asthma, severe allergies, HIV, and diabetes are common chronic medical conditions. Nearly all children with chronic illness will return to their home school. The Individuals with Disabilities Education Act specifies that chronic illness causing an adverse effect on education may be eligible for special education services under the Other Health Impaired category. Moreover, the Diagnostic and Statistical Manual-IV (DSM-IV) contains Axis III that is devoted to identifying medical issues that may be affecting the psychological functioning of patients. However, the educational needs for children with medical issues are complicated by heterogeneous educational, social, and mental health needs across individual case and condition types (Dryfoos, 1994). Collaborative efforts among medical professionals, psychologists, and educators are necessary to address the challenges of children with chronic medical conditions.

Rehabilitation

Psychologists frequently participate in rehabilitation after childhood illness or injury (Talley & Short, 1995). Rehabilitation is a multidisciplinary service intended to reduce the effects of physical, cognitive, and emotional impairments. Although physicians, nurses, and physical and occupational therapists are responsible for physical improvement, school psychologists provide much of the cognitive and emotional rehabilitation in the school setting (Power, Heathfield, McGoey, & Blum, 1999). Counseling and rehabilitation of academic impairments are within the realm of many school psychologists' skills (Shaw et al., 1995). Rehabilitation focusing on academics and social emotional functioning is a significant, yet often forgotten, aspect of children's recovery from illness and injury (Stuart & Goodsilt, 1996).

Although all four levels of service delivery are wholly appropriate for school psychologists, this chapter will focus on children with chronic medical issues. The management and prevention of academic and social problems for children with chronic health problems are activities that nearly all school psychologists will be called upon to address. In order to engage children with chronic health problems, there are several basic considerations that need to be acknowledged before successful service delivery can take place.

BASIC CONSIDERATIONS

There are several important roles for school psychologists in the management of children with medical issues. The roles in which school psychologists are engaged are functions of the training and expertise of the school psychologist. In each role, there are basic considerations to be addressed. These basic considerations have been called "barriers" in the literature (e.g., Shaw et al., 1995). "Prerequisites" to successful service delivery may be a more productive way to think about these issues.

Interprofessional Issues

Effective service delivery to children with medical issues requires collaboration and coordination between school psychologists and medical professionals (Drotar, 1993, 1995). The health care knowledge of medical professionals combined with educational and mental health knowledge of school psychologists in a cooperative, collaborative, interdisciplinary manner has potential to improve the educational, physical, social, and mental health of children with medical issues (Dryfoos, 1994). However, owing to significant barriers to successful consultation relationships, collaboration between these two groups of professionals rarely takes place (Conoley & Conoley, 1991).

The first challenge to collaboration between the two fields is the written findings resulting from evaluations (Drotar, 1998). Terminology is unique to each field and sometimes provides exclusivity to the interpretation of findings. Both professions would benefit from reducing jargon in oral and written communication (Shaw et al., 1995). The inability of professionals in other fields to understand written findings often leads to the dismissal of reports as unusable. Medical reports often do not address specific concerns and challenges manifested in the school and home settings. The treatment suggested in medical reports is usually not educational or behavioral in nature. Such reports often exclude teachers and psychologists from intervening with behavioral or educational strategies on behalf of children, because teachers frequently assume that the problems are only remediable through medical means (Purvis & Whalen, 1992). Moreover, when schools refer children to physicians, educational and psychological reports do not communicate enough medically relevant information to aid physicians in diagnosis or treatment (Drotar, 1993). Rather than interpreting different terminology as providing new information, each profession appears to interpret different terminology as lacking relevance to the referral problem (Resnick & Kruczek, 1996).

A compromise definition of collaboration may be useful: School psychologist and medical professional collaboration is a partnership marked by the exchange of valued information in a coordinated effort to improve the educational, mental health, and medical well being of children. Among the assumptions of this definition of consultation are (a) contributions from both professions are equally useful and valued; (b) assessment and intervention are conducted in a coordinated fashion, rather than by professionals working in isolation; and (c) information is shared in a jargon-free manner to contribute to all professions involved (Reeder et al., 1997). Only when psychologists and medical professionals agree on basic assumptions of collaboration can service delivery for children with medical issues become an enterprise marked by coordination and integration (Miller & Swartz, 1990). There are a growing number of subspecialties that have interprofessional collaboration at the core of their professional identities, such as developmental pediatrics, behavioral pediatrics, pediatric school psychology, and health psychology.

The pressures on medical practices to earn enough revenue to meet the demands of managed care contracts and office overhead make setting aside time for collaboration difficult. Likewise, school psychologists are under time pressures established by the legislation and regulation of the educational system. The goal of collaboration cannot simply be to meet and spend a great deal of professional time to address a child's needs. One of the goals of interprofessional collaboration is to save time and to allow practices to work with more children in a more efficient manner. Ignoring the needs for efficiency will lead professionals neglecting interprofessional collaboration as they succumb to time and financial pressures.

The effort required to surmount all of these barriers to engage in successful collaboration is great. Owing to financial pressures, systems often discourage collaboration, leading to the current situation where collaboration seldom occurs. Individual barriers are likely to fall as each profession becomes familiar with the other's goals, professional challenges, methods, and jargon (Drotar, 1995). With the reduction of barriers comes an increased likelihood that school psychology and medical collaboration will take place (Shaw et al., 1995). Overcoming systemic, training, and individual barriers to collaboration will not be easy. Recall that teachers and school psychologists and clinical psychologists and social workers work together daily, yet still have significant difficulties engaging in collaboration. Likewise, physicians and nurses rarely engage in collaboration despite many commonalties and opportunities.

Interagency Issues

Because most medical problems involve medical, school, and other agencies, there are many practical issues that must be addressed. One issue is definitions. There are over 80 different definitions of learning disabilities used in schools in the United States (Ysseldyke, Algozzine, & Thurlow, 1992). DSM-IV and International Classification of Diseases-9 (ICD-9) also have different definitions of learning disabilities. Medical diagnoses and special education eligibility are often related constructs, but are not interchangeable. Different agencies have different methods of billing. The child's family's type and level of medical insurance is important information. Because Medicaid rations the number of hours of service paid for within certain service delivery categories, careful use of Medicaid funding is important. Finally, internal accountability systems strongly affect the type of services that can be delivered. For example, in school districts where school psychologists are evaluated on the number of assessments, other agencies cannot expect extensive mental health services. Likewise, medical practices that are under financial pressures are unlikely to engage in activities that insurance companies or Medicaid will not reimburse (e.g., prevention). Acknowledging and spanning interagency differences are essential to providing interdisciplinary service delivery.

Child Transition

Children pass through many cognitive and emotional changes as the illness runs its course. Although there are some common issues to all children with medical problems, each medical problem tends to have some unique direct influences on cognition and emotions. An excellent resource is the book, *Health-Related Disorders in Children and Adolescents* (Phelps, 1998), that provides broad descriptions of the cognitive and emotional sequelae of a variety of medical problems. However, not to be overlooked are the indirect influences of medical problems on cognition and emotions.

Direct Influences

Some medical issues directly influence cognitive ability and personality. For example, a brain tumor may cause significant brain tissue loss resulting in deteriorating cognitive ability. Epilepsy, meningitis, later stages of HIV infection, anoxia due to cardiac arrest, some endocrine disorders, alcohol and drug use, and head injuries all may directly cause low cognitive ability and personality change. Moreover, some medications used to treat medical conditions may directly affect cognitive ability (Brown, 1999). Specifically, some, but not all, medications used to control seizure activity have been linked to reduced cognitive ability (Brown, 1999). The short- and long-term cognitive and affective side effects of many (perhaps most) medications have not been studied in detail with children. Although some medical issues may directly cause reduced cognitive ability and personality change, inferring a medical condition based on psychological test scores is inappropriate. Although there is much written about the direct effects of medical issues on cognitive, social, and behavioral functioning, most problems experienced by children with medical issues are due to indirect effects of illness and hospitalization. For example, simply being hospitalized and removed from the routine school setting can be a cause of academic and social problems that may have little to do with the illness or treatment.

Pain

Children with medical issues frequently complain of pain. Pain adversely affects concentration, increases fatigue, and may lead to depression and feelings of helplessness.

Although there is a dearth of quality research on malingering of pain, malingering is a factor in 10–40% of pain cases (Siegel & Smith, 1989). Vague descriptions of diffuse pain or descriptions of pain that do not fit the medical course may be learned behaviors. In other words, the consequences of pain may be positive (e.g., extra attention, pain-killing medications) and pain complaints may be learned. Like any learned behavior, determining the antecedents and consequences of pain complaints is an important step. In many cases, some level of pain is controlled operantly. By changing antecedents and consequences of pain complaints, the levels of the perception of pain can be reduced to a large degree. Integration of behavioral observations from several professionals, clinical interviews, knowledge of treatment and disease course, and instruments should help to reduce being fooled by a malingering child. In some circles, it may be thought cruel to consider that a child with cancer may be malingering. However, an overestimate of actual pain may change or delay the course of treatment or result in an excess of pain-reduction medication. Both may have a negative effect on the overall physical and psychological recovery.

Fatigue

Children with medical issues frequently experience physical and mental fatigue. In many cases, fatigue may also be a sign of malingering or lack of motivation. Consultation with medical personnel can help you to determine the level of physical and mental fatigue placed on the child by the illness or treatment.

Stress and Anxiety

Chronic medical issues often lead to dramatic changes in the life of children. Change of any type causes some stress or emotional distress in children. In the case of medical illness, fear of death, anticipation of painful medical procedures, isolation from peers, change in lifestyle, becoming different from peers, and disruption of normal development causes extreme stress and anxiety. Children and adolescents with medical issues are twice as likely to develop psychiatric disorders as their healthy peers (Katon, Berg, Robins, & Risse, 1986). School problems, adjustment disorders, somatic complaints of unknown origin, panic attacks, hyperactivity, noncompliance with medical treatment, social withdrawal, and peer conflict are common results of medical condition. Depression occurs in 10–30% of children with severe medical problems (Katon et al., 1986). Children experiencing depression co-occurring with medical conditions are at-risk for suicide attempts. The more life threatening the illness, the more likely depression and other psychiatric problems will occur (Katon et al., 1986). Incidence of psychiatric disorders increases when the medical problems involve the central nervous system. The relationship between medical issues and anxiety are not well understood. Family support appears to be a mitigating factor in the development of high levels of anxiety (Katon et al., 1986).

Motivation

Children with medical issues frequently are passive, withdrawn, inattentive, and fail to initiate responses (Lynch, Lewis, & Murphy, 1993). Many clinicians also report that medically involved children are uncooperative, verbally aggressive, and defiant. Lack of motivation is an extremely common complaint among psychologists and teachers working with this population. For most children, this is a phase to be worked through. When children are experiencing life threatening illness, pain, or fear of death, getting an "A" on Friday's spelling test may not be he highest priority. However, focusing on the normality of life and encouraging success in academic and social areas can aid in recovery and assist in helping children to envision and achieve a future.

Quality of Life

Assessment of quality of life is becoming increasingly important as the survival rates associated with chronic diseases increase. Quality of life is a multidimensional construct relating to a child's functioning associated with illness or treatment (Spieth & Harris, 1996). The four basic domains are disease state and physical symptoms, psychological functioning, functional status, and social functioning. Instruments that are used to assess quality of life are either self-report, physician report, or parent informant measures (Spieth & Harris, 1996). Quality of life appears to be an important construct for improving the medical and psychological treatment of children and adolescents, yet assessment instruments of poor psychometric quality hinder the formal assessment of this potentially important construct.

Treatment Adherence

Adherence to medical treatment is one of the challenges that physicians and nurses face. About half of all patients do not adhere to treatment regimens (Burrell & Levy, 1985). This number is higher for children and for persons with chronic illnesses. Even such important treatments such as insulin injection for diabetes (48% compliance) and antiasthmatic treatment (46% compliance) are not often followed (Burrell & Levy, 1985). Psychotropic medications are estimated to have a 35% rate of compliance to treatment.

Approximately 10% of hospital admissions can be traced to failure to use medications properly (Burrell & Levy, 1985). Although there are many methods for assessing adherence such as counting pills in a prescription, biochemical analysis of blood or urine, and physician opinions, the best and simplest method is to ask the patient. When a question is phrased, "Most people have trouble remembering to take their medication. Do you remember to take yours?" most children will answer honestly. Those who admit to having trouble taking their medications are also those who will best benefit from a behavioral adherence-enhancement strategy.

Family Transition Issues

Families with children who have medical issues experience severe stress on the family system. Grief and adjustment issues are two commonly experienced family concerns. Whenever a child is diagnosed with a medical problem, is hospitalized, or is placed on a treatment regimen, there is disruption in family life. In some cases, there is only inconvenience. In cases where a child dies or has a life-threatening medical problem, families are disrupted forever. Working through guilt, fear, and other intense emotions is often necessary for families to continue as a functional unit.

Intervention plans for children with medical issues who have siblings need to address sibling issues. Even young siblings should be included as an important resource in intervention plans. Such an approach provides additional family support to the child with medical issues and educates and empowers the sibling during this frightening and difficult time.

Many medical and educational professions do not appreciate economic stressors on families. Many families have inadequate health insurance. The result is that families often lose their savings, acquire debt, experience the stress of working with collection agencies, and borrowing money from relatives. Financial hardships are a major cause of marital difficulties.

Marital difficulties and divorce are more common in parents of children with chronic medical issues than the general population (Walker, Johnson, Manion, & Cloutier, 1996). Intervention at the level of parent counseling, financial counseling, and guidance through adjustment difficulties has the potential to be a valuable service that reduces risk factors for vulnerable children. Divorce is an additional risk factor for children with medical issues.

School Transition Issues

Teachers and school personnel are rarely prepared for the arrival of a student with medical issues. Medical conditions in children can create fear and avoidance reactions in many teachers that interfere with the instructional relationship. School personnel tend to either overestimate or underestimate the direct effects of the medical issues on children's school performance. Either every social, academic, or behavior problem is attributed to the medical issue or no social, academic, or behavior problem is attributed to the medical issue. In many cases, the medical issue has no functional bearing on children's school functioning. Education of school personnel on the educational sequelae of the specific medical issue and quality assessment of each child's educational needs are major factors in addressing the needs of school personnel.

BEST PRACTICES

School psychologists providing comprehensive service delivery to children with chronic medical problems take on a variety of roles. The training, ability, and willingness to engage in each of these roles and integrate these roles into a cohesive service delivery model define best practices.

Parent Training

When meeting with caregivers, make them aware of the issues that tend to arise with certain medical conditions in school settings. A common problem is that parents stop setting appropriate limits on the child's behavior. Failure to set limits is a frequent issue in vulnerable child syndrome (Katon et al., 1986). A related problem is that families tend to identify a sibling as the problem child who receives the brunt of negative interactions. Families need to be informed of common issues regarding major life changes families undergo when a member of the system has a medical issue. Families often want to know the cognitive and academic prognosis for children with medical issues. In these cases, school psychologists need to recognize the limits of knowledge on long-term effects of many illness and treatments. In addition, school psychologists must be careful not to place limits on a child's future educational achievement. School psychologists also provide a valuable service when they identify for families the types of educational accommodations and support (e.g., special education eligibility and services, legal rights, community agencies, homebound services) that are available for their child.

Compile a list or lists or, if possible, create a notebook of resources in your community as well as those in surrounding communities. These resources include specific professionals, agencies, organizations, parent support groups, and individuals who can address some of the child and family transition issues that are outside the scope of the school psychology service field. Be inclusive and creative when compiling lists, families may need different types of information (e.g., from hospice to respite care to clergy to credit counselors). Do not duplicate work that other agencies have already completed. Ask for existing resource lists from hospitals and other service agencies. Sharing knowledge with parents and among agencies is the key ingredient in interdisciplinary service delivery for children with medical issues.

Child Advocacy

Despite what a school psychologist learns about a child's medical condition, it is important to remember to treat the child and not the disease. As noted previously, automatically attributing behavior or learning problems to the medical issues is inappropriate. Knowledge is power. Children with medical issues often have little power. Therefore, children require as much knowledge about their medical issues and treatment as is available. When possible, allow children to make as many decisions about their health and educational care as is developmentally and medically appropriate. Often significant adults attempt to guard the children with medical issues by withholding information or not discussing the medical condition. Parents must be advised that this is rarely a productive course of action. Children know of the seriousness or level of complexity of their health status simply by their experiences (e.g., frequency of medical visits, changes in surrounding adults' behaviors). School psychologists should also address and highlight for others that non-cognitive issues, such as the fatigue, pain, weakness, and emotional toll related to the disease and not the disease itself could be at the root of academic problems and could be the focus of interventions. School personnel should also seek to make the school life of children with medical issues as normal as possible. For example, if there is an established classroom management program in the child's school then the same consequences and rewards would be applied to children with medical issues, if at all possible.

Assessment

Assessment for diagnosis or eligibility for a program usually requires a psychometric approach to assessment. Nationally norm-referenced standardized tests of intelligence, academic achievement, psychosocial functioning, and adaptive behavior are most appropriate for these goals. If the goal of assessment is to aid in developing an intervention or rehabilitation plan, then measures of current functional skills are required. Adaptive behavior scales, direct observations, and curriculum-based assessment are some of the measures used. Nationally norm-referenced tests are usually not effective for intervention development. An exception is that some diagnostic tests provide task analysis of academic skills. These tests allow examiners to pinpoint exact subskills that are in need of intervention. Without carefully developed hypotheses, the hypothesis- testing model of effective and efficient assessment cannot take place.

Assess Pre-Morbid Functioning

If the goal of assessment is to determine how much ability and skill was lost during the period of medical involvement, then the place to begin is to determine ability and skill before the injury. Hearing a teacher complain that a child's illness or treatment has caused poor reading performance may be reason for alarm. In many cases, children's reading was also poor before the onset of illness. Unless there is a previous psychological report, the determination of pre-morbid skills demands some detective work. A good place to start is an examination of the child's school records. Although teacher-assigned grades tend to be an unreliable source of information, they can provide some useful general data. For example: Was the child performing in a satisfactory manner? Are there specific areas of academic weakness? Were there any problems with deportment, citizenship, or behavior?

Any notes concerning detentions, teacher referrals for special education, referrals to the principal's office, or referrals to the psychologist or counselor should be noted. The most useful aspect of student records is group achievement test scores. Group test scores tend to be reliable, yet quite general. These norm-referenced test scores provide a solid estimate of reading, mathematics, and language skills compared to age peers. Interviewing the child's teacher from before the injury is the next step. How was the child's academic performance compared to classmates? Behavior compared to classmates? How was language development compared to classmates? Any unusual behaviors? And so on. If possible, any work samples, systematic direct observations, or curriculum-based measurement data that the child completed before the illness may be helpful to compare to post-onset of illness work. Parents may also have work samples from previous schooling. Finally, administer a teacher report form of an adaptive behavior checklist to teachers who knew the children before the onset of the medical problem. The teacher should respond based on behaviors presented in class before the injury. Interviewing parents and professionals, who know the child after the injury, may result in biased responses. In this fashion, some estimate of pre-morbid skills can be gleaned.

Assess Trends Over Time

During the course of an illness or treatment, abilities and test performance may change. Repeated testing with intelligence or nationally norm-referenced academic achievement tests will result in practice effects. Practice effects are often significant (ranging from 0.3 to 1.0 standard deviations). As a result repeated testing will confound practice effects with true improvement over time. Direct observation, curriculum-based assessment, and curriculum-based measurement may provide more information for tracking improvement over time. Brief, daily assessments of behavior or academic ability can be plotted on a graph to demonstrate improvement and regression in ability. Each probe or observation is not an especially reliable measure. Yet, these behavioral data effectively assess trends over time and are excellent supplements to standardized, norm-referenced measures. Effective integration of these two types of assessment provides experienced clinicians with assessment information valuable for diagnosis, developing and modifying interventions, and evaluating rehabilitation programs.

Assess Environment

The assessment of children with medical issues often focuses on the obvious medical problems and their psychological and educational sequelae. However, the assessment of the environment is an often forgotten aspect of good assessment. Through direct observations and interviews, the examiner needs to understand antecedents, consequences, and discriminant stimuli of behaviors. Parents, hospital workers, and teachers frequently treat ill children differently than they do healthy peers. As a result, behavior problems, academic difficulties, and lowered cognitive abilities can occur. Even in the case where a medical issue or treatment directly causes brain damage, a stimulating structured environment can aid in effective rehabilitation of impaired functions.

Service Coordination

There is a tendency for a variety of agencies and professionals to provide a wide array of services to a child with chronic medical problems. However, unless these services are coordinated and communication is effective, there is a risk of redundant and ineffective services delivery.

The first matter is establishing a communication system between the three eco-systems of a child's life, home, school, and medical agency (Shields, 1995). One method of establishing such a communication system would be to appoint a medical or transition liaison (Stuart & Goodsilt, 1996). Each school should have a standing medical liaison. Although there are advantages, the liaison does not necessarily have to be the school nurse. The liaison must be an employee of the school district (as opposed to a volunteer), be available daily to the school and medical professionals, and have knowledge of how to work with medical professionals. The liaison needs to have knowledge of medical technology, hospital policies and culture, as well as educational and community resources (Stuart & Goodsilt, 1996). The role of the medical liaison is to serve as the clearinghouse for relevant information about educational concerns for each child and the medical issues. The medical liaison also serves as a vehicle for assisting medical personnel in monitoring the health issues within the framework of the school. The medical liaison keeps communication and correspondence logs. The medical liaison helps to link the medical system, school system, and home system into an integrated treatment unit.

The liaison is involved in a second matter of service delivery. This involves deciding, or advising administrators, as to which professionals need to be involved in service delivery to children with medical issues. At this level, who needs to be involved depends on the questions regarding the child with medical issues. Within the school district these questions are issues of eligibility for special education services, accommodations in the classroom, and the provision of school-based educational and mental health services. The questions arise from three possible scenarios. The first scenario is that there is a continued concern about the child regarding preexisting conditions (e.g., behaviors, academic problems) that are not related to the health issue. A second scenario is that academic problems have been acquired because of the medical condition or treatment. The third scenario is that the medical issue has exacerbated a preexisting condition. Each of these scenarios and their related questions require the establishment of which professionals need to be involved and at what intensity. For example, if the issue is a preexisting condition that has been exacerbated by a medical issue, then the persons who addressed the condition in the past and anyone who could provide information about that condition should be involved.

Counseling

Prevention and treatment of mental health issues is a fundamental component of service delivery to children with chronic health issues. Individual, group, and family counseling can have an ameliorative effect on the child and family transition issues experienced by nearly all children with chronic health problems. School psychologists are in prime positions to provide behavioral consultation to teachers and parent training of behavior management techniques (Power et al., 1998). Prevention programs such as anger management, social skills training, conflict resolution, and diversity training programs can be effective in altering the school milieu to creating a better environment for children with chronic medical issues.

Program Development

Program development and service delivery for children with chronic medical issues has received a great deal of attention in recent years. School-based, school-linked, and clinic-based services have all been described in detail (Dryfoos, 1994; Reeder et al., 1997; Shaw et al., 1995). Each of these models of service delivery requires a great deal of networking between school, health care providers, and the community. Often lobbying and education of school administrators, parent representatives, and community leaders is a major role for psychologists. More than one school-based or school-linked clinic proposal has failed to get off the ground owing to unfounded community fears that the clinic will distribute contraceptives or information about pregnancy termination. Community input and information are critical to provision of health services affiliated with schools funded with public moneys. The development of any program requires funding. Although some school-based and school-linked programs are funded exclusively with public funds, most have foundation support (e.g., Robert Wood Johnson Foundation). Therefore, nearly all school-based and school-linked programs have an individual dedicated to writing and maintaining grants and Medicaid compliance. Without all of these political and fiscal efforts, few programs for children with chronic illness are realized.

Program Evaluation

School psychologists may be the only professionals working with children with chronic medical problems who have research training and experience. Although basic and clinical research may be appropriate in some settings, the research skills of the school psychologists can best be used to evaluate the effectiveness of programs. Often educational, therapy, or rehabilitation programs are initiated because they "make sense," or because the programs are available, or because "we have always done it this way." Rarely are the efficacy, efficiency, and value of these programs evaluated. The same concerns apply to evaluating the efficacy of medical therapies such as stimulant medications for Attention Deficit Hyperactivity Disorder and other pharmacological treatments. Although summative evaluation may be useful for directing programs in future cases, continuous formative evaluation is necessary for making decisions to continue or modify programs.

SUMMARY

Increasingly, school psychologists are addressing the needs of children with chronic medical issues. Some school psychology training programs are offering specializations in pediatric school psychology. The four major journals in school psychology (i.e., *School Psychology Review*, *Journal of School Psychology*, *School Psychology Quarterly*, and *Psychology in the Schools*) have all published numerous papers on service delivery to children with chronic medical issues. School psychology is responding to the need for service delivery to this population.

However, working with children with chronic medical issues is a complex process because this is not a heterogeneous population. In addition, working with this population presents many novel challenges and new roles for schools psychologists. By addressing the major systemic and clinical challenges presented by children with chronic medication problems, new roles and functions can be developed to best meet the needs of these children.

REFERENCES

Brown, R. T. (Ed.). (1999). *Cognitive aspects of chronic illness in children.* New York: Guilford.

Brown, R. T., & DuPaul, G. (1999). Introduction to the mini-series: Promoting school success in children with chronic medical conditions. *School Psychology Review, 28,* 175–181.

Burrell, C. D., & Levy, R. A. (1985). Therapeutic consequences of noncompliance. In *Improving medication compliance: Proceedings of a symposium.* Reston, VA: National Pharmaceutical Council.

Conoley, J. C., & Conoley, C. W. (1991). Collaboration for child adjustment: Issues for school and clinic based child psychologists. *Journal of Consulting and Clinical Psychology, 59,* 821–829.

Drotar, D. (1993). Influences on collaborative activities among psychologists and pediatricians: Implications for practice, training, and research. *Journal of Pediatric Psychology, 18,* 159–172.

Drotar, D. (1995). *Consulting with pediatricians.* New York: Plenum.

Drotar, D. (1998). Training students for careers in medical settings: A graduate program in pediatric psychology. *Professional psychology: Research and Practice, 29,* 402–404.

Dryfoos, J. (1994). *Full service schools.* San Francisco: Jossey-Bass.

Frank, R. G., Thayer, J. F., Hagglund, K. J., Vieth, A. Z., Schopp, L. H., Beck, N. C., Kashani, J. H., Goldstein, D. E., Cassidy, J. T., Clay, D. L., Chaney, J. M., Hewett, J. E., Johnson, J. C. (1998). Trajectories of adaptation in pediatric chronic illness: The importance of the individual. *Journal of Consulting & Clinical Psychology, 66,* 521–532.

Kaplan, R. M. (2000). Two pathways to prevention. *American Psychologist, 55,* 382–396.

Katon, W., Berg, A., Robins, A., & Risse, S. (1986). Depression: Pattern of medical utilization and somatization in primary care. In S. McHugh & T. M. Vallis (Eds.), *Illness behavior: A multidisciplinary model* (pp. 355–364). New York: Plenum.

Lynch, E., Lewis, R., & Murphy, D. (1993). Educational service for children with chronic illnesses: Perspectives of educators and families. *Exceptional Children, 59,* 210–220.

Miller, T., & Swartz, L. (1990). Clinical psychology in general hospital settings: Issues in interpersonal relationships. *Professional Psychology: Research and Practice, 21,* 48–53.

Phelps, L. (Ed.). (1998). *Health-related disorders in children and adolescents.* Washington, DC: American Psychological Association.

Power, T. J., DuPaul, G. J., Shapiro, E. S., & Parrish, J. M. (1998). Role of the school-based professional in health-related services. In L. Phelps (Ed.), *Health-related disorders in children and adolescents* (pp. 15–26). Washington, DC: American Psychological Association.

Power, T. J., Heathfield, L. T., McGoey, K. E., & Blum, N. J. (1999). Managing and preventing chronic health problems in children and youth: School psychology's expanding role. *School Psychology Review, 28,* 40–48.

Purvis, P., & Whalen, R. J. (1992). Collaborative planning between pediatricians and special educators. *Pediatric Clinics of North America, 39,* 451–469.

Reeder, G. D., Maccow, G. C., Shaw, S. R., Swerdlik, M. E., Horton, C. B., & Foster, P. (1997). School psychologists and full-service schools: Partnerships with medical, mental health, and social services. *School Psychology Review, 26,* 603–621.

Resnick, R. J., & Kruczek, T. (1996). Pediatric consultation: New concepts in training. *Professional Psychology: Research & Practice, 27,* 194–197.

Shaw, S. R., Kelly, D. P., Joost, J. C., & Parker-Fisher, S. J. (1995). School-linked health services: A renewed call for collaboration between school psychologists and medical professionals. *Psychology in the Schools, 32,* 190–201.

Shields, J. (1995). The eco-triadic model of educational consultation for students with cancer. *Education and Treatment of Children, 18,* 184–200.

Siegel, L. J., & Smith, K. E. (1989). Children's strategies for coping with pain. *Pediatrician, 16,* 110–118.

Spieth, L. E., & Harris, C. V. (1996). Assessment of health-related quality of life in children and adolescents: An integrative review. *Journal of Pediatric Psychology, 21,* 175–193.

Stuart, J. L., & Goodsilt, J. L. (1996). From hospital to school: How a transition liaison can help. *Teaching Exceptional Children, 28,* 58–62.

Talley, R. C., & Short, R. J. (1995). *School health: Psychology's role. A report to the nation.* Washington, DC: American Psychological Association.

Tarnowski, K. J., & Brown, R. T. (1995). Psychological aspects of pediatric disorders. In M. Hersen & R. T. Ammerman (Eds.), *Advanced abnormal child psychology* (pp. 393–410). Hillsdale, NJ: Erlbaum.

Walker, J. G., Johnson, S., Manion, I., & Cloutier, P. (1996). Emotionally focused marital intervention for couples with chronically ill children. *Journal of Consulting and Clinical Psychology, 64,* 1029–1036.

Ysseldyke, J. E., Algozzine, B., & Thurlow, M. L. (1992). *Critical issues in special education.* Boston: Houghton Mifflin.

ANNOTATED BIBLIOGRAPHY

Brown, R. T. (Ed.). (1999). *Cognitive aspects of chronic illness in children.* New York: Guilford.
This book is an important review of research on the effects of illness and treatments on children with cognitive and behavioral functioning. Chapters on training and collaborative intervention planning are outstanding.

Camic, P. M., & Knight, S. J. (Eds.). (1998). *Clinical handbook of health psychology: A practical guide to effective interventions.* Seattle, WA: Hogrefe & Huber.
This volume is more of a global guide to the field of pediatric psychology as compared to the disease–driven model of the Phelps book. An excellent overview of pediatric psychology.

Phelps, L. (Ed.). (1998). *Health-related disorders in children and adolescents.* Washington, DC: American Psychological Association.
An excellent compilation of rare and common disorders. Each chapter is a four- to six-page summary of a medical disorder and the educational and psychological sequelae of each disorder. This book is the first place to turn when faced with a child with a medical condition, especially a low incidence disorder. Each chapter has an outstanding collection of references and resources.

Rosensky, R. H., Sweet, J. J., & Tovian, S. M. (1997). *Psychological assessment in medical settings.* New York: Plenum.
This book presents assessment approaches for the psychologist who works in medical settings. It provides guidance on how psychologists can be effective and valued members of health care teams. Information is also presented that can aid psychologists in balancing the needs of patients with that of the needs of a health care setting. Throughout the book case studies are presented to illustrate the assessment-diagnostic and critical thinking philosophy proposed by the authors.

93 Best Assessment and Intervention Practices With Second Language Learners

Alicia Paredes Scribner
Southwest Texas State University

OVERVIEW

Since Richard Figueroa's chapter in *Best Practices II* (Figueroa, 1990), much has been written about the difficulties of assessing second language learners. Although there remains great concern about using norm-referenced tests on second language learners, school psychologists continue to "adapt" these instruments by using procedures they consider non-biased (e.g., testing the limits, using interpreters, using nonverbal instruments). These procedures can be insufficient in assisting the school psychologist in making informed recommendations for appropriate interventions. Taken alone, they, in fact, may underestimate the level of native language abilities of the student in question, as well as the student's overall potential to achieve in an English language curriculum.

Who are these second language learners and what educational services are available to them? Second language learners are students from linguistically and culturally diverse backgrounds whose native language is not English, and who have limited English proficiency (LEP). They cut across all grades in public education and enter the American educational system with different levels of academic achievement in their native language and in English. Within a given classroom, the continuum of linguistic competence may vary from monolingual in the first language to some degree of bilingualism. Recent data (Macias, 1998) indicate school enrollment of second language learners more than doubled in the decade between 1987 and 1997, from 1,553,918 to 3,452,073, and continues to grow exponentially into this new millennium. Already nearly half of the nation's school districts enroll second language learners who speak more than 100 languages. While students from Spanish-speaking countries remain the largest group, the growing number of students from Asian Pacific populations has become the next largest group of second language learners (U.S. Immigration and Naturalization Service, 1995). By the year 2026, second language learners from a myriad of different cultures and ethnic groups in our global society are expected to make up nearly a quarter of our student body (Garcia, 1999).

In contrast to the unprecedented growth in the number of second language learners is the limited number of teachers adequately trained to teach those students. Even in some mid-size school districts, fewer than one in five teachers who currently serve second language learners are certified to teach LEP students (Paredes Scribner, 1999). Nearly one-third of LEP students receive no tailored assistance in understanding what is being taught. This means that these students receive limited instruction in how to speak English or in understanding content area subjects. Paralleling the teacher shortage for LEP students is the shortage in related services, such as school psychology. The combined effect of these shortages exacerbates the academic vulnerability of LEP students. Lack of appropriately trained and culturally sensitive assessment personnel, in particular, leads to psycho-educational practices that reinforce deficit assumptions for minority student performance.

Non-biased assessment for second language learners begins by examining the quality of education these students receive. We need to understand how best to develop linguistic competence in LEP students and shift our focus to more consultation and appropriate interventions in regular education. This chapter will present those interventions and assessment practices known to be effective with second language learners. In the Basic Considerations section, the areas in which school psychologists should become more knowledgeable are addressed. These areas include (a) achieving English language proficiency, (b) issues of acculturation that affect achievement, (c) advocacy-oriented assessment practices that reflect advances in the field of psycho-educational evaluation, and (d) instructional interventions and modifications. In the Best Practices section, recommendations are made for the desired competencies to be developed by school psychologists working with second language learners.

BASIC CONSIDERATIONS

Achieving English Language Proficiency

The literature on school reform and academic achievement is replete with examples of how students learn best. We know that learning takes place when teachers set high expectations for their students, when new learning theories guide instruction, when teaching and learning are collaborative, and when there is ample opportunity for listening, speaking, reading, and writing (Garcia, 1999; Paredes Scribner, 1999). Low expectations, on the other hand, perpetuate narrow curricula, which prevent students from developing the aptitudes needed to succeed in academic endeavors. What we have learned about enhancing academic achievement for the general population should also extend to second language learners.

As students become exposed to English as a second language, they first develop conversational skills in the new language where communication is largely mediated by the environmental context in which they find themselves. At this level of proficiency, students appear to be more linguistically competent than they really are because of the context-embedded nature of communicative interactions. Cummins (1984) has refined the concept of language proficiency by distinguishing between "surface level proficiency" and "conceptual-linguistic proficiency" (p. 136). He operationalized this distinction by describing the communicative skills first acquired when learning a new language as basic interpersonal communication skills (BICS), and the more involved cognitive/academic language proficiency skills (CALP), as the ability to manipulate language in decontextualized academic situations. This distinction was also analyzed by Shuy (1978) when he contrasted the quantifiable aspects of formal language (e.g., pronunciation, basic vocabulary, grammar) with the more pragmatic aspects of language proficiency (e.g., semantic and functional aspects of language).

Depending on the programs available in the schools, second language learners may be offered some form of bilingual curriculum, English as a second language (ESL) instruction, transitional bilingual education, and/or immersion programs. Seventy-five percent of second language learners are Spanish-speaking. Those in need of English instruction are primarily served by transitional bilingual programs, which offer a transition from early-grade Spanish instruction to later-grade English-only instruction (Garcia, 1999). For the remainder of second language learners receiving little to no instruction in their native languages, ESL or immersion programs prevail. The latter two programs depend largely on the use of English as the primary mode of instruction and do not require teaching personnel who speak the native language of the students. These programs are usually offered in classrooms in which there are heterogeneous non-English language groups.

Understanding levels of English proficiency and linguistic skills in contextualized and decontextualized settings is critical for the school psychologist working with second language learners. When teachers refer second language learners for psycho-educational evaluations, the school psychologist should be sufficiently knowledgeable about second language acquisition to be able to differentiate the student's level of proficiency in English. When the teacher states that the student knows sufficient English to be tested by a monolingual psychologist, the school psychologist will want to know if the student's proficiency level is surface-level proficiency or conceptual-linguistic proficiency. The school psychologist must ask the right questions to bring relevant, current information for a valid referral. Some questions to consider might include:

1. How long has the family resided in the United States?

2. Does the family live within or identify with the same cultural/linguistic community?

3. What language is used by various members of the family?

4. How well does the family communicate across generations?

5. What is the preferred language of the child at home? In school? With peers?

6. What language programs have been offered to the child? For how long?

Informal assessment procedures (story telling-retelling, interviews using open-ended questioning techniques) will assist the examiner to establish if the student is able to draw inferences, make evaluations, or analyze information with native-like fluency.

Acculturation

Level of acculturation also can impact the assessment process for second language learners. Acculturation refers to the changes that occur as a result of continuous contact between two distinct cultures (Berry, Trimble, & Olmedo, 1986). Educational attainment is a very important aspect of culture. The greater the difference in educational attainment between groups, the greater the cultural differences. Culture is both explicit and implicit. At the explicit level, culture is manifested in overt, customary patterns of behavior and in thinking and feeling patterns. At the implicit level, culture is manifested in covert, unspoken, and mainly unconscious values and assumptions (Gopaul-McNicol & Thomas-Presswood, 1998). Although we talk about cultural differences in assessment of second language learners, there remains a reluctance to incorporate the role of culture in the assessment process, probably as a result of cost factors. It takes longer and costs more to conduct a fair and non-biased assessment of LEP students involving two languages.

Berry, Kim, Power, Young, and Bujaki (1989) developed a model of acculturation that sets forth four modes of acculturation. *Assimilation,* occurs when ethnic groups choose to identify solely with the dominant society. *Integration* occurs when ethnic groups successfully involve themselves with the dominant culture and retain their traditional culture. They are equally comfortable in both cultures. *Separation* occurs when the ethnic group has little or no interaction with the dominant culture. The last, *marginality,* occurs when the ethnic group experiences a loss of its own culture or origin and simultaneously lacks involvement with the dominant society. Marginality creates anxiety so severe it often produces neurotic or deviate behaviors.

The extent to which new immigrants are acculturated into the new society depends in large part on (a) the importance new arrivals place on identifying or maintaining cultural characteristics of their ethnic groups and (b) the importance they attribute to maintaining positive relationships with the larger society and other ethnic groups (Phinney, Chavira, & Williamson, 1992). Depending on conditions of immigrant status and receptiveness by the mainstream culture, second language learners can experience acculturative stress, which is a normal reaction in the process of adaptation. Acculturative stress may manifest itself in learning difficulties as a result of adjustment problems caused by relocation, feelings of isolation or anonymity, and loss of friendships or family relationships left behind, which result in a discontinuity of everything familiar to the individual. Some families experience a conflict of values and role reversals when the more acculturated children assume financial and social responsibilities for the non-English–speaking parents. This leads to problems that range from extreme shyness to acting-out behaviors or more serious psychological problems. Individuals who migrate when in their teens experience higher levels of acculturative stress than those who migrate at a younger age.

Another very important factor when considering cultural differences is the complexity of culture. There can be many different cultures represented within a race or ethnic group, as well as many races and ethnic groups represented within any given culture (Frisby, 1998). We continue to make broad generalizations about "Hispanics," "Native Americans" or "Asians" when these groups comprise many subgroups and subcultures that are very different from one another. Approximately two-thirds of Hispanics are Mexican Americans, concentrated in the southwest and midwest, and these are followed by Puerto Ricans, who are mostly in the northeast, and finally

Central and South Americans and Cubans, found throughout the country (Gopaul-McNichol & Thomas-Presswood, 1998). Most recently, large numbers of Middle Easterners and Eastern Europeans have arrived as a result of political conflicts in their part of the world.

Diversity among these groups is wide-ranging. They may be influenced by other cultures or neighboring countries. Hispanics, for example, may be influenced by Spanish, African, and indigenous cultures. They are diverse in terms of language, education, length of time in the United States, countries of origin, and traditions. First- and second-generation immigrants are different from new immigrant groups. For example, Mexican American students born in the United States may have little in common with newer immigrant students from Mexico.

Most practitioners recognize the dilemma of testing second language learners with instruments that may yield results affected by culture or language difference. Sensitive practitioners will strive to create conditions that will enhance student performance. They must recognize that the examinee possesses certain attributes that cannot be generalized among all students from broadly conceived cultural identifications, such as Hispanic, Asian, Native American, or other ethnic minorities. Then, they must seek an understanding of the acculturative stress the examinee may be experiencing. Finally, they must establish rapport with the examinee, as well as ensure that the examinee has sufficient cognitive/academic proficiency in English so that test scores will be valid. If there is a suspicion that cultural characteristics affect the validity of test scores, then cautious practitioners will avoid basing important decisions on incomplete information and note such concerns in their reports.

Although it is clear that culture and cultural differences are important factors to consider in testing second language learners, it is difficult for practitioners to know what path to follow to comply with ethical and professional standards. The National Association of School Psychologists Ethical Standards encourage members to consider all information in the context of the student's socio-cultural background and the setting in which the student is functioning (National Association of School Psychologists, 2000). The Individuals with Disabilities Education Act (IDEA 1997) and the American Psychological Association (1993) also address issues of language and culture in the provision of psychological services. Yet, there are too many issues to consider and too many ways to approach changing attitudes. It is unrealistic to believe that practitioners will accomplish a new mindset when working with second language learners by simply reading a book chapter. However, the acquisition of incremental knowledge about acculturation, and the opportunity to work collaboratively in teams, will help the school psychologist gain greater sensitivity and become a better advocate for second language learners.

Advocacy-Oriented Assessment

Testing has become an integral part of our educational system. We have discovered much about how children learn, how learning deficiencies manifest themselves, and how testing results can guide instructional interventions. Schools are the largest consumers of testing instruments, and school psychologists, as the trained administrators of such instruments, have helped diagnose academic failures and solved many mysteries in the teaching-learning process. Tests are objective measures without which "we cannot calibrate an individual's level or rate of learning nor can we discover the reasons why the individual does not achieve" (Samuda, 2000, p. 2). Yet, as Samuda points out, these tests have fallen into disrepute when used with minority populations. Well-intentioned teachers, school psychologists, and administrators use testing results to aid in the sorting and labeling function, which results in overrepresentation of second language learners in special education programs. Tests have been known to have dire social and economic consequences for those students who are misdiagnosed and placed in minimal curricular programs (Samuda, 2000).

Although outside the scope of this chapter, the on-going controversy with large-scale district-wide assessments and the achievement levels of second language learners must be mentioned. Minorities as a whole perform less well than their non-minority peers in large-scale testing. Often, the results of large-scale testing present obstacles for minority students that (a) track them into reductionist curricula or (b) result in students dropping out of school (Miramontes, Nadeau, & Commins, 1997; Valencia & Guadarrama, 1996). In some states there are on-going efforts to include second language learners in district-wide assessments. If we are to improve second language student achievement, then these accountability systems must nurture effective practices and lead to effective instruction (Darling-Hammond and Archer, 1991).

Level of language proficiency is a critical factor in assessment of second language learners. When is a child whose native language is not English ready to be tested only in English? Figueroa (1989) contends that no one really knows because the technology of measuring language proficiency in the schools remains imprecise in assisting the school psychologist in differentiating between surface-level and conceptual-linguistic skills. The federal government has provided momentum to reform the entire assessment process. Several states are already advocating for less emphasis on psycho-educational assessment and greater availability of interventions in regular education. The groundwork for this reform stems from the work of Reuven Feuerstein, whose theory of cognitive modifiability supports a shift from a static to a dynamic process of assessing the learning potential of students (Jackson, Lewis, Feuerstein, & Samuda, 2000).

Feuerstein's theory of mediational processes appears to be very appropriate for second language learners. The elements in this theory encompass improvement of less effective cognitive functions, preparation for higher order learning through the establishment of prerequisite functioning, behavioral teaching of cognitive operations and content, provision of performance feedback, and the establishment of appropriate communication skills (Jackson et al., 2000). The student-teacher or student-assessor interactions help students make bridges to support their own learning, thereby making connections between cognitive skills and content materials. In addition, assessment reform can reverse the academic decline of second language learners by examining hidden strengths that traditional testing methods are not likely to discover. In order to achieve this goal, assessment of academic skills in the student's native language *must* be part of the process.

Current assessment procedures used with second language learners fail to accurately measure the student's linguistic competence in both the native language and in English. We must incorporate alternative assessment techniques such as systematic observation, mediated learning experiences, test-teach-test paradigms, and diagnostic teaching as interventions in order to focus more effectively on the process of learning, as opposed to the product of learning (Cummins, 1984; Figueroa, 1990; Garcia, 1999; Gopaul-McNicol & Thomas-Presswood, 1998; Miramontes et al., 1997; Paredes Scribner, 1999; Samuda, 2000).

Instructional Interventions

The current environment and profile of classrooms in the United States is far different than what it was 30 years ago; that is, that many of those teaching today went to school with classmates who were the same as they, a common-enough occurrence. In contrast, today's classrooms can be made up of students of radically different cultures with different native languages. Many school personnel are unprepared for the demands of an increasingly culturally diverse student population (Garcia, 1999). Additionally, in many areas of the country the teacher deficits are so high that classrooms are staffed by teachers holding emergency certificates, which means that questionably qualified teachers are often teaching the poor and minority students (Garcia, 1999).

Probably the most important consideration is the effectiveness of instruction for second language learners, because the areas mentioned earlier in this section are affected by classroom instruction. While some theorists claim that school failure can be explained by a "culture clash" between home and school, others submit unequivocally that lack of school success rests primarily on the failure of instructional personnel to implement effective teaching practices (Garcia, 1999). Consequently, these students, because of their poor English skills, risk being referred for special education services by undertrained and/or inexperienced teachers. Unfortunately, such referrals are made when the problems inherent in low achievement may be pedagogically induced. Owing to limited English language skills, second language learners are typically offered low level courses and English as a second language classes that emphasize segmented skills, worksheets, and little opportunity for oral language development (Paredes Scribner, 1995). When teachers and school psychologists absolve themselves of the responsibility for the education of these students, the chances of students realizing their full potential are further exacerbated.

In summary, a lack of attention to the various issues that affect the achievement of second language learners presents a contradiction between theory and practice. We know sound principles of learning and assessment. We also know that how these principles are implemented often results in faulty practices with second language learners. For example, owing to limited English skills, second language learners are considered to have minimal language or cognitive skills. Native-like fluency is expected with short periods of ESL instruction, with no reinforcement of English skills in the regular classroom. Students are exited from ESL classes typically after 2 years without further support (Miramontes et al., 1997). We know that it takes much longer to achieve fluency.

When we test these students, we do so in areas where they have had little or no academic experience. In essence, we may be penalizing them for their lack of quality instruction. Although we know that oral language development is the key to language and cognitive skills, we separate these students from fluent English speakers who could be effective peer language models (Miramontes et al., 1997). Moreover, many reading and writing interventions ignore the importance of oral language development. Many times these students are taught in their first language by teachers or paraprofessionals who speak the language, but may not read it or write it. Owing to the demands for bilingual personnel in teaching and assessment, these same paraprofessionals may operate with little to no supervision from certified staff (Garcia, 1999).

For assessment, we need to know details about a student's instructional program in order to make decisions about the student's performance and achievement. Owing to limited English proficiency, scores on placement tests or other types of group assessments lead to tracking of these students into reductionist curricula (Miramontes et al., 1997). We must collaborate with teachers and parents to ensure that students are not relegated to low-level or remedial classes, where they may remain indefinitely. Assessment practices should address the individual student's strengths and weaknesses, as well as the instructional requirements, to help all students achieve academically.

Not only are we guided by ethical and professional standards, but also by safeguards and guidelines provided by legislation that dictate how second language learners should be assessed. Court cases, statutes, and federal legislation have dictated that LEP students should be assessed in their native language (*Diana v. State Board of Education*, 1970; *Guadalupe Organization, Inc. v. Tempe Elementary School District*, 1978; IDEA 1997). Tests must evaluate what students are taught and assessment personnel must be appropriately trained to administer non-discriminatory assessments. Placement decisions should not be based on a single factor or a single score. Reevaluations should be timely and student progress should be monitored closely to ensure that instruction is relevant for the student's individual needs (Gopaul-McNicol & Thomas-Presswood, 1998).

To summarize, the school psychologist serving second language learners must

1. Be able to evaluate a student's level of language proficiency

2. Understand how acculturation may affect achievement

3. Perform appropriate and fair assessments

4. Recommend effective instructional procedures for this population of students

The following section further develops the areas of second language acquisition, acculturation, assessment, and instructional interventions by recommending added competencies school psychologists should develop in order to achieve best practices in the assessment of second language learners.

BEST PRACTICES WITH SECOND LANGUAGE LEARNERS

Research studies, investigations and publications that report successful programs for this population of students (Frisby, 1998; Garcia, 1999; Gopaul-McNicol & Thomas-Presswood, 1998; Miramontes et al., 1997; Reyes, Scribner, & Paredes Scribner, 1999; Samuda, 2000) suggest that assessment should be multi-varied and should be used to examine the extent of the student's knowledge and the manner in which the student learns. School psychologists working with second language learners require added competencies to address second language acquisition, acculturation, instructional interventions, and advocacy-oriented assessment. Both acculturation and instructional interventions must be considered *prior* to assessment. When formal assessment is indicated, the school psychologist should base assessment on the documentation generated by the pre-referral interventions, modifications, and the quality of instruction received by the student, using the added competencies listed below.

Competencies for Understanding Second Language Acquisition Programs

One of the major considerations in the assessment of second language learners is how the pre-referral process considers the student's levels of language proficiency, acculturation, and effectiveness of educational environment. Pre-referral intervention implies that all available and appropriate resources have been utilized before referrals for special education services are made. These interventions may include native language instruction in content areas, enhanced English language instruction, and collaborative teaching and learning strategies.

Nature of ESL Programs

When considering appropriate interventions, we must also understand the goals of language programs for second language learners. Many districts have "newcomer" programs designed for recent arrivals to the United States, who have limited proficiency in English, who are below grade level in language skills, who have limited formal education, or who have been in the country for fewer than 3 years (Genessee, 2000). The overall objective of newcomer programs is to help students acquire basic English language skills and to expose them to the culture of the American schools. Newcomer programs also use either sheltered instruction or bilingual instruction. Sheltered instruction refers to specially designed instruction in English that maximizes nonverbal instructional communication, combining content with English-language learning goals (Garcia, 1999).

Transitional bilingual instruction provides initial instruction in literacy and academic content in the native language at the same time that students are learning English through specialized English instruction in non-academic subjects. Transitional bilingual instruction attempts to achieve basic oral English proficiency within 2 years and transitioning to an all English classroom within 3 years. Second language immersion programs are designed for students who already have some English skills (Genessee, 2000). The objective for immersion programs is that students will develop English language skills while acquiring advanced levels of functional proficiency.

Successful programs for second language learners are those that offer support for an additional year or two after the student has been exited from bilingual education, monitoring the student's progress in the English language classroom (Paredes Scribner, 1999). Knowing the differences among the various language support programs and including these observations mean better and more reliable referral questions for non-discriminatory assessments.

Length of Time Required to Acquire Language Proficiency

Acquiring a first or second language is a developmental process. There is a natural progression from simple to complex language functions as children learn to communicate orally. Depending on age, second language learners may have acquired language functions in their native language, which will facilitate second language acquisition. It takes 2 years to acquire BICS and those skills required to function in context-embedded communicative interactions. Under the best of circumstances, it takes 5–7 years to develop full CALP in a second language (Cummins, 1984). CALP skills are those skills fundamental to thinking and learning that the instructional program must foster. In order to provide optimal language learning conditions for the second language learner, the classroom instruction should provide

1. Constant opportunity to use and practice the new language
2. Oral language development as an added dimension of instruction
3. Planned daily instruction to develop critical thinking skills in English
4. Balanced program components so that curriculum is integrated
5. Structured language learning for success in literacy skills

Second language proficiency requires clear, distinct, and meaningful contexts created during instructional time. Proficiency does not mean drilling vocabulary or grammatical structures, but instead means using language to engage students in active exploration and expression of ideas. It is incumbent on assessment personnel to become informed and knowledgeable regarding second language acquisition to be effective consultants to teachers and parents. Some important facts to remember when assessing students who are in the process of acquiring English as a second language follow:

1. It is typical for English skills (vocabulary, grammar, pronunciation, and comprehension) to be less well developed than those of their English-speaking peers.

2. There is a predictable sequence second language learners will follow, similar to younger children learning their first language (listening, speaking, reading, and writing skills).

3. Reduced opportunities to use the native language will result in a loss of competence in the first language.

4. Code-switching or switching back and forth between the two languages is common. The examiner should attend to the level of sophistication exhibited in the student's utterances.

5. Results of language assessments should reflect skills in both the native language and in English.

Competencies for Understanding the Acculturation Process

It is level of acculturation, rather than culture per se, that is likely to affect test performance. Acculturation is experiential background in the new culture and is developmental in nature. We cannot presume that children raised outside the U.S. mainstream culture have had the same experiences, learning opportunities, or exposure to the mainstream culture as those of their American-born peers. An individual's level of acculturation will affect performance; that is, the more familiar he or she is with the American culture, the better he or she is likely to perform in traditional norm-referenced tests. In the process of familiarizing oneself with the new culture and learning a second language, there are factors that enhance or impede the acculturation process and the acquisition of the second language.

Affective Factors

Second language learning can bring about feelings of inadequacy, threaten one's sense of self, and bring about other psychological factors such as culture shock and lack of motivation (Miramontes et al., 1997). Second language learners not only must learn academic content, but must also figure out a new system of language and communication. Negative experiences can affect the process of second language acquisition. Krashen (1982) has described these psychological factors as a type of "affective filter" that can facilitate or impede learner input. These psychological factors are affected positively if the school climate is "additive" or inclusive, or negatively if it is "subtractive" or exclusive. Students' attitudes are shaped by the circumstances they experience as newcomers to a host country.

Although the research on cognitive and perceptual styles is inconclusive, the relationship between culture and learning is worth mentioning in this context. Children come to school with some knowledge about language, how it works and how it is used, and learn higher-level cognitive and metalinguistic skills as they engage in socially meaningful activities. Children's development and learning are best understood as the interaction of linguistic, sociocultural, and cognitive factors. Recognizing that strict generalizations cannot be made, it has been observed that many Hispanic and Asian students tend to be field-dependent learners (Gopaul-McNichol & Thomas-Presswood, 1998). Field-dependent students tend to view things more globally, interact more cooperatively, and pay more attention to the social context in which they are framed.

Another area to consider under acculturation is cognitive processing. Cognitive processing refers to how individuals interpret and learn new information. Two cognitive processing styles have been identified in the literature: verbal/analytic processing (descriptive-analytic) and visual/holistic (inferential-categorical) (Gopaul-McNicol & Thomas-Presswood, 1998). The verbal/analytic learner prefers to split stimuli into discrete entities and to respond to them as separate units, while the visual/holistic learner derives meaning from the pattern of the whole. It is important to differentiate between the two learning styles because second language learners and other minority students typically are raised in environments where they are taught to be flexible and adaptable in their use of language. Information the school psychologist could share with the teacher(s) around these issues might increase a tolerance and an understanding of diverse cultural patterns of behavior. Furthermore, while the verbal-analytic learner is rewarded for individual competitiveness, second language learners and other minority students appear to learn best when allowed to work cooperatively (Gopaul-McNicol & Thomas-Presswood, 1998).

Additive Classroom Environments

The school psychologist can help identify factors over which the teacher can exert a positive impact on students. For example, organizing group size for instruction, instructional organization and strategies to enhance second language acquisition, and providing opportunities for language practice are a few strategies teachers can use to improve the instruction of second language learners. The concept of "cultural capital" (Miramontes et al., 1997) or the background of experience the student draws upon is another area educators can utilize. For healthy human development to occur, second language learners must experience opportunities to construct relationships between what they know and new learning. Ways to build on cultural capital are

1. Create a supportive school-wide climate
2. Create opportunities for student-directed instruction
3. Provide instructional strategies that enhance second language acquisition
4. Provide systematic student assessment
5. Develop collaborative teaching and learning practices
6. Provide on-going, relevant staff development

Competencies for Evaluating Educational Interventions

Successful school environments are characterized by open, friendly, and culturally inviting settings in which instructional arrangements allow students to interact with one another and use collaborative learning techniques. Rather than follow a strict curriculum, successful teachers align themselves by grade level and work together to develop thematic units to reinforce skills across the curriculum (Paredes Scribner, 1999). Other effective interventions with second language learners are enhanced language development and support in content areas, comprehension development, and cooperative learning. Team planning appears to be one of the most important interventions for second language learners. When same grade level teachers, or those working with the same group of students, plan instruction together, they share instructional procedures and strategies, as well as ensure that lesson plans cover and reinforce desired goals. By working and planning together, teachers not only minimize their workload but also develop a sense of community among themselves and their students. In contrast, individuals working alone tend to feel disconnected and unsupported (Miramontes et al., 1997).

Activities That Enhance Language Development

Oral language development is the foundation of literacy skills. There is an interrelatedness between language, thinking, values, and culture that is fostered by effective language development. Second language learners must be provided with the type of linguistic support that will facilitate comprehension for them to succeed in school. The following strengthen language development:

1. Adjusting language demands by presenting material in different modalities, using context clues, and relating instruction to the student's experiences
2. Incorporating principles of second language acquisition to increase student understanding
3. Applying principles of directed reading activities to content areas by pre-teaching concepts and new vocabulary

4. Presenting lessons in a consistent manner so that the student knows what is expected

5. Encouraging students to predict questions, analyze situations, solve problems, offer opinions, and draw conclusions with oral and/or written materials

6. Offering cooperative learning activities

7. Shifting focus of instruction from merely understanding ideas and concepts to the ability to communicate those ideas.

Competencies for Assessment of Second Language Learners

Assessment of second language learners requires, in part, the specialized competencies discussed in the previous sections. Ability to speak the examinee's language alone does not ensure a fair, accurate, and nondiscriminatory assessment. Since few programs in school psychology offer training in bilingual assessment, practitioners must enhance their skills in this area through professional development, in-service training, or self study. Awareness and skill development in the area of bilingual assessment must include (a) an understanding of how language and culture can affect test performance, (b) validity of methods and instruments used on second language learners, and (c) careful consideration of test results within the context of the student's language, level of acculturation, and experiential history. Although pre-referral documentation for any student should include the following recommendations, it is imperative that referrals for second language learners provide the following information:

1. Background and educational history

2. Assessment of literacy skills in the native language

3. Quality and type of native and/or English language instruction

4. Nature of instructional strategies/modifications

5. Duration and effectiveness strategies/modifications

6. Dynamic assessment interventions

7. Clinical observations

8. Other authentic assessment in the classroom

Working as Part of a Professional Team

Owing to the multi-varied aspects of the assessment of second language learners, no single professional can do the job adequately. It is best to approach the assessment and interventions for this population of students from a team perspective. Beginning at the pre-referral level, the school psychologist should work with the classroom teacher(s) and others to recommend appropriate steps in improving the achievement opportunities of the second language learner to rule out a learning disability. Since learning is a process of both dynamic and constructive development, the more mediated the learning experience, the better the information to build on for more learning growth (Garcia, 1999). At this level, the school psychologist and teacher(s) can enhance the active learning opportunities; that is, those meaningful activities that are constructive in nature. The school psychologist can assist the teacher(s) in analyzing the nature of student errors. It is important to differentiate between errors made normally in the process of second language acquisition and semantic or pragmatic errors in language that can be detected in the native language as well as English. To do this, the school psychologist can consult with the teacher(s), the speech/language therapist, and other relevant personnel.

Similarly, professionals can administer Curriculum-Based Assessment and/or other criterion-referenced measures to assess the student's instructional level. Based on this information, the team can determine what skills need to be taught or re-taught to the student to ensure mastery. Of utmost importance will be the need to support the development of critical thinking skills. Second language learners should be given ample opportunity to

1. Interact fully with the instructional content

2. Test and question new ideas

3. Learn to understand the perspective of others

4. Discriminate among ideas

5. Defend their own point of view

Good teaching strategies that develop critical thinking will lead to academic achievement. On the other hand, poor programs and poor educational experiences will bear poor results whether they are conducted in the native language, in English, or in both languages.

Working With Interpreters

Owing to the limited number of trained bilingual school assessment personnel who can perform adequate assessments in languages other than English, many school psychologists must rely on paraprofessionals to serve as interpreters to conduct assessments of second language learners. These paraprofessionals are often untrained for the role they are asked to fulfill, may lack adequate language proficiency in English or the native language, and may be unfamiliar with the assessment process (Figueroa, 1990; Paredes Scribner, 1999). As new instruments are developed that recommend the use of interpreters, we must ensure that the use of such paraprofessionals does indeed improve the assessment of second language learners. The following topics need to be addressed in training for interpreters (Langdon and Cheng, 1992; Paredes Scribner and Fuchs, 1998).

1. The interpreter may be able to serve as a cultural consultant to the assessment team. The interpreter could possibly report to the assessment team the student's native language linguistic skills and level of acculturation. Depending on the student's family's background, the interpreter could possibly assist the assessment team in establishing positive communication with the family, and advise the team on sensitive issues that may hinder communication with the family (e.g., methods of discipline, child-rearing practices). Finally, it may be relevant and helpful to the team if the interpreter can provide information regarding the educational system in the family's country of origin or cultural group.

2. The interpreter should become familiar with legal requirements of non-biased assessment. They should understand the concept of special education, support services, and the nature of learning difficulties so that they may relay this information to the parent(s). Training in due process and parents' rights will ensure that parents are fully informed in their native language.

3. The interpreter should understand and accurately use terminology specific to the assessment in the native language and in English. When translations of instructions are required, these translations should be developed ideally when there are at least three speakers of the same language group. Given the requirements of translation and the dialectical differences within languages, it is necessary to have a system of checks and balances among several speakers of the same language group to ensure the validity and reliability of the translation.

4. The interpreter's role in the assessment process is critical in providing improved services to students and families of second language learners. Since the interpreter may be the first contact with the family, training in interviewing skills is recommended. Understanding issues of confidentiality and neutrality are essential. It would be preferable for the school psychologist to use the same interpreter for a given language group. In all cases, there should be an opportunity to brief the interpreter about the relevant aspects of the case; there should be an opportunity for the school psychologist and the interpreter to discuss elements of the interactions during testing; there should be an opportunity for debriefing, during which the school psychologist and interpreter will discuss impressions, reactions, and any questions they may have.

5. If the interpreter is required to perform alternative assessment in the native language, then the interpreter will need to develop skills in administering such measures (e.g., obtaining natural language samples, conducting informal assessments of literacy skills in the native language). If school districts have to rely on the use of paraprofessionals to conduct more reliable and fair assessment of second language learners, then school psychologists must encourage their school districts to invest in the training of these paraprofessionals.

Choosing Appropriate Batteries

Regardless of test instruments used, the quality of any assessment will be a function of how well the examiner knows the instrument(s), their psychometric properties, and the skillful interpretation of results. To fully understand what intelligence test batteries measure, practitioners must know the theoretical background of tests. For second language learners, clinical evaluation of test performance must take into account not only issues of validity and reliability, but also construct relevance, cultural loading, and linguistic demands of the instrument (Flanagan, McGrew, & Ortiz, 2000). Cultural loading refers to the interaction between test content and the examinee's level of acculturation. Specifically, culture specific knowledge to which the examinee has not previously been exposed can be considered cultural loading (Flanagan et al., 2000).

Many tests presume the examinee to have a high level of linguistic competence (i.e., ability to comprehend instructions, formulate or verbalize responses, or otherwise manipulate linguistic demands in a question/answer mode). There is strong evidence that intelligence tests that have high linguistic demands are biased for second language learners (Cummins, 1984; Figueroa, 1990; Flanagan et al., 2000; Garcia, 1999; Paredes Scribner, 1999).

The evolution of psychometric theory seeks more complete frameworks to evaluate cognitive abilities. As we learn more about how best to measure these abilities, the analysis of fluid and crystallized intelligence (Gf-Gc theory) appears to be a more reliable method when assessing second language learners (Flanagan et al., 2000). The majority of test batteries in use today in academic settings do not adequately measure the complete range of broad abilities. The Gf-Gc theory has driven the development of recent test revisions and has introduced practitioners to the concept of cross-battery assessment and construct relevance. Individual subtests in a test battery frequently are confounded by tapping more than one ability/construct. The concept of construct relevance becomes more critical when testing second language learners because many of the constructs have imbedded linguistic demands and may require varying degrees of cultural experience. Flanagan et al. (2000) offer a comprehensive review of widely used test measures and Gf-Gc theory. Figueroa (1990) called for application of new theoretical methods, and cross-battery assessment appears to answer this call because it offers the practitioner critical information about construct relevance and requires insightful consideration of the instrument's relevancy for this population of students. If school psychologists intend to improve the service delivery system for second language learners, then their assessments must include quantitative and qualitative measures in order to explain the child's past and present educational and cultural experiences. Table 1 summarizes the components necessary in the assessment of second language learners.

SUMMARY

As in all evaluations, best practices in assessment and intervention for second language learners do not begin at the time the school psychologist selects a test bat-

Table 1. Necessary components in the assessment of second language learners

Assessment	*Components*
Pre-referral documentation	• Examination of instructional program • Dynamic assessment of skills/abilities
Language assessment	• Level of native language skills • Level of English language skills
Assessment of literacy skills	• Oral and written skills in native language • Oral and written skills in English
Formal assessment	• Use of reliable and valid psychometric measures • Use of non-psychometric measures
Instructional recommendations	• Type and nature of language support • Monitor classroom language demands • Use various modalities in teaching • Pre-teach concepts/new vocabulary • Teach critical thinking skills • Integrate curriculum components • Offer collaborative learning activities

tery. Rather, best practices call for the school psychologist's intervention much earlier in the process. Through consultation with teachers, parents, and others, the school psychologist can exert much needed attention to the areas highlighted in this chapter. If the second language learner, or any student for that matter, is not receiving appropriate instruction, then the student should not be penalized for what could be construed as pedagogically induced learning difficulties.

This chapter offers insights into what the author feels are best practices based on experience as a practitioner and university trainer. No one person working alone can advocate for this population of students. A recent study of high-performing Hispanic schools (Reyes et al., 1999), found that best practices include a systems approach to intervention, a learning community created for learning to take place. The "community" or school takes into consideration the conditions under which the student is expected to learn by requiring the stakeholders to determine the required knowledge. The "community" considers the cultural elements of those who serve (educators, assessment personnel) and those who are served (students) that affect how the knowledge is to be understood. It then examines the "community's" learning capacity as an organization by considering if the cultural elements become barriers to the academic success of students. Finally, the "community" considers what it knows, what it thinks and feels, and how all the components work together. School psychologists, by skillfully developing the added competencies presented in this chapter, will become effective consultants and advocates for second language learners, and critical links in their own learning communities.

REFERENCES

American Psychological Association (1993). Guidelines for providers of psychological services to ethnic, linguistic, and culturally diverse populations. *American Psychologist, 48*, 45–48.

Berry, J., Kim, U., Power, S., Young, M., & Bujaki, M. (1989). Acculturation attitudes in plural societies. *Applied Psychology: An International Review, 38*, 185–206.

Berry, J., Trimble, J., & Olmedo, E. (1986). The assessment of acculturation. In W. Lonner & J. Berry (Eds.). *Field methods in cross-cultural research*. Beverly Hills, CA: Sage.

Cummins, J. (1984). *Bilingualism and special education: Issues in assessment and pedagogy.* San Diego: College-Hill Press.

Darling-Hammond, L., & Ascher, C. (1991). *Creating accountability in big city school systems.* New York: Columbia University, Teacher's College.

Diana v. State Board of Education, No. C-7037, Rfp (U.S. District Court of Northern California, 1970).

Figueroa, R. A. (1989). Psychological testing of linguistic-minority students: Knowledge gaps and regulations. *Exceptional Children 56*(2), 145–152.

Figueroa, R. A. (1990). Best practices in the assessment of bilingual children. In A. Thomas & J. Grimes (Eds.). *Best practices in school psychology II.* Washington, DC: National Association of School Psychologists.

Flanagan, D. P., McGrew, K. S., & Ortiz, S. O. (2000). *The Wechsler Intelligence Scales and Gf-Gc Theory: A contemporary approach to interpretation.* Boston: Allyn & Bacon.

Frisby, C. L. (1998). Culture and cultural differences. In J. H. Sandoval, C. L. Friscy, K. F. Geisinger, J. Scheuneman, & J. R. Grenier (Eds.). *Test interpretation and diversity: Achieving equity in assessment.* Washington, DC: American Psychological Association.

Garcia, Eugene. (1999). *Student cultural diversity: Understanding and meeting the challenge* (2nd ed.). Boston: Houghton Mifflin.

Genessee, F. (2000). Teaching linguistically diverse students. *Principal 79*(5), 24–27.

Gopaul-McNicol, S., & Thomas-Presswood, T. (1998). *Working with linguistically and culturally different children: Innovative clinical and educational approaches.* Boston: Allyn & Bacon.

Guadalupe Organization, Inc. v. Tempe Elementary School District No. 3, 587, F. 2d 1022, 1027, 1029, 9th Cir. (1978).

Jackson, Y., Lewis, J. E., Feuerstein, R., & Samuda, R. J. (2000). Linking assessment to intervention with instrumental enrichment. In R. J. Samuda, R. Feuerstein, A. S. Kaufman, J. E. Lewis, & R. J. Sternberg (Eds.). *Advances in cross-cultural assessment*. Thousand Oaks, CA: Sage.

Krashen, S. (1982). *Principles and practice in second language acquisition*. New York: Pergamon.

Langdon, H. W., & Cheng, L. L. (1992). *Hispanic children and adults with communication disorders: An assessment and intervention*. Gaithersburg, MD: Aspen.

Macías, R. F. (1998). *Summary report of the survey of the states' limited English proficient students and available educational programs and services, 1996–97*. Washington, DC: National Clearinghouse for Bilingual Education.

Miramontes, O. B., Nadeau, A., & Commins, N. L. (1997). *Restructuring schools for linguistic diversity*. New York: Teachers College Press.

National Association of School Psychologists. (2000). *Principles for professional ethics*. Bethesda, MD: Author.

Paredes Scribner, A. (1995). Advocating for Hispanic high school students: Research-based educational practices. *The High School Journal 78*(4), 206–214.

Paredes Scribner, A., & Fuchs, F. (1998, April). *A training model for the effective use of interpreters in psychoeducational assessment*. Paper presented at the meeting of the National Association of School Psychologists, Orlando, FL.

Paredes Scribner, A. (1999). High-performing Hispanic schools: An Introduction. In P. Reyes, J. D. Scribner, and A. Paredes Scribner (Eds.), *Lessons from high-performing Hispanic schools: Creating learning communities*. New York: Teachers College Press.

Phinney, J. S., Chavira, V., & Williamson, L. (1992). Acculturation attitudes and self-esteem among high school and college students. *Youth & Society, 23*(3), 299–311.

Reyes, P., Scribner, J. D., & Paredes Scribner, A. (1999). *Lessons from high-performing Hispanic schools: Creating learning communities*. New York: Teachers College Press.

Samuda, R. J. (2000). Cross cultural assessment. In R. J. Samuda, R. Feuerstein, A. S. Kaufman, J. E. Lewis, and R. J. Sternberg (Eds.), *Advances in cross-cultural assessment*. Thousand Oaks, CA: Sage.

Shuy, R. W. (1978). Problems in assessing language ability in bilingual education programs. In H. Lafontaine, H. Persky, & L. Golubchick (Eds.), *Bilingual education*. Wayne, NJ: Avery.

U.S. Immigration and Naturalization Service (1995). *Statistical yearbook of the immigration and naturalization service*. Washington, DC: U.S. Government Printing Office.

Valencia, R. R., & Guadarrama, I. (1996). High-states testing and its impact on racial and ethnic minority students. In L. A. Suzuki, P. J. Meller, & J. G. Ponterroto (Eds.). *Handbook of multicultural assessment*. San Francisco: Jossey-Bass.

ANNOTATED BIBLIOGRAPHY

Flanagan, D. P., McGrew, K. S., & Ortiz, S. O. (2000). *The Wechsler Intelligence Scales and Gf-Gc theory: A contemporary approach to interpretation*. Boston: Allyn & Bacon.

This book presents a psychometric profile analysis modernizing the interpretation of the Wechsler Intelligence Scales by using the cross-battery approach. Relevant to this chapter is the information presented on measuring cognitive abilities of linguistically diverse populations by highlighting differences between culture bias versus cultural loading, and language bias versus language loading.

Garcia, E. (1999). *Student cultural diversity: Understanding and meeting the challenge* (2nd ed.). Boston: Houghton Mifflin.

An excellent framework to understand the social, cognitive, linguistic, and instructional needs of second language learners. This book encompasses the home, community, and educational environments, helping instructional personnel realize how they can take an active role in the education of second language learners.

Recommended as a valuable source in classroom consultation.

Reyes, P., Scribner, J. D., & Paredes Scribner, A. (Eds.). (1999). *Lessons from high-performing Hispanic schools: Creating learning communities*. New York: Teachers College Press.
This book is pertinent to the school psychology practitioner as a framework from which to operate collaboratively with other school personnel on behalf of second language learners. Most important is the premise that low expectations and the "deficit" model often attached to Hispanic and other minority students in schools need not exist.

Samuda, R. J., Feuerstein, R., Kaufman, A.S., Lewis, J. E., & Sternberg, R.J. (2000). *Advances in cross-cultural assessment*. Thousand Oaks, CA: Sage.
The authors of this book examine the appropriateness of norm-referenced tests for students whose language and background are different to the mainstream culture. New advances and perspectives presented will heighten the awareness of practitioners and professionals regarding the issues relevant to assessment of second language learners.

WEB SITES FOR ASSESSMENT OF SECOND LANGUAGE LEARNERS

NCBE Library:
http://www.ncbe.gwu.edu/library/assess.htm

Bilingual Assessment:
http://www.earthrenewal.org/Questionnaire.htm

94 Best Practices for Supporting Students With Autism

Martin J. Ikeda
Heartland Area Education Agency 11

OVERVIEW

School Psychologists face *increasing challenges* in the area of Autism than ever before. Although Autism and other diagnoses on the Autism spectrum are considered low incidence disabilities, affecting roughly 22 per 10,000 (Bristol et al., 1996) legal cases surrounding programming for Autism are increasing (Yell & Drasgow, 2000). In addition, parents of children diagnosed with Autism have created advocate groups that are quite assertive, putting pressures on schools to provide services with documented effect rather than settling for mere access to services (Shriver, Allen, & Mathews, 1999).

Effective parental advocacy has led to numerous due process proceedings in the area of Autism. In one case (*G. F. v. East Hanover Board of Education*, 1989), parents of a four-year-old boy contended that the proposed program of the district was not appropriate, and sought reimbursement for summer services. The parents felt that a behavior-oriented program was the only program acceptable to meet their son's needs. Expert testimony on behalf of the parents cited lack of specific goals in the Individual Education Plan (IEP), and infrequent data collection, as evidence that the IEP was not appropriate for meeting the needs of a child with Autism. In this case, the Administrative Law Judge ruled in favor of the district, finding that a "blended" approach was appropriate for meeting the needs of G. F.

In another case (*Union Elementary School District*, 1990), parents of a four-year-old boy sought reimbursement for behavior therapy by a private provider. The district had originally proposed placement in a class for children with visual impairments, subsequently recommended placement in a class for children with severe handicaps. In this case, the district provided no evidence, according to the Hearing Officer, that any of the proposed placements were sufficient to meet the child's individualized needs. The district, while recognizing the severe communication deficits presented by the child, only proposed speech and language services "as appropriate," and did not have a teacher that was specifically trained in Autism. In the original case and in the appeal by the district (*Union School District v. B. Smith*, 1994), the courts ruled in favor of the parents.

The two cases cited above are among the earliest proceedings in the now raging legal battles over Autism. Yell and Drasgow (2000) reviewed and summarized 45 cases resolved in due process hearings between 1993 and 1998. In some cases, the failure of the district to diagnose Autism was a point of contention. However, even when districts failed to properly identify students as Autistic, the more pivotal issue being debated tended to be over whether or not a district will pay for in-home, one-on-one discrete trial instruction for up to 40 hours per week (Yell & Drasgow, 2000).

The courts have applied the standard that came out of the U.S. Supreme Court in the *Board of Education of the Hendrick Hudson Central School District v. Rowley* (1982). The Supreme Court developed a two-part for courts to apply when reviewing cases involving disputes within implementation of the Individuals with Disabilities Education Act (IDEA) (Yell & Drasgow, 2000). First, courts examine if schools complied with the *procedural safeguards* of IDEA. Second, the courts determine if the IEP was *reasonably calculated* to confer *educational benefit*.

In the recent cases in Autism in which school districts have lost, Yell and Drasgow (2000) note procedural violations in the areas of parent participation, evaluation, IEP, placement, and qualifications of school personnel. In the area of assessment of Autism, school psychologists must be knowledgeable about characteristics of Autism, and skilled in evaluating Autism. Without background in Autism, the school psychologist lacks credibility and his or her assessment results may be challenged.

Where procedural violations were not substantive, courts then examined the appropriateness of program (Yell & Drasgow, 2000). Under this circumstance, schools have responded in two ways. First, some schools have responded by trying to place students with Autism in programs without support of professionals knowledgeable in Autism. This response has not worked, because the courts have ruled that students with Autism deserve access to treatment that is either recognized in the literature as an effective treatment or has documented effectiveness as a treatment. In addition, it is accepted that students with Autism should be working with teachers who have been trained to support students with Autism (e.g., *Board of Education of the Ann Arbor Public School District*, 1996). The second response of schools described by Yell and Drasgow (2000) is the argument that growth toward goals on individualized education programs provides evidence that programming is or is not working for individual students with Autism. In this response, schools argue that the diagnosis of Autism should not prescribe treatment. Instead, the diagnosis of Autism describes *characteristics* or *behaviors* that manifest in classrooms. Progress toward goals indicates if the method is effective, and lack of progress toward goals indicates that an instructional change needs to be made.

As a result of the *challenges* schools face in developing *appropriate* programs, school psychologists need expertise in *assessing characteristics* of Autism, as well as in *developing and evaluating effectiveness* of programs for children with Autism.

BASIC CONSIDERATIONS

Understanding the types of behaviors associated with Autism is critical for the school psychologist. However, the diagnosis of Autism is important only if that diagnosis *leads to interventions* in the classroom that have a true and meaningful impact on the student and the student's family (Shriver et al., 1999). Hence, it is important for a school psychologist to recognize behaviors characteristic of the *spectrum* of disorders known as Autism, so that some of the strategies described later in this chapter can be explored for potential benefit for the child. As with any of the behaviors or syndromes in this volume, the school psychologist needs to engage in activities *beyond diagnosis*. Assessments need to provide information about the *significance* of the behaviors exhibited by the child, as well as on whether or not the *interventions* needed to address the behavior need special education resources (Shriver et al., 1999).

Characteristics of Autism

Autism is considered a Pervasive Developmental Disorder (American Psychiatric Association, 1994; Bristol et al., 1996). This class of disorder is characterized by *severe impairment* in the areas of (a) social interaction, (b) communication, and (c) presence of stereotypic, or repetitive, behaviors (Bristol et al., 1996). The professional literature refers to this class as *Autism Spectrum Disorders* (Lord, 2000). This spectrum includes Autism, Rett's Syndrome, Heller Syndrome, Childhood Disintegrative Disorder, Asperger's Syndrome, and Atypical Pervasive Developmental Disorder (Bristol et al., 1996; Freeman, 1997; Sponheim, 1996).

Behaviors affected by Autism include social interactions, communication, and repetitive or stereotypic behavior (Shriver et al., 1999). Compounded with IDEA 97 eligibility requirements that vary from state to state (Shriver et al., 1999), and the contributions of other factors like mental retardation or other disorders, school psychologists need to thoroughly assess factors that are related to suspected Autism, but need to rule out other considerations as well.

Best Practices in Assessing Autism

The acronym *RIOT* is helpful in identifying assessment methods that could be used in assessing Autism: (a) *R*eview of reports and records, (b) *I*nterviews of significant caregivers, (c) *O*bservations of the child in a natural setting, and (d) *T*esting of the child.

Reviews of records and reports, when available, help the school psychologist understand the severity and pervasiveness of the behavior over time, and the types of treatments that were used to address the behaviors of concern. In addition, the school psychologist learns if others have used the diagnoses representative of the Autism Spectrum, or Mental Retardation, in classifying the child.

Interviews can be unstructured or structured. An unstructured interview might consist of the school psychologist taking diagnostic criteria from *Diagnostic and Statistical Manual of Mental Disorders* (4th ed.) (DSM-IV) (American Psychiatric Association, 1994), and asking parents and teachers about the extent to which each behavior is present and the situations in which the behavior is most prevalent. The *Autism Diagnostic Interview-Revised* (ADI-R) (Lord, Rutter, & Le Couteur, 1994) is one of several structured interview formats available commercially (see Shriver et al., 1999, for other structured interviews available commercially). In addition, interview formats that are not specific to Autism could be used. An interview format that is helpful in both assessing severity of the behaviors but also in identifying potential treatment, is the *Functional Assessment Interview* (O'Neill et al., 1997). This interview format helps the school psychologist better understand the conditions under which behaviors are present or absent, and helps generate hypotheses about events that seem to "trigger" the behavior and consequences that could be maintaining the behavior. Functional assessment is an important consideration in treating Autism, and will be discussed in depth later in this chapter.

Behavior observations help in identifying and verifying things such as: (a) the extent to which child plays with other children his or her age, (b) initiation of social interactions through sharing of toys, and (c) response to attempts of children or adults to initiate an interaction with the child (Rogers, 2000). Shriver et al. (1999) provide an excellent summary of observational systems with adequate reliability and validity for use in assessing Autism for eligibility decision making.

The *Childhood Autism Rating Scale* (CARS) (Schopler, Reichler, & Renner, 1988), *Pre-Linguistic Autism Diagnostic Observation Schedule* (PL-ADOS) (DiLavore, Lord, & Rutter, 1995), and *Autism Diagnostic Observation Schedule* (ADOS) (Lord et al., 1989) all were reported by Shriver et al. (1999) to have at least some (if not small), evidence of reliability and validity. An extension of both the PL-DOS and the ADOS, the *Autism Diagnostic Observation Schedule-Generic* (ADOS-G) (Lord et al., 2000), has initial evidence of reliability as a screening measure. An additional assessment system, of which observation is an integral component, is the *Autism Screening Instrument for Educational Planning (Second Edition)* (ASIEP-2) (Krug, Arick, & Almond, 1993).

Of the observational systems mentioned above, the CARS requires the least amount of training to use. The school psychologist observes the child and then rates the child on 15 behaviors. CARS is an indicator of the severity of the behaviors associated with Autism and is considered a screening tool (Shriver et al., 1999), and should be one piece of *convergent* information used to assess special education eligibility for a child suspected of being Autistic.

The PL-ADOS, ADOS, and ADOS-G are structured observation systems. The ADOS was designed to complement the original *Autism Diagnostic Interview* (ADI) (Le Couteur at al., 1989), and was meant primarily for diagnosing Autism for research purposes (Lord et al., 2000). The PL-ADOS, ADI-R, and ADOS-G were developed when it became clear that instruments were needed in clinical applications (Lord et al., 2000). The ADOS-G attempts to broaden the spectrum of diagnoses which can be differentiated using the ADOS-G, instead of focusing only on one component of the Autism spectrum (Lord et al., 2000). Specific activities across several domains are presented to the child, and the response in that situation is recorded. The observations assess severity of behaviors in areas of social behavior and communication. A school psychologist would require supervised training, opportunities for practice, and feedback in order to become proficient at administering these instruments.

The ASIEP-2 is a comprehensive assessment system (Olmi, 1998). Included in the ASIEP-2 is the *Autism Behavior Checklist* (ABC). The ABC is completed by caregivers who know the child well. The other parts of the battery require observing of the child, and typically require more than one administrator. A teacher observation is included as part of the ASIEP-2. Information from the ASIEP-2 is useful for *screening* the types of behaviors associated with Autism presented by the child, and the severity of the behaviors.

The standardized observational systems available for assessing Autism are useful in identifying that a child meets *diagnostic* criteria for Autism. As part of a *multi-method* assessment, the school psychologist and interdisciplinary team will better understand the types of behaviors that are problematic, the severity of the behaviors, and the conditions under which the behaviors are observed. A school psychologist should not feel limited to using a standardized observational system. Any behavior that is carefully defined (Tilly & Flugum, 1995) can be observed, using behavioral assessment methods (Alberto & Troutman, 1999).

Anecdotal reports can be generated by classroom teachers, and analyzed to better understand when and where behaviors are occurring. For more direct observations, event recording, interval recording, time sampling, duration recording, and latency recording can be used (Alberto & Troutman, 1999). Direct observational systems are helpful in identifying instructional *needs* of the learner by observing factors such as the numbers of opportunities the child has to respond to the teacher, the accuracy of those responses, and the amount of time that the learner is actively engaged in their required work. A second strength of direct observational systems is that these systems can be used to measure changes in the learner that result from individualized programming (Alberto & Troutman, 1999).

Testing is the fourth method for assessing Autism. Published, standardized, norm referenced tests can be used to understand where the child is in comparison to a peer group or developmental standard. Specific to Autism, the *Psychoeducational Profile-Revised* (PEP-R) (Schopler, Reichler, Bashford, Lansing, & Marcus, 1990) is often used to test a child suspected of having Autism. Despite its widespread use, the PEP-R lacks evidence of utility in educational decision making (Shriver et al., 1999). Any available published criterion- or norm-referenced test (e,g, Woodcock-Johnson Tests of Academic Achievement, Woodcock & Johnson, 1989) or direct assessment of academic skill (e.g., Shapiro, 1997) can be used with a child with Autism if the school psychologist has reason to believe that the test will provide important information about the eligibility of the child for services, or the educational needs of the child.

Adaptive behavior measures, such as the Vineland Adaptive Behavior Scales (Sparrow, Balla, & Cicchetti, 1984), are often used as part of an assessment battery when working with children with Autism (Handleman & Harris, 1994). Measures like the Vineland provide a normative comparison for the child being assessed, in a variety of relevant domains like communication, motor, and daily living skills. The Vineland and other adaptive behavior measures can also be used to assess growth reported by caregivers over time. The school psychologist must remember, however, that measures like the Vineland are in essence scaled self-reports, and could supplement these measures with direct observations to verify reported growth.

BEST PRACTICES IN PROGRAMMING FOR STUDENTS WITH AUTISM

Much of the controversy in the area of Autism is around the issue of *effective* programming (Gresham & MacMillan, 1997; Yell & Drasgow, 2000). Over the years there has been evidence, using single-case designs and behavior analytic methods, that effective intervention can be implemented for communication, social, and behavior concerns (Shriver et al., 1999). The pressures on schools were increased, however, when advocacy groups began demanding *large-scale* evidence of effective treatment (Gresham, Beebe-Frankenberger, & MacMillan, 1999).

The data around large-scale program effectiveness are much more subject to debate than the data surrounding case reports (Gresham & MacMillan, 1997; Gresham et al., 1999; Smith & Lovaas, 1997). The debate centers around potential biased samples of subjects, the lack of randomization of subjects in most studies, and the ethics of making claims that may not be substantiated given the data (Gresham et al., 1999). Despite the controversy, there appears to be some consensus that effective programs for students with Autism contain components of: (a) curricular activities with sufficient scope to address the behaviors associated with Autism, (b) structured environment, (c) schedules and routines, and (d) a functional approach to assessing problem behaviors (Dawson & Osterling, 1997; Gresham et al., 1999; Harris & Handleman, 1994; Quill, 1997).

Curricular Activities for Students With Autism

Programs that are accepted in the professional literature as effective for helping children with Autism use curricula that emphasize expressive and receptive language, appropriate interactions with toys or objects, initiating and maintaining appropriate social interactions with peers and adults, and effective transitioning (Harris & Handleman, 1994; Gresham et al., 1999; Olley, 1999). While instructional methods vary from discrete-trial format (Lovaas, 1987) to creating opportunities for the child to practice skills in everyday routines (McGee, Daly, & Jacobs, 1994), children with Autism generally need support in one or more of the aforementioned curricular areas. Targeting skills of others the same age helps promote ambitious goal setting, and more positive impact on the life of the child with Autism (Kennedy & Shukla, 1995).

There is also some consensus in the Autism literature that curriculum considerations for students with Autism address (a) self-help, (b) self-management, (c) cognition, and (d) play/social skills (Harris & Handleman, 1994; Olley, 1999). Depending upon the level of functioning of the learner, self-help skills may need to start with compliance. Maurice, Green, and Luce (1996) provide a curriculum for developing self-help skills. While Maurice et al. (1996) advocate for discrete trial instruction outside of a school setting, others (McGee, Daly, & Jacobs, 1994) have successfully taught self-help skills using direct instruction in the classroom. Self-management skills have been effectively taught through use of schedules (McClannahan & Krantz, 1999; Schopler, Mesibov, & Hearsey, 1995).

Harris and Handleman (1994) provide opportunities for programs for young children with Autism to describe cognitive growth achieved by their programs. The May Center for Early Childhood Education (Anderson, Campbell, & O'Malley Cannon, 1994) addresses communication, self-care, pre-academics, social, play/motor, and aberrant behavior. Home-based programming and school transitioning are integral parts of this program. The Delaware Autistic Program (Bondy & Frost, 1994) uses picture exchanges to promote language acquisition and interaction with peers, adults, and the environment. Another program with documented cognitive effects is the UCLA Young Autism Project (Lovaas, 1987) that demonstrated that early intervention consisting of intensive one-to-one instruction of 40 hours per week positively affected cognition.

Play is an important component of a curriculum for young children with Autism (Olley, 1999; Strain & Cordisco, 1994). Improving play can be accomplished in different ways. One effective strategy is to have peers initiate play (Strain, Kohler, & Goldstein., 1996). Baker, Koegel, and Koegel (1998) used the Autistic child's obsessive interest to build opportunities to interact with peers. As children mature, social skills instruction (Gresham, 1995) can help promote peer interactions. To promote more spontaneous peer interaction, instruction should be in the natural context (rather than in contrived situations), and use preferred toy objects (McGee et al., 1994; Strain & Cordisco, 1994).

Structured Environment

A second important consideration for children with Autism is a structured environment (Quill, 1997; Gresham et al., 1999). Structured teaching improves skills of students by using their unique interests as motivators, and to structure the child's setting so that behaviors associated with Autism are minimized (Schopler et al., 1995). Structured teaching capitalizes on the visual processing strengths of students with Autism, and downplays the weaknesses in auditory processing often associated with Autism. Physical structure minimizes distractions, and defines physical boundaries. Using color-coded tape, construction paper, or other visual cues helps the student recognize locations within the classroom and school in which they are expected to perform. Dividers are set up to minimize distractions, and to further define boundaries for the student. Structure can be set up in any classroom, in group activities, play activities, transition activities, independent seat work, and in one-on-one instruction.

Schedules and Routines

Schedules help establish routines. Schedules teach the students what they need to do first, and aid in transitions. Schedules help students gain predictability from their setting by providing a sequence of activities that will occur within a school day. Depending upon the skill level of the child, schedules are developed using physical objects, pictures, line drawings, or words. The child needs to be taught to use the schedule, and to match their schedule with the corresponding object or word that represents where the student is supposed to be at a given time. Teachers keep objects or words handy so that schedules can be changed daily, or even in the middle of the day if an unexpected event (an assembly) occurs. It is important to create a daily schedule that creates a balance of easy-to-difficult, and preferred-to-nonpreferred tasks (Olley, 1999).

Functional Approach to Assessing Problem Behaviors

Students with Autism can present with difficult or challenging behaviors. These are behaviors that interfere with learning and, in some cases, with the child's being able to remain in a public school setting. A functional approach to problem behavior is important in *efficiently* identifying interventions with *higher likelihood* of success than interventions based on less systematic approaches. In order to conduct an adequate functional assessment, the school psychologist needs skills in interviewing and in direct observation of behavior (O'Neill et al., 1997, Tilly, Knoster, & Ikeda, 2000). The school psychologist learns more about the behaviors considered problematic. Instead of focusing on the shape of the behavior, like "hitting," the school psychologist is gathering information to understand the *function* that the behavior serves for the child (O'Neill et al., 1997; Tilly et al., 2000). By teaching the child other ways to escape or obtain certain events, people, or stimuli in the environment, most often the school psychologist assesses if the learner is attempting to escape or obtain: (a) attention, (b) activities, or (c) sensory stimulation (O'Neill et al., 1997).

An example of effective implementation of functional assessment is described in Hintze and Eckert (2000). A 12-year-old girl was presenting with severe noncompliance. Noncompliance is common in children with Autism (Shriver & Allen, 1997), and can have serious impact on a learner's ability to complete tasks in the classroom and on a school district's willingness to keep the learner in school (Hintze & Eckert, 2000). The school psychologist, using the Functional Assessment Interview and Functional Assessment Observation Form (O'Neill et al., 1997), identified instructional demand as an antecedent to noncompliance, and escape from task as the perceived function of the noncompliance (Hintze & Eckert, 2000). An intervention that reinforced alternate behaviors, and did not allow escape from the task demands, was implemented. The intervention was successful in reducing noncompliance, and is a good illustration of how school psychologists *can* implement functional assessment in school settings.

Other Considerations for Supporting Students With Autism

Transitioning from activity-to-activity is often problematic for students with Autism (Olley, 1999). Schedules as described above help with transitions. School psychologists should interview teachers in all settings in which transitions are occurring, and observe the task demands in those settings, to help facilitate transition planning.

Another important consideration for school psychologists is the proliferation of unproven treatments, disproven treatments, or misinformation (Olley, 1999). In the area of Autism, pharmacological treatment using the drug Secretin (Horvath et al., 1998), facilitated communication (Biklen, 1990; Biklen & Schubert, 1991), Auditory Integration Therapy (Rimland & Edelson, 1994) and Sensory Integration Therapy (Ayres, 1972) are therapies often demanded by parents, but whose effectiveness as a treatment is not widely accepted.

In a recent two-part clinical investigation, Chez et al. (2000) investigated whether or not Secretin resulted in changes in behaviors in children with Autism compared to a group receiving placebo. The data indicated that there were no differences between the groups in reported changes in behavior as rated by the CARS. In a response to Chez et al. (2000), Rimland (2000) questioned the interpretation of the data, and suggested that Secretin indeed is a beneficial treatment. Chez and Buchanan (2000) responded in defense of their original conclusion, and challenged the field to provide peer-reviewed data of the efficacy of Secretin. To date, there are no peer-reviewed studies that demonstrate that Secretin has a positive and documented impact on behaviors associated with Autism.

Facilitated communication is a method of communication in which a "facilatator" provides support to the forearm of an individual with a communication impairment, "facilitating" access to letters on a keyboard (Braman, Brady, Linehan, & Williams, 1995). There are a few published, peer-reviewed studies that have found facilitated communication not helpful or even under the control of the facilitator (Hudson, Melita, & Arnold, 1993; Montee, Miltenberger, & Wittrock, 1995; Regal, Rooney, & Wandas, 1994; Wheeler, Jacobson, Paglieri, & Schwartz, 1993). These studies have been criticized by proponents of facilitated communication (Braman et al., 1995) because the studies were too empirical in nature, and did not honor the relationship that the facilitator and facilitatee need in order to be successful.

Using criteria established by Biklen (cf. Braman et al., 1995), Braman et al. examined the use of facilitated communication of three participants. The results of this study, which addressed the question, "Will people with Autism who use facilitated communication demonstrate similar levels of contextual accuracy regardless of whether the content is known or unknown to the facilitator?" found that the responses of the participants were strongly influenced by the facilitator. Braman et al. contend that their results do not disprove facilitated communication as an intervention. Instead, their results simply verify that in some cases, there is bias from the facilitator. Nevertheless, professional organizations such as the American Psychological Association, the American Academy of Pediatrics, and the American Academy of Speech and Hearing all have refuted facilitated communication as a treatment (Campbell, Schopler, Cueva, & Hallin, 1996; Gresham et al., 1999).

In Auditory Integration Training (AIT) (Rimland & Edelson, 1994), sounds and music are presented with certain frequencies filtered to individuals (Heflin & Simpson, 1998). The theory behind AIT is that a sensitivity to certain frequencies makes it difficult to hear. By presenting sounds and filtering out frequencies, the individual learns to adjust to intense sounds (Heflin & Simpson, 1998). The research on AIT typically employs anecdotal reports or behavioral rating scales as the outcome measure. There is little to no evidence using reliable, direct measures of behavior to suggest that AIT is an effective treatment for Autism (Gillberg, Johansson, Steffenburg, & Berlin, 1997; Gresham et al., 1999; Heflin & Simpson, 1998).

Sensory integration (Ayers, 1972) explains behaviors of children with Autism as functional attempts to seek preferred stimuli and avoid other, unpleasant or non-preferred stimulation. Sensory integration suffers from similar research voids as does AIT: no peer reviewed studies using direct measures of behavior as outcomes (Heflin & Simpson, 1998). Given the lack of data on applying sensory integration to children with Autism, and considering the conclusions of the learning disabilities community, this treatment should be viewed as exploratory at best. Genaux and Maloney Baird (1999) in a legal workshop on building defensible programs in Autism include sensory integration in the category of "non-validated practices." As such, school psychologists should be cautious when examining sensory integration as part of a student's programming.

One final consideration for school psychologists in working with children with Autism: listen to their parent(s). Parent-school collaboration, or lack thereof, has been an historical barrier in special education (Wood, 1995). The child with Autism functions in two distinct worlds: that of the school and that of home (Zigler, 1984). Programs should be implemented so that both worlds are affected positively. At school, the child accesses nondisabled peers and the general curriculum to the maximum extent appropriate. At home, the work done by parents and school-based professionals provide the child with access to activities preferred by the family (Wood, 1995). Having strong relationships between home and school allows for meaningful dialogue to occur, so that if conflict resolution must occur, a reasonable middle ground can more likely be found. (Feinberg & Beyer, 1999)

SUMMARY

Autism is a complex disorder that manifests through problems with (a) communication, (b) social interactions, and (c) repetitive displays of behavior. Autism is not a new disorder, although there has been a proliferation of research and theoretical work done in the area in the last 5 years. To best support students with Autism, school psychologists need skills in accurately identifying Autism, assessing the impact of behaviors associated with Autism on learning, and helping teachers and parents develop and evaluate programs to address the problem areas.

The acronym RIOT (Review, Interview, Observe, Test) helps to promote multi-method assessment needed to both (a) identify students as Autistic and (b) identify areas in which individualized programming will be needed. While there are published interviews and observational systems useful in diagnosing Autism, many of these instruments will require specialized training to learn to administer. Unstructured interviews can be used, as can direct observational methods familiar to most school psychologists. If academic skills testing is needed, published tests could be used. An alternative to published, norm referenced tests of achievement, direct assessment of academic skills using functional academic assessments can provide valuable information about student learning needs.

When developing programs for students with Autism, school psychologists need to understand what skills should be taught in a curriculum. Self-help, self-management, cognition, and play/social skills are areas often targeted. Structure is helpful in defining boundaries for children with Autism. Schedules help students understand when tasks start, and what to do or where to go when they have finished an activity. Functional assessment of challenging behaviors is helpful in identifying factors that can be changed in a setting, either before a behavior occurs or after the behavior occurs, so that a student is more successful in the setting.

Perhaps more than other categorical disabilities, Autism carries with it an "aptitude by treatment interaction" mentality. In other words, because the child is Autistic, *X* treatment should be implemented. There is a proliferation of unproven treatments in the area of Autism. School psychologists need information on these unproven treatments, so that they can effectively team with parents in identifying the most appropriate treatment for an individual learner with Autism.

School psychologists bring a variety of skills that can be helpful in supporting Autism. Collaboration, assessment, knowledge of childhood disorders, consultation, and evaluating treatment effects, all are necessary for ensuring that a child with Autism receives an appropriate program. Though the threat of legal action is daunting, a school psychologist with assessment and intervention skills, who supplements their skills by learning more of the specifics surrounding Autism, is an important source of information for the family of the child, a critical support for the teacher of the child, and, most importantly, an effective advocate for the child with Autism. While avoiding claims of "cures" or "recoveries" (Gresham & MacMillan, 1997), the school psychologist can ensure that the child with Autism receives an effective program.

REFERENCES

Alberto, P. A., & Troutman, A. C. (1999). *Applied behavior analysis for teachers* (5th ed.). Upper Saddle River, NJ: Prentice-Hall.

American Psychiatric Association (1994). *Diagnostic and statistical manual of mental disorders* (4th ed.). Washington, DC: American Psychiatric Association.

Anderson, S. R., Campbell, S., & O'Malley Cannon, B. (1994). The May Center for Early Childhood Education. In S. L. Harris & J. S. Handleman (Eds.), *Preschool education programs for children with Autism* (pp. 15–36). Austin, TX: PRO-ED.

Ayers, J. (1972). *Sensory integration and learning disorders*. Los Angeles: Western Psychological Services.

Baker, M. J., Koegel, R. L., & Koegel, L. (1998). Increasing the social behavior of young children with Autism using their obsessive behaviors. *Journal of the Association for Persons with Severe Handicaps, 23*, 300–308.

Biklen, D. (1990). Communication unbound: Autism and praxis. *Harvard Educational Review, 60*(3), 291–314.

Biklen, D., & Schubert, A. (1991). New words: The communication of students with Autism. *Remedial and Special Education, 12*, 46–57.

Board of Education of the Ann Arbor Public Schools, 24 IDELR 621 (SEA MI, 1996).

Board of Education of the Hendrick Hudson Central School District v. Rowley, 458 U S. 176 (1982).

Bondy, A. S., & Frost, L. A. (1994). The Delaware Autistic program. In S. L. Harris & J. S. Handleman (Eds.), *Preschool education programs for children with Autism* (pp. 37–56). Austin, TX: PRO-ED.

Braman, B. J., Brady, M. J., Linehan, S. L., & Williams, R. E. (1995). Facilitated communication for children with Autism: An examination of face validity. *Behavioral Disorders, 21*, 110–119.

Bristol, M. M., Cohen, D. J., Costello, E. J., Denckla, M., Eckberg, T. J., Kallen, R., Kraemer, H. C., Lord, C.,

Maurer, R., McIlvane, W. J., Minshew, N., Sigman, M., & Spence, M. A. (1996). State of the science in Autism: Report to the National Institutes of Health. *Journal of Autism and Developmental Disorders, 26*, 121–157.

Campbell, M., Schopler, E., Cueva, J. E., & Hallin, A. (1996). Treatment of autistic disorder. *Journal of American Academy of Child Adolescent Psychiatry, 35*, 134–143.

Chez, M. G., & Buchanan, C. P. (2000). Reply to B. Rimland's "Comments on 'Secretin and Autism: A two-part clinical investigation.'" *Journal of Autism and Developmental Disorders, 30*, 97–98.

Chez, M., G., Buchanan, C. P., Bagan, B. T., Hammer, M. S., McCarthy, K. S., Ovrutskaya, I., Nowinski, C. V., & Cohen, Z. S. (2000). Secretin and Autism: A two-part clinical investigation. *Journal of Autism and Developmental Disorders*, 30, 87–94.

Dawson, G., & Osterling, J. (1997). Early intervention in Autism. In M. Guralnick (Ed.), *The effectiveness of early intervention* (pp. 307–326). Baltimore: Brooks.

DiLavore, P. C., Lord, C., & Rutter, M. (1995). The prelinguistic autism diagnostic observation schedule. *Journal of Autism and Developmental Disorders, 23*, 355–379.

Feinberg, E., & Beyer, J. (1999). Mediation in the individuals with disabilities education act. Reprinted in K. T. Whatley & E. Shaw (Eds.), *NECTAS Resource Collection on Autism Spectrum Disorders* (pp. 111–114). Chapel Hill, NC: NECTAS.

Freeman, B. J. (1997). Guidelines for evaluating intervention programs for children with Autism. *Journal of Autism and Developmental Disorders, 27*, 641–651.

G. F. v. East Hanover Board of Education, 16 EHLR 141 (1989).

Genaux, M., & Maloney Baird, M. (1999). *Building a blueprint for defensible Autism programs*. Alexandria, VA: LRP.

Gillberg, C., Johansson, M., Steffenburg, S., & Berlin, O. (1997). Auditory integration training in children with autism. *Autism: The International Journal of Research and Practice, 1*, 97–100.

Gresham, F. M. (1995). Social skills training. In A. Thomas & J. Grimes (Eds.), *Best practices in school psychology III* (pp. 1021–1030). Washington, DC: National Association of School Psychologists.

Gresham, F. M., Beebe-Frankenberger, M. E., & MacMillan, D. L. (1999). A selective review of treatments for children with Autism: Description and methodological considerations. *School Psychology Review, 28*, 559–575.

Gresham, F. M., & MacMillan, D. L. (1997). Autistic recovery?: An analysis and critique of the empirical evidence on the Early Intervention Project. *Behavioral Disorders, 22*, 185–201.

Handleman, J. S., & Harris, S. L. (1994). The Douglass Developmental Disabilities Center. In S. L. Harris & J. S. Handleman (Eds.), *Preschool education programs for children with Autism* (pp. 71–86). Austin, TX: PRO-ED.

Harris, S. L., & Handleman, J. S. (1994). *Preschool education programs for children with Autism*. Austin, TX: PRO-ED.

Heflin, L. J., & Simpson, R. L. (1998). Interventions for children and youth with Autism: Prudent choices in a world of exaggerated claims and empty promises. Part I. Intervention and treatment option review. *Focus on Autism and Other Developmental Disabilities, 13*, 194–211.

Hintze, J. M., & Eckert, T. L. (2000). The use of functional assessment and analysis strategies to reduce the noncompliant behavior of a child with Autism. *Proven Practice, 3*, 9–15.

Horvath, K., Stefanatos, G., Sokolski, K. N., Watchel, R., Nabors, L., & Tildon, J. T. (1998). Improved social and language skills after secretin administration in patients with autistic spectrum disorders. *Journal of the Association for Academic Minority Physicians, 9*, 9–15.

Hudson, A., Melita, B., & Arnold, N. (1993). Brief report: A case study assessing the validity of facilitated communication. *Journal of Autism and Developmental Disorders, 23*, 165–173.

Kennedy, C. H., & Shukla, S. (1995). Social interaction research for people with Autism as a set of past, current, and emerging propositions. *Behavioral Disorders, 21*, 21–35.

Krug, D.A., Arick, J. R., & Almond, P. J. (1993). *Autism screening instrument for educational planning* (2nd ed.). Austin, TX: PRO-ED.

Le Couteur, A., Rutter, M., Lord, C., Rios, P., Robertson, S., Holdgrafer, M., & McLennan, J. D. (1989). Autism diagnostic interview: A semistructured interview for parents and caregivers of autistic persons. *Journal of Autism and Developmental Disabilities, 19*, 363–387.

Lord, C. (2000). Commentary: Achievement and future directions for intervention research in communication and Autism spectrum disorders. *Journal of Autism and Developmental Disorders, 30*, 393–398.

Lord, C., Risi, S., Lambrecht, L., Cook, E. H., Leventhal, B. L., DiLavore, P. C., Pickles, A., & Rutter, M. (2000). The Autism Diagnostic Observation Schedule-Generic: A standard measure of social and communication deficits associated with the spectrum of Autism. *Journal of Autism and Developmental Disorders, 20*, 205–223.

Lord, C., Rutter, M., Goode, S., Heemsbergen, J., Jordan, H., Mawhood, L., & Schopler, E. (1989). Autism Diagnostic Observation Schedule: A standardized observation of communication and social behavior. *Journal of Autism and Developmental Disorders, 19*, 185–212.

Lord, C., Rutter, M., & Le Couteur, A. (1994). Autism Diagnostic Interview-Revised: A revised version of a diagnostic interview for caregivers of individuals with possible pervasive developmental disorders. *Journal of Autism and Developmental Disorders, 24*, 659–685.

Lovaas, O. I. (1987). Behavioral treatment and normal educational and intellectual functioning in young autistic children. *Journal of Consulting and Clinical Psychology, 55*, 3–9.

Maurice, C., Green, G., & Luce, S. C. (Eds.). (1996). *Behavioral intervention for young children with Autism: A manual for parents and professionals.* Austin, TX: PRO-ED.

McClannahan, L. E., & Krantz, P. J. (1999). *Activity schedules for children with autism: A manual for parents and professionals.* Austin: TX: PRO-ED.

McGee, G. G., Daly, T., & Jacobs, H. A. (1994). The Walden preschool. In S. L. Harris & J. S. Handleman (Eds.), *Preschool education programs for children with Autism* (pp. 127–162). Austin, TX: PRO-ED.

Montee, B., Miltenberger, R., & Wittrock, D. (1995). An experimental analysis of facilitated communication. *Journal of Applied Behavior Analysis, 28*, 189–200.

Olley, J. G. (1999). Curriculum for students with Autism. *School Psychology Review, 28*, 595–607.

Olmi, D. J. (1998). Review of the Autism Screening Instrument for Educational Planning, Second Edition. In J. C. Impara & B. S. Plake (Eds.), *The thirteenth mental measurements yearbook* (pp. 74–76). Lincoln, NE: The University of Nebraska Press.

O'Neill, R. E., Horner, R. H., Albin, R. W., Sprague, J. R., Storey, K., & Newton, J. S. (1997). *Functional assessment and program development for problem behavior: A practical handbook* (2nd Ed.). Pacific Grove, CA: Brooks/Cole.

Quill, K. A. (1997). Instructional considerations for young children with Autism: The rationale for visually cued instruction. *Journal of Autism and Developmental Disorders, 27*, 697–714.

Regal, R. A., Rooney, J. R., & Wandas, T. (1994). Facilitated communication: An experimental evaluation. *Journal of Autism and Developmental Disorders, 24*, 345–355.

Rimland, B. (2000). Comments on "Secretin and Autism: A two-part clinical investigation," by M. G. Chez et al. *Journal of Autism and Devlopmental Disorders, 30*, 95.

Rimland, B., & Edelson, S. (1994). The effects of auditory integration training on autism. *American Journal of Speech-Language Pathology, 3*, 16–24.

Rogers, S. J. (2000). Interventions that facilitate socialization in children with Autism. *Journal of Autism and Developmental Disorders, 30*, 399–409.

Schopler, E., Mesibov, G. B., & Hearsey, K. (1995). Structured teaching in the TEACCH system. In E. Schopler and G. B. Mesibov (Eds.), *Learning and cognition in Autism* (pp. 243–268). New York: Plenum.

Schopler, E., Reichler, R. J., Bashford, A., Lansing, M. D., & Marcus, L. M. (1990). *Psychoeducational Profile Revised (PEP-R)*. Austin: TX: PRO-ED.

Schopler, E., Reichler, R. J., & Renner, B. R. (1988). *The Childhood Autism Rating Scale (CARS)*. Los Angeles: Western Psychological Services.

Shapiro, E. S. (1997). *Academic skills problems: Direct assessment and intervention* (2nd ed.). New York: Guilford.

Shriver, M. D., & Allen, K. D. (1997). Defining child noncompliance: An examination of temporal parameters. *Journal of Applied Behavior Analysis, 30*, 173–176.

Shriver, M. D., Allen, K. D., & Mathews, J. R. (1999). Effective assessment of the shared and unique characteristics of children with Autism. *School Psychology Review, 28*, 538–558.

Smith, T., & Lovaas, O. I (1997). The UCLA Young Autism Project: A reply to Gresham and MacMillan. *Behavioral Disorders, 22*, 202–218.

Sparrow, S., Balla, D., & Cicchetti, D. (1984). *Vineland Adaptive Behavior Scales*. Circle Pines, MN: American Guidance Service.

Sponheim, E. (1996). Changing criteria of autistic disorders: A comparison of ICD-10 research criteria and DSM-IV with DSM-III-R, CARS, and ABC. *Journal of Autism and Developmental Disorders, 26*, 513–525.

Strain, P. S., & Cordisco, L. K. (1994). LEAP preschool. In S. L. Harris & J. S. Handleman (Eds.), *Preschool education programs for children with Autism* (pp. 225–244). Austin, TX: PRO-ED.

Strain, P. S., Kohler, F. W., & Goldstein, H. (1996). Learning experiences, An alternative program: Peer-mediated interventions for young children with Autism. In E. D. Hibbs & P. S. Jensen (Eds.), *Psychosocial treatments for child and adolescent disorders: Empirically based strategies for clinical practice* (pp. 573–586). Washington, DC: American Psychological Association.

Tilly, W. D., & Flugum, K. R. (1995) Best practices in quality interventions. In A. Thomas & J. Grimes (Eds.), *Best practices in school psychology III* (pp. 485–500). Washington, DC: National Association of School Psychologists.

Tilly, W. D., Knoster, T. P., & Ikeda, M. J. (2000). Functional behavioral assessment: Strategies for positive behavior support. In C. Telzrow & M. Tankersley (Eds.), *IDEA Amendments of 1997: Practice guidelines for school-based teams* (pp. 151–199). Bethesda, MD: National Association of School Psychologists.

Union Elementary School District,16 EHLR 978 (1990).

Union School District v. B. Smith, 20 IDELR 987 (1994).

Wheeler, D. L., Jacobson, J. W., Paglieri, R. A., & Schwartz, A. A. (1993). An experimental assessment of facilitated communication. *Mental Retardation, 31*, 49–60.

Wood, M. (1995). Parent-professional collaboration and the efficacy of the IEP process. In R. L. Koegel and L. K. Koegel (Eds.), *Teaching children with Autism: Strategies for initiating positive interactions and improving learning opportunities* (pp. 147–174). Baltimore: Brookes.

Woodcock, R. W., & Johnson, M. B. (1989). *Woodcock-Johnson Tests of Achievement*. Allen, TX: DLM Teaching Resources.

Yell, M. L., & Drasgow, E. (2000). Litigating a free appropriate public education: The Lovaas hearings and cases. *The Journal of Special Education, 33*, 205–214.

Zigler. E. (1984). Handicapped children and their families. In E. Schopler & G. B. Mesibov (Eds.), *The effects of Autism on the family* (pp. 21–40). New York: Plenum.

ANNOTATED BIBLIOGRAPHY

Maurice, C., Green, G., & Luce, S. C. (Eds.). (1996). *Behavioral intervention for young children with Autism: A manual for parents and professionals*. Austin: PRO-ED.

A data-based approach to programming and instruction is described. The manual offers an objective summary of research, including unproven. Chapters include a discrete trial curriculum, working with school-professionals and the school system, making program decisions based on data, and promoting language acquisition using verbal and augmentative systems.

O'Neill, R. E., Horner, R. H., Albin, R. W., Sprague, J. R., Storey, K., & Newton, J. S. (1997). Functional assessment and program development for problem behavior: A practical handbook. Pacific Grove, CA: Brooks/Cole.
Begins with theoretical underpinnings of functional behavioral assessment. Uses an indirect method of interviewing, combined with direct observation of the behavior and its antecedents and consequences, to support positive behavior by making problem behaviors irrelevant, inefficient and ineffective. Provides interview, direct observation, and behavior diagramming forms.

Reichle, J., York, J., & Sigafoos, J. (Eds.). (1991). Implementing augmentative and alternative communication: Strategies for learners with severe disabilities. Baltimore: Brookes.
After reading thoroughly the 14 chapters in this edited volume, the school psychologist should better understand how to team with teachers, parents, and speech and language pathologists in developing communication skills. There are suggestions for assessment of communication that link to intervention development for both verbal and augmentative communication.

Schopler, E., & Mesibov, G. B. (Eds.). (1995). *Learning and cognition in Autism.* New York: Plenum.
Sixteen chapters describing learning styles of students with Autism. "Part IV: Education and Treatment of Autism," contains chapters on structured teaching, cognitive development, strategies for enhancing socialization and communication, and using communication training to resolve problem behaviors.

AUTHOR NOTE

The author acknowledges the contributions of the Heartland AEA 11/Des Moines Public Schools Autism Resource Team. This team consists of Richard W. Tucker, Barbara E. Rankin, Ann Baird, Bindy Brown, Margaret Cook, John Drinnin, Marilyn Finn, Susan Guest, Patricia Hollinger, Mary Humke, Dee Sorenson, and David Wood. This multi-disciplinary team of dedicated professionals brings to life the reality of serving children with autism in public schools.

The present work was supported in part by Grant No. H024B960027 from the Office of Special Education Programs, U. S. Department of Education. The opinions expressed herein are those of the authors and should not be interpreted as having agency endorsement.

95 Best Practices in the School Psychologist's Role in the Assessment and Treatment of Students With Communication Disorders

Melissa A. Bray, Thomas J. Kehle, and Lea A. Theodore
University of Connecticut

OVERVIEW

In 1989, Telzrow guest edited an issue of *School Psychology Review* (SPR) on communication disorders in preschool and school-aged children. She stated that the special issue provides SPR readers with the state-of-the-art in children's communication disorders. Telzrow (1989) identified the following three themes that were consistent in the five articles that comprised the special issue: (a) communication disorders are pervasive in that they influence several areas of cognitive, academic, and social functioning, (b) assessment indices are limited when used with special populations and therefore may require alternative strategies, and (c) optimal intervention approaches should be long term allowing for emphasis on the children's relative strengths. The intent of this chapter is to summarize what we believe were the most relevant issues raised in the 1989 special issue and to supplement this information with recent advances in the identification and treatment of children's communication disorders relative to the practice of school psychology.

BASIC CONSIDERATIONS

Students that evidence communication disorders have been shown to be at risk for both academic and social/emotional problems (Cantwell & Baker, 1985). Therefore, school psychologists should be aware of the potential influences communication has on academic performance and social functioning with regard to assessment, consultation, and treatment.

Generally, communication disorders are categorized into the broad areas of speech, language, and hearing including central auditory processing disorders (CAPD). The American-Speech-Language-Hearing Association (American-Speech-Language-Hearing Association 1993) defines communication disorder as an impairment in the ability to receive, send, process, and comprehend concepts or verbal, nonverbal, and graphic symbol systems.

Speech disorders include articulation, voice, or fluency/stuttering. Articulation disorders are defined as a typical production of speech sounds characterized by substitutions, omissions, additions, or distortions that may interfere with intelligibility (American-Speech-Language-Hearing Association, 1993, p. 40). A voice disorder is defined by abnormalities of vocal pitch, loudness, duration, quality, and/or resonance. Fluency or stuttering is characterized by repetitions of sounds, words or phrases, sound or syllable prolongations, and/or blocking, which is the inability to move the lips or vocal folds to produce meaningful speech (American-Speech-Language-Hearing Association, 1993).

Language disorders include deficits in the areas of expressive language (speaking or writing), receptive language (listening or reading), or mixed expressive/receptive. According to American-Speech-Language-Hearing Association (1993), expressive and receptive language disorders may be composed of deficits in the following areas: (a) form of language including phonology (sounds and rules governing their combinations), morphology (the smallest segment of a word that denotes meaning), and syntax (grammar); (b) the content of language including semantics (meaning); and (c) function of language including pragmatics (social use of language).

Hearing disorders may impair the development, comprehension, and production of speech and language (American-Speech-Language-Hearing Association, 1993). Hearing disorders may be peripheral or central in nature. Peripheral hearing refers to impairments in actual hearing. Central auditory processing refers to deficits in the ability to process auditory stimuli (American-Speech-Language-Hearing Association, 1993).

BEST PRACTICES FOR LANGUAGE DISORDERS.

Out of all of the communication disorders previously outlined, language deficits are most pertinent to the role and function of the school psychologist. If the school psychologist observes deficits in expressive or receptive language in the areas of phonology, morphology, syntax, semantics, and pragmatics during a psychoeducational assessment, then he or she should (a) interpret these language impairments relative to the student's academic and social functioning and (b) refer the student for a speech and language evaluation. Unfortunately, it is often the case that referral and collaboration with speech language pathologists does not occur.

Generally, indicators of language impairment that may influence academic and social functioning that could be readily detected in the psychoeducational evaluation include the student's limited vocabulary, reduced knowledge of concepts, word-finding difficulties, poor grammar, difficulty with tasks that require memory, following directions, poor comprehension, auditory perception of words, pronunciation, story telling, nonverbal communication, and pragmatic language. In the preschool population, students with language disorders may evidence difficulty with play; counting; reciting the days of the week; colors; following one-, two-, and three-step directions; responding to direct questions; and comprehension of stories (Mercer, 1997).

Children with relatively milder language impairments may not be identified until third grade or later when the academic demands increase (Mercer, 1997). These elementary school students may have difficulty with reading because of impairment in their phonological processing skills. In addition, comprehension of textbook material, verbal expression, formulation, synthesis of ideas, and written language may also be impaired. In adolescence, these students may evidence difficulty with higher-level language such as figurative language, expository writing, listening to lectures, note-taking, and study habits (Mercer, 1997).

Language-Based Learning Disability

There is considerable empirical support for the relationship of language to learning and learning disabilities (LD) as evidenced by the inclusion of it as a criterion in the federal definition of LD. Forty-six percent of all students in special education are classified as learning disabled, 18% are classified as speech and language impaired (U.S. Department of Education, 1996), and it has been estimated that between 40 and 60% have both (Wiig & Semel, 1984). With respect to academic performance, students with language deficits often have the most difficulty with reading. It has been proposed that this is due to their poor phonological processing skills (Mercer, 1997).

Specific Language-Based Learning Disability in Reading

Reading is mainly based on phonological processing or the awareness of the language's sound structure. Phonological processing includes manipulation of sounds, rhyming, blending, segmentation, and deletion (Kaminski & Good, 1998). Furthermore, early language indicators of reading problems include difficultly with letter sound recognition, rapid naming of objects, words, memory, and speaking slowly.

The Dynamic Indicators of Basic Early Literacy Skills (DIBELS) was developed as an assessment tool for school psychologists to use in order to identify preschool, kindergarten, and first-grade students who are at risk for reading failure (Kaminski & Good, 1998). The DIBELS assesses three areas: (a) phonemic segmentation fluency (i.e., the student is required to divide a word into sounds), (b) onset recognition fluency (i.e., the student is required to supply the first letter of a word as depicted in a picture), and (c) letter-naming fluency (i.e., the student is required to name the letters of the alphabet when presented in random order). The purpose of the DIBELS assessment is to identify students in need of early reading skills, to aid in treatment design, and to monitor progress (Kaminski & Good, 1998). Curriculum-based assessment (CBA) and curriculum-based measurement (CBM) would be the appropriate assessment choice for older students with reading difficulties. Finally, students with a language-based learning disability may not only evidence specific learning disabilities in reading, but also may reveal specific learning disabilities in the areas of written language, spelling, and mathematics, particularly with application and word problems.

Language and Social/Emotional Disorders

Students with language difficulties may also exhibit social and emotional deficits. This may be due to their impairment in pragmatic language as evidenced by difficulty with such skills as eye contact, turn taking, and adjusting to the listener's needs. These students also have difficulty joining conversations already in progress. In addition, they misinterpret social cues, have poor peer relations, are impulsive, hyperactive, and have difficulty judging the consequences of their behavior. These deficits in both language and social skills are often the harbinger of isolation from their peers (Mercer, 1997).

In support of the relationship between speech and language deficits and psychiatric disorders, Cantwell, Baker, and their colleagues, on the basis of several studies, found that speech and language impairments are associated with an increased prevalence of LD, attention deficit hyperactivity disorder (ADHD), autism, behavior disorders, anxiety, and depression. Furthermore, Beitchman, Cantwell, Forness, Kavale, and Kauffman (1998) noted that approximately 50% of students with language-learning disabilities also exhibited an Axis I psychiatric disorder.

Assessment of Language Disorders

Riccio and Hynd (1993) suggested indices that school psychologists should consider in the assessment of language disorders relative to the child's academic and social functioning. They included (a) the assessment of pragmatic language with the Test of Pragmatic Skills—Revised (Shulman, 1986) and the Interpersonal Language Skills Assessment (Blagden & McConnell, 1985). (Overall, with regard to pragmatic language, few measurement indices exist.) However, it is important to examine aspects of pragmatic language such as turn taking for speaking, topic management, and responding to and initiating response clarification.); (b) the assessment of adaptive behavior specific to social and communication skills with the Vineland Adaptive Behavior Scale (Sparrow, Balla, & Cicchetti, 1984) and the Behavior Assessment System for Children (BASC) (Kamphaus & Reynolds, 1992); and (c) the inclusion of a developmental interview to obtain information on hearing loss, family history of speech and language disorders, and relevant academic and behavior difficulties.

Furthermore, Downing (1989) described the difficulty in assessing language skills in students with severe multiple handicaps. He recommended, as an adjunct to standardized evaluation, the use of contextual communication assessment that involves the incorporation of the natural setting to accurately assess the communicative needs of the student within the social context. Allen (1989) also argued that formal assessment devices used for expressive language and comprehension are often inadequate and should be augmented with a spontaneous language sample.

Relatedly, Ganschow, Sparks, and Helmick (1992) recommend that in diagnoses, school psychologists, in addition to their traditional battery, should include indices of speech and language. Specifically, they stated that the Wechsler scales should not be the sole criteria for a speech and language referral. However, Sparks, Ganschow, and Thomas (1996) found that oral language, receptive vocabulary, and reading comprehension measures significantly contributed to the explanation of the variance in Verbal IQ on the Wechsler scales. Therefore, the Wechsler scales may offer some assistance in diagnosis of language disorders. However, other additional assessment is recommended. Aaron's (1991) suggestion that a diagnosis of a relative strength in the child's listening comprehension, relative to reading comprehension, could identify reading disabilities. This discrepancy would also suggest possible interventions based on phonemic awareness.

Interventions for Language Disorders

Telzrow, Fuller, Siegel, Lowe, and Lowe (1989) suggested that one of the roles school psychologists may play in treatment was as a consultant to assist the speech pathologists' delivery of services. Furthermore, the school psychologist's knowledge of behavioral and cognitive theories may be beneficial in collaboration with the speech pathologist in the design of language-based treatments.

Creaghead (1999) stated that outcome data are not available to demonstrate which strategies currently used for facilitating children's speech, language, and communication skills are most effective and efficient (p. 335). However, those treatments that are firmly based on behavioral or cognitive-behavioral theory appear most promising (Kehle, Madaus, Baratta, & Bray, 1998).

With regard to receptive language, the school psychologist can provide and reinforce strategies for comprehending written text such as paragraph restatement, story mapping, and creative dramatics. Paragraph restatement requires the student to pause after reading each paragraph and then orally summarize the content of the paragraph. Story mapping requires the student to depict the content read with key words or sentences. Creative dramatics refers to the student's interpreting and physically acting out the meaning of words, sentences, or whole stories.

With respect to listening comprehension, direction retelling, cognitive monitoring, and teaching vocabulary and concepts with a multimodal approach that provides the child with feedback and reinforcement have also been effective (Mercer, 1997).

In consideration of oral expressive language, the school psychologist could provide modeling for correct grammar, create increased opportunities for verbal responses, and have the child retell stories (Mercer, 1997). In addition, Mercer (1977) recommended that the addition of words to child's utterances and pictography promoted oral expressive language.

Specifically, with respect to the adding of words to the child's utterances, Bradshaw, Hoffman, and Norris (1998) employed a form of storybook reading that incorporated expansions and close procedures. The results indicated that the procedure promoted the children's responses to questions about the storybook, interpretations, and use of syntactically more complex language.

Pictography is a notational system that involves the creation of stories where the characters, settings, and sequences are represented by stick-figure drawings (Ukraninetz, 1998). Although focusing on oral narrative is crucial to promoting expressive language, it is difficult to remember, review, and revise. Narrative conveyed through pictography is substantially easier for the student to remember the content. This narrative-type intervention promotes understanding of sequence, quality, length, and clarity of content, substantially more so than simply having the student express themselves orally (Ukraninetz, 1998).

Story mapping, self-instruction, and word processing are the recommended strategies with regard to written expression. Story mapping can be used to outline the content that will eventually be expressed in writing. The student uses key words or sentences as a prompt to facilitate written expression. Self-instruction is defined as an intervention that employs a self-regulated strategy that includes prompts to facilitate the student's written expression. For example the mnemonic DARE, where D prompts determining your premise, A prompts assemble reasons to support your premise, R prompts reject arguments for the opposing view, and E prompts end with a conclusion (Graham & Harris, 1999).

With regard to pragmatic language, the school psychologist should recommend social skills training programs, specifically, modeling appropriate conversational skills, such as eye contact, topic maintenance, initiation, maintenance, and termination of conversation, and turn taking (Mercer, 1997; Riccio & Hynd, 1993). To a degree, these pragmatic language skills can be taught by having the student model appropriate social language. In addition, the uses of role playing and edited self-modeling videotapes have been effective in promoting social language skills (Kehle et al., 1998).

BEST PRACTICES FOR SPEECH DISORDERS

Articulation and Phonology

Articulation is defined as the correct pronunciation of developmentally appropriate speech. Articulation disorders may interfere with academic and social functioning (*Diagnostic and Statistical Manual of Mental Disorders* (4th ed.) (DSM-IV) (American Psychiatric Association, 1994). Furthermore, and most relevant to school psychologists, is recent research that has demonstrated that articulation disorders or lack of intelligibility of speech are related to difficulty in phonological processing and subsequently problems in reading (Mercer, 1997), writing, spelling, and mathematic abilities. It has been estimated that 50–70% of children with phonological disorders also have academic problems throughout their school years. When the student exhibits unintelligible speech, or evidence of a language impairment, the assessment of phonological awareness may be appropriate through the use of the Auditory Conceptualization Test–Revised (Lindamood, Bell, & Lindamood, 1992), or the Goldman-Fristoe Test of Articulation–2 (Goldman & Fristoe, 2000).

Phonology can also be assessed informally by presenting pictures that depict all consonants in the initial and final position in the word. Incorrect pronunciation of the speech sounds relative to the student's developmental age level should be noted (Mercer, 1997). Following this, a direct observation can be accomplished by taking a frequency count of correct speech productions of the target phoneme in a spontaneous speech sample during a 3–4-minute time interval (Diederick, 1971). Methods of direct observations and use of this information for progress monitoring is another area in which school psychologists could assist the speech pathologist in assessment and treatment. In addition, auditory discrimination can also be assessed informally. The student is presented with word pairs such as cat and hat and asked if the words are the same or different. Difficulty in auditory discrimination would be indicated by 10% or more inaccuracy (Mercer, 1997).

Interventions for Articulation and Phonological Disorders

Interventions designed to improve the student's articulation can involve the use of behavior programs that reinforce the student's correct pronunciation. A token economy with a response cost is one such classroom-based program that is relatively easy to implement.

Interventions designed for phonological deficits typically begin with auditory discrimination training. The school psychologist can address these deficits by incorporating auditory discrimination training (i.e., training student to hear differences between environmental sounds, letter sounds, etc.) into recommendations designed to improve the students' academic competencies. Phonological awareness may be enhanced by word segmentation, where the student identifies sounds and words, and blending exercises, where the student practices blending parts of words together. These could be included in recommendations for the treatment of reading.

Stuttering

As with children with language disorders, the speech disorder of stuttering has been associated with academic and social deficits (Bray & Kehle, 1996). This is tenable in that language disorders have been implicated in the etiology of stuttering. Also, as with language disorders, stuttering is related to depression and anxiety. Specifically, Blood and Seider (1981) stated that 68% of elementary school children who stutter also evidenced articulation, language, and emotional problems. The implication for school psychologists is that during assessment it may be beneficial to consider the co-occurrence of stuttering with emotional and academic problems.

Interventions for Stuttering

Some strategies that can be employed in collaboration with the speech pathologist involve relaxation paired with systematic desensitization, positive and negative reinforcement, timeout, successive approximations, differential reinforcement of other behavior, response cost, and habit reversal. Although these inventions have been effective in reducing stuttering, none has evidenced an enduring positive effect after cessation of intervention over the long term. However, one recently developed intervention for stuttering, self-modeling, has documented what appears to be a long-lasting positive effect for more than 2 years (Bray & Kehle, 2001). Self-modeling is defined as the multiple viewing of oneself on edited videotapes that depict exemplary behavior (Bray & Kehle, 1996). Bray and Kehle (1996, 1999) edited videotapes to portray students with stuttering disorders not stuttering in settings that were previously problematic.

Voice Disorders

Voice disorders are characterized by abnormal pitch, loudness, resonance, or duration (American-Speech-Language-Hearing Association, 1993). The causality of these voice disorders include such conditions as vocal nodules, which account for approximately 60% of hoarseness in children (Gray & Smith, 1996), tumors of the vocal tract, and muscular dysfunctions of the larynx. Although these voice disorders may influence academic and social functioning, they are almost exclusively addressed by speech pathologists. However, efforts for generalization of treatment gains can be supported by behaviorally based treatments designed and evaluated by school psychologists.

Hearing and Central Auditory Processing Disorders

Hearing impairments certainly influence speech and language skills. With respect to assessment, item difficulty on the WISC-III differentiates children with hearing impairments from children without hearing impairments, particularly on items that compose the Picture Completion, Information, Similarities, Vocabulary, and Comprehension subtests (Maller, 1997). Gibbins (1989) found that severely/profoundly hearing-impaired children achieve similar performance test scores as the standardization sample. In support of this, Braden (1992) stated that the use of special norms is perhaps not necessary for intellectual assessment of children with hearing impairments. Although audiologists and speech and language pathologists are typically responsible for assessment and intervention, collaboration with school psychologists may promote effective practice. Conversational skills, or pragmatic language, are problematic with children with hearing impairments. Furthermore, and probably because of this relative lack of pragmatic language, children often exhibit social skills deficits similar to those of children with learning disabilities and therefore may benefit from social skills training. Having the child role-play scenarios that focus on active communication and decision-making situations promote conversational speech (Johnson, 1997).

Central auditory processing disorders (CAPD) imply a disorder in the individual's ability to correctly process auditory stimuli. These disorders are not related to the individual's cognitive ability or the physiology of hearing. It is suggested that CAPD involve the individual's ability to correctly deal with acoustic stimuli, including decoding and attaching meaning to its contents (American-Speech-Language-Hearing Association, 1993). Formal testing is usually conducted by an audiologist and speech language pathologist. However, it has been suggested that this testing can function in the identification of a processing disorder with respect to learning disabilities. Finally, collaboration between school psychologists and speech pathologists is warranted based on Riccio and Hynd's (1996) reported similarities in etiology and symptomatology between children with ADHD and CAPD.

SUMMARY

The themes apparent in the communication disorders literature identified by Telzrow in 1989 are still evident: Communication disorders are pervasive in that they affect the student's cognitive, academic, and social functioning; assessment indices are limited and may require alternative strategies; and intervention approaches tend to be long term and emphasize the children's relative strengths.

With respect to all of the communication disorders, of most concern to the school psychologist is language impairment. Students with expressive and language disorders tend to have difficulty with reading. This is probably due to impairment in their phonological processing skills. In addition, verbal expression, formulation, synthesis of ideas, and written language may also be impaired.

Of the 48% of students in special education who are classified as learning disabled, 18% are also classified as speech and language impaired. Students with a language-based learning disability may evidence not only a specific learning disability in reading but also specific learning disabilities in the areas of written language, spelling, and mathematics. Therefore, it is recommended that school psychologists include an assessment of the child's language skills in their psychoeducational evaluations. The psychoeducational evaluation provides a unique opportunity to observe the child's language skills particularly in the areas of oral and written communication, auditory perception, understanding directions, pronunciation, and grammatical errors.

Perhaps because of their impairment in pragmatic language as evidenced by difficulty with such skills as eye contact, turn taking, and adjusting to the listener's needs, students with language difficulties may also exhibit social and emotional deficits. They may misinterpret social cues, are often impulsive and overactive, and have difficulty forming friendships and considering the consequences of their behavior.

Speech and language disorders are associated with an increased prevalence of co-morbid LD, ADHD, behavior disorders, anxiety, and depression. Furthermore, it has been noted that approximately half of students with language learning disabilities also exhibit an Axis I psychiatric disorder. Because of possible impairment in both academic and social functioning, school psychologists should minimally consider incorporating into their overall evaluation assessment of the student's pragmatic language and adaptive behavior, particularly with regard to social and communication skills. Also, the formal assessment of the student's expressive language and comprehension should be supplemented with a spontaneous language sample.

With regard to treatment, the school psychologist should consult and assist the speech pathologist's delivery of services. The school psychologist's knowledge of behavioral and cognitive interventions may be beneficial in collaboration with the speech pathologist in the design of language-based treatments.

In consideration of oral expressive language, the school psychologist could provide interventions that employ modeling correct grammar and increased opportunities for verbal responses. With regard to facilitating written expression, recommended interventions involve self-instruction and word processing.

Social skills training programs have been useful in helping children with communication disorders improve their pragmatic language. Such programs as outlined by Sheridan (1995) may be beneficial with these students. These include having the student model appropriate conversational skills and practice appropriate eye contact, topic maintenance, turn taking, and self-monitoring.

REFERENCES

Aaron, P. G. (1991). Can reading disabilities be diagnosed without using intelligence tests. *Journal of Learning Disabilities, 24,* 178–186.

Allen, D. A. (1989). Developmental language disorders in preschool children: Clinical subtypes and syndromes. *School Psychology Review, 18,* 442–451.

American Psychiatric Association. (1994). *Diagnostic and statistical manual of mental disorders* (4th ed). Washington, DC: Author.

American Speech-Language-Hearing Association. (1993). Definitions of communication disorders and variations. *ASHA, 35,* (Suppl. 10), 40–41.

Beitchman, J. H., Cantwell, D. P., Forness, S. R., Kavale, K. A., & Kauffman, J. N. (1998). Practice parameters for the assessment and treatment of children and adolescents with language and learning disorders. *Journal of the American Academy of Child and Adolescent Psychiatry, 37,* 46–62.

Blagden, C. M. & McConnell, N. L. (1985). *Interpersonal Language Skills Assessment.* Moline, IL: LinguiSystems.

Blood, G. W. & Seider, R. (1981). The concomitant problems of young stutterers. *Journal of Speech and Hearing Disorders, 46,* 31–33.

Braden, J. P. (1992). Intellectual assessment of deaf and hard-of-hearing people: A quantitative and qualitative research synthesis. *School Psychology Review, 21,* 82–94.

Bradshaw, M. L., Hoffman, P. R., & Norris, J. A. (1998). Efficacy of expansions and close procedures in the development of interpretations by preschool children exhibiting delayed language development. *Language, Speech, and Hearing Services in Schools, 29,* 85–95.

Bray, M. A. & Kehle, T. J. (1996). Self-modeling as an intervention for stuttering. *School Psychology Review, 25,* 359–370.

Bray, M. A., & Kehle, T. J. (1999). Self-modeling as an intervention for stuttering: A replication. *School Psychology Review, 27,* 587–598.

Bray, M. A., & Kehle, T. J. (2001). Long-term effects of self-modeling as an intervention for stuttering. *School Psychology Review, 30,* 131–137.

Cantwell, D. P., & Baker, L. (1985). Psychiatric and learning disorders in children with speech and language disorders: A descriptive analysis. *Advances in Learning and Behavioral Disabilities, 4,* 29–47.

Creaghead, N. A. (1999). Evaluating language intervention approaches: Contrasting perspectives. *Language, Speech, and Hearing Services in Schools, 30,* 335–338.

Diederick, W. M. (1971). Procedures for counting and charting a target phoneme. *Language, Speech, and Hearing Services in Schools, 5,* 18–32.

Downing, J. (1989). Identifying and enhancing the communicative behaviors of students with severe disabilities: The role of the school psychologist. *School Psychology Review, 18,* 475–486.

Ganschow, L., Sparks, R., & Helmick, M. (1992). Speech/language referral practices by school psychologists. *School Psychology Review, 21,* 313–326.

Gibbins, S. (1989). Use of the WISC-R performance scale and K-ABC nonverbal scale with deaf children in the U.S.A. and Scotland. *School Psychology International, 10,* 193–198.

Goldman, R., & Fristoe, M. (2000). *Goldman-Fristoe Test of Articulation, 2.* Circle-Pines, MN: American Guidance Service.

Graham, S., & Harris, K. R. (1999). Assessment and intervention in overcoming writing difficulties: An illustration from the self-regulated strategy development model. *Language, Speech, and Hearing Services in Schools, 30,* 255–264.

Gray, S. D., & Smith, M. E. (1996). Voice disorders in children. *NCVS Status and Progress Report, 10,* 133–149.

Johnson, C. E. (1997). Enhancing the conversational skills of children with hearing impairment. *Language, Speech, and Hearing Services in Schools, 28,* 137–145.

Kaminski, R. A., & Good, R. H. (1998). Assessing early literacy skills in a problem-solving model: Dynamic indicators of basic early literacy skills. In M. R. Shinn (Ed.), *Advanced applications of Curriculum-Based Measurement.* New York: Guilford.

Kamphaus, R. W., & Reynolds, C. R. (1992). *Behavior assessment system for children.* Circle Pines, MN: American Guidance Service.

Kehle, T. J., Madaus, M. M. R., Baratta, V. S., & Bray, M. A. (1998). Augmented self-modeling as a treatment for children with selective mutism. *Journal of School Psychology, 36*(3), 377–399.

Lindamood, P. C., Bell, N., & Lindamood, P. (1992). Issues in phonological awareness assessment. *Annals of Dyslexia, 42,* 242–249.

Maller, S. J. (1997). Deafness and WISC-III item difficulty: Invariance and fit. *Journal of School Psychology, 35,* 299–314.

Mercer, C. D. (1997). *Students with learning disabilities* (5th ed.). Englewood Cliffs, NJ: Prentice-Hall.

Riccio, C., & Hynd, G. W. (1993). Developmental language disorders in children: Relationship with learning disability and attention deficit hyperactivity disorder. *School Psychology Review, 22,* 696–709.

Riccio, C., & Hynd, G. W. (1996). Relationship between ADHD and central auditory processing disorder. *School Psychology International, 17,* 235–252.

Sheridan, S. M. (1995). *The tough kid social skills book.* Longmont, CO: Sopris West.

Shulman, B. (1986). *Tests of pragmatic skills, Revised.* Tucson, AZ: Communication Skill Builders.

Sparks, R., Ganschow, L., & Thomas, A. (1996). Role of intelligence tests in speech/language referrals. *Perceptual and Motor Skills, 83,* 195–204.

Sparrow, S. S., Balla, D. A., & Cicchetti, D. V. (1984). *Vineland Adaptive Behavior Scales: Interview edition.* Circle Pines, MN: American Guidance Service.

Telzrow, C. F. (1989). Guest editor's comments. Communication disorders preschool and school-aged children. *School Psychology Review, 18,* 440–441.

Telzrow, C. F., Fuller, A., Siegel, C., Lowe, A., and Lowe, B. (1989). Collaboration in the treatment of children's communication disorders: A five-year case study. *School Psychology Review, 18,* 463–474.

Ukraninetz, T. A. (1998). Stick writing stories: A quick and easy narrative representation strategy. *Language, Speech, and Hearing Services in Schools, 29,* 197–206.

U.S. Department of Education. (1996). *Eighteenth annual report to Congress on the implementation of the Indi-*

viduals with Disabilities Education Act. Washington, DC: Author.

Wiig, E. H., & Semel. E. M. (1984). *Language assessment and intervention for the learning disabled* (2nd ed.). Boston: Allyn & Bacon.

ANNOTATED BIBLIOGRAPHY

Cantwell, D. P., & Baker, L. (1985). Psychiatric and learning disorders in children with speech and language disorders: A descriptive analysis. *Advances in Learning and Behavioral Disabilities, 4,* 29–47.
The Cantwell and Baker article is a concise, informative, and thorough review of the relationship between psychiatric illness and communication disorders.

McGuinness, D. (1997). *Why our children can't read: And what we can do about it.* New York: Simon & Schuster.
This book is intended for a general audience; however, it is clearly based on empirical evidence. She predicates her argument on the failure of the whole language approach, phonics, or the combination of the two, to teaching reading. She proposes in the place of these failed techniques an approach to teaching reading that stresses the ability to hear the sounds of the language correctly and the connection of sounds to the symbols they represent.

Mercer, C. D. (1997). *Students with learning disabilities* (5th ed.). Englewood Cliffs, NJ: Prentice-Hall.
This book offers a comprehensive review of learning disabilities and their relationship to language disorders. Best practices for assessment and remediation are described.

Kaminski, R. A., & Good, R. H. (1998). Assessing early literacy skills in a problem-solving model: Dynamic indicators of basic early literacy skills. In M. R. Shinn (Ed.), *Advanced applications of Curriculum-Based Measurement.* New York: Guilford.
Kaminski and Good provide an excellent presentation of the DIBELS assessment procedure for the identification of early reading skills.

Swanson, H. L., Hoskyn, M., & Lee, C. (1999). *Intervention for students with learning disabilities: A meta-analysis of treatment outcomes.* New York: Guilford.
This text represents a comprehensive overview of over 30 years of intervention research applicable to students with language learning disabilities.

96 Best Practices in School-Based Sexuality Education and Pregnancy Prevention

Adena B. Meyers and Steven Landau
Illinois State University

OVERVIEW

Sexual behavior among adolescents is linked to a variety of undesirable outcomes, such as unplanned pregnancy and exposure to sexually transmitted infections (STIs) including HIV. In this section we provide a brief review of recent trends and statistics relevant to adolescent sexual behavior and related social and health problems. As interested professionals are likely aware, behavioral and epidemiological data in this area are constantly being revised and updated. Thus, to keep abreast of the most current available information, readers are also encouraged to access the various internet sites listed at the end of this chapter.

Although the proportion of adolescents engaging in sexual behavior showed a slight decline during the 1990s, more recent evidence suggests that adolescent sexual activity has again begun to increase (Wilson, 2000). Moreover, despite a recent drop in adolescent pregnancy rates nationwide (Darroch & Singh, 1999), the United States still ranks alarmingly high among developed countries in rates of adolescent pregnancy, childbirth, and STI transmission (Panchaud, Singh, Feivelson, & Darroch, 2000; Singh & Darroch, 2000). Indeed, it is estimated that each year nearly 1 million adolescents in the United States become pregnant, and approximately 3 million contract STIs (Alan Guttmacher Institute, 1999).

These statistics are even more disturbing in light of the serious and often irreversible health and developmental consequences associated with adolescent pregnancy and STI infection. Close to 80% of adolescent pregnancies in the United States are unintended, with about 35% ending in abortion and more than 40% ending in unintended births (Henshaw, 1998). Intended or not, adolescent childbearing appears to be associated with a variety of deleterious outcomes for young mothers and their children. For example, adolescent mothers are more likely than their same-age peers to drop out of school, rely on public assistance, and report high levels of psychological distress (Coley & Chase-Lansdale, 1998). Pregnant adolescents are less likely than older women to obtain adequate prenatal health services, and are more likely to deliver pre-term and low birth-weight infants (Klerman, 1993). Ultimately, their children are at risk for a number of developmental problems including cognitive delay, school failure, and aggressive behavior (Coley & Chase-Lansdale, 1998; Furstenberg, Brooks-Gunn, & Morgan, 1987). Longitudinal evidence suggests that the negative consequences suffered by early child-bearers may diminish over time, but that the disadvantages observed in their children tend to persist and even increase as they grow older (Coley & Chase-Lansdale, 1998; Furstenberg et al., 1987).

While pregnancy can adversely affect an adolescent's life trajectory, STIs can be lethal. In 1998, HIV was the ninth leading cause of death among young people aged 15–24 in the United States (National Center for Health Statistics, 2000). In December 1998, there were more than 3,400 adolescents living with symptomatic AIDS in this country. However, owing to the virus' long latency period, almost all HIV-infected adolescents remain asymptomatic *and undetected* throughout their tenure in the school setting. Indeed, most of these students will not become aware of their HIV-positive status until later in adulthood. Unfortunately, the sexually active HIV-infected teen will be most contagious within 10 days following his or her first exposure to the virus (a time before the emergence of HIV antibodies). Thus, infected students who are sexually active with multiple partners can dramatically affect the epidemiology of this STI (Wodrich, Swerdlik, Chenneville, & Landau, 1999).

The most prevalent STIs among adolescents include chlamydia, gonorrhea, genital warts, and genital herpes. Although these diseases are generally not life-threatening, their symptoms can be extremely serious. If left untreated, chlamydia and gonorrhea may lead to Pelvic Inflammatory Disease (PID) and subsequent infertility in women. Genital herpes and genital warts are both caused by viruses. Although the symptoms are manageable, the viruses remain in the body indefinitely and thus may be passed on to future sex partners. Importantly, the presence of genital warts is associated with an increased incidence of cervical cancer, and both of these viruses may be transmitted to infants in the birth canal and lead to complications during childbirth (Moore & Rosenthal, 1993).

In light of these serious consequences, schools have been called upon to address the problems of early sexual behavior, adolescent pregnancy, and STI transmission by providing sexuality education and pregnancy prevention services. In a recent survey of U.S. public school administrators, the majority (69%) reported that district-wide policies require schools to offer sexuality education (Landry, Kaeser, & Richards, 1999). However, the definition and content of sexuality education varies considerably, particularly with respect to the relative emphasis placed on abstinence as opposed to contraception and other risk-reduction methods. In light of current diversity in practice, Landry et al. (1999) refer to three types of sexuality education policies: (a) *comprehensive* policies discuss abstinence as one option among many pathways to healthy sexual development; (b) *abstinence-plus* policies promote abstinence as the best option for adolescents, but effective methods of contraception and disease prevention are also addressed; and (c) *abstinence-only* policies present abstinence as the only acceptable option outside of marriage, and the discussion of contraception is either prohibited altogether or restricted to information about its failures and shortcomings.

The relative merits and drawbacks of these very different approaches have been the subject of political as well as scholarly debate. Recent legislative mandates favor an abstinence-only approach, yet little evidence of its effectiveness has ever been documented (Donovan, 1998). Regardless of which type of policy may be in effect in a given school district, practitioners are well aware of the enormous difficulty and challenge involved in any attempt to change adolescents' sexual behavior. Effective sexuality education and pregnancy prevention programs address phenomena that cut across multiple areas of functioning including health, mental health, cognitive development, and behavior change. Because of their training and experience relevant to each of these domains, school psychologists are in an excellent position to collaborate with a variety of other school-based professionals such as nurses, social workers, health educators, and guidance counselors in addressing these complex problems. School psychologists may be asked to contribute directly to the design and delivery of school-based pregnancy prevention and sexuality education, or they may be called upon to participate more indirectly, through consultation with parents, teachers, or other school personnel. In any case, it seems likely that school psychologists will become involved in these issues.

BASIC CONSIDERATIONS

Typically, prevention efforts target behaviors that lead to undesirable outcomes or are in themselves maladaptive. Substance abuse and violence, for example, because they cause harm and are considered problems in most if not all contexts throughout the life span, are appropriate targets for prevention. Sexual behavior makes a more complicated intervention target since it is not inherently dysfunctional. Some types of sexual behavior are associated with problems at all ages. Examples include unprotected intercourse with multiple partners or coercive sex with a reluctant or powerless partner. Clearly these behaviors are legitimate targets for prevention programs. In contrast, abstinence-oriented interventions seek to postpone, rather than prevent, behavior that emerges in the course of normal development. Indeed, proponents of such programs explicitly acknowledge that sexual intercourse between married, heterosexual adults is acceptable, even desirable. What is not always clear is how these efforts to prevent early sexual behavior fit into a more general understanding of normal, healthy, sexual development. Thus, school-based professionals involved in sexuality education and pregnancy prevention programs must reconcile personal values with community standards regarding child and adolescent sexuality and the school's role in addressing these inevitable events.

Sexual Development

Sexuality education and pregnancy prevention efforts should be informed by empirical evidence regarding normal sexual development in children and adolescents. In deciding on prevention targets and strategies, it is helpful to know which sexual behaviors are normative among various populations at various ages. The notion that sexuality unfolds over the course of the lifespan, beginning in infancy or early childhood, remains somewhat controversial but is certainly not new. Researchers and scholars have been discussing and describing childhood and adolescent sexuality since the eighteenth century, if not earlier (Money, 1997).

Today, we know that sexual behaviors, such as masturbation and exploratory play with same-sex or opposite-sex peers, are common among young children (Starks & Morrison, 1996). For example, interview data indicate that 49% of boys and 32% of girls have masturbated by the age of 13, and that many begin doing so in early childhood (Arafat & Cotton, 1974). Furthermore, Crooks and Baur (1993) surveyed parents and found that more than 75% had observed their six- and seven-year-old children engaging in some form of sex play with other children. The types of sex games that are considered normal at this age involve looking at or touching another's genitals. However, inappropriate sexual behavior in a child may be a sign of sexual victimization (Kendall-Tackett, Williams, & Finkelhor, 1993). Behaviors such as oral-genital contact, insertion of objects into the vagina or anus, and imitating intercourse are relatively uncommon among prepubescent children and may be cause for concern (Berliner & Elliott, 1996).

During adolescence, the incidence of masturbation increases, particularly among boys, while sexual behavior with a partner begins to take on more mature forms. With respect to masturbation, Sorenson (1973) found that among adolescents older than 15, 70% of boys and 42% of girls had masturbated at least once. Meanwhile, heterosocial interaction increases as adolescents start spending more of their free time with members of the opposite sex. Among younger adolescents, sexual experimentation often occurs in a group context and may involve kissing games such as "spin the bottle." Older adolescents are more likely to participate in paired dating, which typically involves progressively intimate forms of sexual expression (Starks & Morrison, 1996). The progression generally unfolds over several years and follows a predictable pattern, from kissing, to fondling breasts, to genital petting, to intercourse (Moore & Rosenthal, 1993).

While this pattern captures the experience of the majority of American teens, there is evidence of variation within the population. For example, African-American adolescents often engage in intercourse prior to genital petting (Smith & Udry, 1985). Additionally, during adolescence a substantial minority of young people becomes aware of sexual and romantic attraction to members of their own sex. Remafedi, Resnick, Blum, and Harris (1992), for example, found that 10.7% of the high school students they surveyed were unsure of their sexual orientation, 4.5% reported they were primarily attracted to members of their own sex, 0.7% identified themselves as bisexual, and 0.4% as homosexual. Finally, it should be noted that some adolescents elect to remain virgins. Michael, Gagnon, Laumann, and Kolata (1994) report that as many as 5.8% of females and 8.3% of males wait until age 20 or older before initiating intercourse. The above summary offers unambiguous implications for the school psychologist: We must be knowledgeable of child and adolescent sexual development from a normative perspective and realize that various cultural or ethnic subgroups within the population may differ in terms of what is considered normative.

Intercourse

Over the past several decades, the average age at first intercourse has declined while the average age of marriage has increased, thereby contributing to an overall increase in the prevalence of premarital intercourse. For example, Michael et al. (1994) found that 84% of women born between 1933 and 1942 were either virgins or had only had intercourse with one partner when they reached the age of 20, but among women born after 1953, one-half reported having multiple partners by the age of 20. Recent evidence indicates that intercourse among adolescents in the United States, which had been on the rise during the 1970s and 1980s, appears to have stabilized or declined slightly during the 1990s. Still, adolescents are considerably more likely to have sex now than they were 50 years ago. The median age at first intercourse is 16.5 years for adolescents in the United States (Warren et al., 1998), and by age 18 approximately two-thirds have had sex (Alan Guttmacher Institute, 1999).

Adolescent sexual behavior is influenced by a variety of contextual variables. Research reveals that intercourse is probably indicative of social and behavioral problems for some adolescents while it may be a sign of healthy and prosocial development for others. For example, Small and Luster (1994) found that experience with intercourse increases with age and with the presence of a steady boyfriend or girlfriend. In other words, as adolescents mature and enter into exclusive dating relationships, they are more likely to have sex. On the other hand, the same study also revealed that intercourse is associated with alcohol use, low parental monitoring, poor grades, and sexual abuse history. Thus, sexual activity appears more common among adolescents with developmental and behavioral difficulties. Other predictors of adolescent sexual behavior include the perception that peers are having sex (Romer et al., 1994), permissive parental values (Small & Luster, 1994), delinquency, and physical abuse history (Stoiber & Good, 1998).

Intercourse is relatively uncommon among younger adolescents in this country. Before age 13, only 9.4% of boys and 4.5% of girls have had intercourse. However, there exists considerable regional and ethnic variation in these data. For example, in some states, fewer than 4% of young people initiate intercourse before age 13, while in other states more than 20% do so. Also, African-Americans tend to experience intercourse earlier than members of other ethnic groups. This is particularly true of African-American boys, more than half of whom have had intercourse by the age of 14 (Centers for Disease Control and Prevention, 1998; Warren et al., 1998).

These patterns suggest that the developmental significance of early intercourse may depend on the context in which it occurs. Nevertheless, research indicates that early intercourse is generally associated with a variety of psychosocial problems. For example, there is evidence that adolescents with histories of sexual victimization and substance use initiate intercourse earlier than their peers (Mott, Fondell, Hu, Kowaleski-Jones, & Menaghan, 1996; Stock, Bell, Boyer, & Connell, 1997). Also, it appears that many adolescents are coerced into early sexual encounters they do not want. For example, one recent study of 15- to 24-year-old women found that nearly one-fourth of the respondents whose sexual debuts occurred before age 14 reported their experience was not voluntary (Abma, Driscoll, & Moore, 1998).

In summary, school-based practitioners interested in sexuality education and pregnancy prevention must contend with the complexity and diversity that characterize sexual development. Broadly defined, sexual behavior occurs normally throughout childhood and adolescence. In one sense, then, the prevention of adolescent sexual behavior is neither practical nor advisable. However, certain types of sexual behavior, such as sexual intercourse, appear to be maladaptive among some young people in certain contexts. Moreover, while intercourse is normative among older adolescents, it is relatively uncommon among younger teens. Taken together, these observations suggest that adolescents who are likely to engage in sexual intercourse at an early age may benefit from preventive services of some kind. However, given that norms for early sexual behavior appear to vary considerably across subgroups, prevention strategies that are effective and appropriate with one group of young people are unlikely to be equally useful in all contexts. Moreover, it would be a mistake to assume that circumscribed programs aimed at the prevention of early intercourse will ultimately lead to improvements in other areas such as academic achievement and family functioning, and it is highly unlikely that such programs will alleviate the problems associated with a pre-existing history of sexual victimization. Instead, comprehensive preventive efforts that simultaneously target several of these developmental problems may be the most beneficial. Finally, focused interventions have the potential to reduce negative health outcomes that can be caused by discrete behaviors such as unprotected intercourse. We turn now to a discussion of these problems.

The Politics of Preventing Sexual Behavior

In the field of prevention science, few topics are fraught with political and moral undertones and heated debate as those related to the sexual behavior of American adolescents. We have all heard that adolescent pregnancy has reached epidemic proportions, that our teens are in danger of contracting and spreading life-threatening diseases, and that these problems are somehow tied to the moral decay of society and the deterioration of cherished institutions such as marriage, family, and religion. It has been posited by some (e.g., Reppucci, 1987) that the political atmosphere surrounding this topic has clouded our understanding of the relevant issues and may even interfere with efforts to improve outcomes for adolescents. For example, Fine (1988) argues that the public discourse on adolescent sexuality has been limited in its focus on the potentially violent and dangerous elements of sexual behavior, and on certain moral issues, to the exclusion of any discussion of the developing sexual desire that virtually all humans experience as they approach adulthood. Typically, one finds in a sex education curriculum "...(1) the authorized suppression of a discourse of female sexual desire; (2) the promotion of a discourse of female sexual victimization; and (3) the explicit privileging of married heterosexuality over other practices of sexuality" (Fine, 1988, p.30). Female students are not perceived as active sexual agents but as sexual victims devoid of normally developing sexual drives. Inherent in this sexuality-as-violence perspective is the presumption of a causal relationship between official silence regarding student sexuality and a decrement in sexual activity (i.e., if we don't teach about sex, it will not occur) (Fine, 1988).

According to Fine (1988), a curriculum that attends to female sexuality should encourage female students to consider what feels good and what does not, what is desirable and warrants pursuit versus what should be avoided, and these should be discussed in school in the context of individual sexual experience and needs. This approach to sex education is designed to release females from their traditional, passive role in which they are recipients of other people's sexuality to one in which they initiate and negotiate their own sexual behavior based on assessment of pleasure and a cost-benefit analysis. It is obvious this "discourse of desire" is rarely found in U.S. classrooms. Indeed, even though polls throughout the nation indicate that 80–90% of adult respondents support the notion of sex education in schools (with components addressing disease prevention through contraception), most school boards are under intense pressure to ensure the curricular focus on teen pregnancy prevention is through abstinence-only education (Donovan, 1998).

The silencing of this discourse is exemplified in a variety of recently developed programs and policies that may fly in the face of common sense. For instance, Donovan (1998) describes several abstinence-only programs that rely on scare tactics. One curriculum includes a video that attempts to silence desire by telling students that if they want to have premarital sex, they'll "just have to be prepared to die." The Welfare Reform Act provides funding for abstinence-only interventions that promote "a mutually faithful monogamous relationship in the context of marriage is the expected standard of human sexual activity" (DiClemente, 1998, p. 1574), and as of March 1998, 20 state legislatures had enacted abstinence-only sex education bills (Donovan, 1998). Given that most Americans do not marry until their mid twenties or later, this standard is clearly unrealistic, and simply ignores the sexual desires of many mature adults. In recent memory, however, the discourse of desire was most decisively silenced when U.S. Surgeon General M. Joycelyn Elders, M.D., was fired by President Clinton after she made the provocative remark that "...masturbation is something that is a part of human sexuality, and is a part of something that perhaps should be taught" (i.e., as a way to reduce the spread of AIDS) (see Zytkow, 1995, for details). Clearly, many believe that school-based sex education should not address masturbation. School administrators and teachers are feeling intense pressure regarding the debate about these controversial issues, and school psychologists may be in the best position to assist in the resolution of this conflict.

Unfortunately for practitioners, these examples illustrate that what is politically viable may conflict with what is scientifically and logically justifiable. In attempting to intervene on behalf of the health and well being of young people, one may run into formidable obstacles in the form of political, religious, and moral concerns about adolescent sexuality. In an ideal world, we would simply recommend the selection of interventions on the basis of empirically supported effectiveness. However, we recognize that this recommendation is not practical in all contexts, and that political considerations do influence intervention choices. A prevention program may be scientifically "proven" to reduce pregnancy, STIs, or early intercourse, but if its methods are not acceptable to some concerned and vocal parent groups, students, administrators, and community leaders, then its effectiveness will be greatly compromised.

On the other hand, political decisions are sometimes made on the basis of faulty assumptions about majority opinion. For example, there is ample evidence that most parents want their children to be exposed to sexuality education that includes information about STI prevention and contraception (e.g., Algozzine, Berne, & Huberman, 1995; Donovan, 1998), yet many administrators and practitioners may be afraid to implement such programs because they believe parents would complain. In light of these concerns, it seems particularly important that school-based practitioners become informed about what types of interventions their constituents (e.g., parents, students, teachers, administrators, community leaders) want and what they will tolerate. Professionals who are thus informed, and familiar with a variety of intervention strategies, will then be able to select techniques with adequate empirical support as well as social acceptability.

Potential Aptitude-by-Treatment Interactions

The importance of promoting norms that are appropriate to the target audience underscores the general notion that the effectiveness of a given prevention strategy is likely to vary depending on the context in which it is implemented and the characteristics of the participants. What follows is a discussion of several factors that might moderate the effectiveness of different prevention methods.

Demographic Factors

Factors such as age, gender, and ethnicity influence adolescent sexual behavior and should thus be taken into consideration when selecting and developing prevention strategies. For example, there is evidence that older adolescents are more likely than those under age 14 to show improvement in contraceptive use following preventive interventions (Franklin, Grant, Corcoran, Miller, & Bultman, 1997). This result suggests that the age of participants should be taken into account in deciding whether and how to present information about safer sex practices. Gender also plays an important role in sexual risk-taking, which indicates girls and boys may have different problems and different intervention needs. For example, depression is associated with early sexual involvement and nonuse of birth control in girls, but not in boys (Kowaleski-Jones & Mott, 1998). Thus, girls may benefit from strategies aimed at improving their emotional functioning while boys may respond better to other approaches. Ethnicity and cultural context are important because of their influence on norms regarding early sexual behavior and sexual risk-taking. For instance, Newcomb and his colleagues demonstrated that Latina women who are more acculturated to life in the United States engage in more risky sexual behaviors than their less acculturated peers. Importantly, acculturation status was a better predictor of sexual behavior than a number of theoretically derived variables based on the health belief model (Newcomb et al., 1998). This finding implies that certain theory-driven interventions may not be universally applicable.

Sexual Experience

Common sense suggests and evidence confirms that some strategies will work better with sexually experienced youth while others will be more effective with adolescents who have not yet initiated intercourse. For example, in their evaluation of an abstinence-oriented program for young teens, Howard and McCabe (1990) found their program effective in delaying the onset of intercourse among sexually inexperienced students, but ineffective for those students who were already sexually experienced at baseline. Intuitively, one should assume that sexually experienced students will not relate to interventions that stress abstinence. This notion is corroborated by findings from a study comparing the efficacy of an abstinence-oriented intervention to that of a safer sex intervention (Jemmott, Jemmott, & Fong, 1998). Sexually experienced students showed a greater reduction in intercourse frequency and unprotected intercourse if they were exposed to the safer sex intervention rather than the abstinence-oriented intervention.

It should also be noted that sexual victimization history may influence students' responses to prevention programs. Sexual victimization is associated with earlier initiation of intercourse and more risky sexual behavior (Stock et al., 1997). This suggests that children who have been victimized may be in need of more intensive prevention interventions. Furthermore, it is possible that students who have been previously forced to engage in sexual behavior may not respond to programs that emphasize self-control and personal responsibility pertaining to abstinence or safer sex practices. It may be particularly difficult (yet particularly important) to increase self-efficacy among this group of students.

Other Potential Factors

Other factors that may moderate intervention effectiveness include personal experience, academic performance, parent-child relationship variables, religious affiliation, and sexual orientation. Students who are personally familiar with problems such as STIs and adolescent pregnancy may have different responses to preventive interventions relative to their peers. If they have witnessed the effects of AIDS, for instance, they may be more readily motivated to take protective measures. Students who are having academic difficulty in school may not respond as well to traditional classroom-based instructional methods, and school attendance problems could interfere with participation in school-based programs. Furthermore, adolescents whose parents do not monitor their behavior may show more reduction in sexual risk-taking if interventions successfully engage their parents' participation. Students who are affiliated with religious organizations may respond best to programs that promote values and group norms consistent with their religious beliefs. Finally, although it is important for sexually active gay, lesbian, and bisexual youth to adopt safer sex practices, they may not relate well to programs that assume all participants are heterosexual. In general, it would be a mistake to adopt any intervention strategy without first considering the impact of these and other potential intervening variables.

BEST PRACTICES

In recent years, several authors have reviewed research on interventions aimed at adolescent pregnancy prevention (Franklin et al., 1997; Frost & Forrest, 1995) and sexual risk-reduction (Kirby et al., 1994), drawing conclusions about specific programs that have been shown to be effective and the characteristics that differentiate these from less effective approaches. Key findings and conclusions of these reviews are summarized below:

Sexuality Education

One aim of many preventive interventions is to increase adolescents' knowledge about sexuality. This often involves presenting information about physical maturation, reproduction, contraception, and STIs (specifically, symptoms and transmission mechanisms). Although it is well documented that educational efforts can effectively increase adolescents' sexuality-related knowledge, it is also recognized that young people do not change their sexual behavior on the basis of knowledge alone (Schinke, Forgey, & Orlandi, 1996). Nevertheless, effective interventions do tend to include educational components that provide accurate information about risks associated with unprotected intercourse and methods to avoid these risks (Frost & Forrest, 1995; Kirby et al., 1994), suggesting that increased knowledge may be a necessary but not sufficient ingredient in the prevention of unsafe sexual behavior. Kirby et al. (1994) also observe that effective programs tend to use active learning techniques to present sexuality information. Examples include group discussions, role-playing, and *in vivo* skill practice (e.g., going to stores or clinics to practice accessing birth control and prophylactics). Gilchrist, Schinke, and Blythe (1985) point out that actively involving adolescents in the learning process helps them personalize the information that is presented.

A concern about sexuality education raised in many communities is that teaching young people about sex and birth control may convey the message that it is acceptable to initiate intercourse during adolescence, thereby increasing the rates of early sexual behavior. Available evidence suggests that this concern is clearly unfounded. For example, Kirby et al. (1994) examined eight programs with sexuality education components and found that none of these led to increased frequency of intercourse among participants. Similarly, Franklin et al. (1997) conclude that pregnancy prevention programs do not significantly increase rates of sexual activity, and this is the case regardless of whether the programs emphasize abstinence or sexuality education.

Access to Condoms and Other Contraceptives

Frost and Forrest (1995) point out that the majority of effective pregnancy prevention programs provide access to contraceptive services, often through school-based or school-linked clinics. Consistent with this, Franklin et al. (1997) conclude that programs which provide information about *and access to* contraception are more successful than other programs if increasing contraceptive use to reduce pregnancy is the objective. The same concerns that have been raised about sexuality education are also relevant here. Indeed, distributing birth control in schools is a highly controversial strategy, often thought to condone and promote early sexual behavior. However, the research indicates that providing adolescents with access to contraception does not result in increased sexual activity. For example, Schuster, Bell, Berry, and Kanouse (1998) report that after condoms were distributed in an urban high school, the rate of intercourse among students remained stable while the rate of condom use among sexually active students increased.

Interpersonal Skills

Many effective programs include training in interpersonal skills that are of particular relevance to sexual risk reduction. These include decision making, negotiation, communication, and refusal of sexual advances. (Frost & Forrest, 1995; Kirby et al., 1994). Effective training generally involves modeling, instruction, and various types of skill practice.

Intervention Setting

Prevention programs that target sexual behavior are often delivered in schools or community-based clinics or hospitals. Some involve widespread community participation, while others are more circumscribed and may only involve classroom instruction. In their description of effective pregnancy prevention programs, Frost and Forrest (1995) identify effective school- and clinic-based curricula, as well as successful approaches for school/community agency collaboration. Their analysis suggests that effective programs may be conducted in a variety of settings, and that many effective programs are school-based. However, the results of Franklin et al.'s (1997) meta-analysis indicate that community-based and clinic-based programs are more effective than school-based programs in increasing adolescents' use of contraception. These data suggest that collaboration with community agencies, such as health clinics, business leaders, religious organizations, and parents, may facilitate school-based prevention efforts.

Involving Parents

Interestingly, in many of the prevention programs examined in these reviews, the involvement of parents is minimal or nonexistent. This omission seems particularly salient in light of evidence that parent behaviors such as monitoring and communication are important predictors of adolescent sexual risk-taking (e.g., Romer et al., 1994; Small & Luster, 1994). It seems plausible that prevention efforts might be enhanced if parents were to play a greater role. Possible strategies could include educating parents about their potential influence on their children's sexual behavior, training parents to increase their ability to monitor their children's behavior, or providing sexuality education to parents, which might enhance their confidence about discussing sex and birth control with their adolescents.

Role of Values

In general, effective programs are not value-neutral. Kirby et al. (1994) argue that this is one of the most salient differences between effective and ineffective programs. Instead of encouraging students to make individually based decisions about sexual behavior, effective programs take a clear stand regarding what is and is not appropriate, and they actively seek to shape group norms. Frost and Forrest (1995) conclude that effective programs specifically emphasize abstinence as the best way for adolescents to avoid unwanted pregnancy and STIs. This may seem surprising or even contradictory given the role that birth control information and access apparently play in program effectiveness. However, many effective interventions simultaneously advocate abstinence and sexual responsibility. They teach that abstinence is the best choice, but they also encourage adolescents to practice safer sex should they chose to become sexually active.

Importantly, the relative emphasis placed on abstinence as opposed to safer sex varies from program to program. Kirby et al. (1994) point out that effective programs promote the norms and values appropriate for the specific population they target. For example, an intervention aimed at middle-school students who are predominantly virgins places the most emphasis on abstinence (Howard & McCabe, 1990), while interventions aimed at high-risk teens who are predominantly sexually experienced stress condom use and other risk-reduction strategies (e.g., St. Lawrence, Jefferson, Alleyne, & Brasfield, 1995; Walter & Vaughan, 1993).

Summary of Effective Strategies

Since the effectiveness of any particular prevention strategy is likely to depend on a variety of contextual factors, it seems potentially misleading to identify a set of "most effective" program characteristics. What is most effective in one context might be quite ineffective in another. However, some general patterns emerge from the above discussion, and are worth summarizing. In general, school-based practitioners are advised to consider the following program components and strategies (see Kirby et al., 1994, for a similar list of key program characteristics):

- Theoretical basis: Effective programs tend to be theory-driven. Many rely on social learning theories, which emphasize the role of social influences (e.g., peers, mass media), and personally relevant knowledge about risks and risk-reduction strategies.

- Access to contraception: Although some school districts may not allow this, effective programs tend to facilitate (in one way or another) students' access to condoms and/or other contraception methods.

- School versus clinic setting: Evidence is mixed regarding which location is best, but if increased contraception/condom use is a central goal, and school-based distribution of these items is not feasible, then collaboration with school-linked clinics, or community-based preventive services should be considered.

- Sexuality education: Although education alone does not change sexual behavior, it is a prerequisite for behavior change according to most theoretical models. The majority of effective prevention programs include sexuality education components.

- Interpersonal skills training: Effective programs tend to provide training in skills such as communication, negotiation, and refusal.

- Active learning and skill practice: Effective programs tend to offer opportunities for students to participate actively in the learning process and to practice skills in simulated (e.g., role-play) or real-life situations.

- Question of values: Effective programs emphasize values that are appropriate to the needs of the target audience (e.g., abstinence versus safer sex). There is evidence that a totally value-free decision-making approach is less effective than one that presents clear messages about sexual responsibility (Kirby et al., 1994).

- Involving parents: Obviously, parents play an important role in shaping their children's behavior in general and sexual development in particular. Practitioners should consider creating opportunities for parents to participate and collaborate in the selection, development, and implementation of prevention programs.

Recommendations for Selecting Prevention Programs

Needs Assessment

Before adopting an intervention approach, a careful assessment should be conducted to determine the specific sexual risk-reduction needs of the community and any potential obstacles that may interfere with efforts to address these needs. One of the first steps in this process is to identify relevant stakeholders and potential collaborators. At a minimum, these should include students, parents, and school personnel. Other possibilities include health-care providers, public health officials, owners of businesses (particularly those who sell condoms and other contraceptives), religious figures, and other community leaders. Donovan (1998) recommends setting up an advisory board of various school personnel and community members. This strategy will facilitate collaboration, and increase the chances that decisions about prevention goals and intervention methods represent the opinions of various constituent groups.

A number of critical questions should be addressed in the needs assessment. One important goal is to learn as much as possible about the political feasibility of various sexually oriented interventions in the local context. Additionally, it is important to gather information about the sexual norms and behaviors of students in the target population, and relevant contextual variables, such as family composition, ethnicity, and socioeconomic status of community members. It would be useful to determine what (if any) gaps exist in relevant knowledge and resources among parents, teachers, students, and the community in general. Data relevant to all of these questions could be generated by conducting surveys or focus group interviews. Additionally, review of relevant records will prove beneficial. Public health statistics regarding rates of unintended pregnancy, abortion, and STIs among adults and adolescents in the community should be reviewed, and data gathered from reproductive health-care providers to determine the extent to which adolescents are already accessing such services.

Developing Goals and Selecting Intervention Strategies

Information collected during the needs assessment should be used to develop prevention goals appropriate for the community. These goals may relate to specific behaviors (e.g., "increase the proportion of students who wait until age 16 to initiate intercourse" or "decrease the average number of sexual partners that sexually active students report having") or to more general outcomes (e.g., "reduce the rate of adolescent pregnancy") or both. Ideally, the goals will be relevant to the community's needs, and acceptable to its members. Intervention strategies should then be selected that are likely to be effective with respect to the prevention goals and the characteristics of the participants. The model programs described above provide examples of the variety of approaches presently available. Practitioners may choose to adopt one of these models or combine various elements of several different programs.

In cases where community norms are potentially dysfunctional, a school-based practitioner may need to consider implementing a politically unpopular intervention. For example, in a community with high rates of early sexual behavior and STIs, the best practice might be to negotiate with or (if necessary) work in opposition to a vocal community leader who objects to any discussion of condoms with students. In such instances, it may be necessary to educate the community about the seriousness of the risks, and the results of studies demonstrating that educating students about birth control and safe sex does not lead to increases in sexual behavior. In some circumstances, creative solutions may be called for. For example, if it is not politically feasible to discuss sexuality issues with students, then information about the prevalence of adolescent sexual behavior and the risks associated with it can be provided to parents, along with training in how to communicate with their children about these issues.

Assessment of Process And Outcome

Process and outcome assessment should accompany the delivery of any intervention. In the case of prevention programs aimed at the delay or modification of sexual behavior among adolescents, several issues ought to be addressed. Throughout the intervention, the integrity and acceptability of the prevention strategies should be repeatedly assessed. Assessment of intervention effectiveness should focus on whether and to what extent original goals are being met, and should include outcome data beyond student self-report. For example, public health statistics regarding adolescent pregnancies, abortions, and STIs could be examined and compared to pre-intervention rates. Results of both process and outcome assessment should be communicated to community members. For example, a newsletter about the intervention could be sent out at regular intervals to parents and students. Also, local media could be invited to cover the intervention and its results. In some cases, as information about the successes and failures of an intervention come to light, goals may need to be revised and the adoption of new strategies may be warranted.

SUMMARY

In light of continuing concerns regarding adolescent pregnancy and STI transmission, schools are being called upon to deliver sexuality education and pregnancy prevention programming in many communities. Because school psychologists are knowledgeable about health, mental health, cognitive development, and behavior change, they are in an ideal position to contribute to the development and implementation of these interventions. Thus, it may be helpful for school psychologists to know that effective programs tend to be theoretically grounded, provide access to contraception, provide accurate information about sexual health and development, emphasize the development of interpersonal skills, and emphasize appropriate values. In addition, pregnancy prevention and sexuality education efforts may be enhanced through increased parent involvement. School psychologists should select intervention strategies with sensitivity to a variety of (often conflicting) concerns including evidence of intervention efficacy, information about normative sexual development, and community needs and values. Finally, ongoing assessment is recommended to ensure these interventions are implemented in a consistent and effective manner.

REFERENCES

Abma, J., Driscoll, A., & Moore, K. (1998). Young women's degree of control over first intercourse: An exploratory analysis. *Family Planning Perspectives, 30*, 12–18.

Alan Guttmacher Institute (1999). *Facts in brief: Teen sex and pregnancy* [On-line]. Available: http://www.agi-usa.org/pubs/fb_teen_sex.html.

Algozzine, B., Berne, L. A., & Huberman, B. K. (1995). Comparison of beliefs about the family life education curriculum. *The Journal of Educational Research, 88*, 331–337.

Arafat, I. S., & Cotton, W. L. (1974). Masturbation practices of males and females. *Journal of Sex Research, 10*, 293–307.

Berliner, L., & Elliott, D. M. (1996). Sexual abuse of children. In J. Briere, L. Berliner, J. A. Bulkley, C. Jenny, & T. Reid (Eds.), *The APSAC handbook on child maltreatment* (pp.51–71). Thousand Oaks, CA: Sage.

Centers for Disease Control and Prevention (1998). Youth risk behavior surveillance: United States, 1997. *Morbidity and Mortality Weekly Report, 47*(SS-3).

Coley, R. L., & Chase-Lansdale, P. L. (1998). Adolescent pregnancy and parenthood: Recent evidence and future directions. *American Psychologist, 53*, 152–166.

Crooks, R., & Baur, K. (1993). *Our sexuality*. Redwood City, CA: Benjamin/Cummings.

Darroch, J. E., & Singh, S. (1999). *Why is teenage pregnancy declining? The roles of abstinence, sexual activity and contraceptive use*. Occasional Report No. 1. The Alan Guttmacher Institute, New York.

DiClemente, R. J. (1998). Preventing sexually transmitted infections among adolescents: A clash of ideology and science. *Journal of the American Medical Association, 279*, 1564–1575.

Donovan, P. (1998). School-based sexuality education: The issues and challenges. *Family Planning Perspectives, 30*, 188–193.

Fine, M. (1988). Sexuality, schooling, and adolescent females: The missing discourse of desire. *Harvard Educational Review, 58*, 29–53.

Franklin, C., Grant, D., Corcoran, J., Miller, P. O., & Bultman, L. (1997). Effectiveness of prevention programs for adolescent pregnancy: A meta-analysis. *Journal of Marriage and the Family, 59*, 551–567.

Frost, J. J., & Forrest, J. D. (1995). Understanding the impact of effective teenage pregnancy prevention programs. *Family planning perspectives, 27*, 188–195.

Furstenberg, F. F., Jr., Brooks-Gunn, J., & Morgan, S. P. (1987). *Adolescent mothers in later life*. New York: Cambridge University Press.

Gilchrist, L. D., Schinke, S. P., & Blythe, B. J. (1985). Preventing unwanted adolescent pregnancies. In L. D. Gilchrist & , S. P. Schinke (Eds.), *Preventing Social and Health Problems through Life Skills Training* (pp. 55–62). Seattle: University of Washington.

Henshaw, S. K. (1998). Unintended pregnancy in the United States. *Family Planning Perspectives, 30*, 24–29, 46.

Howard, M,. & McCabe, J. B. (1990). Helping teenagers postpone sexual involvement. *Family Planning Perspectives, 22*, 21–26.

Jemmott, J. B., III, Jemmott, L. S., & Fong, G. T. (1998). Abstinence and safer-sex HIV risk reduction interventions for African American adolescents: A randomized controlled trial. *Journal of the American Medical Association, 279*, 1529–1536.

Kendall-Tackett, K., Williams, L. & Finkelhor, D. (1993). Impact of sexual abuse on children: A review and synthesis of recent studies. *Psychological Bulletin, 113*, 164–180.

Kirby, D., Short, L., Collins, J. Rugg, D., Kolbe, L., Howard, M., Miller, B., Sonenstein, F., & Zabin, L. S. (1994). School-based programs to reduce sexual risk behaviors: A review of effectiveness. *Public Health Reports, 109*, 339–360.

Klerman, L. V. (1993). Adolescent pregnancy and parenthood: Controversies of the past and lessons for the future. *Journal of Adolescent Health, 14*, 553–561.

Kowaleski-Jones, L., & Mott, F. L. (1998). Sex, contraception, and childbearing among high-risk youth: Do different factors influence males and females? *Family Planning Perspectives, 30*, 163–169.

Landry, D. J., Kaeser, L., & Richards, C. L. (1999). Abstinence promotion and the provision of information about contraception in public school district sexuality education policies. *Family Planning Perspectives, 31*, 280–286.

Michael, R. T., Gagnon, J. H., Laumann, E. O., & Kolata, G. (1994). *Sex in America: A definitive survey*. Boston: Little, Brown.

Money, J. (1997). *Principles of developmental sexology*. New York: Continuum.

Moore, S., & Rosenthal, D. (1993). *Sexuality in adolescence*. London: Routledge.

Mott, F. L., Fondell, M. M., Hu, P. N., Kowaleski-Jones, L., & Menaghan, E. G. (1996). The determinants of first sex by age 14 in a high-risk adolescent population. *Family Planning Perspectives, 28*, 13–18.

National Center for Health Statistics (2000). Deaths: Final data for 1998. *National Vital Statistics Reports, 48*(11).

Newcomb, M. D., Wyatt, G. E., Romero, G. J., Tucker, M. B., Payment, H. A., Carmona, J. V., Solis, B., & Mitchell-Kernan, C. (1998). Acculturation, sexual risk taking, and HIV health promotion among Latinas. *Journal of Counseling Psychology, 4*, 454–467.

Panchaud, C. Singh, S. Feivelson, D. & Darroch, J. E. (2000). Sexually transmitted diseases among adolescents in developed countries. *Family Planning Perspectives, 32*, 124–132, 45.

Remafedi, G., Resnick, M., Blum, R., & Harris, L. (1992). Demography of sexual orientation in adolescence. *Pediatrics, 89*, 714–721.

Reppucci, N. D. (1987). Prevention and ecology: Teen-age pregnancy, child sexual abuse, and organized youth sports. *American Journal of Community Psychology, 15*, 1–22.

Romer, D., Black, M., Ricardo, I., Feigelman, S., Kalijee, L., Galbraith, J., Nesbit, R., Hornik, R. C., & Stanton, B. (1994). Social influences on the sexual behavior of youth at risk to HIV exposure. *American Journal of Public Health, 84*, 977–985.

Schinke, S. P., Forgey, M. A., & Orlandi, M. (1996). Teenage sexuality. In M. A. Mattaini & B. A. Thyer (Eds.), *Finding solutions to social problems: Behavioral strategies for change* (pp. 267–288). Washington, DC: American Psychological Association.

Schuster, M. A., Bell, R. M., Berry, S. H., & Kanouse, D. E. (1998). Impact of a high school condom availability program on sexual attitudes and behaviors. *Family Planning Perspectives, 30*, 67–72, 88.

Singh, S., & Darroch, J. E. (2000). Adolescent pregnancy and childbearing: Levels and trends in developed countries. *Family Planning Perspectives, 32*, 14–23.

Small, S. A., & Luster, T. (1994). Adolescent sexual activity: An ecological approach. *Journal of Marriage and the Family, 56*, 181–192.

Smith, E. A., & Udry, J. R. (1985). Coital and non-coital sexual behaviors of white and black adolescents. *American Journal of Public Health, 75*, 1200–1203.

Sorenson, R. C. (1973). *Adolescent sexuality in contemporary America: Personal values and sexual behavior ages thirteen to nineteen*. New York: World.

Starks, K. J., & Morrison, E. S. (1996). *Growing up sexual* (2nd ed.). New York: Harper Collins.

St. Lawrence, J. S., Jefferson, K. W., Alleyne, E., & Brasfield, T. L. (1995). Comparison of education versus behavioral skills training interventions in lowering sexual HIV-risk behavior of substance-dependent adolescents. *Journal of Consulting and Clinical Psychology, 63*, 154–157.

Stock, J. L., Bell, M. A., Boyer, D. K., & Connell, F. A. (1997). Adolescent pregnancy and sexual risk-taking among sexually abused girls. *Family Planning Perspectives, 29*, 200–203, 227.

Stoiber, K. C., & Good, B. (1998). Risk and resilience factors linked to problem behavior among urban, culturally diverse adolescents. *School Psychology Review, 27*, 380–397.

Walter, H. J., and Vaughan, R. D. (1993). AIDS risk reduction among a multi-ethnic sample of urban high school students. *Journal of the American Medical Association, 270*, 725–730.

Warren, C. W., Santelli, J. S., Everett, S. A., Kann, L., Collins, J. L., Cassell, C. C., Morris, L., & Kolbe, L. J. (1998). Sexual behavior among U.S. high school students, 1990–1995. *Family Planning Perspectives, 30*, 170–172, 200.

Wilson, S. N. (2000). Sexuality education: Our current status, and an agenda for 2010. *Family Planning Perspectives, 32*, 252–254.

Wodrich, D. L., Swerdlik, M. E., Chenneville, T., & Landau, S. (1999). HIV/AIDS among children and adolescents: Implications for the changing role of school psychologists. *School Psychology Review, 28*, 228–241.

Zytkow, N. (1995, October). *Speaker Joycelyn Elders puts prevention 1st* [On-line]. Available: http://www.spub.ksu.edu/ISSUES/v100/FA/n032/cam-elders-zytkow.html.

ANNOTATED BIBLIOGRAPHY

Donovan, P. (1998). School-based sexuality education: The issues and challenges. *Family Planning Perspectives, 30*, 188–193.

This paper addresses several of the political issues that influence the delivery of preventive sexuality education services in schools. The author provides useful information and advice for practitioners interested in implementing such services.

Franklin, C., Grant, D., Corcoran, J., Miller, P. O., & Bultman, L. (1997). Effectiveness of prevention programs for adolescent pregnancy: A meta-analysis. *Journal of Marriage and the Family, 59*, 551–567.

This study examines the results of 32 published evaluations of adolescent pregnancy prevention programs, focusing on the effects of such interventions on sexual activity, contraceptive use, and pregnancy. The meta-analytic strategy allows the authors to make generalizations about the effects of interventions on these three outcome variables, and to examine the roles of several possible moderating factors such as participant demographics, type of intervention (i.e., abstinence-only versus sex education with no contraception versus sex education with contraceptive knowledge-building and distribution), and locus of intervention (i.e., school vs. community).

Frost, J. J., & Forrest, J. D. (1995). Understanding the impact of effective teenage pregnancy prevention programs. *Family planning perspectives, 27*, 188–195.

This paper focuses on five empirically supported adolescent pregnancy prevention programs (including the School/Community Program for Sexual Risk Reduction Among Teens and the PSI curriculum described in this chapter). The authors present details about each intervention and its evaluation, and draw conclusions about elements that appear to be common among effective programs.

Kirby, D., Short, L., Collins, J., Rugg, D., Kolbe, L., Howard, M., Miller, B., Sonenstein, F., & Zabin, L. S. (1994). School-based programs to reduce sexual risk behaviors: A review of effectiveness. *Public Health Reports, 109*, 339–360.

This review examines the findings of a variety of empirical studies addressing the effects of school-based programs aimed at pregnancy prevention, sex education, and/or STI prevention. Seven of the studies reviewed assess the effects of sex education through national surveys of adolescents, and the other 16 studies are experimental or quasi-experimental evaluations of specific prevention programs (including the PSI and AIDS-preventive curricula described in this chapter). The authors provide details about each of the 16 interventions and evaluations, and they compare the characteristics of effective and ineffective programs.

WEBSITES RELATED TO PREGNANCY PREVENTION AND SEXUALITY EDUCATION

The following internet resources offer current information that may be useful to school psychologists interested in school-based pregnancy prevention and sexuality education.

Alan Guttmacher Institute <www.agi-usa.org>
This site provides access to fact sheets and reports summarizing recent statistics about adolescent sexuality and pregnancy. It also offers, a full-text version of the current issue of *Family Planning Perspectives*.

Centers for Disease Control and Prevention <www.cdc.gov>
Information about health promotion, disease prevention, and epidemiological data compiled by the CDC may be downloaded from this site.

Planned Parenthood Federation of America <www.plannedparenthood.org>
This site contains up-to-date information about contraceptive technology, relevant legal developments (particularly regarding abortion laws and policies), answers to frequently asked questions about sexual health, and information targeted specifically at adolescents. It also provides a list of local Planned Parenthood agencies.

Sexuality Information and Education Council of the United States (SIECUS) <www.siecus.org>
This site offers an array of comprehensive sexuality education resources for adolescents, parents, educators, religious groups, and others.

AUTHOR NOTE

Portions of this chapter previously appeared in Meyers, A. B., & Landau, S. (2000). Preventing early sexual behavior: Sociopolitical issues and the design of empirically supportable school-based interventions. In K. Minke & G. Bear (Eds.), *Preventing school problems– promoting school success: Strategies and programs that work* (pp.299–336). Bethesda, MD: National Association of School Psychologists.

97 Best Practices Working With Students Using Assistive Technology

Julia E. McGivern
Brian C. McKevitt
University of Wisconsin-Madison

OVERVIEW

School psychologists are increasingly called upon to work with students using assistive technology (AT). AT is a broad term used to describe a range of devices and services (Individuals with Disabilities Education Act (P.L. 101-426) 20 U.S.C. Chapter 33. Amended by P.L. 105-17, June, 1997) that can be used with students with limitations in communication, motor control, sensory skills, and learning abilities. These devices and services are intended to enhance students' ability to express needs, learn, demonstrate knowledge, function socially, and achieve success. School psychologists may become involved with AT when assessing a student's skills, planning interventions, working on IEP teams, or consulting with other school professionals and parents. Knowledge of the different types of AT available to students and issues associated with the use of AT is crucial for making informed decisions about student placement, programming, and progress.

More than 1,000 new AT products are introduced every year (Blackstone, 1996). Consequently, "it is impossible for one person or group of people to be familiar with all the technology options currently available" (Scherer & Galvin, 1996, p. 2). *Most school psychologists are not AT experts, nor do they need to be.* However, school psychologists must be prepared to work in collaboration with other school staff members, families, and students themselves to meet the needs of students who use AT. In this chapter, we present information intended to assist school psychologists in providing services to all students. We describe legal mandates and ethical standards pertaining to AT, describe the roles school psychologists may fill while working with students using AT, outline considerations for selection and use of AT in assessment, and focus specifically on AT designed to assist students with communication. We have chosen to focus on AT for communication because this is a technology domain with which many school psychologists interact in the course of direct and indirect service to students with disabilities. Also, please note that because technology is changing so rapidly, we have included few brand name product examples. Please refer to the ABLEDATA resource in the annotated bibliography for current technology availability.

BASIC CONSIDERATIONS

Laws Related to AT

Several federal statutes address the provision of AT in schools. The Technology-Related Assistance for Individuals with Disabilities Act of 1988 (Pub. L. No. 100-407) states that AT devices and services must be available to people with disabilities. The Individuals with Disabilities Education Act incorporated language from the Technology Act and applied it to educational services. IDEA defines AT broadly as both devices and services (see Table 1).

IDEA regulations state that "each public agency shall ensure that AT devices or AT services, or both, are made available to a child with a disability if required as part of (a) special education, (b) related services, or (c) supplementary aids and services" (34

Table 1. Selected Assistive Technology Definitions and Provisions in IDEA

Assistive Technology Device
The term "assistive technology device" means any item, piece of equipment, or product system, whether acquired commercially off the shelf, modified, or customized, that is used to increase, maintain, or improve functional capabilities of a child with a disability (IDEA, 20 U.S.C., §602, 1997).
Assistive Technology Service
The term "assistive technology service" means any service that directly assists a child with a disability in the selection, acquisition, or use of an assistive technology device. Such term includes (a) the evaluation of the needs of such child, including a functional evaluation of the child in the child's customary environment; (b) purchasing, leasing, or otherwise providing for the acquisition of assistive technology devices by such child; (c) selecting, designing, fitting, customizing, adapting, applying, maintaining, repairing, or replacing of assistive technology devices; (d) coordinating and using other therapies, interventions, or services with assistive technology devices, such as those associated with existing education and rehabilitation plans and programs; (e) training or technical assistance for such child, or, where appropriate, the family of such child; and (f) training or technical assistance for professionals (including individuals providing education and rehabilitation services), employers, or other individuals who provide services to, employ, or are otherwise substantially involved in the major life functions of such child (IDEA, 20 U.S.C., §602, 1997).
Use Of Assistive Technology Across Settings
On a case-by-case basis, the use of school-purchased assistive technology devices in a child's home or in other settings is required if the child's IEP team determines that the child needs access to those devices in order to receive FAPE [free appropriate public education] (34 C.F.R. §300.308, 1999).

C.F.R. § 300.308, 1999). When deemed part of special education and necessary for provision of a free and appropriate public education (FAPE), AT devices and/or services are addressed in IEP goals and objectives. Goals and objectives may relate to activities accomplished via AT or to training and use of AT itself. As clarified in IDEA regulations (1999), the use of school-owned AT must be available for the student in settings outside the school if the AT is necessary for the student to receive FAPE (see Table 1).

IDEA 1997 also contains provisions for the inclusion of students with disabilities in statewide and district-wide assessments, stating that "children with disabilities are included in statewide and district-wide assessment programs, with appropriate accommodations and modifications in administration if necessary" (34 C.F.R. § 300.138, 1999). *Testing accommodations* are changes in the way a test is administered or responded to that are intended to offset or correct for distortions in scores that may be caused by a student's disability (McDonnell, McLaughlin, & Morrison, 1997). If participation in general assessment is not appropriate, even with accommodations, an *alternate assessment* must be developed to measure a student's progress (34 C.F.R. 300.138, 1999). Elliott, Kratochwill, and Schulte (1999) identified AT, such as text-talk converters (text-to-speech software), speech synthesizers, visual magnification devices, or auditory amplification devices, as potential accommodations on standardized tests or alternate assessments.

Ethical Standards Related to AT

In addition to legal mandates for using AT, there are ethical obligations school psychologists must meet that pertain to the use of AT. NASP's *Principles for Professional Ethics* (National Association of School Psychologists, 1997) states that school psychologists advocate for their students and they speak up for the needs and rights of their students (National Association of School Psychologists, 1997, Introduction). School psychologists need an understanding of AT devices and services to advocate for students in need of them. Furthermore, school psychologists "are committed to the application of their professional expertise for the purpose of promoting improvement in the quality of life for students, their families, and the school community" (National Association of School Psychologists, 1997, III.A.1.). This mandate describes an ethical responsibility held by school psychologists to use their knowledge to help enhance the well being of *all* children, including children using AT. Finally, school psychologists must use technological devices when appropriate to improve the quality of client services (National Association of School Psychologists, 1997, IV.C.7).

Types of AT

A wide range of devices and services may be considered AT. The complexity of these devices can vary widely. Low technology devices are often simple to use, have few moving parts, and can be handmade. Examples of low technology assistive devices are pencil grips, crutches, adaptive pointers, and communication boards. High technology devices are often computerized or motorized and require a higher degree of skill and/or training on the part of the student to use. Powered mobility devices and some computerized devices would be considered high technology assistive devices.

AT devices may be used by students with mild or severe disabilities who have limited communication, cognitive skills, motor control, vision, or hearing. Students may use AT tools for daily living activities (such as personal care, eating, environmental control), seating and mobility, academics, transportation, sensory needs, recreation, and communication (e.g., Galvin & Scherer, 1996). Students with learning disabilities, such as reading and writing disabilities, may use computer software to assist in learning to read (e.g., Torgesen & Barker, 1995) and write (e.g., De La Paz, 1999).

Roles of the School Psychologist with Students Using AT

School psychologists act as problem solvers in schools, formulating problems, identifying potential solutions, and testing selected alternatives (Deno, 1995). As a function of their diverse roles within a school and district, school psychologists may interact with students who use AT in a variety of ways. The brief case examples below illustrate several roles assumed by school psychologists in which knowledge about AT is critical.

Case 1

Chris is a five-year-old boy with severe cerebral palsy who has just entered kindergarten. Chris has limited motor control and speech. He uses a wheelchair for mobility and indicates yes/no via head movement. Chris's parents are wondering whether Chris is ready for a more sophisticated communication system. The school district's AT team has asked the school psychologist and speech/language pathologist to evaluate Chris's cognitive and communication skills to help in developing an appropriate communication system. The kindergarten teacher is uncertain about the level of Chris's literacy skills.

As illustrated in the example of Chris, the school psychologist may be called upon to evaluate the skills of a student not yet using AT. In this case, the psychologist may need to understand how to use low-level technology to interact with the student and how to evaluate specific skills the student may require in using more advanced technology. To accomplish these tasks, the school psychologist must first understand how to assess Chris's current level of performance (e.g., cognitive, communication, academic). In addition, because the school psychologist is being asked to provide information to help *select* AT devices for use at the completion of the evaluation, the school psychologist must understand factors that influence selection of AT.

Case 2

J.T. is a fourth grader at his local elementary school. He sustained a traumatic brain injury when he was hit by a car while riding his bike two years ago. J.T. is learning to use a sophisticated augmentative communication system, but his teacher does not understand how the device works. The educational assistant who works with J.T. received some training with the device and often helps J.T. complete his assignments and tests. The teacher is not sure how much work J.T. is doing independently. She is frustrated because she is not sure what J.T. knows and where to target her instruction. She has asked the school psychologist, who serves on the school's AT team, for assistance with assessment (including the state-mandated fourth grade tests) and instructional planning.

In the example of J.T., the school psychologist is asked to consult with a teacher about a student already using AT to ensure that instruction is appropriately matched to the student's skills and to facilitate assessment. To address these questions, the school psychologist must understand how the student's use of AT relates to IEP goals and must consult with the teacher about the AT. The school psychologist is also a member of the AT team, which facilitates the selection and implementation of assistive devices. In this case, the school psychologist needs to understand the student's needs and skills and must be familiar with the range of AT devices available.

Case 3

Maria is a tenth grader whose family is moving from one school district to another in the state. Maria is quadriplegic from a diving accident and uses AT for mobility, personal care, and communication. Her former school district is loaning her assistive devices to her new school while the staff reviews Maria's needs and obtains AT for her. The school psychologist is the Local Education Agency (LEA) representative on the IEP team.

In Maria's case, the school psychologist is asked to fulfill an administrative role on the IEP team. In this role, the school psychologist must be knowledgeable about system issues, such as cost, resources, and training needs related to AT.

Different roles may require different types of knowledge about AT. Types of AT knowledge needed by school psychologists include:

- Familiarity with the range of AT tools available
- Understanding of how to use specific devices
- Understanding of specific student skills and preferences affecting device use
- Awareness of family and cultural issues affecting AT use
- Understanding of technology issues (e.g., transportability, safety)
- Understanding of system issues (e.g., cost, training)

Direct service roles, in which the school psychologist evaluates the skills and instructional needs of a student, often require the psychologist to interact with the student's AT. The psychologist needs to understand the function of AT devices the student uses (e.g., positioning and communication AT) that support the student's performance in school. When the school psychologist is evaluating the student's need for AT or is assisting in determining appropriate AT for a student, the school psychologist must be familiar with the types of AT available for consideration and the student skills required to use the device. To fulfill *indirect service roles*, such as administrative roles as in the case of Maria, the school psychologist must understand system factors that influence AT selection and use. Table 2 identifies questions the school psychologist may address to guide practice across direct and indirect service roles with students using AT.

BEST PRACTICES

Considerations for AT Selection

One role school psychologists fill in school districts is membership on AT teams seeking to identify appropriate AT for a student. Numerous authors (e.g., Parette, 1998; Parette & Marr, 1997; Scherer & Galvin, 1996) have identified domains to consider in selecting appropriate AT, including student factors, family issues, cultural perspectives, technology features, and system issues.

Student Factors

To identify appropriate AT, the AT team must first consider the needs, skills, and preferences of the student. AT must be matched to the purpose(s) of its use. Clear identification of purposes the technology will serve is the starting point for identifying useful AT. What exactly do you want to enable the student to do?

A second critical question is what skills and needs does the student exhibit that affect AT use. Many forms of AT require specific student skills (e.g., cognitive, motor, perceptual) to employ the AT effectively. Examples of these skills are presented in Table 3. School psychologists are often highly qualified to help assess student skills. A helpful evaluation tool for assessing these skills is included in the Wisconsin Assistive Technology Initiative (1998) resource manual.

Third, what are the student's preferences regarding AT? Some students are eager to increase their independence and will use whatever device allows them to function more independently. Some students are concerned about the appearance of some devices (e.g., head pointers). Some students are willing to use higher technology devices (such as computers) but are unwilling to use lower level devices (such as communication boards) and vice versa. Some students are reluctant to use any device that singles them out from their peers.

Family Issues

Family preferences and values will also influence whether an AT device is appropriate for a student and the extent to which it will be used out of the home to provide FAPE. An appropriate AT device

Table 2. Questions to Guide Practice Across School Psychologists' Roles With Students Using AT

Direct Service Roles

Assessment and Intervention With Students Using AT

- What AT does the student use and why?
- What is the goal of the assessment/intervention? Can the AT help me attain my goal?
- What exactly do I want the student to do? Does the AT help the student do it?
- What preferences does the student have about AT use?
- Can I communicate reliably with the student?
- Would additional/alternative AT facilitate the student's demonstration of skills?
- What training would the student require to use additional/alternative AT?
- Do I need AT training to work effectively with the student using the AT?
- What other professionals can I consult who have expertise about AT?

AT Selection With Students in Need of AT

- What skills (e.g., motor, cognitive, language, sensory) does the student have?
- What does the student need to be able to do that he or she cannot do without AT?
- How will AT facilitate attainment of IEP goals?
- What AT devices/services might help the student accomplish goals?
- What specific devices are being considered for the student?
- What skills does the student need to use these devices?
- How do the student and family feel about these devices?
- Are there cultural issues that will affect AT selection and use?
- What system issues might influence selection of AT?
- What will the student's back-up AT system be?
- How might the student's needs change over time?

Indirect Service Roles

Consultation With Families and Teachers of Students Using AT

- What are the concerns of the student? Family? Staff? Does AT relate to these concerns?
- What AT does the student use now? Can the student use the AT? Independently?
- Does the AT facilitate attainment of IEP goals and participation in classroom, school, and community activities necessary for FAPE?
- Do the family and teachers understand how to use the AT?
- What student, family, and teacher preferences regarding AT use must be considered?
- Do the student, family, or teachers need AT training?
- How might the student's needs change over time?

Administrative Roles (e.g., IEP team LEA Representative)

- What AT does the student use now?
- What AT devices and services are required for FAPE for the student?
- What needs do student, family, and teachers report that are not met with current AT?
- What are the student, family, and teacher preferences regarding AT use?
- Will the student's needs for AT change over time?
- What AT options might be considered for the student?
- What funding sources are available for the AT?
- What LEA resources must be committed to support the student's AT use?
- What are the legal/ethical requirements regarding AT device and service provision?
- How will student, family, and staff training needs be met?
- How will transitions affect student AT needs and resources?

addresses the concerns of the family for the student and does not disrupt family functioning (Parette, 1998). If a family views a device as too cumbersome or if a device increases the family's stress, then it likely will not be used.

Cultural Perspectives

The cultures of both the family and the school must be considered in selecting appropriate AT. As ethnic, racial, cultural, and linguistic diversity of the U.S. school population increases (e.g., IDEA, 1997),

Table 3. Student Skills Related to AT Use

Student Domains	*Examples of Factors to Consider*
Communication skills	Use of speech and gestures; reliability of communication; comprehension; initiation skills; AT use; specific skills (e.g., pointing, eye gaze, scanning)
Cognitive skills	Cause and effect; representational skills; symbol use; means-end reasoning; sequencing skills; memory; reading level; math level
Visual skills	Acuity; glasses; visual fields; perception; color vision; visual tracking; peripheral vision
Auditory skills	Acuity and range of frequencies (left and right ears); sensitivities to sounds; amplification/aids; interference of background noise
Motor skills/motor control	Spasticity/tremor; voluntary motor control (e.g., arm/hand, head, foot control); overflow movements; handedness
Medical/physical needs	Alertness; fatigue; seizures; eating/drinking needs; Medications/side effects; Toileting needs; Drooling
Positioning needs	Head control; trunk control; table/chair height; physical supports; positioning of materials
Attentional skills	Alertness; fatigue; attention span; distractibility; interests; motivation
Social-emotional needs	Reactions to familiar/unfamiliar people/situations; supports; temperament; interests; reinforcers; dislikes; co-occurring disorders (e.g., depression, anxiety)

education professionals are becoming more aware that families from varied backgrounds may hold different views of disability, education, professional assistance, and technology (e.g., Hourcade, Parette, & Huer, 1997). Parette and Marr (1997) have identified questions to ask to ensure that cultural issues have been addressed prior to selection of an alternative or augmentative communication (AAC) device. These include (Parette & Marr,1997, p. 344):

- Do I understand the family's values, beliefs, customs, and traditions?
- Do I understand the family's attitude regarding disability?
- Does the family accept the idea of assistive technology as a tool to help their child?
- Have I identified important social influences which might affect children or family perception and use of AAC devices?
- Do I understand how the family feels about making direct contact with professionals involved in AAC decision making?
- Have I included the extended family in the AAC assessment process?

Parette and Marr (1997) also note the critical importance of recognizing that many cultures do not value independence and self-sufficiency, which are often goals of the use of AT devices, to the degree that Euro-American cultures do. Some cultural groups may wish to provide direct care and support for their children with disabilities, and they may value the guidance of community or religious leaders more than that of education personnel.

Finally, school professionals, including school psychologists, must examine their own cultural backgrounds, values, and assumptions (e.g., Arredondo et al., 1996). Are these values and assumptions in concert with those of the family? Do these values and assumptions interfere with communication with the family or result in judgments that alienate families?

Technology Features

A steadily increasing array of assistive devices is available today to meet the needs of students with disabilities. Parette (1997) has identified examples of technology features and issues to consider when choosing among available options, including, the following ones: How well does the device address the student's needs and enhance the student's performance? How transportable is the device? How broad/limited are its uses? How easy and comfortable is the device to use? How dependable and durable is the device? Are repair services readily available? How costly are the device and its maintenance? Is the device safe? How does it compare with alternatives?

System Issues

In addition to student, family, culture, and technology factors, there are also school system issues to consider in selecting AT. Two of the most critical system issues to consider are training and funding (Parette, 1997). Many assistive devices require significant training for the student, family, and professional staff interacting with the device. Students may require extensive training over time to understand complex features of sophisticated devices. Teachers, parents, and others, including school psychologists, who interact with the student also need training to understand how the technology can facilitate student performance and how to support and encourage the student's use of the technology. Too often, inadequate training is available to help students, families, and staff members take full advantage of the possibilities AT can provide. Scherer and Galvin (1996) recommend using a spiral curriculum in which training begins by focusing on familiar features of a device or piece of equipment. As training continues, novel features are introduced.

Funding is also a factor that must be considered in AT selection (Smith, 1998). Some low technology devices (e.g., eye gaze frames, head pointers) are very inexpensive and can often be made by school personnel. Other higher technology devices (e.g., computers and mobility devices) are very expensive. Cost of assistive devices must always be considered within the context of student use. To what degree will the device facilitate student performance? If a device significantly increases a student's performance, then it is easier to justify higher cost than if a device only marginally facilitates performance. As computer availability and miniaturization continue (Vanderheiden, 1996), costs of higher technology devices will fall.

Considerations in AT Use in Educational Assessment and Intervention

Traditionally, school psychologists have spent a high proportion of their time in schools in assessment activities (Wilson & Reschly, 1996). However, the focus of assessment is increasingly on its link with intervention and outcomes to produce improved learning and behavior (e.g., Reschly & Ysseldyke, 1995). School psychologists, through assessment and intervention activities, interact directly as problem solvers with students; that is, with students using AT, that means direct interaction with the student's technology, particularly communication technology.

Specific issues and concerns often arise when school psychologists conduct assessment and intervention activities with students using communication AT. These include (a) use of appropriate assessment tools, (b) the fit between the student's AT and goals of the activity, (c) reliability, (d) validity, (e) examiner bias, (f) reporting findings, and (g) collaboration. These are discussed below.

Use of Appropriate Assessment Tools

When assessing the skills of a student who uses AT, the school psychologist must determine the types of assessment tools that will yield the most useful information. This range of tools includes record reviews; interviews of the student, teachers, and family; observations of the student across settings; rating scales; analogue measures (e.g., CBA); teacher-constructed probes; authentic work samples; and standardized, norm-referenced measures. Each of these tools can contribute important information about a student's strengths and needs. The task of the school psychologist is to determine which tools will provide the most guidance for intervention with the student.

The Fit Between the Student's AT and the Activity Goals

Sometimes a student's AT does not allow the type of communication or performance most suited to a particular assessment or intervention activity. For example, many communication devices are intended to *expand* the student's overall communication (initiation, commenting, replying, etc.). However, in many assessment activities (with students with and without disabilities) the examiner *limits* the communication opportunities of the student (e.g., true-false and multiple-choice exams) to allow sampling of content, to facilitate comparisons across students, and to increase reliability. When working with students using AT, the school psychologist must evaluate the type of response he or she wants the student to make and determine whether this response is possible using the student's AT. If not, what alternatives—in both assessment tools and AT—are available? Could the school psychologist rely more on observational data? Interview data? Constructed probes?

Reliability

Reliability here refers to the consistency of the student's responses or performance on a task and the examiner's interpretation of performance. All performance varies somewhat across trials, but our goal, particularly in assessment activities, is to limit error variance which reduces usefulness of measures (Joint Committee on Standards for Educational and Psychological Testing, 1999). Use of communication AT has the potential of introducing error in the assessment process if, for example, the student and/or examiner are not adequately familiar with the AT or if the examiner cannot reliably interpret the responses of the student. As stated in the *Standards for Educational and Psychological Testing*, "precision and consistency in measurement are always desirable. However, the need for precision increases as the consequences of decisions and interpretations grow in importance" (Joint Committee on Standards for Educational and Psychological Testing, 1999, pp. 29–30).

Validity

Systematic errors in assessment affect the validity of measurement (Joint Committee on Standards for Educational and Psychological Testing, 1999). When working with students using communication AT, the school psychologist must attend to possible sources of systematic error, such as observation or interview conditions, test administration conditions, or language levels. In addition, the psychologist must be aware that use of communication AT often places additional cognitive, perceptual, and motor demands on the student (Blackstone, 1996). These demands may increase the difficulty of a task such that comparisons with students not using AT are not valid.

Examiner Bias

At times, interpreting responses of students using AT can be difficult. For example, a student using an eyegaze frame may have only brief eye pointing. The psychologist must be aware of the potential for bias introduced in such situations and use strategies to reduce bias. These include, for example, completing assessment over longer time periods to avoid student fatigue, using multiple forms of assessment, or investigating alternative AT.

Reporting Findings

Findings must be described in sufficient detail to assist others in recognizing factors that facilitate and limit the student's performance. For example, what were environmental conditions during observations of student success? When assessment administration procedures are altered to accommodate the student's communication mode, access, and AT, it is critical for the school psychologist to report such modifications and consider their effects on interpretations of results.

Collaboration

As was stated earlier, most school psychologists are not AT experts. Other professionals, such as physical, occupational, and speech/language therapists, have the training and expertise necessary to meet the needs of many students using AT. Family members also have important information to contribute to evaluation and intervention plans. Working as part of a team addressing the AT needs of the student will increase the school psychologist's effectiveness.

AT for Communication

School psychologists must be able to use augmentative communication devices to carry out direct service roles with students. Communication with students with disabilities can be as simple as talking or as complex as interacting through a sophisticated computer. Blackstone (1996) defines communication as "exchanging, transmitting, and receiving information, thoughts, feelings, and ideas" (p. 97). For communication through an assistive device to be effective, the communication partner (sometimes the school psychologist) must be knowledgeable about the communication process and any devices and strategies the student uses.

Communication Modes and Access

Interpersonal communication includes communication through speech and gestures, reading and writing, and communication via assistive strategies and devices. For individuals who cannot use speech, communication *access*, the way in which the individual selects messages (Blackstone, 1996), is a critical consideration. Communication device access includes two primary strategies: *direct selection*, in which the student indicates by pointing to, looking at, touching or picking up, an item from a set of items; and *scanning*, in which a student selects a desired item from a series of items presented auditorally or visually in a predetermined order. Each of these access modes has certain uses and limitations and issues that arise with their use. Types of communication modes and access, examples, and issues specific to each are summarized in Table 4.

Speech and Gestures

Most people use speech and gestures to communicate. Sometimes students with disabilities (e.g., cerebral palsy) are able to use speech and gestures, but their speech may be difficult to understand and their gestures imprecise because of limited motor control. Issues that arise in communicating with students with limited motor or speech skills include, for example, reliability (*Can the communication partner reliably interpret the student's responses?*), student fatigue (*Is it tiring for the student to talk or use gestures?*), and time (*How much time does it take to communicate by speech and/or gestures?*). Students sometimes use speech to activate assistive devices, such as environmental control of lights, TV, and computers.

Reading and Writing

Students with learning disabilities and those with physical disabilities can benefit from voice-activated and speech-recognition software (e.g., De La Paz, 1999). Reading skills can be enhanced via speech synthesis, which allows the reader to hear text read aloud (e.g., Erickson & Koppenhaver, 1998). Speech-to-text transcription products and spelling devices can be used to assist students with writing disabilities.

Direct Selection

By using direct selection, a student indicates choice of an item from an array of items. Direct selection may take several forms, as discussed below.

Pointing. The student manually points to an object, picture, symbol. *Example: The classroom teacher is concerned about whether the student, who has limited expressive language, understands basic preschool concepts such as between, under, and next to. The school psychologist administers a concept measure that requires only a pointing response.* This form of direct selection is used frequently with low technology communication tools, such as communication boards and books. These devices are usually constructed in response to specific needs and skills of the student. Issues to consider with students using manual pointing include

- Reliability: How precisely can the student point? How clear is the selection?
- Positioning of the student and materials: Where should materials be placed to allow the student access to them? How far apart do the materials need to be to facilitate reliable choice-making? What position should the student be in to select reliably from the array?
- Fatigue and physical pain: How tiring/painful is it for the student to point to his or her choice?

Eye Gaze/Eye Pointing. The student indicates a selection from an array by pointing with his or her eyes. *Example: A school psychologist is helping the teacher assess the student's ability to distinguish among initial consonants. Together they create several sets of words from the student's classroom materials (e.g., mat, sat, cat, hat). The school psychologist displays the sets one at a time on the student's eye gaze frame. She asks the student to look at the word that says, for example, "cat."* Direct selection via eye gaze or pointing is a useful communication access mode for some students with limited motor control and limited speech. The reliability of eye gaze responses may be increased with an assistive device called an eye-gaze frame. This device, which can be made or is available for purchase, usually consists of a simple frame approximately 17" x 22" which supports a clear piece of plastic or polycarbonite vinyl. The communication partner attaches the array of items to the corners of the frame, allowing ample space between them. The eye gaze frame is placed at eye level for the student, who looks at all the options available and then looks at his or her selection. The communication partner looks through the clear plastic to read the student's response. A limitation of eye pointing as communication is that it often requires initiation by the communication partner (e.g., in selecting and dis-

Table 4. Types of Communication Access With Examples and Associated Issues

COMMUNICATION ACCESS	EXAMPLES	COMMUNICATION ISSUES
Speech/Gestures: Student uses limited speech and/or gestures to communicate		
• **Speech:** e.g., single words such as yes, no • **Gestures:** e.g., head nod/shake; eye gaze to indicate yes/no	• Student communicates without AT, but may require partner to elicit communication • Communication partner asks yes/no questions or questions requiring brief responses or gestures	• Intelligibility of speech • Reliability of interpretation by partner • Student fatigue • Time
• **Voice Activated Systems:** student activates assistive technology via speech	• Voice activated environmental control systems (e.g., lights, TV, computer)	• Training • Cost
Reading and Writing: Student uses AT to assist in reading and writing communication activities		
• **Dictation, Speech Recognition, Speech Synthesis, and Spelling Aids:** computer software recognizes speech, produces text from speech, and/or produces speech from text; spelling tools aid written language activities	• Speech recognition software to produce text (e.g., *Naturally Speaking*, Dragon systems) • Word prediction software (e.g., *Co:Writer*, Don Johnston) assists in writing tasks • Speech synthesis allows readers to hear text read aloud (e.g., *Write OutLoud*, Don Johnston) • Spelling tools (e.g., *Franklin Bookman Dictionary and Thesaurus*, Franklin Learning Resources)	• Fatigue and health (e.g., voice clarity) • Portability • Training • Student preferences • Cost
DIRECT SELECTION: *Student directly indicates a selection from a set of items*		
• **Pointing:** student points to objects/pictures placed in front of him/her	• Objects/pictures placed on a surface (e.g., feltboard) • Communication boards (e.g., can be made using *Boardmaker*, Mayer-Johnson) • Foam core strip with Velcro	• Reliability • Precision of pointing • Positioning of student and materials • Student fatigue
• **Eye Gaze/Eye Pointing:** student makes choices from an array by looking at objects/pictures	• Eye gaze frame (e.g., can be made from PVC pipe and clear plastic) • Object board (e.g., can be made by attaching objects to a display using Velcro) • Communication book (e.g., can be made using *Boardmaker*, Mayer-Johnson)	• Reliability related to duration and accuracy • Positioning of student, materials, partner • Examiner bias • Student fatigue • Time • Availability of materials
• **Assisted Direct Selection:** student uses a device to facilitate selection of an item from a set of items	• Finger pointers (e.g., a piece of PVC pipe) • Head pointers • Light/laser pointers (e.g., baseball cap with small flashlight attached)	• Reliability • Motor control (e.g., head control) • Positioning of student and materials • Student preferences

• **Augmentative and Alternative Communication Devices:** student accesses a communication device through physical contact with the device (e.g., touching a button, typing, depressing a switch) or without physical contact (e.g., using eye gaze to activate a switch, using a light pointer, using voice recognition software)	• Simple voice output devices: student selects a message from several choices (*Voice-in-a-box*, Frame Technologies; *Cheap Talk*, Toys for Special Children; *BIGmack*, AbleNet) • Layering devices: device stores sets of messages in layers (e.g., *MaCaw*, Zygo Industries, Inc.) • Icon sequencing devices: student selects series of icons to produce a message (e.g., *Touch Talker*, *Liberator*, Prentke Romich; *Chatbox*, Saltillo) • Dynamic display: pictures are presented on a computer screen; student selects series of screens to produce a message (e.g., *DynaVox*, Sentient Systems Technology)	• Cognitive skills • Reliability • Independence • Issues related to specific access mode (e.g., eye gaze, pointing • Portability of device • Cost
Scanning: Student selects desired item from a series presented auditorally or visually in a predetermined order		
• **Assisted Manual Scanning:** partner indicates (e.g., by pointing to or speaking) items one at a time. Student indicates choice when desired item is presented • **Specific Scanning Technologies:** devices designed specifically to facilitate scanning	• Communication partner offers a series of items/choices; student indicates selection by saying yes/no or nodding/shaking head as each item/choice is presented • Device presents items in sequence; student stops device (e.g., by depressing a switch when selected item is presented; *Compartmentalized Clock Communicator*, Toys for Special Children)	• Reliability • Bias • Student fatigue • Time • Cognitive skills • Limited applicability • Portability • Training
• **Computer-Based Scanning:** computer device presents arrays of choices. Items may be presented in linear or group format. Student selects desired item (e.g., by depressing a switch, using eye gaze, remote mouse, or pointing) when it appears	• Step scanning: student controls presentation of each item by depressing a switch (e.g., using *EZ Keys* software, Words Plus, Inc.) • Inverse scanning: student depresses switch to activate scanning and releases switch when desired item appears • Linear format: device presents items sequentially; student selects desired item when it is presented • Group format: device highlights items in groups (e.g., rows and columns or quadrants); student selects group containing desired item; device then presents each item in group (e.g., *ClickIt!*, IntelliTools) Student independence	• Cognitive skills • Student and staff training • Portability of device • Time • Cost • Training

Notes. Communication access categories based on Blackstone (1996); Lynch, Moehn, and Walser (1997). Tools identified in this table are examples. For a comprehensive listing of AT tools and devices, please see www.abledata.com.

playing the items in the array). Considerations in the reliable use of eye gaze and pointing include

- Visual acuity: What size materials, background, or color will facilitate vision?
- Duration of eye pointing: How long can the student look at an item?
- Positioning of student, partner, and materials: How should the student be positioned to facilitate good head and eye control? How far apart do materials need to be positioned?
- Student fatigue: How tiring is this form of communication access for the student?
- Time: How long does it take to identify and set up items for the array and obtain student responses? Can the student use other forms of access that require less time?
- Bias and/or error: Are the student's responses clear enough that there is reliability across communication partners?

Assisted Direct Selection: The student uses a device to facilitate selection of an item from a set of items. *Example: The school psychologist is buying lunch for his student advisory team today. One student uses a light pointer to indicate which of three sauces she wants with her chicken strips.* Students may be able to select a choice from an array with the assistance of a low technology device, such as a head pointer, finger pointer, or light pointer attached to a hat. In communicating with students using assistive pointing devices, the following considerations arise:

- Motor control: How well can the student control the device. For example, does the student have adequate head control to use a head pointer?
- Positioning of student and materials: What is the optimal position for the student to be in when using the device? Where should materials be placed to increase reliability?
- Reliability: Can the partner consistently read the student's selection?
- Student preferences: Is the student willing to use the device?

Switch Access. Many students with severe motor impairments use switches to activate AT. *Example: A student depresses a switch mounted on his headrest to access his computer and respond to the teacher's question.* Switches can be attached to simple voice output devices or to computers to allow access; and switches can be placed on a laptray or mounted on a wheelchair to be activated by hand, arm, head, chin, mouth, tongue, foot, or even muscle movement. Switch categories include pressure (putting pressure on the device activates the switch), motion (movement over the switch activates it), sound, pneumatic (using air), or photosensitive (light reactive) switches (Lynch, 1997).

Scanning

Scanning is another means of access to communication. Using scanning, a student selects a desired item from a series of items presented auditorally or visually in predetermined order (Blackstone, 1996). *Example: A student uses scanning to spell out a message letter by letter.* Items may be presented by a communication partner or by a communication device.

Partner-Assisted Scanning. Some students are unable to select items when they are presented by a communication device, but they are able to indicate a choice with support from the communication partner. For example, the partner may point to each item in the array as the student indicates yes or no to each item. Student fatigue is a concern in partner-assisted scanning.

Specific Scanning Technologies. Some devices are produced that are specifically designed to facilitate scanning. For example, some students use a clock-like scanning tool that is used with overlays of pictures, words, numerals, or letters organized in a circular pattern. The student depresses a switch when the clock pointer indicates the desired item.

Types of Scanning. Scanning access includes *step* and *inverse* scanning. Arrays of items may be presented in *linear*, *circular*, or *group* formats. Please refer to Table 4 for further description and examples of scanning.

Important considerations in using scanning technologies include

- The student's cognitive skills: Bunn (1998) suggests that students need prerequisite skills to communicate via scanning, including (a) ability to use a switch as a means to an end (which includes object permanence skills, understand of cause and effect, and mean/end understanding), (b) visual and/or auditory perception skills, (c) choice making ability.
- Time: Scanning can be a time-consuming communication means.
- Training: Scanning technology ranges from simple object scanning devices to complex computer software using group scanning. Students, families, and educators need adequate training to support the use of scanning for communication.

AAC Devices

There are several types of communication devices that students may use, ranging from simple communication boards to computers (Lynch, Moehn, & Walser, 1997). Most high technology AAC devices are computers, either dedicated devices designed specifically for communication or off-the-shelf computers adapted to meet communication needs (Blackstone, 1996). Most devices are used with direct or assisted direct selection. Some computerized AAC devices include specific scanning technology.

Communication Boards. These may include objects, pictures, or symbols designed to allow communication. *Example: A student in an early childhood program may use a communication board to indicate her choice of activity during center time. A student who uses a computerized device may use a communication board to indicate basic needs when her higher technology device is unavailable.* Boards may be simple (e.g., containing only a few pictures) or more complex (e.g., symbols or combinations of symbols and pictures). They may serve as a student's primary communication device or as a back-up to higher level technology (Lynch et al., 1997).

Simple Voice Output Devices. These devices present a set of messages (e.g., four pre-programmed responses) to the user. The user depresses a button or key to produce the desired message. *Example: A school psychologist helps a teacher design a system for a student to initiate communication in the classroom. With the student they identify three communication messages to program into a voice output device kept on the student's laptray: "I know the answer," "I need a break," and "This is an emergency."* Students can access these devices directly (e.g., by touching a button) or can activate a switch attached to the device.

Leveling/Layering Devices. These devices allow storage of several layers of messages. *Example: A teacher programs level one for use in reading activities, level two for use in math class, and level three for use during lunch.* A limitation to these devices is that, although the layers of messages can be pre-programmed in advance and changing message layers requires only pushing a button, the picture overlays must be changed manually.

Icon Sequencing Devices. Icon sequencing devices use pictures to represent words. The user depresses several keys in sequence to create a message. *Example: A student presses three icons in a row to produce the message "I want a drink of water."* To use icon sequencing devices a student must be able to remember what the icons and specific icon combinations represent.

Dynamic Display Devices. These devices present symbols or pictures on a computer screen, usually touch activated. Several layers of pictures can be stored. *Example: A student wants to explain to the school psychologist, with whom he is meeting, that he needs to go to his math classroom to take a make-up exam. He selects a picture on his communication device that represents class subjects and selects the math class icon. The device then presents a display of several school activities (e.g., reading, making a presentation, taking a test, etc.). He selects the icon representing test-taking.* Blackstone (1996) notes that an advantage of dynamic display devices is that layers are easily changed via direct selection and the user relies on recognition skills rather than recall of symbol meanings.

Standard Computers as Communication Devices

Some students are able to use standard computers as communication tools with software designed for communication. For example, dynamic display software programs are available for use with standard computers. According to Vanderheiden (1996), there are four strategies for making computers accessible to people with disabilities: (a) built-in or universal design, in which access features are built directly into the operating system or applications and include such features as sticky keys (which act as toggles) and slow keys (which increase the time a key must be depressed before it is read); (b) adaptive interfaces, which are standard products that can be installed to make the computer more accessible; (c) connections to other devices, such as Braille displays, to meet a user's needs; and (d) custom modifications to meet the needs of a specific user.

Lynch (1997) notes that students with disabilities prefer to use hands to access computers when possible. Features such as slow keys or sticky keys allow computer access through a standard keyboard. Software is available to facilitate production of written text via word prediction and keystroke expansion, in which longer words/messages can be represented by just a few keystrokes. Students without adequate hand control may use devices to facilitate head access to the keyboard, such as a head mouse or head mounted stick. Alternately, a student may use toe access or voice activation. Voice recognition technology requires that the user have good speech articulation. Students with severe speech/motor impairments may produce text via scanning.

Considerations that arise in the use of communication devices and computers include

- Training: High-technology devices and standard computers require significant training for the student, family, and school staff. As Todis and Walker (1993) observed, AT training often is conducted by a regional specialist available only on a limited basis, the training may be directed to only one staff member, and training often addresses technical aspects of the AT, but neglects focus on the purpose of the technology. "Staff training must emphasize that the goal is not just to teach the student to use the device but, rather, to show the student how to use the device to complete specified tasks and work toward IEP goals" (Todis & Walker, 1993; p. 11).
- Cost: Although the cost of computers continues to decline, some computers/AAC devices remain expensive, particularly in comparison with low-technology devices.

FACTORS LIMITING THE USE OF AT

Despite the numerous benefits for students AT can afford, there are certain factors that may limit its use and lead to technology abandonment. According to Scherer and Galvin (1996), approximately one-third of AT devices are no longer used after the first three months. The failure to consider user opinions and preferences in the selection of AT devices is the "overarching factor associated with technology abandonment" (Scherer & Galvin, 1996, p. 4). Some other reasons include (a) lack of improvement in student functioning from its use; (b) difficulties with service and repair; (c) difficulty with use of the device; (d) changes in the abilities or activities of the student; (e) lack of training or motivation to use the device; or (f) the way the device looks, weighs, or appears (Scherer & Galvin, 1996; Todis & Walker, 1993). Careful selection of AT devices, adequate training and resources to maintain the equipment, and ongoing evaluation of student progress can ensure that the devices are meeting students' needs.

SUMMARY OF BEST PRACTICES

Awareness

To meet the needs of all students in a school, the school psychologist must be aware of laws regarding the range of AT *devices and services* that might be required to provide the student a free, appropriate, public education. In addition, the school psychologist must be familiar with factors, including student, family, cultural, technology, and system factors, that affect AT selection and use.

Collaboration

The field of AT is growing by leaps and bounds, and most school psychologists are not AT experts. School psychologists must work with family members and other professionals, some of whom may be AT experts, to identify and meet the needs of students using or in need of AT.

Purpose of AT

In selecting or evaluating a student for AT, consider whether the AT facilitates attainment of important, socially and educationally valid goals for the student.

Individualization

Appropriate AT might differ significantly across students with similar limitations. When selecting AT, carefully evaluate the skills and needs of the student, the preferences of student, family, and teachers, and the context in which AT will be used. Make the technology fit the student, not vice versa.

Culture

Consider the cultures of the family and school in selecting AT. Cultural practices (e.g., in play and use of language) vary, and cultures differ in the degree to which they value technology and the independence technology is designed to afford. Also, appropriate computer software is not available in all languages.

Training

One of the primary reasons for abandonment of AT is inadequate training. Be sure appropriate AT training is available for the student, for teachers and other staff members, and for families.

REFERENCES

Arredondo, P., Toporek, R., Brown, S. P., Jones, J., Locke, D. C., Sanchez, J., & Stadler, H. (1996). Operationalization of the multicultural counseling competencies. *Journal of Multicultural Counseling and Development, 24*, 43–78.

Baker, S. K., Kame'enui, E. J., & Simmons, D. S. (1998). Characteristics of students with diverse learning and curricular needs. In E. J. Kameenui & D. W. Carnine (Eds.), *Effective teaching strategies that accommodate diverse learners*. Upper Saddle River, NJ: Prentice-Hall.

Blackstone, S. W. (1996). selecting, using, and evaluating communication devices. In J. C. Galvin & M. J. Scherer (Eds.), *Evaluating, selecting, and using appropriate assistive technology* (p. 97–124), Gaithersburg, MD: Aspen.

Bunn, D. L. (1998, June). Teaching students to scan. Workshop presented at the Wisconsin Assistive Technology Summer Institute, Amherst, WI.

De La Paz, S. (1999). Composing via dictation and speech recognition systems: Compensatory technology for students with learning disabilities. *Learning Disability Quarterly, 22*, 173–182.

Deno, S. L. (1995). School psychologist as problem solver. In A. Thomas & J. Grimes (Eds.), *Best practices in school psychology III* (pp. 471–484).Washington, DC: National Association of School Psychologists.

Elliott, S. N., Kratochwill, T. R., & Schulte, A. G. (1999). *Assessment accommodations checklist*. Monterey, CA: CTB/McGraw-Hill.

Erickson, K. A., & Koppenhaver, D.A.(1998). Developing a literacy program for children with severe disabilities. *The Reading Teacher, 48*, 676–684.

Galvin, J.C., & Scherer, M. J. (Eds.). (1996). Evaluating, selecting, and using appropriate assistive technology. Gaithersburg, MD: Aspen.

Hourcade, J. J., Parette, H. P., & Huer , M. B. (1997). Family and cultural alert: Considerations in assistive technology assessment. *Teaching Exceptional Children, 30*(1), 40–44.

IDEA (1997). Individuals with Disabilities Education Act (Pub.L. No.101-426) 20 U.S.C. Chapter 33. Amended by Pub. L. No. 105-17, June, 1997.

Joint Committee on Standards for Educational and Psychological Testing (1999). *Standards for educational and psychological testing*. Washington, DC: American Educational Research Association, American Psychological Association, National Council on Measurement in Education.

Lynch, K. J. (1997). Overview of physical access to computers. In *Assessing students' needs for assistive technology: A resource manual for school district teams* (1998 Revision, p. 3-8–3-10). Amherst, WI: Wisconsin Assistive Technology Initiative.

Lynch, K. J., Moehn, D., & Walser, P. (1997). Six categories of AAC devices. In *Assessing students' needs for assistive technology: A resource manual for school district teams* (1998 Revision, p. 4-7–4-9). Amherst, WI: Wisconsin Assistive Technology Initiative.

McDonnell, L. M., McLaughlin, M. J., & Morison, P. (Eds.) (1997). *Educating one and all: Students with disabilities and standards-based reform.* Washington, DC: National Academy Press.

National Association of School Psychologists (1997). *Professional Conduct Manual* (3rd ed.). Silver Spring, MD: Author.

Parette, H. P. (1997). Assistive technology devices and services. *Education and Training in Mental Retardation and Developmental Disabilities, 32*(4), 267–280.

Parette, H. P. (1998). Assistive technology effective practices for students with mental retardation and developmental disabilities. In A. Hilton & R. Ringlaben (Eds.), *Best and promising practices in developmental disabilities* (p. 205–224). Austin, TX: PRO-ED.

Parette, H. P., & Marr, D. D. (1997). Assisting children and families who use augmentative and alternative communication (AAC) devices: Best practices for school psychologists. *Psychology in the Schools, 34,* 337–346.

Reschly, D. J., & Yesseldyke, J. E. (1995). School psychology paradigm shift. In A. Thomas & J. Grimes (Eds.), *Best practices in school psychology III* (pp. 17–32). Washington, DC: National Association of School Psychologists.

Scherer, M. J., & Galvin, J. C. (1996). An outcomes perspective to quality pathways to the most appropriate technology. In J. C. Galvin & M. J. Scherer (Eds.), *Evaluating, selecting, and using appropriate assistive technology* (p. 1–26). Gaithersburg, MD: Aspen.

Smith, D. C. (1998). Assistive technology: Funding options and strategies. *Mental and Physical Disability Law Reporter, 22*(1), 115–123.

Technology-Related Assistance for Individuals With Disabilities Act of 1994. P.L. 103-218. (March 9, 1994). 29 U.S.C. 2201 et seq: U.S. Statutes at Large, 108, 50-97.

Todis, B., & Walker, H. M. (1993). User perspectives on assistive technology in educational settings. *Focus on Exceptional Children, 26*(3), 1–16.

Torgesen, J. D., & Barker, T. A. (1995). Computers as aids in the prevention and remediation of reading disabilities. *Learning Disability Quarterly, 18,* 76–87.

Vanderheiden, G. C. (1996). Computer access and use by people with disabilities. In J. C. Galvin & M. J. Scherer (Eds.). *Evaluating, selecting, and using appropriate assistive technology* (p. 237–276). Gaithersburg, MD: Aspen.

Wisconsin Assistive Technology Initiative (1997). *Assessing students' needs for assistive technology: A resource manual for school district teams* (1998 Rev.). Amherst, WI: Author.

Wilson, M. S., & Reschly, D. J. (1996). Assessment in school psychology training and practice. *School Psychology Review, 25,* 9–23.

ANNOTATED BIBLIOGRAPHY

ABLEDATA: sponsored by the National Institute on Disability and Rehabilitation, U.S. Department of Education. www.abledata.com.
ABLEDATA is a federally funded project that provides up-to-date information about AT and rehabilitation equipment. Its website includes a database that contains information on more than 25,000 AT products. The database contains descriptions of the products, prices, and company information.

Galvin, J. D., & Scherer, M. J. (Eds.). (1996). *Evaluating, selecting, and using appropriate assistive technology.* Gaithersburg, MD: Aspen.
This is a comprehensive book about the use of AT with individuals with disabilities. It covers topics such as pol-

icy, legislation, funding, evaluation, selection, and maintenance. Chapters relate to the use of technology in education, employment, and recreation.

Rehabilitation Engineering and Assistive Technology Society of North America (RESNA). www.resna.org. 1700 N. Moore St. Suite 1540, Arlington, VA, 22209-1903.
RESNA is an interdisciplinary association for the advancement of rehabilitation and AT services. Its website contains useful resources about AT devices and services.

Wisconsin Assistive Technology Initiative (WATI). (1998). *Assessing students' needs for AT: A resource manual for school district teams*. Amherst, WI: Author.
This manual is an excellent resource for school personnel working with students using AT. It is organized around the tasks that children perform in schools (e.g., writing, reading, communicating) and includes information about assessment procedures and AT resources. It also contains useful forms that can assist educators in selecting appropriate AT. The manual can be ordered at WATI's website, www.wati.org.

AUTHOR NOTE

The authors would like to thank Joni Nygard, Communication Aids and Systems Clinic, UW-Madison; Penny Reed, Wisconsin AT Initiative; and Brent Odell, Wisconsin Department of Public Instruction, for their helpful comments on an earlier draft of this chapter.

98 Best Practices in Peer-Mediated Interventions

Kathryn E. Hoff
Illinois State University
Sheri L. Robinson
University of Texas-Austin

OVERVIEW

School psychologists have unique training and expertise in assessment and intervention strategies that can be influential in promoting children's educational progress and development. Just as the majority of classroom instruction tends to be teacher-led, interventions for academic and behavior difficulties recommended by school psychologists are also likely to be teacher-directed. Investigations have demonstrated the efficacy of children as agents for peer behavior change, or peer-mediated interventions, as an ideal alternative to more traditional intervention approaches. This chapter will define and review the benefits of using peer-mediated interventions. Next, we will provide an overview of general considerations for school psychologists when implementing direct peer-mediated interventions. Finally, we will provide a brief review of a variety of peer-mediated interventions available to school psychologists.

Definition of Peer-Mediated Interventions

Peer-mediated interventions refer to academic, behavioral, or social strategies that employ peers, rather than adults, as direct or indirect behavior change agents. In this context, a peer is defined as a person who has relatively equal standing, age, or rank with others. Accordingly, a child's peer may include students of similar age, status, grade, knowledge, or developmental level. Four main types of peer-mediated interventions have been documented in the literature: (a) peers as models of selected behaviors; (b) peers as tutors for academic or developmental skills; (c) peers as managers of social or nonacademic behaviors of other children; and (d) peers as participants in group-oriented reinforcement contingencies with other children (Kohler & Strain, 1990). These interventions can be further broken down into direct and indirect interventions. Direct interventions are those procedures where peers directly influence the target behavior of a student, including peer prompting and reinforcement, peer-mediation, peer initiations, and peer tutoring. Indirect interventions include strategies in which peers influence behavior indirectly such as peer modeling, positive peer reporting and group contingencies (Mather & Rutherford, 1991).

Rationale for Peer-Mediated Interventions

Because of the training requirements and the general acceptance of adult-led instruction and interventions, teachers may be reluctant to incorporate peer-mediated interventions. In the following section, we provide a rationale for selecting peers as agents of peer behavior change, considering such issues as peer influence, new legislation, and a shift from a deficit model to a more ecological model.

PEER INFLUENCE

Current theories suggest that children engage in reciprocal relationships with their environment throughout the formation and organization of social relationships (Bandura, 1978). A child's social interactions typically consist of reciprocal and complementary interchanges with peers that support the actions and behaviors of other peer group members (Farmer & Farmer, 1996). Additional research indicates that peers mutually reinforce behaviors, values, and norms that are consistent with their own and exert a strong influence on one another's behaviors and attitudes within that group (e.g., conformity to group pressure) (Dishion, Andrews, & Crosby, 1995).

As children develop, peers play an increasingly central and influential role. For example, by age 11 almost 50% of a child's social activity involves peers, and by middle school children report spending more time talking and interacting with peers than any other activity. To date, much of the research interest is directed at negative behaviors such as consumption of alcohol, cigarette smoking, and delinquent activities. Research from the juvenile delinquency literature indicates that negative peer influences can exacerbate subsequent antisocial behaviors by providing a socially acceptable venue to engage in deviant behavior (Coie, 1997). While the negative effects of peer influence are evident, peers also play a powerful role in the development of positive behaviors. Because peers become increasingly important throughout child development, they are exceptional candidates as positive behavior change agents. Specifically, positive involvement with peers provides increased opportunities for children to engage in prosocial behaviors and may improve social acceptance and academic achievement.

The potential benefits of enlisting children as agents for peer behavior change has not gone unnoticed in our field, resulting in a steady increase of peer-mediated strategies in the literature over the last two decades. Positive results have been reported for various techniques, including class-wide peer tutoring (Greenwood, Maheady, & Carta, 1991), reciprocal peer tutoring (Fantuzzo & Ginsburg-Block, 1998), positive peer reporting (Ervin, Miller, & Friman, 1996), group contingencies (Skinner, Cashwell, & Dunn, 1996), peer-monitoring (Henington & Skinner, 1998), peer-mediation (Schrumpf, Crawford, & Bodine, 1997), and social skills training (Gresham, 1998).

Legal Mandates

Although school psychologists have been committed to developing, implementing, and evaluating effective interventions for youth exhibiting problematic behavior, attention to this subject has intensified with mandates put forth by the 1997 Amendments to the Individuals with Disabilities Education Act (IDEA 97). These amendments require that school personnel develop and implement positive behavioral intervention strategies for children whose behavior impedes his or her learning or the learning of others, or if the child's inappropriate behavior is repetitive or anticipated to re-occur (34 C.F.R. §300.346(a)(2)(i); Appendix A, p. 12479). The new law creates an opening for more proactive strategies, and translates into a need for effective, time-efficient interventions. The most common intervention approach for students with problematic behavior is traditional teacher-led classroom management, which is less effective in environments where resources are limited. Simply put, it is unfeasible to expect a teacher to continuously monitor all students in the classroom. Sole reliance on teachers to implement individualized interventions for all students is also burdensome, leaving less time for other instructional activities. Peer-mediated interventions are a viable alternative and can be as effective as teacher-led programs. Additionally, the time and cost effectiveness of peer-mediated interventions may increase the acceptability of the intervention and the integrity of implementation for both the student and teacher.

Ecological Model

Parallel to the recent changes in legislation is the evolution in practice from a within-child deficit model to a more ecological approach of assessment and intervention. While peers have been used in the past as models for appropriate behavior, much of the earlier literature on peer-mediated interventions has focused on using peers to facilitate the training or the acquisition of a specific skill. Consequently, interventions focused solely on changing a behavior *within* the target individual exhibiting the problem (a deficit model) and ignored the broader environmental context. For example, a discrete skill is selected (e.g., saying "please"), an intervention targeting the deficit is implemented (e.g., teach the child to say "please"), and the occurrence or non-occurrence of this behavior is recorded to document behavior change. Although specific skills continue to be targeted, assessment and intervention have increasingly focused on identifying the function of the behavior and environmental influences that maintain various behaviors. Recognizing that peers are part of the environment and a natural part of intervention programs is consistent with an ecological approach to assessment and intervention (Strain & Hoyson, 2000).

BASIC CONSIDERATIONS

School psychologists are likely to have a variety of roles when using peer-mediated interventions, including intervention facilitator, intervention monitor, consultant, and/ or parent-teacher liaison. Because of the school psychologist's involvement on multiple levels across students, teachers, and parents, it is important to be familiar with the potential advantages and disadvantages of using peer-mediated approaches for all those involved (see Table 1).

Advantages of Using Peers

Accessibility of Peers

From a practical standpoint, classroom peers are readily available and children have more continuous, frequent, and convenient access to their peers than adults. Children also spend time together across a larger variety of settings, many of which preclude adult interaction (e.g., transition times, restroom, lunch, or recess). As such, using peers for interventions capitalizes on the "social and instructional resources of the classroom, school or district to address fundamental needs of children" (Garcia-Vazquez & Ehly, 1995 p. 404).

Table 1. Advantages and disadvantages of peer-mediated interventions

Advantages

- Accessibility of peers
- Adaptability
- Enhanced generalization
- Teacher flexibility
- Increased active engagement and performance feedback
- Academic, cognitive, social, and interpersonal benefits

Disadvantages

- Ethical concerns
- Initial time requirement
- Cost

Adaptability

Peer-mediated interventions can be successfully employed with a wide range of students, including students with disabilities (e.g., autism, learning disabilities, behavioral disorders, severe disabilities), social difficulties (e.g., peer rejection, social isolation), academic concerns, or non-disabled students. Historically, peer interventions were used to facilitate integration and inclusion of students with disabilities into the classroom. Interactions with more advanced peers provided model behavior and encouragement for appropriate behaviors, and promoted the development of social relationships, communicative, and academic skills of students with disabilities. More recently, however, peer-mediated interventions have been extended to non-disabled students, and research has demonstrated gains in cognitive, academic, behavioral, and social performance in both participants (the target and confederate peer).

Enhanced Generalization

Another major advantage of using peers as intervention agents is the facilitation of generalization and maintenance of target behaviors (Greenwood & Hops, 1981). Peer-peer interactions are qualitatively different from adult-child interactions, and provide a natural context for behavior change. Peer-mediated interventions can facilitate generalization by eliciting responding with numerous peers and settings, providing multiple exemplars. Because peers are available in multiple settings, they may serve as cues or common stimuli in the presence of which the target behavior may be more likely to occur in untrained settings. When implementing an intervention, peers naturally vary their response, providing opportunities for students to learn skills under more loosely controlled contexts. Finally, peer interactions during an intervention may serve as a natural reinforcer, potentially enhancing maintenance of intervention effects beyond that of a contrived reinforcement system (Strain, Kohler, & Goldstein, 1996).

Teacher Flexibility

While initial planning requires additional teacher time, peer-mediated interventions permit teachers to spend less time engaged in direct instruction and more time monitoring and providing feedback to individual students. Less time in direct instruction allows for increased individualized instruction or intervention without high demand of teacher time. The use of peer-mediated procedures, either direct (e.g., peer-monitoring of inappropriate behavior) or indirect (e.g., increased engaged time during peer tutoring) also may result in teachers spending less time addressing behavior problems.

Increased Active Engagement and Performance Feedback

Typical teacher-led instruction may be accompanied by as little as 30% active engaged learning time by students (Mathes & Fuchs, 1994). Using peers as intervention facilitators can lead to the subsequent increase in the percentage of active learning time in the classroom. Peer-mediated interventions (e.g., peer-tutoring) facilitate a higher level of attention to task because of increased opportunities to respond, give and receive feedback, be actively engaged, and ask questions. Additionally, a high level of performance feedback can motivate students, thereby enhancing overall performance.

Academic, Cognitive, Affective, and Interpersonal Benefits

Peer-mediated interventions have resulted in academic, cognitive, affective, and social gains across heterogeneous groups of children and settings (e.g., Stern, Fowler, & Kohler, 1988; Tabacek, McLaughlin, & Howard, 1994; Mathes & Fuchs, 1994). For example, Ervin et al. (1996) reported increased positive social interactions and decreased negative exchanges among peers and target children participating in a peer-mediated intervention. Other researchers have reported lower levels of inappropriate behavior, and enhanced cooperation and positive attitudes for participants (Eiserman, 1988; Johnson & Johnson, 1994; Maheady, 1998). The peer-tutoring literature has demonstrated that both peer tutors and tutees demonstrate academic gains (Greenwood, Carta, & Hall, 1988). Finally, participating in peer-mediated interventions may result in affective benefits such as increased self-confidence (Lane, Pollack, & Sher, 1972) and feelings of altruism (Topping & Ehly, 1998).

Disadvantages of Using Peers

Ethical Concerns

The various methods of peer-mediated interventions have led to three general areas of ethical concern: accountability, competence, and informed consent (Garcia-Vasquez & Ehly, 1995). School psychologists should be prepared to respond to parental concerns regarding the learning benefits of peer-mediated learning programs, such as peer-tutoring. Parents of children receiving and delivering instruction may express concern regarding the value and benefits of such programs. Specifically, questions may arise regarding the ability of peers to adequately teach the material, and, conversely, parents may express concern over the use of their child's instructional time for providing instruction to peers. While the benefits of such programs have been documented for both the tutor and the tutee (Greenwood, Carta, & Hall, 1988), it is necessary to include procedures that allow the progress of all students involved to be monitored and documented. Collecting progress data will allow teachers to make any necessary adjustments in the intervention and determine the extent to which participants are benefiting from the program.

Another potential ethical concern is identifying the "less skilled" child, as may be the case in peer-tutoring dyads or social/behavioral interventions. Procedures must be in place to ensure students are not always identified as the tutee or target child by providing opportunities for students to experience both roles.

All of these concerns are valid and may be prevented by (a) providing parents with literature describing the program and its benefits, (b) allowing children and parents to choose participation without coercion, (c) providing adequate training to tutors and tutees, (d) carefully selecting peer tutors and evaluating mastery of necessary skills, and (e) providing careful and consistent monitoring.

Initial Time Requirement

Although peer-mediated interventions can be less time-consuming in the long run, often it does require time up front to select and train peers (Garcia-Vazquez & Ehly, 1995). For example, curriculum adaptations are often necessary for peer-assisted learning strategies such as peer tutoring or cooperative learning. While most objectives and materials can be adapted for peer-mediated approaches, making such adaptations has been noted as one of the most time-consuming components of the program.

Cost

Related to teacher time is the expense of the program, including teacher planning and training time, peer training, program materials, and consultation. While start-up costs must be considered, once peer-mediated programs are in place, they have been found to be more cost-effective than other methods (e.g., teacher aides).

BEST PRACTICES

There are a number of practical considerations for school psychologists to take into account when using peer-mediated interventions. Below are some general guidelines for developing, implementing, and evaluating a peer-mediated intervention.

Prior to the Intervention

To optimize intervention effectiveness, a thorough assessment of the environment should be conducted in order to tailor the intervention to the classroom environment, social context, and the needs of the student (Gresham, 1998). Because a detailed description on the comprehensive assessment of the environment is beyond the scope of this chapter, we refer readers to other chapters in this volume for discussions and readings on these important topics (e.g., Knoster & McCurdy, this volume).

Developing the Intervention

Selecting a Target Behavior/Response

Following a thorough assessment of the environment, appropriate student goals and objectives must be identified. The target skill and subsequent intervention should be directly linked to the assessment information and matched to the student's ability level. If too many new or unknown skills are included, then students may not achieve a sufficient ratio of success for optimal learning. Consequently, it may be helpful to identify conditions where the student already exhibits some level of the behavior. Additionally, the intervention should be matched to the environmental context. For example, a group contingency program designed to increase cooperative interactions may be more effective in a classroom that allows talking and free movement, increasing the likelihood of cooperative play interactions (Strain, Kerr, & Ragland, 1981). Finally, clear and appropriate rules and outcomes should be established. The target skill and response should be specific, and students should be able to easily discern if an answer or response is correct or incorrect, especially if the peer is responsible for delivering a consequence contingent upon exhibiting a behavior (e.g., asking a tutor to decide if a tutee's response to a spelling word or math fact is correct or incorrect and subsequently providing appropriate feedback) (Miller & Kohler, 1993).

Selecting a Peer-Mediated Intervention

Similar to selecting a target behavior and response, the selection of an intervention should be linked directly to the assessment information, individualized, and based on the function of the problem behavior for the student. School psychologists can take advantage of a large body of literature describing effective peer-mediated interventions. Some strategies include using peers for peer-tutoring (e.g., class-wide and reciprocal peer tutoring) (Delquadri, Greenwood, Whorton, Carta, & Hall, 1986; Fantuzzo & Ginsburg-Block, 1998), cooperative learning groups, paired learning activities, counseling and education, peer mediation (Schrumph et al., 1997), modeling appropriate behavior, group contingencies (Skinner et al., 1996), peer-monitoring and assessment (Dougherty, Fowler, & Paine, 1985; Henington & Skinner, 1998).

Selecting Intervention Times

After identifying an intervention, it is necessary to define appropriate times during the week when the intervention will be implemented. Given that teachers' schedules are typically quite busy, the school psychologist can work collaboratively with the teacher to find times during the day he or she may be able to restructure an activity for a peer-mediated intervention, rather than creating an extra activity for the teacher to fit into the day (Maheady, Harper, & Sacca, 1988).

Selecting Peer Facilitators

Peer facilitators are needed for peer assisted learning strategies. The following characteristics have been identified for ideal peer trainers: regular school attendance, exhibits desired skill or behavior, compliant with adult direction, willing to participate in the program, and responsive to adult reinforcement. While the ideal peer model has all of the above characteristics, it is not always possible or even necessary to find facilitators with these characteristics. Tutors or models can be trained to demonstrate mastery of the specific target skill prior to becoming a facilitator.

Training Peers

Peer-mediated interventions should be used only after students have been trained sufficiently in the intervention procedures. Although training of peers can increase the initial time commitment, thorough training is associated with better outcomes. Because this component is so critical, we suggest a structured training session prior to the implementation of the intervention, which should include explicit training steps and procedures for students to follow. To help structure student training and to enable the trainer to quickly provide specific academic, behavioral, or social responses, we recommend using a pre-written training manual (if one is available). Examples of such manuals are provided in reference section of this chapter. If a manual is not available, then written guidelines can be posted in the classroom or attached to students' desks.

Successful training involves deciding who will carry out the training, how and where training will occur, and how often training will be conducted. Generally, the training format should consist of (a) introduction of the skill and/or presentation of the material, (b) modeling of the intervention procedure, (c) role-play of skills with praise and corrective feedback , and (d) monitoring and corrective feedback of the first few initial trials (e.g., Greenwood et al., 1988). Practice of the intervention procedures should continue until mastery is attained (independent of adult instruction), or until a pre-determined criterion is met. There is no generally accepted period of time that is considered optimal. However, research has demonstrated that students can typically learn intervention procedures in two to four sessions. Considerations such as the complexity of the material to be taught and the age and skill of the students will need to be addressed (Harper, Maheady, & Mallette, 1994).

Peers inadvertently may reinforce inappropriate behavior, punish appropriate behavior, or fail to provide the appropriate contingencies, thereby extinguishing the target behavior. Therefore, students should be taught how to administer appropriate consequences and/or error correction procedures based on the occurrence or nonoccurrence of the behavior, or quality of the response (Kohler & Strain, 1990). For example, students can be taught to provide some type of a reward contingent upon a correct response, such as a verbal statement ("Yes, that is correct"; "Good work!") or a tally mark that could be exchanged for a backup reward (Miller & Kohler, 1993).

In addition to the general intervention procedures, training also may incorporate trouble-shooting techniques by teaching students how to respond in situations where a peer provides an incorrect response or fails to respond. For example, in a peer-mediated social intervention for students with autism, peer helpers were taught to be persistent when initiating social contact. As training of the peer helpers progressed, the trainers (acting as a child with autism) made it gradually more difficult for the peers to evoke a correct response by ignoring the child or waiting a progressively longer period of time before responding to the peer initiations (Strain et al., 1996). In a similar example, Kohler and Fowler (1985) trained participants how to respond to target children if they refused play invitations and modeled alternative responses ("Ok, I will ask again later"). For additional strategies and examples, the reader is referred to Kohler, Shearer, and Strain's (1990) *Peer-Mediated Intervention Manual.*

Implementation of the Intervention

Programming Environmental Supports

Classrooms are heterogeneous, which adds to the organizational complexity of any intervention. In many cases, structuring the environment will be necessary to ensure the target behaviors are supported within the natural context and to enhance maintenance and generalization of skills. For example, merely placing children together in play situations may not spontaneously elicit the desired cooperative behaviors or positive interactions among peers. The environment needs to be designed to elicit these behaviors. One necessary environmental arrangement may include increasing and/or structuring the opportunities for the child to engage in the appropriate behavior. Both social and academic interventions require an environment that promotes increased and varied opportunities for the student to engage in the target behavior (Strain & Hoyson, 2000). For example, within peer-tutoring interactions students should be engaged in a high or rapid rate of responding and practice, and students should receive a sufficient number of opportunities to practice each item for mastery (Fuchs, Fuchs, & Burish, 2000). Additional environmental arrangements may include providing feedback and reinforcement, altering structural arrangements or manipulating the composition of groups, and/or providing additional prompting and rewards to further increase desirable behavior. When extending the intervention to non-trained settings, or in settings when fewer adults are present, such as recess or lunch, a more intensive reward program may need to be implemented at the outset.

Monitoring and Evaluating the Intervention

When peer-mediated interventions are employed, the teacher's primary role shifts from directly teaching skills to managing and supervising the intervention. Consequently, teachers must closely monitor the program to determine if additional accommodations or changes are necessary. Practical examples of such monitoring include walking around the room and listening to ensure students understand the task, prompting the necessary skills or responses, ensuring error correction procedures are being used adequately, and making certain students are providing appropriate contingencies. Additionally, teachers should provide specific feedback to students regarding behaviors they are performing well and any changes students should make (Miller & Kohler, 1993).

As with any intervention, data should be collected in order to monitor student progress and the effects of intervention on the target behavior. Monitoring goals should be observable and measurable, and assessed with outcome measures that directly relate to the skills that are taught (see Steege this volume, for further discussion on evaluating interventions). Although it is often not feasible for the school psychologist to directly collect progress-monitoring data, consultation can be provided to help the teacher identify appropriate data collection and recording methods and to help with data analysis (e.g., single-subject design). While the individual objective of interventions will vary, progress monitoring for peer-mediated interventions may include (a) academic performance indicators, such as quiz scores, worksheet accuracy (calculating the percentage of correct responses) or curriculum based measurement; (b) social gains indicators such as the quality of interactions, frequency of social initiations, frequency or duration of interactions, proximity of peers, or sociometric data; or (c) affective gain indicators such as attitudes toward peers, school, or self.

Adjustment of Intervention if Necessary

In the course of progress monitoring, it may be determined that some students are making insufficient progress. A thorough assessment is necessary to determine which intervention components need to be adjusted. For example, if the student is not progressing at an appropriate academic rate, a closer look at the academic environment may indicate certain adjustments should be made, including longer tutoring sessions, more frequent sessions, more intensive training on a particular skill (carrying math facts), or further training in peer-tutoring procedures. Factors outside of the immediate academic task may reveal further problems. For example, routine problems during peer tutoring that often require additional intervention include loud noise levels, cheating during tutoring procedures, arguing or student disruptiveness (Greenwood et al., 1991). If it is determined that the intervention is not successful, then the school psychologist should return to the assessment of the environment or target skill to determine if the intervention is appropriate and what adaptations can be made.

Maintenance of the Intervention

To encourage sustained use over time, peer-mediated procedures must be relatively easy to use, and potentially adaptable for a group or class-wide setting. School psychologists can help maintain the continued use of peer-mediated interventions by providing manuals with detailed instructions and steps to follow, preparing teachers for potential pitfalls and identifying possible solutions, remaining available for trouble-shooting sessions, and by implementing treatment integrity checks (e.g., Greenwood et al., 1988; Schrumph et al., 1997).

PEER-MEDIATED INTERVENTIONS

Peer-Tutoring. There is a long-standing history of peer involvement in the educational curriculum, and numerous examples attest to the effectiveness of peer-mediated academic intervention programs (e.g., cooperative learning, class-wide peer tutoring, reciprocal peer tutoring, peer-assisted learning, and academic coaching). Peer tutoring is one of the most commonly used academic interventions, and is the subject of extensive research (see reviews by Delquadri et al., 1986; Greenwood et al., 1991; Mathes & Fuchs, 1994). A number of peer-tutoring methods have been suggested, varying on a number of factors, including peer-pairing procedures (e.g., same-age versus cross-age, high-status with low status peers, pairing by disability, pairing by classroom type), intervention focus (e.g., individual versus class-wide, cross-age tutoring, reciprocal tutoring, cooperative learning groups), content area (e.g., spelling, reading, vocabulary, and mathematics), and procedural factors (e.g., contingencies) (Greenwood et al., 1991).

Common elements of peer-tutoring interventions include student training, use of a structured set of procedures, high rates of responding and practice, performance feedback, and point earning contingencies (Greenwood et al., 1991). For optimal academic learning, the instructional environment should be arranged so students are afforded repeated opportunities to practice the material. Thus, within peer-tutoring interactions, students should be engaged in a high rate of responding and practice. For example, if the skill to be taught is correct recitation of the 2s and 3s division facts, flashcards allow multiple repetitions within a short period of time. Additionally, students should engage in a sufficient number of opportunities to practice each item for mastery. Consequently, only a small set of skills should be used in each tutoring session. The focus should be on mastery of a smaller set of material, rather than exposure and practice of a broader range of material. Finally, turn taking as a tutor and tutee ensures students practice in both roles (Miller & Kohler, 1993; Fuchs et al., 2000).

Performance feedback is also a necessary component of peer-tutoring interventions. Specifically, tutors should provide immediate, appropriate, and corrective feedback to the tutees. As a consequence, tutors should be taught specific procedures and prompts for situations where the tutee elicits an incorrect response, or fails to respond. Error correction procedures may consist of the tutor stopping the tutee and prompting the tutee for the correct response, or providing the correct answer and engaging the tutee in repeated trials of practicing the correct response ("The answer is 10. Now you try this problem again. What is 5 plus 5?"). In other situations, the tutor may need to prompt the tutee for a response. For example, providing a verbal cue, "Try this math problem." Finally, tutors should provide some type of a reward contingent upon a correct response, such as verbal praise or a secondary reinforcer that can be exchanged at a later time (Miller & Kohler, 1993).

Peer-Mediation. Mediation is one component of conflict resolution that requires the parties in conflict to meet with a neutral third party to resolve the problem (Schrumpf et al., 1997). During the mediation process, the peer-mediator is responsible for creating and maintaining the problem-solving communication between those in dispute. Each party listens to the other's point of view, identifies areas contributing to the conflict, identifies potential solutions, and selects an agreed upon solution.

Perhaps in response to the increased focus on aggression and school violence, conflict resolution and peer-mediation programs are becoming increasingly popular in public schools. In a review of the literature on peer-mediation, there was evidence that following peer-mediation training, students retained the information learned and were able to accurately apply the procedures, reported fewer conflicts, and generalized the skills beyond the training setting (Johnson & Johnson, 1994). However, most of the research is limited to correlational, anecdotal, and self-report data and therefore must be interpreted cautiously.

Positive Peer Reporting. Positive peer reporting (PPR) is a simple peer-mediated technique that involves the use of peer attention and prosocial statements to improve the quality of peer interactions. Specifically, peers publicly report the positive behaviors exhibited by a target child to the teacher for a brief, specified period of time (e.g., last 5 minutes of homeroom). A faux raffle or drawing can be conducted to select a name in order to preserve the identity of target children. During PPR, peers report any prosocial behaviors exhibited by the target child over the course of the day for a specified number of days (e.g., typically 1 week). Peers are rewarded for making comments deemed specific and genuine by the teacher. The underlying rationale for this intervention centers around the powerful influence peers can have on behavior and the premise that public acknowledgement of a behavior from peers may be more reinforcing than when delivered by adults (Ervin et al., 1996).

Repeated demonstrations of improvements in the quality of peer interactions during treatment phases have provided substantial support for PPR as an effective intervention for children with performance deficits in social skills and/or children who are socially rejected or ignored. Table 2 provides the general steps of the procedure.

Social Skills Interventions. Three types of peer-mediated interventions for improving social skills have been identified: (a) proximity procedures, (b) prompt and reinforcement procedures, and (c) peer initiation procedures.

Proximity interventions are characterized by placing socially skilled children with target children to initiate and encourage play, but without any training. Studies using proximity procedures typically have included peer-pairings of high and low accepted children, or higher functioning children and lower functioning children. Peer prompting and reinforcement interventions move beyond proximity by training peers to prompt and then reinforce a desired behavior (e.g., social initiation) of target children. In general, a teacher initially teaches a peer confederate to deliver a peer prompt (e.g., "look at me"), or elicit a social behavior (e.g., "hi"), and then provides reinforcement (e.g., praise). For the third procedure, peer-initiation, peers are trained to initiate social interactions with a target child (e.g., ask to play), thereby providing increased opportunities to respond.

While many of the peer-mediated interventions in the social skills literature have resulted in behavior change, intervention success rarely has been documented over extended periods of time, or outside of the immediate intervention locale to more natural contexts. Gresham (1998) has suggested that in order to improve upon these strategies, school psychologists should (a) engage in careful assessment using socially valid techniques (e.g., friendships) and observation, (b) take advantage of naturally occurring occasions in order to promote generalization, (c) match the training to specific deficits, and (d) develop and teach skills that will work more reliably than competing problem behaviors.

Group Contingencies. Group contingencies maximize on the dynamics of peer influence among children by taking advantage of social contingencies controlled by the peer group (see Skinner, this volume, for additional information). Group contingencies have been found to be at least as effective as individual contingencies, but require less teacher time. There are three types of group contingencies, each with varying degrees of embedded peer influence: independent, interdependent, and dependent. Independent group contingencies allow for each child to receive the same consequence based on individual behavior. Only those children who meet the criteria have access to reinforcement. Peer influence plays the smallest role in independent group contingencies, but is still in effect (e.g., observing a peer receiving reinforcement, competition). Interdependent group contingencies require an entire group to reach a specified level of performance in order to gain access to reinforcement (e.g., an entire class remains quiet while transitioning in order to receive a pizza party). The final type of group contingency is the dependent contingency. With a dependent group contingency, the consequence for a group is determined by the performance of an individual (e.g., "If Joe finishes his assignment, the whole class gets 5 extra recess min-

Table 2. Positive peer reporting

- Identify target student (peers are not aware that there is a target student because all class members can participate)
- Select a location and time period: 5–10 minutes is needed
- Teach and practice specific examples and non-examples of positive behaviors appropriate for reporting (example: Sam passed the ball to me during basketball practice; non-example: I like Sam's new haircut)
- Have class help identify rewards for participation (group contingencies work well)
- Have a drawing to select target students
- Post the name of the target student and class progress toward reward

utes."). It is important to make sure that peer influence does not become pressure or coercion. This can best be prevented by only using reinforcement contingencies (not cost), and setting appropriate, attainable goals.

Peer Monitoring. Peer monitoring involves teaching children to observe and objectively record a specific behavior (e.g., assignment completion). Similar to self-management, peer monitoring procedures (peer observation and recording) also can be extended to include peer evaluation (the comparison of a peer's behavior with a determined standard such as class rules) and reinforcement of peer behavior (Henington & Skinner, 1998). Peer monitoring can be a time-efficient method to collect data on social, academic, appropriate, and inappropriate behaviors. It also may be incorporated into other peer-mediated interventions such as peer tutoring and social skills training. For example, during peer tutoring, peers observe the occurrence or non-occurrence of a target behavior (e.g., spelling a word), record and evaluate accuracy (correct or incorrect spelling), and provide reinforcement (e.g., praise, star, points).

Peer Modeling. Peer modeling involves a target child viewing an appropriate behavior of at least one peer. An advantage of peer modeling is that the similarity of a peer-peer interaction can enhance motivation and self-efficacy for learning and promote academic achievement beyond an adult modeling interaction. Despite the potential effectiveness, peer modeling cannot always stand alone. A student skill may require more than a modeled demonstration of a skill, such as practicing the skill and receiving corrective feedback. Additionally, it may help to highlight the distinctive features of the modeling session to which the students should attend (Schunk, 1998).

Multiple Component Intervention. Peer-mediated techniques can be embedded within a comprehensive intervention package. One intervention example is Learning Experiences: An Alternative Program (LEAP) (see Strain et al., 1996, for a program description). This comprehensive early intervention program for typical preschoolers and preschoolers with autism includes intensive peer-mediation procedures to increase or enhance communication and social interaction, as well as specific training sessions in classroom instruction and family involvement. In the LEAP program example, peers were taught specific peer-initiation procedures such as establishing eye-contact, describing play, initiating joint play, establishing joint attention, repeating, requesting further clarification or expanding on the verbalizations made by the child with autism, and prompting requests. In a recent publication describing the preliminary results of the 18-year study in which the LEAP program was used, data indicate that the level of positive interactions increased from 3 to 23%, comparable to same aged peers (Strain & Hoyson, 2000).

Other Interventions. Other peer-mediated interventions that are beyond the scope of this chapter but may be of interest to readers include peer counseling, peer-mentoring peer-support groups, and peer-education. These additional interventions are often used to prevent or reduce harmful behaviors such as drugs and alcohol use, smoking, or to increase desired behaviors such as abstinence from sexual activity. Readers are referred to Foot, Morgan, and Shute (1990) and Topping and Ehly (1998) for additional information on these topics.

SUMMARY

Owing to limited resources in our schools, interventions are needed that maximize available classroom resources while maintaining or improving learning outcomes. Peers are highly influential in child development and are a valuable resource in the schools. Although a majority of the interventions for academic and behavior difficulties currently recommended by school psychologists are likely to be teacher-directed, peer-mediated interventions are an effective and efficient technique that can be employed. Moreover, results of peer-mediated intervention research demonstrate that peers can apply intervention procedures, provide opportunities for peers to learn from multiple examples, and are at least as effective than adults as intervention agents.

The school psychologist as a problem solver, intervention facilitator, consultant, or parent/teacher liaison can serve a primary role in developing, implementing, and evaluating peer-mediated interventions. Advantages to using peer-mediated interventions, including benefits to both the target and non-target peer, enhanced generalization, and greater flexibility for the classroom teacher make peer-mediated interventions an attractive option for school psychologists to add to their list of interventions. School psychologists who wish to use peer-mediated interventions have a variety of strategies to choose from.

REFERENCES

Bandura, A. (1978). The self-system in reciprocal determinism. *American Psychologist, 33,* 344–358.

Coie, J.D. (1997). *The prevention of conduct disorders.* Lecture series for the Visiting Preventionist Virtual Symposium: Early Career Preventionists Network.

Delquadri, J., Greenwood, C. R., Whorton, D., Carta, J. J., & Hall R. V. (1986). Class-wide peer tutoring. *Exceptional Children, 52,* 535–542.

Dishion, T. J., Andrews, D. W., & Crosby, L. (1995). Antisocial boys and their friends in early adolescence: relationship characteristics, quality, and interactional process. *Child Development, 66,* 139–151.

Dougherty, B. S., Fowler, S. A., & Paine, S. C. (1985). The use of peer monitors to reduce negative interaction during recess. *Journal of Applied Behavior Analysis, 18,* 141–153.

Eiserman, W. D. (1988). Three types of peer-tutoring: Effects on the attitudes of students with learning disabilities and their regular class peers. *Journal of Learning Disabilities, 21,* 249–252.

Ervin, R. A., Miller, P. M., & Friman, P. C. (1996). Feed the hungry bee: Using positive peer reports to improve the social interactions and acceptance of a socially rejected girl in residential care. *Journal of Applied Behavior Analysis, 29,* 251–253.

Fantuzzo, J., & Ginsburg-Block, M. (1998). Reciprocal peer tutoring: Developing and testing effective peer collaborations for elementary school students. In K. Topping & S. Ehly (Eds.), *Peer-assisted learning* (pp. 121–144). Hillsdale, NJ: Erlbaum.

Farmer, T. W., & Farmer, E. M. (1996). Social relationships of students with exceptionalities in mainstream classrooms: Social networks and homophily. *Exceptional Children, 62,* 431–450.

Foot, H., Morgan, M., & Shute, R. (Eds.). (1990). *Children helping children.* New York: John Wiley.

Fuchs, D., Fuchs, L. S., & Burish, P. (2000). Peer-assisted learning strategies: An evidence-based practice to promote reading achievement. *Learning Disabilities Research & Practice, 15,* 85–91.

Garcia-Vazquez, E., & Ehly, S. (1995). Best practices in facilitating peer tutoring programs. In A. Thomas and J. Grimes (Eds.), *Best practices in school psychology III* (pp. 403–411). Washington, DC: National Association of School Psychologists.

Greenwood, C. R., Carta, J. C., & Hall, R. V. (1988). The use of peer tutoring strategies in classroom management and educational instruction. *School Psychology Review, 17,* 258–275.

Greenwood, C. R., Delquadri, J., & Carta, J. J. (1999). *Together we can! Class-wide peer tutoring to improve basic academic skills.* Longmont, CO: Sopris West.

Greenwood, C. R., & Hops, H. (1981). Group-oriented contingencies and peer behavior change. In P. S. Strain (Ed.), *The utilization of classroom peers as behavior change agents* (pp. 189–259). New York: Plenum.

Greenwood, C.R., Maheady, L., & Carta, J. J. (1991). Peer tutoring programs in the regular education classroom. In G. Stoner, M. R., Shinn, & H. M. Walker (Eds.), *Interventions for achievement and behavior problems* (pp. 179–200). Silver Spring, MD: National Association of School Psychologists.

Gresham, F. M. (1998). Social skills training: Should we raze, remodel or rebuild? *Behavioral Disorders, 24,* 19–25.

Harper, G. F., Maheady, L., & Mallette, B. (1994). The power of peer-mediated instruction. In J. S. Thousand, R. A. Villa, & A. I. Nevin (Eds.), *Creativity and collaborative learning: A practical guide to empowering students and teachers* (pp. 229–242) Baltimore: Brookes.

Henington, C. & Skinner, C. H. (1998). Peer monitoring. In K. Topping & S. Ehly (Eds.), *Peer-assisted learning* (pp. 237–254). Hillsdale, NJ: Erlbaum.

Johnson, D. W. & Johnson, R. T. (1996). Conflict resolution and peer mediation programs in elementary and secondary schools: A review of the research. *Review of Educational Research*, *66*, 459–506.

Johnson, R. T., & Johnson, D. W. (1994). An overview of cooperative learning. In J. S. Thousand, R. A. Villa, & A. I. Nevins (Eds.), *Creativity and collaborative learning: A practical guide to empowering student and teachers* (pp. 31–44). Baltimore: Brookes.

Kohler, F. W., & Fowler, S. A. (1985). Training prosocial behaviors to young children: An analysis of reciprocity with untrained peers. *Journal of Applied Behavior Analysis, 18,* 187–200.

Kohler, F. W., Shearer, D., & Strain, P. S. (1990). *Peer-mediated intervention manual.* Pittsburgh, PA: University of Pittsburgh.

Kohler, F. W., & Strain, P.S. (1990). Peer-assisted interventions: Early promises, notable achievements and future aspirations. *Clinical Psychology Review, 10,* 441–452.

Lane, P., Pollack, C., & Sher, N. (1972). Remotivation of disruptive adolescents. *Journal of Reading, 15,* 351–354.

Maheady, L. (1998). Advantages and disadvantages of peer-assisted learning strategies. In K. Topping & S. Ehly (Eds.), *Peer-assisted learning* (pp. 45–66). Hillsdale, NJ: Erlbaum.

Maheady, L., Harper, G. F., & Sacca. M. K. (1988). Peer-mediated instruction: Promising alternative for secondary learning disabled students. *Learning Disability Quarterly, 11,* 108–114.

Mather, S. R., & Rutherford, R. B. (1991). Peer-mediated interventions promoting social skills of children and youth with behavioral disorders. *Education and Treatment of Children, 14,* 227–242.

Mathes, P.G., & Fuchs, L. S. (1994). The efficacy of peer tutoring in reading for students with mild disabilities: A best-evidence synthesis. *School Psychology Review, 23,* 59–81.

Miller, L. J., & Kohler, F. W. (1993). Winning with peer tutoring. *Preventing School Failure, 37,* 14–19.

Schrumph, F., Crawford, D., & Bodine, R. (1997). *Peer mediation: Conflict resolution in the schools.* Champaign, IL: Research Press.

Schunk, D. H. (1998). Peer modeling. In K. Topping & S. Ehly (Eds.), *Peer-assisted learning* (pp. 45–66). Hillsdale, NJ: Erlbaum.

Skinner, C. H., Cashwell, C. S., & Dunn, M. S. (1996). Independent and interdependent group contingencies: Smoothing the rough waters. *Special Services in the Schools, 12*, 61–78.

Stern, G. W., Fowler, S. A. & Kohler, F. W. (1988). A comparison of two intervention roles: Peer monitor and point earner. *Journal of Applied Behavior Analysis, 21*, 103–109.

Strain, P.S. (Ed.). (1981). *The utilization of classroom peers as behavior change agents.* New York: Plenum.

Strain, P. S., & Hoyson, M. (2000). The need for longitudinal intensive social skill intervention: LEAP Follow-up outcomes for children with autism. *Topics in Early Childhood Special Education, 20*, 116–122.

Strain, P. S., Kerr, M. M., & Ragland, E. U. (1981). The use of peer social initiations in the treatment of social withdrawal. In P. S. Strain (Ed.), *The utilization of classroom peers as behavior change agents.* (pp. 101–128). New York: Plenum.

Strain, P. S., Kohler, E W., & Goldstein, H. (1996). Learning experiences ...An alternative program: Peer-mediated interventions for young children with autism. In E. Hibbs & P. Jenson (Eds.), *Psychosocial treatments for child and adolescent disorders* (pp. 573–587). Washington, DC: American Psychological Association.

Tabacek, D. A., McLaughlin, T. F., & Howard, V. F. (1994). Teaching preschool children with disabilities tutoring skills: Effects on pre-academic behaviors. *Child and Family Behavior Therapy, 16*, 43–63.

Topping, K. & Ehly, S. (Eds.). (1998). *Peer-assisted learning*. Hillsdale, NJ: Erlbaum.

ANNOTATED BIBLIOGRAPHY

Foot, H., Morgan, M., & Shute, R. (Eds.). (1990). *Children helping children.* New York: John Wiley.
An edited book with a wide variety of chapters involving peers as mediators. Topics are quite diverse ranging from theoretical and historical to specific interventions and specific populations. The book has 17 chapters and three main sections: peer tutoring, cooperative learning, and social and clinical uses.

Greenwood, C. R., Delquadri, J., & Carta, J. J. (1999). *Together we can! Class wide peer tutoring to improve basic academic skills.* Longmont, CO: Sopris West.
This is an excellent manual that school psychologists can use for implementing class-wide peer tutoring. This 94-page resource provides usable dry-erase charts and step-by-step procedures for implementing class-wide peer tutoring.

Miller, L. J., & Kohler, F. W. (1993). Winning with peer tutoring. *Preventing School Failure, 37*, 14–19.
This article provides practical step-by-step guidelines for implementing a peer-tutoring intervention within a classroom.

Strain, P. S. (Ed.). (1981). *The utilization of classroom peers as behavior change agents.* New York: Plenum.
This text provides a historical perspective and review of peer mediated interventions. Issues of generalization, advantages and disadvantages of peer-mediated interventions, and practical considerations are thoroughly discussed.

Topping, K. & Ehly, S. (Eds.). (1998). *Peer-assisted learning*. Hillsdale, NJ: Erlbaum.
This edited book is an up-to-date and comprehensive book addressing peer-mediated interventions. The book is composed of 17 chapters broken down into five general categories: benefits of peer-assisted learning, peer tutoring, peer facilitation, peer feedback, and extensions of peer-assisted learning. The chapters provide overviews of the various techniques in addition to research on the subject and useful references for additional information.

99 Best Practices in School-Based Vocational Assessment

Edward M. Levinson
Indiana University of Pennsylvania

OVERVIEW

Unfortunately, students are leaving schools without the skills necessary to acquire and maintain satisfying jobs. A report published by the U.S. Department of Labor (1991) concluded that "...more than half our young people leave schools without the knowledge foundation required to find and hold a good job " (p. xv). The U.S. General Accounting Office (1993) reported that one-third of young workers ages 16–24 do not have the skills they need to perform entry-level, semiskilled jobs. A series of nationwide studies commissioned by the National Career Development Association and carried out by the Gallup Organization (Brown & Minor, 1989; Hoyt & Lester, 1995) revealed that only one-third of adults are in their current jobs as a result of conscious planning. The remaining two-thirds entered their jobs because of chance factors, the influence of others, or because they took the only job available. Only about half of these workers reported that they were satisfied with their jobs.

The school population with whom school psychologists work most frequently, individuals with disabilities, may be at even greater risk than the general population when it comes to preparation for work. Studies have consistently demonstrated that compared to their non-disabled peers, individuals with mild disabilities experience a higher rate of unemployment and underemployment, lower pay, and more dissatisfaction with employment (Dunn, 1996).

One factor that has historically contributed to the lack of vocational preparedness among individuals with disabilities is the elevated drop-out rate that characterizes this population. Studies that have compared special education drop-out rates with control group drop-out rates or normative data have consistently demonstrated that students with disabilities leave school more often than students without disabilities (Ysseldyke, Algozzine, & Thurlow, 1992). Students with learning disabilities and emotional disabilities appear to be at particularly high risk of dropping out of school. Drop-out rates for these students have been reported to exceed 40 and 50%, respectively (Gajar, Goodman, & McAfee, 1993).

But why do students drop out of school? One explanation is that for the majority of students who do *not* plan to go on to college, schools are particularly ineffective in addressing their educational and vocational needs. A 1993 Gallup Poll (Hoyt & Lester, 1995) indicated that 60% of American adults said high schools devote enough attention to preparing students for college, but *not* enough attention to helping non-college–bound students get jobs. Most schools direct most of their resources toward preparing students for college. Yet only about 15% of incoming ninth graders go on to graduate from high school and then obtain a 4-year college degree within 6 years of their high school graduation (Morra, 1993). Hence, schools focus their curriculum more on the educational needs of the college-bound minority than on the educational needs of the work-bound majority. Among students with disabilities, the need to address vocational skills rather than the academic skills necessary for entrance into to college is even more pressing. The 21st Annual Report to Congress on the Implementation of the IDEA (U.S. Department of Education, 1999) reported that only 24.5% of students with disabilities ages 17 years and older graduated from high school with a diploma (a prerequisite for college entrance). This report also indicated that students with disabilities were less likely to drop out of school and more likely to be competitively employed after high school if they received adequate vocational education training in high school. The report concluded that at the systems level, major changes are needed in schools, adult service agencies, and in the community if the vocational needs of students with disabilities are to be met. There is little doubt that given the high unemployment and underemployment rates that exist among individuals with disabilities, and the elevated drop-out rate that exists among this population, efforts in the area of special education have not assisted these individuals in making a successful adjustment to work.

To address the problems just outlined, considerable legislation has been passed in the last 10–15 years designed to improve the vocational and career assistance provided to individuals with disabilities. The Vocational Rehabilitation Act, the Education of the Handicapped Act, the Vocational Education Amendments Act, and the Career Education Incentive Act have combined to provide federal funding assistance to assist individuals with disabilities to prepare for work.

More recently, the Carl D. Perkins Vocational Education Act and the Individuals with Disabilities Education Act have contributed to the development of school-based vocational and career assessment services. The Perkins Act requires that information about vocational education opportunities be provided to parents and students no later than the beginning of the ninth grade or at least 1 year before the student enters the grade in which vocational education is offered. The Act also requires that information about eligibility requirements for enrolling in vocational education programs be provided to parents and students, and that once enrolled in vocational education, students receive an assessment of interests, abilities, and special needs and other special services designed to facilitate transition from school to post-school employment or training.

The Individuals With Disabilities Education Act (IDEA) was originally passed in 1990, and amendments to it were passed in 1997. IDEA incorporates requirements for the establishment of services designed to assist students in making a successful transition from school to work and community living. Under this law, plans for a student's transition from school to work and community living must be initiated by age 14.

A necessary first step in transition planning is assessment (Levinson, 1998). Assessment is designed to identify what skills a student needs in order to make a successful transition to work and community living. Given that all transition planning should be based upon assessment, a through and valid vocational assessment of student needs is a necessary, prerequisite, and perhaps most important first step in the transition planning process. Readers who are interested in additional information on transition services are referred to Levinson (1998) and Levinson and Murphy (1999) and/or chapters on transition elsewhere in this volume.

To briefly summarize, students in general, and students with disabilities in particular, are not being adequately prepared for work by our public schools. Though the overwhelming percentage of students, particularly those with disabilities, do not pursue post-secondary education and leave high school in search of employment, our schools typically emphasize an academic program designed to prepare students for post-secondary education. As a consequence, many students, particularly those with disabilities, find that the education they are receiving does not meet their needs and eventually drop out of school.

For the purposes of this chapter, the terms "career assessment," "vocational assessment," "vocational evaluation," and "work evaluation" will be considered synonymous, although distinctions have been made among them in the literature. While the purpose of all of these processes is to generate information that can be used to assist individuals in making decisions regarding career choice, differences have largely to do with the professional group involved in the process, the setting in which the process occurs, or the instrumentation or methodology utilized to complete the process.

Historically, school psychologists have reported spending only a small percentage of their time in vocational activities despite attaching great importance to them (Shepard & Hohenshil, 1983). Studies have indicated that approximately one-third of school psychologists have had some involvement in vocational assessment (Levinson, 1988), though the percentage of time spent by school psychologists in this aspect of assessment has been estimated to be less than 1% (Carey, 1995). Staab (1996) surveyed a randomly selected sample of 602 school psychologists working at the secondary level to determine (a) the functions they performed in the area of transition planning, (b) the importance they attached to transition planning, and (c) the barriers they perceived to exist that prevented them from participating in transition-planning activities. Results indicated that school psychologists were interested in transition-planning activities, perceived these activities to be important, but generally felt unprepared to perform the activities listed. However, the two transition activities that were described as activities that school psychologists "definitely should" perform were associated with vocational assessment: "explain test results to students so that they understand their strengths/needs, and modifications/adaptations needed for successful transition planning and programming" and "completing triennial evaluations to help meet transition planning needs."

Despite limited involvement by school psychologists in vocational assessment activities, the National Association of School Psychologists (NASP) has provided some support for school psychologist involvement in vocational activities, and incorporates both vocational assessment and vocational intervention in its *Professional Conduct Manual*. In its description of Standards for the Provision of School Psychological Services, NASP (1997) states, "Psychological and psychoeducational assessments include evaluation, as appropriate, of the areas of...vocational development, aptitude, and interests" (p.44). In reference to consultation, the standards state, "School psychologists provide skill enhancement activities (such as...vocational development...) to school personnel, parents, and others in the community, regarding issues of human learning, development, and behavior" (p. 44). In reference to direct service, the standards state, "School psychologists design direct service programs to enhance...vocational development" (p. 45).

Hence, if school psychologists are going to practice their profession in a manner consistent with their professional standards, then they must be involved in vocational assessment and programming in the schools. In fact, given their particular expertise as compared to other professionals in the schools, the school psychologist's involvement in the vocational assessment process may be critical to the success of such programs. As I have stated elsewhere (Levinson, 1993, 1995, 1998; Levinson & Murphy, 1999), the school psychologist's psychometric expertise and knowledge of measurement theory can safeguard against the inappropriate selection and use of assessment devices, and the inappropriate interpretation and use of assessment data (historically a problem in school-based vocational assessment programs). Their skills in assessment can be used to generate data (i.e., intelligence, achievement, personality, social skills, etc.) which is critical to vocational planning, and their knowledge of learning and behavior theory and of adolescent psychology can be used in the effective development and implementation of vocational services.

For school psychologists to become significantly involved in vocational assessment activities, however, several important changes need to occur. First, their knowledge and skills in this area must be upgraded. Despite NASP standards that incorporate vocational/career assessment, vocational/career counseling, vocational/career consultation, and vocational/career program development, there is little evidence that accreditation of training programs is at all contingent on *any* of these skills being taught to pre-service school psychologists. Hence, few if any school psychologists who graduate from NASP-approved school psychology programs have been adequately prepared to provide the vocational and transition related activities that NASP itself includes in its standards.

Minimally, school psychologists need to become more informed about career development theory and its application in assessment, counseling, consultation, and program development. School psychologists need to understand transition from a K–12 career development perspective and recognize that there is an important role for them to play in the process, regardless of whether they work at an elementary, middle school, or secondary school level. From an assessment perspective, school psychologists need to become more informed about interest and aptitude assessment, and other more experientially based vocational assessment techniques such as work sampling, situational assessment, and simulated work experiences. Additionally, school psychologists need to become better acquainted with the vocational relevance of the assessment data they currently gather. While some experts will argue that intelligence and academic achievement test data have only minimal relevance to vocational planning, personality assessment data have tremendous relevance and is an integral aspect of most theories of career development. School psychologists need to learn how to gather and use such data in a manner that easily translates into vocational recommendations. Readers are referred to this chapter's annotated bibliography for references that can be used to upgrade knowledge in these areas.

BASIC CONSIDERATIONS

The planning and implementation of vocational assessment services should be guided by two overriding concerns: vocational/career development theory and the skills needed by individuals to make decisions that will lead them into jobs that they both enjoy and in which they perform well. While the latter determines which traits should be assessed as part of a comprehensive vocational assessment, the former determines when these traits should be assessed, and how the resulting data will be interpreted.

Vocational/Career Development Theory

Developmental theory underlies and guides the appropriateness of any assessment or educational intervention. Just as our interpretation of letter reversals and transpositions in writing is influenced by our understanding of perceptual-motor development (that is, we would not be overly concerned about a 6 year old who evidenced letter reversals but would be concerned about a 12 year old who did), so too is our interpretation and use of vocational data influenced by vocational/career development theory. To design and implement a school-based vocational assessment program, one must understand vocational development theory, and use such knowledge in deciding what traits will be measured in a particular individual at any given grade or age level. Similarly, vocational development theory allows results to be placed in perspective, and allows users of the data to generate developmentally appropriate recommendations for the student.

While there are numerous theories of vocational development, Figure 1 depicts the various stages of development that span the school years as suggested by Super (1957) and Ginzberg, Ginsberg, Axelrad, and Herma (1951). Not all individuals progress through the various stages listed at the same rate, and not all students are capable of accomplishing the objectives at each stage without assistance. One purpose of vocational assessment is to determine if a student is progressing through the developmental stages at an acceptable rate or if the student might need assistance in accomplishing the objectives associated with each stage.

During the elementary school years, children begin to learn about themselves and the world of work through play. They fantasize themselves to be police officers, teachers, doctors, ballerinas, etc., and try on various life roles. They also begin to learn about the value and importance of work and how to interact and work with others. As children get older and move into middle school or junior high school, self and occupational awareness is refined, decision-making skills begin to develop, and tentative interests and aptitudes emerge. In high school, students begin to combine their knowledge of themselves with their understanding of occupations and, utilizing their decision-making skills, begin to make tentative career choices.

Skills Needed for Employment

Clearly, different jobs require different sets of skills for success. For example, success as a school psychologist is more dependent upon general cognitive ability and verbal skill than it is upon manual dexterity and spatial aptitude. The opposite is true of success as a carpenter or plumber. However, there are some traits that are universally important for success in any employment setting. The ability to get along with others (social skills) and the ability to make good decisions (decision making skills) are general skills that are important in all jobs.

A comprehensive vocational assessment incorporates an evaluation of psychological, social, educational/academic, physical/medical, and vocational functioning. Figure 2 depicts the domains that should be part of a comprehensive vocational assessment, and the information within each domain which might be gathered. It is important to note that much of the

Figure 1. Developmental tasks by stage of career development and age

STAGE	GROWTH			EXPLORATION		
Substage	*Fantasy*	*Interest (What do I like?)*	*Capacity (What am I good at?)*	*Tentative (What will I do......*	*Transition ....)*	*Trial*
Estimated age range	*0—10*	*11–12*	*13–14*	*15–17*	*18–21*	*22–24*
Tasks		1. Gain awareness of personal qualities and develop a healthy self-concept. 2. Appreciate and consider the broad variety of careers and acquire knowledge of workers, their roles, and the value of work. 3. Develop a broad, flexible, and satisfying sex role identity. 4. Develop attitudes that are conducive to competence, cooperation, and achievement.	1. Gain awareness of aptitudes and values. 2. Develop decision-making, planning, and problem-solving skills. 3. Realize that different occupations have different requirements and provide different rewards. 4. Become aware of imminent academic choices and their relationship to post-high-school alternatives. 5. Assume responsibility for own career-related decisions.	1. Gain awareness of aspiration. 2. Develop tentative career goals and identify vocational options. 3. Explore tentative career goals and vocational options.	1. Specify a choice. 2. Acquire necessary skills for entry-level employment	1. Implement vocational choice (acquire a job).

information that needs to be gathered as part of a comprehensive vocational assessment is typically obtained by school psychologists when conducting psychoeducational evaluations. Intelligence test data, academic achievement test data, personality data, etc., all have relevance in vocational planning. While it is beyond the scope of this chapter to discuss the vocational implications of traditional psychoeducational test data, readers who are interested in a more detailed discussion of this are referred to Levinson (1993, 1998).

A variety of techniques are employed to collect information in vocational assessment programs. Record reviews, interviews, observations, and paper-

Figure 2 . Type of information in vocational assessment

Psychological Functioning

- Emotional Stability
- Needs
- Temperament
- Values
- Intelligence
- Behavioral Tendencies

Social Functioning

- Adaptive Behavior
- Social/Interpersonal Skills
- Independent Living Skills
- Hygiene

Educational/Academic Functioning

- Receptive/Expressive Language (Oral, Written)
- Reading Skills
- Mathematic Skills
- Range of Knowledge (General Information)

Physical/Medical Functioning

- Vision
- Hearing
- Health
- Strength
- Dexterity/Motor Skills
- Endurance

Vocational Functioning

- Vocational Interests
- Vocational Aptitudes
- Work Habits/Attitudes
- Vocational/Career Maturity

and-pencil tests are commonly employed and are techniques with which school psychologists are familiar. Additionally, performance tests, work samples, and situational assessment are often used in such programs. Performance tests are manipulative tasks that minimize the use of language (Anastasi, 1982), and are designed to evaluate a specific ability believed to be related to successful job performance. A performance task may measure manual dexterity, an ability related to the performance of many trade and technical occupations, by requiring a student to assemble a series of nuts and bolts (Anderson, Hohenshil, Buckland-Heer, & Levinson, 1990). Work samples are samples of actual work that allow individuals to experience work activities related to a particular job. An automotive work sample might require an individual to change the oil in a car, and a clerical work sample might require an individual to file papers, type a memo, etc. Work samples usually consist of demonstration, training, and assessment phases. The task is first demonstrated to the individual being assessed; the individual is then trained to perform the task; and, last, the individual performs the task while being observed and evaluated. Performance may be compared to industrial and age-based norms, and interest and motivation to perform the task are observed and measured. Situational assessment techniques are designed to test an individual's interests, aptitudes, and work habits in a real or simulated work situation. A student who is interested in sales occupations might be employed in a school store and observed and evaluated by a business education instructor. A student who is interested in a food service job might be employed in the school cafeteria and observed and evaluated by cafeteria workers and/or an occupational foods instructor.

BEST PRACTICES

The following section will discuss best practices in establishing school-based vocational assessment programs, a recommended program model, and roles for school psychologists in the vocational assessment process. Consistent with the best practice standards listed by the Interdisciplinary Council on Vocational Evaluation and Assessment (of which NASP is a member) (Smith et al., 1995), vocational assessment should (a) be an ongoing and developmental process linked to career development, (b) incorporate multiple assessment methods, (c) involve a variety of professionals, and (d) be an integral part of a larger service delivery system. The nature and type of vocational assessment program to be established will depend on several factors, including the available resources, the characteristics and expertise of available personnel, the population targeted for services, the nature and type of vocational and post-secondary training and placement options available in the community, and the nature of auxiliary services available.

Steps in Program Development and Implementation

In that school-based vocational assessment services should be part of a broader service delivery system designed to meet the educational needs of all students in general, and students with disabilities in particular, time needs to be devoted to carefully planning and implementing a system-wide program. The steps involved in planning and implementing school-based vocational assessment programs encompass three phases: Planning and Development, Implementation, and Evaluation and Improvement (Levinson, 1993). Figure 3 summarizes the program development process.

The first step in program development is to develop a task force that adequately represents all school and community personnel who are likely to be involved in or affected by the assessment program. The task force conducts a needs assessment identifying school and community resources/services that can be utilized within the program and potential obstacles that may exist to successful vocational planning. An assessment model should then be developed that makes use of local resources and minimizes potential obstacles to programming. Formal interagency agreements are established between school and community agencies that clearly identify what services will be provided by which agencies, to which students, and at what point in time. Funding requirements are identified and sources of funding secured, if necessary. A coordinator is appointed to oversee the implementation of the assessment program and, with the assistance of other involved personnel, identifies sites at which assessments will be conducted, develops a manual that clearly describes procedures, selects and purchases equipment, and trains involved personnel. Following workshops designed to acquaint school and community personnel with the program, the pro-

Figure 3. **Steps involved in program development**

Phase 3 – Evaluation

1. Identify Aspects of Program in Need of Evaluation
2. Identify Standards for Evaluation
3. Hire/Identify a Program Evaluator
4. Conduct Evaluation
5. Plan and Implement Program Improvements

Phase 2 – Implementation

1. Hire a Vocational Assessment Program Coordinator
2. Select Vocational Assessment Site(s)
3. Develop a Procedure Manual
4. Select/Purchase Materials and Equipment
5. Train Personnel
6. Conduct In-service Workshops with School Staff/ Community
7. Pilot-Test the Assessment Program
8. Revise and Implement the Program

Phase 1 – Planning and Development

1. Develop a Task Force
2. Conduct a Needs Assessment
3. Develop a Program Model and Establish Objectives
4. Develop Local Interagency Agreements/Action Plans
5. Identify Funding Requirements and Sources

gram is pilot tested on a small select target group, modified and revised, and then fully implemented. After the program has been in operation for a predetermined period, the program is evaluated and revised as necessary.

Program Models

Most school-based vocational assessment programs employ several levels of assessment. At different levels the assessment process has different purposes, is designed to answer different questions (based upon developmental objectives and referral concerns), uses different assessment techniques and strategies, and is designed to gather different types of information. The nature and purpose of assessment at a particular level is directly related to the developmental objectives discussed previously, and to specific referral concerns. Programs usually consist of either two or three levels of assessment. As summarized by Anderson, Hohenshil, Buckland-Heer, and Levinson (1990) (Figure 4), level 1 assessments begin during the elementary school years, focus on a child's understanding of self, interpersonal skills, and decision-making skills, utilize vocational and career exploration activities, and have the goal of building self awareness. Typical assessment questions to be answered at this level include the following ones: Does the student have adequate understanding of their strengths and limitations, has the student acquired necessary social and interpersonal skills, has the student acquired an appreciation for work, and has the student acquired effective decision making skills? Level 2 assessments generally occur during the middle school or junior high school years; focus on interests, aptitudes, work habits and career maturity; utilize record reviews, interviews, observations, and standardized norm referenced assessment instruments; and have the goal of continuing to encourage career exploration and assisting individuals in making tentative choices regarding educational and career goals. Typical assessment questions include the following ones: What are the students interests, what are the students aptitudes, what occupational areas/vocational training programs might be appropriate for the student to explore, what program modifications and support services might the student need to be successful in their chosen program, and is the student ready to make a choice about which vocational program in which to enroll. A level 3 assessment generally occurs during the high school years, often employs more experientially based devices such as work samples and situational assessment, and focuses upon the specific training needed to obtain post-school education or employment. Level 3 assessments are also designed to determine what skills an individual may need in order to make a successful transition from school to work, post-secondary education, and community living. Typical assessment questions include the following ones: What services will the student need to make a successful transition to post-school life, has the student acquired job seeking skills, and what additional training does the student need in order to be employable?

TRANSDISCIPLINARY SCHOOL-BASED VOCATIONAL ASSESSMENT

Though the nature and type of vocational assessment program developed in a particular locale will depend on the factors listed previously, I advocate a transdisciplinary school-based vocational assessment (TVA) program model (Levinson, 1993) as a framework for the development of local programs. TVA is defined as follows:

Figure 4. **Vocational assessment and programming continuum**

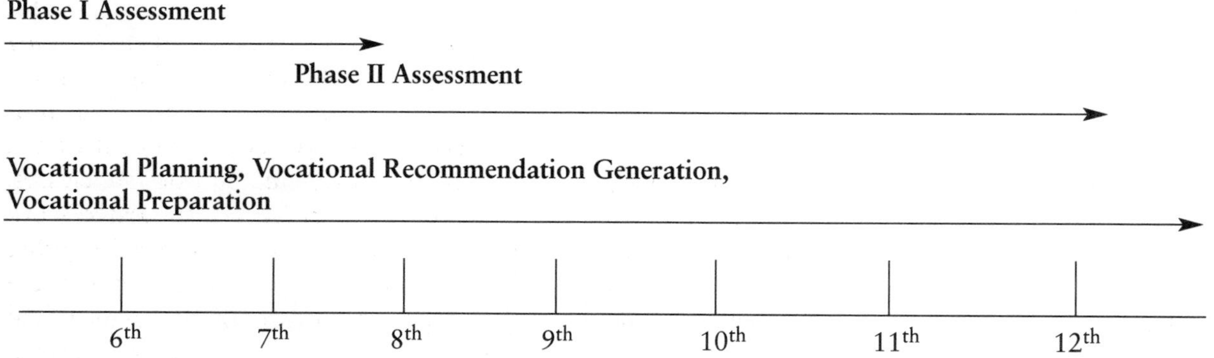

Interfacing of Vocational Assessment with Special Education Triennial Re-Evaluation

Student's Triennial Special Education Re-evaluation	Phase I Assessment	Phase II Assessment
6th Grade	6th Grade	9th Grade - or when needed
7th Grade	6th - 7th Grade	10th Grade - or when needed
8th Grade	7th - 8th Grade	11th Grade - or when needed

A comprehensive assessment conducted within a school setting whose purpose is to facilitate educational and vocational planning in order to allow a student to make a successful adjustment to work, post-secondary education and community living. The assessment is conducted by educational, community agency, and state agency personnel, in cooperation and consultation with the student's parents, and incorporates an assessment of the student's psychological, social, educational/academic, physical/medical, and vocational functioning.

The term "transdisciplinary" is used instead of "multidisciplinary" in order to depict the need to involve professionals "across disciplines" (and outside of the schools) in the vocational assessment and planning process. Figure 5 depicts the transdisciplinary school-based vocational assessment program model that links assessment and intervention, and involves school and community-based professionals in both the planning and development of the program, and in the gathering and use of data. Four phases that embody two levels of assessment are included in the TVA model. Phase 1 involves planning, organizing, and implementing the assessment program. Community agency and school personnel are involved in this planning, which would follow the steps regarding program development discussed previously.

Phase 2 involves an initial level 1 vocational assessment that is conducted at some point between grades 6 and 9. This yields data that are used to establish educational and vocational objectives to be included in student's Individual Education Plans. These data are used to tentatively identify vocational training options for students, options that can form the basis for further vocational exploration. Data are also used to identify residential living options for the student, curricula modifications that might be necessary in order for the student to achieve success in vocational training, and school or community services the student may require to make a successful transition from school to work, post-secondary education, and community living.

Phase 3 occurs during grades 10–12, and consists of specific vocational training (which may occur in a variety of settings). A level 2 vocational assessment may be conducted should additional problems or questions arise about the appropriateness of this training. Following this assessment, a revised educational/vocational plan can be developed for the student, and modifications in training can be initiated. Phase 4 follows this training, and involves placement in a job, a post-secondary institution, and/or a residential living facility. To facilitate successful transition from school to work and community living, follow-up and ongoing support can be provided as part of this phase.

Roles for School Psychologists

The role of the school psychologist in a vocational assessment program will vary depending upon the nature of the vocational services available in the district and the expertise of other involved school personnel. In a best practice scenario, a school-based vocational assessment program similar to the model previously described will be in operation, and the school psychologist will be one of several school and community-based professionals working as a member of a team. Working alongside teachers, counselors, and representatives from Vocational Rehabilitation and Social Services for example, the school psychologist might be responsible for gathering information regarding a student's intellectual, academic, and social functioning and interpret this data from a vocational perspective. When working with adolescents, the school psychologist might include measures of vocational interests and aptitudes in their assessments, review the student's work history and performance in vocational classes, observe the student in work and/or simulated work settings, and conduct clinical interviews to gather vocationally relevant data. As a team member, the school psychologist might use their psychometric and measurement knowledge to assist in the selection of instruments and techniques to be used. The school psychologist's knowledge of learning theory and of adolescent psychology will also allow them to assist in individual vocational planning and to act as consultants for others who are involved in vocational programming.

Where an organized, school-based vocational assessment program is not in operation, the school psychologist might assume the lead in the development of such a program or assist others in such devel-

Figure 5. **Transdisciplinary school-based vocational assessment model**

Vocational Program Planning and Development

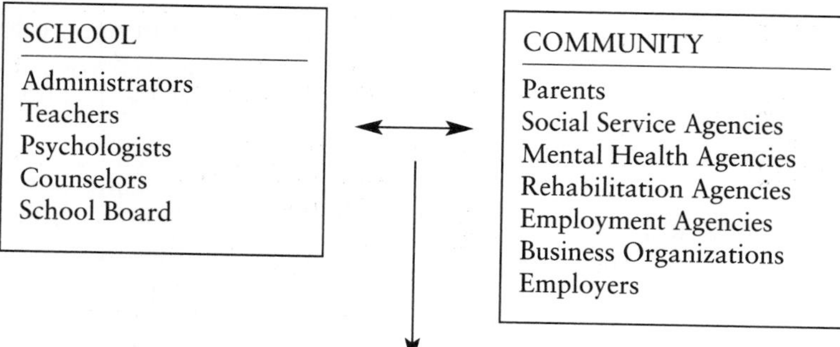

Vocational Assessment and Exploration (Grades 6-9)

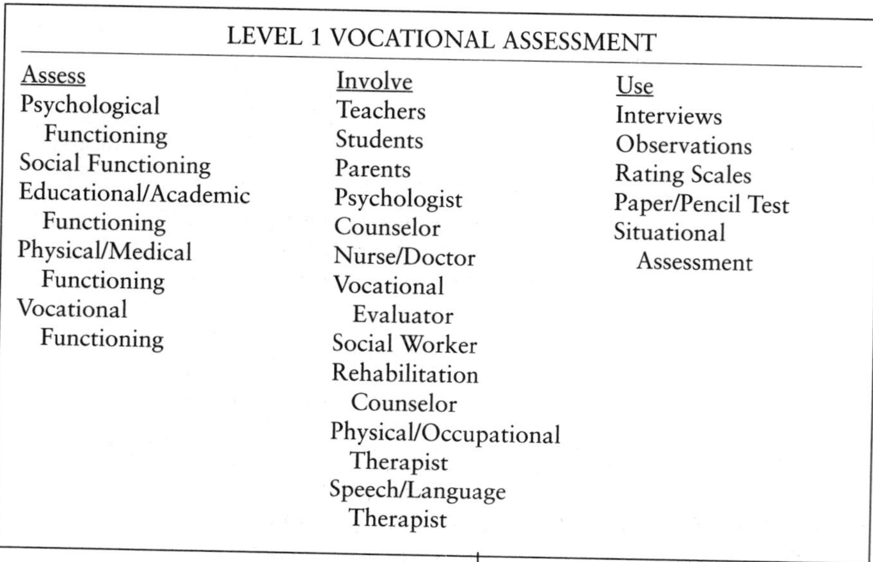

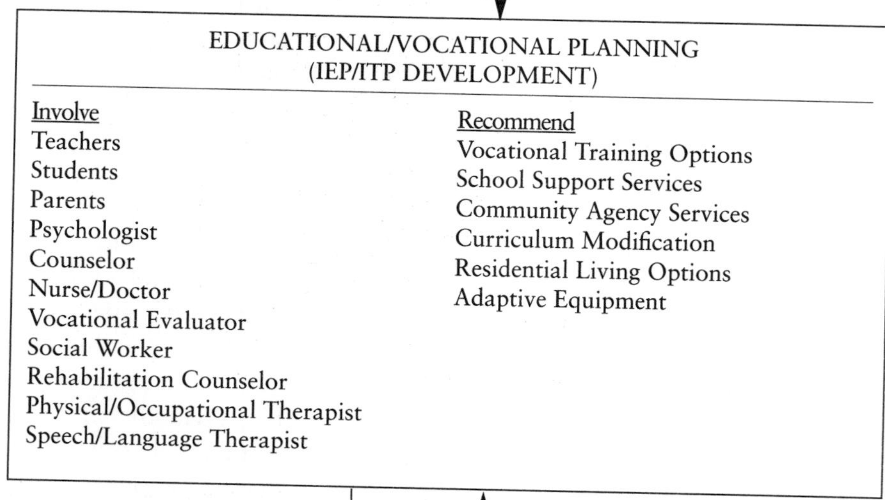

from Level 2 Vocational Assessment

(Figure continues on the following page.)

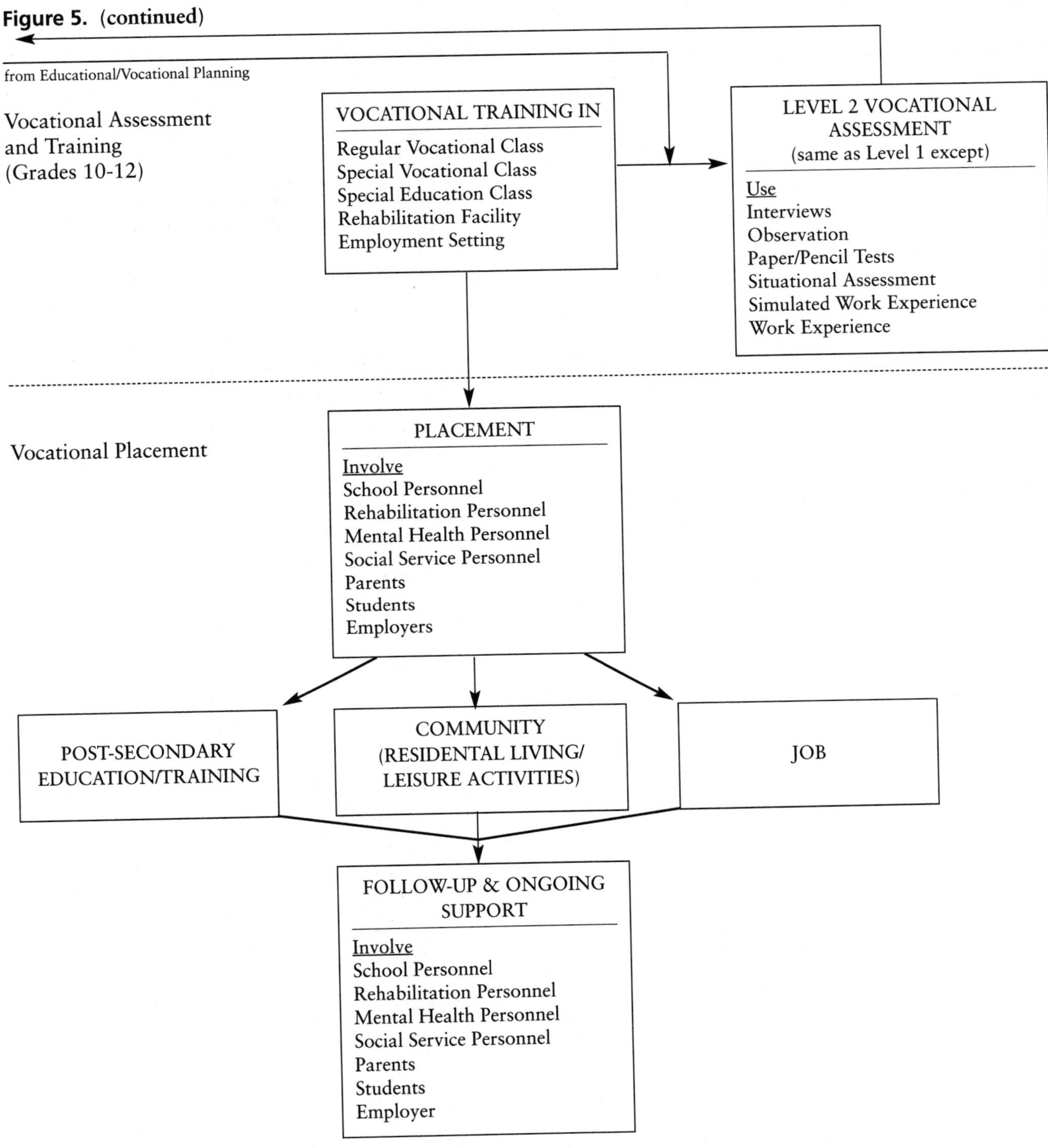

Figure 5. (continued)

opment. The school psychologist's expertise in psychometrics and measurement can be used to design an assessment program that incorporates sound, reliable, and valid instrumentation. If the development of a comprehensive vocational assessment program involving several professionals is not possible, then school psychologists may find themselves as the sole person involved in vocational assessment. Though this is far from a best practice, school psychologists may then wish to consider incorporating a vocational component in each evaluation conducted with an adolescent. Such a component could include measures of vocational interests, aptitudes, work habits, and career maturity, as well as traditional psychoeducational measures. There are many time- and cost-efficient instruments available to assess these traits, and school psychologists are referred to this chapter's annotated bibliography for references summarizing these instruments. In that many school psychologists find themselves in such "a not so best practice" situation, a scenario describing how a school psychologist might function in such a situation is included in Appendix A. Further, readers who are interested in a more thorough description of the roles school psychologists can assume in vocational and transition planning are referred to Levinson & Murphy (1999).

SUMMARY

Work is an integral aspect of American life. The extent to which one successfully adjusts to work influences physical and psychological well being, and overall quality of life. It is important to ensure that individuals develop the skills they need in order to secure and maintain satisfying and productive work once they leave school.

Students in general, and students with disabilities in particular, are not being adequately prepared for work by our public schools. Though the overwhelming percentage of students, particularly those with disabilities, do not pursue post-secondary education and leave high school in search of employment, our schools typically emphasize an academic program designed to prepare students for post-secondary education. As a consequence, many students, particularly those with disabilities, find that the education they are receiving does not meet their needs and eventually drop out of school.

Vocational assessment is designed to provide the information needed by school personnel to facilitate educational and vocational planning of students, the goal of which is to allow students to acquire the skills they need to make a successful transition to work and community life. This assessment involves a variety of school and community personnel, and includes an evaluation of the student's psychological, educational/academic, physical/medical, vocational, and social functioning.

School psychologists have a critical role to play in the vocational assessment process. In particular, the school psychologist's psychometric expertise and knowledge of measurement theory can safeguard against the inappropriate selection and use of assessment devices in assessment programs, and the inappropriate interpretation and use of assessment data; their skills in assessment can be used to generate data (i.e. intelligence, achievement, personality, social skills, etc.), which are necessary for effective vocational planning; and their knowledge of learning and behavior theory and of adolescent psychology can be used in the effective development and implementation of services.

However, if school psychologists are to increase their involvement in vocational and transition related activities, then the profession as a whole must demonstrate greater commitment to the area. While tacit acceptance of the importance of vocational- and transition-related activities is reflected in NASP standards for practice, that school psychologists can graduate from NASP-accredited programs with virtually *no* training in the area suggests a lack of true commitment. Historically, school psychologists have worked with students who have disabilities and in the shadow of special education. The high unemployment and underemployment rates and the elevated drop-out rates that exist among this population of students clearly suggest that traditional service delivery has not resulted in desirable outcomes and that a change in focus is needed. It is time for school psychologists to accept some of the responsibility for these outcomes and to give the vocational and transition needs of students the same emphasis in assessment that they give to the cognitive, academic, and social needs of the students with whom they work.

REFERENCES

Anastasi, A. (1982). *Psychological testing* (5th ed.). New York: Macmillan.

Anderson, W. T., Hohenshil, T. H., Buckland-Heer, K., & Levinson, E. M. (1990). Best practices in vocational assessment of students with disabilities. In A. Thomas & J. Grimes (Eds.)

Best practices in school psychology II. Washington, DC: National Association of School Psychologists.

Brown, D., & Minor, C. W. (Eds.). (1989). *Working in America: A status report*. Alexandria, VA: National Career Development Association.

Carey, K. (1995). *A national study of the role and function of the school psychologist*. Paper presented at the annual meeting of the National Association of School Psychologists, Chicago, IL.

Dunn, C.(1996). A status report on transition planning for individuals with learning disabilities. In J. R. Patton & G. Blaylock (Eds.), *Transition and students with learning disabilities: Facilitating the movement from school to adult life*. Austin, TX: PRO-ED.

Gajar, A., Goodman, L. And McAfee, J. (1993). *Secondary schools and beyond: Transition of individuals with mild disabilities*. New York: Macmillan.

Ginzberg, E., Ginsburg, S. W., Axelrad, S. & Herma, J. L. (1951). *Occupational choice: An approach to a general theory*. New York: Columbia University Press.

Hoyt, K. B. & Lester, J. L. (1995). *Learning to work: The NCDA Gallup survey*. Alexandria, VA: National Career Development Association.

Levinson, E. M. (1988). Correlates of vocational practice among school psychologists. *Psychology in the Schools, 25*(3), 297–305.

Levinson, E. M. (1993). *Transdisciplinary vocational assessment: Issues in school based programs*. Brandon, VT: Clinical Psychology Publishing.

Levinson, E. M. (1995). Best practices in transition services. In A.Thomas & J. Grimes (Eds.), *Best practices in school psychology III*. Washington, DC: National Association of School Psychologists.

Levinson, E. M. (1998). *Transition: Facilitating the post-school adjustment of students with disabilities*. Boulder, CO: Westview.

Levinson, E. M. & Capps. C.F. (1985). Vocational assessment and special education triennial reevaluations at the secondary school level. *Psychology in the Schools, 22*, 283–292.

Levinson, E. M., and Murphy, J. (1999). Transition and school psychology. In S. DeFur & J. R. Patton (Eds.). *Transition and school-based services : Interdisciplinary perspectives for enhancing the transition process*. Austin, TX: PRO-ED.

Morra, L. G. (1993). *Transition from school to work: H.R. 2884 addresses components of comprehensive strategy* (GAO/HRD-93-32). Testimony before the Committee on Education and Labor, U.S. House of Representatives. Washington, DC: General Accounting Office.

National Association of School Psychologists (1997). *Professional conduct manual*. Silver Spring, MD: Author.

Shepard, J. W. & Hohenshil, T. H. (1983). National survey of career development functions of practicing school psychologists. *Psychology in the Schools, 20*(4), 445–449.

Smith, F,. Lombard, R., Neubert, D., Leconte, P., Rothernbacher, C. & Sitlington, P. (1995). *Position paper of the Interdisciplinary Council on Vocational Evaluation and Assessment*. Available at: http:www.vewaa.org/council.html.

Staab, M. J. (1996). The role of the school psychologist in transition planning (Doctoral dissertation, University of Kansas, Lawrence 1996). *Dissertation Abstracts International, 58*, 281.

Super, D. E. (1957). *The psychology of careers*. New York: Harper.

U.S. Department of Education (1999). *Twenty first annual report to congress on the implementation of the IDEA*. Washington, DC: U.S. Government Printing Office.

U.S. Department of Labor (1991). *What work requires of schools: A SCANS report for America 2000*. Washington, DC: U.S. Government Printing Office.

U.S. Government Accounting Office (1993, September). *Transition from school to work: States are developing new strategies to prepare students for jobs*. Report to Congressional Requesters by the General Accounting Office (GAO/HRD-93-139). Washington, DC: Author.

Ysseldyke, J. E., Algozzine, B., and Thurlow, M. L. (1992). *Critical issues in special education* (2nd ed.). Boston: Houghton-Mifflin.

ANNOTATED BIBLIOGRAPHY

Clark, G. B. (1998). *Assessment for transitions planning: A guide for special education teachers and related service personnel.* Austin, TX: PRO-ED.
This book discusses areas that need to be assessed for transition planning. It includes a discussion of instrumentation and different assessment techniques such as computerized assessment, curriculum-based assessment, and medical appraisals. The book discusses accommodations in assessment practices that may need to be made for individuals with disabilities, and roles of various professionals in transition assessment. Appendices are included that summarize assessment instruments and that include transition-planning examples.

Kapes, J. T., Mastie, M. M., and Whitfield, E. A. (1994). *A counselor's guide to career assessment instruments* (3rd ed.). Alexandria, VA: National Career Development Association.
This book summarizes uses and technical characteristics of frequently used vocational assessment instruments. Measures of interests, aptitudes, work values, and career maturity are included, as well as sections on test selection and instruments for use with individuals with disabilities.

Levinson, E. M. (1998). *Transition: Facilitating the post-school adjustment of students with disabilities.* Boulder, CO: Westview.
This book conceptualizes assessment as a necessary first step in transition planning, and discusses assessment within the context of a transdisciplinary transition model. Assessment techniques and domains are discussed as they relate to transition planning, training, placement, and follow-up activities.

Levinson, E. M. and Brandt, J. (1997). Career development. In G. Bear, K. Menke, and A. Thomas (Eds.), *Children's Needs II.* Washington, DC: National Association of School Psychologists.
This chapter summarizes the career development stages through which school age children progress, identifies common career choice problems experienced by the school aged population, and discusses both systemic and individualized actions school psychologists and other school personnel can take to facilitate the career development process of the students with whom they work.

Power, P. W. (2000). *A guide to vocational assessment* (3rd ed.). Austin, TX: PRO-ED.
Though oriented toward rehabilitation rather than school-based professionals, this book addresses issues in developing effective vocational assessment services, and includes chapters on interviewing, interest assessment, aptitude assessment, intelligence testing, and personality assessment.

Seligman, L. (1994). *Developmental career counseling and assessment* (2nd ed.). Thousand Oaks, CA: Sage.
This book discusses the career development needs of individuals at different life stages, and discusses the various assessment instruments and techniques, which are appropriate for use at these different stages. Case studies are provided for each life stage discussed to illustrate the career development issues, assessment techniques, and counseling strategies applicable to each stage. Though not specific to individuals with disabilities, the book provides an overview of career assessment through the life span. Of its 10 chapters, school psychologists may find only two (chapter 8 on Middle Adulthood and chapter 9 on Later Adulthood) that may not be applicable to their practice.

Smith, F,. Lombard, R., Neubert, D., Leconte, P., Rothernbacher, C. & Sitlington, P. (1995). *Position paper of the Interdisciplinary Council on Vocational Evaluation and Assessment.* Available at: http:www.vewaa.org/council.html.
The Interdisciplinary Council on Vocational Evaluation and Assessment is composed of representatives from 11 organizations, including NASP, and represents the issues and concerns of personnel involved in vocational assessment across settings and disciplines. This position paper addresses best practice issues across settings, and identifies competencies that all providers of vocational assessment should possess.

APPENDIX A

A "Not Best Practice But Not Bad Example"

A school psychologist who works in a district with no organized, school-based vocational assessment program is asked to complete a reevaluation on Sharon, a tenth grade student with a learning disability. Sharon had been identified as having a reading disability in the fourth grade and reevaluated in the seventh grade. After reviewing both cumulative and confidential files, the school psychologist notes that Sharon has consistently demonstrated above-average intelligence but slightly below-average academic achievement, particularly in those areas that emphasize reading. Grades in academic classes have consistently been Cs, except in art and music classes where she consistently received As. Previous evaluations had suggested Sharon to be reasonably creative and adept at performing tasks that required visual reasoning and auditory processing (on a WISC-III she demonstrated a significant verbal-performance discrepancy in favor of the performance score; on a WJ-III, her highest score was in Gv; her next highest score was in Ga). However, she was said to be shy and had some difficulty getting along with others.

Given the consistent findings of the two previous intellectual and academic assessments, the school psychologist chose not to conduct another intellectual or academic (other than reading) assessment. Instead, the psychologist began by interviewing Sharon. In the interview, the school psychologist asked Sharon about her post-school plans (she wanted to go to college and major in art or music, but her parents did not think she could and wanted her to work in the family's convenience store), her social relationships and leisure interests (she had one close friend, did not participate much in school activities, and preferred solitary leisure activities like drawing and playing guitar), her independent living skills (she could do everything on her own but her parents baby her), and her previous work experiences (she had cut lawns and had worked in the family convenience store).

Next, the school psychologist interviewed Sharon's parents and addressed these same areas. Her parents indicated that they did not think Sharon could be successful in college because "she cannot read," and expected her to work in the family convenience store and live at home upon graduation. They confirmed that Sharon was shy, had few friends, and preferred solitary activities. They added that based on their observation of her cutting lawns and working in the convenience store, her work habits were not particularly well developed. Interviews with Sharon's teachers confirmed what the school psychologist had previously learned about Sharon. To further assess work habits and with both Sharon's and her parent's permission, the school psychologist conducted an observation at the convenience store where Sharon worked on weekends, contacted families for whom Sharon cut lawns, and interviewed Sharon's teachers. On the basis of the information gathered, the school psychologist chose to conduct an assessment of social skills (Sharon, her parents, and her teachers all completed a social skills questionnaire). Additionally, the school psychologist assessed Sharon's reading by using both standardized norm-referenced tests and informal curriculum-based techniques using her textbooks. Sharon's ability to make vocational decisions on her own was assessed through use of a career maturity measure. Her vocational interests were assessed through interview and use of a paper-pencil inventory appropriate for her reading level. Given Sharon's level of intelligence and her interest in attending college, an attempt was made to identify a list of potential college majors that conformed to her identified interests. Last, a transition planning inventory completed by Sharon, her parents, and her teachers was used to identify any other areas of need across all legislatively mandated transition areas.

In the staffing that followed the assessment, the school psychologist presented his results. He indicated that Sharon had adequate self- and occupational awareness, and seemed capable of making a realistic vocational decision on her own. Further, she seemed to have both the interest and aptitude necessary to be successful and happy in jobs that revolved around her stated interests in art and music. In particular, Sharon seemed best suited for artistic occupations that emphasized her strengths in visual and auditory processing and that generally entailed solitary work. In addition, she seemed to possess the ability to complete the postsecondary education requirements necessary for entry into these fields, if she were to be provided with accommodations for her reading disability. However, shyness (and an inability to advocate for herself), social skills and work habit deficits, and parental expectations were issues that might also impede successful transition and training. The school psychologist recommended that Sharon participate in a social skills training program that he conducted (to improve areas of deficit and to teach advocacy skills that would be necessary for success in any post-secondary educational setting), and recommended that Sharon (with the assistance of the guidance counselor) continue to explore occupational areas of interest by interviewing and shadowing professionals in these areas (and by offering to do volunteer work for these professionals if interested) and by reviewing the educational requirements for the college majors generally associated with entry into these fields. The school psychologist also recommended that Sharon consider volunteering at the high school television or radio station (to explore audio and video production, artistic areas she had little knowledge of, or experience with), join the art club, and consider joining band or chorus. The school psychologist also recommended that Sharon and her parents become familiar with the services offered to students with disabilities at local colleges, and offered to assist in setting up such a meeting. Strategies to assist Sharon in compensating for her reading difficulties were developed. In particular, because Sharon's listening comprehension had consistently been measured as above average, books on tape was one compensatory strategy that seemed promising. The school psychologist also volunteered to enter into a short-term counseling relationship with Sharon and her parents to address parental expectations and post–high school aspirations. On the basis of this meeting, a transition component to Sharon's IEP was developed, with the intent to review, evaluate, and revise it the following year.

100 Best Practices in Transition to Post-Secondary Work

Raymond Witte
Miami University

OVERVIEW

This chapter examines the transition from secondary school to the adult world for individuals with disabilities. In the field of special education at least two major educational transitions are formally acknowledged, although additional transitions exist and are recognized: preschool to elementary and high school to adult life. The notion of school transition has usually been associated with the end of the educational career of a student. In the traditional approach, plans and services, usually provided at the secondary level, served as a connector between the school and the adult world.

Halpern (1992, p. 203) has described the secondary transition phase "as a period of *floundering* that occurs for at least the first several years after leaving school as adolescents attempt to assume a *variety* of adult roles in their communities." He envisions the goals of transition dealing with the broader issues of adult adjustment as opposed to just the area of employment. In addition, a life-span approach to services is seen as beneficial and essential for preparing youth with disabilities if they are to experience satisfaction with both employment as well as adult life. Focus on life-span services and outcomes for successful work transition and employment has increased as transition has been refined to an outcome directed process (Individuals with Disabilities Education Act of 1990 (IDEA 1990)). However, current findings have indicated that students with disabilities often lack the necessary academic and functional work skills necessary for post-school employment or post-secondary education (Phelps & Hanley-Maxwell, 1997).

The transition from school to the adult world is difficult for many identified students. The reality for many special needs students is that their learning and behavioral challenges continue through adulthood and ultimately into the world of work. Acknowledging this "reality" is vital because it serves as an Individual Education Plan (IEP) planning focus point. Long-term educational planning involving the development of essential, functional life skills (e.g., academic, behavioral, and social) throughout a student's educational career must exist along with service continuation after graduation. A long-term perspective is essential if successful adult employment and general life satisfaction are viewed as desired outcomes for special needs learners.

Before addressing model practices and services for adults with disabilities, current knowledge about youth with disabilities and their skills as they enter the workplace will be examined. Past and current legislation will be briefly reviewed followed by current "status" profiles of youth with disabilities. Finally, potential roles and responsibilities school psychologists can have in the transition process will be discussed.

Background

Vocational services for students with disabilities can be traced back 60 years ago to the Second World War. However, major legislative action involving a direct vocational focus occurred during the 1970s primarily through three laws: the Vocational Rehabilitation Act of 1973, the Education for All Handicapped Children Act of 1975, and the Vocational Education Amendments of 1976. This federal legislation, despite limited interagency cooperation and implementation, helped to direct attention and effort toward the vocational preparation of adolescents with disabilities (Szymanski & Danek, 1985).

Emphasis on serving individuals with disabilities was increased in legislative action during the 1990s. The Rehabilitation Act Amendments of 1992 involved the reauthorization of the Rehabilitation Act of 1973, which provided for smoother service integration for identified students leaving public school and obtaining employment (Wood & Test, 1997). The Tech-Prep Act was created from the amended Perkins Vocational and Applied Technology Education Act. It was designed to provide academic instruction that was work or occupation centered and involved a competency-based curriculum focused on functional academic, thinking/higher reasoning, and personal, life skills (Evers, 1996b).

Specific legislative action on work transition involved the School-to-Work Opportunities Act. Passed in 1994, the School-to-Work (STW) program involving school- and work-based learning components along with connecting activities was designed to help all students (including those with disabilities) to obtain vital work skills and experiences before they enter full-time employment or postsecondary education (Evers, 1996a). Under IDEA 1990, all identified students were required to have transition plans within their IEPs by the age of 16. In the Individuals with Disabilities Education Act Amendments of 1997, all students with disabilities are required to have a statement of transition in the IEP by age 14 and by age 16 (or younger as determined by the IEP team) a statement of needed transition services must exist (U.S. Department of Education, 1999; IDEA 1997 Amendments, P.L. 105-17).

The Americans with Disabilities Act (ADA) passed in 1990 included protections designed to prohibit hiring and employment discrimination against individuals with disabilities. The ADA helped to create equal rights and opportunities for individuals with disabilities while increasing public awareness and acceptance to the issues of disability particularly in the workplace. However, despite continued legislative action and upgraded service delivery for school-to-work transition, dropout and unemployment figures for individuals with disabilities have been devastating (D'Amico, 1991; Phelps & Hanley-Maxwell, 1997). Moreover, involvement of special needs students in organized work experience and transition programs such as STW has been disappointingly low (Unger & Luecking, 1998). Considerable evidence has been found that high school vocational training has either been ineffective or nonexistent for individuals with learning disabilities (LD) (Grayson, Wermuth, Holub, & Anderson 1997). Despite legislative support, special needs students transition to work or other post-secondary experiences often lacking well-defined functional life skills, essential work skills, and on-the-job training.

Status of Students With Disabilities

School psychologists view themselves as problem solvers. However, within the problem-solving model, Deno (1995) points out that a proactive position is essential if substantial change is expected between a current and a future state of affairs. Since formal instruction, by design, organizes and eventually directs educational outcomes, a systematic "end-product" focus and standard must exist and be embedded within the special education delivery model. In particular, the desired graduate in special education should possess skills and competencies that would make him or her a competitive employee or post-secondary student along with a competent and functional member of society. This long-term, total package approach requires a proactive problem-solving stance for special needs students and their transition from school to the adult world. Short-sighted, poorly integrated, academic-only focused IEPs are not consistent with the long-term life-span approach that needs to exist for every identified student. School psychologists must ensure that the long-term perspective is acknowledged and maintained through the IEP process along with the continued emphasis of developing functional life skills concomitant with anticipated academic progress.

The current post-secondary picture for students with disabilities is not a pretty one. High school graduation rates for individuals with disabilities vary from state to state because of graduation requirements, exit exams, etc., but they are typically lower than their non-identified peers. According to the twenty-first annual report to Congress (U.S. Department of Education, 1999) 24.5% of all students with disabilities during the 1996–1997 school year graduated with a standard high school diploma, a slight increase from the previous year (24%). Graduation percentages varied according to disability categories:

1. Speech and language impairments, 34.6%
2. Visual impairments, 30%
3. Traumatic brain injury, 30%
4. Specific LD, 29.4%
5. Hearing impairments, 28.5%
6. Other health impairments, 25.7%
7. Orthopedic impairment, 23.7%
8. Emotional disturbance, 21.4%
9. Deaf-blindness, 14.7%
10. Mental retardation, 13.43%
11. Multiple disabilities, 8.94%
12. Autism, 7.5%

Initiated in 1987, the National Longitudinal Transition Study (NLTS) was a 5-year study designed to investigate the educational and postsecondary performance of more than 8,000 special education youth between the ages of 13 and 21. This study represents the largest and most comprehensive study of educational and employment outcomes for students with disabilities (Blackorby & Wagner, 1997). The immediate- and long-term results for these individuals with disabilities were very discouraging.

For students with LD:

1. 28% dropped out of high school
2. 19% of graduates were enrolled in postsecondary academic programs
3. 18% were enrolled in postsecondary vocational programs
4. 34% had independent living status

For students with emotional or behavioral disabilities:

1. 48% dropped out of high school
2. 15% of graduates enrolled in postsecondary academic programs
3. 13% were enrolled in postsecondary vocational programs

For students with mental retardation:

1. 30% dropped out of high school
2. 2% of graduates enrolled in postsecondary academic programs
3. 6% were enrolled in postsecondary vocational programs
4. 15% had independent living status

An employment rate of only 55% for all youth with disabilities was demonstrated (Wagner et al., 1991), and females with disabilities were more likely to become wives and mothers and less likely to be employed when compared with males with disabilities (Blackorby & Wagner, 1996; D'Amico, 1991). However, employment rates for students with LD were comparable with or even exceeded the general population. Approximately 71% of graduates with LD (compared to 55% for all disabilities) were employed 3–5 years post-graduation as compared with 70% of the general population, yet the majority of students with disabilities were employed in low-skill jobs. Unfortunately, the dropout rate was high (almost 30%), and enrollment in post-secondary vocational programs was considerably less for dropouts than for non-dropouts (Blackorby & Wagner, 1997).

Overall, youths with disabilities still lag behind their non-disabled peers in educational attainment, thereby decreasing the likelihood of future employment advancement and earnings. Women with disabilities are less likely to be employed or possess independent living status when compared with men with disabilities, and minority status further limits employment and higher wage possibilities. As Blackorby & Wagner (1997, p. 73) have stated, the NLTS data served as an essential wake-up call for services and policy directions for students with disabilities.

Recently, the Office of Special Education Programs (OSEP) funded seven projects dealing directly with national assessment requirements. One of those seven projects will include the Longitudinal Study of Secondary and Postsecondary Outcomes for Students with Disabilities (NLTS-2). A cohort of students with disabilities will be followed through high school and into early adulthood. School and employment progress will be examined for this group, and the findings from this study will be used to direct educational policy and disability practices (U.S. Department of Education, 1999). Given the educational realities of special needs students it comes as no surprise that these youth continue to struggle with their learning challenges into their adult lives. Skill deficits do not typically fade away. Consequently, academic difficulties persist and may hinder later life and work adjustment.

BEST PRACTICES

In order to begin to change the school-to-adult world picture for special needs youth, the proactive tenet of the problem-solving model must predominate. Each school district, with community input, must generate a standard of expected competencies across all skill domains that each student's progress will be compared with. The educational community must have a very clear notion of what students should be able to do when they finish high school, a desired set of expected outcomes to use as the measuring standard. Throughout this process, the expectancy of reaching for higher levels of proficiency in all life functional skill areas including, for instance, academics, personal and community autonomy, and personal finance, must be recognized. Moreover, it must be understood that service support must be extended beyond the secondary level directly into the adult years as higher levels of autonomy or proficiency are sought. The highest levels of interagency collaboration are necessary in order for this to come about. And that collaboration and service integration must occur early in the educational process.

Transition should not be viewed as a discrete event but as a life-long, never-ending process; a careful, well-planned process that will be years old before the intended outcomes begin to be reached; a process that over time will involve numerous individuals, several administrative teams, professionals from outside agencies, family members, along with the identified student; and a process where all involved parties have responsibility and all share accountability.

Transition involves more than moving an individual with disabilities from the school setting to the adult world. Individual and local planning must coexist and be integrated for every identified student. Individual transition teams are essential at the school level while local core transition teams facilitate interagency school-to-work collaboration and cooperation. As Wehman, Moon, Everson, Wood, and Barcus (1988, p. 50) have stated, "Transition planning that results in improved outcomes of employment, independence, and community integration must be a cooperatively planned and implemented process at a local community level."

Upon review of exemplary state procedures, Furney, Hasazi, and Destefano (1997, p. 352) found that "there is no single recipe for change." However, when considering transition improvement Furney et al. (1997, p. 352–353) suggested examining the following guidelines, (a) "Define and highlight values and beliefs that foster the development and initiation of transition policies and practices," (b) "develop and implement federal and state policies on transition in ways that strengthen existing practice and empower communities to make change," (c) "reinforce a collaborative and comprehensive view of leadership," (d) "add or strengthen collaborative structures at the state and community level to promote high-quality transition practices and services," (e) "implement a variety of capacity-building and evaluation activities that empower local schools and communities to make change," (f) "include research and evaluation activities at all levels of implementation," and (g) "link current transition initiatives to related and future initiatives." Clearly, with transition programs one size does not fit all. Consistent with the tenets of the problem-solving model, individuation must be provided. As schools work toward developing their own programs, careful consideration to system structures and resources must be made.

At the school level, Wehman (1996) recommends a multi-step process for developing and implementing individualized transition plans (ITPs). An ITP involves the operating procedures for the school transition plan. It may include vocational skill profiles (strength oriented), actual transition goals for school and community, transition supports, as well as post-school follow-up procedures (Inge, Wehman, Clees, & Dymond, 1996). First, Wehman advocates for organizing ITP teams for all transition-age students. That would include the student and the school personnel who will serve on the team (e.g., parents, special educators, vocational educator) as well as the adult service representative who should be brought early into the process perhaps as early as 2 years prior to graduation. Next, a student support circle needs to be organized through person-centered planning. The strengths and talents, and not the weakness or identified deficits of the student, must be emphasized in the student's personal profile. Also, key activities that are thought to be essential for continued transition progress must be identified and completed.

Wehman (1996) contends that the transition meeting can be part of the annual IEP meeting; thereby connecting the ITP directly to the IEP goals and providing for a more integrated transition process. Implementing the actual ITP would then follow, acknowledging that some services may be short term while others may be conducted over a series of years. The ITP would have to be updated annually, and contact with adult services would increase as each student moves closer to graduation. Finally, at the end of the student's secondary education, an exit meeting would be necessary. Goals, met and unmet, would have to be examined. In addition, follow-up and follow-along services must be discussed and determined before each student leaves the school environment. Three factors that Wehman (1996, p. 101–102) believes to be critical to successful ITP implementation include " the involvement of ITP members who are knowledgeable about local services, the identification of all desired outcomes within the least restrictive service options, and community agencies providing or obtaining all needed services."

The local interagency core team has the responsibility of assessing, developing, and/or modifying transition procedures and guidelines between the participating agencies. Typical team representation may include at least a school representative, parent advocate, mental health board member, and a vocational rehabilitation representative. As part of this group, these members can review a variety of issues ranging from pre-employment training programs to general public awareness to more formal interagency policies, action plans, and evaluation procedures. Wehman's ITP approach is vocation/work focused but should incorporate other functional/adaptive skill expansion as well. Moreover, it can be directly attached, in procedure and in function, to the IEP. This creates shared importance and significance for this plan and increases institutional accountability regarding its implementation.

Kohler (1993) reviewed 46 transition studies and identified three critical model components: vocational training, parental involvement, and interagency collaboration and service delivery. Minskoff (1996, p. 282) identified the following essential components for transition programs for students with LD:

1. Individual transition plans
2. Vocational education and training
3. Work experience
4. Social skills training
5. Parent involvement
6. Interagency coordination
7. Integration with non-disabled persons in vocational and work settings
8. Academic support
9. Vocational counseling
10. Job seeking and job placement services
11. Personal counseling
12. Supportive services from an advocate
13. Program evaluation involving follow-up and follow-along

Similar components have been identified and recommended by others in the field (Zigmond, 1990; Phelps & Hanley-Maxwell, 1997). The resounding message that has emerged is that each identified student requires an individualized, integrated service delivery model with genuine participation from family, school, and community .

Minskoff (1996, p. 282) contends that a comprehensive transition plan must involve these three stages, "planning for transition, transition within the IEP, and implementation of the IEP." She contends that transition starts as soon as the child is identified with a disability. Therefore, services should be provided over the entire school career and involve several areas including academics, social skills, functional life skills, and career planning. High standards and proficiency are advocated in all areas. School transition plans require collaboration between the school and community. Student and parental involvement/advocacy is strongly encouraged in this process. Although, limited parental participation in transition planning has been reported (Winton, 1990) transition effectiveness is clearly enhanced when parents are involved (Hasazi, Gordon, & Roe 1985). The IEP must be current and present functioning levels known in order to make the best educational decisions. Goals of desired post-secondary outcomes should be developed in several areas such as employment, continuing education, and adult living. Consultation and collaboration between special and vocational education is viewed as essential. Finally, implementation should occur at both the school and post-school levels.

A TRANSITION CASE

Following Minskoff's model program, a transition focus should exist as soon as a child is identified. Therefore, if identified in the second grade, then the child's transition services should start at that time and continue throughout his or her school career and into adulthood. Along with appropriate academic and behavioral IEP goals, separate goals directed toward functional life skills, social and work skills, career exploration and training, post-secondary education, etc., should be considered, identified as part of the ITP, and directly connected and annually reviewed as part of the IEP. The emphasis at the elementary level should be academic with intensive intervention and skill remediation of identified weaknesses and/or delays. Skill deficit issues are better addressed at this time then adulthood when skill training and intervention efforts have minimal effect. Clearly, early intervention provides the greatest window of opportunity for academic recovery and success. Moreover, helping students understand their unique learning issues and responsive adaptive strategies allows them to gain valuable insight into their own learning process at that time, and throughout their educational career.

Although instructional modifications and accommodations may be useful in the classroom setting, caution is noted because these modifications may lead to unrealistic views of learner's abilities and performances. Shorter, easier assignments that sacrifice skill development and enhancement do nothing for students except create false hopes and expectancies. The world of work will not seek out nor long accept workers who have weak processing skills and cannot work collaboratively with their coworkers. Therefore, the highest levels of skill development should be sought out for all identified students and even periodic failure experienced in order to help create a more realistic perception of themselves and their world. Teaching them how to handle failure as well as effective ways to avoid it in the future could be one of the most important lessons they will learn in school.

As identified students advance through elementary school, interpersonal life skills need to be developed and refined. It is essential that we teach children to get along with each other, to listen to each other, and to possess a mutual respect for each other. For example, cooperation, individual and group effort, listening, and general problem solving are all important and essential, and these must be cultivated in combination with their specific academic skills and competencies. Career education should be provided so that all students become exposed to various careers in the community. In addition, parental input into their child's long-term educational outcomes is vital from the onset of services. Transition effectiveness is enhanced when parents serve as active team members.

At the middle school, a career orientation focus should exist. Career inventories should be completed along with individual career profile matches. An analysis can be completed of personal characteristics consistent with particular jobs and careers and based on personal style and trait/temperament issues. Professional contacts with various community workers should be encouraged. E-mail contacts, in addition to job fairs, classroom presentations, and job shadowing, can provide relatively easy connection with professionals in the field.

Continued emphasis on academic and functional life skills should be maintained throughout the middle school experience, especially since students with disabilities are at high risk for dropping out of school. Personal counseling can be critical at this time since students may begin to question their abilities, the utility of school, or their seemingly impossible educational dreams. Psychological support through the school system is vital for both the student and the student's family. This support on some level will likely be needed throughout the student's school career. At this time each identified student should be encouraged to be an active participant in his or her educational plans and intended outcomes of the ITP that should exist as part of the IEP. Discussion of both post-secondary education and potential employment options should occur at this time. A completed vocational assessment should provide valuable information for that discussion. Each student, along with the parents, should have complete knowledge and awareness of those findings so that critical and informed decisions can be made and acted upon with the remaining high school years.

It is a federal requirement that every identified student upon entering high school have an established and functional transition plan in place by age 16 or earlier if necessary. In the model case the transition plan was in place well before high school, which should be the norm and not the exception. Representation on the student's team should broaden at this time to include essential outside agency members (e.g., vocational rehabilitation counselors, social service and/or community college representatives). This must occur in order for a smooth transition of services and support to occur after graduation. For example, since the schools relinquish responsibility and financial obligation upon graduation, the vocational rehabilitation counselor will be instrumental in helping shift institutional responsibility and providing continuing services to any qualified student. The transition plan must stipulate, through clear goals and objectives, anticipated post-secondary outcomes (e.g., work and/or college classes), necessary vocational training, and adult living plans.

One of the critical components in successful transition programs is the work experience component. Half-year to full-year paid work programs, typically during the senior year, have proved to be effective in increasing the likelihood of sustained employment after graduation. Apprenticeship programs should be contacted and thoroughly reviewed by this time.

For students who plan on attending post-secondary institutions, it is paramount that identified students visit their selected institutions early (before the senior year) and contact the appropriate university offices before they enroll in order to receive entitled academic services. Students must provide appropriate documentation of their disability status, typically a full and current (within a year of enrollment) psychoeducational assessment along with a qualification of disability, in order to receive appropriate classroom accommodations and support services outside the classroom. In addition, knowledge of basic civil rights, the ADA, and general procedural safeguards will be needed because students must serve as their own advocate. Gerber (1997, p. 4) has noted, "In order for a person who is learning disabled to navigate in the workplace, self-direction as well as self-advocacy is a must." To formally address this, an education training component on the ADA connected to the IEP can and should be started at the secondary level and carried over into the post-secondary level for those students who continue their formal education.

The school system does not typically take on the "educational responsibility" of informing employers about various disabilities and the special education law that is designed to protect employees in the workplace. And despite greater public awareness and acceptance of disabilities, employers are still not well educated to the needs and legal safeguards of individuals with disabilities. Therefore, work transition plans at the high school level should include information packets for employers and businesses. In addition, personal visits and education seminars can help to increase awareness in these areas.

Owing to the increased opportunities in social engagement whether on the job or outside the work place, the highest levels of social conduct and interpersonal control will be needed. Dealing with daily issues involving stress, anger, self-esteem, etc., are important for everyone and that includes individuals with disabilities. Seeking out and receiving professional assistance especially during periods of work or life adjustment will be necessary for adults with special needs. This kind of training can be initiated in the classroom curriculum and maintained through a continuing education program beyond high school.

Continued learning assistance with basic skills (e.g., reading, mathematics) beyond high school for adults, whether college bound or not, will likely be needed. As was mentioned previously, proficiency in many academic skills will continue to lag and consequently require continued instruction and support services. Adult service programs or flexible "additional year" programs at the secondary level may be used to help address this need. Vocational training programs that have reentry options are needed for adults who seek additional job skills/preparation or advancement. A life-long learning perspective must be held and maintained by both those served as well as the service providers.

Model Programs

The Marriott Foundation's "Bridges... From School to Work" program is a community-based vocational internship work program for students with disabilities (Donovan & Tilson, 1998). Across six cities around the nation a standardized vocational experience, including a 2–5 month competitive paid internship, is provided to seniors possessing a wide range of disabilities (e.g., LD, mental retardation, emotional /behavioral disabilities, sensory disabilities). More than 3,000 students have participated in this program, and a majority of students (86%) have completed their internships and have obtained gainful employment (Donovan & Tilson, 1998). This highly successful program generated four essential principles that must be acknowledged in order to create successful employment outcomes. When setting up an effective transition program, Donovan and Tilson (1998, p. 19–21) list the following: "Competitive, paid work experience plays a significant role in post-school vocational outcomes, lasting relationships grow from complementary needs and capabilities, first-hand experience is vital to building real understanding and commitment, and under promise and over deliver."

The Pathways to Satisfaction (PTS) Model developed by Thomas Holub is utilized in more than 30 school districts throughout the midwest. This program is a student and parent focused program primarily provided through regular education instruction. Individualized plans are initiated during the middle school years with a transition specialist, followed by a comprehensive vocational assessment and career exploration, actual work experience, and appropriate transition experiences, and continued through the post-high school period with follow-up services and evaluation.

Beyond the Classroom

Once a student with a disability leaves the school setting and enters the world of work the need for services and support does not end. In fact, it grows as job-related skill enhancement is required and/or new life adjustment issues are faced. The adult with special needs faces old and new challenges. Brown (1997) contends that the economy in the twenty-first century will require new work and technology skills for all workers including those with disabilities. In particular, employees today must work faster and more often be a part of a team. Also, employees are more empowered to make decisions on their own and may or may not work directly in the office. In addition, young workers must be flexible in learning new systems, approaches, software packages, etc., in the workplace. Students with disabilities must be given opportunities to develop these work skills and habits as well as prepare for the entire job search process.

Moreover, adults with disabilities must become fully informed about their constitutional rights and protections under the ADA. This is critical because current research indicates that adults with LD perceive themselves as having minimal knowledge and understanding of their constitutional rights and safeguards (Witte, in press). Brown (1997, p. 34) has stated that, "Individuals must continuously work to understand and improve themselves." This critical message is for all individuals with disabilities, and it must be followed if meaningful employment is to be found and retained.

Gerber, Ginsberg, and Reiff (1992) examined the successful employment patterns of adults with LD. One essential theme was found for these individuals: the ability to take control and charge of one's life and to effectively adapt to one's environment. The control involved both an internal (e.g., general desire to succeed, setting goals, positive spin on their learning and/or personality style) and external focus (e.g., coping mechanism, a goodness of fit between an individual's abilities and their immediate environment). Clearly, the integration of internal processes and skills matched to an existing and compatible system (e.g., the workplace) can create a best "fit" for adults with LD (Szymanski & Hershenson, 1998).

Also, many of the highly successful adults with LD had personal mentors within their support groups. Based on the interview findings, a process model for vocational success that can be embedded within existing curricula was developed. Gerber et al. (1992, p. 484–485) note that "success begins with a set of internal decisions; then, highly successful adults with LD pursue several ways of adapting themselves to their disability and the world around them. Successful adapting strengthens the desire, produces more goal setting, and helps people through the maze of reframing. And, with strong adapting high levels of control are attainable."

Several essential aspects and components that increase the effectiveness of transition plans have emerged from the current literature. The following is a listing of core elements that a district should consider before developing a transition program.

Key Aspects of Effective Transition Plans

1. Determine the standards (e.g., proficiencies, skill levels, etc.) that special needs graduates will be evaluated against; the "end product" must be known in order for effective planning to occur.

2. Clear organization, from the elementary to the high school levels, along with strong administrative ownership and follow-through are essential for effective transition services.

3. A long-term planning focus complete with periodic progress monitoring is needed; provide services early and consistently throughout the student's educational career.

4. Every identified child must have an individualized transition plan based on their unique needs, issues, and goals.

5. Parents, as well as the identified student, need to be actively involved in the transition planning process as early as possible.

6. The ITP should exist as an inseparable part of the IEP and be reviewed and/or evaluated at least once a year.

7. Focus on multiple domains (e.g., academic skills, functional life skills, interpersonal skills) in the IEP throughout the student's educational career.

8. Career and vocational education and training should start during the middle school period and extend throughout the high school period. Paid work programs and experiences during the junior and/or senior years should be pursued by school districts.

9. A seamless transition of support from high school to adult services must occur. A vocational rehabilitation representative should be a member of the transition team by the time the identified student enters high school. Interagency collaboration is critical for effective transition performance and that coordination should start well before the student exits the educational system. A life–span model must be held as individual needs for services, continuing education, trainings, etc., will emerge as these youth participate more fully in work and society.

10. Every student must be educated regarding his or her rights, protections, and procedural safeguards guaranteed under the ADA.

Roles for School Psychologists

The following suggested roles and responsibilities may or may not fit into the "expected" school psychology position. In the past, school psychologists have had minimal participation and impact in vocational planning and training for students with disabilities (Levinson, 1990). However, as Levinson (1995) has noted, the school psychologist's expertise in human development, applied behavior analysis, learning theory, and assessment (e.g., daily living skills, vocational interest) makes that professional an extremely valuable resource for transition planning. The following roles are essential to effective transition service and match up well with the formal training and expertise of most school psychologists:

1. Serve as a "quality control" coordinator ensuring that the maximum intervention effect is being provided throughout the educational career of the identified student. However, this responsibil-

ity and position should be separate from the case manager position that exists with most identified student teams.

2. Educate team members to the varying learning and human development needs/issues of the identified student as the student transitions (e.g., elementary, middle, high school, vocational, college, work) through the educational life stream. An emphasis on long-term life adjustment and functional work competencies should be maintained.

3. Serve as a school transition specialist (as a possible member of the ITP team) for students leaving the secondary system and entering vocational, college, or direct work settings. Part of this role should be to make sure each student has the proper paperwork and/or documentation completed for the next phase in the transition process. For example, if the student is going off to college and has an identified disability, then a current psychoeducational evaluation will be necessary in order for that student to receive university services and/or accommodations.

4. Provide through formal and informal assessment measures (e.g., aptitude, academic, interpersonal, social) a current student profile that can be directly integrated into the ITP.

5. Serve as a designated business consultant informing and educating employers to various disabilities, characteristics, appropriate accommodations, special education law, civil rights protections, etc.

6. Help design and evaluate the effectiveness of transition program procedures and pre-employment services.

7. Provide periodic inservice and continuing education programs for adults with LD and their service providers.

8. Serve as a professional mentor and consultant for adults in transition.

9. Parents of identified students need to be welcomed and valued by the educational team. The school psychologist is in a prime position to facilitate parental involvement in the transition process.

10. If needed, the school psychologist can provide mental health counseling as part of psychological support services in the transition plan.

11. Teach classes and provide lectures in high school and/or collect resources (e.g., websites) for individuals with disabilities about the ADA and their constitutional rights and protections.

12. Since self-control/adaptation is an identified success ingredient for adults with LD, direct instruction and consultation in personal management techniques to transition students seems warranted and could be provided by the school psychologist.

SUMMARY

Transition can be defined as the passing or moving from one point to another with an eye toward the future. And that future must provide for students with disabilities the opportunity to fully participate in the adult world. Much more work is still required in order for that reality to exist. If a collective "transition picture" can be drawn of youth and adults with disabilities, then it would likely include the following:

1. Skill deficits may remain: Address them with a life-long perspective and plan.

2. Lack of specialized training and/or continued education may limit future employment opportunities: Keep doors open to effective and flexible programs and options for students and adults.

3. Gender and minority status further limit employment opportunities: They are the most at-risk clientele and must not be forgotten.

4. Adults with disabilities, particularly those with LD, may hide their disability, lack true understanding of their rights and protections, and when employed may experience minimal job satisfaction including those who have graduated from college (Witte, Philips, & Kakela 1998): Educate them to the long-term benefits of self-advocacy because they must continue to educate, inform, and influ-

ence the general population about the life-span issues that confront individuals with disabilities.

REFERENCES

Blackorby, J., & Wagner, M. (1996). Longitudinal post-school outcomes of youth with disabilities: Findings from the national longitudinal transition study. *Exceptional Children, 62,* 399–413.

Blackorby, J., & Wagner, M. (1997). The employment outcomes of youth with learning disabilities: A review of findings from the NLTS. In P. J. Gerber & D. S. Brown (Eds.), *Learning disabilities and employment* (pp. 57–74). Austin, TX: PRO-ED.

Brown, D. S. (1997). The new economy in the 21st century: Implications for individuals with learning disabilities. In P. J. Gerber & D. S. Brown (Eds.), *Learning disabilities and employment* (pp. 19–37). Austin, TX: PRO-ED.

D'Amico, R. (1991). The working world awaits: Employment experiences during and shortly after secondary school. In M. Wagner, L. Newman, R. D'Amico, E. D. Jay, P. Butler-Nelson, C. Marder, & R. Cox (Eds.), *Youth with disabilities: How are they doing? The first comprehensive report from the National Longitudinal Transition Study of Special Education Students* (ERIC Document Reproduction Service No. ED 341 228, pp. 8-1–8-55). Menlo Park, CA: SRI International.

Deno, S. L. (1995). School psychologist as a problem solver. In A. Thomas & J. Grimes (Eds.), *Best practices in school psychology III* (pp. 471–484). Washington, DC: National Association of School Psychologists.

Donovan, M. R., & Tilson, G. P. (1998). The Marriott Foundation's "Bridges...From School to Work": A framework for successful employment outcomes for people with disabilities. *Journal of Vocational Rehabilitation, 10,* 15–21.

Evers, R. B. (1996a). The positive force of vocational education: Transition outcomes for youth with learning disabilities. *Journal of Learning Disabilities, 29,* 69–78.

Evers, R. B. (1996b). The positive force of vocational education: Transition outcomes for youth with learning disabilities. In J. R. Patton & G. Blalock (Eds.), *Transition and students with learning disabilities: Facilitating the movement from school to adult life* (pp. 113–129). Austin, TX: PRO-ED.

Furney, K. S., Hasazi, S. B., & Destefano, L. (1997). Transition policies, practices, and promises: Lessons from three states. *Exceptional Children, 63,* 343–355.

Gerber, P. J. (1997). Life after school: Challenges in the workplace. In P. J. Gerber & D. S. Brown (Eds.), *Learning disabilities and employment* (pp. 3–18). Austin, TX: PRO-ED.

Gerber, P. J., Ginsberg, R., & Reiff, H. B. (1992). Identifying alterable patterns in employment success for highly successful adults with learning disabilities. *Journal of Learning Disabilities, 25,* 475–487.

Grayson, T. E., Wermuth, T. R., Holub, T. M., & Anderson, M. L. (1997). Effective practices of transition from school to work for people with learning disabilities. In P. J. Gerber & D. S. Brown (Eds.), *Learning disabilities and employment* (pp. 77–99). Austin, TX: PRO-ED.

Halpern, A. S. (1992). Transition: Old wine in new bottles. *Exceptional Children, 58,* 202–211.

Hasazi, S. B., Gordon, L. R., & Roe, C. A. (1985). Factors associated with the employment status of handicapped youth exiting high school from 1979 to 1983. *Exceptional Children, 51,* 455–469.

Inge, K., Wehman, P., Clees, T. J., & Dymond, S. (1996). Transition from school to adulthood. In P. J. McLaughlin & P. Wehman (Eds.), *Mental retardation and developmental disabilities* (pp. 69–84). Austin, TX: PRO-ED.

Kohler, P. D. (1993). Best practices in transition: Substantiated or implied? *Career Development for Exceptional Individuals, 16*(2), 107–122.

Levinson, E. M. (1990). Vocational assessment involvement and use of the Self-Directed Search by school psychologists. *Psychology in the Schools, 27*(3), 217–227.

Levinson, E. M. (1995). Best practices in transition services. In A. Thomas & J. Grimes (Eds.), *Best practices in school psychology III* (pp. 909–915). Washington, DC: National Association of School Psychologists.

Minskoff, E. H. (1996). Improving employment outcomes for persons with learning disabilities. In N. Gregg, C. Hoy, & A. F. Gay (Eds.), *Adults with learning disabilities: Theoretical and practical perspectives* (pp. 277–297). New York: Guilford.

Phelps, L. A., & Hanley-Maxwell, C. (1997). School-to-work transitions for youth with disabilities: A review of outcomes and practices. *Review of Educational Research, 67,* 197–226.

Szymanski, E. M., & Danek, M. M. (1985). School-to-work transition for students with disabilities: Historical, current, and conceptual issues. *Rehabilitation Counseling Bulletin, 29,* 81–89.

Szymanski, E. M., & Hershenson, B. (1998). Career development of people with disabilities: An ecological model. In R. M. Parker & E. M. Szymanski (Eds.), *Rehabilitation counseling: Basics and beyond* (pp. 327–378). Austin, TX: PRO-ED.

Unger, D. D., & Luecking, R. (1998). Work in progress: Including students with disabilities in school-to-work initiatives. *Focus on Autism and Other Developmental Disabilities, 13,* 94–100.

U.S. Department of Education (1999). *Twenty-first annual report to Congress on the implementation of the Individuals with Disabilities Education Act.* Washington, DC: Office of Special Education Programs.

Wagner, M., Newman, L., D'Amico, R., Jay, E.D., Butler-Nalin, P., Marder, C., & Cox, R. (1991). *Youth with disabilities: How are they doing? The first comprehensive report from the National Longitudinal Transition Study of Special Education Students* (ERIC Document Reproduction Service No. ED 341 228). Menlo Park, CA: SRI International.

Wehman, P. (1996). Individualized transition planning. *In life beyond the classroom: Transition strategies for young people with disabilities* (pp. 77–102). Baltimore, MD: Brookes.

Wehman, P., Moon, M. S., Everson, J. M., Wood, W., & Barcus, J. M. (1988). *Transition from school to work: New challenges for youth with severe disabilities.* Baltimore, MD: Brookes.

Winton, P. J. (1990). Families of children with disabilities. In N. G. Haring, L. McCormick, & T. G. Haring (Eds.), *Exceptional children and youth* (pp. 502–525). New York: Macmillan.

Witte, R. (2002). College graduates with disabilities and the Americans with Disabilities Act (ADA): Do they know their employment rights? *Learning Disabilities: A Multidisciplinary Journal, 11*(1), 27–30.

Witte, R., Philips, L., & Kakela, M. (1998). Job satisfaction of college graduates with learning disabilities. *Journal of Learning Disabilities, 31*(3), 259–265.

Wood, W. M., & Test, D. W. (1997). Transition from school to work for students with severe disabilities: What advocates need to know about the 1992 rehabilitation act amendments. *Journal of Vocational Rehabilitation, 8,* 171–182.

Zigmond, N. (1990). Rethinking secondary school programs for students with learning disabilities. *Focus on Exceptional Children, 23,* 1–22.

ANNOTATED BIBLIOGRAPHY

Adelman, P. B., & Vogel, S. A. (1998). Adults with learning disabilities. In B. Wong (Ed.), *Learning about learning disabilities* (pp. 657–701). New York: Academic.
This chapter provides an exhaustive review of the current literature of adults with learning disabilities. Academic, social, and employment areas are examined and reviewed.

Gerber, P. J., & Brown, D. S. (1997). *Learning disabilities and employment.* Austin, TX: PRO-ED.
This book provides the reader with a better understanding of important pre-employment knowledge, experiences, and practices for adults with learning disabilities. In addition, workplace issues (e.g., job accommodations, technology, ADA issues) are discussed.

Phelps, L. A., & Hanley-Maxwell, C. (1997). School-to-work transitions for youth with disabilities: A review of outcomes and practices. *Review of Educational Research, 67,* 197–226.
This research article provides a comprehensive review of current school-to-work transition outcomes and data-generated practices for youth with disabilities.

Wehman, P. (1996). Life beyond the classroom: *Transition strategies for young people with disabilities.* Baltimore, MD: Brookes.
This text provides a comprehensive overview of transition services for students with disabilities as well as the total transition process. Direct programming applications are provided for youth with various disabilities. A great reference text filled with many practical applications.

WEBSITES

National Transition Alliance Home Page, http://www.dssc.org/nta/html/home.htm.

Parents and the School-to-Work Transition of Special Needs Youth, http://www.kidsource.com/kidsource/content4/special.needs.trans.html.

Transition Services in the IEP, http://www.Idonline.org/Id_indepth/iep/ieppub.html.

Transition Plans Guide to the Future, http://www.sna.com/switp/tgp.htm.

Work Incentives Transition Network-Home Page, http://www.vcu.edu/rrtcweb/witn/ssi.htm.

Transition Planning Parent Brief, http://ici2.umn.edu/ntn/pub/briefs/tplanning.html.

101 Best Practices in Transition Planning for College-Bound Students With Disabilities

Susan M. Vess
The University of Iowa

OVERVIEW

National focus on employment outcomes for all students originated in the 1980s, intensified in the 1990s, and led to legislation promoting school-to-work initiatives (Minskoff, 1996). As an outgrowth of efforts to improve academic and job-related skills for all students, transition planning for students with disabilities (SWD) was included in the Individuals with Disabilities Education Act (IDEA) to enhance those skills in young adults who participated in special education during their school years. The history of school-to-work initiatives for all students, transition planning for SWD, and the dismal educational and employment outcomes of SWD were reviewed by Defur and Reiff (1994) and Minskoff (1996).

Although few SWD include college in their high school transition plans, a growing number have enrolled in college since the early 1970s (Hameister, 1989; Heath Resource Center, 1995; Minskoff, 1996; Rapp, 1997). The college aspirations of SWD, especially those with learning disabilities (LD), are fueled by (a) federal legislation, including Section 504 of the Rehabilitation Act (Section 504), the Americans with Disabilities Act (ADA), and the IDEA (Brinckerhoff, Shaw, & McGuire, 1993; Horn & Bobbitt, 1999); (b) change in the orientation of special education away from remediation and tutoring to instruction in study skills, problem solving, and other learning strategies (Brinckerhoff, Shaw, & McGuire, 1993; Minskoff, 1996); (c) renewed emphasis on educating children with disabilities within the general curriculum and with a focus on post-graduation outcomes (Brinckerhoff et al., 1993; Minskoff, 1996); (d) emphasis on personal skills such as self-advocacy, personal independence, and self-determination needed for both postsecondary education and employment (Defur & Reiff, 1994; McGuire, 1997; Minskoff, 1996); (e) mandated transition planning for successful movement into adulthood and meaningful employment (Brinckerhoff et al., 1993; Defur & Reiff, 1994; Minskoff, 1996; Vogel & Reder, 1998b); (f) improved technology including advances in computer hardware, software, and assistive technology (Brinckerhoff et al., 1993); (g) increased sophistication of the workplace and demands for high academic standards (McGuire, 1997; Minskoff, 1994, 1996); and (h) expanding societal expectations and changing demographic characteristics of college students (Brinckerhoff et al, 1993; Habley, 1995; Synatschk, 1995; Vogel & Reder, 1998a, b).

Compared to special education students not seeking postsecondary education, SWD attending college show mild disabilities and good academic skills (Horn & Bobbitt, 1999; Minskoff, 1994, 1996). Now, about half of postsecondary SWD report LD which is a significant increase in these students numerically and proportionally in the past decade (Henderson, 1999; McGuire, 1998; Minskoff, 1994; Scott, 1997a). LD continues as the largest group of SWD in postsecondary education with rapid increases in students with other *hidden disabilities* (ADHD and chronic health or psychological disorders). In contrast, there are proportionally fewer students with orthopedic disabilities and visual impairments served by campus disability offices (Henderson, 1999; Heyward, 1998).

Despite the importance of transition planning as a means of successfully moving SWD to post-graduation activities, these efforts are not as effective as postsecondary matriculation and graduation rates might suggest. College students with LD demonstrate poor academic skills relative to other college students (Vogel & Reder, 1998b). About one-third of SWD remain in college until a baccalaureate degree is earned compared to 48% of non-disabled students who graduate (Henderson, 1999; Horn & Bobbitt, 1999). However, SWD who do graduate from college are comparable to non-disabled graduates in salaries, employment in areas related to their majors, and matriculation into graduate school (Henderson, 1999; Horn & Bobbitt, 1999).

While movement from secondary to postsecondary education is not a seamless process for any student, this intermediate link between high school and work is fraught with difficulties for SWD. First, although the conceptualization of transition planning expanded to include preparation for postsecondary education, transition efforts often focus on the needs of students moving directly into employment after high school (Defur & Reiff, 1994). Second, high school SWD achieve short-term academic objectives found on IEPs with little regard for the rigors and requirements of postsecondary options (Defur & Reiff, 1994; Rapp, 1997). Finally, secondary students with mild disabilities are believed to move easily into higher education so may receive less attention than other SWD attending high school (Defur & Reiff, 1994; Minskoff, 1994).

BASIC CONSIDERATIONS

Developmental, student, institutional, and legal variables contribute to the challenges SWD face in college. Hameister (1989) reported that all first-year college students, including SWD, experienced developmental crises, such as intellectual and academic competence, establishing and maintaining interpersonal ties, and career choices that match interests, skills, abilities, aspirations, and attitudes. Alternatively, Upcraft and Gardner (1989) identified the following factors associated with successful adjustment to college by first-year students: (a) intelligence and history of academic success; (b) personal attributes such as motivation, emotional stability, and values consistent with those of the institution; and (c) parental support and lack of either family or nonacademic problems such as childcare, money, and disputes about major area of study, career choices, grades, and the personal behavior of students at school. SWD often fall short of these developmental milestones and success indicators because of the mismatch between expected effort and academic demands, reluctance to use support services such as the student disability office, and limited self-awareness.

Independence and self-determination are major developmental issues for college students. For example, students must resist the urge to overuse out-of-class time for socializing instead of studying or to sleep late rather than attend class. For many first-year SWD, independence takes the form of ignoring the presence of a disability that produces a negative impact on learning and/or behavior (Defur & Reiff, 1994).

Like all college freshmen, SWD must not only develop age-appropriate independence, but also learn to function separately from parents and special education case managers who advocated for and often protected them from academic and interpersonal problems in high school (Defur & Reiff, 1994; Minskoff, 1996). Not only do they face the usual hazards of campus life such as disputes with other students, issues related to time and money management, and talking to professors about academic problems, SWD must also disclose their disability to the appropriate institutional officer, request accommodations, and find assistance on campus for resolving non-disability–related academic concerns. SWD using a personal care attendant hire, supervise, and potentially fire that individual. Yet, many SWD have limited experience in independent functioning, self-awareness, and self-advocacy required for these efforts (Defur & Reiff, 1994; Minskoff, 1996; Scott, 1997a).

Students With Disabilities

During the 1995–1996 school year, approximately 6% of undergraduates reported the presence of a disability, and approximately one-third of SWD in this survey identified LD as their disability (Horn & Bobbitt, 1999). In a 1998 survey of first-year, full-time freshmen enrolled in higher education, over 154,000 students or approximately 9% reported at least one disability (Henderson, 1999). This represents more than a 300% growth in the number of freshmen reporting a disability since 1978 (Henderson, 1999).

By using an index composed of (a) grades (GPA of 2.7 or higher in academic classes); (b) class rank at or above the 54th percentile; (c) National Education Longitudinal Study (NELS) composite scores at or above the 56th percentile on the 1992 NELS mathematics and reading aptitude test; and (d) a composite ACT of at least 19 or combined SAT scores above 820, SWD were less likely to be *minimally qualified* for postsecondary education than their non-disabled peers. Students with and without disabilities in the top 10–25% of entering freshmen on the index (*highly qualified for admission*) enrolled in four-year institutions at similar rates. When comparing students who were *moderately qualified* (50–75%), SWD more often enrolled in two-year institutions (Horn & Bobbitt, 1999).

In 1998, college freshmen with disabilities more often aspired to an associate or vocational degree and attended a two-year institution than first-year students without disabilities. The major exception to this was attendance at a four-year private college (Henderson, 1999; Horn & Bobbitt, 1999). Students with LD are the largest disability population attending community colleges (Rapp, 1997).

Despite the intention of transferring to a four-year school after graduating with an associate degree, most students graduating from a two-year college do not enroll in a four-year institution. Consequently, few students who aspire to a baccalaureate degree actually earn one (Horn & Bobbitt, 1999).

Community colleges and other two-year institutions offer certificates in vocational or technical areas or terminal associate degrees, either of which is appropriate for employment requiring education beyond high school, but not a college degree (Rapp, 1997). They have modest or open admissions requirements, coursework that ranges from remedial or developmental to college level, and an employment orientation including pre-service opportunities, career exploration and development, and job search strategies (Rapp, 1997). They offer a range of services for SWD (Minskoff, 1994; Rapp, 1997).

Special educators often believe that community colleges offer vocational training with less academic coursework (Rapp, 1997). Further, they consider this option desirable for SWD who are described as good hands-on learners but have poor academic skills. However, there are three important considerations: (a) matriculation into most programs, even those that are technical, require high school coursework in math, sciences, and other areas; (b) students with limited academic skills may find the academic portions of training beyond their abilities; and (c) a vocational focus combined with limited academic skill and knowledge development may consign SWD to entry-level employment and reduce their opportunity for advancement to supervisory positions, business management, or business ownership (Minskoff, 1996).

When comparing first-year SWD to other freshmen on demographic variables, SWD are more likely to be male, older, and white, non-Hispanic (Henderson, 1999; Horn & Bobbitt, 1999). Both groups show comparable parental levels of education and employment. However, SWD come from families with slightly lower income levels. The above characteristics of SWD are associated with problems in persistence to degree attainment for all students (Horn & Bobbitt, 1999).

Although students with and without disabilities attend postsecondary education to obtain a good job or earn more money, SWD also reported that they enrolled to prove to others they can succeed in college and to improve reading and study skills (Habley, 1995; Henderson, 1999). Additionally, they attend college because of the encouragement of a mentor or role model. Students with and without disabilities indicate preference for the same majors, especially business (Henderson, 1999; Horn & Bobbitt, 1999).

When compared to college-bound secondary students without disabilities, college-bound SWD demonstrate less academic preparation. Although secondary students with and without disabilities averaged four hours weekly on homework, SWD were less likely to study with friends and meet or exceed recommended secondary classes in math, foreign language, and science (Henderson, 1999). They enrolled in remedial math and English classes more often; were equally likely to complete requirements in American history, government, and arts/music; and took advanced placement (AP) courses less often (Henderson, 1999; Horn & Bobbitt, 1999). SWD also achieved lower secondary GPAs, especially a C or D average, and earned lower average scores on college placement exams such as the SAT or ACT (Horn

& Bobbitt, 1999). Finally, when compared to other first-year SWD, freshmen with LD were less likely to complete two years of foreign language in high school and often expressed interest in special programs for SWD at the collegiate level (Horn & Bobbitt, 1999).

According to Habley (1995), first-year college students often inflate degree aspirations, personal characteristics, and academic skills and abilities and underestimate the likelihood of failing a course, changing majors, transferring to another school, leaving college, and seeking personal and career counseling, tutoring, and other services. The majority of first-year students leaves college or stops taking classes for an extended period rather than earn either an associate or baccalaureate degree (Tinto, 1993).

Despite first-year college students' tendency to overestimate abilities, SWD ranked themselves lower on math ability, intellectual self-confidence, academic ability, and writing ability than their non-disabled peers (Henderson, 1999). Minskoff (1994, 1996) attributed problems in academic competency and poor self-esteem to special education modifications in class work and testing that gave SWD an unrealistic, inaccurate appraisal of their skills relative to those of their high school classmates.

Postsecondary Education

Students enhance their potential for success in college by choosing an institution that fits their personal needs and preferences for size, location, curriculum and program options, selectivity, academic rigor, mission, and cost (Heath Resource Center, 1995, 1997; Tinto, 1993; Upcraft & Gardner, 1989). They are further assisted if they understand the culture, structure, requirements, and vocabulary of higher education both generally and specific to the institution they attend (Heath Resource Center, 1995). Success in higher education also depends on a variety of practical skills and attitudes, including (a) reading the college catalog for general information such as course descriptions and campus services and for policies and procedures such as grading and graduation requirements, (b) understanding core academic requirements and those of the major field of study, (c) calculating the GPA and using this information in decision making, (d) determining course sequences over several terms, (e) scheduling semester course loads to balance academic demands and instructor teaching style and expectations with personal interests and skill levels, and (f) knowing and complying with institutional policies, procedures, and requirements for selection of a major area of study, class registration, withdrawal from courses, academic probation and dismissal, graduation, and academic integrity and conduct (Heath Resource Center, 1995).

According to Tinto (1993), persistence until graduation is strongly predicted by academic preparation and aspirations. Students also increase their likelihood of graduating if they transfer prior commitments to high school teachers and friends to new ties at college (Tinto, 1993). For SWD who depended on their parents and former teachers during high school, forming new relationships with postsecondary faculty and service providers and relying on their own skills and initiatives are major hurdles.

Persistence to degree attainment is also enhanced when students can express clear, realistic academic, personal, and career goals (Heath Resource Center, 1995; Tinto, 1993). At all levels of postsecondary education, persistence and retention are tied to motivation to expend personal energy and resources to achieve academic and personal goals (Tinto, 1993). Although ability and academic achievement are directly related to admission and success in higher education, the personal characteristics of students, especially motivation and perseverance, are more important to college retention until degree completion (Heath Resource Center, 1995; Minskoff, 1994; Tinto, 1993). Nevertheless, a strong work ethic does not compensate for inadequate academic skills.

When SWD's low educational aspirations, confidence, and self-esteem are coupled with their limited academic preparation and demographic characteristics, remaining in college until degree attainment is often a problem. SWD are less likely to possess the academic credentials to gain admittance, enroll in courses bearing academic credit needed for graduation, or compete on an equal academic footing with non-disabled classmates (Horn & Bobbitt, 1999). They may have attitudinal, experiential, behavioral, and maturational issues that further delay or deter them from achieving a successful postsecondary outcome. In virtually every respect then, SWD are at a competitive disadvantage when compared to non-disabled students in postsecondary education.

Legal Considerations

Upon high school graduation, SWD transition to a new legal and eligibility status under the ADA and Section 504 (Heath Resource Center, 1997; Heyward, 1998). The ADA and Section 504 protect SWD who are qualified for the activity they are pursuing and meet the legal definition of disability (Heath Resource Center, 1997). At the postsecondary level, these two laws impose obligations and limitations on SWD seeking accommodations.

Although the protections of these laws overlap in postsecondary education, the ADA is often considered more applicable in employment contexts (Minskoff, 1996), and Section 504 historically and currently has greater impact on postsecondary education (McGuire, 1998). These civil rights statutes require equal access and participation of qualified SWD without reduction or modification of standards or provision of special programs for SWD (Gordon & Keiser, 1998; Heath Resource Center, 1995; Heyward, 1998; McGuire, 1997, 1998; Scott, 1994, 1997b). Additionally, neither law requires postsecondary accommodations that are indirectly related to participation and meeting course requirements, even though SWD received a host of interventions in secondary education (Heath Resource Center, 1997; Scott, 1994, 1997a; Wells & Hanebrink, 1997).

SWD who meet essential requirements, with or without accommodations, are described as *otherwise qualified*. If SWD are otherwise qualified, then the ADA and Section 504 guarantee access and participation in all college programs and activities (Heath Resource Center, 1995; Heyward, 1998; Scott, 1997b). SWD must meet all standards required for admissions, retention, and graduation to maintain qualified status (Heyward, 1998; Scott, 1997a, b; Wells & Hanebrink, 1997). Scott (1994) stated that qualified status is determined through review of (a) student characteristics such as disability and its functional impact, (b) essential requirements of the institution or program of study, and (c) whether reasonable accommodations would enable SWD to meet essential requirements.

The application of the ADA and Section 504 requires balancing the rights of SWD to participate and the rights of institutions to maintain academic integrity (Heyward, 1998; McGuire, 1998; Wells & Hanebrink, 1997). Institutions are not required to change essential and technical standards if they are legitimate and reasoned, rationally related to the goals and requirements of the program or institution, and are not applied in a discriminatory manner (Heyward, 1998). Essential and technical requirements usually evolve from professional and accreditation standards, are enjoined on all students, and ensure students with and without disabilities have the knowledge, attitudes, skills, and other prerequisites to participate in a program and its activities (Heyward, 1998; McGuire, 1998; Scott, 1994, 1997a).

In postsecondary institutions, *essential functions* include course work and participation in laboratory and other experiences necessary to acquire the knowledge and skills required to work in a particular field and obtain professional licensure (Heyward, 1998; Scott, 1997b). *Technical standards* are non-academic requirements such as attendance, personal and professional behavior, prior education and experience, physical strength and dexterity, use of appropriate grammar and vocabulary, and compliance with professional practices, standards, and ethics (Scott, 1997b). If SWD meet both essential and technical standards and do not pose an immediate threat to health or safety, it is illegal to deny admissions or participation in a program on the basis of speculations about their disability, limitations, or employability (Heyward, 1998; Scott, 1994, 1997a, b).

The ADA and Section 504 emphasize the similarity of students with and without disabilities in postsecondary education (Heath Resource Center, 1997; Heyward, 1998; McGuire, 1998). Because they are nondiscrimination statutes, they mandate services required for access and equal participation of SWD. Except for accommodating access needs, these laws expect SWD to learn independently, complete the same requirements, and comply with expectations for acceptable academic performance and conduct.

The ADA and Section 504 require SWD to succeed or fail on the merits of their performance. They do not rescue SWD, on the basis of disability, from onerous course or institutional requirements and sanctions and do not require an emergency effort to provide accommodations or to relieve SWD from academic jeopardy due to limited academic skills or low grades, poor attendance, and inadequate test performance. Thus, SWD who argue that they would have met standards but for their disability are not admitted, retained, or graduated.

In all academic decisions from matriculation to graduation, SWD are held to the same policies and procedures as non-disabled students and are rarely given preferential treatment such as tuition refunds, changes in course meeting times, or relief from penalties given for academic integrity or conduct violations. They are unsuccessful when they claim cheating was due to the impulsivity of ADHD or plagiarism was due to LD. SWD are subject to regular disciplinary proceedings rather than manifestation reviews.

Any student may be qualified for admissions, but then flounder and find themselves on academic probation or dismissed for lack of reasonable academic progress. GPA requirements are not waived to admit SWD to a particular major and a minimum grade in a prerequisite class is not ignored so that SWD can move to the next-level course. SWD are usually unsuccessful in appealing academic decisions when they claim that the disability was responsible for their academic difficulties. Any student may be denied graduation because they have not met general or major requirements for graduation or have not earned the necessary GPA. SWD cannot successfully demand waiver of foreign language, math, or other course or graduation requirements even if lack of that element delays degree completion.

According to the ADA and Section 504, a student with a *disability* has a physical or mental condition that *substantially* limits a *major life activity* such as learning, thinking, or concentrating, has a history of a condition, or is regarded as having a condition (Kincaid, 2000). SWD who are currently and significantly impaired are eligible for accommodations; students who fit the *history of* or *regarded as* portions of the definition are protected from discrimination but are not accommodated (Kincaid, 2000).

Unlike the IDEA, the ADA and Section 504 do not specify particular mental or physical conditions as qualifying SWD for their protections. Rather, determination of disability rests on both the *presence* and *severity* of the condition (Gordon & Keiser, 1998; Kincaid, 2000). Significant severity means an inability or considerable difficulty in engaging in one or more major life activities in comparison to the *average* person.

Some activities may be severely limited, but do not fall within the parameters of a basic life activity. Several examples help clarify this distinction: (a) There may be a significant limitation in reading, but a significant limitation in biology is too specific to be a life activity and test anxiety is too broad; (b) there may be a significant limitation affecting a class of jobs, but SWD are not assured the right to major in a particular area such as medicine; and (c) there may be a significant limitation in one or more areas within a unique, superior overall profile (gifted LD) or in comparison to an above-average cohort such as other postsecondary students, but SWD are compared to the *average* person in the general population (Gordon & Keiser, 1998; Kincaid, 2000).

The ADA and Section 504 require an individualized inquiry to determine if a student meets the criteria of the definition, especially the severity of impact and functional limitations (Heyward, 1998). The manifestations and severity of a condition vary by time and circumstances; therefore, these laws require an evaluation of its current, functional limitations under various circumstances (Gordon & Keiser, 1998).

Scott (1994) indicated that eligibility for accommodations was based on four factors: (a) disability, (b) adequate documentation, (c) qualified status, and (d) reasonable modifications. At the postsecondary level, SWD must disclose their disability to the appropriate institutional officer and request accommodations (Heath Resource Center, 1995, 1997; Heyward, 1998; Scott, 1997b).

In response, the institution has the right to request documentation of the disability and adequate time to review it (Heyward, 1998). If requested documentation is incomplete or not sufficiently current to identify accommodations, the institution requires SWD to seek evaluation at personal expense (Heyward, 1998; McGuire, 1998; Scott, 1994, 1997b). The institution determines what accommodations are necessary in view of academic demands and manifestations of the disability (Heath Resource Center, 1995; Heyward, 1998; Wells & Hanebrink, 1997). Accommodations provide access and participation to a particular student, but are not necessarily those recommended by the diagnostician or preferred by that student (Scott, 1994).

Under the ADA and Section 504, *accommodations* are designed to permit access and meaningful participation by removal of architectural and other barriers to learning (Heath Resource Center, 1997; Heyward, 1998). Usually, they involve alterations in how information is communicated in the classroom and how learning is demonstrated on tests (Scott, 1997a).

Only students whose disabilities present a current, severe functional limitation are provided with accommodations (Heyward, 1998). When they argue that their history of disability as demonstrated by their special education record entitles them to accommodations, many SWD are surprised to find that their IEPs, dated psychological reports, or receipt of special education services are insufficient to demonstrate a current, severe functional limitation and trigger accommodations under the ADA and Section 504.

Accommodations are described as *outcome neutral* because they are designed to provide access rather than a specific grade or competency (Gordon & Keiser, 1998; Scott, 1997a, b). Indeed, outcome is not the measure of the effectiveness of an accommodation in postsecondary education (Heath Resource Center, 1995; Scott, 1997b).

SWD facing difficult academic demands or sanctions and expecting immediate relief are frustrated. However, in college, SWD are not guaranteed academic success and accommodations are not retroactive (Well & Hanebrink, 1997).

Effective accommodations are timely and meaningful in view of the manifestations of the disability in a specific context and permit SWD to participate equally with classmates (Heath Resource Center, 1995). There is scrupulous care not to apply accommodations that provide an unfair advantage over classmates. SWD are expected to monitor the effectiveness of accommodations and to notify the appropriate college representative if accommodations are not effective in providing access (Scott, 1997b).

For qualified SWD, accommodations are forged on the basis of an individualized inquiry about the specific functional limitations posed by the disability and the academic and access demands of a particular situation (Heyward, 1998; McGuire, 1998; Scott, 1997a, b; Wells & Hanebrink, 1997). To identify the need for accommodations for particular courses, disability advisors and SWD determine whether the manifestations of the disability in specific situations are sufficiently severe to warrant modifications. Because of the individualized nature of the inquiry, SWD may not necessarily receive accommodations for every course. Moreover, they must conform to all policies and procedures for obtaining accommodations and use them appropriately (Scott, 1997b). For example, those SWD who do not attend class because they receive the accommodation of a note taker do not lose the note taker, but will receive any penalties for nonattendance.

SWD expecting services which assure success in postsecondary education receive accommodations that permit access and foster development of independence, a major developmental goal for all college students. They do not receive personal services or devices such as tutoring, remedial classes, in-class supervisors or coaches, readers for personal use or study, computers or software, assistance with homework and projects such as word processing, care attendants, and reminders to take medicine, attend class, or turn in assignments. SWD do not receive assistance such as case managers, modifications of class work, or different grading standards that they enjoyed in high school (Scott, 1997a; Minskoff, 1996). If SWD require more extensive or intensive services at the postsecondary level, then SWD should seek out a special college for SWD or attend an institution with a for-fee special program for SWD.

BEST PRACTICES

Transitioning is a life-long process rather than an event with clearly demarcated boundaries. Thus, the transition from secondary education to postsecondary education must be based on progressive, planned strategies that began early in SWD's school careers. Minskoff (1994), for example, believes transition planning begins with special education and related services in elementary and secondary school and continues through postsecondary education and vocational training. Specifically, academic preparation and development of social and life skills, self-awareness and self-advocacy, and career knowledge and behaviors are key components of both transition efforts and successful postsecondary and employment outcomes for SWD.

In effect, postsecondary education becomes the period during which adolescents further develop skills, knowledge, and personal attributes leading to a satisfying quality of life, equal opportunity and treatment, and meaningful employment in adulthood. When combining this school-to-work orientation with postsecondary education, three themes in transition planning for college-bound SWD emerge: (a) assets and barriers facing students and adults with disabilities, (b) career planning, and (c) practical considerations.

Assets and Barriers Facing Students and Adults With Disabilities

According to Synatschk (1995) and Heath Resource Center (1995), postsecondary success for SWD, especially those with LD, is associated with high frustration tolerance, average to above average ability, perseverance despite periodic setbacks, and recognition of the need to study more and even take a longer time to earn their degrees than is required of students without disabilities. Preliminary findings about the academic success of students with LD or ADHD in college emphasize factors associated with an active learning style, including motivation, organization, high cognitive abilities, and use of multiple resources (Minskoff, Minskoff, Allsopp, & Hedrick, 2000).

Success in adults with disabilities is related to *self-control* and *self-determination*, including setting attainable goals consciously (*internal decisions*) and engaging in actions to realize those aspirations (*external manifestations*) (Ginsberg, Gerber, & Reiff, 1994; McGuire 1997). While aspiration is critical, persistence leads directly to success (Ginsberg et al., 1994). Discussion of traits of successful adults with LD is found in McGuire (1997) and Ginsberg et al. (1994).

In contrast, factors related to lack of academic progress by college SWD include poor motivation for academic success, primary interest in nonacademic areas such as athletics and fraternities, learned helplessness and reliance on accommodations, cognitive rigidity and/or disorganization, low cognitive and/or academic skills, emotional problems, and difficulty with prescribed medication (Minskoff et al., 2000; Vogel & Reder, 1998a, b). According to Scott (1997a) and Vogel and Reder (1998a), SWD often experience problems with independence, organization, and time management, even if these learning skills were acquired in high school. Further, they may deny personal responsibility for academic problems and transfer blame for academic failure to other individuals or to circumstances (Vogel & Reder, 1998a). Finally, even when they take ownership of problems, SWD may not analyze what went wrong and identify workable, replicable solutions (Vogel & Reder, 1998a). These characteristics are associated with a passive learning style and external locus of control.

School psychologists may understand that SWD enter postsecondary education with inadequate academic preparation and an unrealistic understanding of themselves as learners. Yet, because they lack instructional responsibilities, some question their own contribution to transition planning. However, school psychologists, by virtue of their training, expertise, and professional orientation, can assume the following roles: (a) participant, (b) advocate, and (c) program planner.

Although some IEPs indicate college as a post-graduation outcome, inspection of these documents reveals few concrete actions undertaken to assist SWD in attaining this goal. Unfortunately, it is often assumed that SWD who enroll in the general curriculum will, of necessity, acquire the skills and credits required for postsecondary education. But, as a SWD on a pre-college visit eloquently stated, "I've been screwed by my 504 plan!"

School psychologists can fill the gaps in academic preparation and self-awareness of SWD by actively participating in transition activities designed to help them enter college with comparable skills and attitudes to students without disabilities. They can assist SWD with selecting a curriculum that leads to acquisition of skills and knowledge taught in college-prep English, social studies, science, math, and foreign language, rather than agree that SWD should enroll in basic math, general science, and other classes that limit their academic skills and educational horizons. By using information from research to guide academic planning, school psychologists can help SWD identify classes that focus on the skills and knowledge needed for postsecondary education, rather than choose classes based on uncritical acceptance of educational vogues about self-esteem, foreign language learning by SWD, motivation, etc. They can teach SWD how to learn independently and generalize skills and knowledge acquired in one class to others. School psychologists can track progress in development of college-level academic knowledge and skills and teach SWD how to measure their own learning and skill levels.

These efforts hold the promise of helping SWD become academically competitive and develop self-esteem and motivation that reflect struggle and accomplishment. Thus, school psychologists can contribute to SWD's development of an active learning style.

School psychologists must advocate for SWD by reviewing the legal underpinnings of service delivery in postsecondary education and the attributes of successful SWD and adults and then using this information to assist SWD with learning about themselves; developing independence, self-advocacy, and self-determination; and emancipating themselves from unnecessary accommodations. They should insist that SWD take an active role in IEP and Individual Transition Plan (ITP) development, including discussing academic and transition goals and making decisions based on knowledge of personal strengths and weaknesses, skills, interests, and accommodation needs. They can assist SWD in developing skills in leadership, problem solving, and negotiation. By using information from psychological reports, functional assessment and classroom experience, school psychologists and SWD can discuss academic skills, psychological processes, learning style, career interests and goals, and other related factors and their practical implications. By providing information and fostering self-knowledge, school psychologists can facilitate development of realistic self-awareness and self-advocacy skills that will enable SWD to make informed decisions about themselves and their futures.

Recognizing that passive learners expect extensive accommodations and that IEPs often list an extraordinary number of interventions, school psychologists can wean SWD from assistance that is tangentially related to manifestations of the disability and/or perpetuates dependency on interventions. Instead, they clearly identify significant limitations posed by students' disabilities and recommend accommodations that provide access. Then, school psychologists can assist SWD with trying out accommodations and evaluating their effectiveness.

School psychologists can engage in program planning efforts that enable SWD to develop organization, time management, test taking, social, study, and active reading skills needed for postsecondary education and employment. They can promote skill development and acquisition of learning strategies in applied contexts. For example, they could adopt a model of strategy development such as that proposed by Minskoff et al. (2000). Their program moves SWD through a hierarchy of skills needed in postsecondary education, including (a) understanding course requirements listed on the syllabus, (b) time management, (c) study and test taking skills, and (d) tutoring based on generalization of learning strategies.

Career Planning

Postsecondary education is not the endpoint of life or learning. Instead, it demands comparable skills to those expected by employers, such as (a) interpersonal skills, including working as a team member; (b) communication skills, including speaking, writing, and listening; (c) computer skills, including keyboarding and finding and processing information; (d) problem solving, including the application of basic science; (e) math literacy, including reasoning, problem solving, basic statistics, and arithmetic calculations; (f) functional literacy; (g) knowledge of geography, history, and government; (h) cultural awareness, including foreign language and sensitivity to differences; (i) learning ability, including preparation for changing technology and job demands; and (j) personal management skills, including self esteem, goal setting, time management and motivation (McGuire, 1997; Rapp, 1997). Further, both postsecondary education and employment require the same personal attributes such as self-awareness, self-determination, personal responsibility, self-direction, independence, and self-reliance (Heath Resource Center, 1995; McGuire, 1997; Vogel & Reder, 1998b).

A career focus in postsecondary education requires self-awareness combined with informed, realistic goal setting and subsequent selection of a major leading to employment in an area consistent with skills, interests, attitudes, and behavior. Steps for selecting a career, and a major, involve (a) clear description of the skills and knowledge required by a particular job, (b) appraisal of the current skill levels and training needs, and (c) development of a plan to acquire missing skills or knowledge or to develop realistic career goals within a group of related careers (Minskoff, 1996).

School psychologists should foster implementation of career orientation beginning in elementary school by promoting acquisition of academic skills and development of job-related attitudes and abilities such as punctuality, cooperation, and responding appropriately to supervision and criticism. They can encourage active participation of state Vocational Rehabilitation counselors, secondary vocational teachers, and career counselors in IEP and ITP meetings. Additionally, school psychologists help foster work experiences, participation in experiential learning opportunities, and application of academic skills and job-related attitudes and behavior in a work setting while SWD are still enrolled in high school.

Practical Considerations

Special education is designed to meet the unique learning needs of children with disabilities and enable them to participate in the general curriculum, meet high standards for all students, and prepare for independent living, employment, and post-school activities. Postsecondary education is both an outcome and an intermediate step between secondary education and employment, but it is not a continuation of special education.

SWD are expected to compete on the proverbial level academic playing field with non-disabled students in postsecondary education. Consequently, questions such as what is a good school or an easy major for SWD or what accommodations are available to SWD at a particular institution erroneously focus on disability. Similarly, letters from special educators identifying interventions SWD will need to succeed in postsecondary education miss the key connection between access and accommodations.

Fortunately, most students attend in-state postsecondary institutions, usually within 50 miles of home (Habley, 1995; Henderson, 1999). Therefore, school psychologists are encouraged to meet with regional disability services providers to establish professional relationships and discuss academic expectations, admissions criteria, documentation requirements, the organization of various types of services on campus, provision of reasonable accommodations, and availability of special programs. Additionally, they should accumulate catalogs from nearby institutions and develop information sheets on various institutions and their requirements that are useful in transition planning. Finally, school psychologists could visit a college bookstore to examine the reading demand and length of college-level textbooks.

School psychologists are encouraged to develop ongoing group opportunities that help SWD explore differences between high school and postsecondary education. In preparation for these sessions, they can gather information about expectations and differences in requirements, personal responsibilities, and learning environments from multiple sources such as college catalogs, the A-LEC Home Page (2000), Brinckerhoff et al. (1993), and the Heath Resource Center. They can then use these materials to identify topics and content for group activities.

For example, secondary students spend 30 hours weekly in class and another 4 on homework for a total of 34 hours, most of which are devoted to very clear tasks. In contrast, college students enrolled in 12–15 hours of course work weekly are expected to spend 2–3 hours per course hour engaged in independent reading and study for a total of 36–60 hours. Most college-level study time is not designated for particular activities. Thus, lots of free time in college due to few in-class hours is an illusion for most students. The amount of independent learning time coupled with the need to spend more time studying presents a special challenge to SWD.

School psychologists make an enormous contribution to transitioning SWD from high school to postsecondary education when they provide a psychological evaluation at the end of secondary education, even though assessment may be resisted as expensive and unnecessary for academic planning. The psychological report must document that a disability as defined by the ADA and Section 504 exists, diagnose a condition on the basis of adult procedures and DSM IV criteria, identify substantial, functional limitations on life activities, describe how these limitations produce an important impact on the classroom or examinations, and recommend accommodations that provide access. Generic versions of documentation guidelines for postsecondary students with LD are available from www.ahead.org or www.ldonline.org. Specific documentation requirements are available from college disability services offices. However, irrespective of disability and postsecondary institution, criteria for documentation are sufficiently standard that a comprehensive psychological report is applicable across institutions.

SUMMARY

The following quotation summarizes the rationale for transition planning for SWD pursuing postsecondary education:

> In high school, you may have had special classes or resource room teachers for certain

subjects because of your disability. In college, you are not likely to find such special arrangements. You will be matched with your non-disabled peers, sitting side-by-side in the classroom and expected to compete academically. The instructors will assume that every student in the class has similar educational background and experience. If you come into your classes with less-than-complete academic preparation, you will be at an immediate disadvantage. *Now* is the time to review your preparation and make an honest appraisal of your current knowledge, skills, and abilities (Heath Resource Center, 1997, p. 5).

Current evidence indicates that SWD encounter multiple challenges in postsecondary education because of inadequate academic preparation and learning skills, limited knowledge of their legal rights and obligations, minimal career awareness, and underdeveloped personal/emotional traits. However, the skills and characteristics associated with success in adults with disabilities are considered teachable (Ginzberg, Gerber, & Reiff, 1994). Additionally, SWD who graduate from postsecondary education achieve equivalent outcomes when compared to their non-disabled peers. By engaging in behaviors associated with both traditional and alternative roles, school psychologists will participate in activities for and with SWD that promote successful transition to postsecondary education and realization of career and independent living goals articulated by the IDEA.

REFERENCES

A-LEC Home Page. (2000). How is college different from high school? Available from www.smu.edu/~alec/whyhighschool.html

Brinckerhoff, L. C., Shaw, S. F., & McGuire, J. M. (1993). Introduction. In L. Brinckerhoff, S. Shaw, and J. McGuire (Eds.), *Promoting postsecondary education for students with learning disabilities: A handbook for practitioners* (pp. 1–17). Austin, TX: PRO-ED.

Defur, S., & Reiff, H. B. (1994). Transition of youth with learning disabilities to adulthood: The secondary education foundation. In P. Gerber and H. Reiff (Eds.), *Learning disabilities in adulthood: Persisting problems and evolving issues* (pp. 99–110). Austin, TX: PRO-ED.

Ginsberg, R., Gerber, P. J., & Reiff, H. B. (1994). Employment success for adults with learning disabilities. In P. Gerber and H. Reiff (Eds.), *Learning disabilities in adulthood: Persisting problems and evolving issues* (pp. 204–213). Austin, TX: PRO-ED.

Gordon, M., & Keiser, S. (1998). Underpinnings. In M. Gordon and S. Keiser (Eds.), *Accommodations in higher education under the Americans with Disabilities Act (ADA): A no-nonsense guide for clinicians, educators, administrators, and lawyers* (pp. 3–19). New York: Guilford.

Habley, W. R. (1995). First-year students: The Year 2000. In M. Upcraft and G. Kramer (Eds.), *First-year academic advising: Patterns in the present, pathways to the future* (pp. 3–14). Columbia, SC: University of South Carolina.

Hameister, B. G. (1989). Disabled students. In M. L. Upcraft, J. N. Gardner, and Associates (Eds.), *The freshman year experience: Helping students survive and thrive in college* (pp. 340–351). San Francisco: Jossey-Bass.

Heath Resource Center. (1995). *Getting ready for college: Advising high school students with learning disabilities.* Washington, DC: American Council on Education.

Heath Resource Center. (1997). *How to choose a college: Guide for the student with a disability* (5th ed.). Washington, DC: American Council on Education.

Henderson, C. (1999). *1999 College freshmen with disabilities*. Washington, DC: American Council on Education (Heath Resource Center).

Heyward, S. (1998). *Disability and higher education: Guidance for Section 504 and ADA compliance*. Horsham, PA: LRP.

Horn, L., & Bobbitt, L. (1999). *Students with disabilities in postsecondary education: A profile of preparation, participation, and outcomes*. Washington, DC: U.S. Department of Education (NCES 1999-187).

Kincaid, J. M. (2000, July). *Mission impossible #3: The 10th anniversary of the ADA offers new challenges.*

Paper presented at the annual meeting of the Association on Higher Education and Disability, Kansas City, MO.

McGuire, J. M. (1997). Four-year college programs: Effective practices for developing employment skills. In P. Gerber and D. Brown (Eds.), *Learning disabilities and employment* (pp. 117–141). Austin, TX: PRO-ED.

McGuire, J. M. (1998). Educational accommodations: A university administrator's view. In M. Gordon and S. Keiser (Eds.), *Accommodations in higher education under the Americans with Disabilities Act (ADA): A no-nonsense guide for clinicians, educators, administrators, and lawyers* (pp. 20–45). New York: Guilford.

Minskoff, E. H. (1994). Post-secondary education and vocational training: Keys to success for adults with learning disabilities. In P. Gerber and H. Reiff (Eds.), *Learning disabilities in adulthood: Persisting problems and evolving issues* (pp. 111–120). Austin, TX: PRO-ED.

Minskoff, E. H. (1996). Improving employment outcomes for persons with learning disabilities. In N. Gregg, C. Hoy, and A. Gay (Eds.), *Adults with learning disabilities: Theoretical and practical perspectives* (pp. 277–297). New York: Guilford.

Minskoff, E. H., Minskoff, J. G., Allsopp, D., & Hedrick, L. (2000, July). *Students with LD and ADHD can be effective learners: Results of a model demonstration project.* Paper presented at the annual meeting of the Association on Higher Education and Disability, Kansas City, MO.

Rapp, R. H. (1997). Community college programs: Their role in preparing students with learning disabilities for employment. In P. Gerber and D. Brown (Eds.), *Learning disabilities and employment* (pp. 101–116). Austin, TX: PRO-ED.

Scott, S. S. (1994). Determining reasonable academic adjustments for college students with learning disabilities. *Journal of Learning Disabilities*, *27*, 403–412.

Scott, S. S. (1997a). Accommodating college students with learning disabilities: How much is enough? *Innovative Higher Education*, *22*, 85–99.

Scott, S. S. (1997b). Legal foundations. In S. S. Scott, S. Wells, and S. Hanebrink (Eds.), *Educating college students with disabilities: What academic and fieldwork educators need to know* (pp. 1–8). Bethesda, MD: American Occupational Therapy Association.

Synatschk, K. (1995). *College-bound students with learning disabilities: Assessment of readiness for academic success.* Available from www.ldonline.org

Tinto, V. (1993). *Leaving college: Rethinking the causes and cures of student attrition* (2nd ed.). Chicago: University of Chicago Press.

Upcraft, M. L., & Gardner, J. N. (1989). A comprehensive approach to enhancing freshman success. In M. L. Upcraft, J. N. Gardner, and Associates (Eds.), *The freshman year experience: Helping students survive and thrive in college* (pp. 1–12). San Francisco: Jossey-Bass.

Vogel, S. A., & Reder, S. (1998a). Adults with learning disabilities. In S. Vogel and S. Reder (Eds.), *Learning disabilities, literacy, and adult education* (pp. 5–28). Baltimore: Brookes.

Vogel, S. A., & Reder, S. (1998b). Educational attainment of adults with learning disabilities. In S. Vogel and S. Reder (Eds.), *Learning disabilities, literacy, and adult education* (pp. 43–68). Baltimore: Brookes.

Wells, S., & Hanebrink, S. (1997). Auxiliary aids, academic adjustments, and reasonable accommodations. In S. S. Scott, S. Wells, and S. Hanebrink (Eds.), *Educating college students with disabilities: What academic and fieldwork educators need to know* (pp. 37–51). Bethesda, MD: American Occupational Therapy Association.

ANNOTATED BIBLIOGRAPHY

Gordon, M., & Keiser, S. (Eds.). (1998). *Accommodations in higher education under the Americans with Disabilities Act (ADA): A no-nonsense guide for clinicians, educators, administrators, and lawyers*. New York: Guilford.
This book contains information about implementation of the ADA in postsecondary environments, documentation and accommodation of disability, and discussion of several disabling conditions. It provides an overview and guidelines for postsecondary services that would be help-

ful for professionals preparing secondary students for higher education.

Heath Resource Center. Washington, DC: American Council on Education. (800-544-3284 V/TTY or www. heath-resource-center.org)
The Heath Resource Center, a clearinghouse on postsecondary education of SWD, provides free materials such as *Getting ready for college: Advising students with LD* (GR); *How to choose a college: Guide for the student with a disability* (CAC); *College freshmen with disabilities: A biennial statistical profile* (CF); and *Creating options: A resource on financial aid for students with disabilities* (FA).

Heyward, S. (1998). *Disability and higher education: Guidance for Section 504 and ADA compliance*. Horsham, PA: LRP.
This manual reviews basic differences among the IDEA, Section 504, and the ADA and discusses application of the ADA to admissions, documentation, accommodation, and other topics related to postsecondary education. It includes court citations, OCR rulings, case examples, and red flags making it informative, engaging, and useful.

Scott, S. S. (1994). Determining reasonable academic adjustments for college students with learning disabilities. *Journal of Learning Disabilities*, 27, 403–412.

Scott, S. S., Wells, S, & Hanebrink, S. (Eds.). (1997). *Educating college students with disabilities: What academic and fieldwork educators need to know*. Bethesda, MD: American Occupational Therapy Association.
The article describes the process, procedures, and legal criteria postsecondary institutions follow to determine eligibility for accommodations and provides a clear, comprehensive overview of service delivery in postsecondary education. Trainers will find the book useful in accommodating SWD in school psychology programs.

IV.

Appendices

I Appendix I — NASP Principles for Professional Ethics

I. INTRODUCTION

The formal principles that elucidate the proper conduct of a professional school psychologist are known as *Ethics*. By virtue of joining the Association, each NASP member agrees to abide by the *Ethics*, acting in a manner that shows respect for human dignity and assuring a high quality of professional service. Although ethical behavior is an individual responsibility, it is in the interest of an association to adopt and enforce a code of ethics. If done properly, members will be guided toward appropriate behavior, and public confidence in the profession will be enhanced. Additionally, a code of ethics should provide due process procedures to protect members from potential abuse of the code. The NASP *Principles for Professional Ethics* have been written to accomplish these goals.

The principles in this manual are based on the assumptions that 1) school psychologists will act as advocates for their students/clients, and 2) at the very least, school psychologists will do no harm. These assumptions necessitate that school psychologists "speak up" for the needs and rights of their students/clients even at times when it may be difficult to do so. School psychologists also are constrained to provide only those services for which they have acquired an acknowledged level of experience, training, and competency. Beyond these basic premises, judgment is required to apply the ethical principles to the fluid and expanding interactions between school and community.

There are many different sources of advice for the proper way to behave; local policies, state laws, federal laws, credentialing standards, professional association position statements, and books that recommend "Best Practices" are just a few. Given one's employment situation and the array of recommendations, events may develop in which the ethical course of action is unclear. The Association will seek to enforce the Ethical Principles with its members. NASP's *Guidelines for the Provision of School Psychological Services* are typically not enforced, although all members should work toward achieving the hallmarks of quality services delivery that are described therein. Similarly, "position statements" and "best practices" documents are not adjudicated. The guidance of the *Ethical Principles* is intentionally broad to make it more enduring than other documents that reflect short-term opinions about specific actions shaped by local events, popular trends, or recent developments in the field. The member must use judgment to infer the situation-specific rule from the general ethical principle. The lack of a specific reference to a particular action does not indicate permission or provide a defense against a charge of unethical practice. (For example, the document frequently refers to a school psychologist's relationships with a hypothetical "student/client." Because school psychologists work in a wide variety of settings, there is no single term that neatly identifies the "other" individual in the professional relationship. Therefore, one should apply *Ethical Principles* in all professional situations, realizing that one is not released from responsibility simply because another individual is not strictly a "student" or a "client.")

The principles in this manual are organized into several sections as a result of editorial judgment. Therefore, principles discussed in one section may also apply to other sections. Every school psychologist, regardless of position (e.g., practitioner, researcher, university trainer, supervisor, state or federal consultant, administrator of psychological services) or setting (e.g., public or private school, community agency, hospital, university, private practice) should reflect upon the theme represented in each ethical principle to determine its application to her or his individual situation. For example, although a given principle may specifically discuss responsibilities toward "clients," the intent is that the standards would also apply to supervisees, trainees, and research participants. At times, the *Ethics* may require a higher standard of behavior than the prevailing policies and pertinent laws. Under such conditions, members should adhere to the *Ethics*. Ethical behavior may occasionally be forbidden by policy or law, in which case members are expected to declare their dilemma and work to bring the discrepant regulations into compliance with the *Ethics*. To obtain additional assistance in applying these principles to a particular setting, a school psychologist should consult with experienced school psychologists and seek advice from the National Association of School Psychologists or the state school psychology association.

Throughout the *Principles for Professional Ethics*, it is assumed that, depending on the role and setting of the school psychologist, the client could include children, parents, teachers and other school personnel, other professionals, trainees, or supervisees. Procedural guidelines for filing an ethical complaint and the adjudication of ethical complaints are available from the NASP office or website (*www.naspweb.org*).

II. PROFESSIONAL COMPETENCY

A. General

1. School psychologists recognize the strengths and limitations of their training and experience, engaging only in practices for which they are qualified. They enlist the assistance of other specialists in supervisory, consultative, or referral roles as appropriate in providing services. They must continually obtain additional training and education to provide the best possible services to children, families, schools, communities, trainees, and supervisees.

2. Competence levels, education, training, and experience are declared and accurately represented to clients in a professional manner.

3. School psychologists do not use affiliations with persons, associations, or institutions to imply a level of professional competence that exceeds that which has actually been achieved.

4. School psychologists engage in continuing professional development. They remain current regarding developments in research, training, and professional practices that benefit children, families, and schools.

5. School psychologists refrain from any activity in which their personal problems or conflicts may interfere with professional effectiveness. Competent assistance is sought to alleviate conflicts in professional relationships.

6. School psychologists know the *Principles for Professional Ethics* and thoughtfully apply them to situations within their employment setting or practice. Ignorance or misapplication of an ethical principle is not a reasonable defense against a charge of unethical behavior.

III. PROFESSIONAL RELATIONSHIPS

A. General

1. School psychologists are committed to the application of their professional expertise for the purpose of promoting improvement in the quality of life for children, their families, and the school community. This objective is pursued in ways that protect the dignity and rights of those involved. School psychologists accept responsibility for the appropriateness of their professional practices.

2. School psychologists respect all persons and are sensitive to physical, mental, emotional, political, economic, social, cultural, ethnic and racial characteristics, gender, sexual orientation, and religion.

3. School psychologists in all settings maintain professional relationships with children, parents, and the school community. Consequently, parents and children are to be fully informed about all relevant aspects of school psychological services in advance. The explanation should take into account language and cultural differences, cognitive capabilities, developmental level, and age so that it may be understood by the child, parent, or guardian.

4. School psychologists attempt to resolve situations in which there are divided or conflicting

interests in a manner that is mutually beneficial and protects the rights of all parties involved.

5. School psychologists are responsible for the direction and nature of their personal loyalties or objectives. When these commitments may influence a professional relationship, school psychologists inform all concerned persons of relevant issues in advance, including, when applicable, their direct supervisor for consideration of reassignment of responsibilities.

6. School psychologists do not exploit clients through professional relationships or condone these actions in their colleagues. No individuals, including children, clients, employees, colleagues, trainees, parents, supervisees, and research participants, will be exposed to deliberate comments, gestures, or physical contacts of a sexual nature. School psychologists do not harass or demean others based on personal characteristics. School psychologists do not engage in sexual relationships with their students, supervisees, trainees, or past or present clients.

7. Dual relationships with clients are avoided. Namely, personal and business relations with clients may cloud one's judgment. School psychologists are aware of these situations and avoid them whenever possible.

8. School psychologists attempt to resolve suspected detrimental or unethical practices on an informal level. If informal efforts are not productive, the appropriate professional organization is contacted for assistance, and procedures established for questioning ethical practice are followed:

   a. The filing of an ethical complaint is a serious matter. It is intended to improve the behavior of a colleague that is harmful to the profession and/or the public. Therefore, school psychologists make every effort to discuss the ethical principles with other professionals who may be in violation.

   b. School psychologists enter into the complaint process thoughtfully and with concern for the well-being of all parties involved. They do not file or encourage the filing of an ethics complaint that is frivolous or motivated by revenge.

   c. Some situations may be particularly difficult to analyze from an ethical perspective. School psychologists consult ethical standards from related fields and seek assistance from knowledgeable, experienced school psychologists and relevant state/national associations to ascertain an appropriate course of action.

   d. School psychologists document specific instances of suspected ethical violations (i.e., date, time, relevant details) as well as attempts to resolve these violations.

9. School psychologists respect the confidentiality of information obtained during their professional work. Information is revealed only with the informed consent of the child, or the child's parent or legal guardian, except in those situations in which failure to release information would result in clear danger to the child or others. Obsolete confidential information will be shredded or otherwise destroyed before placement in recycling bins or trash receptacles.

10. School psychologists discuss confidential information only for professional purposes and only with persons who have a legitimate need to know.

11. School psychologists inform children and other clients of the limits of confidentiality at the outset of establishing a professional relationship.

B. Students

1. School psychologists understand the intimate nature of consultation, assessment, and direct service. They engage only in professional practices that maintain the dignity and integrity of children and other clients.

2. School psychologists explain important aspects of their professional relationships in a clear, understandable manner that is appropriate to the child's or other client's age and ability to understand. The explanation includes the reason why

services were requested, who will receive information about the services provided, and the possible outcomes.

3. When a child initiates services, school psychologists understand their obligation to respect the rights of a child to initiate, participate in, or discontinue services voluntarily (See III-C-2 for further clarification). When another party initiates services, the school psychologist will make every effort to secure voluntary participation of the child.

4. Recommendations for program changes or additional services will be discussed with appropriate individuals, including any alternatives that may be available.

C. Parents, Legal Guardians, and Appointed Surrogates

1. School psychologists explain all services to parents in a clear, understandable manner. They strive to propose a set of options that takes into account the values and capabilities of each parent. Service provision by interns, practicum students, or other trainees should be explained and agreed to in advance.

2. School psychologists recognize the importance of parental support and seek to obtain that support by assuring that there is direct parent contact prior to seeing the child on an ongoing basis. (Emergencies and "drop-in" self-referrals will require parental notification as soon as possible. The age and circumstances under which children may seek services without parental consent varies greatly; be certain to comply with III-D-5.) School psychologists secure continuing parental involvement by a frank and prompt reporting to the parent of findings and progress that conforms to the limits of previously determined confidentiality.

3. School psychologists encourage and promote parental participation in designing services provided to their children. When appropriate, this includes linking interventions between the school and the home, tailoring parental involvement to the skills of the family, and helping parents gain the skills needed to help their children.

4. School psychologists respect the wishes of parents who object to school psychological services and attempt to guide parents to alternative community resources.

5. School psychologists discuss with parents the recommendations and plans for assisting their children. The discussion includes alternatives associated with each set of plans, which show respect for the ethnic/cultural values of the family. The parents are informed of sources of help available at school and in the community.

6. School psychologists discuss the rights of parents and children regarding creation, modification, storage, and disposal of confidential materials that will result from the provision of school psychological services.

D. Community

1. School psychologists also are citizens, thereby accepting the same responsibilities and duties as any member of society. They are free to pursue individual interests, except to the degree that those interests compromise professional responsibilities.

2. School psychologists may act as individual citizens to bring about social change in a lawful manner. Individual actions should not be presented as, or suggestive of, representing the field of school psychology or the Association.

3. As employees or employers, in public or independent practice domains, school psychologists do not engage in or condone practices that discriminate against children, other clients, or employees (if applicable) based on race, disability, age, gender, sexual orientation, religion, national origin, economic status, or native language.

4. School psychologists avoid any action that could violate or diminish the civil and legal rights of children and other clients.

5. School psychologists adhere to federal, state, and local laws and ordinances governing their prac-

tice and advocacy efforts. If regulations conflict with ethical guidelines, school psychologists seek to resolve such conflict through positive, respected, and legal channels, including advocacy efforts involving public policy.

E. Other Professionals

1. To best meet the needs of children and other clients, school psychologists cooperate with other professional disciplines in relationships based on mutual respect.

2. School psychologists recognize the competence of other professionals. They encourage and support the use of all resources to best serve the interests of children and other clients.

3. School psychologists should strive to explain their field and their professional competencies, including roles, assignments, and working relationships to other professionals.

4. School psychologists cooperate and coordinate with other professionals and agencies with the rights and needs of children and other clients in mind. If a child or other client is receiving similar services from another professional, school psychologists promote coordination of services.

5. The child or other client is referred to another professional for services when a condition or need is identified which is outside the professional competencies or scope of the school psychologist.

6. When transferring the intervention responsibility for a child or other client to another professional, school psychologists ensure that all relevant and appropriate individuals, including the child/client when appropriate, are notified of the change and reasons for the change.

7. When school psychologists suspect the existence of detrimental or unethical practices by a member of another profession, informal contact is made with that person to express the concern. If the situation cannot be resolved in this manner, the appropriate professional organization is contacted for assistance in determining the procedures established by that profession for examining the practices in question.

8. School psychologists who employ, supervise, or train other professionals, accept the obligation to provide continuing professional development. They also provide appropriate working conditions, fair and timely evaluation, and constructive consultation.

F. School Psychologist Trainees and Interns

1. School psychologists who supervise interns are responsible for all professional practices of the supervisees. They assure children and other clients and the profession that the intern is adequately supervised as designated by the practice guidelines and training standards for school psychologists.

2. School psychologists who conduct or administer training programs provide trainees and prospective trainees with accurate information regarding program sponsorships/ endorsements/accreditation, goals/objectives, training processes and requirements, and likely outcomes and benefits.

3. School psychologists who are faculty members in colleges or universities or who supervise clinical or field placements apply these ethical principles in all work with school psychology trainees. In addition, they promote the ethical practice of trainees by providing specific and comprehensive instruction, feedback, and mentoring.

4. School psychology faculty members and clinical or field supervisors uphold recognized standards of the profession by providing training related to high quality, responsible, and research-based school psychology services. They provide accurate and objective information in their teaching and training activities; identify any limitations in information; and acknowledge disconfirming data, alternative hypotheses, and explanations.

5. School psychology faculty members and clinical or field supervisors develop and use evaluation practices for trainees that are objective, accurate, and fair.

IV. PROFESSIONAL PRACTICES—GENERAL PRINCIPLES

A. Advocacy

1. School psychologists typically serve multiple clients including children, parents, and systems. When the school psychologist is confronted with conflicts between client groups, the primary client is considered to be the child. When the child is not the primary client, the individual or group of individuals who sought the assistance of the school psychologist is the primary client.

2. School psychologists consider children and other clients to be their primary responsibility, acting as advocates for their rights and welfare. If conflicts of interest between clients are present, the school psychologist supports conclusions that are in the best interest of the child. When choosing a course of action, school psychologists take into account the rights of each individual involved and the duties of school personnel.

3. School psychologists' concerns for protecting the rights and welfare of children are communicated to the school administration and staff as the top priority in determining services.

4. School psychologists understand the public policy process to assist them in their efforts to advocate for children, parents, and systems.

B. Service Delivery

1. School psychologists are knowledgeable of the organization, philosophy, goals, objectives, and methodologies of the setting in which they are employed.

2. School psychologists recognize that an understanding of the goals, processes, and legal requirements of their particular workplace is essential for effective functioning within that setting.

3. School psychologists attempt to become integral members of the client service systems to which they are assigned. They establish clear roles for themselves within that system.

4. School psychologists who provide services to several different groups may encounter situations in which loyalties are conflicted. As much as possible, the stance of the school psychologist is made known in advance to all parties to prevent misunderstandings.

5. School psychologists promote changes in their employing agencies and community service systems that will benefit their clients.

C. Assessment and Intervention

1. School psychologists maintain the highest standard for educational and psychological assessment and direct and indirect interventions.

   a. In conducting psychological, educational, or behavioral evaluations or in providing therapy, counseling, or consultation services, due consideration is given to individual integrity and individual differences.

   b. School psychologists respect differences in age, gender, sexual orientation, and socioeconomic, cultural, and ethnic backgrounds. They select and use appropriate assessment or treatment procedures, techniques, and strategies. Decision-making related to assessment and subsequent interventions is primarily data-based.

2. School psychologists are knowledgeable about the validity and reliability of their instruments and techniques, choosing those that have up-to-date standardization data and are applicable and appropriate for the benefit of the child.

3. School psychologists use multiple assessment methods such as observations, background information, and information from other professionals, to reach comprehensive conclusions.

4. School psychologists use assessment techniques, counseling and therapy procedures, consultation techniques, and other direct and indirect service methods that the profession considers to be responsible, research-based practice.

5. School psychologists do not condone the use of psychological or educational assessment tech-

niques, or the misuse of the information these techniques provide, by unqualified persons in any way, including teaching, sponsorship, or supervision.

6. School psychologists develop interventions that are appropriate to the presenting problems and are consistent with data collected. They modify or terminate the treatment plan when the data indicate the plan is not achieving the desired goals.

7. School psychologists use current assessment and intervention strategies that assist in the promotion of mental health in the children they serve.

D. Reporting Data and Conference Results

1. School psychologists ascertain that information about children and other clients reaches only authorized persons.

   a. School psychologists adequately interpret information so that the recipient can better help the child or other clients.

   b. School psychologists assist agency recipients to establish procedures to properly safeguard confidential material.

2. School psychologists communicate findings and recommendations in language readily understood by the intended recipient. These communications describe potential consequences associated with the proposals.

3. School psychologists prepare written reports in such form and style that the recipient of the report will be able to assist the child or other clients. Reports should emphasize recommendations and interpretations; unedited computer-generated reports, pre-printed "check-off " or "fill-in-the-blank" reports, and reports that present only test scores or global statements regarding eligibility for special education without specific recommendations for intervention are seldom useful. Reports should include an appraisal of the degree of confidence that could be assigned to the information. Alterations of previously released reports should be done only by the original author.

4. School psychologists review all of their written documents for accuracy, signing them only when correct. Interns and practicum students are clearly identified as such, and their work is co-signed by the supervising school psychologist. In situations in which more than one professional participated in the data collection and reporting process, school psychologists assure that sources of data are clearly identified in the written report.

5. School psychologists comply with all laws, regulations, and policies pertaining to the adequate storage and disposal of records to maintain appropriate confidentiality of information.

E. Use of Materials and Technology

1. School psychologists maintain test security, preventing the release of underlying principles and specific content that would undermine the use of the device. School psychologists are responsible for the security requirements specific to each instrument used.

2. School psychologists obtain written prior consent or they remove identifying data presented in public lectures or publications.

3. School psychologists do not promote or encourage inappropriate use of computer-generated test analyses or reports. In accordance with this principle, a school psychologist would not offer an unedited computer report as his or her own writing or use a computer-scoring system for tests in which he or she has no training. They select scoring and interpretation services on the basis of accuracy and professional alignment with the underlying decision rules.

4. School psychologists maintain full responsibility for any technological services used. All ethical and legal principles regarding confidentiality, privacy, and responsibility for decisions apply to the school psychologist and cannot be transferred to equipment, software companies, or data-processing departments.

5. Technological devices should be used to improve the quality of client services. School psychologists will resist applications of technology that ultimately reduce the quality of service.

6. To ensure confidentiality, student/client records are not transmitted electronically without a guarantee of privacy. In line with this principle, a receiving FAX machine must be in a secure location and operated by employees cleared to work with confidential files, and e-mail messages must be encrypted or else stripped of all information that identifies the student/client.

7. School psychologists do not accept any form of remuneration in exchange for data from their client data base without informed consent.

F. Research, Publication, and Presentation

1. When designing and implementing research in schools, school psychologists choose topics and employ research methodology, subject selection techniques, data-gathering methods, and analysis and reporting techniques that are grounded in sound research practice. School psychologists clearly identify their level of training and graduate degree on all communications to research participants.

2. Prior to initiating research, school psychologists working in agencies without review committees should have at least one other colleague, preferably a school psychologist, review the proposed methods.

3. School psychologists follow all legal procedures when conducting research, including following procedures related to informed consent, confidentiality, privacy, protection from harm or risks, voluntary participation, and disclosure of results to participants. School psychologists demonstrate respect for the rights of and well-being of research participants.

4. In publishing reports of their research, school psychologists provide discussion of limitations of their data and acknowledge existence of disconfirming data, as well as alternate hypotheses and explanations of their findings.

5. School psychologists take particular care with information presented through various impersonal media (e.g., radio, television, public lectures, popular press articles, promotional materials.). Recipients should be informed that the information does not result from or substitute for a professional consultation. The information should be based on research and experience within the school psychologist's recognized sphere of competence. The statements should be consistent with these ethical principles and should not mistakenly represent the field of school psychology or the Association.

6. School psychologists uphold copyright laws in their publications and presentations and obtain permission from authors and copyright holders to reproduce other publications or materials. School psychologists recognize that federal law protects the rights of copyright holders of published works and authors of non-published materials.

7. When publishing or presenting research or other work, school psychologists do not plagiarize the works or ideas of others and acknowledge sources and assign credit to those whose ideas are reflected.

8. School psychologists do not publish or present fabricated or falsified data or results in their publications and presentations.

9. School psychologists make available data or other information upon which conclusions and claims reported in publications and presentations are based, provided that the data are needed to address a legitimate concern or need and that the confidentiality and other rights of all research participants are protected.

10. If errors are discovered after the publication or presentation of research and other information, school psychologists make efforts to correct errors by publishing errata, retractions, or corrections.

11. School psychologists accurately reflect the contributions of authors and other individuals in

publications and presentations. Authorship credit and the order in which authors are listed are based on the relative contributions of the individual authors. Authorship credit is given only to individuals who have made substantial professional contributions to the research, publication, or presentation.

12. School psychologists only publish data or other information that make original contributions to the professional literature. School psychologists do not publish the same findings in two or more publications and do not duplicate significant portions of their own previous publications without permission of copyright holders.

13. School psychologists who participate in reviews of manuscripts, proposals, and other materials for consideration for publication and presentation respect the confidentiality and proprietary rights of the authors. School psychologists who review professional materials limit their use of the materials to the activities relevant to the purposes of the professional review. School psychologists who review professional materials do not communicate the identity of the author, quote from the materials, or duplicate or circulate copies of the materials without the author's permission.

V. PROFESSIONAL PRACTICE SETTINGS—INDEPENDENT PRACTICE

A. Relationship with Employers

1. Some school psychologists are employed in a variety of settings, organizational structures, and sectors and, as such, may create a conflict of interest. School psychologists operating in these different settings recognize the importance of ethical standards and the separation of roles and take full responsibility for protecting and completely informing the consumer of all potential concerns.

2. School psychologists dually employed in independent practice and in a school district may not accept any form of remuneration from clients who are entitled to the same service provided by the school district employing the school psychologist. This includes children who attend the nonpublic schools within the school psychologist's district.

3. School psychologists in independent practice have an obligation to inform parents of any school psychological services available to them at no cost from the public or private schools prior to delivering such services for remuneration.

4. School psychologists working in both independent practice and employed by school districts conduct all independent practice outside of the hours of contracted public employment.

5. School psychologists engaged in independent practice do not use tests, materials, equipment, facilities, secretarial assistance, or other services belonging to the public sector employer unless approved in advance by the employer.

B. Service Delivery

1. School psychologists conclude a financial agreement in advance of service delivery.

   a. School psychologists ensure to the best of their ability that the client clearly understands the agreement.

   b. School psychologists neither give nor receive any remuneration for referring children and other clients for professional services.

2. School psychologists in independent practice adhere to the conditions of a contract until service thereunder has been performed, the contract has been terminated by mutual consent, or the contract has otherwise been legally terminated.

3. School psychologists in independent practice prevent misunderstandings resulting from their recommendations, advice, or information. Most often, direct consultation between the school psychologist in private practice and the school psychologist responsible for the student in the public sector will resolve minor differences of opinion without unnecessarily confusing the parents, yet keep the best interests of the student or client in mind.

4. Personal diagnosis and therapy are not given by means of public lectures, newspaper columns, magazine articles, radio and television programs, or mail. Any information shared through mass media activities is general in nature and is openly declared to be so.

C. Announcements/Advertising

1. Appropriate announcement of services, advertising, and public media statements may be necessary for school psychologists in independent practice. Accurate representations of training, experience, services provided, and affiliation are done in a restrained manner. Public statements must be based on sound and accepted theory, research, and practice.

2. Listings in telephone directories are limited to the following: name/names, highest relevant degree, state certification/licensure status, national certification status, address, telephone number, brief identification of major areas of practice, office hours, appropriate fee information, foreign languages spoken, policy regarding third-party payments, and license number.

3. Announcements of services by school psychologists in independent practice are made in a formal, professional manner using the guidelines of V-C-2. Clear statements of purposes with unequivocal descriptions of the experiences to be provided are given. Education, training, and experience of all staff members are appropriately specified.

4. School psychologists in independent practice may use brochures in the announcement of services. The brochures may be sent to other professionals, schools, business firms, governmental agencies, and other similar organizations.

5. Announcements and advertisements of the availability of publications, products, and services for sale are professional and factual.

6. School psychologists in independent practice do not directly solicit clients for individual diagnosis, therapy, and for the provision of other school psychological services.

7. School psychologists do not compensate in any manner a representative of the press, radio, or television in return for personal professional publicity in a news item.

PROCEDURAL GUIDELINES FOR THE ADJUDICATION OF ETHICAL COMPLAINTS

Revised in 1997

Section I. Responsibility and Function

The Ethical and Professional Standards Committee shall be responsible for developing and maintaining a clearly defined position for the Association regarding the ethical and professional conduct principles to be adhered to by its members and also the members of the National School Psychology Certification System (NSPCS). The major area of particular ethical concern to the Committee will be that of the protection and general well-being of individuals served by school psychologists, in schools and in private practice, and in institutions or agencies through which the service is rendered. The Committee is further charged to study and make recommendations to the Executive Council when it is alleged that a NASP or NSPCS member has failed to follow the ethical principles of the Association.

Members of the Ethical and Professional Standards Committee recognize that their role is an extremely important one, involving the rights of many people, the reputation of the profession and the careers of individual professionals. They bear a heavy responsibility because their recommendations may alter the lives of others. Therefore, they must be alert to personal, social, organizational, financial or political situations or pressures that might lead to misuse of their influence. The Ethical and Professional Standards committee shall assure the responsible use of all information obtained in the course of an inquiry or investigation. The objective with regard to the individual shall, whenever possible, be constructive, rather than punitive in character.

The function of the Committee in investigating complaints of alleged ethical misconduct involves obtaining a thorough and impartial account of the behaviors or incidents in order to be able to evaluate the character of the behaviors in question. When responding to complaints, members of the Ethics and

Professional Standards Committee have the responsibility to consider the competency of the complainant, to act in an unbiased manner, to work expeditiously, and to safeguard the confidentiality of the Committee's activities. Committee members and their designees have the added responsibility to follow procedures which safeguard the rights of all individuals involved in the complaint process.

Section II. Scope and Authority

The Ethical and Professional Standards Committee shall address issues of ethical misconduct in an investigatory, advisory, educative and/or remedial role. What constitutes ethical misconduct shall be determined on the basis of the provisions of the NASP *Principles for Professional Ethics* and any published advisory opinions that from time to time are developed by the Ethical and Professional standards Committee. In applying the Principles, the authorized opinions of those charged by NASP with the administration and interpretation of the ethical principles shall be binding on all NASP members, individuals who hold a certificate issued by the National School Psychology Certification Board (NSPCB), and on the members of state associations affiliated with NASP.

When investigating and/or responding to a complaint or inquiry, the Ethical and Professional Standards Committee shall conduct itself in a manner consistent with the Bylaws of the Association and the NASP *Principles for Professional Ethics* and shall also be bound by these procedures. The Ethical and Professional Standards Committee shall endeavor to settle cases informally, recommend disciplinary action when unethical conduct has occurred, report regularly to the Delegate Assembly on its activities and shall revise and amend (subject to ratification by the Delegate Assembly) the NASP Principles and these procedures in a timely manner. The Association may at the recommendation of the Ethical and Professional Standards Committee, and in accordance with the Bylaws of the Association, expel a NASP member. The Ethical and Professional Standards committee will also issue a recommendation to the NSPCB regarding charges filed against any nationally certified school psychologist.

When a complaint is received about a non-member, the Ethical and Professional Standards Committee shall respond only if the individual complained against is a member of the National School Psychology Certification System. Otherwise, the committee may act only in an advisory or educative fashion and shall have no authority to investigate the case or to discipline the individual in question.

Complaints that address concerns about professional standards, organizations, employers and the like, shall be referred to the Ethical and Professional Standards Committee. Nevertheless, it should be recognized that in situations where an individual school psychologist is being coerced to behave unethically, he/she bears certain ethical responsibilities and to fail to take appropriate action, e.g., refusing to behave unethically, could eventuate in charges of misconduct against the individual psychologist involved. However, as a rule such "standards" concerns would not fall under the purview of this complaint process.

Complaints received by the Ethical and Professional Standards Committee shall be reviewed and judged on the basis of the *Principles for Professional Ethics* in force at the time of the alleged misconduct. Investigation and adjudication of ethical complaints shall be on the basis of the "Procedural Guidelines for the Adjudication of Ethical Complaints" in force at the time the complaint is received by the Committee.

Section III. Receipt and Acknowledgment of Complaints and Inquiries

A. The Ethical and Professional Standards committee shall recognize and respond to all complaints and inquiries from any responsible individual or group of individuals in accordance with these procedures. The individual who petitions the Committee (hereinafter referred to as the complainant) need not be a member of NASP or the affiliated state association. Anonymous letters and phone calls will not be recognized. Complaints by members which are judged by the committee to be frivolous or revengeful may be cause for action against the complainant.

B. An oral complaint or inquiry may be informally handled, referred elsewhere when appropriate, or an Ethical and Professional Standards Committee chairperson may request that the complaint be formally submitted in writing. Only written statements expressing the details of the alleged misconduct will be accepted for action. Such written statements shall be signed by the complainant and should state, in as much detail as practicable, the facts upon which the complaint is based. NASP will maintain appropriate records regarding the number and nature of all written complaints filed against NASP members and members of the National School Psychology Certification System.All the correspondence, records and activities of the Ethical and Professional Standards Committee shall remain confidential.

C. Within 15 days of receipt of a written statement outlining the details of the alleged misconduct, the chairpersons of the Ethical and Professional Standards Committee shall do the following:

1. Determine if the individual against whom the complaint is made (hereinafter referred to as the respondent), is a member of NASP or an NCSP. If the respondent is not a member of NASP or an NCSP, the complainant shall be so advised and when appropriate, referred to other agencies and/or associations who would have authority in the matter.

2. If the respondent is a member of NASP or an NCSP, the Ethical and Professional Standards Committee chairpersons, with any advisory opinions deemed necessary, shall review the complaint. If it is determined that the alleged misconduct, even if true, would not constitute an actual violation of the NASP Principles, a chairperson shall notify the complainant.

3. If the information obtained from the complainant is insufficient to make a determination regarding the alleged misconduct, the chairpersons may send a written request to the complainant, asking for clarification and/or additional information as would be needed to make such a determination.

4. If it is determined that the alleged misconduct, if substantiated, would constitute an actual violation of NASP Principles, the Ethical and Professional Standards Committee chairperson shall direct a letter to and advise the complainant that the allegation will be investigated by the Committee. The complainant shall be asked to sign a release, authorizing that his/her name be revealed to the respondent.

5. If the complainant refuses to permit his/her identity to be made known to the respondent, such refusal will serve as a basis for forfeiting the complaint process. However, the Ethical and Professional Standards Committee may proceed on its own volition when a member appears to have engaged in ethical misconduct that tends to injure the Association or to adversely affect its reputation, or that is clearly inconsistent with or destructive of the goals and objectives of the Association.

Section IV. Conduct of an Informal Inquiry

A. Within 15 days of receipt of the signed release, the Ethical and Professional Standards Committee shall inform the respondent, in writing, with the envelope marked "confidential," that a complaint has been filed against him/her. This letter shall describe the nature of the complaint, indicate the principle(s) which appear to have been violated, and request the respondent's cooperation in obtaining a full picture of the circumstances which led to the allegations. A copy of the NASP *Principles for Professional Ethics*, these procedures, and any pertinent advisory opinions of the Ethical and Professional Standards committee shall also be enclosed. Ordinarily the respondent shall be informed of the name of the complainant, when written permission to do so has been obtained. (See Section III, C-5 above, for exception.)

B. The respondent shall be asked to provide a written statement outlining his/her view of the situation in order that the Committee may be cognizant of all relevant aspects of the case.

C. Whenever possible, the Ethical and Professional Standards Committee shall attempt to resolve differences privately and informally through further correspondence with all parties involved. An attempt shall be made to bring about an adjustment through meditative efforts in the interest of correcting a general situation or settling the particular issues between the parties involved.

D. If the respondent does not respond to the original inquiry within 30 days, a follow-up letter shall be sent to the respondent by registered or certified mail, marked "confidential," with a return receipt requested.

E. If the respondent refuses to reply to the Committee's inquiry or otherwise cooperate with the Committee, the Committee may continue its investigation, noting in the record the circumstances of the respondent's failure to cooperate. The Committee shall also inform the respondent that his/her lack of cooperation may result in action which could eventuate in his/her being dropped from membership in the Association.

F. As a rule, if the complainant wishes to withdraw the complaint, the inquiry is terminated, except in extreme cases where the Committee feels the issues in the case are of such importance as to warrant completing the investigation in its own right and in the interest of the public welfare or that of the Association. (See Section III, C-5.)

G. The Association will not recognize a respondent's resignation from membership while there is a complaint pending before the Ethical and Professional Standards Committee or before an ethics committee of a state association unless he/she submits an affidavit stating that:

1. The resignation is free and voluntary;

2. He/she is aware of a pending investigation into allegations of misconduct;

3. He/she acknowledges that the material facts upon which the complaint is based are true; and

4. He/she submits the resignation because he/she knows that if charges are predicated on the misconduct under investigation, he/she could not defend him/herself successfully against them.

H. Within 30 days of receipt of the written statement from the respondent, or (in the event the respondent fails to reply or otherwise cooperate), within 30 days of receipt of the return receipt requested from the second notification by the Committee (Section IV, D, E), the chairpersons, through advice of the Committee, shall determine if a violation may have occurred, and if so, what principles have potentially been violated.

I. If, in the opinion of the Committee, the complaint has a basis in fact but is considered likely to be corrected without further action, the chairpersons shall so indicate in the record and shall so inform all parties involved.

J. If, in the opinion of the chairpersons, the issues raised by the complaint would, if true, constitute a violation of the principles, and if it appears that the complaint cannot be resolved by less formal means, the chairpersons, shall, in coordination with the appropriate State Delegate, appoint two impartial NASP members from the state in which the respondent practices to form an Ad Hoc Committee, together with the chairpersons of the Ethical and Professional Standards Committee. The purpose of this Ad Hoc Committee is to investigate the case, to evaluate the character of the behavior(s) in question and to make recommendations to the Ethics and Professional Standards Committee for final disposition of the case.

K. The Ethical and Professional Standards Committee chairpersons shall transmit to the members of the Ad Hoc Committee, by registered or certified mail, in envelopes marked "confidential," copies of the following:

1. The original complaint or material;

2. The letter to the respondent apprising him/her of the nature of the alleged violation;

3. The response from the respondent; and

4. Any such further facts related to the case as the chairpersons can assemble from sources of evident reliability.

L. The Ad Hoc Committee shall then determine whether:

1. The case shall be closed;

2. Further investigation by correspondence is indicated;

3. Future investigation by a Fact-Finding Committee is indicated (see Section V);

4. The respondent and/or complainant shall be asked to appear before the Ad Hoc Committee; or

5. Some other action or a combination thereof shall be taken.

Section V. Recommendations of the Ad Hoc Committee

A. When the Ad Hoc Committee has obtained sufficient information with which to reach a decision, or in any event, in not more than 60 days from the formation of the Ad Hoc Committee, the Ethical and Professional Standards Committee chairpersons shall request that the Ad Hoc Committee vote on the disposition of the case.

B. If, in the unanimous opinion of the Ad Hoc Committee members, a violation of the NASP Principles has occurred and if, in the opinion of the Ad Hoc Committee, the unethical behavior can be terminated by action of the Committee itself, one or more of the following recommendations shall be made:

1. The Ad Hoc Committee shall request, in writing, that the respondent take corrective measures to modify or stop certain activities or practices;

2. The Ad Hoc Committee shall, in writing, censure or reprimand the respondent;

3. The Ad Hoc Committee shall require that the respondent provide restitution to or apologize, in writing, to an individual, or organization harmed by the respondent's unethical conduct;

4. The Ad Hoc Committee shall recommend that the respondent be placed under a period of probation of membership or surveillance under fixed terms agreed to by the respondent;

5. The Ad Hoc Committee may recommend a combination of the above four recommendations. (NOTE - In all cases, supervision of the member's behavior for a period of time will be required component of the corrective action.)

C. Within 5 days, the Ethical and Professional Standards Committee chairpersons shall inform the respondent of the Ad Hoc Committee's determination and recommendations. The respondent shall be notified that he/she may make a request for a hearing on the charges within 30 days from the receipt of a statement of the charges and the Committee's findings and recommendations. Such a request shall be in writing and directed to the President of the Association.

D. The Ethical and Professional Standards committee chairperson shall draft a report summarizing the findings and recommendations of the Ad Hoc Committee, copies of which shall be distributed to the two other Ad Hoc Committee members, the respondent and, at the Committee's discretion, the complainant. This report shall be transmitted in envelopes marked "confidential" in the case of the respondent, by registered or certified mail with a return receipt requested.

E. A summary report shall then be edited by the Ethical and Professional Standards Committee chairpersons, ensuring the confidentiality of all persons involved is strictly maintained, for purposes of reporting to the Delegate Assembly at the next regularly scheduled meeting on the activities and recommendations of the Ethical and Professional Standards Committee and its designees, e.g., any Ad Hoc Committee so convened in the interim.

F. The unanimous decision of the Ad Hoc Committee shall be binding on the Association unless overturned by the Hearing Committee, Executive Council or Delegate Assembly in accordance with the procedures outlined herein. (See Section VIII)

Section VI. Conduct of a Formal Investigation

A. A formal investigation shall be undertaken if any one of the following circumstances prevails:

1. The Ad Hoc Committee finds that it lacks sufficient data with which to proceed;

2. The Ad Hoc Committee is unable to reach consensus;

3. The recommendations of the Ad Hoc Committee do not lead to resolution of the problem; or

4. The facts alleged in the complaint, if substantiated, would likely require action leading to termination of the respondent's membership in the Association, or revocation of a National Certificate.

B. When a formal investigation is warranted under these procedures, the Ethical and Professional Standards Committee chairpersons, in coordination with the President of the Association, shall appoint a Fact-Finding Committee, which shall appoint its own chairperson, to consist of not less than three nor more than five members of the Association, for the specific purpose of more fully investigating the charges. No member previously involved in reviewing the case may serve on the Fact-Finding Committee. The Ethical and Professional Standards Committee chairpersons shall serve on the Fact-Finding Committee in ex-officio status in order to apprise the Fact-Finding Committee of the procedures by which they are bound and to serve in an advisory capacity.

C. The Fact-Finding Committee shall be bound by the same procedures and timelines as outlined in Sections III and IV of these procedures. In addition, the Fact-Finding Committee may, at the discretion of the Executive Council, retain a legal advisor as counsel to the committee while investigating its case.

D. The respondent may seek advice from any individual, including an attorney or another member of the Association, for assistance in preparing and presenting documentary evidence requested by the Fact-Finding Committee.

Section VII. Recommendations of the Fact-Finding Committee

A. If the formal investigation was convened following a decision by consensus of the Ad Hoc Committee, and if the Fact-Finding Committee unanimously concurs with the Ad Hoc Committee's findings and recommendations, all parties shall be so informed and this decision shall be binding on the Association unless overturned by the Hearing Committee, Executive Council or Delegate Assembly, in accordance with the procedures outlined herein.

B. If the case was not resolved at the Ad Hoc Committee level, the Fact-Finding Committee must announce its findings and recommendations within the prescribed timelines. The Fact-Finding Committee may exercise any of the recommendations open to the Ad Hoc Committee (Section V, B) and in addition may also recommend that the respondent's membership in the Association be terminated.

C. Should the Fact-Finding Committee so recommend, the chairpersons of the Ethical and Professional Standards Committee must present the findings and recommendations of the Fact-Finding Committee to the NASP Executive Council and Delegate Assembly. A summary report shall be prepared, such that the confidentiality of all parties involved, i.e., identifying information of the informer, is strictly maintained. The case shall be reviewed in sufficient detail so as to allow the Executive Council and the Delegate Assembly members to vote to concur or overrule the decision of the Fact-Finding Committee.

D. In accordance with NASP Bylaws, cases involving a recommendation for expulsion from the Association by the Ethical and Professional Standards Committee shall be confirmed by a 2/3 vote of the Executive Council, with a majority ratification by the Delegate Assembly. If the expelled NASP member is also a member of the NSPCS, the expulsion shall be reported to the NSPCB along with a recommendation for further action, if any, the NSPCB should take.

E. At the discretion of the Executive Council and Delegate Assembly, the respondent may be allowed to voluntarily resign his/her membership in the Association.

F. Within five days, the Ethical and Professional Standards Committee chairpersons shall inform the respondent of the decision of the Executive Council and Delegate Assembly in the same manner as provided in Section V-C of these procedures.

G. If the Executive Council and/or the Delegate Assembly do not concur with the Committee's recommendation for expulsion from membership, the case shall be remanded back to the Fact-Finding Committee for consideration of a lesser penalty.

Section VIII. Conduct of the Hearing Committee

A. Within 30 days of receipt of a statement of the charges against him/her and a statement of the Committee's findings and recommendations, the respondent has the right to request from the President of the Association a hearing on the charges. This right shall be considered waived if such request is not made in writing within the 30 day period.

B. If the respondent does request a hearing, the President shall select a panel of ten members of the Association, none of whom shall be members of the Ethical and Professional Standards Committee or have had any prior connection with the case. From the panel, the respondent shall have 30 days in which to choose a Hearing committee of five members. If he/she does not make a selection, the President shall choose the five members to comprise the Hearing Committee.

C. The President shall select a chairperson of the Hearing Committee who shall conduct the hearing and assure that the procedures are properly observed. There shall be no communication between the members of the Hearing Committee and the Ethical and Professional Standards Committee or any of its representatives prior to the hearing itself.

D. A date for the hearing shall be set by the President with the concurrence of the respondent. In no event shall the hearing take place later than 90 days from the date of the respondent's request for a hearing.

E. At least 30 days prior to the hearing, the respondent and the Hearing Committee members shall be provided with copies of all documents to be presented and the names of all witnesses that will be offered by the Ethical and Professional standards Committee in support of the charges.

F. Presentation of the case against the respondent shall be the responsibility of the Ethical and Professional Standards Committee, or such others as the Ethical and Professional Standards Committee has designated to investigate the complaint. Legal counsel for the Association may participate fully in the presentation of the case.

G. All evidence that is relevant and reliable, as determined by the chairperson of the Hearing Committee, shall be admissible. Evidence of mitigating circumstances may be presented by the respondent.

H. The respondent shall have the right to counsel, to present witnesses and documents and to cross-examine the witnesses offered by the Ethical and Professional Standards Committee.

I. The hearing may be adjourned as necessary and the Ethical and Professional Standards Committee may introduce rebuttal evidence.

J. In the interest of obtaining a full and accurate record of the hearing, a tape recorder or other transcription device may be used, at the discretion of the Hearing Committee and the respondent.

Section IX. Recommendations of the Hearing Committee

A. At the conclusion of the hearing, the Hearing Committee shall have 30 days in which to issue its report and recommendations.

B. If the Hearing Committee recommends that the respondent be dropped from membership or that the respondent be permitted to resign, the matter shall be referred to the Executive Council. A recommendation that the respondent be expelled or be allowed to resign must be made by 4 of the 5 committee members. Other disciplinary measures would be decided upon per individual case and would require a simple majority vote.

C. Only the disciplinary measures specified by the Ethical and Professional Standard Committee in the formal statement of charges, or a lesser penalty, shall be recommended by the Hearing Committee. Although the Ethical and Professional Standards Committee recommendations may be modified by the Hearing Committee, it may not increase the penalty recommended.

D. The Hearing Committee shall submit its report and recommendations simultaneously to the Executive Council and to the respondent.

E. The respondent shall have 15 days from receipt of the Hearing Committee's report in which to file a written statement with the Executive Council. The Ethical and Professional standards Committee shall then have 15 days in which to file a response.

F. After consideration of the record, the recommendation of the Hearing Committee and any statements that may be filed, the Executive Council shall adopt the recommendations of the Hearing Committee unless it determines that:

1. The NASP Principles and/or the procedures herein stated have been incorrectly applied;

2. The findings of fact of the Hearing Committee as stated in the report are not supported by the evidence; or

3. The procedures followed were in violation of the Bylaws of the Association.

G. The Ethical and Professional Standards Committee shall inform the respondent and, at its discretion, may inform the complainant of any final action taken by the Executive Council. The Ethical and Professional Standards Committee shall report to the Delegate Assembly at its next regularly scheduled meeting, in Executive Session, the names of those members who have been allowed to resign or who have been expelled from membership, and the ethical principle(s) involved. Actions involving individuals who hold a certificate issued by the NSPCB will be reported to the national certification board in a timely manner.

H. The Ethical and Professional Standards Committee shall report annually and in confidence to the delegate Assembly and Executive Council, in Executive Session, the names of members who have been expelled from the Association and the ethical principle(s) involved.

I. In severe cases and when the welfare of the public is at stake, and when the Ethical and Professional Standards Committee deems it necessary to maintain the principles of the Association and the profession, it may also notify affiliated state and regional associations and state and local licensing and certification boards of the final disposition of the case. Other interested parties, including the respondent's employer, may be notified of the final action when, in the opinion of the Ethical and Professional Standards Committee, notification is necessary for the protection of the public or the profession.

PROCEDURAL GUIDELINES FOR THE ADJUDICATION OF ETHICAL COMPLAINTS SUMMARIZED IN CHART FORM

A COMPLAINT IS RECEIVED BY THE COMMITTEE.

Is the complaint anonymous?	If so, take no action
Is the complaint oral?	If so, advise only.
Is the complaint about *Standards*?	If so, advise only.
Is the complaint frivolous or vengeful?	If so, consider action against complainant.
Is the ethical complaint about a NASP member or a member of the National Certification system?	If not, advise complainant that the situation is out of NASP jurisdiction

WITHIN 15 DAYS OF THE COMPLAINT:

The committee reviews the written complaint.	
Is there a potential violation of NASP Ethics?	If not, notify complainant and get more information, or stop.
Complainant is advised that an informal investigation will occur, and is asked for a release so that respondent may know who issued the complaint.	
Is the release obtained?	If not, the committee must decide whether to proceed on its own volition.

WITHIN 15 DAYS OF SIGNED RELEASE:

Inform the respondent, describe the complaint and the principles believed to be involved, request cooperation, and send a copy of the Ethics. Ask for a written response.

Attempt to resolve the situation informally, if possible.

IF NO ANSWER WITHIN 30 DAYS

Follow up with another request for a written response, using a certified letter with return receipt requested.

If there is still no reply, or if the respondent refuses to cooperate, note this in the record and inform the respondent that a lack of cooperation could result in expulsion from NASP.

WITHIN 30 DAYS OF THE WRITTEN STATEMENT:

If the facts seem to suggest that a violation may have occurred, is the situation likely to correct itself without further action?	If so, inform all parties and monitor the situation.

WITHIN THE NEXT 60 DAYS:

Contact the state delegate, appoint two impartial NASP members in the respondent's state, and form an Ad Hoc committee.

Ad Hoc Committee receives copies of the original complaint materials, the committee's letter to the respondent, the respondent's written response, and other pertinent material.

Can the situation be settled at the informal level?	If so, contact parties and monitor the situation.
Can the needed information be obtained through correspondence?	If so, the Ad Hoc committee continues to gather the facts.
Does the Ad Hoc committee need for the complainant and the respondent to appear?	If so, arrange for them to appear before the committee.
Does the Ad Hoc Committee have enough information to decide the issues at hand?	If not, begin fact-finding procedures.
Is the Ad Hoc committee unanimous in its decision?	If not, begin formal investigation procedures.

THE COMMITTEE ISSUES A DECISION, WHICH IS BINDING UNLESS OVERTURNED BY A HEARING; SUPERVISION IS REQUIRED:

Order corrective action.	Censure or reprimand.	Require an apology or restitution.	Require probation.	Determine no violation occurred.

WITHIN 5 DAYS:

Notify the respondent of the decision.

WAIT 30 DAYS FOR RESPONDENT TO REQUEST A HEARING:

If there is no request for a hearing, draft a report and advise the Delegate Assembly of the actions of the committee. Make recommendation to National Certification Board if respondent holds national certification.

FORMAL INVESTIGATION PROCEDURES

Follow these steps if:

- The Ad Hoc Committee lacks the data to proceed.
- The Ad Hoc Committee cannot reach a consensus.
- The solutions available to the Ad Hoc Committee are unlikely to resolve the problem.
- The facts, if substantiated, could lead to the expulsion of a NASP member or a member of the NSPCS.

The chairs of the Ethical and Professional Standards Committee, along with the NASP President, appoint members of a fact finding committee. This committee follows the same basic procedures as the Ad Hoc committee.

Does the fact finding committee concur unanimously with the Ad Hoc Committee?

If so, the Ad Hoc Committee decisions are binding unless overturned by a hearing, Executive Council, or Delegate Assembly.

The fact finding committee reaches its own conclusions. The recommendation may include expulsion.

If expulsion is advised, the Ethical and Professional Standards chairs will present the findings to the NASP Executive Council and the Delegate Assembly, with all due consideration for matters of confidentiality.

Is the expulsion recommendation confirmed by a 2/3rd vote of the Executive Council and ratified by a majority of the Delegates?

If not, have the fact finding committee review the situation and consider a lessor penalty.

WITHIN 5 DAYS:

Notify the respondent.

WAIT 30 DAYS FOR RESPONDENT TO REQUEST A HEARING:

If there is no request for a hearing, draft a report and advise the Delegate Assembly and the National Certification Board (if necessary) of the actions of the committee.

CONDUCT OF THE HEARING COMMITTEE

Upon receipt of a written decision by the Ad Hoc or the Fact Finding Committee, a respondent has thirty days in which to ask for a hearing. Should a hearing be requested within the 30 days.

The NASP President selects a panel of 10 impartial NASP members. From this group, the respondent selects 5 to serve on the committee. The President then selects the Chair.

NO LATER THAN 90 DAYS FROM THE DATE OF THE HEARING REQUEST:

The date for the hearing is set.

AT LEAST 30 DAYS BEFORE THE HEARING:

Hearing committee members and respondent receive copies of all relevant documents.

AT THE HEARING:

The Ethical and Professional Standards Committee chair, or designee, presents the facts in the complaint. The respondent has the right to counsel, to present witnesses and documents, and to cross-examine witnesses. The Ethical and Professional Standards Committee may offer rebuttal.

WITHIN 30 DAYS:

The hearing committee issues a report and recommendations to the respondent and the NASP Executive Council.

WITHIN 15 DAYS:

The Ethical and Professional Standards Committee and the respondent may file comments on the hearing committee report.

AT THE NEXT EXECUTIVE COUNCIL MEETING:

Does the NASP Executive Council believe that there is no evidence of ethical misconduct, or that there was a problem with the application of the principles or procedures for investigation?

Is yes, the matter is ended.

The Executive Council adopts the findings and recommendations of the Hearing Committee.

The Ethical and Professional Standards Committee informs the respondent, and has the discretion to inform the complainant or not. The EB/DA is notified of member expelled and the ethical principles involved. The National School Psychology Certification System will be notified if the proceedings involve an NSPCS member.

When the welfare of the public is at stake, NASP may notify other interested parties of the final disposition of the case.

II Appendix II — Standards for the Provision of School Psychological Services

INTRODUCTION

The *Guidelines for the Provision of School Psychological Services* represent the position of the National Association of School Psychologists (NASP) regarding the delivery of appropriate and comprehensive school psychological services. First written in 1978, revised in 1984, 1992, 1997, and 2000, the *Guidelines* serve as a guide to the organization and delivery of school psychological services at the federal, state, and local levels. The *Guidelines* provide direction to school psychologists, students, and trainers in school psychology, administrators of school psychological services, and consumers of school psychological services regarding excellence in professional school psychology. They also delineate what services might reasonably be expected to be available from most school psychologists and, thus, should help to further define the field. In addition, they are intended to educate the profession and the public regarding appropriate professional practices and, hopefully, will stimulate the continued development of the profession. A principal objective of the *Guidelines* is to inform policy and decision-makers of the major characteristics of comprehensive school psychological services. The first section presents the responsibilities of the individual school psychologist. The second section outlines responsibilities that should be assumed by the unit responsible for providing psychological services within an organization (e.g., school district, community agency) that employs school psychologists. The "unit" is defined as the entity (e.g., the single school psychologist in a small district, a psychological services unit in a large district, a district that contracts with an agency for psychological services) that is responsible for ensuring that schools, students, and families receive comprehensive psychological services.

Not all school psychologists or school psychological service units will be able to meet every standard contained within this document. Nevertheless, it is anticipated that these guidelines will serve as a model of "good practice" for program development and professional practice on a federal, state, and local level. School psychologists will perceive that it is in their own best interest—and that of the agencies, parents, and children they serve—to adhere to and support these *Guidelines*. NASP encourages state and federal legislators, local school boards, and the administrative leaders of federal, state, and local education agencies to support the concepts contained within these *Guidelines*.

NASP acknowledges that the *Guidelines* set requirements for services not presently mandated by federal law or regulation and not always mandated in state laws and administrative rules. Future amendments of such statutes and rules, and the state and local plans resulting from them, should incorporate the suggestions contained in this document. Furthermore, NASP understands that school psychological services are provided within the context of ethical and legal mandates.

Nothing in these *Guidelines* should be construed as superseding such relevant rules and regulations. The *Guidelines* provide flexibility, permitting agencies and professionals to develop procedures, policies, and administrative organizations that meet both the needs of the agency and the professional's desire to operate within recognized professional standards of practice. At the same time, the *Guidelines* have sufficient specificity to insure that services will be provided appropriately and adequately.

PRACTICE GUIDELINES

Practice Guideline 1

School psychologists use a decision-making process in collaboration with other team members to (a) identify academic and behavior problems, (b) collect and analyze information to understand the problems, (c) make decisions about service delivery, and (d) evaluate the outcomes of the service delivery. School psychologists must (a) utilize current professional literature on various aspects of education and child development, (b) translate research into practice through the problem-solving process, and (c) use research design and statistics skills to conduct investigations to develop and facilitate effective services.

1.1 School psychologists define problems in ways that

(a) identify desired goals (e.g., academic/behavioral),

(b) are measurable, (c) are agreed upon by those involved, and (d) are linked appropriately to assessment strategies.

1.2 School psychologists select assessment method(s) that are validated for the problem area under consideration including formal and informal assessment procedures, as appropriate, and include data collected from all settings and persons necessary and appropriate to complete the problem-solving process.

1.3 School psychologists develop and implement effective interventions that are based upon the data collected and related directly to the desired outcomes of those interventions.

1.4 School psychologists use appropriate assessment information to evaluate interventions to determine their effectiveness, their need for modification, or their need for redevelopment. Effectiveness is determined by the relationship between the actual outcome of the intervention and the desired goal articulated in the problem solving process.

1.5 School psychologists apply the problem-solving process to broader research and systems-level problems that result in the identification of factors that influence learning and behavior, the evaluation of the outcomes of classroom, building, and system initiatives and the implementation of decision-making practices designed to meet general public accountability responsibilities.

Practice Guideline 2

School psychologists must have the ability to listen well, participate in discussions, convey information, and work together with others at an individual, group, and systems level. School psychologists must understand the degree to which policy influences systems, systems influence programs, programs and interventions impact consumers, and the methods to facilitate organizational development through strategic change.

2.1 School psychologists use decision-making skills and are proficient in systems consultation to facilitate communication and collaboration with students and school personnel, community professionals, agencies, and families/schools.

2.2 School psychologists participate in public policy discussions and understand the process by which public policy influences systems. By applying decision-making methods to public policy determination, school psychologists facilitate organization development and change.

2.3 School psychologists must be able to present and disseminate information to diverse communities, such as parents, teachers, school boards, policy makers, business leaders, and fellow school psychologists in a variety of contexts, in an organized and meaningful manner.

2.4 School psychologists facilitate the development of healthy learning environments and reduce divisiveness through the use of conflict resolution and negotiation skills.

2.5 School psychologists function as change agents, using their skills in communication, collaboration, and consultation to promote necessary change at the individual student, classroom, building, and district local, state, and federal levels.

Practice Guideline 3

School psychologists (in collaboration with others) develop challenging but achievable cognitive and academic goals for all students, provide information about ways in which students can achieve these goals, and monitor student progress towards these goals.

3.1 School psychologists apply current empirically based theory and knowledge of learning theory and cognitive processes to the development of effective instructional strategies to promote student learning and social and emotional development.

3.2 School psychologists incorporate assessment information to the development of instructional strategies to meet the individual learning needs of children.

3.3 School psychologists use appropriate and applicable assessment techniques to assess progress toward academic goals and assist in revising instructional methodology as necessary.

3.4 School psychologists assist in facilitating and implementing a variety of research-based instructional methods (e.g., cooperative learning, class-wide peer tutoring, cognitive strategy training) to enhance learning of students at the individual, group, and systems level.

3.5 School psychologists assist in the design and delivery of curriculum to help students develop behaviors to support effective learning such as study skills, self-regulation and self-monitoring, planning/organization, time management skills, and making choices that maintain physical and mental health.

3.6 School psychologists promote the principles of student-centered learning to help students develop (when appropriate) their individual ability to be self-regulated learners, including the ability to set individual learning goals, design a learning process to achieve those goals, and assess outcomes to determine whether the goals were achieved.

3.7 School psychologists are informed about advances in curriculum and instruction and share this knowledge with educators, parents, and the community at large to promote improvement in instruction, student achievement, and healthy lifestyles.

Practice Guideline 4

School psychologists make decisions based on multiple theoretical perspectives and translate current scientific information to develop effective behavioral, affective, or adaptive goals for all students, facilitate the implementation of programs/interventions to achieve these goals, and monitor progress towards these goals.

4.1 School psychologists use decision-making models (e.g., functional behavioral assessment) that consider the antecedents, consequences, functions, and potential causes of behavioral problems experienced by students with disabilities, which may impair learning or socialization.

4.2 School psychologists identify factors that facilitate the development of optimal learning environments. Optimal learning environments are characterized as settings where all members of the school or agency community treat one another with respect and dignity. Optimal learning environments are characterized as settings where students' basic needs are assured so that learning can occur and health and mental health are systematically evaluated.

4.3 School psychologists facilitate the development and implementation of strategies that result in instructional environments which foster learning and high rates of academic engaged time and reduce the presence of factors that promote alienation and impact learning and behavioral progress.

4.4 School psychologists demonstrate appropriate knowledge of treatment acceptability and treatment integrity by including these principles in the development, implementation, and evaluation of interventions.

4.5 School psychologists apply the principles of generalization and transfer of training in the development of interventions in such a way that, when appropriate, interventions can be implemented across settings— school, home, and community.

4.6 School psychologists develop and implement behavior change programs (individual, group, classroom) that demonstrate the use of alternative, appropriate approaches (e.g., positive reinforcement, social skills training, academic interventions) to student discipline, ecological and behavioral approaches to classroom management, and awareness of classroom climate.

4.7 School psychologists assist parents and other adult caregivers in the development, implementation, and evaluation of behavior change programs in the home in order to facilitate the learning and behavioral growth of their child.

4.8 School psychologists incorporate appropriate strategies when developing and delivering intervention programs to facilitate successful transitions of students from one environment to another environment. These programs include program to program, early childhood to school, school to school, and school to work transitions.

4.9 School psychologists evaluate interventions (learning/ behavioral) for individuals and groups. These include the skills necessary both to evaluate the extent to which the intervention contributed to the outcome and to identify what constitutes a "successful" outcome.

Practice Guideline 5

School psychologists have the sensitivity, knowledge, and skills to work with individuals and groups with a diverse range of strengths and needs from a variety of racial, cultural, ethnic, experiential, and linguistic backgrounds.

5.1 School psychologists develop academic and behavioral interventions. They recognize that interventions most likely to succeed are those which are adapted to the individual needs and characteristics of the student(s) for whom they are being designed.

5.2 School psychologists recognize (in themselves and others and in the techniques and instruments that they use for assessment and intervention) the subtle racial, class, gender, and cultural biases they may bring to their work and the way these biases influence decision-making, instruction, behavior, and long-term outcomes for students. School psychologists work to reduce and eliminate these biases where they occur.

5.3 School psychologists promote practices that help children of all backgrounds feel welcome and appreciated in the school and community.

5.4 School psychologists incorporate their understanding of the influence of culture, background, and individual learning characteristics when designing and implementing interventions to achieve learning and behavioral outcomes.

Practice Guideline 6

School psychologists demonstrate their knowledge of schools (or other institutional settings) as systems when they work with individuals and groups to facilitate structure and public policies that create and maintain schools and other systems as safe, caring, and inviting places for all persons in that system.

6.1 School psychologists use their knowledge of development, learning, family, and school systems to assist schools and communities to develop policies and practices related to discipline, decision-making, instructional support, staff training, school improvement plans, program evaluation, transition plans, grading, retention, and home-school partnerships.

6.2 School psychologists use their knowledge of organizational development and systems theory to assist in creating climates that result in mutual respect and caring for all individuals in the system, an atmosphere of decision-making and collaboration, and a commitment to quality services.

6.3 School psychologists regularly participate in the development of policies and procedures that advocate for effective programs and services.

6.4 School psychologists are actively involved in the development of systems change plans (such as school improvement plans) that directly impact the programs and services available to children, youth, and their families and that directly impact the ways in which school psychologists deliver their services.

6.5 School psychologists assist in the development of policies and procedures to ensure that schools are safe and violence free. School psychologists participate in the implementation and evaluation of programs that result in safe and violence free schools and communities.

6.6 School psychologists are actively involved in public policy at the local, state, and federal levels as a means of creating systems of effective educational services.

6.7 School psychologists are aware of funding mechanisms that are available to school and communities that support health and mental health services. School psychologists participate in the development of funding strategies to assure that needed services are available to students and their families.

Practice Guideline 7

School psychologists shall appropriately utilize prevention, health promotion, and crisis intervention methods based on knowledge of child development, psychopathology, diversity, social stressors, change, and systems.

7.1 School psychologists shall apply knowledge of child development, psychopathology, diversity, social stressors, change, and systems to the identification and recognition of behaviors that are precursors to school dropouts or the development of mental health disorders such as conduct disorders or internalizing disorders.

7.2 School psychologists shall provide direct counseling and indirect interventions through consultation for students with disabilities and suspected disabilities who experience mental health problems that impair learning and/or socialization.

7.3 School psychologists shall develop, implement, and evaluate prevention and intervention programs based on recognized factors that are precursors to development of severe learning and behavioral problems.

7.4 School psychologists shall collaborate with school personnel, parents, students, and the community to provide competent mental health support during and after crises (for example, suicide, death, natural disasters, murder, bombs or bomb threats, extraordinary violence, and sexual harassment).

7.5 School psychologists promote wellness by (a) collaborating with other health care professionals to provide a basic knowledge of behaviors that lead to good health for children; (b) facilitating environmental changes conducive to good health and adjustment of children; and (c) accessing resources to address a wide variety of behavioral, learning, mental, and physical needs.

Practice Guideline 8

School psychologists have knowledge of family influences that affect students' wellness, learning, and achievement and are involved in public policy that promotes partnerships between parents, educators, and the community.

8.1 School psychologists design and implement and evaluate programs to promote school-family partnerships for the purpose of enhancing academic and behavioral goals for students. These might include (but are not limited to) developing parent education programs, establishing drop-in centers for parents, establishing homework hot-lines, or providing other supports for parents to help them parent successfully and to help them enhance the academic and psychological development of their children.

8.2 School psychologists help parents feel comfortable participating in school functions or activities. These might include providing support for them when participating on special education and I.E.P. teams, encouraging parental involvement in school-wide committees such as school improvement teams, *and* facilitating home-school communication when problems arise and includes assisting parents in accessing community-based services for their family.

8.3 School psychologists educate the school community regarding the influence of family involvement on school achievement and advocate for parent involvement in school governance and policy development whenever feasible.

8.4 School psychologists help create linkages between schools, families, and community agencies and help coordinate services when programming for children involves multiple agencies.

8.5 School psychologists are knowledgeable about the local system of care and related community services available to support students and their families.

8.6 School psychologists work with parent organizations to promote public policy that empowers parents to be competent consumers of the local system of services.

8.7 School psychologists are active participants in public policy by serving on committees, participating in work groups and task forces, and in responding to proposed legislation and rules.

GUIDELINES FOR THE ORGANIZATION AND OPERATION OF THE UNIT

Unit Guideline 1: Organization of Service Delivery

School psychological services are provided in a coordinated, organized fashion and are delivered in a manner that ensures the provision of a comprehensive and seamless continuum of services. Services are delivered following the completion of a strategic planning process based on the needs of the consumers and an empirically supported program evaluation model.

1.1 School psychological services are available and accessible to all students and clients served by the agency and are in proportion to the needs of the client.

1.2 School psychological services are available to all students on an equal basis and are not determined by a specific funding source. Services are provided to students based on their need, not based on their eligibility to generate specific funding.

1.3 School psychological services are integrated with other school and community services. Students and their families should not be responsible for the integration of these services based on funding, setting, or program location. Therefore, school psychological and mental health services are provided through a "seamless" system of care.

1.4 School psychological services units ensure that the services delivered by the unit and provided directly by the school psychologist to consumers are based on a strategic plan. The plan is developed based on the collective needs of the district and community with the primary focus being the specific needs of the population served by individual practitioners.

1.5 School psychological services units conduct regular evaluations of the collective services provided by the unit as well as those services provided by individual practitioners. The evaluation process focuses on both the nature and extent of the services provided (process) and the student/family focused outcomes of those services (product).

1.6 The school psychological services unit provides a range of services to their clients. These consist of direct and indirect services that require involvement with the entire educational system as well as other services systems in the community. The consumers of and participants in these services include: students, teachers, administrators, other school personnel, families, caretakers, other community and regional agencies, and resources that support the educational process.

Unit Guideline 2: Climate

It is the responsibility of the unit to create a climate in which school psychological services can be delivered with mutual respect for all parties. Employees of the unit have the freedom to advocate for the services that are necessary to meet the needs of consumers and are free from artificial, administrative, or political constraints that might hinder or alter the provision of appropriate services.

2.1 Providers of school psychological services maintain a cooperative relationship with colleagues and co-workers in the best mutual interests of clients. Conflicts are resolved in a professional manner.

2.2 The potential negative impact of administrative constraints on effective services is kept to a minimum. The school psychologist will advocate for administrative policies that support the school psychologist in seeking the needed services and will provide mechanisms for referral and consultation regarding unmet health and mental health needs.

2.3 Members of the unit advocate in a professional manner for the most appropriate services for their clients without fear of reprisal from supervisors or administrators.

2.4 School psychological services units are aware of the impact of work environment on the job satisfaction of unit employees and on the quality of services provided to consumers. Measures of work climate are included when the unit conducts self-evaluations.

2.5 School psychological services units promote and advocate for balance between professional and personal lives of unit employees. Unit supervisors monitor work and stress levels of employees and take steps to reduce pressure when the well-being of the employee is at risk. Supervisors are available to employees to problem solve when personal factors may adversely affect job performance and when job expectations may adversely affect the personal life of the employee.

Unit Guideline 3: Physical, Personnel, and Fiscal Support Systems

School psychological services units ensure that (a) an adequate recruitment and retention plan for employees exists to ensure adequate personnel to meet the needs of the system; (b) all sources of funding, both public and private, are used and maximized to ensure the fiscal support necessary to provide adequate services; (c) all employees have adequate technology, clerical services, and a physical work environment; and (d) employees have adequate personnel benefits necessary to support the work of the unit including continuing educational professional development.

3.1 School psychological services units assume the professional responsibility and accountability for services provided through the recruitment of qualified and diverse staff and the assurance that staff members function only in their areas of competency.

3.2 School psychological services units support recruitment and retention of qualified staff by advocating for appropriate ratios of school psychology services staff to students. The ratio of staff to students should not exceed one staff person for every 1000 students.

3.3 School psychological services units utilize advanced technologies (e.g., computer-assisted) in time management, communication systems, data management systems, and service delivery.

3.4 School psychological services units have access to adequate clerical assistance, appropriate professional work materials, sufficient office and work space, adequate technology support (e.g., e-mail, computer) and general working conditions that enhance the delivery of effective services. Included are test materials, access to private telephone and office, secretarial services, therapeutic aids, and professional literature.

Unit Guideline 4: Communication and Technology

The school psychological services unit ensures that policies and practices exist which result in positive,

proactive communication and technology systems both within the unit, its central organizational structure, and those organizational structures with which the unit interacts.

4.1 School psychological services units provide opportunities for members of the unit to communicate with each other about issues of mutual professional interest on a regular basis.

4.2 School psychological services units maintain a formal system of communication channels with other units within the parent organization and between the unit and other agencies with whom it interacts on behalf of clients. The unit engages in decision-making and strategic planning with other units and agencies in order to ensure optimal services are provided to mutual clients.

4.3 School psychological services units ensure that staff members have access to the technology necessary to perform their jobs adequately and to maintain communication with service providers and clients within and outside the unit. The requirement for confidentiality is respected, with adequate resources available to service providers to ensure confidential communication.

4.4 School psychological services units' policy on student records is consistent with state and federal rules and laws and ensures the protection of the confidentiality of the student and his or her family. The policy specifies the types of data developed by the school psychologist that are classified as school or pupil records. The policy gives clear guidance regarding which documents belong (consistent with FERPA or similar state/court regulations) to the school and the student/guardian and which documents (such as clinical notes) are the personal property of the school psychologist.

4.5 Parents may inspect and review any personally identifiable data relating to their children that were collected, maintained, or used in his/her evaluation. Although test protocols are part of the student's record, school psychologists protect test security and observe copyright restrictions. Release of records and protocols is done consistent with state/federal regulations.

Unit Guideline 5: Supervision

The school psychological services unit ensures that all personnel have levels and types of supervision adequate to ensure the provision of effective and accountable services. Supervision is provided through an ongoing, positive, systematic, collaborative process between the school psychologist and the school psychology supervisor. This process focuses on promoting professional growth and exemplary professional practice leading to improved performance by all concerned including the school psychologist, supervisor, students, and the entire school community.

5.1 A supervisor of a school psychological services unit holds or meets the criteria for the Nationally Certified School Psychologist (NCSP) credential and has been identified by an employing agency and/or school psychological services unit as a supervisor responsible for school psychology services in the agency or unit. Supervisors hold a state school psychologist credential and have a minimum of three years of experience as a practicing school psychologist. Training and/or experience in the supervision of school personnel are desirable.

5.2 When supervision is required for interns, beginning school psychologists, or others for whom supervision is necessary, such supervision will be provided at least 2 hours per week for persons employed full-time.

5.3 Supervisors lead school psychological services units in developing, implementing, and evaluating a coordinated plan for accountability and evaluation of all services provided in order to maintain the highest level of effectiveness. Such plans include specific, measurable objectives pertaining to the planned effects of services. Evaluation is both formative and summative. Supervisors provide leadership by promotion of innovative service delivery systems that reflect best practices in the field of school psychology.

5.4 Supervisors lead school psychological services units in developing, implementing, and evaluating a coordinated plan for accountability and evaluation of all services provided by individual staff members and by the unit as a whole in order to maintain the highest level of services. Such plans include specific, measurable objectives pertaining to the planned effects of services on all relevant elements of the system and the students it serves. Evaluation is both formative and summative.

5.5 The school psychological services unit continues to provide supervision or peer review for its school psychologists after their first year of employment to ensure continued professional growth and development and support for complex or difficult cases.

5.6 Supervisors coordinate the activities of the school psychological services unit with other professional services units through review and discussion of 1) intervention planning and outcomes; 2) comprehensive, systemic procedures and special concerns; and 3) discrepancies among views of various professional service providers or employing agencies.

5.7 Supervisors ensure that practica and internship experiences occur under conditions of appropriate supervision including 1) access to professional school psychologists who will serve as appropriate role models, 2) provision of supervision by an appropriately credentialed school psychologist, and 3) provision of supervision within the guidelines of the training institution and NASP *Standards for Training and Field Placement Programs in School Psychology.*

5.8 Supervisors provide professional leadership through participation in school psychology professional organizations and active involvement in local, state and federal public policy development.

Unit Guideline 6: Professional Development and Recognition Systems

Individual school psychologists and the school psychological services unit develop professional development plans annually. The school psychological services unit ensures that continuing professional development of its personnel is both adequate for and relevant to the service delivery priorities of the unit and that recognition systems exist to reflect the continuum of professional development activities embraced by its personnel.

6.1 All school psychologists within the unit actively participate in activities designed to continue, enhance, and upgrade their professional training and skills to help ensure quality service provision.

6.2 The school psychological services unit provides support (e.g., funding, time, supervision) to ensure that school psychologists have sufficient access to continuing professional development and supervision activities at a minimal level necessary to maintain the NCSP.

6.3 School psychologists develop a formal professional development plan and update this plan annually. The goals, objectives, and activities of the plan are influenced by the following factors in order of priority: (1) the most pressing needs of the population and community served; (2) the knowledge, skills, and abilities required to implement initiatives sponsored by the unit; and (3) the individual interest areas of the school psychologists employed by the unit.

6.4 School psychologists seek and use appropriate types and levels of supervision as they acquire new knowledge, skills, and abilities through the professional development process.

6.5 School psychologists document the type, level, and intensity of their professional development activities. The school psychological services unit provides technology and personnel resources to assist in these activities.

6.6 School psychologists individually seek appropriate levels of advanced recognition (e.g., advanced degrees, levels established by district, state, or national recognition bodies) to reflect on-going professional development.

6.7 School psychological services units provide levels of recognition (e.g., salary, opportunity to use new skills) within the unit that reflect the professional development of the school psychologists in the unit.

Unit Guideline 7: Contracted/Independent Provider Services

The school psychological services unit is responsible for providing psychological services. These services can come from district employed school psychologists, from psychologists employed in independent practice, or through other agencies. Regardless of whether personnel are employed or contracted, it is the responsibility of the unit to ensure the same level and quality of services as those provided by personnel from within the unit.

7.1 Contractual school psychological services encompass the same comprehensive continuum of services as is provided by regularly employed school psychologists. These services include opportunities for follow-up and continuing consultation appropriate to the needs of the student. Individual contracts for services may be limited as long as the school psychological services unit ensures comprehensive services overall.

7.2 Contractual school psychological services are not used as a means to decrease the amount and quality of school psychological services provided by an employing agency. They may be used to augment and enhance programs, as in the case of retaining needed expertise, to coordinate with other community health services, and to assure that services are available to students and their families.

7.3 Contracted services may be used as a mechanism to maximize available resources. However, any such models of service must provide comprehensive psychological services and must assure quality services of equal or greater value when compared to services provided by school-based personnel.

7.4 Contractual school psychological services are provided in a manner that protects the due process rights of students and their parents as defined by state and federal laws and regulations.

7.5 Psychologists providing contractual school psychological services provide those services in a manner consistent with these Guidelines, NASP *Principles for Professional Ethics*, and other relevant professional guidelines and standards.

7.6 Persons providing contractual psychological services are fully credentialed school psychologists as defined by these or other (e.g., state certification boards) recognized standards. In specific instances, however, services by credentialed psychologists in other specialty areas (e.g., clinical, industrial/organizational, neuropsychology) might be used to supplement school psychological services and should be coordinated with school psychological services.

7.7 Psychologists providing contractual school psychological services will require regular evaluation of the quality of services provided as well as the continued need for contracted services.

7.8 A credentialed school psychologist who has completed a school psychology training program that meets the criteria specified in the NASP *Standards for Training and Field Placement Programs in School Psychology* and two full-time years (one of which may be internship) of satisfactory, properly supervised experience is considered qualified for personally supervised, independent practice with peer review, regardless of work setting. (NOTE: "Independent practice" as used in this paragraph refers to autonomous functioning within the employing school or agency. Contrast this with the licensure rules of various states for "private practice.")

7.9 A credentialed school psychologist or an organized group of credentialed school psychologists may engage in independent practice outside of a school agency or unit pursuant to existing rules regarding the independent practice of psychology within a given state. Units will support public policy that will provide for the independent practice of school psychology.

III Appendix III — Standards for Training and Field Placement Programs in School Psychology

The mission of the National Association of School Psychologists (NASP) is to promote educationally and psychologically healthy environments for all children and youth by implementing research-based, effective programs that prevent problems, enhance independence, and promote optimal learning. This is accomplished through state-of-the-art research and training, advocacy, ongoing program evaluation, and caring professional service. The NASP *Standards for Training and Field Placement Programs in School Psychology* contribute to the development of effective services through the identification of critical training experiences and competencies needed by candidates preparing for careers in school psychology. These *Standards* serve to guide the design of school psychology graduate education by providing a basis for program evaluation and a foundation for the recognition of programs that meet national quality standards through the NASP program approval process.

I. PROGRAM CONTEXT/STRUCTURE

School psychology training is delivered within a context of program values and clearly articulated training philosophy/mission, goals, and objectives. Training includes a comprehensive, integrated program of study delivered by qualified faculty, as well as substantial supervised field experiences necessary for the preparation of competent school psychologists whose services positively impact children, youth, families, and other consumers.

1.1 The program provides to all candidates a clearly articulated training philosophy/mission, goals, and objectives. An integrated and sequential program of study and supervised practice clearly identified as being in school psychology and consistent with the program's philosophy/mission, goals, and objectives are provided to all candidates.

1.2 A commitment to understanding and responding to human diversity is articulated in the program's philosophy/mission goals, and objectives and practiced throughout all aspects of the program, including admissions, faculty, coursework, practica, and internship experiences. Human diversity is recognized as a strength that is valued and respected.

1.3 Candidates have opportunities to develop an affiliation with colleagues, faculty, and the profession through a continuous full-time residency or alternative planned experiences.

1.4 The program possesses at least three full-time equivalent faculty. At least two faculty members (including the program administrator) shall hold the doctorate with specialization in school psychology and be actively engaged in school psychology as a profession (e.g., by possessing state and/or national credentials, having experience as a school psychologist, participating in professional school psychology associations, and/or contributing to research, scholarly publications, and presentations in the field). Other program faculty possess the doctoral degree in psychology, education, or a closely related discipline with a specialization supportive of their training responsibilities in the school psychology program.

1.5 The program provides, collaborates in, or contributes to continuing professional development opportunities for practicing school psychologists based on the needs of practitioners.

Requirements for Specialist-Level Programs Only (1.6-1.7)

1.6 Specialist-level programs consist of a minimum of three years of full-time study or the equivalent at the graduate level. The program shall include at least 60 graduate semester hours or the equivalent, at least 54 hours of which are exclusive of credit for the supervised internship experience. Institutional documentation of program completion shall be provided.

1.7 Specialist-level programs include a minimum of one academic year of supervised internship experience, consisting of a minimum of 1200 clock hours.

Requirements for Doctoral Programs Only (1.8-1.10)

1.8 Doctoral programs provide greater depth in multiple domains of school psychology training and practice as specified in these standards (see Standard II). (Note: Programs are encouraged to provide opportunities for doctoral study for practicing school psychologists and, to the greatest extent possible, credit for prior training.)

1.9 Doctoral programs consist of a minimum of four years of full-time study or the equivalent at the graduate level. The program shall include a minimum of 90 graduate semester hours or the equivalent, at least 78 of which are exclusive of credit for the doctoral supervised internship experience and any terminal doctoral project (e.g., dissertation) and shall culminate in institutional documentation.

1.10 Doctoral programs include a minimum of one academic year of doctoral supervised internship experience, consisting of a minimum of 1500 clock hours.

II. DOMAINS OF SCHOOL PSYCHOLOGY TRAINING AND PRACTICE

School psychology candidates demonstrate entry-level competency in each of the following domains of professional practice. Competency requires both knowledge and skills. School psychology programs ensure that candidates have a foundation in the knowledge base for psychology and education, including theories, models, empirical findings, and techniques in each domain. School psychology programs ensure that candidates demonstrate the professional skills necessary to deliver effective services that result in positive outcomes in each domain. The domains below are not mutually exclusive and should be fully integrated into graduate level curricula, practica, and internship. Domains are more fully illustrated on page 1652.

2.1 **Data-Based Decision-Making and Accountability:** School psychologists have knowledge of varied models and methods of assessment that yield information useful in identifying strengths and needs, in understanding problems, and in measuring progress and accomplishments. School psychologists use such models and methods as part of a systematic process to collect data and other information, translate assessment results into empirically-based decisions about service delivery, and evaluate the outcomes of services. Data-based decision-making permeates every aspect of professional practice.

2.2 **Consultation and Collaboration:** School psychologists have knowledge of behavioral, mental health, collaborative, and/or other consultation models and methods and of their application to particular situations. School psychologists collaborate effectively with others in planning and decision-making processes at the individual, group, and system levels.

2.3 **Effective Instruction and Development of Cognitive/ Academic Skills:** School psychologists have knowledge of human learning processes, techniques to assess these processes, and direct and indirect services applicable to the development of cognitive and academic skills. School psychologists, in collaboration with others, develop appropriate cognitive and academic goals for students with different abilities, disabilities, strengths, and needs; implement interventions to achieve those goals; and evaluate the effectiveness of interventions. Such interventions include, but are not limited to, instructional interventions and consultation.

2.4 **Socialization and Development of Life Skills:** School psychologists have knowledge of human developmental processes, techniques to assess these processes, and direct and indirect services applicable to the development of behavioral, affective, adaptive, and social skills. School psychologists, in collaboration with others, develop appropriate behavioral, affective, adaptive, and social goals for students of varying abilities, disabilities, strengths, and needs; implement interventions to achieve those goals; and evaluate the effectiveness of interventions. Such interventions include, but are not limited to, consultation, behavioral assessment/intervention, and counseling.

2.5 **Student Diversity in Development and Learning:** School psychologists have knowledge of individual differences, abilities, and disabilities and of the potential influence of biological, social, cultural, ethnic, experiential, socioeconomic, gender-related, and linguistic factors in development and learning. School psychologists demonstrate the sensitivity and skills needed to work with individuals of diverse characteristics and to implement strategies selected and/or adapted based on individual characteristics, strengths, and needs.

2.6 **School and Systems Organization, Policy Development, and Climate:** School psychologists have knowledge of general education, special education, and other educational and related services. They understand schools and other settings as systems. School psychologists work with individuals and groups to facilitate policies and practices that create and maintain safe, supportive, and effective learning environments for children and others.

2.7 **Prevention, Crisis Intervention, and Mental Health:** School psychologists have knowledge of human development and psychopathology and of associated biological, cultural, and social influences on human behavior. School psychologists provide or contribute to prevention and intervention programs that promote the mental health and physical well-being of students.

2.8 **Home/School/Community Collaboration:** School psychologists have knowledge of family systems, including family strengths and influences on student development, learning, and behavior, and of methods to involve families in education and service delivery. School psychologists work effectively with families, educators, and others in the community to promote and provide comprehensive services to children and families.

2.9 **Research and Program Evaluation:** School psychologists have knowledge of research, statistics, and evaluation methods. School psychologists evaluate research, translate research into practice, and understand research design and statistics in sufficient depth to plan and conduct investigations and program evaluations for improvement of services.

2.10 **School Psychology Practice and Development:** School psychologists have knowledge of the history and foundations of their profession; of various service models and methods; of public policy development applicable to services to children and families; and of ethical, professional, and legal standards. School psychologists practice in ways that are consistent with applicable standards, are involved in their profession, and have the knowledge and skills needed to acquire career-long professional development.

2.11 **Information Technology:** School psychologists have knowledge of information sources and technology relevant to their work. School psychologists access, evaluate, and utilize information sources and technology in ways that safeguard or enhance the quality of services.

III. FIELD EXPERIENCES/INTERNSHIP

School psychology candidates have the opportunities to demonstrate, under conditions of appropriate supervision, their ability to apply their knowledge, to develop specific skills needed for effective school psychological service delivery, and to integrate competencies that address the domains of professional preparation and practice outlined in these standards and the goals and objectives of their training program.

3.1 Supervised practica and internship experiences are completed for academic credit or are otherwise documented by the institution. Closely supervised practica experiences that include the development and evaluation of specific skills are distinct from and precede culminating internship experiences that require the integration and application of the full range of school psychology competencies and domains.

3.2 The internship is a collaboration between the training program and field site that assures the completion of activities consistent with the goals of the training program. A written plan specifies the responsibilities of the training program and internship site in providing supervision, support, and both formative and summative performance-based evaluation of intern performance.

3.3 The internship is completed on a full-time basis over one year or on a half-time basis over two consecutive years. At least 600 hours of the internship are completed in a school setting. (Note: Doctoral candidates who have met the school-based internship requirement through a specialist-level internship or equivalent experience may complete the doctoral internship in a non-school setting if consistent with program values and goals. Program policy shall specifically define equivalent experiences and explain their acceptance with regard to doctoral internship requirements.)

3.4 Interns receive an average of at least two hours of field-based supervision per full-time week from an appropriately credentialed school psychologist or, for non-school settings, a psychologist appropriately credentialed for the internship setting.

3.5 The internship placement agency provides appropriate support for the internship experience including: (a) a written agreement specifying the period of appointment and any terms of compensation; (b) a schedule of appointments, expense reimbursement, a safe and secure work environment, adequate office space, and support services consistent with that afforded agency school psychologists; (c) provision for participation in continuing professional development activities; (d) release time for internship supervision; and (e) a commitment to the internship as a diversified training experience.

IV. PERFORMANCE-BASED PROGRAM ASSESSMENT AND ACCOUNTABILITY

School psychology training programs employ systematic, valid evaluation of candidates, coursework, practica, internship, faculty, supervisors, and resources and use the resulting information to monitor and improve program quality. A key aspect of program accountability is the assessment of the knowledge and capabilities of school psychology candidates and of the positive impact that interns and graduates have on services to children, youth, families, and other consumers. Further guidance regarding the assessment of candidate performance is provided in a companion NASP document, *Guidelines for Performance-based Assessment and Program Accountability and Development.*

4.1 Systematic, valid procedures are used to evaluate and improve the quality of the program. Different sources of process and performance information (e.g., instructional evaluation, performance portfolios, field supervisor evaluations, candidate/ graduate performance on licensing/certification examinations, alumni follow-ups) are used, as appropriate, to evaluate and improve components of the program.

4.2 The program applies specific published criteria, both objective and qualitative, for the assessment and admission of candidates to the program at each level and for candidate retention and progression in the program. The criteria address the academic and professional competencies, as well as the professional work characteristics needed for effective practice as a school psychologist (including respect for human diversity, communication skills, effective interpersonal relations, ethical responsibility, adaptability, and initiative/ dependability).

4.3 The program employs a systematic, valid process to ensure that all candidates, prior to the conclusion of the internship experience, are able to integrate domains of knowledge and apply professional skills in delivering a comprehensive range of services evidenced by measurable positive impact on children, youth, families, and other consumers.

V. PROGRAM SUPPORT/RESOURCES

Note: Programs in units/institutions accredited or undergoing review by the National Council for Accreditation of Teacher Education (NCATE) do not need to provide a response to the standards in Section V as part of the NASP program review process. Adequate resources are available to support the training program and its faculty and candidates. Such resources are needed to assure accomplishment of program goals and objectives and attainment of competencies needed for effective school psychology practice that positively impact children, families, and other consumers.

5.1 Faculty loads take into account program administration, supervision, scholarship, service, and assessment associated with graduate level school psychology faculty responsibilities. Faculty teaching and supervision loads are no greater than 75% of that typically assigned to those teaching primarily undergraduate courses. The program administrator receives at least 25% reassigned time for administrative duties.

5.2 In order to ensure sufficient candidate access to program faculty instructors, mentors, and supervisors, the program maintains a no greater than 1:10 FTE faculty to FTE student ratio in the overall program, as well as in practica and internship.

5.3 Program faculty receive support for ongoing learning and professional experiences relevant to assigned training responsibilities. This includes support for continuing professional development in school psychology, involvement with professional organizations, and similar involvement in the profession, research, and related activities important to maintaining and enhancing knowledge, skills, and contributions to the profession.

5.4 Candidates receive ongoing support during training that includes faculty advisement and supervision, the availability of university and/or program support services, and opportunities for funding and/or related assistance needed to attain their educational goals (e.g., assistantships, fellowships, traineeships, internship stipends).

5.5 Adequate physical resources are available to support faculty and candidates in school psychology. These resources include adequate office space, clinical and laboratory facilities, data and information processing facilities and equipment, instructional resources, audiovisual materials, and technology needed for effective instruction.

5.6 The program provides reasonable accommodations for the special needs of candidates and faculty with disabilities.

5.7 Adequate library and information resources and services are available to support instruction, independent study, and research relevant to school psychology. Resources include access to major publications and periodicals in the field.

5.8 The program meets established approval standards for the appropriate state credentialing body(s) and is located in a unit/institution that meets regional accreditation standards.

EXPANDED DESCRIPTIONS OF DOMAINS OF SCHOOL PSYCHOLOGY TRAINING AND PRACTICE

The expanded descriptions of the "Domains of School Psychology Training and Practice" are adapted from pages 7-9 of Ysseldyke, J., Dawson, P., Lehr, C., Reschly, D., Reynolds, M. & Telzrow, C. (1997). *School Psychology: A Blueprint for Training and Practice II.* Bethesda, MD: National Association of School Psychologists. Adapted with permission of copyright holder.

2.1 **Data-Based Decision-Making and Accountability: School psychologists have knowledge of varied models and methods of assessment that yield information useful in identifying strengths and needs, in understanding problems, and in measuring progress and accomplishments. School psychologists use such models and methods as part of a systematic process to collect data and other information, translate assessment results into empirically-based decisions about service delivery, and evaluate the outcomes of services. Data-based decision-making permeates every aspect of professional practice.**

EXPANDED DESCRIPTION: Data-based decision-making and accountability should be the organizing theme of and permeate school psychology training and practice. School psychologists have knowledge of effective data-based decision-making and problem-solving processes. They systematically collect information to identify and define strengths and needs and use the information to make decisions, plan services, evaluate the outcomes of services, and facilitate accountability for the decisions that have been made. School psychologists collect considerable data on individual students, educational and health programs, classroom environments, and other aspects of schools and other agencies to evaluate problems and needs, assess current status, and measure the effects of a decision-making process.

School psychologists have knowledge of varied models and methods of assessment, or a process of testing, observing, and interviewing, to collect data for making decisions. They are well-versed in a variety of psychological and educational assessment methods validated for the problem area under consideration, including formal and informal test administration, behavioral assessment, curriculum-based measurement, interviews, and/or ecological or environmental assessment. They collect data about environments, including school and home, as well as cognitive, emotional, social, and behavioral factors that have a significant impact on children's school achievement and personal competence. School psychologists evaluate the components of environments that facilitate or impede learning or behavioral changes for children and identify how environmental factors and children's characteristics interact to affect academic and social/behavioral outcomes. They have knowledge of methods to link assessment results with intervention and use data to design and implement effective direct and indirect intervention services that promote children's competence and prevent difficulties or disabilities. They evaluate the outcomes of intervention services, with effectiveness determined by the relationship between the actual outcome of the interventions and the desired goals articulated in the decision-making process.

School psychologists assist school and other agency administrators with assessment and data-based decision-making designed to meet accountability responsibilities. School psychologists apply their knowledge of decision-making and problem-solving processes to broader research and systems-level problems that result in (a) identification of factors that influence learning and behavior; (b) evaluation of the outcomes of classroom, building, and system initiatives; and (c) implementation of problem solving practices designed to meet general public accountability responsibilities.

2.2 **Consultation and Collaboration: School psychologists have knowledge of behavioral, mental health, collaborative, and/or other consultation models and methods and of their application to particular situations. School psychologists collaborate effectively with others in planning and decision-making processes at the individual, group, and system levels.**

EXPANDED DESCRIPTION: School psychologists have knowledge of and employ effective behavioral, mental health, collaborative, and/or other consultation approaches. They apply their knowledge of consultation and collaboration in numerous situations in their practice. School psychologists function as change agents, using their knowledge and skills in consultation and collaboration to promote change at the levels of the individual student, classroom, building, district, and/or other agency. School psychologists use consultation and collaboration to facilitate development of harmonious environments in schools and other settings, to reduce the divisiveness and disenfranchisement often found in troubled schools, and to promote the kinds of principles necessary to achieve consensus.

School psychologists have the knowledge and skills necessary to facilitate communication and collaboration with children and youth and among teams of school personnel, families, community professionals, and others. School psychologists have positive interpersonal skills and listen, adapt, address ambiguity, and are patient in difficult situations. They have knowledge of the important features of collaboration and use effective collaboration skills with individuals of diverse backgrounds and characteristics. In addition to their knowledge and skills in communication and collaboration, school psychologists clearly present and disseminate information to diverse audiences, such as parents, teachers, school boards, policy makers, community leaders, colleagues, and others in a variety of contexts.

2.3 **Effective Instruction and Development of Cognitive/Academic Skills: School psychologists have knowledge of human learning processes, techniques to assess these processes, and direct and indirect services applicable to the development of cognitive and academic skills. School psychologists, in collaboration with others, develop appropriate cognitive and academic goals for students with different abilities, disabilities, strengths, and needs; implement interventions to achieve those goals; and evaluate the effectiveness of interventions. Such interventions include, but are not limited to, instructional interventions and consultation.**

EXPANDED DESCRIPTION: School psychologists have knowledge of learning theory and cognitive strategies and their application to the development of effective instructional strategies to promote student learning. They have knowledge of the cognitive and academic skills of students with different abilities, disabilities, strengths, and needs and of assessment and instructional strategies for use with students with diverse backgrounds and experiences. School psychologists are knowledgeable about principles of student-centered learning and use the principles to help students develop their abilities to be self-regulated learners. They assist children with developing behaviors to support effective learning, such as study skills, self-monitoring, planning/organization, and time management skills.

School psychologists have a current, professional knowledge base of empirically-demonstrated components of effective instruction and alternative instructional methodologies for students with diverse strengths and needs. They assist in implementing a variety of assessment techniques and instructional methods to enhance the learning of students at the individual, group, and systems levels. School psychologists, in collaboration with others, set individual learning goals, design a learning process to achieve those goals, and assess outcomes to determine whether the goals are achieved. School psychologists maintain current information and research about advances in curriculum and instruction and share this information and research with educators, parents, and the community at large to promote improvement in instruction and student achievement.

School psychologists help schools and other agencies develop appropriate cognitive and academic goals for all children, with variations in standards and expectations for individual students and alternative ways to monitor and assess individual student progress toward the accomplishment of goals and standards. They also assist State Education Agency and Local Education Agency personnel who design state and local accountability systems. School psychologists link assessment information to the development of instructional strategies in order to meet the individual learning needs of children. They have knowledge of and use appropriate assessment techniques to assess progress toward academic goals and assist in revising instructional methodology as necessary. They apply techniques to evaluate the extent to which the instructional or intervention strategy contributed to the outcome and to identify the factors that constitute a "successful" outcome. School psychologists are knowledgeable about and routinely use methods to assess treatment integrity (the extent to which treatment or programs are being implemented in the ways in which they were intended).

2.4 **Socialization and Development of Life Skills: School psychologists have knowledge of human developmental processes, techniques to assess these processes, and direct and indirect services applicable to the development of behavioral, affective, adaptive, and social skills. School psychologists, in collaboration with others, develop appropriate behavioral, affective, adaptive, and social goals for students of varying abilities, disabilities, strengths, and needs; implement interventions to achieve those goals; and evaluate the effectiveness of interventions. Such interventions include, but are not limited to, consultation, behavioral assessment/intervention, and counseling.**

EXPANDED DESCRIPTION: School psychologists have a current professional knowledge base about development processes in behavioral, social, affective, and adaptive domains. They are knowledgeable about sound principles of assessment and behavior change within these domains and apply these principles through the provision of effective consultation, behavioral assessment, intervention, and counseling services. School psychologists have knowledge of the socialization and life skills of children with different abilities, disabilities, strengths, and needs and knowledge of direct and indirect intervention strategies for use with children with diverse backgrounds and experiences.

School psychologists have knowledge and skills in consultation, behavior management, and counseling strategies that enhance appropriate student behavior. They develop methodologies, such as conflict resolution and social problem-solving/decision-making approaches, that will assist teachers and families in teaching pro-social behavior. School psychologists apply the principles of generalization and transfer of training to the development of interventions in such a way that, when appropriate, interventions can be implemented across settings (e.g., school, home, community). School psychologists provide leadership in creating environments for children that reduce alienation and foster the expression of appropriate behavior, as well as environments in which all members treat one another with respect and dignity. They assist teachers, families, and others with helping children become responsible for their own behavior. School psychologists assist parents and other adult caregivers with the development and implementation of behavior change programs in the home in order to facilitate the learning and development of their children.

School psychologists have knowledge of and facilitate the development and implementation of strategies that result in optimal instructional environments, foster learning and high rates of students' academic engaged time, and reduce the presence of factors that promote alienation and have a negative impact on children's learning and behavioral progress. School psychologists have knowledge of research on classroom climate and of ecological and behavioral approaches to classroom management. They use ecological and behavioral approaches to develop and implement behavior change programs (individual, group, classroom, etc.). They incorporate appropriate strategies when developing intervention programs to facilitate successful transitions of students from one environment to another environment. These intervention programs include program to program, early childhood to school, and school to work transitions.

School psychologists link assessment information to the development of strategies in order to address individual behavioral, affective, adaptive, and social goals for children. They have knowledge of and use appropriate assessment techniques to assess progress toward goals and assist in revising intervention strategies as necessary. They apply techniques to evaluate the extent to which the intervention strategy contributed to the outcome and to identify the factors that constitute a "successful" outcome. School psychologists are knowledgeable about and assess treatment integrity (the extent to which treatment or programs are being implemented in the ways in which they were intended).

2.5 Student Diversity in Development and Learning: School psychologists have knowledge of individual differences, abilities, and disabilities and of the potential influence of biological, social, cultural, ethnic, experiential, socioeconomic, gender-related, and linguistic factors in development and learning. School psychologists demonstrate the sensitivity and skills needed to work with individuals of diverse characteristics and to implement strategies selected and/or adapted based on individual characteristics, strengths, and needs.

EXPANDED DESCRIPTION: School psychologists recognize that students in today's schools and their families come from a variety of backgrounds. They have knowledge of the potential influences of biological, social, cultural, ethnic, experiential, socioeconomic, gender-related, and linguistic factors in children's development and learning and incorporate this knowledge when designing and implementing interventions to achieve learning and social/ behavioral outcomes. School psychologists have knowledge of individual differences, abilities, and disabilities and assist with acknowledging, supporting, and integrating the activities and talents of all students into instructional programs and other settings. School psychologists recognize that experiential and linguistic differences can also result in learning difficulties and apparent disabilities for children, and they assist schools in identifying what is needed for students to succeed and what instructional or other modifications are required to address children's difficulties. School psychologists develop academic and social/behavioral interventions that reflect knowledge and understanding of children and families' cultures, backgrounds, and individual learning characteristics. School psychologists recognize that interventions most likely to succeed are adapted to the individual needs and characteristics of the students for whom they are designed.

School psychologists promote practices that help children and families of all backgrounds feel welcome and appreciated in the school and community. School psychologists recognize in themselves and others the subtle racial, class, gender, cultural, and other biases they may bring to their work and the way these biases influence decision-making, instruction, behavior, and long-term outcomes for students.

2.6 School and Systems Organization, Policy Development, and Climate: School psychologists have knowledge of general education, special education, and other educational and related services. They understand schools and other settings as systems. School psychologists work with individuals and groups to facilitate policies and practices that create and maintain safe, supportive, and effective learning environments for children and others.

EXPANDED DESCRIPTION: School psychologists have a current professional knowledge base of school and systems structure and organization and of general education and regular education. They use their knowledge to assist schools and other agencies in designing, implementing, and evaluating policies and practices in areas such as discipline, problem-solving, instructional support, staff training, school and other agency improvement plans, program evaluation, transition plans, grading, retention, and home-school partnerships. School psychologists have knowledge of and apply effective principles of organizational development and systems theory to assist in promoting learning, preventing problems, creating climates that result in mutual respect and caring for all individuals in the system, facilitating decision-making and collaboration, and fostering a commitment to quality, effective services for all children, youth, and families.

School psychologists regularly contribute to the development of school, agency, community, and/or public policies and procedures that advocate for effective programs and services and benefit all children, youth, and families. They have the knowledge and skills to assume leadership roles in the development of systems change plans and/or public policies (e.g., state or local school improvement plans) that directly impact the programs and services available to children, youth, and their families in schools and communities and that directly impact the ways in which school psychologists deliver their services. School psychologists assist in the development of policies and procedures to ensure that schools are safe and violence free. They participate in the implementation and evaluation of programs that result in safe and violence free schools and communities.

2.7 Prevention, Crisis Intervention, and Mental Health: School psychologists have knowledge of human development and psychopathology and of associated biological, cultural, and social influences on human behavior. School psychologists provide or contribute to prevention and intervention programs that promote the mental health and physical well-being of students.

EXPANDED DESCRIPTION: School psychologists have knowledge of current theory and research about child and adolescent development; psychopathology; human diversity; biological, cultural, and social influences on behavior; societal stressors; crises in schools and communities; and other factors. They apply their knowledge of these factors to the identification and recognition of behaviors that are precursors to academic, behavioral, and serious personal difficulties (e.g., conduct disorders, internalizing disorders, drug and alcohol abuse, etc.). They have knowledge of effective prevention strategies and develop, implement, and evaluate programs based on recognition of the precursors that lead to children's severe learning and behavior problems. School psychologists have knowledge of crisis intervention and collaborate with school personnel, parents, and the community in the aftermath of crises (e.g., suicide, death, natural disasters, murder, bombs or bomb threats, extraordinary violence, sexual harassment, etc.).

School psychologists are key participants in health programs for children and promote mental health in schools and other agencies. They have knowledge of and address diverse health issues such as diet, eating disorders, teenage pregnancy, AIDS prevention, and stress management. They collaborate with other health care professionals to promote behaviors that lead to good health for children. They facilitate environmental changes that support the health and adjustment of children. They have knowledge of and routinely access resources to address a wide variety of behavioral, learning, mental, and physical problems.

2.8 Home/School/Community Collaboration: School psychologists have knowledge of family systems, including family strengths and influences on student development, learning, and behavior, and of methods to involve families in education and service delivery. School psychologists work effectively with families, educators, and others in the community to promote and provide comprehensive services to children and families.

EXPANDED DESCRIPTION: School psychologists have a current knowledge base about (a) family systems and their influences on students' cognitive, motivational, and social characteristics that affect their development and/or academic performance; (b) family involvement in education; (c) methods to promote collaboration and partnerships between parents and educators that improve outcomes for students; (d) cultural issues that impact home-school collaboration; and (e) other family, home, and community factors that work to support learning and achievement in school. School psychologists apply this knowledge to design, implement, and evaluate programs that promote school, family, and/or community partnerships and enhance academic and behavioral goals for students. For example, school psychologists provide or collaborate with others in the development of educational and support programs that assist parents in efforts to enhance the academic and social/behavioral success of their children.

School psychologists provide support and assistance for parents when participating in school functions or activities and help them become comfortable, active, effective participants. For example, they provide support for parents when participating on special education and IEP teams, they encourage parent involvement in school wide committees and improvement teams, and they facilitate home-school communication and collaboration when problems arise. School psychologists have knowledge of and apply methods to facilitate collaboration between schools and parents in designing school curriculum and interventions for students.

School psychologists educate schools and communities regarding the influence of family involvement on children's development and achievement and advocate for parent involvement in school governance whenever feasible. They are knowledgeable about school and community resources; help create links between schools, families, and community agencies; and help coordinate services when programming for children, including multiple agencies. School psychologists work within the local system of care to provide for the health and mental health needs of children.

2.9 Research and Program Evaluation: School psychologists have knowledge of research, statistics, and evaluation methods. School psychologists evaluate research, translate research into practice, and understand research design and statistics in sufficient depth to plan and conduct investigations and program evaluations for improvement of services.

EXPANDED DESCRIPTION: School psychologists have knowledge of basic principles of research design, including single subject design and quantitative and qualitative research techniques, and apply the principles in their own research and as consumers of others' research. They differentiate acceptable from inadequate research and evaluate research in terms of its internal and external validity. They have knowledge of research and statistics in sufficient depth to evaluate published research and to plan and conduct their own investigations. They have knowledge of evaluation techniques and methods and integrate their knowledge of research, statistics, and evaluation when collecting data about school and community programs and in other program accountability activities. School psychologists have knowledge of measurement principles and psychometric standards and apply the knowledge when selecting and using assessment techniques and published tests. They review and evaluate validity research and psychometric properties when selecting the best assessment methods to use in data-based decision-making.

School psychologists maintain a professional knowledge base of research findings, professional literature, and other information relevant to their work and apply the knowledge base to all components of their work. They base their practice on sound research and translate new research findings into service delivery improvements. School psychologists have knowledge of and apply findings from intervention research when designing educational, mental health, or treatment programs for children.

School psychologists provide leadership in schools and other agencies in understanding and using research and evaluation data. They apply their knowledge and skills in statistics and measurement to assist school or agency personnel with valid interpretation and use of school and/or district data. School psychologists provide information about relevant research findings to school personnel, parents, and the public.

2.10 School Psychology Practice and Development: School psychologists have knowledge of the history and foundations of their profession; of various service models and methods; of public policy development applicable to services to children and families; and of ethical, professional, and legal standards. School psychologists practice in ways that are consistent with applicable standards, are involved in their profession, and have the knowledge and skills needed to acquire career-long professional development.

EXPANDED DESCRIPTION: School psychologists have knowledge of the standards, models, methods, and practices of their profession and apply their knowledge to all aspects of their professional services. They have knowledge of the history and foundations of school psychology, as well as psychology, education, special education, health care, and related fields and use this understanding in work with children, parents, and professionals in schools and other agencies. They have knowledge of all appropriate ethical, professional, and legal standards, and they practice in schools and other settings in ways that meet standards, both to enhance the quality of services and to protect the rights of all parties. School psychologists promote due process guidelines in all decisions affecting students; maintain accepted standards in assessment, consultation, intervention, and general professional practice; and fulfill all legal requirements, as in response to law and court decisions. They have knowledge of the processes and procedures for public policy development. School psychologists use their knowledge of professional and legal standards to advocate for the rights and welfare of children and families and to promote new public policies and practices in schools and other settings.

School psychologists recognize that their own learning and development must continue throughout their careers. They have knowledge of and apply methods to routinely evaluate their own knowledge, professional competencies, and outcomes of their services and use their evaluation to determine specific needs for their continuing professional development. They recognize their own limitations and biases, as well as those areas in which they have training and expertise. School psychologists plan and implement systematic and effective techniques to enhance their professional development throughout their careers, and they acquire training to meet current needs in schools and other settings. School psychologists maintain certification or licensure and attend continuing professional development activities. They work with other school psychologists and school or agency staff to advocate for continuing professional development opportunities for all personnel.

2.11 Information Technology: School psychologists have knowledge of information sources and technology relevant to their work. School psychologists access, evaluate, and utilize information sources and technology in ways that safeguard or enhance the quality of services.

EXPANDED DESCRIPTION: School psychologists recognize that advances in technology have many positive impacts on the dissemination of information, on their professional practice, and on services for children. School psychologists use the latest technological advances in their work, but also recognize the need to use technology in ways that safeguard or enhance the quality of services. School psychologists have knowledge of information sources and technology and of methods and standards for using information technology to enhance services. School psychologists wisely use information resources such as digital medium (e.g., CD-ROM), the World Wide Web, e-mail, interactive television, distance learning technology, etc. to acquire information, current research findings, and continuing professional development. School psychologists have knowledge and skills in using word processing, spread sheets, test scoring software, and other computer resources to function more effectively and efficiently. School psychologists have current knowledge about technology resources for children (e.g., instructional software, adaptive technology for individuals with disabilities) and use the resources when designing, implementing, and evaluating instructional programs or interventions for children.

DEFINITIONS OF TERMS USED IN *STANDARDS FOR TRAINING AND FIELD PLACEMENT PROGRAMS IN SCHOOL PSYCHOLOGY*

Integrated, sequential program of study—a planned sequence of related courses and field experiences designed around program goals. Course prerequisites, a required program sequence, and/or similar methods ensure candidates complete the program in a systematic, sequential manner.

Practica—closely supervised on-campus or field-based activities designed to develop and evaluate a school psychology candidate's mastery of distinct professional skills consistent with program and/or course goals. Practica activities may be completed as part of separate courses focusing on distinct skills or as part of a more extensive experience that covers a range of skills.

Internship—a supervised, culminating, comprehensive, pre-degree field experience through which school psychology candidates have the opportunity to integrate and apply professional knowledge and skills acquired in prior courses and practica, as well as to acquire new competencies consistent with training program goals.

School setting—a setting in which the primary goal is the education of students of diverse backgrounds, characteristics, abilities, disabilities, and needs who are enrolled in grades P-12. The school setting has available an internal or external pupil services unit that includes at least one credentialed school psychologist and provides a full range of student services.

Program faculty—faculty with primary teaching, supervisory, and/or administrative responsibilities in the school psychology program. Program faculty, as opposed to other faculty who may teach one or more program courses, participate in program decision-making, planning, and evaluation processes.

Continuing professional development—formal post-degree activities designed to enhance the knowledge and/or skills of practicing professionals or to provide opportunities to acquire new knowledge of skills.

Residency—a university or program requirement that a specified minimum number of credit hours be completed within a minimum time period. At the graduate level, full-time enrollment is typically defined as at least nine semester hours or the equivalent during any one semester. Thus, one academic year of "continuous" residency is typically defined as enrollment in at least nine semester hours per semester for a period of one academic year or two consecutive semesters.

Alternative planned experiences—planned experiences designed to accomplish many of the same goals as full-time, continuous residency. Examples include required attendance at regularly scheduled program/department seminars, participation with other candidates and faculty in professional organization meetings, participation with other candidates and faculty in ongoing research, program development and/or service activities, and similar regularly scheduled activities that provide opportunities for candidates to develop an affiliation with colleagues, faculty, and the profession.

Institutional documentation of program completion—"official" documentation provided by the higher education institution (or by a unit of the institution) that an individual has completed the entire required program of studies, including the internship. Institutional documentation is typically in the form of a degree or diploma, certificate of advanced graduate studies, transcript notation indicating program completion, or similar documentation.

Degree specialization in school psychology—a degree specifically in school psychology or a degree in an allied field (e.g., educational or counseling psychology), but with a formal, identifiable specialization in school psychology. A specialization is typically noted on the diploma or academic transcript.

FTE—full-time equivalent. The ratio of FTE candidates to FTE faculty consists of candidates enrolled full-time in the program to full-time program faculty, and/or a pro-rated proportion of part-time candidates and/or part-time faculty. Interns may be pro-rated based on the semester hours enrolled and the amount of supervision provided by program faculty.

Specialist level internship or equivalent experience—completion of a supervised internship as part of one's specialist level program or similar, supervised field experience. Experiences considered equivalent to such an internship must be defined by the program.

Graduate semester hours—units of graduate credit based on a semester course schedule. In cases in which a quarter schedule system is used, three quarter hours equals two semester hours. Thus, 90 quarter hours of credit are essentially equivalent to 60 semester hours.

Public policy—a dynamic process reflecting the nature, values, and operations of a political system such as the government or one of its subparts (e.g., schools), and includes the positive and negative consequences of government action. The process includes the establishment of priorities and the allocation and reallocation of available resources to specific plans, goals, or tasks to achieve these priorities. As such, public policy serves to create, improve, or dissolve the very systems within which school psychologists work. (Adapted from: Dye, T. R. (1995). *Understanding public policy.* Englewood Cliffs, NJ: Prentice-Hall.)

IV Appendix IV — Standards for the Credentialing of School Psychologists

Credentialing is the process that authorizes the use of the title, "School Psychologist," or related titles, by those professionals meeting accepted standards of training and experience who seek to provide school psychological services. The purpose of this document is to provide guidelines to state and national bodies for the establishment of, and procedural processes involved in, implementing credentialing standards. These guidelines were developed and approved by the National Association of School Psychologists (NASP) pursuant to its mission to promote educationally and psychologically healthy environments for all children and youth and to advance the standards of the profession of school psychology.

The National School Psychology Certification System (NSPCS) was created by NASP to establish a nationally recognized standard for credentialing school psychologists. The title to be used by persons accepted into the NSPCS is "Nationally Certified School Psychologist," or NCSP. Among the purposes of this national credentialing system are to promote uniform credentialing standards across states, agencies, and training institutions and to facilitate credentialing of school psychologists across states through the use of equivalency.

The NASP *Standards for the Credentialing of School Psychologists* are used by the NSPCS and are considered appropriate for states to use in executing their authority in credentialing school psychologists.

CREDENTIALING STRUCTURE

1. Legal Basis for Credentialing

1.1 Credentialing is the process whereby a state authorizes the provision of school psychological services and the use of the title, "School Psychologist," (or related titles, such as "School Psychology Specialist") by professionals who meet accepted standards of training and experience. The basis of a state's credentialing authority is found in its statutory laws. Under these laws, all providers of school psychological services and all users of the title "School Psychologist" must hold a current credential, and legal sanctions and sanctioning procedures are provided for violators.

2. Credentialing Body

2.1 The state legislature empowers one or more bodies to administer the credentialing (certification and/or licensure) process. Administrative codes and regulations adopted by such bodies will comply with these *Standards for the Credentialing of School Psychologists* (or their equivalent) and carry the weight of law.

3. Nature of the Credential

3.1 The credential is issued in writing and expressly authorizes both the practice of school psychology as defined by NASP's *Guidelines for the Provision of School Psychological Services* and the exclusive use of the title "School Psychologist" in all settings.

3.2 The credential is issued for a minimum period of three years.

3.3 Where a state empowers more than one body to issue more than one type of credential, such as for the separate regulation of school psychological services in the public schools and in independent practice, the lowest entry levels of all such credentials conform to these standards.

3.4 Upon completion of one academic year of post-degree supervision, the credential will allow school psychologists to have professional autonomy in determining the nature, scope, and extent of their specific services in all settings. These services will be consistent with NASP definitions of school psychological services and will be delivered within the bounds of the school psychologist's training, supervised experience, and demonstrated expertise as specified in NASP's *Guidelines for the Provision of School Psychological Services and Principles for Professional Ethics.*

CREDENTIALING REQUIREMENTS

4. Criteria for Credentialing

4.1 The minimum requirement for credentialing will be a sixth year/specialist program, with a 60 graduate semester hour minimum, consisting of coursework, practica, internship, and an appropriate graduate degree from an organized program of study that is officially titled "School Psychology." Criteria for each area will be consistent with NASP's *Standards for Training and Field Placement Programs in School Psychology.*

4.2 Domains of Professional Practice
The applicant will complete an integrated and sequential program of study that is explicitly designed to develop knowledge and practice competencies in each of the Domains of Professional Practice. Competency requires both knowledge and skills. School psychology programs ensure that candidates have a foundation in the knowledge base for psychology and education, including theories, models, empirical findings, and techniques in each domain. School psychology programs also ensure that candidates demonstrate the professional skills necessary to deliver effective services that result in positive outcomes in each domain. The domains on the following page are not mutually exclusive and should be fully integrated into graduate level curricula, practica, and internship. Domains of Professional Practice are more fully illustrated on page 22 of NASP's *Standards for Training and Field Placement Programs in School Psychology.*

1. **Data-Based Decision-Making and Accountability:**
School psychologists have knowledge of varied models and methods of assessment that yield information useful in identifying strengths and needs, in understanding problems, and in measuring progress and accomplishments. School psychologists use such models and methods as part of a systematic process to collect data and other information, translate assessment results into empirically-based decisions about service delivery, and evaluate the outcomes of services. Data-based decision-making permeates every aspect of professional practice.

2. **Consultation and Collaboration:** School psychologists have knowledge of behavioral, mental health, collaborative, and/or other consultation models and methods and of their application to particular situations. School psychologists collaborate effectively with others in planning and decision-making processes at the individual, group, and system levels.

3. **Effective Instruction and Development of Cognitive/ Academic Skills:** School psychologists have knowledge of human learning processes, techniques to assess these processes, and direct and indirect services applicable to the development of cognitive and academic skills. School psychologists, in collaboration with others, develop appropriate cognitive and academic goals for students with different abilities, disabilities, strengths, and needs; implement interventions to achieve those goals; and evaluate the effectiveness of interventions. Such interventions include, but are not limited to, instructional interventions and consultation.

4. **Socialization and Development of Life Skills:**
School psychologists have knowledge of human developmental processes, techniques to assess these processes, and direct and indirect services applicable to the development of behavioral, affective, adaptive, and social skills. School psychologists, in collaboration with others, develop appropriate behavioral,

affective, adaptive, and social goals for students of varying abilities, disabilities, strengths, and needs; implement interventions to achieve those goals; and evaluate the effectiveness of interventions. Such interventions include, but are not limited to, consultation, behavioral assessment/intervention, and counseling.

5. **Student Diversity in Development and Learning:**
   School psychologists have knowledge of individual differences, abilities, and disabilities and of the potential influence of biological, social, cultural, ethnic, experiential, socioeconomic, gender-related, and linguistic factors in development and learning. School psychologists demonstrate the sensitivity and skills needed to work with individuals of diverse characteristics and to implement strategies selected and/or adapted based on individual characteristics, strengths, and needs.

6. **School and Systems Organization, Policy Development, and Climate:** School psychologists have knowledge of general education, special education, and other educational and related services. They understand schools and other settings as systems. School psychologists work with individuals and groups to facilitate policies and practices that create and maintain safe, supportive, and effective learning environments for children and others.

7. **Prevention, Crisis Intervention, and Mental Health:**
   School psychologists have knowledge of human development and psychopathology and of associated biological, cultural, and social influences on human behavior. School psychologists provide or contribute to prevention and intervention programs that promote the mental health and physical well-being of students.

8. **Home/School/Community Collaboration:**
   School psychologists have knowledge of family systems, including family strengths and influences on student development, learning, and behavior, and of methods to involve families in education and service delivery. School psychologists work effectively with families, educators, and others in the community to promote and provide comprehensive services to children and families.

9. Research and Program Evaluation: School psychologists have knowledge of research, statistics, and evaluation methods. School psychologists evaluate research, translate research into practice, and understand research design and statistics in sufficient depth to plan and conduct investigations and program evaluations for improvement of services.

10. **School Psychology Practice and Development:** School psychologists have knowledge of the history and foundations of their profession; of various service models and methods; of public policy development applicable to services to children and families; and of ethical, professional, and legal standards. School psychologists practice in ways that are consistent with applicable standards, are involved in their profession, and have the knowledge and skills needed to acquire career-long professional development.

11. **Information Technology:** School psychologists have knowledge of information sources and technology relevant to their work. School psychologists access, evaluate, and utilize information sources and technology in ways that safeguard or enhance the quality of services.

4.3 Practica will consist of a sequence of closely supervised on-campus or field-based activities designed to develop and evaluate a candidate's mastery of distinct professional skills consistent with program and/or course goals. Practica activities may be completed as part of separate courses focusing on distinct skills or as part of a more extensive experience that covers a range of skills.

4.4 The internship experience will consist of a full-time experience over one year, or half-time over two consecutive years, with a minimum of 1200 clock hours, of which at least 600 hours must be in a school setting. A comprehensive internship experience is required for candidates to demonstrate, under supervision, the ability to integrate knowledge and skills in the professional practice domains and to provide a broad range of outcome-based school psychological services. Internship experiences are provided at or near the end of the formal training period, are designed according to a written plan that provides a broad range of experiences, occur in a setting appropriate to the specific training objectives of the program, are provided appropriate recognition through the awarding of academic credit, occur under conditions of appropriate supervision, are systematically evaluated in a manner consistent with the specific training objectives of the program, and are conducted in accordance with current legal and ethical standards for the profession.

4.5 Professional Work Characteristics
The candidate's professional work characteristics will be evaluated and verified by the school psychology training program through information collected during courses, practica, internship, and other appropriate means. Professional work characteristics will include:
1. Respect for human diversity
2. Communication skills
3. Effective interpersonal relations
4. Ethical responsibility
5. Adaptability
6. Initiative and dependability

CREDENTIALING PROCEDURES

5. Implementation of Credentialing Criteria

5.1 Graduates of NASP approved programs, or programs consistent with NASP's *Standards for Training and Field Placement Programs in School Psychology,* and graduates of school psychology programs that, at the time of the applicant's graduation, were accredited by an agency approved by the U.S. Department of Education and met the internship requirement specified in Standard 4.4, are eligible for credentialing. (A complete listing of NASP approved programs, *Approved Programs in School Psychology,* is published annually.)

5.2 Each program that meets the criteria in Standard 5.1 is responsible for assessing a candidate's professional work characteristics and competency in the domains of professional practice.

5.3 All assessment methods used by the credentialing body or training program rely on the most objective, quantifiable, and reliable procedures available. Performance-based assessment uses multiple methods of assessment including multiple data sources, environments, and domains.

5.4 The responsibility for the final determination of professional competencies in all areas rests with the credentialing body.

6. State Credential

6.1 The state credential is granted to individuals who meet the requirements described in Standard 4, including completion of an appropriate graduate degree, demonstration of professional work characteristics, completion of applied professional practice, and competency in the domains of professional practice.

6.2 Persons who hold the credential Nationally Certified School Psychologist (NCSP) meet the criteria for an initial state credential.

6.3 Upon initial granting of the state credential, the individual arranges supervision and mentoring to assure that entry-level qualifications are translated into ongoing competency in the provision of school psychological services. Supervision consists of a minimum of two hours per week, in a face-to-face format, for the initial academic year of full-time practice or the equivalent.

6.4 Supervision and mentoring will be provided by a credentialed school psychologist with a minimum of three years of experience. For any portion of the experience that is accumulated in a non-school setting, supervision and mentoring will be provided by a psychologist or school psychologist appropriately credentialed for practice in that setting.

6.5 Initial renewal of the state credential will be granted to applicants meeting the following criteria:
   A. Evidence of public, private, or university-based practice for a minimum of one academic year of full-time equivalent (FTE) experience during the previous three years.
   B. Evidence of continuing professional development for a minimum of 75 clock hours in the previous three year period during which the credential was in effect.

7. Nationally Certified School Psychologist

7.1 The credential, Nationally Certified School Psychologist (NCSP), is granted to persons who have successfully met national training standards by:
   A. Achieving a passing score on the Educational Testing Service's (ETS) School Psychology Examination as determined by the National School Psychology Certification Board, and
   B. Graduation from a NASP approved program, or
   C. Completion of a sixth-year/specialist level program or higher in school psychology, with a 60 graduate semester hour minimum or equivalent, consisting of course work, practica, internship, and an appropriate graduate degree from an organized program of study that is officially titled "School Psychology," and
   D. Successful completion of a 1,200 clock hour supervised internship in school psychology, at least 600 hours of which must be in a school setting, and
   E. Demonstration of competency in the domains of professional practice as specified in Standard 4.2.

7.2 Renewal of the NCSP will be granted to applicants who complete at least 75 contact hours of continuing professional development activities within a three-year period.

8. Withdrawal/Termination of the Credential

8.1 The credentialing body has the right to cancel, revoke, suspend, or refuse to renew the credential of any school psychologist, or to reprimand any school psychologist, upon proof that the school psychologist has engaged in unprofessional conduct as defined by NASP's *Principles for Professional Ethics* or *Guidelines for the Provision of School Psychological Services.* Such action must be based on a formal finding of guilt by the appropriate adjudicating body after following a documented procedure ensuring that the due process rights of all parties involved have been fully observed.

APPENDIX A

Definition of Terms Used in *Standards for the Credentialing of School Psychologists*

STANDARD 3.1:
NASP *Guidelines for the Provision of School Psychological Services*: The current standards document from the National Association of School Psychologists (NASP) describing the delivery of appropriate and comprehensive school psychological services for administrative and employing agencies.

STANDARD 3.4:
NASP *Principles for Professional Ethics*: The current document of principles from the National Association of School Psychologists (NASP) describing guidelines for ethical behavior including professional competency, professional relationships and responsibilities, and professional practices in public and private settings.

STANDARD 4.1:
NASP *Standards for Training and Field Placement Programs in School Psychology*: The current standards document from the National Association of School Psychologists (NASP) describing procedural standards supporting the comprehensive training of school psychologists at the doctoral and sixth year/specialist levels.

STANDARD 4.4:
School Setting (from Appendix A of NASP *Standards for Training and Field Placement Programs in School Psychology*): A setting in which the primary goal is the education of P-12 students of diverse backgrounds, characteristics, abilities, disabilities, and needs. The school setting has available an internal or

external pupil services unit that includes at least one credentialed school psychologist and provides a full range of student services.

STANDARD 5.1:
***Approved Programs in School Psychology*:** The National Association of School Psychologists (NASP) publishes annually a list of training programs in school psychology that have been determined to meet NASP *Standards for Training and Field Placement Programs in School Psychology.* A copy of the Approved Program list can be obtained by contacting the National Association of School Psychologists at 4340 East West Highway, Suite 402, Bethesda, Maryland 20814, by e-mail at *cert@naspweb.org*, or can be found at the NASP website: *www.naspweb.org*

V Appendix V — National School Psychology Certification System

NCSP RENEWAL MATERIAL

The contents were approved by the NASP Executive Board in January 1992. Revisions were approved by the National School Psychology Certification Board in September 1996. Editorial and format changes were made by the NASP Professional Development Committee in November 1996. Revisions were approved by the National Association of School Psychologists Executive Council in July 2001.

Additional copies are available on the web: www.nasponline.org

INTRODUCTION

National Association of School Psychologists (NASP) assumes that all school psychologists, and particularly those participating in the National School Psychology Certification System, have a common ethic and goal to grow professionally. It is a professional obligation to remain current regarding developments in research, training, and professional practices that benefit children, family, and schools (*Standard for the Provision of School Psychological Services*, *Professional Conduct Manual*, 2000). Membership in professional organizations, attendance at professional conferences, reading of professional literature, and discussion of professional issues with colleagues are essential components of any school psychologist's overall professional development activities. Because the knowledge base of the field is broad, training and skill levels are varied, and the professional role has many dimensions, school psychologists will want to have a personal plan for professional development. The plan should be designed to include a broad range of experiences and topics and should be unique to the needs of each individual.

Participation in the NASPs' Professional Development Program requires 75 hours of continuing professional development (CPD) activities within a three-year period. Nationally Certified School Psychologists (NCSP) are expected to document and maintain records of their CPD activities.

It is expected that school psychologists will enhance their skills in a variety of areas. Although activities covering specific skill areas are not required for the NCSP renewal, expanding one's knowledge in less familiar areas is an important aspect of professional growth. Continuing professional development should involve a variety of learning activities covering a wide range of topics.

Inasmuch as school psychologists function in a variety of job assignments in many diverse locations, NASP recognizes the importance and availability of formal and informal in-service opportunities. The intent of the CPD requirement, therefore, is not to limit the school psychologist's continuing professional development by approving only specific activities but rather to acknowledge and encourage participation in the variety of activities that are available.

SUBMITTING YOUR RENEWAL FOR PROCESSING

As of September 1, 2001, a new process for submitting your NCSP renewal is in effect. NCSPs are no longer required to submit documentation of CPD credits unless audited. The rules for the audit process are listed separately in this document.

The renewal process now consists of the following four steps:

1. Complete and maintain the documentation identifying the activities completed for the required 75 contact hours of continuing professional development. Information on proper documentation can be found later in this booklet under **Guidelines for Documentation of CPD Activities. KEEP THIS DOCUMENTATION** for your own records. Do not send it with your renewal documentation.

2. Sign the affidavit attesting to participation in the required CPD activities and agreeing to an audit if notified.

3. Fill out the Directory Information Listing and Renewal Questionnaire forms.

4. Submit the appropriate payment, including any late fees that may have accrued.

Copies of the necessary forms are included with this booklet. The renewal documentation forms are available on the web at www.nasponline.org.

FEES

Current fees for the NCSP credential renewal are located on the Directory Information form.

Late fees for renewal are assessed one calendar month after the NCSP credential expires. To avoid being assessed the late fee, the renewal must be received in the NASP office on or before the last day of the month after it expires. The late fee is listed on the Directory Information form. Any NCSP submitting a renewal that will be received one calendar month after the expiration date must include the appropriate late fees with the renewal.

AUDIT GUIDELINES

NCSPs are required to maintain proper documentation of their CPD activities. This will be in the form of the documentation discussed under "Submitting Your Renewal for Processing." Individuals will be subject to a random audit of their CPD documentation. The audit will ensure that the number of contact hours of CPD activities was accomplished as stated on the signed affidavit and that proper documentation of CPD activities is being maintained. An individual will be notified of an audit in writing. This notification may be sent at any time after the individual renews his/her NCSP credential. In general, approximately 15% of the renewals submitted will be subject to an audit.

An individual selected for audit has 60 days from the date of the notice to submit documentation of 75 CPD credits. CPD credits will meet the guidelines listed below. The NCSP will be considered expired if the individual fails to respond within the 60-day time limit.

Once the documentation of credits has been received and processed, the NCSP will be notified of the audit results. If it is determined that the NCSP has any deficiencies, the NCSP will be given 60 days to correct the deficiency. Any deficiency not corrected within the 60-day period will cause the immediate expiration of the NCSP credential.

Documentation submitted for an audit will not be returned. Copies of the documentation are acceptable; please do not submit your originals.

GUIDELINES FOR CONTINUING PROFESSIONAL DEVELOPMENT ACTIVITIES

Develop a Personal Plan

Activities should be chosen as part of an overall professional development plan devised by each school psychologist to enhance knowledge in several foundation areas. While submission of a formal plan is not required, participants are encouraged to devise such a plan for themselves.

Plan for a variety of activities that emphasize learning including workshop experiences, coursework, presentations, self study, program development, or research. These activities should exceed the ordinary aspects of employment.

Evaluate the Benefit

School psychologists may evaluate and select CPD activities and claim the activities for CPD credit without contacting NASP for pre-approval of these activities. There are four questions to ask when evaluating an activity to determine if it may be claimed for CPD credit. A "Yes" to all four of the following questions means the NCSP may claim CPD credit for the activity:

1. **Did the activity enhance or upgrade my professional skills or add to my knowledge base?**

2. **Was the activity relevant to the professional practice of school psychology?**
3. **Did the activity fit into my personal plan for continuing professional development?**

4. **Did the activity go beyond the ordinary aspects of my employment?**

Questions regarding the acceptability of a specific activity should be directed to the NASP Professional Standards Program at the NASP office.

GUIDELINES FOR DOCUMENTATION OF CPD ACTIVITIES

All NCSPs are required to maintain proper documentation of participation in CPD activities. If an NCSP is notified of an audit this documentation must be submitted to the NASP office within sixty (60) calendar days.

Continuing Professional Development Activity Categories

Consistent with the NASP *Standards for the Provision of School Psychological Services* (2000), participation in activities designed to maintain and expand skills and to ensure quality service provision is the continuing obligation of school psychologists. With this in mind, NASP offers CPD credit for the following activities:

GROUP A	Workshops, Conferences, and In-service Training
GROUP B	College/University Courses
GROUP C	Teaching and Training Activities
GROUP D	Research & Publications
GROUP E	Supervision of Interns
GROUP F	Post-Graduate Supervised Experiences
GROUP G	Program Planning/Evaluation
GROUP H	Self Study –Sequenced Programs –Informal Programs
GROUP I	Professional Organization Leadership

CPD Credit

One (1) CPD credit is defined as one (1) contact hour or an actual clock hour (60 minutes) spent in direct participation in a structured educational format as a learner. Some organizations award CPD activities using a standard called Continuing Education Units (CEUs). One CEU may be equivalent to 10 contact hours or 10 CPD credits. It depends on the number of clock hours you spent in the activity.

CPD credits are considered expired after three (3) years. The three-year period is counted backward from the month the renewal is submitted to the NASP office. For example, if the renewal is submitted in June of 2003, credits earned from June of 2000 through June of 2003 would be accepted for that renewal cycle. Credits from a previous renewal cycle may *not* be resubmitted. Credits above the required 75 hours may *not* be carried over to the next renewal cycle.

Proper Documentation Guidelines

Refer to the Summary Table of CPD Credit Allowances and Ceilings to determine the required documentation for each activity. The Summary Table is located near the end of this document. Several forms of documentation are acceptable:

Certificate of Attendance	Certificates of attendance or log sheets of participation provided by the CPD sponsor are required
Official Transcripts	Official transcripts are required for college or university credit
Summary Reports	Summary Reports can be used in states where professional development is required for maintenance of certification or licensure or in school districts or other agencies/organizations where professional development is required.
Activity Documentation Form	Any activity not otherwise documented per the above instructions can be documented with this form

Participation in CPD activities must be documented properly. Documentation of CPD activities should include the following information:

- Name of participant
- NCSP or membership number
- Category or type of activity
- Date of activity
- Hours of participation
- Title or topic of activity
- Activity sponsor

CPD Categories and Credit Allowances

The NASP Continuing Professional Development Program allows a variety of activities that have potential for enhancing a school psychologist's knowledge and skills.

Some activities earn one hour of CPD credit for each contact hour of participation and have no ceiling limits in terms of the number of credits that can be accumulated. Other activity categories have a maximum credit allowance and restrictions on the frequency in which credit can be claimed.

CATEGORY A: WORKSHOPS, CONFERENCES, IN-SERVICE TRAINING

This category also includes seminars/workshops taken via web cast, ITTS (interactive television), and distance learning programs.

Credit Allowances — One hour of participation = 1 CPD credit

Ceiling Limit — None

Required Documentation — Certificate of Attendance or Activity Documentation Form. Program flyers, handouts, agendas, and brochures are not acceptable forms of documentation. Please use an Activity Documentation Form if only a program flyer or agenda is available.

CATEGORY B: COLLEGE/UNIVERSITY COURSES

Distance learning courses resulting in college/university credit are included in this category.

Credit Allowances — This category refers to courses completed beyond those required for entry-level certification/ licensure.
1 quarter hour = 10 CPDs
1 semester hour = 15 CPDs

Ceiling Limit — None

Required Documentation — Official college/university transcript

CATEGORY C: TEACHING AND TRAINING ACTIVITIES

Credit Allowances — One hour of participation = 1 CPD credit except as noted. CPD credits should not be claimed for activities such as workshops or in-service training that are part of the school psychologist's regular job requirements. However, credit may be claimed for those teaching/training activities that go beyond the normal demands of each psychologist's job setting.

Ceiling Limit — Although the course or in-service training may be repeated, credit may only be claimed once.

Required Documentation — Copy of an Activity Documentation Form or course syllabus and/or program flyer with category C, the hours of CPD credit, date of training and sponsor included on the documentation.

CATEGORY D: RESEARCH & PUBLICATIONS

Credit Allowances — Research and publications are valuable professional activities. To claim credit in this category, it is necessary for the participant to reasonably estimate the amount of time spent and claim those actual hours up to the maximum specified.

Ceiling Limit — Unpublished research = 10 CPD credit maximum per project
Research and publication or presentation on a topic = 25 CPD credits maximum per project

Non-research-based published articles with references or poster presentation at a state or national convention = 10 CPD credits maximum per project
Published theoretical or editorial articles = 5 CPD credits maximum per project

All participants in this category should claim credit *only once for any project.*

Required Documentation — Activity Documentation Form and abstract of article if possible.

CATEGORY E: SUPERVISION OF INTERNS

Credit Allowances — For purposes of claiming CPD credit, field-supervisors of school psychology interns should consider the extent to which this role leads to professional growth on the part of the supervisor.

Supervision of one intern for one academic year = 10 CPD credits maximum.

Ceiling Limits — 20 CPD credits (no more than two interns in a three year period)

Required Documentation — Activity Documentation Form

CATEGORY F: POST-GRADUATE SUPERVISED EXPERIENCE

Credit Allowances — Following completion of their school psychology degrees, many school psychologists participate in supervised fellowships, internships, or other experiences to acquire new knowledge and skills. The supervised experiences may occur in settings outside the school psychologist's regular job setting or may occur as part of a planned and sequential program on the job. For purposes of claiming CPD credit for this activity category, school psychologists should consider the extent to which the supervised experience leads to professional growth and new knowledge and skills. CPD credit may *not* be claimed for regular supervised experiences that are required as part of the school psychologist's employment. CPD credit may be claimed according to the percentage of the school psychologist's time spent in the supervised experience, according to the following:

1/4 time = 5 CPD maximum — 1/2 time = 10 CPD maximum
3/4 time = 15 CPD maximum — full time = 20 CPD maximum

Ceiling Limits — Credit for supervised experiences may be claimed no more than twice (for two years) during a three-year renewal period.
Note: If the experience is taken for university/college course credit, Activity Category B should be used instead of Category F. In addition, some activities during the supervised experience, such as attendance at conferences or in-service training or informal programs of self-study, may earn CPD credit in other activity categories.

Required Documentation — Activity Documentation Form

CATEGORY G: PROGRAM PLANNING/EVALUATION

Credit Allowances — Program planning/evaluation may be claimed when it is not an ordinary aspect of one's employment.
One hour of participation = 1 CPD credit

Ceiling Limits — 25 CPD credits maximum. Only one project may be submitted in a three-year period.

Required Documentation — Activity Documentation Form

CATEGORY H: SELF STUDY

Credit Allowances — Two types of self-study are valid for CPD credit:

Sequenced Programs are self studies developed and published to provide training in specific knowledge or skill areas. A test is typically given at the end of the course and usually a certificate of completion is issued. This could also include a course taken on the Internet and is issued a credit.
One Topic= 15 CPD credits (unless otherwise specified and documented in self-study publication)

Informal Programs involve systematically studying a topic of interest by reviewing the literature and becoming familiar with the available resources. Included in this category would be book, journal, and manual reading.
One topic = 15 CPD credit maximum

Ceiling Limits — Sequenced Program = no more than 30 CPD credits in a three year period
Informal Programs = no more than 2 topics or 30 CPD credits during a three year period

Required Documentation — Certificate of Completion or Activity Documentation Form (including four professional sources per self study topic)

CATEGORY I: PROFESSIONAL ORGANIZATIONAL LEADERSHIP

Credit Allowances — A school psychologist who holds a position in a local, state, or national professional organization may earn CPD credit.
President = 10 CPD credits
Other Officer = 5 CPD credits
Delegate Representative, Delegate, or Committee Chair = 5 CPD credits

Ceiling Limit — Credit may be obtained for no more than one position, per year, per organization with a maximum 20 CPD credits in 3 years.

Required Documentation — Activity Documentation Form

NATIONAL CERTIFICATION RENEWAL POLICY

The following policies, along with the previously stated guidelines, apply to the renewal of the NCSP credential:

1. The credential is valid for three years unless revoked.

2. The NCSP credential must be renewed by the expiration date, else the credential is considered expired.

3. An individual is given a grace period of one calendar month to renew the credential before a late fee is assessed.

4. If an individual earns the required 75 hours of CPD credit prior to his/her expiration date and wishes to renew prior to the expiration date, the renewal materials will be accepted by the NASP office. The full renewal fee must accompany the renewal. The individual's renewal month will be changed to the month the renewal is submitted. This allows flexibility for an individual who wishes to use future CPD credits in his/her next renewal cycle. For example, assume that an individual has earned his/her 75 CPD credits by June 2002 and they do not expire until December 2002. The individual may renew in June 2002, receive an expiration date of June 30, 2005 and use all credits earned during and after June 2002 for their next renewal cycle. (Remember credits from a previous renewal cycle may *not* be resubmitted and credits above the required 75 hours may <u>not</u> be carried over to the next renewal cycle.)

5. Once the NCSP credential expires, the individual has three (3) years to renew. The appropriate late fees must be paid with the renewal. CPD credits are considered expired after three (3) years. The three years are counted backward from the month the renewal materials are received in the NASP office. When an NCSP renews late, the expiration date of the credential is changed to the month the renewal is received. For example, assume an individual's NCSP credential expired on December 31, 2002. The individual submits renewal material along with the late fees in June 2003. CPD credits that were earned from June 2000 through June 2003 must be submitted, and the individual's new expiration date will be June 30, 2006.

6. An individual who fails to renew the NCSP credential within three (3) years of his/her expiration date must re-apply for the NCSP under the current standards at the time of re-application. The current NCSP Application must be submitted with all supporting documentation; the ETS National School Psychology Examination (#10400) must be retaken and the scores submitted to NASP.

7. The NCSP credential expires 36 months (3 years) from the month the renewal is received and processed. The expiration date is always the last day of the month. (See examples listed in #4 and #5 previously.)

8. A new certification card will be sent as verification of renewal.

9. Please refer to your NCSP certification card for your certification number and expiration date

RETIRED STATUS

The NCSP (Retired) designation allows retired NCSP to continue to identify themselves as persons who have met the national standard of their profession. The official title of this designation is "Nationally Certified School Psychologist (Retired)" or "NCSP (Retired)."

ELIGIBILITY

Nationally Certified School Psychologists are eligible for NCSP (Retired) status when the following requirements are met:

- All public or private remunerative activity as a school psychologist has ceased.
- The applicant has been an NCSP for at least six (6) years.
- The applicant is an NCSP in good standing at the time the application is received in the NASP office.

REINSTATEMENT

Should an NCSP (Retired) decide to re-enter the workforce, he/she can convert their NCSP (Retired) status to a full NCSP by completing the current CPD requirements and paying the appropriate renewal fee.

SUMMARY TABLE
CPD CREDIT ALLOWANCES AND CEILINGS

Activity Category	*Cpd Credit Allowances*	*Ceiling Limits*	*Required Documentation*
A. Workshops/ Conferences/ In-Service Training	One hour = 1CPD CREDIT	NONE	Certificate of Attendance or Activity Documentation Form
B. College/University Courses	One quarter hour = 10 CPD CREDITS One semester hour = 15 CPD CREDITS	NONE	Official Transcript
C. Teaching and Training Activities	One hour = 1 CPD CREDIT	Credit may be claimed only first time content is taught.	Copy of course syllabus *or* copy of program flyer *or* Activity Documentation Form
D. Research and Publications	Actual hours, up to maximum specified All maximums specified for this category are per project.	Unpublished Research = 10 CPD CREDIT MAX. Research & Publication or Presentation = 25 CPD CREDIT MAX. Article Published or Poster Presented = 10 CPD CREDIT MAX. Theoretical/editorial article = 5 CPD CREDIT MAX. Each project may only be claimed once.	Activity Documentation Form and abstract of program, if possible
E. Supervision of Interns	1 year of supervision = 10 CPD CREDITS	20 CPD CREDIT MAX. No more than 2 interns in 3 years	Activity Documentation Form
F. Post-Graduate Supervised Experiences	1/4 time = 5 CPD CREDITS MAX. 1/2 time = 10 CPD CREDITS MAX. 3/4 time = 15 CPD CREDITS MAX. full time = 20 CPD CREDITS MAX.	No more than 2 supervised experiences in 3 years	Activity Documentation Form
G. Program Planning/ Evaluation	One hour = 1 CPD CREDIT	25 CPD CREDITS MAX. No more than 1 project in 3 years	Activity Documentation Form
H. Self-Study	Sequenced: 1 topic = 15 CPD CREDITS MAX. Informal: 1 topic = 15 CPD CREDITS MAX.	Sequenced = 30 credits in a 3 year period. Informal = no more than 2 topics or 30 credits in a 3 year period.	Certificate of completion *or* Activity Documentation Form
I. Professional Organization Leadership	President = 10 CPD CREDITS Other Officer = 5 CPD CREDITS Delegate Representative / Delegate/ Committee Chair = 5 CPD CREDITS	No more than one activity per organization per year. No more than 20 CPD CREDITS in a 3-year period.	Activity Documentation Form

AFFIDAVIT OF CONTINUING PROFESSIONAL DEVELOPMENT CREDITS

National Association of School Psychologists
4340 East West Highway, Suite 402, Bethesda, MD 20814
ph: 301-657-0270 fax: 301-657-0275 e-mail: cert@naspweb.org

I hereby attest that the following information is true and accurate. If audited I will provide documentation of all Continuing Professional Development Credits listed. I am keeping and maintaining proper documentation of all Continuing Professional Development Credits earned.

Signature ______________________ Date ______________________

PLEASE PRINT CLEARLY OR TYPE:

Name: ______________________ Certification Number: ______________

Address: ____

City: ______________ State: __________ Zip: ______________

Activity Category	*Credit Allowances*	*Ceiling Limits*	*Total Hours Earned*
A. Workshops/Conferences/ In-Service Training	1 hr = 1 CPD	None	
B. College/University Courses	1 qtr hr = 10 CPD 1 sem hr = 15 CPD	None	
C. Teaching and Training Activities	1 hr = 1 CPD	Credit may be claimed only first time content is taught	
D. Research and Publications	Actual hours, up to maximum specified. All maximums specified for this category are per project. Each project may only be claimed once.	Unpublished research = 10 CPD Max Research & Publication or Presentation = 25 CPD Max Article Published or Poster Presentation = 10 CPD Max Theoretical/Editorial Article = 5 CPD Max	
E. Supervision of Interns	1 yr supervision = 10 CPD	20 CPD Max No more than 2 interns in 3 years	
F. Post-Graduate Supervised Experience	.25 time = 5 CPD Max .5 time = 10 CPD Max .75 time = 15 CPD Max full time = 20 CPD Max	No more than 2 supervised experiences in 3 years	
G. Program Planning/ Evaluation	1 hr = 1 CPD	25 CPD Max No more than 1 project in 3 years	
H. Self Study	Sequenced: 1 topic = 15 CPD Max Informal: 1 topic = 15 CPD Max	Sequenced = 30 CPD Max Informal = 30 CPD Max No more than 2 topics or 30 credits in a three year period	
I. Professional Organization Leadership	President = 10 CPD Max Other Office = 5 CPD Max Delegate Rep. /Delegate/ Committee Chair =5 CPD Max	No more than one activity per organization per year. No more than 20 CPD in a 3-year period.	
		TOTAL CPD HOURS CLAIMED	

REQUIRED: CPD Hours Earned* from (month/year)______________ **to** (month/year)______________

*Credits older than three years are considered expired. The three years is counted backward from the month the renewal is submitted.

Rev.: August, 2001

DIRECTORY INFORMATION

National Association of School Psychologists
4340 East West Highway, Suite 402, Bethesda, MD 20814
ph: 301-657-0270 fax: 301-657-0275 e-mail: cert@naspweb.org

I hereby give my permission for the following information to appear in the NCSP Directory. The Directory is posted on the NASP web site under the NCSP Only Secured page.

________________________________ ____________________
Signature Date

CERTIFICATION NUMBER : ____________________

PLEASE PRINT CLEARLY OR TYPE
(Required information: this information is also used to update your record for future mailing)

Name: ________________________________

Address: ________________________________

City: ________________ State: __________ Zip: __________

(Optional information for directory listing)

Work Phone: ________________ Home Phone: ________________

E-Mail Address: ________________________________

Place of Employment: ________________ Title: ________________

If changes or additions are made in degree, state certification, or state licensure, you must enclose documentation (copies of transcript, certificate or license) to verify these changes or additions.

States Certified: ________________ States Licensed: ________________

Highest Degree Held: ________________ Language Spoken (Other than English): ________________

RENEWAL FEES:

	NASP Members	Non-NASP Members	Quantity	Total
Renewal Fee	$80.00	$115.00	1	
Late Fees* (for every six months the renewal is late)	$13.00	$ 19.00	____	
			Total Amount Due:	

* Late fees for renewal accrue one calendar month after the NCSP credential expires. To avoid being assessed the late fee, the renewal must be received in the NASP office on or before the last day of the month.

Please make check payable to NASP and attach check to this form or complete the charge card information.

Charge to: ☐ Visa ☐ MasterCard Card No: ____________________

Exp. Date: (Month/Year) __________ Signature: ____________________

Rev.: August, 2001

NCSP RENEWAL QUESTIONNAIRE

National Association of School Psychologists
4340 East West Highway, Suite 402, Bethesda, MD 20814
ph: 301-657-0270 fax: 301-657-0275 e-mail: cert@naspweb.org

Name: ______________________________ Certification No.: __________________

Address: ______________________________ Daytime Phone No.: __________________

City, State, Zip: __________________________ Fax No.: ______________________

E-Mail: ____

1. Have you ever been found in violation of ethical principles by an ethics or professional practices board?

   ☐ YES ☐ NO

2. Have you ever voluntarily surrendered a professional credential in response to an ethics charge?

   ☐ YES ☐ NO

3. Have you ever received disciplinary action from an ethics or professional practices board?

   ☐ YES ☐ NO

4. Have you ever had a professional credential revoked, suspended or limited by an ethics or professional practices board?

   ☐ YES ☐ NO

5. Have you ever been convicted of or pleaded guilty or nolo contendere to a felony or other offense, other than a minor traffic offense, in a federal, state, or municipal court?

   ☐ YES ☐ NO

6. Have you ever received formal disciplinary action by an employer or supervisor based wholly or in part on ethical issues?

   ☐ YES ☐ NO

If the answer to any of the above questions is "yes," please provide a complete explanation on a separate page(s).

I verify that the information herein is true and accurate. I further affirm that I will abide by NASP's Principles for Professional Ethics and agree to submit to NASP procedures for adjudication of any alleged violations of same.

______________________________ ____________________

Signature Date

Rev.: August, 2001

ACTIVITY DOCUMENTATION FORM

National Association of School Psychologists
4340 East West Highway, Suite 402, Bethesda, MD 20814
ph: 301-657-0270 fax: 301-657-0275 e-mail: cert@naspweb.org

INSTRUCTIONS: This documentation form is to be used to report activities for which no other standard documentation exists. A separate form must be used for each activity.

Name: ______________________ Certification No.: ______________

Address: ______________________ Daytime Phone No.: ______________

City, State, Zip: ______________________ Fax No.: ______________

E-Mail: ____

Title of Activity: ____

Date(s) of Activity: (month/day/year) ______________ Sponsor: ______________

Description of Activity:

Type of Activity: ____

Actual Number of Clock Hours of Participation: ______________________

CPD Credits Earned (See credit allowances/limits in the CPD table): ______________

I affirm that this activity merits CPD credit in that it meets the following criteria:

1. This activity enhanced my professional skills and/or added to my knowledge base.
2. This activity was relevant to the professional practice of school psychology.
3. This activity is within my personal plan for continuing professional development.
4. This activity exceeded the ordinary aspects of my employment.

The activities reported on this form reflect actual activities in which I participated. I understand that falsification of this information is an ethical violation and may result in my being ineligible for future certification and/or legal actions may be taken against me.

______________________ ______________
(Signature) (Date)

– Reproduce This Form as Needed –

Rev.: August, 2001

VI Appendix VI — Position Statements

Ability Grouping

To ensure educational equity and excellence for all America's youth, NASP supports the creation of inclusive classrooms that are based on the belief that all students can learn—a core value of all schools in a democracy. NASP believes that tracking, or whole class ability grouping, is not consistent with that core value. Extensive research on ability grouping has documented the following negative effects:

- Students with lower ability achieve less in lower track classes than in mixed ability classes.
- Students with higher ability do not achieve more in tracked classes than in mixed ability classes.
- Placing students with lower ability in tracked classrooms reduces self-esteem, with a particularly negative effect on students' sense of their own academic competence.
- Tracking students reduces the likelihood that students placed in lower track classes will choose college preparatory courses.
- Tracking students reduces opportunities to develop relationships among students from other racial, ethnic, and socioeconomic groups and has a negative effect on race relations.
- The placement decision concerning ability grouping is often made very early in a student's school career, is often based on questionable data, and is enduring.

NASP believes that grouping students heterogeneously offers advantages unavailable in schools that track. When implemented appropriately, heterogeneous grouping:

- gives all students equal access to an enriched curriculum and the highest quality instruction schools have to offer;
- avoids labeling and stigmatizing students with lower ability;
- promotes higher expectations for student achievement;
- reduces inschool segregation based on socioeconomic status, race, gender or ethnicity, or disability;
- encourages teachers to accommodate individual differences in students' instructional and social needs;
- enables students to learn from their peers, including students whose background may be very different from their own; and
- emphasizes effort more than ability.

NASP recognizes that heterogeneous grouping will not automatically guarantee all students a quality education. "Watering down" the curriculum or "teaching to the middle" will create disadvantages for able students and should be avoided. While NASP believes that all students can benefit from a more challenging curriculum, we also strongly support the development of a curriculum which recognizes and accommodates individual differences in learning styles, abilities, and interests. To be successful, mixed ability grouping must occur within the context of such a curriculum.

NASP also recognizes that heterogeneous classes require instructional and organizational innovations to accommodate a wide range of learners. Such approaches include cooperative learning groups, peer tutors, flexible grouping practices, team teaching, multiage groupings, and instruction in higher order thinking and problemsolving skills. Where teachers do not currently possess competencies to enable them to work effectively with mixed ability classes, a commitment to further training is essential.

NASP believes that "untracking" schools requires careful planning and collaboration among constituent groups, including teachers, administrators, support personnel, students, and parents. Planned change can best take place using a model that includes the following:

- a steering committee composed of educators, parents, community members and school board representatives whose task is to study grouping practices and make policy recommendations to the school board;

- local self-study to assess the impact of grouping practices within the school community;

- wide dissemination of local and national studies of ability grouping effects;

- a board-approved policy statement on grouping for instruction; and

- implementation of a strategic plan that allows for a phase-in process and ensures monitoring, trouble-shooting, and evaluation.

NASP believes that school psychologists can play a central role in helping schools develop appropriate alternatives to tracking. School psychologists have access to research, understand good instructional practices that enhance learning for all students, and possess group problem-solving skills that make them valuable as members of steering committees and strategic planning groups and as staff trainers.

School psychologists can contribute to the process of untracking schools by:

- making research available to administrators and central office personnel;

- leading informal study groups to explore alternative grouping practices;

- becoming members of steering committees assembled to study tracking and to develop policy recommendations; and

- participating in strategic planning and staff development to prepare for untracking.

NASP recognizes that schools cannot simply eliminate tracking but must develop viable alternatives. Developing alternatives to tracking will take patience and careful planning. In order for schools to live up to the promise of educating all students to become productive citizens of the 21st century, NASP believes these alternatives must be characterized by fairness and challenge, with equity and excellence equally available to all learners.

Adopted by the NASP Delegate Assembly, April 17, 1993
Reapproved by the NASP Delegate Assembly, July 25, 1998

This position statement drew on material from George, P. (1992). How to untrack your school. Alexandria, VA: Association for Supervision and Curriculum Development.

Advocacy for Appropriate Educational Services for All Children

P.L. 94-142 (The Education of All Handicapped Children Act) has achieved major goals in serving handicapped children, many of whom had been previously excluded from appropriate educational programs. Since its enactment in 1975, all handicapped children have been guaranteed a free and appropriate education, the right to due process, and individualization of program according to need. We strongly support the continuation of legislation which has mandated these guarantees.

We also recognize that serious problems have been encountered as school districts strive to meet these mandates and that quality education is still an elusive goal. Some of these problems reflect difficulties within special education; others appear to be special education issues but have their origins in the regular education system.

One major set of problems involves reverse sides of the issue of access to appropriate education:

(1) On the one hand, access to special education must be assured for all significantly handicapped children who need and can benefit from it.

(2) Conversely, children are being inappropriately diagnosed as handicapped and placed in special education because of: (a) a lack of regular education options designed to meet the needs of children with diverse learning styles, (b) a lack of understanding, at times, of diverse cultural and linguistic backgrounds, and (c) inadequate measurement technologies which focus on labels for placement rather than providing information for program development.

It is not a benign action to label as "handicapped" children who are low achievers but are not, in fact, handicapped, even when this is done in order to provide them with services unavailable in general education. School personnel often resort to labeling because it seems the only way to obtain needed services for children. This is an unfortunate result of categorical models which attach funding to classifications. Other problems originating in the classification system include:

- Labels that are often irrelevant to instruction needs.

- Categories,based on deficit labels, that are rather arbitrarily defined, particularly for mildly handicapped and low achieving students, but which come to be accepted as "real" and may prevent more meaningful understanding of the child's psychoeducational needs. The intent of this statement is not necessarily to endorse mixing children with different moderate to severe handicaps in a single special education classroom.

- Reduced expectations for children who are placed in special needs programs.

- Assessment processes aimed at determining eligibility which often deflects limited resources from the determination of functional educational needs and the development of effective psychoeducational programs.

- A decreased willingness on the part of regular education, at times bordering on abdication of responsibility to modify curricula and programs in order to better meet the diverse needs of all children.

As increasing numbers of children are classified as handicapped and removed from regular classrooms for special instruction, there has been a dramatic reduction in the range of abilities among children who remain within the general education system.

Concurrently, as national standards for excellence are being raised, the number of children at risk for school failure is growing dramatically. Without provisions to prepare students for higher expectations through effective instructional programs, many of these children may also be identified as handicapped and placed in special education. This climate, in which children are tested and labeled as failures or as handicapped in increasing numbers, creates an urgent need for reexamination and change in the system which provides access to services.

In view of these problems, and based upon the commitment to see that all children receive effective and appropriate education irrespective of race, cultural background, linguistic background, socio-economic status, or educational need, we believe:

- All children can learn. Schools have a responsibility to teach them, and school personnel and parents should work together to assure every child a free and appropriate education in a positive social environment.

- Instructional options, based on the individual psychoeducational needs of each child, must be maximized within the general education system. Necessary support services should be provided within general education, eliminating the need to classify children as handicapped in order to receive these services.

- Psychoeducational needs of children should be determined through a multi-dimensional, non-biased assessment process. This must evaluate the match between the learner and his or her educational environment, assessing the compatibility of curriculum and system as they interact with the child, rather than relying on the deficit based model which places the blame for failure within the child. Referral to the assessment and placement process must always relate directly to services designed to meet psycho-educational needs.

- In addition to maintaining current protection for handicapped children, protections and safeguards must be developed to assure the rights of children who are at risk for school failure and require services while remaining in general education without classification as handicapped.

We propose a new national initiative to meet the educational needs of all children:

We propose the development and piloting of alternatives to the current categorical system. This requires reevaluation of funding mechanisms, and advocacy for policy and funding waivers needed for the piloting of alternative service delivery models. It also requires the development of increased support systems and extensive retraining of all school personnel to enable them to work effectively with a broad range of children with special needs within the regular education system.

This initiative will encourage greater independence for children by enabling them to function within the broadest possible environment, and independence for school personnel by providing them with training and support so they can help a wide range of children.

The types and extent of change we are suggesting should be made cautiously. Targeted funds intended for children with moderate and severe handicapping conditions must be protected. Similarly, resources for children who are not handicapped, but who experience learning difficulties, must be protected even though these children are served within general education. We need to assure that no child is put at risk for loss of services while the change process is occurring.

Our task is to reduce the rigidities of the current system without taking away the protections offered by P.L. 94-142. All experimentation and research must take place within a framework of maximum protection for children. It is highly likely that this may require the development of temporary parallel systems — the traditional system of classification and placement under P.L. 94-142, and a system of experimental programs, primarily within general education — until satisfactory models can be developed which meet the requirements of accountability, due process, and protection of students' and parents' rights, and provide funding for students in need of services. In addition, while these recommended modifications might reduce the risk of misclassification due to cultural or linguistic differences, we caution that these issues must continue to be monitored and discussed during the transition period and beyond.

Because of the complexity of these issues, the generation of effective solutions will require a national effort of interested persons and organizations which we hope to generate through this task force. We will actively work toward the collaboration of a wide variety of individuals and organizations, joining together to develop a strong base of knowledge, research, and experience in order to establish new frameworks and conceptualizations on which to base decisions, design feasible service delivery options, advocate for policy and funding changes needed to implement these alternatives, and coordinate efforts and share information for positive change. We invite you to join us.

This statement issued jointly by the National Association of School Psychologists and the National Coalition of Students.

School Psychologists' Involvement In The Role of Assessment

The National Association of School Psychologists promotes educational and mental health services for all children and youth. Assessment, linked to prevention and intervention, is an important part of ensuring that all children and youth receive needed services. School psychologists, through training, continuing professional development, research activities and experience, are experts in assessment. They can provide local education agencies, as well as state education agencies, with the knowledge, skills, and techniques needed to restructure schools in positive ways. Thus, NASP endorses assessment practices that are tailored to the needs of the individual student in the context of a comprehensive delivery system which facilitates educational progress for all children.

Evidence from practice and research indicates that:

- specialized training and skills in areas of psychological and educational assessment are needed by those engaged in such practices;
- assessment and intervention should be designed to produce positive outcomes for the student;
- multidisciplinary team assessment must include multiple sources of information, multiple procedures, and multiple settings in order to yield a comprehensive understanding of student's abilities;
- assessment and intervention must be multidimensional and based on the needs of the student;
- family systems and home environments substantially influence the development of all students and should be addressed in assessment;
- parent-professional and where appropriate student collaboration is crucial to decision making as well as to the identification of students' and families' needs;
- longitudinal assessment is needed to evaluate and document progress or response to interventions; and
- assessment information should guide intervention strategies.

Therefore, the National Association of School Psychologists endorses assessment practices that are:

- linked to efforts to resolve the problem through intervention and/or early intervention;
- based on the characteristics of students and related environments;
- relevant to the referral question;
- comprehensive in addressing the educational, cognitive, and mental health needs of the student;
- directly linked to relevant intervention designs for the student;
- not limited to any single methodology or theoretical framework;
- nondiscriminatory in terms of ethnicity, gender, native language, family or socioeconomic status;
- technically appropriate and used for the purposes for which they were developed and/or validated.

The National Association of School Psychologists encourages all school psychologists and their service delivery units to assure that ethical standards are maintained in the use of assessment procedures and that such assessment techniques are used only by qualified personnel.

NASP promotes efforts to establish empirical foundations for all assessment procedures. School psychologists, because of their training and experience in psychometric theory and practices, should apply their expertise to the use and interpretation of all methods of evaluating student performance and program effectiveness. All approaches to assessment, including, but not limited to techniques such as performance-based assessment, standardized measures of intelligence and academics, curriculum-based assessment, psychological, personality, social-emotional measures, behavior rating scales, ecological assessment, portfolio review, etc., can be useful and should receive empirical examination. School psychology training programs are encouraged to assist students in developing research concerning all aspects of assessment methodologies and their application to meet the needs of children and youth.

Position statement adopted by NASP Delegate Assembly, July 1994.

School Psychologists: Assessment Experts for Restructured Schools

School psychologists have long been recognized for their expertise in developing, conducting, and interpreting individual and program assessment procedures; and

School psychologists are specifically trained in psychometric theory, assessment procedures and the applications of assessment data to educational decisions; and

School psychologists have expertise in norm-referenced assessment techniques that are well grounded in research; and

School psychologists promote the use of technically adequate assessment tools which are directly linked to instruction and intervention; and

Initiatives for school restructuring, such as inclusion, outcome-based education, and site-based management, have significant implications for the evaluation of student and program outcomes; and

New models of schools may require new approaches to student and program evaluation; and

The current empirical base for new approaches such as authentic assessment is very limited; and

Furthermore, be it resolved that the National Association of School Psychologists will work with school psychologists to refine the appropriate use of norm-referenced assessment techniques and expand their understanding and utilization of alternative assessment techniques. NASP will work with training programs to ensure that alternative models of assessment are included in the revision and updating of core curriculum to prepare school psychologists for their roles in restructured schools. NASP affirms its commitment to ensure that practicing school psychologists have opportunities to learn and develop skills in functional and problem-solving assessment through ongoing professional development.

Adopted by the NASP Delegate Assembly, April 17, 1993

Students With Attention Problems

The National Association of School Psychologists advocates appropriate educational and mental health services for all children and youth. NASP further advocates noncategorical models of service delivery within the least restrictive environment for students with disabilities and students at risk for school failure.

NASP recognizes that some students with academic and adjustment problems exhibit a constellation of behaviors commonly associated with Attention Deficit Hyperactivity Disorder (ADHD). NASP believes that these behaviors exist along a continuum from mild to severe and that appropriate interventions will vary depending on the nature and severity of the behaviors of concern.

Longitudinal data suggest that the behaviors associated with ADHD typically present at an early age, may change over time, and may persist into adulthood. Therefore, NASP believes that interventions must be designed within a developmental framework. Furthermore, recognizing that these students are at particular risk for developing social-emotional and learning difficulties, NASP believes problems should be addressed early to reduce the need for long- term special education. NASP believes that students with severe attention problems can be provided appropriate special education services under current disability categories of the IDEA or with accommodations in regular education through Section 504 of the Rehabilitation Act of 1973.

Diagnosis of ADHD should be done with care and with the understanding that attention problems are also symptoms of other psychological conditions. Because attention problems can co-exist with other significant problems or be symptomatic of very different disorders, it is essential that a thorough, differential evaluation be conducted prior to diagnosis and treatment, and that this assessment should include direct input from school and home. Further, NASP strongly believes that assessment of attention problems should be linked to interventions and recommends that intervention assistance to students, teachers and parents is provided early and for as long as such support is necessary to assure optimal performance.

NASP believes that effective interventions should be tailored to the unique strengths and needs of every student. For children with attention problems, such interventions will often include the following:

1) Classroom modifications to enhance attending, work production, and social adjustment;

2) Behavior management systems to reduce problems in areas most likely to be affected (e.g., unstructured settings, large group instruction, independent seatwork, etc.);

3) Direct instruction in study strategies and social skills, with explicit strategies for enhancing generalization to natural environments such as the classroom, playground, etc.;

4) Collaboration and consultation with families to ensure that parents' expertise in managing their child is fully utilized, to support parents' behavior management at home, and to facilitate the use of consistent approaches across home, school, and community settings;

5) Monitoring by a case manager to ensure effective implementation of interventions, to provide adequate support for those interventions, and to evaluate the effectiveness of programs in meeting behavioral and academic goals;

6) Education of school staff in characteristics and management of attention problems to enhance appropriate instructional modifications and behavior management;

7) Access to special education services when attention problems significantly impact school performance;

8) Collaboration with community agencies providing medical and related services to students and their families;

9) Interventions to help these students to appreciate their unique abilities and to develop their self esteem.

Research indicates that medication can be an effective treatment for many students with attention problems and can enhance the efficacy of other interventions. NASP believes that a decision to use medication rests with parents and is not an appropriate contingency for school placements and interventions. A thorough, differential assessment is essential prior to pharmacological intervention to assure that the most appropriate medication (if any) is prescribed. Furthermore, medication should be considered only after attempting or ruling out alternative, less invasive treatments. When medication is considered, NASP strongly recommends:

1) That behavioral and academic data be collected before and during blind medication trials to assess baseline conditions and the efficacy of medication; and

2) That communication between school, home, and medical personnel emphasize mutual problem solving and collaborative teamwork; and

3) That the student's health, behavior and academic progress while on medication are carefully monitored and communicated to appropriate medical providers.

NASP believes school psychologists have a vital role to play in developing, implementing, and monitoring effective interventions with students with attention problems. As an Association, NASP is committed to publishing current research on ADHD and to providing continuing professional development opportunities to enhance the skills of school psychologists to meet the diverse needs of students with attention problems.

This revision was adopted by the NASP Delegate Assembly, July, 1998.

Employing School Psychologists for Comprehensive Service Delivery

The National Association of School Psychologists supports policies and practices that enhance the education of all students. In its 1997 Standards for the Provision of School Psychological Services[1], NASP promotes school psychological services that "are provided in a coordinated, organized fashion and are deployed in a manner that ensures the provision of a comprehensive continuum of services..." (Standard 3.1). In addition to these professional standards, the federal mandates of the Individuals with Disabilities Education Act (IDEA) require that the evaluation and placement of students with disabilities is comprehensive, multi-faceted and determined by a multi-disciplinary team. This process stresses the need for educational specialists to work with each other in the educational environment and to gather input from numerous sources, including observation of the student within the learning environment, consultation with school personnel regarding educational performance, consultation with parents and individualized assessment of the student's skills.

During times of economic crisis and personnel shortages, school districts may consider alternatives to employing their own school psychologists, such as contracting out for specific services or general staff reductions. The increased availability of third-party reimbursement may make arrangements with private providers more attractive. NASP is concerned about staffing policies that are detrimental to the best interests of the child, family and school system as a whole. Therefore, it is essential that administrators and policymakers understand the nature and potential limitations of these options and the importance of maintaining professional standards in order to make cost-effective decisions that do not sacrifice the quality or availability of services to students.

Independent contracting for school psychological services includes a variety of arrangements, such as privatization and subcontracting through other public agencies. Some school districts have implemented contracts with agencies or individuals which shift the delivery of services from the public to the private sector, or may contract services through public cooperative (intermediate) units, or may supplement or supplant school-based services with "co-located" services of community agencies.

NASP does not oppose the provision of comprehensive school psychological services through intermediate educational agencies or community providers, as long as such services do not supplant the services of district-employed school psychologists. In fact, NASP recognizes that such alternatives often represent the most viable means of insuring appropriate, comprehensive services. Further, NASP recognizes that the provision of limited contractual services (such as for a specific service) may augment available district resources and contribute toward the delivery of comprehensive services overall. However, NASP opposes independent contracting if it compromises the delivery of comprehensive services as required by professional standards and federal law and if contracting supplants or decreases the availability of comprehensive services delivered by district-employed school psychologists (Standard 3.4.4).

Both NASP and the American Psychological Association recognize the specialized training in school psychology as different from the training in other specialty areas, such as clinical and industrial psychology. As stated in NASP's Standards (3.4.3), "persons providing contractual psychological services are fully credentialed school psychologists..." The independent contractor who is not a trained school psychologist may be a skillful clinician but may lack essential knowledge, expertise and experience to gather appropriate data in the school context and to facilitate a collaborative, comprehensive approach with the other members of the educational team.

School psychologists employed by school districts:

- offer cost-effective services including early prevention, intervention and wellness activities which can eliminate the need for many costly evaluations and placements;
- are readily available to school personnel, students and the community for crisis prevention and intervention services;
- understand school issues from a systems perspective;
- are sufficiently familiar with the students, staff, legal requirements and policies of the school system to facilitate communication and defuse potentially dangerous or adversarial situations;
- provide accessible mental health services to children and families, including evaluation, group and individual counseling, and consultation regarding mental health and educational issues;
- provide a wide range of services not easily or cheaply purchased via private contracts, such as reviews of records; consultation with parents and school personnel; ongoing, systematic classroom observations; inservice training; program planning and evaluation; and participation on multidisciplinary teams.

Contractual services may be appropriate in limited circumstances in which an outside contractor supplements the regular services of the district's school psychologists or provides comprehensive services which are otherwise unavailable or impractical. Such circumstances include:

- specific situations where specialized training and experience beyond what is typically available in the school district are required in order to provide appropriate service to the student or district, such as with low incidence disabilities or the provision of clinical home-based services through shared funding;
- situations where a very small district is unable to support the funding of a full-time psychologist and must seek an alternative arrangement such as contracting through an independent provider or intermediate agency;
- situations where a personnel shortage creates a temporary need to obtain services from available sources such as private providers;
- situations where a second opinion or outside service is warranted due to conflict between family and school regarding a school-based service.

Psychologists hired under independent contract to provide services in the schools should hold at least the same credentials and should be expected to practice within the same professional and ethical standards as school-employed psychologists. Any contractual agreement should meet the standards established by NASP (Standards for the Provision of School Psychological Services, 1997, Section 3.4, "Contractual Services") and insure that:

- the welfare and best interests of the student are the primary concern of the service provider;
- the amount and quality of psychological services are increased, not decreased;
- due process rights of students are upheld; and
- the agreement does not result in any loss of legitimate employee rights, benefits or wages.

The National Association of School Psychologists is committed to enhancing educational opportunities for all students through the organized delivery of comprehensive school-based psychological services. NASP further recognizes that such services can be delivered in a variety of ways without compromising the rights and needs of students. However, in most situations, the most cost-effective, professionally accountable services will be those delivered by school psychologists employed by the school district.

Therefore, NASP urges school administrators and school board members to consider the legal, educational and long-term financial ramifications of any shift of services away from the school district, and to seek more cost-effective models of service delivery that do not decrease the availability of school-based psychologists. NASP further urges school psychologists to work with administrators, collective bargaining units and professional associations to help develop strategies for the delivery of cost-effective services that enhance educational outcomes for all students while maintaining their rights as employees.

Finally, NASP urges school psychologists and other educators to empirically evaluate the cost-effectiveness of current and proposed models of service delivery and to establish ongoing program evaluation of all providers of school-based psychological and mental health services.

---

1. Standards for the Provision of School Psychological Services. National Association of School Psychologists, 1997.

— Original statement adopted by the NASP Delegate Assembly, April 18, 1993

— Revision adopted by the NASP Delegate Assembly, April 10, 1999

Corporal Punishment in Schools

The use of corporal punishment has been declining in U.S. schools. Waning public acceptance, increased litigation against school boards and educators regarding its use and legislative bans have led to the decline. More than half of the states ban its use. In states where it is allowed, many school boards voluntarily prohibit it. Yet, over 250,000 children are being hit yearly in public schools with a disproportionate number being minority children and children with disabilities. Corporal punishment is any intervention which is designed to or likely to cause physical pain in order to stop or change behavior. In the United States, the most typical form of school corporal punishment is the striking of a student's buttocks with a wooden paddle by a school authority because the authority believes the student has disobeyed a rule.

Discipline is important and schools have a strong role in teaching children to be self-disciplined. Self-discipline is the ability to understand a situation, to make appropriate decisions about one's behavior in that situation and to ordinarily perform the appropriate behavior when unsupervised by adults. Effective discipline is primarily a matter of instruction rather than punishment. Many means of effective and safe discipline are available. Punishment contingencies in general tend to have negative side effects including leading students to be sneaky and to lie about their behavior in order to escape punishment. Corporal punishment is a technique that can easily be abused leading to physical injuries. Evidence indicates that corporal punishment negatively effects the social, psychological and educational development of students and contributes to the cycle of child abuse and pro-violence attitudes of youth. The National Association of School Psychologists (NASP) reaffirms its opposition to the use of corporal punishment in schools and will actively support removal of legal sanctions for its use. NASP resolves to educate the public about the effects of corporal punishment and alternatives to its use, and will encourage research and the dissemination of information about corporal punishment effects and alternatives.

Alternatives to Corporal Punishment

Effective discipline includes programs and strategies for changing student behavior, for changing school or classroom environments, and for educating and supporting teachers and parents. Effective discipline includes prevention and intervention programs and strategies. It is empirically based rather than relying on custom or habit. The following are alternatives which can be initiated and developed or supported by school psychologists and other educators and which help provide an atmosphere where learning can take place and where students learn to be self-disciplined:

- Help students achieve academic success through identification of academic and behavioral deficiencies and strengths and help get them appropriate instruction

- Use behavioral contracting

- Encourage positive reinforcement of appropriate behavior

- Use individual and group counseling

- Encourage disciplinary consequences which are meaningful to students and have an instructional and/or reflection component

- Provide social skills training

Alternatives for changing the school and classroom environment:

- Encourage programs that emphasize early diagnosis and intervention for school problems including problems of staff and problems of students
- Encourage programs that emphasize values, school pride and personal responsibility and support the mental health needs of children
- Encourage development of fair, reasonable and consistent rules
- Support strong parent/school and community/school communications and ties

Alternatives for educating and supporting teachers (as preventive measures):

- Provide information on effective discipline programs and resources
- Provide inservice programs on communication, classroom management, understanding of behavior and individual differences, and alternative ways for dealing with misbehavior
- Network with community groups and mental health agencies to provide programs and support for school staff
- Assist with development and monitoring of behavioral intervention programs - schoolwide, classwide or individual

Alternatives for educating and supporting parents:

- Provide parenting classes on effective discipline particularly as it relates to such issues as homework, school grades, peers, learning problems, developmental expectations and undesirable behavior
- Provide school-based consultation to parents on effectively managing child behavior
- Encourage home visitation programs for parents of babies and toddlers - programs which focus on developmental expectations, resources and discipline
- When corporal punishment is allowed, help parents to protect children by informing them about exemptions to corporal punishment that may exist such as written notification or amending the IEP as well as what actions parents should take if a child is injured (seeing a physician, contacting child protection authorities and the police, taking color photos of the injury and contacting advocacy organizations)

The Role of School Psychologists

School psychologists can take leadership roles in encouraging school districts to ban corporal punishment, if it is allowed, and in helping to develop effective discipline programs. They are trained in identifying learning and behavior problems which often lead to school discipline problems if undiagnosed and untreated. They are trained in developing appropriate programs and interventions for children with learning and behavior problems. Education programs for parents and teachers which focus on appropriate ways to deal with misbehavior and ways to foster self-discipline can be provided by school psychologists. Other direct services which can be provided by school psychologists include counseling of students and consultation with parents and school staff. School psychologists can bring to schools research about the development and evaluation of disciplinary codes, social skills training and the effectiveness of alternative discipline methods. School psychologists can bring to educators, the community, and policy makers information about the effects of corporal punishment and the need to eliminate its use.

Summary

NASP reaffirms its opposition to the use of corporal punishment in schools because of its harmful physical, educational, psychological and social effects on students. Corporal punishment contributes to the cycle of child abuse and pro-violence attitudes of youth by teaching that it is an acceptable way of controlling the behavior of others. Discipline is important and effective alternatives are available to help students develop self-discipline. These are primarily instructional in nature rather than punitive. School psychologists provide many direct services to improve discipline of individual children as well as services which improve classroom and schoolwide discipline. NASP will continue to work actively with other organizations to educate the public and policy makers about the effects of corporal punishment and alternatives to its use and will seek its complete prohibition in schools.

— Original Statement Adopted by NASP Delegate Assembly, April, 1986

— Revision adopted by NASP Delegate Assembly, April 18, 1998

— Revision adopted by NASP Delegate Assembly, July 21, 2001

Early Childhood Assessment

The National Association of School Psychologists believes that early identification of developmental and learning problems in preschool and primary grade children is essential because of children's broad and rapid development. Intervention services for these children's psychological and developmental difficulties are essential, beneficial, and cost-effective. Because the accurate and fair identification of the developmental needs of young children is critical to the design, implementation, and success of appropriate interventions school psychologists must play a key role.

Evidence from research and practice in early childhood assessment indicates that issues of technical adequacy are more difficult to address with young children who have short attention spans and go through periods of variable, rapid development. Therefore, standardized assessment procedures should be used with great caution in educational decision-making because such tools are inherently less accurate and less predictive when used with young children.

Multidisciplinary team assessments must include multiple sources of information, multiple approaches to assessment, and multiple settings in order to yield a comprehensive understanding of children's skills and needs. Therefore, assessments should center on the child in the family system and home environment, both substantial influences on the development of young children. Similarly, families' self-identified needs should drive the decision-making process concerning the identification of child and family services.

Because categorical identification of infants, toddlers, and young children is ineffective in meeting the special needs of young children, assessment of infants and young children requires specialized training and skills beyond those required for the assessment of older children. Longitudinal and functional assessment of behavior and development of infants, young children, and families in a variety of settings is needed to evaluate and document progress and response to intervention over time, and must guide early intervention strategies in meaningful ways.

Therefore, the National Association of School Psychologists will promote early childhood assessment practices that are:

- developmentally appropriate, ecological, comprehensive, skills-based, and family-focused;
- conducted by a multi-disciplinary team;
- linked to intervention strategies designed for young children, rather than to categorical classification;
- based upon comprehensive, educational and/or behavioral concerns, rather than isolated deficits identified by individual assessments;
- nondiscriminatory in terms of gender, ethnicity, native language, family composition, and/or socio-economic status; and
- technically adequate and validated for the purpose(s) for which they are used, including the provision of norms for minority children and children with physical disabilities.

Role of the School Psychologist

NASP encourages the adoption of the philosophy of "parents as partners" and families as the focus to promote assessments and interventions for young children that include full integration of parents and families into the assessment and intervention components of early childhood services. This mandates methods of naturalistic and systematic observation and information gathering, including work sampling procedures and the involvement of the family, home environment, daycare/preschool, and the community ecology as part of the comprehensive assessment to gather information and input from parents and caregivers. School psychologists should provide leadership to the multidisciplinary team in ensuring that all information gathered through the assessment is clearly understood by parents so that they can make fully-informed decisions about interventions for their children.

NASP also advocates for pre-service and in-service education for school psychologists and other professionals to address the following issues:1) normal as well as atypical developmental patterns of infants and young children; 2) practices, procedures, and instrumentation appropriate for screening and assessment of young children, their families, and their environments; 3) the selection of assessment techniques and utilization of findings from such assessments for the design, implementation, and efficacy evaluation of interventions; 4) and standards for early childhood psychological and educational assessment, including legal, ethical, and professional issues — all in the context of noncategorical service delivery for young children and their families.

Summary

NASP supports early childhood assessment practices that allow for accurate and fair identification of the developmental needs of infants, preschoolers, and young children and facilitate interventions that involve parents and other caregivers. Sound early childhood assessment should involve a multi-disciplinary team, including school psychologists with specialized training in the assessment of the young child, and who view behavior and development from a longitudinal perspective.

— Original version adopted by NASP Delegate Assembly, March 24, 1991

— Revision adopted by NASP Delegate Assembly, July 24, 1999

Annotated Bibliography

Gridley, Betty. (1995). Preschool Screening. In A. Thomas & J. Grimes (Eds.), Best practices in school psychology - III, (pp 213-226). Washington, DC: National Association of School Psychologists.

This chapter discusses the purposes of screening, the importance of parental input to appropriate screening practices, commonly used screening instruments, and practical activities for parents to do to facilitate development and learning in their child.

Gullo, Domnic, F. (1994). Understanding assessment and evaluation in early childhood education. Teachers College Press: New York, NY.

This book will help early childhood practitioners develop the essential understanding required for appropriate use of informal and formal assessment and evaluation information. Appendices contain a glossary of assessment instruments in early childhood education and a case study of an alternative assessment program.

Harrington, Robert, H., & Tongier, Jane. (1993). The compatibility between state eligibility criteria for developmental delays and available early childhood assessment instrumentation. Diagnostique 18(33), 199-217.

This paper discusses the results of a survey of 50 state consultants in early childhood special education in the United States to evaluate whether they perceive available developmental assessment instrumentation to be satisfactory for the identification of children with developmental delays in the 3 through 5 year old range. Results showed a need for instruments that facilitate parent involvement and a need for special norms for minority children and children with physical disabilities.

Katz, L. (1997). A developmental approach to assessment of young children. Champaign, IL: ERIC Clearinghouse on Elementary and Early Childhood Education.

This paper describes the concept of developmental appropriateness as it applies to the assessment of young children. The various purposes of assessing individual children are discussed. A match between plans, strategies, and assessment instruments and specific assessment purpose is mandated.

McClean, M.E. (1993). Practices for Young Children with and without disabilities: A comparison of DEC and NAEYC Identified Practices. Topics in Early Childhood Special Education, 13(3), 274-292.

This article summarizes practices that represent consensus of professionals and consumers in the field of early childhood education and early intervention relative to useful practice. Practices identified through the work of the Division for Early Childhood (DEC) Task Force on Recommended Practice are compared with practices identified through the work of the National Association of the Education of Young Children (NAEYC). Similarities and differing emphases in the areas of inclusion, family involvement, assessment, program planning, curriculum and intervention strategies, service delivery models, and transition are discussed.

Neisworth, John. (1993). Assessment: DEC recommended practices. In DEC recommended practices: Indicators of quality in programs for infants and young children. (EC 301 933).
This paper lists practices recommended by the Division for Early Childhood for assessment in early intervention and early childhood special education programs for infant and young children with special needs and their early families. Introductory text examines the role of assessment, materials, and procedures used, and assessment principles, including: assessment must clearly identify developmental or behavioral objectives for change; assessment should help to select and guide treatment activities; assessment should contribute to evaluating intervention or program efficacy, assessment should identify goals and objectives that are judged as worthwhile and important; assessment methods and materials themselves should be judged as acceptable; assessment decisions must be based on a wide base of information; assessment batteries should contain several types of scales and include observation and interviews; assessment should include data and reports from parents and other significant individuals; and assessment must be done on multiple occasions.

Preator, Karleen, K., & McAllister, J.R. (1995). Assessing infants and toddlers. In A. Thomas & J. Grimes (Eds.), Best practices in school psychology - III, (pp775-788). Washington, DC: National Association of School Psychologists.
This chapter discusses basic considerations when assessing infants and toddlers, particularly under the requirements of federal legislation. The role of the school psychologist in working with the medical community and working with families as team members, as well as how to formulate assessment strategies with this population are also included.

SERVE: Southeastern Regional Vision for Education. (1991). Assessment in Early Childhood Education: Status of the Issue. Office of Educational Research and Improvement: Washington DC (ED 368 507).
This research brief argues that standardized testing has been over-used and misinterpreted, particularly when tests do not have established reliability and validity, when readiness tests are substituted for screening tests, and when tests are used for purposes they were not designed for. The National Association for the Education of the Young Child recommends that the most important consideration in evaluating and using standardized tests with young children is utility. Staff must be trained to recognize what specific tests can and cannot measure. Assessment systems that can be used cooperatively by parents and teachers is recommended. On-going evaluation should consist of criterion -referenced checklists. portfolio collection of the child's work, and summative teacher report forms.

Schweinhart, Lawrence. (July, 1993). Observing young children in action: The key to early childhood assessment. Young Children 48(5), 29- 33.
This article discusses practices such as performance-based assessment that are consistent with early childhood profession's process goals. Appropriate assessment practices are described including the use of observational methods that use anecdotal notes to complement assessments with developmental scales of established reliability and validity.

Shephard, L., Kagan, S., & Wurtz,E. (1998) Principles and recommendations for early childhood assessments. Washington DC: National Education Goals Panel. http://www.negp.gov
This booklet discusses best practices for assessment of young children considering their unique development, recent abuses of testing, and legitimate demands for clear and useful information. General principles of assessment included address benefits, reliability and validity, age level appropriateness and language, and parent role in assessment.

Early Childhood Care and Education

The National Association of School Psychologists recognizes that the futures of children are affected by many factors that occur early in life. One such factor is child care. Affordable, high quality early childhood care and education represent major needs of today's and tomorrow's children and families. Although the role of parents in children's care and upbringing remains of primary importance, most families need good child care options. The availability of high quality child care can benefit children, families, and society in terms of prevention of later learning and behavior problems, increased family self-sufficiency, and reduced costs for special education, welfare, and other public assistance.

The need for available, affordable, high quality early childhood care and education is supported by the following findings:

The majority of families in the United States have two parents or a single head of household who work outside the home because of economic necessity. A total of 7.7 million children under the age five are cared for during the day by someone other than a parent.

Most families need child care for their young children.

Many children are left unsupervised or in poor quality child care and may be vulnerable to psychological and physical risks that affect their development and safety. Most state and local regulations are limited and do not ensure that all child care programs are of good quality. About 70% of child care programs are of poor to mediocre quality. Kindergarten teachers are concerned that many children entering kindergarten are not prepared to participate in learning and social activities in the classroom. For school-age children, estimates indicate that only 33% to 52% of public schools offer before-school and after-school programs.

Many children and families in the United State are poor, even when both parents or a single head of household are employed. Poverty rates remain inexcusably high, especially for children. In 1995, 21% of all children lived in households below the poverty level. For single parent families, financial resources are often limited by multiple factors, including, in many cases, failure of non-custodial parents to pay child support.

Governmental funding for child care is inadequate. Many families, particularly low income and single parent families, cannot afford good quality child care. The typical yearly child care costs of $4,000 per child represents about 35% of the annual income for one parent working at minimum wage. Child care costs for infants are often higher than costs for toddlers and preschoolers, and many child care facilities cannot offer infant programs because of personnel costs. The high cost of child care results in a system in which low income families have few child care choices.

Inadequate child care options can have a broad and costly social impact by contributing to some parents' inability to acquire or maintain employment, inability to participate fully in job assistance programs, and higher absenteeism and lower productivity on the job.

It is recognized that families have a variety of child care needs, ranging from occasional in-home care to part-time or full-time out-of-home day care programs. The availability of affordable, high quality early childhood care and education can increase options for many families and provide benefits for children, families, and society. Research supports that higher quality child care programs have greater benefits than lower quality programs. Criteria for high quality child care include appropriate group size, adequate adult-child ratios, developmentally-appropriate curriculum, interactions with adults that are caring and stimulating for children, and comprehensive training and education of the staff.

Family involvement and other services for families can also be effective components of early child care programs. Positive outcomes of high quality child care and education programs are found for children and families of all income levels and can be pronounced for children and families of lower income levels. Examples of positive outcomes include the following:

Children

Participation in high quality early childhood programs can result in enhanced social and cognitive behaviors of young children, including increased self-regulation, verbalization, and competence in play and exploration.

Participation in high quality early childhood programs can have long-term educational benefits for children who are at-risk, including decreased placement in special education and lower failure and drop-out rates.

Families

Participation in high quality early childhood programs, particularly those which provide family services, can result in factors such as more positive attitudes and modeling for parents regarding their children and themselves and better parent-child interactions.

Availability of affordable early childhood programs can promote increased family financial self-sufficiency.

Society

Availability of good early childhood programs can result in reduction to costs to society, such as costs related to special education and public assistance.

Availability of affordable early childhood programs can result in increased business productivity related to less turnover and absenteeism and improved job productivity in parents.

The need for early childhood care and education cannot be denied; furthermore, the availability of affordable, high quality child care can promote the success of children and their families. Most families in the United States need better child care programs and more options for the safe care of their young children. Therefore, the National Association of School Psychologists will:

1. Support programs and government funding that provide equal access to affordable, high quality early childhood care and education for all children and their families. Tax rebates and credits are not substitutes for comprehensive government support of accessible, well-designed programs.

2. Encourage the development, implementation, and ongoing evaluation of stringent standards for quality in child care programs, including:
   - developmentally appropriate curricula
   - appropriate group sizes and adult-child ratios, adequate staff selection, education, training, and compensation
   - appropriate physical facilities
   - responsiveness to individual differences and cultural and language diversity
   - appropriate access to special and related educational and health services and specialists, non-discriminatory practices.

3. Support and assist with the implementation of alternative forms of child care, including both in-home and out-of-home care, that meet the preferences and needs of families,

4. Support public regulation of all forms of out-of-home child care to ensure the quality of programs and safety of children.

5. Support comprehensive programs, beginning at the prenatal period, that include many services for parents and families and health, nutrition, education, and related services.

6. Support the implementation of programs that provide effective services and accommodations for children and families with special needs. Children with, for example, disabilities, developmental delays, chronic health problems, and childhood illnesses — and their families — should have equal access to high quality child care programs.

7. Encourage the establishment of partnerships between communities, schools, and other agen-

cies to provide accessible, comprehensive programs for young children. These programs should include subsidized child care services for infants and toddlers, pre-kindergarten programs in public schools and other settings, and well-supervised before-school and after-school programs.

8. Support and recognize the efforts of employers and corporations that have family-oriented policies and services, such as flex-time and on-site child care, and that afford families more options to meet the needs of their children and demands of their employment responsibilities. Men and women today are active in their parenting roles, and corporate and government policies that support parenting efforts reduce the needs for many families to rely on outside day care.

9. Encourage the development of programs that help families identify their child care needs and goals and evaluate the quality of child care programs in their communities.

10. Support continued research investigating factors related to child care, including effects of child care and family dynamics on children's development, methods of improving child care, effects of alternative forms of child care and family services, long-term benefits of child care for children and families, benefits of before-school and after-school programs, and economic benefits of child care for society.

Notes:
Data in this document were obtained from The State of America's Children: Yearbook 1997 by the Children's Defense Fund, Washington, DC; the special daycare issue of the journal Young Children (May, 1995); and "Extended Day Programs in Elementary and Combined Schools" by Robert Rossi and others (1996, ERIC Document Reproduction Service No. ED 395 721).

Parents and professionals who are interested in guidelines for selecting high quality child care programs are encouraged to read "A Good Preschool for Your Child" and other publications available from the National Association of the Education of Young Children, 1509 16th Street, NW, Washington, DC 20036, 800-424-2460 (www.naeyc.org).
— Adopted by the NASP Delegate Assembly, April 18, 1998.

Early Intervention Services

The National Association of School Psychologists is committed to serving the educational and mental health needs of all children and youth, including infants and young children. Research has shown that early intervention with infants, toddlers and preschool children with disabilities or who are at-risk for developmental problems benefits both children and families and accrues long-term cost savings to both school districts and society. Research also indicates that early intervention is most effective when the families of children are actively involved.

Many public schools are involved in the provision of special education and related services to young children as a result of federal and state legislation. The National Association of School Psychologists supports the expansion and improvement of services to children, toddlers, and preschool children who have disabilities or who are at-risk.

NASP encourages school psychologists and others to take part in efforts at the national, state, and local levels to advocate for high quality early intervention services from birth through age 5. We must work with school administrators, teachers, and families to develop comprehensive intervention programs that attend to total development, including cognitive, motor, self-help, socio-emotional, and communication skills, and actively involve parents and caregivers in intervention. Programs for young children should be based on their unique developmental needs. To ensure this we must:

- Promote and assist in "Child Find" or "Child Check" programs to identify children who may be at risk or have a disabling condition as early as possible and use only unbiased, reliable, and valid screening procedures with thorough follow-up assessment when appropriate.

- Use team approaches that include parents, families, and other caregivers as team members.

- Support the provision of services to children based on their individual needs without labeling or categorical procedures.

- Establish programs that include the child in natural environments whenever possible with appropriate assistance and consultation provided to the teacher.

- Actively and vigorously advocate for the provision of state and federal funding of early intervention programs and ensure that such funding allows for the careful evaluation of program outcomes to continually improve services to infants, toddlers, and preschool children.

We must also ensure that all service providers obtain professional development experiences that offer adequate preparation to serve young children and their families. University programs, professional organizations, public schools and other continuing education providers should be encouraged to provide professional development in these areas. Similarly, it is essential to establish a communication network among multiple service agencies that work with young children to ensure that effective and efficient collaborative services are provided to families.

Summary

NASP supports the establishment of comprehensive early intervention programs that begin as soon as possible, that actively involve parents and other caregivers in planning intervention and decision-making activities that serve children according to their unique needs in natural environments. NASP encourages governmental policies that work to meet these goals by providing funds to prepare professionals to serve young children, to support research in the efficacy of intervention approaches, and to increase effective collaboration among service agencies.

— Original statement adopted by the NASP Delegate Assembly, September, 1987
— Revision adopted by the NASP Delegate Assembly, April 10, 1999

Annotated Bibliography

Barnett, D.W., Ehrhardt, K. (1995). Early intervention design, In A. Thomas & J. Grimes (Eds.), Best practices in school psychology – III (pp 999-1008). Bethesda, MD: National Association of School Psychologists.
This chapter describes an alternative model to traditional placement of young children with disabilities in special education classes. The model discussed is guided by intervention design principles. This model involves ongoing parent-teacher problem-solving and intervention research.

Barrett, W.S. (1995). Long-term effects of early childhood programs on cognitive and school outcomes. The Future of Children, 5 (8), 25-50.
This article reviews the extent to which early childhood programs produce long-term benefits in children's cognitive development, socialization, and school success. Thirty-six studies of both model demonstration projects and large scale public programs are included. Results indicate that early childhood programs can produce large short-term benefits for children on intelligence quotient (IQ) and sizable long term effects on school achievement, grade retention, placement in special education, and social adjustment. Variability among programs exists perhaps due to funding and quality differences.

Campbell, F.A., Taylor, K. (May, 1996). Early childhood programs that work for children from economically disadvantaged families. Young Children, 51 (4), 74-80.
This article presents a study which surveyed how parents and children derived benefits from early childhood intervention programs for low income families. Such programs were found to provide appropriate and stimulating environments for young children and support the roles of parents. Participants have higher academic achievement and parents made positive changes in their own educational and employment levels. Child abuse and neglect also decreased.

Entwisle, D.R. (1995). The role of schools in sustaining early childhood program benefits. The Future of Children 5(3), 133-144.
This article discusses links between children's educational experience in elementary school and preschool settings which foster school success.

Frede, E.C. (1995). The role of program quality in producing early childhood program benefits. The Future of Children 5(3), 115-132.
This article analyzes early childhood program practices associated with effectiveness, with recommendations for policy, practice, and research. Effective programs were characterized by small class size with low teacher-student ratios; teachers who received support regarding reflective practice; long-lasting or concentrated interventions; ongoing, focused child-centered communication between school and home; and some curriculum content and classroom processes that are similar to traditional schooling.

Guralnick, M.J. (1991). The next decade of research on the effectiveness of early intervention. Exceptional Children 58(2), 174-183.
This article reviews the effectiveness of early intervention programs for children with developmental disabilities and for children at biologic risk. A general pattern indicating important effects of early intervention programs was noted. The ability of early interventions to minimize declines in development was identified as a significant outcome.

Gomby, D.S., Larner, M.B., Stevenson, C.S., Lewit, E.M., & Behrman, R. (1995). Long-term outcomes of early childhood programs: Analysis and recommendations. The Future of Children 5(3), 6-24.
This article provides an analysis of varying approaches to early childhood programs, including family-focused and child-focused. It concludes with recommendations for strengthening programs.

Effective Parenting: Positive Support for Families

The issue of how to provide appropriate and adequate parenting and discipline is of great concern to the educational community. Parents want well-behaved children. They want children to grow up to be contented, productive, responsible and self disciplined. Some children's behaviors are particularly challenging. Noncompliance and aggressive behaviors can bring out the worst in parents. Neither extremes of severe physical punishment nor limitless freedom will lead to long-term behavior change. School psychologists can help parents and caregivers develop practical and effective ways of disciplining and parenting children.

Discipline is a word that makes most people uncomfortable. It is typically used as a synonym for punishment, often for physical punishment. Discipline comes from the Latin word disciplina meaning instruction or teaching. Discipline, so defined, places the parent as the leader or teacher and the child as the student. A parent teaches values, good judgment, self control and caring for others through daily interactions with children. A parent sets limits and makes appropriate responses when a child does something that is in conflict with parental wishes. Effective parenting is safe, nurturing and instructive. Physical punishment can be harmful physically, emotionally and socially. It is usually ineffective because it does not teach appropriate behaviors, but teaches that hitting is acceptable in dealing with others. The National Association of School Psychologists supports the use of both verbal and nonverbal discipline practices that treat children with respect and shape children's behavior to encourage self-control and caring for others.

Preventing Behavior Problems

The National Association of School Psychologists believes that the following parenting practices help prevent the development of behavior problems in children:

- **Developing a trusting relationship**
  When children feel loved and respected by parents, they want to please them. Parents form trusting relationships with their children by exhibiting predictable and mature behavior and by protecting them from harm. Children who feel safe to make mistakes can learn to make better decisions in the future. A trusting relationship between parents and children is the cornerstone of effective discipline.

- **Developing appropriate expectations**
  Children need to understand the expectations their parents have for them, and they need to feel they can meet those expectations. These expectations must be appropriate for the child's age, temperament, and abilities. Children with learning or behavioral disabilities provide additional challenges to parents who must adjust their expectations to their child's unique needs and developmental patterns.

- **Setting limits**
  Limits can help children feel that the world is orderly, predictable and safe. Parents should consider the child's age and development when setting limits. Limits should be enforced consistently, and there should be clear and appropriate consequences when those limits are challenged.

- **Offering praise**
  Praising children's appropriate behavior will increase that behavior. Praise for specific behaviors is the basis for effective behavior management and should be used abundantly.

- **Effective Ways of Dealing with Misbehavior**
The National Association of School Psychologists urges school psychologists to promote the development of effective discipline practices through the following interventions:

- **Early intervention programs**
Home visitation programs for parents of newborns are an effective means of teaching and supporting parents in the difficult job of raising children. These programs provide parents with knowledge about normal development, realistic expectations, and how to keep babies healthy and safe. School psychologists can take a leadership role in developing community support for these programs.

- **School-wide programs to encourage effective discipline**
Peer mediation, conflict resolution, and social skills training are all proven ways to help children develop responsible behavior. By incorporating regular communication with parents and opportunities for their participation, the effectiveness of these programs can be enhanced. School psychologists can bring leadership, research, and management skills to the development of these programs.

- **Consultation to parents**
School psychologists have unique opportunities to talk with parents about discipline. In consulting with parents on children's learning and behavior problems, school psychologists can provide a) behavioral expectations appropriate to the child's age and development, b) alternative methods of behavior management such as time out, logical consequences, behavioral contracting, positive reinforcement, and privilege systems, and c) information about school and community resources such as parenting programs and professional help available beyond school services.

- **Parent education classes**
School psychologists are in an ideal position to provide parent training using a variety of research-supported parent education programs. They can help parents develop positive approaches to behavior management including limit setting, use of praise and reinforcement, giving effective commands, reducing negative parent-child interactions, and using negotiating and mediation. School psychologists can also provide guidance for parents on school-related concerns such as homework, report cards, and peer relationships.

Summary

Raising self-disciplined children is one challenge among many facing parents in American society today. Parents have little or no training in effective parenting and they are often removed from extended families which have in the past been available to provide support and relief from the stress of child rearing. Discipline is too often viewed as "punishment" which may lead parents to equate more discipline with harsher punishments.

The National Association of School Psychologists encourages school psychologists and other professionals working with children and families to help parents develop effective discipline practices that are positive, safe, and instructive. School psychologists can help parents by supporting, developing, and implementing school and community programs which build healthy parent-child relationships and strengthen the home to enable children to become caring and responsible members of society.

— Adopted by NASP Delegate Assembly, April 18, 1998
Revision adopted by NASP Delegate Assembly, July 21, 2001

Students with Emotional and Behavioral Disorders

The National Association of School Psychologists is committed to promoting effective services to meet the educational and mental health needs of all students. Emotional and behavioral disorders interfere with the acquisition of academic, vocational, and social skills and negatively affect adult adjustment. Therefore, early identification and intervention for students with emotional and/or behavioral problems is essential. Students with emotional and/or behavioral problems are frequently underserved by the educational and mental health systems of the United States. It is the position of the National Association of School Psychologists that children with these disorders should receive comprehensive assessment and intervention services in a collaborative family- and community-oriented fashion. Services to students with emotional and behavioral disorders should be sensitive to the need for the involvement and perspectives of persons from diverse cultural backgrounds.

Definition

The National Association of School Psychologists recognizes that children may exhibit emotional or behavioral problems for a variety of reasons, including developmental or environmental stressors and the presence of a longer -term disorder. These difficulties also exist along continuums of intensity, duration and frequency of occurrence. For the identification of students who are in need of specialized educational services in the school, the Association has endorsed the following definition of Emotional and Behavioral Disorders developed by the National Mental Health and Special Education Coalition:

- Emotional or Behavioral Disorder (EBD) refers to a condition in which behavioral or emotional responses of an individual in school are so different from his/her generally accepted, age appropriate, ethnic or cultural norms that they adversely affect performance in such areas as self care, social relationships, personal adjustment, academic progress, classroom behavior, or work adjustment.
- EBD is more than a transient, expected response to stressors in the child's or youth's environment and would persist even with individualized interventions, such as feedback to the individual, consultation with parents or families, and/or modification of the educational environment.
- The eligibility decision must be based on multiple sources of data about the individual's behavioral or emotional functioning. EBD must be exhibited in at least two different settings, at least one of which is school related.
- EBD can co-exist with other handicapping conditions.
- This category may include children or youth with schizophrenia, affective disorders, anxiety disorders, or who have other sustained disturbances of conduct, attention, or adjustment.

Assessment and Identification

The goals of the assessment process are to (a) gather relevant information about the student in the social and instructional environments, (b) assimilate the data to create a comprehensive picture of concerns, and (c) develop initial short and long term goals and strategies for intervention. It is important that the assessment identify both the strengths and needs of the individual and the people and systems with whom the student interacts. The assessment should insure that the child's difficulties are not primarily due to transient developmental or environmental variables, cultural or linguistic differences, or influences of other handicapping conditions. Referral for special services should not be used as a disciplinary action or an effort to resolve conflicts between individuals or agencies. The results of the assessment should provide information about the following factors:

- Specificity: The student's difficulties must be identified in a functional, objective and observable fashion;
- Environmental Factors: The relationship between the instructional, social and community environment and the specific difficulties demonstrated by the student. The assessment should identify those persons and systems that impact on the student;
- Strengths: Identify the strengths and resources of the student, family, teacher(s) and school setting;
- History: The duration of the difficulties, their relationship to specific developmental or situational stressors and previous attempts to resolve the difficulties;
- Intensity: The level of severity of the difficulties as they affect academic achievement, acquisition and execution of social skills, and/or interpersonal relationships within the school setting;
- Pervasiveness: The number of settings in which difficulties occur in the school, family or community;
- Persistence: The extent to which difficulties have continued despite the use of well-planned, empirically-based and individualized intervention strategies provided within lesser restrictive environments; and
- Developmental and cultural data: Identify the student's current developmental status. Determine the extent to which the student's behavior is different from the behavior expected for children of the same age, culture, and ethnic background.

Information should be obtained from a variety of sources that can provide data about the child's difficulties across various settings. Information from family members, community treatment providers, teachers and other school personnel, social service workers, combined with a thorough review of records may all prove useful. The assessment should gather information about a child's behavioral and emotional functioning, developmental history, areas of significant impairment in school adaptive behavior and achievement, impairment outside the school setting in areas such as vocational skills, and social skills or interpersonal relationships. Because biological and neurological factors may contribute to, cause or trigger problematic behaviors, consultation with medical care providers and consideration of relevant student and family medical history is important.

Formal methods for gathering information may include behavior checklists, standardized self-reports, structured interviews, rating scales, and other appropriate assessment techniques. Informal methods, such as behavior observation and analysis of work samples can also be useful. The potential effects of identifying a child as having an emotional or behavioral disorder necessitate the use of highly reliable and explicitly valid instruments. Norms should be representative, current and appropriate for the individual being assessed in terms of age, ethnicity, and gender. Functional behavior assessment procedures are recommended to gather information about the child's behavior in relationship to the instructional and social environment.

Intervention

Eligibility for services under the category of emotional/behavioral disorders should not automatically imply placement in a categorical special education program. Since emotional and behavioral disorders have multidimensional influences, interventions for children with these disorders must be multifaceted and comprehensive. Interventions should be planned by a team which includes the parent, the child whenever possible, the school psychologist and other student services personnel, teachers, administrators, and community service providers. Intervention plans should take into account the strengths of the child, the family, the child's teacher(s), and the school. Most schools exist primarily as an educational setting rather than a treatment setting, so children with significant emotional or behavioral disorders may frequently need interventions outside of those provided in the schools. Collaboration and coordination of services provided in the school and community will be required.

The following intervention approaches should be considered in developing a comprehensive school intervention plan for children and youth with emotional or behavioral disorders.

- **Individualized academic and curricular interventions.** Children with emotional or behavioral problems frequently achieve below grade expectations in academic areas. Academic difficulties often take a back seat to the student's behavioral difficulties. Students may benefit from adaptations to the curriculum, alteration of the pace of delivery, improvements to the instructional and organizational ecology, and instruction in learning and study skills.

- **Consultation with teachers and other support services.** Teachers may benefit from consultation directed at understanding the needs of the student and applying the most effective strategies to help the child improve behavior. Teachers will also benefit from the psychosocial support component of consultation in dealing with the frustration and isolation that often is present when working with children with significant problems.

- **Consultation and partnership with parents.** Parents will benefit from consultation directed at understanding their child's difficulties, developing and implementing effective behavior management strategies, and working collaboratively with other caregivers. The parent may also need assistance with negotiating the array of services available in the community.

- **Individual and group counseling.** Counseling may help the student improve social and school adjustment. Students frequently need assistance in dealing with the stresses in their environment, and understanding responsibility and self-directedness.

- **Social skills training.** Students with emotional and behavioral disorders frequently have deficits in the acquisition or execution of social skills. Training that is aimed at increasing social skills in the child's multiple environments is often helpful.

- **Crisis planning and management.** Crises should be anticipated and plans for dealing with crises should be a part of the student's intervention plan.

- **Specialized educational settings.** Children should be provided services in the least restrictive environment that meets the student's academic, psychological and social needs. Many students' needs can be effectively addressed through consultation with teachers and parents, short term counseling, and interventions in the regular classroom setting. School psychologists should encourage alternatives to categorical placement and help ensure that only those students who cannot be served appropriately in the regular classroom, based upon reliable and valid data, are considered for more restrictive programs.

- **Career, vocational and transitional planning.** Interventions addressing career exploration, the development of pre-vocational and vocational skills, and transition to the post- secondary education world should be included for all adolescents with emotional and behavioral disorders.

The Role of The School Psychologist

School psychologists' knowledge of learning, development and emotional functioning make them especially qualified to assess children suspected of having EBD and assist other members of the educational team in developing and executing comprehensive intervention plans. School psychologists can provide consultation, counseling, assessment, intervention programs, and crisis intervention. School psychologists can also be a resource for families and community providers.

Summary

Early identification and intervention for students with emotional and/or behavioral problems is essential to reduce the negative effects on academic and social adjustment. School psychologists play an important role in ensuring that these students receive comprehensive assessment and intervention services in a collaborative family- and community-oriented fashion.

References

Adelman, H. S., & Taylor, L. (1998). Mental health in the schools: Moving forward. School Psychology Review, 27, 175-190.

Batsche, G. M., & Knoff, H. M. (1995). Best practices in linking assessment to intervention. In A. Thomas & J. Grimes (Eds.), Best practices in school psychology-III. Washington, DC: NASP. pp. 569-586.

Illback, R. J., Nelson, C. N. (1996). Emerging school-based approaches for children with emotional and behavioral problems: Research and practice in service integration. New York: The Haworth Press.

McConaughy, S. H., & Ritter, D. R. (1995). Best practices in multidimensional assessment of emotional or behavioral disorders. In A. Thomas & J. Grimes (Eds.), Best practices in school psychology-III. Washington, DC: National Association of School Psychologists. Pp. 865-877.

Quinn, K. P., & McDougal, J. L. (1998). A mile wide and a mile deep: Comprehensive interventions for children and youth with emotional and behavioral disorders and their families. School Psychology Review, 27, 191-203.

Stage, S. A., & Quiroz, D. R. (1997). A meta-analysis of interventions to decrease disruptive classsroom behavior in public education settings. School Psychology Review, 26, 333- 368.

Stroul, B. A. (1996). Children's mental health: Creating systems of care in a changing society. Baltimore, MD: Brookes.

— Original statement adopted by NASP Delegate Assembly, April 18, 1993
— Revision adopted by the NASP Delegate Assembly, April 10, 1999

Gay, Lesbian, and Bisexual Youth

Youth who become aware of a minority sexual orientation within themselves during childhood or adolescence are at greater risk for a number of dangerous or harmful situations or activities. The most prominent risks include suicide, physical and verbal harassment, exposure to the HIV virus, and substance abuse. In addition, these youth are often rejected, emotionally and physically, by their families and may become homeless as a result of the disclosure of their sexual orientation. Society's attitudes and behaviors toward these youth render them invisible. As a result, this group suffers from a lack of resources to deal with the problems caused by the internalized sense of inadequacy and low self-esteem. Gay, lesbian, and bisexual youth who also have disabilities or are members of other minority groups have additional barriers to receiving appropriate education and mental health care within the school system and society as a whole.

The National Association of School Psychologists supports equal access to education and mental health services for sexual minority youth within public and private schools. This can be accomplished through: 1) education of students and staff, 2) direct counseling with students who are experiencing difficulties within themselves or with others due to actual or perceived minority sexual orientation, 3) advocacy for such youth within the school and the community settings, 4) support of research on evaluations of interventions and programs designed to address the needs of gay, lesbian, and bisexual youth in schools, and 5) support of programs for HIV prevention directed at gay, lesbian, and bisexual youth.

Violence and intimidation directed at sexual minority youth, whether aimed at an individual through direct harassment or at the entire group through antigay statements or biases, violate the right of these students to receive equal educational opportunities. NASP believes that school psychologists are ethically obligated to ensure that these students have an equal opportunity for the development of their personal identity in an environment free from discrimination, harassment, violence, and abuse. To achieve this goal, efforts must be made through education and advocacy for these youth to reduce discrimination and harassment against sexual minority youth by both students and staff.

Creating Safe Schools for Sexual Minority Youth

Schools must maintain campuses that are safe and conducive to learning for all students. NASP believes that efforts to create safe schools for sexual minority youth should include but not be limited to education of all students and staff, direct intervention with victims and perpetrators of harassment and discrimination of those at risk, and promoting societal and familial attitudes and behaviors that affirm the dignity and rights of gay, lesbian, and bisexual youth.

Education of students and staff. Because many gay, lesbian, and bisexual students choose not to reveal their sexual orientation for fear of harassment, other students and staff are often not aware of their presence. Staff and students who are aware and supportive may fear openly speaking out for sexual minority youth because of the possibility of being discriminated against themselves. Even among those who are aware of the existence of sexual minority youth in their school, many maintain misconceptions regarding these youth and may be unsure how to address their needs. NASP supports educating students and staff regarding the existence and needs of sexual minority youth through inservice training on the risks experienced by these youth, research relevant to these youth, and appropriate ways of addressing harassment and discrimination directed toward any student. In addition, issues pertaining to sexual orientation can be infused in the curriculum, such as presenting theories regarding the development of sexual orientation in a science class, reading works of famous gay, lesbian, or bisexual authors in a literature class, or discussing the gay rights movement in historical context with other civil rights movements in a social studies class. Sexual minority youth must also be educated to reduce unsafe behavior such as substance abuse and exposure to HIV. In addition, educating these youth can reduce the isolation they often feel as a result of perceiving themselves as invisible or as misunderstood.

Direct intervention with victims and perpetrators of harassment and discrimination. As with any instance of school violence, harassment and discrimination against sexual minority youth should be addressed both through applying consequences and educating the perpetrator and by supporting and protecting the victim. Both goals can be achieved through nonjudgmental counseling for students who have been victims of such harassment or who are questioning their sexual orientation and may become targets of harassment in the future by disclosing their status as gay, lesbian, or bisexual. Counseling and education should also be provided to the perpetrator to help prevent future episodes of harassment. Because school staff may, knowingly or unknowingly, discriminate against sexual minority youth, NASP believes that education and support for sexual minority youth must occur at all levels of schooling. This education should include students, teachers, support staff, and administrators and should stress that discrimination and harassment must be addressed regardless of the status of the perpetrator.

Promoting societal and familial attitudes and behaviors that affirm the dignity and rights within educational environments of gay, lesbian, and bisexual youth. By educating students and staff, school psychologists can help change negative or indifferent attitudes toward sexual minority youth. However, a much more powerful agent of change may be the example of the school psychologist who refuses to allow slurs or discrimination to occur and who is willing to provide services to all students regardless of sexual orientation or other minority status. Within their own schools and in society as a whole, school psychologists can promote attitudes that affirm the dignity and rights of sexual minority youth by removing biases from their own practice . They can also point out the actions or statements of other school staff who discriminate or neglect the needs of sexual minority youth and attempt to address these issues in a fair way. In particular, school policies should mandate fair treatment of all students and equal access to educational and mental health services within the schools. School psychologists can provide expert opinions and research-based information to assure that such policies are in place and enforced. Finally, school psychologists can encourage local, state, and national organizations to disseminate information to parents and other groups that need to be aware of the issues related to gay, lesbian, and bisexual youth in the schools.

Role of the School Psychologist

Because they work directly with students as well as staff and administrators, school psychologists are uniquely positioned to affect policies and practices within the schools. They can also teach by example. School psychologists can explicitly inform students that they are available to all students regardless of sexual orientation. In counseling sessions, they can be mindful that not every student is heterosexual and that sexual minority status can affect self-esteem and peer relationships. School psychologists can address issues of sexual orientation in inservice sessions as well. In presenting material on sexual harassment or discrimination, for example, they can take care to include examples and information involving sexual minority youth. School psychologists are also in a position to educate students on a number of issues related to high risk behaviors that are especially frequent among gay, lesbian, and bisexual youth, targeting both the school population in general and sexual minority youth in particular.

Summary

NASP recognizes that students who are of a minority sexual orientation, or are perceived to be, are at risk of a number of dangerous and destructive behaviors as well as harassment, discrimination, and low self-esteem. A successful program to address these issues educates both those who discriminate and those who are discriminated against because of sexual orientation. This education can occur on a number of levels: intervention with individual students, schoolwide inservice training, and modeling behaviors attitudes and behaviors by school psychologists in daily interactions with all students and staff. Any program designed to address the needs of sexual minority youth should also include efforts to educate parents and the community through involvement with other organizations committed to equal opportunity for education and mental health services for all youth. Schools can only be truly safe when every student, regardless of sexual orientation, is assured of access to an education without fear of harassment or violence.

References

Besner, H., & Spungin, C. (1995). Gay and lesbian students: Understanding their needs. Washington, DC: Taylor & Francis.

Garofola, R., Wolf, R.C., Kessel, S., Palfrey, J., & DuRant, R.H. (1998). The association between risk behaviors and sexual orientation among a school-based sample of adolescents. Pediatrics, 101(5), 895-902.

Hunter, J. (1990). Violence against lesbian and gay male youths. Journal of Interpersonal Violence, 5(3), 295-300.

Kourany, R.F.C. (1987). Suicide among homosexual adolescents. Journal of Homosexuality, 13(4), 111-117.

Marzuk, P. M., Tierney, H., Tardiff, K., et al. (1988). Increased risk of suicide in persons with AIDS. Journal of the American Medical Association, 259, 1333-1337.

Morales, E. (1990). Ethnic minority families and minority gays and lesbians. In Bozett, F. & Sussman, M. (eds.) Homosexuality and family relations. Binghamton, NY: Harrington Press.

Owens, Jr., R.E. (1998). Queer kids: The challenges and promise for lesbian, gay, and bisexual youth. New York: Harrington Park Press.

Remafedi, G. (1993). The impact of training on school professionals' knowledge, beliefs, and behaviors regarding HIV-AIDS and adolescent homosexuality. Journal of School Health, 63(3), 153-157.

Remafedi, G. (1994). The state of knowledge on gay, lesbian, and bisexual youth suicide. In G. Remapped (Ed.) Death by denial: Studies of suicide in gay lesbian teenagers. Boston: Alyson Publications, Inc.

Remafedi, G., Farrow, J. A., & Deisher, R. W. (1991). Risk factors for attempted suicide in gay and bisexual youth. Pediatrics, 87(6), 869-875.

Remafedi, G., French, S., Story, M., Resnick, M.D., & Blum, R. (1998). The relationship between suicide risk and sexual orientation: Results of a population-based study. American Journal of Public Health, 88(1), 57-60.

Rosario, M., Hunter, J., & Gwadz, M. (1997). Exploration of substance use among lesbian, gay, and bisexual youth: Prevalence and correlates. Journal of Adolescent Research, 12(4), 457-476.

Ryan, C., & Futterman, D. (1998). Lesbian and gay youth: Care and counseling. New York: Columbia University Press.

Schneider, A. G., Farberow, N. L., & Kruks, G.N (1989). Suicidal behavior in adolescent and young adult gay men. Suicide and Life-Threatening Behavior, 19(4), 381-394.

Shaffer, D. (1993, May 3). Political science. The New Yorker, p. 116.

The Governor's Commission on Gay and Lesbian Youth (1993). Making schools safe for gay and lesbian youth: Breaking the silence in schools and in families (Publication No. 17296-60-500-2/93-C.R.). Boston, MA: Author.

Tremble, B., Schneider, M., & Appathurai, C. (1989). Growing up gay or lesbian in a multicultural context. Journal of Homosexuality, 17(3/4), 253-267.

Unks, G. (Ed.) (1995). The gay teen: Educational practice and theory for lesbian, gay and bisexual adolescents. New York: Routledge.

— Adopted by the NASP Delegate Assembly, April 10, 1999

HIV/AIDS

HIV/AIDS is a serious health and psychosocial crisis affecting not only adults, but children and adolescents as well. By the end of 1996, nearly 8,000 cases of pediatric AIDS (i.e., children under age 13) were reported by the U. S. Centers for Disease Control and Prevention (CDC). At least 90% of these involved infants born to mothers with HIV infection. Because treatment medications continue to improve, an increasing number of infected children are now living to reach school age, and public schools must prepare for their enrollment. With the greatest increase in annual incidence of HIV occurring among young adult females, it is expected that the number of infected children will grow dramatically. Furthermore, because the typical incubation period between HIV infection and symptomatic AIDS is 10 years, AIDS in young adulthood most often results from risk-taking behaviors during adolescence, a time when most individuals are in school. The National Association of School Psychologists believes communities must develop policies and procedures to address the HIV needs of children and adolescents in our schools.

Consequences of Pediatric HIV

Medical consequences. Eighty percent of children infected by their mothers develop full-blown symptoms of AIDS by two years of age. Because the virus interrupts in-utero brain development, the child with HIV often has extensive brain damage, and cognitive impairment increases as the disease progresses. Possible consequences include visual and auditory short-term memory difficulties, motor, speech, and language delays, as well as attention deficits. The child with HIV who lives to reach school age is likely to have serious academic problems.

In the case of adolescent infection, HIV affects a fully-developed, intact nervous system. Thus, the profound neurological deficits associated with pediatric HIV are not as apparent in adolescent cases, and the illness progresses at a much slower rate. Indicators of neurological involvement in adolescents and adults include general mental slowness, impaired concentration, mild memory loss, and motor skills impairment.

Psychoeducational consequences. Children with HIV present complex, individual differences regarding central nervous system (CNS) disease, as well as changing patterns of functioning across time. Impairments will differ greatly depending on the areas of the brain affected. However, these impairments are not unique to HIV disease, and children can benefit from existing early intervention and special education services for those with other developmental disabilities.

Psychosocial consequences. The psychological and social issues associated with HIV are compelling. Children with HIV have higher rates of depression and anxiety, and some have been labeled "autistic-like" because of severely withdrawn behavior. HIV forces the child to confront an abbreviated life of chronic illness, including fear of death, loss of abilities, social stigma, plus the likelihood of others at home with the same disease. To complicate matters, HIV is most prevalent in economically and socially oppressed communities; many infected children did not receive sufficient prenatal and postnatal care, and many had in-utero exposure to heroin, cocaine, alcohol, and/or nicotine.

The stigma associated with AIDS presents a major problem for the family of a child with HIV. The dread of ostracism can delay detection and efforts to access needed services. In addition, extended family members may fear catching the virus, remain distant, and offer little support. Thus, the resulting loss of the family's support network may further exacerbate the vulnerability of the child. Also, media accounts reveal that many parents are loath to have their son or daughter in the same classroom with a student with HIV, and intense emotional reactions in some communities have precluded more reasoned response. Recent data indicate that exposure to psychosocial stressors, such as those described above, can worsen the medical course of pediatric HIV. Role of the School Psychologist: In response to the HIV/AIDS crisis, school psychologists have two critical roles to play: they should be at the forefront both of prevention efforts to reduce the risk of infection and intervention efforts to meet the needs of all people in the school community affected by HIV/AIDS.

Prevention

Prevention efforts should include:

Safety precautions. All members of the school community—including school psychologists—should receive training in the CDC's Universal Precautions regarding exposure to blood and other bodily fluids. This training should occur regardless of the known presence of a student with HIV.

HIV/AIDS education for students. Schools must address all social and health problems relevant to a student's learning. NASP supports the CDC recommendation that age-appropriate AIDS education be dispensed at all grade levels to increase the likelihood that high-risk behaviors can be prevented before they become firmly established and highly resistant to change. NASP believes that an AIDS prevention curriculum should:

- be jointly developed by school psychologists, parents, teachers, school administrators, health educators, and appropriate community representatives;
- be infused into a more general health education program;
- be taught by regular classroom teachers in the elementary grades and qualified health educators in secondary grades;
- describe the benefits of sexual abstinence for young people and, for teenagers becoming potentially sexually active, should address ways to reduce the risk of HIV infection and other sexually transmitted diseases (including the judicious use of condoms);
- be guided by empirical demonstrations of program efficacy, monitored periodically to determine effectiveness, and modified as necessary;
- should include guidelines to address the epidemic of HIV/AIDS stigma. School-based curricular efforts typically stress prevention but often overlook social reactions to those already infected. NASP believes that the stigma surrounding HIV may be the most formidable obstacle in prevention education and recommends that psychological and social issues be infused throughout AIDS programming in the school.

HIV/AIDS education for school personnel and parents. NASP strongly believes that all school personnel should be educated about physical, psychosocial, and developmental aspects of HIV. School personnel and parents must recognize and address their own feelings and personal concerns regarding AIDS. HIV/AIDS Education can alleviate fears and, thus, promote tolerance of children with HIV. Furthermore, school personnel and parents who are knowledgeable about HIV/AIDS are in a better position to educate children and model appropriate behavior and attitudes. Given their training in psychological and educational principles, school psychologists are in an ideal position to implement HIV/AIDS training programs that emphasize prevention education and the psychosocial issues surrounding AIDS.

Intervention

Intervention efforts should include:

Confidentiality/disclosure. NASP recommends that only those who have a legitimate need to know be informed regarding a child's HIV status. In some cases, this may mean that classroom teachers and school psychologists will not have access to this information unless it can be documented that such disclosure will benefit the child and a parent has consented to its dissemination. Disclosure of a child's HIV status often reveals information about parental intravenous (IV) drug use, sexual orientation, and marital fidelity, thereby reflecting on the entire family system. Regardless of individual decisions regarding disclosure, school personnel must be formally prepared to handle the rapid spread of HIV-related rumors among students and staff.

Psychoeducational interventions. NASP recommends that multidisciplinary teams be involved in the assessment, intervention planning, and evaluation of children with HIV. Because of the progressive nature of the disease and deteriorating CNS functioning, NASP recommends that a longitudinal perspective be used when assessing children with HIV and when planning and evaluating interventions. This must include a comprehensive neuro-developmental assessment to determine areas of impaired functioning as well as data on family and developmental history, current cognitive functioning, psychosocial status, physical impairments, receptive and expressive language, attention, memory, perceptual-motor skills, academic skills, and adaptive behavior. NASP affirms the rights of children with HIV to a free and appropriate education in the least restrictive environment. Where special education services are needed, preschool children with HIV should qualify under IDEA due to high likelihood of developmental delay and school-age children should qualify due to cognitive and physical impairments.

Psychosocial interventions. NASP recommends that issues of social contamination and stigma be considered in all decisions regarding children with HIV and their families. Negative reactions from classmates and school staff must be addressed through proper education. School psychologists can reduce the child's social isolation by gaining greater knowledge of HIV/AIDS and by training others through in-service presentations designed to reduce the fear of contagion. NASP believes that schools must work to protect the child with HIV from the ostracism that frequently accompanies HIV/AIDS. Additionally, schools must recognize that AIDS affects entire families. Pediatric HIV typically indicates the presence of AIDS in other family members, and intense emotional strain, social stigma, and bereavement are experienced by all. NASP believes that schools must address family issues, and school psychologists should contribute to the school's response to HIV/AIDS in the community.

Therapeutic interventions. The health of the school-aged child with HIV is likely to decline over time, ultimately leading to a departure from school for hospital-based care. NASP believes that school psychologists must assist children with bereavement issues at school. These issues may include students' bereavement due to the death of a classmate, AIDS-related deaths of teachers and other school staff, as well as deaths of family members of school children. School psychologists should be knowledgeable about children's developmental differences in understanding death and specific helping behaviors to use in school. In addition, the school psychologist must recognize that the child with HIV is at risk for a disintegrated family. AIDS not only creates orphans, it causes other major stressors for children, such as witnessing the conspicuous deterioration of a loved one, moving to live with an extended family member, and/or legal battles regarding custody.

Research and training. NASP believes school psychology should contribute to the limited research base regarding psychoeducational and psychosocial consequences of HIV/AIDS among children and adolescents. This research is essential to better serve children with HIV, as well as to meet the needs of others indirectly affected by the illness and its stigma. School psychologists, especially those in academic settings, should also accept this mission by sensitizing colleagues and training graduate students about the complex issues surrounding HIV disease.

Summary

NASP recognizes that schools can no longer react to the urgencies of society by focusing exclusively on academics. The changing needs of the community, plus increased political and social pressure for health care reform, require that public schools also address the general health of its students and their families, including the impact of HIV/AIDS. School psychologists have a critical role to play in combating the devastating effects of an epidemic that touches the lives of too many children and families throughout the United States. NASP strongly urges its members to work with schools and communities to slow the spread of this deadly disease and to improve the lives of all those affected by it.

NASP believes that the use of safety precautions and school-based curricular interventions (e.g., AIDS education) are the best defenses against the spread of HIV/AIDS. Secondly, school psychologists must intervene in the lives of students and families affected by HIV/AIDS. Because of the complexity of issues and concerns, the school psychologist will only be one among many professionals who must respond to the needs of a child with HIV.

Original version adopted by NASP Delegate Assembly, April, 1988

Revision adopted by NASP Delegate Assembly, July, 1999

Home-School Collaboration: Establishing Partnerships to Enhance Educational Outcomes

The National Association of School Psychologists is committed to increasing the academic, behavioral and social competence of all students through effective home-school partnerships. Such partnerships involve collaboration among families, educators and community members to support students' educational and mental health needs. Unlike traditional "parent involvement" activities that emphasize passive support roles for parents, family-school collaboration involves families and educators actively working together to develop shared goals and plans that support the success of all students.

Benefits of Collaboration

When families are involved in education, there are significant benefits for students, educators, and families. Students demonstrate more positive attitudes toward school and learning, higher achievement and test scores, increased homework completion, and improved school attendance. Teachers report greater job satisfaction and higher evaluation ratings from parents and administrators. Parents experience better understanding of schools and improved communication with their children. Although it cannot be shown that family participation causes these benefits, these positive outcomes have been documented across families from diverse ethnic and socio-economic backgrounds.

Challenges of Collaboration

Despite these many benefits, family-school collaboration is very difficult to attain. Families and educators often differ in their expectations, goals, and communication patterns, sometimes leading to frustration and misunderstanding among students, families and educators. When these differences are not recognized and addressed, a lack of communication between home and school further divides and separates the two most vital support systems available to the student. Open communication is essential in order for educators and families to understand and respect each other's perspectives.

Establishing Effective Partnerships

The role of schools

Working together toward shared goals with shared power is the essential characteristic of effective home-school collaboration. The process requires ongoing planning, development, and evaluation. It also requires the allocation of adequate resources to assist families and teachers in fulfilling their partnership roles. Schools must take the lead in providing opportunities for collaborative partnerships to be developed and sustained through:

Providing a positive environment: It is the school's responsibility to provide a welcoming environment for all families. The school must send consistent messages to families that their contributions to forming effective partnerships are valued. Efforts are made to work collaboratively with all families, including those whose primary language is not English and those with limited literacy skills.

Supporting the efforts of families and educators: Family participation increases when such participation is promoted by the school. Schools can encourage collaboration by eliciting and understanding families' perspectives and expectations. Multiple options for participation should be made available, with the recognition that individual families will support their children in different ways. Schools can foster an open dialogue between home and school and should provide opportunities for families to have decision-making roles in school governance. Resources must be provided by the school to support the collaborative efforts of families and educators (e.g., release time for teachers to meet with families in the community, development of a family support room in the school).

Increasing the understanding of diversity: Families come in many shapes and sizes with multiple perspectives, expectations, and communication styles. Schools need to provide education to staff and families that encourages understanding and celebration of diverse family forms, cultures, and ethnicities. When schools and families make the effort to understand and educate each other, they often find more similarities than differences. Collaboration is based in the assumption that families, children, and educators are doing the best they can; efforts are made to understand others' behavior and intentions rather than judge them as right or wrong.

Promoting a view of education as a shared responsibility: Home-school collaboration is not an activity; it is a process that guides the development of goals and plans. When collaboration is characterized by open communication, mutually agreed upon goals, and joint decision-making, education becomes a shared responsibility. Together, families and educators can discuss expectations for student achievement and their respective roles in helping students meet these expectations; they can develop programs to promote effective home-school- community partnerships that support positive academic, behavioral and social competencies in all students; and they can engage in efforts to increase mutual respect, understanding, caring and flexibility among families and the school community. When problems arise, they are addressed jointly by families, students, and educators in a respectful, solution-focused manner.

The role of families

Child-rearing is both complex and difficult. Individual families face multiple challenges with unique sets of resources, skills, and preferences. Therefore, it is unrealistic and potentially damaging to family-school relationships to take a "one size fits all" approach to collaboration. Roles for families should be broadly conceived, but individually applied. That is, educators and families should work together to develop an array of opportunities for families to participate meaningfully in their children's education. Such opportunities should be offered with the knowledge that families will differ in their choices; these differences must be understood to reflect individual families' needs and preferences. Potential avenues for family participation may include, but are not limited to:

- Active involvement in school decisions and governance
- Participation at school as volunteers and committee members
- Encouragement of leisure reading with their children
- Participation in school functions, athletics, and other extra-curricular activites
- Monitoring homework completion
- Regular communication with school personnel about their child's progress
- Frequent communication with their children about academic and behavioral expectations and progress
- Participation as fully informed, decision-making members of problem-solving teams (e.g., IEP teams)
- Participation in adult educational opportunities offered by the school
- Active support of the school through communication, sharing resources and seeking partnership with educators

The role of the school psychologist

NASP encourages school psychologists to take part in national, state and local efforts to define parent involvement in education as true collaborative partnerships among homes, schools and communities. School psychologists need to advocate for increased home-school collaboration and identify strategies to encourage family participation by:

- Establishing school-based teams consisting of parents, educators and community members that assess needs, develop priorities and plans, and implement joint efforts to improve educational outcomes for students

- Serving as a liaison to support communication among homes, schools and communities
- Ensuring the meaningful participation of families in special education processes by providing decision-making opportunities for families in assessment, intervention, and program planning activities
- Providing direct service to families regarding strategies that promote academic, behavioral and social success across environments
- Working with administrators to ensure that sufficient resources are allocated to family-school collaboration efforts
- Pursuing and promoting continuing education on topics such as family interventions, multicultural issues, models of home-school collaboration and parent education

Summary

Home-school collaboration leads to improved student achievement, better behavior, better attendance, higher self-concept and more positive attitudes toward school and learning. Successful home-school collaboration is dependent upon educators, families and community members working together to understand each others' perspectives and to develop shared goals. NASP is committed to supporting collaboration among families, educators and community members to promote positive educational outcomes for all children and youth.

Resources

Henderson, A., & Berla, N. (Eds.). (1994). A new generation of evidence: The family is critical to achievement. Washington, DC: National Committee for Citizens in Education.

Minke, K. M., & Vickers, H.S. (1999). Family-school collaboration. In S. Graham & K. R. Harris (Eds.), Teachers Working Together: Enhancing the Performance of Students with Special Needs (pp. 117-150). Cambridge, MA: Brook Line.

Swap, S. M. (1993). Developing home-school partnerships: From concepts to practice. New York: Teachers College Press.

Note
"Parent" is defined as any adult who fulfills a parenting role for a child; it should not be interpreted to mean only birth parents. "Educators" is used to emphasize that collaboration involves the entire school community, not just teachers.

— Adopted by the National Association of School Psychologists Delegate Assembly, April 1999.

Inclusive Programs for Students with Disabilities

The 1997 Individuals with Disabilities Education Act (IDEA 97) created significant educational opportunities for students with disabilities and established important safeguards that ensure the provision of a free, appropriate public education to students with special needs. NASP strongly supports the continuation and strengthening of this mandate. NASP also recognizes the need to continually evaluate the effectiveness of all aspects of our educational system and to promote reform when needed.

A Call for Inclusive Schools

NASP, in its continuing commitment to promote more effective educational programs for all students, advocates the development of inclusive programs for students with disabilities. Inclusive programs are those in which students, regardless of the severity of their disability, receive appropriate specialized instruction and related services within an age appropriate general education classroom in the school that they would attend if they did not have a disability. NASP believes that carefully designed inclusive programs individualized to meet the needs of students with disabilities represent a viable and legitimate option on the special education continuum that must be examined for any student who requires special education. Inclusive education is within the continuum of special education services, and must be based upon the individual needs, goals, and objectives determined by IEP teams.

Potential Benefits

Some of the benefits of inclusive programs include:

- typical peers serving as models for students with disabilities;
- the development of natural friendships within the child's home community;
- learning new academic and social skills within natural environments, facilitating generalization of skills;
- students with disabilities existing in "natural" proportions within the school community;
- all students learning to value diversity; and
- general education classrooms that are better able to meet the needs of all students as a result of additional instructional resources, staff development for general and special educators, a more flexible curriculum, and adapted instructional delivery systems.

Developing Inclusive Programs

In advocating for the development of these programs, NASP takes the position that:

- Inclusive programs must provide all the services needed to ensure that students make consistent social, emotional, and academic gains.
- General education teachers, special education teachers, school psychologists, other related services providers, and parents must collaborate to ensure appropriate services for all students and to ensure that all programs are based upon a careful analysis of each student's needs. Decisions regarding services must be made on an individual child basis.
- Outcome-based data on inclusive programs must be collected to ensure that students with and with-

out disabilities are making consistent educational progress. Ongoing empirical examination and further research are needed.

- All educators and administrators involved in implementing inclusive programs must participate in planning and training activities. When developing inclusive programs, adults with disabilities serving as experts and/or advocates, in addition to the students themselves, need to be included as much as possible.

- Knowledge and skills in effective collaboration, curriculum adaptation, developing supportive social relationships, and restructuring special services are but a few of the areas in which skills are needed.

- Preservice and inservice training based upon the needs of the staff involved in planning these programs is essential. The active involvement of general educators and administrators in staff development is critical for successful inclusion.

- School districts with limited resources may have difficulty meeting the needs of all students, particularly those with low incidence or severe disabilities. It may be necessary to provide planning and training for the provision of reasonable accommodations to students with low incidence or severe disabilities attending their neighborhood schools.

The Role of the School Psychologist

School psychologists can provide effective leadership in the development of inclusive programs. School psychologists have training and experience in collaborative consultation, behavioral and academic intervention design, curriculum adaptation, modification of learning environments, program evaluation, peer mediated learning, facilitating friendships, and other issues critical to effective inclusive programs. Because of this expertise, school psychologists are in a unique position to assist schools in assessing student needs, reallocating existing resources, and restructuring service delivery systems to better meet the educational and mental health needs of all students. School psychologists can foster the development of inclusive schools by:

- gathering and providing information regarding the strengths and needs of individual students;

- providing meaningful support and consultation to teachers and other educators implementing inclusive programs;

- distributing articles and research to fellow educators and district committees responsible for educational restructuring;

- leading or serving as members of groups that are evaluating or restructuring education programs;

- planning and conducting staff development programs that support inclusion;

- offering training and support to teachers, students and families;

- developing new resources through grant writing and collaboration with other community agencies, and other activities;

- providing information on needed changes to legislators and state and federal policy-makers; and,

- collecting and analyzing program evaluation and outcome based research.

Concerns Regarding the Traditional Special Education System

Certain aspects of traditional special education include a number of problems that create unintended negative outcomes for students:

- A referral and evaluation system that does not function as originally intended. Some of the weaknesses of this system include:

- Over reliance upon a classification system of disability categories that lacks utility and reliability for this purpose, and lacks acceptance by many parents and professionals.

- A lack of empirical research showing that students with mild disabilities grouped by category learn differently or are taught differently.

- Inequities in implementation of the least restrictive environment and access to general education curriculum provisions of IDEA 97. Data suggest that the restrictiveness of many special education placements is not based upon the severity of students' disabilities, but may instead result from the configuration of the service delivery system that is available in the community.

- Concerns that traditional special education programs are not effective in terms of learner outcomes.

- Overly restrictive special education programs housed in separate schools or "cluster" sites that result in social segregation and disproportionate numbers of students with disabilities being grouped together. For example, some students, especially those with more severe disabilities, must attend separate schools to receive special services, rather than being provided appropriate services in his/her neighborhood school. Many parents and professionals feel that it is inherently inequitable that some students must leave their neighborhood schools and communities to receive appropriate services. Although neighborhood schools may be the best decision for most students, decisions must be made on an individual basis.

Changing our Schools

NASP recognizes that the traditional framework of special education policies and regulations is often incompatible with inclusive programs. Consequently, NASP joins with the National Association of State Boards of Education in calling for a fundamental shift in the policies which drive our compensatory education system. Changes are suggested in:

- The system used to identify and evaluate students with special needs. This should be made more reliable and less stigmatizing. Noncategorical services (Rights without labels) may be appropriate for inclusive education.

- The traditional special education funding system. The link between funding and placements must be severed. Many aspects of the funding system are driven by labels and program locations rather than by student needs. Special education funding systems must be based on the provision of services to students and not on the maintenance of programs, facilities, personnel, etc.

- School improvement planning. School improvement /restructuring plans must include students with disabilities. The integration of general and special education issues must be reflected in building and district level improvement plans. This requires collaboration and staff development for both general and special educators in order to address the needs of all students.

- NASP recognizes that the shift toward more inclusive schools will require profound changes in the ways in which schools are organized. We are committed to working with parents, other professional groups, and state and national policy-makers in creating new funding and regulatory mechanisms that promote effective programs within neighborhood schools and ensure that students with special needs continue to receive appropriate resources. We endorse a process of planned change that involves all stakeholders in research, planning, and training to ensure that our nation's schools can attain excellence for all of our children.

References

Baker, E.T., Wang, M.C., & Walberg H.J. (1994). The effects of inclusion on learning. *Educational Leadership, 52*(4), 33-35.

Falvey, M.A. (Ed.). (1995). *Inclusive and heterogeneous schooling. Assessment, curriculum, and instruction.* Baltimore, MD: Paul H. Brookes.

National Association of State Boards of Education. (1992). *Winners all: A call for inclusive schools.* Alexandria, VA: Author.

National Association of State Boards of Education. (1995). *Winning ways: Creating inclusive schools, classrooms, and communities.* Alexandria, VA: Author.

National Information Center for Children and Youth with Disabilities (NICHCY). (1995) *The national study of inclusive education.* New York: National Center on Educational Restructuring and Inclusion, The Graduate School and University Center, The City University of New York.

Rogers, J. (1993) The inclusion revolution. *Research Bulletin*, no. 11. Bloomington, IN: Phi Delta Kappan Center for Evaluation, Development, and Research.

Salisbury, C.L., Pumpian, I., Fisher, D., Roach,V., & McGregor, G. (1995). A framework for evaluating state and local policies for inclusion. Consortium on Inclusive Schooling Practices.[On-line]. Available: http://www.icdi.wvu.edu/others.htm#g10

Stainback, S. & Stainback, W. (Eds.). (1996). *Inclusion: A guide for educators.* Baltimore, MD: Paul H. Brookes.

Staub, D. & Peck, C.A. (1994). What are the outcomes for nondisabled students? *Educational Leadership, 52*(4), 36-40.

Thompkins, R. & Deloney, P. (1995) Inclusion: The pros and cons. *Issues About Change,* 4, 3. Southwest Educational Development Laboratory.

Waldron, N.L. (1997). Inclusion. In G.G. Bear, K.M. Minke, & A.Thomas (Eds.), *Children's needs II: Development, problems and alternatives.* Bethesda,MD: National Association of School Psychologists.

— Adopted by the NASP Delegate Assembly, 1993
Revision adopted by NASP Delegate Assembly, April 1, 2000

Interagency Collaboration to Support the Mental Health Needs of Children and Families

Recognizing the link between children's mental health and academic performance, the National Association of School Psychologists is committed to the development of partnerships between schools and other child-serving agencies to build a coordinated, comprehensive system of care to meet the educational and mental health needs of children and their families. Children with mental health problems are often unable to receive the services that they need due to limited resources and lack of coordination between agencies. Collaboration among agencies is essential in order to create a comprehensive service delivery system based on child and family strengths that reduce barriers to learning.

Fragmentation, poor communication, and inefficient and ineffective practices among schools and community agencies result in gaps in and duplication of services. Research shows that collaborative efforts improve working relationships between schools and community mental health, juvenile justice, and other child-serving agencies and result in improved outcomes for children and their families. In addition to improved service delivery, streamlining of services through collaboration avoids duplication, provides for a continuum of service delivery options, and is cost-effective. Increased academic performance, improved attendance, increased engagement in academic activities, and fewer disruptions to the learning environment are a few of the many outcomes documented when systems design a continuum of services that includes prevention, early intervention, and treatment of severe and chronic mental health problems.

The NASP mission, Strategic Goals and Training and Practice Standards support the role of school psychologists as mental health service providers, as well as their active involvement in building collaborative relationships and promoting public policies that impact the education and mental health of children.

Most school psychologists provide prevention and intervention activities, such as staff and parent consultation, individual counseling, group counseling, and staff and parent training. In advocating for such services to support children's mental health needs, school psychologists should promote communication with relevant agencies to facilitate collaborative efforts that enhance healthy outcomes.

The Role of the School Psychologist

Schools serve most children/youth in familiar settings that are often less stigmatizing than other community agency settings; therefore, schools have become the key focal point for coordinated service delivery. School psychologists are at the forefront of mental health service delivery in the schools and are uniquely trained to help bridge the gap between schools and community agencies. With training in both education and mental health, school psychologists provide an important perspective for systems reform. School psychologists are trained or have the resources available to function as change agents who utilize skills in systems consultation and in advocacy of public policies to support the education and mental health needs of children. School psychologists facilitate communication and collaboration with students and school personnel, community professionals, agencies, families, and schools, which result in positive academic, behavioral, and mental health outcomes for children/youth.

School Psychologists as Partners: As a partner on interagency and school teams, school psychologists provide services within the prevention/intervention continuum, such as:

- Consulting with school staff and/or parents regarding the social/emotional/behavioral needs of children/youth.

- Consulting with administrators, teachers and other staff regarding a coordinated plan of psychological services for students as mandated in IDEA.
- Consulting with school staff regarding school-wide approaches to address student behavior and learning.
- Consulting with school staff to develop positive behavior supports and interventions.
- Consulting with parents regarding the implications of their child's academic and behavioral challenges and strategies to support these challenges.
- Coordinating referral of children/families to other service agencies, to provide for mental health needs.
- Assisting in the needs assessment and design of school safety plans.
- Assisting in the development and implementation of crisis plans.
- Providing staff development on topics such as positive behavior supports and intervention, prevention of violence, and crisis intervention.
- Providing resources, training, and information to school staff and/or parents regarding characteristics, intervention, and treatment of learning and behavior disorders and mental health problems.
- Screening, evaluation, identification and referral for appropriate services for children exhibiting emotional disturbances.
- Conducting functional behavior assessments to assist in the development of positive behavior supports.
- Assessing, planning and implementing appropriate academic and other educational supports.
- Measuring progress and improvement both for individuals and also for programs.
- Monitoring progress of students in collaboration with parents and private practitioners.
- Providing interventions for students with chronic behavior/emotional needs.
- Providing classroom-based instruction in prosocial skills.
- Providing small group and/or individual counseling for such issues as social skills and anger control.

School Psychologists as Facilitators of Collaboration: School psychologists can foster collaborative relationships that facilitate the creation of a system of care by engaging in the following activities:

- Identifying (mapping) the available resources in the community and at the school.
- Developing a working relationship with practitioners in other agencies.
- Developing a common vision for collaborative outcomes with community practitioners and develop a common philosophy of service delivery.
- Helping agencies develop an understanding of each community agency's role and how each agency can expand services or eliminate duplication that may exist.
- Working with community agency staff and parents to identify needs of families in the community.
- Working with community agencies to develop written policies and procedures for managing issues of confidentiality and referral between agencies.
- Promoting interagency agreements and understanding of legal/ethical issues that exist between school-based policies/practice and agency-based policies/practice
- Developing clearly defined outcomes of the collaboration effort such as increased student attendance, decreased suspensions, and improved academic performance.

- Providing cross-agency training by inviting agency personnel to participate in inservice programs focused on developing complimentary services and effective collaboration.

- Inviting community agency personnel to present information to the school staff regarding their services and ways to access their resources.

- Providing information to parents about the services that school psychologists can provide, as well as services available from community agencies.

- Providing information to school administrators, other agencies, and policy makers on the training and role of school psychologists in providing mental health services.

Collaboration Support

NASP has a vested interest in fostering the collaborative approach and in promoting the benefits of school-based services and programs, both in the workplace and in the policy arena. NASP will provide assistance and support to school psychologists in obtaining the resources necessary to effectively facilitate collaborative efforts. To further encourage collaborative partnerships, NASP requests other child-serving providers and organizations to join in efforts to establish working relationships that enhance service delivery and to address children's needs. The goal of collaborative relationships among schools, agencies and parents is to create a comprehensive and integrated system of care to support the mental health needs of children.

References

Adelman, H.S., & Taylor, L. (1997). Guidebook: Mental health and school-based health centers. Los Angeles: Center for Mental Health in Schools.

Adelman, H. S. (1996). Restructuring education support services and integrating community resources: Beyond the full service school model. *School Psychology Review, 25*(4), 431-445.

Building Collaboration in Systems of Care, 1998 Series, Volume VI. Washington, D.C.: Center for Effective Collaboration and Practice, American Institutes for Research.

Curtis, M.J., Hunley, S.A., Walker, K.J. & Baker, A.C. (1999). Demographic characteristics and professional practices in school psychology. *School Psychology Review, 28*, 104-115.

Mental Health: A Report of the Surgeon General, Department of Health and Human Services, 1999.

Nastasi, B.K. (Ed.). (1998). Mini-Series: Mental Health Programming in Schools and Communities. *School Psychology Review, 27* (2).

Standards for the Provision of School Psychological Services. NASP, July, 2000.

Standards for Training and Field Placement Programs in School Psychology. NASP, July, 2000.

The Role of Education in a System of Care: Effectively Serving Children with Emotional or Behavioral Disorders, 1998 Series, Volume III. Washington, D.C.: Center for Effective Collaboration and Practice, American Institutes for Research.

— Adopted by NASP Delegate Assembly, July 21, 2001

Mental Health Services in the Schools

"Children are the messages we send to a time we will not see."

— Neil Postman

The National Association of School Psychologists recognizes that school success is facilitated by factors in students' lives such as psychological health, supportive social relationships, positive health behaviors, and schools free of violence and drugs. A collaborative and coordinated effort is needed among schools, families, and communities to meet the needs of children and adolescents so that as a result of their years in school, students will have achieved as many positive academic and behavioral outcomes as possible. One of the most important of these positive outcomes is psychological competence, a set of skills and attitudes that lead to positive mental health and a strong sense of well-being.

To that end, NASP advocates the inclusion of effective, comprehensive mental health services in the schools. Mental health services must be included in school reform efforts in order to help students overcome barriers to learning, many of which are the result of poverty, family difficulties, and/or emotional and social needs.

School psychologists are at the forefront of mental health service delivery in the schools. Throughout the United States, school psychologists provide mental health services including - assessment, counseling, mental health and behavioral consultation services and crisis intervention in partnership with teachers, parents, school administrators, and other members of the school community to assist in developing effective interventions to service students in need. School psychologists are also serving students directly through individual and group counseling services, and as members of school based mental health programs.

The Need for Mental Health Services in Schools

The effect of mental health on school success, and achievement is well documented. Factors such as healthy self-esteem and positive relationships are important to students' success. Research emphasizes the importance of positive student behaviors and attitudes as being elements in promoting effective schools.

Unfortunately, in today's society, too many students are unable to benefit from educational experiences due to environmental or personal difficulties. Statistics regarding poverty, family disintegration, violence and substance abuse are staggering indications of barriers to learning and school success.

Addressing Student Mental Health Needs Within the Context of the Schools

Schools are the logical point of entry to increase the efficacy of mental health services to children and adolescents. School based services can be designed to address students' mental health needs using a range of service options from prevention to intervention. The key to making mental health services effective is to ensure that they are comprehensive, coordinated, and accessible to students and families.

Although providing for the mental health needs of students is a community responsibility, there are several advantages to providing such services in the schools:

1. Schools are the optimal place to develop psychological competence and to teach children about making informed and appropriate choices concerning their health.

2. Schools are the best place to integrate and coordinate the efforts of teachers, families, mental health service providers, and administrators to foster the mental health of students.

3. Accessible, affordable mental health services are most easily provided in the educational setting. Problems of transportation, accessibility, and stigma are minimized when such services are provided in schools.

The Role of School Psychologists as Mental Health Service Providers in the Schools

School psychology is a distinct profession that integrates a base of knowledge and skills in providing psychological services with training in learning, child development and an understanding of educational systems. School psychologists are well-qualified to provide comprehensive, cost-effective mental health services given this broad-based training and experience. School psychological services include but are not limited to: consultation, counseling, assessment, the development of prevention or intervention programs, behavioral plans and crisis intervention. School psychologists also assist schools, administrators, teachers, families, and other community agencies in direct and indirect service delivery, systems level planning, and program evaluation.

Given the Significant Need for School Psychological Services

1. NASP advocates coordinated and comprehensive school-based mental health services emphasizing prevention, education, and early intervention. Intervention services provided by school psychologists are a cost-effective means by which to deliver mental health services to children, adolescents, families and communities.

2. NASP advocates for increased federal, state and private funding for mental health services in the schools.

3. NASP supports and works to ensure that mental health services are as available as other health services with parity in insurance coverage.

4. NASP supports school reform that eliminates barriers to students' learning and includes school psychological services as an integral component of effective schools. NASP promotes culturally competent school psychological services that are sensitive to the individual needs of students, their families, and their communities.

5. NASP considers the following to be hallmarks of exemplary mental health programs in the schools and supports inclusion of the following factors. The mental health program:
   a. Integrates theory, research, and practice;
   b. Is based on an ecological-developmental model;
   c. Demonstrates a collaborative-participatory model;
   d. Makes a continuum of mental health services available; and
   e. Evaluates program acceptability, integration, and efficacy.

References

Nastasi, B.K., Varjas, K., Bernstein, R. & Pluymert, K. (1997). *Exemplary mental health programs: School psychologists as mental health service providers*. Bethesda, M.D. NASP.

Nastasi, B.K. (Ed.). (1998). Mini-Series: Mental Health Programming in Schools and Communities. *School Psychology Review*, 27 (2).

— Adopted by the NASP Delegate Assembly, July 1998

Minority Recruitment

One of the purposes of the National Association of School Psychologists is to serve the mental health and educational interests of all youth. In order to effectively accomplish this task, NASP resolves to work actively to increase the number of culturally and linguistically diverse school psychologists who work directly with children and who are trainers in school psychology programs. NASP believes that efforts to recruit culturally and linguistically diverse school psychologists can take many forms, and is a challenging task. Essential actions include but are not limited to the use of established recruitment procedures that are known to be successful, membership assistance in recruiting culturally and linguistically diverse individuals into the profession, the development of training programs in geographically relevant areas, and the use of research to develop more effective recruitment strategies.

Cultural and Linguistic Diversity Among the School-Age Population

Underscoring the need to recruit culturally and linguistically diverse school psychologists is the rate at which the culturally and linguistically diverse school-age population is growing. Through natural population growth and immigration, the overall U.S. population is forecast to increase by almost 50% by the year 2050. The Caucasian (White Not of Hispanic Origin) population will experience the smallest proportional increase. This is in sharp contrast to the large proportional increase forecast for the African-American, Asian/Pacific Islander, Hispanic, and Native American populations during the same time period.

Recent immigration patterns alone provide an example of the diverse student population served through the public schools. During the past decade, more people have immigrated to the United States than any other time since the turn of the century. In addition to the cultural diversity and unique life experiences common to individuals entering the United States from other parts of the world, the vast majority of children are from home countries which have a primary language other than English. This combination of cultural and linguistic diversity necessitates unique skills on the part of school psychologists, which are developed by participating in appropriate training programs.

Cultural and Linguistic Diversity Among School Psychologists

There are disproportionately few culturally and linguistically diverse school psychologists available to serve both regular and special education students. In order to provide appropriate psychoeducational services to such a heterogeneous population, it is critical that a greater number of culturally and linguistically representative school psychologists be recruited to work with children and serve as trainers in school psychology programs. As the proportion of culturally and linguistically diverse students in the total school population increases, the need for representative school psychology service delivery will be increasingly magnified. NASP, therefore, remains committed to the recruitment of members from culturally and linguistically diverse groups and recommends the implementation of the following strategies:

Strategies for Increasing Minority Recruitment

NASP advocates for the use of established recruitment procedures related to enrollment in training programs that are known to be successful, including:

- Flexible admission standards. Flexible multifaceted admission standards provide greater strength to the admission process than single, rigid criteria.

- Flexibility during the admission process may include strategies such as the recognition of various professional and life experiences prior to the pursuit of an advanced degree as a complement to entrance examination requirements and/or grade point average requirements.

- Flexible training options. Training programs may endeavor to meet the needs of working students by offering part-time training opportunities for some of the student's graduate education. In addition, some key coursework may be offered in the evenings or during the summer. This may serve to encourage individuals who would be qualified candidates, such as teachers currently working in the schools, to consider re-training in the field of school psychology.

- Financial support. Comprehensive financial support may take the form of waived or reduced application fees, the availability of special financial aid including grants, fellowships, and/or loans, and the use of special scholarships for eligible culturally and linguistically diverse students (e.g., NASP Minority Scholarship).

- Active outreach efforts. Outreach efforts targeting culturally and linguistically diverse populations may include the use of special brochures, media advertisements, personal contacts, and the use of current and past student ambassadors.

NASP encourages its membership to assist school psychology training programs in recruiting culturally and linguistically diverse group members into the profession through:

- Mentoring. NASP members may serve as mentors for students interested in pursuing careers in education and psychology. Through this grass roots effort, many talented high school and undergraduate students may become informed about the profession of school psychology and the various duties and requirements involved.

- Nominating. NASP members are encouraged to nominate talented students to regional and national school psychology training programs.

- Advocating. NASP members may choose to serve as advocates for talented students throughout the application and admission process. This may be accomplished through letters of recommendation, a willingness to provide information regarding various application procedures, and ongoing support and encouragement.

NASP supports the development of school psychology training programs in geographically relevant areas. In order to increase the total recruitment pool and provide educational opportunities for a greater number of individuals, cities and states with a sufficiently diverse population are encouraged to develop training programs which focus on the recruitment and training of culturally and linguistically diverse students.

NASP also encourages school psychology training programs to conduct research and develop the most appropriate strategies to recruit, train, and graduate greater numbers of culturally and linguistically diverse individuals from their programs.

Summary

NASP is firmly committed to the recruitment of greater numbers of culturally and linguistically diverse individuals. Culturally and linguistically diverse school psychologists are needed to serve the mental health and educational interests of all youth and to train the practitioners of tomorrow. NASP believes that the application of recruitment strategies which remove barriers from the path of prospective students and involve both association members and school psychology training institutions are those which will prove most effective.

— Revision adopted by NASP Delegate Assembly, July 25, 1998.

Pupil Services: Essential to Education

Schools are unique learning environments staffed by specialists, including pupil services teams, who are charged with the design and delivery of programs to facilitate formal and informal development of desired abilities and to help remove obstacles that may prevent success. With the new century, along with the traditional tasks, pupil services specialists are faced with the challenges of designing programs to ensure equal access and service delivery to all children in our society, and responding to a broad societal concern about the overall quality of life. The National Association of School Psychologists (NASP) recognizes that school psychologists play a key role in the delivery of these services.

Definition of Pupil Services

The professional education team has long included specialists from various helping professions. Historically, pupil services and school populations have been shaped by community, state, and federal mandates, including the original Elementary and Secondary Education Act (ESEA, U.S. Congress, 1965), the amended Individuals with Disabilities Education Act (IDEA, U.S. Congress, 1997) and initiatives in Section 504 of the Rehabilitation Act of 1973 (PL 93-112; U.S. Congress, 1973) with components infused into the Americans with Disabilities Act (ADA; U.S. Congress, 1990). These changes have resulted in an increased diversity in the services that students receive, the way in which services are accessed, and the professional fields responsible for the delivery of these services. Such progress has provided fertile ground for the emergence of a variety of pupil services specializations.

The pupil services team is typically defined to include school psychologists, school counselors, school social workers, school health professionals, and other qualified professional personnel involved in providing assessment, therapeutic (e.g., counseling, speech/language), educational remediation, strategy instruction and general curriculum support, program coordination and accountability, and other necessary services as part of a comprehensive program to meet student needs. The organization of these specialists results in highly functional transdisciplinary teams working with special and regular education teachers, families, students and community agency personnel to provide the most successful educational opportunities for all students.

Objectives for Pupil Services

The following are critical elements in design and delivery of pupil services programs:

1. Programs should be developed from identified needs of students, recognizing potential contributions from all stakeholders, including parents, special service providers, teachers, administrators, and other support personnel.

2. Effective programs necessitate a comprehensive approach, including a focus on developmental, preventative, and remedial activities which facilitate the educational process for students.

3. Effective programs recognize that not all services can be provided in the school and include effective linkages with various community resources.

4. Accountability through consistent, continuing, and effective program evaluation is crucial in both development of effective programs and insuring continuing community support.

Role of the School Psychologist

The role of the school psychologist in the delivery of pupil services is unique in the provision of psychological evaluations. School psychologists are also prepared, along with other pupil service specialists, to deliver direct intervention services, case consultation, program service development and monitoring, and system wide preventative activities. It is essential that a coordinated team approach to the delivery of these overlapping services be instituted in all of our schools. While federal and state regulations have shaped what professional services must be provided, the boundaries between the specialty areas have often been blurred. The school psychologist in collaborative effort with other specialists is proactive in advocacy for support of programs to meet special student needs and for coordinated delivery of such programs.

Summary

NASP supports the concept that effective delivery of pupil services is essential to education and recognizes that meeting the diversity of student needs requires a transdisciplinary team approach utilizing trust, open communication, mutual respect, and ongoing collaboration of professionals from each specialty area. Because all pupil services are related, the sometimes overlapping areas of expertise can serve to strengthen the overall program and be an ongoing resource for consultation and support. Regardless of the administrative structure employed, it is the coordination of pupil services that becomes most essential when meeting the commitment to serve this country's school-aged youth, and enhance the communication of the critical importance of the services to the constituencies which provide financial support.

References

U.S. Congress. (1965). PL 89-10 – Elementary and Secondary Education Act.

U.S. Congress. (1973). PL 93-112 – Rehabilitation Act.

U.S. Congress. (1990). PL 101-336 – Americans with Disabilities Act.

U.S. Congress. (1997). PL 105-17 – Individuals with Disabilities Act Amendments.

— Original version adopted by NASP Delegate Assembly, 1989

— Revision adopted by NASP Delegate Assembly April 10, 1999

Racism, Prejudice, and Discrimination

The National Association of School Psychologists is committed to promoting the rights, welfare, educational, and mental health needs of all students. This can only be accomplished in a society which ensures that all people, including children and youth, are treated equitably without reference to race or ethnicity. NASP believes that racism, prejudice, and discrimination are harmful to children and youth because they can have a profoundly negative impact on school achievement, self-esteem, personal growth, and ultimately the welfare of all American society.

A discussion of multicultural issues requires a definition of terms. The following definitions apply to the terms used in this position statement (adopted from the Multicultural Project for Community Education, Cambridge, MA and Washington D.C.).

Prejudice: Prejudice is an attitude, opinion, or feeling formed without prior knowledge, thought, or reason.

Discrimination: Discrimination is differential treatment that favors one individual, group, or object over another. The source of discrimination is prejudice, and the actions are not systematized.

Racism: Racism is racial prejudice and discrimination supported by institutional power and authority used to the advantage of one race and the disadvantage of other race(s). The critical element of racism which differentiates racism from prejudice and discrimination is the use of institutional power and authority to support prejudice and enforce discriminatory behaviors in systematic ways with far reaching outcomes and effects.

Research indicates that many students who are the victims of racism, prejudice, and discrimination: develop feelings of worthlessness; deny membership within their own group; identify with the dominant group; develop prejudice against other ethnic minorities; achieve less in school and have lower aspirations for the future; and drop out of school in increased numbers (e.g., Hale-Benson, 1990; Mabbutt, 1991; Taylor, 1996).

As a nation, we must be committed to replacing racism, discrimination, and prejudice with attitudes and behaviors that reflect fairness and cooperation. Children must learn tolerance and cooperation, and this learning must begin at an early age. The National Association of School Psychologists urges all educators and community leaders to:

- promote policies to establish and maintain racial, cultural, and linguistic diversity among school personnel;
- take an active role in teaching students tolerance and pluralistic values, using
- strategies such as cultural sensitivity training, cooperative learning, and conflict resolution training;
- discuss racism, prejudice, and discrimination with students of all ages;
- provide students with an opportunity to learn about culturally, ethnically, and linguistically diverse groups;
- promote and employ curricula which give students the opportunity to explore issues of self identity; and
- develop programs for all students designed to promote self-respect and respect for others.

Role of the School Psychologist

As mental health professionals, school psychologists must understand the effects of racism, discrimination, and prejudice, how they impact their professional work, and how they affect every facet of the lives of children and adults in America. The practice of school psychology must be informed by this knowledge and understanding, and NASP supports all efforts, at both a preservice and inservice level, to ensure that this occurs. NASP believes that school psychologists have a critical role to play in making schools culturally sensitive environments and directly supports this endeavor through the NASP Minority Scholarship, the promotion of racially, culturally, and linguistically sensitive training standards, and through the development of Tolerance Curriculum materials. Ultimately, the welfare of all students and our nation is at stake.

References

Hale-Benson, J. (1990). Achieving equal educational outcomes for Black children. In A. Barona & E. E. Garcia (Eds.), Children at risk: Poverty, minority status, and other issues in educational equity (pp.201-216). Washington, D.C.: National Association of School Psychologists.

Mabbutt, R. (1991). Reducing bias: Research notes on racism in America. Boise, ID: Idaho Human Rights Commission.

Taylor, R. (1996). Family as an agent in the education process: A test of a theory of underachievement of African-American adolescents. Philadelphia, PA: National Research Center on Education in the Inner Cities.

— Originally adopted by NASP Delegate Assembly, April 1993

— Revision adopted by NASP Delegate Assembly, April 1999

Rights Without Labels

The Rights Without Labels concept has been developed to address problems associated with the classification and labeling of children as "handicapped" for educational purposes. This classification establishes certain legal rights for children and parents, often including funds for schools offering specialized services.

Problems permeate this system: unreliability of classification; lack of instructional relevance for some classifications; exclusion of children from regular education; and the stigmatization of classified children. Moreover, removing these classifications and labels to return a student to regular education has proved very difficult.

The Rights Without Labels guidelines presented here have special significance for children with academic and/or behavioral difficulties who are frequently classified as learning disabled, educable mentally retarded or behavior disordered/emotionally disturbed. Our intention, however, is to apply these guidelines to as broad a range of exceptionalities as is feasible and in no way to diminish opportunities for even the severely/profoundly handicapped student to be served in settings with their non-handicapped peers.

The Rights Without Labels guidelines are based on the assumption that it would be desirable at this time to conduct programs wherein efforts are made to serve children who have special needs without labeling them or removing them from regular education programs. Research indicates that several factors are critical to the success of such experimental programs.

Pre-referral Screening/Intervention

Attempts must be made at the very outset to ameliorate educational difficulties through the use of pre-referral screening/intervention methods conducted by regular school personnel with the support of resources typically limited to special education (i.e., school psychologists, teachers, social workers, speech therapists, etc.). This benefits all children, especially those experiencing educational problems, while helping to identify students with characteristics consonant with legal definitions of handicapped conditions. Such practices will engender an abiding respect for students' rights under the law not to be evaluated in the absence of genuine suspicion of a handicap.

Curriculum Based Assessment

Secondly, identification and evaluation methods must include curriculum based assessment procedures. Research demonstrates these procedures provide reliable measures of student performance and produce relevant information for instructional planning. Most importantly, they fulfill the evaluation protection criteria set out in P.L. 94-142. The primary purpose of these procedures is not to classify or label children, but rather to identify specific curriculum and instructional deficits and strengths in order to provide a framework to develop appropriate educational programs. Individualized Education Programs (IEPs) continue to be required, as well as related services provided in accordance with current legal guidelines.

Special Resources in Regular Settings

The traditional array of special education supplementary aids, services and resources (including teachers/aides) are available to children only outside the regular classroom. Our goal is to broaden the classroom situation within which special education resources can be used and to reverse the practice of moving handicapped students to special education situations outside regular classes and schools. Instead, special education resources can be transferred into the non-categorically identified students' regular classroom setting.

RIGHTS WITHOUT LABELS GUIDELINES

These guidelines are stated positively as principles for programs which professionals, advocates and parents may wish to examine. The checklist format is provided for use in developing experimental programs in local or state systems.

GUIDELINES FOR ASSURING RIGHTS WITHOUT LABELS IN REGULAR/SPECIAL EDUCATION PROGRAMS

I. ASSURANCES: Any proposed alternatives non-categorical program or system shall:

A. Ensure that the fundamental rights afforded handicapped students and their parents under P.L. 94-142 are maintained and safeguarded. These include, but are not limited to:

1) Standards for fair and unbiased identification and evaluation of children who would qualify as "handicapped" in a categorical system.

2) Individualized Education Programs (IEPs) for all students who would otherwise qualify under a categorical system.

3) Specialized instruction and related services for students who would otherwise qualify under a categorical system.

4) Least Restrictive Environment (LRE) standards in determining educational placements.

5) Appointment of surrogate parents when appropriate.

6) Non-discriminatory discipline procedures.

7) All timeline standards governing the above practices and procedures.

8) Parental rights in the identification, evaluation, IEPs and placement of students who would otherwise qualify under a categorical system.

9) Due Process rights for parents and students who wish to pursue concerns/complaints regarding educational evaluations, programs and placements.

10) Local advisory boards to assist (LEAs) in planning for the provision of appropriate educational services.

B. Provide parents of handicapped students with an alternative to selecting a traditional categorical approach to classification.

C. Provide full disclosure of the non-categorical system to parents including an explanation of resources, services and rights that will be afforded students in this system.

II. GENERAL QUALITY OF ALTERNATIVE PROGRAM: Any proposed non-categorical program or system shall:

A. Employ pre-referral screening/intervention measures and utilize evaluation procedures that include curriculum based assessments.

B. Employ methodology known to be associated with effective teaching/learning (for example, provide students with orderly and productive environments, ample learning/teaching time, systematic and objective feedback on performance, well sequenced curricula, etc.).

C. Focus attention on basic skills as priority areas for instruction (for example, language, self-dependence, reasonable social behavior, mathematics, health and safety, etc.).

D. Provide procedures to identify and respond to the individual needs of all students, and in particular, those who may need modifications in their school programs.

E. Provide for special education aids, services and resources to be delivered in regular education settings.

III. ASSESSMENT OF OUTCOMES: Any proposed non-categorical program shall:

A. Have an objective methodology for assessing the educational progress of students in major curriculum domains (including academic, social, motivational and attitudinal variables) and for comparing such progress with results in traditional programs.

B. Contain and utilize a cost-benefit analysis to compare costs with traditional programs.

IV. TEACHING STAFF AND FACILITIES: Any proposed non-categorical program shall:

A. Include instruction and services by teachers and staff who are qualified in accordance with current state certification standards.

B. Include a delivery system that provides continuing staff development responsive to the training needs of the teaching staff and administrative personnel who will be implementing the requirements of the non-categorical program.

C. Include appropriate instructional materials and other resources.

D. Include assurances that funding levels and personnel allocations will not be decreased during the experimental period or as a result of successful alternative service delivery.

---

*To provide these assurances, it is assumed that as part of the experimental procedures, it would be common to conduct a dual classification system, whereby, for example, a student who might be classified as "learning disabled" in a traditional system would actually be so identified. Although the student's record would reflect the traditional classification, the student would be considered in need of "supplemental services" (i.e., regular and special education services) for purposes of his/her participation in the non-categorical program. Only by such a dual system could assurances concerning "rights" be offered and safeguarded. Over the long term, the traditional classification system might be modified if all stake-holders are satisfied about the new procedure.

Preventing and Responding to School Violence

Introduction

National studies report that districts have recently reduced violence on school campuses as demonstrated by a 70% reduction of school-associated deaths between 1992-93 and 2000-01 and a 42% reduction of student-reported weapon possession between 1991 and 1999. Despite these encouraging trends, whenever violence occurs in schools, it challenges assumptions that society holds about the role of schools. When parents leave their daughters and sons at the schoolhouse door each day, they trust that their children will be cared for and safe. They believe that schools will minimize exposure to all sources of harm, be it tragic campus shootings, chronic bullying, name-calling, sexual harassment, or social exclusion. When violence occurs at school, trust is violated, which thereby diminishes schools' efforts to attain their primary mission of educating all students. For this reason, the National Association of School Psychologists (NASP) believes that schools must continue to strive to be havens of safety and security that permit all youth to thrive academically, socially, and emotionally.

NASP also recognizes that all forms of violence at school threaten the physical, psychological, and emotional well being of students and school staff. Schools must ensure that no harm comes to anyone on school campuses at any time. To achieve this goal, efforts need to be made to eliminate obvious aggressive and illegal acts. Other behaviors are not illegal - such as mean-spirited teasing - but may nevertheless damage students' development and negatively affect school climate.

NASP further recognizes that teachers and other educators, including school psychologists, have the potential to be resources for children and youth who experience multiple, chronic risk factors in their lives. The relationships that these children form with adults in the school setting can help them cope with challenges and avoid violence perpetration and/or victimization. It is important to consider the role of such attachment and bonding in promoting and enhancing school violence prevention.

Role of the School Psychologist

NASP supports school psychologists' initiative to assume a leadership role in encouraging schools to develop comprehensive approaches to violence reduction and crisis response. School psychologists are trained to:

- implement prevention and intervention programs designed to reduce aggressive behaviors among youths and others;
- consult with school staff implementing social skills programs and other programs designed to teach peaceful ways to resolve conflicts;
- provide group process and consultation to help schools form effective safety planning teams;
- participate in needs assessment and program evaluation at the school and district levels;
- counsel victims of violence; and
- help communities respond to crises spawned by violence.

In addition, school psychologists are the mental health professionals who can conduct informative socioemotional assessments of students involved with aggressive behavior at school. These are essential components of a comprehensive school safety plan. To help ensure that school psychologists are well prepared to provide leadership in school violence prevention, NASP supports efforts to ensure that school psychologists have the requisite knowledge and skills to design and implement violence prevention and school crisis preparation programs.

Creating Safe Schools

NASP vigorously promotes and supports efforts to help rid America's schools of the destructive influences of violence in all of its forms. Efforts to reduce school violence can be successful when they use multiple strategies selected to be appropriate for each school's needs; these include:

Creating School-community safety partnerships. No school district or individual school can implement a comprehensive, school violence prevention program without engaging in a systematic planning process to understand its school safety problems and opportunities. School psychologists assist schools by helping them to engage in such systematic team building and problem identification process.

Establishing comprehensive school crisis response plans. Meeting the needs of victims appears self-evident. However, research shows that most schools respond to antisocial and aggressive behaviors through disciplinary action against the perpetrators, while neglecting to provide appropriate support and counseling for victims. Children who have been the victims of school violence perceive schools as failing to protect them, and as a result they may feel threatened and unsafe while at school. These children display many characteristics common to individuals with Post-traumatic Stress Disorder, including blocked learning and symptoms of serious emotional problems. NASP strongly supports the availability of counseling and recovery programs for the victims of school violence.

Enhancing classroom climate, school climate and promoting positive school discipline and support. Some programs may not focus on specific violent behaviors directly but seek to change the conditions that may be conducive to violent acts. Individualized instruction and remedial support where needed can reduce academic failure and frustration. Programs to decrease racism and other forms of intolerance have the effect of also increasing appreciation of diversity and improve levels of trust among the school community. Such programs can also decrease violence by creating a climate of acceptance and understanding and improve the quality of the relationships among and between students and staff. While school violence may engender a desire to discipline the aggressors harshly, NASP encourages school personnel to balance disciplinary responses with efforts to promote cooperation, positive social skills, and peaceful means of resolving conflicts. Addressing school violence must go beyond increasing campus security and punishing students who have violated school rules. A comprehensive campaign to end school violence must also encompass efforts to increase support, trust, and caring among students and staff.

Using nonstigmatizing school violence prevention programs. Attention to early behavioral and emotional distress signals from students will help to ensure that students are provided prevention and support services as early in their school careers as possible - in most cases prior to the need for extreme disciplinary response. NASP does not support assessment procedures that claim to identify or profile students as being at risk of committing acts of violence because of the potential for high false identification rates (many students have emotional or behavior difficulties, but relatively few commit serious violent acts). As alternatives to practices such as corporal punishment and ceasing educational services, NASP promotes the use of positive methods of school discipline such as solution-focused approaches that include the application of behavior management principles and strategies.

Promoting anti-violence initiatives that include prevention programs for all students. NASP advocates the use of a multi-level model of school violence prevention such as discussed in the federal document, *Safeguarding our Children: An Action Guide*. At the most general level, interventions include school-wide violence prevention programs. These activities encourage all students to experience positive emotional development and to use non-violent means to resolve their personal conflicts. NASP encourages programs designed to teach peacemaking, peer mediation, and conflict resolution. Such programs are natural bridges between interventions that focus on individual change and those seeking to change the ecology of the school.

Providing support for students exhibiting early warning signs of disruptive behavior. Not all students respond to school wide programs, therefore, violence prevention efforts also must target students who have shown aggressive behavior at school. As a result of public demands to respond punitively to threats of violence at school through "zero-tolerance" programs, schools often focus disciplinary actions on the perpetrators of violence. Policies that focus only on catching and punishing violent behaviors fall far short of the goal of creating a safe school environment. These efforts have recently been associated with the development of procedures to identify students thought to be "at risk" of committing violent acts. NASP supports schools efforts to thoughtfully consider a broad range of risk indicators as illustrated in the *Early Warning, Timely Response: A Guide to Safe Schools* document as well as contextual (family, school, and community) that may influence a student's behavior.

Intervening with students who experience significant school behavioral adjustment problems. Schools must also make efforts to modify the behavior of students who have engaged in or are at risk of engaging in violent behavior. NASP strongly supports systematic efforts to implement strategies that teach social skills and self-control to children and youth as part of a school-wide plan to create a safe and healthy climate conducive to learning. In addition, for many of these students, the complex problems they face require the coordination of interventions across school and community agencies. Schools alone cannot address the myriad needs of these students. For this small proportion of students, with these complex needs, cooperative agreements will be needed with community mental health, juvenile probation, child welfare services, alcohol and drug treatment, and other youth and family-serving agencies.

Summary

NASP recognizes that violent acts at school, although rare, have complex origins and profound consequences. Efforts to reduce violence at school, therefore, must be multi-faceted. A successful program will ensure the ongoing safety of all students and staff both by creating conditions that discourage violence and by responding quickly and effectively when violence occurs. To be truly comprehensive, however, violence reduction programs must influence student attitudes toward violence, teach students and school staff effective conflict resolution skills, and create a climate that promotes tolerance and understanding among students and staff. School safety programs are most effective when integrated with other violence prevention efforts involving local law enforcement, juvenile probation, public health personnel, and other parent and community groups. When an entire community commits to reducing violence, the health and well being of its children and youth are enhanced.

Resources

Bear, G. C., Webster-Stratton, E., Furlong, M. J., & Rhee, S. (2000). Preventing school violence. In K. M. Minke & G. C. Bear (Eds.), *Preventing school problems - Promoting school success: Strategies and programs that work* (pp. 1-69). Bethesda, MD: National Association of School Psychologists.

Dwyer, K., Osher, D., & Warger, C. (1998). *Early warning, timely response: A guide to safe schools.* Washington, DC: U. S. Department of Education.

Dwyer, K., & Osher, D. (2000). *Safeguarding our children: An action guide.* Washington, DC: U. S. Departments of Education and Justice, American Institutes for Research.

Furlong, M. J., Kingery, P. M., & Bates, M. P. (2001). Introduction to the special issue on the appraisal and prediction of school violence. *Psychology in the Schools, 38,* 89-92.

Furlong, M. J., Pavelski, R., & Saxton, J. (in press). The prevention of school violence. In S. Brock, P. Lazarus, & S. Jimerson (Eds.), *Best practices in school crisis planning.* Bethesda, MD: National Association of School Psychologists.

Larson, J., Smith, D. C., & Furlong, M. J. (in press). Best practices in school violence prevention. In A. Thomas (Ed.), *Best practices in school psychology IV.* Bethesda, MD: National Association of School Psychologists.

Poland, S. (1997). School crisis teams. In A. P. Goldstein & J. C. Conoley (Eds.), *School violence intervention: A practical handbook* (pp. 127-159). New York: Guilford.

United States Departments of Education and Justice. *2000 annual report of school safety.* Washington, DC: Authors. (Available Online at: www.ed.gov/offices/OESE/SDFS/annrept00.pdf).

— Original version adopted by NASP Delegate Assembly, July 1996
— Revision adopted by NASP Delegate Assembly, July 21, 2001

Sexuality Education

Education lasts a lifetime and plays a significant role in the decisions we make about our lives. Learning about sexuality is a normal and healthy part of this lifelong process. NASP believes that a comprehensive sexuality education program helps young people develop positive views of sexuality, gives them accurate information regarding health and sexuality, and assists them in acquiring the skills to make healthy decisions regarding their own sexuality now and in the future.

Sexuality education occurs in many settings and requires a collaborative effort by parents, teachers, religious leaders, and medical personnel. The common goal should be to give young people the information they need to develop their own values, to enhance their self-esteem, to provide insight into their relationships with members of both genders, and to better understand their obligations and responsibilities to themselves and others.

Comprehensive Sexuality Education

NASP believes sexuality education should begin early in life and should follow a curriculum that:

- Is part of a comprehensive, K-12 school health education program;
- Is developmentally appropriate with respect to content and instructional methods;
- Respects the diversity of values, beliefs, and cultures within the community;
- Has the support of the school administration, the governing school board, and the broader community;
- Addresses a wide range of factors related to sexuality such as: AIDS and other sexually transmitted diseases; the abuse of alcohol and other drugs and their effect on personal health; pregnancy prevention; parenting skills; reproductive and sexual health care; accurate information about sexual orientation; healthy decision-making; and effective communication skills, including the skills necessary to refuse unwanted sexual contact;
- Includes the prevention of high risk behaviors. Research shows that successful prevention programs provide both accurate information and instruction in the skills necessary to cope with difficult problems and situations. Abstinence Plus programs, which impart accurate information and comprehensive social skills training in addition to sending a strong abstinence message, have been shown more effective than Abstinence Only programs; and
- Is taught by qualified teachers who have had specialized training in human sexuality and who receive ongoing training and supervision by qualified supervisors.

Role of the School Psychologist

With their training in human development and behavior, psychological and learning processes, and educational systems, school psychologists can play an important role in the integration of appropriate sexuality education into the school system. Recognizing that the issue of sexuality education is controversial, NASP encourages all school psychologists to become informed about the issues and to use their expertise to facilitate effective sexuality education and to provide appropriate related services to high-risk students.

In collaboration with other support and educational personnel, school psychologists can:

- Assist in developing, implementing and evaluating a sexuality education curriculum that is appropriate for the ages, developmental levels, and cultural identities of the student population;
- Provide counseling for students on issues related to sexuality as needed;
- Facilitate parental and community involvement in sexuality education in the home, school, and community;
- Help teachers, administrators, and parents articulate their feelings and concerns regarding sexuality education; and
- Respond to those in the broader community who are concerned about sexuality education and its impact on student behavior.

NASP believes comprehensive sexuality education is essential to preserve the health of our children. In the absence of this education, students base their decisions regarding sexual activity, abstinence, birth control, dating, and relationships on the misinformation provided them by peers, television, movies, and what they read in novels and the popular press. Without the intervention of responsible and caring adults, the decisions they make may stem from myth or ignorance. Given the lifelong impact that decisions regarding sexuality can have, NASP believes that comprehensive sexuality education should be an integral part of the school curriculum.

— Adopted by the NASP Delegate Assembly, July 1997.

Student Grade Retention and Social Promotion

The academic underachievement of American school children is a widespread and increasingly severe problem. The recent movement to mandate academic "standards" and ensure accountability has rekindled public debate on the use of retention as a means to remedy academic deficits. While some professionals and organizations are calling for an end to "social promotion," evidence from research and practice highlights the importance of seeking alternatives that will enhance educational outcomes.

The National Association of School Psychologists promotes the use of interventions that are effective and research-based and discourages the use of practices which, though popular or widely accepted, are either not beneficial or are harmful to the welfare and educational attainment of America's children and youth. Through many years of research, the practice of retaining children in grade has been shown to be ineffective in meeting the needs of children who are academically delayed. However, despite the evidence, published estimates indicate that the rate of retention has increased by approximately 40% over the last twenty years, with as many as 15% of all American students held back each year and 30%-50% held back at least once before ninth grade. Furthermore, the highest retention rates are found among poor, minority inner city youth. Given the frequent use of this ineffective practice, NASP therefore urges schools and parents to seek alternatives to retention that are more beneficial to children and address more effectively the specific instructional needs of academic underachievers.

Research Findings

The research on the effects of retention is extensive. While admittedly of varying quality, the preponderance of the research demonstrates:

In elementary school:

- Some groups of children are more likely to be retained than others. Those at highest risk for retention are male, Black or Hispanic; have a late birthday, delayed development and/or attention problems; live in poverty, in a single-parent household or have parents with low educational attainment; or have changed schools frequently.

- While delayed entry and readiness classes may not hurt children in the short run, there is no evidence of a positive effect on either school achievement or adjustment. Furthermore, by adolescence, these early retention practices are associated with numerous health and emotional risk factors.

- Retention is generally associated with poorer academic achievement when groups of retained children are compared to groups of similar children who are promoted. The most notable deficit for retained students is in reading, the primary academic problem for which students are retained.

- Initial achievement gains may occur during the retention year, but the consistent trend across many research studies is that achievement gains decline within 2-3 years of retention such that retained children either do no better or perform more poorly than similar groups of promoted children. This is true whether children are compared to same-age or same grade students who were promoted.

- Children who are the most delayed are most likely to be harmed by retention. Particularly at the first grade level, large percentages of retained children are either subsequently retained again or are placed in special education.

- Retention appears to have no significant impact on overall school adjustment as measured by self-esteem inventories; however, retention is associated with significant increases in behavior problems as measured by behavior rating scales, with problems becoming more pronounced as the child reaches adolescence.

AT THE SECONDARY LEVEL:

- Students who were retained or had delayed kindergarten entry are more likely to drop out of school compared to students who were never retained, even when controlling for achievement levels. The probability of dropping out increases with multiple retentions. Even for single retentions, the most consistent finding from decades of retention research is the high correlation between retention and dropping out.

- Retained students have increased risk of health-compromising behaviors such as emotional distress, cigarette use, alcohol use, drug abuse, driving while drinking, use of alcohol during sexual activity, early onset of sexual activity, suicidal intentions, and violent behaviors. Furthermore, students who themselves were not retained but who attend schools with a higher proportion of old-for-grade students are also at risk for increased substance abuse.

IN ADULTHOOD:

- Grade repeaters as adults are more likely to be unemployed, living on public assistance or in prison than adults who did not repeat a grade.

Benefits of Retention

The research on retention at all age levels and across studies is based on group data. While there may be individual students who benefit from retention, no study has been able to predict accurately which children will gain from being retained. Under some circumstances, retention is less likely to yield negative effects:

- Students who have positive self concepts, good peer relationships, and have adequate skills to catch up easily are less likely to have negative retention experiences.

- Students who have difficulty in school because of lack of opportunity for instruction rather than lack of ability may be helped by retention. However, this assumes that the lack of opportunity is related to attendance/health or mobility problems that have been resolved and that the student is no more than one year older than classmates.

- Students who perform within one standard deviation of the mean on achievement tests and do not have serious social, emotional or behavioral deficits might benefit from retention, although such students are not likely to be referred for retention as their needs can generally be met with minor modifications in instruction.

- Retention is more likely to have benign or positive impact when students are not simply held back, but receive specific remediation to address skill or behavioral deficits. Such remediation is also likely to benefit students who are promoted.

Alternatives to Retention/Social Promotion

Both retention and social promotion are failed practices. Neither repeating a grade nor merely moving on to the next grade provide students with the supports they need to improve academic and social skills. NASP encourages school districts to consider a wide array of well-researched, effective and responsible strategies in lieu of retention or social promotion. Specifically, NASP recommends that school districts:

- actively encourage parents' involvement in their children's schools and education

- adopt age-appropriate and culturally sensitive instructional strategies that accelerate progress in all classrooms

- establish multi-age groupings in classrooms where teachers have been trained to work with mixed-age and ability populations

- provide effective early reading programs such as Success for All, Reading Recovery and Direct Instruction

- implement effective school-based mental health programs such as The Primary Mental Health Project
- use teacher assistance teams to identify specific learning or behavior problems, design interventions to address those problems, and evaluate the efficacy of those interventions
- appropriately provide special education services for children with educational disabilities
- offer extended year and extended day programs
- implement tutoring programs with peer, cross-age, or adult tutors
- establish full-service schools to provide a community-based vehicle for the organization and delivery of educational, social and health services to meet the diverse needs of at-risk students.

For children experiencing academic difficulties, neither grade retention nor social promotion offer effective remedies. If American schools are committed to helping all children achieve academic success and reach their full potential, we must discard these practices in favor of programs and interventions designed to address the factors that place students at risk for school failure. NASP encourages school psychologists to take an active part in helping their school districts develop effective alternatives to retention and social promotion.

Supporting resource

Dawson, P. (1998, June). A primer on student grade retention: What the research says. *Communiqué*, 26 (8), 28-30.

— This revision was adopted by the NASP Delegate Assembly on April 17, 1998.

Three-Year Reevaluations for Students with Disabilities

The National Association of School Psychologists is committed to promoting standards of best practice in conducting three-year reevaluations of students in special education programs, as well as supporting compliance with the requirements of P.L. 105-17 (1997 Amendments to the Individuals with Disabilities Education Act). NASP supports, and federal regulations allow, a flexible approach to three-year reevaluations based on the unique needs of the student and the specific questions that need to be answered. The reevaluation is an opportunity to critically examine the current educational environment and evaluate student progress, instructional needs, the Least Restrictive Environment, and long term goals. As such it requires the collaborative involvement of the multi-disciplinary team, including teachers, the family, and the student.

Developing A Three-year Reevaluation Plan

Federal guidelines and professional standards call for meaningful, individualized, multifaceted reevaluations which serve the best interests of students. The purposes and specific questions for reevaluation should guide the selection of assessment methods and instruments. Three broad purposes of reevaluation are:

1) **Accountability.** The effectiveness of the student's individual education program should be analyzed. Reevaluations should include a review of progress by examining data on past and present levels of performance. Data may include grades, school discipline records, curriculum- based measures, and norm-based measures. Lack of progress should stimulate IEP changes in curriculum, instructional techniques, behavioral strategies, or the educational environment or a reassessment of the nature of the disability.

2) **Planning.** Evaluation information should be utilized to determine whether modifications to the special education services received are needed in order for the child to meet the annual goals and participate, as appropriate, in the general curriculum. Factors such as behavior, current skill levels as compared to regular education peers, and communication skills should be considered. Future needs must be addressed, especially at transition points in the child's educational program. Transition planning might address confirmation of disability, community living skills, vocational training, or plans for post-secondary education.

3) **Qualification.** Under IDEA it is assumed that the initial identification of an educational disability and qualification for special education services are valid processes. Therefore the emphasis of reevaluation need not be to reconfirm eligibility, but to gauge the effectiveness of interventions and determine future programming needs. IDEA clearly states that additional formal assessments to reconfirm the disability are not required unless a change in disability is suspected or the parent requests assessment in areas of development. An evaluation must be conducted, however, before determining that a child no longer has a disability. If, at the time of the reevaluation, the student's progress suggests that he or she may no longer have a disability requiring special education, the assessment should address the student's needs and programming when exiting special education.

In reviewing existing data to determine the components of the reevaluation for the individual student, parental input is essential. Further, the team should consider factors that influence the choice of specific assessment procedures including the student's age; degree of language proficiency in English; severity and nature of disability; progress in school; years of support from special education; and the consistency of the results of previous evaluations. Existing information, such as classroom-assessments, norm-based measures, curriculum-based measures, observations by related service professionals, and interviews with teachers, family and student may provide critical data from which the team can determine the questions to be addressed by the reevaluation. Finally, the reevaluation should emphasize the collection of functional data—data readily linked to instructional strategies. The outcome of the reevaluation should be a better understanding of the student's current levels of performance and needed modifications in instruction to match the goals of the general education curriculum to the extent feasible.

Role of the School Psychologist

NASP encourages school psychologists, school administrative units, and state education agencies to develop flexible and meaningful approaches to reevaluation. School psychologists have unique training and expertise in gathering and reviewing data, and their knowledge is crucial in the selection of appropriate, reliable, and valid assessment procedures.

As part of the IEP team, they should assist in coordinating a review of the student's progress that considers the efficacy and appropriateness of the student's current program. School psychologists should work with parents, student, and teachers in determining future program needs, especially at transition times. Program changes or the continuation of special education services should be addressed when the student has made significant progress in remediating or compensating for learning or behavioral deficits.

School psychologists should assist in developing appropriate instructional strategies and behavioral interventions so that students with disabilities may successfully be educated in their least restrictive environments with optimal exposure to the general education curriculum.

References

U.S. Congress. (1997). Individuals with Disabilities Education Act Amendments, P.L. 105-17.

— Original version adopted by NASP Delegate Assembly, April 1998

— Revised version approved by NASP Delegate Assembly, July 1999

VII

Appendix VII — University Training Programs in School Psychology

Alex Thomas
Miami University

There are approximately 220 institutions currently providing school psychology training that culminates in a minimum of a state credential to practice school psychology. Many of the programs also have program approval and/or accreditation at the national level. This appendix provides pertinent information for university training programs that is current as of December 2001. Individuals wishing to obtain information may contact the individual university program through the available website, e-mail, phone, or postal address provided.

On the following chart, the following abbreviations are used:

APA = American Psychological Association

Accred. = Accreditation

D = Doctoral

DA = Degrees awarded

EN = Student enrollment

FA = Percentage of students receiving financial assistance

NN = NASP/NCATE

S = Specialist

YG = Approximate yearly graduates

School/Address/Web site	Accred.	Director	Dept.	Application Info.	Prim. Faculty	EN	FA	DA	YG
—ALABAMA—									
Auburn University 2084 Haley Center Auburn, AL 36849 www.auburn.edu/academic/education/ccp/au_ccp		Joseph A. Buckhalt Ph: 334-844-2875 Fax: 334-844-2860 buckhja@auburn.edu	Counseling & Counseling Psychology	Dept of Counseling & Counseling Psychology, ATTN: Admissions	Joseph Buckhalt, Elizabeth Brazelton	S 3, D 6	50%	M.Ed., Ed.S., Ph.D.	S 1, D 2
University of Alabama Professional Studies, PO Box 870231 Tuscaloosa, AL 35487-0231 www.bamaed.ua.edu	S: NN D: NN	Jeff Laurent Ph: 205-348-7575 Fax: 205-348-0683 jlaurent@bamaed.ua.edu	Educational Studies in Psychology, Research Methodology, and Counseling	Graduate School, University of Alabama, Box 870118 Tuscaloosa, AL 35487-0118	Jeff Laurent, Patti Harrison, Pat Logan, James Collier	S 4, D 12	35%	M.A., Ed.S. , Ph.D.	S 2, D 3
University of Alabama - Birmingham Room 201 EB Birmingham, AL 35294 www.uab.edu		Gary L. Sapp Ph: 205-975-8315 Fax: 205-975-8040 gsapp@uab.edu	Human Studies	UAB Graduate School, Rm 511 Hill University Center, 1400 University Blvd, Birmingham, AL, 35294-1150	Gary Sapp, Maxie Kohler	S 6	20%	Ed.S.	S 2
—ARIZONA—									
Arizona State University Div of Psychology in Education, College of Education Tempe, AZ 85287-0611 http://seamonkey.ed.asu.edu/~gail/programs/spy1.htm	D: NN, APA	Ray Kulhavy Ph: 602-965-3384 Fax: 602-965-0300 DPE@ASU.edu	Psychology in Education	Program and Graduate College Admissions, ASU, Tempe, AZ, 85287-1003	Ray Kulhavy, Andres Barona, Jerry Harris, Maura Roberts, Maryann Santos de Barona, Mary Stafford	D 42	45%	Ph.D.	D 3
Northern Arizona University Educational Psychology, CEE 5774, Northern Arizona University Flagstaff, AZ 86011 www.nau.edu/~cee/academics/EPS	D: NN	Ramona Mellott (Chair), Mary McLellan (Prog. Coor.) Ph: 520-523-6534 Fax: 520-523-1929 Ramona.Mellott@nau.edu	Educational Psychology Area	Program	Mary McLellan, Lena Gaddis, Kathy Bohan	S 25, D 21	70%	M.A., Ed.D	S 12, D 5
University of Arizona Department of Special Education, Rehabilitation, and School Psychology Tucson, AZ 87521-0069 www.ed.arizona.edu/html/serppsych.html	S: NN D: APA	Richard Morris Ph: 520-621-3086 Fax: 520-621-3821 morrisr@u.arizona.edu	Special Education, Rehabilitation, and School Psychology	Program	Richard Morris, John Obrzuit, Shitala Mishra, Jan Lord-Maes	S 14, D 32	75%	M.A, Ed.S., Ph.D	S 3, D 4
—ARKANSAS—									
University of Central Arkansas Department of Psychology and Counseling, Box 4915, UCA Conway, AR 72035 www.uca.edu	S: NN	John Murphy Ph: 501-450-3193 Fax: 501-450-5424 jmurphy@mail.uca.edu	Psychology and Counseling	Program	John Murphy, Ron Bramlett, Billy Smith, Joan Eichler	S 18, D 6	50%	M.S., Ph.D.	S 6
—CALIFORNIA—									
California State University - Chico Dept of Psychology (234), California State University Chico, CA 95929-0234 www.csuchico.edu/catalog/psy/	S: NN	Denise Worth, James Wolfe Ph: 530-898-5147 Fax: 530-898-4740 dworth@facultypo.csuchio.edu, jwolfe@csuchico.edu	Psychology	Graduate School, CSU - Chico, Chico, CA 95929-0875	Denise Worth, James Wolfe, Neil Schwartz	S 28	Standard univ. fin. aid opportunities	M.A.	S 7

California State University - Fresno 5310 Campus Drive, Department of Psychology, M/S PH11 Fresno, CA 93740-8019 www.csufresno.edu/gradstudies/gradfolder/psy	S: NN	Karen T. Carey Ph: 559-278-2478 Fax: 559-278-7910 karen_carey@csufresno.edu	Psychology	Program and CSU Fresno Graduate Admissions	Karen Carey, Marilyn Wilson, Beth Harn	S 21	41%	M.S.	S 11
California State University - Hayward Department of Educational Psychology, California State University Hayward, CA 94542 www.csuhayward.edu/ecat	S: NN	Mary diSibio Ph: 510-885-7430 Fax: 510-885-4798 mdisibio@csuhayward.edu	Educational Psychology	Program	Mary diSibio, Theodore Alper, Greg Jennings	S 55	50%	M.S.	S 19
California State University - Long Beach Dept of Ed. Psychology, Administration, & Counseling 1250 Bellflower Long Beach, CA 90840 www.csulb.edu/~edpsychg/academic.html#edpsych		Kristin Powers Ph: 562-985-9287 Fax: 562-985-4534 kpowers@csulb.edu	Educational Psychology, Administration and Counseling	Program	Kristin Powers, Thomas Kampwirth, Michael Bernard	S 60	30%	M.A., M.S.	S 7
California State University - Los Angeles 5151 State University Drive Los Angeles, CA 90032-8140 http://web.calstatela.edu/dept/edac	S: NN	Margaret Garcia Ph: 323-343-4448 Fax: 323-343-4252 mgarcia2@calstatela.edu	Administration and Counseling	Program	Margaret Garcia, Pauline Mercado, G. Roy Mayer, George Hong, Michael Carter , Glenda Vittimberga	S 69	25%	M.S.	S 20
California State University - Northridge Department of Psychology, California State University Northridge, CA 91330 www.csun.edu		Jean Elbert Ph: 818-677-2827 Fax: 818-677-2829 eva.wahlroos@csun.edu	Psychology	Program	Jean Elbert, Joseph Morris, Marian Schiff	S 25	30%	M.A.	S 12
California State University - Sacramento School of Education, California State University, 6000 J. Street Sacramento, CA 95819-6079 http://edweb.csus.edu/eds/schpsy.htm	S: NN	Catherine Christo Ph: 916-278-6649 Fax: 916-278-5904 christo@csus.edu	Special Education, Rehabilitation and SchoolPsychology	Program	Catherine Christo, Leslie Cooley, Stephen Brock	S 65	50%	M.S.	S 18
California State University - San Bernardino 5500 University Parkway San Bernardino, CA 92407 http://soe.csusb.edu/2b_specred.html		Dudley Wiest Ph: 909-880-5699 Fax: 909-880-7040 dwiest@csusb.edu	Educational Psychology and Counseling	Program	Dudley Wiest, Dwight Sweeney	S 15	5%	Pupil Personnel Services Credential	

School/Address/Web site	Accred.	Director	Dept.	Application Info.	Prim. Faculty	EN	FA	DA	YG
Chapman University One University Drive Orange, CA 92866 www.chapman.edu		Michael Hass Ph: 714-628-7217 Fax: 714-744-7035 mhass@chapman.edu	School of Education	Program	Michael Hass, John Brady	S 68	28%	Ed.S	S 12
Fresno Pacific University 1717 South Chestnut Fresno, CA 93702 http://www.fresno.edu/dept/grad/PPS.html		Dale E. Matson Ph: 559-453-2096 Fax: 559-453-2001 dematson@fresno.edu	Pupil Personnel Services		Dale E. Matson, Diane Talbot	S 45	5%	M.A.	S15
Humboldt State University Psychology Department, Humboldt State University Arcata, CA 95521 sorrel.humboldt.edu/~gradppsi	S: NN	Brent Duncan Ph: 707-826-5261 Fax: 707-826-4993 bbd1@humboldt.edu	Psychology	Program	Brent Duncan, Rich Langford, Susan Frances, Jan Paulus, William Reynolds	S 28	60%	M.A.	S 9
La Sierra University Educational Psychology and Counseling, 4700 Pierce St Riverside, CA 92515 www.lasierra.edu		Roger Handysides Ph: 909-785-2267 Fax: 909-785-2205 djewett@lasierra.edu	Educational Psychology and Counseling	Admissions Office, La Sierra University, 4700 Pierce St, Riverside, CA, 92515	Roger Handysides, Chang-Ho Li, Lennard Jorgensen	S 11	30%	Ed.S.	S 5
Loyola Marymount University School of Education, School Psychology Program, 7900 Loyola Blvd. Los Angeles, CA 90045 www.lmu.edu/acad/gd/edhuman		Scott W. Kester Ph: 310-338-2863 Fax: 310-338-1976 skester@lmumail.lmu.edu	Human Services	Program	Scott Kester, Brian Leung	S 35	90%	M.A	S 11
San Diego State University SDSU School Psychology Program, MC 1179 San Diego, CA 92182-1179 http://edweb.sdsu.edu/CSP/sp	S: NN	Valerie Cook-Morales Ph: 619-594-7730 Fax: 619-594-7025 schpsych@mail.sdsu.edu	Counseling and School Psychology	Program	Valerie Cook Morales, Carol Robinson-Zañartu,Colette Ingraham, Tam O'Shaughnessy	S 31	100%	M.S	S 10
San Francisco State University Psychology Department, 1600 Holloway Ave. San Francisco, CA 94132 www.sfsu.edu/~psych/psybul.htm	S: NN	Diane Harris Ph: 415-338-2711 Fax: 415-338-2398	Psychology	Program	Diane Harris, Eric Gallencamp, Frank Treadway, Mary McGrath, Deborah Estell, Amira Mostaya	S 16	Contact Office of Student Financial Aid 415-338-6000	M.S., P.P.S. Credential	S 5
University of California - Berkeley School of Education, University of California Berkeley, CA 94720-1670 www-gse.berkeley.edu/program/SP/	D: APA	Nadine M. Lambert Ph: 510-542-7581 Fax: 510-642-3555 nlambert@socrates.berkeley.edu	Cognition and Development	Admissions Office, Graduate School of Education, University of California, Berkeley, CA 94720-1670	Nadine Lambert, Carolyn Hartsdugh, Kamenji Singh,Gary Yarbroue, Kate Perry, Lin Cerles	D 34	60%	Ph.D.	D 5

University of California - Davis Division of Education, One Shields Avenue Davis, CA 95616-8579 http://education.ucdavis.edu/		Jonathan Sandoval Ph: 530-752-3198 Fax: 530-752-5411 jhsandoval@ucdavis.edu	Education	Contact Karen Bray, 530-752-0761	Jonathan Sandoval, Patricia Gandara	D 7	50%	Ph.D	D 2
University of California - Riverside School of Education, University of California Riverside, CA 95616 www.education.ucr.edu/GradEd/PhDSPsyOvr		Frank M. Gresham Ph: 909-787-4516 Fax: 909-787-3942 edfmg@ucrac1.ucr,edu	School of Education	Program	Frank M. Gresham, Lee Swonson, Don MacMillan	D 10	100%	Ph.D.	D 3
University of California - Santa Barbara UCSB, Gevirtz Graduate School of Education Santa Barbara, CA 93106 http://education.ucsb.edu/~ccspweb/	S: NN D: APA	Gale Morrison, Mike Furlong Ph: 805-893-3375 or 805-893-3338 Fax: 805-893-7264 gale@education.ucsb.edu or mfurlong@education.ucsb.edu	Education	Program	Gale Morrison, Michael Furlong,Shane Jimerson	S 17, D 15	100%	M.Ed, Ph.D	S 7, D 3
University of the Pacific Benerd School of Education, 3601 Pacific Ave Stockton, CA 95211 www.uop.edu/education/cpsych		Linda Webster Ph: 209-946-2559 Fax: 209-946-3110 lwebster@uop.edu	Educational and Counseling Psychology	Program	Linda Webster, Lydia Flasher, Judith Van Hoorn, Rachelle Kisst-Hackett	S 10, D 7	50%	M.A., P.P.S. Credential, Ed.D	S 5, D 5
—Colorado—									
University of Colorado - Denver School of Education Campus Box 106, PO Box 173364 Denver, CO 80217-3364 www.soe.cudenver.edu	S: NN	Robyn Hess Ph: 303-556-6784 Fax: 303-556-4479 robyn_hess@ceo.cudenver.edu	Professional Learning and Advancement Networks	Program	Robyn Hess, Steven Zucker	S 90	25%	Ed.S.	S 16
University of Denver 2450 S. Vine St., College of Education Denver, CO 80208 www.du.edu/education/		Gloria Miller Ph: 303-871-3340 Fax: 303-871-4456 glmiller@du.edu	Educational Psychology	Program	Gloria Miller, Mark Lyon, Martin Tombari	S 8, D 24	80%	Ed.S, Ph.D	S 2, D 4
University of Northern Colorado Programs in School Psychology, McKee 248, Box 131 Greeley, CO 80639 www.edtech.univnorthco.edu/coe/PPSY/schpsy.html	S: NN D: NN, APA	Rik Carl D'Amato Ph: 970-351-2731 Fax: 970-351-2625 talexand@edtech.unco.edu	Professional Psychology Division	Admissions Secretary, Program in School Psychology, Division of Professional Psychology, University of Northern Colorado, Greeley, CO 80639	Rik Carl D'Amato, Achilles Bardos, Ellis Copeland, Michelle Schicke, Franci Crepeau-Hobson, David Gonzalez	S 43, D 30	30%	Ed.S, Ph.D	S 20, D 5

School/Address/Web site	Accred.	Director	Dept.	Application Info.	Prim. Faculty	EN	FA	DA	YG
—CONNECTICUT—									
Fairfield University Graduate School of Education and Allied Professions Fairfield , CT 065430-7524 www.fairfield.edu/academic/gradedu/gseap_index		Paula Gill Lopez Ph: 203-254-4000 x2632 Fax: 203-254-4047 plopez@fair1.fairfield.edu	Psychology Graduate	Program	Paula Gill Lopez, Faith-Ann Dohm	S 50	80%	M.A, C.A.S.	S 12
Southern Connecticut State University Counseling and School Psychology, DA 126, 501 Crescent Street New Haven, CT 06515 scwww.ctstateu.edu	S: NN	Joy Fopiano Ph: 203-392-5910 Fax: 203-392-5917 fopiano@scsu.ctstateu.edu	Counseling and School Psychology	Program	Joy Fopiano, Michael Martin	S 79	7%	M.S., Sixth Year Professional Diploma	S 10
University of Connecticut Department of Educational Psychology, 249 Glenbrook Road, U-64 Storrs, CT 06269 www.ucc.uconn.edu/~wwwcpu	S: NN D: NN	Thomas J. Kehle Ph: 860-486-0166 Fax: 860-486-0210 kehle@uconnvm.uconn.edu	Educational Psychology	Program	Thomas Kehle, Melissa A. Bray, Sandra Chafouleas	S 4, D 27	90%	M.A, Ed.S., Ph.D.	S 4, D 3
University of Hartford Dept of Psychology, University of Hartford, 200 Bloomfield Avenue West Hartford, CT 06117 www.hartford.edu/graduate/as	S: NN	Tony D. Crespi Ph: 860-768-4544 Fax: 860-768-5292 crespi@uhavax.hartford.edu	Psychology	Program	Tony Crespi, John Schloss, Len Millins, Mary Steir	S 35	25%	M.S., Specialist Distinction	S 9
—WASHINGTON, DC—									
Gallaudet University Psychology Department, Gallaudet University, 800 Florida Avenue NE Washington, DC 20002 www.gallaudet.edu/	S: NN	Lynne Blennerhassett Ph: 202-651-5540 Fax: 202-651-5747 lynne.blennerhassett@gallaudet.edu	Psychology	Program	Tammy Weiner, Lynne Blennerhassett, Tania Thomas-Presswood, Bryan Miller	S 22	90%	M.A., Psy.S.	S 8
Howard University Dept of Human Dev. & Psychoeducational Studies, Urban School Psychology, 2400 6th St NW Washington, DC 20059 www.howard.edu		LaMonte G. Wyche, Sr. Ph: 202-806-7350 Fax: 202-806-7018 lwyche@howard.edu	Human Development and Psychoeducational Studies, Urban School Psychology	Program	LaMonte G. Wyche, Sr.	S 2, D 17	50%	M.Ed, M.A., C.A.G.S., Ed.D, Ph.D	S 2, D 3
—DELAWARE—									
University of Delaware School of Education, College of Human Resources Newark, DE 19716 www.udel.edu	S: NN	Kathleen Minke Ph: 302-831-1648 Fax: 302-831-4445 minke@udel.edu	School of Education	Program	Kathleen Minke, George Bear, Joseph Glutting	S 13, D 2	100%	M.A., Ph.D	S 6

—Florida—									
Barry University Department of Psychology, 11300 N.E. 2nd Avenue Miami Shores, FL 33161 www.barry.edu	S: NN Conditional	Agnes E. Shine Ph: 305-899-3991 Fax: 305-899-3279 ashine@mail.barry.edu	Psychology	Div. of Enrollment Services. Graduate Admissions	Agnes E. Shine, Christopher Starratt, Linda M. Peterson, Marie-France Desrosiers, Kayreen Burns, Lenore Szuchman	S 14	30%	M.S., S.S.P.	S 6
Florida A & M University College of Arts & Sciences, GECC, Room 305 Dept of Psychology Tallahassee, FL 32307 http://www.famu.edu/cas/psychology.html		Seward Hamilton Ph: 850-599-3014 Fax: 850-561-2540	Psychology	Office of Admissions, Florida A & M University, Tallahassee, FL 32307-0077	Seward Hamilton, Yvonne Bell, Joseph Baldwin, Raeford Brown, John Chambers, H. Jackson-Lowman, Oladipo Aroyewun, Clarice Hall	S 21	30%	M.S.	S 3
Florida International University School Psychology Training Program, University Park,EB 238-A Miami, FL 33199 www.fiu.edu/~edpsy/sch_psychhome.htm		Philip J. Lazarus Ph: 305-348-2725 Fax: 305-348-4125 philaz1@aol.com	Educational Psychology and Special Education	Program and Graduate Admissions, Florida International University, University Park Campus, Miami, FL 33199	Philip Lazarus, Pat Del Valle, Jeff Toomer, Adriana Garcia McEachern, Maureen Kenny, Martha Palaez-Nogueras, Marisol Gavilan	S 40	20%	Ed.S	S 12
Florida State University Psychological Services in Education, HSS/COE, 215 Stone Bldg. Tallahassee, FL 32306 www.coe.fsu.edu/departments/hss/schoolpsy.html	D: APA	Frances Prevatt Ph: 850-644-2854 Fax: 850-644-4335 fprevatt@coe.fsu.edu	Human Services and Studies	Program	Frances Prevatt, Briley Proctor	S 22, D 38	75%	Ed.S, Ph.D	S 10, D 5
University of Central Florida College of Education Orlando, FL 32816 http://www.ucfed.ucf.edu.schpsy	S: NN	Carl Balado Ph: 407-823-2054 Fax: 407-823-3859 cbalado@mail.ucf.edu	Child, Family, and Community Sciences	Program	Carl R. Balado, Gordon Taub	S 48	25%	Ed.S.	S 16
University of Florida School Psychology Program, 1403 Norman Hall Gainesville, FL 32611-2053 http://nersp.nerdc.ufl.edu/~founded/handbk2.htm	S: NN D: NN, APA	John H Kranzler Ph: 352-392-0723 Fax: 352-392-5929	Educational Psychology	Program	John Kranzler, Thomas Oakland, Tina Smith, Nancy Waldron, Jennifer Asmus	S 40, D 20	95%	M.Ed, Ph.D	S 10, D 4
University of South Florida Dept of Psychological Foundations, FAO 100 U, Room 270 Tampa, FL 33620 www.coedu.usf.edu/deptpsysoc/psych	S: NN D: NN, APA	George M. Batsche Ph: 813-974-3246 Fax: 813-974-5814 batsche@tempest.coedu.usf.edu	Psychological Foundations	Program	George Batsche, Howard Knoff, Kathy Bradley-Klug, Kelly Powell-Smith, Linda Raffaele, Michael Curtis	S 22, D 46	100%	M.A., Ed.S., Ph.D.	S 10, D 4
—Georgia—									
Georgia Southern University P.O. Box 8131 Statesboro, GA 30460-8131 www2.gasou.edu/coe/medpsych.htm www2.gasou.edu/coe/edspsych.htm		Robert Martin Ph: 912-681-5051 Fax: 912-486-7104 bobmart@gasou.edu	Leadership Technology and Human Development	College of Graduate Studies, P.O. Box 8113, Georgia Southern U, Statesboro, GA 30460	Robert Martin, Patricia McAfee	S 37	70%	M.Ed., Ed. S.	S 11

School/Address/Web site	Accred.	Director	Dept.	Application Info.	Prim. Faculty	EN	FA	DA	YG
Georgia State University Department of Counseling and Psychological Services Atlanta , GA 30303-3089 www.gsu.edu/~wwwaae/eds/SPS	D: NN, APA	Gary Evans Ph: 404-651-4856 Fax: 404-651-1160 cpsjge@langate.gsu.edu	Counseling and Psychological Services	Office of Academic Assistance, College of Education, Georgia State University 300 Education Building, University Plaza, Atlanta, GA 30303-3089	Gary Evans, Rich Gilman, Kris Varjas, Joel Meyers, Robin Gordon	S 24, D 20	30%	M.Ed., Ed.S., Ph.D.	S 22, D 2
University of Georgia 329 Aderhold Hall, Dept of Educational Psychology Athens, GA 30602 www.coe.uga.edu/edpsych/schoolpsych/index.html	D: NN, APA	Randy W. Kamphaus Ph: 706-542-0014 Fax: 706-542-4240 rkamp@arches.uga.edu	Educational Psychology	Program	Randy Kamphaus, Roy P. Martin, Michele Lease, Leslie Munson	D 43	88%	Ph.D.	D 6
Valdosta State University Department of Psychology and Counseling Valdosta, GA 31698-0100 www.valdosta.edu/~lhilgert/spsyc	S: NN Conditional	Larry Hilgert Ph: 912-333-5930 Fax: 912-259-5576 lhilgert@valdosta.edu	Psychology and Counseling	Valdosta State University, Graduate Studies, Valdosta, GA 31698-0005	Larry Hilgert, Kerry Hinkle, Daniel Kaeck, David Wasielski	S 23	50%	Ed.S.	S 5
—Idaho—									
Idaho State University Box 8059, Idaho State University Pocatello, ID 83209 www.isu.edu/departments/educ/special/psycho	S: NN	Gerald Nunn Ph: 208-236-3499 Fax: 208-236-4224 spadgera@isu.edu	Counselor Education and Special Education	Program	Gerald Spadafore, Gerald Nunn	S 12	90%	M.Ed., Ed.S	S 6
University of Idaho School Psychology Program, College of Education, PO Box 443083, University of Idaho Moscow, ID 83844-3083 www.uidaho.edu/ed/divisions.html	S: NN	Thomas N. Fairchild Ph: 208-885-6838 Fax: 208-885-6869 thomasf@uidaho.edu	Division of Adult, Counselor and Technology Education	Program	Tom Fairchild, Tom Trotter, Nicole Konen	S 51		Ed.S.	S 10
—Illinois—									
Eastern Illinois University Psychology Department, Eastern Illinois University Charleston, IL 61920 www.eiu.edu/~psych/schoolpsych.htm	S: NN	Mike Havey Ph: 217-581-3523 Fax: 217-581-6764 cfjmh@eiu.edu	Psychology	Program	Mike Havey, Gary Canivez, Assege Hailemariam, Gary Cates	S 27	100%	S.S.P.	S 10
Governors State University Department of Psychology and Counseling, Governors State University University Park, IL 60466-0975 www.govst.edu/users/glysbuyer/PandS.html	S: NN	Leisa A. Williams Ph: 708-534-4840 Fax: 708-534-8451 l-williams2@govst.edu, lawphd@prodigy.net	Psychology and Counseling	Program	Leisa Williams, Trista Huckleberry, Gabriele van Lingen	S 120	4%	M.A.	S 24
Illinois State University Department of Psychology, Campus Box 4620 Normal, IL 61790-4620 www.cas.ilstu.edu/psychology	S: NN D: NN, APA	Mark E. Swerdlik Ph: 309-438-8701 Fax: 309-438-5789 meswerd@Ilstu.edu	Psychology	Program	Mark Swerdlik, Karla Doepke, Kathryn Hoff, Steven Landau, Adena Meyers	S 18, D 37	100%	S.S.P., Ph.D.	S 6, D 6

Loyola University of Chicago 820 North Michigan Ave Chicago, IL 60611 www.luc.edu/schools/education	S: NN	Ronald R. Morgan Ph: 847-853-3332 Fax: 847-853-3375 rmorgan@luc.edu	CIEP	Program	Ronald Morgan, Pamela Fenning, David Prasse, Joy Rogers, Nancy Scott, Martha Wynne, Jack Kavanagh	S 38, D 32	25%	M.Ed., Ph.D.	S 15, D 5
National-Louis University Educational Psychology Department, 2840 Sheridan Road Evanston, IL 60201-1796 www.nl.edu	S: NN	Diane Salmon Ph: 800-443-5522 x 2724 Fax: 847-256-1057 aday@evan1.nl.edu	Educational Psychology	National College of Education, Graduate Admissions Office, National-Louis University	Diane Salmon, Marjorie Roth Leon, Rita Weinberg, Robert Clark, Barbara Leys, Philip Garber, Shani Beth-Halachmy	S 54, D 14	12%	M.Ed., M.S.Ed, Ed.S., Ed.D.	S 15, D 1
Northern Illinois University Department of Psychology, Northern Illinois University DeKalb, IL 60115-2892 www.niu.edu/	S: NN	Gregory Waas Ph: 815-753-3508 Fax: 815-753-8088 gwaas@niu.edu	Psychology	Program	Gregory Waas, Elise Masur, Michelle Demuray, Christine Malecki	S 15, D 8	95%	M.A., Ph.D.	S 6, D 1
Southern Illinois University - Edwardsville Psychology Department, Box 1121, Southern Illionois University Edwardsville, IL 62026 www.siue.edu/PSYCHOLOGY/htm	S: NN	Emily J. Krohn Ph: 618-650-3646 Fax: 618-650-5087 ekrohn@siue.edu	Psychology	Program	Emily Krohn, Andrea Rotzan, Robert Lamp, Jeremy Jewell, Bryce Sullivan, Anthony Traxler	S 17	100%	M.S., S.S.P.	S 10
Western Illinois University Department of Psychology Waggoner Hall, 1 University CIrcle Macomb, IL 61455 www.wiu.edu/users/mipsy/	S: NN	Paula S. Wise Ph: 309-298-2652 Fax: 309-298-2179 Paula_Wise@ccmail.wiu.edu	Psychology	Department of Psychology, Western Illinois University, Macomb, IL 61455	Paula Wise, Ruth Kelly, Tracy Cruise	S 23	28%	S.S.P.	S 7
—Iowa—									
Iowa State University No program Ames, IA 50011-3180 http://psych-server.iastate.edu/grad/homepage.htm		Daniel J. Reschly Ph: 515-294-1742 Fax: 515-294-6424 dreschly@iastate.edu	Psychology	Program	Daniel J. Reschly, Carla Peterson, William Panak, Camilla Benbow	S 11, D 8	100%	S.S.P., Ph.D.	S 3, D 1
University of Iowa 362 Lindquist Center Iowa City, IA 52242 www.uiowa.edu/~coe2/divisions/pandq/schoolpsych/	D: NN, APA	Kathryn Gerken Ph: 319-335-5333 Fax: 319-335-6145 kathryn-gerken@uiowa.edu	Psychological and Quantitative Foundations	Program	Kathryn Gerken; Stewart Ehly, Kenneth Merrell, Christine Novak	D 36	95%	Ph.D.	D 5
University of Northern Iowa 617 Schindler Education Center, University of Northern Iowa Cedar Falls, IA 50614-0607 http://www.uni.edu/pubrel/catalog/ma-special-dr.htm	S: NN	Annette M. Carmer Ph: 319-273-2694 Fax: 319-273-6997 barry.wilson@uni.edu	Educational Psychology and Foundations	Program	Annette M. Carmer, Don Schmits, Ralph Scott	S 13	72%	Ed.S.	S 6

School/Address/Web site	Accred.	Director	Dept.	Application Info.	Prim. Faculty	EN	FA	DA	YG
—INDIANA—									
Ball State University Educational Psychology, Teachers College 524, Ball State University Muncie, IN 47306 www.bsu.edu/teachers/departments/edpsy	S: NN D: NN, APA	Ray Dean/Josh Hall Ph: 765-285-8500 Fax: 765-285-5988/285-3653 rdean@bsu.edu or jhall2@bsu.edu	Educational Psychology	Program	R. S. Dean, J. Hall, B.E.Gridley, B. A. Rothlisberg, D. McIntosh	S 17, D 32	90%	M.A., Ed.S., Ph.D.	S 4, D 7
Indiana State University School of Education, Room 606 Terre Haute, IN 47809 http://web.indstate.edu:80/	S: NN D: NN, APA	Lisa Bischoff Ph: 812-237-3588 Fax: 812-237-7613 epbisch@befac.indstate.edu	Educational and School Psychology	Program	Lisa Bischoff, Edward Kirby, Chris MacDonald, P.G. Aaron, Michael Bahr	S 17, D 33	64%	M.Ed., Ed.S., Ph.D	S 6, D 5
Indiana University 201 N. Rose Avenue, W.W. Wright School of Education Bloomington, IN 47405-1006 http//education.indiana.edu/cep/sphmpg.html	S: NN D: NN, APA	Thomas J. Huberty Ph: 812-856-8332 Fax: 802-856-8333 or 812-856-8440 huberty@indiana.edu	Counseling and Educational Psychology	Program	Thomas Huberty, Jack Cummings, Russell Skiba, Karen Gavin	S 10, D 38	90–95%	Ed.S., Ph.D.	S 4, D 3
Valparaiso University Department of Education, Valparaiso University, 221 Miller Hall Valparaiso, IN 46383 http://www.valpo.edu/psych/Grad.htm		Maryann Dudzinski Ph: 219-464-5473 Fax: 219-464-6878 maryann.dudzinski@valpo.edu	Education	Division of Graduate Studies, 115 Kretzmann Hall, Valparaiso University, Valparaiso, IN 46383	Maryann Dudzinski, Christina Grabarek, Doris Cole, Ed Hackett, Joyce Burgener	S 19	0%	Ed.S.	S 4
—KANSAS—									
Emporia State University Box 4031, Emporia State University Emporia, KS 66801 www.emporia.edu/psyspe/school.htm	S: NN Conditional	Sharon Karr Ph: 316-341-5819 Fax: 316-341-5801 karrshar@emporia.edu	Psychology and Special Education	Emporia State University, Office of Graduate Studies and Research Box 4003, Emporia, KS, 66801-5087	Sharon Karr, Jim Persiuger, Cooper Holmes, Paul McKnab, Frank Mullins	S 24	42%	M.S., Ed.S	S 7
Fort Hays State University Department of Psychology, Fort Hays State University 600 Park St. Hays, KS 67601-4099 www.fhsu.edu/psych/index		Steven F. Duvall Ph: 785-628-4405 Fax: 785-628-5861 rmarkley@fhsu.edu	Psychology	Program	Steven Duvall	S 8	95%	M.S., Ed.S.	S 4
Pittsburg State University Department of Psychology and Counseling Pittsburg, KS 66762-7551 www.pittstate.edu/psych/		Rick Lindskog Ph: 316-235-4522 Fax: 316-235-4520 clindsko@pittstate.edu	Psychology and Counseling	Program	Rick Lindskog	S 27	49%	M.S., Ed.S	S 7
University of Kansas Department of Psychology and Reserch in Education, 621 Pearson Hall, 1122 West Campus Road Lawrence, KS 66045 www.soe.ukans.edu/programs/schoolpsyc.html	S: NN D: NN, APA	Steven W. Lee Ph: 785-864-3931 Fax: 913-864-3820 swlee@ku.edu	Psychology and Research in Education	Program	Steven Lee, Marvin Fine, Robert Harrington, Shane Lopez, Richard Simpson	S 21, D 22	100%	Ed.S, Ph.D	S 8, D 2

Wichita State University Campus Box 123, 1845 Fairmount Wichita , KS 67260 www.twsu.edu/~coewww	S: NN	Nancy McKellar Ph: 316-978-3326 Fax: 316-978-3102 mckellar@wsuhub.uc.twsu.edu	Administration, Counseling, Educational and School Psychology	Program	Nancy McKellar, Marci Girton	S 40	50%	M.Ed., Ed. S.	S 6
—Kentucky—									
Eastern Kentucky University Department of Psychology, 127 Cammack, Richmond KY 40475-0937 www.eku.edu./psy	S: NN	Jim Batts Ph: 606-622-1105 Fax: 606-622-5871 jim.batts@eku.edu	Psychology	Program	Jim Batts, Dan Florell, Myra Bundy	S 27	70%	Psy.S.	S 10
Murray State University Department of Educational Studies, Leadership and Counseling, P.O. Box 9 Murray, KY 42071-3818 http://campus.murraystate.edu/academic/faculty/marty.dunham/home.html		Mardis Dunham Ph: 270-762-2791 Fax: 270-762-3799 marty.dunham@coe.murraystate.edu	Educational Studies, Leadership and Counseling	Program	Mardis Dunham, Gabriele van Linger, Thomas Holcomb, Thomas Wagner		20%	Certification only	
University of Kentucky School Psychology Clinic, 641 Maxwelton Court Lexington, KY 40506-0349 www.uky.edu/education/edphead.html	S: NN D: NN, APA	Stephen T. DeMers Ph: 859-257-1381 Fax: 859-257-1191 sdemers@pop.uky.edu	Educational and Counseling Psychology	School Psychology Program, Educational and Counseling Psychology, Director of Graduate Studies, 245 Dickey Hall, Lexington, KY, 40506-0017	Stephen DeMers, Harriet Ford, H.Thompson Prout	S 22, D 25	60%	M.S.Ed, Ed.S, Ph.D	S 9, D 2
Western Kentucky University Department of Psychology, WKU, 1 Big Red Way Bowling Green, KY 42101 http://edtech.tph.wku.edu/~psych/areas/school	S: NN	Carl Myers Ph: 270-745-2695 Fax: 270-745-6934 carl.myers@wku.edu	Psychology	Program	Carl Myers, William Pfohl, Elizabeth Jones	S 28	100%	Ed.S.	S 7
—Louisiana—									
Louisiana State University Department of Psychology, 236, Audubon Hall Baton Rouge, LA 70803-5501 http://bitwww1.psc.lsu.edu	D: APA	Joseph C. Witt Ph: 504-388-4111 Fax: 504-388-4125 pswitt@lsu.edu	Psychology	Program	Joseph Witt, George Noell, Dorthea Lerman, John Northup	D 12	100%	Ph.D	D 4
Louisiana State University - Shreveport Psychology Department, One University Place Shreveport, LA 71115 www.lsus.edu	S: NN	Merikay M. Ringer Ph: 318-797-5046 Fax: 318-798-4171 mringer@pilot.lsus.edu	Psychology	Program	Merikay Ringer, P. Stanley, R. Nolan	S 30		Psy.S	S 5
McNeese State University Department of Psychology, McNeese State University Lake Charles, LA 70609 http://www.mcneese.edu/colleges/education/index.htm		Jerry Whiteman Ph: 318-475-5457 Fax: 318-475-5467	Psychology	McNeese State University, Registrar,Lake Charles, LA 70609	Jerry Whiteman, L.S. Dilks, Lynette Fisher	S 10	10%	M.A.	S 4

School/Address/Web site	Accred.	Director	Dept.	Application Info.	Prim. Faculty	EN	FA	DA	YG
Nicholls State University Department of Psychology and Counselor Education, PO Box 2075 Thibodaux, LA 70310 www.nicholls.edu	S: NN Conditional	J. Steven Welsh Ph: 504-448-4370 Fax: 504-448-4926 psyc-sjw@nich-nsunet.nich.edu	Psychology and Counselor Education	Program	J. Steven Welsh, Carmen Dupree Broussard, Larry Stout	S 34	60%	S.S.P.	S 6
Tulane University School Psychology Program, Dept of Psychology, 2007 Stern Science Center New Orleans, LA 70118 www.tulane.edu/~psych/psychome.html	D: APA	C. Chrisman Wilson Ph: 504-865-5331 Fax: 504-862-8744 c.wilson@tulane.edu	Psychology	Program	C. Chrisman Wilson, Michael Cunningham, Barbara Moely, Margaret Dempsey, Jeffrey Lockman, Melanie McGrath, Stacy Overstreet	D 15	100%	Ph.D.	D 2
University of Louisiana at Monroe Department of Psychology Monroe, LA 71209-0260 www.ulm.edu/~chutto/gradpsy.html	S: NN	Veronica Evans Lewis Ph: 318-342-1330 Fax: 318-342-1240 pslewis@ulm.edu	Psychology	Program	Veronica Lewis, Patty Wilhite, David Williamson, Jean Cottingham	S 22	65%	M.S., S.S.P	S 8
—MAINE—									
University of Southern Maine 400 Bailey Hall, University of Southern Maine Gorham, ME 04038 http://www.usm.maine.edu/~coe/program/sp2.htm	S: NN	Mark W. Steege Ph: 207-780-5309 Fax: 207-780-5043 msteege@usm.maine.edu	Human Resources	University of Southern Maine, Advising & Admission Office, 118 Bailey Hall Gorham, ME 04038	Mark Steege, Rachel Brown-Chidsey	S 40	33%	M.S.	S 8
—MARYLAND—									
Towson State University Psychology Department, Towson University, 8000 York Rd. Towson, MD 21252 www.towson.edu	S: NN Conditional	Susan Bartels Ph: 401-704-3070 Fax: 410-704-3800 sbartels@towson.edu	Psychology	Graduate School, Towson University, Towson, MD 21252	Susan Bartels, Stanley Zweback, Bruce Mortenson	S 45	20%	M.A., C.A.S	S 10
University of Maryland 3214 Benjamin Bldg, Dept of Counseling & Personnel Services College Park, MD 20742-1125 www.education.umd.edu/spsy	S: NN D: NN, APA	William Strein Ph: 301-405-2858 Fax: 301-405-9995 ws30@umail.umd.edu	Counseling and Personnel Services	Program	William Strein, Hedwig Teglasi, Sylvia Rosenfield	S 5, D 34	100%	M.A., C.A.G.S., Ph.D.	S 1, D 3
—MASSACHUSETTS—									
American International College 1000 State St, Box 16L Springfield, MA 01109-3189 www.aic.edu/		Antoinette Spinelli-Nannen Ph: 413-205-6302 Fax: 416-205-3598	Graduate Psychology	Program	Antoinette Spinelli-Nannen, Richard Sprinthall, John DeFrancesco,Paul Quinlan, Lorna Murphy	S 60		M.A, C.A.G.S	S 6
Northeastern University Dept of Counseling and Applied Educational Psychology, 203 Lake Hall Boston, MA 02115 www.bouve.neu.edu/department/crs/caepdegrees.html or www.dac.neu.edu/cp/sp	S: NN, D: APA	Louis Kruger (CAGS); Karin Lifter (Ph.D.) Ph: 617-373-3276 Fax: 617-373-8892 counsel@neu.edu	Department of Counseling and Applied Educational Psychology	Graduate School, Bouve College Health Sciences, 203 Mugar, Boston, MA 02115	Louis Kruger, William Sanchez, Chieh Li, Karen Lifter, Emanuel Mason, Debbie Greenwald, Barbara Okun, Carmen Armengold, Ena Vazuez-Nuttall	S 44, D 12	66%	M.S., C.A.G.S., Ph.D.	S 20, D 2

Tufts University Department of Education, Tufts University Medford, MA 02155 ase.tufts.edu/education	S: NN	Caroline Wandle Ph: 617-627-2393 Fax: 617-627-3901 caroline.wandle@tufts.edu	Education	Program	Caroline Wandle, Steven Luz-Alterman, Amy Pobst, Terry Davis	S 45	80%	M.A., C.A.G.S	S 15
University of Massachusetts - Amherst School of Education, University of Massachusetts Amherst, MA 01003-4150 http://www.umass.edu	S: NN Conditional D: NN, APA (inactive)	Gary Stoner Ph: 413-545-3610 Fax: 413-545-1523 gstoner@educ.umass.edu	Student Development and Pupil Personnel Services	Program	Gary Stoner, Bill Matthews, Brunilda DeLeon, John hintze	S 15, D 15	90%	M.Ed., C.A.G.S., Ph.D	S 4, D 3
University of Massachusetts - Boston Graduate College of Education, Wheatley Hall, 100 Morrissey Blvd Boston, MA 02125-3393 http://mirror.www.umb.edu/EXPLORE_ACADEMIC_PROG/graduate_programs/	S: NN	Varda Konstam Ph: 617-287-7619 Fax: 617-287-7664 konstam@umbsky.cc.umb.edu	Counseling and School Psychology	Program	Varda Konstam, Peter Entwistle, Virginia Harvey, Joan Struzziero, Carol Leavell, Mary Ann Ham	S 55	10%	M.Ed., C.A.G.S.	S 33
—Michigan—									
Andrews University Educational and Counseling Psychology Berrien Springs, MI 49104 www.educ.andrews.edu		Sheryl A. Gregory Ph: 616-471-3473 Fax: 616-471-6374 ecp@andrews.edu	Educational and Counseling Psychology	Program	Sheryl A. Gregory, Elsie Jackson, Lenore Brantley		25%	Ed.S., Ph.D., Ed.D.	S 4, D 1
Central Michigan University 139 Sloan Hall, Department of Psychology Mt Pleasant, MI 48859 www.cmich.edu	S: NN D: NN	Sharon Bradley-Johnson Ph: 989-774-6464 Fax: 989-774-2553 sharon.bradley.johnson@cmich.edu	Psychology	School Psychology Program, 101 Sloan, Psychology Dept., Mt Pleasant, MI 48859	Sharon Bradley-Johnson, Tim Hartshorne, Susan Jacob, Sandra Morgan, Katrina Rhymer	S 26, D 7	60%	S.S.P., Ph.D	S 6, D 2
Michigan State University 455 Erickson Hall, CEPSE East Lansing, MI 48824 http://ed-web3.educ.msu.edu/schpsych/	D: NN, APA	Evelyn R. Oka/Jean A. Baker Ph: 517-432-0843 Fax: 517-353-6393 evoka@msu.edu, jbaker@msu.edu	Counseling, Educational Psychology and Special Education (CEPSE)	Program	Jean A. Baker, Evelyn R. Oka, John S. Carlson	S 14 D 27	65%	Ed.S, Ph.D	S 5, D 3
University of Detroit - Mercy College of Liberal Arts, 8200 Outer Dr., PO Box 19900 Detroit, MI 48219-0900 http://www.udmercy.edu		Mary Elizabeth Hannah Ph: 313-993-6167 Fax: 313-993-6397 HannahME@UDMercy.edu	Psychology	Program	Mary Elizabeth Hannah, Judy McCown, Douglas MacDonald	S 40	45%	S.S.P.	S 8
Wayne State University College of Special Education, Room 331, Wayne State University Detroit , MI 48202 http://WWW.COE.Wayne.Edu/org/TBF/grad/grad.html		Guy T. Doyal Ph: 313-577-1614 Fax: 313-577-5235	Educational Psychology	Program	Guy Doyal, Stephen Hillman, Cheryl Somers, Jina Yoon	S 36, D 60		M.A., Ph.D.	S 18, D 7

School/Address/Web site	Accred.	Director	Dept.	Application Info.	Prim. Faculty	EN	FA	DA	YG
Western Michigan University Department of Psychology, Western Michigan University, 1903 W. Michigan Ave. Kalamazoo, MI 49008-5439 unix.cc.wmich.edu/~dalye/schoolpsychology/schoolpsych.htm	S: NN	Edward Daly Ph: 616-387-4469 Fax: 616-387-4550 edward.daly@wmich.edu	Psychology	Program	Edward Daly, Kristal Ehrhardt, Ruth Ervin	S 16, D 10	41%	Ed.S., Ph.D.	S 9
—Minnesota—									
Moorhead State University School Psychology Program, 1104 7th Ave. So. Moorhead, MN 056563 www.mnstate.edu/gradpsyc	S: NN	Margaret L. Potter Ph: 218-236-2802 Fax: 218-236-2168 potter@mnstate.edu	Psychology	Program	Margaret Potter, Olivia Melroe, Lisa H. Stewart	S 18	100%	M.S., Ed.S.	S 7
University of Minnesota School Psychology Program,350 Elliott Hall, 75 East River Road Minneapolis, MN 055455 http://www.coled.umn.edu/EdPsy/SchPsy/default.html	S: NN D: NN, APA	Scott McConnell Ph: 612-624-4156 Fax: 612-624-0879 lavoi003@tc.umn.edu	Educational Psychology	Program	Sandra Christenson, James Ysseldyke, Scott McConnell, Marika Ginsburg-Block, Daria Courtney, Matthew Lau	S 14 D 42	100%	Ed.S., Ph.D.	S 9, D 6
—Mississippi—									
Mississippi State University Allen Hall, Rm 508, Mississippi State University Miss. State, MS 39762 http://www.msstate.edu/dept/COE/CEdEPy/cedepy.html	S: NN D: NN, APA	T. Steuart Watson Ph: 662-325-3426 Fax: 662-325-3263 tsw2@ra.msstate.edu	Counselor Education and Educational Psychology	The Graduate School, P.O Box G, Mississippi State, MS 39762	T.S Watson, C. Hennington, Tony Doggett	D 21	**100%**	Ed.S, Ph.D	S 1, D 5
University of Southern Mississippi Department of Psychology, Box 5025 Hattiesburg, MS 39406-5025 www.dept.usm.edu/~psy/school/home.htm	D: NN, APA	Daniel H. Tingstrom Ph: 601-266-4177 Fax: 601-266-5580 daniel.tingstrom@usm.edu	Psychology	Program	Daniel Tingstrom, Ron Edwards, D.Joe Olmi, Heather Sterling-Turner	D 24	**95%**	M.A., Ph.D	D 6
—Missouri—									
University of Missouri - Columbia 16 Hill Hall, University of Missouri-Columbia Columbia, MO 65211 www.tiger.coe.missouri.edu/~schpsy	D: APA	Rick Jay Short Ph: 573-882-7731 Fax: 573-884-5989 rshort@tiger.coe.missouri.edu	Educational and Counseling Psychology	Program	Rick Jay Short, James Koller, Craig Frisby, Greg Holliday, Maria Gutierrez	S 6, D 21	**75%**	Ed.S, Ph.D	S 4, D 2
—Montana—									
University of Montana Psychology Department, University of Montana Missoula, MT 59812 www.umt.edu/grad	S: NN	George C. Camp Ph: 406-243-4521 Fax: 406-243-6366 psycgrad@selway.umt.edu	Psychology	Program	George Camp	S 16	44%	M.A., Ed.S	S 6

—Nebraska—									
University of Nebraska - Kearney Department of Counseling and School Psychology, Founders Hall Room 2102 Kearney, NE 68849 www.unk.edu	S: NN	Max McFarland Ph: 308-865-8318 Fax: 308-865-8097 mcfarlandm@unk.edu	Counseling and School Psychology	Program	Max McFarland, Jean Ramage, Theresa McFarland, Teana Archuanety	S 50	20%	Ed.S.	S 10
University of Nebraska - Lincoln 117 Bancroft Hall, Depatment of Educational Psychology Lincoln, NE 68588-0345 www.unl.edu/schpsych	S: NN D: NN, APA	Terry B. Gutkin Ph: 402-472-1154 Fax: 402-472-8319 tgutkin@unlserve.unl.edu	Educational Psychology	Graduate Admissions Office, 116 Henzlik Hall, Lincoln, NE 68588-0385	Terry Gutkin, Sue Sheridan, Susan Swearer, Beth Doll, Harold Keller	S 22, D 29	45%	Ed.S., Ph.D.	S 4, D 4
University of Nebraska - Omaha Department of Psychology, 347 Arts & Sciences Hall, 60th at Dodge Omaha, NE 68182 http://crd.unomaha.edu/~psychweb	S: NN	Robert H. Woody Ph: 402-554-2592 Fax: 402-554-2556 rwoody@cwis.unomaha.edu	Psychology	Program	Robert Woody, Lisa Kelly-Vana, Norm Hamm	S 25	10%	M.A., M.S., Ed.S.	S 3
—New Jersey—									
Fairleigh Dickinson University Psychology Department, Fairleigh Dickinson University, 1000 River Rd, T-WH1-01 Teaneck, NJ 07666 www.fdu.edu		Ron Dumont Ph: 201-692-2464 Fax: 201-692-2304 dumont@mailbox.fdu.edu	Psychology	Program	Ron Dumont, Judith Kaufman, Linda Reddy	S 55, D 38	10%	M. A., Psy.D.	S 7
Georgian Court College Department of Psychology, Georgian Court College, 900 Lakewood Ave Lakewood, NJ 08701 www.georgian.edu		Lorraine Licata, Coordinator Ph: 732-364-2200 Fax: 732-367-7301 licata@georgian.edu	Psychology	Program	Lorraine Licata , Linda James, Christopher Trigani, Joseph Springer	S 8	0%	M.A.	S 3
Kean University Department of Psychology Union NJ 07083-9982 www.kean.edu/~schpsych/school_psychology.html	S: NN	Dennis R. Finger Ph: 908-527-2181 Fax: 908-629-7044 schpsych@turbo.kean.edu	Psychology	Graduate Admissions, Office of Graduate Studies, Kean University,Union, NJ 07083	Dennis Finger, Adrienne Garro, Rosa Bianco, Robert Roth, Rhoda Feigenbaum	S 66	18%	M.A., Professional Diploma	S 9
Montclair State University Psychology Department Upper Montclair, NJ 07043 www.chss.montclair.edu/psychology/		Ofelia Rodriguez-Srednicki Ph: 973-655-7925 Fax: 973-655-5121 rodriguezo@mail.montclair.edu	Psychology	Graduate Office, Montclair State University, Upper Montclair, NJ 07043	Ofelia Rodriguez-Srednicki, Anthony D'Urso,Timothy Lionetti	S 68	15%	M.A .	S 10
New Jersey City University 2039 Kennedy Blvd Jersey City, NJ 07305 www.njcu.edu		Jim Lennon Ph: 201-200-3309 Fax: 201-200-3082 jlennon@njcu.edu	Psychology	Program	James Lennon, Andrew Getzfeld, Linda Lyons	S 18		Professional Diploma in School Psychology	S 6

School/Address/Web site	Accred.	Director	Dept.	Application Info.	Prim. Faculty	EN	FA	DA	YG
Rider University 2083 Lawrenceville Road Lawrenceville, NJ 08648 http://www.rider.edu		Kathleen McQuillan Ph: 609-895-5486 Fax: 609-896-5362 kmcquillan@rider.edu	Graduate Education	Program	Kathleen McQuillan, James Murphy	S 30	0%	Ed.S.	S 7
Rowan University Special Education Department, Robinson Hall, 201 Mullica Rd. Glassboro, NJ 08244 http://spider.rowan.edu/mars/depts/speced/maschpsy.htm	S: NN	John W. Klanderman Ph: 609-256-4500 x 3797 Fax: 609-926-8452 klanderman@rowan.edu	Special Education	The Graduate School, Memorial Hall, Rowan University, 201 Mulica Hill Road Glassboro, NJ 08028	John Klanderman, Roberta Dihoff, Hector Rios, Barbara Williams, Rosemary Mennuti , Mark Chapel	S 62	34%	M.A., Ed.S.	S 15
Rutgers University 152 Frelinghuysen Road Piscataway, NJ 08855-0819 gradstudy.rutgers.edu	D: APA	Kenneth Schneider Ph: 732-445-2008 Fax: 732-445-4888 kirchner@gsapp.rutgers.edu	Applied Psychology	Rutgers University, Graduate Admissions, 18 Bishop Place, New Brunswick, NJ 08901	Kenneth Schneider, Nancy Fagley, John Kalafat, Charles Maher, Cary Cherniss, Karen Haboush, Judith Springer	D 58	75%	Psy.D	D 10
Seton Hall University Dept of Professional Psychology & Family Therapy South Orange, NJ 7079 http://www.shu.edu/academic.html		Thomas Massarelli Ph: 973-761-9450 Fax: 973-275-2188 massarth@shu.edu	Professional Psychology and Family Therapy	Program	Thomas Massarelli, Cheryl Thompson, Arnold Derosa	S 40		M.A., Ed.S.	S 8
—New Mexico—									
New Mexico State University Department 3SPE, Box 30001, New Mexico State University Las Cruces, NM 88003-8001 www.nmsu.edu/~colgeduc/Dept_Fac/Spec_Ed/		Robert Rhodes/Enedina Vazquez Ph: 505-646-5972 Fax: 505-646-7712 rorhodes@nmsu.edu	Special Education/Communication Disorders and Counseling and Educational Psychology	Program	Robert Rhodes, Enedina Vazquez, Eric Lopez , Louis Vazquez	S 21	25%	Ed.S.	S 6
—Nevada—									
University of Nevada - Las Vegas College of Education, UNLV Las Vegas, NV 89154 http://www.nscee.edu/unlv/Colleges/Education/EP/pse.htm	S: NN	Joe N. Crank Ph: 702-895-3205 Fax: 702-895-0984 crank@nevada.edu	Special Education	Graduate College, UNLV, 4505 Maryland Parkway, Box 451017, Las Vegas, NV 89154	Joe N. Crank, Sherri Strawser	S 40	20%	Ed.S.	S 10
University of Nevada - Reno Department of Counseling and Educational Psychology Reno, NV 89557-0214 http://www.unr.edu/colleges/educ/cep/edsedpsc.html		Steven Harlow Ph: 702-784-6637 Fax: 702-784-6298 sdh@unr.edu	Counseling and Educational Psychology	Program	Steven Harlow, Rhonda Cummings, Gary Fisher, Mary Maples, LaMont Johnson, Cleg Maddux, Livia D'Andrea, Jack Casey	S 12, D 3	20%	Ed.S., Ed.D., Ph.D.	S 5, D 1
—New York—									
Alfred University Division of School Psychology, Saxon Drive Alfred, NY 14802-1232 www.alfred.edu	S: NN D: APA	Edward Gaughan Ph: 607-871-2212 Fax: 607-871-2342 fgaughan@alfred.edu	School Psychology Program	Graduate Admissions Office, Alfred University, Saxon Drive, Alfred, NY 14802	Edward Gaughan, John Cerio, Jana Atlas, Nancy Evangelista, Mark Fugate, Timothy Keith	S 42, D 35	100%	M.A , C.A.S., Psy.D	S 18, D 6

City University of New York - Brooklyn College 2900 Bedford Avenue, School of Education, School Psychology Program, 1105 James Hall Brooklyn, NY 11210 http://depthome.brooklyn.cuny.edu/schooled	S: NN	Laura Barbanel Ph: 718-951-5876 Fax: 718-951-4232 barbanel@brooklyn.cuny.edu	Education	Program	Laura Barbanel, Florence Rubinson, Grace Elizaldi-Utnick	S 85		M.S., Certificate	S 20
City University of New York - GSUC Graduate Center, 365 Fifth Ave. New York, NY 10016 www.gc.cuny.edu	D: APA	Philip A. Saigh Ph: 212-817-8292 Fax: 212-817-(unknown) rpalant@email.gc.cuny.edu	Educational Psychology	Program	Philip Saigh, Georgiana Shick-Tryon, Marian Fish, Joseph LiPuma	D 45		Ph.D.	D 6
City University of New York - Queens College Graduate Program in School Psychology Division of Education Flushing, NY 11367 www.qc.edu/ECP/schpsych/index.htm	S: NN	Marian Fish Ph: 718-997-5230 Fax: 718-997-5248 mfish@gc.cuny.edu	Educational and Community Programs	Graduate Admissions Office, Queens College, CUNY, Flushing, NY 11367	Marian Fish, David Goh, Emilia Lopez, Roslyn Ross	S 95	15%	M.S., Certificate	S 22
College of New Rochelle 29 Castle Place New Rochelle, NY 10805 http://www.cnr.edu/grs.htm		Claire Lavin Ph: 914-632-5561 Fax: 914-654-5593 clavin@cnr.edu	Human Services Division	Program	Claire Lavin, Robert Arko, James Magee	S 60	25%	M.S.	S 20
Columbia University - Teachers College Box 120, Teachers College, Columbia University, 525 W 120 th St New York, NY 10027 http://www.tc.columbia.edu/depts/9depts.html	D: APA	Stephen Peverly Ph: 212-678-3942 Fax: 212-678-4048 stp4@columbia.edu	Health and Behavior Studies	Office of Admissions, Box 302, Teachers College, Columbia University, New York, NY 10027	Stephen Peverly, Marla Brassard, Ursula Kirk	S 46, D 43	25%	Ed.M., Ed.D.	S 10, D 5
Fordham University Graduate School of Education, 113 West 60th St New York, NY 10023 www.fordham.edu	S: NN D: NN, APA	Vincent C. Alfonso Ph: 212-636-6481 Fax: 212-636-6416 alfonso@fordham.edu	Psychological and Educational Services	Office of Admissions, Graduate School of Education, Rm 1115	Vincent C. Alfonso, Anthony Cancelli, Karen Brobst, Giselle Esquivel, Abigail Harris , Laura Kestemberg	S 62, D 70	14%	Professional Diploma, Ph.D	S 11, D 3
Hofstra University 127 Hofstra University, Psychology Department Hempstead, NY 11550 www.hofstra.edu	D:NN, APA	Vincent Guarnaccia Ph: 516-463-5662 Fax: 516-463-6052 psyvjg@hofstra.edu	Psychology	Apply to above address	V. Guarnaccia, H. Kassinove, P. Ohr, A. Akin-Little M. Schare, K.Salzinger, R. O'Brien	D 137	15%	Ph.D.	D 24
Marist College Department of Psychology, Dyson Center Poughkeepsie, NY 12601-1387 www.marist.edu		Paul Egan Ph: 845-575-3000 x2135 Fax: 845-575-3695 paul.j.egan@marist.edu	Psychology	Graduate Admissions, Marist College, Poughkeepsie, NY 12601	Paul Egan, William Van Ornum, Joseph Canale	S 54	50%	M.A.	S 16

School/Address/Web site	Accred.	Director	Dept.	Application Info.	Prim. Faculty	EN	FA	DA	YG
New York University School Psychology, NYU, 239 Greene Street, Rm 537 New York, NY 10003 www.nyu.edu/education/appsych	D: NN, APA	Iris Fodor Ph: 212-998-5367 Fax: 212-260-8719 ief@nyu.edu	Applied Psychology	Program	Iris Fodor, Judith Alpert, Lawrence Balter, Ester Buchholz, Gilbert Trachtman, Marilyn Varadi	S 8, D 115	35%	M.A, Certification in S.P., Psy.D., Ph.D.	S 1, D 17
Pace University Psychology Department, 1 Pace Plaza New York, NY 10038 http://www.pace.edu/dyson/dyson.html	D: APA	Barbara A. Mowder Ph: 212-346-1506 Fax: 212-346-1618 bmowder@pace.edu	Psychology	Graduate Admissions, Pace University	Barbara Mowder, Leonard Bart, Beth Hart, Jack Herman, John Stokes, June Chisholm	S 60, D 92	65%	M.S.Ed, Psy.D.	S 20, D 20
Plattsburgh State University Psychology Dept, 101 Broad St. Plattsburgh, NY 12901 http://www.plattsburgh.edu/psy/gradprog.html		James B. Hale Ph: 518-564-3395 Fax: 518-564-3397 james.hale@plattsburgh.edu	Psychology	Admissions Office, Kehoe Building, SUNY-Plattsburgh, 101 Broad St. Plattsburgh, NY 12901	James Hale, Gregg Macmann, Jeanne Ryan		10%	M.A.	MA/CAS: 8
Rochester Institute of Technology 1 Lomb Memorial Drive School Psychology Program Rochester, NY 14623-5604 www.rit.edu	S: NN	V.K. Costenbader Ph: 716-475-6701 Fax: 716-475-6715 vkcgsp@ritvax.1sc.rit.edu	School Psychology	Office of Admissions, Bauch & Lomb Center, 60 Lomb Memorial Drive Rochester, NY 14623-5604	Virginia Costenbacher, Jennifer Lukomski, Paul McCabe	S 40	100%	M.S./ Certificate of Advanced Study	S 18
St. John's University Department of Psychology, 8000 Utopia Parkway Jamaica, NY 11439 www.stjohns.edu/academics/programs/grad_programs.html	S: NN	Raymond DiGuiseppe Ph: 718-990-1546 Fax: 718-990-5926 digiuser@stjohns.edu	Psychology	Graduate Admissions Office, St. John's University	R. DiGiuseppe, D. Flanagan, Z. Zhou, M. Tejersen, M. Beasley, S. Ortiz	S 108, D 62	25%	M.S., Psy.D.	S 22
State University of New York - Buffalo 409 Baldy Hall, Department of Counseling & Education, SUNY Buffalo, NY 14260 http://www.gse.buffalo.edu/DC/CEP/CEP_SP.htm	S: NN D: APA	LeAdelle Phelps Ph: 716-645-3154 Fax: 716-645-6616 Phelps@acsu.buffalo.edu	Counseling and Educational Psychology	Program	LeAdelle Phelps, Pat Logan, Steve Truscott, Nancy Zoeller	S 24, D 12	100%	M.A., Ph.D.	S 8, D 3
State University of New York - Oswego CPS #13, SUNY Oswego, NY 13126 http://www.oswego.edu/~gradoff/FieldofStudy.html	S: NN	Betsy Waterman Ph: 315-341-4051 Fax: 315-341-3198 waterman@oswego.edu	Counseling and Psychological Services	Program	Thomas Cushman, Janet Carlson, Betsy Waterman, Gerald Porter	S 45	80%	M.S./ C.A.S.	S 15

Syracuse University Psychology Department, 430 Huntington Hall Syracuse, NY 13244-2340 http://psychweb.syr.edu.html	D: APA	Brian K. Martens Ph: 315-443-3835 Fax: 315-443-4085 bkmarten@psych.syr.edu	Psychology	Graduate Admissions Office, Syracuse University, Syracuse, NY 13244	Brian Martens, Lawrence Lewandowski, Tanya Eckert, Benita Blachman	D 24	100%	M.S., Ph.D.	D 5
Touro College 27 W. 23rd St., Room 536 New York, NY 10010 www.touro.edu/edgrad		Carol S. Lidz Ph: 212-463-0400 x777 Fax: 212-462-4889 zdilsc@aol.com	School Psychology	No longer accepting new students	Carol S. Lidz, Boris Gindis	S 21		M.A., Certificate	S 12
University at Albany-Suny 1400 Washington Avenue-Education 232 Albany, NY 12222 www.albany.edu/schoolpsych	D: APA	Douglas K. Smith Ph: 518-442-5052 Fax: 518-442-4953 smeissner@uamail.albany.edu	Educational and Counseling Psychology	Graduate Admissions - UAB 121, 1400 Washington Ave., Albany, NY 12222	Douglas K. Smith, Deborah Kundert, Joan Newman, David Miller, Maureen Cohan, Denise De Zolt	S 6, D 43	100%	C.A.S., Psy.D.	S 3, D 5
Yeshiva University Ferkauf Graduate School of Psychology, 1300 Morris Park Ave Bronx, NY 10461 www.education.wisc.edu/edpsych.index.html	D: NN, APA	Abraham Givner Ph: 718-430-3945 Fax: 718-430-3960 givner@aecom.yu.edu	Psychology	Program	Abraham Givner, Barbar Gerson, Gilbert Foley, Louise Silverstein, Susan Warshaw, Joyce Weil, Lillian Zach, Esther Stavrov	D 125	70%	Psy.D.	D 30
—North Carolina—									
Appalachian State University Department of Psychology, Appalachian State University Boone, NC 28607 www.appstate.edu/dept/psych	S: NN	Jim Deni Ph: 828-262-2728 Fax: 704-262-2974 denijr@appstate.edu	Psychology	Appalachian State University, Graduate School, B.B. Dougherty Administration Building, Boone, NC 28607	Jim Deni, Eric Hatch, Pam Kidder Ashley	S 34	100%	M.A/ C.A.S	S 10
East Carolina University Department of Psychology, Rawl 105 Greenville, NC 27834-4353 www.ecu.edu/psyc/grad/school	S: NN	Michael B. Brown Ph: 252-328-4170 Fax: 252-328-6283 brownmi@mail.ecu.edu	Psychology	Program	Michael B. Brown, Larry Bolen	S 22	75%	M.A., C.A.S.	S 8
North Carolina State University Department of Psychology Box 7801 Raleigh, NC 27695-7801 www.ncsu.edu/psychology/graduate/conc/school/	D: NN, APA	William P. Erchul Ph: 919-515-2251 Fax: 919-515-1716 william_erchul@ncsu.edu	Psychology	Graduate Admissions, North Carolina State University, 104 Peele Hall, Box 7102 Raleigh, NC 27695-7102	William P. Erchul, Patricia Horan, Mary Haskett, Ann Schulte, Marcia Bingham, Patricia Collins	D 20	100%	M.S., Ph.D.	D 3
University of North Carolina - Chapel Hill 112 Peabody Hall. Education CB #3500 Chapel Hill, NC 27599-3500 http://www.soe.unc.edu/depts/ed/schpsy	S: NN D: NN, APA	Walter B. Pryzwansky Ph: 919-962-8689 Fax: 919-962-1533 walterbp@email.unc.edu	School Psychology	Web Page, Graduate School, UNC-CH	Walter Pryzwansky, Martha Petoskey, Rune J. Simeonsson, John Brantley,Barbara Hanna Wasik	S 17, D 25	70%	M.A/ M.Ed, Ph.D	S 6, D 5

School/Address/Web site	Accred.	Director	Dept.	Application Info.	Prim. Faculty	EN	FA	DA	YG
Western Carolina University Department of Psychology, 311 Killian Building Cullowhee, NC 28723 www.wcu.edu/cc/onlineRes/infosheets/spsspc.html	S: NN	Candace Boan Ph: 704-227-7361 Fax: 704-227-7388 cboan@wcu.edu	Psychology	Graduate School, Western Carolina University, Cullowhee, BC 28723	Candace Boan, Mickey Randolph, Harrison Kane, Shawn Acheson, Bruce Henderson, Hedy White, Robin Kowalski	S 19	100%	M.A.	S 6
—North Dakota—									
Minot State University 500 West University Avenue Minot, ND 58707 www.minotstateu.edu	S: NN	Alisha Ford Ph: 701-858-3099 Fax: 701-858-4262 fordalis@minotstateu.edu	Psychology	Dr. Brent Askvig, Director of Graduate Studies, Memorial Hall, Minot, ND 58707	Philip Hall, Alisha Ford	S 23	100%	Ed.S.	S 6
—Ohio—									
Bowling Green State University EDSE #403, Education Building, Bowling Green State University Bowling Green, OH 43403-0255 http://edap.bgsu.edu/EDSE/	S: NN	Audrey Ellenwood Ph: 419-372-9848 Fax: 419-372-8265 aellenw@bgnet.bgsu.edu	Division of Intervention Services	Program	Audrey Ellenwood, Edward Fiscus	S 25	100%	M.Ed	S 9
Cleveland State University Department of Psychology, 2300 Chester Ave Cleveland, OH 44115-3696 http://www.asic.csuohio.edu/psy/grad.html	S: NN	Kathy McNamara Ph: 216-687-2521 Fax: 216-687-9294 k.mcnamara@csuohio.edu	Psychology	Office of Graduate Admissions, RT 204, Campus Box G, Cleveland State University, Cleveland, OH 44115	Kathy McNamara, Colleen McMahon, Norma Cofresi, Leigh Ann Forsyth, Stephen Slane, Deborah Plummer	S 29	100%	M.A., Psy.S.	S 8
John Carroll University Administration Bldg., Department of Education and Allied Studies University Hts, OH 44118 http://www1.jcu.edu/educatio/programs.htm	S: NN	Jeanne E. Jenkins Ph: 216-397-4656 Fax: 216-397-3045 jjenkins@jcu.edu	Education and Allied Studies	Graduate School, John Carroll University, Administration Building, University Heights, OH 44118	Jeanne Jenkins, John Guidibaldi	S 27	24%	M.Ed	S 8
Kent State University 405 White Hall, Kent State University Kent, OH 44242 spsy.educ.kent.edu	S: NN D: NN, APA	Cathy Telzrow Ph: 216-672-0606 Fax: 330-672-2512 ctelzrow@educ.kent.edu	Educational Foundations and Special Services	Program	Cathy Telzrow, Caven Mcloughlin, Kara McGoey	S 47, D 16	100%	M.Ed., Ed.S., Ph.D.	S 15 D 2
Miami University 201 McGuffey Hall Oxford, OH 45056 www.muohio.edu/edp/	S: NN	Alex Thomas Ph: 513-529-6621 Fax: 513-529-3646 thomasa@muohio.edu	Educational Psychology	Program	Alex Thomas, Raymond Witte, Katherine Wickstrom	S 33	100%	M.S., Ed.S.	S 10
Ohio State University 1945 North High Street, 356 ARPS Hall Columbus, OH 43210 www.coe.ohio-state.edu	S: NN D: NN	Antoinette Miranda Ph: 614-292-5909 Fax: 614-292-4255 miranda.2@osu.edu	School of Physical Activity and Educational Services	Office of Student and Academic Programs, 215 Pomerene Hall, 1760 Neil Ave., Columbus, OH 43210 614-292-6787	Antoinette Miranda, Laurice Joseph	S 14, D 9	58%	M.A., Ph.D.	S 10, D 3

University of Cincinnati School Psychology Program, PO Box 210002 Cincinnati, OH 45221-0002 www.education.uc.edu	S: NN D: NN, APA (on probation)	Janet Graden Ph: 513-556-3335 Fax: 513-556-3898 janet.graden@uc.edu	Human Services	Program	Janet Graden, Sarah Allen, David Barnett, Kevin Jones, Francis Lentz	S 22, D 37	100%	M.Ed., Ph.D.	S 10, D 5
University of Dayton 300 College Park Dayton, OH 45469-0530 www.udayton.edu/edu/departments/edc/schoolpsych.html	S: NN	Sawyer A. Hunley Ph: 937-229-3644 Fax: 937-229-1055 sawyer.hunley@notes.udayton.edu	Counselor Education and Human Services	Program	Sawyer A. Hunley, James Evans	S 44	25%	M.S., Ed. S.	S 10
University of Toledo College of Health and Human Services, 2801 West Bancroft St Toledo, OH 43606-3390 cmhs.utoledo.edu		Jerome Zake Ph: 419-530-2718 Fax: 419-530-7879 jerome.zake@utoledo.edu	Counseling and Mental Health Services	Suzanne Martin, Counseling and Mental Health Services, #119, University of Toledo, 2801 W. Bancroft St. Toledo, OH 43606-3390	Jerome Zake, Robert Wendt	S 23, D 2	18%	M.Ed., Ed. S., Ph.D.	S 8, D 1
—Oklahoma—									
Oklahoma State University School of Applied Health and Educational Psychology, 434 Willard Hall Stillwater, OK 74708 www.pio.okstate.edu	S: NN Conditional D: NN, APA	Terry A. Stinnett Ph: 405-744-9629 Fax: 405-744-6756 tas@okstate.edu	Applied Health and Educational Psychology	Graduate Records, COE, Attn. Cindy Jones, 327 Willard, Okalahoma State University	Terry Stinnett, Judy Oehler-Stinnett	S 6, D 20	90%	Ed.S., Ph.D.	S 5, D 5
University of Central Oklahoma Department of Psychology, 100 N. University Drive Edmond, OK 73034 www.ucok.edu		Peggy Kerr, Ph.D Ph: 405-974-5477 Fax: 405-974-3822 pkerr@ucok.edu	Psychology	Program	Peggy Kerr	Certification: 53	5%	M.A., Certification	Certification: 10
—Oregon—									
Lewis and Clark College MSC 86, 0615 Palatine Hill Rd., Portland, OR 97219 Portland, OR 97219 www.lclark.edu/dept/cpsy	S: NN Conditional	Mary Henning-Stout Ph: 503-768-6060 Fax: 503-768-6065 cpsy@lclark.edu	Counseling Psychology	Program	Mary Henning-Stout, Peter Mortola, Amy Rees	S 55	90%	M.S.	S 15
University of Oregon School Psychology Program, 5208 University of Oregon Eugene, OR 97403-5208 interact.uoregon.edu/DSECR/sp.htm	D: NN, APA	Roland H. Good III Ph: 541-346-5501 Fax: 541-346-2897 RHGood@darkwing.uoregon.edu	Special Education Area	Program	Roland Good, Ruth Kaminski, Deanne Crone, Nancy Bank	S 5, D 43	Varies	M.S., Ph.D.	S 1, D 5
—Pennsylvania—									
Bryn Mawr College Department of Psychology, 101 N. Merion Ave Bryn Mawr, PA 19010 www.brynmawr.edu		Leslie Rescorla Ph: 610-527-5190 Fax: 610-527-2879 lrescorl@brynmawr.edu	Psychology	S - Program; D - Grad School of Arts and Sciences, 101 N. Merion Ave, Bryn Mawr, PA 19010	Leslie Rescorla, Kim Cassidy, Robert Wozniak, Marc Schulz	S 2, D 12	S - 0%; D - 100%	M.A., Ph.D.	S 2, D 7

School/Address/Web site	Accred.	Director	Dept.	Application Info.	Prim. Faculty	EN	FA	DA	YG
Bucknell University School Psychology Program, 459 Olin Science Lewisburg, PA 17837 www.bucknell.edu/departments/education		Candace R. Logan Ph: 5700-577-1324 logan@bucknell.edu	Education	Program	Candace R. Logan; Leslie Babiuski; Steve Knotek	S 24	100%	M.S.Ed	S 8
California University of Pennsylvania 250 University Ave, Psychology Dept, Box 65, LRC 317 California, PA 15419 http://www.cup.edu/		Kirk R. John Ph: 412-938-4100 Fax: 724-938-4406 John_K@cup.edu	Psychology	California University of PA, School of Graduate Studies, 250 University Ave, Box 91, California, PA 15419	Kirk John, Elizabeth Mason, Sam Lonich, Gail Ditkoff, Richard Scott, Nickolas Martin, Holiday Adair, Dennis Sweeney, Richard Cavasina	S 42	20%	M.S.	S 11
Duquesne University Dept of Counseling, Psychology and Special Education, Canevin Hall Pittsburgh, PA 15282 http://schoolpsych.duq.edu	S: NN Conditional	Joseph C. Kush Ph: 412-396-4794 Fax: 412-396-5585 kush@duq.edu	Counseling, Psychology and Special Education	Program	Joseph Kush, Jeffrey Miller, Tammy Hughes, Kim Blair	S 65	80%	M.S.Ed., C.A.G.S	S 12
Edinboro University of Pennsylvania 114B Butterfield Hall Edinboro, PA 16444 http://www.edinboro.edu/cwis/acaff/gradstudy/gradhome.html		Joel Erion Ph: 814-732-2200 Fax: 814-732-2268 jerion@edinboro.edu	Special Education and School Psychology	Office of Graduate Studies, Edinboro University of Pennsylvania, Edinboro, PA 16444	Joel Erion, Ed Snyder	S 50	25%	Ed.S	S 12
Immaculata College Box 500, Immaculata College Immaculata, PA 19345 www.immaculata.edu		Jed Yalof/ Pam Abraham Ph: 610-647-4400 x 3464 Fax: 610-993-8550 pabraham@immaculata.edu	Graduate Psychology	Sandra Rolleson, Director, Graduate Admissions, Immaculata, PA 19345	Pamela Abraham, Jed Yalof	S 43, Psy.D 5	0%	M.A., Certification	S 14
Indiana University of Pennsylvania 246 Stouffer Hall, Department of Educational and School Psychology Indiana, PA 15705 www.iup.edu/ep/	S: NN D: NN	John P. Quirk/ Victoria B. Damiani Ph: 724-357-2316 Fax: 724-357-6946 jpquirk@grove.iup.edu or vdamiani@grove.iup.edu	Educational and School Psychology	Program	John Quirk, Victoria Damiani, Gurmal Rattan, Robert Hoellein, Edward Levinson, Mary Ann Rafoth	S 34, D 79	100%	M.Ed., Ed.D.	S 14, D 6
Lehigh University School Psychology Program, College of Education, 111 Research Drive, Iococca Hall Bethlehem, PA 18015-8765 www.lehigh.edu/~ineduc/SPmain.html	S: NN D: NN, APA	George DuPaul Ph: 610-758-3256 Fax: 610-758-6223 gjd3@lehigh.edu	Education and Human Services	Program	George DuPaul, Edward Shapiro, Christine Cole, James C. DiPerna, Patricia Manz, David Miller	S 18, D 36	100%	Ed.S., Ph.D.	S 4, D 3
Marywood University McGowan Center, Marywood University Scranton, PA 18509-1598 http://www.marywood.edu/gas/counsel.htm		Kathleen A. Marjinsky Ph: 570-348-6211 ext. 2315 Fax: 717-961-4744 marjinsky@es.marywood.edu	Psychology and Counseling	Graduate School of Arts & Sciences, Psychology & Counseling Department School Psychology Program, 2300 Adams Ave, Scranton, PA 18509-1598	Kathleen Marjinsky, Ronald Miller, Rita Miller	S 33	5%	M.A.	S 5

Millersville University of Pennsylvania Department of Psychology, Byerly Hall Millersville , PA 17551 www.millersville.edu	S: NN	Katherine Green Ph: 717-872-3709 Fax: 717-871-2480 katherine.green@millersville.edu	Psychology	Program	Katherine Green, Helena Tuleya Payne	S 50	10%	M.S.	S 10
Pennsylvania State University 227 Cedar Building, Penn State University University Park, PA 16802-3109 espse.ed.psu.edu/spsy/spsy.ssi	D: NN, APA	Marley Watkins Ph: 814-865-1881 Fax: 814-863-1002 mww@psu.edu	Educational and School Psychology and Special Education	Program	Marley Watkins, Frank Worrell, Robert Hale, Barbara Schaefer	D 31	80%	M.S., Ph.D.	D 5
Temple University Rittler Annex 269, 1301 Cecil B. Moore Philadelphia, PA 19122 www.temple.edu/education/pse/schpsypgm.html	S: NN D: NN, APA	Joseph G. Rosenfeld Ph: 215-204-8075 Fax: 215-204-6013 schpsych@temple.edu	Psychological Studies in Education	Program	Joseph Rosenfield, Irwin Hyman, Catherine Fiorello, Joseph Ducette, Frank Farley, T. Chris Tillman, Louisa Lurkis	S 8, D 98	13%	M.Ed/CSP, Ph.D.	S 3, D 13
University of Pennsylvania Graduate School of Education, 3700 Walnut St Philadelphia, PA 19104-6216 www.upenn.edu/gse/	D: APA	Raymond P. Lorion Ph: 215-898-7367 Fax: 215-573-2115 lorion@gse.upenn.edu	Psychology in Education	Program	Raymond P. Lorion, Paul McDermott, John Fantuzzo, Amy Sichel, Howard Stevenson, Dianne Salter, Jeanne Stanley	D 16		Ph.D.	D 4
—Rhode Island—									
Rhode Island College Department of Counseling and Educational Psychology, 108 Adams Providence, RI 02908 www.ric.edu/academics/		Mifrando Obach Ph: 401-456-8023 Fax: 401-456-9628 mobach@ric.edu	Counseling and Educational Psychology	School Psychology Program, 600 Mt. Pleasant Ave, Providence, RI 02908	Mifrando Obach, Krista Robertson, Mary Wellman	S 49		M.A./Certificate of Advanced Graduate Study	S 9
University of Rhode Island Department of Psychology, 10 Chafee Road, Suite 8 Kingston, RI 02881-0808 www.psy.uri.edu/artsci/psy/schpsy	S: NN Conditional D: NN, APA	Paul Bueno de Mesquita Ph: 401-874-4216 Fax: 401-874-2157 jkulberg@uriacc.uri.edu	Psychology	Program	Paul Bueno de Mesquita, Susan Brady, W.Grant Willis, Margaret Rogers, Danel Koonce, Nansook Park, Janet Kulberg	S 9, D 27	86%	M.S., Ph.D.	S 0, D 2
—South Carolina—									
Francis Marion University Dept of Psychology and Sociology, P.O Box 100547 Florence, SC 29501-0547 http://aplha1.fmarion.edu/psych		Sam F. Broughton Ph: 803-661-1638 Fax: 803-661-1628 sbroughton@fmarion.edu	Psychology and Sociology	Program	Sam Broughton, Robert Bridger, John Hester	S 29	48%	M.S.	S 5
The Citadel Department of Psychology, 171 Moultrie St Charleston, SC 29409 www.citadel.edu/	S: NN	Nancy Bell Ph: 843-953-5320 Fax: 843-953-6797 nancy.bell@citadel.edu	Psychology	College of Graduate and Professional Studies, Bond Hall, 171 Moultrie St., Charleston, SC 29409	Nancy Bell, Michael Politano, K. Lassiter, A. Finch	S 50	50%	M.A., Ed.S	S 14

School/Address/Web site	Accred.	Director	Dept.	Application Info.	Prim. Faculty	EN	FA	DA	YG
University of South Carolina Department of Psychology, Barnwell College Columbia, SC 29208 http://www.cla.sc.edu/PSYC/schprog.htm	D: NN, APA	Richard J. Nagle Ph: 803-777-4137 Fax: 803-777-9558 nagle@sc.edu	Psychology	Department of Psychology, Graduate Admissions, Attn: Doris Davis Barnwell College, USC, Columbia, SC 29208	Richard Nagle, Frederic Medway, James Evans, Laurie Ford, Scott Huebner, Marion Burns, Pauline Pagliocca, Julia Mendez, Lorraine Taylor, Bradley Smith	D 7	100%	Ph.D.	D 5
Winthrop University Psychology Department, 135 Kinard Hall, Winthrop University Rock Hill, SC 29733 www.winthrop.edu	S: NN	Joseph Prus Ph: 803-323-2117 Fax: 803-323-2347 prusj@winthrop.edu	Psychology	Office of Graduate Studies, Winthrop University, Rock Hill, SC 29733	Joseph Prus, Gary Alderman, Antigo Martin, Letha Maxton	S 25	90%	M.S., S.S.P.	S 8
—South Dakota—									
University of South Dakota Counseling and Psychology in Education, School of Education Vermillion, SD 57069 www.usd.edu/cpe/school%20psych/spsy.html	S: NN	Hee-sook Choi Ph: 605-677-5250 or 606-677-5847 Fax: 605-677-5438 hchoi@usd.edu	School Psychology	Program	Hee-sook Choi, Patricia Work, Bruce Proctor, Dale Pietrzak	S 16, D 6	52%	Ed.S., Ph.D.	S 7, D 2
—Tennessee—									
Austin Peay State University PO Box 4537, APSU, Psychology Department Clarksville, TN 37044 www.apsu.edu		Maureen McCarthy Ph: 931-648-7233 Fax: 931-648-6267 mccarthym@apsu.edu	Psychology	Program	Maureen McCarthy, Patti Wilson, Rick Greive	S 2	80%	M.A., Ed.S	S 3
Middle Tennessee State University Box 533, MTSU Station Murfreesboro, TN 37132 www.mtsu.edu/~psycholo/	S: NN	James O. Rust Ph: 615-898-2319 Fax: 615-898-5027 jorust@mtsu.edu	Psychology	Graduate College, Middle Tennessee State University, Murfreesboro, TN 37132	James Rust, Susan Sobel, Gloria Hamilton, Ellen Slicker	S 15	25%	M.A., Ed.S.	S 8
Tennessee State University Psychology Department, 3500 John A. Merritt Blvd Nashville, TN 37209-1561 www.tnstate.edu		Lynn M. Boyer Ph: 615-963-1559 Fax: 615-963-5140 LBoyer@tnstate.edu	Psychology	Program	Lynn Boyer, Cornell Lane	S 10, D 14	25%	Ed.S., Ph.D.	D 1
Tennessee Technological University Box 5031 Cookeville, TN 38505 www.tntech.edu		Jann D. Cupp Ph: 931-372-3457 Fax: 931-372-3722 jcupp@tntech.edu	Counseling and Psychology	Dean of Graduate Studies, Box 5036, TTU, Cookeville, TN 38505	Jann D. Cupp, Michael Rohr	S 17	20%	M.A., Ed.S	S 3
University of Memphis Department of Psychology, The University of Memphis, Room 202 Memphis, TN 38152-3230 http://www.psyc.memphis.edu/psych.htm	S: NN	Thomas K. Fagan Ph: 901-678-4676 Fax: 901-678-2579 tom-fagan@mail.psyc.memphis.edu	Psychology	Program	Tom Fagan, Randy Floyd	S 17, D 7	40%	M.A., Ed.S., Ph.D.	S 3, D 2

University of Tennessee - Chattanooga Graduate Studies Division, College of Education and Applied Professional Studies Chattanooga, TN 37403 www.utc.edu/gradstudies/edsschpsy.html		George Helton Ph: 423-755-4272 Fax: 423-755-5380 George-Helton@utc.edu	Graduate Studies Division	Graduate Studies, 114 Race Hall, 615 McCallie Avenue, Chattanooga, TN 37403-2598	George Helton, Pamela Guess, Ted Miller	S 15	25%	Ed.S.	S 6
University of Tennessee - Knoxville Claxton Complex A-525 Knoxville, TN 37996-3400 http://www.coe.utk.edu/units/pes/programs.html	S: NN D: NN, APA	Christopher H. Skinner Ph: 865-974-8145 Fax: 865-974-0135 cskinne1@utk.edu	Educational Psychology	Graduate Admissions, College of Education, University of Tennessee Knoxville, TN 37996-3400	Christopher Skinner, R. Steve McCallum, Sherry K. Bain, Bob Williams, Luther Kindall, Tom George, Ron Carlini, Kathy Greenburg	S 4, D 27	93%	Ed.S., Ph.D.	S 2, D 5
—TEXAS—									
Abilene Christian University 210-D Chambers Bldg., ACU Box 28011, Dept of Psychology Abilene, TX 79699 www.acu.edu/psyc		Robert McKelvain Ph: 915-674-2280 Fax: 915-674-6968 mckelvainr@acu.edu	Psychology	Program	T. Scott Perkins, Joann Campbell, Edwin Headrick	S 17	50%	M.S.	S
Baylor University Baylor University, Box 97301 Waco, TX 76798-7301 http://www.baylor.edu/~EDP/baylor_school_psychology.html		Patricia Woods Prewitt Ph: 254-710-6113 Fax: 254-710-3265 patricia_prewitt@baylor.edu	Educational Psychology	Program	Patricia W. Prewitt, Eric Robinson, Thomas Proctor, Terrill F. Saxon	S 21	25%	Ed.S.	S
Our Lady of the Lake University 411 S.W. 24th St San Antonio, TX 78207 http://www.ollusa.edu/academic/secs/default.htm		Cynthia Gonzalez Ph: 210-431-6711 x8152 Fax: 210-436-0824 gonzcy@lake.ollusa.edu	Psychology	OLLU, Office of Admissions	Cynthia Gonzalez, J. Biever, C. de las Fuentes, G. Gardner	S 26	10%	M.S.	S 4
Sam Houston State University Psychology Department Huntsville, TX 77341 www.shsu.edu/~psy_www/	S: NN Conditional	Marsha Harman Ph: 409-294-3875 Fax: 409-294-3798 edu_mjh@shsu.edu	Psychology	Dr. Rowland Miller, Graduate Advisor, Department of Psychology and Philosophy, PO Box 2447, SHSU, Huntsville, TX 77341-2447	Marsha Harman, Richard Eglsaer, Cheryl Hiscock	S 11	20%	M.A.	S 4
Southwest Texas State University Department of Educational Administration & Psychological Services San Marcos, TX 78666 www.swt.edu	S: NN	Alicia Paredes Scribner Ph: 512-245-3083 Fax: 512-245-8872 as08@swt.edu	Educational Administration and Psychological Services	Program	Alicia Paredes Scribner, Cindy Plotts, Edward Scholwinski, S.Sue McCullough, Christabel Jorgenson	S 85	10%	M.A.	S 26
Texas A & M University Department of Educational Psychology College Station, TX 77843-4225 http://www.coe.tamu.edu/~edpsy/	D: NN, APA	Mike Ash Ph: 409-845-1831 Fax: 978-845-1875 mash@tamu.edu	Educational Psychology	Academic Advisor, Department of Educational Psychology TAMU, College Station, TX 77843-4225	Michael Ash, Cecil Reynolds, Jan Hughes, Cynthia Riccio, Jan Hasbrouck, Salvador Hector Ochoa, Karla Anhalt	D 49	100%	Ph.D.	D 4

School/Address/Web site	*Accred.*	*Director*	*Dept.*	*Application Info.*	*Prim. Faculty*	*EN*	*FA*	*DA*	*YG*
Texas A & M University - Commerce School Psychology Program, Texas A&M University Commerce, TX 75429 www.tamu-commerce.edu/coe/psy/schpsym.html		William G. Masten Ph: 903-886-5594 Fax: 903-886-5510 William_Masten@tamu-commerce.edu	Psychology	Program	William Masten, Steve Ball, Dean Ginther	S 15	50%	M.A.	S 5
Texas Woman's University Department of Psychology and Philosophy, PO Box 425470 Denton, TX 76204-0996 www.twu.edu/AS/psyphil/sppc/	S: NN D: NN	Daniel C. Miller Ph: 940-898-2303 Fax: 940-898-2301 dmiller@twu.edu	Psychology and Philosophy	Dr. Hamilton, Admissions Committee Chair	Daniel Miller, Sandra Jimenez, Frank Vitro, Basil Hamilton	S 10, D 33	15%	M.A., Ph.D.	S 2, D 4
The University of Texas Pan American Department of Educational Psychology Edinburg, TX 78539 http://www.panam.edu/colleges/coe.cfm		Ralph Carlson Ph: 210-381-3466 Fax: 210-381-2184 rcarlson@panam.edu	Educational Psychology	Program	Ralph Carlson, JoAnn Burns, Terry Overton, Mary Valerio, Cheryl Fielding	S 38	71%	M.A.	S 6
Trinity University 715 Stadium Drive, Education Department San Antonio, TX 78212-7200 http://www.trinity.edu/departments/education/ma.htm	S: NN	Terry Migliore Ph: 210-999-7595 Fax: 210-999-7592 terry.migliore@trinity.edu	Education	Program	Terry Migliore	S 38	100%	M.A.	S 14
University of Houston - Clear Lake 2700 Bay Area Blvd Houston, TX 77058 http://www.cl.uh.edu/hsh/main/BehSciSchoolPsyc.html	S: NN	Gail Cheramie Ph: 281-283-3392 Fax: 281-283-3397 cheramie@cl.uh.edu	Behavioral Sciences	Program	Gail Cheramie, Emily Sutter	S 35		M.A.	S 12
University of North Texas School Psychology Program, Terrill Hall, Rm 351, Psychology Department Denton, TX 76203 www.psyc.unt.edu		Sander Martin Ph: 940-565-2671 Fax: 940-565-4682 smartin@terrill.unt.edu	Psychology	Gina Miller, Graduate Coordinator, Psychology Dept, Denton, TX 76203	Sander Martin, Vincent Ramospad, David Baker, Raphael Toledo, Persephone Silverthorn, Wayne Hresko	S 15	50%	M.A., M.S.	S 6
University of Texas Department of Educational Psychology, SZB 504 Austin, TX 78712 www.utexas.edu/ or edpsych.edb.utexas.edu	D: NN, APA	Kevin D. Stark Ph: 512-475-7641 Fax: 512-471-4155 kevinstark@mail.utexas.edu	Educational Psychology	website	Kevin Stark, Deborah Tharinger,Cindy Carlson, Peg Semrud-Clikeman, Sheri Robinson, Richard Valencia	D 77	90%	Ph.D.	D 16
University of Texas - Tyler Department of Psychology, 3900 University Blvd Tyler, TX 75799 www.uttyler.edu		Ronald B. Livingston Ph: 903-566-7130 Fax: 903-565-5656 rlivings@mail.uttyl.edu	Psychology	Program	R. Livingston, R.F. McClure, F.G. Mears, S. Jones, C. Grothues, P. Lundberg	S 15	50%	M.S.	

—UTAH—									
Brigham Young University 320-A MCKB, BYU Provo, UT 84602 www.byu.edu/cse		Ron Bingham Ph: 801-378-3857 Fax: 801-378-3961 ron_bingham@BYU.edu	Counseling Psychology and Special Education	School of Education, 328 MCKB, Provo, UT 84602-5093	Ron Bingham, Annette Jerome, Melissa Allen, Timothy Smith		52%	M.S.	S 15
University of Utah 1705 E Campus Center Drive, Rm 327 Salt Lake City, UT 84112 www.gse.utah.edu/edpsy/schpsy.htm	D: NN, APA	Elaine Clark Ph: 801-581-7968 Fax: 801-581-5566 clark@gse.utah.edu	Educational Psychology	Program	Elaine Clark, William Jenson, Dan Olympia, Lora Tuesday Heathfield, Janice Pompa	S 8, D 32	25%	M.S., Ph.D.	S 2, D 6
Utah State University Department of Psychology, Utah State University Logan, UT 84322-2810 www.coe.usu.edu/psyc/	S: NN D: APA	Gretchen A. Gimpel Ph: 435-797-0721 Fax: 435-797-1448 ggimpel@coe.usu.edu	Psychology	Program	Gretchen Gimpel, Carolyn Barcus, Donna Gilbertsson	S 23	90%	M.S.	S 8
—VIRGINIA—									
College of William and Mary School of Education, PO Box 8795 Williamsburg, VA 23187-8795 www.wm.edu/education/index.html	S: NN	Sandra Ward Ph: 757-221-2326 Fax: 757-221-2988 scbrub@wm.edu	School Psychology and Counselor Education	Program	Sandra Ward, Lynn Pelco, John Lavach	S 33	50%	M.Ed., Ed.S.	S 14
George Mason University Psychology Department, George Mason University, 4400 University Dr. Fairfax, VA 22030-4444 www.gmu.edu/deparments/psychology/homepage/schlma.html	S: NN	John Blaha Ph: 703-993-1342 x 2 Fax: 703-993-1359 grad_psychology@gmu.edu	Psychology	Admissions	John Blaha, Scott Merydith, Susanne Denham, David Weisman, Virginia Smith, Edythe Wiggs, Jerome Bruns	S 30	30%	M.A.	S 9
James Madison University Dept of Psychology , Johnston Hall - MSC 7401 Harrisonburg, VA 22807 cep.jmu.edu/schoolpsyc	S: NN D: APA	Anthony Paolitto Ph: 540-568-3373 Fax: 540-568-3322 paolitaw@jmu.edu	Psychology	Program	Anthony Paolitto, Patricia Warner, Tammy Gilligan, Ashton Trice	S 18	95%	M.A., Ed.S., Psy.D.	S 10, Psy.D.
Radford University Box 6946 Department of Psychology Radford, VA 24142 www.runet.edu	S: NN	Robert Hiltonsmith Ph: 540-831-5972 Fax: 540-831-6113 bhiltons@radford.edu	Psychology	Program	Robert Hiltonsmith, Dianne Friedman, Joseph Montuori	S 28	75%	Ed.S.	S 8
University of Virginia Curry School of Education, University of Virginia, PO Box 400270 Charlottesville, VA 22904-4270 http://curry.edschool.Virginia.EDU/curry/dept/edhs/	D: NN	Ronald E. Reeve Ph: 434-924-0790 Fax: 434-924-1433 rer5r@virginia.edu	Human Services	Admissions Office	Ronald Reeve, Richard Abidin, Robert Pianta, Ann Loper, Antoinette Thomas	D 43	100%	M.Ed., Ph.D.	D 8

School/Address/Web site	Accred.	Director	Dept.	Application Info.	Prim. Faculty	EN	FA	DA	YG
—Washington—									
Central Washington University Psychology Department, Central Washington University Ellensburg, WA 98926 http://www.cwu.edu/%7Epsych/mdegrees.html	S: NN	Gene Johnson Ph: 509-963-2501 Fax: 509-963-2307 johnsong@cwu.edu	Psychology	Graduate Studies & Research, CWU Mail Stop 7510, Ellensburg, WA 98926	Gene Johnson, Lisa Weyandt, Stephanie Stein, Phil Diaz	S 20	30%	M.Ed.	S 9
Eastern Washington University Department of Psychology, 151 Martin Hall, Eastern Washington University Cheney, WA 99004-2423 www.ewu.edu	S: NN Conditional	Mahlon Dalley Ph: 509-359-6147 Fax: 509-359-6325 mdalley@owl.ewu.edu	Psychology Dept and Counseling, Educational, and Developmental Psych Dept	Program	Mahlon Dalley, Gretchen Jefferson, David Hatfield		12%	M.S.	
Seattle Pacific University School of Education, 3307 Third Ave West Seattle, WA 98119-1997 http://www.spu.edu/depts/soe/psych.html		Janine Jones Ph: 206-281-2369 Fax: 206-281-2756 janine@spu.edu	School Counseling and Psychology	Roger Long, Graduate Enrollment and Program Manager	Janine Jones, William Rowley , Christopher Sink	15		Ed.S., Ed.D	6
Seattle University School of Education, Seattle University Seattle, WA 98122-4340 www.seattleu.edu	S: NN	Kristin Guest Ph: 206-296-5776 Fax: 206-296-1982 kguest@seattleu.edu	Counseling and School Psychology	Office of Admissions, Seattle University, Broadway & Madison, Seattle, WA 98122-4340	Kristin Guest, Kay Beisse	S 45	60%	Ed.S.	S 12
University of Washington 322 Miller, Box 353600 Seattle, WA 98195-3600 http://www.educ.washington.edu/COE/ed-psych/index.html	S: NN D: NN, APA	Scott Stage Ph: 206-543-1846 Fax: 206-543-8439 vwb@u.washington.edu	Educational Psychology	Shirley Shimada, 206 Miller Hall, Box 353600, University of Washington, Seattle, WA 98195-3600	Scott Stage, Virginia Berninger, James Mazza	S 22, D 12	76%	M.Ed., Ph.D.	S 8
—West Virginia—									
Marshall University Graduate College 100 Angus Peyton Drive S. Charleston, WV 25303-1600 http://www.mugc.edu/Academic/sepd/psych.htm		Stephen L. O'Keefe Ph: 304-746-1932 Fax: 304-746-8951 sokeefe@marshall.edu	School Psychology	Admissions Office, Marshall University Graduate College, South Charleston, WV 25303-1600	Stephen O'Keefe, Fred Krieg, Elizabeth Kelley Boyles	S 40	20%	Ed.S.	S 9
—Wisconsin—									
University of Wisconsin - Eau Claire School Psychology Program, Dept of Psychology Eau Claire, WI 54702-4004 www.uwec.edu	S: NN	William Frankenberger Ph: 715-836-5733 Fax: 715-836-4892 Frankewr@uwec.edu	Psychology	Program	William Frankenberger, Richard Fuhrer, Kimberly Knesting, Larry Morse, Barbara Lozar	S 24	90%	M.S.Ed., Ed. S.	S 8

University of Wisconsin - La Crosse Psychology Department, 1725 State St La Crosse, WI 54601 www.uwlax.edu	S: NN	Milton Dehn Ph: 608-785-8441 Fax: 608-785-8443 dehn.milt@uwlax.edu	Psychology	School Psychology Program, 341 Graff Main Hall, University of Wisconsin — La Crosse 1725 State St, La Crosse, WI 54601	Milton Dehn, Betty Miller, Robert Dixon	S 28	92%	M.S.Ed., Ed. S.	S 9
University of Wisconsin - Madison 1025 W. Johnson St Madison, WI 53706-1796 www.education.wisc.edu/edpsych/gradprog/schpsych	D: NN, APA	Thomas R. Kratochwill Ph: 608-262-1427 Fax: 608-265-4559 edpsych@facstaff.wisc.edu	Educational Psychology	Barb Lienau, Admissions Secretary	Tomas R. Kratochwill, Jeff Braden, Steve Elliott, Maribeth Gettinger, Julie McGivern, Steve Quintana	D 26	100%	M.S., Ph.D.	D 5
University of Wisconsin - Milwaukee Department of Educational Psychology, PO Box 413 Milwaukee, WI 53201 www.uwm.edu/dept/soe	D: NN, APA	Anne Teeter Ellison Ph: 414-229-4767 Fax: 414-229-4939 teeter@uwm.edu	Educational Psychology	Program	Anne Teeter Ellison, Karen Stoiber, Michael Vanderwood, Dawn Reinemann	S 51, D 20	50%	M.A., Ph.D.	S 9, D 0
University of Wisconsin - River Falls Department of Counseling and School Psychology, 410 S. Third St River Falls, WI 54022 www.uwrf.edu	S: NN	Donald Lee Stovall Ph: 715-425-3889 Fax: 715-425-3242 donald.lee.stovall@uwrf.edu	Counseling and School Psychology	College of Education and Graduate Studies, University of Wisconsin - River Falls, 410 S. Third St, River Falls, WI 54022	Donald L. Stovall, Mike Bonner, John Lecapitaine	S 35	10%	M.S.	S 10
University of Wisconsin - Stout 419 EHS Menomonie, WI 54751 www.uwstout.edu	S: NN	Denise E. Maricle Ph: 715-232-2229 Fax: 715-232-1400 maricled@uwstout.edu	Education, Counseling and School Psychology	Program	Denise E. Maricle, Jacalyn Weissenburger, Scott Orme, Mary Beth Tusing	S 40		M.S., Ed.S.	S 15
University of Wisconsin - Superior McCaskill 111, PO Box 2000 Superior, WI 54880 http://www.uwsuper.edu/tis/gradprog.htm	S: NN Conditional	Suzanne C. Griffith Ph: 715-394-8316 Fax: 715-394-8146 sgriffit@staff.uwsuper.edu	Counseling and Psychological Profession	Graduate Studies Office, Old Main 137, 1800 Grand Avenue, Superior, WI 54880	Suzanne C. Griffith, Rob Dixon, Nancy Minahan	S 16	100%	Ed.S.	S 8
University of Wisconsin - Whitewater Department of Psychology, 800 W. Main St Whitewater, WI 53190 www.uww.edu.psychology/schpsych/school_psychology	S: NN	James Larson Ph: 262-472-5412 Fax: 262-472-1863 larsonj@uwwvax.uww.edu	Psychology	Program	James Larson, Randy Busse	S 45	30%	M.S.Ed., Ed.S.	S 12

Index

A

B

C

D

E

F

I

J

K

L

M

O

P

Q

R

S

T

U

V

W

Y

Z